D1327979

BEST AMERICAN PLAYS

1918-1958 Supplementary Volume

Other Books by JOHN GASSNER

BEST PLAYS SERIES
Edited by John Gassner
(Containing the complete texts of the plays, introductory matter, etc.)

25 BEST PLAYS OF THE MODERN AMERICAN THEATRE
Early Series, 1916-1929

20 BEST PLAYS OF THE MODERN AMERICAN THEATRE, *1930-1939*

BEST PLAYS OF THE MODERN AMERICAN THEATRE
Second Series, 1939-1946

BEST AMERICAN PLAYS—THIRD SERIES, *1945-1951*

20 BEST EUROPEAN PLAYS ON THE AMERICAN STAGE

BEST AMERICAN PLAYS—FOURTH SERIES, *1951-1957*

THE THEATRE IN OUR TIMES

MASTERS OF THE DRAMA

PRODUCING THE PLAY

OUR HERITAGE OF WORLD LITERATURE

A TREASURY OF THE THEATRE (3 VOLS.)

ENGLISH COMEDIES

COMEDIES OF MOLIÈRE

HUMAN RELATIONS IN THE THEATRE

FORM AND IDEA IN THE MODERN THEATRE

TWENTY BEST FILM PLAYS

BEST FILM PLAYS OF 1943-44

BEST FILM PLAYS OF 1945

THEATRE AT THE CROSSROADS

M ±1393668
Keep S- 5367553 / 7464111
multiple
copies 3/17/06
        A Byrd

PN
6112
.B47
1918-58
copy 2

Best AMERICAN Plays

SUPPLEMENTARY VOLUME

1918—1958

DISCARDED

NORMANDALE COMMUNITY COLLEGE
9700 FRANCE AVENUE SOUTH
BLOOMiNGTON, MINNESOTA 55431

EDITED, WITH AN INTRODUCTION BY

John Gassner

Crown Publishers, Inc., NEW YORK

To the Memory of
DUDLEY NICHOLS
(1895-1960)

Seventh Printing, December 1976

DISCARDED

© 1961, BY CROWN PUBLISHERS, INC.

LIBRARY OF CONGRESS CATALOG CARD NUMBER: 57-12830
ISBN: 0-517-504502
NOTE: All plays contained in this volume are fully protected under the copyright laws of
the United States of America, the British Empire, including the Dominion of Canada,
and all other countries of the Copyright Union. Permission to reproduce, wholly or in part,
must be obtained from the copyright owners or their agents.

PRINTED IN THE UNITED STATES OF AMERICA

Acknowledgments

I should like to express special indebtedness to the following individuals for their generous assistance in the preparation of the present volume:

To Paul Green and Elmer Rice who supplemented the previously printed texts of THE HOUSE OF CONNELLY and THE ADDING MACHINE with hitherto unpublished scenes.

To John Patrick for permitting the republication of THE TEAHOUSE OF THE AUGUST MOON and reading proof on the text.

To Leah Salisbury, Abbott Van Nostrand, and Harold Freedman for effectuating clearances of several important plays.

To Herbert Michelman of Crown Publishers and his assistant editor Mrs. Naomi Rosenbach for her help in clearing permissions, tracking down scripts, and organizing the material.

And to an ever-patient wife, Mollie Gassner, for guidance, editorial labors, and much spadework.

John Gassner

February, 1961

CONTENTS

Introduction

AMERICAN SUPPLEMENT

by JOHN GASSNER

Perhaps there is too little to be said in general terms about the present volume to justify an Introduction, and a mere Preface would do. My object in compiling the present *Best American Plays Supplement*, consisting of plays (up to 1958) that are not in my previous *Best Plays* volumes, was to salve my conscience and to fill a gap. Now that the plays, seventeen in number and all of them full-length, are between covers, it is apparent to me that my conscience remains unsalved and that the gap is still not filled. Time allowing, and my publishers and the copyright owners of the plays willing, I shall simply have to put together a second and perhaps even a third Supplement, for the American theatre will not be thoroughly enough represented until a considerable number of other plays, some withheld at present for special reasons, join the series—among them certain plays by Eugene O'Neill Thornton Wilder, John Howard Lawson, Emmet Lavery, Arthur Laurents, John Wexley, Robert Ardrey, Samson Raphaelson, Virgil Geddes, Albert Bein, and Dan Totheroh.

In the meantime, I can at least console myself with the reflection that I have supplied readers of the *Best Plays* series, including the present Supplement, with a total of 113 items, all but a handful of which are full-length plays. And if the American adaptations in *20 Best European Plays on the American Stage* (published in 1957) are added, as they should be, the number would soar above 120. I have, in addition, supplied introductions of varying length to the individual plays in their proper places. If readers will turn to these, they will realize I have not entirely shirked my editorial responsibilities. But there is a still better reason for turning to these pages: I sometimes digress into information that may be useful to those who propose to stage or study any of the selections.

Exactly why these particular plays should be made available, apart from the reason that they were not presented in previous *Best Plays* volumes, is a legitimate query. Taking the plays in their chronological order, I think I can dispose of the question briefly, if not always briskly.

Clarence, the seemingly oddest of my choices, stands here as an example of the genial type of American comedy favored early in our century. Booth Tarkington as author has become a nostalgic memory, but Alfred Lunt, who played the title part, fortunately remains a living presence for playgoers, seen most recently in the noteworthy and for our times characteristically pessimistic Duerrenmatt morality *The Visit*. Tarkington's optimistic comedy, innocent of the slings and arrows of our most outrageous nuclear-age fortune, provides a springboard for the conscientious reader's plunge into the turbulence of the 1920's and the succeeding decades.

Rain appears in this collection as one of the most intelligently conceived melodramas of the 1920's, if not indeed of subsequent decades, too. John Colton's dramatization of the Somerset Maugham South Seas story was timely, telling as it did of a missionary's undoing through his own libido's masquerading as righteousness. It encompassed the Freudian interest and the anti-puritan crusade presided over by H. L. Mencken, who ate hypocrites for breakfast and washed them down with Dionysian potations. If the presence of *Rain* should also revive memories of Jeanne Eagels, the Miss Thompson of the original production, so much the better.

The theatre has much to forget, but also a lot more to remember than literary critics tend to realize and playgoers are allowed to remember by the business of living.

In the case of *The Adding Machine*, explanations are perhaps less necessary for the serious-minded reader than for lighthearted playgoers. Many of the latter probably overlooked Elmer Rice's dramatic experiment when the venturesome young Theatre Guild directors presented it. It did not appear that the ranks of the Guild's subscribers were swelled by refugees from normal Broadway show business when the play had its relatively short run in 1923. In its time, *The Adding Machine* was written no less in revolt against humdrum realistic playwriting than against the standardization of life that appeared to be growing with our affluence after World War I. Today, both the substance and style of the play make it more rather than less meaningful. And although its expressionistic form lacks the novelty it once had in our theatre, it may receive at least a nod from the admirers of Ionesco's *Rhinoceros*. It is obvious, besides, that we cannot keep too much imaginative American work in retirement—we produce so little of it nowadays.

We may observe, too, that the Elmer Rice play exemplifies our realistic bias even in stylized theatre. Before 1918, advanced groups such as the Washington Square Players, the parent organization of the Theatre Guild, made a noble effort to sponsor an "esthetic" symbolist type of drama, chiefly by producing the quasi-mystical plays of Maeterlinck. They made little headway. American playwrights reacted more favorably to expressionism, mainly I suppose because its progenitor, Strindberg, fused symbolism with naturalism, as did the later Central European expressionists represented by the Theatre Guild of the twenties. I refer to social-minded expressionists like Georg Kaiser, Karel Capek, and Ernst Toller rather than ultra-subjective playwrights. O'Neill accomplished the same fusion in *The Emperor Jones* and *The Hairy Ape*, which the Provincetown Players produced in Greenwich Village before the Guild presented *The Adding Machine* on Broadway. John Howard Lawson, and George Kaufman in collaboration with Marc Connelly, followed the same procedure in *Roger Bloomer* (1923) and *Beggar on Horseback* (1924) respectively, as did Sophie Treadwell later in the twenties in *Machinal*, successfully revived in New York during the 1959-60 season. This is a familiar observation and it was well expressed in a University of Kansas City Playhouse *Newsletter* (in March, 1951): "The American expressionists. . . . hewed closer to naturalism [than Maeterlinck-inspired symbolists], seeking a more realistic, 'lifelike' portrayal than had their literary godfather, and seldom did their plays show any Maeterlinckian dreamlike quality. When many of these dramatists later turned away from expressionism, all but a few went back to the purely realistic drama rather than to the symbolically obscure dream-play." This statement clearly pertains to Elmer Rice, who went on to write *Street Scene*, as well as to O'Neill, whose last plays are among the best and most realistic he ever wrote.

A helpful observation concerning the Elmer Rice experiment was offered by Joseph Wood Krutch, when he wrote in his *American Drama Since 1918* that "the very monotonous insistence of its vulgarity hypnotizes the imagination, and one passes easily into the world of half-insane fantasy where the main action takes place." Mr. Krutch added that "the formal unity and hence the artistic success of the piece depends upon the fact that the spell of the nightmare is never broken and no attempt is made to interpret it in fully rational terms." Never broken for a very good reason, since *The Adding Machine* is projected through the arid mind and diminished sensibility of the commonplace bookkeeper Mr. Zero, which reflect the world that produces a Mr. and Mrs. Zero.

From the nineteen-thirties we have a variety of work that seems to me worth preserving; anthologizing is, after all, a form of preservation—and, let us trust, not always akin to embalming. *Green Grow the Lilacs* may surprise the reader only with its title. Assisted, I expect, by his still green memories of *Oklahoma!*, he will find the Lynn Riggs play of the year 1930 more than a trifle familiar. To the studious or the simply curious, I offer an opportunity to compare the book of that celebrated musical, which began the resurgence of our popular theatre, with the less known play upon which it was based. And the play, we may observe, also constitutes popular theatre, in a sense. *Green Grow the Lilacs* was steeped in the life of a region and is one of the classics of our so-called regional theatre. It comes from "the people," albeit through the mediation of a poet, and belongs to them. As for the poet himself, he can be allowed here to speak for a number of sensitive writers such as Dan Totheroh, Virgil Geddes, and George O'Neil, who came into our theatre in the bright-as-day 1920's and found it difficult then, as well as later, to adapt themselves to the flinty surface of show business. Above all, they wanted organic theatre; they did not want to force dramatic action for effect. "My beliefs," wrote Lynn Riggs in his preface to *Green Grow the Lilacs*, "run counter to the current notions. . . ." As for "true drama," he wrote, perhaps echoing the father of modern poetic drama, Maeterlinck (*The Tragical in Daily Life*), "Two people in a room, agreeing or not agreeing, are to me truly dramatic. The edges of their being can never be in accord; psychically, as well as physically, they are assailed by an opposing radiation. And the nature of the flow of spirit from each determines both the quality of their conflict, and the shape of their story." Quite a credo for show business to assimilate!

The House of Connelly also comes from a region remote from Broadway, and it is significant that it should have reached the New York stage as the first important production of the Group Theatre, a company committed to dealing with social reality and living up to that commitment in terms of individual characterization rather than of collective depersonalization, which is often the case with sociologists in literature. One of the first "social dramas" of the socially slanted theatre of the thirties, *The House of Connelly* qualifies historically for inclusion here, and at the same time it qualifies as an authentic work of playwriting.

The play, moreover, is the first and most highly regarded of Paul Green's climactic contributions to the Broadway stage before he decided to devote most of his energies to the creation of symphonic epic productions in the South and gave us the nearest thing to a national theatre founded on the American heritage. A wide-ranging poet and visionary of the theatre, Paul Green's stature as man and artist makes pygmies of most aspirants to the profession in New York. When, after returning from military service in World War I and assuming a teaching position at the University of North Carolina, Green found himself lacking a ferment for his writing, he floundered, according to report (*Readers' Digest*, July, 1960), until he asked his university students, "Why is it that it takes us so long to *believe* in this democracy we give lip service to?" And he answered: "Let's give everyone around us—rich or poor, white or Negro—room enough to reach for fulfillment. For what sin can be greater than to cause a man to miss his life?" The question and the answer are characteristic of Paul Green; they account, in part, for virtually everything he wrote even before *In Abraham's Bosom.*

My tribute to Paul Green, as well as to Lynn Riggs, is not intended, however, to brush aside the merits of professional theatre as an urbane occupation when it is truly urbane—bucolic fervor does not carry me that far. In the present anthology two plays represent the cosmopolitan theatre that its devotees like to call sophisticated. Widely disparate in subject matter, Mayer's *Children of Darkness* and Behrman's *Biography* have two indispensable qualities of theatrical cosmopolitanism—namely, "style" in the principal character and wit in the writing.

In *Children of Darkness*, the author suitably adopted an eighteenth-century finish for both his protagonist and his dialogue. But he achieved something more than a period piece about the dubious cosmopolitanism of a London prison where aristocracy mingled with the riffraff. In the period of the thirties charged not only with social conflict but liberal righteousness, Mayer performed the perverse feat of producing an *amoral* romantic tragi-comedy—a comedy compounded of corruption and cynicism that exalts life while debasing it, a work luminous at the same time that it is satanic. This bizarre composition may well be the delectation of all who prefer caviar to corn bread in the theatre. Inevitably, I suppose, it also proved "caviar to the general" when first produced in 1930, and it was actually that again when it won plaudits for the author and the cast more than a quarter of a century later at the Circle in the Square Theatre in Greenwich Village. Popularity cannot, however, be the measure of merit, and the relatively novel pleasure of encountering an American play that not only acts but reads well is not to be slighted.

Biography represents S. N. Behrman, one of our two most distinguished writers of high comedy in some forty years of Broadway "modernity" (the other is, obviously, Philip Barry). Its stylistic merits and the judiciousness of Behrman's observation of "temperament" or character are as evident today as they were when the Theatre Guild first presented *Biography* with the inimitable Ina Claire in the principal role. *Biography* was also the first of Behrman's wryly comic encounters with the social conscience of the 1930's; or, if you will, with the still timely problem of commitment to a cause that Jean-Paul Sartre trumpeted in the 1940's as "engagement." The problem happens to be no less important to art, especially the art of comedy—as Behrman himself observed in the later play *No Time for Comedy*—than to citizenship and the preservation of civilization.

Anywhere, but especially in a democracy, it would be futile to expect that more than a fraction of comedy would be strictly "high." Two homespun comedies of exceptional vitality, *On Borrowed Time* and *Morning's at Seven*, one an adaptation and the other an original work by the same author, Paul Osborn, came out of the 1930's when identification with the common folk became an article of faith. *On Borrowed Time* also belongs to the imagination, with its fantasy of getting Death up a tree. The special delight of the work resides, however, not in its fancy but in the vivid reality of characters as familiar as backyard neighbors—especially, of course, the salty octogenarian Gramps, whom Dudley Digges and Victor Moore made endearing when they played the role a decade or so apart. *On Borrowed Time* is fantasy as Americans know it, and if its conclusion is anything but comic, there can be no doubt that it was the folksy humor that made the pathos endurable and the play attractive.

Without actually being regional, *Morning's at Seven* is essentially provincial comedy, and the barbed tongue of the lone intellectual in Mr. Osborn's play only serves to underline the provincialism of the majority of the characters. It would seem fairly easy to compose this kind of comedy, but the abundance of dithering plays about the folks back home shows that although in America the temptation to write such comedy has been strong, the talent to do so has been meager. The theatre's experience with this type of comedy since *Morning's at Seven* opened on Broadway in 1939 requires no revision of this statement. In 1955, when the play was successfully revived in Greenwich Village, Brooks Atkinson probably spoke for the general public in writing: "After sixteen years, *Morning's at Seven* is still an original portrait of human folly." Everyman, Mr. Atkinson thought, could "see glimpses of his own reflection in one part or another of Mr. Osborn's mirror."

But the land has long been a source of tragedy as well as delight, especially the stony land of New England. The Owen and Donald Davis dramatization of *Ethan*

Frome conveyed its dour subject effectively, and the play and Edith Wharton's original story are likely to remain outstanding in their field. It would be difficult to find another play that represents so well our dark pastoralism. The play *Ethan Frome*, despite the stiffness of its structure, which, since it agrees with the stark drama, helps as well as hurts, has become almost as much of a classic in our theatre as the Edith Wharton novella has been in our non-dramatic literature. The novelist herself, reading the dramatization in the south of France, was of the opinion that it had given her work a new lease on life. She would have been certain of this if she had seen the Guthrie McClintic production with Pauline Lord, Ruth Gordon, and Raymond Massey in the principal parts.

Even this dramatization of a tale of the past became, in the mid-thirties, something more than a purely private tragedy. It acquired another dimension in the writing and staging and in the sensibility of at least a part of its public. The present writer recalls his own response when he wrote the following paragraph—a quarter of a century ago!—in the pages of the *New Theatre Magazine* (March, 1936):

> This tale makes a bitter story of frustration and puritanic inhibitions. There is further tragedy, for those who understand it, in the abysmal poverty of its people, and in the harshness of the encroaching factory system which is throwing its shadow across their fields. Those who concentrate on the love-tragedy in *Ethan Frome* see only half of the play, only one plane of action, only one collection of protagonists. One cannot separate Zenobia Frome's hypochondria, Ethan's suppressed spirit, and Mattie's birdlike pecking at a few crumbs of life, from the bleak poverty which has haunted these characters and has hounded them throughout their existence. The tragedy that ensues arises to a considerable degree from these circumstances, which perhaps might have been underscored more unambiguously. The grim effectiveness of *Ethan Frome* is produced by a compound picture of man and environment.

Awareness of social pressures was of course the order of the day, and it undoubtedly accounted for some of the interest aroused by the primarily medical drama *Men in White*. It was appropriately produced by the Group Theatre, although the Sidney Kingsley play was too mild to please radical members of the acting company. *Men in White* became the Group's first popular success, although more for its personal drama than for any collective issue, as well as for Lee Strasberg's authentic production and Mordecai Gorelik's suggestive settings. The production of *Men in White* introduced Sidney Kingsley as one of the young hopefuls of the new theatre of that time—that is, a theatre of charged realism.

Sidney Howard did not, of course, have to be introduced to Broadway; he had been quite at home there ever since the early 1920's. But *Yellow Jack* showed our ablest playwright-craftsman turning to what was for him a new field, fusing science and social responsibility in a play about the conquest of disease through the collaboration of scientists and common men. A new idealism of factualness appeared in Howard's work and ranged him on the side of the playwright-evangelists who seemed to be taking over our theatre of the "popular front" thirties. But *Yellow Jack* qualifies here especially because in treating a scientific subject, he went on to create a form of documentary drama. The form, no less than the subject matter, should be important to any theatre that pretends to reflect the modern age. For a time, the documentary form of drama was, in fact, explored and presented as "living newspapers" on a large scale by the short-lived Federal Theatre of the New Deal. The "living newspapers" on TVA and slum clearance (*Power* and *one third of a nation*, respectively) proved to be amazingly vivid drama. The more humanized documentary created by Howard in *Yellow Jack* was a more personal creation, and is the best example we have had thus far of a playwright making a *play* out of a wide assortment of facts or *art* out of reportage.

An inevitable selection, *Awake and Sing!* epitomizes the second major decade of our theatre. Every striving special to the theatre of the 1930's appears in this play which introduced Clifford Odets as a Broadway playwright in 1935. An optimism wrung from defeat and desperately maintained infuses the work, and the victims of a soul-confining and demeaning society, of a depressed economy and a bourgeois ethic, are called upon, in the words of the Hebrew prophecy, to "awake and sing." We see in the play, regardless of whatever extravagances attend a youthful work based on a vaguely held ideology, a combination of realism and idealism and of pity and protest. It is a work of memory and hope, spontaneous yet organized, and strongly felt if not altogether clearly thought out. There is rebellion in it against the middle-class family and, by projection and implication, against the middle-class world. At the same time, there is understanding and pity for the young and the old, for children and parents alike. The subject is poverty, both material and spiritual. Odets wrung poetry from the common man's colloquialism, pathos from his stale-mate, passion from his restiveness. Environment plays an important part in the work; it is a dramatic factor rather than mere background. And the author's concern with the role of economic forces represents a strong identification with the common man. The revolt against the bourgeois family is a sort of dress rehearsal for revolutionary action against bourgeois society, which is equated with materialism, lovelessness, and inhumanity. "The revolution," in so far as it is implied in *Awake and Sing!* is homemade, and the revolutionists of the future are educated in the home where they first encounter frustration. *Awake and Sing!* is a work of inchoate genius made cohesive by dramatic form and leftist doctrine, with neither of these factors destroy-ing the human vitality of the characters. It is no wonder that Odets was acclaimed as the O'Neill of a new generation. In the acclaim lay much of the aspiration and hope of the generation of the 1930's. And in what happened to the applauded author after 1939, we see evidence of the decline of apostolic fervor in American society and the American theatre except for a brief period of war-inspired liberalism. With Odets' play we can close an important chapter in the history of the American stage.

The historical position of *Awake and Sing!* is not an invention of hindsight. The author's colleagues and contemporaries were aware of it, and so was the young Odets himself. He retained that viewpoint up to the end of the thirties, when he said to his readers, in a preface to his collected plays, "If you have acquired by now the distressing sense that I am situating myself historically, correct!"

Philip Barry preferred to locate the somber side of his talent—his vision of good and evil—in timeless reality rather than in history or in the historical moment. This is evident in *Here Come the Clowns*, his weightiest, if hardly his most successful, play. It was timely to write a morality play for the age at a moment when evil, complete with swastikas and fasces, was pushing the world to the brink of disaster. The play may be taken as a veritable summation of fear and faith as time was running out for men of good will in the thirties. Philip Barry's symbolism was a distillation of the times, and the practical result was a quasi-allegorical play. This made for a neces-sary, if not necessarily gratifying, abstractness, and the experienced playwright took the precaution of fleshing out the characters and giving the action a specific habita-tion. The personnel of vaudeville had two limitations—those of commonplaceness and littleness; and although the commonplaceness of many of the characters could be overcome to a degree by their bizarreness, what could not be overcome, except in moments of maximum tension when good and evil obtain their greatest intensity, was their littleness.

Only the Devil-figure Pabst, the music-hall illusionist, attains appreciable stature in the latter part of the play—proving, as William Blake said of Milton, whose most impressive character is Satan, that the writer was of the Devil's party whether he knew it or not. In reviewing an off-Broadway 1960 revival for the *New York Times*, Howard Taubman understandably asked, "Why do playwrights so often give the devil the better dramatic case?" *Here Come the Clowns* (produced originally in 1938 by Eddie Dowling), despite its various limitations—for me the greatest are the weakness of the Job-figure Clancy and a general want of soaring language equal to the author's thematic elevation—has continued to challenge the exertions of the theatrical groups that have presented it in defiance of determined minority dissent, like that of the *New Yorker* reviewer in 1960, who resented its "squidlike bursts of melancholy," and consigned the play "to permanent oblivion." In the present anthology, *Here Come the Clowns* represents Philip Barry's striving to express the fullness of his sensibility and his noblest effort to pitch his talent above the Mayfair of modish comedy.

After the ardors of the twenties and the thirties, the dread goddess—Anticlimax! On the whole, the forties and fifties were not particularly eventful in the American theatre but for the emergence of a number of playwrights whose youthful works won various degrees of respect or enthusiasm. Among the writers most likely to be recalled are William Saroyan, Tennessee Williams, Arthur Miller, William Inge, Arthur Laurents, Paddy Chayefsky, and Robert Anderson. The writers of the previous generation were vanishing or their energy declining. Harassed by a major warperiod of some five years, and rattled on the one hand by postwar crises while lulled on the other by prosperity-born complacency, the 1940-60 period consisted largely of reprise, rejection, and resuscitation. Most of the major productions of these years have already been represented in my previous *Best Plays* volumes (*Best American Plays*, Second, Third, and Fourth Series) with some comment on the individual playwrights and the collective enterprise of the theatre.

Out of respect for individual effort and accomplishment, in these volumes I have bowed sufficiently in the direction of the post-1940 playwrights and their persevering elders. In my estimates of their work, I may indeed have erred on the side of generosity. But even so, I think it is correct to say that with extremely few exceptions, the 1940-60 period brought neither conspicuous advances nor marked departures—except in the area of stage production, where theatre-in-the-round or arena-theatre productions made headway. Among the exceptions (up to the 1957-58 season, which is as far as I go in the present collection), I have thus far failed to present only Thornton Wilder's *The Skin of Our Teeth* (1942), a work I have greatly admired but have been unable to secure from the original publishers. For the most recent period, therefore, I here supply only *Harvey*, *The Teahouse of the August Moon*, and *The Diary of Anne Frank*.

Each of these plays has its obvious justification in the Supplement. *Harvey* is here for its warmth and imaginativeness, *Teahouse* for its charm and good will in reflecting America's role in the world after V-J day, and *The Diary* for its re-creation of the conscience of the world, on the stage. A suitable summation will be found in Brooks Atkinson's preface to the published play, in which he writes that the dramatization "reminds us that the Nazis murdered not only lives but life," and adds that in killing Anne Frank, "they murdered a radiant part of the future."

With *The Diary* the present Supplement ends chronologically. It is no great indulgence for me to reflect that, in terms of chronology, the Supplement begins with youth in *Clarence* and closes with youth in *The Diary*—but with a formidable difference in substance and implication. And the intervening period that gave us what the late Barrett H. Clark once called "our new adult American drama" records the intervening changes. In the midst of modish decadence, Alexandrian intellectualism, and the opportunism of show business, the present volume is launched here with no greater claims than that it reflects changes and fluctuations in some forty years of the American theatre. And at the same time it enables the publishers and myself to amplify the coverage of the *Best Plays* series and repair some omissions of plays and some injustices to playwrights.

As for the concluding generalization usually required of a prefatory essay—I am not prepared to say that American drama since 1918 has been "good." But I would maintain that our theatre has produced during this period many good and nearly good plays sufficient unto the day, if not patently sufficient unto the ages. Some of these plays* are submitted to readers and potential producers in *Best American Plays Supplement*.

---

* I am pleased to report that a number of the plays contain helpful modifications or additions supplied by the playwrights themselves. Thus, *The House of Conelly* is presented here with alternate closing scenes, and *The Adding Machine* contains a scene omitted in the original production of the play.

CLARENCE

Booth Tarkington

Clarence was first produced under the direction of George C. Tyler at the Hudson Theatre, New York City, on September 20, 1919. The play was staged by Frederick Stanhope. The cast was as follows:

MRS. MARTYN ...... Susanne Westford
MR. WHEELER .... John Flood
MRS. WHEELER .... Mary Boland
BOBBY WHEELER ...... Glenn Hunter
CORA WHEELER .... Helen Hayes
VIOLET PINNEY .... Elsie Mackay
CLARENCE .... Alfred Lunt
DELLA .... Rea Martin
DINWIDDIE .... Barlowe Borland
HUBERT STEM .... Willard Barton

THE SCENES

ACT ONE: The anteroom to Mr. Wheeler's private office, New York.

ACT TWO: Living room of Mr. Wheeler's home, Englewood, N.J.

ACT THREE: The same. That evening.

ACT FOUR: The same. Next morning.

Copyright 1921, by N. Booth Tarkington. Also copyright in Great Britain and the Dominion of Canada, 1921, by N. Booth Tarkington. Copyright 1948 (in renewal), by Susannah K. Tarkington.

CAUTION: Professionals and amateurs are hereby warned that *Clarence*, being fully protected under the copyright law of the United States of America, the British Empire, including the Dominion of Canada, and all other countries of the Copyright Union, is subject to royalty. All rights, including but not limited to professional, amateur, motion picture, recitation, lecturing, public reading, radio broadcasting, television, and the rights of translation into foreign languages, are strictly reserved. Particular emphasis is laid on the question of readings, permission for which must be secured from the author's agent in writing.

All inquiries concerning rights (other than amateur rights for the United States and Canada) should be addressed to the author's agent, Harold Freedman, Brandt & Brandt Dramatic Department, Inc., 101 Park Avenue, New York 17, New York, without whose permission in writing no performance of the play may be made.

The amateur acting rights of *Clarence* are controlled by Samuel French, Inc., 25 West 45th Street, New York 36, New York, without whose permission in writing no amateur performance of the play may be made.

Booth Tarkington (1869-1946) first gained popularity in 1900 with his eight-eenth-century romance *Monsieur Beaucaire*, which consisted mainly of the adventures of a French nobleman disguised as a barber. This had been preceded by a novel about a country editor's struggle against local political corruption, *The Gentleman from Indiana* (1899), and Tarkington actually won a reputation as a serious writer only with the more or less "social" novels that succeeded this realistic work. Two of these, *The Magnificent Ambersons* (1918), a chronicle of three generations of an Indiana family, and *Alice Adams* (1922), gained Pulitzer Prizes for Tarkington, who also pursued a successful career as the author of books about American youth, such as *Penrod* (1914) and *Seventeen* (1916). But *Monsieur Beaucaire* was the first of Tarkington's works to display his flair for theatricality. He wrote, and collaborated in the writing of, a number of plays after his dramatization of *Monsieur Beaucaire* in 1901 (in which the celebrated Richard Manfield played the romantic role); of these the best known was *Clarence* in 1919. Although the first-mentioned is now a dated romance (it has lent itself to successful spoofing in films), the latter retains the vivacity of natural comedy.

Clarence comes from the first new theatrical season that followed World War I and ushered in the fabulous nineteen-twenties. It was an exciting boom season in New York, with returning veterans and visitors jamming the theatres of such successful managements as the Shuberts, Belasco, Ziegfeld, Henry Miller, and the firm of Cohan and Harris—that is, George M. Cohan and Sam H. Harris. It was also a season to be long remembered for the strike of the New York actors effectively organized for the first time in an Actors' Equity Association led by Frank Gillmore. In the annals of the New York stage, however, both *Clarence* and the 1919-20 season are also remembered for the emergence of the young Alfred Lunt. His talents had impressed Tarkington in Boston, where the actor was performing in the touring company of the author's *American Cousin* (1917). Tarkington decided to write a play for him, and *Clarence* was the result. After discouraging experience with other plays, Tarkington at last had an unqualified success as a playwright and his principal actor enjoyed the first of his many triumphs on Broadway. With other roles filled by Helen Hayes, Mary Boland, and Glenn Hunter, the production was not only successful but memorable.

Clarence did not qualify Tarkington for a major role in the modernization of the American drama. But the romance of adolescence, a familiar ingredient in Tarkington's writing, and the farcicality of the plot in this comedy were not only attractively set forth but invigorated by satire and enlivened by the best dialogue Tarkington was capable of writing. The play can still interest those who are able to visualize it on the stage and enjoy its blithe view of life, which now suggests an all-but-vanished innocence. Tarkington wrote about a dozen other plays after *Clarence*, many in collaboration with Harry Leon Wilson and Julian Street, but without ever approximating its success.

ACT ONE

SCENE.—*The time is any day, nowadays. A room in the President's suite of offices of an impressive financial Institution, on the top floor of the Institution's building in Nassau Street, New York. This is not a business play; but the details follow actuality. There are no maps on the walls, no signs on the doors, no papers on the table, there is no token of business, or of any other form of activity. There is almost nothing in the room, which is in two shades of brown—a "dull-finish" wood paneling up to seven or eight feet on all four walls, and above that a "dull-finish" plaster. The back wall is broken by a door* C., *the* R. *wall has a fireplace* C., *and a mantel of brown wood, in type with the paneling, with a clock upon it. There is a second door; it is in the* L. *wall* C.

Against the back wall are two high-backed settles, or upholstered benches with backs, one up R. *the other up* L., *flanking the door* C., *and another such settle is placed at right angles with the* R. *wall, and just up of the fireplace* R.C. *Another settle is placed at right angles to this one, and facing the fire, forming an* L-*shape nook. These settles are uniformly upholstered in dull green stuff. There is a chair, similarly upholstered, near the fireplace, down* R. *There is a chair at a small table up* L. *The table is of dull wood; plain and expensive—with nothing on it. Another chair, similar,* L.C. *A fire burns in the fireplace, but no coal-hod or fire-irons are seen. When this fire is tended, a person in uniform brings the implements with him and takes them away with him when he goes. (As such a person, however, will not be shown in the play, the matter could be explained to the critics between the acts, in the lobby of the theatre.)*

No one is seen for a moment or two. Then there is the sound of a distant buzzer. A moment or two after this, MRS. MARTYN *enters up* L. *She is a distinguished looking, intelligent woman of middle age, very quietly dressed in black, not a new dress; she wears glasses. She has no hat, and her air is that of a person at home. She goes directly to the chair at the table up* R. *and sits, letting her hands rest in her lap, her manner patiently expectant, as by a familiar routine.*

Several moments elapse; then WHEELER *enters* C. *He is in later middle age, a thoughtful man-of-affairs—large affairs. His hair is still plentiful, but not wavy, though there is a somewhat careless front lock that curves down enough for a cartoonist to seize in a caricature. He is healthy-looking and robust, but his head and shoulders stoop a little. He wears glasses;*

his sack suit is of dark, rough material; his collar is winged in front, his tie is dark with a figure, or a diagonal stripe. He does not wear a white false collar with his waistcoat. He has a short mustache, of course, and is preoccupied. He comes in neither briskly nor languidly, and goes to the fire, where, not stooping, he warms his hands, and chafes the palm of each with its own fingers. He greets MRS. MARTYN *as he is crossing from the door to the fire. This is a daily program and there is no liveliness about it.*

WHEELER. Good morning, Mrs. Martyn.

MRS. MARTYN (*placidly*). Howd'ya-do, Mr. Wheeler. (*Then, as he warms his hands,* WHEELER *goes* R.) I suppose it must be cold, motoring in from the country these mornings.

WHEELER (*with preoccupied geniality*). No, there's a heater in the car. It's just habit for a man to go to a fireplace.

MRS. MARTYN. I hope Mrs. Wheeler's cold is better.

WHEELER (*at fireplace* R., *faintly surprised, absently*). I don't think my wife has a cold. (*Frowns a little.*)

MRS. MARTYN (*explaining*). The other day when she came to take you out to lunch I got the impression she said she wasn't very well.

WHEELER (*thoughtfully, with a very slight note of annoyance*). Oh, she's well enough, I think. May have been disturbed about something. (*As he speaks he has crossed to* C.) Have I appointments with any of those people waiting? (*Crosses to door* L.)

MRS. MARTYN. No; I haven't made any appointments at all for you this morning. At one o'clock you go to Mr. Milly's lunch for the Secretary of the Interior; you have a directors' meeting at three— the Unity—and the Pitch Pine consultation at three-thirty. (*She does not consult a notebook, nor display a pencil or fountain pen.*) Mr. Lindsay and Mr. Vance will do for all the people in the anteroom. (*She seems to stop; he turns to exit* L. *Then, with a faint frown and half-smile, she adds.*) Except one, perhaps.

WHEELER. Who's that?

MRS. MARTYN (*beginning*). It's a soldier who—

WHEELER. In a private's uniform— rather a sickly-looking fellow?

MRS. MARTYN. Yes.

WHEELER. I noticed him waiting out there yesterday too.

MRS. MARTYN. They sent him to Mr. Vance, but he wouldn't tell what he wanted; said he had to see you. Of course Mr. Vance told him that was impossible; he didn't even have a letter of introduction.

WHEELER (*briefly, carelessly*). Oh, well, he's a soldier; see what he wants. (*Turns to go.*)

MRS. MARTYN. Very well. (WHEELER *starts to go out* L., *abruptly thinks better of it and halts.*)

WHEELER (*frowning*). Oh—uh—(*Hesitates momentarily.*) It's possible my daughter and her governess, Miss Pinney, will come in town this morning to see me. Miss Pinney spoke to me just as I was leaving the house, and I understood her to say—I'm not just sure I caught her meaning—(*His manner is the least bit confused;* MRS. MARTYN *looks surprised. He continues.*) She spoke in a low voice, for some reason . . .

MRS. MARTYN. Your daughter did?

WHEELER (*very slightly uncomfortable*). No, my daughter's governess—uh—Miss Pinney. I understood her to say that she wanted to see me in private. . . . I think she meant she wanted to talk with me about my daughter.

MRS. MARTYN. I understand.

WHEELER. I ink she implied that she and my dau' er might come in town and turn up re at the office . . . (*Leaves this tentative.*)

MRS. MARTYN. I'll look out for them.

WHEELER. Thanks. (*Exits* L.).

(MRS. MARTYN *sits looking thoughtfully after him for a moment or two, then rises and moves toward the door up* L. *Just before she reaches it, it is rather impetuously thrown open and* MRS. WHEELER *enters in a state of controlled excitement. She is a pretty young woman,* WHEELER'S *second wife . . . wearing a fashionable dark street dress and hat, with a veil and fur coat.* MRS. MARTYN *utters an exclamation of surprise at sight of her.*)

MRS. MARTYN. Why, Mrs. Wheeler— (*Moves as if to go to door* L.).

MRS. WHEELER (*at door* C., *checking her quickly*). Good morning, Mrs. Martyn. Don't disturb my husband, please. How long has he been here?

MRS. MARTYN. He just came.

MRS. WHEELER. Has Bobby been here?

MRS. MARTYN (*puzzled*). No. I thought he was away at school.

MRS. WHEELER (*with a slight grimness*). He's been home for several days, and he's not going back—at least not to *that* school.

MRS. MARTYN. Mr. Wheeler hasn't mentioned—

MRS. WHEELER (*with a strained smile*). Mr. Wheeler didn't mention that he was expecting *any* of us here this morning?

MRS. MARTYN. I'm sure your coming in town so soon after he did will be a surprise to him, Mrs. Wheeler. Won't you let me . . .

MRS. WHEELER (*quickly*). No. Not now. I really don't want to disturb him, especially as he's probably just got to concentrating on his work. (*Turning to door up* C.) I'm going to run along and do some things I came in town for. (*Turning with her hand on the knob of the door up* C. *and speaking with an anxiety she seeks to veil.*) I don't suppose he's expecting any of the rest of the family? (*Pauses an instant.* MRS. MARTYN *follows* MRS. WHEELER *up* C.). Not my daughter—or—her governess— Miss Pinney?

MRS. MARTYN (*beginning impulsively*). Why—(*Checks herself, then moves toward* R.). Won't you let me ask him, Mrs. Wheeler? I'm sure he'd want to . . .

MRS. WHEELER (*quickly*). Oh, *please* don't—(*Comes down.*) It's one of the things I pride myself on in being the wife of an important man; I *don't* interfere with his work! (*Goes up.*) Please don't mention my . . . my dropping in. I just thought maybe I'd find Bobby here. (*Nods, then exits* C. *A moment later, the door* L. *opens and* WHEELER *appears there, his expression rather disturbed.*)

MRS. MARTYN. Very well, Mrs. Wheeler. (*Closes door.*)

WHEELER. Was that my wife here?

MRS. MARTYN. Yes; she . . .

WHEELER. I *thought* I heard her voice.

MRS. M. She wouldn't let me disturb you. She wanted to know if your son had been here.

WHEELER (*reflectively*). So! Ask Mr. Lindsey to telephone. I shall not be able to attend the luncheon party for the Secretary of the Interior.

MRS. M. Very well.

(WHEELER *retires, closing the door* L. MRS. MARTYN *turns toward door up* C., *when it is again somewhat impetuously thrown open and another member of the* WHEELER *family appears, also under the influence of excitement. He is hovering on the elder side of sixteen; his hair is to the mode of New York, according to the interpretation of his years, and so is his costume, which includes an overcoat. He also wears a pair of pale spats, too large for his shoes—he is strongly conscious of them at times, and also of a large hook-handled cane, too long for him. He removes his hat at sight of* MRS. MARTYN. *At all times he is deathly serious; and speaks quickly; when he doesn't stammer. This is* BOBBY.)

BOBBY (*hastily as he enters*). Howd'y'do. Listen. Look, Mrs. Martyn, have any the fam'ly been here yet?

MRS. MARTYN. Is it Bobby? Bobby Wheeler?

BOBBY (*coming down*). Yes'm, I'm Robert. I . . . Didn't you know me?

MRS. M. You grow so fast! The last time I saw you you'd just got your *first* long trousers.

BOBBY. Well, I do grow a bit; but my first long trousers were practically a lifetime ago.

MRS. M. Yes. A couple of years at *least*!

BOBBY. Listen! I'm glad you're still here, Mrs. Martyn, after all these years.

MRS. M. Oh, yes; I *have* been here practically a lifetime. By the way, your mother was just here. Didn't you meet her as she went out?

BOBBY (*hastily*). No, I didn't. I guess she came in her limousine. I came in on the ten-eleven. *They* were comin' in the tourin'-car. Listen. What *I* want to find out; have they been here yet?

MRS. M. Who?

BOBBY. Why, my sister Cora and— (*Suddenly gulps.*) . . . look! I mean my sister Cora and . . . (*Gulps again.*) . . . and Violent. I don't mean Violent . . . (*Hurrying on in helpless confusion, but with abysmal gravity.*) Listen! I mean her and Cora. Look! I mean Cora and Miss Pinney. Miss Pinney. Cora's governess, Miss Pinney. Pinney.

MRS. M (*shaking her head wonderingly*). No. they haven't been here.

BOBBY. Well, they'll be here pretty *soon* then. I don't want my father to know I'm here if it's convenient. (*Crosses to* R. *Goes to the fireplace.* MRS. M *sits up* R.) We haven't got along too well lately and besides I took his spats. Look, do you suppose he'll care? He's never had 'em on; I don't think he likes to wear 'em. It's right, isn't it? I mean you don't haf to be very old to wear spats, do you?

MRS. M (*gravely*). Oh, I don't think so.

BOBBY (*with added earnestness*). Look; they haven't gone *out* in New York, have they? I been away at school for practick'ly a lifetime; and I haven't had a good chance yet to see what they're wearing.

MRS. M. I didn't know you were interested in "what they're wearing." The last time I saw you . . .

BOBBY. Well, I said that was about a lifetime ago! Look; I used to go around like a scarecrow, but you can't do that all the time because, look; why, how do you look if you do? Do you think it's right to carry a stick over your arm like this? (*Hooks it on his arm.*) With shammy gloves? Or do you think you ought to kind of lean on it?

MRS. M (*gravely*). Oh, I'd lean on it.

BOBBY (*nervously*). Look; I think a single eyeglass may be all right, but look, I think it's kind of silly to *wear* one, don't you?

MRS. M. I suppose it all depends.

BOBBY (*fumbling nervously in his waistcoat*). Look; I guess it wouldn't be any harm to *own* one, would it? Another thing I was goin' to ask somebody, well, f'r instance, s'pose I found a lens that dropped out of a pair of somebody's spectacles, listen: Do you think it would damage your eyes any if you had a hole put in it for a string and kind of practiced with it in your own room? What I mean; look, if you don't wear it all the *time* it wouldn't damage your eyes any, would it? I guess it wouldn't look too well to have it on when—well, look, what I mean . . .

(*There is a tapping upon the door* C., BOBBY *goes* R. *adjusting attire, then adjusts attire generally in some agitation. Two pretty girls are revealed in the doorway. The elder,* VIOLET—MISS PINNEY—*the governess, is well dressed in dark winter clothes, a hat, wrap, and veil; she is about twenty-two or twenty-three. The younger,* CORA, *is a piquant little beauty, a year one side or the other of her brother's age; she is gaily in the fashion, being fond of color, and is equipped to have driven to town in an open car. She speaks cheerfully, as soon as the door is opened.*)

CORA. Hello, Mrs. Martyn! Oh, Violet, *look*! There's *Bobby*! (*They come in.*)

VIOLET (*coming down to* MRS. MARTYN. *Seriously, as they enter*). Mrs. Martyn, did Mr. Wheeler say . . .

MRS. M (*going* L.). Yes. He's expecting you, I think. (*Exits* L. *behind table.*)

BOBBY (*nervous*). Violet . . . (*Gulps.*)

CORA (*turning. Crossly*). What do you mean calling Miss Pinney "Violet"? You've only known her these four days since you got fired from this *last* school, and certainly . . .

BOBBY (*interrupting sternly*). You show a little delicacy, please! (*Crosses to* VIOLET. *With emotion to* VIOLET, *who stands looking at the door* L. *in serious expectancy, biting her lip.*) Vio—Violent . . . Violet . . . I only ask you to show me at least this much consideration that you would certainly observe to a mere—dog!

VIOLET (*turning quickly*). I'm not going to speak to your father about *you* at all, Mr. Wheeler.

CORA. "Mister" Wheeler! Miss Pinney, *do* call the child "Bobby"!

BOBBY (*sternly to her*). Haven't you got any sense at all? (*Goes up* C. MRS. MARTYN *enters quickly* L.)

MRS. M. He will see you and Cora now, Miss Pinney.

VIOLET. I wanted to see him alone first. (*Goes over to* MRS. M.)

MRS. M (*nodding*). That's all right, I'm sure.

VIOLET. Thank you. (*Exits* L. MRS. MARTYN *at the same time exits up* C. CORA *goes across to the door* L. *and listens.*)

BOBBY (*sitting* L.C., *bitterly*). That's a woman's honor, *that* is! Eavesdropping!

CORA (*coming away from the door, crosses to* C.). Door's too thick to hear, anyhow. That's *papa's* stick. The idea of a child of your age—oh! (*Shouting.*) *Look!* (*Pointing.*) Those are papa's *spats*, too! Well, aren't you ashamed of yourself!

BOBBY (*haughtily*). You tend to your own petty affairs.

CORA (*glancing ruefully* R.). Golly! I wish they *were* petty! She's come to tell papa on me!

BOBBY. What about?

CORA (*coldly*). You 'tend to your own petty affairs.

BOBBY. Whyn't she discipline you herself?

CORA. She thinks I'm getting so dissolute something in the father-line has to be done. She'll get into a scrape, all right.

BOBBY (*incredulous*). *How* will she?

CORA. Mama'll have a fit if she finds out about her coming here to papa's office.

BOBBY. Why will she?

CORA (*cryptic, pursing her lips*). School boys needn't ask too many questions.

BOBBY (*sharply*). I'm not a school boy!

CORA (*earnestly. On table*). No; that's so! Bobby, what *did* they fire you for? Papa wouldn't tell me.

BOBBY (*crosses to* CORA *at* C., *loudly*). I want to know why will Miss Pinney get in a scrape.

CORA (*lightly*). Oh—mama thinks Miss Pinney's too young and pretty to be a governess, anyhow!

BOBBY (*growling, not comprehending*). What you talkin' about?

CORA. Of course *I'm* not goin' to tell mama we made this secret excursion to tell on me and discuss how my character's to be saved . . . but when she finds *out* . . . whoopee!

BOBBY. Why can't you even talk so a man can understand?

CORA. A "man"?

BOBBY (*sternly*). Never mind! (*Anxiously, comes forward.*) Are you *sure* it's you and not me, they're talkin' about?

CORA (*not sympathetically*). Why, you aren't in any *new* trouble, are you? Not in just these few *days* since you got sent home?

BOBBY (*loftily, severely*). Never mind, I tell you.

CORA (*goes to* BOBBY *at* C. *Curiously*). Yesterday I heard you saying something to Miss Pinney about Della, that Irish housemaid at our house.

BOBBY (*breathing wildly*). Look here! Were you listening at the lib'ary keyhole?

CORA. No . . . at the sunroom window. What *were* you telling Miss Pinney about Della? I only heard you say something that sounded just horrible.

BOBBY (*fiercely*). What was it?

CORA. I heard you say something about this housemaid, Della, and then you said "a mere passing fancy isn't the love of a lifetime," and then mama called me. What on earth did that have to do with Della? Is she the love of your lifetime?

BOBBY (*bitterly*). If I had a daughter like you, do you know what I'd do with her?

CORA (*gaily*). Feed her on sugar and spice? (BOBBY *turns and goes on to settle. Moving in a half-dancing mockery.*) What are little girls made of? Sugar and spice! What are little *boys* made of? Rats and snails! And puppy-dog's tails! (*Curtsies and pirouettes, as he flings himself down on the settle by the fireplace, desperate with exasperation. She hums dance-music.*)

BOBBY (*with distended nostrils*). You tend to your own petty affairs, I tell you! (*The opening of the door* C. *by* MRS. MARTYN *interrupts* CORA'S *continued evolutions and humming.* MRS. M. *doesn't quite close the door behind her, but stands tentatively prepared to open it again.*)

MRS. M (*at* C.). Do you children mind if I see somebody for your father in here? It's a soldier that's been waiting two days to see him; he seems rather queer; and there are so many people in the anterooms it's hard to talk out there.

CORA. Why, this *is* your place for seeing people, isn't it, Mrs. Martyn?

MRS. M (*smiling*). Not when Mr. Wheeler's own family . . .

CORA (*interrupting earnestly*). *Do* go ahead. I want to study how you do it so *I* can be a woman of affairs some day.

BOBBY (R. CORA, R.C. BOBBY, *pessimistic about this*). Oh, murder!

(CORA *goes to the settle* R., *but kneels on it, looking over the back of it, facing* L. BOBBY *is on the other settle, unseen.*)

MRS. M (*opening the door and speaking to off up* R.). Step in here, please.

(THE SOLDIER *shambles in slowly, his hat in his hand. He is very sallow; his hair is in some disorder; he stoops, not only at the shoulders, but from the waist, sagging forward, and, for a time, to the left side; then, for a time, to the right; his legs "give" slightly at the knees, and he limps somewhat vaguely. He wears the faded old shabby khaki uniform of a private of the Quartermaster's department, and this uniform was a bad misfit for him when it was new. A large pair of spectacles shield his blinking eyes; his hands are brown; and altogether he is an unimposing figure.* CORA *watches him closely, as he comes down* C. *and stands, turning the rim of his army hat in his hands with an air of patience. He seems unaware of anybody, and continues so throughout the next speeches. This is* CLARENCE. MRS. MARTYN *goes to the table* R. *and sits.*)

MRS. M. I am Mr. Wheeler's secretary . . .

CORA (*interrupting gravely*). She's papa's *confidential* secretary. It's just the same as talking to papa.

MRS. M. We didn't want to keep you waiting any longer, when there's no opportunity . . .

CORA (*interrupting her impulsively, but not unsympathetically*). What makes you sag so much to one side?

CLARENCE (*turning his head to look at her solemnly*). It's my liver.

CORA (*blankly*). Oh! (*Crosses to settle.*)

MRS. M (*raising her voice a little emphatically, to put an end to* CORA'S *talking*). You see, Mr. Wheeler himself *can't* see *everybody*; and as you haven't even a letter to him, wouldn't it be the simplest thing for you to state your business to me?

CLARENCE (*hesitating rather forlornly*). Wuw . . . well . . . I haven't any business . . . exactly.

MRS. M (*dryly*). Well, your desires, then.

CLARENCE (*adding a melancholy doggedness to his former manner*). Well—I thought I'd better see *him.*

MRS. M (*with a thought*). Have you ever *met* Mr. Wheeler?

CLARENCE. Not—not yet.

MRS. M (*frowning*). Of course we want to show consideration to any *soldier* . . . (*As she speaks she takes a notebook and a fountain pen from a drawer of the desk.*) What is your name, please?

CLARENCE. Clarence Smum. (*Bang drawer on Smum. He does not actually say "Smum"; this word represents* MRS. M.'S *impression of what she hears. His voice disappears casually, as it were, during the pronunciation of his surname, though he pronounces "Clarence" distinctly enough.*)

CORA (*speaking at the same time so that her voice blurs his*). I do think . . . Clarence is a poetic name! Some people don't, but I think it is.

MRS. MARTYN (*a little embarrassed*). Clarence what, please?

(CORA, *after blurring* CLARENCE'S *reply by speaking at the same time as* CLARENCE, *continues the thought of the preceding speech.*)

CORA. There used to be Dukes of Clarence in history, you know, very wealthy people that the King drowned in a barrel of cider or something. There could hardly be a nicer name than Clarence, no matter what people say. (CORA *still in the same position.*) Were you in the war? (*Her voice is eager and serious.*)

CLARENCE (*looking at her again*). I was in the—army. (*Noncommittal.*)

(BOBBY *rises and looks over the settle at him.*)

BOBBY (*rises, sternly, in a low voice*). You don't know him.

CORA (*quickly*). It's right to speak to soldiers. (*Appealing to* CLARENCE.) Isn't it?

CLARENCE (*solemnly*). If you . . . don't mind . . . what they say . . . back.

CORA (*to* BOBBY). *I* told you.

MRS. MARTYN. Now, if you please, Mister . . .

(*She mumbles after this, covering her difficulty with his last name, though she frowns and glances at her book as if for help.*)

CLARENCE (*in his former manner*). Well, I thought I'd better see *him*.

MRS. MARTYN. If you're looking for a position, I'm sorry. We've taken on more returned soldiers, really, than we have places for. It would only waste your own time . . .

CLARENCE. Well—I thought I'd better—

MRS. MARTYN (*bothered*). I know Mr. Wheeler would never *decline* to see you, but—(*Looking at book.*) your first opportunity, even for a few minutes, wouldn't come until about Wednesday of next week.

CORA (*going to* MRS. MARTYN *at* L. *Impulsively*). Oh, yes, it could! When Miss Pinney gets through telling about *me* in there, I'll *cheerfully* give this soldier *my* time with papa!

MRS. M (*bothered*). My dear, that wouldn't—

CORA (*quickly. Crosses to* R. *of table*). Why, yes, it would! It'd be the best thing that could happen for everybody! (*Determinedly.*) I actually *insist* on it, Mrs. Martyn. (*To* CLARENCE.) It's all right. Why don't you sit down?

CLARENCE (*solemnly*). I will. (*He sits near* R.C. *With great care, as if the action might disjoint some internal connection,* MRS. M. *shuts drawer.*)

CORA. Do you have to take pretty good care of yourself like that?

CLARENCE (*nodding slightly*). I do.

CORA (*with great interest*). Do you wear spectacles because your eyes got gassed?

CLARENCE. No. They say the liver affects the eyes very much.

(*At this* MRS. MARTYN *gives up. She throws the book back in the drawer and closes the latter sharply. Then, in response to a buzzer off, she rises and goes out decisively* C.)

(CORA *is profoundly interested in* CLARENCE's *disclosures. She walks in a semicircle around him to up* R., *looking at him all the time, her expression concentrated and serious; and still looking at him, she drags* MRS. MARTYN's *chair from the table to near him, and seats herself.* BOBBY, *meanwhile, kneels on the settle to face* CLARENCE.)

CORA. How did it *feel* when you first enlisted?

CLARENCE. It felt all right. There was nothing the *matter* with it then.

CORA (*hastily*). I don't mean your liver. I mean how did *you* feel when you first enlisted?

CLARENCE. I was drafted.

CORA. Were you just a private all the time?

CLARENCE. Yes, all the time after I was drafted, I was.

BOBBY. I hope there'll be another war in about a couple o' years or so.

CLARENCE (*simply*). You want another war?

BOBBY. You bet! (*He is severe.*)

CLARENCE. So you could be in it?

BOBBY. Yes, *sir!*

CLARENCE (*gravely*). I wish you'd been in this one. What would you do?

BOBBY. Flying Corps. That's the life!

CORA (*eagerly to* CLARENCE). What did *you* do in the war?

CLARENCE (*with a faint note of pathos*). I drove a mule.

CORA (*astounded*). What in the world did you do that for?

CLARENCE. Somebody *had* to.

CORA. But what *for*?

CLARENCE. They won't go where you want 'em to unless you drive 'em.

BOBBY. Did you meet Major Brooks-Carmel in France? He's a cousin of ours.

CLARENCE. No. I didn't meet him.

CORA. Did you meet Lieutenant Whitcomb?

CLARENCE. What was *his* first name?

CORA. Hobart. Lieutenant *Sir* Hobart Whitcomb really. He was English—

—in the Royal Flying Corps.

CLARENCE. No. I didn't meet him.

BOBBY. Did you meet Captain Arthur McKinley?

CLARENCE. I don't *think* I did.

CORA (*seriously hoping to establish a point of social contact*). Or Flight Commander Larcher? (CLARENCE *shakes his head.*) Or Captain T. P. Schuyler of Englewood? (*He shakes his head.*) Let's see . . . (*Discouraged, she considers.*) Well, I don't know *him* myself, but did you meet General Pershing?

CLARENCE (*shaking his head, seriously*). General Pershing? No.

CORA. Where do you live when you're home?

CLARENCE. Well, nowhere precisely.

BOBBY. Where was your home before the war?

CLARENCE. It was wherever I was boarding.

CORA. How *inter*'sting! Where did your mother and father bring you up?

CLARENCE (*simply*). I was brought up by some cannibals.

CORA. Oh, my goodness! When you were little?

CLARENCE. Yes. That is, my nurse was a cannibal.

BOBBY. My gosh!

CORA (*eagerly*). Didn't your nurse ever try to eat you?

CLARENCE (*as with scrupulous exactness*). No . . . not *me*.

CORA. But didn't they ever try to eat your *fam'ly*?

CLARENCE. No—not my *family*.

CORA. Well, who *did*—

BOBBY (*annoyed, to* CORA). You don't haf to ask so many *personal* questions, do you?

CORA (*earnestly and confidently to* CLARENCE). It's *right* to be personal to soldiers, isn't it—so as to look after their welfare?

CLARENCE (*mildly*). It's very public-spirited.

CORA (*impulsively*). I think our American uniform is *so* becoming, don't you?

CLARENCE (*faintly, plaintive*). Do you mean you think I'd look worse in other clothes?

CORA (*untouched*). No, but I *would* like to know why you drove a mule.

CLARENCE. I didn't *select* that branch of the service myself. (*A faint emphasis on "select."*)

CORA. You mean somebody told you to?

CLARENCE. Yes; I thought it was better to do what they said.

COEA (*earnestly curious*). Did you have to learn to swear at the mules to make them obey?

CLARENCE (*thoughtfully*). No. No, I didn't.

CORA (*brightly eager, rises and goes over to* C.). Were you ever wounded?

CLARENCE (*grimly*). Yes, I was.

CORA (*excitedly to* BOBBY). Oh, he was wounded! (*To* CLARENCE.) Where was it?

CLARENCE. At target practice! (*His voice breaks to falsetto on the word "target," so extreme is his resentment of this shaft of destiny.*)

CORA (*large-eyed*). Was it artillery?

BOBBY (*in despair of her intelligence*). Oh, my! Artillery! (*Throws up his hands and turns away.* CLARENCE *looks at him mildly, then at* CORA.)

CLARENCE (*grimly*). It was. It was artillery.

CORA (*moving toward him in her excitement*). Oh, that must have *hurt.*

(BOBBY *again manifests his opinion of her by a repetition of his gesture. At the same time the door* L. *opens and* VIOLET, *gravely concerned, somewhat severe, stands there.*)

VIOLET. Cora. (CLARENCE *rises carefully.*) Your father will speak to you now, Cora.

CORA (*rising gloomily*). Oh, murder! (*To* CLARENCE.) Here's where *I* get wounded! (*She goes out* L.).

(BOBBY *crosses to* R.C. VIOLET *follows* CORA, *closing the door.* CLARENCE *again carefully sits.*)

BOBBY (*quickly*). See here—

(BOBBY *approaches* CLARENCE, *bringing forth a box of small, gold-tipped cigarettes.*)

BOBBY (*spaciously, referring to his sister*). See here. (*Puts a cigarette, unlighted, in his own mouth, and brings forth a patent lighter from a pocket, at the same time offering, with his free hand, the box to* CLARENCE.) Have a coffin-nail? (*He likes this reckless word.*)

(CLARENCE *bends his head over the box, peering at the cigarettes through his spectacles.*)

CLARENCE. No, no, thanks.

BOBBY (*hopefully*). Oh, you better!

CLARENCE. I believe not.

BOBBY (*disappointed*). Don't you smoke?

CLARENCE. I believe I won't here. You

see, I want to make a good impression on your father.

BOBBY (*glancing* R., *disappointed*). Well —I guess I'll haf to give up the idea. (*Puts up his materials and sits gloomily.*) The family don't know I smoke yet, and if I couldn't lay the smell to somebody else father might make trouble.

CLARENCE (*looking at him without gratitude*). I see.

BOBBY (*producing a pair of dice*). Ever roll the bones? (*Rolls them at his feet.*)

CLARENCE. I doubt if we'd better.

BOBBY (*puzzled, as he picks up the dice*). Don't you shoot 'em? I thought *everybody* in the *army*—

CLARENCE. Well, for one thing, I haven't any money.

BOBBY. Blow in all your pay?

CLARENCE. No; not any. They're still saving mine for me in Washington.

BOBBY (*innocently*). Why, I didn't know they did that. Do they keep it for you?

CLARENCE. Yes, they usually keep it for you—until you don't need it.

BOBBY (*gravely important*). I'll tell you somep'n, if you'll keep it to yourself. (*Showing the dice.*) This is what I got fired for from my last school, too. I've been fired from three schools for it.

CLARENCE (*frowning*). Why, that's just autocracy!

BOBBY (*pleased, but gloomy*). I can't seem to quit it. Once I get a habit fastened on me I can't seem to give it up. Listen: you been in the army. I'd like to ask your advice about somep'n. (*Gets up thoughtfully, facing* CLARENCE.)

CLARENCE (*gravely*). I hope you've come to the right man.

BOBBY. Listen; I'd like to ask you because, look, you been in the army and I can tell by your conversation you been around a good deal. (*Sits.*) Listen, do you think when a man's taken advantage of a woman's inexperience and kissed her, he's bound to go ahead and marry her even is he's in love with another woman?

CLARENCE (*gravely*). Did you kiss somebody?

BOBBY. Yes. I wouldn't again; not her, I mean.

CLARENCE. Was it against her will?

BOBBY. She claims so. (*No especial emphasis on claims.*)

CLARENCE. Does she claim you ought to marry her?

BOBBY. She says if I don't, she'll tell the whole family, because, look, the person that was engaged to her saw this thing happen, and he got mad at her, and she says I either got to pay her damages or run off and marry her. Well, I haven't any money for damages. I wouldn't tell this to everybody.

CLARENCE. No; I wouldn't, either. Who *did* you tell?

BOBBY. Well, I told Cora's governess, Miss Pinney—that just came in here for her. (*Gestures to door* L.).

CLARENCE. What did you tell Miss Pinney for?

BOBBY. Well, I told her because, listen, this *other* affair, it was just a passing fancy, but, look. I think when something higher and more spiritual comes into your life, why, look, you're just hardly responsible for what you do, don't you?

CLARENCE. You mean when the higher love comes, then you get really wild?

BOBBY (*earnestly emphatic*). That's it. You see when this first thing happened I'd hardly even noticed what Miss Pinney *looked* like.

CLARENCE. Miss Pinney is the spiritual—? (*Leaves it unfinished, and* BOBBY *nods solemnly.*) And this other person that has a claim on you—(BOBBY *shudders.*)

BOBBY. It's horrible! Look, you been in the army and everything, what would you do about it?

CLARENCE. I'd go away to school again.

BOBBY. Yes, but look, when you've been fired from three prominent schools, you get kind of a reputation, and, listen, it's kind of hard to get you in. Father's already had quite a rebuff from *one* Principal and he says himself I'm about as big a responsibility for him as anyone in the family.

CLARENCE (*glancing* L. *uncomfortably*). He does?

BOBBY. Oh, yes, and besides, well, look, I don't want to go 'way just when this *other* thing's happened to me. It's the biggest thing in my *life*.

CLARENCE. You want to stay near Miss Pinney. (*Assenting.*)

BOBBY (*simply*). Sure. Wouldn't you?

CLARENCE (*glancing at door* L). Yes, I think I should. (*Then a smile.*)

BOBBY. Because, listen, if I don't, why, look—

(*He is interrupted by the entry of* CORA, L.

She enters quickly and decisively, being in a state of controlled fury. She is almost oblivious of CLARENCE *and* BOBBY, *as she strides to the chair she has formerly occupied and flings herself down in it. Again* CLARENCE *rises painfully and sits.*)

CORA (*as she enters, and not pausing when she sits*). They can go to thunder! If two people ever made me tired, it's papa and Miss Pinney! Puritans!

BOBBY (*superior*). Oh, they got through with you pretty quick, considerin' what you prob'ly been doin'.

CORA (*sharply*). They're not through with me. They're "consultin' "; inventin' the "discipline" they'll haf to put me through! Narrow-minded—

BOBBY (*quickly, shrewdly, and severely interrupting*). I b'lieve you been up to somep'n again with that ole grass-widower!

CORA (*sharply*). He's *not* old!

BOBBY (*triumphant and severe*). That's it! It's that ole grass—

CORA (*interrupting fiercely*). Hush up! (*Rapidly.*) He's one of the most perfect characters that ever came into my life. (*To* CLARENCE, *with rapid and indignant and pathetic appeal.*) I leave it to *you* if grass-widowers aren't just as perfect as the other kind of widowers.

CLARENCE (*heartily*). Yes, just about.

CORA (*oblivious of his comment, going on as before*). I *did* go out motoring with him and I did dine at his country club with him, and danced there till twelve o'clock —and then Miss Pinney came and got me, but I leave it to you: is there any harm in that?

BOBBY (*immediately*). Well, of all the vile confessions—

CORA. You hush up! Of course I *said* I was going to spend the evening with a girl-friend, but Miss Pinney found out— and what I want to know . . . If *you* were my father . . . (*To* CLARENCE.) Would you go into thirty-five fits over a thing like that?

CLARENCE. No. Not that many.

CORA. Why, you ought to *see* those two in there; you'd think they were Judges of the Ex-treme Court of the United States in Washington! What I'm afraid of, they'll never let me see him again! (*Sits, sobs suddenly.*)

BOBBY (*sharply*). They ought to drown you; I never heard such a disgusting story in all my . . .

CORA (*not noticing him except for the two words; it is all poured out rapidly to* CLARENCE). Hush up! She dee-lib'rutly comes to father with this just because mama's only our stepmother and hasn't got any idea of discipline—and you just ought to *hear* her in there, the way she goes on about being responsible for the shaping of my character because she's my governess! She'll get papa so prejudiced against me . . . (*Voice rising to end.*)

BOBBY (*interrupting*). At that, I bet she hasn't told him half she knows about you! (*To* CLARENCE *appealing.*) Don't some women make you sick sometimes? (*With a gesture at* CORA.)

CLARENCE. No; to me she seems attractive. You see, she isn't *my* sister.

CORA (*quickly, earnestly*). Listen; you've been in the army and all that. What would you do if *you* were a girl and in a fix like that?

CLARENCE (*shaking his head, sincerely*). I don't know what I'd do if I were a girl in a fix like that; I don't even know what I'd do if I were a girl.

CORA (*appreciatively*). Well, anyway, I think you're awf'ly nice and sympathetic.

BOBBY (*frowning*). Aw, fluuf, leave it out! *He* don't care what *you* think!

CORA (*rises. Straightening up to look crossly at* BOBBY). How do you know? You don't know him any better than I do.

BOBBY. I *don't?*

CORA. You don't know him as well.

BOBBY. Aw, blub!

CORA (*to* CLARENCE, *with earnest, pathetic naïveté, quickly*). I kept trying to talk to papa about *you* all the time. I told him again and again there was a soldier waiting to see him, but they wouldn't let me change the *subject!* I tried to tell 'em about the cannibals, and how you'd been wounded, and about your liver, and I *did* tell 'em how you could drive mules without swearing—

CLARENCE. That wasn't what I said. I said I didn't have to learn how to swear at 'em. But did your father believe you when you *said* I could do it without?

CORA (*plaintive to tears*). He didn't say: he switched the subject right back to me. Never mind! (*Vindictively.*) They'll be in a fix, all right, if *mama* hears about it!

BOBBY (*scornfully*). *How* will they?

CORA. Why, they can't *tell* her they

ignored her in the matter because she's merely an incompetent *stepmother*, can they? Besides that, there's somep'n else about mama and Miss Pinney and papa. (*Significant and ominous.*)

BOBBY. What?

CORA. I told you once and you were too dumb to understand. I'm not goin' to tell you again.

BOBBY. Aw, blub!

CORA (*vindictively*). You'll see! Just let 'em wait!

(*The door* L. *opens and* VIOLET *comes in, very serious in expression. She leaves the door open.* CLARENCE *rises.*)

VIOLET (*as she comes*). We'll go now, Cora. (*Exit up Center.*)

BOBBY (*with a private significance to* CLARENCE; *taps on shoulder*). Look. (*To* VIOLET.) Vi—Miss Pinney, I'd like to have you meet my friend, Mister—uh—Clarence. (*Coughs. He has gone ahead with considerable confidence passing the word* "Clarence.")

CLARENCE. How do you do?

VIOLET (*gravely offering her hand*). How do you do? (*He takes her hand for a moment; she smiles on him.*) I think Cora said you'd been wounded. I hope—

CLARENCE. It's my liv—(*Checks himself.*)

CORA (*earnestly. At* R. *of table*). Tell her about it. You make it *so* interesting.

CLARENCE. No! I—ah—think perhaps —I don't believe I can.

VIOLET. You were wounded in France?

CLARENCE. No, no, I never got out of Texas.

(WHEELER *enters left.*)

WHEELER. Oh, you're the soldier that's been waiting to see me?

CLARENCE. Yes, two days. I've sat longer than that, other places. I've found it's no use seeing anybody anywhere unless you see the top man.

WHEELER (*not unkindly, but preoccupied*). I suppose you want a position here?

CLARENCE. I want one anywhere.

WHEELER (*shaking his head*). I'm sorry; I wish I had something to offer you, and I wish I had time to talk with you.

CORA (*bitterly*). You always say that! You've got plenty of time to talk with *me!*

VIOLET (*indignantly*). Cora!

(WHEELER *ignores this, though his frown deepens.*)

WHEELER (*to* CLARENCE, *with faint, grim humor*). My daughter has informed me that you can drive mules without swearing; I'm sorry I can't go into your other efficiencies, too. If you'll pardon us—Good day! (*Turns away.*)

CLARENCE (*gulping, nods, speaks resignedly*). Good day. (*Starts to go up* C.)

CORA (*vehemently*). Well, if that isn't rotten mean! (*Fiercely to* CLARENCE.) You wait. (*He halts, undecided.* CORA *goes on with some vehemence to* WHEELER.) You're getting to act just this way about everything, Papa! (*There is a threat of a sob in her voice; she speaks with great rapidity.*)

WHEELER (*quickly*). Get her down to the car, Miss Pinney.

CORA. I won't! You expect me to be taken out home and disciplined and not allowed to see anybody, even if he *is* a grass-widower—

WHEELER (*profoundly annoyed, hastily interrupting under his breath*). D'you realize there's a stranger still in the room?

CORA. He's not! He knows all about it. I told him!

WHEELER (*wholly disgusted, also disquieted*). Oh, Lord!

CORA. I told him *everything!* (*Bursting into tears, but continuing fast and vehement.*) Yes, and I told him how cruel you're goin' to be to me and not let me see *him* any more—oh!

WHEELER. Miss Pinney! Get her in the other office. (*Pointing to* CLARENCE, *speaks frowningly, quickly.*) Wait, young man. (*Pointing to the fireplace settle* L.) Sit down, please. (*Turning to follow* CORA *and* MISS PINNEY L.) For heaven's sake be quiet!

(CORA *is moving* L. *under* MISS PINNEY's *guidance, sobbing* "I will see him! What if he is a grass-widower? I will, too." *They go out* L., WHEELER *last. He closes the door.* CLARENCE *during this has gone to the settle by the fireside and taken his seat there.*)

BOBBY (*with solemn, slow vehemence*). If ever I have a child like that—(*He leaves this horrid contingency in the air, leans on the other settle and looks at* CLARENCE.)

CLARENCE. Well, you *may* not.

BOBBY. I guess father was embarrassed havin' you hear all that family scandal and wanted a chance to ask you not to tell it, before you go.

CLARENCE. I'm *afraid* that's all he wanted.

BOBBY. Look, do you consider the army the best preparation for the after life?

CLARENCE. No; I don't think it's particularly good for that—but of course when there's a war, the after-life is what you're very liable to have happen.

BOBBY. No; what I mean by the after-life is when you marry and enter business.

CLARENCE. I see your point of view.

BOBBY (*solemn*). You know what I told you—about the one that claims—*you know*—

CLARENCE. Yes. I remember. Her young man saw you kissing her—

BOBBY. Well, I'd like to get your advice; you been in the army. How would you *treat* her if you were in my position?

CLARENCE. Do you see her very often?

BOBBY (*gulping*). She's one of our housemaids.

CLARENCE (*impressed with the desperate nature of the situation*). Then, I'd be very polite to her.

(*Sob from* CORA *off* L.)

BOBBY (*sighs*). Well—there's one satisfaction. (*Looks* L.) I guess *Cora's* getting the grand mazoo-mie-zaboo in *there*, all right! (*Amused.*) I expect what makes papa about as sick as anything is your happening to hear so much of the family private affairs this way. He's *awful* strong on self-reserve and privacy and all such stuff.

CLARENCE. I'm afraid he'll hold it against me.

BOBBY. You can't tell *what* he'll do; he's as peculiar a man as I ever knew.

(*The door* C. *opens quickly and* MRS. WHEELER *comes in; her excitement has increased; she controls it, however, and speaks with crisp decisiveness.*)

MRS. WHEELER (*as she enters*). Bobby—
BOBBY. Hello, mama.
MRS. WHEELER. Our open car's waiting down there. Did you come in it?
BOBBY. No, I came on the—

MRS. WHEELER (*with slightly raised voice*). Did Miss *Pinney* come in it?
BOBBY. Why, yes, she—came in it.
MRS. WHEELER. Oh, she *did!* (*Comes down.*)
BOBBY. Sure.
MRS. WHEELER (*pointing at the door* L.). Is she in there with your father now?
BOBBY (*contentedly*). Yes. She's in there.
MRS. WHEELER (*stung*). Oh!
BOBBY. Her and Cora.
MRS. WHEELER (*bitterly*). Oh, she brought *Cora* along?
BOBBY (*grimly*). I should say she did!
MRS. WHEELER. Has Cora been in there with them all the time? (*She does not emphasize this vulgarly; she is jealous, but is, "technically," a lady; and her emotion, though considerable, is not raucous in expression.*)
BOBBY. No, not all.
MRS. WHEELER. I fancy not! (*Walks up and down.*)
BOBBY. They let her out once, but they had to take her back.
MRS. WHEELER (*in a disgusted, low voice*). What a farce!
BOBBY. It certainly was! (*Then, beginning to perceive something.*) What's the matter with you, Mama; you're kind of excited?
MRS. WHEELER (*with quiet bitterness*). Oh, no; I'm not.
BOBBY (*diagnosing*). I s'pose Cora makes you perty mad—
MRS. WHEELER (*speaking quickly*). No, she doesn't. I love Cora; I love both of you, Bobby. It's only that being a stepmother's an unfortunate position. One has to leave "discipline" to fathers and—governesses—which means that fathers and governesses have to consult, very frequently!
BOBBY (*genially*). Cora was sayin' somep'n about that herself. She said: How could they ever tell you it was no use putting it up to you about her, but she thought herself it was goin' to make you perty mad.
MRS. WHEELER (*with increasing emotion*). So, even Cora thought I had a right to be angry, did she? Oh, Bobby—(*With a sudden break in her voice.*)
BOBBY. Why, what's the matter?
MRS. WHEELER (*just barely keeping the sobs from becoming vociferous*). Oh, Bobby, don't any of you see what I have to suffer? Don't you understand what I have to bear every day from your father

and—these "consultations for discipline"? He and Miss Pinney— (CLARENCE *interrupts this emotional confidence with a loud, diplomatic cough. Too preoccupied with her own feelings to be much startled.*) Is someone— (CLARENCE *rises.*)

BOBBY. Papa told him to wait there. (*Formally.*) I would like you to meet my friend, Clarence.

CLARENCE (*bowing as well as his liver will let him*). How do you do? (*He rests his hands on the back of the settle, looking at her.*)

MRS. WHEELER (*touching her eyes with her handkerchief, nods meekly*). Have you been in here most of the morning?

BOBBY (*reassuringly*). Oh, he knows everything that's been goin' on.

MRS. WHEELER (*ruefully*). I should think he would! (*With a pathetic smile to* CLARENCE.) Well you've been in the army; I don't suppose there's any real reason to mind your having seen that we're a rather measly family.

BOBBY (*reasonably*). Why, no, we aren't. I don't see anything to worry the *rest* of you.

MRS. WHEELER (*swallowing*). Well, some of the rest of us do worry, I'm afraid. (*Smiles pathetically.*) Don't let me keep you standing. (CLARENCE *has begun to sag.*)

BOBBY: It's his liver.

CLARENCE (*to him, gratefully*). Thanks. (*Completes his sagging in a sitting position on the settle, where he is again unseen from the greater part of the room.*)

MRS. WHELEER (*to* BOBBY, *sniffing*). He's very tactful.

BOBBY (*as a matter of course*). Sure. (*Regards her placidly.*)

MRS. WHEELER (*tapping her foot*). Have you seen your father at all this morning? Has he been out here at all? (*She speaks rapidly, in a lowered voice, almost a whisper.*)

BOBBY. He came out once.

MRS. WHEELER. Only once?

BOBBY. What *is* the matter?

MRS. WHEELER (*in the same voice, panting*). I don't believe I can stand this *much* longer!

BOBBY. You got somep'n you want to see papa about?

MRS. WHEELER. Yes, I have! (*Going towards door* L.) I can't let things go on like this! (*She intends to open the door and go into the room, but is stopped by a long,* loud wail in that quarter. Then the door is opened, and CORA comes out, her handkerchief to her eyes, wailing, followed by VIOLET, somber, and WHEELER, stern and indignant. When he sees his wife he confronts her with the air of a man who is angrily bearing enough but expects more. Her expression justifies his anticipations. CLARENCE again laboriously arises and after politely coughing, during the next bit of dialogue, without attracting anybody's attention, subsides again into his seat.*)

CORA (*as she comes, sobbing*). I we-yull! You were a widower yourself once, papa. Yes, you were! If you . . . (*Sobs.*) . . . write him to stay off (*Sobs.*) the place—

MRS. WHEELER (*in a sharp, loud voice*). Cora! what is it?

CORA (*with the cry of a refugee flinging herself in* MRS. WHEELER'S *arms, sobbing*). Mama! They say I can't even see Mr. Stem again! They're treating me like a mere dog! I hope you'll just give them fits!

(*Enter* WHEELER L.)

WHEELER (*to* VIOLET). Get her home.

MRS. WHEELER. Never mind, Miss Pinney. I'm only a stepmother, but the *child* seems to turn to me instead of to the governess. That seems strange, of course, considering the *father's* preference!

VIOLET (*her hand to her eyes as if she had been struck*). Oh! (*She turns away quickly.*)

WHEELER (*under his breath to* MRS. WHEELER, *with sharp denunciation*). Shame, Fanny! (*Louder.*) We can't have this going on *here!* Cora! I'll give you five seconds to begin acting like a human being. (*He swings her away from* MRS. WHEELER, *who stands stung and insulted.*) Pull down your veil! (*To* VIOLET.) Miss Pinney, pull it down *for* her, here!

VIOLET (*her voice shaking*). Mr. Wheeler, I can't—

WHEELER (*in sharp appeal*). For heaven's sake, don't *you* get upset! Get her out! Get her home! Bobby, you take your *mother* home, d'you hear me?

(VIOLET *is urging the stricken* CORA *to the door* C.)

MRS. WHEELER (*bitterly*). Thank you, no! It happens that one person prefers me to Miss Pinney. If it's only poor little Cora!

WHEELER (*desperately*). Heaven help

me! (CORA *has instantly begun to sob louder.*) Stop her! Don't take her out there while she's . . . (MRS. WHEELER *begins to sob.* WHEELER *addresses her desperately.*) This is an *office;* don't you understand? (*To* BOBBY.) Bobby, can't you help Miss Pinney quiet your sister? (*He swings back to* MRS. WHEELER, *sternly repeating the expostulatory name.*)

MRS. WHEELER (*sobbing*). Always neglected—

WHEELER. Fanny! Fanny! Fanny! (*She sobs louder.*)

(BOBBY *has gone instantly to* CORA *and* MISS PINNEY *up* C. *and begun shaking his first in* CORA'S *face.*)

BOBBY. You shut up! You *bet* you'll never see him again! (CLARENCE *rises again.*)

WHEELER. Oh, murder! (*He strides desperately away from her toward* R., *and with horror confronts* CLARENCE *across the back of the settle. This is an astounding climax for* WHEELER.) What are you . . . (*Abruptly shifting.*) Have you been here all through this? Oh, murder, I forgot you!

CLARENCE. I don't wonder at all. (*They all have turned to look at him.*)

CORA (*semi-hysterically and pathetically, but quickly*). Clarence, you ought to know, you're a soldier. What would you do if you were treated like this?

CLARENCE (*with considerable significance*). I'd go home with Miss Pinney.

CORA (*choking down her sobs*). All right, but they'll *see*—(*She goes up* C. *with* VIOLET, *pulling down her veil.* MRS. WHEELER *looks at* CLARENCE, *and decides to regulate her agitation for the present, as he seems a fixture.*)

MRS. WHEELER (*with dignified pathos*). Bobby, will you give me your arm?

BOBBY. Why, cert'nly. (*Goes to* MRS. WHEELER *as* CORA *and* VIOLET *go quickly out up* C. MRS. WHEELER *and* BOBBY *start up* C., *she with her head bent forward.* WHEELER *looks at them, frowning, then strides decisively, importantly, at* CLARENCE.) Tell you some more about that, next time I see you. (*Exit with* MRS. WHEELER *up* C. CLARENCE *subsides into his seat.*)

(*Buzzer off.* MRS. MARTYN *enters up* C., *crosses and exits* L. *Silence.* CLARENCE *shakes his head. Decides he's wished away from there. He gets up slowly and forlornly goes up a few*

steps, *having given up.* MRS. MARTYN *enters* L., *a box of cigars in her hand.*)

MRS. MARTYN. Where are you going, Mr.—Mr.—

CLARENCE. I thought he—forgotten me again. He seemed to have several other things on his mind—so I—

MRS. MARTYN. He wants you to sit down, please.

CLARENCE (*sitting* C.). Thanks.

MRS. MARTYN (*offering cigars*). He said perhaps you'd like—

CLARENCE (*accepting*). Thanks.

MRS. MARTYN. He thinks he can find a position for you. But first—he wants me to ask you if it's really true you can drive mules without swearing? (*Seriously, earnestly.*)

(CLARENCE, *preparing to light the cigar, abandons that idea for the present; he looks at her, then at the door up* C., *through which the disturbed family have gone out; then he looks at her again.*)

CLARENCE. Does that mean he expects to give me a position—at his house?

MRS. MARTYN (*dryly*). I think it must! (*Exits.* CLARENCE *half rises; then sits again.*)

(CORA *throws open the door. She is still emotional, is breathless with haste; leaves the door open.*)

CORA (*all in breath*). Clarence, if papa brings you home with him, I want you to promise to be my only friend. (*Hurriedly swallowing a sob.*) You'll *love* it out there, Clarence!

(VIOLET *has entered just before the conclusion of this speech; she is almost running.*)

VIOLET (*seizing* CORA'S *hand and taking her quickly to the door*). Cora! Come along! Come along home, Cora! (*The trick accent which has just barely tinged her former utterances elusively is somewhat more pronounced in this exigency.*)

CORA. Don't forget, Clarence!

(*Exit with* VIOLET, *who closes the door decisively, not releasing* CORA. VIOLET, *as she gets to door, turns and nods pleasantly.* CLARENCE *with a dreamy smile, repeats* VIOLET'S *accent "Come along."*)

CURTAIN

ACT TWO

SCENE.—*A drawing room or living room, and in connection with it a solarium—the 1912-1919 rendition of a conservatory. The walls are paneled, ivory-colored—and the architecture and decoration are altogether symmetrical. Down* C., *in* R. *wall, are double doors of glass, moderate-sized panes, the glass shielded by thin material.*

In the wall space to R. *of this opening is a dark, oval portrait, a decoration merely . . . and there is a similar portrait in the corresponding space* L. *of the opening.*

There is a baby grand piano up R. *on stage by steps* C.—*the other furniture is comfortable, harmonious, and not pronounced or eccentric, or even clever—the tone is kept light, and there is no varnished wood or high polish.*

At back is platform with balustrade on either side and steps. Center down archways R. *and* L. *are the entrances to this room; there are pillars* C. *which opening leads beyond to glass doors* C. *which open to garden.*

This is a sunroom.

In the drawing room the lamps are not lit, and the curtains of the sunroom are pulled back, showing an autumn day beyond . . . mainly the trees (pines and oaks) of a large suburban yard . . . a yard of several acres, with perhaps the glimpse of the rather distant roof of an opulent neighbor.

In the sunroom, with a mop and bucket, is DELLA, *washing the tiles of the floor.* DELLA *is about thirty—not at all like a "French maid"—but very like an American-Irish one at $7.00 a week. She is rather robust and not particularly plain of face—it is possible to understand why* BOBBY *kissed her. At times, finding something obdurate upon the tiles, she kneels and works with a scrubbing brush from the bucket. She is in this position at the beginning of the Act, and is conversing with an unseen person a room or so distant to her* L. *This person makes no visible entrance either now or later, but has a thin voice, higher and older than* DELLA'S, *and also, like* DELLA'S, *there is the faint remnant of an almost worn-out brogue.*

———

THE VOICE. Della?

DELLA. I hear ye, Rosie.

VOICE. D'he say how his liver is to-day? —the poor sojer-boy?

DELLA. He did not.

VOICE. I want to know: what is he?

DELLA (*rising to the mop*). Well, some o' the time he runs the typewriter in the boss's lib'ry upstairs.

VOICE. He do?

DELLA. He fixed the hot water heater in the basement, day before yesterday; he's a bit of a plumber I think.

VOICE. Well, then what'll he be?

DELLA. He'll be anything you ask him to be. (*Sentimentally.*) He's a sweet nature.

VOICE. He'd be better lookin' if it wasn't fer . . .

DELLA. Hush, Rosie!

(CLARENCE *enters* R.—*he is still in his old uniform—he still somewhat stoops and sags at times, but there is an improvement in his appearance. He walks without limping—is straighter; he is no longer sallow or hollow-eyed—his hair is more orderly. His expression is one of patience, as if his army experience and his liver, and the consequences of both, as well as his present situation, were things to be accepted with resignation. He has dispensed with his spectacles. He carries a small, crumpled leather cylinder in his hand, and places it upon the piano. He lifts the piano lid, and sighs.*)

(DELLA *comes down—casually—leans on piano.*)

DELLA. You're lookin' better, Clarence. *What's become of yer spectacles?* (*Pauses in her work.*)

CLARENCE. They told me to wear 'em until I got so I could see without 'em. I could, yesterday. (*He unfolds the leather, displaying a set of small tools.*)

DELLA. Where'd you git them tools?

CLARENCE. I borrowed 'em from the Swede.

DELLA. What kind of tools are they?

CLARENCE (*taking out some of the tools*). Automobile tools. (*He begins to tune the piano with them.*)

DELLA (*simply inquiring*). Are they good fer a piano?

CLARENCE (*explaining mildly*). That would depend on what you did to a piano with 'em.

DELLA (*exclaiming*). You ain't a piano-tuner, now!

CLARENCE. Yes, *now*. (*Scales.*) I noticed one or two of the keys were off. . . . I thought I could make 'em sound better.

DELLA (*impressed*). How d'ju know how?

CLARENCE (*absently*). Well, you see, I've been in the army . . . (*As if this were a part of an explanation to follow.*)

DELLA (*protesting*). Why, Miss Cora says you drove a *mule* in the army!

CLARENCE. Well, I know just as much

about tuning piano as I did about driving a mule.

DELLA (*puzzled*). Clair'nce, what line was you in *before* you went in the army?

CLARENCE. I was working in a laboratory.

DELLA. Oh? In a hotel, I s'pose? (*Then amused.*) Rosie was wonderin' if we ought to call you "*Mister* Clair'nce"! (*Then seriously interested, gently.*) Have y'iver been married, Clair'nce? (*He shakes his head, operating upon the piano. She goes on ominously. Music.*) What a body sees in *this* house wouldn't put 'em much in a mind fer marryin', I guess! (*Music.*) Young lady o' the house under watch to keep her from runnin' away wit' a grass-widdywer; the Missuz crazy wit' jealousy; the boss in love wit' the governess . . . (CLARENCE *strikes a thunderous chord that makes her jump.*)

CLARENCE (*Chord!*). Yes, and the young son of the house threatened with breach-of-promise by a housemaid! It *is* shocking, Della!

DELLA (*astounded*). Who told you that, Clair'nce? (CLARENCE *loudly plays the beginning of "Here comes the Bride," not looking at* DELLA, *but at the arch* R. *appears a man-servant,* DINWIDDIE, *who carries a tailor's double carton of considerable size. He wears a dark sack-coat, black trousers, black bow tie. He enters in a human manner, but freezes with repugnance at sight of* DELLA. *He approaches* CLARENCE. CLARENCE *plays "Here Comes the Bride." Dulcet. Crosses to* L.) What have ye there now, Mister Dinwiddie?

DINWIDDIE. Cook says they're yours. Clarence. She says you brought 'em in and left 'em in the back hall. See you've got your pay from the Guvment, and gone to squander'n' it first thing. Bought yourself some clothes.

CLARENCE (*preoccupied with piano*). Yes. Would you mind putting them in my room for me, Dinwiddie?

DINWIDDIE (*sincerely*). Well, I'm not sure it's my place to do that, Clarence. You been here about three weeks now, and the domestic side of the household ain't able to settle what you are.

CLARENCE. What *I* are?

DINWIDDIE. I mean, are you one of us, or do we treat you as one o' the family?

CLARENCE (*gives him an absent-minded glance, continuing, preoccupied*). It doesn't matter.

DINWIDDIE (*perplexed, but kindly*). I'll take them up for you this time, anyhow. (DELLA *crosses to* L. DINWIDDIE *crosses to* R. *Starts out* R., *but stops halfway and speaks placidly, without looking at either* CLARENCE *or* DELLA.) I'm sorry to see you in loose company, Clair'nce. (*Goes straight out through glass doors down* R.)

DELLA (*going to* C., *bitterly. Comes toward him, angrily agitated*). Clair'nce, would you talk like that of Miss Pinney jist because you'd happened to see somebody a-kissin' of *her?*

CLARENCE (*at piano. Stung*). What? When did anybody . . .

DELLA (*cutting him off*). I said *if* ye did? Now listen: If somebody caught ye bein' kissed ag'inst yer will wouldn't you say *somebody* had to do the right thing by ye?

CLARENCE (*shaking his head*). Oh, if that happened to *me* . . . I'd be very upset . . . I don't know.

DELLA (*goes up* C., *mopping in doorway—emphatically*). Well, it *did* happen to *me*, I *do* know! (*Exits arch* L.)

(BOBBY *opens door* L., *anxious—he keeps out of* DELLA'S *sight.*)

BOBBY (*enters* R. *In hoarse whisper*). Could you get her to "greet" anything? (*Goes up, sees* DELLA—*dodges back* L. *of* CLARENCE.)

CLARENCE. I thought better not try yet. She seems right bitter.

BOBBY (*nervously depressed*). Well, stick by me, Clarence; I cert'nly need help! (*A bell sounds off.* BOBBY *exits hastily* R. *Bell.* DELLA *stands with her cheek against a window in the sunroom, peering to off* R., *getting an oblique view of the principal entrance to the house, evidently.*)

DELLA (*looking off* R.). Well, if that ain't a bold man!

CLARENCE. Bold?

DELLA. It's that grass-widdywer. Miss Cora's. Ain't he callin' at the very front door! (*Turns away.*)

CLARENCE. What's his name?

DELLA. Mr. Hubert Stim.

CLARENCE (*thoughtfully*). Stim?

DELLA (*down to* CLARENCE). He's rich, and he's had the experience o' wan wife; he'd be a good match fer anybody. (*Enter* DINWIDDIE. *Goes up* L.)

DINWIDDIE (*coldly*). Callers? This is no place for all the loose help. (*Music.*)

DELLA (*impotent to avenge herself*). It's a bad world! (*Exit to off* L. *up, with her bucket and mop.*)

(*At the same time* VIOLET *enters up* C. *She wears a quiet, pretty afternoon dress. As she comes in,* CLARENCE *rises from the piano bench.*)

VIOLET (*enters with hat from garden. To* DINWIDDIE). I'll see him in here. (CLARENCE *rises. Exit* DINWIDDIE *up* L.) No, please go right on tuning the piano, if that *is* what you're doing. (*Puts hat on table. She is quick and decisive in manner; somewhat perturbed, too.* CLARENCE *has begun to lower the lid. He turns to her gravely.*)

CLARENCE. You mean you want me to go on tuning the piano while you talk to—?

VIOLET (*smiling*). Yes, I do.

CLARENCE (*restoring the lid to its highest position*). I'll be glad to. (*Sits and resumes his work.* VIOLET *goes down* L.C.)

(MR. HUBERT STEM *enters.* MR. STEM *is about twenty-six, cheerful, good-looking, smart—he wears a homespun or tweed sack suit, and is daintily haberdashed. Goes to* VIOLET.)

STEM. Good afternoon, Miss Pinney. (*He glances at* CLARENCE *with some surprise.*)

VIOLET (*gravely*). How do you do?

STEM. You got my note?

VIOLET. That's why I am seeing you. (*Music.*)

STEM. Ah . . . isn't there somewhere we could go?

VIOLET (*shaking her head*). Nowhere else, I'm afraid.

STEM. Well . . . if this is my only chance to see you . . .

VIOLET (*biting her lips*). Please listen. Mr. Wheeler agreed with me—

STEM (*interrupting cheerfully*). Yes. Mr. Wheeler always agrees with you, doesn't he? (CLARENCE'S *sounding of a key becomes a little more emphatic.*)

VIOLET (*her voice somewhat sharper*). He agreed with me that I'd better see you the next time you came and explain to you clearly . . . (*Music.*)

STEM (*glancing at* CLARENCE, *who seems all the while profoundly occupied with the piano*). This is a splendid chance for a clear explanation!

VIOLET. It won't disturb me in what I have to say.

STEM. That's another thing shows how remarkable you are!

VIOLET. Mr. Wheeler prefers not to see you *this* time himself. (*Music.*)

STEM. I should think he might prefer that! (*Referring to* CLARENCE'S *music.*)

VIOLET (*quietly but grimly*). He wished me to say that in *future*, if you call here, he *will* see you himself, and that if there are notes or telephone messages, *he* will receive them and reply. (*Music.*)

STEM (*hopefully*). But why wouldn't he let *you* be the one to see me and receive notes and telephone messages from me? That would be what I've been working for.

VIOLET (*primly*). I have told you what he asked me to.

STEM (*eagerly*). But you haven't answered my question. (*Music.*) You know what it's about?

VIOLET. No.

STEM (*becoming loverlike—crosses to* VIOLET, *close*). It's about *you*; it's all been just an excuse for that. You've kept yourself out of my way; well, I'm inventive. I'll I'll tell you a secret—it was I that telephoned you. Cora and I were at the Country Club dance. I did it all . . . just for a glimpse of *you!* (*Music.*)

CLARENCE (*as if profoundly concentrated in his work*). B flat. Same old B flat.

STEM (*huskily to* VIOLET). This is intolerable (*Goes* L.)

VIOLET (*as if about to rise*). There's no need to prolong it; I've said all I need. (*Half rising.*)

STEM (*suddenly desperate, goes to her*). No! If you *will* see me with a piano-tuner in the room, why I don't care, you'll have to listen! *You* know why I've taken the only means I could find to even get a *glimpse* of you now and then! Violet, how long are you going to keep me . . . (CLARENCE *bangs the piano.*) Confound it! (*He walks over to* CLARENCE.) See here, my friend . . .

CLARENCE (*rising politely*). It's Mr. Stim, I believe?

STEM (*sharply*). Mr. *Stem*, not Stim! Mr. Hubert *Stem!* Let me say, I'm usually *glad* to see the returned soldiers getting their old positions back, but they do take a holiday sometimes, don't they?

CLARENCE (*innocently*). You mean you'd rather I did this some other time?

STEM (*showing him a bill, unseen by* VIOLET). There'll be this in it: Get your hat and coat and go back to the city: you can tune this piano some other time.

CLARENCE (*mildly*). Tune it? I finished tuning it quite a while ago. All this last you've heard: I was playing.

STEM (*taken aback—he looks at* VIOLET *as if to inquire whether she has noticed that the turner is perhaps insane; then shows the bill again to* CLARENCE). Just get your things and go back to town.

CLARENCE (*amiably*). I can't; I live here.

STEM. What?

VIOLET (*rising*). Oh, this is one of Mr. Wheeler's secretaries, Mr. Stem.

CLARENCE (*rising again quickly, shakes hands*). How- dy'-do, Mr. Stem? It was an Irish person told me it was "Stim." You're not interested in music?

STEM (*dryly*). No. Are you?

CLARENCE (*crouching and again sitting on the piano bench*). Oooh! (*He whispers this, appreciating that* STEM *has scored.*)

STEM (*turning to* VIOLET). Miss Pinney, won't you come out for a breath of air?

VIOLET (*shaking her head*). Thanks. (*Music.*)

STEM (*desperately to* CLARENCE). Won't *you* come for a breath of air?

CLARENCE (*mildly surprised*). You want *me* to take a walk with you?

STEM. Well, if you'd go ahead, I'd come after you, and take you over and show you my place. Aren't you interested in Nature?

CLARENCE (*shaking his head*). No. All I care for's my music.

STEM. Your what?

CLARENCE (*politely*). Perhaps you'd rather I didn't . . . (*With a gesture to the keys.*) Shall I . . .?

VIOLET. Do.

STEM (*entreating hoarsely*). Violet, won't you?

(*She shakes her head, and places a piece of sheetmusic before* CLARENCE *on the rack.* VIOLET *goes up to piano and kneels on settee.*)

VIOLET. Do you know this?

CLARENCE (*quickly changing the air*). Well, I can *try* it. (*Does so.*) It's pretty, isn't it? Kind of sad.

STEM (*going up step and on platform. Controlling himself*). I think I'll say good afternoon!

(VIOLET *nods.* CLARENCE, *half-rising, bows graciously.* STEM *strides out* R. CLARENCE *resumes the air he is playing.*)

CLARENCE (*playing*). I couldn't tell, but it seemed to me almost as if you wanted to get rid of him.

VIOLET (*dryly*). Did I? (*Goes down stage of piano, arranging sheet music on the piano.*)

CLARENCE (*turning from the keys*). It seemed almost as if you'd taken some prejudice against him.

VIOLET (*sinks into seat at piano*). Well, don't you think it's pretty odious of a man, when he knows a girl dislikes him, to pursue her by pretending to pursue a younger girl who's in her charge?

CLARENCE. Are you consulting me on this point because I've been in the army, or more on the ground that I'm a person?

VIOLET (*smiling faintly*). More on *that* ground.

CLARENCE. That surprised me. However, speaking to your point that a pursuer belonging to the more cumbersome sex becomes odious to a fugitive of the more dexterous sex, when the former affects the posture of devotion to a ward of the latter . . . (*He paused, judicially, for a moment—and she interrupts him, amused.*)

VIOLET (*simply curious*). Were you a college professor before the war?

CLARENCE (*conscientiously*). Not a *professor.*

VIOLET. Surely not just a student?

CLARENCE. No. Not a *student.*

VIOLET. Well, then, what . . .

CLARENCE (*earnestly*). What I was leading to was, that I, personally, am indifferent to your reason for finding this young man, or any other young man odious.

VIOLET (*somewhat offended*). Thank you. I didn't put it on *personal* grounds. I believe. (*Rises and goes* C.).

CLARENCE (*rises*). The *reason*, I say, is indifferent to me. I merely experience the pleasure of the *fact.*

VIOLET (*surprised and puzzled*). What fact?

CLARENCE. That you don't like him. (*Returns to piano and tools.*)

VIOLET (*staring*). I believe you are the queerest person I ever met.

CLARENCE (*nodding*). That's what my grandmother always said of my grandfather, and they *had* been married sixty-one years. (*Gathers his tools.*)

VIOLET (*impressed*). Your grandfather was as queer as that?

CLARENCE. No. Only to grandmother. (*Starting to go out* R.).

VIOLET. Are you *very* much like him? (CLARENCE *stops abruptly and turns to her.*)

CLARENCE. I'm just as much like my grandmother; you see, I'm descended just as much from her as I am from him.

VIOLET. I never thought of that. (*Laughs.*)

CLARENCE (*earnestly*). Well, after this, won't you think of me as just as much like her as like him?

VIOLET (*rather stiffly*). Isn't *that* a little *personal?*

CLARENCE. Personal? Good gracious! You've just been discussing *my* most intimate family affairs: my grandfather, my grandmother ...

VIOLET (*checking him impatiently*). Never *mind!* I *will* think of you as just as much like your grandmother as your grandfather!

CLARENCE. It's very kind of you to think of me.

VIOLET (*sharply*). I didn't say ...

CLARENCE (*cutting her off, rapidly*). It's kind because you've got so many to think of: I want you to think of me; Mr. Stim ... Stem! ... wants you to think of him; Bobby wants you to think of him; Mr. Wheeler wants you to think ...

VIOLET (*interrupting angrily*). That will do, please!

CLARENCE. Well, but doesn't ...

VIOLET (*sharply—quickly*). You *know* my position in this house; do you think it's manly to refer to it?

CLARENCE. I don't know about "manly"; maybe this is where I'm more like my grand*mother*. My idea was merely that since so many want you to think about them, if you'd just concentrate your thoughts on somebody that had been in the army, it might avoid ... complications.

VIOLET (*bitterly*). Do you suppose I'd stay in this house another hour, if I hadn't given my word to Mr. Wheeler I'd stand by Cora, until she comes through this nonsense? He asked me to just stick it out until the child's come to herself again, and I gave him my word I'd do it. It seems *you* take Mrs. Wheeler's view of me!

CLARENCE. But, Mr. Stem ... he's ...

VIOLET (*sharply*). If I told Cora the truth about him, she'd only hate me. If I left her, she'd do the first crazy thing she could think of. She's *really* in *love;* it's a violence, but it may last a long while.

CLARENCE. She tells *me* it's "forever"! I'm her only friend and she made me her only confidant ... except her stepmother, and Della, and Dinwiddie, and both of the chauffeurs. She told us that when she first saw him, she knew it was forever. (*Amiably.*) Do you think it's advisable, Miss Pinney, for ... anybody to fall in love ... permanently?

VIOLET (*turning away coldly, then facing him*). I don't think I feel like holding a discussion with you about such things ... or anything else.

CLARENCE (*looks at her, his head on one side, philosophically*). That must be all, then. (*Starts out R, but pauses as she speaks.*)

VIOLET. When you first came here, I thought you were another friendless person, like me; pretty well adrift in the world, so that you had to make yourself useful in whatever you could find, just as I did. I did make that mistake; I thought I'd found a friend!

CLARENCE. Couldn't I keep on ... being found?

VIOLET (*decisively, but with feeling*). Thank you, no! Not after what you said a moment ago! I'm glad you said it, though, because I like to know who my enemies are! (*Crosses L., then up to window.*)

CLARENCE (*blankly*). Oh? (*He puts his head on one side, looking at her. She sits R.*).

(CORA *is heard off up L., in the sunroom, calling.*)

CORA (*off up L.*). Clarence! Clair-*uh*-unce! (VIOLET *turns up. She comes in seriously and eagerly up R., in the sunroom, wearing a modish afternoon dress.*) Clarence, Dinwiddie says you've been throwin' your money around on clothes. (*As she comes down.*) I wonder how you *will* look out of a uniform! Funnier than ever, I expect, don't you? (*Genially.*) Don't you think maybe you will, Clarence?

CLARENCE. No. I think it'll be an improvement.

CORA. Bobby says you wouldn't know what kind of clothes to order, Clarence.

CLARENCE. That is, he thinks they'd be different from his?

CORA. Do put 'em on.

CLARENCE. Why, I was going to. (*Goes R.*)

CORA. We all want to see you in 'em. (*She imperfectly suppresses a giggle.*)

CLARENCE (*at door, nodding*). So do I.

(VIOLET *goes to couch and sits.*)

CORA. You know, Clarence, you always did seem an awfully peculiar kind of a soldier.

CLARENCE. That's what the officers kept telling me.

(CLARENCE *exits* R.)

CORA. Isn't he the queerest ole thing? He's awful sympathetic and useful around the place, and so mysterious and likable; but I overheard mama telling papa last night she thinks he must be crazy for hiring him just because he could drive mules without swearing, and nobody knows a *thing* about him. Papa said it was mostly because Clarence was a stranded soldier and he didn't have any place for him except to dictate his letters to when he was home, but he guessed maybe he *was* crazy to do it. (*Pauses.*) What's the matter with you?

VIOLET. Nothing.

CORA. You look the way you do when you're teaching me Latin. Did you know Clarence had begun tutoring Bobby in Math? Bobby says Clarence is a Wiz. at Math. Oh, yes, and I . . . (*Sits.*) overheard Della talkin' to Bobby, and then Bobby talkin' to Clarence, and Bobby's put all his affairs in Clarence's hands. (VIOLET *sits.*) Clarence said he'd do the best he *could*, but he thought Bobby belonged in Salt Lake City, whatever he meant by that. Isn't he *weird!*

VIOLET (*frowning*). Yes; I think he is . . .

CORA. By the way, who was here a while ago?

VIOLET. Someone called on *me*.

CORA (*beginning to be suspicious*). Who was it?

VIOLET. Cora, don't you understand —when a person says "someone," that means not to ask?

CORA (*more suspicious*). I believe I'll ask Dinwiddie. (*Rises, goes* C.)

VIOLET. It won't do you any good; he won't tell you.

CORA. Why won't he? Did anybody give him orders not to tell me?

VIOLET. Never mind that, Cora.

CORA. *You* did!

VIOLET. If I did, I had authority for it.

CORA (*sharply*). Then it *was* Hubert Stem! You can't deny it!

VIOLET (*stiffly*). I'm not called upon to "deny" anything to you, Cora.

CORA (*goes up to window* C. *Loudly*). It *was!* He was *here!* It was *him!*

VIOLET (*wearily, but sharply*). It was "he," Cora. You *must* begin to look after your pronouns.

CORA (*coming down again. Loudly, almost tearfully*). What do I care for your old pronouns! You *know* he was *here!* He was here, tryin' to see me, and you kept him *from* it. You drove him away, I know you did! You drove him away!

VIOLET (*gravely, quickly*). No. I *wanted* him to go, but if anybody drove him away, I think it was Clarence.

CORA (*furiously*). That upstart? He dared to drive out a guest of mine? Then just wait till I get a chance at *him!* Does Clarence think he's *master* around here? (*Instantly becoming emotionally pathetic, her voice loud and tremulous.*) Which chair did he sit in when he was here?

VIOLET (*coldly*). He sat on the piano bench. (*Crosses down to seat* R.C.)

CORA (*loudly plaintive*). Oh! (*She sinks to the floor by the piano bench, her arm caressingly over it.*) Oh, Hubert! Poor Hubert! You came to find *me*, in spite of everything, didn't you? And they treated you so cruelly, so . . .

VIOLET (*sharply*). Mr. Stem stood over *here!* It was Clarence on the piano bench.

CORA (*jumping away from the bench with an outcry, as if it had stung her*). Ah! (*Jumping up.*) What did you *tell* me Hubert sat there for?

VIOLET. You're not going to go through it *again* are you, with the couch?

CORA (*heaving angrily*). What did that horrible Clarence *do* to him to drive him out?

VIOLET (*gravely*). Well, he didn't use profanity. You know, that's one thing your father said he engaged Clarence for; because he said he could *drive* without strong language.

CORA (*outraged*). Do you mean to insinuate that Mr. Stem is a mere mule?

VIOLET (*quickly*). Oh, get hold of yourself, Cora.

(*Enter* BOBBY *from up* L. *on balcony.*)

CORA. I won't! (*Determinedly.*) I'll let *everybody* understand this much: If there's got to be any insinuations about drivin' mules in this family, I can be just as mulish as anybody! Yes, and I *will* be too!

(BOBBY, *during this speech, is in a state of exasperation.*)

BOBBY (*coming down*). You certainly will! Oh, I heard you, but you're wrong! I guess if there's goin' to be any mulishness in this fam'ly, it'll be from me! How often do I have to tell you you're not speak to Violet like this? Shame on you!

CORA (*her eyes wide with fury*). Why, you mere, miserable little . . .

BOBBY (*vehemently cutting her off*). Don't you know that this is one of the most spiritchal and highminded women that ever lived? (*Gesticulating at* VIOLET.) The idea of your troubling *her* about your petty amours with that Hubert Stem . . . (*He is interrupted in full gesture.* DELLA *has followed him, and at this moment makes her appearance at the* R. *side of the sunroom opening, up* C. *Except for her head, she is only partially seen.*)

DELLA (*rather ominously*). Could I have another word wit' ye, Mr. Robert?

BOBBY (*looking over his shoulder fiercely*). No, you can't! Go 'way from there! (DELLA *withdraws. He returns instantly to the attack on* CORA.) Let me tell you, if there's goin' to be any mules in this fam'ly—

CORA (*violently*). You hush up! (*She flings herself into a chair, kicking her heels up and down on the floor, and repeating.*) Hush up! Hush up!

BOBBY (*indignantly*). I'll make myself heard! You never did have any more idea of behavior than the merest scum! Why, look at *me* . . . (*Glancing to where* DELLA *has appeared.*) why, I got more troubles in my private life than people would have any conception of . . . you don't hear *me* howlin' around like some frowsy cuttlefish, do you?

CORA. Hush up!

BOBBY. I tell you when you attack this lady, that soils her soul by bein' your governess, you simply an' positively put a stain on your whole vile sex!

VIOLET (*quickly, crossly*). Bobby! I can do my own defending, please, and I'm a member of the same sex.

BOBBY (*vehemently*). No, you're not! I'd never believe it! There may be *some* women the same sex as Cora, but not you! It was only the third or fourth time I ever saw you, a kind of a somepin' came over me and I wanted to live a

higher life. (CORA *bursts into wild laughter. He instantly whirls upon her, shouting.*) You hush up! What you laughing about? I believe you're historical.

(MRS. WHEELER *has entered up* C. *from up* R. *during this. She speaks quickly.*)

MRS. WHEELER (*annoyed*). What *is* the din? Really Miss Pinney, if you can't keep better order than this . . .

CORA (*jumping up, laughing loudly*). Bobby says a somepin' came over him when he saw Violet . . .

MRS. WHEELER (*quickly*). Yes; that's not unusual, it seems!

(*The scene is played rather rapidly.*)

CORA (*going in*). And he wants to live a higher life!

MRS. WHEELER. That's not *always* her effect!

BOBBY. Well, what if I do? That's no disgrace, is it?

CORA (*at* BOBBY). I know something on you! (BOBBY *wheels.*) Not any higher life, either! (*This is a vicious threat.*) You wait till papa comes!

BOBBY. If *I* ever catch that Hubert Stem around this place . . .

CORA (*choking at the name, crosses to* MRS. W.). Oh, mama! He was here! (*Emotional again.*) He came to try to see me! That little brute of a Clarence drove him *out!*

MRS. WHEELER (*incredulously*). Clarence did?

VIOLET. I take the responsibility for that!

MRS. WHEELER (*loudly*). You take a great deal of responsibility, Miss Pinney!

BOBBY (*hotly*). Well, papa wants her to, doesn't he?

MRS. WHEELER (*emphatically*). Yes! He does!

BOBBY. Who else but Miss Pinney has *any* control over this . . . this . . . this . . . (*His denunciatory finger leveling at* CORA.)

CORA (*shouting*). I'll get you, Bobby Wheeler! (*She shouts "Hush up!" throughout the following speech.*)

BOBBY (*bawling*). I'll take that Hubert Stem, and I'll pull his legs and arms off like a mere spider!

(WHEELER *enters up* R. *He has just come from his office, and has on his hat and overcoat; a folded newspaper is in his hand. Neither* CORA *nor* BOBBY *are aware of him.* CORA *continues to shout "Hush up!" and* BOBBY *goes on.*)

BOBBY. You threaten *me*, and I'll show

you who's master in this house! You got the worst disposition . . .

(WHEELER *strikes the newspaper several times, quickly and sharply, into the palm of his hand for silence, which stops them. He is indignant, disgusted, and tired.*)

WHEELER. Stop it, stop it! I could hear you at the front door!

CORA (*goes to* WHEELER *at* C.). Papa, I found out today Bobby kissed Della, and she says he's got to marry her or breach o' promise, an' she'll tell the fam'ly on him! *Now* he's in love with Violet! (*Whirling on* BOBBY. *Goes up* R.) Didn't think I knew that, did you?

BOBBY (*hoarsely*). Cuttlefish!

(MRS. WHEELER *crosses to couch, sits.*)

WHEELER (*sternly to him*). I'll speak to you later. (*Taking off hat and coat.*)

BOBBY (*alarmed, but vindictive. Crosses to* WHEELER). Her grass-widower was here again. We had to drive him out, and she got convulsions.

CORA (*beginning to wail*). Oh! (*This sound continues.*)

WHEELER (*handing his hat and coat to* BOBBY, *decisively*). Take these out.

BOBBY (*bitterly*). I'll do it. (*Passes behind* WHEELER *and up off* R.)

WHEELER. Cora, either stop that, or go to your room and wash your face.

CORA (*going up with extreme pathos, weeping*). Wash my face, wash my face, wash my face . . . (*Up off* R.)

WHEELER (*up* R.C., *frowning*). I'll go over this with you, Miss Pinney.

MRS. WHEELER (*on couch* R. *Burlesquing politeness*). Oh? With Miss *Pinney?* Do excuse me! It's so unusual—your wanting to be alone with her! I didn't understand for the moment you wished *me* to leave the room!

WHEELER (*drearily and disgustedly appealing with a gesture, but not rising or turning to her*). Oh, please, Fanny!

MRS. WHEELER (*angry, yet plaintive*). As it seems *I'm* nothing in *anybody's* life, I—

WHEELER (*interrupting sharply*). Oh, for pity's sake!

MRS. WHEELER (*sharply, breathing quickly*). Oh, I'll not interfere with this charming—interview! (*Exit up* C. *to off* L.)

(VIOLET *swallows painfully, her lip quivers; she controls herself and comes near* WHEELER, *who still sits rubbing his head.*)

VIOLET (*in a low, quick voice*). Mr. Wheeler, I think you'll have to relieve me of my promise.

WHEELER (*not changing*). No, I can't do it. (*Painfully, but as if absently.*)

VIOLET. I really think you'll have to. I can't go on—I really can't.

WHEELER (*in same manner*). No. You said you'd stick to the job and see the children through. I can't depend on anybody but you. I've got to keep you to your word. (*Slight emphasis on "got."*)

VIOLET. But it's getting beyond my strength—and my temper.

WHEELER. I know. I know. The children get beyond your strength and my wife gets beyond your temper—(*No pause.*)

VIOLET (*in a low voice, affirmatively*). Yes. (*No pause.*)

WHEELER. But I've got to keep you. Sit down. will you? (*He begins to pace, across and back.*) Let's see if we can think what's to be done. Was that man Stem here?

VIOLET. I gave him your message.

WHEELER. Did he try to hang about and see Cora?

VIOLET. He tried to hang about. Clarence got rid of him.

WHEELER (*musing absently and gloomily*). Odd thing about—Clarence. I don't know just why I took him up and brought him out here. Crazy sort of impulse—anything but like me to do that. He seems all right, does he?

VIOLET. Yes, I think so. (*Noncommittal. Then she bites her lip, remembering her enmity.*)

WHEELER (*still absently*). Friendly sort of friendless creature. I had a—a feeling —if he could drive an army mule with such courtesy—well, I don't know just what it was—a feeling that in some way he'd be a good influence—here. (*Turning toward her.*) Is Cora's story true about that damn boy?

VIOLET. About Bobby? (*Pauses.*)

WHEELER. Oh! You don't want to tell on him? Is it his behavior—that makes you want to leave?

VIOLET. No. But I think I must go, Mr. Wheeler.

WHEELER. Where would you go? Have you a chance at another position?

VIOLET. No.

WHEELER. What would you do?

VIOLET. Look for one, I suppose.

WHEELER (*abruptly*). I can't let you do that. (*She looks up, somewhat startled by his tone.*)

VIOLET. What did you say—

WHEELER (*swallowing, speaks with sorrowful feeling, simply*). I said I couldn't let you do that. See here; I suppose I've seemed to you just a commercial machine—head of a big business and head of an unhappy, rowing family, like so many of us machines. Well, I'm *not*—not altogether. (*Sits on couch* R.) I'm a pretty tired man. The naked truth is I'm pretty tired of the big business and pretty tired of the family. It's so. Sometimes I don't know whether I'm an old man or just a sort of worn-out boy; I only know the game I play isn't worth the candle, and that I want to get away from the whole thing. (*His voice trembles a little.*) I don't think I *could* stay with it, if *you* don't stay and help me.

VIOLET (*touched*). Oh, *poor* Mr. Wheeler!

WHEELER. If you give *me* up, I'll give everything up. (*His tone is quiet throughout, but he is in desolate, utter earnest.*)

VIOLET (*gentle but troubled and a little breathless*). Oh, I don't think you should quite say that, should you?

WHEELER. I've never seen how people could get away from the truth. I've got people I can rely on in *business*—but you're the only person I can fall back on out *here*.

VIOLET. Oh, no!

WHEELER. And a man's house is more important than his business, too. What am I going to do about it?

VIOLET (*in a low, troubled voice*). I—don't know. (*She stands with her head bent, turned away. He is profoundly grave.*)

WHEELER. If you can't stand it here—

VIOLET (*feebly, blankly*). What?

WHEELER (*his voice husky, but somewhat louder than it has been*). If you can't stand it, *I* can't! If you quit, we both quit.

VIOLET (*rises, plaintive*). I don't think I understand that. I'm free to go, Mr. Wheeler, but—

WHEELER (*rising. With a kind of husky, but not noisy, desperation*). Well, I can be free, too.

VIOLET (*entirely taken aback*). Oh—(*She falls back from him, her hand to her cheek, staring at him. At the same time a long, strange wail is heard up off* L. *The two remain in their present attitudes, freezing with horror. The wail continues, growing louder. It issues from the throat of* MRS. WHEELER, *it appears. She comes in from the arch* L., *weeping, still wailing.*)

MRS. WHEELER (*her wail becoming verbal*). I heard every word! You needn't run away—I'll go! Drive *me* out; *I* haven't got anyone to go with me! (*Loudly.*) Oh, I'd *take* him if I had! Oooh—(*The wail increases. She flings herself in a chair* L.C.)

WHEELER (*desperate, wailing himself*). Ah, murder! Who was talking about going *with* anyone? (*Another wailing, not unlike* MRS. WHEELER's *in quality, is heard off up* R. *It likewise approaches, though slowly; the two sounds mingle.*) Oh, my soul! I can't stand this! (WHEELER *comes down. To* VIOLET *passionately.*) Could you stop Cora just this once?

VIOLET (*goes down* R., *sharply*). It isn't Cora's voice.

WHEELER. It's Cora! (*To* MRS. WHEELER). For pity's sake, Fanny, pull yourself together! (*He starts up* C., *shouting fiercely.*) Cora! Stop it! Stop it! Cora!

(DELLA *appears in the sunroom, walking backward from off* R. *She is in a high state of excitement, lifting and dropping her arms in a strange rhythm, as if keeping time to some grotesque stimulant.* WHEELER, *without pausing, shouts at her.*)

WHEELER. Tell Cora she's got to stop it! Tell her I say—

DELLA (*shouting*). It ain't her! It ain't Miss Cora! (*Struck by this, and by the peculiar nature of the approaching sound,* WHEELER *falls back.*)

WHEELER. What!

DELLA. It's *him!* It's Mister Clair'nce all dressed up and wastin' his money on musical instruments!

WHEELER (*hoarsely, crosses down* R.). Oh, my soul!

(*The sound has now resolved itself into the loud cry of a saxophone rendering a march.* CLARENCE *marches on in the sunroom; he is the musician. Behind him* CORA *prances, clashing the silver covers of two dishes together for cymbals, and loudly singing the air. Behind her* DINWIDDIE *pompously dances, beating a tray with a large spoon, and whistling. This procession evidently intends to move along the sunroom from off* R. *to off* L., *but is arrested by* WHEELER's *vehemence.*)

WHEELER (*bellowing*). What in the name of—(*They stop; so does the music.* MRS. WHEELER *has stopped crying and has risen.*)

DINWIDDIE (*alarmed*). Oh! (*He bolts to off* R.)

WHEELER (*gasping*). What in the—

CLARENCE (*removing the saxophone from*

his mouth). We didn't know there was anybody here.

CORA (*enthusiastically*). *Look* at him, papa! (CLARENCE *has made a remarkable change in his appearance; he wears a beautifully fitting new suit of exquisite gray or fawn material, and he has been at pains to brush his hair becomingly; has a scarf-pin in his tie, and altogether is a most dashing figure.* CORA *goes on, without pausing.*) Isn't he *wonderful*, Mama?

MRS. WHEELER (*seriously and emphatically*). Why, *yes!* He *is!*

CORA (*bringing him down, holding his sleeve*). He went and bought *those* (*his clothes.*) and the most *glorious* evening things all out of what he made in the war, and he borrowed the Swede's saxophone and never even told us he could play it! Just look at him! Turn around! (*Obeying her gesture, made as she speaks, he solemnly turns round, so that they may see his back.* CORA *is carried away by helpless admiration. She almost moans this; then as he faces front again.*) Oh, Clarence!

(BOBBY *enters up* L.C. *from off up* L. *and approaches* CLARENCE.)

CLARENCE. I'm afraid we disturbed— (*He stops, meeting* BOBBY'S *estimating eye.*)

(BOBBY *walks all round him,* CLARENCE'S *eyes following him wonderingly until* BOBBY *passes behind him. Then* CLARENCE *looks over the other shoulder as* BOBBY *comes round on that side.*)

BOBBY (*condescendingly*). Pretty good! Pretty good!

CLARENCE (*blankly*). What—

BOBBY (*with a gesture to mean the new outfit*). Pretty good.

CORA (*vehement*). Nobody ever knew he could play at *all!* He never *said* a thing—

CLARENCE (*interrupting solemnly*). They transferred me from the band to the— mule-team.

CORA (*jumping up and down*). Come on; we've got to play some more—(*She pulls at his sleeve. Takes* CLARENCE *to piano.*) Come play his accompaniment, Violet.

VIOLET (*controlling her agitation, answers hastily*). No. I can't. (*Crosses* R.)

CLARENCE. I'm afraid we might disturb—(*He looks from* VIOLET *to* WHEELER.)

MRS. WHEELER (*sharply*). No, you won't disturb *anybody!*

(WHEELER *comes down to chair* R.)

CLARENCE. I'm afraid—we might—

MRS. WHEELER (*seriously, almost pas-*

sionately). It's beautiful! It's the most beautiful music I ever heard in my life. *I'll* play your accompaniment, Clarence. I'd adore to! (*Goes to piano.*)

CORA (*pulling him to the piano*). C'm on! C'm on!

CLARENCE. What is it?

CORA. William Tell!

MRS. WHEELER. In B flat.

CLARENCE. Same old B flat.

(WHEELER *crosses to settee* L. *and sits.* MRS. WHEELER *plays loudly upon the piano.* CLARENCE *does likewise upon the saxophone.*)

DELLA (*she has remained hovering in the sun parlor. She now edges into the room, leans against the balustrade, and lifts her eyes in rapture before speaking*). Oh—ain't it hivinly!

(CLARENCE *looks solemnly round at her, not ceasing to play, and turning his whole body to keep the instrument in position.* WHEELER *also looks at her, then back at his paper.* CLARENCE *turns to the piano again.* CORA, *looking up at him, sings the air, and* BOBBY, *having joined the group, condescendingly adds his voice. After a moment or two,* VIOLET, *who is* R., *opens the door* R. *and goes out. The saxophone stops abruptly.* CLARENCE *has been watching her out of the corner of his eye.*)

CORA (*with quick solicitude*). What's the matter, Clarence? (*This is as if some illness threatened her only child.*)

CLARENCE. Nothing. (*Solemnly resumes playing.*)

CORA. Oh, Clarence! (*She sings again and the music continues.*)

CURTAIN

ACT THREE

SCENE: *The same. The lamps are lit. The curtains in the sunroom have been pulled over the glass. The doors* R. *are wide open.*

DELLA, R.C., *is looking off through these doors in a manner expressing the warmest and most sympathetic admiration of something she is watching. She clasps her hands in a Madonna gesture beside her cheek, her eyes uplifted.*

DELLA (*fondly muttering*). Ah! (*Pause.*) Ah, now! (*She becomes haughty and repellent.*) Whoosh! (*Tosses her head and moves slowly* R.C.)

(*The cause of her change of manner is the approach of* DINWIDDIE. *He comes in* R., *dressed for dinner service, with a silver tray, silver coffeepot, and sugar, cups, and saucers. He looks sternly at* DELLA, *then takes the tray to a table. She again looks off through the door* R. *from her position* C., *and resumes her fond gesticulations.* DINWIDDIE *looks at her several times with extreme disapproval; then he looks intently at the ceiling.*)

DINWIDDIE (DELLA *turns in contempt to* DINWIDDIE. DINWIDDIE *addressing the ceiling*). I don't speak to no one here present, but if they was a little bird I could see up there in the sky—

DELLA (*interrupting, plausibly*). In the sky? It's the ceiling. Even if you was outdoors, it's dark an' you couldn't see no birds.

DINWIDDIE (*persisting*). If they was a little bird up there—(*Looks at her, then up again.*)—I would speak to him and I would say: (*Coldly.*) Bird, the fam'ly is comin' out from dinner in a minute or so, an' this ain't no place fer domestics of smirched reputations. (*Puts tray on table* L.C. *Concludes looking at her.*)

DELLA. *You* better run then!

DINWIDDIE (*sternly*). I am as pure . . .

DELLA. Are ye talkin' t' the bird? (*He utters a sound of pain and fiercely arranges the tray. She responds with a short laugh, and resumes her admiring interest of off* R., *going on rapturously.*) You can see right through t' the dining-room. From here you can see him eatin'—just as plain! (*She indicates her joyous contempt of this measure by the briefest sketch of an undignified dance.*)

DINWIDDIE. Sickening!

DELLA (*jeeringly*). Speakin' to me?

DINWIDDIE (*lifting his eyes*). I'm speaking to the bird!

DELLA (*runs across, opens one of the doors slightly, looks through and becomes rapturous again*). He's eatin' his dessert!

DINWIDDIE (*explosively*). Who *is* this Clair'nce? Nobody knows! (*Still looking up.*) Nobody knows a thing about him—not a thing!

DELLA (*unheeding, clasping her hands in soft rapture*). He eats so pritty!

DINWIDDIE (*fiercely, looking at her*). Oh, my Guh—(*He catches himself in the middle of the word, looks up, and without pausing, goes on.*) Oh, bird!

(BOBBY, *in his dinner clothes, hastily enters* R., *he has a cautious manner, yet nervous and quick.*)

BOBBY (*to* DINWIDDIE). D'ju take Miss Pinney's dinner up to her room for her?

DINWIDDIE. She sent word she didn't wish any.

BOBBY (*crosses to* DINWIDDIE). Mamma says for you to go up and ask her from *her* if she won't please come down here as a favor.

(DINWIDDIE *exits* L.)

DELLA (*looking off* R.). You could never believe it!

BOBBY (*suspiciously*). Believe what?

DELLA. That Mr. Clarence used to be a washroom man in a hotel. Of course, there's tips. . . .

BOBBY (*incredulous*). You say he worked in a hotel *lavatory?*

DELLA. He told me so.

BOBBY. Why, that's horrible! The fam'ly ought to know about this.

DELLA. Little Ainjill! (*Looking* R.)

BOBBY. Now, see here! I don't want any endearmalents from you. All that was mere sensuosity on my part, and nothing permanent at all. If you come around here callin' me "angel"—

DELLA (*exclaiming in denial*). Oh, bird!

BOBBY. I'm tired of all this blackmail; the fam'ly know about it, anyhow. You can't call me "bird" nor "angel" nor—

DELLA (*with a wan laugh*). I didn't mean you, Mister Robert! (*She is looking off* R.)

BOBBY (*staggered*). Who *did* you mean? (*Earnestly, with an inspiration after a glance over his shoulder to* R.) Did you mean Clarence?

DELLA (*dreamily*). Oh, yes!

BOBBY (*earnestly*). Well, if he's taken this burden onto himself off o' my shoulders he's done *some* good if he *was* a lavatory porter! After usin' these terms over another man, you can't dogmatize *me* any more!

DELLA (*with a sweet, dreamy look*). All but the most willin' thoughts has gone out o' my mind. (*Goes up.*)

BOBBY. Well, that's a relief to *me,* whatever you mean.

(VIOLET *enters* L., *wearing the same dress seen in the second act. Her expression is serious.*)

VIOLET (*quickly, as she enters*). Mrs. Wheeler sent for me.

(*Exit* DELLA *up* C. *to off* R.)

BOBBY (*instantly*). Oh, Violet! (*This is

in a voice of dreamy inexpressibleness, but is spoken quickly. He starts toward her.) Oh, Vio . . .

(*He is checked by* MRS. WHEELER'S *entrance* R. *She is in a handsome evening gown with jewels, camelias in her corsage, a pretty evening scarf over her shoulders, a fan in her hand. She looks radiant! Comes in briskly and speaks quickly.*)

MRS. W (*as she enters*). Run away a minute, Bobby, please. (BOBBY *goes out* R. *quickly.* MRS. W. *stands* R.C. *near the coffee table, smiling graciously, and going on at once.*) Miss Pinney, I'm going to be very direct. I want you to forget that little scene this afternoon if you will.

VIOLET (*standing by a couch* L.C., *her hands moving slightly upon the top of the back of it, her eyes cast down.*) I'm afraid I can hardly do *that*, Mrs. Wheeler.

MRS. W (*coming to couch—amiably*). Mr. Wheeler *is* rather worn out, and he forgot himself for a moment and said things he didn't mean—and—(*Sits on couch with a little laugh.* VIOLET *sits* R. *end of couch*)—so, perhaps, did I, I'm afraid. *You* said nothing at all that I could object to. That's all there was *of* it. Somehow everything seems so much cheerfuller in this house, this evening, than it has for a long time. I've told my husband that I'm not in the least angry with him —why should I be? I hope we're all going to be—happier; we all need *something* in our lives. And about this afternoon, well, it was a *mistake;* that's all— suppose we just pass it over?

VIOLET (*profoundly perplexed*). I'm afraid I—(*Rises, goes* R.)

MRS. W (*cheerfully, goes behind table* C.). Tut, tut, now! Now, please, you wouldn't have any dinner; you'll at least have your coffee?

VIOLET (*at* C.). I . . .

MRS. W. I'm sure you will, just to please your friends, we're all friends this evening. (*Calling.*) Come back, Bobby! (*She pours the coffee.* BOBBY *appears in the doorway* R. *At* R. *of couch. Nodding gaily.*) Tell them their coffee's getting cold. Take this to Miss Pinney, dear. (BOBBY *takes the cup of coffee she hands him to* VIOLET, *who accepts it perplexedly and both sit* R. MRS. WHEELER, *pouring other cups, calls to off* R.) Aren't you coming? (WHEELER, *in dinner clothes, very serious, enters* R., *smoking a cigar*

just lit. MRS. WHEELER *addresses him amiably.*) Come in, poor, dear man! Here! (*She gives him a cup.*) Go and sit by poor Miss Pinney and cheer her up. (*Goes on pouring, not looking up.*)

WHEELER (*going to* MRS. W., L. *heavily embarrassed*). Thanks. I'm smoking— I'll—uh— (*Goes up to sunroom.* BOBBY *sits by* VIOLET.)

MRS. W (*beamingly to* R.). Waiting for you.

CORA *enters* R. *She is in a very pretty evening dress appropriate to her age, and her expression is wanly solemn. She comes in slowly, halts just in the room, and sighs inaudibly but not visibly, as she opens her mouth to do it. This is facing front; then she looks* R.)

CORA (*crosses* L. *In an earnest, solicitous, solemn voice*). Aren't you coming in here, Clarence?

CLARENCE (*door* R. *Entering* R.). Yes, oh, yes. (*He wears new dinner clothes, has a camelia in his buttonhole. He is somewhat apprehensive.*) Oh, thank you! (*Speaking across the room.*) Good evening, Miss Pinney. (*She nods slightly.*) I'm sorry to hear you had a headache. (*She acknowledges this faintly.*) I hope it's very much better. . . . I hope you haven't any at *all* by this time. I hope . . . (*Starts to sit by* MISS PINNEY *at* R.)

CORA (*reprovingly, in a hushed voice, solemnly, huskily*). Let's sit down. Let's sit down *here*, Clarence. (*Divan* L.C.)

CLARENCE (*crosses to couch* L.). Oh, yes, thanks. (*He sits upon the* R. *side of divan, facing front.* CORA *sits exactly at the same time he does, to* L. *of him, facing him, her profile to front, her elbow on the back of the divan, her hand to her cheek.* MRS. WHEELER *puts a cup and saucer in his hand, smiling benevolently.*)

MRS. W (*gently*). There, Clarence. Is it right?

CLARENCE. Thanks.

CORA (*not moving, speaks sacredly*). He takes one lump in the evening, Mama. He takes two in the morning. He told me so, himself. Didn't you, Clarence?

CLARENCE. Yes.

MRS. W (*putting a lump of sugar in* C's *cup, gently*). Is this right, Clarence?

CORA. Yes, Mama.

CLARENCE. Thanks. I'm sorry Miss Pinney's headache . . .

CORA (*dreamily*). Oh, Clarence! (*He turns to look at* CORA. *Her fixed look at him is embarrassing.*)

CLARENCE (*solicitously to* CORA). Mayn't I give *you* some coffee?

CORA (*unchanging*). No. No. No coffee. (*To avoid her gaze, he turns and smiles feebly to* MRS. WHEELER. *Her instantly responsive smile is such that his own fades, and he looks forward blankly.*)

MRS. W (*smiling solicitously*). Is there *any*thing you want, Clarence?

CLARENCE. Oh, no!

BOBBY (L. *near* VIOLET). I expect he'd like Cora to quit lookin' at him. (*Speaks slowly and with calm bitterness. There is a pause. Then, earnestly marveling, he adds to* VIOLET.) My goodness, she didn't even try to make any repartee!

CORA (*unchanging, in a monotone throughout*). Clarence? Clarence? (*He looks at her; he has been trying to look at* VIOLET.) Clarence, aren't you going to play some more for us? I want you to play. I want you to play right away. (*Still unchanging.*) Bobby, run up to Clarence's room and get his saxophone for him.

BOBBY (*calmly but doggedly*). I will not. (WHEELER *goes to table and* MRS. W. *takes cup.*)

CORA (*unchanging except for the slightest note of plaintiveness*). Papa, won't you please go get his saxophone for him?

WHEELER (*up* C. *Mildly incredulous*). What did you say?

MRS. W (*amiably*). Do, Henry.

WHEELER (*coming down a little way*). Do what?

MRS. W (*pleasantly*). Won't you go and get Clarence's sax—

CLARENCE (*coughing hastily*). Oh, no, no! I don't think I play really at all well.

(WHEELER *turns up again.*)

CORA. Then if you won't play, will you answer me one question, Clarence?

CLARENCE (*a little suspicious*). What is the question?

CORA (*wistfully*). It's simply, Clarence, what *was* the matter with your liver?

CLARENCE. If I answer you this time, will you promise never to ask me again?

CORA (*quickly*). Yes. What *was* the matter with your liver, Clarence?

CLARENCE. I was *shot* in it!

MRS. W (*with eager loudness*). At Château Thierry?

CLARENCE (*explosively, his voice breaking with protest*). No! At *target* practice!

(MR. WHEELER *sits up* L. *in armchair.*)

CORA (*after a pause*). What else did you do that was heroic, Clarence?

CLARENCE (*despairingly*). I beg your pardon?

CORA. What was the next thing you did in the war?

CLARENCE. That was the *last* thing I did. I didn't do any more after that.

CORA (*unable to express her dreamy wistfulness*). Oh, Clarence!

(*He sighs and sets his cup on the table.* BOBBY *rises, crosses and puts cup on table.*)

BOBBY. Has Hubert Stem been telephoning or anything this evening, Cora? (*Apparently casual.*)

CORA (*not looking at him, speaks carelessly*). Who?

BOBBY. That ole grass-widower Stem.

CORA (*vaguely*). "Stem?" (*As if the name were unknown.*) What about him? (*Impulsively,* BOBBY *crosses to* R.) Clarence, you must have been standing somewhere in the way of the target!

CLARENCE. I heard—afterwards— that I had been.

MRS. W (*cheerfully to him*). Sha'n't we all go and see if it's moonlight on the veranda, Clarence? (*Rises.* WHEELER *notices this with surprised annoyance.*)

CLARENCE (*blankly*). I should be delighted. (*Rises, preparing to go.* WHEELER *comes down a little.*)

CORA (*dreamily*). No. Let's stay just like this.

MRS. W (*in an ordinary, pleasant tone*). Yes. It's lovely here. I suppose moonlight is in one's heart, after all . . . in any heart that's found something to put moonlight about. (WHEELER *comes down, by piano.*) That's the *hard* thing: to find someone to pour moonlight out on. But when you do, it doesn't matter where you are. Don't you think that's true, Clarence?

CLARENCE (*after a somewhat disturbed glance at* WHEELER). I'm sure it must be.

CORA. Clarence, I do want you to play again. Papa, won't you *please* run and get—

CLARENCE (*hastily*). I really don't think I should. You see, it's only an accident that I ever knew how to play at all. (WHEELER *is down.*)

WHEELER (*dryly*). How was that? How could you learn to play the saxophone by accident?

CLARENCE. Why, we used to see whether certain species of beetles found in Montana are deaf, or if they respond to peculiar musical vibrations.

(BOBBY *rises, and comes down; he and* WHEELER *glance at each other.*)

CORA (*dreamily*). Beetles! How wonderful! How could you tell if the beetles responded to the vibrations?

CLARENCE. We placed them in a dish filled with food that they were passionately fond of, and then I played to them. If they climbed out of the dish and left this food and went away we knew they'd heard the music.

BOBBY (*rises, very serious*). Are the *hotels* good out in Montana? (*He has risen on* CLARENCE's *speech.*)

CLARENCE. I don't know. I was living in a tent.

WHEELER. (*dryly*). Hunting those beetles?

CLARENCE. Yes. They live outdoors.

BOBBY (*staring*). And you were playing the saxophone to 'em?

CLARENCE. Yes. Hours and hours at a time—to the deaf ones. It got very tedious.

(WHEELER *and* BOBBY *mark this as another incredible statement.*)

CORA. I wish I'd been one.

BOBBY (*huskily*). You wouldn't haf to *change* much!

CORA. Were there any cannibals in Montana, Clarence?

(WHEELER *looks from* CORA *to* CLARENCE.)

CLARENCE (*mystified*). No. Almost everything else but no cannibals.

WHEELER (*to* CORA, *severely*). What do you mean? Cannibals in Montana?

CORA (*to all, casually*). You know he was brought *up* by the cannibals.

WHEELER (*gravely incredulous*). He was?

CORA (*going on quickly*). And they never tried to eat him or his family. He told me the first time we met him. They tried to eat almost everybody else, but they never tried to eat him or his family. *Did* they, Clarence?

(BOBBY *and* WHEELER *turn up to the sunroom; disappear thence to off* L. *Exit.*)

CLARENCE. No! But that wasn't precisely what I intended to convey to your mind!

CORA (*with gentle reproach*). It was that day in Papa's office, Clarence, you said the cannibals— (*She is interrupted, to the mystification of herself,* MRS. WHEELER,

and CLARENCE, *by* VIOLET, *who breaks into irrepressible laughter. They look at her, and* CLARENCE *rises.*)

MRS. WHEELER (*staring in surprise*). Miss Pinney! (CLARENCE *walks across and looks solemnly at her: then he looks at* MRS. W, *then back at* VIOLET, *who rises, trying to control her mirth, but not succeeding.*) Is she hysterical?

VIOLET. I'm *not* hysterical!

CLARENCE (*gravely, to* MRS. WHEELER). She says not.

VIOLET (*turning from him, still out of control*). Please go away! (*He takes a step back, utterly mystified.*)

CORA (*rising, incredulous and indignant*). Is she laughing at *Clarence?*

VIOLET (*protesting almost hysterically*). Oh, never! Never! I could never do anything like *that!*

MRS. W (*going* C., *smiling*). It might be tactful of us to go and see if it really *is* moonlight on the veranda, don't you think so? (*To* CLARENCE.)

CORA (*quickly and decidedly, as she goes up*). I'm coming, too, Mama!

MRS. W (*dryly*). Of course, dear. (*Smiling and extending her hand toward* CLARENCE.) Aren't you coming?

CLARENCE (*blankly*). Oh—thanks— (*He goes up; each takes one of his arms.*)

MRS. W (*happily*). It *is* moonlight out there!

CORA (*leaning back to look at him better*). Oh, Clarence! (*This is always quiet and wistful.*)

CLARENCE (*hurriedly*). That reminds me; something I forgot— (*Detaching himself.*)

MRS. W (*quickly*). We'll send and get it.

CLARENCE. Well, in fact, it's something I forgot to ask Miss Pinney. I'll come in *just* a moment.

MRS. W (*amiably, a little bothered, going*). Oh, of course.

(*Exit up* L. CLARENCE *starts down.*)

CORA (*going*). Not a *long* moment?

CLARENCE (*reassuringly, stopping*). No, no. (*Exit* CORA *up* L., *giving him a wistful final look.* CLARENCE *turns to* VIOLET). Of course when you told me to go away—

VIOLET (*interrupting*). That's why you —*didn't?*

CLARENCE. Well, of course when a lady declines to eat her dinner on account of a headache, and then laughs at you out of a clear sky and tells you to go away, why—no— In fact—you don't!

VIOLET. You mean you stayed because you're curious about why I laughed. (*Half question, half assertion.*)

CLARENCE. No. I just mean I stayed.

VIOLET (*looking up at him with hidden amusement*). Don't you want to know why I laughed?

CLARENCE (*uneasily*). I'm not *sure!* I'm not at all sure I do; people aren't usually made much cheerfuller by finding out why other people laugh at them!

VIOLET (*with an inclination of her head toward up* L.). You told *them* you had a *question* to ask me. (*Gravely.*) You oughtn't to keep them waiting.

CLARENCE. A question? Yes. You said this afternoon we couldn't be friends any more. My question is: If that wasn't just an afternoon rule that we could consider not operating in the evening.

VIOLET. Hardly!

CLARENCE. Couldn't?

VIOLET. It was on account of what you said this afternoon that I laughed at you this evening. (*In a lower voice, turning from him.*) You have so many to think of, you know!

CLARENCE (*puzzled*). I? To "think" of!

VIOLET (*with indignant amusement*). Doesn't it seem rather funny, even to you: *your* giving me that little lecture this afternoon about the people that you said wanted me to "think" of them?

CLARENCE (*enlightened*). Oh, you mean when I said I wanted you to think of *me!*

VIOLET (*scornfully*). Oh!

CLARENCE. You mean you got to thinking about that this evening, and that's what made you laugh. You thought it was so funny my wanting you to think of me.

VIOLET (*gaily*). No; I thought it was so funny your giving me that lecture; *you* see, *you* seem to have so many to think of that I *don't* want you to think of *me!*

CLARENCE (*earnestly*). I'd like to do what you want: I don't know. I don't know whether it could be stopped or not. A person goes around thinking —it wouldn't make any *noise*, just thinking. It needn't disturb you at all.

VIOLET (*with scornful amusement*). I think you'll be able to stop it.

CLARENCE (*plaintively*). But it's the only pleasant thing I do!

VIOLET (*scornfully*). Oh!

CLARENCE (*going on plaintively*). It seems unreasonable to be asked to give it up. I'd even rather give up my music!

VIOLET (*emphatically*). Oh, believe me! *That*, you'll *not* be allowed to give up!

CLARENCE (*apprehensively*). Don't you think I will? I don't think Mr. Wheeler cares for it particularly.

VIOLET. Neither do I; but I'm sure you'll have to keep on with it, that and your wonderful stories about beetles and—

CLARENCE (*interrupting*). Those weren't stories; it was perfectly true.

VIOLET (*with feeling*). I *hope* it was truer than what you said to me this afternoon, when you—when you thought fit to bring—to bring Mr. Wheeler's name into your lecture.

CLARENCE. I only meant to—well, I thought a friendly warning might—

VIOLET (*smoldering*). You meant that this—friendliness—to me was troubling his wife. (*Indignantly and pathetically.*) As if I could—help—

CLARENCE. If you cried—I—couldn't stand it!

VIOLET (*going on brokenly*). As if I— knew which way—to turn—or what to do—

CLARENCE. If you cry I'll do something queer!

VIOLET (*her indignation getting the better of pathos*). *I* sha'n't cry! I only want you to imagine that *Mrs.* Wheeler's—friendliness—to you—had already begun to attract her husband's attention—and to annoy him!

CLARENCE (*somewhat stiffly*). Ordinarily I'd want to imagine anything you wanted me to imagine, but I could hardly imagine *that!*

VIOLET. No? You couldn't?

CLARENCE (*more stiffly*). Certainly not!

(BOBBY *enters quickly up* C. *from off* L.)

VIOLET (*seeing him*). I think you're wanted! (*significantly*.)

CLARENCE (*stiffly*). I beg your pardon.

VIOLET (*more significantly*). I think you're sent for.

(CLARENCE *turns, following her glance, and sees* BOBBY.)

BOBBY (*very serious*). Mama wants to know how long before you're coming.

CLARENCE (*bothered*). Ah—does she?

BOBBY. So does Cora.

VIOLET (*quietly*). You mustn't keep them waiting. (CLARENCE *looks at her coldly.*)

BOBBY (*coming down*). There's just one thing I want to say. I don't mind speakin' of it before Miss Pinney because I already told her all the worst in my nature, and it's better to be aboveboard anyhow, isn't it?

VIOLET (*looking at* CLARENCE). Yes. *I* think it is.

CLARENCE (*sharply*). Why, certainly it is!

BOBBY. Well, it's just this: I might of paid mighty dear for a mere imprudence, if Della hadn't got the way she is over you, Clarence.

CLARENCE. *Della?*

BOBBY. Whatever happens to you, I want to thank you for that.

CLARENCE (*astounded*). Thank *me* for—for the way—*Della*—"*is*—over *me*"?

BOBBY. That's practically all I had to say. Whatever it is about you that's got Mama and Cora so upset, why Della acts just about the same as they do and it's certainly a great relief to *me!* So now I've thanked you, and it's pretty cold out on that veranda, and they told me to say —(*He is interrupted by* CORA, *who has just come on from up* L. *and stands up* C. *She wears a wrap.*)

CORA (*sweetly plaintive*). Clarence, Mama says maybe you don't *want* to come—

CLARENCE (*desperately—crosses* L.). Miss Pinney—

VIOLET. They're waiting for you! (*Crosses* L. *up to* L. *of table. He gives her an indignant look.*)

CORA (*dreamily*). Aren't you coming, Clarence?

CLARENCE (*in an agonized voice*). Oh, yes; thanks! (*He goes up to her.*)

CORA (*cosily as they move* L.). You like us all, don't you, Clarence?

(*Exeunt up* L.)

BOBBY (*after a glance at this departure*). It's just as well for you, you didn't come down to dinner; you could hardly have eaten any anyway, the way Cora was sayin', "Oh, Clarence!" and Mama *almost* as terrible. I and Father hardly could, ourselves!

VIOLET (*with amused distaste*). And you say *Della*— (*Turns down to* BOBBY.)

BOBBY. I caught her callin' him an angel. Oh, not *to* him; but she can't hamper *my* career after that! She says he told her he used to work in a hotel washroom—

VIOLET (*not believing it*). Oh, no.

BOBBY. Well, anyway, it's only another of his stories about himself. Look, whenever he says anything about himself it's somp'n a body can hardly believe, or else disgraceful like that. I and Father been havin' a talk about him and we both think it'll be better if you don't have any more to do with him, Violet.

VIOLET. Why?

BOBBY. Look; the way *I* look at it is simply, well, simply look at the way Cora and Mama and Della *are!* Look, you don't want to get like that; you got an awful high nature. It brings out all the most spirichul things I got *in* me, and *we* think this is gettin' to be a serious matter.

VIOLET (*puzzled*). Clarence is?

BOBBY (*even more earnestly*). Look; don't even let him talk to you. (*Casually.*) Course we don't feel it makes so much difference about Cora and Mama— (*Becoming earnest again.*)—but with your spirichul nature, Violet, and all this and that, and he telling about these Montana beetles, and them listening to a saxophone, and being brought up by cannibals, and this mule story without bad language, and then workin' in a hotel lavatory— (WHEELER *enters up* C. *from off* L. BOBBY *and* VIOLET *do not see him*)—and all thus and so, why, *we* think it's time somep'n'll haf to be done about it!

VIOLET. What like? (*Somewhat troubled.*)

BOBBY. Well, I and Father—

WHEELER (*up* C., *interrupting*). Never mind, Bobby. (VIOLET *moves to go out.*) Please, Miss Pinney— (*Coming down* C. *This detains her.*)

BOBBY (*sits*). I guess we better talk it over frankly, now we're all three here.

WHEELER (*gives him a thoughtful glance*). No. I'm going to ask you to step out for a moment, Bobby.

BOBBY (*getting up, gravely surprised*). Me? Well, all right. I only want to say just one thing, listen: When my *own* son is practically a grown man, I *think* I shall know how to value him! (*Exit coldly* C.L.)

VIOLET (*in a low voice — goes to* WHEELER). What *is* it about Clarence?

WHEELER (*much troubled, but quiet*). Just a moment. I see now that whatever I decide to do with my own life, I've got first to straighten out my mistake in bringing him here. But I want to tell you I *was* "overwrought" this afternoon—I suppose I am still, for that matter—but I meant every word I said.

VIOLET (*troubled, looking down*). Oh, no, Mr. Wheeler.

WHEELER (*doggedly*). Yes, I did. (*She shakes her head.*) Oh, yes.

VIOLET (*quietly, not looking up*). You don't know how sorry I am for you. (*Moves away a little.*)

WHEELER (*with feeling, but quietly*). I felt I simply couldn't stand the situation here, unless I could rely on your helping me.

VIOLET (*looking up seriously*). I think things have just got too much for you, Mr. Wheeler.

WHEELER (*with a controlled desperation*). If they were that, this afternoon, they're *more* than that tonight, don't you think? (*More loudly.*) I've never seen anything like it! You couldn't have helped but notice my wife's behavior with this fellow Smun.

VIOLET. With whom?

WHEELER (*impatiently*). With this Smun!

VIOLET (*frowning*). Who?

WHEELER. Clarence. Clarence Smun.

VIOLET. But his name isn't "Smun."

WHEELER. Yes. S-M-U-N Smun.

VIOLET. No. His name's Moon. M-double O-N Moon. Clarence Moon.

WHEELER (*annoyed*). Oh, but I *know*. My secretary took his name when he applied in my office. I'm not quite such an idiot as to put a man in my house and not even know his *name!* It's Smun.

VIOLET. Have you ever spoken to him by that name? Calling him "Mr. Smun," I mean?

WHEELER (*at* C.). Why, certainly! I don't know—maybe I haven't. No. Perhaps not. Bobby and Cora started in calling him Clarence, and the rest of us just dropped into that. (*Goes over to* VIOLET.) But have *you* ever called

him "Mr. Moon?"

VIOLET (*a little consciously*). I believe I've just called him "you."

WHEELER. I thought so! It's Smun. I may be in a bad state of nerves, but at least I know a name of four letters when I see it!

VIOLET (*skeptically*). Did he write it for you?

WHEELER. No! But Mrs. Martyn *did!*

VIOLET (*coldly*). Oh, she was mistaken.

WHEELER (*emphatically*). Mrs. Martyn is *never* mistaken!

VIOLET (*with serene doggedness*). His name's Moon, though!

WHEELER (*sharply*). I really don't see what's the use of being so obstinate about it!

VIOLET (*offended*). Mr. Wheeler!

WHEELER (*with a flinging out of hands, he swings away from her*). Oh, well; good gracious, what's the good of quarreling about a thing like that? It is *Smun!* (*Turns up.*)

(BOBBY *enters up* C.)

VIOLET (*shaking her head slightly*). No. Moon.

WHEELER (*whirling upon her*). I said— (*Checks himself, his mouth open. He sees* BOBBY.) I asked you—

(BOBBY *passing up;* WHEELER *calls to him.*)

BOBBY (*reprovingly*). *Look;* you said, "Step out a *moment.*" (*Going off.*)

WHEELER. Wait a minute. (BOBBY *comes in.*) What do you understand Clarence's name to be?

BOBBY (*with suspicion that either he is being insulted or his father is becoming an idiot*). What do I understand Clarence's *name* to be?

WHEELER (*testily*). That's what I asked you!

BOBBY (*in the same state of mind, testily*). Why, what do you mean, asking me such a question?

WHEELER (*angrily*). What?

BOBBY (*a light striking him*). Oh, you mean his *last* name?

WHEELER (*savagely*). I do! Do you *know* it?

BOBBY (*with dignified asperity*). Cert'nly I know it. His name's Clarence Smart.

VIOLET (*with a quiet triumph*). I told you it wasn't "Smun." It's Moon.

WHEELER (*turning up, despairing of everything*). Oh, dear! Oh, dear!

BOBBY (*mildly*). His last name's Smart,

Violet.

VIOLET. No. It's Moon.

(CORA *sings off* L.)

BOBBY (*surprised*). Oh, is it? Well—all right. It's Moon. (*Sits philosophically.* WHEELER *turns and stares at him.*)

VIOLET (CORA *enters* C., *still humming, starts to exit up* R.). Well? What *about* him?

BOBBY. Well, in the first place—

WHEELER (*up* C.). Wait. (*Frowning.*) Cora. (*He comes down.*)

CORA (*halting at door*). Whatcha want, Papa?

WHEELER. What is Clarence's last name?

CORA (*preoccupied, but the slightest bit surprised*). Clarence? I never thought of his having one. (*Begins to hum again and exits* R., *still much preoccupied.*)

BOBBY (*mildly explaining*). You see, she hasn't got *any* sense.

(*A bell is heard.*)

WHEELER (*almost moaning*). Perhaps we might agree to continue to speak of him just as "Clarence." The important thing is to— (*He breaks off as* DINWIDDIE *enters* R. WHEELER *looks at him in frowning inquiry.*)

DINWIDDIE (*not stopping, crossing to* L.C.) Door, sir.

WHEELER. Not at home. (DINWIDDIE *starts out* R. *Front of* WHEELER, *back of* VIOLET) Dinwiddie? (DINWIDDIE *turns.*) You distribute the mail in the house; you've seen Smun's letters—

DINWIDDIE. Whose, sir?

WHEELER (*goes up to* DINWIDDIE— *testily*). Clarence's! How is his last name spelled on the letters that come for him?

DINWIDDIE. There haven't any come for him since he's been here, sir.

WHEELER. All right.

DINWIDDIE. Yes, sir.

(*Exit up* C. *to* R.)

WHEELER (*at* L.C. *Going on rather irritably*). Been here three weeks and hasn't had a letter; that's pretty queer!

BOBBY. Well, yes!

WHEELER. I'm willing to waive his *name*—though, of course, it *is* Smun.

VIOLET (*rises—interrupting*). But, Mr. Wheeler, *nobody's* name ever was "Smun."

WHEELER. It happens *his* is. Mrs. Martyn—

VIOLET. There isn't such a name. It's Moon.

WHEELER (*gulping down a sharp expostulation*). Well, let's get to what has to be *done* about him! I don't like this three weeks without a letter. A young man of that sort gets letters. It looks as if he'd taken measures *not* to get 'em.

BOBBY. Well, you *brought* him here, Father.

WHEELER (*at* C.). All of us have our foolish day *sometime*, when we do the thing we've never before. *Afterwards* it was so embarrassing to ask him questions about himself that I've put it off from day to day. I won't put it off *now!* (*Enter* DINWIDDIE *from* R.) What do you want? (*This is to* DINWIDDIE.)

DINWIDDIE. It's Mr. Hubert Stem, sir. He asked for you, sir.

WHEELER (*sharply*). What!

VIOLET. I made it clear to him this afternoon, Mr. Wheeler, that if he came here again, *you* would see him.

DINWIDDIE. That's what he said, sir, when I told him "Not at home."

WHEELER (*sharply, as if to go out* R.) Is Miss Cora out there?

DINWIDDIE. No, sir; she's upstairs.

WHEELER (*grimly breathing hard*). Tell him to come in. (*Exit* DINWIDDIE R.) I'll finish *this* one first! Just— (*Goes up* C.) Please, Miss Pinney—

(*He motions to them to go up, and they do as* STEM *enters* R. *He is in dinner clothes and overcoat, no hat, and is repressing some excitement.* DINWIDDIE *closes the door without entering.* BOBBY *goes up on veranda.*)

WHEELER. Now, Mr. Stem—

STEM (*quickly as he enters*). Now, wait, Mr. Wheeler, before you say anything you'll be sorry for!

WHEELER (*grimly*). Then perhaps you'd better speak quickly, Mr. Stem.

(STEM *comes down.*)

STEM (*quickly, earnestly*). I came here to do your family a *service.* (*Enter* CORA R.) I know—

WHEELER (*sharply*). Wait, if you please.

(CORA *is heard for an instant humming* R. *The same song. She is carrying* CLARENCE'S *saxophone. Seeing nobody, she goes rhythmically with her humming to up* C. *Suggests, merely, a dance thought accompanying the air.*)

BOBBY (*at* L.C. *on platform. Seriously and significantly*). Cora, don't you see Mr. Stem?

CORA (*not stopping, glances back at*

STEM *with an utterly blank semicircular sweep of her eye, speaks in an absent monotone*). Howja do. (*Instantly humming again, exits gaily up* C. *Short pause.*)

BOBBY (*plaintively*). Well, that's the way they are, sometimes!

WHEELER (*sternly to* STEM). Go on, sir, if you please.

STEM. I'm going to be brutally frank. I want first to apologize for my thoughtlessness about Miss Wheeler. I know she's not "out" and I did get her to do a rather absurd thing, but it was my only way to force another lady to pay some attention to my existence. I mean Miss Pinney.

WHEELER (*incredulous*). Miss Pinney?

VIOLET. You couldn't leave me out of it?

STEM. No. (*To* WHEELER.) I tell you candidly I'm here now on Miss Pinney's account. The only reason I've *ever* been here is on Miss Pinney's account.

BOBBY (*coming down to* R. *of* STEM. *Severely*). Look here! *This* is *serious!*

VIOLET (*looking all the while at* STEM). Mr. Stem knows that I've always been unable to like him: he's not very pleasant in the means he uses to "force" my "attention to his existence."

WHEELER (*to* STEM, *impatiently*). What do you want to say?

STEM. When I saw her this afternoon, there was a very unattractive young man in a soldier's uniform drumming on the piano here.

WHEELER. Well, what about him?

STEM. I'm sorry to say I thought Miss Pinney seemed quite—under his spell. (VIOLET *laughs.*) Since then I've made some inquiries about him. (VIOLET *laughs again.*)

WHEELER. How?

STEM (*smiling faintly*). Well, for one thing, my servants know yours.

WHEELER. Well?

STEM. If yours know the facts—and I think they do—you brought this man here without knowing anything whatever about him.

WHEELER (*grimly*). Well, we know his *name.* It's Clarence Smun.

VIOLET. Mr. Wheeler, will you ask him, himself?

WHEELER. I decline! Have a man three weeks in my house and then go up and ask his *name?*

VIOLET. It's Clarence Moon.

STEM. Oh, no. I think you'll find it's not even Clarence.

VIOLET. What nonsense!

STEM. Is it? (*To* WHEELER.) He said he drove mules, and he wears the uniform of a private in the Quartermaster's Department, doesn't he? (*Taking a newspaper from his pocket.*)

WHEELER. Yes. He did.

STEM. He's been here three weeks.

WHEELER. Just about.

STEM (*opening the paper*). "Charles Short, *wagoner* in the Quartermaster's Department. Deserted three weeks ago, sought both by War Department and divorced wife seeking alimony. Also wanted in Delaware." There's his picture.

WHEELER. But it doesn't *look* like him.

STEM (*promptly*). Newspaper pictures never *do.* I got the idea as soon as I saw it. It looks *something* like him.

VIOLET (*taking the paper*). More like me! It might *just* as well be my picture! (*Then with great earnestness.*) What an *awful* fool you are! (*She hands paper to* BOBBY, *who looks at it.*)

STEM (*angrily triumphant*). There! That's *one* thing I wanted to find out!

VIOLET. What is?

STEM. How much interest you *do* take in him!

VIOLET (*contemptuously*). As a matter of fact I'm extremely *un*interested in him! (*Turns to window. Indignantly.*)

BOBBY (*pleased. Following* VIOLET *up to window*). Are you, Violet? (*Turns to* VIOLET.)

STEM (*sharply, crosses to* WHEELER). Mr. Wheeler, have you any objection to my asking him point-blank if he's this Charles Short?

WHEELER (*profoundly annoyed by everything, pacing the floor*). Oh, ask him, ask him! Point-blank or any other way! We've got to do *something* about him!

STEM (*decisively*). I'll do it! (VIOLET *laughs; he turns to her, expostulating.*) Wait till you hear what he says. Watch to see if he doesn't quibble. (*Going up.*) Is he out there? I'll ask him now.

BOBBY (*goes up* C.). You *can't* now. Listen—It's terrible.

(*The saxophone and an alto and soprano are heard off* L. *in the air* CORA *has been humming. The effect is not bad, but fails to please those in room.* WHEELER *paces.* VIOLET R.C. STEM *stands* R.C.)

BOBBY (*with feeling*). Why, I haven't heard Mama even try to sing for anyway four or five years, have you, Papa?

WHEELER (*halting*). No; I haven't. (*His frown deepens.*)

BOBBY. It might be *kind* of—better, if Cora wouldn't—they must feel terribly happy to be able to stand makin' sounds like those!

WHEELER (*waving toward him angrily*). It's gone far enough! Tell them to come in here.

BOBBY (*shouting to off* L.). Hey! Take a rest! Quit! Come *in* here! Papa wants you to come in here! (*Music stops.*) Yes, he does! Yes! In *here!*

(*Laughing voices are heard off up* L., *then* CORA *appears up* C., *still wearing her wrap, carrying the saxophone affectionately.* CLARENCE *follows, his coat closed over his chest, the collar turned up.* MRS. WHEELER *clings happily to his arm; she has a fur wrap about her.* STEM *goes down* R. VIOLET *to piano,* WHEELER *above table.*)

CORA (*as she comes*). You want us to come in? (*As in dreamy surprise.*)

MRS. W (*smiling brightly. Passes* CORA). Howdy'do, Mr. Stem? (*To* WHEELER, *mildly surprised.*) Did you want *us?* Miss Pinney's · here. (*Crosses down to* C. *She relinquishes* CLARENCE'S *arm, coming down, letting her wrap fall to her arm.*) Do hope our little operetta didn't disturb—

WHEELER. Never mind, Fanny! Mr. Stem has a question he wants to ask, I believe.

MRS. W (*frowning, amused*). Of me?

STEM (*nervously, but sharply, pointing to* CLARENCE, *who is up* R.C. *with* CORA). No. Of that person there!

CLARENCE (*surprised, pausing as he turns down his collar*). Of *this* person? (*Comes down.*)

STEM (*loudly*). Yes, sir! You!

CLARENCE (*puzzled, coming down,* CORA *following him*). You wanted to ask me about something?

(CORA *halts when he does, the saxophone in her arms, her eyes always fixed upon him.*)

STEM (*sharply.* BOBBY *crosses to* L.). I wanted to ask you a simple, direct question. I see you've left off your uniform since this afternoon.

CLARENCE. Why, that isn't a simple, direct question. It isn't a question at all. It's an observation.

STEM (*exasperated*). I'm *coming* to my question, but first I want to know: Didn't you leave off your uniform after the arrival of this evening's paper?

CLARENCE (*with some indignation*). No. I left off my uniform after the arrival of my other clothes.

STEM (*angrily*). Isn't that quibbling?

CLARENCE. Why, do *you* dress by the paper?

STEM (*fiercely*). My question is simply and plainly this: Did you ever hear the name of Charles Short?

CLARENCE (*quickly*). Charles Short? Yes.

STEM (*approaching a triumph*). Do you know anybody by the name of Charles Short?

CLARENCE. Of course I do.

STEM (*crescendo*). Do you know anybody by the name of Charles Short *well?*

CLARENCE. Charles Shortwell? I do not.

STEM. But you *do* know a person named Charles *Short?*

CLARENCE. Yes. Don't you? What do you mean? *Everybody* knows somebody named Charlie Short!

STEM (*loudly, and gesticulating like a lawyer*). I'm talking about the one *you* know!

CLARENCE (*quickly*). I know three!

STEM (*furious*). I mean the one we're talking about!

CLARENCE. Well, good heavens, my dear sir, which one of them *are* we talking about? *I'm* not talking about any of 'em. If you want to ask me a simple, direct question about somebody named Charlie Short, surely you ought to be able to say something more about him than that he's the one we're talking about.

STEM. More quibbles! Quibbles!

CLARENCE. "Quibbles?" I'm trying if possible to reach your mind! It seems you think we have a mutual acquaintance named Charlie Short and you want to find out something about him from *me,* and you immediately proceed to lose your temper because your own powers of description are too limited for you to tell me which of the three *I* know is the one *you* know!

CORA (*in a breath, with dreamy enthusiasm.*

Comes down). Clarence, that's the most wonderful logic! Let's go out on the porch and play some more—this is "awf'ly tedious."

MRS. W (*about to rise from where she sits near table*). Let's do!

WHEELER· (*loudly, angrily*). No! We'll finish this!

STEM. I'll tell you which Charles Short I mean: I mean the one that was in the army!

CLARENCE (*despairing of him, plaintively to the others*). We had four million men in the American Army: I suppose he'd— (*Meaning* STEM.)—think it singular if I told him that so far as I can guess probably all three of the Charles Shorts I know either enlisted or got drafted!

STEM (*loudly*). I claim his evasions are more and more suspicious! (*Crosses to table, picks up paper. Seizing it and thrusting it under* CLARENCE'S *eyes, slapping it.*) THIS is the Charles Short *I* mean! Charles Short, deserter!

CLARENCE. Oh, that's the one *you* know? Charles Short, deserter?

STEM. I ask the point-blank question, yes or no. *DO YOU KNOW HIM?*

CORA (*on this, plaintively*). Clarence, won't you play just *once* more? This is getting so *tedious!*

(*Her voice rises high in complaint on the last word.* STEM *is in despair at the interruption.* CLARENCE *looks at her.* STEM *goes down* C. *disgusted.*)

STEM (*his own voice strained*). I say I want to know—

CLARENCE (*turning his head from* CORA *to look at the paper, which he has taken*). You want to know if I know this one? (*Turning to look at* STEM.) They were *all* homely. Was the one you knew—

STEM. I say do you know that face?

CLARENCE. It could just as well be a picture of *me* as anyone else. (STEM *looks at* WHEELER.) Or Mr. Wheeler, or you.

STEM (*ominously, shaking his head*). No. That's not a picture of me! Or of Mr. Wheeler!

CLARENCE. It *could* be, I said. Of course, it *isn't*, because evidently it's a picture of the Short that you know: at least, I suppose you do! (*Exasperated.*) What *is* it about him? What do you want to know about him? Why in the world do you ask *me* about him?

VIOLET (*rises, comes to up* C.). Let ME tell you. In the first place, they want to

know if you know him.

CLARENCE (*despairingly*). I've been able to—gather that much from Mr. Stem! How on earth could a person tell if he knew another person from a picture like *that?*

VIOLET. You couldn't, but—

CLARENCE (*going on*). And what about it if I *did* know him? What do they want me to *do* about him?

VIOLET. They think you *are* this Charles Short!

CLARENCE. They what? They think *I* am this Charles Short?

VIOLET (*sharply*). Yes. Mr. Stem does!

CLARENCE. Do *you* think so? You seemed to think a lot of other things— do you—

VIOLET (*sharply*). Yes. I think the other things, but I don't think this one!

CLARENCE. I'd rather have you think this one and not the others.

STEM (*vehemently*). Aren't you *this Charles Short?*

CLARENCE (*violently*). Let me get this straight. You want to know whether I know *this* Charles Short and then, whether I know him or not, you want to know whether I *am* this Charles Short and *not* one of the other two Charles Shorts? Is *that* what you mean?

STEM (*fiercely*). I want to know—

CLARENCE (*cutting him off fiercely*). Well, I'll answer you: No! I'm not this Charles Short! I'm not this one here in the paper, understand! About my being either of the other two, or both of 'em, I won't commit myself, but I'm not *this* one!

STEM (*furiously*). Isn't that quibbling, Mr. Wheeler?

CLARENCE (*turning sharply on* WHEELER). Does Mr. Wheeler think— (*Incredulously to him.*) Have you been sharing Mr. Stem's suspicions as to his friend, this Mr. Charles Short?

WHEELER (*emphatically*). I have not. It might have been possible, so I let him ask you. I'm glad it came up, because we certainly need to know more about you than we do. We need to know just *who you are!*

CLARENCE (*incredulous*). You need to know who I *am!* Why, I supposed you *did* know from the time I gave my name to Mrs. Martyn in your office!

WHEELER (*vehemently*). Well, I didn't! We don't know anything about you!

CLARENCE (*in an equally vehement tone*). Why, good heavens, all you had to do was to look me up in the last edition of *Who's Who*—I don't mean that I'm a great man, but I certainly *am* one of the authorities on the coleoptera!

WHEELER (*angrily*). On the *what?*

(DINWIDDIE *enters* L., *stands there.*)

CLARENCE (*shouting*). On the COLE-OPTERA!

DINWIDDIE (*sharply and quickly, in one breath*). The hot water plant's busted again and no plumbers. Mister Clair'nce, if you don't come and fix it the house'll be flooded with ice-water. It's an eight-hour job. I'll lend ye some overalls. (*Exit* DINWIDDIE.)

(CLARENCE *strides to up* R. VIOLET *drops back to down* R.C.)

CORA (*plaintively*). Clarence, couldn't you play just *once* more?

CLARENCE (*at door* L.). No, I'm afraid I can't! Not for eight hours!

(*Exit* CLARENCE L., DINWIDDIE *following him.* MRS. WHEELER *stands looking after him wistfully, but* CORA, *close to her, sits sorrowfully upon the floor as he says "eight hours."* VIOLET *exits* R. *simultaneously when* CLARENCE *exits* L. *They look across at each other just before.*)

BOBBY (*coming down importantly*). Well, wha'daya *think* about it, Father? Don-'cha think he's prob'ly crazy?

WHEELER (*sweeping him away with a gesture, exasperated and perplexed beyond measure*). I don't know! Go get me a dictionary! And a copy of *Who's Who*!

(*Begins to pace the floor,* BOBBY *going up* C. MRS. WHEELER *and* CORA R.C.)

CURTAIN

ACT FOUR

SCENE: *The same. The curtains of the sun-room have been pulled back, showing a bright morning outdoors. In the sunroom are:* CORA, *in pretty country-clothes for autumn, but not wearing a hat; and* MRS. WHEELER *in a becoming morning negligee. They sit, examining with interest some large books, turning the pages; other books, including a new "Who's Who," are on a table near them.* WHEELER *enters* R. (*The doors there are open.*) *He wears* the same clothes shown in Act One and Two, and glasses; has "Sun" and "Times." He is going to sit in the sunroom and read; but halts upon seeing MRS. WHEELER, on couch L. He doesn't see CORA at R. of steps.

MRS. WHEELER (*pleasantly*). Good-morning, Henry! (*Nods smilingly.*) I hope you slept well? (*Looks again at her book; exchanges it for another;* CORA *doing the same.*)

WHEELER (*gravely*). Thanks. (*Goes to settee by piano.*)

MRS. WHEELER. I told 'em not to put too much sugar on your grapefruit again. Was your breakfast all right?

WHEELER. Thanks. It's quite surprising.

MRS. W (*looking at her book*). What is?

WHEELER (*gravely*). Your being so— amiable.

MRS. W (*indulgently*). You mean in the morning?

WHEELER (*casually*). Yes—or evening. (*Sits by piano on settee* R.C., *lifting one of the papers to read.*)

MRS. W (*amiably*). Oh, we're *all* cheerful now. (*Sits* L.C.) Isn't Miss Pinney down yet?

WHEELER (*quietly*). I don't know. Is— Clarence?

MRS. W. No. Dinwiddie says the poor boy didn't go to bed till after four—but he kept at it till he got that dreadful heating plant repaired—!

CORA (*dreamily, at back*). Isn't he wonderful?

WHEELER (*mutteringly*). Oh, are *you* there, Cora? I didn't see you.

MRS. W. I thought you didn't.

CORA (*alluding to book*). This is "Bon-Con," Mama. There's nothing that sounds (*Comes down.*) like it here. It couldn't be Coaling Stations of course? You don't think it was Coaling Stations he said, do you? I know it was coal-something, wasn't it, Papa?

WHEELER (*gruffly*). Wasn't *what* "coal something?"

CORA. What Clarence said.

WHEELER (*touched on a sore spot*). I don't know and I don't care to know. (*Reading his paper again.*)

CORA (*coming down, carrying a large book. Crosses to* WHEELER). Yes, Papa; *you* know when he said last night he was one of the authorities on coal-something and you sent Bobby for the dictionary and got so mad because by the time he came back with it you couldn't remember this coal-something-word to look it up; so you couldn't, and went off to bed with a headache powder. It was coal-something wasn't it, because *you* can remember anyhow *that* much, *can't* you, Papa?

WHEELER. No. I cannot; and I don't care to!

CORA (*going back to the sunroom*). Well, I know it *was*. (*Plaintively.*) But the encyclopedia's abslootly more than useless whenever you need it the most. You can't get any help out of it at *all* unless you know just what you want to look up! (*Goes up and gets "Who's Who."*) *I'd* have *willingly* gone and asked Clarence last night while he was working in the cellar, only you wouldn't let me.

MRS. W. (*pleasantly*). I don't just see why you couldn't have asked him yourself, Henry.

WHEELER (*irascibly*). Don't you? I suppose you think I'm so ridiculous already I needn't have minded making myself more so!

MRS. W (*soothingly*). But I don't see the ridiculousness—

WHEELER. You don't see the ridiculousness of going down in the cellar to ask a man you've been badgering and who's repairing a heating plant for you —to ask him what a word was that he'd already *told* you *twice!*

CORA (*comes down* C. *with book*). Well, you couldn't sit up till four o'clock to ask him; at least, Miss Pinney wouldn't let me. (*Emphasizing the last two words.*) How *could* you be so absurd as to think Clarence's name was Smun, Papa?

MRS. W (*quietly reproving*). Your father's always accurate, Cora.

(WHEELER *stares at her, and sits again.*)

CORA. Well, so's Violet. *She* heard him give his name in the office and she says it's Moon.

MRS. W (*absently*). Hush! Your father's right, of course.

CORA (*putting her book on the table*). There's a whole book on Coal in the library. I'm goin' to get it. (*Runs off* L.)

WHEELER (*rises—crosses to table for paper*). Do you mind being quite frank? Why have you suddenly become so amiable with me?

MRS. W (*smilingly*). Don't you think anybody can be amiable if she can find even just one pleasant thing to think

about—at home? I suppose we all need —*something!*

WHEELER (*frowning*). Yes. There's one pleasant thing *I* think about *you*, Fanny.

MRS. W (*amiably*). You've *found* one?

WHEELER. I mean to say; you're not obstinate—about names, for instance—

MRS. W (*lightly but seriously*). Oh, no. I only think of what he *is*.

WHEELER (*striking his paper impatiently*). "What he *is?*" You can't! We don't know any more about that than we did before I questioned him!

MRS. W (*pleasantly*). "Questioned him"? Why, you didn't even ask him his name!

WHEELER (*breaking out*). My Lord, do you suppose I could have a man in my house three weeks and then ask him his *name?* His name's Smun.

MRS. W (*indulgently*). There isn't any Smun in *Who's Who*. Or any Clarence Moon either.

WHEELER. I didn't *expect* to find him in *Who's Who!* You don't suppose anybody in *Who's Who* would have been looking for a job the way he—(*Louder with the new thought.*) Why hasn't he had any letters since he's been here?

MRS. W (*casually, as she looks in a book*). Probably because he hasn't written to anybody. (*Struck by this idea, and annoyed by it,* WHEELER *rubs his head. Going on absently.*) That usually *is* the way, isn't it?

WHEELER (*mumbling*). I dunno! I dunno! (*Reads again.*)

(CORA *enters* L., *bringing another book.*)

CORA (*as she comes in*). I've *almost* remembered what he said: it was something like "coal and potteries"—I'm sure there was something about potteries in it. (*She is at table.*) Don't you think there was something like "potteries" in it, Papa?

WHEELER (*almost shouting*). I don't *know!*

CORA. Well, Violet didn't know, herself, and she's supposed to tutor me in *French* an' ev'rything—so it *can't* be *any*thing in *French* or anything. *That* makes it seem as if it might be coal and potteries, doesn't it?

(BOBBY *enters from* L., *dressed as in Act Two. He speaks briskly as he enters.*)

BOBBY. Well, have you found out what he was talkin' about yet? (WHEELER *utters a sound of exasperation, rises and goes up, taking his papers with him. Goes round* R.

of table and up into sunroom. BOBBY *enters* L. *Going on.*) I don't think it *was* a word myself. Look! I think it was just somep'n he made up, because, listen, if it was a word, why *Father'd* of known it. (WHEELER *gives him a look and goes out up* L. *garden quickly.* BOBBY *looks after him.*) Listen! I wonder what makes him so nervous?

MRS. W (*thoughtfully*). Maybe we all do. (*She goes quietly out up* C. *to* L. *garden after* WHEELER.)

BOBBY. You don't suppose she means his fam'ly upsets him.

CORA (*goes up* C. *with a book. To* BOBBY, *virtuously reproving*). I guess she means the behavior of *some* o' the fam'ly does! (VIOLET *enters* R., *dressed as in Act One, but without a wrap. She wears a hat.* CORA *doesn't pause.* BOBBY *doesn't see* VIOLET, *goes up* C.) *You* wouldn't even let him read his paper in peace an' quiet.

BOBBY (*indignantly*). Me! Why, it was you! I'm goin' to *ask* him. (*Going* L.) Papa, wasn't it Cora that—

CORA (*going* L.). I'll ask him first! Papa wasn't it Bobby that—

(*They go out angrily up* L., *clamoring together. Exit* C. *to* L., *then cross to* R.) "Papa, wasn't it (Cora) (Bobby) that disturbed you?" (WHEELER'S *voice is heard loudly protesting off* L., *but not his words, and a moment later* CORA *and* BOBBY *return, retreating across the sunroom from up* L. *to up* R. *in serious discomfiture, talking loudly, simultaneously, not pausing. What* BOBBY *says is:*) 'Twas your fault! Never heard him speak like that before! C'm out 'n the yard! (*What* CORA *says is:*) Well, I never was so insulted by my own father in my life! (*Both these speeches are finished off* R. DELLA *enters* R—*carrying a small vacuum cleaner just as the two are crossing.* VIOLET *goes up and looks after them; then off* L. *thoughtfully.*)

WHEELER (*off*). Oh, damn it—let me alone!

DELLA (R. *benevolently, alluding to* R.). He's eatin'.

VIOLET. What? (*Comes down part way.*)

DELLA. He's eatin' his breakfast; one cup coffee; one slice toast. Never nothin' more. It only takes um a minute an' three-quahters; he's a comfortin' man to have in a house. Now he's through. Jist like that.

(VIOLET *goes up, looking at the books.* CLARENCE *enters* R., *dressed as in the latter part of the second act.*)

CLARENCE (*cheerfully*). Good morning, Miss Pinney. (DELLA *stops and turns. She nods, not looking fully at him.*) Good morning, Della.

DELLA (*half amused, half languishingly*). Good mornin', Mister Clair'nce. (*Goes* L. *as on reluctant duty. Looking back.*)

CLARENCE. Oh—Della—

DELLA. Yes? Yes, sir?

CLARENCE. Ah—did you understand me to say that before I was in the army I'd been employed in a—washroom—in a hotel?

DELLA. You didn't *say* in a hotel, sir, but I knew you'd never 'a' been contented wit' less. You says in a lavatory, sir.

CLARENCE. Oh! (*Gravely.*) Well, I'd have done as well as I could in a position in a lavatory, I hope; but what I said was "laboratory."

DELLA (*matter-of-course*). Yes, sir. What is the difference, sir?

CLARENCE. Well, in a laboratory you have to do some work.

DELLA (*commiserating him*). Trust you for findin' the hard jobs, Mister Clair-'nce.

CLARENCE. Thank you, Della.

DELLA (*gently*). Yes, sir.

(*Exits* C. *to* L. *with the vacuum cleaner.* CLARENCE *crosses over to look at* VIOLET. VIOLET *comes down.*)

CLARENCE (*alluding to* VIOLET'S *hat*). Are you going out this morning? So am I.

VIOLET (*quietly, rather coldly*). I'm going *away*, this morning.

CLARENCE (*going nearer her*). "Going *away* this morning." So am I. That's peculiar.

VIOLET (*dryly, with a glance at him and away*). Yes, it *would* be, if *you* were going! I'm afraid you'd have it take—several—people with you! (*Looking away from him.*) Why do you think of going?

CLARENCE. "*Why?*" Don't you think for an employee to remain in a position a certain amount of connivance on the part of his employer is almost a necessity?

VIOLET. But *Mrs.* Wheeler won't let you go.

CLARENCE. I know the repartee for that, but—

VIOLET (*interrupting quickly*). Mr. Wheeler won't let *me*. (*With a slight laugh.*) Don't fear; we had the most absurd argument over a foolish point last night and—well, I'm sure he thinks me outrageously feminine!

CLARENCE. What was the foolish point?

VIOLET. It was too foolish to tell you. (*Comes down a little. Both speak seriously.*)

CLARENCE (*frowning*). Well, I suppose the important thing is that we're both going away—and don't know where. You've never told me. Haven't you got any father or mother or anything?

VIOLET (*not gloomily*). No. I've got a second cousin in Belfast—I've never met him.

CLARENCE. I've got an aunt—in Honolulu. She used to write to me for money sometimes. I don't believe she'd be much help.

VIOLET. Not in an emergency, I should think.

CLARENCE (*cheerfully*). Yes—we—seem to have an emergency.

VIOLET (*looking up at him*). "We?" I'm simply going in town to an agency and wait till they find something for me.

CLARENCE. Suppose your—funds—didn't hold out till they did?

VIOLET. Oh, but they *will!* (*She means they must.*)

CLARENCE. Mine wouldn't. I wonder if Della happens to *know* of a good hotel where they need—

VIOLET (*sincerely*). I have a full month's check; paid this morning. I'll lend you half of it till you find out.

CLARENCE (*stares at her; then speaks rather huskily*). You will?

VIOLET (*quietly*). Why, of course.

CLARENCE. Be careful; I might do something queer!

VIOLET (*with dry naïveté*). "Be careful" —of my money?

CLARENCE. No. Be careful now. Of talking about lending me half of it.

VIOLET. Don't you suppose I meant it?

CLARENCE. Yes. That's why I might do something queer. (*She looks up at him in increasing puzzlement.*)

VIOLET. Queer? (*Turns a little.*)

CLARENCE (*profoundly in earnest*). Don't worry. I'm all right again. There's something I want to tell you. It's about myself. I don't believe I've mentioned it. I *have* mentioned a lot of things about myself—

VIOLET. Well, not a lot—but—some.

CLARENCE. Nothing's so stupid as a man going about telling everyone all about his private affairs—I'm afraid I talk about myself too much altogether. Of course, it was disgustingly conceited on my part to think Mr. Wheeler had looked me up—but wasn't it natural to think he'd do that when Mrs. Martyn had my *name?* I suppose I often forget I'm a specialist and that businessmen, of *course*, don't know much about such people as entomologists.

VIOLET (*not knowing, herself*). I—suppose they—don't.

CLARENCE (*going on with an enthusiasm that increases*). On the other hand, doesn't it seem strange they don't? My subject is of the most august proportions in the world. The coleoptera are the largest division of the animal kingdom. They outnumber mere human beings by billions of billions. Not held in check, they would sweep the whole of mankind from the earth like a breath!

VIOLET. They would?

CLARENCE (*going on with still greater spirit and enthusiasm*). I say I am an expert on them; that only means I know most of the little we know about them: our ignorance is still of the dark ages! Mr. Wheeler is an expert on dollars. Anybody can know *all about* dollars. Put all the wealth of all the nations together and you get a sum that can be spoken in hundreds of billions, whereas the coleoptera consist of *eighty thousand species* and the population of a *single one* of those eighty thousand species alone outnumbers the dollars of all the nations of the earth as stupendously as the dollars of those nations outnumber the dollars in Mr. Wheeler's pocket! No, no; there's no reason for *him* to feel superior. No, no, indeed! *Nobody* need set up to be snobbish about *beetles!*

VIOLET (*startled*). Beetles! Are the cocoleoptera—are they just *beetles?*

CLARENCE (*amazed*). Why! Didn't you know?

VIOLET. I—I don't believe many people—do.

CLARENCE. No. I suppose they don't. Each man to his trade—I've heard a politician get as excited about politics—or a minister about his congregation—as I do about the coleoptera! You wouldn't believe it, but—

VIOLET (*interrupting*). Yes, I believe it. I believe everything you say—but you said you wanted to tell me something

about your private affairs. You didn't
mean the co-leoptera, did you?

CLARENCE (*remembering*). Yes; in a way
their affairs are mine. What I wanted to
tell you is that it's possible we shan't need
to worry about money.

VIOLET (*frowning*). Possible that "*we*"
shan't?

CLARENCE. We *might* not, after this
morning's mail. You see, before the war I
was on potato-bugs—

VIOLET (*disturbed*). You were?

CLARENCE. Oh, yes; I was a *long* time
on potato-bugs.

VIOLET. Are *they* co-le-op—

CLARENCE. Absolutely. You see, by
finding their worst enemies—

VIOLET. Enemies? You mean people
that hate potato-bugs?

CLARENCE. No! Other *bugs* that hate
'em. At least they don't get on with them.
The enemies are altogether too much for
the potato-bugs, you see; and by getting
the potato-bugs and their enemies *together*, of course you save the potatoes.

VIOLET. But I should think their enemies might—

CLARENCE. No. Their enemies don't
like potatoes.

VIOLET (*sincerely*). How strange!

CLARENCE (*enthusiastically*). It's one of
the most fortunate things in the world!
If they *both* liked 'em there wouldn't be
any potatoes. Now, the potato-bug—
(*As if lecturing.*)

VIOLET (*interrupting*). But surely this
isn't what you wanted to tell me about
yourself?

CLARENCE. Yes, it is. (*In the same tone as
before.*) Now, the potato-bug—the potato-bug has several acknowledged authorities, and I was one of 'em.

VIOLET (*nodding*). Of course.

CLARENCE. My assistant was even
more so! *I'm* more a general authority;
he's all potato-bug; he's spent *sixteen
years* on potato-bugs; and he's the oldest
potato-bug man in the world today! He
is! He's a good general bug man, too, a
fine all-round bug man, but when it
comes to potato-bugs, he can eat any
other bug man alive!

VIOLET (*seriously*). He can?

CLARENCE. Yes, when I went into the
army, this assistant of mine was appointed to the position *I'd* held; and it
was what he deserved. When I got out of
the army, I knew if I went back there the

trustees would put me in again, and
he'd be dropped, so I decided it was
only decent not to disturb him, but I
had spent a lot of money on outside
experiments, and I had to do something.
However, I discovered that during a
period of economic reconstruction after
a world war there are extremely limited
openings for a specialist on the coleoptera.

VIOLET (*gently, her eyes lowered*). You
had a pretty hard time—

CLARENCE. Not compared to some of
the others.

VIOLET. But I understood you to say
you might be all right if you get a letter
you're expecting by this morning's mail.

CLARENCE. No. I said "we." I said
we might be all right.

VIOLET (*genuinely perplexed*). But I
don't see—

CLARENCE. Why, yes. It will all
depend on the letter. You see, several
days ago the papers said my assistant
had been called to Washington by the
Department of Agriculture and he'd
accepted. So you see where that might
put *us*, right away.

VIOLET. "Put us"? I don't see where
it might put anything!

CLARENCE. But my *dear*—

VIOLET (*turning, not angrily, but disturbed of mind*). What?

CLARENCE. My dear Miss *Pinney*—

VIOLET. Oh! (*Meaning "Oh, I see!"*)

CLARENCE. Don't you see; that left
me free to write the laboratory that I was
out of the army—so I *did* write 'em
yesterday, and if they think half as
much of me as a coleopterist, as I do of
myself, they'll have my re-appointment
in this morning's mail and we'll be all
right.

VIOLET (*impatiently*). But "we," "we"!
You keep saying "we"!

CLARENCE. Well, by that I mean us.
I couldn't ask for a better salary.

VIOLET (*bothered, but not cross*). Oh,
it's *you* that are going to lend money
now—if your letter comes? Would you
lend me—half of it?

CLARENCE. I thought probably—the
best way would be—would be for you
to take charge of all of it—as it comes
in—and let me have what I need when
I need it!

VIOLET (*incredulous*). You thought—

CLARENCE. Yes. Wouldn't you do that?

VIOLET (*turns from him, then again to him*). That's a curious speech for a man to make, when only last night I was told I was mistaken about his very name!

CLARENCE. Why, how could you have been mistaken about my name?

VIOLET. I couldn't, of course; but Mr. Wheeler thought I was. That's the "foolish point" I told you we were both disagreeable about. He thinks your name is Smun.

CLARENCE. Why, *nobody's* name is Smun! It can't *be!*

VIOLET. That's what I told him—so often he began to hate me, I think! But he insisted Smun was the name you gave Mrs. Martyn.

CLARENCE. Naturally, *you* knew better.

VIOLET. Naturally! I told him what it was; but why did Mrs. Martyn tell him it was Smun?

CLARENCE. I suppose I must have mumbled it; people with ordinary names nearly always do.

VIOLET. I don't think your name's very "ordinary."

CLARENCE (*anxiously*). Don't you? People usually do, but I'm glad *you* don't.

VIOLET. Of course I don't.

CLARENCE. Do you think—beetles—are all right, too? At least, I hope you could enjoy them?

VIOLET (*seriously, not shyly*). I don't know enough about them to say.

CLARENCE. I could tell you a little; it wouldn't take long.

VIOLET. How long?

CLARENCE. About as long as I live.

VIOLET (*quickly*). Oh, no!

CLARENCE (*quickly*). You can only tell a little about beetles in a lifetime. Of course, we'd *often* speak of other things —or wouldn't we?

VIOLET (*seriously and quickly*). Why, we'd—have to.

CLARENCE (*quickly*). Then we *will*. Is your bag packed?

VIOLET (*breathlessly*). It's right by the door of my room.

CLARENCE. I'll get 'em both. Where's your trunk?

VIOLET (*gulping*). It's—ready.

CLARENCE. We'll *send* for *it!* (*Exit rapidly* L. VIOLET *sinks down in a corner of the sofa, looking dazed.*)

(DINWIDDIE *enters up* R. *in the sunroom with letters, rolled magazines, and circulars on a tray; he sets this upon piano, and goes out up* R. BOBBY's *voice is heard off up* R. DINWIDDIE *exits* C. *to* R. *garden.*)

BOBBY (*off*). Morning mail in, Dinwiddie?

DINWIDDIE. Yes, sir, on the piano.

CORA (*off*). Hoop-la! (*She runs on up* R. *Halts in the sunroom staring* L. BOBBY *follows her.*)

BOBBY (*amazed staring* L. *also*). Why, look at Father and Mama!

CORA. I *am* looking at 'em!

BOBBY. He's got his arm around her!

CORA (*slowly and dreamily*). That's all Clarence's influence.

BOBBY. Well, you cert'nly have got an imagination! (*Shouting.*) Hey! Papa! Morning mail's here!

CORA (*indignantly*). Is that your idea of what to do when you see anybody with their arm around somebody? Why couldn't you leave 'em alone? (*Coming down to piano.*)

BOBBY. I don't like to see Papa gettin' so soft. (*Coming down to piano.*)

CORA. I guess he wouldn't be *your* father if he wasn't pretty impressionable!

BOBBY (*examining letters with her*). It's you he inherits *that from!* Here's a couple of circulars for—(*Taking them to* VIOLET, *speaks tenderly.*)—for—*you*— Violet.

(VIOLET *rises and goes toward piano.*)

CORA (*huskily commenting*). He certainly ought to be in school. (*Almost musingly.*)

VIOLET (*in a low, absent voice, not looking at him*). Thanks. (*Takes them absently; not opening them. He returns to the table.* CORA *stands near the piano with magazines. Comes and sits chair* L.C. *opens them. In a troubled voice*). Is there a letter there for—for Mr. Moon?

BOBBY. Who?

CORA (*sharply*). For Clarence! (*To* VIOLET.) I think it's wonderful; all this mystery about him and the cannibals and the saxophone and everything. He's perfectly certain to turn out to belong to an old Knickerbocker millionaire family with a yacht and all the old clubs—and a valet.

BOBBY. His name's Smun!

CORA. It is not! It's Moon! (*Crosses up* C.)

BOBBY (*crossly*). Well, there isn't any letter here for *either* of 'em!

VIOLET (*gently*). Are you sure?

BOBBY (*calmly*). I'm always sure. (VIOLET *crosses down* R.)

CORA (*comes down* C. *to* BOBBY. *Looking at him with concentration*). My! I'll be sorry for the woman that marries you; you already talk just like a regular little *man!* (*Crosses to* C. MRS. WHEELER *enters up* L.; *stands in sunroom unobserved.* CORA *goes on.*) If you want me to explain that, I'll merely mention it's meant for an insult. (*Plaintively.*) I *don't* know how I live in the same house with you! (*Crosses to table.*)

MRS. WHEELER (*amiably, coming down*). You're not going to, Cora, very long. Your father's decided on a school for you—next week.

CORA. He has? Well, if it weren't for —for just one thing—I'd say "Father's right for once!"

BOBBY. What "one thing"?

CORA (*gulping*). Well—it's a person.

MRS. W (*going to* VIOLET, *who rises*). Clarence has just spoken to us—out there. (*Takes her hand.*) He tells us you're going. I'm *really* sorry!

BOBBY (*startled*). Who's going?

VIOLET (*gently*). I am.

BOBBY. When?

VIOLET. Why—this morning.

BOBBY (*gulping*). Why, when am I goin' to see you again?

VIOLET (*gently, gravely*). Why, whenever you like, when you have a vacation.

MRS. W. You're going, too, tomorrow, Bobby.

BOBBY (*dazed*). I am?

MRS. W (*nodding amiably*). Your father's got the school to take you back. (*Crosses to* L. *Enter* WHEELER *and* CLARENCE, *carrying hat, overcoat, and gloves.*)

BOBBY (*his voice breaking*). He did? (CORA *giggles irrepressibly. He whirls fiercely on her.*) You hush up! (*She dodges him gaily; he sinks morbidly into a chair.*)

CORA (*merrily taunting*). Oh, Bobby!

WHEELER. Miss Pinney . . .

VIOLET. Yes, Mr. Wheeler?

WHEELER. Clarence has just told me you've decided—you've both decided —on taking a step much more important than merely leaving this house. (CLARENCE *comes down.*)

CORA (*mystified but not troubled*). What's Papa talking about? (*She is by the table.*)

VIOLET (*troubled, to* WHEELER). I'm afraid part of his plan may have to—be postponed.

CLARENCE. If any part of my plan is postponed, it won't be *that* part of it!

VIOLET (*troubled*). Your letter—didn't come.

CLARENCE (*dismayed*). It didn't? (*Turning up a little to the table.*) Why, it had to!

CORA (*shaking her head—goes up to piano*). No. There wasn't any letter for you, Clarence. There were two for Violet and some magazines and circulars, and all the rest is for Papa and Mama.

CLARENCE. But it's *got* to be there.

CORA. No. That's all there is; there isn't a single solitary other letter except just this one that'll have to be sent to the Dead Letter Office because it's addressed to somebody that doesn't live here at all. It's addressed "C. Smith, Esquire," care of Papa.

CLARENCE. But, good heavens, that's *it!*

CORA (*loudly*). What!

CLARENCE (*taking it*). "C. Smith," Clarence Smith. Of *course* it's it! You gave me a fright! (*There is a general exclamation of profound amazement.* CORA *immediately runs up to table for "Who's Who."*)

WHEELER. Smith? Clarence Smith!

VIOLET (*dazed*). Smith!

(*She whispers the words, staring front; her mouth remains open as she sinks into a settee.* CLARENCE *is seriously occupied reading the letter.* CORA *comes down to the table with "Who's Who," rapidly turning the pages.*)

CORA. It's a 1916 *Who's Who in America* — before the war, that is. S — S Satterthwaite — Smalley — (*Loudly and emphatically.*) Smith! Clarence Smith! He's the very first Smith there is in it! (*Reading.*) "Clarence Smith, zoologist. Born, June, 13th, 1890, at Zubesi Mission Station, Congo River, Africa— (*Looking up.*) Well, I should say he *did* have cannibals! (*Reading again.*) Son of Gabriel C., Medical Missionary, and Martha S., Grad. Coll. Physical Science Newcastle-on-Tyne, England. Postgrad. Polytechnique, France. D.S.C.— (*Repeating.*) "D.S.C."

BOBBY. It means he's a Doctor of Science. I had a prof. was one—ole Doc. Toser!

CORA (*reading*). "Doctor of Science.

Chief en—en—tomologist"— (*Looking up inquiringly.*)

CLARENCE (*absently, not looking up from his letter*). Entomologist. It means somebody that studies bugs.

CORA (*gravely*). Bugs? How lovely! (*Reading again.*) Chief ento-tomologist and curator of entomology, Sturtevant Biological Laboratories. Fellow N. Y. Acad. Sciences; mem. N. Y. Zoological Soc—society—Address Sturtevant Biological Laboratories, N. Y. (*Looking up, dazed.*) Did you ever hear anything like it? And that just means Clarence!

VIOLET (*huskily*). Smith! Clarence Smith! (*Rising.*)

(CLARENCE *has finished the letter and hears her. He comes to her.*)

CLARENCE (*slowly*). Why, *you* knew it was Smith, didn't you?

VIOLET (*still dazed, shakes her head dumbly before speaking, huskily*). No. I didn't.

CLARENCE. Is it—is it going to make a difference?

VIOLET (*groping forward—rises*). I couldn't—I couldn't—

CLARENCE. You mean you couldn't—because it's Smith?

VIOLET (*just over a whisper, brokenly*). Smith's—beautiful!

CLARENCE (*gently*). Yes—it *will* be. (*She looks up at him.*)

CORA (*disturbed, to* MRS. WHEELER). What *are* they talking about?

MRS. WHEELER (*smiling*). Sh! They're going to be married. (*Almost a whisper, but briskly.*)

CORA (*in a feeble voice*). What?

(BOBBY *comes down.*)

CLARENCE. I've got our things at the door, and I telephoned for a car. It's here.

VIOLET (*tremulously, pathetically*). Do you think I can go 'way with you like this—when I've just found out your name? (*She gives him her hand for an instant.*)

CLARENCE. Oh, Violet! (*He means it, profoundly, as a lover, but it has unintentionally much the effect of* CORA'S "*Oh, Clarence!*")

BOBBY (*approaching*). Violet— (*Gulps. She looks at him; he is unable to bear it. Speaks hastily, with a choke.*) I'll go help—carry out your baggage! (*Exits hurriedly* L.)

CLARENCE (*heartily, shaking hands with* WHEELER). Good-by and thank you, Mr. Wheeler!

WHEELER (*earnestly*). Good luck to you, Doctor Smith! (*No emphasis on "Doctor."*)

VIOLET (*gasping*). Doctor—

WHEELER. Why, certainly; Doctor of Science. He's called "Doctor," of course.

CLARENCE (*crosses in front of* VIOLET—*shaking* MRS. WHEELER'S *hand*). You've been so kind, Mrs. Wheeler. (*Quickly going on to* CORA.) Good-by, Cora.

CORA (*looking straight front, her hands already behind her*). I won't. (*Speaks quickly but not loudly.*)

MRS. W (*quickly and cordially*). Oh, we're all coming out to see you off. (*They all move to* L. *except* CLARENCE *and* CORA.) We'll say good-by out there!

(*Exit* L., *taking* WHEELER'S *arm at the door.* VIOLET *runs back and kisses* CORA *on the cheek, hurriedly, and then runs out* L. CORA *is unchanged in adamantine attitude, though a very short sniff is heard from her.*)

CLARENCE. Good-by, Cora.

CORA. I won't.

CLARENCE. Won't you say good-by to me?

CORA (*unchanging*). I won't! I hate engaged men! I hate 'em, I hate 'em, I hate 'em!

CLARENCE. Won't you say good-by to me, dear?

CORA. I won't. (*Then suddenly, but still looking straight forward.*) What'd *Violet* say if she heard you were already around callin' other women "dear"?

CLARENCE. Well—(*Moves* L.)—if you won't say good-by I'll have to go and confess it to her! (*He looks back from the doorway.*) Good-by?

CORA (*not moving anything but her eyes, which follow him sidelong*). I hate 'em, I hate 'em, I hate 'em! (CLARENCE *makes a gesture of farewell and resignation; Exit* L. CORA *sinks into a chair* L.C. *just behind her, unchanged, repeating mechanically*) I hate 'em, I hate 'em, etc.

(MRS. WHEELER *enters* L., *smiling, but with tears in her eyes.* CORA *continues.*)

MRS. WHEELER (*as she comes*). They *were* dears! Wasn't he lovely? Cora! Didn't you tell them good-by? (CLARENCE *is seen outside the sunroom window up* C. *in bright sunshine. He raises the window.* MRS. WHEELER *goes up, exclaiming*) Oh, look; it's Clarence; he wants you to—

CLARENCE (*calling in*). Good-by, Cora dear!

(CORA *leaps up suddenly.*)

CORA (*in a loud, tremulous, sweet voice*). Oh, good-by! (*She runs up, waving her handkerchief. He waves his hat, shouting* "*Good luck! Good-by!*" *and runs off to* L. *outside.* MRS. WHEELER *goes to window, waving her handkerchief.* CORA *comes down, not weeping but swallowing. She sits again. Swallowing, gently.*) Oh, Clarence!

CURTAIN

RAIN

John Colton and Clemence Randolph

(founded on W. Somerset Maugham's story "Miss Thompson")

Rain was first produced in the United States by Sam H. Harris at the Maxine Elliott Theatre, New York City, on November 7, 1922. The play was staged by John D. Williams. The cast was as follows:

NATIVE GIRL . . . . . . Kathryne Kennedy	SERGEANT O'HARA,
NATIVE POLICEMAN . . Bhana Whitehawk	U.S.M.C. . . . . Robert Elliott
NATIVES . . . . Oka Bunda,	JOE HORN . . . . Ripley Holmes
Llano Panlo	DR. MACPHAIL . . . . Fritz Williams
AMEENA . . . . Emmie Wilcox	MRS. MACPHAIL . . . . Shirley King
PRIVATE GRIGGS,	MRS. DAVIDSON . . . . . . Catharine Brooks
U.S.M.C. . . . . Kent Thurber	QUARTERMASTER BATES . . Harry Quealy
CORPORAL HODGSON,	SADIE THOMPSON . . . . Jeanne Eagles
U.S.M.C. . . . . Harold Healy	REV. DAVIDSON . . . . Robert Kelly

The action of the play takes place in the living room of Joe Horn's hotel-store in the port of Pago Pago on the Island of Tutuila in the South Seas, during the rainy season. The time is the present.

ACT ONE: Early morning.
ACT TWO: Two days later. Night.
ACT THREE. *Scene One:* Four days later. Night. *Scene Two:* Early the following morning.

Copyright 1923, by Liveright, Inc.
Copyright (acting edition) 1948, by Samuel French, Ltd.
All rights reserved.

CAUTION: Professionals and amateurs are hereby warned that *Rain*, being fully protected under the copyright laws of the United States of America, the British Empire, including the Dominion of Canada, and all other countries of the Copyright Union, is subject to a royalty. All rights, including professional, amateur, motion pictures, recitation, public reading, radio and television broadcasting, and the rights of translation into foreign languages, are strictly reserved. Inquiries should be addressed to American Play Company, 52 Vanderbilt Avenue, New York 17, N.Y.

JOHN COLTON is best remembered for *Rain*, his dramatization of Somerset Maugham's short story *Miss Thompson*. His collaborator on this immensely successful enterprise was Miss Clemence Randolph, who owes her sole distinction in the theatre to this early anti-puritan melodrama which arrived on the American scene in 1922, in time to be enlisted in the new generation's assault on puritanism. Somerset Maugham was by then, of course, a well-known writer of fiction (*Of Human Bondage* had appeared in 1915 and *The Moon and Sixpence* in 1919), as well as playwright known for such productions as *Frederick* (1907), *The Land of Promise* (1914), *Home and Beauty* (1919), and *The Circle* (1921).

John Colton was born in Minnesota in 1891, but was taken to Japan by his parents while still an infant. His father being occupied at the time with collecting art treasures for the firm of Vantine and Company, the future playwright became quite a traveler in the East, visiting China and India as well as Japan. Although educated by tutors in the Orient, as well as in France and England, he failed to survive as an undergraduate at Columbia University in New York and went west in search of a career. After marking time for about two years, he found a berth on a newspaper in Minneapolis and also got a stock company production for an unidentified early play. In pursuit of a profitable profession he then moved to Hollywood, and it was here that he met Somerset Maugham, from whom he got permission to dramatize *Miss Thompson*. The magazine *Cosmopolitan*, normally hospitable to Maugham's writings, had found the story too risqué to publish when Maugham submitted it to the chief editor, Ray Long. It was published instead by George Jean Nathan in the *Smart Set*, the lively predecessor of *The American Mercury* which Nathan edited at that time with H. L. Mencken.

When Maugham gave his proofs from the the *Smart Set* to Colton to read, the latter concluded that the story was excellent material for a play. Going back to New York and taking on Miss Randolph as a collaborator, Colton soon sold his dramatization to the Broadway producer John D. Williams on the basis of an incomplete handwritten draft. In search of an actress to play the heroine Sadie Thompson, Williams took the script to other producers. A. H. Woods tried to get Marjorie Rambeau for the part, but was turned down by Hugh Dillman, her husband, who disliked the play. Sam H. Harris had Jeanne Eagels under contract; he produced the play, with Williams directing it at first but later relinquishing the reins to Sam Forrest. With difficulties developing during the tryout stage, Sam Harris not only changed directors midstream but brought in the expert playwright Eugene Walter, remembered for his daring drama *The Easiest Way*, whose ministrations in Philadelphia do not appear to have been particularly important. But when *Rain* opened in New York at the Maxine Elliot Theatre, the excitement in the audience amounted to a demonstration, especially when Sadie denounced the Reverend Davidson at the end of the second act and in the last scene of the third. (Ward Morehouse gives a good account of the event in his *Matinee Tomorrow: Fifty Years of Our Theatre*, 1949.) The play became a tremendous success, and Jeanne Eagels played Sadie Thompson for five years. *Rain*, which was unsuccessfully turned into a musical play in the 1940's, stands, along with *What Price Glory?*, the Stallings and Anderson anti-war comedy, as a landmark in the American theatre's march toward freedom of expression in the early 1920's.

Colton, who had had a difficult time of it during the Philadelphia tryout, was able to score so successfully in our theatre only once again, even though he remained a conscientious craftsman and a man of broad sympathies. I recall reading an appealing adaptation he made of the German dramatist Georg Kaiser's *The Soldier Tanaka*, an anti-militaristic drama about a Japanese soldier during World War II. It might have succeeded on Broadway during this period of crisis when we were at war with Japan, but it failed to get a production. In 1933 he had a romantic adaptation of a Hungarian play on the boards under the curious title of *Saint Wench*, but even the presence of Helen Menken in the principal part could not keep the play running longer than two weeks. In the same season he rewrote a murder-case melodrama, *Nine Pine Street*, and Lillian Gish played the part of the heroine who, losing her reason after her mother's death and her father's remarriage, murdered both her father and his second wife. Colton got only twenty-eight performances for this melodrama. His one successful play after *Rain* came in 1926. *The Shanghai Gesture* was received with some derision by critics. Nevertheless, it ran for nearly three years under the management of A. H. Woods, with Florence Reed in the role of Mother Goddam, the former Manchu princess who discovers that a dissolute girl in her brothel is her own child by a faithless English lover.

ACT ONE

The SCENE of the play is the public living-room of JOE HORN'S hotel-store in the port of Pago Pago in the South Seas.

It is to be presumed that the hotel-store is a frame building of two stories with broad verandas on both floors. It stands on a little incline, a short distance from the wharf at which steamers touch. Apart from the government buildings and a small U.S. Naval Station, it is the only occidental habitation in this tiny island.

The audience views the room from a slight angle, enabling them to see the veranda, which extends across the stage at R. The veranda is railed in iron-work painted yellow, supported by wooden pillars upholding a roof of corrugated iron.

The floor of the room is covered with greasy matting, and the walls are papered only in vague patches with paper that at one time or another had gold markings on it. Where the paper has peeled, crumbling plaster and whitewashed laths show through. From the ceiling, at C., hangs a lamp worked by chains. The lamp is framed in a tin and glass arrangement, and when lit casts on the floor an oval pool of reddish-gold light.

The center of the back wall is broken by a rickety staircase, projecting out into the room. The stairs reach a half-landing on stage, then turn and lead to a higher landing offstage to R.

Upstage in the L. wall are swing doors. By the sign over them we learn that they lead into the general store of Pago Pago, of which JOE HORN is the proprietor. Downstage in the L. wall is another door, recessed, and covered by a bedraggled Japanese bead curtain, stringy, bitten, and very old. This leads into the room which SADIE THOMPSON occupies later.

On the walls are lithographs of Queen Alexandra and President Garfield and an old map of American Samoa.

In the R. upstage corner is a shabby sofa upholstered in maroon plush. Near it, an ornate oak table, on which is a fat German lamp with a shade on which poppies have been painted.

At L.C., somewhat downstage, is a narrow dining table with a shabby red cloth. It is littered with dreary castors, salt cellars, and sugar bowls, protected from insects by swathings of mosquito netting. Five iron café chairs, painted green, are set at this table.

At R.C. is a dilapidated rattan deck-chair in which JOE HORN habitually reclines. By it is a stool or coffee table, on which are a box with a few cigars, and a battered volume of Nietzsche.

There is an upright rattan chair below and R. of Horn's chair, and another down R., and by this a small café table.

There is a long step to the veranda, extending almost the entire length of the entrance. Below the downstage end of the step is a hatrack and a receptacle containing a large and battered umbrella for the use of visitors. On the veranda are two rattan or painted iron chairs, set near the rail.

Beyond the veranda we see a vista of sky, sea, beach, and distant mountains. Nearby, bright green palm trees lift their branches, and brilliant flowers grow in riotous confusion.

When the curtain rises, the scene is bathed in the intense sunlight of early morning. Insects buzz and birds sing. In the distance we hear the low chanting of natives at work, broken once or twice by the booming blast of a steamer's siren.

Then a native girl enters from down R., on the veranda. She wears the lava lava, the native costume of the South Seas, and carries on her head a basket of pineapples. She crosses indolently and gracefully to L., and enters the store. She is followed by a native boy, and an old man, also wearing the lava lava. The boy carries fruit and the old man a basket of toys and ferocious masks of Kanaka workmanship. They are all chattering and laughing good-humoredly. After them comes an old woman, chewing betel-nut and balancing on her back a pole to which are attached fish bladders and pieces of dried shark.

They all enter the store and chatter is heard within. The ship's siren is heard again. The natives emerge from the store, cross to the veranda and sit about; some of them begin to make wreaths from a basket of flowers. As the action of the play proceeds, they disappear aimlessly and unobtrusively. From afar comes the plaintive wail of a native flute and the low strumming of a stringed instrument.

As the natives reach the veranda, there enters from the store AMEENA, who is MRS. JOE HORN. She is a large and darksome lady, the color of deep café au lait, and ten years ago she was very pretty. Now she is enormously fat and oozes rather than walks. Her bare feet are thrust into carpet slippers and her oily black hair is skewered into a wizened knot at at the back of her head. She crosses to the *veranda and looks off, shading her eyes from the too bright sun. The siren is heard again and she turns, and waddles back towards the store.*

She opens the door and calls shrilly.

———

MRS. HORN. Joe! Joe! Why-for you ain't up, hein? The boat comes already to the jett-ee . . . get yourself dressed.

(*She returns to the. table, surveys it, fanning herself. She then moves away to* L.C. *At this moment two Marines enter via the veranda. They are* PRIVATE GRIGGS *and* CORPORAL HODGSON, U.S.M.C. *Both are clean-cut, fresh-skinned, good-humored young lads, dressed in the bleached khaki uniforms of the Tropics.*)

HODGSON. Hullo! Tell us, mamma— Where's you old man?

MRS. HORN (*with scorn; coming to* R. *of the table*). My old man? Hui He! (*She gestures with her shoulders, expressing helplessness.*)

GRIGGS (*moving in with* HODGSON). Lay off the moans, old lady—cheer up! (*He slaps her back and she begins to smile broadly.*) Much better—much better—she's real fascinating when she smiles, ain't she, Bill?

HODGSON (R. *of the deck-chair; winking at* GRIGGS). Garod, what a valentine!

MRS. HORN (*regaining her good humor*). Get along, you scamps—what you want —hein?

GRIGGS. Bring out a white man's cigarette for the love of God!

MRS. HORN (*with an empty gesture*). Cigarettes! Not got yet.

HODGSON (*astonished*). Not got yet! The boat's in, ain't it? Jack here and I are 'bout ready to commit murder for a Lucky.

MRS. HORN. The boat is in. Yes . . . (*Points to the store.*) But what does he care—that man—my husband? He sleeps.

GRIGGS. I tell you, mamma, if we don't get a human smoke pretty soon we'll get fierce. Where is he?

(MRS. HORN *gestures in the direction of the store, folds her hands, closes her eyes, and gives a snore.*)

GRIGGS. Asleep, huh? Just wait—(*He starts for the store.*)

HODGSON. We'll have that bird on his feet and down to the dock—chop-chop pronto! (*He crosses* L., *after* GRIGGS.)

MRS. HORN (*jeeringly*). I think so—no!

HODGSON (*at the door*). I tnink so, yes.

(*They clatter into the store noisily.* MRS. HORN *laughs and sits* R. *of the table.*)

(SERGEANT TIM O'HARA *enters,* R. *He is a tall, well-set-up fellow of about thirty-five —stalwart, tanned, pleasing to look at. He is fair with kindly blue eyes and jolly smile, and very spick and span in his morning whites.*)

MRS. HORN. Hello—there, you O'Hara—

O'HARE. Morning, mamma. (*Moving in, to* R.C.) How is it by you today?

MRS. HORN (*sniffing*). Not so good.

O'HARA. Not so bad, I guess—

MRS. HORN. Mebbe a bit good. Plenty bad.

O'HARA (*crossing below* MRS. HORN, *to* L.C.). What's the trouble? Old man acting up again?

MRS. HORN (*indignantly, rising*). How you talk—What you say—my husband is very, very good man—sleep too much —mebbe—drink—sometimes a little mebbe too, sometimes not come home— mebbe no—but always he is very, very good man, my husband—

(O'HARA *laughs.* GRIGGS *and* HODGSON *enter, lugging with them* JOE HORN, *the trader of Pago Pago.* HORN *is a monstrously large man. He has tousled white hair and a broad, good-humored, shrewdly tolerant countenance. He stands rubbing his eyes—a somewhat ludicrous figure in dirty white dungaree trousers and pajama coat. His bare feet are thrust into broken-down, laceless shoes.*)

HORN. Not so fast—not so fast—what's all this? Where am I?

MRS. HORN. Where is he—he asks. (*She turns up, above the table.*)

HORN (*smiling and rubbing his eyes*). To be sure—as usual we find ourselves at home. Bosom of the family. Greetings, fair one, greetings.

MRS. HORN (*sniffing*). Greetings. He gives his wife greetings!

HORN (*to* O'HARA, *moving to below the table*). Naturally I greet my blossom of delight—Damn fine woman, Mrs. Horn. Excellent woman. Sometimes I wish she was in Hell.

MRS. HORN. Always he jokes like that. My Joe—Such a man he is for fun!

HORN (*agreeably*). Well, what are we waiting for? (*Crossing to* R.C.) Why this tension? What's expected of me?

O'HARA. The *Orduna's* in, Joe—been in for an hour.

HORN. What of it? (*He sits in the deck-chair.*)

MRS. HORN (*screamingly, moving down* R. *of the table*). What of it! What of it—the store is empty, no calico, no sardines, no peaches, no corned beef! No nothing!

(GRIGG *and* HODGSON *have moved* R., *to above the deck-chair.*)

HORN (*lazily*). Old Mother Hubbard—

GRIGGS (R. *of the chair, hoisting* HORN *to his feet*). On your feet, mate, we want cigarettes!

HORN (*sitting again and lighting a cigarette calmly*). Go away! It is much too early in the morning for life's burdens—let me first accustom myself to the fact that another day has come to join eternity—besides, this is Sunday, is it not—six days shalt thou labor—

GRIGGS. Bush-wa!—You should talk of Sunday.

(*He and* HODGSON, *who is* L. *of the chair, propel* HORN *out of it.*)

HORN (*wearily*). If I must—I must. (*He chucks* MRS. HORN *under the chin, then pauses in ponderous mischief.*) Wait a minute! Did you boys ever hear of Dr. Johnson?

GRIGGS. Sure! He was surgeon on the *Utah.*

HORN (*scornfully*). No, my boy, no! Dr. Samuel Johnson!

HODGSON (*wearily*). Well, what did he do, Joe?

(HORN, HODGSON, *and* GRIGGS *start for the veranda,* HORN *in the lead.* HORN *suddenly stops again and turns towards* HODGSON *and* GRIGGS.)

HORN (*beginning to pontificate*). Great works, says Dr. Johnson are not performed by strength alone, but by perseverance—

GRIGGS (*urging him to keep moving*). Yeah, that's right, Joe.

HORN (*deliberately walking as slowly as possible toward the veranda*). He who walks three hours a day will in seven years circle the globe.

(GRIGGS *and* HODGSON *propel* HORN *with difficulty out of the scene. They disappear beyond the veranda.*)

O'HARA (*reflectively; sitting on the edge of the table*). Nothing like few wants and thorough satisfaction with what one's got, and every man is his own king.

MRS. HORN (*nodding amiably, following the others off with her eyes*). King! Sure, my father one time King Pago Pago here. I princess. I marry Joe Horn, Christian way, now Joe all same King. Alu he ca mi kapi.

O'HARA (*rising strolling toward the veranda*). You gonna tell me all that again? I've heard it a million times!

MRS. HORN (*tartly*). What you know? You only sailor man. Hui!

O'HARA (*leaning on the veranda rail, looking aff down* R.). Here's some people coming, mamma, off the *Orduna.*

MRS. HORN (*waddling toward him*). Pipple come—pipple come here?

O'HARA. Yeah—look like missionaries.

MRS. HORN. Mee-sion-arry! (*Turning and hurrying* L.) God dam! I run! (*She exits into the store.*)

O'HARA. Me too. (*He hastens after her.*)

(*A moment later* MRS. DAVIDSON *enters, followed by* DR. *and* MRS MACPHAIL. MRS. DAVIDSON *is a little woman with dull brown hair, stiffly arranged. Her face is long, like a sheep's, but she gives no impression of foolishness, rather of extreme alertness—she has the quick movement of a bird. She is dressed in black china silk and wears around her neck a gold chain from which dangles a small cross. Her prominent blue eyes look forth sharply from behind gold-rimmed pince-nez. Her voice is high, metallic, and without inflection. It falls on the ears with a hard monotony, irritating to the nerves, like the clamor of a pneumatic drill.*)

MRS. DAVIDSON. This is the trader's place, I believe.

(*She gestures to* DR. *and* MRS. MACPHAIL, *who have lingered on the veranda observing the landscape. They enter.* DR. MACPHAIL *is a man of forty, thin, pinched, with a bald patch on his crown. He is a man of humor and reticence. One likes him instinctively.* MRS. MACPHAIL *is a woman a little younger than her husband. She is the indefinite type of person, who looks like everyone else—polite, acquiescent, rather sweet, and not at all sure of herself.*)

DR. MACPHAIL (*to his wife; on her* R.). Now don't worry about the baggage, dear. It will be taken care of in plenty of time. (*Seeing sign, he reads:*) "Pago Pago General Store, Joe Horn, Prop."

MRS. MACPHAIL (*looking about curiously*). No one seems to be about! (*Moving into the room.*) I do hope we can get some lunch here, Robert. We breakfasted so early I feel rather faint.

MRS. DAVIDSON. The trader's wife

serves meals here I believe—they're very bad I'm told, but we can't expect very much from Pago Pago. Thank heaven we shan't be here for long.

DR. MACPHAIL (*crossing up* L.). Well, anyway I'll see what I can do. (*He exits into the store.*)

MRS. MACPHAIL (*to* MRS. DAVIDSON). Is this a hotel?

MRS. DAVIDSON. Well, not exactly, (*She sits* R. *of the table.*) This man Horn accommodates people from time to time while they're changing boats, that's all, I believe.

MRS. MACPHAIL. Oh, you've been here before, then?

MRS. DAVIDSON. Oh yes, Mr. Davidson and I were here on our way to America a year ago.

MRS. MACPHAIL (*moving to the upstage end of the veranda, looking off*). How beautiful it all is. I hope we'll have time for a walk, after lunch.

MRS. DAVIDSON (*rising and moving up* R.). Oh, there's nothing to see but a few native huts and the Naval Station and the Governor's house. (*She points.*) That's it. Just around the corner.

MRS. MACPHAIL (*astonished*). Is *that* the Governor's house? Why, it's only a bungalow.

MRS. DAVIDSON (*turning back into the room*). As I say, there's nothing to see, but when my husband comes back we'll take a turn about—it can't take him long to transfer our baggage.

(MRS. MACPHAIL *moves down and they both seat themselves at the dining-room table.*)

MRS. MACPHAIL (*seated* R. *of the table*). I must confess I rather dread the rest of the trip on the schooner.

MRS. DAVIDSON (*seated above the table*). You well may! But think of Mr. Davidson and myself! We shall have ten days more on the schooner when we leave you at Apia. (*She pauses, then remarks sharply.*) I'm sorry, though, you're getting your first impressions of the South Seas from these Islands.

MRS. MACPHAIL (*innocently*). Why?

MRS. DAVIDSON (*as though imparting a dreadful fact*). They're far below the moral standard—the steamers touching here make the people unsettled. Then there's the Naval Station—that's bad for the natives. (*Shaking her head at the awful thought.*) Oh! It's almost a hopeless task for the missionaries here.

MRS. MACPHAIL (*curiously*). Really!

MRS. DAVIDSON (*very earnestly*). Your husband's coming is most timely, Mrs. MacPhail! Mr. Davidson was saying only last night that at last the Institute had sent the right man for the right job. Diseased conditions here are terrific!

MRS. MACPHAIL (*as though to change the subject*). I suppose we'll be stationed several months in Apia. What's it like there?

MRS. DAVIDSON (*determined the subject shall continue*). It's a dreadful place! The missionaries haven't as much power as they ought to have, and the place is overrun with American prostitutes.

MRS. MACPHAIL (*taken aback*). How horrible!

MRS. DAVIDSON (*drawing her chair closer to* MRS. MAC PHAIL *and speaking almost in a whisper*). You remember what we were talking about the other night? Have you told Dr. MacPhail yet?

MRS. MACPHAIL (*hesitatingly*). You mean about what their marriage customs used to be? Yes!

MRS. DAVIDSON (*with relish*). What did he say?

MRS. MACPHAIL (*slowly*). Well—he never says very much, but I'm sure he thought it was perfectly awful.

MRS. DAVIDSON (*eagerly continuing*). You made it all clear to him I hope? About what the old men and women used to do—about the common house—about the festivals?

MRS. MACPHAIL (*rather flustered*). I—tried—to—

(*Her speech is broken by* DR. MAC PHAIL, *who enters from the store, followed by* MRS. HORN.)

DR. MACPHAIL (L. *of the table, to his wife and* MRS. DAVIDSON). This is our hostess, Mrs. Horn—she has promised us some lunch. (*To* MRS. HORN.) About twelve you said, didn't you?

MRS. HORN (*lauguidly; above the* L. *end of the table*). Oh, a long time. I go send girl now—kill chicken—come home by'n-by. (*She crosses,* R., *and exits.*)

DR. MACPHAIL. H-m! Colorful, if not aesthetic!

MRS. DAVIDSON (*to* DR. MACPHAIL). Well? I hear that Mrs. MacPhail has been telling you some of the things about these islands which I couldn't, even though you are a doctor.

DR. MACPHAIL (*mildly interested*). What

things?

MRS. DAVIDSON (*warming to her subject*). About the moon dancing, the sugarcane festival, etcetera!

DR. MACPHAIL (*rather amused*). Ah, yes, yes . . .

MRS. DAVIDSON. Can you imagine such depravity! Such dances!

DR. MACPHAIL (*whimsically, as he strolls to the deck-chair*). Tell me, Mrs. Davidson, when you were a little girl did you ever dance around the Maypole?

MRS. DAVIDSON (*mystified*). It's quite possible that I did. Why?

DR. MACPHAIL (*turning to her, enjoying himself immensely*). Oh nothing, except that I believe the custom of the Maypole had its origin in festivals somewhat similar to those you have been telling my wife about.

MRS. DAVIDSON (*totally lost as to what it's all about*). I haven't the slightest idea what you're talking about.

DR. MACPHAIL (*sitting in the deck-chair; with satisfaction*). Yes, that's possible.

(SERGEANT O'HARA *makes his appearance, urging before him two natives who seem determined to take their own good time.*)

O'HARA. You boys hurry up. Go down dock running. Many fella want cigarettes. Hurry up! Plenty rain soon coming. (*He exits.*)

MRS. MACPHAIL (*rising, and moving to the veranda*). It can't be going to rain, can it?

MRS. DAVIDSON (*rising, and joining her*). Very likely. This is the beginning of the rainy season.

MRS. MACPHAIL (*on the veranda step, upstage end*). But the sky is so blue!

MRS. DAVIDSON (*pointing toward the sky*). Do you see those fleecy little gray clouds? The shape of spoons—they look like puffs of smoke.

MRS. MACPHAIL (*looking as directed*). Yes.

MRS. DAVIDSON. Note how they are gathering together. We shall certainly have rain in a little while.

(SERGEANT O'HARA *re-enters down* R., *on the veranda.*)

O'HARA (*calling off to the natives*). Hurry up, now! Go beach runnun! Make bring damn double quick! (*He turns to enter.*)

MRS. DAVIDSON (*to* O'HARA). Young man, do you know whether our baggage has been taken from the ship?

O'HARA (*touching his hat*). No ma'am. I don't know a thing about it.

MRS. DAVIDSON (*exasperated*). Oh! the procrastinations of these people are terrible! (*She moves back into the room.*)

O'HARA (*ironically*). Yes ma'am, they are terrible. (*Turning to the veranda.*) Terrible indeed! (*He lounges against the veranda rail.*)

(MRS. DAVIDSON *sits* R. *of the table.* MRS. MACPHAIL *follows to above the table.*)

DR. MACPHAIL (*to* MRS. DAVIDSON). Hadn't I better go down to the dock and see what's happening?

MRS. DAVIDSON. I wish you would.

DR. MACPHAIL. I shall.

(*He exits downstage via the veranda, fanning himself with his hat.* MRS. HORN *enters from the upstage end of the veranda.*)

MRS. HORN (*amiably, coming to* R.C.). Girl kill chicken now—by'n-by you get eating lunch.

MRS. DAVIDSON. Lunch *will* be welcome.

O'HARA (*standing erect*). Here's more company coming, mamma!

MRS. HORN (*turning to him*). More company coming? (*To the upstage end of the veranda step.*) What you say?

O'HARA. Yeah. More company—I'd say there was.

(PRIVATE GRIGGS *rushes in, from down* R.)

GRIGGS (*on the veranda*). Oh buddy! You ought to see the dame the *Orduna's* quartermaster's got in tow! They're both heaving this way—full rigged—all sails set!

(HODGSON *appears and joins* GRIGGS.)

HODGSON. Wait till you see this baby, Tim! Wait till you see it!

GRIGGS (*whacking* O'HARA *on the back*). Get your prettiest smile on, me hearty—get it on.

O'HARA. Hey, lay off that, or I'll swab the decks with you—what's the matter with you?

HODGSON (*hugging* O'HARA *and pointing off down* R.). Wait till you see it! Wait till you see it!

(GRIGGS *and* HODGSON *go into helpless laughter.*)

O'HARA. Stow that, you cubs! For God's sake act like you had some sense. Are you crazy?

GRIGGS (*still laughing, and crossing* O'HARA *to above him*). Sure. The heat's gone to our head.

(*Offstage we hear a woman's laughter—shrill, throaty, good-natured, then into the scene comes* MISS SADIE THOMPSON, *hanging on the arm of* QUARTERMASTER BATES *of the S.S. "Orduna."* MISS THOMPSON *is a slim, blondish young woman, very pretty, very cheery, very rakish. She has a tip-tilted nose and merry eyes. She walks easily, without self-consciousness. There is something of the grace of a wild animal in her movements, something primitive perhaps, even as her clothes suggest savage and untutored responses to cut and color. It is undoubtedly her best hat and frock that she has on. It is the sort of hat and frock a lady of her species anxious to be taken notice of would wear for appearance at the race tracks in Honolulu or Yokohama or Shanghai. High button shoes,* MISS SADIE THOMPSON *wears, and open-work stockings, and she carries a not very new parasol which does not match her dress. When she moves there is a rattling sound, due to the many imitation silver, gold, and jade bangles on her wrists. On entering, she pauses and clutches her companion's left arm.* QUARTERMASTER BATES, MISS THOMPSON'S *companion, is a wizened little man with a large mustache. He is several inches shorter than the effulgent* MISS THOMPSON—*but he is blithely unaware of this discrepancy. He is highly pleased at the fine figure he believes he cuts, and his whole attitude is that of one who is entirely convinced that he is quite a dashing dog and a devil with the ladies. He twirls his mustache—as* MISS THOMPSON *lets go his arm and gestures with her fringy parasol.*)

SADIE (*loudly, as she enters*). So—I'm to be parked here, am I, dearie? (*She looks about her with bright interest, standing on the veranda step.*)

MRS. DAVIDSON (*in a tense whisper to* MRS. MACPHAIL). That's the girl from the second class he was dancing so outrageously with at the captain's ball last night!

MRS. MACPHAIL. Yes, I thought it rather daring to bring her up to the first cabin, didn't you?

BATES (*gallantly, to* SADIE, *standing below the veranda step*). Make yourself right at home, Sadie.

SADIE (*clicking her heels together*). I will! Well, well! (*She comes in and then turns, pointing with her parasol to the veranda.*) Rail to put one's feet on, 'n everything. (*Seeing the three Marines, she does a step of the hornpipe, then waves her parasol at them.*)

Ha! "Join the Navy and see the world." Good boys—that's right—nothing like this where you come from I'll bet. (*She points to the landscape—the three Marines remain speechless—*MRS. HORN *waddles down* R.C.)

BATES (*turning to her*). How de do Mrs. Horn. How's Joe?

(SADIE *turns to see* MRS. HORN. O'HARA *moves in, to down* R.)

MRS. HORN. Allo Quartermaster! Joe —he damn fine.

BATES. How's all the kids? No new ones since my last trip?

(*He pokes her amiably and winks—at this* MRS. HORN *laughs, highly pleased, and* SADIE *exclaims heartily.*)

SADIE (*turning to* BATES). Any of them yours, little honeysuckle?

(MRS. HORN *and* BATES *find this remark tremendously funny.* MRS. HORN *holds her fat sides with laughter. Between gasps she manages to speak, pointing to* SADIE.)

MRS. HORN. Who is these—mebbe you bring back wife this trip—eh?

BATES. Get that, Sadie? She thinks you're my wife—

SADIE (*taking a pace to* MRS. HORN). Say, do I look that weak of intellect, do I look that artless? Should I marry the little husband of all the world? No lady, no matter what I am, I'm no pansy stick pin, I broke out of my plush case years ago! (*At this remark we see the rigid back of* MRS. DAVIDSON *become more rigid.* MRS. MACPHAIL *draws a little closer to* MRS. DAVIDSON. *These two ladies do not speak, but they look volumes.* SADIE *now strolls towards* O'HARA, *who is standing down* R., *apart from his companions. She smiles at him in a friendly way.*) Hello, Handsome! When did you leave Kansas?

(GRIGGS *and* HODGSON, *on the veranda step, howl with laughter.*)

GRIGGS. Ha, ha, the lady's got your number, Tim, it's written all over your map.

HODGSON. Ha, ha! She got you that time, kid.

SADIE (*turning to* GRIGGS *and* HODGSON, *her hands on her hips*). Say, little high-school boys, cover your books. I was addressing this gentleman. Run back to recess or the girls will get the basketball. (*She turns and observes* O'HARA *shrewdly, offering her hand.*) How are you?

O'HARA (*shyly, taking her hand*). Fine— very pleased to meet a lady.

(GRIGGS *and* HODGSON *howl*.)

SADIE. What's the matter with these two colts? (*She regards them severely.*) They act as though they had too much oats. (*She turns to* O'HARA.) I'd ration their feed if I was you—bad thing to jump 'em from milk too fast. Young things like that should be put out to grass first. I'm a farmer's daughter, so I know.

(BATES *howls at this sally, and* GRIGGS *and* HODGSON *look discomfited.* O'HARA *smiles in increasing embarrassment.*)

BATES (*gallantly*). Take a seat, Sadie—make yourself comfortable. Meet these ladies—(*He attempts to lead her over to* MRS. DAVIDSON.)

SADIE (*bringing him up short*). No, little cute one. Now I've got my bearings I think I will go out into the sunshine. Who's coming with me? (*To* BATES.) You, buttercup?

BATES. Can't do it, Sadie—I've got to buy some stores for the ship. Why don't one of you boys take Sadie out!

GRIGGS (*on the veranda step*). I am a wonderful little guide.

HODGSON (*on* GRIGGS' R.). Don't believe him, ma'am, I wrote the book he guides by—

SADIE. Yes, I bet you did! (*Turning to* O'HARA.) I'm taking Handsome—(*crossing and linking her arm in his*). Tag in back if you like but don't get run over. (*To* QUARTERMASTER BATES.) We'll be back for lunch, dearie. Don't forget that swell feed you promised me on shore? No shark steak or raw eels, please—but all the rest of the atmosphere—and plenty of that cocoanut hooch you mentioned.

BATES. Where are you going, Sadie?

SADIE. I want to see the cannibals and everything. *A tout à l'heure*, little one—that's French for *au revoir*, if you know the language. (*She exits with* O'HARA, *down* R., *followed by the Marines, waving her parasol as she goes.*)

MRS. HORN (*at* R.C.; *admiringly to* BATES). Nice, grand lady—who is she?—Hien?

BATES (*on her* R., *twirling his mustache*). Friend of mine. Her name is Miss Sadie Thompson.

MRS. HORN. Where she come from?

BATES. Came aboard at Honolulu—

MRS. HORN. She go Apia?

BATES. Yeah—got a job down there—cashier in sugar godown—

MRS. HORN. She make change boat here—hien?

BATES. Yeah, she is waiting for the schooner—you fix us up one tip-top lunch—see?

MRS. HORN. A'right—I do—(*She starts to exit, nudges him, winks.*) Aw—you davill! (*She crosses up* L., *and exits into the store.*)

(*During all the above*, MRS. DAVIDSON *and* MRS. MACPHAIL *have been sitting in silence.* MRS. DAVIDSON'S *sharp eyes gleaming behind her pince-nez.* MRS. MACPHAIL *is interested and undecided.* MRS. DAVIDSON'S *long upper lip is tightly pressed against her lower lip, and* MRS. MACPHAIL *from time to time is concerned with the attitude of mind she will be expected to take.* BATES *now approaches them, moving to above the* R. *end of the table.*)

BATES. Well, ladies, I bet you're glad to be on shore again—

MRS. DAVIDSON (*sharply*). We are very well, thank you. Tell me, have you seen Mr. Davidson anywhere?

BATES. He is aboard the schooner, I think. If I see him, shall I tell him you want him?

MRS. DAVIDSON. Do not trouble—

BATES. No trouble—I'll be taking Miss Thompson's things over soon.

MRS. DAVIDSON. Miss Thompson?

BATES. The young lady that was just here.

MRS. DAVIDSON. She was in the second class, wasn't she?

BATES. Yes—but it'll be all one class to Apia—you'll meet her there—she's full of life.

MRS. DAVIDSON (*dryly*). I believe it!

BATES. If I see Reverend Davidson I shall be glad to—

MRS. DAVIDSON. It will not be necessary—

BATES. Just as you say, ma'am.

MRS. DAVIDSON (*turning her back on* BATES, *and speaking to* MRS. MACPHAIL). I think that we will be more comfortable in those cane chairs . . . (*She rises, followed by* MRS. MACPHAIL, *and sits in the deck-chair.* MRS. MACPHAIL *sits on the chair on her* R. BATES *exits into the store. To* MRS. MACPHAIL.) These ship quartermasters are always so dreadfully officious.

(*Note:—During the above conversation it has steadily grown darker. A greenish yellow aspect has crept over earth and sky—the clean sunlight of the opening scene has become heavy and turgid. Now the wind begins to moan faintly and a gray pall settles over the scene.*)

MRS. MACPHAIL. How dark it's getting —and it is hotter than ever! (*Fans herself.*)

MRS. DAVIDSON. You must expect it, this time of year.

(*Voices are heard off* R. *The* REV. DAVIDSON *enters, followed by* DR. MACPHAIL. DAVIDSON *is a man of singular aspect. He is very tall and thin, with long limbs loosely jointed, hollow cheeks, and curiously high cheek bones; he has so cadaverous an air that it is a great surprise to note how full and sensual are his lips. He wears his hair very long. His eyes, set deep in thin sockets, are large and tragic; his finely shaped hands give him a look of great strength. The most striking thing about him is the feeling he gives of suppressed fire. His is a personality that is impressive and vaguely troubling.* NOTE: *With the entrance of* DAVIDSON *the rain begins to fall, not heavily but lightly, touching the tin roof with a strange sighing refrain. There is a scurry of bare feet on the veranda. The natives appear and start to let down the bamboo rain shutters.*)

MRS. DAVIDSON. What's the matter, Alfred? Has anything happened?

REV. DAVIDSON (*clearing his throat*). Unwelcome news. (*Moving to above and* L. *of the deck-chair.*) We can't start for Apia today.

(DR. MACPHAIL *is between the two chairs.*)

MRS. DAVIDSON. Not start today? (*She rises.*) Why—what—

REV. DAVIDSON (*moving down* L.C., *below the table*). One of the sailors aboard the schooner has come down with cholera. (*Turning to them.*) We can't sail until it is certain that none of the rest of the crew are affected. It means a delay of several days.

MRS. MACPHAIL (*rising*). But where can we stay? Not here, certainly.

REV. DAVIDSON. Here, certainly. There is no other accommodation in Pago Pago. We shall have to be thankful there is a roof over our heads, a bed to sleep on.

MRS. DAVIDSON (*moving to above the* R. *end of the table*). Can nothing be done?

REV. DAVIDSON. It is barely possible that I may be able to persuade the Governor to make an exception in our case. (*Crossing to the veranda.*) I am going to see him now.

MRS. DAVIDSON. Take an umbrella, Alfred.

REV. DAVIDSON. No. (*He exits.*)

(*The others watch him go.* MRS. DAVIDSON *sighs deeply.* MRS. MACPHAIL *joins her and looks at her husband weakly.*)

DR. MACPHAIL. I doubt whether he can do much. (*Moving to below the table,* L.C.) Peculiar chaps these governors. Their jobs are so easy, they have to make them look difficult.

(MRS. MACPHAIL *sits* R. *of the table.*)

MRS. DAVIDSON (*grimly*). Mr. Davidson usually gets what he sets out to get. (*She moves to the veranda and looks out.*)

DR. MACPHAIL (*dryly*). He is luckier than most of us then.

(*Two natives enter from the veranda with boxes of merchandise on their heads. They cross the scene and exit into the trader's store.* MRS. DAVIDSON *draws back a pace on their appearance.*)

DR. MACPHAIL (*watching them, speaking generally*). A fine race, aren't they? Make us all look awkward. Notice how their muscles mold into the flesh without one ugly line?

MRS. DAVIDSON (*moving across to above the table*). I am not an artist, Dr. MacPhail. I am not concerned with their bodies. It is my business to think of their souls. (*Pauses, then says sharply.*) Thank God we have practically eradicated the *lava lava* in our district.

MRS. MACPHAIL. What is that?

MRS. DAVIDSON. The native costume! Mr. Davidson thinks that it ought to be prohibited by law. How can you expect a people to be moral when they wear nothing but a strip of cloth around their loins?

DR. MACPHAIL (*mopping his brow*). Suitable enough for the climate, I should say. (*He turns up, above the chair* L. *of the table.*)

(MRS. MACPHAIL, *troubled, rises and moves slowly down* L., *and turns there as* HORN *enters from the veranda. He is wet, and carries a box of cigars. A native carrying a box of tobacco follows him. The native crosses up* L. *into the store and* HORN *sinks into his rattan deck-chair wearily.*)

HORN. Tough luck for you folks this about the cholera. Looks as though you were in for a stay here. (*He puts the cigars on the stool.*)

DR. MACPHAIL. Any chance of this rain letting up today?

(MRS. MACPHAIL *moves up and stands by her husband.*)

HORN. Not for long, the rainy season's on, and Pago Pago is about the rainiest place in the Pacific when it rains. Sometimes we don't see the sun for weeks this time of year. You get so used to the infernal downpour you can hear a pin drop.

MRS. DAVIDSON (*breaking in*). We may as well settle about accommodations at once. Have you any rooms that you can let us have?

HORN. You will want two sleeping rooms, I take it, for your party?

MRS. DAVIDSON. Yes.

HORN. Best I can do is put you upstairs.

MRS. DAVIDSON. How much will the rooms be?

HORN. Oh—about four dollars a day, meals included.

MRS. MACPHAIL (*nervously*). Could—could we look at them?

HORN (*calling, loudly*). Ameena—Ameena!

MRS. HORN (*off* L.). Yes—I come!

MRS. DAVIDSON (*sotto-voce to* DR. *and* MRS. MACPHAIL). Don't expect much, I know what these places are; we will be lucky if the roof doesn't leak. As for the rest—it is bound to be awful—so don't be disappointed.

(MRS. HORN *enters, from the store, up* L., *and crosses to* R.C.)

HORN. Ah—my spouse. Conduct these ladies upstairs to the—er—royal suite—point out all the comforts and elegances. (*To* MRS. DAVIDSON.) The roof leaks only a little. It is wise of you to resolve not to be disappointed.

MRS. HORN (R. *of the table, addressing* MRS. DAVIDSON *and* MRS. MACPHAIL). All right ladies—I put you in—come 'long—upstairs.

(MRS. HORN *starts upstairs, smiling hospitably.* MRS. DAVIDSON *and* MRS. MACPHAIL *exchange looks and then follow* MRS. HORN. MRS. DAVIDSON *stalks ahead.* MRS. MACPHAIL *draws her skirts carefully about her legs and looks resigned.*)

HORN. Try a cigar. New stock came in today.

DR. MACPHAIL (*moving to* R.C., *above the table*). Thanks—I stick to a pipe. (*He takes out his pipe.*)

HORN (*fumbling under his chair and producing a bottle of square face*). Drink? (DR. MACPHAIL *shakes his head.* HORN *pours a drink and smacks his lips.*) Sight-seeing?

DR. MACPHAIL (*moving down,* R. *of the table*). Not exactly.

HORN (*pausing and regarding* DR. MACPHAIL *with a scrutinizing eye*). You are not a missionary, I can see that.

DR. MACPHAIL (*sitting on the* R. *lower corner of the table*). No, I'm not a missionary—you're right.

HORN. Can't exactly place you, though.

DR. MACPHAIL. I'm a doctor.

HORN. Much better.

DR. MACPHAIL. You sound prejudiced.

HORN. Prejudiced? Oh no; damned fine people, missionaries! Got plenty of good friends among 'em. Some traders are afraid of them, but I've always found 'em all right. My only objection to them is—eh, well they're kind of shy on humor.

DR. MACPHAIL. Is that a necessary qualification for the job?

HORN. It helps—in any job.

DR. MACPHAIL. Persuading your neighbors to believe what you believe is a serious business, friend.

HORN (*gulping a drink.*) Gotta have a single track mind for it, anyway.

DR. MACPHAIL. Just so. There's no place for the light touch in reform.

HORN (*spitting a bit of cigar out of his mouth*). That's a word I can't listen to without spitting. It's my belief these reform folk fighting public depravity are only fighting their own hankering for indulgences they suspect others of! (*He gulps a drink.*)

DR. MACPHAIL (*smiling*). Just so! They chase you with a hatchet because they'd like a drink too? Is that it?

HORN. Shouldn't wonder! (*Leaning toward* DR. MACPHAIL.) Take these islanders, Doctor! They're naturally the happiest, most contented people on earth—they asking nothing of life save to be allowed to sing and eat, dance and sleep—thinking gives them a headache—the trees and the sea give 'em all the food they want, so they don't have to fight—they're satisfied with their gods of wind and wave. Then along comes Mr. Missionary in broadcloth and spectacles and tells 'em they're lost souls and have to be saved whether they want to be or not!

DR. MACPHAIL (*reflectively, as he rises and moves down* L.C.). Too bad that man couldn't develop a soul without losing the Garden of Eden . . . (*He turns up* L. *of the table.*)

HORN (*smiling*). You're a real philosopher, Doctor MacPhail.

(SADIE'S *laugh is heard offstage down* R.)

DR. MACPHAIL (*looking across at* HORN). Call me an observer of life, rather!

HORN. Ditto, brother—an observer of life who sees the joke!

(*During the last two speeches we hear, offstage, a succession of staccato squeals and laughing shrill cries. Now* MISS SADIE THOMPSON *comes into view; she rushes across the veranda and into the scene. Close at her elbow is* O'HARA, *and hard at her heels* GRIGGS *and* HODGSON; *after them hurries* QUARTERMASTER BATES. HORN *turns in his chair to glance at them.* DR. MACPHAIL *watches from above the table.* SADIE *has lifted her skirts above her head to protect her hat from the rain. She stands up* R.C., *laughing and pulling down her dresses. The men, standing on the veranda step, are carrying* SADIE'S *luggage—an oddly assorted multitude of objects hastily thrown together in shawls and large handkerchiefs. There is one very old and battered suitcase.*)

SADIE. Hell! That was sudden—and me in the only decent togs I've got to my name. (*To her escorts.*) Put that stuff down anywhere, boys. (*They deposit her luggage at the back of the room and stand wiping the rain from their eyes.*) Behold— the Wreck of the Hesperus! (*She crosses down* L., *removing her hat and flicking the ostrich feathers.*) H'm! That plume has waved its last. Farewell, pretty one— farewell. I guess any idea of me looking neat and chipper when I get to Apia is shot to pieces, eh, what?

BATES (*crossing to above the* R. *end of the table*). Don't worry, Sadie, you'll dry out.

SADIE (*carelessly*). Shi-cat-a-gani. Shi-cat-a-gani. That's what the Japs in Honolulu say when they mean "I should worry."

BATES (*moving to* HORN). How are you, Joe?

HORN (*not rising*). Never better, Quartermaster. (*They shake hands.*)

BATES (*to* SADIE, *easing away from the chair*). Shake hands with Joe Horn, Sadie —Miss Sadie Thompson, Joe.

SADIE (*crossing* R., *laughing*). Your climate's bum, Mr. Horn. (*She shakes hands with* HORN, *who rises.*)

HORN. Sorry, it's the best we've got. (*He sits again.*)

SADIE (*between* HORN *and* BATES). Oh, I am not blaming you. What is this about the delay? How long am I booked for this burg, do you know?

HORN. Well, I'd compose myself for a two weeks' stay.

SADIE. Two weeks. That being the case, what can't be helped can't be helped, as the canary said when the cat swallowed it.

BATES. Don't fret about that job in Apia, Sadie, they'll keep it for you.

SADIE. I never fret, little one. Make the best of things today—they're bound to be worse tomorrow. (*She turns up* R. *to the Marines, in good humor.*) Anyway, I like the boys here.

BATES (*easing towards* HORN). You will find Sadie some place to sleep, won't you, Joe?

HORN. All the upstairs is let. There's kind of a storeroom down here, though. (*Pointing to the door down* L., *covered by bead curtains.*) It is a pretty fair size, and I guess we can rig up a bed.

BATES (*confidentially to* HORN). You know how it is—being short when one is traveling. Sadie left Honolulu kind of sudden—she's a square kid, down on her luck a bit. She can't pay more than a dollar a day. You got to take her for that, Joe.

SADIE (*eargerly*). I was telling the Quartermaster I'll board myself—I got a burner with me. I don't eat so much.

HORN. Oh, that'll be all right. Mrs. Horn will fix you up. Take a look at the room if you like. (*Drinks.*)

SADIE. Much obliged. (*She crosses to the room,* L., *parts the curtains and peeps in.* BATES *crosses to* DR. MACPHAIL, *who has been watching the foregoing scene with quiet amusement.*)

BATES. You and your folks fixed up O.K.?

DR. MACPHAIL. Yes, we're upstairs. I see the *Orduna's* getting up steam.

BATES. Captain's taking no chance of getting stuck here. We're leaving just as soon as we get our clearance papers.

SADIE (*having peeped into the room, returning*). I'll do fine there. Home with me is where my other pair of shoes is.

BATES (*to* DR. MACPHAIL). You ain't met Miss Sadie Thompson, have you, Doctor.

DR. MACPHAIL. No, I have not had the pleasure.

(SADIE *smiles and bows.*)

BATES. If you get sick, Sadie, yell for Dr. MacPhail.

SADIE (*scornfully*). Get sick? Never in my life: I'm so healthy that it hurts. Well, now that it's settled where I flop, let's all have a shot of hootch; I have some rye with me that's not long for this world—it's far too good. (*Calling to* O'HARA, *who is perched with* GRIGGS *and* HODGSON *on the sofa at the back of the room.*) Say, Handsome, in that parcel you're resting on you'll find an object tied up in a red handkerchief. Bring it out. (O'HARA *begins to undo the parcel, which is tied up in a blanket.* DR. MACPHAIL *starts to move to the veranda;* SADIE *stops him.*) That includes you, too, Doc. What are you rushing off for? Seeing we're all stranded here, why not get friendly?

MACPHAIL (*smiling at her, then moving* R.). Thanks—it is a little early for me. (*To* HORN.) I'll take this umbrella if I may, and meet Davidson. (*He takes the umbrella in the barrel down* R., *and exits.*)

SADIE (*watching him go*). I'd say that's one wise old bird. (*To* O'HARA.) If the red-eye isn't in that parcel, it's in the brown box.

BATES. You sure are a live wire, Sadie.

SADIE (*moving to above the table*). Oh, I believe in living while one can. We're all going to be a long time dead.

BATES (*to* HORN). Yay Ha! She sure can stir things up, this kid here, can't she?

SADIE (*patting* BATES' *shoulder and speaking to* HORN). I suppose I'll find it pretty quiet down in Apia, won't I?

HORN (*gallantly*). Things ought to brighten up considerable after you get there, anyway!

SADIE (*in a simpery voice*). O-h-h . . . Mis-ter ... Ho-ho-horn! (*She winks at him, then turns to* O'HARA.) Say, you are slow! I'd have thought you'd be thirsty enough to locate by instinct. Here—I'll look. (*She crosses up* R., *and begins to rummage.*)

GRIGGS (*looking over her shoulder as she delves into her belongings*). Twist the devil's tail—if this ain't a gramophone!

SADIE. Yep! Brought it along for company. Never can tell when one's going to be lonesome.

HODGSON (*delightedly*). Golly. Got any records?

SADIE. Lots. Wrapped up in my dirty clothes. Hah! Here's the shy Kentucky refugee. I knew I stowed it safe somewhere. (*She finds the bottle and holds it up.*) Who has a corkscrew?

(*She returns to the table,* L. *of* BATES. *The Marines follow and group above and on her* L.)

BATES (*producing a corkscrew from his pocket*). Now ain't that a purty sight!

SADIE (*handing him the bottle*). Truly very winsome, very winsome, Mr. Bates! (*To* GRIGGS, *who is taking out the gramophone.*) Look out, Plainfield, that's filled with lingerie.

BATES (*pulling the cork*). Here you are.

(GRIGGS *puts the gramophone on the table and opens it.*)

BATES (*passing the bottle to* SADIE). You first, dearie.

SADIE (*raising the bottle to her lips*). Friend of mine slipped me that before I left Honolulu. "Not that you'll need it, Sadie," said he, "you were born hooched." I sure was! Why not? Saves a lot of jack these days.

BATES. No, you sure don't need hootch to pep up.

O'HARA (*at the* L. *end of the table*). I'll find a glass for you, Miss Thompson.

SADIE. Down the hatch! What for!

(*She takes a swallow, makes a face, coughs, hands bottle to* BATES, *who drinks and hands it to* HORN. GRIGGS AND HODGSON *are examining the records.*)

GRIGGS (*finding a record*). Holy Willie—"The Wabash Blues"!

SADIE. Put it on! Music and a nip of likka—that's what a rainy day is for, says I. (*To* O'HARA.) Can you dance, Handsome?

(BATES *gets the bottle from* HORN *and passes it to* SADIE, *who passes it to the boys.*)

O'HARA. No, Miss Thompson, I'm a clubfoot! I never could twist my legs right.

(*The boys take drinks and start the gramophone.*)

SADIE. I'll learn you before I leave— that's a threat. (*Laughs.*) The Quartermaster here is a great stepper. You ought to see him shake a shoulder. For one of his size and years, you'd be surprised. (*To* BATES.) Come on, Ethelbert, and show these island boys how hip meets hip in the gay cafés of Honolulu.

(*The Quartermaster gaily seizes* SADIE *around the waist. He is a little higher than her ears. She puts him in position.*)

BATES. Nothing too fancy now, Sadie.

SADIE. We'll begin trifling and light.

(*They start to dance down* R.C. *and across* L., *below the table, to the huge delight of the Marines.* HORN *watches amusedly.*)

GRIGGS. Look — Batesy's one jump ahead of a fit.

HODGSON. One frantic kangaroo!

SADIE (*as they dance at* L.). Easy there— easy there—whoa. (MRS. HORN *comes downstairs with a feather duster, watches in amazement, then smiles broadly.*) Don't bounce—take it easy and smooth—the word to remember is "glide," dearie. It isn't the dance that counts, it's the rhythm.

(MRS. DAVIDSON *suddenly appears, her eyes dark with disapproval.* MRS. MACPHAIL *follows her.* MRS. DAVIDSON *comes down-stage,* R.C. *Then she speaks, doing her best to keep her anger under control.*)

MRS. DAVIDSON. Young woman . . .

(BATES *hops himself out of step and presently stumbles.* SADIE *pushes him away* L., *ignoring* MRS. DAVIDSON. *The music continues.* HODGSON *throws his hat on the floor and steps forward bravely. He seizes* SADIE *and whirls her about so vehemently that her hair falls down.*)

SADIE (*delightedly, as they dance towards down* C.). Good news from home! Batesy, go hide your head.

(*The speed of the dance is accelerated.* MRS. DAVIDSON *now comes determinedly into the scene.*)

MRS. DAVIDSON (*coming toward them*). Young woman—have you no respect for the Lord's Day?

SADIE (*without stopping*). What? (*They dance away towards* L.)

MRS. DAVIDSON. This is Sunday. Young woman.

SADIE (*slowing up her dance at* L.C. *To* MRS. DAVIDSON). Were you speaking to me?

MRS. DAVIDSON. I am just reminding you that this is the Sabbath.

SADIE (*amiably*). Let's see, yesterday was Saturday, right you are, sister! (*She goes on dancing, paying no further attention to* MRS. DAVIDSON.)

MRS. DAVIDSON (*following the dancers*). I protest! I protest! This must stop. (*They bump into* MRS. DAVIDSON.)

HODGSON. Are we disturbing you, ma'am?

MRS. DAVIDSON (*curbing her fury as she fixes on her glasses again*). Whether I have been disturbed or not is of no consequence. There are six days in the week to dance, if you must dance. (*Turning to* HORN.) Is this sort of thing general in your hotel on Sunday, Mr. Horn?

HORN. Well, it's a general store, ma'am.

SADIE. 'Nough said—the complaint's registered. We'll withdraw to my private suite if you've no objection, Mr. Horn.

HORN. No objection—as far as I'm concerned.

SADIE (*to* HORN). Atta nice landlord! (*To* GRIGGS *and* HODGSON.) Come on boys, we're moving. (*To* O'HARA.) You take the records, Handsome. (*To* BATES.) And you, the hooch, little one. (*To* HORN.) Drop in later, if you feel like it, Mr. Horn—always glad to see you!

(*She crosses to the door, holds back the bead curtain while* O'HARA, GRIGGS, HODGSON, *and* BATES *enter.* MRS. DAVIDSON *stares at* SADIE *with unwinking expressionless eyes.* SADIE *returns the stare with saucy amusement; then with a little swagger she exits into the room, rattling the bead curtains as she goes.* MRS. HORN *exits up* L., *laughing.* MRS. DAVIDSON *turns sharply on* HORN, *who is laughing and lounging deep in his chair.*)

MRS. DAVIDSON (R. *of the table, to* HORN). Who is that young woman?

HORN (*drinking*). Her name, ma'am, is Thompson, so far as I know.

MRS. DAVIDSON. I mean—what is she?

HORN. I didn't inquire. She was on the *Orduna*, wasn't she?

MRS. DAVIDSON (*biting her lips*). I am aware she was. (*She turns her back on him and crosses to* MRS. MACPHAIL, *who has been a meek observer of the scene, standing above the table. From* SADIE's *room a ragtime tune now comes bellowing merrily. To* MRS. MACPHAIL.) I am afraid that Mr. Davidson will not like this at all.

MRS. MACPHAIL. I must say that I don't think she is very suitably dressed.

MRS. DAVIDSON. She is an extremely common woman. I dislike being under the same roof with her.

(HORN *rises, gives a loud laugh, and lounges across* L., *below the table and off into the store.*)

MRS. DAVIDSON (*watches him go disapprovingly. She turns to* MRS. MACPHAIL *with set lips, very angry*). Did you notice—that man was almost insolent! I tell you on our island we have the traders trained. A man like this whisky-bibbing Horn would not be tolerated. Mr. Davidson would drive him out at once.

MRS. MACPHAIL. How?

MRS. DAVIDSON (*giving a short laugh and easing away down* R.C.). You do not know Mr. Davidson. (*Turning.*) There was a man by the name of Fred Olsen once . . . (*She stops and smiles.* MRS. MACPHAIL *looks at her inquiringly.* MRS. DAVIDSON's *smile increases in grimness.*) It is a rather long story. I will let Mr. Davidson tell it sometime.

(*The gramophone changes offstage to a wild Spanish tango.* MRS. DAVIDSON *listens with set lips. The record is suddenly removed.* MRS. MACPHAIL *sighs her relief.*)

MRS. MACPHAIL. I'm glad she's stopped that music.

MRS. DAVIDSON. She is probably only changing the record. (*Moving to above the chair* R. *of the table.*) It didn't take her very long to get acquainted here, did it?

MRS. MACPHAIL. Well, you know people of that class aren't very particular. I daresay she's harmless enough.

(MRS. DAVIDSON *gives a short unpleasant laugh.*)

MRS. DAVIDSON. I'm not so sure. I'm not so sure.

(*Off stage are heard the voices of* REV. DAVIDSON *and* DR. MACPHAIL, *who enter.* MACPHAIL *closes the umbrella and puts it in the barrel.* DAVIDSON *comes toward his wife.*)

REV. DAVIDSON. I've argued it out with the Governor but he says there is nothing to be done. He is an obstinate man, afraid to do anything without official sanction.

MRS. DAVIDSON. That means ten days here.

REV. DAVIDSON. Two weeks probably.

MRS. DAVIDSON (*sitting above the table*). Well, I've prepared for the worst and taken rooms upstairs for us. Each room is provided with a chair, a bed and a washstand—we can make out.

MRS. MACPHAIL (*sighing*). But wait until you see the beds, Robert. (*She sits at the* L. *end of the table.*)

MRS. DAVIDSON. Fortunately there's mosquito netting. I have managed to pin together some of the worst rents. Tomorrow, Mrs. MacPhail, you and I must sew them. If we do not, the night will be unendurable.

DR. MACPHAIL (R. *of the deck-chair* R.C.).

Why not today? I have no fancy for being eaten up tonight. (*He sits in the deck-chair* R.C.)

MRS. DAVIDSON. I prefer not to do any sewing on the Sabbath if I can avoid it. It would be different if one were indecently exposed by a tear in one's clothes, for instance, but under the circumstances it might be a bad example to set before the natives.

(*At this point the gramophone in* SADIE's *room starts again—this time a very crazy dance record. There is a sound of laughter and moving about, not disturbing or loud.* MR. DAVIDSON *starts,* MRS. DAVIDSON *looks apprehensive. Offstage we hear the siren of the "Orduna.")*

REV. DAVIDSON (*putting his fingertips together, moving between the table and the deck-chair*). This enforced inactivity is likely to prove wearisome. The only thing to do is to portion out the day to different occupations. (*The music becomes louder and the noise of voices more penetrating.* DAVIDSON *checks, listen, then continues.*) Certain hours each day we had better put aside for study, certain hours for exercise, rain or shine . . . (*He pauses; it is evident the music is now irritating him. Again the "Orduna" siren is heard.*) Then, too, certain hours must go for recreation. (*The music crashes. He rises, his lips set, walks to the veranda and back to the table.*)

DR. MACPHAIL. Recreation may be hard to find.

(SADIE *laughs loudly in the room* L.)

REV. DAVIDSON. Someone appears to have found it.

MRS. DAVIDSON (*her eyes on the door* L.). Yes. That is a person from the second class—very flashily dressed—exceedingly common. In fact, she looks rather fast to me. (*Turning to* MR. DAVIDSON.) Perhaps you noticed her on the boat.

REV. DAVIDSON. No.

DR. MACPHAIL (*quietly*). I met her. Rather a good-natured girl, on her way to a position in Apia.

REV. DAVIDSON. What kind of a girl?

DR. MAC PHAIL. Oh, just an ordinary human being—not over-prosperous, I should say.

(*The music becomes a little louder.* DAVIDSON *with an effort controls a growing irritation.*)

MRS. DAVIDSON (*to* MRS. MACPHAIL). I must say that I think it outrageous of her to keep this music up, don't you? (*She half rises.*)

REV. DAVIDSON (*quietly, to his wife, signing her to sit*). If she wishes to play her own machine, it is not our right to interfere. (*Suddenly the music stops.* DAVIDSON *in relief turns to* MACPHAIL.) By the way, Doctor, I can show you a case of advanced elephantiasis in the hospital tomorrow, if you're interested.

DR. MACPHAIL. Um! A strange disease. Doctors are divided as to its origin.

(*There is now a sound of singing from* SADIE'S *room.* REV. DAVIDSON *listens. This is followed by laughter and voices. We see that* DAVIDSON *is listening to* DR. MACPHAIL *with only one ear.*)

REV. DAVIDSON (*absently*). The origin of any disease, Doctor, is overindulgence. (*To his wife.*) There seem to be others in that room, too!

MRS. DAVIDSON (*indignantly*). Yes—she has the ship Quartermaster in there, and three or four Marines.

(*It is apparent that* DAVIDSON'S *mind is not on what* MACPHAIL *is saying—that he is annoyed and upset by the hub-bub in the next room. There is loud clapping and shuffling.*)

DR. MACPHAIL (*bringing the subject back*). But all nature, Mr. Davidson, is first indulgence, then elimination, is it not?

REV. DAVIDSON (*above the chair* R. *of the table*). I have no patience with the Darwinian Theory, Doctor. In my opinion it should be prohibited by law. (*He stops, and then speaks to his wife.*) This girl, you say, was on the *Orduna?*

MRS. DAVIDSON (*acidly*). Yes—but Dr. MacPhail has met her—he can tell you more than I can.

DR. MACPHAIL (*impatiently*). She isn't anybody of importance. (*To* DAVIDSON.) I am interested, Davidson, in your theory of disease.

REV. DAVIDSON. I believe any disease tendency can be brought under control, just as weakness of the moral structure can. (*Speaking generally.*) Music of this sort is deteriorating, isn't it?

DR. MACPHAIL. Your theory would be easy, Mr. Davidson, if any of us ever were—ever could be—certain of ourselves.

REV. DAVIDSON (*sharply*). I disagree with you. Why can't we be certa⁣ᶠ ourselves?

DR. MACPHAIL (*coolly*). Because ⁣ ⁣each

and every one of us are hidded blights, erratic formations, undiscovered infirmities. An athlete, seemingly fit as a fiddle, crumples suddenly. Why? A faulty heart valve gives way! Not one of us can ever know ourselves until the moment of ultimate pressure—that's the pity of it!

(DR. MACPHAIL's *speech is cut short by the sharp blast of the "Orduna's" siren.*)

MRS. DAVIDSON. The *Orduna* must be going out before her schedule time.

MRS. MACPHAIL. I sort of hate to have her go. She seems our last link with home somehow!

(*The door of* SADIE'S *room suddenly opens and* BATES *comes unsteadily, adjusting his cap. His step is jaunty, however, and he smiles in vast contentment. From the room beyond comes the sound of laughter and of muffled song.* SADIE *appears at the door.*)

SADIE. Better hurry or you'll get left, little one.

BATES. S-sorry can't wait for l-l-lunch —S-sadie—s-ee you again sometime— you're a good kid.

SADIE. Write me a nice little loving postcard—now don't you forget.

BATES. Sure—nize li'l postcard. (*He puts his arm around her waist and gives her a resounding kiss.*) Bye-bye.

SADIE. Toodle-loo.

HORN. Aloha-oa.

SADIE. Sayonara.

(BATES *approaches* MR. *and* MRS. DAVIDSON *and* DR. *and* MRS. MACPHAIL, *and bows gallantly.* SADIE *stands in the doorway, watching as he proceeds unsteadily towards* R., *below the table.*)

BATES (*turning at* R.C.). Well, I'm off. Good luck to all you folks. (*He makes a sweeping gesture with his cap and the "Orduna's" siren is again heard.*)

REV. DAVIDSON (*decisively*). You had better get aboard, Quartermaster, as fast as you can.

BATES. Sure, got to be going—must get on—gotta hurry—boat's leaving— 'bye friends.

(*He moves* R. *jauntily.* SADIE *begins to laugh at his uncertain gait.* O'HARA *and the other Marines appear behind her.*)

SADIE. Look at the list on the little one.

O'HARA (*calling across*). Trim your sails to leeward, old-timer, or you'll founder.

BATES (*turning on the veranda step; singing*).

Way up here in the frozen north,
In the land of the Eski-moo!

I got stranded on the "Sarah Jane"
And I guess I'll never get home again.
The Queen up here is named Gumdrop
                                    Sal
And she's mighty fine to me—
The King's in wrong and I'm in right
And the King goes out most every night
And the nights are six months long.
(*During the above, he exits with short, dignified, and uncertain steps.*)

(*They wave at him, laughing uproariously.* REV. DAVIDSON *rises and watches the proceeding with gloomy eyes. Suddenly* SADIE *notices his eyes are fixed on her. She straightens and a flicker of defiance crosses her face.* SADIE *and* DAVIDSON *look at one another for a full, tense moment.* SADIE'S *eyes are the first to drop. She turns and walks into her room, rattling the curtains as she goes, remarking in a loud voice:*)

SADIE. A guy out there gave me the dirtiest look!

(*After* SADIE *exits,* REV. DAVIDSON *remains standing, looking at the door through which she has gone. His eyes are far away, a deep frown on his forehead. The* MACPHAILS *move restlessly;* MRS. DAVIDSON *watches her husband anxiously. The rain increases. On the veranda all the shutters are left down save one, which is still halfway up. Beyond this we see a gloomy vista of obscured landscape. There is a moment's silence, broken only by the monotonous beat of the rain on the tin roof.*)

DR. MACPHAIL. The rain is getting worse. (*Picking up a book from the stool.*)

MRS. MACPHAIL. Yes. Much worse.

REV. DAVIDSON (*moving to the* R. *end of the table, pulling the chair away*). How long has this sort of thing been going on?

MRS. DAVIDSON. All morning.

REV. DAVIDSON. Where did those sailors come from?

MRS. DAVIDSON. They just appeared from nowhere, in her wake. If there is to be a fortnight of this, I don't know what we shall all feel like at the end of it. (REV. DAVIDSON *gives a sudden sharp cry and strikes the table in front of him with his fist. Rising.*) Alfred, what's the matter?

MR. DAVIDSON (*in a dreadful voice*). Of course—it's just occurred to me—the woman's out of Iweili.

MRS. DAVIDSON (*in the same voice*). Iweili—Iweili. (*She turns to* MRS. MACPHAIL *almost triumphantly.*) The thought came to me when I first saw her but I dared not speak of it.

MRS. MACPHAIL. What do you mean by Iweili?

MRS. DAVIDSON. The plague spot of Honolulu. The red light district.

MRS. MACPHAIL (*rising, horrified*). Oh —oh—(*She turns up* L. *of her chair.*)

MRS. DAVIDSON. It is obvious that she has come out here to carry on her trade.

DR. MACPHAIL. I think you're wrong. She had a position waiting for her in Apia.

MR. DAVIDSON. I am not wrong—I know the look of Iweili. One cannot mistake it. I went there once—the faces of its women have haunted me ever since. She is as clearly out of Iweili as though the fact were written in scarlet letters on her brow.

DR. MACPHAIL. Still, one has no right to assume a thing like that unless—

REV. DAVIDSON (*working himself into a state of strange and curious excitement; his lips moving, his fingers twitching*). I tell you that I went there—saw the place—carried away with me the awful memory. Shall I tell you of it? It lay on the edge of the city. To reach it you went down side streets, near the harbor, in the darkness, across rickety bridges, through deserted roads, then suddenly you came into the light of its shame.

(MRS. MACPHAIL *gives a frightened gasp.*)

DR. MACPHAIL (*quietly*). We can easily imagine the sort of place it was, Davidson.

REV. DAVIDSON. It was the crying scandal of the Pacific, yet it was impossible to avail against it. You know the arguments of the police, that vice is inevitable, consequently the best thing to do is to localize it and control it. The truth is that they were paid—paid! They were paid by the saloon-keepers, the bullies, paid by the women themselves, but, thank God, at last they were forced by public opinion to do something.

DR. MACPHAIL (*impatiently*). Yes, I read about it in the papers that came aboard at Honolulu. Politics, wasn't it?

REV. DAVIDSON. For once a new mayor dared to live up to his election platform. Iweili with its sin and shame ceased to exist on the day that we arrived in Honolulu. The whole population was brought before the Justice and (*he points to* SADIE'S *door.*) this is one who probably managed to escape.

MRS. MACPHAIL (*in a faint voice*). I remember seeing her come aboard just before we sailed. (*She sits again.*) I thought at the time that she had just barely made it—her luggage was tied up in shawls and handkerchiefs.

(MR. DAVIDSON *starts to cross, below the table, towards* SADIE's *door.*)

MRS. DAVIDSON (*in a low voice; rising*). Alfred, what are you going to do?

REV. DAVIDSON (*moving on, to* L.). What do you expect me to do? (*Turning to them.*) I'm not going to have this house turned into a brothel. I am going to stop her.

DR. MACPHAIL. She has a number of men in there. Isn't it rather rash of you to go in now?

(DAVIDSON *gives* MACPHAIL *a contemptuous look, but makes no response. He is now at* SADIE's *door.*)

MRS. DAVIDSON. You know Mr. Davidson very little if you think that fear of physical danger will stop him in the performance of his duties.

(REV. DAVIDSON *opens the door of* SADIE's *room and stalks in.* MRS. DAVIDSON *gives a little gasp, then clenches her hands tightly. The others sit in tense silence waiting to see what will happen. The singing stops suddenly.*)

SADIE (*off*). I beg your pardon! What's the idea? (*Noice of music screeches and dies away.*) Hey! What's going on here?

(*Noise of gramophone thrown on the floor, and* DAVIDSON's *voice,* SADIE's *voice, and those of the Marines, viz.*, "Where d'you think you are? In your own home?" "Here, quit that!" *etc., ad lib. Then* DAVIDSON's *voice louder, and scuffling. A moment later* SADIE's *door flung open, and* O'HARA *and* DAVIDSON *appear, struggling.* O'HARA *has* DAVIDSON *by the back of the collar. They lurch on to the stage, and* SADIE's *angry face appears behind them.*)

SADIE (*shrilly*). Say, the next time you bust into a lady's room maybe you'll get someone to introduce you! My God! The nerve of him! Where does he think he is anyway!

O'HARA. There—if you know what's good for you, get out and stay out!

(MR. DAVIDSON *falls to the floor, down* L.C. O'HARA *and* SADIE *exit, slamming her door. The persons on the stage watch* DAVIDSON *rise. His eyes are terrible. Without a word he turns upstage and starts to mount the stairs very slowly.*)

MRS. DAVIDSON (*calling*). Alfred—Al-

fred . . .

(REV. DAVIDSON *makes no answer. He continues upstairs and disappears.*)

MRS. MACPHAIL (*in a scared whisper to* MRS. DAVIDSON). What will he do?

MRS. DAVIDSON. I don't know. All I know is that I would not be in that girl's shoes for anything in the world.

(*There is a burst of laughter from* SADIE's *room. We again hear voices. The gramophone recommences. We hear the clink of glasses. Someone begins to sing. The people on the stage sit silent as*

the CURTAIN *falls.*

ACT TWO

The SCENE *is same as the preceding act. It is late afternoon, two days later.*

It has stopped raining for the time being. On the veranda the rain curtains are drawn halfway up, revealing an angry sullen sky in which a streak of red zigzags amongst ominous, piled-up clouds. The landscape is indistinct and misty. The gloom of late day is settling over the scene.

As the curtain rises, we find HORN, *the trader, asleep in his inevitable cane chair, his face swathed in mosquito netting; by his side is a whisky bottle. From the distance comes the sound of the natives chanting as they drag the fisher nets out of the sea.* HORN's *sleep is restless and uneasy. He squirms and slaps at the mosquitoes which buzz about his head.*

———

HORN (*muttering*). Pestiferation! Seize these devils—ur—damnation! (HORN *strikes out, slaps his ankle, then curses softly and changes his position.*)

(MACPHAIL *enters from the veranda. He comes in to* L. *of the deck-chair and stands looks looking at* HORN. *He is smoking his usual pipe.* HORN *opens his eyes and wakes slowly, yawning and stretching his arms.*)

HORN. Beelzebub and his hosts! Who—what! Oh, it's you is it. Hello, Doc!

DR. MACPHAIL. Hello!

HORN (*sleepily*). Been out for a walk?

DR. MACPHAIL. Only two steps—got as far as the Governor's gate. Like walking through hot pea soup. (*He wipes his moist face with his wide silk handkerchief.*)

HORN (*yawning*). What time of day is it, anyway?

DR. MACPHAIL (*looking at his watch*).

Going on six—whole hour to put in before dinner.

HORN. Been to the hospital today?

DR. MACPHAIL. No—can't get at my instruments. Nothing left to do but twiddle my thumbs. (*He sits at the* R. *end of the table.*)

HORN. Why twiddle? (*He brings the bottle out from under his chair.*)

DR. MACPHAIL. Enforced idleness makes 'em restive!

HORN (*quaffing and smacking his lips*). Native brew—satisfying. What was I saying?

DR. MACPHAIL. The subject, I believe, was the evil of too much work.

HORN. There's a lot too much misdirected energy in the world, Dr. MacPhail.

DR. MACPHAIL (*amused*). Are you speaking biographically or autobiographically?

HORN (*accepting the doctor's joke*). No, confidentially! (*He pauses and wags his finger.*) You might as well make up your mind that none of you folks can get away from each other for two weeks—and most of that time it's going to rain like hell! Don't be too energetic—it starts the throat-cutting.

DR. MACPHAIL (*puzzled*). Throat-cutting?

HORN (*he drinks*). Just between ourselves, that was a mighty foolish thing the Reverend Davidson did! That girl Sadie Thompson wasn't doing any harm.

DR. MACPHAIL (*nodding his head*). Um! I see what you're getting at.

HORN (*slowly*). He's been after me for letting her have a room.

DR. MACPHAIL. It's your own house, isn't it?

HORN. Yes. (*Doubtfully.*) But the missionaries are all in with one another. I've never had any trouble with 'em myself, but I know traders that have. If they get down on a trader he may as well shut up shop and quit.

DR. MACPHAIL. How can that be?

HORN. Oh, they have ways.

DR. MACPHAIL. Surely he isn't asking you to turn this girl out into the rain?

HORN. No—not exactly. He knows there'd be no place for her to go except a native hut. Not but what I think she'd do better to go into one than stay here, now that he is on to her.

DR. MACPHAIL. Just what *does* he want you to do?

HORN. He said he wanted to be fair to her and to me, but he wouldn't stand for any "doings."

DR. MACPHAIL. Er—what do you think, Horn—is she—er—out of Iweili, that Honolulu red light district?

HORN (*complacently*). I don't know. And I don't care. (*He looks up at* MACPHAIL.) What if she is? We've all crossed thresholds we don't brag about.

(MACPHAIL *gives a slight cough as the truth of this statement reaches him and somewhat embarrasses him. He starts to cross back to his seat by the table, then pauses in his walk and listens intently as* HORN *continues.*)

HORN. Just because she has a few gaudy rags and a bum gramophone, what right has he to conclude that she's out of Iweili? You know, Dr. MacPhail, the whole trick in thinking is, what vision have you? (*Pauses.*) If you have a low horizon, God pity you! Davidson has that! (*He waves his hand in a deprecatory manner.*) This girl hasn't any—that's why I like her. Poor thing! Davidson's sort of got her wondering.

DR. MACPHAIL. How so?

HORN. She's wondering what he's up to! You noticed when the boys came around last night to see her, she got them out on the porch pretty quick and talked to them there?

DR. MACPHAIL (*dryly*). Yes—I noticed! It wasn't the most cheerful of evenings either! (*Rising and moving up* R., *looking off.*) What with the rain and everything, we'd all been happier, I think, if Miss Thompson had been in her room with her friends.

HORN. She felt it too, I guess. (*Examining the contents of his cigar box.*) I hear she went to a half-caste family this morning and tried to get 'em to take her in, but they wouldn't.

DR. MACPHAIL. Why not? (*He comes down,* L. *of* HORN's *chair.*)

HORN (*succinctly, taking a cigar and closing the box*). Afraid to! Must have heard somewhere that the missionaries had got their knives in her. (*He pauses; then continues in confidence.*) Maybe you don't know, but he's been at the Governor to have her sent back to the States. (*He lights his cigar.*)

DR. MACPHAIL (*removing his pipe*). I thought he was up to something like that.

HORN. Yeah, he's got his mind made up to get her out of these islands, no matter what! And she's got wind of it somehow, too!

DR. MACPHAIL (*slowly; moving to* L.C., *above the table*). You know I felt rather sorry for her last night. After her sailor friends left she went into her room without looking at any of us. Just as we were ready for bed she put on her gramophone. Somehow it sounded dismal—like a cry for help.

(*At this moment from* MISS THOMPSON'S *room comes the sound of the gramophone—shrill, discordant, as though put on as a final resort.* HORN *and* MACPHAIL *listen.* HORN *points to* MISS THOMPSON'S *room, puts his finger to his lips, and shrugs his shoulders.* MACPHAIL *changes his position slightly. They both listen. There is a moment's silence. Suddenly the record is snatched off and another is substituted.*)

HORN. There it goes again!

DR. MACPHAIL (*moving down* L. *of the table, to below it, and sitting*). Hard business, trying to cheat one's loneliness.

HORN. Take it from me, she's scared as well as lonely! Not that she'd show it—she's got nerve! But she don't know what Davidson's doing and it makes her anxious. Where is he now, anyway?

DR. MACPHAIL. He's been coming and going from the Governor's all afternoon—whatever that may mean. (*He knocks the ashes from his pipe suddenly as the rain begins to patter lightly on the iron roof.*)

HORN. You're jumpy.

DR. MACPHAIL. Maybe. This rain—it's starting up again.

HORN. Yes, it goes on pretty steady in the rainy season. We have three hundred inches in the year—it's the shape of the bay.

DR. MACPHAIL. Damn the shape of the bay! (*He rises and stalks to the veranda and back to up* R.C., *then back to the veranda again.*)

HORN (*regarding him in amusement*). It's getting you!—all this lush, dripping world—outside, everything growing with a sort of savage violence! Tomorrow you will see strange flowers where yesterday there were only roots. For myself I like it. This rain you hate—it wipes out, it kills—and it begins . . .

(*During the above speech the gramophone stops.* MACPHAIL *moves down* R. *The bead curtains outside* SADIE'S *room part and she enters, in a sudden nervous way. She wears a not very new dress of limp red gingham. There is considerable cotton lace about the dress, which is the sort of garment one might see in a third-rate department store window devoted to summer styles. Around her neck she wears a string of cheap beads. She affects a brave assumption of cheer and good fellowship.*)

SADIE. Evening, everybody! My, the merry water sprites sure do carry on, don't they? (MACPHAIL *nods a little embarrassedly.* HORN *salutes with gallantry.* SADIE *smiles at both in a friendly manner. She comes forward, fanning herself.*) Don't let's mention the heat. Let's talk of Greenland's icy mountains! (*Neither* MACPHAIL *nor* HORN *speaks, and* SADIE *continues, trying hard to keep up her good cheer, moving below the table to* R. *of it.*) You don't mind, do you, seeing we're here by ourselves, if I sit down with you boys and have a smoke? (*She takes out a cigarette and lights it.*)

HORN. Sure. Sit down, light up.

SADIE (*seating herself in the chair* R. *of the table*). You haven't seen that Marine Sergeant I call Handsome 'round anywhere today, have you.

HORN. No—he hasn't been around today.

SADIE. It don't matter. I just wanted to ask him something. If you do see him, tell him to drop around this evening.

HORN. I—er—er—you know what I said to you last night? (SADIE *nods.*) As friend to friend, get me? I'd go slow on company for a day or two.

SADIE. I see. Until Reverend Davidson gets over his terrible experience, eh? (*She gives a short laugh.*) You'd think I'd been to blame for what happened.

HORN. I'm not blaming anyone.

SADIE. What else could he expect, that Reverend Davidson, pushing himself in on us in that way. It's a wonder one of the boys didn't show him what a real crack is! As it was they only handed him a love tap and hustled him out. He's a great missionary, I'll announce, if he's trying to take it out on us just because he got what was coming to him. (*She continues working herself up to a sense of lively indignation.*) What harm were we doing? Just talking and singing—everything happy and pleasant, then bang went the door and in came Reverend Davidson, and began to bawl us all out. The boys thought he'd just naturally gone crazy, so they put the skids under him.

HORN (*soothingly*). I know . . . Anyway, I wouldn't attract his attention any more than I had to, just now.

(MACPHAIL *eases quietly upstage by the veranda steps, to watch.*)

SADIE (*indignantly*). Attract his attention! Well, if it comes to that, he'd better not attract mine! I've never known anyone like him and I don't want to! (*She pauses, then asks confidentially.*) Say, what kind of an egg is the Governor of this place?

HORN. The Governor? Let's see. Pretty good sort, I'd say. Why?

SADIE. I just wanted to know, that's all. The nerve of that Reverend Davidson going to see him about me! Did you ever hear the like of it?

HORN. How do you know Davidson went to see the Governor about you?

SADIE. O'Hara told me. He's reported O'Hara to his officer for drinking. I don't want that boy to get into trouble through me.

HORN. Oh, I guess O'Hara can take care of himself.

SADIE (*rising*). Well, so can I, if it comes to that! (*Moving toward* HORN, *angrily.*) If that Davidson gets gay with me again, I'll tell him who his mother was. Possibly he don't know! (*She gives a loud, derisive laugh.*)

HORN. Miss Thompson—I'd be careful . . .

SADIE. Of what?

HORN. I'd be careful for my own good. One can't tell what . . .

SADIE (*impatiently, moving away to* C.). God give me strength! (*Turning to* HORN.) How many times have I got to tell you that old sin-buster doesn't mean a thing to me. If he minds his own business, I'll mind mine, and if he's looking for trouble, I'll see he gets it! That's all! (*She stops suddenly and cups her hand over her ear.*) Methinks I hear the winds of religion whistling down the chimney! (*Voices are heard offstage;* SADIE *moves away* L. *with mock trepidation.*) Whereat the low hussy frolics off to buy her dinner! (*Turning at* L., *to* HORN.) Where do you keep your tamales, old partner?

HORN. If there's any left, they're on the shelf by the door.

(SADIE *crosses up to the door of the store with an attempt at rakishness, then pauses and looks back at* HORN *and* MACPHAIL *a little doubtfully.*)

SADIE. Anyway, there's no ill feeling between any of us, is there? (*To* MACPHAIL.) The doctor hasn't been saying much. (*She shrugs her shoulders, then laughs nervously.*) Life just teems with quiet fun, don't it? (*She exits into the store.*)

(MACPHAIL *moves toward the* R. *end of the table.*)

HORN (*to* MACPHAIL). There—what did I tell you? She's frightened.

(MACPHAIL *sighs and does not respond.* HORN *rises and moves slowly* L., *below the table. There is an increased patter of rain on the roof, and the scene darkens. Two natives appear on the veranda and begin to draw the shutters. There is a moment's silence during which we hear only the rain and the slip-slop of native feet and the low murmur of their voices. Then* MRS. DAVIDSON *enters from outside, followed by* MRS. MACPHAIL.)

MRS. DAVIDSON (*to* HORN). Has Mr. Davidson arrived?

HORN (*turning up* L.). No, ma'am. (*He exits into the store.*)

DR. MACPHAIL (*moving down* L., *below the table*). How far did you ladies go?

MRS. MACPHAIL (*crossing to* C., *above the table*). Only as far as the wharf. We watched the clouds pile up. Such curious black shapes as they were taking. I got a little afraid. So Mrs. Davidson thought we'd better get back. (*She sits, above the table.*)

DR. MACPHAIL (*to* MRS. DAVIDSON.) How's the headache? Any better?

MRS. DAVIDSON. Very little. (*She sits,* R. *of the table.*) Mr. Davidson has had no sleep for two nights. When he doesn't sleep, I cannot sleep. At four this morning he got up and got dressed and went out. He came back wet through, but he wouldn't change. (*She sighs.*) It's that thing that happened the other day! It's preying on his mind.

DR. MACPHAIL (*sitting* L. *of the table*). She—that girl—Miss Thompson was in here just before you came. I think—I have an idea she is sorry for what happened. I am sure she could be easily persuaded to apologize.

MRS. DAVIDSON. There is no question of apology. I do not know what will happen. I know only this. He will conquer this girl, perhaps quickly, perhaps slowly—but in the end completely.

(SADIE *enters from the trader's store, talking to* HORN, *who enters with her. She is carrying a can of tamales and a pitcher.* HORN *follows her.* MRS. DAVIDSON *gives* SADIE *a swift look, then speaks to* MRS. MACPHAIL.)

MRS. DAVIDSON. Do not look around! Here she comes now!

SADIE (*moving down* L., *flushing with anger*). Yes, here I come now! Why shouldn't I come now? See here, let's settle this. I'm paying for my own room with the privilege of getting my own meals. Is that so, Mr. Horn?

HORN (*down* L., R. *of* SADIE, *anxious to escape the scene*). That's so, Miss Thompson.

SADIE. Then will you kindly tell these ladies I have as good a right here as they have?

HORN. Now, Miss Thompson, there isn't anyone saying you haven't. (*He pats her soothingly and exits into the store.*)

MRS. DAVIDSON (*to* MRS. MACPHAIL). Don't look at her—don't speak to her.

SADIE. No—I wouldn't if I were you. But seeing you started the conversation by talking at me, I may as well be polite. How's your husband today? If I may say so, he wasn't looking any too well when I saw him gumshoeing down the road this morning.

DR. MACPHAIL. Miss Thompson, please . . .

SADIE (*viciously*). What your husband needs, I think, is a good dose of salts! (*She turns down to her door.*)

MRS. DAVIDSON (*in a voice choking with fury*). Don't you dare speak to us again, you dreadful woman! If you insult me I shall have you turned out of here . . .

SADIE (*turning at her door*). Say! Did I ask Mr. Davidson to make my acquaintance in the first place? Did I?

MRS. MACPHAIL. Don't answer her!

SADIE. I assure you the overtures to know *me* have been entirely on your side of the fence! (*She exits, closing her door with a bang.*)

MRS. DAVIDSON. She's brazen—outrageous! (*She puts her hands to her head as though about to choke.*)

MRS. MACPHAIL (*rising and going to her*). Don't. You'll only harm yourself—and all for that creature. (*Turning toward* MACPHAIL.) Robert—

MRS. DAVIDSON (*feebly*). It's foolish, I know, but this is the first time I have ever had words with a woman of that

sort. Well, there's one comfort, we shan't have to suffer this sort of thing much longer! (*She smiles in rather a grim and terrible manner.*) No! Mr. Davidson is attending to that!

MRS. MACPHAIL (*curiously*). What do you suppose he is doing?

MRS. DAVIDSON. When Mr. Davidson is on the Lord's work I do not question him.

(MRS. DAVIDSON *clenches and unclenches her hands.* MRS. HORN *enters from the store with a lamp, which she takes to the table upstage by the sofa, and lights it.*)

MRS. HORN. Dinner soon now—mebbe one hour—one hour half. (*She crosses back to the door up* L.)

MRS. DAVIDSON (*sighing*). I only hope I can persuade Mr. Davidson to eat something tonight.

(MRS. HORN *exits.*)

MRS. MACPHAIL. He doesn't think of himself at all, does he?

MRS. DAVIDSON (*slowly, tensely*). Never! He is so without thought or fear for himself that often he is like a man possessed.

(MACPHAIL *has been sitting quietly during the above conversation—a somewhat quizzical expression on his face. Now he jerks himself forward in his chair suddenly and strikes at his ankle.*)

DR. MACPHAIL. Damn those mosquitoes!

MRS. MACPHAIL (*reprovingly*). Robert! (*She moves to* L. *of the chair above the table.*)

DR. MACPHAIL. Sorry! I've always been touchy about the ankles! They seem to know it! (*He looks off and sees* DAVIDSON *approaching.*) Hello, Davidson.

(DAVIDSON *enters, coming into the room from the porch. He shakes the rain from his hat and removes an oilskin cape.*)

MRS. DAVIDSON (*rising and going to him at* R.). Alfred, please change your wet clothes!

REV. DAVIDSON (*crossing her, to up* R.C.). No—I shall be going out again probably.

MRS. DAVIDSON. Again! Oh, you must try to get a little rest. Alfred—you must! (*She sits in the deck-chair.*)

REV. DAVIDSON (*almost tenderly, turning to her*). My wife, like Martha, "thou hast troubled thyself about many things"— and mostly about me! (*He smiles but his eyes are far away; then he turns, speaking to* MACPHAIL.) I do not know what I could ever have done without my dear wife. In the early days of our island ministry when my heart sank and I was near despair, it was she who gave me strength and courage to go on. It was she who put her work aside and read to me from the Bible until peace came and settled upon me like sleep upon the eyelids of a child —and when at last she closed the book, she would say, "We will save them in spite of themselves!" Then I would feel strong again and answer, "Yes, with God's help I will save them. I must save them!"

(*During the above,* MRS. DAVIDSON *is deeply affected, too. She takes off her glasses and wipes them; she holds back her tears with a great effort.*)

DR. MACPHAIL (*dryly*). Save who?

MRS. MACPHAIL (*quickly*). The islanders, Robert! (*She moves to* R. *of the table and sits.*)

(*From* SADIE THOMPSON'S *room comes the sound of the gramophone—harsh, wheezy.* DAVIDSON *listens.* MRS. MACPHAIL *looks nervous.* MRS. DAVIDSON *bites her lips.* DR. MACPHAIL *puffs his pipe.*)

MRS. DAVIDSON (*to* DAVIDSON). Alfred, just before you got back that girl was in here; she jeered and screamed at us. What are you going to do about her?

REV. DAVIDSON (*putting his hand to his temple*). I must give her every chance first—every chance—before I act.

(MRS. HORN *enters with a tray of dinner dishes, which she places on the table, after first laying down the slovenly cloth.*)

DR. MACPHAIL. Hamburg steak tonight again, Mrs. Horn?

MRS. HORN (*clattering the dishes*). Hamburg steak, I give you—bananas fried—mebbe.

DR. MACPHAIL (*gloomily*). Strange how one's thoughts run to food when there is nothing else to think of.

REV. DAVIDSON. As it happens, there is a great deal to think of. (*To* MRS. DAVIDSON.) You say this Thompson woman spoke to you?

MRS. DAVIDSON. She thrust herself in upon us with low insults.

REV. DAVIDSON. H'm! The Governor tells me the affair is no concern of his, but if I find her incorrigible I shall see to it he *acts*. I am afraid he has no backbone.

DR. MACPHAIL (*attempting facetiousness*). I suppose that means he won't do exactly as you want—whatever it is you want him to do?

REV. DAVIDSON. I only want him to do what is right!

DR. MACPHAIL (*laconically*). There may be differences of opinion about what is right.

REV. DAVIDSON. If a man had a gangrenous foot, would you have patience with anyone who hesitated to cut it off?

DR. MACPHAIL. But gangrene is a matter of fact . . .

REV. DAVIDSON. And is not evil?

DR. MACPHAIL (*quietly*). To me it has always seemed a matter of opinion. Anyway the poor thing will only be here until the boat for Apia goes.

REV. DAVIDSON. And after she gets to Apia?

DR. MACPHAIL. I can't see how that concerns us.

REV. DAVIDSON (*moving to above the chair* R. *of the table*). That's where you and I differ. (*He stops, looks hard at* MACPHAIL *and continues.*) You don't mind my turning you out of here for a little while, do you? I want to speak to this woman alone. (*To* MRS. DAVIDSON.) I think it would be best if you went too.

(DR. *and* MRS. MACPHAIL *rise silently, cross* R., *and disappear along the veranda, upstage.*)

MRS. DAVIDSON. Alfred, why do you see her?

REV. DAVIDSON. I cannot act until I've given her every chance.

MRS. DAVIDSON. She'll insult you.

REV. DAVIDSON. Let her insult me. Let her spit on me. She has an immortal soul and I must do all that is in my power to save it.

(*During the above scene* MRS. HORN *has been busy at the table.* DAVIDSON *now turns to her and speaks.*)

REV. DAVIDSON. Ask Miss Thompson if she will step out of her room for a moment.

MRS. HORN (*coming forward*). You want spik with Miss Thompson? (*She points to* SADIE'S *room.*)

REV. DAVIDSON. Yes. Ask her to kindly come out for a minute.

MRS. DAVIDSON. I tell you, Alfred, she has gone too far.

REV. DAVIDSON. Too far for the mercy of the Lord? (*His eyes light up and his voice grows mellow and soft.*) Never! The sinner may be deeper in sin than the depth of hell itself, but the love of the Lord Jesus can reach him still.

(MRS. DAVIDSON *turns and goes out up-*

stairs. MRS. HORN *knocks on* SADIE'S *door.* SADIE *answers,* "Come." *The music stops and after a moment she enters.*)

SADIE (*moving down* L., *munching a banana*). What is it? (*She looks inquiringly at* MRS. HORN, *who points with her thumb to where* DAVIDSON *stands.*)

MRS. HORN. He wan make talk wit you. (MRS. HORN *exits into the store.*)

SADIE (*half hesitates on seeing* DAVIDSON, *then squares her shoulders and stands against the doorway, her eyes fixed on him. To* DAVIDSON). You want to see me?

REV. DAVIDSON. Yes, I want to talk to you, Miss Thompson.

SADIE. I'm eating my supper. (*Her mouth is full of banana.*)

REV. DAVIDSON. I'll wait until you're through.

SADIE. Oh, the supper can stand by if it's important.

REV. DAVIDSON. It is important—very important.

(SADIE *comes forward, her eyes on* DAVIDSON. *He motions her to a seat. She sits nervously,* L. *of the table. He stands looking at her strangely.*)

REV. DAVIDSON. Sadie Thompson, I have brought you out here to make you a gift—the most precious gift life can offer you.

SADIE (*uncertainly*). You want to give me something?

REV. DAVIDSON. The gift I offer is free.

SADIE (*with a nervous titter*). I'm glad of that. I'm pretty short on cash. (*She throws the banana skin on the table.*)

REV. DAVIDSON (*moving to below the chair* R. *of the table*). The gift I'm offering you is the infinite mercy of our Lord Jesus Christ.

SADIE (*suspiciously*). Just what is the idea, Reverend Davidson—making me these presents?

REV. DAVIDSON. The time has come, Sadie Thompson, for you to make your choice. The broad bosom of our Lord, His tender arms, His all-consoling whisper in your ear, His healing fingers on your weary eyes—all these are yours for the asking.

SADIE (*with dignity*). I don't know why I get all this attention from you, Reverend Davidson. I guess you mean well, but I think I can worry along just as I've been worrying along these several years without your help. I go my own way and don't ask any favors.

REV. DAVIDSON (*pleasantly*). Those who have the key of salvation offered them, and fail to open that door, must be destroyed.

SADIE (*cheerfully*). I see what you mean! But I won't get destroyed. I always make out one way or another! (*She rises.*) If that's all, Reverend Davidson, I guess I'll go back and eat—I'm hungry. (*She moves away* L.)

REV. DAVIDSON. You are hungry for the bread of the Spirit. You are thirsty for the waters of eternal life.

SADIE (*turning*). You mean right by me, Reverend Davidson—and I sure am grateful, especially after what happened the other day. (*She comes towards him in a half-shy, half-confidential manner.*) You know, just between ourselves, I had sort of a feeling you were laying to get me for that little trouble we had—you know! When you busted the gramophone and the boys bawled you out. I felt awful bad about it. I've been wanting to apologize.

REV. DAVIDSON (*patiently*). You are mistaking me—but I do not think willfully.

SADIE (*below the chair* L. *of the table*). They all told me you were sore, but I just couldn't think a man as big as you would hold a grudge over a little misunderstanding.

REV. DAVIDSON. All this is beside the point, Miss Thompson. The only thing that concerns me now is that you must be given your chance before I act.

SADIE. My chance for what?

REV. DAVIDSON. Your chance to be saved.

SADIE (*carelessly, sitting against the lower edge of the table*). Oh, I'm all right—don't you bother about me a bit! You see (*She smiles in a frank, friendly manner.*) I'm a happy-go-lucky kind of a fellow! I'll be all right as soon as I get to Apia. I've got friends there.

REV. DAVIDSON (*slowly*). You have friends in Apia? What sort of friends?

SADIE. Oh, just friends! A girl I used to work with is there. She wrote me I could have a job as cashier. I'm pretty quick at figures.

REV. DAVIDSON. For some time past you have lived in Honolulu, haven't you? What did you do there?

SADIE (*evasively*). Well, part of the time I had sort of a singing job. (*She smiles.*) My voice isn't so awful if you don't listen too hard.

REV. DAVIDSON. Before you went to Honolulu, where were you?

SADIE. Where do I come from, do you mean? (*Their eyes meet. He regards her gloomily. She forces herself to return his stare. Her nervousness reveals itself in the tensity of her fingers as they twist the dress she wears.*) I was born in Keneshaw, Kansas—if that means anything—but pa and ma got the California fever, so they sold the farm and bought a little ranch outside Los Angeles. I was about fifteen then I guess. Then ma died and pa and I didn't get along so well, so I went up to San Francisco. I was working there up to to to the time I went to Honolulu . . .

REV. DAVIDSON. What made you go away to Honolulu?

SADIE (*nervously*). I—I don't know. I wanted a change I suppose . . .

REV. DAVIDSON. Ah! You wanted a change. Well, Sadie Thompson . . . (*There is a long pause in which* DAVIDSON's *gloomy eyes seem to chisel into* SADIE's *soul.*) This gift I offer you—what are you going to do about it?

SADIE. Do about it? I don't know. I don't know what you're talking about! I can take care of myself. Up or down—in jack or broke! What's the odds! Wherever night overtakes me, that's my resting place—that's my way. (*She rises and eases* L., *then turns to him.*) Thank you for your interest, though—it's kind of you after what happened. I'm mighty glad you aren't sore at me. I like to keep friends with everybody.

REV. DAVIDSON (*firmly*). Sit down, Miss Thompson, I see I must be very patient. (SADIE *sits,* L. *of the table.*) I see I must make you understand. My poor lost child, what happened the other day is of no importance. Do you imagine what you or those sailors said to me made any difference?

SADIE (*greatly relieved*). You certainly are all to the good, Mr. Davidson, and I want to say this. Don't be afraid but that I'll keep to myself. I know oil and water don't mix. The ladies in your party won't even know I'm under the same roof with them. I'll be as quiet as a mouse! (*She rises and moves down* L.)

REV. DAVIDSON (*firmly, moving to below the table*). Don't go, Miss Thompson. You must listen to me.

SADIE (*wearily, moving past him to down* R.C.). Reverend Davidson—why do you worry about me.

REV. DAVIDSON (*moving up, by the chair* R. *of the table*). You've had your own soul in trust and you failed. It is now my business to show you the way to redeem it.

SADIE (*turning at* R.C.). And haven't I anything to say about myself then?

REV. DAVIDSON. Yes—you can choose one of two paths.

SADIE (*with a flash of "pep"*). What's second choice?

REV. DAVIDSON (*in a final voice*). Destruction!

SADIE. And who's going to destruct me?

REV. DAVIDSON. The forces which find no place for evil.

SADIE (*in a half whisper*). And you—what are you going to do?

REV. DAVIDSON. Only my duty.

SADIE. What might that be?

REV. DAVIDSON. Infectious diseases must be quarantined. Sin must be segregated until it can be stamped out.

(*A long look passes between them; an expression of terror comes into* SADIE's *eyes. She backs against the deck-chair like an animal at bay.*)

SADIE (*shrilly*). I know; you went to see the Governor about me, didn't you? Oh, don't say you didn't. I got it straight. Some of the boys told me. They didn't know what you said, but they told me to look out for you! Now I understand what they meant.

REV. DAVIDSON. You are right. I have been to the Governor. (*Rushing along.*) I shall not let you go to Apia, Sadie Thompson. You are an evil woman, you have lived an evil life. You have come here only to carry your infamy to other places. You are a harlot out of Iweili!

SADIE. You're a liar!

REV. DAVIDSON (*moving down nearly level with* SADIE, *on her* L.). Look at me.

SADIE. Who the hell do you think you are—standing there, calling names!

REV. DAVIDSON. Look at me. Do you deny that you escaped from Iweili?

SADIE (*hysterically*). I've listened all I'm going to listen to you. Now you listen to me. You just told me to be careful. Be careful yourself! Lay off me or I'll show you what it means when I start to get mad. It'll be the worse for you, if you don't.

REV. DAVIDSON. The devil in you is strong, poor Sadie Thompson. Evil has claimed you as its own.

SADIE. You take care of your own evil, and I'll take care of mine. (*With a horrid laugh.*) I know what you want! You want another scalp to hand to the Lord. Well, you don't get mine, old tit-bit!

REV. DAVIDSON (*passionately breaking in*). Lord!—Hear Thou my prayer for this lost sister. Close Thy ears to her wild and heedless words. (*He puts his hand on her arm. She draws it away.*)

SADIE. You Bible-backs don't fool me. I've met you before! Make me go over your way, would you? Just try it!

(*DAVIDSON grasps her arm and tries to force her to kneel.*)

REV. DAVIDSON. Kneel, Sadie Thompson, God is waiting. He is waiting.

SADIE (*pulling away*). You let go of me!

REV. DAVIDSON (*reaching for her*). This is your last chance, Sadie Thompson. Kneel with me and pray.

(*He grabs her wrist. She allows him to hold it for a second. She looks right into his eyes. Then she gives a peal of sudden laughter and tosses his hold away from her wrist.*)

SADIE (*crossing him quickly to* C.). Oh-h! You make me laugh!

REV. DAVIDSON (*in an awful voice*). Sadie Thompson, you're doomed!

(*SADIE turns to him. For a moment they face each other. Again SADIE laughs; then suddenly she spits full in DAVIDSON's face, turns, rushes into her room, and slams the door, leaving DAVIDSON alone. DAVIDSON's eyes are dark and fearful and his hands work convulsively. He breathes heavily. MRS. DAVIDSON comes hastily down the stairs.*)

MRS. DAVIDSON (*moving down to above the* R. *end of the table*). Alfred! What happened?

(*DAVIDSON slowly turns up toward his wife.*)

REV. DAVIDSON (*in an awesome voice*). I have given her every chance. I have exhorted her to repent. Now, I shall take the whips with which the Lord Jesus drove the usurers and the money changers out of the temple of the Most High. (*He paces* R. *and back in wild exaltation. His wife watches him in fear.*) Even if she fled to the uttermost parts of the earth, I should pursue her! (*He picks up his hat and goes* R. *The gramophone in* SADIE's *room breaks into the "Dance of the Marionettes."*)

MRS. DAVIDSON (*taking a step after him*). Alfred!

(*DAVIDSON does not heed her. He stalks out* R. *She makes a futile gesture, then, ignored and hurt, she stands irresolute.*

MRS. DAVIDSON. Alfred!

(*As she says this, she sinks into a chair, her hands clasped uselessly in her lap.* O'HARA *enters through the veranda. Having just collided with the unseeing* DAVIDSON, *he rubs his shoulder and smiles.*)

O'HARA (*moving to* R.C.). There was some big breeze! (*On seeing* MRS. DAVIDSON, *he stops and mumbles.*) Evening!

(*MRS. DAVIDSON turns on hearing* O'HARA. *She rises and faces him. Once more she is the missionary. This is her chance to do something. She is alert and brisk.*)

MRS. DAVIDSON. Young man, I should not come here if I were you.

O'HARA. Why?

MRS. DAVIDSON. You are likely to get into more trouble than you're in already!

O'HARA. This isn't my first year away from home ma'am—and I haven't got run over yet!

MRS. DAVIDSON. Do you know what kind of a girl this Sadie Thompson is?

O'HARA. I don't ask anything of anybody except to be square.

(SADIE's *door opens and* SADIE *comes out. She stops, standing in her doorway.*)

MRS. DAVIDSON. My advice to you is, keep away from bad company!

SADIE (*breaking in on* MRS. DAVIDSON). Bad company! (*She salutes and clicks her heels.*) Present!

(MRS. DAVIDSON *gives* SADIE *a look of withering disgust. Then she turns and without a word marches upstairs.* SADIE *and* O'HARA *watch her until she is out of sight. Then* SADIE *turns to* O'HARA *and snaps her fingers with a weary gesture.*)

SADIE. Such is joy! (*Her expression changes as she sinks into the chair* R. *of the table with a bitter sigh.*)

O'HARA (*to* SADIE). What's the matter? You look low!

SADIE. Low? Maybe. It's this rain, I guess.

O'HARA. You ought to try getting out for a walk.

SADIE. I was out this morning. I went to that half-caste family you told me about last night. I asked them if they wouldn't take me in to board. They closed the door in my face so fast you'd have thought I had smallpox.

O'HARA. Don't you care. You're better off here.

SADIE (*dryly*). I'm not so sure! (*A moment's silence, save for the rain.*) Listen to it. Don't it make you want to scream? And when you do scream, what good does it do you? You haven't got any strength left—you're hopeless—you're miserable!

O'HARA. That's no way to talk, Miss Sadie. Don't sound like you.

SADIE (*rising*). Forget it. I've got the fantods. I'll get over 'em—you see. (*She hesitates—moves a little L. below the table—then returns to O'HARA.*) I—I—I've just had a run-in with that Davidson.

O'HARA (*moving to below the deck-chair*). Yeah! What about?

SADIE. He's not going to let me go to Apia—so he says. (*She pauses.*) And anybody can see with two glass eyes that this side of the Equator the reverend's in right and I'm in wrong. What I'm trying to figure out is what devil's trick he'll use to stop me.

O'HARA. I don't see what he can do.

SADIE. Neither do I—but we don't say it with bells—either of us! (*Pauses.*) There's something about that crow that isn't human. He's deep—he's creepy! I guess it's his eyes—they look right into you—seem to know what you're thinking. Something tells me I'm going to need friends soon, Handsome. I'm far from home!

O'HARA. Well, any time you call for help, I'm right here, don't forget that, and if there's any help needed . . .

SADIE (*with a half-smile*). Thanks! Thanks!

O'HARA. Looka here! If something should go wrong—that is, about your getting to Apia—what'll you do? You might as well make plans.

SADIE. What'll I do? That means you're afraid something will go wrong?

O'HARA. No! No! But if the old nose-pusher gets around the Governor somehow, and they do stop you somehow, what'll you do?

SADIE. I don't know.

O'HARA. Go back to the States, I suppose?

SADIE. No—no! (*She gives a sudden movement of terror*). There's no way they can make me go back to the States, is there?

O'HARA. I don't see how, unless you want to! (SADIE's *eyes have suddenly become round and fixed as though a great fear had seized her. She sits R. of the table, gazing into space. Suddenly she buries her head in her hands.*) Why, what's the matter, Miss Sadie?

SADIE (*through her teeth*). I won't go back to the States. They couldn't make me go, could they?

O'HARA. You don't want to go to Honolulu either, I suppose?

SADIE (*disgusted*). No—no!

(*There is a pause. She stares out before her.*)

O'HARA (*sitting on the R. corner of the table, above her*). You could go to Sidney. Work's easy to get. Living's cheap, they say. I'd head that way instead of Apia if I were you. There's a boat twice a month. That's where I'm bound as soon as I shed these hash marks—that'll be one month and three days.

SADIE (*without turning*). What are you going to do there?

O'HARA. Going into the building business. Old shipmate of mine has his own place and wants a partner—these three years Biff's been at me to get my discharge and come in with him. You'd like this Biff. We joined the service same time, sixteen years ago.

SADIE. I'm glad you're fixed, Handsome, and you ought to do fine!

O'HARA. Then there's another thing. If you go to Sidney now, I'll be hoving in sight in a few weeks. Not that that might mean so much to you, maybe.

SADIE (*turning slowly in her chair and giving him a curious look*). Mean so much? I haven't many friends, Handsome, but what I could do with one more. (*She smiles a strange, wistful, tender smile.*) You're an awful funny fellow, Handsome.

O'HARA. I guess I'm the dumbbell king, all right.

SADIE (*thoughtfully, her chin in her hands*). I thought I knew most all there was to know about men, until you came along, but . . .

O'HARA (*after a pause*). How about it?

SADIE. About what?

O'HARA. Changing your route and going to Sidney anyway.

SADIE (*slowly*). Yes, why not? (*She rises, and moves a pace R.*) I guess no one can stop me from doing that! (*She swings round to face O'HARA with a laugh and seems to throw off her despondency.*) God! What a poor simp I was to get the wind up all over nothing! There was I jumping with the shakes and nervous as a witch just because that dismal crumb Davidson wouldn't let me go to Apia. (*Moving* L. *below the table.*) Well, Apia my foot—it's Sidney for mine!

(*A native appears at the veranda. He wears a raincoat of rushes over his lava lava and a dripping straw hat.*)

O'HARA (*crossing to the native*). What belong you want—lookum see.

NATIVE. I belong make fetch Governor's letter. (*He holds letter out to* O'HARA.)

O'HARA (*taking the letter and scanning the envelope, then moving toward* SADIE). It's— for you.

SADIE (*moving toward* O'HARA *and taking it gingerly*). For me—who's sending me a letter? (*She looks at it, then at* O'HARA.) It's—it's from the Governor's office. (*She holds it fearfully; her hand trembling.*)

O'HARA (*turning to the native*). Sahulanua mi—make go. (*The native exits. To* SADIE.) Better open it.

(SADIE *opens the letter with nervous twistings. She reads it in silence.*)

SADIE (*having read letter, reads it aloud in a monotonous voice*). Listen to this!—"It has been brought to the attention of the Governor that your presence in Pago Pago is not best for the public good. An order of deportation has therefore been issued, in compliance with which you will leave this Island on the first boat. A passage from this port to San Francisco . . . (*her voice falters a second, but she goes on bravely*) . . . San Francisco, on the *S.S. Cumberland*, leaving Pago Pago on the 6th inst., will be procured for you, and a sufficient sum of money given for the necessities of the journey.

"Signed, JOHN C. ROSS,
"*Secretary*."

(*She stands motionless, mechanically refolding the letter with a vague stare. Then, enraged with a growing sense of injustice.*) I won't go back to 'Frisco—they can't make me. There's reasons I can't tell you! I've got some rights, haven't I . . .? (*She stops, unable to continue.*)

O'HARA (*soothingly*). Now don't get nervous. I tell you what. Go see the Governor yourself right away. Ask him as a favor to let you stay here until the Sidney boat goes. That'll only mean three or four days more.

SADIE. Will he see me?

O'HARA. Hurry up before he goes for dinner—it's only two steps!

SADIE. All right, I'll make him listen! He's got to listen!

O'HARA. Want me to go with you?

SADIE. Wait till I get my hat.

(SADIE *rushes into her bedroom with a whirl of the bead curtains, leaving* O'HARA *on the stage. He eases further* L. DAVIDSON *appears on the veranda and enters the room. A second later* SADIE, *slamming a hat on her head, reappears. She stops short on seeing* DAVIDSON. *He gives no evidence of seeing her, but continues across the room as though to go upstairs. Her eyes flashing,* SADIE *crosses up and intercepts him.*)

SADIE. So you're back, are you? You low-down skunk, what have you been saying—to the Governor about me?

REV. DAVIDSON (*up* R.C., *in a quiet voice*). I've been hoping to have another talk with you, Miss Thompson.

SADIE (*between her teeth*). You miserable snail snatcher. I wouldn't talk with you, if you and me were the only people left on earth. You're so doggone mean, it makes me sick even to look at you. That's what I think of you, coming to me with all that guff you spilled about salvation —then going and having me deported on top of it—you low-lived . . .

O'HARA. Sadie—for God's sake! (*He goes up, to above the* L. *end of the table, as if to check her.*)

REV. DAVIDSON. I am wholly indifferent to the abuse you think fit to heap on me, Miss Thompson—but I am puzzled as to the cause of it.

SADIE. You know what you've been and done—filling the Governor up with a lot of filthy lies about me—and now this comes—and I've got to beat it on the next boat. (*She crumples the Governor's order in her fist, waving it at* DAVIDSON.)

REV. DAVIDSON. You could hardly expect him to let you stay here under the circumstances.

SADIE (*screaming*). What did the Governor know or care about me until you went and hauled your hooks into me? It's you that did it—you did it all!

REV. DAVIDSON. I don't want to deceive you, Miss Thompson. I urged the Governor to take the only steps consistent with his obligations.

SADIE. Why couldn't you let me be? Was I doing you any harm—was I?

REV. DAVIDSON. You may be sure if

you had, I would be the last man to resent it.

SADIE. You don't think I *want* to stay in this rain hole, do you?

REV. DAVIDSON (*smiling grimly*). In that case, I don't see what cause for complaint you have! You are being given every opportunity of getting out. (*He makes for the stairs.*)

O'HARA (*moving up and pulling at* SADIE's *arm*). Sadie—Sadie—come on—don't talk any more.

SADIE (*shaking off* O'HARA *and following* DAVIDSON; *putting herself directly in front of him and shrieking, words tumbling pell-mell*). You! You! I know your kind, you dirty two-faced mutt! I'll bet when you were a kid you caught flies and pulled their wings off—I bet you stuck pins in frogs, just to see 'em wiggle and flap while you read 'em a Sunday School lesson. I know you! You'd tear the heart out of your grandmother if she didn't think your way, and tell her you were saving her soul — you — you — you psalm-singing _____!

(*Her crazy words end in an inarticulate shriek of rage. During the above, as though drawn by* SADIE's *clamor,* MRS. DAVIDSON *runs down the stairs.* DR. *and* MRS. MACPHAIL *appear behind her;* HORN, *astonished out of his usual calm, enters from the store,* MRS. HORN *also peers through the door. They watch the finish of the scene between* SADIE *and* DAVIDSON *in fearful wonder. Following her outburst,* SADIE *breaks into sobs and is pulled out of the scene by* O'HARA. SADIE *and* O'HARA *cross* R. *to the veranda noisily, and exit.*)

(*No word is spoken on the stage.* DAVIDSON *stands in terrible silence. His wife, her hands clasped, watches him.* HORN *signals his wife.* MRS. HORN *withdraws, followed by* HORN. *On the stage are the* MACPHAILS *and the* DAVIDSONS *only.*)

MRS. DAVIDSON. Alfred—this sort of thing must stop. It can't go on—it's wearing you out. That woman is possessed of devils.

REV. DAVIDSON. Yes—she is possessed of devils. (*In a deliberate voice.*) However, you will be glad to hear that the Governor has acted at last. Miss Thompson will leave on the first boat that goes.

(MRS. MACPHAIL, *followed by the* DOCTOR, *moves down,* L. *of the table.*)

DR. MACPHAIL (*wearily*). How soon will that be?

REV. DAVIDSON. The San Francisco boat is due here from Sidney next Tuesday. She's to sail on that.

DR. MACPHAIL (*with a sigh*). Four days more!

REV. DAVIDSON (*looking at his watch*). It's half past six. (*To* MRS. DAVIDSON.) Are you ready, Hester? (*He goes to the stairs slowly.*)

MRS. DAVIDSON. Yes, Alfred. (DAVIDSON *mounts the stairs and exits. To* MRS. MAC PHAIL.) No matter where we are, always we make it a point to read a chapter of the Gospel either after tea or before retiring for the night. Then we study it with the commentaries and discuss it thoroughly. It's a great training for the mind. (MRS. DAVIDSON *mounts the stairs and exits.*)

(*The* MACPHAILS *exchange glances.* DR. MACPHAIL *drags on his pipe and turns to his wife.*)

DR. MACPHAIL. That settles Miss Thompson's hash, I guess. (*He moves* R., *above the table.*)

MRS. MACPHAIL (*sighing*). These incessant scenes are very trying. I don't understand them. They horrify me. (*She sits above the table and opens her needlework bag.*)

DR. MACPHAIL (*by the deck-chair,* R.C., *puffing*). Um-m—But who's to blame? Even a rabbit, you know, tears at the trap closing over it. (*He sits in the deck-chair.*)

(MRS. MACPHAIL *sighs and stitches on her comforter. Somewhere from above there comes a voice lifted in prayer. It reverberates above the steady downpour of the rain.* MACPHAIL *gestures to his wife. His finger is at his lips. She nods.*)

MRS. MACPHAIL. Yes! I heard him last night. The partition between the room is so thin. I thought he'd never stop.

DR. MACPHAIL. I suppose he's praying for the soul of Sadie Thompson.

MRS. MACPHAIL. No wonder Mrs. Davidson looks like a ghost. She's so sensitive to sin. She tells me she hasn't closed her eyes since we came, thinking of that unmentionable woman under the same roof with her.

DR. MACPHAIL. Hm! The founder of her religion wasn't so squeamish.

MRS. MACPHAIL. Don't joke about such things please, Robert.

(*She bites her thread in virtuous, wifely reproof.* SADIE *and* O'HARA *are now seen entering the veranda.* O'HARA *is half-support-*

ing SADIE,, *who, on seeing that the room is occupied by* DR. *and* MRS. MACPHAIL, *sinks into a chair by the veranda rail.* O'HARA *enters the room and crosses to* L. *of* MACPHAIL.)

O'HARA (*in a low voice*). Excuse me, Doctor — but — Miss Thompson isn't feeling well. Will you see her for a moment?

DR. MACPHAIL (*rising*). Certainly.

O'HARA. She's right out there. I'll bring her in. (*He eases* R., *and beckons to* SADIE.) Sadie, here's Doctor MacPhail. Tell him what you want. (SADIE *enters.* O'HARA *moves towards her and speaks in a lower voice.*) I've got to get back for inspection now. I'll come around later. See you later—now keep your chin up. (*They shake hands.* O'HARA *exits quickly at the veranda.*)

(SADIE *crosses slowly to* DR. MACPHAIL, *who sets the chair for her* R. *of the table.* SADIE *sits, looking nervously at* MRS. MACPHAIL.)

DR. MACPHAIL. This is my wife—Miss Thompson.

(MRS. MACPHAIL *glances quickly at her husband, who pantomimes her to be pleasant.* SADIE *nods;* MRS. MACPHAIL *does likewise.*)

MRS. MACPHAIL (*nervously gracious*). I—I—believe we are fellow lodgers.

SADIE (*apathetically*). Yes.

(*There is an embarrassed pause.* MACPHAIL *signals for his wife to go.*)

MRS. MACPHAIL (*rising*). Has the rain lessened at all?

SADIE. No-o—not much.

MRS. MACPHAIL (*crossing above the table to the veranda*). Last night there was a tiny bit of sunset shining through from somewhere—perhaps there is tonight. I'm going to see. (MRS. MACPHAIL *exits* R., *with nervous flutterings.*)

DR. MACPHAIL. Sorry to hear you're not feeling well.

SADIE (*tensely*). Oh, I'm well enough —not really sick. O'Hara said that because I just had to see you. (*She clasps her hands until the knuckles show white.*)

DR. MACPHAIL (*gently, as he moves to the deck-chair and sits*). Yes, Miss Thompson?

SADIE. It's this, Doctor! I've been ordered to clear out of here on a boat that's going to San Francisco.

DR. MACPHAIL. So I understand.

SADIE (*hoarsely*). Well, it isn't convenient for me to go back to San Francisco now. I've just been to see the Governor about it. He didn't want to speak to me, I'll say, but I wouldn't let him shake me

off. Finally he said he had no objection to my staying here until the next boat to Sidney goes, if the Reverend Davidson would stand for it.

DR. MACPHAIL (*dubiously*). I don't know exactly what I can do.

SADIE (*desperately*). Well I thought maybe you wouldn't mind asking the Reverend Davidson if he'd let me go to Sidney instead. I swear to go; I won't start anything here—if he'll only let me stay. I won't go out of my room if that will suit him. It's only three or four days longer.

DR. MACPHAIL (*touched by her apparent desperation*). I'll ask him.

SADIE. Tell him I can get work in Sidney—straight stuff. (*Rising.*) It isn't asking much. I know I've talked to him awful—but he got me so mad. But I'll admit he's got me beat now. Tell him I just can't go back to San Francisco—there's reasons—I just can't! (*She goes to the deck-chair and catches* MACPHAIL's *hand in hers.*) Please—please!

DR. MACPHAIL. When I see him I'll do what I can. (*He rises.*)

SADIE (*inarticulately*). Thank you—thank you! (MACPHAIL *turns up toward the veranda as though to follow his wife.* SADIE *sees he is not going to do it immediately. She goes after him.*) Oh—couldn't you do it now? I can't settle to a thing until I know the dope one way or another.

DR. MACPHAIL. Oh well, all right.

(*He crosses up reluctantly and mounts the stairs.* SADIE *crosses after him and listens.*)

DR. MACPHAIL (*calling*). Oh, Davidson!

REV. DAVIDSON (*heard off, upstairs*). What is it Doctor?

DR. MACPHAIL. I want to speak to you about something. Shall I come up?

REV. DAVIDSON. No, I'll come right down!

(*During the above* SADIE *stands by the staircase listening tensely. On hearing this she scurries down* L. *towards her doorway.* DR. MACPHAIL *descends.*)

SADIE (*moving up and frantically tugging at* MACPHAIL's *arm*). Tell him I ask his pardon—tell him I'm sorry.

DR. MACPHAIL. Yes—yes! Better get into your room, Miss Thompson.

(*He motions her to go into her room.* DAVIDSON *is heard descending.* SADIE *hurries to obey.* DAVIDSON *appears and descends. A flicker comes into his eye as he notices that the bead curtain into* SADIE's *room is still moving.*)

REV. DAVIDSON (*coolly*). Well, Doctor, what can I do for you? (*He comes to above the table.*)

DR. MACPHAIL (L. *of the table*). It's—er —it's about Miss Thompson. (DAVIDSON *stands frigidly waiting for* MACPHAIL *to continue.*) The Governor has told her that if you have no objection he will allow her to remain here until she can take the boat for Sydney.

REV. DAVIDSON. I'm sorry, Dr. MacPhail, but it is useless to discuss the matter.

DR. MACPHAIL. It appears the girl has reasons for not wanting to return to San Francisco. I don't see that it makes any difference if she goes to Sydney instead. It's only a matter of a few days.

REV. DAVIDSON (*slowly*). Why is she unwilling to go back to San Francisco?

DR. MACPHAIL. I didn't inquire—and I think one does better to mind one's own business.

REV. DAVIDSON. You mean this interference for the best, Doctor, but my mind is made up.

DR. MACPHAIL (*very slowly; moving to* DAVIDSON). If you want to know what I think—I think you are harsh and tyrannical.

REV. DAVIDSON (*with a gentle smile*). I'm terribly sorry you should think that of me, Dr. MacPhail. (*Easing* R. *of the table and turning there.*) Believe me, my heart bleeds for that unfortunate woman— but I cannot find it in my conscience to change the decision. If the Governor wishes to do so on his own account, that is his business.

DR. MACPHAIL. He won't—and you know why. (*A long look passes between the two.*)

REV. DAVIDSON (*with a melancholy smile*). Please don't bear malice toward me because I cannot accede to your wish. I respect you very much, Doctor, and I should be sorry if you thought ill of me.

DR. MACPHAIL (*coldly*). I have no doubt you have a sufficiently good opinion of yourself to bear mine with equanimity.

REV. DAVIDSON (*with a gloomy chuckle*). That's one on me! (DAVIDSON *turns and exits upstairs.*)

(SADIE's *door opens fearfully. She comes out. A pause.*)

DR. MACPHAIL (*averting his eyes from hers.*) I'm sorry. (*He shakes his head. A sob breaks from* SADIE. *She covers her face and stands shaking before him.*)

SADIE. Oh!—Oh!—Oh!

DR. MACPHAIL (*in sudden pity*). Don't give up hope. I think it is a shame the way they're treating you. I'll go and see the Governor myself.

SADIE (*brokenly*). Will you? Will you? Now?

DR. MACPHAIL (*going toward the veranda*). Now!

SADIE (*inarticulately*). You're awful good—awful good!

(MRS. MACPHAIL *enters from the veranda.*)

MRS. MACPHAIL. Where are you going, Robert?

DR. MACPHAIL (*at* R.C., *curtly*). Just a step. I'll be back in two minutes.

MRS. MACPHAIL. Dinner's nearly ready. (SADIE *shudders and sobs.*)

DR. MACPHAIL (*turning to look at her*). Don't cry, Miss Thompson—I think I can do something.

SADIE (*struggling for composure*). God bless you—Doctor—God bless you— you don't know what this means to me.

(MACPHAIL *exits.* SADIE *sinks into the chair* L. *of the table.* MRS. MACPHAIL *is evidently deeply curious but she says nothing; she unrolls her sewing, sitting* R. *of the table.* SADIE *sits in stony silence, twisting her hands drearily.*)

MRS. MACPHAIL (*attempting to be charitable*). Everything is so damp, my needle has rusted in just these few minutes.

SADIE (*in a desolate voice*). Yes—even your bones would rust around here.

(*The silence is punctured by the rain. Off* L. *we hear the clatter of* MRS. HORN *and the children.* MRS. HORN *enters with more dishes. She waddles to the table.*)

MRS. HORN (*to* MRS. MACPHAIL). Dinner very soon happen!—mebbe five, mebbe ten minutes now—better you make ready. (*She sets the dishes down noisily.*)

(HORN *enters up* L., *from the store.*)

HORN (*crossing* R., *above the table*). The din of my spouse, and the spluttering of Hamburg steak—not to mention the odor of indifferent grease—have detached me from my slumbers. (*He sprawls into his cane chair and continues in elaborate mockery as he sniffs.*) I detect our menu! The Hamburg steak of our luxurious table d'hote you are surely familiar with by this time, Mrs. MacPhail. As a flanking dish we offer you fried bananas, I believe. My fair Ameena, here, rarely varies the diet—she has deduced that it is substantial, satisfying, and easy to prepare. She is a wise woman—she knows that ten minutes after consummation it won't matter whether one has dined on truffled grouse or Hamburg steak, so why bother. Isn't that so, my beloved?

(*Arms akimbo, nodding with pride,* MRS. HORN *listens to this oration. She smiles a vast, beaming smile.*)

MRS. HORN (*proudly*). That man—my husband—he talk damn fine—what? (*Wisely.*) Hui!—That's right—That's right.

HORN. See! She concurs! No more need be said.

MRS. MACPHAIL (*for the purpose of making conversation*). At that I quite agree with you, Mr. Horn. Most of us think too much about our stomachs. Take Mr. Davidson, he scarcely eats anything—but he is a very strong man—unusually strong—

(*Nodding wisely, her head cocked to one side,* MRS. HORN *listens to the above. Now she breaks in excitedly.*)

MRS. HORN. Muihichia! Me tell you something. Meestaire Davidson belong damn big Ju-ju-ija!

HORN (*pretending reproof*). My dear Ameena!

MRS. HORN. All I same I know! He Ju-ju-ija!

MRS. MACPHAIL (*biting her thread*). What *is* she saying?

HORN (*with amused mockery*). My wife in her gentle Polynesian way is tendering a high compliment to the Reverend Davidson—she says Mr. Davidson reminds her of a Ju-ju-ija!

MRS. MACPHAIL. Whatever does she mean?

HORN. My knowledge of the Ju-ju-ija is limited. When we got civilized here most of the Ju-ju-ijas packed off to remote places to weave their spells in peace. (*He turns to* MRS. HORN.) He ate up devils, didn't he, Ameena?

MRS. HORN. Yes—Yes—Ju-ju-ija he ate plenty devil—know everything—see everything—my father's time, plenty Ju-ju-ija—now all gone! (*She exits into the store.*)

HORN. A species of wizard, you perceive! (*He smiles maliciously.*) Knew everything! Saw everything! Lived by the power of thought! A grilled goat chop had no charms for him. When hungry

he simply ferreted out a devil and ate him up for tea.

SADIE (*jumping to her feet*). God! It gives me the willies to hear that kind of talk.

(SADIE *crosses* R. *nervously toward the veranda, looking out in the direction of the Governor's house. While her back is turned,* HORN *and* MRS. MACPHAIL *exchange glances, pregnant with meaning. The rain beats down pitilessly. In the silence we hear again the rumble of* DAVIDSON's *voice, coming from above. He is praying.* SADIE, *returning, begins to shiver. She shakes so that it is noticeable to* MRS. MACPHAIL. *Reaching the table, she takes a glass of water and tries to drink. The glass drops from her trembling hand and crashes to the floor.*)

SADIE (*shaking*). Oh! I'm sorry—I'm sorry!

MRS. MACPHAIL (*half rising*). You are ill, Miss Thompson.

SADIE (*moving away to* R.C.). No—I'm all right—this rain chills you—don't it?

HORN (*producing his bottle*). Here—drink this.

SADIE (*taking the bottle*). Thanks! (*She gulps the drink, returns the bottle to* HORN, *and asks in a hushed voice.*) That's Reverend Davidson upstairs, isn't it?

HORN. Sounds like his voice.

SADIE. Give me another—please. (HORN *hands her the bottle. She gulps it.*) What's he saying?

(*She jerks her head in the direction of upstairs. We hear* DAVIDSON's *voice saying* "Amen." *The praying finishes.*)

HORN (*ironically*). He said "Amen!"

SADIE. Either I'm jinxed or this stuff is, Horn. I can't seem to feel it! Maybe your wife's Juijua is after me! (*She laughs a little crazily.*) What's that the old jig does? Sees everything—knows everything? (*She drinks again.*) Well, that's the kind of eye the Reverend Davidson has, all right! He'd look right into you and know what you were trying to hide. It wouldn't be any use to try to keep much from him, would it? (*She gives the bottle to* HORN.)

(*A* NATIVE GIRL *enters with an old cowbell, which she rings vigorously, announcing dinner.* MRS. HORN *follows with two steaming platters.* HORN *rises lazily.*)

HORN. Ha, the feast is served!

MRS. MACPHAIL (*rising, crossing to* L. *of the table, and sitting there*). For myself, I doubt whether I can eat a bite.

(MRS. DAVIDSON *is seen descending the*

stairs. SADIE *sees her coming, pauses irreso-lutely, undecided what to do. Then she turns and walks quickly off via the veranda.* MRS. DAVIDSON *makes no comment on* SADIE'S *flight. She takes her place* L. *of the table in silence.* MRS. HORN *gives orders to the native girl and they exit up* L.)

(DAVIDSON *appears and begins to descend. As he comes into the room he notes that* MACPHAIL *is absent.*)

REV. DAVIDSON (*amiably, to* MRS. MAC-PHAIL). Isn't your husband dining?

MRS. MACPHAIL (*nervously*). He just stepped out for a minute.

REV. DAVIDSON (*with a peculiar smile*). Where has he gone?

MRS. MACPHAIL. I couldn't say exactly.

REV. DAVIDSON (*almost amused*). Ah! I think I can guess! (*He seats himself above the table and bows his head. The others follow suit. There is a second's silence while grace is said.*)

(MACPHAIL *and* SADIE *appear on the veranda. The change in* SADIE *is extraordinary. Her hair is disheveled and her eyes glare with fear. The tears stream down her face.* MAC-PHAIL *is silent and depressed. The two stand waiting patiently until grace is over.*)

REV. DAVIDSON (*lifting his head and seeing* SADIE; *speaking in a pleasant cordial voice*). Can I do something for you, Miss Thompson?

(MACPHAIL *moves down* R. *of the deck-chair.* SADIE *comes toward* DAVIDSON *with a horrible cringing movement. She checks at up* R.C.)

SADIE. I'm sorry for what I said to you today. For everything that's happened—I ask pardon.

REV. DAVIDSON (*smiling*). I guess my back's broad enough to bear a few hard words.

SADIE. You've got me beat, I'm all in. For God's sake don't make me go to 'Frisco. I'll go anywhere else you say.

(DAVIDSON'S *genial manner vanishes and his voice grows hard and stern. He leaves the table and comes to her.*)

REV. DAVIDSON. Why don't you want to go back there?

SADIE (*craftily*). It's this way, Reverend Davidson. I'm trying to go straight now. If I go back to San Francisco I can't go straight.

REV. DAVIDSON. What will prevent you from going straight—if you really want to?

SADIE. There's a man in San Francisco who won't let me.

REV. DAVIDSON. Who is this man?

SADIE (*at random*). Sort of politician. He's bad man. I'm scared of him.

REV. DAVIDSON. San Francisco is a big place. It should not be difficult to keep out of his way—if you want to.

SADIE (*wildly*). He'll know, though—He'll know! All the boats coming in are being watched.

REV. DAVIDSON. Do you mean to tell me that every boat coming into the port will be watched, on the chance you are on it!

SADIE. Yes—Yes!

REV. DAVIDSON (*in a terrible voice*). Come, Miss Thompson, these evasions are getting you nowhere. Why are you afraid to return to San Francisco?

SADIE. I've told you. I can't go straight there.

REV. DAVIDSON (*rising and towering over* SADIE, *who puts her hands up to her face and cringes*). Shall I tell you why you are afraid to go back?

MRS. MACPHAIL (*to* MRS. DAVIDSON). I think you and I had better leave!

(MRS. DAVIDSON *nods and the two ladies rise, move up, and exit upstairs.* HORN *taps* MACPHAIL *on the shoulder and the two men sneak off via the veranda.* SADIE *and* DAVID-SON *are now alone.* SADIE *cowers before him.*)

REV. DAVIDSON. You have told me lies. Now I shall tell you the truth. This politician you fear is a politician in uniform—and he wears a badge! (*He takes her by the shoulders and his great shining eyes seem to bore into her soul.*) What you fear is—the penitentiary.

(SADIE *gives a sudden cry, then weakens at the knees and falls, clasping his legs.*)

SADIE. Don't send me back there. I swear to you before God, I'll be a good woman. I'll give all this up.

(DAVIDSON *leans over her, lifts her face, forces her to look at him.*)

DAVIDSON. Is that it—the peniten-tiary?

SADIE (*faintly*). I was framed! But I got away before they caught me. They'll nab me the moment I step off the ship, and it's three years for mine—three years—three years. (DAVIDSON *lets go of* SADIE *and she falls in a heap on the floor, sob-bing bitterly. After a second, between her sobs.*) Give me a chance—one chance.

REV. DAVIDSON (*with shining eyes*). I'm going to give you the finest chance you've ever had.

SADIE (*taking hope, half rising*). I don't have to go back, you mean?

REV. DAVIDSON. Yes, you'll have to go back. You will sail for San Francisco on Tuesday, as the Governor has ordered. (SADIE *gives a groan of horror, sinks on the floor again, and bursts into low, hoarse moans, scarcely human.*) If you are truly repentant you will gladly accept this punishment. You will offer it to God as the atonement for your sins. (*The missionary's lips move silently in prayer. Then, gently.*) When you want me, Sadie Thompson, call for me— I will come. (DAVIDSON *is extraordinarily moved. Tears run down his cheeks.*) At any hour—day or night—when you need me I will come. I shall be waiting for your call.

(*He turns and slowly starts toward the stair.* SADIE's *shuddering moans become fainter. They are now deep, tortured sighs.* DAVIDSON *begins to mount the stairs.* SADIE *rouses herself. She gives a little cry.* DAVIDSON *pauses.*)

SADIE (*struggling to her feet*). Reverend Davidson—wait a minute! (*A flicker of craft comes into* SADIE's *eyes—the craft of desperation. Her expression indicates that her mind is working rapidly. She crosses up* C., *below the banisters and clasps her hands.*) Reverend Davidson—you're right. I am a bad woman, but I want to be good, only I don't know how. So you let me stay here with you, then you can tell me what to do, and no matter what it is I'm going to do it for you.

REV. DAVIDSON (*looking down on her, shaking his head*). No, you can't stay here. You've got to go back to San Francisco; you've got to serve your time.

SADIE (*looking at him, astonished after her offer*). You mean to say, if I repent and I want to be good—I still have to go to the penitentiary? (*Clutching the banisters, throwing her last plea.*) But I was framed, I tell you! I was framed!

REV. DAVIDSON. Innocent or guilty, you must serve your sentence! It's the only way you can prove to God that you are worthy of His mercy.

SADIE. Innocent or guilty? What kind of a God are you talking about? Where's your mercy? Ah, no, Reverend Davidson, I guess that repentance stuff is off. (*She turns away, moving down* R.C.)

REV. DAVIDSON. Was it ever on, Miss Thompson?

SADIE (*turning to face the stairs*). Whether it was or not, it's off now! The way you figure out God, He's nothing but a cop.

REV. DAVIDSON. You've got to go back to San Francisco!

SADIE (*throwing discretion to the winds*). Straight orders from your private heaven, eh? Ah, no, Reverend Davidson, your God and me could never be shipmates, and the next time you talk to Him (*She steps up a pace or two and shouts in his face.*) you tell Him this for me: Sadie Thompson is on her way to Hell!

REV. DAVIDSON (*drawing himself up to full height and shouting back at her*). Stop! This has gone far enough!

SADIE (*in wild hysteria*). No! It hasn't gone far enough! You've been telling me what's wrong with me. Now I'll tell you what's wrong with you. You keep yelling at me—be punished! Go back and suffer! (*Turning down* R.C.) How do you know what I have suffered? You don't know, you don't care: you don't even ask, and you call yourself a Christian. (*Turning to face him.*) You're nothing but a miserable witch-burner— that's what you are—you believe in torture. You know you're bit and you're strong and you've got the law on your side—and the power to hang me. All right! But I want to tell you this: I've got the power to stand here and say to you—Hang me and be damned to you! (*She stampedes* L. *and into her room, sobbing hoarsely.*)

DAVIDSON's *lips move in prayer as*

the CURTAIN *falls.*

ACT THREE

SCENE ONE

The SCENE *is the same as the preceding. It is night; four days later.*

The rain is beating persistently on the roof. On the veranda the shades are drawn. Indoors, the center lamp is lit, casting a circle of reddish light on the floor below. The chairs above the table are pushed in. The corners of the room are heavily in shadow. Blending with the sound of the rain, as from a distance, we hear the ominous beating of festival drums.

As the curtain rises, HORN *and his wife are alone on the stage.* HORN *is seated on the deck-chair under the lamp, reading.* MRS.

HORN *is snoozing in the chair* L. *of the table, her head nodding, a palm-leaf fan slipping from her fingers.*

———

HORN (*reading aloud from his book*). Everything goeth—everything returneth—eternally rolleth the wheel of existence! Everything dieth—everything blossometh forth again. Eternally runneth on the year of existence! Thus spake Zarathustra! (*He smacks his lips as though enjoying the sonorous rolling of the words.*) Good old Nietzsche!

(*There comes a faint cry from* SADIE'S *room—the cry of a person awakening from an uneasy sleep.*)

SADIE (*calling from her room*). Reverend Davidson! Reverend Davidson!

(HORN *lays aside his book, and* MRS. HORN *opens one eye.*)

MRS. HORN. Ohm! (*She struggles into an upright position and listens.*) She wake up! Mebbe I go look-see, what?

HORN (*wearily*). No! Don't do anything. If God is good she is only turning over!

MRS. HORN (*sleepily*). Alumen—ta—mih—bah! Tomorrow she go! Trouble all finish, zazut!

HORN. Tomorrow she goes! That episode endeth!

(*They both listen. The sound from* SADIE'S *room is repeated.* MRS. HORN *rises and crosses to the* L. *door, opening it gently.* SADIE'S *voice is heard.*)

SADIE (*crying from her room*). Reverend Davidson! Reverend Davidson!

MRS. HORN (*at door*). He soon be coming. He soon be coming.

SADIE (*her voice is like a child's*). Hasn't he got back yet?

MRS. HORN (*consolingly*). He come soon now. You go sleep!

SADIE. Oh—dear!

MRS. HORN. You good girl now—nothing be 'fraid . . .

(MRS. HORN *closes the door and returns to her chair. She rocks and* HORN *reads. There is a moment's silence. Then a loud knock is heard, seeming to come from the store.* MRS. HORN *starts.* HORN *sits erect and listens. The knock is repeated.*)

HORN. Who in creation's that?

MRS. HORN. Mamut! Mamut! Who?

HORN. Go see, Ameena!

MRS. HORN (*fearfully*). Me no like go! Too many bad things happen.

HORN. Damn! (*He rises lazily, crosses* L., *and opens the store door.* O'HARA *enters.*) Oh, it's you, is it? Why the back way?

O'HARA. Nix—will you. (*He holds up a warning hand.*)

HORN (*returning to* R. *of the table*). Where you been all week?

O'HARA (*grimly, as he moves down to above the table*). In the brig.

HORN (*with a smile*). Yep! I heard you was demi-tassing in the guardhouse.

O'HARA (*angrily*). I'm out tonight, all right, though, they'll all find out.

HORN. About time you come around. (*He sits,* R. *of the table.*) Nice doing we've been having.

O'HARA. I'll bet you have! (*Sitting on the upper edge of the table.*) Where's all your swell company?

HORN. Whole caboodle's gone over to that native witch dance on Tangu Island.

O'HARA (*bitterly*). I had a hunch they'd go there. The Reverend couldn't pass up a chance like that, to get a few words in. Bet he busts the show up when the dancing starts.

HORN. Yeah. He'll be needing new brands to snatch from the burning now he's nipped poor Sadie Thompson out of the flames.

O'HARA. He can't get back before midnight, anyway—so we've got happy moments for a couple of hours. (O'HARA *pauses, then says in a different voice, pointing to* SADIE'S *room.*) How is she?

HORN (*shaking his head.*) Not so good.

O'HARA. What's he been doing to her?

HORN. Praying.

O'HARA. Praying?

HORN. Praying!

O'HARA. Got her beached with his psalm stuff—what?

HORN. Beached and delirious, I'd say.

O'HARA (*standing*). He took damn good care to get me stowed away before he started, didn't he? Well, I beat him to it tonight.

HORN. How did you get out?

O'HARA (*with a short laugh, crossing* R.). Walked out through the mess window. Little Griggs and Hodgson helped me—good boys, both of them—they ought to be here any minute now. (*He moves down* L. *of the deck-chair.*)

HORN. Um! What's a-doing, O'Hara? You arouse my curiosity.

O'HARA. If I was you, I'd ease off to bed with my old lady—and not have any curiosity.

HORN. You would, would you—and why would you do that?

O'HARA (*winking*). I'd do that so's I wouldn't get blamed for anything, in case anything happened.

(HORN *gestures to his wife to leave them alone, in obedience to which she rises and waddles off into the store.*)

HORN (*with mock mournfulness*). Sounds like another row is starting! Most unlucky day of my life—that day the *Orduna* came into port. (*He pauses, then goes on with elaborate mournfulness.*) I like my comfort! For five days now this whole household has centered on that tormented Thompson girl in there while Davidson and Old Nick wrestled for her soul! It's got me nervous!

O'HARA (*shortly*). Cheer up. It won't center round her much longer! What's she doing now—sleeping?

HORN. I haven't heard her yell for Davidson for at least ten minutes, so let's hope so.

O'HARA (*sharply*). Get her out for me! I'll tend to the rest of this.

HORN (*rising*). Gladly, gladly. My mind's a blank save for one fact—tomorrow Miss Sadie Thompson'll be on the high seas. (*He crosses below the table to* SADIE's *door.*)

O'HARA (*grimly*). You'll bet she'll be!

HORN (*rapping on* SADIE's *door*). Are you asleep, Miss Thompson? (*An inarticulate sound from* SADIE's *room.*) This is Horn. Will you come out a moment? You're wanted.

SADIE (*listlessly*). All right.

(HORN, *with a shrug of relief, exits up* L. *hastily with a backward look at* O'HARA *of mingled mirth and pity.* SADIE's *door slowly opens. She stands there, her hand over her eyes, like a person waked from sleep. Her hair is uncurled and hangs straight about her shoulders and down her back. She wears an old white dressing-gown of toweling. Over her shoulders is thrown a knitted shawl. She stands vaguely, uncertainly, in her doorway. Her feet are thrust into bedroom slippers. Her eyes are tragic and dark-ringed, her face ghastly. The ghost of a smile comes to her mouth as she sees* O'HARA.

O'HARA (*shocked at her appearance*). Sadie! (*Moving toward her.*) You look awful sick.

SADIE (*moving in a little*). I was wondering whether I'd see you before I left.

You've been awful kind to me. I'll never forget it. I want to thank you.

O'HARA (*shortly; moving to her,* L. *of the table*). Look here, Sadie—how long'll it take you to get packed?

SADIE. I'm pretty well packed up now. Mrs. Horn helped me get ready after dinner.

O'HARA. That's good. Griggs and Hodgson'll be along any minute now, they're to tote your bags. You hurry up now and get dressed as fast as you can.

SADIE. Get dressed?

O'HARA. You're leaving this place tonight.

SADIE. But the boat don't get in until tomorrow morning.

O'HARA. Your boat's going out tonight —and I'm going to see you get aboard her.

SADIE (*crossing him to* R. *of the table*). But I must wait for Mr. Davidson. He was going to see me on board. I . . .

O'HARA. Mr. Davidson isn't going to see you off.

SADIE (*getting frightened*). He isn't going to see me on board? What's happened? Where is he? (*She sinks into the chair* R. *of the table.*)

O'HARA (*moving up to above the table*). You're not going back to San Francisco —that's what's happened. You're leaving in a few minutes for the Samarkind Islands on a junk. You're going to wait there until the Sydney boat comes along. Then you're going to Sydney.

SADIE. Did Mr. Davidson say so?

O'HARA (*moving to above the* R. *end of the table*). I say so! You didn't think I was going to stand by and do nothing while they railroaded you back somewhere you didn't want to go, did you. (SADIE *does not answer.* O'HARA *continues rapidly.*) Hurry up, now, and get your clothes on. We've got time but none to spill. (SADIE *still does not rise. She stares at* O'HARA *in a distracted way.* O'HARA *continues gently.*) Now don't get scared—it's all fixed. You're going as far as the Samarkinds on a ginseng junk, and all you'll have to do is to lie low there for a few days until the Sydney boat comes along.

SADIE (*hazily; her hand at her head*). What do you suppose Reverend Davidson would think if he came back and found me gone?

O'HARA. Huh! You know the old shouter better than I do. (*Chuckles.*) But

I don't mind admitting that a sight of his face at that moment would slip me considerable quiet fun. (*He pauses. She does not respond to his chuckle. He looks at her tenderly.*) You've had a pretty bad time, I guess, these last few days. Just forget 'em. From now on everything's going to be fine. Just go put on a hat and dress, so's you'll be ready to start soon as the boys come.

SADIE. It's mighty sweet and fine of you to go to all this trouble for me.

O'HARA. Fine—fine nothing! This ain't one small bit what I'd like to do for you—if I got the chance.

SADIE. Your doing this—it makes me kind of want to cry—but . . .

O'HARA. What's the but?

SADIE. I can't do it.

O'HARA. Why can't you do it?

SADIE. I'm going through with what I've got to go through with.

O'HARA (*grimly*). Are you afraid of Davidson? He'll never get hold of you again. I'll see to that.

SADIE. No, no, that isn't it at all. It would be awful hard for me to make you understand what's come over me. I can't understand myself. (*A look almost of ecstasy comes into her face.*) Listen, Handsome! That day—remember—it seems years ago—that day the Governor's letter came—I lost my nerve. I ran around like a chicken with its head cut off. I was all over sweat—and I thought —I thought, I'll see if I can't fool him— so I told him a lie as to why I didn't want to go back to San Francisco—but he saw right through me—he looked right into me—he knew—he knew. (*She stops, then goes on rapidly, pantingly.*) Seemed to me then a great net was catching me. I knew nothing was any use—but I tried again. I called him back. I told him I had been a bad woman and I wanted to repent. That was a lie. I'd figured out things long ago and I didn't think I was bad, so there wasn't anything to repent about. I'd doped it out that some folks have luck, some haven't—all folks can't be the same, anyway—who knows what's good or what's bad? Nobody. So I let it go at that—and didn't think too much. I'm not saying, of course, there hadn't been tough moments when you had to think. (*She clings to* O'HARA'S *arm, shaken by memories.*)

O'HARA. Sadie—Sadie—you're get-

ting all upset. Please, baby, don't go on so.

SADIE (*not heeding the interruption*). Well, I told Davidson I'd repent. I thought maybe he'd be easier on me if he thought I'd fallen for his line. But he saw through that, too. Then I lost my head and talked to him terrible but he didn't mind. He followed me into my room and asked me if I would kneel down and pray, and I was so desparate that I said "Yes." Oh, Handsome! He knelt down and began to pray. He prayed a long time—hours! I didn't pay much attention at first. The rain was coming down straight and heavy. Outside, everything was damp and clammy. I kept wishing the mosquitoes would stop humming—I was kind of numb. There was some dreadful fear catching at me—but all at once I began to listen—sort of in spite of myself—Oh, Handsome . . . (*Her voice breaks she cannot go on.*)

O'HARA (*gently; moving round above and* R. *of her chair*). Go on—go on—spill it all. (*He pats her shoulder.*)

SADIE. Mr. Davidson prayed and prayed—and all of a sudden there was I out in a big, bright, beautiful place. Seemed to me all my life I had been in a fog and hadn't known it. He prayed for hours and hours. I was awful tired—but sort of happy. I knew I could be saved if I wanted, and I did want to repent. I told Mr. Davidson how I'd tried to fool him first about repenting—but he said he'd known it all along. (*She pauses, then goes on excitedly.*) Then it came, Handsome! I *did* feel sorry for what I'd been— there was nothing phony about it! I saw myself just as I was. Oh, God! Oh, God! (SADIE *begins to cry in nervous exhaustion. Her tears are the tears of strain, weariness and tension; her sobs, jerky and wretched.*)

O'HARA (*very gently*). Sadie—this thing don't make you happy. You don't realize—it ain't yourself. You've got to forget Mr. Davidson and come with me.

SADIE. No—No—I couldn't—I couldn't. You don't know what you're saying.

O'HARA. They're not going to send you back there with no one to take care of you . . .

SADIE (*putting her hands to her ears*). I won't listen—I won't listen—stop!— stop!

O'HARA. What's to hinder you repenting in Sydney—just as well as in

San Francisco—if you've got to repent? SADIE. You don't understand. I've got to go back and be punished for what I've been—there's no other way out. I've got to serve my time—then God will forgive me. It's the sacrifice I've got to offer up for the life I've led. Oh, if it would only begin at once. It's this waiting for it to start, that's so bad—all these days and days I'll be alone on the boat. I'm weak. I'm afraid. I'm dreadfully afraid. You've got to be very strong, Handsome, to live at all. (*Almost as if to herself.*) It will be much easier in the penitentiary.

O'HARA (*in a strange, shocked voice*). What's that you're saying? The penitentiary?

SADIE (*with a curious smile*). When I get to San Francisco, Handsome, I've got to go to the penitentiary for—three years.

O'HARA (*staring back; under his breath*). God!

SADIE. Reverend Davidson says it doesn't make any difference whether I was innocent or guilty, of what they framed me for. He says that is God's way of letting me square myself. He says I've got to accept an unjust punishment by man as a sacrifice to God.

O'HARA. You just listen to me. Get into your room and throw your clothes on as fast as you can. (*He pulls her from her chair.*)

SADIE. Let go of me—let go! (*She frees herself ferociously; turns on him angrily.*) Don't you dare do that again! I want you to go away. Do you hear? Get right out!

O'HARA (*brokenly*). Sadie—Sadie!

SADIE (*wildly, going* R.). I mean it! Get right out! Go away—go away.

O'HARA. Sadie—listen—please . . .

SADIE (*frantically; turning at* R.) Don't you come near me. Go away!

(*There is a sound on the veranda of the rain-shutters being pulled aside, and hushed voices.* SADIE *and* O'HARA *listen. Then* O'HARA *moves to up* R.C. GRIGGS *and* HODGSON *enter cautiously. The former carries a basket of ripe pineapples. On seeing the tensity of the situation between* O'HARA *and* SADIE, *they pause irresolutely.*)

O'HARA (*in a firm low voice*). Here's the two high-school boys, Sadie—come to say good-by to you. They're going to put your things aboard the junk for you. (*His voice is soothing; the voice one uses to a tired fretful child.*)

(*Suddenly* SADIE *begins to cry again; she sinks into the deck-chair* R., *and sobs violently*

and hoarsely. O'HARA *motions to* GRIGGS *and* HODGSON *to get* SADIE's *baggage. The lads nod, cross quietly* L., *and enter* SADIE's *room.*)

O'HARA (*when they have disappeared*). Sadie . . . listen, Sadie . . .

SADIE. Reverend Davidson! Reverend Davidson! Why don't he come? Why don't he come . . .?

(GRIGGS *comes out with an old carpetbag in one hand and a shawl bundle in the other. He crosses to* O'HARA *and sets them down on the floor.*)

GRIGGS (*to* O'HARA, *in a low voice*). Most of the stuff is tied up pretty good—but how about the gramophone?

O'HARA. Never mind. I'll bring that.

(HODGSON *enters with several large nondescript parcels of bulging shape.* SADIE *turns and sees* GRIGGS *and* HODGSON *moving her luggage.*)

SADIE (*crying out*). Oh, what are they doing? (*Moving towards the veranda.*) They mustn't. They mustn't. (*She gives a scream.*) Reverend Davidson! Reverend Davidson!

O'HARA. Sadie! Someone'll hear you! Don't for God's sake!

SADIE (*turning to face them*). Go away—all of you. Go away! Mr. Davidson!

O'HARA (*to* GRIGGS). See if there isn't a coat or something in there. That old peeler's got her tranced. (GRIGGS *goes quickly into* SADIE's *room. To* HODGSON.) We're taking her whether she wants to go or not.

(GRIGGS *re-appears with a coat belonging to* SADIE *over his arm. He gives it to* O'HARA.)

SADIE. They're taking my things. They mustn't take my things! (*Pleadingly.*) Go away, please. Please let me be. Oh, Handsome, why do you make it so hard for me?

(GRIGGS *and* HODGSON *exit* R. *with* SADIE's *things.*)

O'HARA (L. *of* SADIE; *feelingly*). Don't you know, Sadie? You ain't yourself!

SADIE (*earnestly*). I am myself! I am myself! That's what I've been trying to tell you! (*Easing* R.) Reverend Davidson's a holy man—the Spirit of God is in him. He's different from you and me. He has made me different. (*Turning slowly to* O'HARA.) I've been born all over again—don't you see, Handsome?

O'HARA. Yes—I see, and I see something else. (*He moves toward her.*) Remember, I told you if you ever needed a friend, I'd be here. Well, you need a friend—right now.

SADIE. Reverend Davidson's my friend.

O'HARA. Now, Sadie, you've got to listen to me. (*He waves a hand toward the direction the boys have taken.*) Those boys are waiting for us out there in the boat. They are going to row you out to the junk. You're going on that to the Samarkind Islands and then you're going to wait there until the Sydney boat comes along. And then you're going to take that to Sydney.

SADIE (*wildly*). I'm going back to San Francisco!

O'HARA. You're not going to San Francisco, you're going to Sydney. (SADIE *looks at* O'HARA *with a strange new fright.*) Sadie! Out there you've got your whole life before you. We'll go away, where this damn rain or anything else can't follow us. Just you and me—like Biff and Maggie—fifty-fifty. You'll be Mrs. Tim O'Hara. It's Sydney and us— the whole damn works against the penitentiary. And I'm taking you whether you want to go out or not!

(SADIE *struggles to resist, but pleading, coaxing, cajoling, he is slowly but surely urging her toward the veranda.*)

SADIE (*despairingly*). You mustn't— you mustn't! I'm saved I tell you. You'll send me to Hell! (*Her voice now fairly rings with fear.*) Reverend Davidson! Reverend Davidson!

(*The tall form of* DAVIDSON *suddenly appears on the veranda. He casts his hat and umbrella on the porch floor and strides into the room.*)

REV. DAVIDSON. Here I am, Miss Thompson. It seems I got here just about in time.

(O'HARA *stops in his effort to get* SADIE *from the room and stares threatingly at* DAVIDSON. SADIE *is between them.*)

SADIE. Oh—oh!

(SADIE *slips from* O'HARA's *suddenly relaxed arms. There is something awesome about* DAVIDSON's *appearance. Although out of breath as from running, his movements now are slow and decisive and his voice, when he speaks, sure and contained.*)

REV. DAVIDSON. It seems I got here just about in time, Miss Thompson. (*He pauses, looks at* O'HARA, *then back to* SADIE.) All evening I had a peculiar feeling you were in danger. It was almost as though God were whispering in my ear to hurry back.

O'HARA (L. *of* SADIE). Sadie—Sadie— don't pay any attention to him.

REV. DAVIDSON (*turning to* O'HARA). I'm sorry for you, O'Hara. What you are trying to do is a serious offense.

O'HARA (*heedlessly*). What you're trying to do would make a hyena cry.

REV. DAVIDSON. You are trying to abduct Sadie Thompson. You have made an attempt to defeat the law. It's likely to go hard with you.

O'HARA. That's my lookout. God, what kind of man are you, anyway! Picking on this poor kid here. Getting her so she's half-crazy. Sending her back to where she's got to go to prison. You're one choice specimen, Reverend Davidson. I'll say that for you. They don't make your kind every day!

REV. DAVIDSON. You are a reckless, headstrong man, O'Hara—you are given to loud language and strong drink. Your officers apparently have no control of you. You are breaking barracks now, and attempting a high-handed crime. You defy the authority of State and God. You cannot go on the way you're going —and I shall see to it that you do not!

O'HARA. Begging your pardon, might I ask what you think you're going to do about it?

REV. DAVIDSON (*sternly*). Get back to your barracks as fast as you can, O'Hara. Report here to me tomorrow, after Miss Thompson has gone.

O'HARA. To you? Where do you get these ideas, anyway? What are you? God's pet what-not? Eh? If it's good advice you want to ladle out—keep it! Your bunk gives me an earache! On such rare moments as I think, I think for myself.

REV. DAVIDSON. All this is not helping your case. Watch what you say.

O'HARA. I'm here to watch out that Sadie don't make a fool break. You've got to do some settling with me before she does any sailing.

SADIE (*breaking in*). You're wrong! I know what I'm doing. I'm sorry, Handsome, but I see clear.

O'HARA. See clear! Why this old gadget's got you so it's like you're doped.

(*The rain diminishes.*)

SADIE (*crossing* O'HARA *slowly toward the table*). I see what you don't see—what's happened to me don't happen to everybody. I was nothing. I was nobody. Now

I'm something. I'm somebody. (*Standing by the chair,* R. *of the table.*) Reverend Davidson's shown me! I'd have gone through my whole life never knowing I was anything if it hadn't been for him. It's a wonderful thing to know you've been made of some account—the only thing I can't see is how it happened to me!

(*The rain stops.*)

O'HARA (*up* R.C., *hesitatingly*). Is that the way it is, Sadie?

SADIE. That's the way it is.

O'HARA. What do you want me to do?

SADIE. I don't want you to do anything, except just not say anything more.

O'HARA (*huskily*). All right! I'll tell the boys to bring your things back. (*A pause.*) If you and me never see each other again I want to say this: I'll not forget you—ever.

SADIE (*inaudibly*). Good-by.

(O'HARA *exits* R. *by the veranda, ignoring* DAVIDSON. SADIE *turns, to see* O'HARA *disappear, then faces front again.* DAVIDSON *moves to above the table, by the* L. *end of it.*)

SADIE (*turning up above the chair* R. *of the table*). Don't blame O'Hara, Reverend Davidson—it was all my fault.

REV. DAVIDSON. My poor child, it was not your fault. Far down the beach I heard your cry for help. I heard you call my name. I left MacPhail to take care of the canoe and bring in the women.

SADIE. O'Hara thought he was helping me. He didn't understand.

REV. DAVIDSON. You may be sure, Miss Thompson, I shall give him every chance before I act.

SADIE (*desperately*). Reverend Davidson—O'Hara's an awful simple fellow. He seems rough and all that, but I've met lots of men—and I've never known one so good, take it all through, as him. Please don't do anything to him. I just can't bear to think of him—suffering—and in trouble. He wouldn't know what to do. It's all right for *me*—it was coming to me—but I can't bear to think that I've brought anything on to O'Hara.

REV. DAVIDSON. Can't you see that indirectly you are responsible for the finest thing that could happen to O'Hara. He is to have his chance—just as you had yours! (*He stops; his eyes glow.*)

SADIE (*hopefully*). Can't — can't — what's coming to me do for both of us?

REV. DAVIDSON (*shaking his head*). No

one can pay another's reckoning—each one must pay his own.

SADIE. Yes. (*She pauses.*) But—you told me—maybe I can't understand right yet—you told me Christ took the punishment for all of us—when they crucified Him.

REV. DAVIDSON (*as to a child; moving to her*). Sadie—Christ saved the world for us, but each of us must bear his share of the cross—it wouldn't be fair to leave the whole weight on His shoulders would it?

SADIE. No—I suppose it wouldn't! When you're here, everything is so clear! Everything's all right—but when you're away, I'm afraid! I get to thinking of how wicked I used to be—and I just can't believe it's all forgiven. (*Crossing down and to* L., *below the table.*) The days aren't so bad—but the nights! That's when I begin to think and wonder! If they're bad now, what are they going to be when you can't come any more—when I'm all alone. (*She gives a shudder of fear and a low cry of utter woe, and sinks into the chair* L. *of the table.*)

REV. DAVIDSON (*moving to below her chair*). When you are alone, my strength will come to you through prayers, which will be always on my lips. Little by little you yourself will grow stronger, surer—and presently the time will come when sin and terror are powerless to penetrate the great love God has wrapped around you. Then will you be redeemed—the kingdom and the glory will be yours.

SADIE (*in ecstasy*). Yes—yes—when you talk to me like that—I'm not afraid. That old life I led don't seem to belong to me at all—it was someone else—it wasn't me. When I feel that way, Reverend Davidson, does that mean I'm redeemed?

REV. DAVIDSON (*gently*). Yes, Sadie. In the last few days you have become very close and dear to God. He has tested you and found you true. Tonight he sent the devil to tempt you—but you thrust away the devil. Once your soul lay like a stagnant pool in the lowest pit of the deepest valley. Tonight it has been lifted up to the sun—stagnant no longer, but cleansed, glorified, as the rain of heaven!

SADIE (*shaking her head sadly*). I guess people don't get things when they're tired.

REV. DAVIDSON (*gently*). And tomorrow will be a very busy day. You'll need all your strength. Try to get some sleep now!

SADIE (*covering her face with her hands*). Tomorrow! Oh! (*She gives a little moan. Then she rises and crosses to her door.*) If I wake up tonight and get afraid, will you come and pray with me?

REV. DAVIDSON (*moving down L. of the table*). When I hear you call—I will come!

SADIE (*parting her curtains*). Yes—I'm pretty tired. (*She exits weakly into her room.*)

(DAVIDSON's *lips move in prayer. There is a look of great ecstasy in his eyes. Footsteps are heard on the veranda.* DR. *and* MRS. MAC-PHAIL *and* MRS. DAVIDSON *enter and remove their straw waterproofs.*)

DR. MACPHAIL (*taking off his galoshes*). A disagreeable experience! But now that episode is closed, I want to make one final observation. If heaven were promised me if I could get there in a canoe, I know where I would really land! (*He puts the umbrella in the barrel* R.)

MRS. DAVIDSON (*moving to up* C.). I hope you found nothing wrong, Alfred?

REV. DAVIDSON (*turning and moving down* R.C.). No! (*Exultantly.*) A great happiness has come to me tonight! I have had proof that Sadie Thompson has been reborn; that I have been privileged to bring a lost soul into the loving arms of Jesus! Truly the marvels of the Lord are demonstrated in strange ways! I should never have known this so surely if it had not been for another's attempted sin.

(*He stands below the deck-chair.* MRS. DAVIDSON *moves down on his* L. MRS. MAC-PHAIL *crosses to up* L.C. *and sits in the* L. *chair above the table.*)

DR. MACPHAIL (*dryly, moving across to join his wife*). Since this sin has worked a benefit, isn't it a bit unkind to call it sin?

REV. DAVIDSON (*turning; in a pleasant voice*). It seems to me, Doctor, you rather enjoy refusing to understand me. (*He sits in the deck-chair.*)

DR. MACPHAIL (*above the* R. *end of the table*). Not at all. It was only that your statement seemed to prove to me that every piece of good must be first contrasted to a piece of bad to make it a piece of good—but of course I'm only a doctor and these matters may be quite beyond my grasp.

REV. DAVIDSON (*sharply*). Precisely!

DR. MACPHAIL. What is beyond my grasp, is how you have the heart to send that poor thing back to three years in an American prison.

REV. DAVIDSON. Don't you see? It's necessary! Do you think my heart doesn't bleed for her. I love her as I love my wife and sister. All the time she is in prison I shall suffer all the pain she suffers!

DR. MACPHAIL. Bunkum! (*He sits on the upper corner of the table.*)

REV. DAVIDSON. You don't understand because you don't want to! She's sinned and she must suffer. I know what she'll endure. So does she! Her remorse for all her sins is beautiful. I am humble and afraid. I am not worthy to touch the hem of her garment.

DR. MACPHAIL (*drawing his pipe*). We agree at last.

(DAVIDSON, *first in a reverie, makes no response to this. In fact, it is as though he has not really heard* MACPHAIL. *After a second he smiles at* MACPHAIL *as one would at a foolish child, picks up his hat, rises, and starts toward the veranda.*)

MRS. DAVIDSON (*anxiously following* DAVIDSON). Alfred, you aren't going out, are you?

REV. DAVIDSON (*taking her hand in his with one of his rare demonstrations of affection*). Go to bed, my wife. It is getting late. You look wan and pale.

MRS. DAVIDSON (*her voice changing almost to one of pleading*). Alfred, don't go out again tonight, please don't; it's not healthy. It has rained for four days now and the air is full of poison from rotting plants. Besides, I want to talk to you. I—I—have not had a word alone with you, Alfred, for a long time.

REV. DAVIDSON. My poor wife. I know—I know—but I must! I must! (*He exits through the veranda.*)

MRS. DAVIDSON (*turning; unhappily*). He prayed with Miss Thompson last night until she went to sleep. It was nearly three o'clock when he came upstairs. Then he threw himself down on the bed exhausted—but he only slept in snatches. He has strange dreams that puzzle him. (*Sitting in the deck-chair.*) He'll have a breakdown if he doesn't take care. This morning he told me he had been dreaming about the mountains of Nebraska.

DR. MACPHAIL (*reflectively*). H-m! That's odd!

MRS. DAVIDSON. I don't believe anyone but myself realizes what an enormous amount of emotional force my husband puts into his work.

DR. MACPHAIL. Work is the one outlet for his tremendous energy that Mr. Davidson allows himself. He should look out.

MRS. DAVIDSON (*in a low voice*). The Lord's work is Mr. Davidson's life! (*She pauses.*) On our wedding night Mr. Davidson explained to me his ideals of our marriage. He believed it should be a union free from earthly indulgence, devoted entirely to the salvation of others.

DR. MACPHAIL (*rising and moving to above the chair R. of MRS. MACPHAIL*). A noble doctrine, Mrs. Davidson, but to a medical man like myself, everyday experience proves that flesh and blood are not things apart from the spirit—each is mutually dependent upon the other—and their highest expression, strangely enough, is quite identical.

MRS. DAVIDSON (*sharply*). What do you mean?

DR. MACPHAIL (*moving R.C. towards the veranda*). What I mean is this! Natural emotions can never be denied—only disguised. (*He looks out across the veranda.*)

MRS. DAVIDSON. You are quite wrong. Both Mr. Davidson and I have high views on matters commonly accepted as part of human nature. I can safely say our marriage is entirely a contract of the spirit.

MRS. MACPHAIL (*anxious to smooth out a difficult moment*). And obviously a happy one. All marriages are happy where people have the same ambitions.

MRS. DAVIDSON (*becoming soft and human for the only time in the play*). Perhaps I had looked forward to a marriage of another sort. (*Her face grows wistful and sad.*) Like all women—I believe—I—wanted children. (*Long pause.*) But that was long ago. (*Her eyes are bright with tears.*) Sometimes I wonder a little. Two people as isolated and solitary as Mr. Davidson and myself . . . (*She pulls herself together.*) But no! Mr. Davidson is right. (*She rises.*) There is only one course for those who work for others—immolation of self—and sacrifice. (*She becomes her old, stiff, masked self.*) Good night. (*She goes off upstairs quickly.*)

MRS. MACPHAIL (*a little awed*). I declare—I never realized that Mrs. Davidson was human.

DR. MACPHAIL (*turning*). It's highly probable she was born human. Most of us were!

MRS. MACPHAIL (*rolling up her sewing*). I think you are unfeeling, Robert, in your hard and fast diagnosis of others.

DR. MACPHAIL (*puffing his pipe as he moves to C.*). It is my business to diagnose, my dear. I am a doctor. (*He sits, thinking in the chair R. of the table.*)

MRS. MACPHAIL (*rising and going over to him and yawning*). Well, you needn't work overtime on your friends.

DR. MACPHAIL (*patting her arm*). Everybody's conversation about everybody else is a diagnosis, my dear. In fact, you and I are now diagnosing each other—and my conclusion about you is: to bed, to bed, you sleepy head. Shoo!

MRS. MACPHAIL (*kissing his bald spot*). Serious, silly old darling—Good night! (*She exits upstairs.*)

(*A pause.* MACPHAIL *rises and crosses to the door of the store, opens it and looks in.*)

DR. MACPHAIL. Hello! You still up, Horn?

HORN (*answering*). Yep—reading. Want anything?

DR. MACPHAIL. No—I'm off to bed.

(HORN *enters. His feet are bare. He wears frowzy pyjamas. He carries a bottle in one hand, a book in the other. He yawns and stretches. The two men listen to the rain.*)

DR. MACPHAIL. Seems to be an uncanny concentration of malignancy about the rain tonight.

HORN (*crossing down and to R.*). H-m! Perhaps. (*He goes to turn off the lamp.*) Everyone in?

DR. MACPHAIL. Davidson's still out—can't sleep—has uneasy dreams his wife tells me. (*He goes as far as the stairs and starts to mount.*)

HORN. Can you see the landing?

MACPHAIL. Yes. (*He stops.*) Eh, Horn, did you ever go through Nebraska on the train?

HORN. Twenty years ago.

DR. MACPHAIL. Notice the mountains?

HORN. Molehills, you mean.

DR. MACPHAIL. Call 'em what you like. They rose from the plain abruptly, remember—rounded, smooth. (*He starts toward stairs.*)

HORN (*turning the light very low*). Yep—what of it?

DR. MACPHAIL. Didn't it strike you they were curiously like a woman's breasts? (MACPHAIL *exits upstairs.*)

(HORN *proceeds to turn out the lamp as he leisurely digests* MACPHAIL's *last remark. A flicker of understanding crosses his face. He takes a long look at* SADIE's *door, then gives a short laugh, as though to say "Well, well, well!" He blows out the lamp and exits, leaving the stage in darkness. The stage is empty for a full minute. Through the increasing fury of the rain the plaintive whine of the reed instruments persists. Then the door of* SADIE's *room opens and she totters out. She carries a little hand lamp. In the wan light of the lamp her face is ghastly with suffering. She makes her way to the staircase and calls up pitifully.*)

SADIE (*calling up the stairs*). Reverend Davidson! Reverend Davidson!

(*There is no answer.* SADIE *crosses the stage to the hatrack, notes that* DAVIDSON's *hat is gone. She sighs, seats herself on* HORN's *deckchair, her chin in her hands, staring at nothing.* DAVIDSON *enters from the veranda. He is like a man in a trance, his eyes glazed.* SADIE *gives a little cry and rises, seeing him as he crosses to* C. *He is hatless and rain-soaked.*)

REV. DAVIDSON. Is that you, Miss Thompson? (*Moving down* L. *of* SADIE.) What are you up for?

SADIE. I couldn't sleep—this rain—and those drums—and then thinking about tomorrow. I couldn't seem to stand it in there another moment. I don't seem to be able to do much by myself, do I?

REV. DAVIDSON. Not yet, maybe, but every prayer is going to make you stronger.

SADIE (*sinking into the chair again*). This time tomorrow I'll be on the sea—all by myself. I don't suppose I'll ever see you again.

REV. DAVIDSON. Not in this life, Sadie, probably.

SADIE. I'll be in prison three years. That's a long time. What'll I do when I come out? What'll I be? For hours and hours I've been wondering.

REV. DAVIDSON (*giving her a strange look*). Out there in the rain (*he points*) I walked and wondered too. The darkness was full of eyes. I saw things I never saw before. I looked into the awful groves of Ashtoreth where Solomon went—to find the secrets of joy and terror. I saw Ashtoreth herself—I saw Judas. Sadie, you don't have to go back to San Francisco.

SADIE (*giving him a blank stare*). I don't

have to go back? What do you mean?

REV. DAVIDSON. I repeat—you do not have to go back . . . unless you truly want to.

SADIE. But I do want to. What sacrifice can I make to God but that? I haven't got anything else to offer. It's the only thing that I've got to give. I want to give it—I must!

REV. DAVIDSON (*in a voice shaken with emotion*). Thank God! Thank God!

SADIE. Why do you say that, Mr. Davidson?

REV. DAVIDSON. Because you said what I knew you'd say. My every prayer has been answered. I prayed that there might come into your heart so passionate a desire for this punishment which you now lay as a thank-offering at your Redeemer's feet, that even if I offered to let you go, you would refuse.

SADIE (*faintly*). I hope I'll be strong enough to go through with it right!

REV. DAVIDSON. From now on you will be strong—there's to be no more fear. (*He now speaks as though in ecstasy.*) Beautiful, radiant, you will be one of the daughters of the King. (*He bends over her and speaks in a curiously hoarse whisper.*) That's what you are now, Sadie—one of the daughters of the King—radiant—beautiful.

SADIE (*tottering to her feet*). I'm going to see if I can't get some sleep. Good night! (*She picks the lamp from the stool and exits slowly.*)

DAVIDSON *stands as though hypnotized, watching her. For a brief moment he seems to gain control of his emotions, then strides toward her door and stops abruptly outside it. Suddenly his head droops, his hands clasp convulsively, and a bitter struggle between* DAVIDSON, *the man of* GOD, *and* DAVIDSON, *human creature, takes place. His head and shoulders now square and with studied deliberation he grasps the handle of* SADIE's *door, opens it, and steps inside, slowly closing the door after him. The rain is now almost a cloudburst and*

the CURTAIN *falls.*

SCENE TWO

It is morning when the curtain lifts again. The night and the rain have passed. The place is flooded in sunshine. Immediately one is aware of hub-bub within and without.

At the veranda rail stand two natives. They are pointing and crying out. Some horrible object lying on the ground below is the cause of this commotion. Into the scene rushes a native POLICEMAN *from down* R. *He crosses the stage and enters* HORN'S *store. We hear his excited news and* HORN'S *exclamations of horror.*

————

HORN (*offstage*). Ki-Kai-Awana.

POLICEMAN (*offstage*). Fi-lo-kipi-ma-nuva.

HORN (*offstage*). Mona-lava. Far-fali-oka.

POLICEMAN (*offstage*). Ki-kai-Awana.

(*The store door opens and* HORN *enters, followed by the* POLICEMAN.)

HORN. Oh! Talofi-Talofi. Dreadful, dreadful! (*He stumbles upstairs calling.*) Dr. MacPhail! Dr. MacPhail!

(*Piercing cries are heard, and a* NATIVE GIRL *rushes in from the veranda.*)

NATIVE GIRL (*on the veranda step*). Jujuouija kepi lay manuva!

(*The girl's eyes are dilated with fear. There is chaotic clamoring from all the natives, who join her on the step. The* POLICE-MAN *roughly pushes them out of the scene.*)

HORN (*at the top of the stairs*). Doctor! Doctor!

DR. MACPHAIL (*upstairs, offstage*). Yes, yes! What is it?

HORN (*disappearing up the stairs*). Get up! Right away!

DR. MACPHAIL. What is it?

HORN (*off*). Hurry up! Get up right away!

DR. MACPHAIL (*offstage*). All right, just a minute.

HORN (*re-appearing and coming down the stairs*). Hurry, Doctor!

DR. MACPHAIL (*offstage*). All right! All right! I'll be right down!

(HORN *stumbles downstairs again. Following him comes* DR. MACPHAIL *in pajamas and raincoat, his hair sleepily tousled. He carries a medicine kit which he has picked up in his rush.*)

HORN. Hurry—hurry—hurry!

DR. MACPHAIL. All right! Here I am! What is it?

HORN. It's Davidson! Something terrible has happened!

(HORN *rushes out to the veranda, followed by* MACPHAIL. HORN *stands looking out over the veranda. The* DOCTOR, *after a quick glance over the veranda rail, hurriedly exits*

down R. HORN *shouts to the natives below.*)

HORN. Boys! Don't touch that body until the Doctor gets there!

NATIVE VOICES (*offstage*). O-lan-sta-doctor.

(*The door of the store opens and* MRS. HORN *waddles on. She starts to cross to the veranda but is intercepted by* SERGEANT O'HARA, *who comes tearing around the up-stage veranda entrance at that moment. He is still dressed in his blue denim and is visibly excited.*)

O'HARA (*up* R.C., *to* MRS. HORN). Where's Miss Thompson?

MRS. HORN. She sleep I think.

O'HARA. Sure?

MRS. HORN. I make knock, what?

O'HARA. No! If she's asleep, let her sleep.

(*He crosses to the stairway and looks upstairs.* MRS. HORN *continues to the veranda.*)

MRS. HORN (*on the veranda; wringing her hands*). Mamut! Mamut!

HORN (*calling from the veranda*). Doctor! How long has he been dead?

DR. MACPHAIL (*responding offstage*). Three or four hours, I should judge.

HORN (*turning back into the room and crossing to* R. *of the table*). I hope they don't bring him in here. I don't like men who die that way. They don't rest easy. (MRS. HORN *exits down* R. *to the scene of the tragedy, sniveling as she goes*—HORN *turns and sees* O'HARA.) Pretty rotten business this. How did you know about it?

O'HARA (*coming down to above the table*). One of the mess boys—out fishing early —saw him and came for me. I got over here as fast as I could in case Sadie needed me. (*An apprehensive look comes over his face.*) You don't think (*brokenly*)—there isn't any chance Sadie did it?

HORN (*waving his hand reassuringly*). No! Some native fisherman saw him do it himself. They brought the body here.

O'HARA (*relieved*). Thank God! How long has he been dead?

HORN. Three or four hours MacPhail says. (*He becomes greatly agitated and mops his brow.*) I've got to get Mrs. Davidson.

(MRS. MACPHAIL *is heard coming downstairs.*)

O'HARA (*quickly*). Get her to do it!

MRS. MACPHAIL (*rushing into the room from the stairs. Her hair is frowsy and she is still hooking up her dress*). What has happened? Where's Dr. MacPhail gone! (*She comes down between* HORN *and* O'HARA.)

HORN. He's down on the beach, ma'am. (*Both men try to avoid her eyes.*)

MRS. MACPHAIL (*persistently*). What has happened?

O'HARA (*evasively*). There's been an accident, ma'am.

MRS. MACPHAIL. Is it Miss Thompson?

O'HARA. No!

(MRS. MACPHAIL *suddenly rushes for the veranda. Both men make a belated effort to follow and stop her. She reaches the veranda and leans over and looks down the beach.* O'HARA *and* HORN *stand watching her.*)

MRS. MACPHAIL. What is that crowd doing? (*Suddenly she screams and rushes back into the room, her hands over her eyes.* HORN *puts out his hand and pulls her toward him, trying to calm her. She looks up at* HORN's *face.*) I was afraid of this!

HORN (*astonished*). You were afraid?

(HORN *and* MRS. MACPHAIL *are now* R.C. O'HARA *is above and on their* R.)

MRS. MACPHAIL (*almost convulsively, as* HORN *takes her down to the deck-chair*). Yes. Mrs. Davidson heard you come up for Dr. MacPhail. She's just been in my room and in a dreadful state. Mr. Davidson hasn't been to bed at all, she said. She heard him leave Miss Thompson's room about three. He came upstairs for something—then he went right out. (DR. MACPHAIL *enters hurriedly from the veranda and crosses* L.C. *He places his medicine kit on the table. She rushes to* DR. MACPHAIL.) Is he dead?

DR. MACPHAIL (*in a quiet and professional tone*). Yes! Go and get Mrs. Davidson at once!

MRS. MACPHAIL (*tearfully*). Oh, but I hate to!

DR. MACPHAIL (*curtly*). You must, my dear! (*As she hesitates.*) Be quick.

(MRS. MACPHAIL *goes upstairs in terrified obedience.* DR. MACPHAIL *turns to the two men. He extends his clenched fist to* HORN, *as though indicating something in it.* HORN *moves up to him.*)

DR. MACPHAIL. The razor was still in his hand. (HORN *and* O'HARA *nod understandingly.*) The Naval doctors are with him now. They'll probably take him to the mortuary.

(MACPHAIL *walks to the foot of the stairs and stands waiting for* MRS. DAVIDSON. HORN *and* O'HARA *give each other searching looks.*)

O'HARA (*looking over the veranda*). Look at the crowd. Bad news travels, don't it?

HORN. Yes. (*Looks quizzically at* O'HARA.) He was a strange fellow. I wonder why he did it.

DR. MACPHAIL (*turning to* HORN *and* O'HARA). Be quiet! Here comes Mrs. Davidson.

(*All three men stand by quietly as* MRS. DAVIDSON *enters down the stairway, followed by* MRS. MACPHAIL. *She is dressed in black, her face is blanched and drawn. She stands on the lower stairs, looking at* DR. MACPHAIL, *who is facing her.*)

MRS. DAVIDSON (*brokenly*). Where am I —to go?

DR. MACPHAIL (*offering her his hand and speaking very kindly*). Come with me, Mrs. Davidson. (*He looks up at his wife.*) Better come too, Margaret. It may be necessary.

(*They start toward the veranda.* MRS. MACPHAIL *haltingly following* MRS. DAVIDSON *and* DR. MACPHAIL. HORN *and* O'HARA *watch them silently. As the trio exit,* O'HARA *turns to* HORN.)

O'HARA. Pretty cool, I'll say.

HORN (*shaking his head*). No—she's trembling like a leaf.

O'HARA (*as though to himself*). I wonder how she'll take it.

HORN. I wonder!

(*Suddenly the raucous sound of the gramophone is heard from* SADIE's *room. Both men start, listen, and then turn to each other with a look of tempered horror.*)

HORN. My God! Listen to that!

O'HARA. You see—she don't know yet.

HORN (*excitedly*). But—man—why is she playing it?

O'HARA. One of us ought to go in and tell her what's happened.

HORN (*giving* O'HARA *a keen look*). She hasn't touched that thing since Davidson went after her. (*He takes a step toward* O'HARA *and looks intently into his face.*) What's she playing it now for?

O'HARA (*shifting uneasily on his feet, his head down and speaking almost solemnly*). I don't know.

HORN (*trying to arrive at a conclusion and pointing his words*). Look-a-here! Last night she was frightened and all-in about going back to San Francisco. (*He pauses and fires his question.*) Why is she playing that thing first thing this morning when at noon she's leaving on a journey she's scared to make? (*He pauses and almost shouts.*) Why?

O'HARA (*looking at him doggedly*). How should I know?

HORN (*quizzically*). What do you infer?
O'HARA (*roughly*). I am not inferring!
HORN. Who's going to tell her? You?
O'HARA. It'll come better from you.
HORN (*sighs resignedly*). All right! Go see where the others are.

(HORN *shuffles up to* SADIE'S *door.* O'HARA *waits an instant as though undecided as to what to do. Then, thrusting his chin up determinedly, he crosses to the veranda and exits.*)

HORN. Miss Thompson! (*He knocks on the door.*)

SADIE (*from within her room*). Yes! (*Loudly.*) What is it?

HORN. Let me in. It's Horn!

SADIE (*from within the room*). Oh, no you don't! You stay where you are! I'll be out in a minute.

HORN (*above* SADIE'S *doorway*). It's most important, Miss Thompson.

SADIE (*from within her room*). All right! I'm coming right out!

(HORN *shuffles to a position in front of the sofa as* SADIE'S *door opens and* SADIE *makes her appearance. She is dressed in the costume in which we first beheld her. Her face is tragic beneath its rouge. She carries her parasol. As she enters the room* O'HARA *comes across the veranda and, upon seeing* SADIE, *he halts at* R.C., *as though stupefied.*)

SADIE (*to* HORN). Hello, Horn! What's going on? (*She turns and sees* O'HARA. *With a forced smile.*) Hello, O'Hara! What are you doing up so early? (*She crosses* HORN *to* L. *of the table.*)

O'HARA (*looking dazedly at* SADIE). Sadie!

SADIE (*smiling, but one corner of her mouth seems rather down*). Surprised to see me all dolled up, eh? Well, why not? (*She is making a desperate attempt to be cheerful.*) Had to put on my best, didn't I? This gay and glorious morning. Besides (*her face hardens*) I'm radiant—I'm beautiful. You didn't know that, did you? (*She laughs harshly.*) Couldn't believe my eyes when I saw that sun this morning. Do I feel fine? I do! I'd race you down to the beach if it wasn't for these pesty heels. (*She flicks her heels to the tip of her parasol, moving to above and* L. *of the table.*)

O'HARA (*moving to above the table*). Sadie! For God's sake turn off that gramophone!

SADIE (*coolly*). And why—for God's sake should I turn off the gramophone?
O'HARA. They'll be back any minute.

SADIE. Who?
O'HARA. Mrs. Davidson.

SADIE (*assuming an attitude of studied indifference*). And why should I turn off my gramophone because Mrs. Davidson is coming back? (*An almost snarling sneer comes into her voice.*) I am not concerned with what Mrs. Davidson thinks, and for that matter (*She turns and looks at* HORN.) with what your Reverend Davidson thinks! (*She faces downstage and speaks deliberately.*) My advice to him is to pin on his wings and try the air!

O'HARA (*suddenly to* HORN). Joe, turn off that gramophone, quick! (HORN *starts to* SADIE'S *door.*)

SADIE (*turning quickly to* HORN *as he reaches the door*). Stay out of my room, Horn! That gramophone stays on.

O'HARA (*pleading*). Sadie! Something has happened!

SADIE (*in a voice black with loathing*). Yes! You're right! Something *has* happened. You men! Something *has* happened! (*To* HORN.) You men—you're all alike. (*Hoarsely.*) Pigs! Pigs! I wouldn't trust one of you! (*She turns quickly toward* O'HARA.) No offense to you in that last remark, old pardner. (*She pauses.*) And I'm going to Sydney if that invitation of yours still holds good.

O'HARA (*his voice broken with emotion*). You bet it does! (HORN *motions to* O'HARA *to tell* SADIE *what has happened.* O'HARA *continues.*) Sadie—Davidson's killed himself—

SADDIE (*dully*). What?

O'HARA. They found him on the beach this morning in the water with his throat cut.

(*As the import of what* O'HARA *has said penetrates* SADIE'S *whirling brain, she staggers, then slowly recovers herself.*)

SADIE (*in a strange voice, moving down below the table to* R.C.). So—he killed himself, did he? Then I can forgive him. I thought the joke was on me—all on me! (*Pauses.*) I see it wasn't.

(O'HARA *moves to above the* R. *end of the table.* DR. MACPHAIL *rushes in, gesticulating angrily.*)

DR. MACPHAIL (*on the veranda step*). What the devil are you doing? Stop that damn machine! Mrs. Davidson's coming!

SADIE (*weakly, turning up* R.C.). Yes—turn it off—off. (HORN *rushes into* SADIE'S *room and stops the gramophone.*)

(MRS. DAVIDSON *enters, followed by* MRS. MACPHAIL. MRS. DAVIDSON *walks straight toward* SADIE, *crossing below the table. There is intense silence on the stage. The two women gaze intently at each other.*)

MRS. DAVIDSON (*sadly*). I understand, Miss Thompson. I'm sorry for him and I'm sorry for you.

(MRS. DAVIDSON *passes her, hastily, covers her face and walks upstairs. All the people on the stage watch her until she is out of sight.*)

SADIE (*in a low, sick voice*). I'm sorry for everybody in the world! Life's a quaint present from somebody, there's no doubt about that. (*Moving to* O'HARA.) Maybe it will be easier in Sydney.

(*She clutches* O'HARA'S *arm and breaks into sobs as the* CURTAIN *falls.*

THE ADDING MACHINE

Elmer L. Rice

The Adding Machine was first produced by the Theatre Guild at the Garrick Theatre, New York City, on March 19, 1923. The play was staged by Philip Moeller, with settings by Lee Simonson and incidental music by Deems Taylor. The cast was as follows:

MR. ZERO . . . . Dudley Digges	MRS. FOUR . . . . Edith Burnett
MRS. ZERO . . . . Helen Westley	MR. FIVE . . . . William W. Griffith
DAISY DIANA DOROTHEA	MRS. FIVE . . . . Ruby Craven
DEVORE . . . . Margaret Wycherly	MR. SIX . . . . Daniel Hamilton
THE BOSS . . . . Irving Dillon	MRS. SIX . . . . Louise Sydmeth
MR. ONE . . . . Harry McKenna	POLICEMAN . . . . Irving Dillon
MRS. ONE . . . . Marcia Harris	JUDY O'GRADY . . . . Elise Bartlett
MR. TWO . . . . Paul Hayes	YOUNG MAN . . . . Gerald Lundegard
MRS. TWO . . . . Theresa Stewart	SHRDLU . . . . Edward G. Robinson
MR. THREE . . . . Gerald Lundegard	A HEAD . . . . Daniel Hamilton
MRS. THREE . . . . Georgiana Wilson	LIEUTENANT CHARLES . . . Louis Calvert
MR. FOUR . . . . George Stehli	JOE . . . . William W. Griffith

SCENE ONE: A bedroom.   SCENE FIVE: A death cell.
SCENE TWO: An office.   SCENE SIX: A graveyard.
SCENE THREE: A dining room.   SCENE SEVEN: A pleasant place.
SCENE FOUR: A court of justice.   SCENE EIGHT: Another office.

NOTE. For the present publication of *The Adding Machine*, the author has obligingly restored a scene that had been omitted in the Theatre Guild production of 1923 (and in the published text until now) but has been staged in some later productions of the play. This is the prison scene, concerning which Mr. Rice wrote me in June 1960 that it is "an integral part of the play, and enhances both its reading and performance value." He added, "I strongly urge you to include it in your edition. When the play was done at the Phoenix Theatre [in New York], a few years ago, this scene was included and it came off very well."   —J. G.

Copyright 1922, 1929, by Elmer L. Rice.
Copyright 1923, by Doubleday, Page & Company.
Copyright 1949, 1950, 1956 (in renewal), by Elmer L. Rice.
All rights reserved.

CAUTION: Professionals and amateurs are hereby warned that *The Adding Machine*, being fully protected under the copyright laws of the United States of America, the British Empire, including the Dominion of Canada, and all other countries of the Copyright Union, is subject to a royalty. All rights, including professional, amateur, motion pictures, recitation, public reading, radio and television broadcasting, and the rights of translation into foreign languages, are strictly reserved. Amateurs may produce this play upon payment of a royalty of Fifty Dollars for each performance one week before the play is to be given to Samuel French, Inc., at 25 W. 45th St., New York 36, N.Y., or 7623 Sunset Blvd., Hollywood 46, Calif., or if in Canada, to Samuel French (Canada) Ltd., at 27 Grenville St., Toronto, Ont.

Fashions change. A generation ago, his admirers were certain that Elmer Rice would be chiefly remembered for *Street Scene;* today, they are more likely to invest their expectations in his non-realistic play *The Adding Machine*. They would do better perhaps to invest them in both plays and in both facets of their author's playmaking. Many modern playwrights—Ibsen and Strindberg, O'Casey and O'Neill, among them—have alternated between realistic and non-realistic dramaturgy in expressing the range of their thought and feeling.

Playwriting has always been something of an adventure for Mr. Rice, particularly so in the case of a realistic work such as *Street Scene* as well as of a flight of fancy such as *The Adding Machine*. And there has surely been no contradiction in his labors. He has been consistent in the very duality of his stylistic allegiances. In order to find some reflection of itself in the theatre, our century has needed a minimum of *two* styles. It has required the two mirrors of realism and theatricalism, and it is not at all certain in actual practice that the image of modern man has been more distorted by the latter than the former. (The usual Hollywood mode of realism has given us more fantastic versions of reality than have the expressionist styles of O'Neill and Rice in such plays as *The Hairy Ape* and *The Adding Machine*.) In much of his work, moreover, Elmer Rice has consistently maintained a realistic point of view by means of an imaginative technique. In *The Adding Machine* in particular, we find him fancifully urging a realistic indictment of modern society even more sharply than in *Street Scene*.

Mr. Rice's creditable oscillation between imaginativeness and photography was foreshadowed as early as 1914 in his very first successful play, the melodrama *On Trial*, famous for its use of the flashback method on the stage. One might say that trial-and-evidence drama that attracted the twenty-two-year-old author (he was born in New York City in 1892), who was then a novice lawyer, would suggest the flashback method once it was even slightly in use in the early films. But when he next turned to imaginative theatre in *The Adding Machine* in 1923, he did so under the powerful influence of conviction as well as the example of European expressionists. During World War I, he had written two pacifistic plays (*The House of the Free*, 1917, and *The Iron Cross*, 1917) that had been unsuccessful but represented the thoughtful playwright better than his next success, *For the Defense* (1919). Mr. Rice took a serious and somewhat jaundiced view of the increasing standardization of life and the decline of individuality and original opinion in our postwar society of Prosperity and "Normalcy."

The Adding Machine was not particularly successful in 1923, but its originality was acknowledged in advanced circles and the play has continued to attract experimental groups throughout the country ever since. Its author had previously collaborated on two other plays (*Wake Up, Jonathan* in 1921 and *It is the Law* in 1922), and went on to write *The Mongrel*, an adaptation from the German, in 1924, *Close Harmony*, a collaboration with Dorothy Parker, also in 1924, and *Cock Robin*, a collaboration with Philip Barry, in 1928. Then, in January, 1929, came his realistic masterpiece *Street Scene*, for which the author was awarded the Pulitzer Prize.* After two distinctly less well received productions in 1929 (*See Naples and Die* and *The Subway*), the prolific playwright had two attractive pieces on Broadway in 1931. They were *The Left Bank*, an intelligent treatment of Left-Bank expatriation, and *Counsellor-at-Law*, a sharply drawn character study set in the midst of the familiar social realities of the legal profession, snobbery, and polished anti-Semitism, and youthful radicalism.

---

* See *Twenty-Five Best Plays of the Modern American Theatre*, ed. by John Gassner, Crown Publishers, pp. 566-611.

Less fortune attended *Black Sheep* and *The House in Blind Alley* in 1932, and other subsequent productions of the author, who was for a time also his own producer. His talents and energies by no means limited to playwriting, he became an excellent director of his own and other writers' plays, organized the Playwrights' Producing Company with Sidney Howard, Robert Sherwood, Maxwell Anderson, and S. N. Behrman in 1938, and assumed leadership in numerous literary and liberal causes. But stirred by the tensions of the times, now rising to a peak with the economic depression and Nazism, Mr. Rice wrote several timely plays that had a great deal more merit as well as pertinence than most Broadway hits. This is the least one can say for the Depression drama *We, the People* (1933), the Reichstag fire melodrama *Judgment Day* (1934), and the political conversation piece *Between Two Worlds*, also in 1934. About this time, too, he began to return to experimentation with fantasy and expressionism. His revived interest in theatricalism produced a Pirandellian play about the theatre itself, *Not for Children*, in 1935, and the imaginatively augmented social drama *American Landscape*, in 1938, in which ghosts from the American past (including the deported Moll Flanders herself!) offer advice and encouragement.

In 1940, an attractive little romantic excursion in a Manhattan setting, *Two on an Island*, showed the genial side of its author, as did his playful staging of the piece. But the same war year also brought us the anti-Nazi drama *Flight to the West*, essentially a play of ideas that did justice to the earnest and hard-thinking writer the public had known for a quarter of a century. A finely ground piece of argument in this work was the distinction drawn by one character between the ultimately doomed "rational madness" of the Nazis and the "irrational sanity" of the democracies. After a second, less intriguing bout with social realism in *A New Life* (1943), Mr. Rice entranced Broadway with the comedy *Dream Girl*,* in which he was able to give his expressionistic facility pleasant employment in dream sequences.

In 1947, Elmer Rice collaborated with the famous composer Kurt Weill on a "music drama" based on *Street Scene*, a work of compassion as well as vivid local color that fared less well on Broadway than it deserved. Two plays in the 1950's, *The Winner* (1954) and *Cue for Passion* (1959), also fared poorly, but by then Mr. Rice was an elder statesman of theatre. Without having, of course, to renounce expectations for the rest of his career, he could look back upon many labors, a goodly number of them well accomplished and most of them nobly intended. And to the above-given account of his work the scrupulous bibliographer would have had to add two pamphlets and four novels. In 1959, Mr. Rice fittingly published a summation of his experience and opinion, *The Living Theatre*, based on a course of lectures he had given in 1957–58 in the Graduate School of Arts and Sciences of New York University. The book contained many wise observations, but it is especially characteristic of this persistent professional of the theatre, acquainted with its failures as well as its successes, that he closed with the affirmation: "There is nothing else like the theatre and nothing can ever take its place in answering the needs of the human spirit."

In *The Living Theatre*, Elmer Rice makes a helpful reference to *The Adding Machine*. He recalls that when he was asked, on the occasion of the original Theatre Guild production, what expressionism was, he replied: "It attempts to go beyond mere representation and to arrive at interpretation. The author attempts not as much to depict events faithfully as to convey to the spectator what seems to be their

---

* This play is reprinted in *Best American Plays*, Second Series, ed. by John Gassner, Crown Publishers, 1947.

inner significance. To achieve this end, the dramatist often finds it expedient to depart entirely from objective reality and to employ symbols, condensations and a dozen devices which to the conservative must seem arbitrarily fantastic."

Barnard Hewitt (in his excellent book, *Theatre, U.S.A., 1668–1957*, McGraw-Hill Book Co., 1959, p. 353) reprints a vivid description of the performance of the great Abbey Theatre actor Duddley Digges in the role of Mr. Zero. Edmund Wilson, writing in the May issue of the *Dial*, noted that the actor gave his "poor henpecked overworked boob a relentlessly tragic dignity." Mr. Wilson found the same humanization in the office scene "in which he has to render not only the smarting backfire of his bicker with his fellow clerk, but at the same time the undercurrent of desire and fear which is running in his weary brain"; in Zero's "doglike servility" to his employer, who is about to discharge him, in "his dazed return home after the murder and his gentle surrender to the police," and in his pathetic attempt to explain his conduct to the jury. It is a question only whether this interpretation of Mr. Zero did not lose too much of the satiric force of this part of the play, because Edmund Wilson went on to criticize the Elysian Fields scene as an anticlimax, writing that "having once believed in Mr. Zero's dignity, the author proceeds to take it all away from him . . ." He set it down as a mistake on the part of the author "to begin a play with revolt and end it with a dreary subsidence." Other productions, such as the one given by the Phoenix Theatre in the 1950's, apparently did not create the same impression of divided mood and anticlimax.

To readers of *The New York Times* shortly after the premiere of the play, Mr. Rice gave the following comment in a letter: "In *The Adding Machine* form and content are indissolubly wedded. It may very well be that the same story could have been developed just as effectively in another medium, or that another story could have been better suited to the device. That is not the point. The point is that I wrote the play just as I conceived it, without thought of theories of technique; in fact, without rationalizing about it at all. As proof of this I may add that from the moment I first conceived the play until the moment the manuscript was completed exactly seventeen days elapsed . . ."

The director of the production, Philip Moeller, who was one of our theatre's real geniuses and had a brilliant colleague in his designer, Lee Simonson, also proffered comment. "The 'expressionist' school," wrote Moeller in a foreword to the published play, "is concerned with the difference between interpreting a character from the objective and the subjective point of view. Now, if 'expressionism' is objective seeing, as all observation must be, it is *subjective* projection; that is, all the half-understood 'hinterland' thoughts, all the yearnings and unknown suppressions of the mind, are exposed, so to speak, in spite of the character, just as an X-ray exposes the inner structure of a thing as against its outer, more obvious and seeming form."

Philip Moeller went on to say that the author of *The Adding Machine* had exposed the minds and souls of his characters: "Pitilessly and pityingly, with a curious conglomeration of tenderness and scorn, he has studied the rich barrenness and the ridiculous unbeauty of these 'white-collar' slaves. How many machine-forced minds are there who as the grind goes on and on are wishing to others these calamities of hate and for themselves these escapes in stumbling and half-articulate dreams . . . [and] how many souls are there who here, or hereafter, will be able to live up to a paradise—if there is one either here or hereafter—where everything will be of a bliss, of a sort, that such souls can profit by it and understand." He concluded his effort to introduce a play that was too *avant-garde* for Broadway in 1923 with a ringing tribute to Elmer Rice: "What he has done, and with withering insight, is to expose the starved and bitter littleness and at the same time the huge universality of the Zero type, of the slave type, that from eternity to eternity expresses the futility and the tragedy of the mediocre spirit." If these words serve to remind us that both the author and the director of the play were young men and members of the 1920 generation of rebels, no harm is done, of course. On the contrary, if *The Adding Machine* belongs to our own times, this is at least partly so because it first belonged to its own.

Scene One

SCENE: *A bedroom.*

A small room containing an "installment plan" bed, dresser, and chairs. An ugly electric light fixture over the bed with a single glaring naked lamp. One small window with the shade drawn. The walls are papered with sheets of foolscap covered with columns of figures.

MR. ZERO *is lying in the bed, facing the audience, his head and shoulders visible. He is thin, sallow, under-sized, and partially bald.* MRS. ZERO *is standing before the dresser arranging her hair for the night. She is forty-five, sharp-featured, gray streaks in her hair. She is shapeless in her long-sleeved cotton nightgown. She is wearing her shoes, over which sag her ungartered stockings.*

MRS. ZERO (*as she takes down her hair*). I'm gettin' sick o' them Westerns. All them cowboys ridin' around an' foolin' with them ropes. I don't care nothin' about that. I'm sick of 'em. I don't see why they don't have more of them stories like *For Love's Sweet Sake*. I like them sweet little love stories. They're nice an' wholesome. Mrs. Twelve was sayin' to me only yesterday, "Mrs. Zero," says she, "what I like is one of them wholesome stories, with just a sweet, simple little love story." "You're right, Mrs. Twelve," I says. "That's what I like, too." They're showin' too many Westerns at the Rosebud. I'm gettin' sick of them. I think we'll start goin' to the Peter Stuyvesant. They got a good bill there Wednesday night. There's a Chubby Delano comedy called *Sea-Sick*. Mrs. Twelve was tellin' me about it. She says it's a scream. They're havin' a picnic in the country and they sit Chubby next to an old maid with a great big mouth. So he gets sore an' when she ain't lookin' he goes and catches a frog and drops it in her clam chowder. An' when she goes to eat the chowder the frog jumps out of it an' right into her mouth. Talk about laugh! Mrs. Twelve was tellin' me she laughed so she nearly passed out. He sure can pull some funny ones. An' they got that big Grace Darling feature, *A Mother's Tears*. She's sweet. But I don't like her clothes. There's no style to them. Mrs. Nine was tellin' me she read in *Pictureland* that she ain't livin' with her husband. He's her second, too. I don't know whether they're divorced or just separated. You wouldn't think it to see her on the screen. She looks so sweet and innocent. Maybe it ain't true. You can't believe all you read. They say some Pittsburgh millionaire is crazy about her and that's why she ain't livin' with her husband. Mrs. Seven was tellin' me her brother-in-law has a friend that used to go to school with Grace Darling. He says her name ain't Grace Darling at all. Her right name is Elizabeth Dugan, he says, an' all them stories about her gettin' five thousand a week is the bunk, he says. She's sweet, though. Mrs. Eight was tellin' me that *A Mother's Tears* is the best picture she ever made. "Don't miss it, Mrs. Zero," she says. "It's sweet," she says. "Just sweet and wholesome. Cry!" she says. "I nearly cried my eyes out." There's one part in it where this big bum of an Englishman—he's a married man, too—an' she's this little simple country girl. An' she nearly falls for him, too. But she's sittin' out in the garden, one day, and she looks up and there's her mother lookin' at her, right out of the clouds. So that night she locks the door of her room. An' sure enough, when everybody's in bed, along comes this big bum of an Englishman an' when she won't let him in what does he do but go an' kick open the door. "Don't miss it, Mrs. Zero," Mrs. Eight was tellin' me. It's at the Peter Stuyvesant Wednesday night, so don't be tellin' me you want to go to the Rosebud. The Eights seen it downtown at the Strand. They go downtown all the time. Just like us—nit! I guess by the time it gets to the Peter Stuyvesant all that part about kickin' in the door will be cut out. Just like they cut out that big cabaret scene in *The Price of Virtue*. They sure are pullin' some rough stuff in the pictures nowadays. "It's no place for a young girl," I was tellin' Mrs. Eleven, only the other day. An' by the time they get uptown half of it is cut out. But you wouldn't go downtown—not if wild horses was to drag you. You can wait till they come uptown! Well, I don't want to wait, see? I want to see 'em when everybody else is seein' them an' not a month later. Now don't go tellin' me you ain't got the price. You could dig up the price all right, all right, if you wanted to. I notice you always got the price to go to the ballgame. But when it comes to me havin' a good time then it's always: "I ain't got the price, I gotta start savin'." A fat lot you'll ever save! I got all I can do now makin' both ends meet an' you talkin' about savin'. (*She seats herself on a chair and begins removing her shoes and stockings.*) An' don't go pullin' that stuff about bein' tired. "I been workin' hard all day. Twice a day in the subway's enough for me." Tired! Where do you get that tired stuff, anyhow? What about me? Where do I come in? Scrubbin' floors an' cookin' your meals an' washin' your dirty clothes. An' you sittin' on a chair all day, just addin' figgers an' waitin' for five-thirty. There's no five-thirty for me. I don't wait for no whistle. I don't get no vacations neither. And what's more I don't get no pay envelope every Saturday night neither. I'd like to know where you'd be without me. An' what have I got to show for it?—slavin' my life away to give you a home. What's in it for me, I'd like to know? But it's my own fault, I guess. I was a fool for marryin' you. If I'd 'a' had any sense, I'd 'a' known what you were from the start. I wish I had it to do over again, I hope to tell you. You was goin' to do wonders, you was! You wasn't goin' to be a book-keeper long—oh, no, not you. Wait till you got started—you was goin' to show 'em. There wasn't no job in the store that was too big for you. Well, I've been waitin'—waitin' for you to get started—see? It's been a good long wait, too. Twenty-five years! An' I ain't seen nothin' happen. Twenty-five years in the same job. Twenty-five years to-morrow! You're proud of it, ain't you? Twenty-five years in the same job an' never missed a day! That's somethin' to be proud of, ain't it? Sittin' for twenty-five years on the same chair, addin' up figures. What about bein' store-manager? I guess you forgot about that, didn't you? An' me at home here lookin' at the same four walls an' workin' my fingers to the bone to make both ends meet. Seven years since you got a raise! An' if you don't get one

to-morrow, I'll bet a nickel you won't have the guts to go an' ask for one. I didn't pick much when I picked you, I'll tell the world. You ain't much to be proud of. (*She rises, goes to the window, and raises the shade. A few lighted windows are visible on the other side of the closed court. Looking out for a moment.*) She ain't walkin' around to-night, you can bet your sweet life on that. An' she won't be walkin' around any more nights, neither. Not in this house, anyhow. (*She turns away from the window.*) The dirty bum! The idea of her comin' to live in a house with respectable people. They should 'a' gave her six years, not six months. If I was the judge I'd of gave her life. A bum like that. (*She approaches the bed and stands there a moment.*) I guess you're sorry she's gone. I guess you'd like to sit home every night an' watch her goin's-on. You're somethin' to be proud of, you are! (*She stands on the bed and turns out the light. . . . A thin stream of moonlight filters in from the court. The two figures are dimly visible. MRS. ZERO gets into bed.*)

You'd better not start nothin' with women, if you know what's good for you. I've put up with a lot, but I won't put up with that. I've been slavin' away for twenty-five years, makin' a home for you an' nothin' to show for it. If you was any kind of a man you'd have a decent job by now an' I'd be gettin' some comfort out of life—instead of bein' just a slave, washin' pots an' standin' over the hot stove. I've stood it for twenty-five years an' I guess I'll have to stand it twenty-five more. But don't you go startin' nothin' with women— (*She goes on talking as the curtain falls.*)

SCENE TWO

SCENE: *An office in a department store. Wood and glass partitions. In the middle of the room, two tall desks back to back. At one desk on a high stool is* ZERO. *Opposite him at the other desk, also on a high stool, is* DAISY DIANA DOROTHEA DEVORE, *a plain, middle-aged woman. Both wear green eye-shades and paper sleeve-protectors. A pendent electric lamp throws light upon both desks.* DAISY *reads aloud figures from a pile of slips which lie before her. As she reads the figures,* ZERO *enters them upon a large square sheet of ruled paper which lies before him.*

DAISY (*reading aloud*). Three ninety-eight. Forty-two cents. A dollar fifty. A dollar fifty. A dollar twenty-five. Two dollars. Thirty-nine cents. Twenty-seven fifty.

ZERO (*petulantly*). Speed it up a little, cancha?

DAISY. What's the rush? To-morrer's another day.

ZERO. Aw, you make me sick.

DAISY. An' you make me sicker.

ZERO. Go on. Go on. We're losin' time.

DAISY. Then quit bein' so bossy. (*She reads.*) Three dollars. Two sixty-nine. Eighty-one fifty. Forty dollars. Eight seventy-five. Who do you think you are, anyhow?

ZERO. Never mind who I think I am. You tend to your work.

DAISY. Aw, don't be givin' me so many orders. Sixty cents. Twenty-four cents. Seventy-five cents. A dollar fifty. Two fifty. One fifty. One fifty. Two fifty. I don't have to take it from you and what's more I won't.

ZERO. Aw, quit talkin'.

DAISY. I'll talk all I want. Three dollars. Fifty cents. Fifty cents. Seven dollars. Fifty cents. Two fifty. Three fifty. Fifty cents. One fifty. Fifty cents.

(*She goes bending over the slips and transferring them from one pile to another.* ZERO *bends over his desk, busily entering the figures.*)

ZERO (*without looking up*). You make me sick. Always shootin' off your face about somethin'. Talk, talk, talk. Just like all the other women. Women make me sick.

DAISY (*busily fingering the slips*). Who do you think you are, anyhow? Bossin' me around. I don't have to take it from you, and what's more I won't.

(*They both attend closely to their work, neither looking up.*)

ZERO. Women make me sick. They're all alike. The judge gave her six months. I wonder what they do in the workhouse. Peel potatoes. I'll bet she's sore at me. Maybe she'll try to kill me when she gets out. I better be careful. Hello Girl Slays Betrayer. Jealous Wife Slays Rival. You can't tell what a woman's liable to do. I better be careful.

DAISY. I'm gettin' sick of it. Always pickin' on me about somethin'. Never a decent word out of you. Not even the time o' day.

ZERO. I guess she wouldn't have the nerve at that. Maybe she don't even know it's me. They didn't even put my name in the paper, the big bums. Maybe she's been in the workhouse before. A bum like that. She didn't have nothin' on that one time—nothin' but a shirt. (*He glances up quickly, then bends over again.*) You make me sick. I'm sick of lookin' at your face.

DAISY. Gee, ain't that whistle ever goin' to blow? You didn't used to be like that. Not even good mornin' or good evenin'. I ain't done nothin' to you. It's the young girls. Goin' around without corsets.

ZERO. Your face is gettin' all yeller. Why don't you put some paint on it? She was puttin' on paint that time. On her cheeks and on her lips. And that blue stuff on her eyes. Just sittin' there in a shimmy puttin' on the paint. An' walkin' around the room with her legs all bare.

DAISY. I wish I was dead.

ZERO. I was a goddam fool to let the wife get on to me. She oughta get six months at that. The dirty bum. Livin' in a house with respectable people. She'd be livin' there yet, if the wife hadn't o' got on to me. Damn her!

DAISY. I wish I was dead.

ZERO. Maybe another one'll move in. Gee, that would be great. But the wife's got her eye on me now.

DAISY. I'm scared to do it, though.

ZERO. You oughta move into that room. It's cheaper than where you're livin' now. I better tell you about it. I don't mean to be always pickin' on you.

DAISY. Gas. The smell of it makes me sick.

(ZERO *looks up and clears his throat.*)

DAISY (*looking up, startled*): Whadja say?

ZERO. I didn't say nothin'.

DAISY. I thought you did.

ZERO. You thought wrong.

(*They bend over their work again.*)

DAISY. A dollar sixty. A dollar fifty. Two ninety. One sixty-two.

ZERO. Why the hell should I tell you?

Fat chance of you forgettin' to pull down the shade!

DAISY. If I asked for carbolic they might get on to me.

ZERO. Your hair's gettin' gray. You don't wear them shirt waists any more with the low collars. When you'd bend down to pick somethin' up—

DAISY. I wish I knew what to ask for. Girl Takes Mercury After All-Night Party. Woman In Ten-Story Death Leap.

ZERO. I wonder where'll she go when she gets out. Gee, I'd like to make a date with her. Why didn't I go over there the night my wife went to Brooklyn? She never woulda found out.

DAISY. I seen Pauline Frederick do it once. Where could I get a pistol though?

ZERO. I guess I didn't have the nerve.

DAISY. I'll bet you'd be sorry then that you been so mean to me. How do I know, though? Maybe you wouldn't.

ZERO. Nerve! I got as much nerve as anybody. I'm on the level, that's all. I'm a married man and I'm on the level.

DAISY. Anyhow, why ain't I got a right to live? I'm as good as anybody else. I'm too refined, I guess. That's the whole trouble.

ZERO. The time the wife had pneumonia I thought she was goin' to pass out. But she didn't. The doctor's bill was eighty-seven dollars. (*Looking up*): Hey, wait a minute! Didn't you say eighty-seven dollars?

DAISY (*looking up*). What?

ZERO. Was the last you said eighty-seven dollars?

DAISY (*consulting the slip*): Forty-two fifty.

ZERO. Well, I made a mistake. Wait a minute. (*He busies himself with an eraser*): All right. Shoot.

DAISY. Six dollars. Three fifteen. Two twenty-five. Sixty-five cents. A dollar twenty. You talk to me as if I was dirt.

ZERO. I wonder if I could kill the wife without anybody findin' out. In bed some night. With a pillow.

DAISY. I used to think you was stuck on me.

ZERO. I'd get found out, though. They always have ways.

DAISY. We used to be so nice and friendly together when I first came here. You used to talk to me then.

ZERO. Maybe she'll die soon. I noticed she was coughin' this mornin'.

DAISY. You used to tell me all kinds o' things. You were goin' to show them all. Just the same, you're still sittin' here.

ZERO. Then I could do what I damn please. Oh, boy!

DAISY. Maybe it ain't all your fault neither. Maybe if you'd had the right kind o' wife—somebody with a lot of common sense, somebody refined—me!

ZERO. At that, I guess I'd get tired of bummin' around. A feller wants some place to hang his hat.

DAISY. I wish she would die.

ZERO. And when you start goin' with women you're liable to get into trouble. And lose your job maybe.

DAISY. Maybe you'd marry me.

ZERO. Gee, I wish I'd gone over there that night.

DAISY. Then I could quit workin'.

ZERO. Lots o' women would be glad to get me.

DAISY. You could look a long time before you'd find a sensible, refined girl like me.

ZERO. Yes, sir, they could look a long time before they'd find a steady meal-ticket like me.

DAISY. I guess I'd be too old to have any kids. They say it ain't safe after thirty-five.

ZERO. Maybe I'd marry you. You might be all right, at that.

DAISY. I wonder—if you don't want kids—whether—if there's any way—

ZERO (*looking up*): Hey! Hey! Can't you slow up? What do you think I am—a machine?

DAISY (*looking up*): Say, what do you want, anyhow? First it's too slow an' then it's too fast. I guess you don't know what you want.

ZERO. Well, never mind about that. Just you slow up.

DAISY. I'm gettin' sick o' this. I'm goin' to ask to be transferred.

ZERO. Go ahead. You can't make me mad.

DAISY. Aw, keep quiet. (*She reads*): Two forty-five. A dollar twenty. A dollar fifty. Ninety cents. Sixty-three cents.

ZERO. Marry you! I guess not! You'd be as bad as the one I got.

DAISY. You wouldn't care if I did

ask. I got a good mind to ask.

ZERO. I was a fool to get married.

DAISY. Then I'd never see you at all.

ZERO. What chance has a guy got with a woman tied around his neck?

DAISY. That time at the store picnic—the year your wife couldn't come—you were nice to me then.

ZERO. Twenty-five years holdin' down the same job!

DAISY. We were together all day—just sittin' around under the trees.

ZERO. I wonder if the boss remembers about it bein' twenty-five years.

DAISY. And comin' home that night—you sat next to me in the big delivery wagon.

ZERO. I got a hunch there's a big raise comin' to me.

DAISY. I wonder what it feels like to be really kissed. Men—dirty pigs! They want the bold ones.

ZERO. If he don't come across I'm goin' right up to the front office and tell him where he gets off.

DAISY. I wish I was dead.

ZERO. "Boss," I'll say, "I want to have a talk with you." "Sure," he'll say, "sit down. Have a Corona Corona." "No," I'll say, "I don't smoke." "How's that?" he'll say. "Well, boss," I'll say, "it's this way. Every time I feel like smokin' I just take a nickel and put it in the old sock. A penny saved is a penny earned, that's the way I look at it." "Damn sensible," he'll say. "You got a wise head on you, Zero."

DAISY. I can't stand the smell of gas. It makes me sick. You coulda kissed me if you wanted to.

ZERO. "Boss," I'll say, "I ain't quite satisfied. I been on the job twenty-five years now and if I'm gonna stay I gotta see a future ahead of me." "Zero," he'll say, "I'm glad you came in. I've had my eye on you, Zero. Nothin' gets by me." "Oh, I know that, boss," I'll say. That'll hand him a good laugh, that will. "You're a valuable man, Zero," he'll say, "and I want you right up here with me in the front office. You're done addin' figgers. Monday mornin' you move up here."

DAISY. Them kisses in the movies—them long ones—right on the mouth—

ZERO. I'll keep a-goin' right on up after that. I'll show some of them birds where they get off.

DAISY. That one the other night—*The Devil's Alibi*—he put his arms around her—and her head fell back and her eyes closed—like she was in a daze.

ZERO. Just give me about two years and I'll show them birds where they get off.

DAISY. I guess that's what it's like—a kinda daze—when I see them like that, I just seem to forget everything.

ZERO. Then me for a place in Jersey. And maybe a little Buick. No tin Lizzie for mine. Wait till I get started—I'll show 'em.

DAISY. I can see it now when I kinda half-close my eyes. The way her head fell back. And his mouth pressed right up against hers. Oh, Gawd! it must be grand!

(*There is a sudden shrill blast from a steam whistle.*)

DAISY AND ZERO (*together*). The whistle!

(*With great agility they get off their stools, remove their eye shades and sleeve protectors and put them on the desks. Then each produces from behind the desk a hat—*ZERO, *a dusty derby,* DAISY, *a frowsy straw. . . .* DAISY *puts on her hat and turns toward* ZERO *as though she were about to speak to him. But he is busy cleaning his pen and pays no attention to her. She sighs and goes toward the door at the left.*)

ZERO (*looking up*). G'night, Miss Devore.

(*But she does not hear him and exits.* ZERO *takes up his hat and goes left. The door at the right opens and the* BOSS *enters—middle-aged, stoutish, bald, well-dressed.*)

THE BOSS (*calling*). Oh—er—Mister—er—

(ZERO *turns in surprise, sees who it is, and trembles nervously.*)

ZERO (*obsequiously*). Yes, sir. Do you want me, sir?

BOSS. Yes. Just come here a moment, will you?

ZERO. Yes, sir. Right away, sir. (*He fumbles his hat, picks it up, stumbles, recovers himself, and approaches the* BOSS, *every fibre quivering.*)

BOSS. Mister—er—er—

ZERO. Zero.

BOSS. Yes, Mr. Zero. I wanted to have a little talk with you.

ZERO (*with a nervous grin*). Yes sir, I been kinda expectin' it.

BOSS (*staring at him*). Oh, have you?

ZERO. Yes, sir.

BOSS. How long have you been with us, Mister—er—Mister—

ZERO. Zero.

BOSS. Yes, Mister Zero.

ZERO. Twenty-five years today.

BOSS. Twenty-five years! That's a long time.

ZERO. Never missed a day.

BOSS. And you've been doing the same work all the time?

ZERO. Yes, sir. Right here at this desk.

BOSS. Then, in that case, a change probably won't be unwelcome to you.

ZERO. No, sir, it won't. And that's the truth.

BOSS. We've been planning a change in this department for some time.

ZERO. I kinda thought you had your eye on me.

BOSS. You were right. The fact is that my efficiency experts have recommended the installation of adding machines.

ZERO (staring at him). Addin' machines?

BOSS. Yes, you've probably seen them. A mechanical device that adds automatically.

ZERO. Sure. I've seen them. Keys—and a handle that you pull. (He goes through the motions in the air.)

BOSS. That's it. They do the work in half the time and a high-school girl can operate them. Now, of course, I'm sorry to lose an old and faithful employee—

ZERO. Excuse me, but would you mind sayin' that again?

BOSS. I say I'm sorry to lose an employee who's been with me for so many years—

(Soft music is heard—the sound of the mechanical player of a distant merry-go-round. The part of the floor upon which the desk and stools are standing begins to revolve very slowly.)

BOSS. But, of course, in an organization like this, efficiency must be the first consideration—

(The music becomes gradually louder and the revolutions more rapid.)

BOSS. You will draw your salary for the full month. And I'll direct my secretary to give you a letter of recommendation—

ZERO. Wait a minute, boss. Let me get this right. You mean I'm canned?

BOSS (barely making himself heard above the increasing volume of sound). I'm sorry—no other alternative—greatly regret—

old employee—efficiency—economy—business—business—BUSINESS—

(His voice is drowned by the music. The platform is revolving rapidly now. ZERO and the BOSS face each other. They are entirely motionless save for the BOSS's jaws, which open and close incessantly. But the words are inaudible. The music swells and swells. To it is added every offstage effect of the theatre: the wind, the waves, the galloping horses, the locomotive whistle, the sleigh bells, the automobile siren, the glass-crash. New Year's Eve, Election Night, Armistice Day, and the Mardi-Gras. The noise is deafening, maddening, unendurable. Suddenly it culminates in a terrific peal of thunder. For an instant there is a flash of red and then everything is plunged into blackness.)

CURTAIN

SCENE THREE

SCENE: The ZERO dining room. Entrance door at right. Doors to kitchen and bedroom at left. The walls, as in the first scene, are papered with foolscap sheets covered with columns of figures. In the middle of the room, upstage, a table set for two. Along each side wall, seven chairs are ranged in symmetrical rows.

At the rise of the curtain MRS. ZERO is seen seated at the table looking alternately at the entrance door and a clock on the wall. She wears a bungalow apron over her best dress.

After a few moments, the entrance door opens and ZERO enters. He hangs his hat on a rack behind the door and coming over to the table seats himself at the vacant place. His movements throughout are quiet and abstracted.

MRS. ZERO (breaking the silence). Well, it was nice of you to come home. You're only an hour late and that ain't very much. The supper don't get very cold in an hour. An' of course the part about our havin' a lot of company to-night don't matter. (They begin to eat.) Ain't you even got sense enough to come home on time? Didn't I tell you we're goin' to have a lot o' company to-night? Didn't you know the Ones are comin'? An' the Twos? An' the Threes? An' the Fours? An' the Fives? And the Sixes? Didn't I tell you to be home on time? I might as well talk to a stone wall.

(They eat for a few moments in silence.) I

guess you musta had some important business to attend to. Like watchin' the scoreboard. Or was two kids havin' a fight an' you was the referee? You sure do have a lot of business to attend to. It's a wonder you have time to come home at all. You gotta tough life, you have. Walk in, hang up your hat, an' put on the nose-bag. An' me in the hot kitchen all day, cookin' your supper an' waitin' for you to get good an' ready to come home!

(*Again they eat in silence.*) Maybe the boss kept you late to-night. Tellin' you what a big noise you are and how the store couldn't 'a' got along if you hadn't been pushin' a pen for twenty-five years. Where's the gold medal he pinned on you? Did some blind old lady take it away from you or did you leave it on the seat of the boss's limousine when he brought you home?

(*Again a few moments of silence*). I'll bet he gave you a big raise, didn't he? Promoted you from the third floor to the fourth, maybe. Raise? A fat chance you got o' gettin' a raise. All they gotta do is put an ad in the paper. There's ten thousand like you layin' around the streets. You'll be holdin' down the same job at the end of another twenty-five years—if you ain't forgot how to add by that time.

(*A noise is heard offstage, a sharp clicking such as is made by the operation of the keys and levers of an adding machine.* ZERO *raises his head for a moment, but lowers it almost instantly.*)

MRS. ZERO. There's the doorbell. The company's here already. And we ain't hardly finished supper. (*She rises.*) But I'm goin' to clear off the table whether you're finished or not. If you want your supper, you got a right to be home on time. Not standin' around lookin' at scoreboards.

(*As she piles up the dishes,* ZERO *rises and goes toward the entrance door.*) Wait a minute! Don't open the door yet. Do you want the company to see all the mess? An' go an' put on a clean collar. You got red ink all over it.

(ZERO *goes toward bedroom door.*) I should think after pushin' a pen for twenty-five years, you'd learn how to do it without gettin' ink on your collar.

(ZERO *exits to bedroom.* MRS. ZERO *takes dishes to kitchen, talking as she goes.*) I guess I can stay up all night now washin' dishes. You should worry! That's what a man's got a wife for, ain't it? Don't he buy her her clothes an' let her eat with him at the same table? An' all she's gotta do is cook the meals an' do the washin' an' scrub the floor, an' wash the dishes, when the company goes. But, believe me, you're goin' to sling a mean dish-towel when the company goes to-night!

(*While she is talking* ZERO *enters from bedroom. He wears a clean collar and is cramming the soiled one furtively into his pocket.* MRS. ZERO *enters from kitchen. She has removed her apron and carries a table cover, which she spreads hastily over the table. The clicking noise is heard again.*)

MRS. ZERO. There's the bell again. Open the door, cancha?

(ZERO *goes to the entrance door and opens it. Six men and six women file into the room in a double column. The men are all shapes and sizes, but their dress is identical with that of* ZERO *in every detail. Each, however, wears a wig of a different color. The women are all dressed alike, too, except that the dress of each is of a different color.*)

MRS. ZERO (*taking the first woman's hand*). How de do, Mrs. One.

MRS. ONE. How de do, Mrs. Zero.

(MRS. ZERO *repeats this formula with each woman in turn.* ZERO *does the same with the men, except that he is silent throughout. The files now separate, each man taking a chair from the right wall and each woman one from the left wall. Each sex forms a circle with the chairs very close together. The men—all except* ZERO—*smoke cigars. The women munch chocolates.*)

SIX. Some rain we're havin'.

FIVE. Never saw the like of it.

FOUR. Worst in fourteen years, paper says.

THREE. Y'can't always go by the papers.

TWO. No, that's right, too.

ONE. We're liable to forget from year to year.

SIX. Yeh, come t' think, last year was pretty bad, too.

FIVE. An' how about two years ago?

FOUR. Still this year's pretty bad.

THREE. Yeh, no gettin' away from that.

TWO. Might be a whole lot worse.

ONE. Yeh, it's all the way you look at it. Some rain, though.

MRS. SIX. I like them little organdie dresses.

MRS. FIVE. Yeh, with a little lace trimmin' on the sleeves.

MRS. FOUR. Well, I like 'em plain myself.

MRS. THREE. Yeh, what I always say is the plainer the more refined.

MRS. TWO. Well, I don't think a little lace does any harm.

MRS. ONE. No, it kinda dresses it up.

MRS. ZERO. Well, I always say it's all a matter of taste.

MRS. SIX. I saw you at the Rosebud Movie Thursday night, Mr. One.

ONE. Pretty punk show, I'll say.

TWO. They're gettin' worse all the time.

MRS. SIX. But who was the charming lady, Mr. One?

ONE. Now don't you go makin' trouble for me. That was my sister.

MRS. FIVE. Oho! That's what they all say.

MRS. FOUR. Never mind! I'll bet Mrs. One knows what's what, all right.

MRS. ONE. Oh, well, he can do what he likes—'slong as he behaves himself.

THREE. You're in luck at that, One. Fat chance I got of gettin' away from the frau even with my sister.

MRS. THREE. You oughta be glad you got a good wife to look after you.

THE OTHER WOMEN (*in unison*). That's right, Mrs. Three.

FIVE. I guess I know who wears the pants in your house, Three.

MRS. ZERO. Never mind. I saw them holdin' hands at the movie the other night.

THREE. She musta been tryin' to get some money away from me.

MRS. THREE. Swell chance anybody'd have of gettin' any money away from you.

(*General laughter.*)

FOUR. They sure are a loving couple.

MRS. TWO. Well, I think we oughta change the subject.

MRS. ONE. Yes, let's change the subject.

SIX (*sotto voce*). Did you hear the one about the travelin' salesman?

FIVE. It seems this guy was in a sleeper.

FOUR. Goin' from Albany to San Diego.

THREE. And in the next berth was an old maid.

TWO. With a wooden leg.

ONE. Well, along about midnight—

(*They all put their heads together and whisper.*)

MRS. SIX (*sotto voce*). Did you hear about the Sevens?

MRS. FIVE. They're gettin' a divorce.

MRS. COUR. It's the second time for him.

MRS. THREE. They're two of a kind, if you ask me.

MRS. TWO. One's as bad as the other.

MRS. ONE. Worse.

MRS. ZERO. They say that she—

(*They all put their heads together and whisper.*)

SIX. I think this woman suffrage is the bunk.

FIVE. It sure is! Politics is a man's business.

FOUR. Woman's place is in the home.

THREE. That's it! Lookin' after the kids, 'stead of hangin' around the streets.

TWO. You hit the nail on the head that time.

ONE. The trouble is they don't know what they want.

MRS. SIX. Men sure get me tired.

MRS. FIVE. They sure are a lazy lot.

MRS. FOUR. And dirty.

MRS. THREE. Always grumblin' about somethin'.

MRS. TWO. When they're not lyin'!

MRS. ONE. Or messin' up the house.

MRS. ZERO. Well, believe me, I tell mine where he gets off.

SIX. Business conditions are sure bad.

FIVE. Never been worse.

FOUR. I don't know what we're comin' to.

THREE. I look for a big smash-up in about three months.

TWO. Wouldn't surprise me a bit.

ONE. We're sure headin' for trouble.

MRS. SIX. My aunt has gall-stones.

MRS. FIVE. My husband has bunions.

MRS. FOUR. My sister expects next month.

MRS. THREE. My cousin's husband has erysipelas.

MRS. TWO. My niece has St. Vitus's dance.

MRS. ONE. My boy has fits.

MRS. ZERO. I never felt better in my life. Knock wood!

SIX. Too damn much agitation, that's at the bottom of it.

FIVE. That's it! too damn many strikes.

FOUR. Foreign agitators, that's what it is.

THREE. They ought be run outa the country.

TWO. What the hell do they want, anyhow?

ONE. They don't know what they want, if you ask me.

SIX. America for the Americans is what I say!

ALL (*in unison*). That's it! Damn foreigners! Damn dagoes! Damn Catholics! Damn sheenies! Damn niggers! Jail 'em! shoot 'em! hang 'em! lynch 'em! burn 'em!

(*They all rise.*)

ALL (*sing in unison*). "My country' tis of thee, Sweet land of liberty!"

MRS. FOUR. Why so pensive, Mr. Zero?

ZERO (*speaking for the first time*). I'm thinkin'.

MRS. FOUR. Well, be careful not to sprain your mind.

(*Laughter.*)

MRS. ZERO. Look at the poor men all by themselves. We ain't very sociable.

ONE. Looks like we're neglectin' the ladies.

(*The women cross the room and join the men, all chattering loudly. The doorbell rings.*)

MRS. ZERO. Sh! The doorbell!

(*The volume of sound slowly diminishes. Again the doorbell.*)

ZERO (*quietly*). I'll go. It's for me.

(*They watch curiously as* ZERO *goes to the door and opens it, admitting a policeman. There is a murmur of surprise and excitement.*)

POLICEMAN. I'm lookin' for Mr. Zero.

(*They all point to* ZERO.)

ZERO. I've been expectin' you.

POLICEMAN. Come along!

ZERO. Just a minute. (*He puts his hand in his pocket.*)

POLICEMAN. What's he tryin' to pull? (*He draws a revolver.*) I got you covered.

ZERO. Sure, that's all right. I just want to give you somethin'. (*He takes the collar from his pocket and gives it to the policeman.*)

POLICEMAN (*suspiciously*). What's that?

ZERO. The collar I wore.

POLICEMAN. What do I want it for?

ZERO. It's got bloodstains on it.

POLICEMAN (*pocketing it*). All right, come along!

ZERO (*turning to* MRS. ZERO). I gotta go with him. You'll have to dry the dishes yourself.

MRS. ZERO (*rushing forward*). What are they takin' you for?

ZERO (*calmly*). I killed the boss this afternoon.

(*Quick Curtain as the policeman takes him off.*)

SCENE FOUR

SCENE: *A court of justice. Three bare white walls without door or windows except for a single door in the right wall. At the right is a jury box in which are seated* MESSRS. ONE, TWO, THREE, FOUR, FIVE, *and* SIX *and their respective wives. On either side of the jury box stands a uniformed* OFFICER. *Opposite the jury box is a long, bare oak table piled high with law books. Behind the books* ZERO *is seated, his face buried in his hands. There is no other furniture in the room. A moment after the rise of the curtain, one of the officers rises, and going around the table, taps* ZERO *on the shoulder.* ZERO *rises and accompanies the officer. The* OFFICER *escorts him to the great empty space in the middle of the courtroom, facing the jury. He motions to* ZERO *to stop, then points to the jury, and resumes his place beside the jury box.* ZERO *stands there looking at the jury, bewildered and half-afraid. The* JURORS *give no sign of having seen him. Throughout they sit with folded arms, staring stolidly before them.*

———

ZERO (*beginning to speak; haltingly*). Sure I killed him. I ain't sayin' I didn't, am I? Sure I killed him. Them lawyers! They give me a good stiff pain, that's what they give me. Half the time I don't know what the hell they're talkin' about. Objection sustained. Objection overruled. What's the big idea, anyhow? You ain't heard me do any objectin', have you? Sure not! What's the idea of objectin'? You got a right to know. What I say is if one bird kills another bird, why you got a right to call him for it. That's what I say. I know all about that. I been on the jury, too. Them lawyers! Don't let 'em fill you full of bunk. All that bull about it bein' red ink on the bill-file. Red ink nothin'! It was blood, see? I want you to get that right. I killed him, see? Right through the heart with the bill-file, see? I want you to get that right —all of you. One, two, three, four, five, six, seven, eight, nine, ten, eleven, twelve. Twelve of you. Six and six. That makes twelve. I figgered it up often enough. Six and six makes twelve. And five is seventeen. And eight is twenty-five. And three is twenty-eight. Eight and carry two. Aw, cut it out! Them damn figgers! I can't forget 'em. Twenty-five years, see? Eight hours a day, exceptin' Sundays. And July and August half day

Saturday. One week's vacation with pay. And another week without pay if you want it. Who the hell wants it? Layin' around the house listenin' to the wife tellin' you where you get off. Nix! An' legal holidays. I nearly forgot them. New Year's, Washington's Birthday, Decoration Day, Fourth o' July, Labor Day, Election Day, Thanksgivin', Christmas. Good Friday if you want it. An' if you're a Jew, Young Kipper an' the other one—I forget what they call it. The dirty sheenies—always gettin' two to the other bird's one. An' when a holiday comes on Sunday, you get Monday off. So that's fair enough. But when the Fourth o' July comes on Saturday, why you're out o' luck on account of Saturday bein' a half-day anyhow. Get me? Twenty-five years— I'll tell you somethin' funny. Decoration Day an' the Fourth o' July are always on the same day o' the week. Twenty-five years. Never missed a day, and never more'n five minutes late. Look at my time card if you don't believe me. Eight twenty-seven, eight thirty, eight twenty-nine, eight twenty-seven, eight thirty-two. Eight an' thirty-two's forty an'—Goddam them figgers! I can't forget 'em. They're funny things, them figgers. They look like people sometimes. The eights, see? Two dots for the eyes and a dot for the nose. An' a line. That's the mouth, see? An' there's others remind you of other things—but I can't talk about them, on account of there bein' ladies here. Sure I killed him. Why didn't he shut up? If he'd only shut up! Instead o' talkin' an' talkin' about how sorry he was an' what a good guy I was an' this an' that. I felt like sayin' to him: "For Christ's sake, shut up!" But I didn't have the nerve, see? I didn't have the nerve to say that to the boss. An' he went on talkin', sayin' how sorry he was, see? He was standin' right close to me. An' his coat only had two buttons on it. Two an' two makes four an'—aw, can it! An' there was the bill-file on the desk. Right where I could touch it. It ain't right to kill a guy. I know that. When I read all about him in the paper an' about his three kids I felt like a cheapskate, I tell you. They had the kids' pictures in the paper, right next to mine. An' his wife, too. Gee, it must be swell to have a wife like that. Some guys sure is lucky. An' he left fifty thousand dollars just for a rest-room for the girls in the store. He was a good guy, at that. Fifty thousand. That's more'n twice as much as I'd have if I saved every nickel I ever made. Let's see. Twenty-five an' twenty-five an' twenty-five an'—aw, cut it out! An' the ads had a big, black border around 'em; an' all it said was that the store would be closed for three days on account of the boss bein' dead. That nearly handed me a laugh, that did. All them floor-walkers an' buyers an' high-muck-a-mucks havin' me to thank for gettin' three days off. I hadn't oughta killed him. I ain't sayin' nothin' about that. But I thought he was goin' to give me a raise, see? On account of bein' there twenty-five years. He never talked to me before, see? Except one mornin' we happened to come in the store together and I held the door open for him and he said "Thanks." Just like that, see? "Thanks!" That was the only time he ever talked to me. An' when I seen him comin' up to my desk, I didn't know where I got off. A big guy like that comin' up to my desk. I felt like I was chokin' like and all of a sudden I got a kind o' bad taste in my mouth like when you get up in the mornin'. I didn't have no right to kill him. The district attorney is right about that. He read the law to you, right out o' the book. Killin' a bird—that's wrong. But there was that girl, see? Six months they gave her. It was a dirty trick tellin' the cops on her like that. I shouldn't 'a' done that. But what was I gonna do? The wife wouldn't let up on me. I hadda do it. She used to walk around the room, just in her undershirt, see? Nothin' else on. Just her undershirt. An' they gave her six months. That's the last I'll ever see of her. Them birds— how do they get away with it? Just grabbin' women, the way you see 'em do in the pictures. I've seen lots I'd like to grab like that, but I ain't got the nerve—in the subway an' on the street an' in the store buyin' things. Pretty soft for them shoe-salesmen, I'll say, lookin' at women's legs all day. Them lawyers! They give me a pain, I tell you—a pain! Sayin' the same thing over an' over again. I never said I didn't kill him. But that ain't the same as bein' a regular murderer. What good did it do me to kill him? I didn't make nothin' out of it. Answer yes or no! Yes or no, me elbow! There's some things you can't answer yes or no. Give me the once-over, you guys. Do I look like a murderer? Do I? I never did no harm to nobody. Ask the wife. She'll tell you. Ask anybody. I never got into trouble. You wouldn't count that one time at the Polo Grounds. That was just fun like. Everybody was yellin', "Kill the empire! Kill the empire!" An' before I knew what I was doin' I fired the pop bottle. It was on account of everybody yellin' like that. Just in fun like, see? The yeller dog! Callin' that one a strike—a mile away from the plate. Anyhow, the bottle didn't hit him. An' when I seen the cop comin' up the aisle, I beat it. That didn't hurt nobody. It was just in fun like, see? An' that time in the subway. I was readin' about a lynchin', see? Down in Georgia. They took the nigger an' they tied him to a tree. An' they poured kerosene on him and lit a big fire under him. The dirty nigger! Boy, I'd of liked to been there, with a gat in each hand, pumpin' him full of lead. I was readin' about it in the subway, see? Right at Times Square where the big crowd gets on. An' all of a sudden this big nigger steps right on my foot. It was lucky for him I didn't have a gun on me. I'd of killed him sure, I guess. I guess he couldn't help it all right on account of the crowd, but a nigger's got no right to step on a white man's foot. I told him where he got off all right. The dirty nigger. But that didn't hurt nobody, either. I'm a pretty steady guy, you gotta admit that. Twenty-five years in one job an' I never missed a day. Fifty-two weeks in a year. Fifty-two an' fifty-two an' fifty-two an'— They didn't have t' look for me, did they? I didn't try to run away, did I? Where was I goin' to run to! I wasn't thinkin' about it at all, see? I'll tell you what I was thinkin' about—how I was goin' to break it to the wife about bein' canned. He canned me after twenty-five years, see? Did the lawyers tell you about that? I forget. All that talk gives me a headache. Objection sustained. Objection over-ruled. Answer yes or no.

It gives me a headache. And I can't get the figgers outta my head, neither. But that's what I was thinkin' about— how I was goin' t' break it to the wife about bein' canned. An' what Miss Devore would think when she heard about me killin' him. I bet she never thought I had the nerve to do it. I'd of married her if the wife had passed out. I'd be holdin' down my job yet, if he hadn't o' canned me. But he kept talkin' an' talkin'. An' there was the bill-file right where I could reach it. Do you get me? I'm just a regular guy like anybody else. Like you birds, now.

(*For the first time the* JURORS *relax, looking indignantly at each other and whispering.*)

Suppose you was me, now. Maybe you'd 'a' done the same thing. That's the way you oughta look at it, see? Suppose you was me—

THE JURORS (*rising as one and shouting in unison*). *GUILTY!*

(ZERO *falls back, stunned for a moment by their vociferousness. The* JURORS *right-face in their places and file quickly out of the jury box and toward the door in a double column.*)

ZERO (*recovering speech as the* JURORS *pass out at the door*). Wait a minute. Jest a minute. You don't get me right. Jest give me a chance an' I'll tell you how it was. I'm all mixed up, see? On account of them lawyers. And the figgers in my head. But I'm goin' to tell you how it was. I was there twenty-five years, see? An' they gave her six months, see?

(*He goes on haranguing the empty jury box as the curtain falls.*)

SCENE FIVE*

In the middle of the stage is a large cage with bars on all four sides. The bars are very far apart and the interior of the cage is clearly visible. The floor of the cage is about six feet above the level of the stage. A flight of wooden steps lead up to it on the side facing the audience. ZERO *is discovered in the middle of the cage seated at a table above which is suspended a single naked*

* This scene, which follows the courtroom scene, was part of the original script. It was omitted, however, when the play was produced, and was performed for the first time (in its present revised form) when the play was revived at the Phoenix Theatre in New York in February, 1956.

electric light. Before him is an enormous platter of ham and eggs, which he eats voraciously with a large wooden spoon. He wears a uniform of very broad black and white horizontal stripes.

A few moments after the rise of the curtain a man enters at left, wearing the blue uniform and peaked cap of a GUIDE. *He is followed by a miscellaneous crowd of* MEN, WOMEN, *and* CHILDREN—*about a dozen in all.*

———

THE GUIDE (*stopping in front of the cage*). Now ladies and gentlemen, if you'll kindly step right this way! (THE CROWD *straggles up and forms a loose semicircle around him.*) Step right up, please. A little closer so's everybody can hear. (*They move up closer.* ZERO *pays no attention whatever to them.*) This, ladies and gentlemen, is a very in-ter-est-in' specimen—the North American murderer, Genus *home sapiens*, Habitat North America. (*A titter of excitement. They all crowd up around the cage.*) Don't push. There's room enough for everybody.

A TALL LADY. Oh, how interesting!

A STOUT LADY (*excitedly*). Look, Charley, he's eating!

CHARLEY (*bored*). Yeh, I see him.

THE GUIDE (*repeating by rote*). This specimen, ladies and gentlemen, exhibits the characteristics which are typical of his kind—

A SMALL BOY (*in a little Lord Fauntleroy suit, whiningly*). Mama!

HIS MOTHER. Be quiet, Eustace, or I'll take you right home.

THE GUIDE. He has the opposable thumbs, the large cranial capacity, and the highly developed pre-frontal areas which distinguish him from all other species.

A YOUTH (*who has been taking notes*). What areas did you say?

THE GUIDE (*grumpily*). Pre-front-al areas. He learns by imitation and has a language which is said by some eminent philologists to bear many striking resemblances to English.

A BOY OF FOURTEEN. Pop, what's a philologist?

HIS FATHER. Keep quiet, can't you, and listen to what he's sayin'.

THE GUIDE. He thrives and breeds freely in captivity. This specimen was taken alive in his native haunts shortly after murdering his boss.

(*Murmurs of great interest.*)

THE TALL LADY. Oh, how charming.

THE NOTE-TAKING YOUTH. What was that last? I didn't get it.

SEVERAL (*helpfully*). Murdering his boss.

THE YOUTH. Oh—thanks.

THE GUIDE. He was tried, convicted, and sentenced in one hour, thirteen minutes, and twenty-four seconds, which sets a new record for this territory east of the Rockies and north of the Mason and Dixon line.

LITTLE LORD FAUNTLEROY (*whiningly*). Ma-ma!

HIS MOTHER. Be quiet, Eustace, or Mama won't let you ride in the choo-choo.

THE GUIDE. Now take a good look at him, ladies and gents. It's his last day here. He's goin' to be executed at noon.

(*Murmurs of interest.*)

THE TALL LADY. Oh, how lovely!

A MAN. What's he eating?

THE GUIDE. Ham and eggs.

THE STOUT LADY. He's quite a big eater, ain't he?

THE GUIDE. Oh, he don't always eat that much. You see we always try to make 'em feel good on their last day. So about a week in advance we let them order what they want to eat on their last day. They can have eight courses and they can order anything they want—don't make no difference what it costs or how hard it is to get. Well, he couldn't make up his mind till last night, and then he ordered eight courses of ham and eggs.

(*They all push and stare.*)

THE BOY OF FOURTEEN. Look pop! He's eatin' with a spoon. Don't he know how to use a knife and fork?

THE GUIDE (*overhearing him*). We don't dare trust him with a knife and fork, sonny. He might try to kill himself.

THE TALL LADY. Oh, how fascinating!

THE GUIDE (*resuming his official tone*). And now, friends, if you'll kindly give me your kind attention for just a moment. (*He takes a bundle of folders from his pocket.*) I have a little souvenir folder which I'm sure you'll all want to have. It contains twelve beautiful colored views relating to the North American Murderer you have just been looking at. These include a picture of the murderer, a picture of the murderer's wife, the blood-stained weapon, the murderer at the age of six, the spot where the body was found, the little red schoolhouse where he went to school, and his vine-covered boyhood home in southern Illinois, with his sweet-faced white-haired old mother plainly visible in the foreground. And many other interesting views. I'm now going to distribute these little folders for your examination. (*Sotto voce.*) Just pass them back, will you? (*In louder tones.*) Don't be afraid to look at them. You don't have to buy them if you don't want to. It don't cost anything to look at them. (*To the* NOTE-TAKING YOUTH, *who is fumbling with a camera.*) Hey, there, young feller, no snapshots allowed. All right now, friends, if you'll just step this way. Keep close together and follow me. A lady lost her little boy here one time, and by the time we found him he was smoking cigarettes and hollering for a razor.

(*Much laughter as all follow him off left.* ZERO *finishes eating and pushes away his plate. As* THE CROWD *goes at left,* MRS. ZERO *enters at right. She is dressed in mourning garments. She carries a large parcel. She goes up the steps to the cage, opens the door, and enters.* ZERO *looks up and sees her.*)

MRS. ZERO. Hello.

ZERO. Hello, I didn't think you were comin' again.

MRS. ZERO. Well, I thought I'd come again. Are you glad to see me?

ZERO. Sure. Sit down. (*She complies.*) You're all dolled up, ain't you?

MRS. ZERO. Yeh, don't you like it? (*She gets up and turns about like a mannequin.*)

ZERO. Gee. Some class.

MRS. ZERO. I always look good in black. There's some weight to this veil though, I'll tell the world. I got a fierce headache.

ZERO. How much did all that set you back?

MRS. ZERO. Sixty-four dollars and twenty cents. And I gotta get a pin yet and some writin' paper—you know, with black around the edges.

ZERO. You'll be scrubbin' floors in about a year, if you go blowin' your coin like that.

MRS. ZERO. Well, I gotta do it right. It don't happen every day. (*She rises and takes up the parcel.*) I brought you somethin'.

ZERO (*interested*). Yeh, what?

MRS. ZERO (*opening the parcel*). You gotta guess.

ZERO. Er—er—gee, search me.

MRS. ZERO. Somethin' you like. (*She takes out a covered plate.*)

ZERO (*with increasing interest*). Looks like somethin' to eat.

MRS. ZERO (*nodding*). Yeh. (*She takes off the top plate.*) Ham an' eggs!

ZERO (*joyfully*). Oh, boy! Just what I feel like eatin! (*He takes up the wooden spoon and begins to eat avidly.*)

MRS. ZERO (*pleased*). Are they good?

ZERO (*his mouth full*). Swell.

MRS. ZERO (*a little sadly*). They're the last ones I'll ever make for you.

ZERO (*busily eating*). Uh-huh.

MRS. ZERO. I'll tell you somethin'—shall I?

ZERO. Sure.

MRS. ZERO (*hesitantly*). Well, all the while they were cookin' I was cryin!

ZERO. Yeh? (*He leans over and pats her hand.*)

MRS. ZERO. I just couldn't help it. The thought of it just made me cry.

ZERO. Well—no use cryin' about it.

MRS. ZERO. I just couldn't help it.

ZERO. Maybe this time next year you'll be fryin' eggs for some other bird.

MRS. ZERO. Not on your life.

ZERO. You never can tell.

MRS. ZERO. Not me. Once is enough for me.

ZERO. I guess you're right at that. Still, I dunno. You might just happen to meet some guy—

MRS. ZERO. Well, if I do, there'll be time enough to think about it. No use borrowin' trouble.

ZERO. How do you like bein' alone in the house?

MRS. ZERO. Oh, it's all right.

ZERO. You got plenty room in the bed now, ain't you?

MRS. ZERO. Oh, yeh. (*A brief pause.*) It's kinda lonesome though—you know, wakin' up in the mornin' and nobody around to talk to.

ZERO. Yeh, I know. It's the same with me.

MRS. ZERO. Not that we ever did much talkin'.

ZERO. Well, that ain't it. It's just the idea of havin' somebody there in case you want to talk.

MRS. ZERO. Yeh, that's it. (*Another brief pause.*) I guess maybe I use t'bawl you out quite a lot, didn't !?

ZERO. Oh, well—no use talkin' about it now.

MRS. ZERO. We were always at it, weren't we?

ZERO. No more than any other married folks, I guess.

MRS. ZERO (*dubiously*). I dunno—

ZERO. I guess I gave you cause, all right.

MRS. ZERO. Well—I got my faults too.

ZERO. None of us are perfect.

MRS. ZERO. We got along all right, at that, didn't we?

ZERO. Sure! Better'n most.

MRS. ZERO. Remember them Sundays at the beach, in the old days?

ZERO. You bet. (*With a laugh.*) Remember that time I ducked you. Gee, you was mad!

MRS. ZERO (*with a laugh*). I didn't talk to you for a whole week.

ZERO (*chuckling*). Yeh, I remember.

MRS. ZERO. And the time I had pneumonia and you brought me them roses. Remember?

ZERO. Yeh, I remember. And when the doctor told me maybe you'd pass out, I nearly sat down and cried.

MRS. ZERO. Did you?

ZERO. I sure did.

MRS. ZERO. We had some pretty good times at that, didn't we?

ZERO. I'll say we did!

MRS. ZERO (*with a sudden soberness*). It's all over now.

ZERO. All over is right. I ain't got much longer.

MRS. ZERO (*rising and going over to him*). Maybe—maybe—if we had to do it over again, it would be different.

ZERO (*taking her hand*). Yeh. We live and learn.

MRS. ZERO (*crying*). If we only had another chance.

ZERO. It's too late now.

MRS. ZERO. It don't seem right, does it?

ZERO. It ain't right. But what can you do about it?

MRS. ZERO. Ain't there somethin'—somethin' I can do for you—before—

ZERO. No. Nothin'. Not a thing.

MRS. ZERO. Nothin' at all?

ZERO. No. I can't think of anything. (*Suddenly.*) You're takin' good care of that scrapbook, ain't you. With all the clippings in it?

MRS. ZERO. Oh, sure. I got it right on the parlor table. Right where everybody can see it.

ZERO (*pleased*). It must be pretty near full, ain't it?

MRS. ZERO. All but three pages.

ZERO. Well, there'll be more tomorrow. Enough to fill it, maybe. Be sure to get them all, will you?

MRS. ZERO. I will. I ordered the papers already.

ZERO. Gee, I never thought I'd have a whole book full of clippings all about myself. (*Suddenly.*) Say, that's somethin' I'd like to ask you.

MRS. ZERO. What?

ZERO. Suppose you should get sick or be run over or somethin'—what would happen to the book?

MRS. ZERO. Well, I kinda thought I'd leave it to little Beatrice Elizabeth.

ZERO. Who? Your sister's kid?

MRS. ZERO. Yeh.

ZERO. What would she want with it?

MRS. ZERO. Well, it's nice to have, ain't it? And I wouldn't know who else to give it to.

ZERO. Well, I don't want her to have it. That fresh little kid puttin' her dirty fingers all over it.

MRS. ZERO. She ain't fresh and she ain't dirty. She's a sweet little thing.

ZERO. I don't want her to have it.

MRS. ZERO. Who do you want to have it then?

ZERO. Well, I kinda thought I'd like Miss Devore to have it.

MRS. ZERO. Miss Devore?

ZERO. Yeh. You know. Down at the store.

MRS. ZERO. Why should she have it?

ZERO. She'd take good care of it. And anyhow, I'd like her to have it.

MRS. ZERO. Oh you would, would you?

ZERO. Yes.

MRS. ZERO. Well, she ain't goin' to have it. Miss Devore! Where does she come in, I'd like to know, when I got two sisters and a niece.

ZERO. I don't care nothin' about your sisters and your niece.

MRS. ZERO. Well, I do! And Miss Devore ain't goin' to get it. Now put that in your pipe and smoke it.

ZERO. What have you got to say about it? It's my book, ain't it?

MRS. ZERO. No, it ain't. It's mine now—or it will be tomorrow. And I'm goin' to do what I like with it.

ZERO. I should have given it to her in the first place—that's what I should have done.

MRS. ZERO. Oh, should you? And what about me? Am I your wife or ain't I?

ZERO. Why remind me of my troubles?

MRS. ZERO. So it's Miss Devore all of a sudden, is it? What's been goin' on, I'd like to know, between you and Miss Devore?

ZERO. Aw, tie a can to that!

MRS. ZERO. Why didn't you marry Miss Devore, if you think so much of her?

ZERO. I would if I'd of met her first.

MRS. ZERO (shrieking). Ooh! A fine way to talk to me. After all I've done for you. You bum! You dirty bum! I won't stand for it! I won't stand for it! (In a great rage she takes up the dishes and smashes them on the floor. Then, crying hysterically, she opens the cage door, bangs it behind her, comes down the steps, and goes off toward left.)

(ZERO stands gazing ruefully after her for a moment, and then with a shrug and a sigh begins picking up the pieces of broken crockery.)

(As MRS. ZERO exits at left, a door in the back of the cage opens and a man enters. He is dressed in a sky-blue, padded silk dressing-gown, which is fitted with innumerable pockets. Under this he wears a pink silk union-suit. His bare feet are in sandals. He wears a jaunty Panama hat with a red feather stuck in the brim. Wings are fastened to his sandals and to the shoulders of his dressing-gown. ZERO, who is busy picking up the broken crockery, does not notice him at first. THE MAN takes a gold toothpick and begins carefully picking his teeth, waiting for ZERO to notice him. ZERO happens to look up and suddenly sees THE MAN. He utters a cry of terror and shrinks into a corner of the cage, trembling with fear.)

ZERO (hoarsely). Who are you?

THE MAN (calmly, as he pockets his toothpick). I'm the Fixer—from the Claim Department.

ZERO. Whaddya want?

THE FIXER. It's no use, Zero. There are no miracles.

ZERO. I don't know what you're talking about.

THE FIXER. Don't lie, Zero. (Holding up his hand.) And now that your course is run—now that the end is already in sight, you still believe that some thunderbolt, some fiery bush, some celestial apparition, will intervene between you and extinction. But it's no use, Zero. You're done for.

ZERO (vehemently). It ain't right! It ain't fair! I ain't gettin' a square deal!

THE FIXER (wearily). They all say that, Zero. (Mildly.) Now just tell me why you're not getting a square deal.

ZERO. Well, that addin' machine. Was that a square deal—after twenty-five years?

THE FIXER. Certainly—from any point of view, except a sentimental one. (Looking at his wrist watch.) The machine is quicker, it never makes a mistake, it's always on time. It presents no problems of housing, traffic congestion, water supply, sanitation.

ZERO. It costs somethin' to buy them machines, I'll tell you that!

THE FIXER. Yes, you're right there. In one respect you have the advantage over the machine—the cost of manufacture. But we've learned from many years' experience, Zero, that the original cost is an inconsequential item compared to upkeep. Take the dinosaurs, for example. They literally ate themselves out of existence. I held out for them to the last. They were damned picturesque—but when it came to a question of the nitrate supply, I simply had to yield. (He begins to empty and clean his pipe.) And so with you, Zero. It costs a lot to keep up all that delicate mechanism of eye and ear and hand and brain which you've never put to any use. We can't afford to maintain it in idleness—and so you've got to go.

ZERO (falling to his knees, supplicatingly). Gimme a chance, gimme another chance!

THE FIXER. What would you do if I gave you another chance?

ZERO. Well—first thing I'd go out and look for a job.

THE FIXER. Adding figures?

ZERO. Well—I ain't young enough to take up somethin' new.

(THE FIXER takes out a police whistle and blows shrilly. Instantly two guards enter.)

THE FIXER. Put the skids under him boys, and make it snappy. (He strolls *away to the other side of the cage, and taking a nail clipper from a pocket, begins to clip his nails as the* GUARDS *sieze* ZERO.)

ZERO (*struggling and shrieking*). No! No! Don't take me away! Don't kill me! Gimme a chance! Gimme another chance!

GUARD (*soothingly*). Ah, come on! Be a good fellow! It'll all be over in a minute!

ZERO. I don't want to die! I don't want to die! I want to live!

(*The* GUARDS *look at each other dubiously. Then one of them walks rather timidly over to the* FIXER, *who is busy with his nails.*)

GUARD (*clearing his throat*). H'm!

THE FIXER (*looking up*). Well?

GUARD (*timidly*). He says he wants to live.

THE FIXER. No. He's no good.

GUARD (*touching his cap, deferentially*). Yes sir!

(*He goes back to his companion and the two of them drag* ZERO *out at the back of the cage, still struggling and screaming.*

THE FIXER *puts away his nail clippers, yawns, then goes to the table and sits on the edge of it. From a pocket he takes an enormous pair of horn-rimmed spectacles. Then from another pocket he takes a folded newspaper, which he unfolds carefully. It is a colored comic supplement. He holds it up in front of him and becomes absorbed in it.*

A moment later the door at the back of the cage opens and a tall, brawny, bearded MAN *enters. He wears a red flannel undershirt and carries a huge blood-stained axe.* THE FIXER, *absorbed in the comic supplement, does not look up.*)

MAN (*hoarsely*). O. K.

THE FIXER (*looking up*). What?

MAN. O. K.

THE FIXER (*nodding*). Oh, all right. (*The* MAN *bows deferentially and goes out at the back. The* FIXER *puts away his spectacles and folds the comic supplement carefully. As he folds the paper:*) That makes a total of 2137 black eyes for Jeff.

(*He puts away the paper, turns out the electric light over his head, and leaves the cage by the front door. Then he takes a padlock from a pocket, attaches it to the door, and saunters off as the*
CURTAIN FALLS.)

SCENE SIX

SCENE: *A graveyard in full moonlight. It is a second-rate graveyard—no elaborate tombstones or monuments—just simple headstones and here and there a cross. At the back is an iron fence with a gate in the middle. At first no one is visible, but there are occasional sounds throughout: the hooting of an owl, the whistle of a distant whippoorwill, the croaking of a bullfrog, and the yowling of a serenading cat. After a few moments two figures appear outside the gate—a man and a woman. She pushes the gate and it opens with a rusty creak. The couple enter. They are now fully visible in the moonlight—*JUDY O'GRADY *and a* YOUNG MAN.

———

JUDY (*advancing*). Come on, this is the place.

YOUNG MAN (*hanging back*). This! Why this here is a cemetery.

JUDY. Aw, quit yer kiddin'!

YOUNG MAN. You don't mean to say—

JUDY. What's the matter with this place?

YOUNG MAN. A cemetery!

JUDY. Sure. What of it?

YOUNG MAN. You must be crazy.

JUDY. This place is all right, I tell you. I been here lots o' times.

YOUNG MAN. Nix on this place for me!

JUDY. Ain't this place as good as another? Whaddya afraid of? They're all dead ones here! They don't bother you. (*With sudden interest.*) Oh, look, here's a new one.

YOUNG MAN. Come on out of here.

JUDY. Wait a minute. Let's see what it says. (*She kneels on a grave in the foreground, and putting her face close to headstone, spells out the inscription.*) Z-E-R-O Z-e-r-o. Zero! Say, that's the guy—

YOUNG MAN. Zero? He's the guy killed his boss, ain't he?

JUDY. Yeh, that's him, all right. But what I'm thinkin' of is that I went to the hoosegow on account of him.

YOUNG MAN. What for?

JUDY. You know, same old stuff. Tenement House Law. (*Mincingly.*) Section blaa-blaa of the Penal Code. Third offense. Six months.

YOUNG MAN. And this bird—

JUDY (*contemptuously*). Him? He was mama's whitehaired boy. We lived in the same house. Across the airshaft, see?

I used to see him lookin' in my window. I guess his wife musta seen him, too. Anyhow, they went and turned the bulls on me. And now I'm out and he's in. (*Suddenly.*) Say—say—(*She bursts into a peal of laughter.*)

YOUNG MAN (*nervously*). What's so funny?

JUDY (*rocking with laughter*). Say, wouldn't it be funny—if—if—(*She explodes again.*) That would be a good joke on him, all right. He can't do nothin' about it now, can he?

YOUNG MAN. Come on out of here. I don't like this place.

JUDY. Aw, you're a bum sport. What do you want to spoil my joke for?

(*A cat yammers mellifluously.*)

YOUNG MAN (*half-hysterically*). What's that?

JUDY. It's only the cats. They seem to like it here all right. But come on if you're afraid. (*They go toward the gate. As they go out.*) You nervous men sure are the limit.

(*They go out through the gate. As they disappear,* ZERO's *grave opens suddenly and his head appears.*)

ZERO (*looking about*). That's funny! I thought I heard her talkin' and laughin'. But I don't see nobody. Anyhow, what would she be doin' here? I guess I must 'a' been dreamin'. But how could I be dreamin' when I ain't been asleep? (*He looks about again.*) Well, no use goin' back. I can't sleep, anyhow. I might as well walk around a little. (*He rises out of the ground, very rigidly. He wears a full-dress suit of very antiquated cut and his hands are folded stiffly across his breast.*)

ZERO (*walking woodenly*). Gee! I'm stiff! (*He slowly walks a few steps, then stops.*) Gee, it's lonesome here! (*He shivers and walks on aimlessly.*) I should 'a' stayed where I was. But I thought I heard her laughin'.

(*A loud sneeze is heard.* ZERO *stands motionless, quaking with terror. The sneeze is repeated.*)

ZERO (*hoarsely*). What's that?

A MILD VOICE. It's all right. Nothing to be afraid of.

(*From behind a headstone* SHRDLU *appears. He is dressed in a shabby and ill-fitting cutaway. He wears silver-rimmed spectacles and is smoking a cigarette.*)

SHRDLU. I hope I didn't frighten you.

ZERO (*still badly shaken*). No-o. It's all right. You see, I wasn't expectin' to see anybody.

SHRDLU. You're a newcomer, aren't you?

ZERO. Yeh, this is my first night. I couldn't seem to get to sleep.

SHRDLU. I can't sleep, either. Suppose we keep each other company, shall we?

ZERO (*eagerly*). Yeh, that would be great. I been feelin' awful lonesome.

SHRDLU (*nodding*). I know. Let's make ourselves comfortable.

(*He seats himself easily on a grave.* ZERO *tries to follow his example but he is stiff in every joint and groans with pain.*)

ZERO. I'm kinda stiff.

SHRDLU. You mustn't mind the stiffness. It wears off in a few days. (*He seats himself on the grave beside* ZERO *and produces a package of cigarettes.*) Will you have a Camel?

ZERO. No, I don't smoke.

SHRDLU. I find it helps keep the mosquitoes away. (*He lights a cigarette.*)

SHRDLU (*suddenly taking the cigarette out of his mouth*). Do you mind if I smoke, Mr.—Mr.—?

ZERO. No, go right ahead.

SHRDLU (*replacing the cigarette*). Thank you. I didn't catch your name.

(ZERO *does not reply.*)

SHRDLU (*mildly*). I say I didn't catch your name.

ZERO. I heard you the first time. (*Hesitantly.*) I'm scared if I tell you who I am and what I done, you'll be off me.

SHRDLU (*sadly*). No matter what your sins may be, they are as snow compared to mine.

ZERO. You got another guess comin'. (*He pauses dramatically.*) My name's Zero. I'm a murderer.

SHRDLU (*nodding calmly*). Oh, yes, I remember reading about you, Mr. Zero.

ZERO (*a little piqued*). And you still think you're worse than me?

SHRDLU (*throwing away his cigarette*). Oh, a thousand times worse, Mr. Zero—a million times worse.

ZERO. What did you do?

SHRDLU. I, too, am a murderer.

ZERO (*looking at him in amazement*). Go on! You're kiddin' me!

SHRDLU. Every word I speak is the truth, Mr. Zero. I am the foulest, the most sinful of murderers! You only murdered your employer, Mr. Zero. But I—I murdered my mother. [*He covers his face with his hands and sobs.*)

ZERO (*horrified*). The hell yer say!

SHRDLU (*sobbing*). Yes, my mother!— my beloved mother!

ZERO (*suddenly*). Say, you don't mean to say you're Mr.—

SHRDLU (*nodding*). Yes. (*He wipes his eyes, still quivering with emotion.*)

ZERO. I remember readin' about you in the papers.

SHRDLU. Yes, my guilt has been proclaimed to all the world. But that would be a trifle if only I could wash the stain of sin from my soul.

ZERO. I never heard of a guy killin' his mother before. What did you do it for?

SHRDLU. Because I have a sinful heart—there is no other reason.

ZERO. Did she always treat you square and all like that?

SHRDLU. She was a saint—a saint, I tell you. She cared for me and watched over me as only a mother can.

ZERO. You mean to say you didn't have a scrap or nothin'?

SHRDLU. Never a harsh or an unkind word. Nothing except loving care and good advice. From my infancy she devoted herself to guiding me on the right path. She taught me to be thrifty, to be devout, to be unselfish, to shun evil companions, and to shut my ears to all the temptations of the flesh—in short, to become a virtuous, respectable, and God-fearing man. (*He groans.*) But it was a hopeless task. At fourteen I began to show evidence of my sinful nature.

ZERO (*breathlessly*). You didn't kill anybody else, did you?

SHRDLU. No, thank God, there is only one murder on my soul. But I ran away from home.

ZERO. You did!

SHRDLU. Yes. A companion lent me a profane book—the only profane book I have ever read, I'm thankful to say. It was called *Treasure Island*. Have you ever read it?

ZERO. No, I never was much on readin' books.

SHRDLU. It is a wicked book—a lurid tale of adventure. But it kindled in my sinful heart a desire to go to sea. And so I ran away from home.

ZERO. What did you do—get a job as a sailor?

SHRDLU. I never saw the sea—not to the day of my death. Luckily, my mother's loving intuition warned her of my intention and I was sent back home. She welcomed me with open arms. Not an angry word, not a look of reproach. But I could read the mute suffering in her eyes as we prayed together all through the night.

ZERO (*sympathetically*). Gee, that must 'a' been tough. Gee, the mosquitoes are bad, ain't they? (*He tries awkwardly to slap at them with his stiff hands.*)

SHRDLU (*absorbed in his narrative*). I thought that experience had cured me of evil and I began to think about a career. I wanted to go in foreign missions at first, but we couldn't bear the thought of the separation. So we finally decided that I should become a proof-reader.

ZERO. Say, slip me one o' them Camels, will you? I'm gettin' all bit up.

SHRDLU. Certainly. (*He hands* ZERO *cigarettes and matches.*)

ZERO (*lighting up*). Go ahead. I'm listenin'.

SHRDLU. By the time I was twenty I had a good job reading proof for a firm that printed catalogues. After a year they promoted me and let me specialize in shoe catalogues.

ZERO. Yeh? That must 'a' been a good job.

SHRDLU. It was a very good job. I was on the shoe catalogues for thirteen years. I'd been on them yet, if I hadn't— (*He chokes back a sob.*)

ZERO. They oughta put a shot o' citronella in that embalmin'-fluid.

SHRDLU (*he sighs*). We were so happy together. I had my steady job. And Sundays we would go to morning, afternoon, and evening service. It was an honest and moral mode of life.

ZERO. It sure was.

SHRDLU. Then came that fatal Sunday. Dr. Amaranth, our minister, was having dinner with us—one of the few pure spirits on earth. When he had finished saying grace, we had our soup. Everything was going along as usual—we were eating our soup and discussing the sermon, just like every other Sunday I could remember. Then came the leg of lamb—(*He breaks off, then resumes in a choking voice.*) I see the whole scene before me so plainly—it never leaves me—

Dr. Amaranth at my right, my mother at my left, the leg of lamb on the table in front of me and the cuckoo clock on the little shelf between the windows. (*He stops and wipes his eyes.*)

ZERO. Yeh, but what happened?

SHRDLU. Well, as I started to carve the lamb—Did you ever carve a leg of lamb?

ZERO. No, corned beef was our speed.

SHRDLU. It's very difficult on account of the bone. And when there's gravy in the dish there's danger of spilling it. So Mother always used to hold the dish for me. She leaned forward, just as she always did, and I could see the gold locket around her neck. It had my picture in it and one of my baby curls. Well, I raised my knife to carve the leg of lamb—and instead I cut my mother's throat! (*He sobs.*)

ZERO. You must 'a' been crazy!

SHRDLU (*raising his head, vehemently*). No! Don't try to justify me. I wasn't crazy. They tried to prove at the trial that I was crazy. But Dr. Amaranth saw the truth! He saw it from the first! He knew that it was my sinful nature—and he told me what was in store for me.

ZERO (*trying to be comforting*). Well, your troubles are over now.

SHRDLU (*his voice rising*). Over! Do you think this is the end?

ZERO. Sure. What more can they do to us?

SHRDLU (*his tones growing shriller and shriller*). Do you think there can ever be any peace for such as we are—murderers, sinners? Don't you know what awaits us—flames, eternal flames!

ZERO (*nervously*). Keep your shirt on, Buddy—they wouldn't do that to us.

SHRDLU. There's no escape—no escape for us, I tell you. We're doomed! We're doomed to suffer unspeakable torments through all eternity. (*His voice rises higher and higher.*)

(*A grave opens suddenly and a head appears.*)

THE HEAD. Hey, you birds! Can't you shut up and let a guy sleep?

(ZERO *scrambles painfully to his feet.*)

ZERO (*to* SHRDLU). Hey, put on the soft pedal.

SHRDLU (*too wrought up to attend*). It won't be long now! We'll receive our summons soon.

THE HEAD. Are you goin' to beat it or not? (*He calls into the grave.*) Hey, Bill, lend me your head a minute.

(*A moment later his arm appears holding a skull.*)

ZERO (*warningly*). Look out! (*He seizes* SHRDLU *and drags him away just as* THE HEAD *throws the skull.*)

THE HEAD (*disgustedly*). Missed 'em. Damn old tabby cats! I'll get 'em next time. (*A prodigious yawn.*) Ho-hum! Me for the worms!

(THE HEAD *disappears as the curtain falls.*)

SCENE SEVEN

SCENE: *A pleasant place. A scene of pastoral loveliness. A meadow dotted with fine old trees and carpeted with rich grass and field flowers. In the background are seen a number of tents fashioned of gay-striped silks, and beyond gleams a meandering river. Clear air and a fleckless sky. Sweet distant music throughout.*

At the rise of the curtain, SHRDLU *is seen seated under a tree in the foreground in an attitude of deep dejection. His knees are drawn up and his head is buried in his arms. He is dressed as in the preceding scene.*

A few minutes later, ZERO *enters at right. He walks slowly and looks about him with an air of half-suspicious curiosity. He, too, is dressed as in the preceding scene. Suddenly he sees* SHRDLU *seated under the tree. He stands still and looks at him half fearfully. Then, seeing something familiar in him, goes closer.* SHRDLU *is unaware of his presence. At last* ZERO *recognizes him and grins in pleased surprise.*)

———

ZERO. Well, if it ain't—! (*He claps* SHRDLU *on the shoulder.*) Hello, Buddy!

(SHRDLU *looks up slowly; then, recognizing* ZERO, *he rises gravely and extends his hand courteously.*)

SHRDLU. How do you do, Mr. Zero? I'm very glad to see you again.

ZERO. Same here. I wasn't expectin' to see you, either. (*Looking about.*) This is a kinda nice place. I wouldn't mind restin' here a while.

SHRDLU. You may if you wish.

ZERO. I'm kinda tired. I ain't used to bein' outdoors. I ain't walked so much in years.

SHRDLU. Sit down here, under the tree.

ZERO. Do they let you sit on the grass?

SHRDLU. Oh, yes.

ZERO (*seating himself*). Boy, this feels good. I'll tell the world my feet are sore. I ain't used to so much walkin'. Say, I wonder would it be all right if I took my shoes off; my feet are tired.

SHRDLU. Yes. Some of the people here go barefoot.

ZERO. Yeh? They sure must be nuts. But I'm goin' t' leave 'em off for a while. So long as it's all right. The grass feels nice and cool. (*He stretches out comfortably*). Say, this is the life of Riley all right, all right. This sure is a nice place. What do they call this place, anyhow?

SHRDLU. The Elysian Fields.

ZERO. The which?

SHRDLU. The Elysian Fields.

ZERO (*dubiously*). Oh! Well, it's a nice place, all right.

SHRDLU. They say that this is the most desirable of all places. Only the most favoured remain here.

ZERO. Yeh? Well, that let's me out, I guess. (*Suddenly*). But what are you doin' here? I thought you'd be burned by now.

SHRDLU (*sadly*). Mr. Zero, I am the most unhappy of men.

ZERO (*in mild astonishment*). Why, because you ain't bein' roasted alive?

SHRDLU (*nodding*). Nothing is turning out as I expected. I saw everything so clearly—the flames, the tortures, an eternity of suffering as the just punishment for my unspeakable crime. And it has all turned out so differently.

ZERO. Well, that's pretty soft for you, ain't it?

SHRDLU (*wailingly*). No, no, no! It's right and just that I should be punished. I could have endured it stoically. All through those endless ages of indescribable torment I should have exulted in the magnificence of divine justice. But this—this is maddening! What becomes of justice? What becomes of morality? What becomes of right and wrong? It's maddening—simply maddening! Oh, if Dr. Amaranth were only here to advise me! (*He buries his face and groans*).

ZERO (*trying to puzzle it out*). You mean to say they ain't called you for cuttin' your mother's throat?

SHRDLU. No! It's terrible—terrible! I was prepared for anything—anything but this.

ZERO. Well, what did they say to you?

SHRDLU (*looking up*). Only that I was to come here and remain until I understood.

ZERO. I don't get it. What do they want you to understand?

SHRDLU (*despairingly*). I don't know— I don't know! If I only had an inkling of what they meant—(*interrupting him*). Just listen quietly for a moment; do you hear anything?

(*They are both silent, straining their ears.*)

ZERO (*at length*). Nope.

SHRDLU. You don't hear any music? Do you?

ZERO. Music? No, I don't hear nothin'.

SHRDLU. The people here say that the music never stops.

ZERO. They're kiddin' you.

SHRDLU. Do you think so?

ZERO. Sure thing. There ain't a sound.

SHRDLU. Perhaps. They're capable of anything. But I haven't told you of the bitterest of my disappointments.

ZERO. Well, spill it. I'm gettin' used to hearin' bad news.

SHRDLU. When I came to this place, my first thought was to find my dear mother. I wanted to ask her forgiveness. And I wanted her to help me to understand.

ZERO. An' she couldn't do it?

SHRDLU (*with a deep groan*). She's not here! Mr. Zero! Here where only the most favoured dwell, that wisest and purest of spirits is nowhere to be found. I don't understand it.

A WOMAN'S VOICE (*in the distance*). Mr. Zero! Oh, Mr. Zero!

(ZERO *raises his head and listens attentively*).

SHRDLU (*going on, unheedingly*). If you were to see some of the people here—the things they do—

ZERO (*interrupting*). Wait a minute, will you? I think somebody's callin' me.

THE VOICE (*somewhat nearer*). Mr. Ze-ro! Oh! Mr. Ze-ro!

ZERO. Who the hell's that now? I wonder if the wife's on my trail already. That would be swell, wouldn't it? An' I figured on her bein' good for another twenty years, anyhow.

THE VOICE (*nearer*). Mr. Ze-ro! Yoo-hoo!

ZERO. No. That ain't her voice.

(*calling, savagely.*) Yoo-hoo. (*To* SHRDLU.) Ain't that always the way? Just when a guy is takin' life easy an' havin' a good time! (*He rises and looks off left.*) Here she comes, whoever she is. (*In sudden amazement.*) Well, I'll be—! Well, what do you know about that!

(*He stands looking in wonderment, as* DAISY DIANA DOROTHEA DEVORE *enters. She wears a much-beruffled white muslin dress which is a size too small and fifteen years too youthful for her. She is red-faced and breathless.*)

DAISY (*panting*). Oh! I thought I'd never catch up to you. I've been followin' you for days—callin' an' callin'. Didn't you hear me?

ZERO. Not till just now. You look kinda winded.

DAISY. I sure am. I can't hardly catch my breath.

ZERO. Well, sit down an' take a load off your feet. (*He leads her to the tree.*)

(DAISY *sees* SHRDLU *for the first time and shrinks back a little.*)

ZERO. It's all right, he's a friend of mine. (*To* SHRDLU.) Buddy, I want you to meet my friend, Miss Devore.

SHRDLU (*rising and extending his hand courteously*). How do you do, Miss Devore?

DAISY (*self-consciously*). How do!

ZERO (*to* DAISY). He's a friend of mine. (*To* SHRDLU.) I guess you don't mind if she sits here a while an' cools off, do you?

SHRDLU. No, no, certainly not.

(*They all seat themselves under the tree.* ZERO *and* DAISY *are a little self-conscious.* SHRDLU *gradually becomes absorbed in his own thoughts.*)

ZERO. I was just takin' a rest myself. I took my shoes off on account of my feet bein' so sore.

DAISY. Yeh, I'm kinda tired, too. (*Looking about*). Say, ain't it pretty here, though?

ZERO. Yeh, it is at that.

DAISY. What do they call this place?

ZERO. Why—er—let's see. He was tellin' me just a minute ago. The—er—I don't know. Some kind o' fields. I forget now. (*To* SHRDLU). Say, Buddy, what do they call this place again? (SHRDLU, *absorbed in his thoughts, does not hear him. To* DAISY). He don't hear me. He's thinkin' again.

DAISY (*sotto voce*). What's the matter with him?

ZERO. Why, he's the guy that murdered his mother—remember?

DAISY (*interested*). Oh, yeh! Is that him?

ZERO. Yeh. An' he had it all figgered out how they was goin' t' roast him or somethin'. And now they ain't goin' to do nothin' to him an' it's kinda got his goat.

DAISY (*sympathetically*). Poor feller!

ZERO. Yeh. He takes it kinda hard.

DAISY. He looks like a nice young feller.

ZERO. Well, you sure are good for sore eyes. I never expected to see you here.

DAISY. I thought maybe you'd be kinda surprised.

ZERO. Surprised is right. I thought you was alive an' kickin'. When did you pass out?

DAISY. Oh, right after you did—a coupla days.

ZERO (*interested*). Yeh? What happened? Get hit by a truck or somethin'?

DAISY. No. (*Hesitantly.*) You see—it's this way. I blew out the gas.

ZERO (*astonished*). Go on! What was the big idea?

DAISY (*falteringly*). Oh, I don't know. You see, I lost my job.

ZERO. I'll bet you're sorry you did it now, ain't you?

DAISY (*with conviction*). No, I ain't sorry. Not a bit. (*Then hesitantly*). Say, Mr. Zero, I been thinkin'— (*she stops.*)

ZERO. What?

DAISY (*plucking up courage*). I been thinkin' it would be kinda nice—if you an' me—if we could kinda talk things over.

ZERO. Yeh. Sure. What do you want to talk about?

DAISY. Well—I don't know—but you and me—we ain't really ever talked things over, have we?

ZERO. No, that's right, we ain't. Well, let's go to it.

DAISY. I was thinkin' if we could be alone—just the two of us, see?

ZERO. Oh, yeh! Yeh, I get you. (*He turns to* SHRDLU *and coughs loudly.* SHRDLU *does not stir.*)

ZERO (*to* DAISY). He's dead to the world. (*He turns to* SHRDLU). Say, Buddy! (*No answer*). Say, Buddy!

SHRDLU (*looking up with a start*). Were you speaking to me?

ZERO. Yeh. How'd you guess it? I was thinkin' that maybe you'd like to walk around a little and look for your mother.

SHRDLU (*shaking his head*). It's no use. I've looked everywhere. (*He relapses into thought again*).

ZERO. Maybe over there they might know.

SHRDLU. No, no! I've searched everywhere. She's not here.

(ZERO *and* DAISY *look at each other in despair.*)

ZERO. Listen, old shirt, my friend here and me—see?—we used to work in the same store. An' we got some things to talk over—business, see?—kinda confidential. So if it ain't askin' too much—

SHRDLU (*springing to his feet*). Why, certainly! Excuse me!

(*He bows politely to* DAISY *and walks off.* DAISY *and* ZERO *watch him until he has disappeared.*)

ZERO (*with a forced laugh*). He's a good guy at that.

(*Now that they are alone, both are very self-conscious, and for a time they sit in silence.*)

DAISY (*breaking the silence*). It sure is pretty here, ain't it?

ZERO. Sure is.

DAISY. Look at the flowers! Ain't they just perfect! Why, you'd think they was artifical, wouldn't you?

ZERO. Yeh, you would.

DAISY. And the smell of them. Like perfume.

ZERO. Yeh.

DAISY. I'm crazy about the country, ain't you?

ZERO. Yeh. It's nice for a change.

DAISY. Them store picnics—remember?

ZERO. You bet. They sure was fun.

DAISY. One time—I guess you don't remember—the two of us—me and you—we sat down on the grass together under a tree—just like we're doin' now.

ZERO. Sure I remember.

DAISY. Go on! I'll bet you don't.

ZERO. I'll bet I do. It was the year the wife didn't go.

DAISY (*her face brightening*). That's right! I didn't think you'd remember.

ZERO. An' comin' home we sat together in the truck.

DAISY (*eagerly, rather shamefacedly*). Yeh! There's somethin' I've always wanted to ask you.

ZERO. Well, why didn't you?

DAISY. I don't know. It didn't seem refined. But I'm goin' to ask you now, anyhow.

ZERO. Go ahead. Shoot.

DAISY (*falteringly*). Well—while we was comin' home—you put your arm up on the bench behind me—and I could feel your knee kinda pressin' against mine. (*She stops.*)

ZERO (*becoming more and more interested*). Yeh—well—what about it?

DAISY. What I wanted to ask you was —was it just kinda accidental?

ZERO (*with a laugh*). Sure it was accidental. Accidental on purpose.

DAISY (*eagerly*). Do you mean it?

ZERO. Sure I mean it. You mean to say you didn't know it?

DAISY. No. I've been wantin' to ask you—

ZERO. Then why did you get sore at me?

DAISY. Sore? I wasn't sore! When was I sore?

ZERO. That night. Sure you was sore. If you wasn't sore why did you move away?

DAISY. Just to see if you meant it. I thought if you meant it you'd move up closer. An' then when you took your arm away I was sure you didn't mean it.

ZERO. An' I thought all the time you was sore. That's why I took my arm away. I thought if I moved up you'd holler and then I'd be in a jam, like you read in the paper all the time about guys gettin' pulled in for annoyin' women.

DAISY. An' I was wishin' you'd put your arm around me—just sittin' there wishin' all the way home.

ZERO. What do you know about that? That sure is hard luck, that is. If I'd 'a' only knew! You know what I felt like doin'—only I didn't have the nerve?

DAISY. What?

ZERO. I felt like kissin' you.

DAISY (*fervently*). I wanted you to.

ZERO (*astonished*). You would 'a' let me?

DAISY. I wanted you to! I wanted you to! Oh, why didn't you—why didn't you?

ZERO. I didn't have the nerve. I sure was a dumbbell.

DAISY. I would 'a' let you all you wanted to. I wouldn't 'a' cared. I know it would 'a' been wrong but I wouldn't 'a' cared. I wasn't thinkin' about right an' wrong at all. I didn't care—see? I just wanted you to kiss me.

ZERO (*feelingly*). If I'd only knew. I wanted to do it, I swear I did. But I didn't think you cared nothin' about me.

DAISY (*passionately*). I never cared nothin' about nobody else.

ZERO. Do you mean it—on the level? You ain't kiddin' me, are you?

DAISY. No, I ain't kiddin'. I mean it. I'm tellin' you the truth. I ain't never had the nerve to tell you before—but now I don't care. It don't make no difference now. I mean it—every word of it.

ZERO (*dejectedly*). If I'd only knew it.

DAISY. Listen to me. There's somethin' else I want to tell you. I may as well tell you everything now. It don't make no difference now. About my blowin' out the gas—see? Do you know why I done it?

ZERO. Yeh, you told me—on account o' bein' canned.

DAISY. I just told you that. That ain't the real reason. The real reason is on account o' you.

ZERO. You mean to say on account o' me passin' out—?

DAISY. Yeh. That's it. I didn't want to go on livin'. What for? What did I want to go on livin' for? I didn't have nothin' to live for with you gone. I often thought of doin' it before. But I never had the nerve. An' anyhow I didn't want to leave you.

ZERO. An' me bawlin' you out, about readin' too fast an' readin' too slow.

DAISY (*reproachfully*). Why did you do it?

ZERO. I don't know, I swear I don't. I was always stuck on you. An' while I'd be addin' them figgers, I'd be thinkin' how if the wife died, you an' me could get married.

DAISY. I used to think o' that, too.

ZERO. An' then before I knew it, I was bawlin' you out.

DAISY. Them was the times I'd think o' blowin' out the gas. But I never did till you was gone. There wasn't nothin' to live for then. But it wasn't so easy to do, anyhow. I never could stand the smell o' gas. An' all the while I was gettin' ready, you know, stuffin' up all the cracks, the way you read about in

the paper—I was thinkin' of you and hopin' that maybe I'd meet you again. An' I made up my mind if I ever did see you, I'd tell you.

ZERO (*taking her hand*). I'm sure glad you did. I'm sure glad. (*Ruefully*). But it don't do much good now, does it?

DAISY. No, I guess it don't. (*Summoning courage*.) But there's one thing I'm goin' to ask you.

ZERO. What's that?

DAISY (*in a low voice*). I want you to kiss me.

ZERO. You bet I will! (*He leans over and kisses her cheek*).

DAISY. Not like that. I don't mean like that. I mean really kiss me. On the mouth. I ain't never been kissed like that.

(ZERO *puts his arms about her and presses his lips to hers. A long embrace. At last they separate and sit side by side in silence.*)

DAISY (*putting her hands to her cheeks*). So that's what it's like. I didn't know it could be like that. I didn't know anythin' could be like that.

ZERO (*fondling her hand*). Your cheeks are red. They're all red. And your eyes are shinin'. I never seen your eyes shinin' like that before.

DAISY (*holding up her hand*). Listen—do you hear it? Do you hear the music?

ZERO. No, I don't hear nothin'!

DAISY. Yeh—music. Listen an' you'll hear it.

(*They are both silent for a moment.*)

ZERO (*excitedly*). Yeh! I hear it! He said there was music, but I didn't hear it till just now.

DAISY. Ain't it grand?

ZERO. Swell! Say, do you know what?

DAISY. What?

ZERO. It makes me feel like dancin'.

DAISY. Yeh? Me, too.

ZERO (*springing to his feet*). Come on! Let's dance! (*He seizes her hands and tries to pull her up.*)

DAISY (*resisting laughingly*). I can't dance. I ain't danced in twenty years.

ZERO. That's nothin'. I ain't, neither. Come on! I feel just like a kid!

(*He pulls her to her feet and seizes her about the waist.*)

DAISY. Wait a minute! Wait till I fix my skirt. (*She turns back her skirts and pins them above the ankles.*)

(ZERO *seizes her about the waist. They dance clumsily but with gay abandon.*

DAISY's *hair becomes loosened and tumbles over her shoulders. She lends herself more and more to the spirit of the dance. But* ZERO *soon begins to tire and dances with less and less zest.*)

ZERO (*stopping at last, panting for breath*). Wait a minute! I'm all winded.

(*He releases* DAISY, *but before he can turn away, she throws her arms about him and presses her lips to his.*

ZERO (*freeing himself*). Wait a minute! Let me get my wind!

(*He limps to the tree and seats himself under it, gasping for breath.* DAISY *looks after him, her spirits rather dampened.*)

ZERO. Whew! I sure am winded! I ain't used to dancin'.

(*He takes off his collar and tie and opens the neckband of his shirt.* DAISY *sits under the tree near him, looking at him longingly. But he is busy catching his breath.*)

Gee, my heart's goin' a mile a minute.

DAISY. Why don't you lay down an' rest? You could put your head on my lap.

ZERO. That ain't a bad idea.

(*He stretches out, his head in* DAISY's *lap.*)

DAISY (*fondling his hair*). It was swell, wasn't it?

ZERO. Yeh. But you gotta be used to it.

DAISY. Just imagine if we could stay here all the time—you an' me together—wouldn't it be swell?

ZERO. Yeh. But there ain't a chance.

DAISY. Won't they let us stay?

ZERO. No. This place is only for the good ones.

DAISY. Well, we ain't so bad, are we?

ZERO. Go on! Me a murderer an' you committin' suicide. Anyway, they wouldn't stand for this—the way we been goin' on.

DAISY. I don't see why.

ZERO. You don't! You know it ain't right. Ain't I got a wife?

DAISY. Not any more you ain't. When you're dead that ends it. Don't they always say "until death do us part?"

ZERO. Well, maybe you're right about that but they wouldn't stand for us here.

DAISY. It would be swell—the two of us together—we could make up for all them years.

ZERO. Yeh, I wish we could.

DAISY. We sure were fools. But I don't care. I've got you now. (*She kisses his forehead and cheeks and mouth.*)

ZERO. I'm sure crazy about you. I never saw you lookin' so pretty before, with your cheeks all red. An' your hair hangin' down. You got swell hair. (*He fondles and kisses her hair.*)

DAISY (*ecstatically*). We got each other now, ain't we?

ZERO. Yeh. I'm crazy about you. Daisy! That's a pretty name. It's a flower, ain't it? Well—that's what you are—just a flower.

DAISY (*happily*). We can always be together now, can't we?

ZERO. As long as they'll let us. I sure am crazy about you. (*Suddenly he sits upright*). Watch your step!

DAISY (*alarmed*). What's the matter?

ZERO (*nervously*). He's comin' back.

DAISY. Oh, is that all? Well, what about it?

ZERO. You don't want him to see us layin' around like this, do you?

DAISY. I don't care if he does.

ZERO. Well, you oughta care. You don't want him to think you ain't a refined girl, do you? He's an awful moral bird, he is.

DAISY. I don't care nothin' about him. I don't care nothin' about anybody but you.

ZERO. Sure, I know. But we don't want people talkin' about us. You better fix your hair an' pull down your skirts.

(DAISY *complies rather sadly. They are both silent as* SHRDLU *enters.*)

ZERO (*with feigned nonchalance*). Well, you got back all right, didn't you?

SHRDLU. I hope I haven't returned too soon.

ZERO. No, that's all right. We were just havin' a little talk. You know—about business an' things.

DAISY (*boldly*). We were wishin' we could stay here all the time.

SHRDLU. You may if you like.

ZERO AND DAISY (*in astonishment*). What!

SHRDLU. Yes. Any one who likes may remain—

ZERO. But I thought you were tellin' me—

SHRDLU. Just as I told you, only the most favored do remain. But anyone may.

ZERO. I don't get it. There's a catch in it somewheres.

DAISY. It don't matter as long as we can stay.

ZERO (*to* SHRDLU). We were thinkin'

about gettin' married, see?

SHRDLU. You may or not, just as you like.

ZERO. You don't mean to say we could stay if we didn't, do you?

SHRDLU. Yes. They don't care.

ZERO. An' there's some here that ain't married?

SHRDLU. Yes.

ZERO (*to* DAISY). I don't know about this place, at that. They must be kind of a mixed crowd.

DAISY. It don't matter, so long as we got each other.

ZERO. Yeh, I know, but you don't want to mix with people that ain't respectable.

DAISY (*to* SHRDLU). Can we get married right away? I guess there must be a lot of ministers here, ain't there?

SHRDLU. Not as many as I had hoped to find. The two who seem most beloved are Dean Swift and the Abbé Rabelais. They are both much admired for some indecent tales which they have written.

ZERO (*shocked*). What! Ministers writin' smutty stories! Say, what kind of a dump is this, anyway?

SHRDLU (*despairingly*). I don't know, Mr. Zero. All these people here are so strange, so unlike the good people I've known. They seem to think of nothing but enjoyment or of wasting their time in profitless occupations. Some paint pictures from morning until night, or carve blocks of stone. Others write songs or put words together, day in and day out. Still others do nothing but lie under the trees and look at the sky. There are men who spend all their time reading books and women who think only of adorning themselves. And forever they are telling stories and laughing and singing and drinking and dancing. There are drunkards, thieves, vagabonds, blasphemers, adulterers. There is one—

ZERO. That's enough. I heard enough. (*He seats himself and begins putting on his shoes.*)

DAISY (*anxiously*). What are you goin' to do?

ZERO. I'm goin' to beat it, that's what I'm goin' to do.

DAISY. You said you liked it here.

ZERO (*looking at her in amazement*). Liked it! Say, you don't mean to say you want to stay here, do you, with a lot of rummies an' loafers an' bums?

DAISY. We don't have to bother with them. We can just sit here together an' look at the flowers an' listen to the music.

SHRDLU (*eagerly*). Music! Did you hear music?

DAISY. Sure. Don't you hear it?

SHRDLU. No, they say it never stops. But I've never heard it.

ZERO (*listening*). I thought I heard it before but I don't hear nothin' now. I guess I must 'a' been dreamin'. (*Looking about*). What's the quickest way out of this place?

DAISY (*pleadingly*). Won't you stay just a little longer?

ZERO. Didn't yer hear me say I'm goin'? Good-bye, Miss Devore. I'm goin' to beat it.

(*He limps off at the right.* DAISY *follows him slowly.*)

DAISY (*to* SHRDLU). I won't ever see him again.

SHRDLU. Are you goin' to stay here?

DAISY. It don't make no difference now. Without him I might as well be alive.

(*She goes off right.* SHRDLU *watches her a moment, then sighs, and seating himself under the tree, buries his head on his arm. Curtain falls.*)

SCENE EIGHT

SCENE: *Before the curtain rises the clicking of an adding machine is heard. The curtain rises upon an office similar in appearance to that in* SCENE TWO *except that there is a door in the back wall through which can be seen a glimpse of the corridor outside. In the middle of the room* ZERO *is seated completely absorbed in the operation of an adding machine. He presses the keys and pulls the lever with mechanical precision. He still wears his full-dress suit but he has added to it sleeve protectors and a green eyeshade. A strip of white paper-tape flows steadily from the machine as* ZERO *operates. The room is filled with this tape—streamers, festoons, billows of it everywhere. It covers the floor and the furniture, it climbs the walls and chokes the doorways. A few moments later,* LIEUTENANT CHARLES *and* JOE *enter at the left.* LIEUTENANT CHARLES *is middle-aged and inclined to corpulence. He has an air of world-weariness. He is bare-footed, wears a Panama hat, and is dressed in bright red tights which are a very bad fit—too tight in some places, badly wrinkled in others.* JOE *is a youth with a smutty face dressed in dirty blue overalls.*

CHARLES (*after contemplating* ZERO *for a few moments*). All right, Zero, cease firing.

ZERO (*looking up, surprised*). Whaddja say?

CHARLES. I said stop punching that machine.

ZERO (*bewildered*). Stop? (*He goes on working mechanically.*)

CHARLES (*impatiently*). Yes. Can't you stop? Here, Joe, give me a hand. He can't stop.

(JOE *and* CHARLES *each take one of* ZERO's *arms and with enormous effort detach him from the machine. He resists passively—mere inertia. Finally they succeed and swing him around on his stool.* CHARLES *and* JOE *mop their foreheads.*)

ZERO (*querulously*). What's the idea? Can't you lemme alone?

CHARLES (*ignoring the question*). How long have you been here?

ZERO. Jes' twenty-five years. Three hundred months, ninety-one hundred and thirty-one days, one hundred thirty-six thousand—

CHARLES (*impatiently*). That'll do! That'll do!

ZERO (*proudly*). I ain't missed a day, not an hour, not a minute. Look at all I got done. (*He points to the maze of paper.*)

CHARLES. It's time to quit.

ZERO. Quit? Whaddye mean quit? I ain't goin' to quit!

CHARLES. You've got to.

ZERO. What for? What do I have to quit for?

CHARLES. It's time for you to go back.

ZERO. Go back where? Whaddya talkin' about?

CHARLES. Back to earth, you dub. Where do you think?

ZERO. Aw, go on, Cap, who are you kiddin'?

CHARLES. I'm not kidding anybody. And don't call me Cap. I'm a lieutenant.

ZERO. All right, Lieutenant, all right. But what's this you're tryin' to tell me about goin' back?

CHARLES. Your time's up, I'm telling you. You must be pretty thick. How many times do you want to be told a thing?

ZERO. This is the first time I heard about goin' back. Nobody ever said nothin' to me about it before.

CHARLES. You didn't think you were going to stay here forever, did you?

ZERO. Sure. Why not? I did my bit, didn't I? Forty-five years of it. Twenty-five years in the store. Then the boss canned me and I knocked him cold. I guess you ain't heard about that—

CHARLES (*interrupting*). I know all about that. But what's that got to do with it?

ZERO. Well, I done my bit, didn't I? That oughta let me out.

CHARLES (*jeeringly*). So you think you're all through, do you?

ZERO. Sure, I do. I did the best I could while I was there and then I passed out. And now I'm sittin' pretty here.

CHARLES. You've got a fine idea of the way they run things, you have. Do you think they're going to all of the trouble of making a soul just to use it once?

ZERO. Once is often enough, it seems to me.

CHARLES. It seems to you, does it? Well, who are you? And what do you know about it? Why, man, they use a soul over and over again—over and over until it's worn out.

ZERO. Nobody ever told me.

CHARLES. So you thought you were all through, did you? Well, that's a hot one, that is.

ZERO (*sullenly*). How was I to know?

CHARLES. Use your brains! Where would we put them all? We're crowded enough as it is. Why, this place is nothing but a kind of repair and service station—a sort of cosmic laundry, you might say. We get the souls in here by the bushelful. Then we get busy and clean them up. And you ought to see some of them. The muck and the slime. Phoo! And as full of holes as a flour-sifter. But we fix them up. We disinfect them and give them a kerosene rub and mend the holes and back they go—practically as good as new.

ZERO. You mean to say I've been here before—before the last time, I mean?

CHARLES. Been here before! Why, you poor boob—you've been here thousands of times—fifty thousand, at least.

ZERO (*suspiciously*). How is it I don't remember nothin' about it?

CHARLES. Well—that's partly because you're stupid, But it's mostly because that's the way they fix it. (*Musingly.*) They're funny that way—every now and then they'll do something white like that—when you'd least expect it. I guess economy's at the bottom of it, though. They figure that the souls would get worn out quicker if they remembered.

ZERO. And don't any of 'em remember?

CHARLES. Oh, some do. You see there's different types: there's the type that gets a little better each time it goes back—we just give them a wash and send them right through. Then there's another type—the type that gets a little worse each time. That's where you belong!

ZERO (*offended*). Me? You mean to say I'm gettin' worse all the time?

CHARLES (*nodding*). Yes. A little worse each time.

ZERO. Well—what was I when I started? Somethin' big?—A king or somethin'?

CHARLES (*laughing derisively*). A king! That's a good one! I'll tell you what you were the first time—if you want to know so much—a monkey.

ZERO (*shocked and offended*). A monkey!

CHARLES (*nodding*). Yes, sir—just a hairy, chattering, long-tailed monkey.

ZERO. That musta been a long time ago.

CHARLES. Oh, not so long. A million years or so. Seems like yesterday to me.

ZERO. Then look here, whaddya mean by sayin' I'm gettin' worse all the time?

CHARLES. Just what I said. You weren't so bad as a monkey. Of course, you did just what all the other monkeys did, but still it kept you out in the open air. And you weren't women-shy—there was one little red-headed monkey—Well, never mind. Yes, sir, you weren't so bad then. But even in those days there must have been some bigger and brainier monkey that you kowtowed to. The mark of the slave was on you from the start.

ZERO (*sullenly*). You ain't very partic-ular about what you call people, are you?

CHARLES. You wanted the truth, didn't you? If there ever was a soul in the world that was labeled slave it's yours. Why, all the bosses and kings that there ever were have left their trademarks on your backside.

ZERO. It ain't fair, if you ask me.

CHARLES (*shrugging his shoulders*): Don't tell me about it. I don't make the rules. All I know is you've been getting worse—worse each time. Why, even six thousand years ago you weren't so bad. That was the time you were hauling stones for one of those big pyramids in a place they call Africa. Ever hear of the pyramids?

ZERO. Them big pointy things?

CHARLES (*nodding*). That's it.

ZERO. I seen a picture of them in the movies.

CHARLES. Well, you helped build them. It was a long step down from the happy days in the jungle, but it was a good job—even though you didn't know what you were doing and your back was striped by the foreman's whip. But you've been going down, down. Two thousand years ago you were a Roman galley-slave. You were on one of the triremes that knocked the Carthaginian fleet for a goal. Again the whip. But you had muscles then—chest muscles, back muscles, biceps. (*He feels* ZERO's *arm gingerly and turns away in disgust.*) Phoo! A bunch of mush! (*He notices that* JOE *has fallen asleep. Walking over, he kicks him in the shin.*)

CHARLES. Wake up, you mutt! Where do you think you are! (*He turns to* ZERO *again.*) And then another thousand years and you were a serf—a lump of clay digging up other lumps of clay. You wore an iron collar then—white ones hadn't been invented yet. Another long step down. But where you dug, potatoes grew and that helped fatten the pigs. Which was something. And now—well, I don't want to rub it in—

ZERO. Rub it in is right! Seems to me I got a pretty healthy kick comin'. I ain't had a square deal! Hard work! That's all I've ever had!

CHARLES (*callously*). What else were you ever good for?

ZERO. Well, that ain't the point. The

point is I'm through! I had enough! Let 'em find somebody else to do the dirty work. I'm sick of bein' the goat! I quit right here and now! (*He glares about defiantly. There is a thunderclap and a bright flash of lightning.*)

ZERO (*screaming*). Ooh! What's that? (*He clings to* CHARLES.)

CHARLES. It's all right. Nobody's going to hurt you. It's just their way of telling you that they don't like you to talk that way. Pull yourself together and calm down. You can't change the rules—nobody can—they've got it all fixed. It's a rotten system—but what are you going to do about it?

ZERO. Why can't they stop pickin' on me? I'm satisfied here—doin' my day's work. I don't want to go back.

CHARLES. You've got to, I tell you. There's no way out of it.

ZERO. What chance have I got—at my age? Who'll give me a job?

CHARLES. You big boob, you don't think you're going back the way you are, do you?

ZERO. Sure, how then?

CHARLES. Why, you've got to start all over.

ZERO. All over?

CHARLES (*nodding*). You'll be a baby again—a bald, red-faced little animal, and then you'll go through it all again. There'll be millions of others like you— all with their mouths open, squalling for food. And then when you get a little older you'll begin to learn things—and you'll learn all the wrong things—and learn them all in the wrong way. You'll eat the wrong food and wear the wrong clothes and you'll live in swarming dens where there's no light and no air! You'll learn to be a liar and a bully and a braggart and a coward and a sneak. You'll learn to fear the sunlight and to hate beauty. By that time you'll be ready for school. There they'll tell you the truth about a great many things that you don't give a damn about and they'll tell you lies about all the things you ought to know—and about all the things you want to know they'll tell you nothing at all. When you get through you'll be equipped for your life-work. You'll be ready to take a job.

ZERO (*eagerly*). What'll my job be? Another adding machine?

CHARLES. Yes. But not one of these antiquated adding machines. It will be a superb, super-hyper-adding machine, as far from this old piece of junk as you are from God. It will be something to make you sit up and take notice, that adding machine. It will be an adding machine which will be installed in a coal mine and which will record the individual output of each miner. As each miner down in the lower galleries takes up a shovelful of coal, the impact of his shovel will automatically set in motion a graphite pencil in your gallery. The pencil will make a mark in white upon a blackened, sensitized drum. Then your work comes in. With the great toe of your right foot you release a lever which focuses a violet ray on the drum. The ray playing upon and through the white mark, falls upon a selenium cell which in turn sets the keys of the adding apparatus in motion. In this way the individual output of each miner is recorded without any human effort except the slight pressure of the great toe of your right foot.

ZERO (*in breathless, round-eyed wonder*). Say, that'll be some machine, won't it?

CHARLES. Some machine is right. It will be the culmination of human effort—the final triumph of the evolutionary process. For millions of years the nebulous gases swirled in space. For more millions of years the gases cooled and then through inconceivable ages they hardened into rocks. And then came life. Floating green things on the waters that covered the earth. More millions of years and a step upward—an animate organism in the ancient slime. And so on—step by step, down through the ages—a gain here, a gain there—the mollusc, the fish, the reptile, then mammal, man! And all so that you might sit in the gallery of a coal mine and operate the super-hyper-adding machine with the great toe of your right foot!

ZERO. Well, then—I ain't so bad, after all.

CHARLES. You're a failure, Zero, a failure. A waste product. A slave to a contraption of steel and iron. The animal's instincts, but not his strength and skill. The animal's appetites, but not his unashamed indulgence of them. True, you move and eat and digest and excrete and reproduce. But any microscopic organism can do as much. Well—time's up! Back you go—back to your sunless groove—the raw material of slums and wars—the ready prey of the first jingo or demagogue or political adventurer who takes the trouble to play upon your ignorance and credulity and provincialism. You poor, spineless, brainless boob—I'm sorry for you!

ZERO (*falling to his knees*). Then keep me here! Don't send me back! Let me stay!

CHARLES. Get up. Didn't I tell you I can't do anything for you? Come on, time's up!

ZERO. I can't! I can't! I'm afraid to go through it all again.

CHARLES. You've got to, I tell you. Come on, now!

ZERO. What did you tell me so much for? Couldn't you just let me go, thinkin' everythin' was goin' to be all right?

CHARLES. You wanted to know, didn't you?

ZERO. How did I know what you were goin' to tell me? Now I can't stop thinkin' about it! I can't stop thinkin'! I'll be thinkin' about it all the time.

CHARLES. All right! I'll do the best I can for you. I'll send a girl with you to keep you company.

ZERO. A girl? What for? What good will a girl do me?

CHARLES. She'll help make you forget.

ZERO (*eagerly*). She will? Where is she?

CHARLES. Wait a minute, I'll call her. (*He calls in a loud voice.*) Oh! Hope! Yoo-hoo! (*He turns his head aside and says in the manner of a ventriloquist imitating a distant feminine voice.*) Ye-es. (*Then in his own voice.*) Come here, will you? There's a fellow who wants you to take him back. (*Ventriloquously again*). All right. I'll be right over, Charlie dear. (*He turns to* ZERO.) Kind of familiar, isn't she? Charlie dear!

ZERO. What did you say her name is?

CHARLES. Hope. H-o-p-e.

ZERO. Is she good-lookin'?

CHARLES. Is she good-looking! Oh, boy, wait until you see her! She's a

blonde with big blue eyes and red lips and little white teeth and—

ZERO. Say, that listens good to me. Will she be long?

CHARLES. She'll be here right away. There she is now! Do you see her?

ZERO. No. Where?

CHARLES. Out in the corridor. No, not there. Over farther. To the right. Don't you see her blue dress? And the sunlight on her hair?

ZERO. Oh, sure! Now I see her! What's the matter with me, anyhow? Say, she's some jane! Oh, you baby vamp!

CHARLES. She'll make you forget your troubles.

ZERO. What troubles are you talkin' about?

CHARLES. Nothing. Go on. Don't keep her waiting.

ZERO. You bet I won't! Oh, Hope! Wait for me! I'll be right with you! I'm on my way! (*He stumbles out eagerly.*)

(JOE *bursts into uproarious laughter.*)

CHARLES (*eyeing him in surprise and anger*). What in hell's the matter with you?

JOE (*shaking with laughter*). Did you get that? He thinks he saw somebody and he's following her! (*He rocks with laughter.*)

CHARLES (*punching him in the jaw*). Shut your face!

JOE (*nursing his jaw*). What's the idea? Can't I even laugh when I see something funny?

CHARLES. Funny! You keep your mouth shut or I'll show you something funny. Go on, hustle out of here and get something to clean up this mess with. There's another fellow moving in. Hurry now.

(*He makes a threatening gesture.* JOE *exits hastily.* CHARLES *goes to chair and seats himself. He looks weary and dispirited.*)

CHARLES (*shaking his head*). Hell, I'll tell the world this is a lousy job! (*He takes a flask from his pocket, uncorks it, and slowly drains it.*)

CURTAIN

GREEN GROW THE LILACS
Lynn Riggs
Dedicated to Barrett H. Clark

Green Grow the Lilacs was produced by the Theatre Guild at the Guild Theatre on January 26, 1931. The play was staged by Herbert J. Biberman, with settings by Raymond Sovey. The cast was as follows:

CURLY MC CLAIN . . . . . Franchot Tone
AUNT ELLER MURPHY . . . Helen Westley
LAUREY WILLIAMS . . . . June Walker
JEETER FRY . . . . Richard Hale
ADO ANNIE CARNES . Ruth Chorpenning
A PEDDLER . . . . Lee Strasberg
OLD MAN PECK . . . . Tex Cooper
A COWBOY . . . . Woodward Ritter
ANOTHER COWBOY . . . . Paul Ravell

AN OLD FARMER . . . . . William T. Hays
A YOUNG FARMER . . . . . . A. L. Bartolot
MARTHY . . . . Jane Alden
FIDDLER . . . . William Chosnyk

BANJO PLAYER . . . . . Everett Cheetham
OTHER FARMERS . . . Carl Beasley, Joe Wilson, Roy Ketcham, Gordon Bryant, Everett Cheetham, Elmo Carr, Tommy Pladgett.
COWBOYS . . . Slim Cavanaugh, Chick Hannan, Norton Worden, Jack Miller, Pete Schwartz, J. B. Hubbard.
GIRLS . . . Jean Wood, Lois Lindon, Orlanda Lee, Alice Frost, Faith Hope, Eleanor Powers, Peggy Hannan.

Green Grow the Lilacs is laid in Indian Territory in 1900. Oklahoma, which was admitted to the Union as a state in 1907, was formed by combining Indian and Oklahoma Territories.

SCENE ONE: The "front" or living room of the Williams' farmhouse, a June morning.
SCENE TWO: Laurey's bedroom.
SCENE THREE: The smokehouse. (Scenes Two and Three are simultaneous.)

SCENE FOUR: The porch of Old. Man Peck's house, that night.
SCENE FIVE: The hayfield, a month later.
SCENE SIX: The "front" room, three nights later.

The author added the following note to the published play: "This reading version of Green Grow the Lilacs is a little fuller, a little more complete, especially in Scenes Five and Six than the version so admirably produced by the Theatre Guild."

Copyright 1930, 1931, by Lynn Riggs.
Copyright 1957, 1958 (in renewal), by Howard E. Reinheimer, Executor.
All rights reserved.

CAUTION: Professionals and amateurs are hereby warned that Green Grow the Lilacs, being fully protected under the Copyright Laws of the United States of America, the British Empire, including the Dominion of Canada, and all other countries of the Copyright Union, is subject to a royalty. All rights, including professional, amateur, motion pictures, recitation, public reading, radio and television broadcasting, and the rights of translation into foreign languages, are strictly reserved. Amateurs may produce this play upon payment of a royalty of Fifty Dollars for each performance one week before the play is to be given to Samuel French, Inc., at 25 W. 45th St., New York 36, N.Y., or 7623 Sunset Blvd., Hollywood 46, Cal., or if in Canada to Samuel French (Canada) Ltd., at 27 Grenville St., Toronto, Ont.

The songs in Green Grow the Lilacs are old and traditional. The specific acknowledgments concerning the arrangements used are to:

Margaret Larkin for Sam Hall, Hello, Girls, I Wish I Was Single Again, and Home on the Range. (From her collection Singing Cowboy, published by Alfred A. Knopf.)
Oscar J. Fox for Goodbye, Old Paint (published by Carl Fischer).
Everett Cheetham for Strawberry Roan and Blood on the Saddle.
The Company of Green Grow the Lilacs for Chisholm Trail and Next Big River.
The other songs are from the original script of the play.

Lynn Riggs was one of the most gifted writers ever to write for the American stage, to which he brought a vivid memory, a compassionate spirit, and a poet's soul. It was impossible for him to cut his cloth to the requirements of show business, and I cannot recall anything he ever wrote, including scripts that failed to reach Broadway, to which it was possible to attribute anything less than total integrity of observation and imagination. If he had but meager success in the metropolitan market place in many years of arduous writing for the stage, he had, however, at least one compensation. He was held in high esteem as an artist whether his plays succeeded or failed. With his lively yet fine regional feeling, he also helped to give the American theatre some status for a while as a national institution rooted in the land, rather than a big-city lottery. Toward the end of his life, he had the satisfaction of seeing his folk-play *Green Grow the Lilacs* become one of the most successful and estimable musical comedies of the American theatre. The royalties accruing to him from *Oklahoma!*, which Rodgers and Hammerstein derived from *Green Grow the Lilacs*, probably also compensated him for the many apparently lean years when Broadway remained apathetic toward his singular talent, which often struck New Yorkers as somewhat esoteric and considerably withdrawn.

Born in 1899 in Indian Territory, which became part of the state of Oklahoma when he was eight, Lynn Riggs came honestly by his regionalism. His father had been a cowboy and had become a farmer. The boy worked on the farm, and the first time he left the region for a big city, it was on a train taking cattle to Chicago. A feeling for the land and its robust, dialect-speaking people never left this country-bred writer. Evidently, however, he felt an early attraction to the theatre, too. He worked as a singer in a local movie theatre, and after Chicago, he moved on to New York to investigate the possibilities of building a career. Making no particular headway there (he read proofs and worked successively for Macy's and the American Express Company), he returned to Oklahoma and found a job on the Tulsa Oil and Gas Journal. Then he entered the University of Oklahoma and spent three years seeking an education and writing verse in great quantities. He published a volume of his early poetry under the title *The Iron Dish*.

Lynn Riggs had his first New York production at Richard Boleslavsky's "Laboratory Theatre." The play, a love-tragedy entitled *Big Lake*, had no success, but it called attention to its author's nascent talent. Another play by Riggs, *Sumpin' Like Wings*, was staged at the Detroit Playhouse and sold to Broadway producers three times—without getting a production there during the Depression that was in full swing by 1930. Still another, *A Lantern to See By*, had much the same fate at this time; it was optioned for production but did not reach Broadway. Still, Riggs made his debut there in 1930 when the distinguished New York producer Arthur Hopkins produced his colorful and robust frontier comedy *Roadside*. This rather overstrained play was a failure, but its author was pronounced one of the most promising of young American playwrights. He received a Guggenheim Fellowship, went to France for a year, and while there completed *Green Grow the Lilacs*, a colorful, if somewhat lagging, love story set in Oklahoma at the turn of the century. The Theatre Guild, then at the height of its prestige, accepted this folk-play and gave it a rousing production, with many authentic cowboys in the cast collected by the Guild's casting director, Cheryl Crawford. The production added to Riggs's reputation, but it failed to rouse the public to sufficient fervor, although it did run for 64 performances and went on tour. It was to be remembered by the late Theresa Helburn of the Theatre Guild when she started looking around for a good subject for a musical comedy. She arranged a match between Richard Rodgers, whose brilliant librettist Lorenz Hart was failing in health, and Oscar Hammerstein II, who hadn't had a success in ten years. The fabulous result of this collaboration, in 1943, was *Oklahoma!*, the most successful musical in the American theatre; it brought a deserved resurrection to *Green Grow the Lilacs* while its author was serving with the Army Air Forces in World War II.

Mr. Riggs prefaced the published *Green Grow the Lilacs* with some extremely pertinent notations that assist appreciation of the text. They may also have helped the creators of *Oklahoma!* in arriving at the tone and color of their glowing musical treatment. Remarking that his play might well have been retitled *An Old Song*, Riggs wrote that his intent had been "to recapture in a kind of nostalgic glow . . . the great range of mood which characterized the old folk songs and ballads" he used to hear in his Oklahoma childhood—"their quaintness, their sadness, their robustness, their simplicity, their hearty or bawdy humors, their sentimentalities, their melodrama, their touching sweetness." For this reason he considered it wise "to throw away the conventions of ordinary theatricality—a complex plot, swift action, etc.—and try to exhibit luminously, in the simplest of stories, a wide area of mood and feeling." He said he thought of the first three scenes as "The Characters" and the last three scenes as "The Play"—so that "after the people are known . . . I let them go ahead acting out their simple tale, which might have been the substance of an ancient song."

Mr. Riggs was not idle during the interim between his 1931 and 1943 Theatre Guild productions. A collection of his one-acters called *The Cherokee Night* richly represented the life of people of Indian descent in the Southwest; the play was produced by Jasper Deeter at his Hedgerow Theatre near Philadelphia, where another play by Riggs, *The Son of Perdition*, was staged. *The Cherokee Night* was also staged at the University of Iowa and by the Federal Theatre in New York in 1935. In 1936, the playwright got a moderately successful Broadway production for his *Russet Mantle*, a delicate comedy of romance under unfavorable economic circumstances. This Depression comedy had a run of 117 performances in New York and was also staged in little theatres across the country. His other plays, however, missed success, although one of them, *The Cream in the Well*, produced on Broadway by Martin Gabel in 1941, had affecting characterization and atmosphere. Luckily he managed to make a living during the lean years by writing for Hollywood when he was not secluded in Santa Fe working on his plays.

"A playwright, to be any good," Lynn Riggs once declared, "must also be a poet—and use whatever he has of a poet's equipment to see more clearly and to reveal more eloquently than ever before." He tried to live by this belief, and it removed him from Broadway more often than it brought him to the Main Stem. Even *Green Grow the Lilacs*, a Southwest idyl, removed him until *Oklahoma!* brought him reflected glory and a share of bumper royalties. He took up residence then on Shelter Island, off Long Island, and lived there, for the most part, until his untimely death in a New York City hospital on June 30, 1954.

SCENE ONE

It is a radiant summer morning several years ago, the kind of morning which, enveloping the shapes of earth—men, cattle in a meadow, blades of the young corn, streams—makes them seem to exist now for the first time, their images giving off a visible golden emanation that is partly true and partly a trick of imagination focusing to keep alive a loveliness that may pass away.

The unearthly sunlight pours through the crocheted curtains of a window in the living room—the "front room"—of a farmhouse in Indian Territory. It rests upon, and glorifies, scrubbed floors of oak, bright rag rugs, rough hide-bottomed hairy chairs, a rock fireplace, a settee, an old organ magnificently mirrored, ancestral enlargements in their gilt and oval frames. A double sliding door of pine, now closed, is at the back of the room; other heavier doors of oak lead to other parts of the house and to the outside. Somewhere a dog barks twice and stops quickly, reassured; a turkey gobbler makes his startled, swallowing noise.

And, like the voice of the morning, a rich male voice outside somewhere begins to sing.

———

VOICE

As I walked out one bright sunny
              morning,
I saw a cowb⌐ way out on the plain.
His hat was u⌐owed back and his
              spurs was a-jingling,
And as I passed by him, he was
              singing this refrain:

Ta whoop ti aye ay, git along, you
              little dogies!
Way out in Wyoming shall be your
              bright home
A-whooping and a-yelling and
              a-driving those dogies,
And a-riding those bronchos that are
              none of my own.

The people all say we're goin' to have
              a picnic,
But I tell you, my boy, they've got 'er
              down wrong,
For 'f it hadn't a-been for those
              troublesome dogies,
I never woulda thought of composing
              this song.

Ta whoop ti aye ay, git along, you
              little dogies!

Way out in Wyoming shall be your
              bright home—
A-whooping and a-yelling and
              a-driving those dogies,
And a-riding those bronchos that are
              none of my own.

(Before the first verse is finished, part of the singer comes into sight at a window—a tall, waggish, curly-headed young cowboy in a checked shirt and a ten-gallon hat. He looks about the room singing. Just as he finishes he withdraws, hearing footsteps. A moment later, AUNT ELLER MURPHY, *a buxom, hearty woman about fifty, with a tall wooden brass-banded churn in her arms, comes in from the kitchen. She puts the churn down quickly by the fireplace, goes over to the window and looks out, squinting. She grins, good-humoredly.)*

AUNT ELLER. Oh, I see you, Mr. Curly McClain! Don't need to be a-hidin' 'hind that horse of your'n. Couldn't hide them feet of your'n even if yer head wasn't showin'. So you may as well come on in.

(She turns away from the window, takes off her apron, and comes back into the room. CURLY *appears again at the window.)*

CURLY. Hi, Aunt Eller.

AUNT ELLER *(shortly)*. Skeer me to death! Whut're you doin' around here?

CURLY. Come a-singin' to you only you never give me no time to finish.

(Their speech is lazy, drawling, not Southern, not "hick"—but rich, half-conscious of its rhythms, its picturesque imagery.)

AUNT ELLER. Go on and finish then. *(She smiles at him.)* You do sing purty, Curly.

CURLY. Nobody never said I didn't.

AUNT ELLER. Yeah, purty. If I wasn't an old womern, and if you wasn't so young and smart-alecky—why, I'd marry you and git you to set around at night and sing to me.

CURLY. No, you wouldn't, neither. If I was to marry—anyone—I wouldn't set around at night a-singin'. They ain't no tellin' *whut* I'd do. But I wouldn't marry you ner none of yer kinfolks, I could he'p it.

AUNT ELLER *(wisely)*. Oh! None of my kinfolks neither, huh?

CURLY. And you c'n tell 'em that, *all* of 'em, includin' that niece of your'n, Miss Laurey Williams, if she's about anywhurs.

AUNT ELLER. Mebbe I will, and mebbe

I won't. Whut you doin' over this-a-way, Curly? Thought you was over at Skidmore's ranch, tother side of Justus. Well, air you comin' in or gonna stay there like a Jack-in-the-box?

(CURLY *vaults into the room. He wears dark trousers stuffed into high boots. His heavy roweled spurs clink against the floor.*)

CURLY (*deliberately*). Aunt Eller, if you was to tell me whur Laurey was at—*whur* would you tell me she was at?

AUNT ELLER. I wouldn't tell you a-tall, less'n you sung me another song.

CURLY. Must think I'm a medicine man a-singin' and passin' the hat around, the way you talk! Got to save my voice, got to take keer of it, so I'll have it. Don't want to do the way ole man Comer done. When he was a kid he squalled so much, and when he was growed he sung so much, now he's a ole man he cain't git a squawk out of him, nary a squawk. 'Cept a whistle. And a whistle don't mean nuthin'—the way a song do.

AUNT ELLER (*unimpressed*). Sing me a song, Curly McClain.

CURLY. Aw, I *cain't* sing now! I *told* you. Not if I tried and tried, and even et cat-gut. And even 'f I drunk the gall of a turkey gobbler's liver, I couldn't sing a-tall.

AUNT ELLER. Liar and a hypocrite and a shikepoke! Ain't I heared you? Jist now. *You sing!* Er I'll run you off the place.

CURLY. I cain't sing, I told you! 'Ceptin' when I'm lonesome. Out in the saddle when it ain't so sunny, er on a dark night close to a fa'r when you feel so lonesome to God you could die. Looky here, you're old, my, you're old, you'd orter be so smart! Whur you been, anyhow, whose side meat you been eatin' all yer life, not to know nobody cain't sing good 'ceptin' when he's lonesome?

AUNT ELLER. Lonesome? Then if I was you I'd be a-singin' and a-singin' then. A long song, with forty 'leven verses and a chorus 'tween ever' verse. Fer as fur as I c'n make out, Laurey ain't payin' you no heed a-tall. You might jist as well be ridin' the rails as ridin' that range of your'n. So sing yer head off, you lonesome dogie, 'cause you shore have got into a lonesome side-pocket 'thout no grass, you dehorned maverick, you!

CURLY. Whut'd I keer about that? (*He takes cigaret papers out of his hat-band, Bull Durham from his shirt pocket, and begins to roll a cigaret, with elaborate unconcern.*)

AUNT ELLER. She goes around with her head some'eres else, don't she?

CURLY. How'd I know? Ain't looked at her nary a time since Christmas.

AUNT ELLER. 'Twasn't yore fault though, if you didn't. (*Jeering, good-naturedly.*) She don't see you, does she, Mr. Adam's Off Ox! You've got onto the wrong side of the wagon tongue!

CURLY. Go on, you mean ole womern! Brand a steer till you burn a hole in his hide!

AUNT ELLER. *Mr.* Cowboy! A-ridin' high, wide, and handsome, his spurs a-jinglin', and the Bull Durham tag a-whippin' outa his pocket! Oh, *Mr.* Cowpuncher! 'Thout no home, ner no wife, ner no one to muss up his curly hair, er keep him warm on a winter's night!

CURLY (*swelling up, defensively*). So she don't take to me much, huh? Whur'd you git sich a uppity niece 'at wouldn't pay no heed to *me?* Who's the best bronc buster in this yere state?

AUNT ELLER. You, I bet.

CURLY. And the best bull-dogger in seventeen counties? *Me*, that's who! And looky here, I'm handsome, ain't I?

AUNT ELLER. Purty as a pitcher.

CURLY. Curly-headed, ain't I? And bow-legged from the saddle fer God knows how long, ain't I?

AUNT ELLER (*agreeing*). Couldn't stop a pig in the road.

CURLY. Well, whut else does she want then, the damn she-mule?

AUNT ELLER. I don't know. But I'm shore sartin it ain't *you*.

CURLY. Anh! Quit it, you'll have me a-cryin'!

AUNT ELLER (*triumphantly*). You better sing me a song then, like I told you to in the first place!

CURLY. Aw, whut'll I sing then?

AUNT ELLER. "A-ridin' ole Paint."

CURLY. And nen whut'll I sing?

AUNT ELLER. Lands, you better git one sung 'fore you start in on another'n!

(*But* CURLY *has already leaned against the wall with his head thrown back, and his feet crossed, and begun to sing in his rich, liquid, mock-heroic voice.*)

CURLY (*singing*).

A-ridin' ole Paint and a-leadin' old Dan,
I'm goin' to Montana for to throw
              the hoolian.

They feed in the hollers and they
          water in the draw,
Their tails are all matted and their
          backs are all raw.

Ride around the little dogies, ride
          around them slow,
For the fiery and the snuffy are
          a-rarin' to go.

Ole Bill Jones had two daughters
          and a son,
One went to Denver and the other
          went wrong,
One was killed in a pool room fight,
But still he goes singing from morn
          till night:

Ride around the little dogies, ride
          around them slow,
For the fiery and the snuffy are
          a-rarin' to go.

When I die take my saddle from
          the wall,
Put it on my pony, lead him out
          of his stall,
Tie my bones to the saddle, turn our
          faces to the west,
And we'll ride the trail that we love best.

Ride around the little dogies, ride
          around them slow,
For the fiery and the snuffy are
          a-rarin' to go.

Now whur's Laurey at?

AUNT ELLER (*pointing*). Settin' in there in her room a-sewin' er sump'n, when she orta be in here a-churnin' like I told her. Ain't you gonna sing another song?

CURLY. Ain't you a bother though—keep on a-pesterin'! You go and tell Laurey to drop a stitch, and see whut Sandy Claus brung her.

AUNT ELLER. Meanin' you, I guess. Whut'd you want with her, Curly, no-how? I'm her aunt, so you better tell me first, and see if I like the looks of it.

CURLY. You're jist nosy. Well, if you have to know my business, ole man Peck over acrost Dog Crick's givin' a play-party and I come to ast if Laurey ud go with me.

AUNT ELLER. And me, too, huh?

CURLY. Yeow, you too. If you'll go and knock on the door there, and bring Laurey out whur a man c'n git a look at her.

AUNT ELLER (*knocking*). Laurey! Peck's is givin' a play-party.

LAUREY (*inside*). Who's givin' a play-party.

AUNT ELLER. Ole man Peck acrost Dog Crick.

LAUREY. Cain't hear a word you say. Who?

AUNT ELLER (*shouting*). Come on out. Someone's come to see you. He'll tell you.

LAUREY. Who's come to see me? Who's givin' a party?

AUNT ELLER. Well, open up the door, you crazy youngun, I cain't holler my head off!

(*The door slides back, and* LAUREY *comes out. She is a fair, spoiled, lovely young girl about eighteen in a long white dress with many ruffles. She sees* CURLY.)

LAUREY. Oh! Thought you was some-body. (*To* AUNT ELLER.) Is this all that's come a-callin' and it a'ready ten o'clock of a Satiddy mornin'?

CURLY (*sullenly*). You knowed it was me 'fore you opened the door.

LAUREY. No sich of a thing.

CURLY. You did, too! You heared my voice and knowed it was me.

LAUREY. I did not, I tell you! Heared a voice a-talkin' rumbly along with Aunt Eller. And heared someone a-singin' like a bullfrog on a pond—

CURLY. I don't talk rumbly. And I don't sing like no bullfrog—

LAUREY. Bullfrog in a pond, I told you. But how'd I know it was you, Mr. Curly McClain? You ain't so special. All men sounds alike to me.

CURLY (*doggedly*). You knowed it was me, so you set in there a-thinkin' up sump'n mean to say. I'm a good mind not to tell you nuthin' about the play-party now. You c'n jist stay at home, for yer tongue. Don't you tell her wheer it is, Aunt Eller. Me'n you'll go and leave her at home.

LAUREY. If you *did* ast me, I wouldn't go with you. Besides, how'd you take me? You ain't bought a new buggy with red wheels onto it, have you?

CURLY. No, I ain't.

LAUREY. And a spankin' team with their bridles all jinglin'?

CURLY. No.

LAUREY. 'Spect me to ride on behind ole Dun, I guess. You better ast that ole Cummins girl you've tuck sich a shine to, over acrost the river.

CURLY. If I was to ast you, they'd be a way to take you, Miss Laurey Smarty.

LAUREY. Oh, they would?

CURLY. A bran' new surrey with fringe on the top four inches long—and *yeller!* And two white horses a-rarin' and faunchin' to go! You'd shore ride like a queen settin' up in *that* carriage! Feel like you had a gold crown set on yer head, 'th diamonds in it big as goose eggs.

LAUREY. Look out, you'll be astin' me in a minute!

CURLY. I ain't astin' you, I'm *tellin'* you. And this yere rig has got four fine side-curtains, case of a rain. And isinglass winders to look out of! And a red and green lamp set on the dashboard, winkin' like a lightnin' bug!

LAUREY. Whur'd you git sich a rig at? (*With explosive laughter.*) Anh, I bet he's went and h'ard it over to Claremore, thinkin' I'd go with him!

CURLY. 'S all you know about it—

LAUREY (*jeering*). Went and h'ard it! Spent all his money h'arin' a rig, and now ain't got nobody to ride in it.

CURLY. Have, too! Did *not* h'ar it. Made the whole thing outa my head—

LAUREY. What! Made it up?

CURLY. Dashboard and all!

LAUREY (*flying at him*). Oh! Git outa the house, you! Aunt Eller, make him git hisself outa here 'fore I take a stove arn to him! Tellin' me lies—!

CURLY (*dodging her*). Makin' up a few —Look out, now! Makin' up a few purties ain't agin no law 'at I know of. Don't you wish they *was* sich a rig, though? Nen you could go to the party and do a hoe-down till mornin' 'f you was a mind to. Nen drive home 'th the sun a-peekin' at you over the ridge, purty and fine.

LAUREY. I ain't wantin' to do no hoe-down till mornin'. And whut would I want to see the sun come up fer, a-peekin' purty and fine—alongside of you, any-how?

AUNT ELLER. Whyn't you jist grab her and kiss her when she acts that-a-way, Curly? She's jist achin' fer you to, I bet.

LAUREY (*with mock fury*). Oh! I won't even *speak* to him, let alone 'low him to kiss me, the braggin', saddle-awk'ard, wish-'t-he-had-a-sweetheart bum! (*She flounces into her room, and bangs the sliding door.*)

AUNT ELLER (*turning to* CURLY, *sagely*). She likes you—quite a little.

CURLY. Whew! 'F she liked me quite a *lot*, she'd sic the dogs onto me, or shoot me full of buckshot!

AUNT ELLER. No, come 'ere, Curly, while I tell you sump'n. A womern that won't let you tetch her 'th a ten foot pole like that is jist dyin' fer you to git closer'n *that* to her.

CURLY. Mebbe. But they's women and women. And some of 'em is accordin' to the rules, and some of 'em ain't never *heared* no rules to be accordin' *to*. Guess I better be movin' my camp some'eres else.

AUNT ELLER. No, look here, Curly. I've knowed Laurey all her born days, ain't I? And since her paw and maw died five years ago, I been paw and maw both to her. And whutever I tell you about her way of feelin' is the truth. Er if it *ain't*, I'll give her a everlastin' good spankin', nen it *will* be! Fer I don't know whur her eyes was set in her head 'f she didn't see you, you purty thing, right from the start, the time you come over of a Sunday a year ago and broke them three broncs all in one evenin', 'thout tetchin' leather er yellin' calf-rope. 'Member?

CURLY (*feeling a little better*). Yeah, I remember. Mean as sin they was, too! That one-eyed un 'th the star in his fore-head liked to set me over his head right smack into them lilac bushes the first crack outa the bucket, didn't he? Yeah, onct I break 'em, they're purty apt to stay broke, fer a fact. (*Cryptically.*) You c'n *count* on a horse. (*Suddenly.*) Look here, Aunt Eller, I wanta know sump'n and if you lie to me, I'll ketch thirteen bulgy-eyed toad-frogs and put 'em in yer bed—

AUNT ELLER. Laws a-mercy!

CURLY. Er make you chew Indian turnip till yer tongue feels like a thousand needles run through it, and no way of pullin' 'em out—

AUNT ELLER. Feel 'em a'ready.

CURLY. Listen, whut low, filthy, sneak-in' man has Laurey got her cap set fer?

AUNT ELLER. You.

CURLY. Now!—

AUNT ELLER. Fer a fact, I'm tellin' you! From the way she flew at you jist now, I got my mind all made up. 'F she don't git *you*, Curly, she'll waste away to the shadder of a pinpoint. Yes, sir. Be put in a sateen coffin dead of a broke heart.

CURLY (*ironically*). I wouldn't want her to do *that*. I'd consider lettin' her *have* me, 'f that ud keep her from dyin'.

AUNT ELLER (*wisely*). She's a young girl—and don't know her mind. She don't know her feelin's. You c'n he'p her, Curly—and they's few that can.

CURLY. They must be plenty of men a-tryin' to spark her. And she shorely leans to one of 'em, now don't she?

AUNT ELLER. Ain't no one a-sparkin' her. Well, they is that ole widder man at Claremore, makes out he's a doctor er a vet'nary. And that fine farmer, Jace Hutchins, jist this side of Lone Ellum—

CURLY. That's whut I thought!

AUNT ELLER. Not to say nuthin' about someone nearer home that's got her on his mind most of the time, till he don't know a plow from a thrashin' machine—

CURLY. Who'd you mean by that?

AUNT ELLER. Jeeter.

CURLY. Jeeter who?

AUNT ELLER. Don't you know Jeeter Fry, our h'ard hand?

CURLY. What! That bullet-colored growly man 'th the bushy eyebrows that's alwys orderin' the other hands how to work the mowin' machine er sump'n!

AUNT ELLER. Now you don't need to go and say nuthin' agin him! He's a big help around here. Jist about runs the farm by hisself. Well, two women couldn't do it, you orta know that.

CURLY. Laurey'd take up 'th a man like that!

AUNT ELLER. I ain't said she's tuck up with him.

CURLY. Well, he's around all the time, ain't he? Eats his meals with you like one of the fambly, don't he? Sleeps around here some'eres, don't he?

AUNT ELLER. Out in the smokehouse.

CURLY. Laurey sees him all the time, then, don't she? Whyn't you say so in the first place! Whur is this Jeeter, till I git a look at him and mebbe black his eyes fer him?

AUNT ELLER (*slyly*). Thought you'd moved yer camp some'eres else?

CURLY (*with exaggerated bravado*). My camp's right here till I git ready to break it. And moreover—whoever puts his foot in it's liable to git shot fer a stinkin' skunk er a sneakin' wildcat!

(*As if waiting for this declaration, the front door bangs open, and the bullet-colored, growly man, with an armful of wood for the fireplace, comes in. He throws the wood in the woodbox, and turns to* AUNT ELLER.)

JEETER. Whur's Laurey at?

AUNT ELLER. In her room there.

(JEETER *gives a surly grunt by way of response, and without another word goes out again, leaving the door wide open behind him.*)

CURLY. Now is that Jeeter?

AUNT ELLER. Yeah.

CURLY. Thought it was. (*He goes over and looks out after him.*) Why ain't he a-workin'?

AUNT ELLER. It's Satiddy.

CURLY. Oh! I'd forgot. He's went in the smokehouse.

AUNT ELLER. It's *his* house. Used to be the *dog*house.

CURLY (*chuckling*). That's the place fer him!

(*The sliding door opens a crack, and* LAUREY *sticks her head out.*)

LAUREY. I forgot to tell you, Aunt Eller, you'll have to do the churnin' yerself, less'n you c'n git someone to do it fer you.

AUNT ELLER. Why, you lazy youngun, I'll do no sich of a thing! I got dinner on the stove—

LAUREY. It takes time fer a girl to git herself fixed up, it looks to me like. I'm goin' to a party tonight.

AUNT ELLER. To a party?

LAUREY. Well, stand there 'th yer mouth open! Didn't I tell you?—At ole man Peck's over acrost Dog Crick.

AUNT ELLER. Now whoever went and —Did you, Curly?

LAUREY. I heared about it a week ago. Jeeter told me. I'm goin' with Jeeter.

(*She withdraws.* CURLY *stands very still.*)

CURLY (*after a moment*). Ever hear that song, Aunt Eller?

AUNT ELLER (*frowning*). A thousand pins it takes 'em to dress—

CURLY (*grins, ruefully*). Now wouldn't that jist make you bawl!

(*He goes over, touches a few chords on the organ soberly, and then recovering, seats himself, and after a moment begins to sing, half-satirically. But by the time he has reached the first chorus, the song with its absurd yet plaintive charm has absorbed him. And he sings the rest of its sentimental periods, his head back, his eyes focused beyond the room, beyond himself—upon the young man having his sad say, the young man who'll go into the army, by God, and put an end to his distemper, his unrequited fervor.*)

CURLY (*singing*).

I used to have a sweetheart, but now
                  I've got none,
Since she's gone and left me, I care
                 not for one,
Since she's gone and left me,
             contented I'll be,
For she loves another one better than me.

Green grow the lilacs, all sparkling
                with dew,
I'm lonely, my darling, since
            parting with you,
And by the next meeting I hope to
              prove true
To change the green lilacs to the red,
          white and blue.

I passed my love's window, both
           early and late,
The look that she gave me, it made
          my heart ache,
The look that she gaves me was
          harmful to see,
For she loves another one better than me.

Green grow the lilacs, all sparkling
                with dew,
I'm lonely, my darling, since parting
              with you,
And by the next meeting I hope to
            prove true
To change the green lilacs to the red,
          white and blue.

I wrote my love a letter in red rosy lines,
She sent me an answer all twisted in
              twines,
Saying "Keep your love letters and I
           will keep mine,
Just write to your sweetheart and I'll
          write to mine."

Green grow the lilacs, all sparkling
                with dew,
I'm lonely, my darling, since parting
              with you,
And by the next meeting I hope to
            prove true
To change the green lilacs to the red,
          white and blue.

(*He swings off the organ stool, miraculously healed, and makes for the door.*)

AUNT ELLER (*following him over*). Now don't you be discouraged none, Curly. Laurey's good. She's got sense. She don't let you know too much—keeps you guessin'. And you shore got *her* to wonderin', too! You're shore a pair—full of life—made for each other! Got to have each other. *Got to.* (*She laughs.*) Thought I'd die when you made up all that about the rig and told her—

CURLY (*whistles softly*). Jesus! (*He turns round with a grin.*) Well, we got a date together, you and me, Aunt Eller.

AUNT ELLER. We have?

CURLY. We shore have. We goin' to that party we've heared so much about.

AUNT ELLER. How we goin', Curly? In that rig you made up? (*She chuckles.*) I'll ride a-straddle of them lights a-winkin' like lightnin' bugs, myself!

CURLY. That there rig ain't no made-up rig, you hear me? I h'ard it over to Claremore.

AUNT ELLER. Lands, you did!

CURLY. And when I come callin' fer you right after supper, see that you got yer beauty spots fastened onto you proper, so you won't lose 'em off, you hear? Now then. (*He strides away to the door again, enigmatically.*) I think I'll jist go out here to the smokehouse a while.

AUNT ELLER (*puzzled*). Whur Jeeter's at?

CURLY. Yeow, whur Jeeter's at. Thought mebbe I'd play a game of pitch with him, 'fore I mosey on home. You reckon he'd like that?

(*He goes out the door.* AUNT ELLER *stares after him, figuring out things.*)

CURTAIN

SCENE TWO

LAUREY's *bedroom, behind its sliding doors, is small, primitive, but feminine. There's a bed covered with a beautiful crazy-quilt, a dresser, very ornate, with little souvenir shell boxes, combs, hair receivers, hairpins, a vase of buttercups and daisies, etc. There's a small table with pitchers of water under it, and comfortable chairs. A small window looks out into the brillant day. At the left is a door which goes out to the swept yard in front of the kitchen. The walls are papered, and several small photographs are tacked up—one of a man on horseback, obviously for the first time, one of a young girl with enormous sleeves in her dress.*

LAUREY *is combing her hair. She seems, in this setting, younger, more glowing, more complete than before, as if the room were necessary to her. It is immediately after Scene One.* AUNT ELLER *has come in from the door at the left to see what* LAUREY *is up to.*

AUNT ELLER. Is that all you got to do?

LAUREY (*abstractedly*). When I was a little girl I had my hair in pigtails. It hung down and down, till I'd wrap it around my head. Nen I'd look like sump'n crawled out of a hole.

AUNT ELLER. I ain't got time to listen to sich craziness.

LAUREY. When I got a little older, I cut it off. Maw licked me.

AUNT ELLER. Well, she'd orta licked you.

LAUREY. Why?

AUNT ELLER. Fer cuttin' yer hair off. Don't you know that ain't right?

LAUREY. I ast you fer a answer and all I git is another question.

AUNT ELLER. Oh, I'm goin' back in the kitchen. You ain't started on that churnin'. I jist come in to see what you was up to so long. Here I find you a-primpin' and a-talkin' crazy.

LAUREY. Wait a minute. Why don't you set down here a minute?

AUNT ELLER. They's work to do. Ain't time to set.

LAUREY. Then redd up that table if you won't set. And put some fresh water onto them flowers I picked day before yistiddy. Them buttercups. In the meader back of the wheat field—walkin' in the tall grass and the sumakes, you know what I seen? A snake 'th its tail in its mouth—

AUNT ELLER. And a terrapin carryin' a elephant, too, didn't you?

LAUREY. Won't hurt you none to put some water on them flowers.

AUNT ELLER (*acquiescing, judicially*). Well. You ain't alwys so lazy, I must say.

LAUREY. Dance at yer weddin'.

AUNT ELLER. I don't know whut's got into you, though.

LAUREY. You don't?

AUNT ELLER (*wisely*). Yes, I do.

LAUREY (*cryptically*). I thought you did. (*Silence.* AUNT ELLER *fills the vase.* LAUREY *combs her hair slowly, and begins to sing.*)

One morning as I rambled o'er
The fields I took my way
In hopes of meeting my miner boy
And for a while to stray,
In hopes of meeting my miner boy,
My hope, my joy, my own.
My heart was blessed, it could find no rest
For the thoughts of my miner boy.

The mother to her daughter,
"I'll comfort you to your room,
You never shall marry a miner boy,
It will certainly be your doom.
They're never, never satisfied,
But always on a drunk.
And all they have in this wide wide world
Is a satchel and a trunk."

The daughter to her mother,
"What makes you be unkind?
I never shall marry another one
But the one that suits my mind.
His trousers are made of corduroy,
His jacket of true blue.
I'd rather marry a miner boy
As to reign with the waters true."

Then fill your glasses to the brim,
Let's all go merry round,
And drink to the health of the miner boy
Who works down in the ground,
When work is o'er comes whistling home
With a heart so full of joy,
And happy, happy is the girl
That marries a miner boy.

Would you marry a miner boy, Aunt Eller?

AUNT ELLER. I don't know no miner boys.

LAUREY. Oh, 'f you did, you would, I bet. (*After a moment.*) Wish 't I lived in the White House, and had diamonds on my shoes, and a little nigger boy to fan me—when it was hot. Does it git hot in the White House, Aunt Eller?

AUNT ELLER. How do I know?

LAUREY. Er I wish 't I lived in Virginia or Californie. In Californie, they's or-anges growin', and snow fallin' at the same time. I seen a pitcher of it. In the Verdigree bottom the other day, a man found thirty-three arrow heads—thirty-three—whur they'd been a Indian battle—

AUNT ELLER. Whut's that got to do with the White House and livin' in Californie?

LAUREY. Who said anything about

Californie?

AUNT ELLER (*whistles*). Land's alive! (*After a moment.*) Curly's out in the smoke-house.

LAUREY. Who is?

AUNT ELLER. Curly. Him and Jeeter.

LAUREY (*as if she hadn't heard*). Bet they'll be a hundred people at Peck's. They'll come in buggies and surries, a-horseback, in the wagon, and some'll come afoot. Gracie Denham will come all the way from Catoosie to be there, I bet. When she married Dan Denham, everbody thought—"Good-by, good times"—fer Gracie. She fooled 'em, though. How big is Indian Territory, Aunt Eller?

AUNT ELLER. Oh, big.

LAUREY. It's a funny place to live, ain't it?

AUNT ELLER. Whut's funny about it?

LAUREY. Well, take me—if paw and maw hadn't come here, I'd a-been livin' in Missouri now, 'stid of here. I'd a-had education, I'll bet. (*She puts down her comb and stares thoughtfully out the window.*) I lied about the White House, Aunt Eller. I'd ruther be married to a man—if he was a real good man—than to live in the old White House.

AUNT ELLER (*chuckling*). Hope you do one of the two!

LAUREY. Wouldn't you, Aunt Eller?

AUNT ELLER. I've done about all the marryin' I'm gonna do. Onct is quite a plenty. (*She chortles with delight.*) Less'n I marry Curly and bring him up right. Me and Curly, we're a-goin to that there party—

LAUREY (*jumps up, runs over and begins shaking the astounded* AUNT ELLER). You ain't, you air not! He ain't got no way to take you to no party. You got to go with Jeeter and me—

AUNT ELLER. Curly's h'ard a rig. That un he told you about. (LAUREY *drops her hands, backs away, and looks at* AUNT ELLER *with such an amazed and startled expression, that the older woman cries out:*) Why, you look so funny!—Like you'd saw sump'n. (LAUREY *goes over to the window, hangs on to the curtains.*) Besides, you turned him down. (*Teasing her.*) If you jist *got* to go with Jeeter, they ain't no way out of it, I reckon. Well, me'n Curly, we'll make out—

LAUREY (*quietly, strangely*). Onct I passed by a farmhouse and it was night.

Paw and maw and me was in a covered wagon on our way to here. And this farmhouse was burnin' up. It was burnin' bright too. Black night, it was, like I said. Flames licked and licked at the red-hot chimbley and finally it fell, too, and that was the last of that house. And that was turrible! I cried and cried. (*A sudden slightly-hysterical note in her voice.*) And the farmer's wife jist set there by the side of the road, moanin' and takin' on. Had on a sunbonnet, a *sunbonnet*, and it night! She kept sayin' over and over—"Now my home's burnt up. 'F I'd jist a-give him a piece of cold pork or sump'n. If I'd jist a-fed him!—" (*She shakes her head, as if shutting it out.*) Now ain't that silly!— Don't you listen to a word I said. Ever onct in a while sump'n makes me think about it, the way that womern cried, and said whut she did. Don't you pay no attention to me—

AUNT ELLER. I b'lieve to my soul you got sump'n worryin' on yer mind. Never seen you ack before like a chicken 'th its head cut off, Laurey.

LAUREY (*flippantly*). Worried to death.

AUNT ELLER. Whut about? Now tell yer ole Aunt. Whut is it, honey?

LAUREY. Ain't got a thing to wear to-night.

AUNT ELLER. You make me so mad—!

LAUREY. Well, I ain't. That ole flowered dewdad of a dress looks like sump'n the cat drug in. And my sash is tore. Sylvie Roberts has got a new kind of a shoe with high heels onto 'em like stilts— and I ain't got none.

AUNT ELLER. You'd shore look purty a-wearin' stilts—like a sandhill crane a-wadin' shaller water! That ain't whut's a-worryin' you, though—

LAUREY. I thought it was. Listen to that mockin' bird a-singin'! Ever' mornin' he sets in that ellum and sings like a tree full of birds all by hisself.

AUNT ELLER. He's lonesome.

LAUREY. He's hungry.

AUNT ELLER. Well, it's the same thing.

LAUREY (*with real passion*). If we ever had to leave this here place, Aunt Eller, I'd shore miss it. I like it. I like that thicket down by the branch whur the 'possums live, don't you? And the way we set around in the evenings in thrashin' time, a-eatin' mushmelons and singin', and oh! lots of things! Runnin' to the cellar in a storm, and them yeller trumpet tomaters even, you make jam out of, and the branch and the pond to skate on— They's only one thing I don't to say *like*. And that's Sunday in fall, when it's windy, and the sun shines, and the leaves piles up thick agin the house. I'm 'fraid of my life to go from here to the kitchen—like sump'n was gonna ketch me!

AUNT ELLER. Well, you *air* a silly.

LAUREY. But I'd shore hate to leave here, though, and go some'eres else— like to a town or some place—

AUNT ELLER. Well, the ole Scratch! Whut makes you keep talkin' about leavin' here?

LAUREY. Whut if we had to?

AUNT ELLER. Won't have to. We got money in the bank.

LAUREY. Bank might break.

AUNT ELLER. Well, let it. It's gonna be another good year fer corn and oats, like it's been now fer three year—

LAUREY. Whut if sump'n happened?

AUNT ELLER. Like whut?

LAUREY. Oh, things change. Things don't last the way they air. Besides, whut if they'd be a prairie f'ar—like the one that burnt up a thousand acres by Chambers School House five year ago?

AUNT ELLER. Ain't apt to be no prairie f'ar.

LAUREY. Or a cyclone ud come, like that un did at Sweetwater. Made hash outa three whole sections.

AUNT ELLER. Cain't stop a cyclone by worryin'.

LAUREY. No? Well, whut if Jeeter ud set the house on f'ar?

AUNT ELLER. Jeeter set the—Whut in the name of Jerusalem air you talkin' about! Jeeter set the—My goodness, git yer things ready, gonna start you right off to Vinita to the crazy house!

LAUREY. Well, I told you, anyway—

AUNT ELLER. Git 'em ready!

LAUREY. You don't have to listen.

AUNT ELLER. Whut if I'd put rat poison in the turnip greens? Now whut on earth would Jeeter want to set the house on f'ar fer?

LAUREY. I jist said he might.

AUNT ELLER. Might take a notion to rope a freight train, too. Fiddlesticks! I got my dinner on the stove a-cookin'. (*She makes for the door, slows her pace, and turns around again.*) Now, whut do you mean, anyway—Jeeter set the house

on f'ar?—

LAUREY. They's a horse and buggy turnin' off up the road this-a-way.

AUNT ELLER. I won't look till you tell me whut you're a-meanin'.

LAUREY. It's a roan horse 'th a long tail. He's string-haltered. Look at the way he walks—

AUNT ELLER. Not *gonna* look, I tell you!

LAUREY. You know whut a f'ar is, don't you? And you know Jeeter?

AUNT ELLER. That's jist it.

LAUREY (*gravely, queerly*). Sump'n funny about him. Sump'n black a-pilin' up. Ever since a year ago. Sump'n boilin' up inside of him—*mean*.

AUNT ELLER (*relieved*). Is that it! Well, I guess you don't mind that so much— goin' to parties with him, and all.

LAUREY (*her face white—in a low voice*). I'm afraid to tell him I won't, Aunt Eller. 'F I done what I wanted to, I'd f'ar him off the place so quick! Whut're we gonna do, Aunt Eller! He'd do sump'n turrible, he makes me shiver ever' time he gits close to me—(*With a frightened look around, as if he were in the room.*) Have you ever looked out there in the smoke-house—whur he sleeps?

AUNT ELLER. Course I have, plenty of times.

LAUREY. Whut'd you see?

AUNT ELLER. Nuthin'—but a lot of dirt. Why, whut's out there?

LAUREY (*her voice tight with excitement— creating it*). I don't know, sump'n awful. I hook my door at night and fasten the winders agin it. Agin *it*—and the sound of feet a-walkin' up and down out there under that tree, and around the corner of the house, and down by the barn—and in the front room there!

AUNT ELLER. Laurey!

LAUREY (*as before*). I wake up and hear the boards creakin', I tell you! The rafters jist over my head here shakes a little—*easy*. Next mornin', he comes to his breakfast and looks at me out from under his eyebrows like sump'n back in the bresh some'eres. I know what I'm talkin' about—

AUNT ELLER. Why, I didn't have an idy you felt that-a-way about him! Why, we'll run him off the place if you're skeered of him—

LAUREY (*with deep premonition*). Don't you do it! Don't you say nuthin' to him! *That's* whut skeers me—he'd do sump'n

I tell you! He'd set the house on f'ar, like I told you!

AUNT ELLER. Land's sakes! Jist let me ketch him at it! (*She laughs.*) Now you've went and made all this up, and I don't believe a word of it

LAUREY. You'll find out someday—

AUNT ELLER. Onct when you was a little girl you know what you done? Looked outa the winder and seen a cow standin' in the tool shed, and you said to yer Maw, "I knowed it, I knowed it! I knowed the cow ud eat the grindstone up!" Didn't you? But the cow didn't, though!

LAUREY (*smiling with great relief*). No, the cow didn't.

AUNT ELLER. *Well*, then! You didn't know's much's you thought you did. (*She goes and looks out the window.*) Now who'd you reckon that is drove up? (*A dog begins barking angrily.*) Why, it's that ole pedler! The one that sold me that egg-beater. Jist let me git my hands onto him—'f I don't fix him—! (*She rushes toward the door.*)

LAUREY. He's got someone with him. Why, it's Ado Annie Carnes! Now ain't she a sight! Ridin' around with that ole pedler.

AUNT ELLER. I'll th'ow him in the branch, that's whut I'll do to him! You know whut he done? Told me that egg-beater ud beat up eggs, and wring out dish rags, and turn the ice cream freezer, and I don't know whut all! (*She dashes out the door.*)

LAUREY (*leaning out the window*). Yoo-hoo! Ado Annie! C'm here. And bring yer pedler man in too, 'f you ain't afeard I'll take him away from you. (*She snickers with delight.*) I want to buy some things. (*She flies to the dresser, catches up her hair in the back, straightens her dress, and by the time* ADO ANNIE CARNES *appears in the door is humming softly to herself, apparently having forgotten her uneasiness of the moment before.*)

ADO ANNIE (*coming in*). Hi.

(*She is an unattractive, stupid-looking farm girl, with taffy-colored hair pulled back from a freckled face. Her dress is of red gingham, and very unbecoming.*)

LAUREY. Hi, yerself. Ridin' a piece?

ADO ANNIE (*noncommittally*). Rode over yere.

LAUREY. Well, set. Whur's yer pedler?

ADO ANNIE (*hiding a grin*). Aw, he ain't *mine*. He's out there fightin' with Aunt Eller 'bout that ole egg-beater.

LAUREY (*teasing her*). Now listen here, have you tuck up with a pedler that ud sell a pore old womern a egg-beater that wasn't no good? Ado Annie Carnes, I'm plum ashamed of you! You ort to be strapped.

ADO ANNIE. Ain't tuck up with him. Rode a piece in his ole buggy for I was comin' over here, anyway, to ast about—to ast you sump'n.

LAUREY. Whut was you gonna ast me, then?

ADO ANNIE. 'F you was goin' to that there party over to Peck's.

LAUREY. Course I am.

ADO ANNIE. Well.

LAUREY. Don't I go to all the parties?

ADO ANNIE. I guess. You got fellers, lots of fellers.

LAUREY. Three hundred and fifty.

ADO ANNIE. Oh, you ain't!

LAUREY. Oh, I have.

ADO ANNIE. I kinda wondered 'f you wouldn't take *me*.

LAUREY. *Me*, take *you*? (*She becomes strange and thoughtful.*)

ADO ANNIE. Well, someone's takin' you, ain't they? You could take me along.

LAUREY. Why, my goodness! (*She beams ecstatically.*) Why, I'd jist love to have you, Ado Annie! You git yerself over here to supper all diked up and fancy, and I'll see that you got a way to go, all right. I'll put myself out! (*She has another brilliant idea, which amuses her very much.*) Oh, and I'm gonna buy you sump'n so purty the fellers'll all fall over a wagon tongue a-lookin' at you! Whur *is* that man! (*She rushes to the door, in a fever of delight.*) Aunt Eller, Aunt Eller! Quit a-botherin' that man from his business! I want to buy some of his dewdads. (*To* ADO ANNIE, *with mock gravity.*) You don't want to git to like a pedler man *too* good, Annie. You hear me? They got wives in ever' state in the union.

ADO ANNIE. Oh, foot!

LAUREY. They have! And other places besides. Why, Alaska's jist full of women a-livin' in ice houses, and freezin' to death 'cause of pedlers runnin' off and leavin' 'em 'thout no kindlin' er nuthin'—

ADO ANNIE. Aw!

LAUREY. A man *told* me! Shore as shootin'! He knowed a Eskimo womern that a pedler up there went off and left, and she had to sell her hair—a hundred hairs at a time—jist cut it right off—to keep from starvin' to death. Finally, she looked like a ole shave head, bald-headed as a turkey buzzard, and she tuck cold and died.

ADO ANNIE. *Who* did?

LAUREY. The *womern!*

ADO ANNIE. My goodness!

(AUNT ELLER *and the* PEDLER *come in. He is a little wiry, swarthy Syrian, neatly dressed, and with a red bandanna around his neck. He is very acquisitive, very cunning. He sets down his bulging suitcases, his little beady eyes sparkling professionally. He rushes over and, to* LAUREY's *alarm, kisses her hand.*)

PEDLER. My, oh, my! But you are grown lady, Miss Laurey! (*He gives a grunt of surprised pleasure. His speech is some blurred European tongue with Middle Western variations, from dealing almost entirely with farmers.*)

LAUREY (*backing away*). Heavens and earth!

PEDLER. Growed up, and sich a be-*youty*, too! My, oh my! I don't see you in a whole year. Last time you was little, like that, all sunburnt and bony, and now you've turned into a be-*you*tiful young lady. Yum, yum! (*He kisses her hand again.*)

LAUREY. Quit it, a-bitin' me! 'F you ain't had no breakfast go and eat yerself a green apple. Lands a goodness! You'd think I was angel food cake er sump'n. (*But she is a little pleased, in spite of herself.*)

PEDLER. Angel cake, that's jist whut you air! Angel cake, and jist hot outa the oven!

LAUREY. My, listen at him! Shet up yer mouth, and show me sump'n. Is that the way he talks to you, Ado Annie?

ADO ANNIE. Aw, he don't talk to me!

LAUREY. Mercy, whut does he *do* to you!

PEDLER. Now Aunt Eller, jist listen at the way she does me—

AUNT ELLER (*snapping at him*). I ain't yer *Aunt Eller!* Don't you *call* me Aunt Eller, you little wart! I'm mad at you.

PEDLER. Don't you go and be mad with me. Tell you what. I'll give you sump'n—give you another egg-beater.

AUNT ELLER. Don't you go and say *egg-beater* to me *again!*

PEDLER. Well, I'll give you sump'n—sump'n purty.

AUNT ELLER. Whut'll it be, and it'd better be good?

PEDLER. You wait. Sump'n purty for to wear.

AUNT ELLER (*snorting*). Foot! I got things for to wear. Wouldn't have it. Whur is it?

PEDLER. You wait. I'll show you.

AUNT ELLER. Biggest liar I ever knowed! You'll be tellin' me next you got it hid some'eres, tied onto the horse's belly band—

PEDLER. That's whur it is, exactly! You guessed it!

AUNT ELLER. Lands, you big—I won't listen at you, won't stay in the same room whur you're at. (*She marches out of the room and slams the door. Then she opens it and comes back in.*) Thought I was gone, didn't you? Well, I ain't. I'm gonna stay right here, fer spite. Not gonna leave you and two girls in no bedroom, all by yerselves. (*She sits down, in the corner.*)

LAUREY (*in a kind of abstracted ecstasy*). Want some hair-pins, a fine-tooth comb, a pink un. Want a buckle made out of shiny silver to fasten onto my shoes! Want a dress with lace! Want pe'fume, face whitenin'! Wanta be purty, wanta smell like a honeysuckle vine!

AUNT ELLER (*from her corner*). Give her a cake of soap.

LAUREY (*her mood rising*). Want things I c'n see and put my hands on. Want things I've heared of and never had before—pearls in a plush box, diamonds, a rubber-t'ard buggy, a cut glass sugar bowl. Want things I caint tell you about. Caint see 'em clear. Things nobody ever heared of. (*Passionately, in a low voice.*) Not only things to look at and hold in yer hands. Things to *happen* to you! Things so nice if they ever did happen yer heart ud quit beatin', you'd fall down dead. They ain't no end to the things I want. Everything you got wouldn't be a starter fer me, Mister Pedler Man! (*Breaking off.*) So jist give me a bottle of shoe blackin', and make it quick!

PEDLER (*on his knees, at his suitcases, handing them out*). Some nice garters? Silk in 'em, real silk, too, and bows on 'em! Look at 'em. Made in Persia. Brought to this country—

AUNT ELLER (*satirically*). Brought to this country at great riskin' of life and limb—like them Monsters from Madagascar. (*She giggles.*) Lemme look at 'em.

LAUREY (*taking them*). Jist whut I was a-wantin'—

PEDLER. Try 'em on.

LAUREY. Fer Ado Annie.

ADO ANNIE (*overcome*). Aw!

PEDLER. Four bits apiece.

LAUREY. Four bits a pair.

PEDLER. Apiece.

LAUREY. Keep 'em, then.

PEDLER. Oh, take 'em.

LAUREY (*taking them*). Here, Ado Annie. Put 'em on when no one ain't a-lookin'. (*To the* PEDLER.) You got any face withenin'?

PEDLER (*finding it*). The best they is, Miss Laurey. Liquid powder. Smells like the Queen of Egyp'! Put it on you, they cain't no one stay away from you. Reg'ler love drops! And only six bits a bottle— with a sponge throwed in.

LAUREY. Lemme see it. C'm here, Ado Annie. (*She puts* ADO ANNIE *in a chair.*) Now be still, I'm gonna try it on you. Now don't scrooge around like you had a ringworm or sump'n. Gonna hide them freckles 'f I have to put it on a inch thick.

(*She begins putting the liquid powder on a sponge and dabbing at* ADO ANNIE's *face.* AUNT ELLER *leans back in her chair and begins to sing, in derision.*)

AUNT ELLER (*singing*).
Young men they'll go courting, they'll
                 dress up so fine,
To cheat the poor girls is all their design,
They'll hug and they'll kiss and they'll
                 cheat and they'll lie,
They'll keep the girls up till they're
                 ready to die.
    Sing down, hidery down!

Those girls will get angry, they'll
                 rise up and say:
"I am so sleepy, I wish you'd go 'way."
Those boys will get angry to hear the
                 girls' scorn—
Before they'll go home, they'll sleep
                 in some barn.
    Sing down, hidery down!

Oh, early next morning those laddies
                 will rise,
Brush off the straws and rub up their eyes,
They'll saddle their horses and away
                 they will ride
Like all true lovers dressed up in
                 their pride.
    Sing down, hidery down!

Let us turn from those boys and turn
                 from those lads

And turn to those girls which are
                 twice as bad.
They'll flour up their faces and comb
                 up their hair
Till they look like an owl in the
                 bresh, I'll declare!
    Wo, larry, wo!

It's two long hours they'll stand at
                 the glass,
And a thousand pins it will take
                 them to dress,
They'll dress up so neat, and vanish away,
The devil himself couldn't look half
                 so gay..
    Wo, larry, wo!

You can tell a good girl wherever she
                 goes—
No foolish marks about her clothes,
No ribbons or rings or any such things,
But an old straw bonnet tied under
                 her chin.
    Wo, larry, wo!

Of all the good lives 'tis bachelor's best.
Be drunk or be sober, lie down and
                 take rest,
No wife to scold, no children to squall—
How happy's the man that keeps
                 bachelor's hall.
    Wo, larry, wo!

(*She gets up from her chair to see what* LAUREY *is doing.*) Let's see whut you're a-doin' to her. (*She turns* ADO ANNIE *about in her chair, and bursts into a loud guffaw.* ADO ANNIE's *face is plastered with white.*) Mercy! She's plum whitewashed you! Look like a nigger angel turned all white and shinin'. Whur's yer wings at, Angel?

ADO ANNIE (*scrubbing at her face*). I'll take ever' bit of it off! Won't have no sich of a mess on me. I'm goin' right home! You've made a plumb sight outa me! (*She makes for the door, flustered to death.*)

LAUREY (*holding on to her*). Don't you b'lieve her, Ado Annie! Why, you look purty as one of them rider ladies in the circus—'cept fer not havin' on no pink tights. Well, jist look in the lookin' glass, you don't believe me.

(*There is a muffled pistol shot somewhere outside. They all start violently.*)

AUNT ELLER. Now, whut in the name of—

PEDLER. Shootin'—

ADO ANNIE. I'm goin' home—

LAUREY (*her face white*). Wait a minute! Whur was that shot, Aunt Eller? It wasn't out there—out there—?

AUNT ELLER. Sounded like it come from the smokehouse—

LAUREY. Don't you say it! It couldn't be, couldn't!

AUNT ELLER. It *was*, I tell you.

(*There is another shot.*)

LAUREY (*shaken with fear*). Curly!

AUNT ELLER (*looking at her in alarm*). Why, you're 's white as a sheet, Laurey!

LAUREY (*rushing toward the door*). Why'd you let him go out there whur Jeeter is!

AUNT ELLER. It couldn't be nuthin', honey!

LAUREY. We got to go see!

(*She hurries out the door,* AUNT ELLER *and the* PEDLER *following.* ADO ANNIE *takes out her garters, puts them on hastily, and flies out after them.*)

CURTAIN

SCENE THREE

It is immediately after Scene One—at the same time as Scene Two.

The smokehouse is a dark, dirty building where the meat was once kept. But now, the floor is full of holes; at night the field mice scurry about the room. The rafters are worn and decayed, smoky, covered with dust and cobwebs. On a low loft, many things are stored—horse-collars, plowshares, bridles, jars of fruit, a saddle, binder twine, a keg of nails. Under it, the fourposter bed is grimy and never made. A pair of muddy shoes and a pair of gum boots are lying on their sides under the bed. On the walls, of unpainted two-by-twelves, soiled clothes are hanging, also tobacco advertisements, an enlisting poster, a pink cover off the Police Gazette, a large framed picture of Dan Patch, several postcard pictures of teams pulling heavy loads of logs, etc. In one corner, there are hoes, rakes and axe. In another, a bale of hay covered with a red saddle blanket. In the room also, a tool box, several rough chairs, a table, a spittoon, a washstand, several farm lanterns, a rope, a mirror for shaving. A small window lets in a little light, but not much. The door at back is closed.

JETTER *sits in a low chair looking at some postcards, leaning forward now and then to spit at the spittoon. He is about thirty-five, with a curious earth-colored face and hairy hands. He wears heavy brogans, a greasy pair of trousers, two shirts open at the neck, and both dirty. He is always absorbed, dark, and sullen. Hearing a knock, he shifts about in his chair, spits again, shoves the pictures quickly back into his pocket, and speaks crossly.*

JEETER. Well, cain't you open it?

(CURLY *opens the door and comes in.*)

CURLY. Howdy—

JEETER (*unpleasantly*). Is that yore plug tied to that peach tree?

CURLY. 'F you mean that horse, that's my horse. He ain't no plug.

JEETER. Plug or no plug, you mighta tied him some'eres else.

CURLY. They ain't nary a peach on that tree.

JEETER. And they *won't* be, if everbody's gonna tie his saddle horse to it.

CURLY. I'll go and move him.

JEETER. 'S too late, pardner. I done moved him.

CURLY. Whur'd you put him at?

JEETER. Turned him a-loose.

CURLY (*unruffled*). That's all right.

JEETER. He's prob'ly tuck off up the road by this time, and serve you right.

CURLY. Left the reins a-draggin', didn't you?

JEETER. Yes, I did.

CURLY. Well, that's a cow pony, that is. He'll stand all day if the reins is down.

JEETER (*disappointed*). You orten't to go around a-tyin' him to peach trees.

CURLY. You know, I don't know a peach tree from a corn stalk.

JEETER. Better learn, then. Whut'd you want around here, anyhow?

CURLY. I done got th'ough my business—up here at the house. I jist thought I'd come in and see you.

JEETER. I ain't got time to see no one. I'm a-takin' a bath.

CURLY (*facetiously*). Thought you was balin' hay.

JEETER. How's that?

CURLY. I say, that's a good-lookin' rope you got there. (*He points.*) Buy it at Claremore?

JEETER. Cain't see that that's none of *yore* business.

CURLY. I know you didn't steal it.

JETTER (*shortly*). That rope was *give* to me. It's a used un.

CURLY. Ort to spin, then. (*He goes over,*

takes it down, and begins spinning it.) You know Will Parker?

JEETER. Never heared of him.

CURLY. Ole man Parker's boy up here by Claremore? He can shore spin a rope. Chews gum when he spins it. Gum ain't healthy, I always say. (*Holding on to one end of the rope, he tosses the other over a rafter, and catches it. He pulls down on both ends, tentatively.*) 'S a good strong rafter you got there. You could hang yerself on that, Jeeter.

JEETER. I could—what?

CURLY (*cheerfully*). Hang yerself. It ud be easy as fallin' off a log! Fact is, you could stand on a log—er a cheer if you'd ruther—right about here, see, and put this here around yer neck. Tie that good up there first, of course. Then, all you'd have to do would be to fall off the log— er the cheer, whichever you'd ruther fall off of. In five minutes, er less, with good luck, you'd be dead as a door nail.

JEETER (*suspiciously*). Whut'd you mean by that?

CURLY. The folks ud all gether around and sing. *Sad* songs, of course. And some of 'em ud say whut a good man you was, and others ud say what a pig-stealer and a hound dog you was, and you'd orter been in the penitentiary long ago, fer orneriness.

JEETER. You better be keerful, now!

CURLY. *I* ain't sayin' it. I'm sayin' *they'd* say it. You know the way people talks—like a swarm of mud wasps. (*Looking about the room.*) So this is whur *you* live? Always like to see whur a man's a-livin' at. You got a fine place here, Mr. Jeeter. Matches you.

(*He grins mischievously.* JEETER *gets up, goes over close to him, dangerously.*)

JEETER. I don't know who you air er nuthin'—but I think you'd better tell me whut you come bustin' in here fer, makin' free 'th my things and talkin' the way you talk.

CURLY. Why, my name's Curly. Thought you knowed. Curly McClain. Born on a farm in Kansas. Cowpuncher by trade and by profession. I break broncs, mean uns. I bull-dog steers. I ain't never been licked, and I ain't never been shot. Shot *at*, but not *shot*. I got a good disposition, too, and when anything seems like to me it's funny, why I let loose and laugh till my belt breaks in two and my socks falls down. Whut

on earth air *you* doin' 'th a pitcher of Dan Patch? (*He points to the picture.*)

JEETER (*nonplussed*). Got a right to have a pitcher of Dan Patch, ain't I?

CURLY. Yeah, and you shore have. And that there pink pitcher there, now that's a naked womern, ain't it?

JEETER. Yer eyes don't lie to you.

CURLY. Plumb stark naked as a jaybird! No. No, she ain't, not *quite*. Got a couple of thingumabobs tied on to her.

JEETER. That's a cover off the Police Gazette.

CURLY. Wouldn't do fer me to have sich a pitcher around.

JEETER. Whut's wrong with it?

CURLY. I never seen sich a pitcher! That ud give me idys, that would!

JEETER (*at home now and at ease with his guest*). Shucks, that ain't a thing to whut I got here! (*He draws out his postcards.*)

CURLY (*covering his eyes*). I'll go blind! Whew! Lose my eyesight in a minute! I wonder now if we couldn't have a little game of pitch?

JEETER. Look at this here un. That's a dinger, that is!

CURLY (*looking at it gravely*). Yeah, that shore *is* a dinger.

JEETER. The girls these is tuck of can shore make it interestin' for a man! God, cain't they! Over at Tulsa. I had me another whole pack of these—but I lost 'em—

CURLY. That's too bad. That was sump'n to lose.

JEETER. Yeah, stole off me over to a dance at Bushyhead. Shore, I'll play a game of pitch with you, all right. Here, set down.

(*They sit at the table.* JEETER *fishes in the drawer and pulls out two pistols and a pack of dirty Bicycle playing cards, and lays them on the table.*)

CURLY. You—you got pistols, too?

JEETER. Good uns. Colt .45.

CURLY. Whut do you do 'th pistols?

JEETER. Shoot things.

CURLY. Oh. You deal.

JEETER. No, you deal.

CURLY. Shore, I'll deal. (*He shuffles the cards and begins to deal.*) Is this draw?

JEETER. Suit yerself.

CURLY. Draw, then. With the Jick, and not the left Jack. It's yore first bid.

JEETER. Two.

CURLY. Three.

JEETER. It's your'n.

CURLY. Spades. (*He takes up the deck again.*) How many?

JEETER. One.

(CURLY *deals one to* JEETER, *two to himself, picks up his hand. They begin to play.*)

CURLY (*with lyric warmth—for he is stating something about his own life—and his feeling about life*). Outside, the sun's jist crazy 'th the heat, beatin' on the prairie and the corn stalks. Passed a field in the bottom this mornin' whur the backwater had been. Ground all cracked and blistered and bakin' in the sun. Likin' it, though! Likin' it good. The crawfish put up their pinchers and hustled about, 'cause their holes is all goin' dry. Seen fields of wheat and oats —fine as a fiddle! The crows went to honkin' at me when I rode th'ough the Dog Crick timber, and I could see hundreds of squirrels friskin' in the blackjacks. I could smell them green walnuts, too, whenever old Dun ud tromp on 'em. Shore the purtiest mornin' in a long time! Felt like hollerin' and shoutin'. I raired away back in my saddle and ole Dun stepped out a-prancin' and we come th'ough Claremore like a streak of forked lightnin'! An' it's shore a funny end to a fine mornin' to find yerself shet up in a dark hole bent over a table a-fingerin' a pack of cards 's greasy 's a ole tin spoon, ain't it? Yeah, that's the way it is, though, in this here life. Got to git used to it. (*He begins to sing.*)

Oh, my name it is Sam Hall, it is Sam
　　　　　　　　　　　　　Hall,
My name it is Sam Hall, it is Sam
　　　　　　　　　　　　　Hall,
My name it is Sam Hall, and I hate
　　　　　　　　you one and all,
I hate you one and all, damn yer eyes!

To the gallows I must go, I must go,
To the gallows I must go, I must go,
To the gallows I must go, for I've
　　　　　killed a man you know,
Because he loved her so, damn his
　　　　　　　　　　　　　eyes!

I must hang till I am dead, I am dead,
I must hang till I am dead, I am dead,
I must hang till I am dead, for I killed
　　　　　　　a man, they said,

And I left him there for dead, damn
　　　　　　　　　　　his eyes!

I saw Mollie in the crowd, in the
　　　　　　　　　　　crowd,
I saw Mollie in the crowd, in the
　　　　　　　　　　　crowd,
I saw Mollie in the crowd, and I
　　　　　hollered right out loud:
"Hey, Mollie, ain't you proud, damn
　　　　　　　　　　yer eyes!"

(*As he sings the game goes slower and slower,* CURLY *interested in the song and in* JEETER, JEETER *frowning and strangely excited. Suddenly a dog begins barking angrily.* JEETER *goes to the door quickly and looks out.*)

JEETER. Who would that be, I wonder? In a buggy. Got a girl with him. Oh! (*He is relieved.*) It's that Syrian pedler. Yeah, that's who. (*He closes the door and comes down again. After a moment.*) Did that—did that Sam Hall kill the feller? (CURLY *nods.*) He'd orta killed the girl, too.

CURLY. They wouldn't a-been much fun in that.

JEETER. Fun! Whut was fun about it, anyway! (*Strangely, darkly, his tongue unloosed.*) I knowed a feller onct killed a girl. He'd been keepin' comp'ny with her and aimed to marry her. One day he found her up in the barn loft with another man. He didn't do nuthin' at first. But this girl lived on a farm with her folks. One night her paw and maw couldn't sleep fer the dog a-barkin' so. Next mornin' the old man went down to feed the stock like he always did, and when he come to the horse troft, he seen sump'n white a-layin' there. It was his daughter, in her nightgown, layin' there in the water all covered with blood, dead. They never did find out who done it. But I met up with a man onct on the road-gang a-makin' that road from here to Collinsville, and he told me he done it. Only—you know what he done? Made out this murder tuck place ten year ago back in Missouri. It didn't, though! It was up here by Sweetwater not two year ago—and I'd saw all about it in the paper! But I didn't let on. Whut a liar he was!

CURLY. And a kind of a—a kind of a murderer, too, wasn't he?

JEETER (*absorbed*). I couldn't make out why he cut her throat and then throwed her in the horse troft, too. Less'n—he thought—why, that's why! He'd got blood all over him, and he couldn't stand havin' blood on him, so that's why he done it! I knowed another case, too, of a man got a girl in trouble—

CURLY. I was jist goin' to ast you 'f you didn't know some other stories.

JEETER. This man was a married farmer, and he knowed this girl. It had been goin' on a long time till the man it looked like he couldn't live 'thout her. He was kinda crazy and wild if she'd even speak to anyone. One night, it was moonlight, and they'd met out back of an old mowin' machine left in the meader a-rustin'—She told him about the way she was, gonna have a baby. He went jist hog-wild, and found a piece of old rope in the tool box of the mowin' machine, tied her hands and feet with it, nen throwed her up on top of a stack of hay, and set f'ar to it. Burned her to death! Do you know why? He didn't keer about her goin' to have the baby, that wasn't it. He jist didn't know how he was goin' to live 'thout *havin'* her all the time while she was carryin' it! So he killed her. Yeow, it's funny the things people do, like that.

(CURLY *gets up, goes over, throws the door open. A shaft of brilliant sunlight pours in, alive with millions of dust motes.*)

CURLY. Git a little air in here. (*He goes back and sits down.*) Yore mind seems to run on two things, don't it? Before you come here to work fer the Williams', whur did you work?

JEETER (*hostile again*). I don't know as that concerns no one but me.

CURLY. That's right, pardner. That's yore lookout.

JEETER. I'll tell you, though. Up by Quapaw. And before that over by Tulsa. Bastards to work fer, both of 'em!

CURLY. Whut'd they do?

JEETER. Alwys makin' out they was *better*. Yeah, *lots* better! Farmers they was, like me, wasn't they? Only not half as good.

CURLY. And whut'd you do—git even?

JEETER (*looks up at him, suspiciously*). Who said anything about gittin' even?

CURLY. No one, that I recollect. It jist come in my head.

JEETER. Oh, it did? (*He gets up, goes over and shuts the door, turns in the gloom, comes and sits down again, and looks at* CURLY.) Whut was that business you had up here at the house?

CURLY (*after a moment*). I don't know as that concerns you, does it?

JEETER. It does, though! If it's anything to do with this farm.

CURLY. I forgot you owned it.

JEETER. Never mind that! It couldn't be to buy hay, fer you got plenty of hay.

CURLY. How'd you know that?

JEETER. You work for Skidmore, don't you, tother side of Justus?

CURLY. Thought you didn't know me.

JEETER. I know you, all right. If he's sent you over to buy up the oat crop, why it's done spoke fer.

CURLY. Glad to find that out.

JEETER. We ain't got no cattle to sell, ner no cow ponies, you know that. And the farm ain't fer sale, and won't be.

CURLY. You shore relieved my mind considerable.

JEETER. They's only one thing left you could come snoopin' around here fer. And it ud better not be that!

CURLY (*easily*). That's exactly whut it is!

JEETER (*white with anger*). Better not be!

CURLY. It *is*, I tell you.

JEETER. I wouldn't come on the place if I was you! I wouldn't come here—

CURLY. Whut'll happen if I decide that's jist the right thing fer me to do?

JEETER. I'd git on my horse and go quick! Don't you come around that girl, you hear me?

CURLY (*scornfully*). You shore got it bad. So you're takin' her to that party tonight? Jesus! She's got a taste. I don't know as it's worth fightin' about if she'd ruther go with you. I step out—cheerful as anything. You're welcome. (*Thoughtfully.*) Only—somebody ort to tell her whut you air. And fer that matter somebody ort to tell you onct about yerself.

JEETER. I've had jist about enough!

CURLY. If you'd like to do anything to me, now's the best chanct you'll ever have. (*Softly.*) You got two pistols, good uns, all loaded and ready to bark. They's a axe a-standin' in the corner.

A bright bright sickle, right off the grindstone hangs over there on a nail and shines. Yer hoes is sharp, yer razor's got two edges onto it, and nary a one of 'em is rusty. And it ain't light in here, is it? Not half light enough. A feller wouldn't feel very safe in here 'th you, 'f he didn't know you. (*Acidly*.) But I *know* you, Jeeter. I've knowed you fer a long time.

JEETER (*half rising*). You don't know a thing about me—

CURLY. The country's full of people like you! I been around. (*His voice rises dramatically*.) In this country, they's two things you c'n do if you're a man. Live out of doors is one. Live in a hole is the other. I've set by my horse in the bresh some'eres and heared a rattlesnake many a time. Rattle, rattle, rattle!— he'd go, skeered to death. Skeered— and *dangerous!* Somebody comin' close to his hole! Somebody gonna step on him! Git his old fangs ready, full of pizen! Curl up and wait! Fer as long's you live in a hole, you're skeered, you got to have pertection. You c'n have muscles, oh, like arn—and still be as weak as a empty bladder—less'n you got things to barb yer hide with. (*Suddenly, harshly, directly to* JEETER.) How'd you git to be the way you air, anyway—settin' here in this filthy hole—and thinkin' the way you're thinkin'? Why don't you do sump'n healthy onct in a while, 'stid of stayin' shet up here a-crawlin' and festerin'!

JEETER. Shet up, you!

CURLY. You'll die of yer own pizen, I tell you!

JEETER. Anh!

(*He seizes a gun in a kind of reflex, a kind of desperate frenzy, and pulls the trigger. The wall across the room is splintered by the shot.*)

CURLY. Jesus! What was you shootin' at, Jeeter?

JEETER (*his hands on the two pistols, hoarsely*). Never mind, now!

CURLY (*in a high excitement, but apparently cool and calm*). You orta feel better now. Hard on the wall, though. I wish 't you'd let me show you sump'n. Jist reach me one of them pistols acrost here a minute— (JEETER *does not move, but sits staring into* CURLY's *eyes.*) They's a knot-hole over there about as big as a dime. See it a-winkin'?

I jist want to see if I c'n hit it. (*He leans over unhurriedly, with catlike tension, picks up one of the pistols, turns in his chair, and fires at the wall high up. He turns in triumph.*) Didn't make a splinter! Bullet right through the knot-hole, 'thout tetchin', slick as a whistle, didn't I? I knowed I could do it. You saw it, too, didn't you? Somebody's comin', I 'spect. It's my play, ain't it?

(*He throws down a card.* JEETER *looks at the floor.* LAUREY, AUNT ELLER, *and the* PEDLER, *followed a moment later by* ADO ANNIE, *come running in at the door without knocking.*)

AUNT ELLER (*gasping for breath*) Whut's this? Who's been a-shootin'? Skeer the liver and lights out of a feller! Was that you, Curly? Don't set there, you lummy, answer when you're spoke to!

CURLY. Well, I shot onct.

AUNT ELLER. What was you shootin' at?

CURLY. See that knot-hole over there?

AUNT ELLER. I see lots of knot-holes.

CURLY. Well, it was one of them.

AUNT ELLER. Don't tell me you was shootin' at a knot-hole!

CURLY. I was, though.

AUNT ELLER (*exasperated*). Well, ain't you a pair of purty nuthin's, settin' here a-pickin' away at knot-holes 'th a pair of ole pistols and skeerin' everybody to death! You've give that ole turkey gobbler conniption fits. Ort to give you a good Dutch rub and arn some of the craziness out of you! Come 'ere, you all, they ain't nobody hurt. Jist a pair of fools a-swappin' noises.

ADO ANNIE (*dumbly*). Did someone shoot, Aunt Eller?

AUNT ELLER. Did someone *shoot!*

ADO ANNIE. Whut'd they shoot *at*, Aunt Eller?

AUNT ELLER. Yer grandmaw, silly! (*She goes out.*)

ADO ANNIE. My lands!

(*She follows her out.* LAUREY *and the* PEDLER *stand in the door.*)

LAUREY (*after a moment*). Curly.

CURLY. Yeah.

LAUREY. Did you *hit* that knot-hole?

CURLY. How's that?

LAUREY. I say, did you *hit* that knot-hole?

CURLY (*puzzled*). Yeah, I—I hit it.

LAUREY (*cryptically*). Well. That was good, wasn't it?

(She goes out, smiling. The PEDLER *bounds into life and comes forward with great animation.)*

PEDLER. Well, well. Mr. Jeeter! Don't trouble yerself. Fine day, and a good crop comin'. You too, Mr. Curly. *(Lowering his voice.)* Now then, we're all by ourselves, I got a few little purties, private knick-knacks for to show you. Special for the menfolks. *(He winks mysteriously, and draws out of his inside coat pocket a thin flat box and opens it out on the table.)* Yes sir, special. The things you cain't get and 've got to have. All them little things a man needs in his business, eh? *(He points.)* Jist look at them things. Agin the law, ever one of 'em! There's brass knucks, lay a man out· jist like he was dead in one good hard hit. Fit any knuckle and break any head. And—in the little package, well, I won't tell you!— Jist open her up, and you'll see— The little dinguses that you got to have. Fancy! Lots of colors and jiggers onto 'em. French! Yes, sir! French—right out of Paris. And jackknives and frog-stickers. Steel and never rusty. Kill a hog or a bastard eh, it's all the same to them little ones! And postcards! Kansas City Best. Made right. Take 'em away, they're hard on the eyes! And here's dice, playing cards. Everything you need, everything a man could want. Look 'em over and if they's any little thing you need, jist point, jist make the signs, and I'm right here— Now then, how's that?

JEETER *(rousing himself)*. How much is that frog-sticker?

PEDLER *(taking out a long wicked-looking knife and opening it)*. That frog-sticker. That's reasonable, reasonable. I won't charge you much for a knife like that. 'F you got it in Claremore, you know whut you pay? Twice my price, jist twice. 'F you could get it. That's a good frog-sticker, that is, and I'm sellin' it cheap to you, Mr. Jeeter— fer a man hadn't ort to be *without* a good frog-sticker, it ain't safe, he might need it. He never knows why and he never knows when. Don't see nuthin' to interest you, Mr. Curly?

CURLY *(slowly)*. I was jist thinkin' myself—that mebbe—jist fer the looks of the thing—and to kinda have it around—I might consider—buyin'—if they're good and not too high—and can

be depended on—a nice hard pair of them brass knucks you got there— *(He reaches over and picks them up.)*

CURTAIN

SCENE FOUR

Lead her up and down the little brass
         wagon,
Lead her up and down the little brass
         wagon,
Lead her up and down the little brass
         wagon,
For she's the one, my darling!

One wheel off and the axle draggin',
One wheel off and the axle draggin',
One wheel off and the axle draggin',
For she's the one, my darling!

Spokes all broke and the tongue
        a-waggin',
Spokes all broke and the tongue
        a-waggin',
Spokes all broke and the tongue
a-waggin',
For she's the one, my darling!

Blistered brakes and sides all saggin',
Blistered brakes and sides all saggin',
Blistered brakes and sides all saggin',
For she's the one, my darling!

The party is in full swing in the back yard of OLD MAN PECK'S *place across Dog Creek. There are a few benches on the porch and a large coalstove. A primitive, rough-hewn built-in cabinet runs along one end of the porch and on it are piled all manner of miscellaneous things—ropes, cans of nails, a vinegar bottle, sacks of salt and sugar, home-dried apricots and peaches, a guitar, a fiddle, jars of home-made preserves. On the walls are hanging strings of popcorn on the cob, red peppers, onions hanging by their tops, the dried pelt of a possum, etc. Kerosene lanterns hung to the wall light up the yard. Light streams out from the house. Around the corner of the house can be seen the stone well with its wide arch of iron and its pulley, a tremendous walnut tree and the night sky.*

The farm boys and the cowboys have forgotten their corn plowing, their day in the hay field, their day on the range. They have put up the mules, doused themselves at the pump, bolted a supper of fried salt pork, potatoes and gravy and hot biscuits, and now in their store clothes and their chaps and their overalls they grin and sweat and stomp, their voices loud and harsh in the singing. Those who are not playing at the moment lounge in the doorway, chewing tobacco and smoking; some have gone out behind the barn or to their buggies and saddle pockets for a shot of liquor.

Most of the girls are dressed in white and wear bright bows. Some have tiny watches pinned to their dresses, and carry handkerchiefs. OLD MAN PECK *is clapping his hands. He is an old-timer, grizzled and genial, about seventy. He has gone to play-parties and dances now for fifty years, and knows every trick, every extra stomp, every variation in the songs, every sly elaboration of the* do si do.

The voices crack on the high notes, the feet pound, hands clap, the jars on the high cabinet rattle, dust clouds the air. "The Little Brass Wagon" ends in a burst of high, excited, exhausted laughter. Immediately, on a peak of gaiety, hardly stopping to mop their brows, the men begin getting partners for a square dance, calling loudly, grabbing the girls carelessly around the waist, and getting slapped for their temerity.

OLD MAN PECK (*leaping out into the middle of the floor and holding up his hands*). Hey! Boys and gals! Git in the kitchen fer the candy pullin'.

(*The crowd breaks, and dashes in the house noisily.* OLD MAN PECK *is about to follow.*)

AUNT ELLER (*calling from the darkness off left*). Lands sake, I'm all tangled up in it. Curly, help me, cain't you?

CURLY (*off*). Well, be still, quit a-buckin' up.

AUNT ELLER. Mr. Peck! Mr. Peck, you ole fool, come an' help a lady, cain't you!

OLD MAN PECK. Is that you, Aunt Eller? Whut's the matter?

AUNT ELLER (*entering with* CURLY). Matter! Say, do you have to have barbed w'ar layin' around all over the yard? Gettin' me all tangled up in it! 'F it hadn't a-been fer *me* I'd a-lost a leg. Whur's Mary?

OLD MAN PECK. Oh, I got the ole

womern out in the smokehouse.

AUNT ELLER. Doin' all the work, I bet.

OLD MAN PECK. Yep, that's right. You're kinda late, ain't you?

AUNT ELLER. Got here quick's I could make it. Say, is this whur the party's at —out here in the yard?

OLD MAN PECK. It's too hot in the house.

AUNT ELLER. Well, it's kinda purty out here, I must say. Here—hang this up.

OLD MAN PECK (*taking the lamp she holds out*). Whur'd you get that?

AUNT ELLER (*grinning*). Pulled it off the dashboard. Guess I'll go in and take off my fascinator. (*Taking* CURLY *by the arm.*) How'd you like my feller I went and ketched?

CURLY (*smiling, and taking her by the arm*). How'd you like my girl I went and ketched?

OLD MAN PECK. Both of you is all right, I reckon. Whur's Laurey at?

CURLY (*pausing as he realizes what this means*). Laurey, ain't she here yit?

OLD MAN PECK. *Course* not. Thought you was gonna bring her.

CURLY (*concerned*). They ort to be here, Aunt Eller. Whutta you reckon's happened? They started 'fore we did— half a hour before.

AUNT ELLER (*quieting him*). Aw, they're jist poky. They're drivin' Old Eighty, and that fool mare is alwys wantin' to graze 'long side the road. Now don't look so worried, Curly, they'll git here. Come on in, and le's se *who's* come with *who*.

(*They go in. A burst of greeting floats out.*)

SHORTY (*a cowboy, staggers in, drunk*). Say, Mr. Peck, is that yore big old white cow standin' out there by the grainery?

OLD MAN PECK. Hi, Shorty. Yeah, she's mine. Give two gallon and a half a day.

SHORTY. Whew, she like to skeered me to death. Thought she was a ghost— till she said *Moo.*

OLD MAN PECK. You must be drinkin' a little, Shorty.

SHORTY (*speaking as he makes for the door*). Me? I ain't drinkin'. I'm drunk. (*He goes into the house.*)

OLD MAN PECK (*spying* JEETER, ADO ANNIE *and* LAUREY. JEETER *is carrying a lighted lantern which he hangs up*). Oh, here you air. We been wonderin' whur you was.

ADO ANNIE *and* LAUREY. Hi, Mr. Peck.

OLD MAN PECK. Most everbody's here that's comin', I 'spect. I got to go out to the smokehouse, and see about the ice cream freezin'. Go on in, and git yer pardners for the next set.

(*He disappears around the corner of the house.* LAUREY *starts in the house.*)

JEETER (*stopping her*). I wanta see you.

LAUREY (*a little frightened*). Well, here I am, so look yer eyes full.

JEETER. Ado Annie, go inside.

LAUREY (*grabbing her*). Ado Annie, you stay here a minute.

ADO ANNIE (*pulling loose*). Shoot! I wanta see 'f I cain't git me a pardner, 'fore they're all gone. (*She dashes in.*)

JEETER. Whut'd you ast that Ado Annie to ride with us fer?

LAUREY. She didn't have no way to go.

JEETER. That ain't yore lookout. Why don't you wanta be with me by yerself?

LAUREY. Why, I don't know whut you're talkin' about! I'm with you by myself now, ain't I?

JEETER. You wouldn't a-been, you coulda got out of it.

LAUREY (*impatiently*). Well, now 'at I *am*, whut'd you want?

JEETER. Nuthin'—but—

LAUREY. Well, fer land's-a-livin'! (*She makes for the door.*) Of all the crazies!

JEETER (*getting in front of the door*). Mornin's you stay hid in yer room all the time. Nights you set in the front room and won't git outa Aunt Eller's sight— (*In a strange hoarse excitement.*) Ain't saw you by yerself in a long time! Why ain't I? First time was last year's thrashin'. You was watchin' the chaff fly and them knives a-cloppin' at the bundles. I come around the corner of the stack and you stood there a-wavin' yer sunbonnet to keep some of the dust offen you, and you said to me to git you a drink of water. I *got* you a drink of water. I brung the jug around. I give it to you. I *did* give it to you, didn't I?

LAUREY (*frightened*). I don't know whut you mean.

JEETER (*as before*). Last time it was winter 'th snow six inches deep in drifts when I was sick. You brung me that hot soup out to the smokehouse and give it to me, and me in bed. I hadn't

shaved in two weeks. You ast me 'f I had any fever and you put yer hand on my head to see. Why'd you do that? Whut'd you tetch me for! (*He suddenly seizes her in his arms, his voice thick with excitement.*) You won't git away from me—!

LAUREY (*trying to free herself*). You better le' me alone!

JEETER. You've kep' outa my way, and kep' outa my way—

LAUREY. Quit it, quit it—!

JEETER. Cain't think of nuthin' else! It's killin' me. Lay awake at nights. God damn you, quit a-tryin' to git away—I got you now — (*He holds her closer.*)

LAUREY (*in revulsion*). Oh! (*She turns her head aside, frightened and shaken.*)

JEETER. So goddamned purty!

(*She frees an arm and strikes him in the face, with desperate strength. He releases her, and stands uncomprehending, tranced. She backs away, watching him.*)

LAUREY (*almost hysterically*). Now le' me go, le' me outa here 'fore I holler and tell on you!

JEETER (*after a moment, slowly*). You hit me— (*Breaking out, violently.*) Like 'em all! I ain't good enough, am I? I'm a h'ard hand, ain't I? Got dirt on my hands, pig slop— Ain't fitten to tetch you! You're better, so goddamned much better! Yeah, we'll see who's better—we'll see who's better, Miss Laurey! Nen you'll wish 't you wasn't so free 'th yer airs, you're sich a fine lady—!

LAUREY (*suddenly so angry, all her fear vanishes*). Air you makin' threats—to *me?* Air you standin' there tryin' to tell me 'f I don't 'low you to slobber over me like a hog, why you're gonna do sump'n a about it! Why, you're a mangy dog and somebody'd orta shoot you! (*With enormous scorn.*) Yeah, I ort to 'low you yer own way, I reckon. Sich a great, big, fine strappin' man so full of dazzle I ort to git down on my knees to him! Christ all hemlock! (*Sharply, her eyes blazing.*) You think so much about bein' h'ard hand. Well, I'll jist tell you sump'n that'll rest yer brain, Mr. Jeeter! You ain't a h'ard hand fer me, no more! You c'n jist pack up yer duds and scoot! Oh, and I even got better idys 'n that! You ain't to come on the place again, you hear me? I'll send yer stuff any place you say, but don't you 's much 's set foot inside the pasture gate or I'll sic the dogs onto you! Now then, next time you go makin' threats to people, you better think a few thinks first and spit on yer hands fer good luck!

JEETER (*standing quite still, absorbed, dark, his voice low*). Said yer say. Brought it on yerself. (*In a voice harsh with an inner frenzy.*) Cain't he'p it, I tell you! Sump'n brung it on you. On me, too. Cain't never rest. Cain't be easy. That's the way it is. Ay, I told you the way it was! You wouldn't listen—

(*He goes out, passes the corner of the house, and disappears.* LAUREY *stands a moment, held by his strangeness, then she starts toward the house, changes her mind and sinks onto a bench, a frightened little girl again.* ADO ANNIE *bounds out of the house, excited. She sees* LAUREY.)

ADO ANNIE (*worried*). Laurey, I got sump'n to tell you.

LAUREY (*standing up quickly*). Ado Annie, is Curly in there?

ADO ANNIE. Yes he's in there, but . . . Laurey, now look, Laurey, it's turrible— I gotta tell you—

LAUREY (*starting swiftly towards the house*). Don't bother me.

ADO ANNIE (*catching at her*). Now, Laurey, please—my lands, it's all yore fault, so you gotta tell me whut to do.

LAUREY. Well, whut is it?

ADO ANNIE. Them ole garters is s' tight they 'bout cut my laigs plum in two.

LAUREY. Well, take 'em off.

ADO ANNIE. Take 'em off? Have my stockings rollin' down onto my shoes? Wouldn't I be a purty sight?

LAUREY. You'd have all the boys a-runnin' after you right, you done that.

ADO ANNIE. You shore?

LAUREY. Shore, I'm shore.

ADO ANNIE. Aw, I wouldn't do it fer nuthin'.

LAUREY. Well I told you whut to do, you won't mind me. (*She makes for the door.*)

ADO ANNIE (*stopping her*). Laurey! Them ole boys worries me. The minute I got in the house they started grabbin' at me. Whut'd they mean a-tellin' me, "Come out 'hind the barn 'th me?" That ole Payne boy said that.

LAUREY. Whyn't you ast him whut he meant?

ADO ANNIE. I was skeered he'd tell me.

LAUREY. Fiddlesticks! (*She starts again for the door, turns quickly, struck with an idea.*) Ado Annie, will you do sump'n fer me?

ADO ANNIE. 'F it ain't too hard.

LAUREY. Go in there and find Curly, and tell him to come out here. I want to see him, I got to see him!

(*A man runs out of the house calling out* "Whee! Here's my girl! Come on here, Ado Annie, I'm goin' to swing you till you're dizzy as a loon!" *He whirls her around and around.* LAUREY, *distressed, starts for the house.*)

A MAN (*coming out boisterously*). Here, Laurey's *my* partner. Come on, Laurey, you promised me away back last August, purt' near. (*He swings her into position for the next dance.*)

OLD MAN PECK (*coming from the house*). Git yore pardners like you done before, Two big rings in the middle of the floor.

(*The others all sweep out, paired off, and take their places for the square dance.*)

CROWD (*falling into position*).
I hope there'll be a big fight!
Be lots of work for the shoemaker, to-morrow!
Watch yer honey, watch her close,
When you meet her, double the dose!
Eight hands up, and circle to the west!

(*They start to dance.*)

OLD MAN PECK (*stopping them before they begin*). Whoa, whoa, back, Maud! My, you're like a gang of mule colts! Quiet down, cain't you, they ain't no a-stoppin' you! Wanta tell you sump'n!

CROWD.
Let' 'er rip, grampaw!
Say yer say and git it outa you 'fore you choke on it!
Open up yer mouth and holler yer head off, see 'f I keer!

OLD MAN PECK. Now then, listen to me a minute! We gonna have a little singin' to give us a rest. You all 'll be so broke down in a minute you'll be blowin' like a thrashin' machine. Quiet down now, see 'f we cain't git somebody to sing sump'n —Time we sing a little bit, got a s'prise for you. You all know whur the smoke-house is, don't you?

CROWD.
'Hind that ellum out there.
Shore, we know. Settin' on its foundations!

OLD MAN PECK. Well, I got the ole womern out there a-turnin' the ice cream freezer, and a-makin' popcorn balls. And jist as soon as we sing a little bit, everthing ort to be ready. Er 'f it *ain't* ready, take a scantlin' to the ole womern, I will, and blister her good! Now then, who'll give us a song?

CROWD.

Sing one yerself, Mr. Peck.
You ain't winded, air you?
Sing one of them ole ballets—
Sing "The Dyin' Cowboy." Oh, bury me not on the lone prairee!
Sing that there un 'bout the blind child, while we cry and take on, the pore little son of a gun, didn't have no mammy!

OLD MAN PECK (*humorously*). Aw, I'm bashful 's a blushin' bride! Anyways, all I know is sad songs, make you cry. No, cain't I git someone else—how 'bout you, Lizzie?

CROWD.

The sadder the better!
Go on, you start things, git everbody limbered up—!

OLD MAN PECK. Tell you whut I'll do, then! Sing you "Custer's Last Charge" an' 'f I ketch airy grin on any of you, gonna do sump'n, I'm tellin' you. And you better keep quiet and respectable-like, 'cause this yere is a serious piece.

CROWD.

Go to it, Mr. Peck!
Serious 's a church.
Got my mouth sewed up like a but-tonhole.
Sh!

OLD MAN PECK (*singing in a high, thin voice*).

'Twas just before brave Custer's charge,
Two soldiers drew the rein,
In parting words and clasping hands,
They may never meet again.

One had blue eyes and curly hair,
Just nineteen years ago,
With rosy cheeks and down on his chin,
He was only a boy, you know.

The other was a tall and a dark slim form
With eyes that glittered like gold,
With coal-black hair and brown
                    moustache,
Just twenty-five years old.

The tall dark form was the first to speak,
Saying, "Charley, our hour has come,
We will ride together up on yonder's hill,
But you must ride back alone.

"We have rode together on many a raid,
We have marched for many a mile,
But, comrade dear, I fear the last
Has come with a hopeless smile.

"I have a face, it's all this world to me,
And it shines like a morning's light,
Like a morning's light it has been to me
To cheer my lonesome life.

"Like a morning's light it has been to me
To cheer my lonesome life,
And little did I care for the flow of fate
When she promised to be my wife.

"Write to her, Charley, when I am gone,
Send back this fair-formed face,
And gently tell her how I died
And where is my resting place.

"And tell her I'll meet her on the
                    other shore,
In the bordering land between
Yes, heaven and earth, I'll meet her
                    there,
And it won't be long, I mean."

Then tears filled the eyes of the
                    blue-eyed boy
And his kind heart filled with pain—
"I'll do your bidding, my comrade dear,
Though we never meet again.

"If I get killed and you ride back,
You must do as much for me,
For I have a praying mother at home,
She is all the world to me.

"She has prayed at home like a
                    waiting saint,
She has prayed both night and morn,
For I was the last the country called,
She kissed and sent me on."

Just then, the orders came to charge,
An instant with clasped hands,
Then on they went, then on they rode,
This brave and devoted band.

They rode till they come to the crest of
                    the hill
Where the Indians shot like hail,
They poured death's volley on Custer's
                    men,
And scalped them as they fell.

They turned from the crest of the
                    bloody hills

With an awful gathering gloom,
And those that were left of the faithful
                                    band
Rode slowly to their doom.

There was no one left to tell the
                        blue-eyed girl
The words that her lover said,
And the praying mother will never know
That her blue-eyed boy is dead.

(*The crowd applauds and exclaims.*)

CROWD.
Shore a good un!
Sings plumb like a church choir, don't
he?
Whur's Curly McClain?
Git him to sing.
Here you, Curly, you c'n sing—one of
them cowpuncher ones.

CURLY (*appearing from the crowd*). Well.
Hand me down that guitar, will you?
(*Someone gets the guitar off the cabinet,
and hands it to him. He drags forward a stool
and sits down.*)
CROWD.
"Railroad Man."
"Levee Dan."
"Whistlin' Rufus."
"The Girl I Left Behind Me."
"The Pore Lost Dogie."
"Shoot the Buffalo."
Sump'n lively!
"The Mohawk Trail."
CURLY (*he strums a few notes, and begins
to sing, very simply*)
There is a lady, sweet and kind,
Was never face so pleased my mind,
I did but see her passing by,
And yet I love her till I die.

Her gestures, motion, and her smiles,
Her wit, her voice, my heart beguiles,
Beguiles my heart I know not why,
And yet I love her till I die.

Cupid is wingèd and doth range
Her country so my love doth change,
But change she earth or change she sky,
Yet will I love her till I die.

CROWD (*applauding*).
Sing another'n, Curly.
You shore fooled us. Funny song fer
you to be a-singin'!
Now, Aunt Eller—

Aunt Eller, come on, you, it's yore time.
AUNT ELLER. Ketch me a-singin'! Got
a frog in my throat—I'm t'ard, too. Got
a ketch in my leg and cain't sing. Land's
alive! Whyn't you git Ado Annie—?
Here, Ado Annie, sing one of them songs
of your'n.
(*They drag* ADO ANNIE *forward, squirm-
ing.*)
CROWD. Here, quit it a-pullin' back,
you don't git out of it—
ADO ANNIE (*awkwardly, standing first on
one foot, then on the other*). Done forgot!
Done forgot!
CROWD. Well, hurry up and re-
member—
ADO ANNIE. Don't know none, nary a
one. Done forgot ever one, I tell you!
CROWD. Well, whistle then, you got to
do sump'n.
AUNT ELLER. Forgot yer foot! Sing
that un about when you was young and
single—
ADO ANNIE. Shoot! My th'oat's plumb
sore—
AUNT ELLER. Sump'n else 'll be sore
you don't start. Hurry up, now—
ADO ANNIE (*singing in a flat mournful
voice*).
When I was young and single,
At home by my own f'ar side,
With my loving brother and sister,
My mother she never would chide.

Then there came a young man
His smiles enticèd me.
—And I was young and foolish
And easy led astray.

I don't see why I love him,
He does not keer for me,
But my thoughts are alwys of him
Wherever he may be.

They tell me not to believe him,
Say "He don't keer fer you."
How little I think that ever
Them words would ever come true!

Some say that love is pleasure.
What pleasure do I see?
For the one I love so dearly
Has now gone back on me!

The night is dark and dreary,
A little incline to rain—
O God, my heart is weary
For my lover's gone off on a train!

OLD MAN PECK. All out fer the smokehouse now! Git some ice cream in you, you feel better! Got vanilla and strawberry both, so don't be bashful!

(*The crowd begins to stream noisily out, disappearing past the corner of the house.*)

LAUREY (*catching* CURLY *away from his partner, and dragging him back till the others are all gone*). Curly!

CURLY (*astonished*). Now what on earth is ailin' the belle of Claremore? By gum, if you ain't a-cryin'!

(LAUREY *runs over to him, leans against him.*)

LAUREY. Curly—I'm 'fraid of my life—!

CURLY (*in a flurry of surprise and delight*). Jumpin' toadstools! (*He waves his hat, then throws it away wildly, and puts his arms around* LAUREY, *muttering under his breath.*) Great Lord—!

LAUREY. Don't you leave me—

CURLY. Great Godamighty—!

LAUREY. Don't mind me a-cryin', I cain't he'p it—

CURLY. Jesus! Cry yer eyes out—!

LAUREY. Oh, I don't know whut to do!

CURLY. Here. I'll show you. (*He lifts her face and kisses her. She puts her arms about his neck. He exclaims softly.*) Laurey, Laurey—! (*He kisses her again and again, then takes a step away from her, disengaging her arms gently.*)

LAUREY (*in alarm*). Curly—

CURLY. My goodness! (*He shakes his head as if coming out of a daze, gives a low whistle, and backs away.*) Whew! 'Bout all a man c'n stand in public—! Go 'way from me, *you*!

LAUREY. Oh, you don't like me, Curly—

CURLY. *Like* you? My God! Git away from me, I tell you, plumb away from me!

(*He strides across the porch and sits down on the stove.*)

LAUREY (*crying out*). Curly! You're settin' on the stove!

CURLY (*leaping up*). Godamighty! (*He turns round, puts his hand down gingerly on the lids.*) Aw! 'S cold 's a hunk of ice! (*He sits down again.*)

LAUREY (*pouting*). Wish 't ud burnt a hole in yer pants—

CURLY (*grinning at her, understandingly*). You do, do you?

LAUREY (*turning away, to hide her smile*). *You* heared me.

CURLY. Laurey, now looky here, you stand over there right whur you air, and I'll set over here—and you tell me whut you wanted with me.

LAUREY (*grave again*). Well—Jeeter was here. (*She shudders.*) He skeered me— he's crazy. I never saw nobody like him—

CURLY (*harshly*). Whut'd he do? Aunt Eller told me all about the way you felt —whyn't you tell *me*—why didn't you? Whut'd he do?

LAUREY. Tried to kiss me—Wouldn't let me out of here. Said he'd tried to see me all by myself fer months. He talked wild—and he threatened me.

CURLY. The bastard!

LAUREY. I f'ard him! Told him not to come on the place again. I got mad to see him standin' there like a black cloud, and I told him whut! I wish 't I hadn't-a! They ain't no tellin' whut he'll do now! 'F I'd jist a-kep' my head! Now whut am I gonna do!

CURLY. You f'ard him?

LAUREY. Yes, but—

CURLY. *Well*, then! That's all they is to it! He won't do nuthin'! Tomorrow, I'll git you a new h'ard hand. I'll stay on the place myself tonight, 'f you're nervous about that hound dog. (*Putting an end to it.*) That's the end of Jeeter, and about time. Now quit yer worryin' about it, er I'll spank you. Hey, while I think of it—how—how 'bout marryin' me?

LAUREY (*flustered*). Gracious, whut'd I wanta marry *you* fer?

CURLY (*getting down off the stove and going to her, gravely, like a child*). Laurey, please, ma'am—marry me. I—I don't know whut I'm gonna do if you—if you don't.

LAUREY (*touched*). Curly—why, you— why, I'll marry you—'f you want me to—

CURLY (*he takes her in his arms, kisses her gently*). I didn't think you would, I didn't dream you'd ever—!

LAUREY. Sh!

(*He leads her over, and lifts her up on the stove. Then he lets down the oven door and sits on it, at her feet.*)

CURLY (*humbly*). I ain't got no right to ast you—a good-fer-nuthin' cowpuncher like me—

LAUREY. Don't say things like that.

CURLY. If I'd ever a-thought—! Oh, I'd orta been a farmer, and worked hard at it, and saved, and kep' buyin' more land, and plowed and planted, like somebody—'stid of doin' the way I've done! Now the cattle business'll soon be over with. The ranches are breakin' up fast. They're puttin' in barbed w'ar, and plowin' up the sod fer wheat and corn. Purty soon they won't be no more grazin'—thousands of acres—no place fer the cowboy to lay his head.

LAUREY. Don't you worry none, Curly—

CURLY. Yer paw done the right way. He knowed. He could see ahead.

LAUREY. But Pap ain't alive now to enjoy it. But we're alive, Curly. Alive! Enjoy all we can! Case things happen.

CURLY. Nuthin' cain't happen now— nuthin' bad—if you—if you love me— and don't mind a-marryin' me.

LAUREY. Sh! I'll marry you. Somebody's comin', don't you reckon?

CURLY. I don't keer. When *will* you marry me?

LAUREY. Oh, purty soon. I'll have to ast Aunt Eller, first.

CURLY. I'll ast her myself! (*Gaily.*) Oh, I 'member the first time I ever seen you! You was pickin' blackberries long side the road here years and years ago—you was a little tyke. (*He laughs.*) You'd been a-eatin' berries as fast as you could pick 'em, and yer mouth was black as a coal shovel!—'F you wasn't a sight!

LAUREY (*embarrassed*). Curly!

CURLY. Nen I seen you onct at the Fair—a-ridin' that little gray filly of Blue Starr's, and I says to someone— "Who's that little thing with a bang down on her forehead?"

LAUREY. Yeow, I 'member. You was ridin' broncs that day, and one th'owed you.

CURLY. Did *not* th'ow me!

LAUREY. Guess you jumped off, then.

CURLY. Shore I jumped off.

LAUREY. Yeow, you shore did!

CURLY (*lyrically, rapturously*). Anh, and I seen you once—the Sunday a year ago, I'll never forget. I come over to break them broncs. You'd been out a-pickin' flowers next to that sorghum mill standin' in the cane patch. And you had a whole armful of Sweet Williams and wild roses and mornin' glories, and I don't know whut all. My, I nearly fell off my horse a-lookin' at you! And I thought to myself—"if this yere bronc th'ows me, I won't land anywhurs near no Sweet Williams and wild roses. No sir! No sich luck! I'll find myself 'th my face plowin' up a patch of cuckle burrs and jimson weeds—er most likely a ole cow pile!"

LAUREY. Curly! The way you talk!

CURLY (*as before*). Be the happiest man a-livin', soon 's we're married! (*Frowning.*) Oh, but I'll shore be a unsettled man, though, you're so blame purty, worried somebody'll run off with you! 'F I ever have to leave home to be gone all day, gonna shore tie you up to the hitchin' post, so you'll be there 'gin I git back, you hear? (*He shakes her playfully.*) Ain't gonna take no chances! (*Mischievously.*) And looky here, whut're you gonna give me fer a weddin' present? Well, you gonna marry a good-fer-nothin' cow hand, 'thout a red cent in his breeches, 's yer own fault, they come high! How 'bout a pair of spurs? Er a nice new saddle blanket, eh, 'th red stripes onto it, and 'nitials stitched inside of a bleedin' heart on the corner? Whut's the use of gettin' married, don't git a saddle blanket er sump'n purty out of it!—

LAUREY. Curly! Now I'll know why you married me—to git a saddle blanket!

CURLY. Yeow, out in the open, that's me! A man's got to watch out fer hisself even 'f he has to marry him a homely critter like you—'th a face like a windmill, make you dizzy to look at it! Come 'ere and kiss me, why don't you?

LAUREY (*gravely, touching his hair shyly*). I jist set here and listen at you, and don't keer whut you say about me. Say I'm homely 's a mud fence, you want to—why then, I *am* homely 's a mud fence. 'F you say I'm purty, why I'm purty as anything, and got a voice like Jenny Lind. I never thought of anything like this! But I always wondered and wondered, after the first time I ever seen you— (*Her eyes fill with tears, absurdly.*) And here we set, you and me, on the kitchen stove like a pair of skillets, and I don't know whut's come over us to act so silly—and I'm gonna cry in a minute—and it's all yore fault, you orten't to a-made love to me this-a-way—

(CURLY *jumps up, puts his arms around her.*)

CURLY. Laurey— Cry 'f you want to, then. (*He kisses her tenderly.*) Laurey, sweet— (*After a moment.*) Now, then. (*Crying out, suddenly.*) Why, my lands of goodness! I plumb forgot! You ain't had nothin' to eat! No popcorn er ice cream er nuthin'! You pore thing! Wait a minute. I'll git you sump'n 'fore it's all gone! (*He runs and looks down the well, and comes back quickly very much amused.*) Hey! Look in the cupboard there and see 'f you cain't find two glasses. (*He goes back to the well and can be seen hauling up a rope.*)

LAUREY. Whut're you up to, Curly? (*She flies to the cupboard, finds some glasses.* CURLY *has drawn up a small tin bucket, detached it from the rope, and come back, the bucket dripping. He sets it down on the stool, takes off the cover.*)

CURLY. Cream! Good ole rich cream, right outa the well! Cold as ice! Freeze yer wishbone, might' nigh, a-slidin' down yer throat!

(LAUREY *brings the glasses. He pours them full. They are drinking when the* CROWD, *already paired off, sweeps down into the yard hilariously.*)

CROWD (*calling out in excitement*).

Hey! Whut's this!

Two little love birds!

Jist a-dyin' to git on the nest, too, from the look of 'em!

Gonna be a weddin'—

Gonna be a shivoree—

How'd a girl ever take to a feller like you, Curly?

AUNT ELLER (*appearing*). Land sakes, I feel turrible! I went and ketched me a feller and here he is makin' up to another girl!

A MAN. Let's start the lovin' couple off right!

(JEETER *has leaned against a post and stands brooding. He has been drinking and has a bottle in his hand.*)

JEETER (*with dark scorn*). Yay, start 'em off right! To the bride and groom— (*He lifts the bottle, darkly, insultingly, and hurls it across the yard, where it breaks with a loud crash.* CURLY *starts toward him angrily,* LAUREY *clinging to him.* OLD MAN PECK, *seeing the situation, grabs the hands of the people nearest him, and they form a circle which quickly grows, shunting* CURLY *and* LAUREY *off from* JEETER *on one side of the yard. Someone begins to sing; the crowd joins in.* LAUREY *and* CURLY *are* hoisted up on chairs, the circle around them. CROWD (*singing*):

Gone again, skip to my Lou,
Gone again, skip to my Lou,
Gone again, skip to my Lou,
Skip to my Lou, my darling!

Cain't git a redbird, bluebird'll do,
Cain't git a redbird, bluebird'll do,
Cain't git a redbird, bluebird'll do,
Skip to my Lou, my darling!

My girl wears a number ten shoe,
My girl wears a number ten shoe,
My girl wears a number ten shoe,
Skip to my Lou, my darling!

Flies in the buttermilk, two by two,
Flies in the buttermilk, two by two,
Flies in the buttermilk, two by two,
Skip to my Lou, my darling!

CURTAIN

SCENE FIVE

A July moon is over the hayfield, making silver tents of the mounds of unbaled hay which recede in irregular formation far into the distance, crossing a low hill. A gaunt wire rake with enormous wheels stands at one side. The sky is powdered with stars, but low clouds drift often in front of them and the moon, blotting out the stubble. A soft summer wind, creeping about the meadow, lifts the spears of grass that have escaped the sickle. A low haystack, very near, has a ladder leaning against it.

After a moment, CURLY *and* LAUREY *steal into sight, looking around cautiously. They stop, move forward a little, breathless, begin to speak in hushed voices.*

CURLY (*softly*). D'you hear anything?

LAUREY (*softly*). No.

CURLY. Listen. (*They listen. Then he turns to her with relief.*) Not a sound. We've give 'em the slip.

LAUREY. Sh! Whut was that?

(*There is not a sound.*)

CURLY. Don't hear nuthin'.

LAUREY (*relieved*). Jist the wind, I guess.

CURLY. Listen. We'll leave Old Eighty standin' whur we tied her. We cain't drive up to the house, 'cause 'f anybody's watchin' out fer us, they'd see us. We'll sneak acrost the hayfield and th'ough the plum thicket—and go in the back door. Come on now. Watch whur you step.

LAUREY (*taking his hand, stopping him, hesitantly*). Curly—if they ketch us, whut'll happen? Will it be bad?

CURLY (*soberly*). You know about shivorees, honey. They git purty rough.

LAUREY. I'm afeard.

CURLY. Don't be afeard, honey. Aunt Eller says fer shore nobody seen us gittin' hitched.

LAUREY. They might a s'pected sump'n, though. (*Her voice low.*) That's the ketch about gittin' married—

CURLY (*reassuringly*). But here we air, honey. Married—and purt' nigh home. And not a soul in sight.

LAUREY (*after a moment of registering this, relievedly*). Yeah. We fooled 'em, didn't we?

CURLY. Shore we did.

LAUREY. Course. (*Her voice full of wonder.*) Curly—we're—we're married now.

CURLY (*softly*). Yeah. Plumb hitched.

LAUREY. Was you skeered when the preacher said that about "Will you take this here womern—"?

CURLY. Skeered he wouldn't *say* it.

LAUREY. I was skeered you'd back out on me.

CURLY. I *couldn't* back out on you—'f I *wanted* to. Could you *me*?

LAUREY (*smiling tenderly*). Not if I tried and tried.

(*They kiss, and embrace for a moment. Then, still holding her hand, CURLY turns, looking out over the moonlit field.*)

CURLY (*lyrically, feeling the moment*). Look at the way the hayfield lays out purty in the moonlight. Next it's the pasture, and over yander's the wheat and the corn, and the cane patch next, nen the truck garden and the timber. Ever'thing laid out fine and jim dandy! The country all around it—all Indian Territory—plumb to the Rio Grande, and north to Kansas, and 'way over east to Arkansaw, the same way, with the moon onto it. Trees ain't hardly a-movin'. Branch bubbles over them limestone rocks, you c'n hear it. Wild flower pe'fume smellin' up the air, sweet as anything! A fine night fer anyone to remember fer a weddin' night! A fine night—fer anyone.

(*Caught up in the spell of the night and their feelings, they move softly away across the stubble, and disappear. There is a moment of silence.*

Then there is a subdued titter, followed by shishing sounds, then more titters and smothered laughter. There pop into sight on top of, and from behind the stacks, dozens of men carrying noise-making instruments—tin lids, pots, washboilers, cow bells, gourd rattles, tambourines, pans, iron triangles, whistles, drums. They are an excited, huddled, whispering group, nervous at their long wait for the return of the bride and groom from town, disturbed and hysterical with conjecture on the marital scene they have come to despoil. Veterans of the "shivoree," hardly a bridal couple within twenty miles around, for years and years, has escaped their bawdy ministrations. They look off toward the retreating and oblivious couple, holding their voices down.)

1ST MAN. Sh! They'll hear you!

3RD MAN (*satirically, mockingly*). "Fine night to remember fer a weddin' night!"

(*Laughter.*)

5TH MAN. Fine night fer anyone! Whee! (*Hushing them.*) Quiet down now! They'll hear you 'fore they git to the house!

9TH MAN. Tee hee! Bet they'll go to bed in the dark!

(*Laughter.*)

10TH MAN (*severely*). Be keerful! They'll hear us, you hoodlums!

1ST MAN. Sh!

7TH MAN. Cain't you keep yer mouth still a minute!

3RD MAN. Whee! High ole doin's!

5TH MAN. Ketch 'em in the act!

YOUNG FARMER. Whut're we waitin' fer?

OLD FARMER. Give 'em time to git to the house, cain't you?

CORD ELAM. Don't want to give 'em too much time!

10TH MAN. Wish't I uz in his shoes. Godamighty!

3RD MAN. He shore got him sump'n there!

1ST MAN. Couple of sections!

2ND MAN. Grazin' and timber and plowed land!

4TH MAN. Money!

6TH MAN. Scads of it in the bank, and more comin'!

5TH MAN. And God! She's a purty un, too!

3RD MAN. Got a face fer kissin'!

7TH MAN. Hands white as snow!

5TH MAN. And that ain't all, brother!

YOUNG FARMER. No, and that ain't all! Jesus! Wish't I uz in Curly's shoes! 'F I uz Curly, ud be in my bare feet by this time!

1ST MAN (*in great excitement*). Look! They's a light!

(*The crowd in an excited frenzy begins jumping off the stacks.*)

3RD MAN. In the bedroom!

4TH MAN. Look at the way them curtains blow!

2ND MAN. Lace curtains!

3RD MAN. Blowin' out like a shirt-tail a-poppin' in the breeze!

CORD ELAM. Wonder whut they're a-seein', them curtains?

1ST MAN. Bridal couple! Onct in a lifetime—

3RD MAN. By theirselves!

4TH MAN. Night come on!

YOUNG FARMER. Ay, the good ole black night—'th nobody to spy on you, nobody to see whut you're up to!

8TH MAN. Look at them shadders a-movin'!

1ST MAN. It's them, they're there! See that *there* un!

2ND MAN. Gittin' ready!

3RD MAN. Got to hurry now, 'come on! Give 'em a s'prise!

CORD ELAM. Don't fergit now, right by this here stack whur the ladder is, like we said!

3RD MAN. Don't make so goddamned much noise!

(*They go out. An* OLD MAN *stumbles into the moonlight, shaking his head, dismally.*)

OLD MAN. Listen at that ole owl a-hootin' in the timber, and that there coyote away off yander towards the Verdigree River!

(*He goes out. A* YOUNG FARMER, *flushed and drinking, staggers darkly out of the gloom.*)

YOUNG FARMER. Bridegroom a-waitin' and a-waitin'! Don't you wait now, Mr. Bridegroom! The moon's a-shinin'! Yer time has came! Yes, sirree, bob! No time to wait now. Time to git goin'. See that there bride a-glimmerin' there in her white! Waitin' fer you. Been a-standin' there with her hair down her back and her lips a-movin'! Git next to her, brother! Gonna be high ole times, gonna be Jesus into yer heart!

(*The sound of raucous noise and excitement begins.* CORD ELAM *runs from around a stack shoving the* YOUNG FARMER *out of the way.*)

CORD ELAM. Git outa the way now, Homer! (*To the approaching noisy party.*) Hey! Over this-a-way. Yere's the place!

(*The noise of the shivoree grows louder and louder. Voices rise out of the bedlam, in sharp exclamations and cries.*

A few men drag CURLY *in, struggling and angry, his hair in his eyes. His shirt has been ripped off in the struggle.*)

CURLY. God damn you, leave her alone! Don't ary son of a bitch put his hands onto her, I'll kill him—!

A MAN. Aw, nobody's a-hurtin' her, Curly—

CURLY. Better hadn't. I tell you. Make 'em git away from her, plumb away from her!

A MAN (*shouting off*). Git away from her, you all! Bring her on in!

(CURLY *relaxes, but his captors still hold him tightly.*

A wide circle of men, shouting, whistling, beating their various noise implements, advances across the stubble. In the middle of the group, walking alone, pale and shaken is LAUREY, *in a nightgown, her hair down about her shoulders. The crowd goes over to the foot of the ladder and stops.*)

5TH MAN. Quiet down now, a minute! (*To* LAUREY.) Right up the ladder with you purty thing!

(*The noise stops.*)

6TH MAN. Go on, boost her up!

7TH MAN. Right up on the stack—!

8TH MAN. Make out it's a bed, why don't you!

(LAUREY *looks around at* CURLY, *then climbs up the short ladder, the crowd shouting at her.*)

9TH MAN. Watch it!

10TH MAN. Put yer foot in the right place.

CORD ELAM. Don't wanta fall and break yer neck—cheat pore Curly outa his rights!

10TH MAN. All right, Curly—

6TH MAN. You're next.

10TH MAN. Bring him on over here.

(THE MEN *holding* CURLY *lead him over to the foot of the ladder, and let go of him.* THE CROWD *begins to call out in more jubilant, crazier derision.*)

1ST MAN. Go, on, Mr. Bridegroom, there's yer bride!—

3RD MAN. Purty's a new bronc a-standin' and a-lookin', cain't hardly keep off her!

7TH MAN. Mane like silk and eyes a-shinin'!

CORD ELAM. Git on, there, cowpuncher —! (*After a moment,* CURLY *starts up the ladder, the crowd continuing to shout.*) 'F you ain't a world-beater fer bashful!

3RD MAN. Better be glad we didn't ride you on no fence rail!

1ST MAN. Th'ow the ladder down when he gits up.

10TH MAN. Try to git off, you'll break yer neck, so watch out!

(CURLY *reaches the top. Someone throws the ladder down.*)

CURLY (*deeply troubled*). Laurey, honey —(*She looks at him, in dumb misery.*) I'd give my eyesight, honey—! Try to stand it—I done all I could. I cain't he'p it—

(*He takes her in his arms. The men break out into derisive and lascivious guffaws, and begin the deafening noises again, circling the haystack, kicking up their heels, in an orgy of delight.*)

3RD MAN. Give us a little kiss, honey lamb, do a man good, taint a-askin' much!

CORD ELAM. Give us a lick and a promise!—Quick's these bad ole mens goes away—they ain't no a-tellin', no, siree!

5TH MAN. 'Taint right to stand there like that—Blush to look at you!

7TH MAN. Ain't no right to be in no nightgown!

10TH MAN. Go on, Mr. Moon Man, hide yer face fer shame!

YOUNG FARMER. How's it feel to be married, Laurey, sugar, all safe and proper, to sich a fine purty man with curly hair and a dimple on his chin! Whee! Got you whur I want you—!

1ST MAN. Scrunch you to death, purt' near!

CORD ELAM. Bite them shoulders—

3RD MAN. Eat 'er alive!

5TH MAN. Yay, Curly, and it's one more river to cross!

(*One of the men cries out, excitedly, snickering.*)

A MAN. Hey, Curly! Hey, Laurey! One baby! (*He tosses a grotesque straw baby high in the air and onto the stack.*) Two! (*He tosses another quickly.*) Three! (*He tosses another.*)

ANOTHER MAN (*holding up admonishing hands, grinning delightedly*). Hold it! Not so many! That'll give Curly idys, that will!

(*There is raucous laughter, and beating of instruments.*

The glow and smoke of something burning which has already crept quietly over the hayfield, now leaps up. A haystack is burning.)

CURLY (*startled, pointing*). Look! Fer God's sake, that hay stack's on fire! (THE MEN *rush toward it.*) Get us a ladder someone, quick! The whole hayfield 'll be on fire!

(*Suddenly a dark figure comes into sight, carrying a flaming torch. It is* JEETER.)

JEETER (*crying out*). Yanh, you thought you had it over me so big, didn't you? And you, too, Missy! Wanted sump'n purtier to sleep with. Yanh, you won't be a-havin' it long. Burn you to cracklin's!

(*He springs forward like a maddened animal to apply the torch to the stack.* LAUREY *screams.* THE MEN *start rushing back, as* CURLY *leaps down, knocking the torch out of* JEETER's *hand.*)

CURLY. Godamighty!

(*They struggle. The crowd exclaims.*)

1ST MAN. It's Jeeter Fry! Thought he'd flew the country!

3RD MAN. Drunk as a lord—

3RD MAN. Godamighty, he's crazy drunk!

5TH MAN. He was sweet on her too, they tell me. Stop him, somebody!

7TH MAN. Man seen him last week 'way off in Joplin.

8TH MAN. Jeeter, you goddamned—

(A MAN *beats at the torch with his bare hands, till* ANOTHER MAN *runs up and smothers it quickly with his coat. Someone picks up the torch, stamping out the flames, and runs out to the branch with it.*

JEETER *has backed away in the struggle, and drawn out a knife. He throws himself upon* CURLY. *The crowd mutters in excitement and fear. The men struggle over the knife, their arms gripping each other desperately. Suddenly,* JEETER *trips and they go down on the stubble.* JEETER *groans and whimpers and lies very still.*)

CURLY. Now, now—Christ— (*He shakes his hand, crazily, helplessly, in horror.*) Look at—look at him! Fell on it— Stuck it th'ough his ribs!

(*He backs away, shaken, horrified. Some of* THE MEN *bend over the prostrate man.*)

YOUNG FARMER. Pull that knife out!

MEN.
What's the matter?
Don't you tech it!
Turn him over—

He's breathin', ain't he?

Feel his heart.

How'd it happen?

9TH MAN (*wildly*) Anh, it's went right th'ough his heart—

4TH MAN. Whut'll we do? Ain't he all right?

10TH MAN. 'S he jist stunned?

CORD ELAM (*pushing into the crowd*). Git away, some of you! Lemme look at him. (*He bends down, the men crowding around.* CURLY *has slumped back against the stack, like a sick man.* LAUREY *stands dazed, watching. After a moment, standing upright.*) Cain't do a thing now. Try to git him to a doctor, but I don't know—

9TH MAN (*hysterically*). Pull the knife out, cain't you? Leave a knife stuck in a—! (*He springs forward.*)

CORD ELAM (*grabbing him*). You can't pull it out, you fool! Git away from there! (*The man staggers away, weakly.*) Here, you, some of you! Carry him down to the branch. Quick! I'm 'fraid it's too late!

(*The men lift* JEETER *up.*)

10TH MAN. Handle him easy!

6TH MAN. Don't shake him!

3RD MAN. Hold on to him careful, there!

5TH MAN. Godamighty! Whut a thing to happen!

(*They carry him out.*)

CORD ELAM (*to* CURLY). I don't know, Curly. You better give yerself up, I 'spect. They ain't no a-tellin'. You better go in with me, as I go, and tell 'em how it was. Tonight. It might go hard with you, you don't. (CURLY *stands dazed, as if unhearing.*) 'D you hear me, Curly? You know the way ever'body feels about shivoreein'. You got to take it right.

CURLY (*in desperation*). But far—*far!* He was tryin' to burn us up!

CORD ELAM. I know. But you got to tell the *law.* It'll be easier that way. I'll come back fer you. (*He goes out toward the branch.*)

LAUREY (*in a fever of horror*). Curly, Curly—

CURLY (*hardly able to speak*). Laurey—

LAUREY. Is he—is he—?

CURLY. Don't say anything—

LAUREY. It cain't be that-a-way!

CURLY. I didn't *go* to.

LAUREY. *Cain't* be! Like that—to happen to us!

CURLY. Sh! Be quiet!

LAUREY. Whyn't they do sump'n? Why'd they let him—lay there—? Cain't git over the way he—

CURLY. Laurey, Laurey!

LAUREY (*in mounting hysterical feeling*). He laid there in the stubble, so quiet, 'th his eyes open, and his eyeballs white and starin'! He laid there in the stubble—'th his eyes open—!

(*She buries her face in her hands, shuddering.*

CURLY *turns away, numb, speechless, his shoulders hunched up, like one shielding himself from the wind. The howl of a coyote drifts in on the summer air—near and desperate and forlorn.*)

CURTAIN

SCENE SIX

A few nights later ADO ANNIE *and* AUNT ELLER *are sitting in the front room, sewing. An oil lamp makes an amber pool of light about them. The sliding doors are closed, but a thin crack of light comes from underneath.* ADO ANNIE, *with a piece of plaid across her knees, is snipping at it with scissors.* AUNT ELLER *is very busy over a flour sack; she pushes her iron spectacles up off her nose and looks over at* ADO ANNIE.

AUNT ELLER (*in astonishment*). In the name of Doodlebug—whut *air* you a-doin'?

ADO ANNIE (*looking up from her work*). Makin' a buttonhole, cain't you see?

AUNT ELLER. A *round* buttonhole?

ADO ANNIE. Course.

AUNT ELLER (*amused*). Whyn't you make a square one? Er I tell you—make one looks like a four-leaf clover, why don't you?

ADO ANNIE (*shortly*). Guess I know how to make buttonholes.

AUNT ELLER. Yeah, you shore do. Cuttin' a round hole in that plaid. (*They sew in silence. After a moment* AUNT ELLER *glances up toward the closed door, and says:*) She ain't went to bed yit.

ADO ANNIE. 'S nine o'clock about.

AUNT ELLER (*shaking her head*). Worried about her. She don't eat ner sleep sence Curly was tuck away.

ADO ANNIE. She'll git pore she don't eat.

AUNT ELLER. Well, *course* she'll git pore.

ADO ANNIE. That's whut I said.

AUNT ELLER (*slightly irritated*). I *heared* you say it.

ADO ANNIE (*blandly*). Well.

AUNT ELLER. Looky here, Ado Annie Carnes, don't you ever marry.

ADO ANNIE (*self-consciously*). Gracious, who'd I marry?

AUNT ELLER. Don't you *ever! I* did. And *look* at me. (*Half-seriously.*) First yer man—*he'll* die—like mine did. Nen the baby—*she'll* die. The rest of yer young-uns'll grow up and marry and leave you, the way mine did. Nen you'll be all by yerself. Time you're old as me, you'll be settin' around, jist the way *I* am, 'th a wooden leg and a bald head, and a-rip-pin' up old flour sacks to make yerself a pair of drawers out of. (*She holds up her work for* ADO ANNIE *to see.*)

ADO ANNIE (*overcome with mirth*). Hee! Hee!

AUNT ELLER. Trouble shore starts, you git married. Look at Laurey. Better *not* git married, I tell you.

ADO ANNIE. Well, I won't then, if you say so.

AUNT ELLER. Anh, but trouble starts nohow, so you might jist as well *git* married as to *not.*

ADO ANNIE (*bewildered*). Well, which'll I do, then?

AUNT ELLER. *Both! I* mean—I don't *keer!* (*Her voice sinking to a grave half-whisper, as she says what is really on her mind.*) They *cain't* stick him—

ADO ANNIE. Stick who?

AUNT ELLER. Curly. They *cain't* stick him. Self-defense. Plain's the nose on yer face. Wish't they'd git it over with, that's whut I wish—

ADO ANNIE. Did—did Curly *kill* Jeeter —'th that old knife?

AUNT ELLER. Naw! 'Course not! Jeeter *fell* on his ole knife—and died. And he *ort* to 'a.

ADO ANNIE. They ain't no fair a-holdin' Curly fer it, then?

AUNT ELLER. 'Course it ain't fair! It's jist the law. They got to have their old hearin' first. Them *town* fools! First the shivoreein'—that was bad enough. And on top of it—Jeeter. Now Laurey all broke up, and Curly settin' in the cooler

at Claremore. Shore a happy weddin', I *must* say. Why, them two ain't *railly married* yit.

ADO ANNIE (*her mouth open*). Ain't they married, Aunt Eller!

AUNT ELLER. Well, they're married, all right, but they ain't—My, 'f you don't know whut I mean, I shore ain't gonna tell you! (*She gets up, and goes over to the window.*) Looks blackened up over yander. "More rain, more rest, more niggers from the West." Hope it don't come a rain er a big windstorm 'th all that forty of wheat in the shock. Ort to a-stacked it, I reckon. (*She turns back.*) Does yer Maw need you tomorrow, Ado Annie?

ADO ANNIE. Naw, she said I could stay all week, 'f you ud feed me.

AUNT ELLER. I'll feed you, all right. Grease-eye gravy and cracklin' corn-bread! And roas'n'ears. Tomorrow we'll start in to can them peaches—clings and all. 'Spect we better be gittin' to bed. Only, I kinda hate to go to bed 'th Laurey still— (*She taps softly at* LAUREY's *door, and calls gently.*) Laurey—

LAUREY (*after a moment, inside*). Yes.

AUNT ELLER. Ain't you gone to bed yit, honey?

(*The door slides back and* LAUREY *stands there in the lamplight, looking very pale and changed, years older, a woman now.*)

LAUREY. I cain't sleep—so—they ain't no sense in goin' to bed. (*She comes down into the room.*) Whut're you makin', Ado Annie?

ADO ANNIE. Me a dress. Ain't it purty?

LAUREY. Yes. (*Gravely.*) Aunt Eller, did they—Whut *did* they say?

AUNT ELLER. I *told* you, honey. Jist said the hearin' was comin' up tomorrow. Now, I don't want you to worry about it no more. They'll let him off, all right, they got to.

LAUREY. Curly ort to a-let me went into Claremore with him like I wanted to—to testify for him.

AUNT ELLER. Don't you know they wouldn't a-let you say nuthin', Laurey? You're his wife, ain't you?

LAUREY (*slowly*). Yes. I'm his wife.

AUNT ELLER. Well.

(LAUREY *sinks back in her chair with a disheartened little moan.*)

LAUREY. Oh, I don't see why—I don't see why—when ever'thing was so fine, this had to happen!

AUNT ELLER (*comfortingly*). Oh, Laurey —now nuthin' ain't happened.

LAUREY (*distressed*). Ain't no tellin' whut they'll do to him! And he couldn't he'p it. He *couldn't*. (*Seeing it again.*) It was over in a minute, and Jeeter lay there—dead. He'd a-killed Curly. He *tried* to kill him.

AUNT ELLER (*soothingly*). Now, now—

LAUREY. Why'd they have to th'ow Curly in jail? Anyone could see how it happened—

AUNT ELLER. Shore they could, honey. But you know the way everbody feels about shivoreein'. They got a right to somehow. And a thing like this a-happenin' in the middle of a shivoree—why, it looks *bad*, that's all. But Curly'll go free. Why, it's only been three days. They jist got to git everthing straight. (*She gestures to indicate freedom and happiness for them both.*)

LAUREY. You shore, Aunt Eller?

AUNT ELLER. *Course* I am!

LAUREY. I cain't stand to think of Curly bein' in jail!

AUNT ELLER. Why, it won't be no time now, till it's all over with—and forgot.

LAUREY (*strangely, a new element coming into her concern*). No, *not* over with, *not* forgot. You didn't see. Other things. Things you cain't git outa yer mind. (*She shudders.*)

AUNT ELLER. What is it, honey?

LAUREY. Over and over! The way them men done. The things they said. Oh—why'd it have to be that-a-way!

AUNT ELLER. Don't let yer mind run on it. Men is always like that at shivorees. Sump'n gits into 'em.

LAUREY. The one time in a body's life—

AUNT ELLER. Sh! I know. It musta been bad.

LAUREY. Cain't ferget it, I tell you! I've tried and tried!

AUNT ELLER (*gravely, wisely*). Don't try, honey. Don't *try*. They's things you cain't git rid of—lots of things. Not if you live to be a hundred. You got to learn. You got to look at all the good on one side and all the bad on the other, and say: "Well, all right, then!" to both of 'em.

LAUREY (*unheeding*). On top of everthing!

AUNT ELLER (*with great compassion*). Yeah, you've had yer troubles. I know, Laurey. But they's been good things, too. Think about that. You ain't had to slave away a-workin' fer others, the way some girls has to do—things like that. You've had you a good home—

LAUREY (*her mind temporarily diverted to another trouble*). Paw and maw—

AUNT ELLER. Yeah, right when you needed 'em most, both gone. But you lived on, didn't you? You been happy since, ain't you? Course. You been strong about it. Why, when yer Paw died—and you thought the world of him—you was all by yerself here—and you stood it. When they sent fer me to Pryor, 'fore I could git here, why he was dead, and in his coffin.

LAUREY (*raising her head, and looking back into the room*). It set right there—on two cheers. The head towards the door.

AUNT ELLER. Yeah. (*Quietly, without self-pity, stating the fact.*) When yore Paw died, and laid there—it was *my* brother in his coffin, too. Oh, and they's lots more, Laurey! I couldn't tell you all. Yer Uncle Jack, the children, both of my sisters, my paw and maw. Troubles thick and fast, you got to put up with. My husband—yer Uncle Jack. When *he* died. 'D you know how? A crazy way to die. No use in it! He'd bought some hogs off Lem Slocum, and they turned out to be full of cholery— and all died. Jack walked over jist acrost the pasture to see Lem about it. Didn't show up and it got night. I tuck a lantern and went out to see. When I come to the worm fence, I found him, in a corner, all huddled down, all bloody from a gunshot. Laid there all doubled up—dead—in a patch of yeller daisies. Lem Slocum musta shot him. I didn't know *who* done it. All I knowed was—*my husband was dead*. Oh, lots of things happens to a womern. Sickness, bein' pore and hungry even, bein' left alone in yer old age, bein' afraid to die—it all adds up. That's the way life is—cradle to grave. And you c'n stand it. They's one way. You got to be hearty. You *got* to be.

LAUREY (*moved*): Oh, Aunt Eller, I'm sich a baby—

AUNT ELLER. There, there!

LAUREY. Ashamed of myself! I want to be the way you air.

AUNT ELLER (*breaking off*). Fiddlesticks! *Fat*—and *old?* You couldn't h'ar me to be the way *I* am! Why, in a year's time, you'll git so t'ard even of lookin' at me, you and Curly'll run me off the place, 'th a tin can tied onto my tail—

(LAUREY *half-smiles at the spectacle, and leaning over, gives Aunt Eller an affectionate hug.*)

LAUREY (*through tears*). Oh, whut ud I do 'thout you, you're sich a crazy—

AUNT ELLER. Shore's you're borned—

LAUREY. I never could live. I never could. (*Rising, happier.*) I'll go to bed now.

AUNT ELLER. And sleep, huh?

LAUREY (*smiling*). Tight.

AUNT ELLER. And eat hearty from now on, huh? Fried chicken and everthing?

LAUREY. Tomorrow.

AUNT ELLER. Tomorrow, yer foot! (*She gets an apple out of a basket on the organ.*) Here, eat that.

LAUREY. I don't want it.

AUNT ELLER. *Eat* it, I said.

(LAUREY *takes it, nibbles at it. A dog begins to bark. They all stop abruptly, listening.*)

AUNT ELLER. Now, who could that—(*She stands up, looks at* LAUREY, *questioningly.*) This hour of night—

(LAUREY *stands up, quite still, straight and pale.*)

LAUREY. Curly—

AUNT ELLER. Couldn't be Curly, 'th ole Shep a-actin' up like a—He's stopped barkin'. (*The dog's barks stop suddenly.* AUNT ELLER *goes over to the window.* ADO ANNIE *has put down her work. All three women are in a breathless tranced state—suspended, curiously conjecturing.*) It's pitch black—

LAUREY (*with quiet conviction*). 'S Curly come back.

ADO ANNIE (*with a nervous giggle*). Ole Shep stopped a-barkin' like he was shot!

AUNT ELLER (*angrily—because of her nervous apprehension*). Sh! Be still, cain't you!

LAUREY. It's Curly!

AUNT ELLER. 'Taint *no* one. That dog's jist got the colic, I bet. (*There is a noise as of someone trying the door.*) What's that!

ADO ANNIE (*rising*). I'm goin' home.

AUNT ELLER. Be still. (*She picks up a shovel standing in the fireplace. She calls out sharply.*) Now then. Whoever's there, answer, and answer quick!

(*The door opens quickly, and* CURLY, *disheveled and worn, appears there.*)

CURLY. Laurey!

AUNT ELLER (*joyfully*). Why, it's Curly!

LAUREY. Curly!

(*She runs to meet him halfway across the room as he comes forward. They go into each other's arms, and cling to each other.*

AUNT ELLER (*with extravagant delight*). My, oh my! Look whut the old cat's drug in! Thought we had him safe in jail and here he turns up like a bad penny! Laws a me! Whutta you mean tryin' to skeer us wall-eyed?

ADO ANNIE (*astonished*). Why, it's Curly!

AUNT ELLER (*gaily*). Naw! It's Sandy Claus, cain't you see nuthin'! They've let him off! I knowed they would, I knowed it, I knowed it!

(CURLY *backs out of* LAUREY's *arms, looks round quickly.*)

LAUREY. Curly! Whut is it!

CURLY. Whut was that noise?

LAUREY (*with premonitory alarm*). Whut's the matter? Everything's all right, ain't it? They've let you off, ain't they? Curly! Tell me and be quick, I—

CURLY. No. They ain't let me off.

LAUREY. Curly! (*Running to him.*) They couldn't a-sent you up! It wasn't yore fault. They couldn't, I won't let 'em—I won't, I—

CURLY. Sh! (*As they become silent.*) They're after me. (*He goes swiftly across and pulls down the window shade.*)

AUNT ELLER. Never heared of sich a— Who's after you, the old Booger Man?

LAUREY. Curly!

CURLY. When I clumb th'ough the fence jist by that little bridge, I seen lights 'way over towards Claremore. I knowed they'd got onto which way I was headin', so I run acrost the back of the—

AUNT ELLER. Whut *air* you jabberin' about? (*Light dawning on her.*) Oh! I mighta knowed a curly-headed cowhand like him ud come to a bad end! He's went and broke outa jail.

CURLY (*quickly*). I *had* to see Laurey. I *had* to! I knowed she'd be a-worryin' about everthing, and I couldn't stand it her a-worryin' and nobody to help her none— (*He takes* LAUREY *in his arms again.*)

AUNT ELLER (*severely*). Worryin'! I ort to take a hick'ry to you and beat you plumb to a frazzle! Here you'd a-got off tomorrow, you crazy youngun—everbody *said* so. Now you'll prob'ly git sent up fer five year fer breakin' loose—and I hope you do!

LAUREY. Aunt Eller, they cain't send him up, they *cain't!*

AUNT ELLER. Oh, cain't they? You wait and see. (*To* CURLY.) Didn't you know they'd know whur you was headin' fer, and find you 'fore a cat could lick his front paw?

CURLY. I didn't think.

AUNT ELLER. I reckon you hain't got nuthin' to think with. (*Giving him a swat.*) I'd like to give you a good beatin'! (*Smiling at him tolerantly.*) Aw, I reckon you jist had to see yer girl, didn't you?

CURLY. My wife.

AUNT ELLER. Yeow? Well, *call* her that 'f it does you any good. How fur back was it you seen 'em comin' after you?

CURLY. 'Bout half a mile.

AUNT ELLER. You got jist about two minutes to tell Laurey good-by then.

CURLY. They won't ketch me! Hide me till mornin', Aunt Eller. I cain't let 'em take me now, Aunt Eller!

AUNT ELLER. You'll stay *right* here till they come! You've already caused enough trouble to last us all out to doomsday. Now then. Ado Annie, come on out in the kitchen, and git yerself sump'n to eat. Bet you're hungry.

ADO ANNIE. I hain't hungry, Aunt Eller. I jist had a piece of—

AUNT ELLER. Not hungry! Why, you're all fallin' to staves. Feel ever' rib you got! (*She shoves* ADO ANNIE *out and follows her. As she goes out.*) They'll come any minute now.

CURLY (*after a moment, not knowing how to begin*). You all right, honey?

LAUREY. Yes. I guess. (*She puts her hand to her forehead as if brushing away her darkness.*) I git to thinkin'.

CURLY (*gently*). I know. Me, too. Thinkin' and thinkin' about you—and me bringin' sich trouble on you. All my fault.

LAUREY. Nobody could he'p it.

CURLY. Listen, Laurey. (*She goes to him, questioningly, disturbed at something in his manner.*) I had to see you 'fore the hearin' tomorrow. That's why I broke out. Fer whut if they'd send me up,

and I not see you fer a long time?

LAUREY. Curly! It *couldn't* be. Don't you say that.

CURLY. *Anything* can be. You got to be ready.

LAUREY (*alarmed*). Have you heared anything, Curly? Tell me, whut'd you hear?

CURLY. Nuthin', honey. Ain't heared nuthin'—but *good.*

LAUREY (*with glad relief*). Oh, it's all right, then!

CURLY (*gravely*). That ain't it. I'm shore myself, honey. Er I *was* shore, till I broke out. I never thought whut *that* might do. But sump'n's always happenin' in this here world. Cain't count on a thing. So you got to promise me sump'n. Whutever happens—*whutever* it is—you got to bear up, you hear me? (*Smiling.*) Why, I'm a purty one to go a-losin' sleep over, ain't I?

LAUREY (*ruefully*). Oh, a fine start *we* got, ain't it? (*With an effort, painfully working it out in her mind.*) Oh, I've worried about you, shet up in that filthy jail—

CURLY. Don't mind about that.

LAUREY. —And I've thought about that awful night, too, till I thought I'd go crazy—

CURLY. Pore Laurey.

LAUREY. Looked at it time and again, *heared* it—ringin' in my ears! *Cried* about it, cried about everthing! A plumb baby! And I've tried to figger out how it ud be if sump'n *did* happen to you. Didn't know how I could stand it. That was the worst! And nen, I tried to figger out how I'd go on. Oh, I've went th'ough it all, Curly, from the start. Now I feel shore of sump'n, anyway—I'll be growed up—like everbody else. (*With conviction.*) I'll put up with everthing now. You don't need to worry about me no more. Why, I'll stand it—if they send you to the pen fer life—

CURLY (*with mock alarm*). Here! Don't know's I like that very well!

(LAUREY *bursts out into a peal of amused, hearty, infectious laughter.*)

LAUREY. The look on yore face! 'S the first time I laughed in three days!

CURLY (*his old self again*). *I* ain't goin' to no pen fer life—a-poundin' up rocks, and a-wearin' stripes around my legs!

LAUREY. Wouldn't you look purty!

CURLY (*with delight*). You *air* a devil,

ain't you? I don't think you even *like* me.

LAUREY (*playfully*). Like you? Oh, I like you a little bit. (*They stand looking at each other, shyly, happily.*) Whur on earth'd you git them clothes you got on?

CURLY (*gaily*). Old Man Peck went and got 'em fer me. Shore a good ole man! Thinks the world of you. Shirt come outa Rucker's Dry Goods Store. Brand new, too! He thought I must be a-needin' clean clothes, I reckon, shet up in that ole jail! My, they's things a-crawlin' there, got legs on both sides! Cell next to mine's got a couple of horse thieves into it, the A. H. T. A. caught up by Sequoyah. They gimme a blanket and one of 'em said, "Tain't so purty-fer-nice but it's hell-fer-warm."

LAUREY (*amused*). Curly!

CURLY. 'Nother cell's got a womern into it that smokes and cusses like a mule driver. Caught her stealin' from the Turf Exchange. Don't know whut's got into Indian Territory nohow! They puttin' everbody in jail—women and all!

LAUREY. I think you like yer ole jail!

CURLY. Jist rairin' to git back. Cain't wait! Lay back on that arn cot and dream about featherbeds!

LAUREY (*softly, happily*). Ever time I pass by the barn lot, ole Dun lopes acrost and nickers at me, fer all get-out! Shows his teeth. He's astin' about you, I reckon.

CURLY. Oh, he's apt to fall dead of the heaves when he hears about me—settin' in jail 'stid of on the range! Feels like I ain't set in the saddle in a month of Sundays! Listen, Laurey. I been a-thinkin'—Everthing from now on is gonna be different.

LAUREY. Different?

CURLY. It come to me settin' in that cell of mine. (*Dreamily, out of a visionary absorption—like a song, growing in intensity.*) Oh, I got to learn to be a farmer, I see that! Quit a-thinkin' about dehornin' and brandin' and th'owin' the rope, and start in to git my hands blistered a new way! Oh, things is changin' right and left! Buy up mowin' machines, cut down the prairies! Shoe yer horses, drag them plows under the sod! They gonna make a state outa this, they gonna put it in the Union! Country a-changin', got to change with it! Bring up a pair of boys, new stock, to keep up 'th the way things is goin' in this here crazy country! Life jist startin' in fer me

now. Work to do! Now I got you to he'p me— I'll 'mount to sump'n yit! Come here, Laurey. Come here, and tell me good-by 'fore they come fer me and take me away.

LAUREY (*wryly*). All we do is say "Howdy" and "So long." (*Gravely.*) Good-by, Curly. If you come back to-morrow, I'll be here a-waitin'. If you don't come back, I'll be here a-waitin' anyhow.

CURLY. I'll come back, honey. They couldn't hinder me 'th bird-shot!

LAUREY. Promise me.

CURLY. Oh, I hate to go away and leave you! I cain't. (*He takes her in his arms, hungrily. After a moment, there are* VOICES *and sounds of an approaching party. The couple listen breathlessly.*) They're here. Oh, I cain't go, I cain't leave you!

LAUREY (*anguishedly, clinging to him*). I cain't let you go.

(AUNT ELLER *comes in.*)

AUNT ELLER (*gravely*). Well, here they air, I guess. They's a whole crowd. I seen the lanterns. You all ready, Curly?

CURLY (*in anguish*). I guess—I—

AUNT ELLER (*tenderly*).Good-by,honey. I'm sorry it has to be like this. (*There is a knock at the door.* AUNT ELLER *goes over and calls, her hand on the latch.*) Who is that a-knockin'?

VOICE (*outside*). It's me, Ed Peck—and I got to see you about—

AUNT ELLER (*opening the door, in astonishment*). Why, Mr. Peck! Come on in. Whutta *you* want around here?

OLD MAN PECK (*coming in, his eyes going to* CURLY). Curly knows whut I want. I've *come* fer him.

AUNT ELLER. *You* have? You ain't no marshal.

OLD MAN PECK. I know. But Mr. Burnett, the federal marshal, deputized me and some of the boys to come out and find Curly and bring him back. Come on, Curly.

AUNT ELLER. Well, I *must* say! Sidin' with the federal marshal!

OLD MAN PECK. I ain't sidin' with him, Aunt Eller. Curly's hearin' ain't come up yit, and he hadn't no right to run off this-a-way.

AUNT ELLER. No right! Say, looky here, he wanted to see his wife. That ain't agin the *law* in this country, is it?

OLD MAN PECK. No. But breakin' outa *jail* is agin the law.

AUNT ELLER (*disgusted*). Well, of all the —When'd you go and git so respectful of the law? Looky here, if a law's a *good* law—it can stand a little breakin'. And them out there—Who's out there? Hey, you all! (*She has gone to the window and thrown up the shade.*) Go on home. Nobody's wantin' *you* around here!

VOICES (*outside*). We've come fer Curly, Aunt Eller. We got to take him back. (*Snickering.*) He's a plumb criminal, he is, breakin' outa jail this-a-way!

AUNT ELLER. Who's that? That you, Zeb? I mighta knowed! Say, you're a purty nuthin'—a ole pig-stealer like you tryin' to represent the govament!

VOICE (*outside, offended, protesting*). Who's a pig-stealer?

AUNT ELLER. *You* air, Mr. Zeb Walkley.

VOICE. I ain't, either!

AUNT ELLER. You *air!* Why, you gittin' so that—'stid of talkin'—you plumb grunt like a ole sow! And say, Dave Tyler—you'll feel funny when I tell yer wife you're carryin' on 'th another womern, won't you?

VOICE (*outside*). I ain't carryin' on 'th no one.

AUNT ELLER. Mebbe not. But you'll shore feel funny when I tell yer *wife* you air.

VOICES.

Now, Aunt Eller, we've come fer Curly.

We cain't stand here and listen to you—

Send him out!

AUNT ELLER (*indignantly*). Oh, you'll listen to me! I'm gittin' mad! You cain't *take* Curly, that's all they is to it!

VOICES.

We *got* to, Aunt Eller.

He'll git off tomorrow, won't he?

Make him come on out, and le's git started!

AUNT ELLER (*severely*). All right, 'f you won't listen to me, I plumb warsh my hands of all of you. I thought you was a fine bunch of neighbors. Now I see you're jist a gang of fools. Tryin' to take a bridegroom away from his bride! Why, the way you're sidin' with the federal marshal, you'd think us people out here lived in the United States! Why, we're territory folks—we ort to hang together. I don't mean *hang*—I mean *stick*. Whut's the United States? It's jist a furrin

country to me. And *you* supportin' it! Jist dirty ole furriners, ever last one of you!

VOICES (*outside, grumbling, protesting*). Now, Aunt Eller, we hain't furriners.

My pappy and mammy was *both* borned in Indian Territory! Why, I'm jist plumb full of Indian blood myself.

Me, too! And I c'n prove it!

AUNT ELLER (*full of guile*). Well, maybe you *ain't* furriners. I musta made a mistake. (*Slyly, smiling.*) Anyway, I ain't astin' you to let Curly *off*. That's up to them ole United Statesers at the hearin'. *I* mean—you don't have to take Curly back *tonight*. Take him in the mornin' jist as well.

VOICES (*uncertainly*).

Well, I don't know—

I ain't no furriner!

Whut does Mr. Peck say?

He's the boss. Ast *him*.

I wouldn't wanta stand in the way of lettin' Curly—

AUNT ELLER (*triumphantly, to* MR. PECK). See there! They said it was all right to let him stay tonight.

OLD MAN PECK. No, they didn't.

AUNT ELLER. Did too! Cain't you hear nuthin'? I'll take a blacksnake whip to you!

OLD MAN PECK (*sheepishly*). Well, I— If my men is gonna back out on me this-a-way—I reckon I better let Curly stay.

AUNT ELLER (*overjoyed*). I knowed you'd see daylight, I knowed it, I knowed it!

OLD MAN PECK (*self-consciously, not looking at* CURLY, *and twirling his hat in his hands, sheepishly*). I was young onct myself. (*He hugs* AUNT ELLER.)

AUNT ELLER. Why, you ole devil! Tell yer wife on you!

CURLY. 'D you want me to stay, Laurey?

(*She backs away, flushed and embarrassed and joyous at the same time, flings an arm about his neck and kisses him quickly, whirls over to* OLD MAN PECK, *gives him a quick hug and flies into her room.* CURLY *grins and starts after her.*)

OLD MAN PECK (*as* CURLY *reaches the door*). Curly. I'll be here right after breakfast to fetch you. I'll be here bright and early.

(CURLY *goes in. The door shuts.*)

AUNT ELLER (*slyly, owlishly*). Well, not too early. (*Then, gravely.*) Younguns has a turrible time, don't they? (*She throws it off.*) Oh, well—they git to be old-timers soon enough. *Too* soon. (*She shows* MR. PECK *out with a lantern. She marches over to the window, calling out.*) Hey, you all! Go on home. They ain't nuthin' *you* c'n do around here. Curly's *stayin'*! (*She jerks the shade down.*)

(*The voices outside exclaim delightedly and move away. From the bedroom has come the sound of* CURLY *beginning to sing softly,* "Green Grow the Lilacs.")

AUNT ELLER (*going to the window*). Mr. Peck! (*With delight.*) Listen to that fool cowpuncher! His weddin' night—and there he is singin'!

CURTAIN

GLOSSARY

dogies—specifically, an orphaned calf, but used often, affectionately, as a synonym for cattle.

shikepoke—a mythical Middle West bird, whose activities (unprintable) are embarrassing to everyone. A term of opprobrium.

side meat—bacon.

maverick—an unbranded, and hence ownerless, calf or steer.

off-ox—the ox on the off-side (the right side) of the wagon tongue.

bronc buster—a rider of bucking bronchos.

bull-dogger—one who leaps off a running horse, swings on the horns of a bull or steer, and throws and ties him.

stove arn—that is, stove iron, or handle for lifting the lids.

tetchin' leather—to ride a bronc without touching leather is to ride without hanging on to the saddle horn or any other part of the saddle.

yellin' calf-rope—to yell calf-rope signifies defeat.

to change the green lilacs to the red, white and blue—means, "I'm going to join the army."

string-haltered—a corruption of spring-halted, a convulsive movement of the hind legs of a horse.

Dan Patch—a celebrated racing horse, a pacer.

Jick—the joker in a pack of cards.

bottom—that is, river bottom, the low land along a river.

backwater—the water backed up, from being unable to empty into a swollen stream now higher than its tributaries.

shivoree—a corruption of the French *charivari*, a wedding celebration.

the A. H. T. A.—the Anti-Horse Thief Association.

THE HOUSE OF CONNELLY
Paul Green

The House of Connelly was first produced by the Group Theatre, Inc., under the auspices of the Theatre Guild, at the Martin Beck Theatre, New York City, on October 5, 1931. It was staged by Lee Strasberg and Cheryl Crawford, with settings by Cleon Throckmorton. The cast was as follows:

BIG SIS	Fanny De Knight	CHARLIE	Walter Coy
BIG SUE	Rose McClendon	JODIE	William Challee
PATSY TATE	Margaret Barker	ALEC	Clement Wilenchik
WILL CONNELLY	Franchot Tone	RANSOM	Philip Robinson
JESSE TATE	Art Smith	REUBEN	Clifford Odetts (Odets)
GERALDINE CONNELLY	Stella Adler	ISAAC	Friendly Ford
EVELYN CONNELLY	Eunice Stoddard	TYLER	Gerrit Kraber
ROBERT CONNELLY	Morris Carnovsky	ALF	Robert Lewis
MRS. CONNELLY	Mary Morris	HENRY	Herbert Ratner
DUFFY	J. E. Bromberg	SERENADERS	Phoebe Brand,
VIRGINIA BUCHANAN	Dorothy Patten		Virginia Farmer, Sylvia
ESSIE	Ruth Nelson		Fenningston, Clifford Odetts
JAKE	Lewis Leverett		(Odets), etc.

TIME: The early years of the twentieth century. PLACE: An old aristocratic plantation somewhere in the southern part of the United States.
ACT ONE. *Scene One:* A field on the Connelly plantation. Christmas afternoon. *Scene Two:* The dining room in Connelly Hall. Evening, a few hours later. *Scene Three:* The ruined garden of Connelly Hall. A night in spring several months later.
ACT TWO. *Scene One:* The dining room. Midmorning, a few days later. *Scene Two:* The dining room. Summer, a few months later. *Scene Three:* The dining room. Christmas evening, one year after Scene Two in Act One.

There's grapeshot and musket and the cannon's rumble loud;
There's many a mangled body, a blanket for their shroud;
There's many a mangled body left on the field alone,
And I'm a rebel soldier far from my home.

—Uncle Bob Connelly's favorite
song when drunk

A NOTE ON THE TEXT: For reasons that will be apparent to the reader of the Introduction on the next page, Mr. Paul Green sent me the original ending of his play, and I am reproducing this scene in the text along with (or rather, in front of) the alternate scene used in the Group Theatre production. I do this with the approval of the author, who wrote me, "I certainly look forward to seeing them published, together." I should add that the dialect of the original play has been somewhat reduced by Mr. Green on his own initiative.   J. G.

Copyright 1930, by Paul Green.
Copyright 1939, by Paul Green in *The House of Connelly and Other Plays.*
Copyright 1957, 1958 (in renewal), by Paul Green.
All rights reserved.

CAUTION: Professionals and amateurs are hereby warned that *The House of Connelly*, being fully protected under the copyright laws of the United States of America, the British Empire, including the Dominion of Canada, and all other countries of the Copyright Union, is subject to a royalty. All rights, including professional, amateur, motion pictures, recitation, public reading, radio and television broadcasting, and the rights of translation into foreign languages, are strictly reserved. Amateurs may produce this play upon payment of a royalty of Twenty-Five Dollars for each performance one week before the play is to be given to Samuel French, Inc. at 25 West 45th Street, New York 36, N. Y., or 7623 Sunset Blvd., Hollywood 46, Calif., or if in Canada, to Samuel French (Canada) Ltd., at 27 Grenville St., Toronto, Ont.

The House of Connelly, in 1930, was the first major production of the Group Theatre, the acting company that made theatrical history during the decade of the thirties. Held by the Theatre Guild but turned over to its young splinter group aspiring toward socially based art, *The House of Connelly* was indeed a most suitable play for the infant Group Theatre. Although it is not certain that Group actors as a body could do justice to the work at this early stage in their career, they had in Paul Green's drama a meaningful study of character and milieu, with Chekhovian qualities added for good measure. The play when first printed in 1931 was described on the flyleaf, with attention to the social analysis then fashionable, as "a play which interprets the struggle between the old and the new South—the old South of culture and lost causes, and the new South of the bourgeoisie and a future filled with hopes."

The flyleaf scribe, who may well have been the critic Barrett H. Clark, conscientiously added that the two main characters, Will Connelly and Patsy Tate, "are representative of these two opposing classes of a social system that was drawing to a close about the beginning of the twentieth century." It is to be doubted that this description would entirely suit the author. Paul Green himself would have favored a less schematic definition and preferred a more poetic interpretation than the intellectual climate of the 1930's favored and urged upon him. His original ending for the play, modified in the Group Theatre production, was not conducive to social optimism and culminated, instead, on a note of stark fatality. Nevertheless, the realities of social transition that concerned the Group cannot be overlooked, and the historical outlook of *The House of Connelly* is not radically invalidated by a tragic rather than a sociological view of the work.

It was not the first time that the author could be found at the frontiers of the theatre, where he effected a successful marriage between social and regional drama. Paul Green was born in 1894 near the village of Lillington in North Carolina. The son of a farmer, himself a champion cotton-picker and a ballplayer before entering the University of North Carolina at the late age of twenty, he was from the start of his writing career a "regionalist" lover of local color on the one hand and a social critic on the other. He taught philosophy later at the state university, and remained associated with its dramatic activities under Professor Frederick Koch, the founder of the Carolina Playmakers; he has also remained a confirmed resident of Chapel Hill, where the university is located; he "belongs" by every kind of commitment, to his land and his people. And he "belongs" primarily as both a poet and a realist, both an imaginative writer and a liberal sociologist. This was apparent to the discerning even in his remarkable early short plays, *The No 'Count Boy* (winner of the Belasco "Little Theatre Tournament" trophy in 1925) and a number of other one-act plays published in two distinguished collections, *The Lonesome Road* (1926) and *In the Valley* (1928). The former contains the famous one-act drama *White Dresses*, based on racial relations in the South.* Within a decade, Paul Green supplied the New Theatre movement of the 1930's with its most trenchant protest next to *Waiting for Lefty*—namely, *Hymn to the Rising Sun*. It is a stunning chain-gang drama, and would rank among the outstanding one-act plays of the English language even without any claim to topical interest or "social significance."

Effectively combining a number of episodes into the tragic chronicle of an educated Negro (the illegitimate son of a white man) who stands unhappily suspended between the white and colored people of the South, Paul Green gave the Province-town Players the Pulitzer Prize play *In Abraham's Bosom*. And here, too, he drew equally upon his region and his conscience. He apparently owed the genesis of this work to an incident in childhood, when he saw a train engineer strike a Negro teacher in the face with a walking stick for asking an innocent question. The sicken-

* Reprinted in *Twenty-Five Best Plays of the Modern American Theatre*, ed. by John Gassner, Crown Publishers, pp. 741-48.

ing event was recalled by Paul Green in a letter to the journalist and critic Ward Morehouse, who reprinted it in his book *Matinee Tomorrow: Fifty Years of Our Theatre* in 1949. The closing sentences tell us more about Paul Green than any fine-combing criticism can: "The schoolteacher of that spring morning long ago still lives—now a very old man. A bad scar still shows on his face, running from his forehead down across his chin. And there must be a scar in his heart too. There is in mine, and always will be."

In Abraham's Bosom was followed in 1927 by a fascinating play that was less successful on Broadway, *The Field God;* and after *The House of Connelly,* Mr. Green had another Broadway setback in 1934 with *Roll, Sweet Chariot,* a play of Negro life rendered in symbolic as well as realistic terms. It would seem that the fault was with Broadway rather than with the author, whose original version of this work, published several years before (in 1931) under the title of *Potter's Field,* has impressed me in a recent reading as one of the most powerful works of the American theatre. The author's next play, the rueful, pacifistic drama *Johnny Johnson,* presented by the Group Theatre in 1936, was better received. It was a runner-up in the contest for a New York Drama Critics Award in 1937, with Stark Young and myself as its special advocates. (Readers will find the play in my anthology *Twenty Best Plays of the Modern American Theatre,* 1939.) Its full power was not quite realized in the New York production despite the rollicking caricature of a psychiatrist by Morris Carnovsky and the moving impersonation of a Wilsonian idealist by Russell Collins. *Johnny Johnson,* which consists of numerous episodes rendered in a variety of dramatic styles, was an American version of "epic theatre" in the style of Erwin Piscator and Bertolt Brecht; it required more training in stylization than Group actors had.

In 1937, with the production of *The Lost Colony* on Roanoke Island, the supposed site of the first English settlement in America, Paul Green started a second career as the author of a relatively new type of drama, the outdoor historical pageant or, as Mr. Green has preferred to call it, "symphonic drama." The production started a popular form of summer theatre in the South and a trend toward regional drama that has had national ramifications in subject matter and principle. Finding considerable gratification in this new style of play, largely created by himself, Mr. Green went on to write *The Common Glory,* a Revolutionary War drama, for Williamsburg, Virginia. His *Wilderness Road* was a moving Civil War drama set in the mountains of Kentucky among a tragically divided people. It was first produced in the summer of 1955 as part of the centennial celebration of Berea College in the foothills near Berea, Kentucky. A later symphonic work by him, based on the life of Robert E. Lee, appeared in 1958 at Virginia Beach under the title of *Confederacy.* These and other symphonic dramas, including a more recent one on Stephen Foster, exemplified the imaginativeness their author had already displayed in such earlier plays as *Tread the Green Grass,* a folk-fantasy ("with Interludes, Music, Dumb-show, and Cinema"—so reads the subtitle) first published in 1929, and *Shroud My Body Down* (1935), not produced by Broadway managements.

These experiments and the successful pageant plays displayed their author's interest in dramatic stylization which took him to the Far East; concerning this and related subjects, Mr. Green expressed himself provocatively in a collection of essays *The Dramatic Heritage,* published by Samuel French in 1953. It must not be assumed, however, that in his justifiable disappointment with Broadway, Paul Green withdrew completely from the New York theatre, even if he has always scorned show business, as he did in the 1920's when he wrote: "The American professional stage . . . is an industry and not an art . . . it is a business run to the pattern of supply and demand . . ." He gave Broadway one of its most exciting social dramas when he dramatized Richard Wright's *Native Son,* which Orson

Welles staged in 1941 as a sort of "epic theatre" trial drama, and he supplied an adaptation of Ibsen's *Peer Gynt* for an experimental production program by ANTA (American National Theatre and Academy) staged by Lee Strasberg, with John Garfield in the title role.

Many pertinent observations have been made concerning *The House of Connelly*. The most instructive comment is perhaps Alan Downer's (in his excellent review, *Fifty Years of American Drama*, 1951): "*The House of Connelly* (1931) combines the realistic treatment of a family of decaying Southern aristocrats with rhythmical interludes of Negro life. . . . Big Sis and Big Sue, the two field women who form a chorus for his [Paul Green's] action, are at once images of the doom that hangs over the house and symbols of the eternal rhythm of life which the Connellys have denied." This opinion relates to an early observation by Edith J. Isaacs, who in reviewing *The Lord's Will and Other Plays* remarked that the author "likes to make fate, religious ecstasy, and rooted prejudice service him as actors in his plays." Another thoughtful critic, the late Barrett Clark, who was Paul Green's editor and friend, stressed the poetic character of the play, coupling it with so different a work as the comparatively tenuous *Tread the Green Grass*.

A contradictory opinion on the part of the radically positivistic young Group Theatre led to a simplification or, if you will, reduction of the play and to the elimination of a scene restored in the present text. Harold Clurman describes the Group's opinion in his indispensable book *The Fervent Years* (Alfred A. Knopf, 1945). He recalls that "*The House of Connelly* had originally been written with the tenant farm girl, Patsy, strangled to death at the end by the two old Negro maid-servants of the Connelly house—remnants of the slave past—who were presented as Fates, *Macbeth*-fashion. This ending we thought false; a stock device to round off a rather somber play. It struck us as historically and humanly untrue and in conflict with what we felt to be the theme of the play." The hero, the Group Theatre thought, should be given a chance to redeem his life with the help of the tenant girl. Mr. Clurman goes on to observe that the author resisted this criticism "because though basically a sound, affirmative nature, he has never been able wholly to overcome a pessimistic drag on his spirit, a bafflement before evil."

It is possible to wonder whether the author might not lift an eyebrow today in reading this and the next sentence: "Our own sense of the perfectibility of man, or at least, the inevitability of the struggle against evil, not only made us impatient with the play's violent ending, but roused Paul's own verve and decision in our direction." Regardless of our own decision in this argument, this much is certain: We respond only to half the play, and not the best half either, if we find the message and miss the poetry in *The House of Connelly*.*

* Mr. Green's recollection of the revised ending of the play is contained in a letter he wrote me on June 7, 1960, which reads as follows: "I remember the argument I had with Harold Clurman and Cheryl Crawford of the Group Theatre about the change. And I finally gave in to their 'optimism' because I could also take the cue from life for that as well as for the other. In some cases in the South the old order has throttled new life and in some new life has regenerated the old. [The word *throttled* is obviously a metaphorical analogue of the actual strangling of the heroine by the family's old retainers in the original version of the play.] So it was and is. Recently an off-Broadway group showed interest in the play, and I had some copies of the original-ending version typed for them."

ACT ONE

SCENE ONE

A late winter afternoon is over the fields, and across the land to the west a murky cloud creeps up the sky, lighted along its edge by a bluish tinge from the hidden sun. The air is raw and has the feel of snow in it. A rail fence grown up with an unkempt hedgerow of dead fennel weeds, poke stalks, and sassafras bushes crosses the foreground, rotten and spraddled, with a disused stile near the center. Close beyond it in the field, three stack-poles, now empty and gaunt, stand up like black gallows trees, with ragged wisps of hay clinging to the cross-pieces above. The decaying stalks and weeded hedge exude the rot of death into the air, and the mood of a heavy loneliness is over the earth.

Two old sibyl-like Negro women come in from the right, one carrying a hoe and the other a tow sack, and both chewing tobacco in their toothless jaws. They are huge creatures, sexual and fertile, with round moist roving eyes and jowled faces smooth and hairless as a baby's. The mark of ancient strength and procreation still remains in their protuberant breasts and bulging hips. Under old coats their broad shoulders and arms are muscled like men's.

BIG SIS (*as if talking into the air*). There. (*She gestures toward an uprooted stump behind the hedge where a clump of sassafras grows.*)

BIG SUE (*answering likewise*). Yah. (*They lumber through the hedgerow, the rotten rails breaking under them.* BIG SIS *turns and strikes the fence with her hoe.* BIG SUE *lets out a teasing cackle.*)

BIG SIS (*snarling in simulated anger as she goes behind the stump and begins digging*). Hee-hee! Laugh, laugh! (*A twisting smile creeps around the corners of her mouth.*)

BIG SUE (*softly, her gaze stopping on the haypoles*). Look at them haypoles—like the gallows where they hung nigger Purvis on.

BIG SIS (*now looking up with a wakeful eye*). G'won—Yah, do—gallows where the old General Connelly hung nigger Purvis on.

BIG SUE. Like bunches of hair hanging on 'em too—Jesus!

BIG SIS. Old General stood up in his long robes and said silence in the court—Purvis to be hung by the neck till dead—and Lord have mercy on your poor soul!—uhm.

BIG SUE (*gazing restlessly about her*). Uhm—yah, and the sky look black same like when they killed the Son o' God.

BIG SIS. Poor Purvis!

BIG SUE. Poor General!

BIG SIS. Own flesh and blood make no difference. The law say hang.

BIG SUE. The General say hang.

BIG SIS. Purvis can't say "pappy."

BIG SUE. General can't say "son," no, Lord, no!

BIG SIS (*half-musing as she digs*). Uhm—poor Purvis—that nigger twist about like a worm on a fishhook the day they hang him.

BIG SUE. Uhm—didn't he? And people everywhere—setting on tops of houses like buzzards—uhm—and some of 'em fainted and fell off when he 'gun wriggle on that rope.

BIG SIS. Old General riding by in his great carriage with his head bent down.

(*A gun is fired off far down in the field. They listen a moment without saying anything. Then in unison and without looking at each other, they point their forefingers in the direction of the sound and make a falling-hammer motion with their thumbs, after which they break into a peal of laughter.*)

BIG SUE. Poor nigger. Some of 'em say they hear him whisper, "Give me some air under this black cap, sweet Lord Jesus."

BIG SIS. But like the deadfall of the grave they had him though—Old General Connelly and the law, yeh, had him. (*Digging furiously.*) Come out of that 'ere ground, old root. I gwine boil you and drink your sap. (*She wrenches a root out and hands it up to her sister. The gun goes off again down in the field.*)

BIG SUE. Shoot them doves, Mr. Will Connelly! You can't hit 'em and they feets red with blood. Oughter know it.

BIG SIS. Where they trompled in the blood of the Saviour—nunh-unh.

BIG SUE. Mr. Will couldn't hit 'em if they feets were black like Satan. (BIG SIS *bursts into a peal of laughter.*) Whyfore?

BIG SIS (*straightening up and looking at her sister with a merry glistening eye*). He can't shoot. Can't like his pappy.

BIG SUE (*laughing till her broad bosom heaves*). Popgun.

BIG SIS (*spitting*). Pop goes the weasel. (*With sudden anger she lifts a huge fist and makes a sweeping gesture over the earth.*) He can't do nothing. Creep about. Let the world rot down. Can't do nothing.

BIG SUE. Yah. (*Softly.*) But Lord, his daddy.

BIG SIS. Old General Connelly was a shooting man. (*She slaps her thigh at some far-off remembrance.*)

BIG SUE. Shoot to kill. (*After a moment —slyly.*) Tu-chu, a hoss-man too and heavy riding man. (*They double over in great gales of laughter.*)

BIG SIS. Yah, and knowed the law. (*Now with sudden mournfulness again.*) But he done gone—gone to his long home.

BIG SUE (*forlornly*). Yah—yah—and the Old Man is there where Purvis is.

BIG SIS (*prying among the roots and singing in the deep voice of a man, to which her sister adds a low melodious alto*).
In the cold earth the sinful clay
Wrapped in a sheet is laid away—hah!—
Rock to the hill to the trees do mourn
Pity poor man ever were born—hah!

BIG SUE (*with moody, overcast countenance*). He were good though—in the heart. The Old Man were good. When us wanted meat he give it to us. (*Touching* BIG SIS *on the shoulder and gesturing to the right with her head.*) Look who there.

BIG SIS. Hunh, 'fore God!

BIG SUE. That new tenant gal picking old pokeberries. Unh-unh, sees us.

BIG SIS. Sees everything.

BIG SUE. Do that. Been moved on this plantation three weeks and see everything.

BIG SIS. Us sees too—unh-unh. Hee-hee.

BIG SUE. Do—yeh, us do. Hoo—hoo.

BIG SIS (*digging and grunting*).
They grabble his eye, they work in his head,
Man don't feel 'em, three days dead—hah!—
And all up above him the wind do mourn
Pity poor man ever were born—hah!

BIG SUE (*wrenching a broken rail out of the fence and standing it up*). Ho-ho, now she watch us snatch firewood.

BIG SIS. You done said.

BIG SUE. Poor white trash.

BIG SIS. Like all of 'em—scrouging and a-gouging—Poor white trash!

BIG SUE. Pushing up in the world— reaching and a-grabbing at the high place of the quality and the roof over our heads!

BIG SIS. Uhm—

PATSY (*coming in at the right with a bucket*). Tearing down the fence, Big Sue?

BIG SUE (*singing*).
The sparrow sot with her head in her wing—

(PATSY *is a lithe full-figured girl of twenty or more, with cheeks pink in the cold and dark gipsy-like eyes—eyes which at times have a bright hard look. She wears a cloak buttoned close up under her throat and a stocking cap pulled down over her ears.*)

BIG SUE (*snickering*). Heigh-ho, Miss Patsy.

PATSY. The hogs'll get through that hole.

BIG SUE. Yeb'm, that's so.

PATSY. Better put it back.

BIG SUE (*mumbling*). Yeb'm. (*She replaces the rail with infinite and sassy slowness.*)

PATSY. What's the matter, got no firewood?

BIG SIS (*snickering also*). Nob'm.

PATSY (*impatiently*). There's plenty of it in the woods. (*She begins picking the scattered berries from among the dead stalks and leaves along the hedge.*)

BIG SIS (*facetiously*). Thought the birds had them berries all by this time.

BIG SUE (*softly*). Her make no answer. (*They snicker in disrespect as she moves off toward the right.*)

PATSY (*calling back*). You seem to be feeling good.

BIG SUE. Yeb'm.

BIG SIS. Yeb'm.

BIG SUE (*after a moment, as* PATSY *starts away again*). Gwine find the hunter?

PATSY. What hunter?

BIG SIS. Hunter down in the cornfield there—shooting.

BIG SUE. But can't hit nothing.

(*Again as before they hee-haw with laughter.*)

PATSY (*returning along the hedge towards them*). Why you laugh so?

BIG SIS (*jumping about with her hoe*). Us feeling good.

PATSY. Do you?

BIG SIS (*with mock forlornness*). Us feel bad, feel lonesome then with nobody to love us.

BIG SUE (*picking up a handful of damp holly leaves*). Us tell your fortune about loving.

PATSY (*coming nearer—with slight airiness*). Can you?

BIG SIS. Us both can.

BIG SUE. Us don't miss um neither.

(*Prancing before her and holding a leaf up.*)
Name one them p'ints your sweetheart's
name.

PATSY (*glancing at her sharply*). Hm—
m—

BIG SUE (*sweetly, mammy-like*). Gwine
tell your fortune, honey.

BIG SIS. Yah, name your man, honey.

BIG SUE (*shambling away*). All right then
—now listen, folkses, and catch the
truth.

BIG SIS. That's right, speak it, Sister.

BIG SUE. Done made many a match
with a holly leaf. Toodle-de-doo. And
broke up many one.

PATSY. Oh, yes.

BIG SIS. Yeb'm.
All of us turn and face the west,
See who the man that she love best.

(*They turn and face toward the left, and
presently* PATSY, *smiling, does likewise.* BIG
SUE *brings her arm over in a circle and touches
each point of the leaf.*)

BIG SUE.
Heenery-hinery-hikum-ho,
Answer my answer there below,
Speak with my finger, say with my
                                                voice—
Shall this woman have her choice?
(*Softly.*) None them p'ints show any
urgement yet. (*Chanting.*)
Slimmery-slissum-slickum-slo,
Answer my answer there below,
Who is the man this woman'll wed—
(*She poises her hand in the air, listening.*)

BIG SIS (*grunting*). Who she gonna keep
warm with in bed?

BIG SUE. Don't hear no answer, sump'n
wrong.
Mischief-meevery-miny-mo,
Answer my answer there below,
Gimme some motion, gimme some
                                                sound—

(WILL CONNELLY *comes in at the right and
stands watching them, partly concealed by the
hedge. He is a gentleman farmer of thirty or
thirty-five, with slightly stooping shoulders
and thin clean-shaven face. A gun hangs loosely
from the crook of his arm.* BIG SUE *has again
poised her hand in the air and waits as if for
an answer.*)

BIG SIS (*starting and crying out*).
Death gwine take her church-wedding
                                                bound.

BIG SUE (*tearing the leaf in two and throwing it down*). There. (*With humorous malice.*) You name one man and us tell you
another—hee-hee.

PATSY (*narrowly*). That's funny.

BIG SIS (*loudly again*). Mought's well
take your mind off'n him.

BIG SUE. Off'n the hunter. Sure God
had.

PATSY (*snapping her fingers above her
head*). Hah.

BIG SUE. Her say hah—hee-hee.

BIG SIS. Walk about and look greedy.
(*Now snapping her fingers likewise.*) Done
got her cap sot, by golly.

(WILL, *who has been wiggling himself uneasily, comes forward.*)

WILL. Sis!

BIG SIS. Lord Jesus, Mr. Will! (*She
begins digging quickly among the bushes.*)

BIG SUE (*dropping on her knees and scratching among the leaves*). Us just getting sassafras roots, Mr. Will. (*In a lightning flash
the cunning of their nature has disappeared,
and to the casual observer they are no other than
two obsequious and ignorant old Negro wom-
en.*)

WILL (*his voice full of indulgent and fatherly
patronage*). Ah-hah.

BIG SIS (*softly to her sister*). Let's be going. This'll make tea for a long spell.

BIG SUE (*coming out of the hedge, now shin-
ingly bland and subservient*). Couldn't give
us a quarter for this Christmas Eve,
could you, Mr. Will?

WILL (*after a moment, leaning languidly
on his gun*). Reckon I could.

(*He pulls out a coin and tosses it towards
them. It rolls under the leaves, and they fall
down on their knees searching for it.*)

BIG SIS. Where is you, new money?
Ehp, here she is.

(*They clamber to their feet.*)

BIG SUE. Ain't got no little drinkum stuff
for us at the big house, has you?

WILL. Come around, I'll see.

THE TWO. Thanky, suh, thanky suh.
Us'll be there.

(*Bowing and scraping they go out at the
left. Presently in the distance they are heard
roaring with laughter, then silence.*)

WILL (*partly to himself*). A little thing
makes 'em happy as larks. Poor creatures. (*He gazes at the ground a moment as
if absorbed in thought, and then stares after
them with a gentle whimsical smiling.*)

PATSY (*watching him and trying to hide her
confusion*). Yes, poor things.

WILL. Pathetic! Helpless like children.
(*Musingly.*) All the Negroes on this plantation are.

PATSY (*neutrally*). Yes. (*As if pondering.*)

Who are they?

WILL. Big Sis and Big Sue?

PATSY. Yes.

WILL. Connelly Negroes. They were slaves of my father's. Everybody knows Big Sis and Big Sue.

PATSY. Are they crazy?

WILL.Gracious, no! Why you ask that?

PATSY. They look at you funny, don't they? (*Hesitating.*) I mean at me funny.

WILL (*presently*). Pshaw, they tell fortunes and that sort of stuff, but they don't mean any harm.

PATSY. No?

WILL (*glancing at her*). Of course not.

PATSY (*wiping her stained fingers with her handkerchief and smiling at him with sudden brightness*). Kill anything?

WILL (*still as if his mind were away*). Shot at some doves far off. Just to scare 'em. (*Presently.*) I wouldn't like to kill a dove, you know.

PATSY. Yes. They're hard to hit too, ain—aren't they?

WILL. They fly like the wind. (*Setting his gun down and leaning on it—musingly.*) I killed one once.

PATSY (*watching his bowed head*). You did?

WILL. Never wanted to since.

PATSY. They are pretty things.

WILL. It started out of its eyes—so— (*Starting.*) Aren't you cold?

PATSY. Look. (*She touches him on the arm.*) There's a line of doves coming this way. (*In a kind of quick excitement.*) Shoot 'em.

(WILL *raises his gun and follows the flight of birds across the sky, then lowers it without firing.*)

WILL (*sheepishly*). I won't shoot 'em now. They're going to their roost down in the pasture. (*Uncomfortably, as he searches for something to say.*) How do you find the house?

PATSY. Fine.

WILL. You're not too crowded?

PATSY. We can get along.

WILL. How do your father and your little brothers like it?

PATSY. All right, I guess.

WILL. It ought to've been repaired before you came.

PATSY. Father and I have fixed it up a lot.

WILL. Yes, I know. The yard looks nicer. The house too. I saw it yesterday—and—things all look nicer. (*Staring before him, he awkwardly tips his cap and starts away.*)

PATSY. Look, there's another line of them! (*She suddenly pulls the gun out of his arm, aims at the flying doves, and fires twice in quick succession.*)

WILL. Gracious!

PATSY (*looking up at him with flushed face.*) What do you think of that?

WILL. There, they're falling down. There—in the edge of the field—two of them—gracious!

PATSY (*unbreaching the smoking gun and taking out the shells*). They fly fast and are hard to kill. Their feathers are so thick.

WILL (*staring at her in a kind of blinking intentness*). You're a good shot.

PATSY. Used to I'd win turkeys at the shooting-matches—eighty yards. I'll run and get them. (*She hands him the gun.*)

WILL (*sharply*). No, let them be. (*Turning around.*) I'll be going now. (*Stopping.*) What are you doing with those berries?

PATSY (*with a flashing bright smile*). Your young tenant people are going on a Christmas serenade tonight.

WILL. Are? Why, they haven't serenaded in years. Ah, no they haven't. (*Stopping again.*) And will you be wearing—doughfaces we used to call them?

PATSY. Yes. Some of us will paint up with this berry juice and look terribly funny. Come and go with us tonight.

WILL. Granny's children play at that! I did long ago.

(JESSE TATE, *a heavy-set farmer of fifty with swarthy face and iron-gray hair comes in at the left. He carries a knob-gnarled cudgel in his hand, and walks and talks with heavy and lightless deliberance.*)

TATE (*slightly touching the rim of his hat with his forefinger*). Howdy, Mr. Connelly.

WILL (*looking around*). Evening, Mr. Tate.

TATE (*slowly, after a moment*). Any luck, hunting, sir?

WILL. Your daughter here has just shot two doves. No, I haven't killed anything.

TATE (*pecking at the ground with his stick*). She's about as good as Daniel Boone when it comes to guns. She is that. (*He stares at the ground as if absorbed with something he sees there.*)

PATSY. Pshaw. Father raised me up same as a boy to ride and hunt, Mr. Will.

WILL. Yes. Good training, I reckon. (*Pulling his coat tight.*) Cold weather, like snow. (*His gaze travels around the field and he fingers his gun.*)

TATE (*with his heavy observation*). Don't know. The sky's got a sort of glassy glaze to it, don't look like a muggy, thickish snow cold.

WILL. No. (*After waiting for someone to speak.*) Hope you're not too disappointed in the farm.

TATE. Well, no. I been down looking over that tract you spoke of my tending.

WILL. Hope you can handle it.

TATE. I'll have to, won't I? It's washed about and bogged up with briars and bushes, but I'll clean that out by March.

WILL (*hurriedly*). Well, don't freeze in this cold, Miss Patsy. Good evening. (*Again he tips his cap in half-embarrassment as he starts off.*)

PATSY AND TATE. Good evening.

(WILL *walks away at the right.*)

TATE (*presently.*) Seems like a nice sort of landlord.

PATSY (*turning to her berry picking*). Yes.

TATE (*pushing his stick down into the ground*). But he ain't no farmer. I knew the Connelly farm when I lived in this neighborhood as a boy. I wished you could have seen it then.

PATSY. I do.

TATE. He's no more like his father than black is white. The old General Connelly was a ripsnorter. Things moved around him. (*Sighing*). Still, he was right much of an ungodly person, and I reckon the world evens up somehow, I don't know. Yes, I reckon so.

PATSY. They say Mr. Will is one of the best men in the neighborhood.

TATE. But a man old as him ought to have a family and be making things go along.

PATSY. I don't know. Oh, well, that's not our business, is it?

TATE. No, there's nobody good enough for him, and never will be, according to his mother—and his sisters. Never was anybody good enough for a Connelly. (*Looking off to the left.*) There they all set in that great house. (*Turning back, his eyes sweeping the wide stretch of half-fallow land.*) If I had this farm—(*Muttering to himself.*) Well, no matter, I say.

PATSY. What?

TATE (*thinking to himself*). Walking over these fields today I'd a-give anything, anything in good honesty to have owned them. (*Half-murmuring.*) It's purty land,

purty land and level as a table, two thousand acres of it.

PATSY. You'll have your own farm yet—some of these days you will.

TATE (*with a touch of moroseness*). No, I won't. I'll die the other fellow's man—a tenant. (*After a moment.*) You will too.

PATSY (*sharply*). I won't.

TATE. Oh, but you'll come to it.

PATSY. No.

TATE. Let's go home.

(*He climbs over the stile and goes diagonally away at the left, bumping his stick on the ground before him.* PATSY *stands looking after him a moment, and then turning, stares across the fields to the left, gradually growing absorbed in thought about something. Presently she tosses her head and, whistling, turns once more to picking berries.* BIG SIS *and* BIG SUE *creep back along the hedge at the left and begin digging sassafras roots again, acting all the while as if in ignorance of her presence.*)

PATSY. What you want now?

BIG SIS (*swinging her hoe*). Raise her up—hah—bring her down—hah.

PATSY (*eyeing them*). Hope you work like that when chopping cotton time comes.

BIG SUE (*tearing her piece of rail out of the fence*). I stick this up for a head board at the grave. Already I sticks it up, and watch her rouse mad. (*She jabs it into the earth and watches it swaying as if reading some mystic meaning there.*)

PATSY (*bursting into a laugh*). That's right, tear the old fence down. We'll put up a wire one where it was.

BIG SUE. And the wind and the rain can write the name.

(PATSY *watches them wryly and half-perplexed a moment and then walks away to the left. Just as she goes out of the scene she begins jiggling her bucket and whistling, apparently in high spirits.*)

BIG SIS (*winking and singing*).

The sporrer sot with her head in her
                                                    wing,
The snake crope up and begun to
                                                    sing—

(*As if with simultaneous understanding they turn and thumb their noses after* PATSY, *then at the sky, wagging their heads and breaking into loud blasphemous laughter. Between their staccato guffaws,* PATSY *is heard whistling in the distance.*)

Scene Two

A few hours later supper is being laid in the old Connelly mansion. The tall candles and the firelight in the dining room illumine an interior once pretentious but now falling to decay. The walls, panelled and decorated in proud Georgian style, are yellowed and cracked, and the portraits of the Connelly ancestors hang mouldering in their frames. The furniture is early eighteenth century, with mahogany table, sideboard, chairs, and tapestries here and there. A wide fireplace is at the left, set between fluted pilasters and under an ornate mantel. At the rear a heavy door opens to a latticed side portico, with airy windows on either side. The room is decked with stray bits of Christmas holly and mistletoe. If once the frilled and pompous gentlemen spent many a joyous evening here in the days gone by—when the guests sat to the board and slaves handed on goblets of liquor and wine, as they said—it is so no longer. For now the grace of hospitality is gone, the jovial host is gone, gone is the slave. The furniture is falling to pieces, the brass candlesticks on the walls and the useless chandelier hanging over the table are cankered and green. The ivory wood trimmings are peeling off in brickish patches, and great gaping cracks run leeringly across the plastered ceiling. The dead Connellys erect in their frames wait for the end.

The two surviving daughters of Connelly Hall, now late-middle-aged spinsters, are laying supper in this dining room, fetching dishes of food from the kitchen at the left. GERALDINE *is tall and somewhat prim, with pallid aristocratic features;* EVELYN *is a few years younger and less austere.*

GERALDINE. I heard a gun shoot twice. And I looked out and saw her and Will standing together there in the fields.

EVELYN. Pshaw, Deenie, there's no harm in that, is there?

GERALDINE (*tapping the knuckles of one hand against the palm of the other, a habit she has when she is worried or undecided about something*). I thought I'd speak of it to you, that's all.

EVELYN. Oh, he was talking to her about the farm. Uncle Bob says there never was such a person for farming.

GERALDINE. We don't know what sort of woman she is—I mean—you know, Evelyn.

EVELYN (*bending over and smelling the ham*). Oh, isn't that heavenly? Well, anyway, she's about as pretty a poor white girl as I ever saw.

GERALDINE (*with a faintly peculiar intonation*). She's handsome if that's what you mean. (*She busies herself at the table.*)

EVELYN (*examining the ham*). It browned splendidly, didn't it? (*With a low half-hearted laugh.*) Now Uncle Bob will be sick at his stomach again. (*Picking up the leather-headed gong stick.*) Shall I ring now?

GERALDINE (*standing back and appraising the table.*) Our Christmas supper is ready at last. Yes, ring.

(EVELYN *turns to the sideboard and strikes the gong with slow, measured strokes. The two women grow still in their tracks, listening as the soft musical tones go echoing through the house.*)

EVELYN. I never get tired of listening to it.

GERALDINE (*softly*). Yes, it's beautiful.

EVELYN. Something so lonely beautiful in it. (*Half-musing.*) For a hundred years it has called our people into this dining room. (*Softly also.*) A hundred years.

GERALDINE (*turning with quick nervousness towards the door at the left*). I was forgetting the coffee.

(*She goes into the kitchen, and* EVELYN *moves over to the hearth and leans her head against the mantel. After a moment* GERALDINE *returns with the coffeepot, which she places on the table.*)

EVELYN (*staring at the fire*). Through all the rooms it goes calling. (*Echoing the gong with sentimental and heartaching mournfulness.*) Nobody. Nobody.

GERALDINE. Of course there's somebody.

EVELYN (*with sudden and tearful melancholy*). How warm this fire is. It burned just like this Christmas years ago. I was standing here and Father came in from town. He'd brought me a new fur coat— You remember that coat, Deenie?

GERALDINE. Let's think of tonight, not some other night. Now that's it.

EVELYN. Oh, there was so much fun then. We had so many friends.

GERALDINE (*with a touch of sharpness*). We have friends now, Evelyn.

EVELYN. Yes, Mother, and Will, and Uncle Bob, and you and me. There were so many more then. Father—grandfather—Aunt Charlotte and Uncle Henry. Soon there'll be Uncle Bob and Will and you and me; then you and me and Will; then—

GERALDINE (*gazing about the room as if willing herself into the attitude of an interior decorator*). These ivy leaves look better in the center of the table. (*She moves them from the sideboard.*)

EVELYN (*gazing about the room also*). It looks beautiful, Deenie—beautiful and sad.

GERALDINE (*aloofly and as if conscious that the portraits heard*). This room is always beautiful—and happy to me.

EVELYN (*lighting the candles*). Sad like a funeral. (*Childishly.*) Why don't you ever say so? You know it is.

GERALDINE. Set out the wine please, Evelyn. Mother says we must have some tonight.

EVELYN (*going to the window at the rear and looking out*). It's getting dark and you can't see anything down in the garden there. (*With her face against the pane.*) Remember the Christmas we had the orchestra from Richmond? You danced with a naval officer that night—hours.

GERALDINE (*with a little laugh*). You remember a lot.

EVELYN. Sometimes I do.

GERALDINE. Come away from the window, silly, you'll catch cold.

EVELYN (*turning impulsively toward her*). Deenie!

GERALDINE. Go see if Uncle Bob is ready.

EVELYN. Yes, I will.

(*Dabbing her eyes with her handkerchief, she goes out at the right.* GERALDINE *stands lost in thought a moment, and then brings glasses from the corner cupboard and fills them with water.* WILL CONNELLY *comes in from the door at the rear. He is dressed in the same dark suit as before, except that he has dispensed with his hunter's leggings. He comes up to the fire without a word and stands warming himself, his head bent over in its usual sag.*)

GERALDINE. Any mail?

WILL. A letter or two and some circulars—papers, a few Christmas cards, too. Cousin Vera sends her regular "Merry Christmas" and nothing more. Where's Evelyn?

GERALDINE. Gone to hurry Uncle Bob. Shall I take the mail to Mother?

WILL. Do, I'll be along to fetch her in a minute if she's to eat with us.

GERALDINE. She is.

(*She takes the letters and goes out at the right.* WILL *looks into the kitchen, then turns and starts out at the right as* EVELYN *returns.*)

EVELYN (*coming in*). Supper's ready, Will.

WILL. I was looking for you. (*Stepping outside the rear door and bringing in a package.*) Here you are.

EVELYN. For me?

WILL. Yes.

EVELYN (*with almost a cry*). Thank you, Will!

WILL. It's not from me. Your loving neighbor sent it.

EVELYN. Will.

WILL. Sid Shepherd of course. Oh, I don't mean to tease you. (*She starts to lay the package in the sideboard drawer*). Open it. He came by on the road and asked me to give you this Christmas present with his compliments. (*He looks at her with a touch of fond amusement.*)

EVELYN. Thank you and him both. (*She opens it and takes out a flashy toilet set.*) In spite of the—taste, it's nice.

WILL. Taste nothing. (*Hurriedly.*) Sid Shepherd's all right—if he did grow up from poor white folks.

(*He goes out.* EVELYN *handles the package a moment, her face a mixture of feeling. Then she puts it away and stands by the fire. Presently she picks up the stick and strikes the gong as before, the blows seeming to wait and listen in themselves.* GERALDINE *returns.*)

GERALDINE (*sharply.*) There's no need to ring again, Evelyn.

EVELYN. Oh, excuse me, Deenie.

GERALDINE (*brightly*). Here's Uncle Bob and I'm surprised.

(UNCLE BOB *creaks in from the right and stands surveying the supper. He is a run-down old Southern gentleman of sixty-five or seventy—dressed in moth-eaten evening clothes of the style of the seventies—with a ragged mustache, pointed scraggly beard, and the pale mottled face of a consistent drinker. His eyes are soft and womanish.*)

UNCLE BOB (*in a high thin voice as he pulls out his watch and surveys the table*). Hah, eight o'clock. Is supper ready? (*Putting a spray of ivy in his coat and singing as no one answers him*).

Hop light, ladies, on the ballroom
           floor,
Never mind the weather if the wind
           don't blow.

EVELYN. Merry Christmas to you.

UNCLE BOB. Merry Christmas. You're looking fine, cheeks pink. Purty as that new Tate gal. Merry Christmas, Geraldine. What, don't hear me?

GERALDINE (*starting*). Merry Christmas, Uncle Bob. Could you lay that large log on, please?

UNCLE BOB. Where's your mother? Shall I bring her?

GERALDINE. No, she's coming with Will.

UNCLE BOB. Is she feeling better?

GERALDINE. I think she'll be able to sit to the table. She says so. (*He gets the log on but rips his coat.*)

UNCLE BOB (*resting on his knees and peering around at* GERALDINE). It hath been proved of old times—one coat will not last a man his three score and more. (*Spying the wine.*) Heigho, the old Madeira shows up again, ho?

GERALDINE. Come in, Mother.

(WILL *helps* MRS. CONNELLY *in from the right and seats her at the head of the table. She is near Uncle Bob's age but appears much older, a shell of a woman, but with something of the dignity and strength of the matriarch yet remaining to her. Her head dodders with palsy, but her mouth is firm, even stern at times, and her eyes are alert. She is crippled and walks with the aid of a crutch. Her dress of heavy black silk, surmounted by a lace cap, comes down voluminously around her.*)

MRS. CONNELLY (*when she is settled in her chair*). Merry Christmas, Robert.

UNCLE BOB (*getting up from his knees and kissing her hand gallantly*). Same to you, Ellen. How're you feeling?

MRS. CONNELLY. Better, thank you.

UNCLE BOB. Good, good. You'll throw away that crutch when spring comes.

MRS. CONNELLY. You're always so nice. Thank you. You are indeed. (EVELYN *comes in and they all arrange themselves quietly and with conscious dignity at the table.*)

WILL (*with an embarrassed laugh*). Well, this is nice, Mother, to have you with us.

MRS. CONNELLY. Thank you. (*To* GERALDINE *and then* EVELYN.) How splendidly you girls have arranged things! (*After a moment, bowing her head and reciting in a quavering singsong.*) On this hallowed evening we bow our heads before thee. Bless us, bless this food to our use and to thy name's honor and glory. Bless this house. Teach us to hold sacred its memory and the memory of our fathers. We humbly beg in the name of the blessed Redeemer, Amen.

(*For a moment they sit in silence.*)

UNCLE BOB (*rubbing his hands*). Well, here we are—the napkins folded and the crystal goblets and all.

EVELYN. And I've never tasted better ham, if we did cook it.

UNCLE BOB. A festive board. *Dum Roma deliberat Saguntum* starves to death. (WILL *begins carving the ham.* EVELYN *and* GERALDINE *preside over the other dishes.*)

WILL. That's for you, Mother.

UNCLE BOB (*genially*). If this keeps up you'll have to go in for big farming again, William Byrd. But *carpe diem*, I say with Horatius.

WILL. Hardly a second time, Uncle Bob. Geraldine. (*He hands on a plate.*)

UNCLE BOB (*shivering*). It's cold in here. The fire hardly warms us.

EVELYN (*elated*). Yes, let's have some wine, Deenie. And we have some lovely wine whey for you, Mother.

MRS. CONNELLY (*laughing*). Am I as ill as that? Open a bottle.

(GERALDINE *pours the wine.*)

UNCLE BOB. Once more we gather 'mid scenes of delight.

EVELYN. Yes, once more. (*Holding a glass between her and the fire, her face flushed with happiness.*) What wonderful flames dance in it.

UNCLE BOB (*admiringly*). The color of your face, ah—Better as it nears the end. Hence, melancholy. Rustle up another pirate uncle in the vineyards of the Barbados.

GERALDINE. None of the Connellys ever were pirates, Uncle Bob. (*She smiles at him with her fine, weary eyes.*)

UNCLE BOB. They should have been. (*Smiling likewise.*) Well, whoever furnished it, here's to him. (*He drains down his glass, gesturing slightly with his free hand towards* GERALDINE.) I can remember back in '87 when Ed Waddell and me—the honorable Ed, he came to be in Congress—put away a whole cask of this same stuff and went out to 'dress the Democrats. I laid Zeb Vance in the shade that day.

MRS. CONNELLY (*presently*). Help Uncle Bob again, Geraldine.

(GERALDINE *pours him a second glass, now prim again as if faintly offended at his boorishness.*)

UNCLE BOB. Thanks. (*He raises his glass to his lips and then stops.*) A toast. (*There is no answer, and he rises.*) On this Christmas Eve, marking the one hundred and fiftieth year—(*He draws out the words in deep oratorical sonority.*)—this house has stood, we lift our cup to the present keeper of its ancient hearth—one who bears the sacred name of Mother, one who shared her husband's—(*With a gesture toward the portrait above the mantel.*)—accomplishments and his glory, one who is the proud possessor of all the virtues known to womanhood and not one blemish—(*His voice full of real and genuine feeling.*)—one whose life has been an inspiration to us all; to you, Ellen, we drink.

(*They rise, clink their glasses, and drink.*)

MRS. CONNELLY (*in a low voice*). Thank you, thank you.

(*They reseat themselves and go on eating. Someone heigh-hoes beyond the door at the rear.*)

WILL (*calling out*). Come in! (*A middle-aged Negro opens the door and stands with his cap in his hand and a tow sack on his shoulder.*)

NEGRO (*embarrassed, but artfully obsequious*). I want to see Mr. Will a minute.

WILL (*glancing at* MRS. CONNELLY). Warm yourself by the fire. I'll be through directly. (*He comes in, a ragged nondescript fellow, and sits down meekly on the edge of a chair near the fire. They go on with their supper.*)

MRS. CONNELLY (*graciously and yet the perfunctory mistress*). How's your baby, Duffy?

DUFFY. Right peart.

EVELYN. What's Santa going to bring them all?

DUFFY (*snickering*). Got so many he can't do much visiting this year.

UNCLE BOB. Why you niggers have so many young'uns anyhow?

DUFFY (*hidding a grin behind the bag*). The Good Book say 'splenish the earth, Mr. Bob.

WILL (*pushing himself back from the table*). I'll finish later. Excuse me. How much meat you want, Duffy?

DUFFY. Much as you kin spare, suh.

WILL. Is that all right, Mother?

MRS. CONNELLY. Let him have fat back if you have it.

WILL. That's all gone.

MRS. CONNELLY. Well, whatever's there.

DUFFY. Thanky, ma'am.

(WILL *and the Negro go out.*)

GERALDINE (*motionless*). We must do something about that, Mother.

MRS. CONNELLY. He has to eat.

EVELYN. And we too.

UNCLE BOB. Pray for a miracle. (*Raising his pudgy fist aloft, his voice full of sudden anger.*) Oh, I'd step in and give Duffy's old woman the worst beating she'd ever had. I'd say, get out of that bed, you old whelp, and get to work, you and your puppies. And then I'd fall in on Duffy, and then I'd stretch three or four of his young'uns out cold.

EVELYN. It's not slave days any more, Uncle Bob.

UNCLE BOB (*excitedly, his voice high and thin*). That's it! A Yankee or a Jew—I don't know which is slickest. The Yankees first sold us nigger property, then took it away from us in the name of Christianity and paid us nothing for the loss. But they kept the money they'd got for the trade, b'God! (GERALDINE *suddenly pours her mother a glass of wine.*) The Yankees, the damned Yankees. All that shall go in my book. The truth has never been told. (*He falls to eating again, and no one says anything.*)

WILL (*coming in at the rear and going quietly to the table*). Oh, yes—the book. Still working on it?

UNCLE BOB. My Lord, feeding a nigger on ham!

WILL. I'm the Good Samaritan. (*He smiles wanly at* UNCLE BOB.)

UNCLE BOB. Why don't you get fat back for him at the store?

WILL. Lend me ten dollars and I will.

UNCLE BOB. As soon as they straighten my pension.

(MRS. CONNELLY *makes a slight gesture of impatience.*)

GERALDINE. Sugar, Evelyn?

EVELYN. No, thanks. The butter, please, Uncle Bob.

(WILL *drops his knife and fork on his plate and leans his head on his hand.*)

MRS. CONNELLY. Pass Will the jam.

WILL. I'm not very hungry, Mother.

UNCLE BOB (*in mock sympathy as he regains his spirits*). Not hungry for Christmas dinner? Must be in love. Any bad news in the mail, Will?

WILL. The bank would like to see me. (*Hurriedly.*) Oh, well, let's talk of that later. (*He takes up his knife and fork again.*) By the way, the paper says we may have snow tonight or tomorrow.

EVELYN. And let's get out that old sled, Will. (*To* GERALDINE.) You remember that big snow when Will and Duffy killed so many rabbits—we were riding on the sled and you stuck that awful splinter in your hand. (*Putting an arm around her af-*

fectionately.) But you didn't cry one bit. No, you didn't, Deenie.

GERALDINE. I remember.

UNCLE BOB. Look out, honey, that wine's mighty strong. Any mail come for me, Will?

WILL. Nothing, Uncle Bob.

UNCLE BOB (*feeling his drinks*). Used to I got it by the carload, office piled full of it, running over in the courthouse—to the Honorable Robert Randolph Connelly, Solicitor, Third District, Legislator. (*Eyeing them.*) Oh, yes!

(MRS. CONNELLY *bows her head a trifle in shame for him.*)

GERALDINE (*to* EVELYN). Virginia Buchanan writes she is coming in the spring.

EVELYN. Isn't that lovely? We—

UNCLE BOB (*with dogged and conscious perversity*). I fought the battle of the Wilderness—at Gettysburg I fought. I yielded up my arms at Appomattox. But I never was whipped. I'm not whipped now. (*Foolish and ashamed.*) Ah, Ellen.

MRS. CONNELLY (*smiling*). Of course not.

EVELYN. We must begin to plan for Virginia's visit.

GERALDINE. We could have the Grahams up from Wilmington.

UNCLE BOB (*emboldened again*). Our day is not over. Chance, luck that makes the great, makes success. A heavy rain is what beat the Confederacy. Our guns were stuck below the hill. It happened to rain. But our day will come. (*Drawing up his shoulders.*) And when it does a Jeff Davis won't have to hide in a woman's clothes then. Nor will a Robert E. Lee have to pray to God so much. It'll be minnie balls and not prayer.

MRS. CONNELLY. Perhaps so, Robert. (*Turning to* EVELYN.) Virginia says she's looking forward to being here.

UNCLE BOB. Pass me the wine, Geraldine. Virginia Buchanan, you say? *Te morituri salutamus.* She's worth two million sweated out of the niggers of South Ca'liny.

MRS. CONNELLY (*with a touch of impatience in her voice*). Now, Robert.

UNCLE BOB (*drawing his coat about him*). Selah.

WILL (*dropping his knife with a clatter*). Talk, talk.

GERALDINE (*after a moment*). Will!

WILL. Yes, I said, talk, talk. God help me. God help all of us!

(*They eye him in astonishment and* MRS. CONNELLY *now sits up straight and offended.*)

UNCLE BOB. God? Thou hast not read the Stoics, son. Pass the pickles, Evelyn.

WILL (*angrily*). Stoics, Epicureans, Atomists! Cicero, Horace! They don't tell you how to feed hungry niggers, how to meet overdrafts and pay mortgages. Do they?

MRS. CONNELLY. Lift me up, Robert. (*Agitated.*) I—I must lie down.

UNCLE BOB. No, no, forgive us, Ellen. Will, what in the name of goodness!

MRS. CONNELLY. Never mind, I'm tired —that's all.

WILL. Mother—I'm—sorry—

MRS. CONNELLY (*in a low disturbed voice*). Tomorrow I have some little gifts for you. I'm sorry I can't finish. (*They all rise except* WILL.) No, don't bother. (*With sudden sharpness.*) The Connellys have stood more than poverty without losing their pride. Good night.

WILL (*contritely—jumping up*). I'll help you, Mother. Here, this way—gently.

(*He takes her by the arm and quietly goes out with her,* GERALDINE *leading the way with a candle.*)

UNCLE BOB (*his face haggard and drawn*). Sleep well, Ellen! Good night. (*To himself.*) Sleep—ah. *De mortibus*—ah—

EVELYN (*bursting into tears*). Now—now— (*Furiously.*) Why couldn't you talk of something pleasant? Mother's sick.

UNCLE BOB. What's got into Will? He's laughed at my joking before. Now—Oh, don't cry, honey. (*With sharp self-hate.*) Fool! (*Rising.*) I'll go to her—No, I'll sit right down again.

(EVELYN *sits down by the fire, her face buried in her hands. Presently she springs up again.*)

EVELYN. I can't stand to live like this.

UNCLE BOB. Well, Sid Shepherd's a rich farmer. He'd marry you in a minute.

EVELYN. And that beautiful Dauphine pudding wasted!

UNCLE BOB. That's what's wrong. The damned Connellys are too proud to live in this world. Pudding? We'll eat it. (*Sighing and going to the fire.*) *Desicco, desiccare*—huhm, principal parts—dry, by God—dry and proud!

EVELYN. And I'm glad we are proud.

WILL (*coming in—smiling*). Is that Livy talking again, Uncle Bob?

UNCLE BOB. And what's swelled up your spleen this Christmas Eve?

WILL. I'm sorry you missed your toast to the general—(*Glancing up surreptitiously like a boy.*)—who in the front of war hath held—(*He turns and pokes the fire hurriedly and aimlessly.*)

UNCLE BOB (*gazing up at the portrait draped in the Confederate flag above the mantel*). He can spare it and I can too.

WILL (*pouring himself a large glass of wine*). Good. (*He stirs the fire faster, holding the wine untasted in one hand.*)

UNCLE BOB (*softly*). Let's all take poison and die. Burn up the house. Leave the crickets and the field mice to their inheritance. You hear me?

(EVELYN *goes into the kitchen.* WILL *throws out his hands in a gesture and sits down by the fire, looking through the newspaper and sipping his wine.*)

WILL (*wearily*). Yes, Uncle Bob.

UNCLE BOB. And I can tell you how to change it, if you would.

WILL. Yes.

UNCLE BOB. Turn the farm over to old man Tate and his gal, Patsy. Or turn it over to her.

WILL. They've only been on the plantation three weeks.

UNCLE BOB. I knew Jesse Tate years ago. He was a good farmer then.

WILL. He doesn't seem to have prospered—coming back here as a tenant.

UNCLE BOB. And of course you've prospered, sonny. It would pay you to quit, if you want my advice. You can—oh—ho—ride around and look at the purty girls in the evening time.

WILL. Don't let the wine make you mean, Uncle Bob.

UNCLE BOB. And another thing. Get married.

WILL. Here now. Really?

UNCLE BOB. When Virginia Buchanan comes up here—

WILL (*throwing down his paper in vexation*). Virginia Buchanan—and I beg her pardon—never had a thought but for blue blood and the Confederate flag and something she thinks her folks did on the battlefields of Virginia.

UNCLE BOB. Ho-ho-ho! (*Narrowly.*) Did you and Miss Patsy kill any game this evening? I saw you banging away together there by the hedgerow. Sweet, ain't she?

WILL (*going to the kitchen door*). Can I help you with the dishes?

EVELYN (*within*). No, thank you. (*After a moment* EVELYN *comes in and stands with her head leant on the mantel.*)

WILL. Have a headache?

EVELYN. No.

UNCLE BOB (*twiddling his thumbs and talking half to himself*). Pray with this penknife prick thou this vein. And let there be no tears, tears. The ivy creeps in at the doors, the beams yield under the roof, the beetles bore with their sharp little augers, and the flood pours in. Hold fast the laces, preserve the frills, though the heavens fall. (*Singing in squeaky dolefulness.*)

In-teg-er vi-tae, sce-le-ris-que pu-rus—
Non e-get Mau-ris ja-cu-lis nec ar-cu.

(*He picks up the newspaper which* WILL *has dropped and begins reading.*)

EVELYN (*clearing the table,* WILL *aiding her*). Want any more supper?

WILL. No, much obliged.

UNCLE BOB. And a little Greek becomes it—*Menin aeide thea—Peleia—dos Achilleus oulomen—en—*

(GERALDINE *returns and helps* EVELYN, *going back and forth into the kitchen with dishes.*)

WILL. You're very witty tonight, Uncle Bob. (*Smiling.*) Not that I mind it.

UNCLE BOB. Selah. (*Outside and far away come the sounds of bells and horns intermingled with the faint music of guitars and fiddles.*) Listen. Serenaders, bless my life! (*Excitedly.*) First time I've heard them in years, Will. (*The music is heard more distinctly a moment and then is silent. Disappointed.*) Gone on by, I reckon. (*He returns to his paper.* BIG SIS *and* BIG SUE *open the door at the rear and creep in.*)

WILL. What is it?

BIG SIS. We came for our little drinkum stuff, Mr. Will.

WILL. Go into the kitchen. Evelyn, give Big Sis and Big Sue a little wine.

BIG SIS AND BIG SUE. Thanky suh, thanky, Mr. Will.

UNCLE BOB. What's all that racket out there, Big Sis?

BIG SIS. Serenaders coming up the gyarden with bull fiddle and bells. Yes, suh.

(GERALDINE *takes a bottle of wine and two glasses and follows the Negro women into the kitchen.*)

EVELYN. Won't that be fine! (*Outside there is a sudden burst of horns, ringing of bells and yells let loose.*)

GERALDINE (*coming in*). That will disturb Mother. Stop them, Will. (*She too listens a moment and then goes out at the right.*)

UNCLE BOB. There's the spirit—hah—hah!

(*Presently the clamor dies down, the rude country string band strikes up a ballad, and the serenaders join in singing, led by a young woman's clear voice.*)

EVELYN (*listening, her face full of naïve delight, then half-singing with the girl's voice outside, forgetful for the moment of her surroundings*).
The Brown Girl she has house and lands,
Fair Elinor she has none,
It's my advice to you, my son,
Go bring the Brown Girl home.

(UNCLE BOB *goes to the rear door, opens it and waves unsteadily to the serenaders outside.*)

UNCLE BOB. Heigh, heigh, boys!

(*The music suddenly stops and a group of singers come up under the portico, snarling and snapping in joyous abandon at* UNCLE BOB *like a gang of dogs. He steps back into the room and they stand in the door, loath to come in, yelling, ringing their bells and tooting their guano bugles. They are dressed in all sorts of outlandish garbs—some wearing their clothes backward, some with masks or doughfaces on, and others painted like Indians on the warpath.*)

A BOY (*ringing his bell above his head*). Wake up, it's Christmas!

OTHERS (*yelling and tooting*). Christmas, merry Christmas, everybody!

UNCLE BOB (*catching sight of someone through the door*). Heigh you, Mack Lucas, bring in that fiddle! (MACK LUCAS, *a shy stoop-shouldered man, wearing a stage-villain's mustache, slips just inside the door. He carries a fiddle in his hand.*) Give us a piece. (*Waving his hand unsteadily over them.*) A piece, musicianers! (*His head doddering.*) Christmas comes but once a year. (*Singing.*)
Hop light, ladies, on the ballroom floor,
Never mind the weather if the wind
                    don't blow.

(*The serenaders titter and giggle, and the country musicians strike up a country favorite, "Noah's Ark." UNCLE BOB listens awhile and then pulls EVELYN out into the room and pushes her through a step or two.*)

CROWD. Hooray!

EVELYN (*confused and embarrassed*). Let me go. (*She shakes herself loose from him and flees to the fireplace.*)

UNCLE BOB (*surveying the crowd as he begins cutting steps*). Come on, partner, where are you hiding?

(*The serenaders gradually move into the room, but show all the while that they are somewhat timid about it, no matter how much noise they make outside.*)

A VOICE The old bird's right.

VOICES. Patsy, come in here!

(*Now with shouts and laughter they push* PATSY *through the group and into the room. She is dressed in the garb of a a gipsy with a scarlet band around her head, a flouncy flowing dress, and with stained lips and cheeks, and painted eyebrows and lashes.* WILL *turns around in his chair and looks up at her in mild astonishment.*)

UNCLE BOB (*clapping his hands gleefully as he moves towards her*). Ho—ho—and what's the matter? Don't run back.

VOICES. Dance with him, Patsy.

PATSY (*with a glance that passes by* WILL). We'd better go, maybe. We all didn't mean to come in and disturb you so. (*She apparently tries to push her way through the door, but now emboldened they hold her back.*)

VOICES. Dance off that piece for him.

UNCLE BOB (*still clapping his hands to the music*). Dance all around. (*He snatches a girl, with a pigtail hanging down over her forehead, from the crowd and begins dancing up and down the room. Those not dancing begin to clap their hands rhythmically.* WILL *sits bowed over in his chair, staring at the floor.* PATSY *becomes a partner to a youth wearing his clothes reversed, a flour sack over his face and a mask surmounted by a cap tied on the back of his head. Another fantastic gnarl-visaged fellow makes his way over to* EVELYN *and drags her unwillingly into the dance. After a moment she partially enters into the spirit of the occasion.* WILL *stands up, eyeing* EVELYN *and the roisterers in embarrassment.* UNCLE BOB, *aroused with wine and excitement, wheezes and shouts as he thumps about.*) Let her roll. Swing your partner. Sashay to the right, sashay to the left. Promenade all! Hands all around—Rah-rah for our side! (*He lets go his partner and pulls* PATSY *into his arms as she passes.*)

VOICES. That's a dancing man. (PATSY *and* UNCLE BOB *pass close to* WILL.)

PATSY (*half-teasing*). Come on play, Mr. Will. (*He makes no answer.*)

UNCLE BOB (*blowing*). A regular fox-chase.

(PATSY *falls to doing a sort of crude gipsy dance in the middle of the room.*)

VOICES. Hooray, hooray! (*A firecracker is shot off outside. The serenaders turn for an instant towards the door and yell.*) Merry

Christmas!

A BOY (*with a high cry*). God the Saviour is born!

(*The music changes from "Noah's Ark" to the ballad of "Gipsy Davie." The others stop dancing and stand watching* PATSY. EVELYN, *as if suddenly upset by her part in the shindig, turns abruptly and leaves the room.*)

PATSY (*weaving her hands around her and singing*).
It was all upon a cold river bank,
The water was deep and a-muddy O,
The tears ran down his face like rain,
When first he saw his a-lady O.
(*The others join in.*)
Last night I lay on a warm feather bed,
My arms were around my a-baby O.
Tonight I'll lie on some cold river bank,
In the arms of my Gipsy a-Davie O.

UNCLE BOB (*singing*). For she's gone with the Gipsy a-Davie O. (*Squealing.*) Purty bird in my cup—Jenny Wren! (*Full of devilment he catches* PATSY *by the hand and leads the singing dancers in a circle around* WILL.) Mack Lucas, saw on your strings! Great God!

VOICES (*singing*).
Pull off, pull off them fine kid gloves,
All made of Spanish leather O,
And give to me your lily-white hand,
And we'll shake hands together O.

(*They shake hands and the boys kiss the tips of the girls' fingers and bow. A country boy, dwarfish and idiotic, springs out into the floor with a squeal. He begins dancing round and round by* WILL, *giggling and leering at him. The serenaders roar with laughter.*)

WILL (*suddenly grabbing the boy by the collar*). Stop that laughing.

(*The serenaders stop and look around sheepishly, giggling, murmuring, and begin to move toward the door at the rear.*)

UNCLE BOB (*pouring himself a glass of wine*). A toast, ladies and gentlemen. (WILL, *ashamed, releases the boy, who slinks back to his companions, gurgling foolishly.*) To all of ye a merry Christmas and a happy New Year! (*He climbs up on a chair and raises his glass.*)

SERENADERS (*tittering and nodding at him*). He's gonna speak. (MRS. CONNELLY, *supported by* GERALDINE *and* EVELYN, *appears in the doorway at the right.*)

MRS. CONNELLY. What is this! What are you doing here? (*The serenaders back away before her.*)

UNCLE BOB (*waving his hand to her and gesturing with his glass at the portrait above the mantel*). Saul hath slain his thousands, David his tens of thousands, and on this blessed Christmas Eve, ladies and gentlemen, I lift this cup to the blessed—(*Again the serenaders snicker and murmur among themselves, and some laugh aloud.*)

WILL (*whirling upon them wrathfully*). Be quiet!

UNCLE BOB (*staring intently at* MRS. CONNELLY). To the blessed memory of a gallant soldier and a great gentleman—the dead husband of our dear lady and erstwhile master of this house. (*As he goes on,* MRS. CONNELLY *moves farther into the room, and she and her two daughters stand holding hands and looking up at the portrait.* WILL *has again dropped his head on his chest and is staring at the floor. The serenaders, as if awed by some uncomprehended ritual, begin to steal out of the room one by one.* UNCLE BOB, *oblivious to all around him, slowly continues, his voice deepening with emotion*). To him we drink who in the face of death mounted the Stars and Bars above the rampart of the enemy; the first at Manassas, last at Appomattox, furthest at Gettysburg—to thee we lift this cup—(*As if addressing a living person.*) To thee, suh, jurist, patriot, soldier, citizen, we drink—General William Hampton Connelly of Connelly Hall!

VOICES (*outside*). Hah, hah, hah! Hooray!

(UNCLE BOB *drinks and after a moment steps heavily down from the chair, looking round the room, from which all the serenaders save* PATSY *have gradually gone.*)

MRS. CONNELLY. Thank you, Robert.

EVELYN (*clapping her hands*). Uncle Bob. (*She runs up to him and kisses him on the cheek.*)

GERALDINE (*catching* EVELYN's *arm and continuing to gaze at the portrait.*) Don't.

UNCLE BOB. *Arma virumque cano.* How great a thing to have an honored name. Ah, we shall not look upon his like again. (*He moves to the fireplace and stands looking closely at the portrait. Lifting his arm, disclosing a wide rip in his coat, he goes on in the voice of one at prayer.*) In our poor way we honor thee. (*Stretching his other hand back toward* WILL, *who looks up somewhat sheepishly.*) And may this, thy son, wear the mantle of his father, with profit and renown. May he become conscious of the name he bears, and from this day forth determine by the help of God—(*He stops and sits down in an armchair near the fire, his head bent over.*)

VOICES (*outside*).Come on,Patsy,le's go!

MRS. CONNELLY. We will excuse you.

PATSY. I—all right. Thank you, ma'am. (*Now ignoring* MRS. CONNELLY.) Come on, Mr. Will, and go with us a-serenading.

WILL (*starting up*). Me? (*Foolishly.*) Hah-hah-hah.

GERALDINE. You can go out this way.

PATSY. We're going to stop at the millpond and have an egg-fry. All of you come.

UNCLE BOB. I'll go.

PATSY (*controlling the tremor in her voice*). The young folks told me to ask you. (*As no one says anything.*) I'm sorry we disturbed you, sorry we disturbed you. (*Impetuously.*) Why're you all so—so solemn? (*She turns and walks with dignity from the room. As she passes* GERALDINE *at the door, she looks up and nods with a smile.*)

MRS. CONNELLY (*after a long silence*). Please see to the fire before you go to bed tonight, Will.

WILL. All right, Mother.

MRS. CONNELLY Help me to my room, will you, Geraldine? (GERALDINE *helps her out.*)

UNCLE BOB. Old and solemn, mournful as whippoorwills. (EVELYN *goes into the kitchen and leaves them. He pours himself another glass of wine and gestures heavily towards the portraits.*) Ladies—(WILL *suddenly picks up his hat and starts out at the rear.*) Where to, Galahad?

WILL. I'll look about the barn a minute.

UNCLE BOB (*staring after him and spanking his thigh*). Ho, ho! (*Calling.*) Don't fall in the millpond. By Jesus! (*Gesturing around again at the portraits.*) Gentlemen—

SCENE THREE

A night in early spring several months later. The ruined garden of Connelly Hall with the moonlit fields showing off to the right. Rose brambles, briers, and honeysuckles grow in unkempt profusion among the ragged trees. In the foreground is an old scraggly myrtle tree with a garden seat under it, to the right of which is a stone pool grown up into a mush of lilies and flags. Farther back in the distance the tombstones of the family burying ground glitter in the moonlight, the sarcophagus of General William Hampton Connelly standing lordly above the rest. Between the pool and the garden seat is an old wooden pump, and beyond the pump in the background the gaunt form of a lightning-blasted cypress lifts itself out of the underbrush like a gnarled, disfigured hand. A path leads in from the right foreground through the grass and briers, passes by the pump, and goes crookedly off toward the side portico, the steps and columns of which can be dimly seen at the left rear. The garden is partially illuminated through the lighted windows of the mansion. Contrasting with the mournfulness of the decaying garden and the pallid light of the moon are the gay strains of a waltz coming from an orchestra in the house. Once again a ball is being given in Connelly Hall and the rooms are alive with youthful laughter and music. Twinkling feet go up and down the broad staircase, hands are squeezed, and hearts are fluttered as was told of in the old days.

BIG SIS *and* BIG SUE *come up the path from the right and stop by the pump. They are dressed in long loose wrappers.*

———

BIG SIS. Bet there's muskrats in that pool big as the old black sow.

BIG SUE. Mought be other varmints in this old Connelly garden—ghostes. Look at them tombstones.

BIB SIS. And that poor moon hanging sick with grief.

BIG SUE. Tchee-tchee—but listen at that music. Ain't no grief there.

BIG SIS. Plenty loving. (*Standing by the myrtle tree.*) Lord, they's cutting up there. Sure giving that Miss Virginia a blowout—uhm!

BIG SUE (*coming over and standing with her*). That Miss Virginia sure God is a queen. Look how she sashay!

BIG SIS. Sashay her tail off, do her no good with Mr. Will.

BIG SUE (*hugging her sister and prancing about*). Lord, look like old days done come back to Connelly Hall.

BIG SIS (*grabbing* BIG SUE *by the arm*). There that huzzy bitch Patsy!

BIG SUE. Jesus, hugging up with the quality.

BIG SIS. Gwine get hugged up—eigh Lord.

BIG SUE. Uh-huh, now! (*She catches her sister's hand and they cut a step or two, their wrappers flapping about their bare shanks, and* BIG SIS *moaning softly.*)

BIG SIS.
Rank-tuh-ma-tank, I'm gwine to the fair,
To see them ladies comb their hair.

BIG SUE (*Mocking the fiddles in the house*). Tweedle-duh-dee.

BIG SIS. S'lute yo' pardner. (*The music in the house stops, followed by applause and the chattering of many voices.*) There come somebody.

(*They hurry along the path to the rear as* WILL CONNELLY *emerges from the thicket at the left, hatless and dressed in ill-fitting evening clothes.*)

WILL. Who's that?

(*He waits a moment, and hearing no reply, rolls a cigarette and lights it. He paces up and down muttering to himself. Presently he goes over and stands looking down into the pool. A light form glides through the trees, and* VIRGINIA BUCHANAN *comes out into the clearing.*)

VIRGINIA (*in a cool drawling voice*). Heigh-ho, Will?

WILL. Yes, Virginia.

VIRGINIA (*coming over to the garden seat*). Isn't this the quietest place? I've been out in this garden hours since I came. Yesterday I sat here and read *Lorna Doone* half through and nothing came to disturb me. That's the sweetest story.

WILL. Yes, it's quiet here.

VIRGINIA. Quiet and lovely.

WILL. Yes.

(VIRGINIA *is a tall, gracious woman of twenty-five, somewhat irregularly featured, with a girlish giddy voice that goes prattling along like a bubbling brook. But underneath her giddiness there now and then show through a weariness and subtlety that she strives constantly to keep concealed. She is wearing a filmy white evening dress with a light scarf thrown over her shoulders and a bouquet of carnations at her waist. Sitting down, she makes way for* WILL.)

VIRGINIA. Oh, of course some things came to disturb me.

WILL. Yes, they usually do.

VIRGINIA. A girl can't get away from her thoughts, you know.

WILL. What was worrying you?

VIRGINIA (*leaning over and tapping the toe of her shoe with her fan*). Lor, you'll think I'm foolish.

WILL. I reckon not.

VIRGINIA. I was thinking about you. (*Archly.*) Now don't say I'm too forward.

WILL (*with hidden wryness*). I won't.

VIRGINIA. Look, there's the moon again. A new moon.

WILL (*rolling another cigarette*). Yes, there it is again.

VIRGINIA. Late, late yestre'en I saw the old moon With the new moon in its arms. I fear, I fear, my master dear— Do you know that poem? It's beautiful. Oh me, I believe it's the new moon that has the old moon in its arms, isn't it? Please sit down and cool your fevered thoughts.

(*He sits down awkwardly beside her.*)

WILL. I'm not very well up on poetry and the moon.

VIRGINIA. I declare you haven't said three words to me the whole evening. What's the matter?

WILL. Haven't I? I'm sorry.

VIRGINIA. You haven't said much to me the whole week. I didn't know you smoked.

WILL. I've taken it up lately. Oh, may I?

VIRGINIA. That's all right. But Father used to say a true Southern gentleman chewed tobacco or smoked nothing weaker than cigars.

WILL. I'm not a true Southern gentleman, maybe.

VIRGINIA. Oh, Will!

WILL. Am I?

VIRGINIA. Of course you are. What's the matter? What is it worries you so? I'll declare. You seem worried all the time.

WILL (*turning and looking at her intently*). All right, then, I won't be.

VIRGINIA. That's nice now. Who is that country girl in there, Will?

WILL. Who?

VIRGINIA. Patsy Tate, or some such name?

WILL. She's a girl lives on the plantation.

VIRGINIA. A tenant girl?

WILL. Yes.

VIRGINIA. What's she doing at the dance?

WILL. Everybody's not as proud as you and Geraldine.

VIRGINIA. Oh Lor, I don't care. I just wondered who she was. (*Whistling softly to herself.*) You're not glad to have me up here, are you? I looked forward to it for months.

WILL. Of course I'm glad.

VIRGINIA. La, oh, I declare. (*Looking off to the left also.*) Don't those white dresses look perfect against those old columns?

WILL. Aren't you cold? Shall I bring your wrap?

VIRGINIA. Oh no! I think Connelly Hall is the loveliest place. I've fallen in love with its sad, ancient grandeur.

WILL. Sad?

VIRGINIA (*touching his arm timidly*). You're not happy, Will. You're tired. There's something worrying you. (*Laughing again.*) You ought to come to Charleston and take a vacation. The old homes and lovely gardens there would cheer you up. Lor, I guess for sheer beauty they're not to be equaled anywhere. Still there's something about this place— Did you ever see such boxwood! (*Laughing.*) I never did in my life. I wonder how high those at the front are?

WILL. Some over thirty feet.

VIRGINIA. It's the loveliest place. I declare it is.

WILL (*looking at her*). A Northern man offered me five hundred dollars apiece for them.

VIRGINIA. How foolish! Money couldn't buy them, of course. (*Half singing.*) Late, late yestre'en, I saw the old moon—You don't like poetry, do you? Do you know Longfellow's "Excelsior"?

WILL. I learned it the year Uncle Bob ran for the Legislature.

VIRGINIA. Isn't he the funniest man? He's having the time of his life. (*As the music starts up again.*) Listen at the waltz. Have you ever been to Vienna?

WILL. I should say not.

VIRGINIA (*laying her hand gently on his arm.*) Don't be mournful.

WILL (*standing up quickly*). Mournful little boy—hah?

VIRGINIA (*starting back*). Of course not.

WILL. Well then, that's nice of you, really.

VIRGINIA. There Patsy is by the window with her black eyes, Will—and outlandish dress. (*Laughing.*) I declare. But she doesn't seem to mind though.

WILL. I don't reckon she minds.

VIRGINIA. She's forward, don't you think?

WILL. How do you mean?

VIRGINIA. A bit—you know—coming.

WILL. Well, that would not be so bad—maybe.

VIRGINIA. Oh my, I've dropped my fan. (*He picks it up and hands it to her.*) Thank you.

WILL. Don't mention it. (VIRGINIA *breaks into a peal of laughter.*) I lack style, Virginia. I wasn't born for a courtier.

VIRGINIA. I'll declare you're funny. (*She touches him lightly on the cheek with her fan.*)

WILL. I know it.

VIRGINIA (*looking out before her*). Cousin Geraldine said that hollow down there is where you used to have the race track.

WILL. It's nothing but a canebrake now.

VIRGINIA. Do you ever think of getting it in shape again? It would be wonderful to do it. I'll declare. Think of the people from Richmond and Washington, Charleston and Savannah, all coming here and betting their money! It would be perfectly lovely. And the jockeys all dressed in their funny clothes and caps! And the marvelous crowds!

WILL. Great goodness!

VIRGINIA. It could be done. And it would be more fun than a little. Please sit down.

WILL. Does this place look like there's any money to spend on race tracks, Miss Virginia?

VIRGINIA. "Miss Virginia." Will—I declare, I call you Will like I'd known you all my life.

WILL. Everybody calls me Will—you can. (*He sits down again.*)

VIRGINIA. Shows people like you.

WILL. Really. (*Bitterly.*) Hah?

VIRGINIA. Of course I've known the Connellys through Father for a long time. (*Laughing.*) Didn't you know he used to kind of love Cousin Geraldine?

WILL. Well, I know something about it. He used to come here when I was a little boy.

VIRGINIA. I wonder why it never went any further. I've heard Mother tease him about the aristocratic Miss Geraldine.

WILL. (*sharply*). Aristocratic over the dead! That explains a lot.

UNCLE BOB (*calling from off the left*). Virginia, come in! We want you to sing for us!

VIRGINIA. I don't understand you, Will.

WILL. And your little moon shines on the tombstones. That's the poetry of it. (*As if quoting into the night.*) And all the great past that comes to dust.

VIRGINIA (*with sudden vehemence*). No!

UNCLE BOB (*calling again*). Come on and sing, Virginia! (*Other voices call her.*)

WILL. No, you can't tell me anything about it. I've already thought it out. You'd better go in now.

VIRGINIA. Come in and I'll sing for you then.

WILL (*standing up*). The great Connellys are all dead. The fools and the weak are left alive. Good night.

VIRGINIA (*half-angrily*). Now you are being silly. I go in alone?

WILL. Virginia, stop this mockery!

VIRGINIA. Silly boy, you're not the only one that's had bitter thoughts. We have something in common, Will. (*Laughing but with a touch of anger left.*) *Au revoir.*

WILL (*resentfully*). Oh, yes. Good night. (*She turns and goes quickly out by the myrtle tree to the left.* WILL *sits hunched over with his head in his hands. After a while* UNCLE BOB *comes waddling along the path from the portico. He is pulling* PATSY *by the hand.*)

UNCLE BOB (*peering forward*). They're gone now. Just ask her to sing and she'll come a-running. A voice like a goose in March.

PATSY. What do you want?

UNCLE BOB (*pulling her on*). Wait a minute, sweet Arabia.

PATSY. This is far enough.

UNCLE BOB. There's a seat over there. (WILL *rises and wanders off into the shrubbery back of the pool.* UNCLE BOB *and* PATSY *come in. He is dressed in the same old moth-eaten evening clothes as before.* PATSY *wears a dark dress cut low across her bosom. A single bedraggled flower is in her hair. Still holding her hand, he sits down.*) Phew, I've cut up like a boy tonight. (*Singing.*)
A wounded snake I was, and now
          a fleet greyhound.
(*Tugging at her hand.*) Sit down. (*She does so and he tries to put his arm around her.*) You've put new life in this old hulk. Real life this time, it ain't whiskey.

PATSY (*pushing him away*). Why did you say I was invited to the party when I wasn't?

UNCLE BOB. Will wanted you to come. He's too timid—you know. So I asked you. It's right, honey, he's glad you're here. Ah, Patsy, you'd put new life into any man, even mournful Will.

PATSY. You had something to tell me?

UNCLE BOB (*teasing and laughing at her*). Maybe it was and maybe not.

PATSY. Then I'm going home. (*She tries to move along the path towards the right, but he pulls her back.*)

UNCLE BOB. Yes, I have, real important. Now sit down and listen to your Uncle Robert.

PATSY (*sitting down apart from him*). Go ahead then.

UNCLE BOB. Ho, who could a-thought it? Forty-odd years ago I sot here on a bench and made love to another gal—not nigh as purty as you. Still going strong—unh?

PATSY (*laughing*). You ain't making love to me, I can tell you.

UNCLE BOB. Ain't I? (*He pushes himself close against her.*)

PATSY. What was it? Go on tell me.

UNCLE BOB. Still interested—unh?

PATSY. I wouldn't a-come out here if you hadn't said it was so important.

UNCLE BOB (*grinning at her amorously*). *Ego amo te.*

PATSY (*laughing again*). What's that, the Lord's prayer?

UNCLE BOB. Man's prayer. (*He suddenly grabs her hand and kisses it.*)

PATSY. Let me a-loose.

UNCLE BOB. *Ego amo te,* I love you.

PATSY (*giggling*). Lord a-mercy!

UNCLE BOB (*with a threatening growl*). You laugh at me—hanh? (*She claws at his face and he holds her tight.*)

PATSY (*panting*). Let me a-loose—oh!

UNCLE BOB. So you come a-walking in the dark—anh? Humhn-uhn—you're soft as a kitten. (*She frees one hand and strikes him in the face.*) This is one of the old boys, honey! The bull of the woods! (WILL *bounds through the shrubbery at the left and snatches* PATSY *from him.*)

WILL (*sputtering with helpless anger.*) Get away—get away from here quick!

UNCLE BOB (*clattering to his feet*). Can't you see we're at private—

PATSY (*to* WILL—*laughing*). That's all right, I'm not afraid of him.

UNCLE BOB. God A'mighty, you won't do nothing! Well for Christ's sake, he's got a puny arm around her!

WILL (*moving toward him*). Say another word and I'll kill you.

UNCLE BOB (*staring at him in astonishment*). You will, hanh?

WILL (*flying at him*). You old hog, get

away from here! (*He springs upon him and knocks him down.*)

PATSY (*rushing between them*). Please, Mr. Will, please.

UNCLE BOB (*crawling up on his haunches*). Now you see—now—(*Spluttering.*) I'll get my gun—I ought to shoot you like a dog for that—I ought to—Will Connelly, are you gone crazy?

WILL (*his voice breaking between a sob and a whine*). Get away from here—right quick—

UNCLE BOB (*backing away from him*). All right—all right. I'm going— (*Tauntingly.*) Let the moon shine, let it be dark around, you'd do nothing with her.

WILL. Don't say another word to me, Uncle Bob!

UNCLE BOB (*sneering*). Hah, you happen to knock an old man down and it turns your stomach. Now take her, see'f there's any blood in you, sissy! (*He throws up his hands in an indecent gesture and goes off at the left.*)

PATSY (*bursting into a laugh*). You sure laid him out flat.

WILL. I don't think it's funny at all. I don't see a thing to laugh at.

PATSY (*soberly*). It's not funny. (*After a moment.*) Why do you want to hurt my feelings, Mr. Will? (*She sinks down close to him on the seat.*)

WILL. What have I done now?

PATSY. I wouldn't have come to the party if I'd a-known you didn't want me.

WILL. Well, maybe I wanted you to come.

PATSY. Mr. Bob said you did, or I wouldn't.

WILL (*furiously*). That's just it. He wanted you to come so he could do what—(*Grieving like a boy.*) I hit him right in the face with my fist. Lower and lower. Now we fight like dogs.

PATSY. What a strong man you are, Mr. Will!

WILL. My hands are trembling. It scared me—I'm ashamed of myself.

PATSY (*taking one of his hands in hers*). Your hand is big and strong too. You didn't hurt my feelings by what you said.

WILL. Oh, I don't know what I said —My head's all to pieces now. (*Looking at her.*) Why do you do that?

PATSY (*softly*). Please don't mind.

WILL (*brokenly*). Your hand is nice— it's cool.

PATSY. I'm glad it's so. I feel sorry

because you're sad—you weren't sad the night you went serenading with us. You had a lot of fun.

WILL (*stammering, as he draws his hand away*). I stood in the shrubs and heard it all and I was scared. I didn't know what to do. And then something seemed to go all over me—it made me blind of a sudden and the next thing I knew I was out here and had hit him. (VIRGINIA *is heard singing in the house—"After the ball is over, after the break of day."*) Oh, God, what a mess! Let me tell you something, I'm done.

PATSY (*sharply*). What do you mean?

WILL. I'm going to work in town somewhere. The farm may go to hell and all with it.

PATSY. No.

WILL. Listen there! Fools, fools we are. Borrowing our last cent to give Virginia a big party, having an orchestra and— My God! I'm done—done!

PATSY (*catching his hand in hers*). Let me help you, Will.

WILL. I wish you could, I do.

PATSY (*in a low voice*). I can.

WILL (*raising his head*). No, you're like the rest. You pity me. I am nothing. Even the niggers laugh at me.

(*She bends down suddenly and kisses him on the lips. Incredulous, he stands awkwardly up and then sits down again, nervously fingering his coat.*)

PATSY. I could help you. (*Hesitating.*) And you could help me. You'd be running away like a coward if you left. You'll do it. I'll help you—we'll do it— work—work—together. (*Throwing out her hands.*) I know how to work with the earth. (*Gazing at him with intensity.*) I know her ways. I could teach you. (*Bending vehemently over him as he looks at her with a forlorn smile.*) See, I talk to you—I pour out my heart for you.

WILL. Patsy. (*Murmuring.*) You make it almost real. With you—yes—I might do something—But I'm numbed, cold, empty. I've stayed in this old house too long—

PATSY. No, you must live—live! Wipe away all these gullies and broomstraw patches—and waste—waste.

(*In the background the two Negro women are seen creeping softly forward through the trees and watching them.*)

WILL (*staring at her in a sort of stupefaction*). It seems strange—like a dream.

Yes, I could—Maybe we could. (*Suddenly starting.*) No, I don't know you. No—

PATSY (*catching him by the shoulders*). Yes, yes, you do. (*Putting her arms suddenly around his neck.*) I love you, I do, Will. (*Tugging at his arm and whispering.*) Come with me. (*The Negro women have crept up the path nearer, listening.*) We'll walk in the fields.

WILL (*almost with a pleading shout as he sweeps her suddenly into his arms*). Yes! Out of this death and darkness—into the light! (*He starts out with her, impelled by his burst of feeling, and then stops.* PATSY *puts her arm around him and with her head upon his shoulder leads him on. The Negro women wobble in by the myrtle trees.*)

BIG SIS. This darkness, bless God!

BIG SUE. That light, hallelujah!

BIG SIS. Ehp, her don't know that Connelly blood her messing with mebbe.

(*They hug each other over the pump.*)

BIG SUE. Her think that sassafras water.

BIG SIS (*tossing her head*). Water can turn to blood.

(UNCLE BOB *comes blundering through the underbrush at the left.*)

UNCLE BOB. O little moon, what have I seen? Cock-a-doodle-do! (*He crows like a rooster and flaps his arms up and down.*)

BIG SIS AND BIG SUE. Uhp! (*He cuts a goatish step before them.*) Us done see and foresee.

UNCLE BOB (*like a crier*). William Byrd Connelly is now out farming. Oh yus! Oh yus! (*Calling after* WILL *and* PATSY.) Ain't no fences round your crops—ehp! Let the hogs root.

BIG SIS AND BIG SUE (*guffawing*). Uhp—Lord!

UNCLE BOB (*beginning to pat his hands*). Go to it, old squealers. (*They begin hopping up and down, their wrappers flopping about.*) Great doings ahead. Amen.

BIG SIS AND BIG SUE (*as they dance*). Mischief-meevery-miney-mo, Answer my answer there below.

(*They begin doing a hoochee-koochee dance facing each other.* UNCLE BOB *rolls around on the ground clapping his hands and peering at their huge flashing legs and joggling bodies.*)

UNCLE BOB. Hurrah! (*He rises to his knees, beating time and reaching out his hands to the night in a drunken blasphemous call.*) Our Father who art in heaven, hallowed be the sin which now doth flourish forth to salvation. Ecch, set to it, old cows,

we'll all go home at milking time. (*He goes on foolishly clapping his hands. Presently, emitting a long sigh, he stretches himself out flat on the ground.*)

ACT TWO

SCENE ONE

A few days later, in the Connelly dining room. It is midmorning and still cold enough to have a fire going. WILL CONNELLY, *dressed in rough outdoor clothes, is seated at the table finishing his breakfast.* ESSIE, *a mulatto girl about eighteen years old, comes in with a plate of biscuits.*

ESSIE. The vittles warm enough?

WILL. All right.

ESSIE. Everything 'bout to get cold waiting.

WILL (*taking a biscuit*). I've had a lot to do.

ESSIE (*laughing*). You sho' got an appetite, Mr. Will.

WILL. Yes. Have the others eaten?

ESSIE. The ladies done et early to get to the station.

WILL. Duffy drive Miss Virginia over?

ESSIE. Miss Deenie and Miss Evelyn went too. They waited to say good-by, but you didn't come.

WILL. Yes.

ESSIE. Yessuh, I told 'em you'd gone round to the tenants on business.

(*He goes on eating, saying nothing, and she watches him with merry half-closed eyes.*)

WILL (*after a moment*). Clear everything away. I'll need the dining room. (*He pulls out a notebook and figures in it as she goes about stacking up the dishes.*)

ESSIE. Gonna bring them menfolks in here?

WILL (*handing her a key*). And go down in the cellar and fetch up a jug of wine.

ESSIE. Yessuh.

(UNCLE BOB *comes in at the right.*)

UNCLE BOB. Essie, Mrs. Connelly wants her breakfast in her room.

ESSIE. Yessuh. (*She gathers up the dishes on a tray and goes into the kitchen.*)

UNCLE BOB. She'd like to see you too, Will.

WILL. All right, later. How's she feeling?

UNCLE BOB. Not so spry after the stir

this morning. Oh, saw ye fair Inez as she gaed into the South. You've just played hell, ain't you?

WILL (*smiling*). Not that I know of.

UNCLE BOB.

The Brown Girl she has house and lands, Fair Elinor she has none—

Danged if you ain't becoming a moon-eyed ladies' man.

WILL (*laughing*). Poetic, by God!

UNCLE BOB (*angrily*). And it ain't funny.

WILL. Isn't it?

UNCLE BOB. Must be an interesting little book there.

WILL. Getting ready to address my constituency.

UNCLE BOB. Running for constable? (*Looking out at the rear.*) Your tenant gang. What's up?

WILL. Having a meeting about the crops.

UNCLE BOB. Hustling landlord, like Sid Shepherd, ain't ye?

WILL (*with a glance at him*). Going to put everybody to work.

UNCLE BOB. And what holy transubstantiation has happened to you?

WILL. Your words are too long for business.

UNCLE BOB. Ho-ho! Going to labor under the sign of Venus—eh?

WILL. Go to hell.

UNCLE BOB (*gleefully*). Jesus my Savior, he's getting fiery!

A VOICE (*outside*). Heigh, Mr. Will!

WILL (*going to the door and opening it*). You all come in here.

(UNCLE BOB *goes over and stands by the fireplace. Fifteen or twenty tenant farmers troop in, the Negroes behind the whites, and old* JESSE TATE *in the lead. They all take off their hats as they enter and arrange themselves around the room. With the exception of old* TATE *they are a scurvy, nondescript crew. Three or four ancient ebony darkies with faces wizened as aged monkeys beneath their flaring white hair stand respectfully near the table.* WILL *pushes chairs toward them.*)

WILL. Uncle Reuben, you and Uncle Isaac sit down.

(*They sit down and stare about them with dull, blinking eyes. There are a few middle-aged white men with ragged mustaches and beards, thin gaunt fellows, hollow-eyed and hopeless, their faces burnt like leather by the wind and sun. Some of the Negroes are middle-aged, tattered and mournful like* DUFFY. *And the others are younger, more greasy and merry,* with bold gleaming eyes that roll in their sockets as they take in the splendor of the room. One of the Negroes is taller and more dignified than the rest. He is dressed in the garb of a preacher with a high celluloid collar coming up under his chin and a bluish coat that reaches below his knees. Most of the Negroes are mulattoes. They speak to* WILL *as they enter, some shyly and with embarrassment, others more boldly and with little or no respect in their voices.*)

TATE. Good morning, Mr. Will.

WILL. How're you, Mr. Tate?

TATE. Well, I thanky.

OTHERS. Good morning, Mr. Will— Good morning. Howdy. Right here on the dot.

WILL. Good, Make yourselves comfortable.

OTHERS. Howdy, Mr. Bob.

UNCLE BOB. Howdy, all. (WILL *looks around in some embarrassment at the pinched and weary faces, and nervously fingers his notebook. Then he sits down at the table, turning through it, making notations, very businesslike. The tenants are themselves ill at ease until* UNCLE BOB *goes around among them, shaking hands, asking after their health and the health of their families.*) Well, help my life, Reuben. Isaac, how are you? (*They rise and shake his hand with a dignity that hides all their knowledge of his sins and meannesses.*)

UNCLE REUBEN AND UNCLE ISAAC. Still here, suh, still hanging on.

UNCLE BOB (*making his way among them like a lord*). How're you, Alf? Good morning, Duffy, And here's the preacher— the orator of Shady Grove. (*He shakes hands with the Negro preacher.*) Who'll ask after my soul when you are gone? Ah, Alec, how's your windpipe?

ALEC (*overwhelmed with delight*). Getting her down now so she'll roar, suh.

UNCLE BOB. More like your mammy every day. (*There is a giggling and snickering among the group.*) Well, he is, folkses. Coming to hear you preach in August, Alec. The last time I heard you you had the sinners on the floor licking sweat. It's good to see you all. (*He shakes hands with a thin sad-faced white man.*) How you, Jodie?

JODIE. Purty well, Mr. Bob.

UNCLE BOB. How's your wife?

JODIE. Ain't mended none lately.

UNCLE BOB. Get her some Pluto water to drink—that'll fix up her stomach. Swamp root's good too. Morning, Henry.

Howdy, Tyler.

HENRY AND TYLER (*two fellows with long plow-handle arms*). Howdy, sir, howdy, sir.

WILL (*standing up*). I won't keep you long, not long.

UNCLE BOB. See you got business to attend to. This young landlord'll be running for the legislature next. Glad all my friends looking so well. *Vale et vatque.* Vote for him. (*He goes through the rear door, and regretfully they watch him leave.*)

ALF (*a sad fellow, to his neighbor*). All right!

NEIGHBOR (*tapping his head*). Something in there besides shucks.

WILL (*his embarrassment disappearing as he goes on*). I asked you to come over here so we can talk about the plantation together. Some of you see me now with my work clothes on perhaps for the first time. (*Smiling intimately.*) Ain't it so?

A YOUNG WHITE FELLOW (*wearing galluses and with a mop of mangy hair protruding over his forehead like a cap*). That's about so, Mr. Will.

WILL (*as several of the men nod to one another and some of the Negroes snicker*). Go ahead and laugh. Well, I'm going to work. I want to talk to you and I want you to talk to me. This is the first time we've ever got together and that's what it's for. What's been the matter with this farm? Somebody tell me. (*Nobody says anything.*) What would you say, Ransom?

RANSOM (*a middle-aged white man, with long drooping mustaches and stooped shoulders*). I don't know. I don't just know, Mr. Will.

WILL. There's something been wrong, ain't there?

RANSOM. Seems like it.

A NEGRO (*in the rear—softly*). Sho' God is.

WILL. Who was that?

VOICES. Charlie over here.

WILL. All right, Charlie, what's been wrong?

CHARLIE (*a little dried-up Negro of thirty or forty*). Nothing, Mr. Will. Sho' ain't nothing! Everything fine!

WILL. Don't be afraid to talk out. (*He waits and no one says anything.*) Well, I'll tell you. We ain't been working. Year after year we've lived from hand to mouth. We've let the soil wash away, bushes grow up in the fields, half-plowed the land. (*With nervous impetuosity.*) I've

been a damn poor manager.

VOICES. You been all right, Mr. Will.

A WHITE MAN. You sure have.

OTHER VOICES. Good Lawd, sho' he has!

A NEGRO. Sho' the truth, Mr. Will.

WILL. Maybe I been too good to you, good and no backbone. But that's not all the trouble. We sleep too much on this place.

A NEGRO (*as if in alarm*). Uh-uh!

WILL (*tapping the table*). From this day we're going to change. Ransom, you got children—grown boys and girls somewhere in a factory. They couldn't stand this dead place. They oughta be here with us. We oughta made it so they'd stay. And Jodie's got boys, gone from home, he don't know where they are. The young folks run away from this place like partridges from a hen. Why? We got no life here, that's why. I been figuring on all these things and we're going to take a new start. We're going to be real farmers. We got a lot of land broke but we're going to break a lot more and break it deep. Next week I'll have new plows and more stock. The first thing we'll do is to clean up the hedgerows, patch the fences, and shrub the bushes out of the fields. Everybody's got to work. I'm going to work—we're all going to work. Work won't hurt any of us, will it? And everybody works will get rations. I'm going to start a commissary to furnish you. And I'll see who deserves to eat and who don't.

UNCLE BOB (*applauding in the hall*). Hooray! (*He is heard clapping his hands. The farmers chuckle and murmur among themselves.* WILL *controls his impatience and turns to* TATE.)

WILL. Is that right?

TATE (*solemnly*). Sounds right.

WILL. Yes. Well, there's no reason why we can't make this land pay. How does it compare with the land further south, Mr. Tate?

TATE (*more solemnly still*). The land's all right. Just needs work. (*Monotonously.*) It just needs work and peas and clover now and then.

WILL. I'll get the money to swing this, and if I don't get the money I'll get the credit somehow. (*He stops suddenly and looks at them.*)

A NEGRO (*softly*). Sounds mighty good.

ANOTHER NEGRO. Sound right.

A THIRD NEGRO. I don't mind work.

A FOURTH NEGRO. Me neither— Work, work, I don't mind work. Just so I gets my rations. (*He makes a sound of spitting on his hands preparatory to swinging an ax.*)

FIRST NEGRO (*softly*). Rations.

WILL. Anybody want to say anything?

VOICES (*after a moment*). No, suh, Mr. Will.

WILL. Go ahead and talk out. (*But they look at him dumbly.*) All agree to that?

VOICES. That's right. That's all right. We're satisfied.

WILL (*now at ease—laughing boyishly*). Does it suit you, Alec? You're a preacher, but you don't have to preach till August.

ALEC. Yes, suh, yes suhree. (*He stands bowing up and down in confusion as a roar of laughter bursts around him.*)

WILL. You'll have to get off that long coat and collar, Alec. Can't plow in them. (*A fleeting glimpse of wrath crosses ALEC's face, but he goes on bowing and grinning.*)

ALEC. Yes, suh, yes suhree.

WILL. I'll come around and see each one of you separately. I've already figured out the number of acres you ought to tend and what you ought to make on them. And remember—everybody that works gets his rations. I'll put an oath on it. Every damn one of you that don't, don't eat, and he don't stay on this land either.

ALEC (*with a touch of grim piety*). Now, now.

VOICES. Uh-uh!

WILL. Any questions? All right, meeting's adjourned to the back porch where we'll have a taste of wine. (*He goes to the kitchen door and calls.*) Essie, get out some glasses in there. (*With the exception of OLD TATE, all the men go out and are heard laughing and talking outside. WILL turns back.*) Have some wine, Mr. Tate?

TATE. Thankee, I don't drink. (*Looking around the room.*) Sure is a fine place here, Mr. Will.

WILL. Thank you.

TATE. Don't blame you to wanter keep it going.

WILL. We've started, haven't we?

TATE. They know you mean business now. You've got 'em going. They'll work.

WILL. I meant what I said, too.

TATE. It was all right. Well, I got to get back to my plow. Good day. (*He puts on his hat.*)

WILL. Good day. (TATE *goes out, and* WILL *walks out onto the porch after him.*)

TATE. Count on me to help when I can.

WILL (*outside*). Thank you. (*To the men.*) I'll be around to see you all later in the day.

VOICES. All right, Mr. Will. Yes suh.

(*They are heard guffawing and uttering joking cries.* MRS. CONNELLY *comes in at the right, helped along by* UNCLE BOB. *He settles her in an armchair by the fire and puts a hassock under her feet.*)

UNCLE BOB. I wouldn't talk to him now, Ellen.

MRS. CONNELLY. I'm all right. Tell him to come in, please.

UNCLE BOB. He's all set up over his plans.

MRS. CONNELLY. I'll speak to him now.

UNCLE BOB (*at the rear door*). Will, come here a moment, please.

(WILL *comes in with a glass of wine in his hand.*)

WILL. I was coming to your room, Mother. You feeling better?

MRS. CONNELLY. I'm very well, thank you. (*She waits a moment.* UNCLE BOB *goes out at the rear and closes the door behind him.*) Sit down.

WILL (*going to the fire*). Let me stand up if you don't mind.

MRS. CONNELLY. I've got to be plain with you.

WILL. What's the matter, Mother?

MRS. CONNELLY. You've hurt us all terribly. I want you to know that.

WILL. I'm sorry.

MRS. CONNELLY. Virginia's gone home. You weren't even here to tell her good-by.

WILL. I told her good-by last night. I had to be away this morning.

MRS. CONNELLY. Why, why do you act this way? Please tell me.

WILL. Well. We just didn't get along together and that's all. It's past now.

MRS. CONNELLY. She's asked you to come down hunting in the fall. I want you to go.

WILL. The harvest will be on then. (*Fumbling his notebook.*) I have a lot to do now, Mother. (*He drinks down his wine and comes over and pats her on the shoulder, as if to leave the room.*)

MRS. CONNELLY. Please don't go. It's not that I've offended you in some way, is it?

WILL. Why no.

MRS. CONNELLY (*agitated*). Don't you have any love for this plantation and the carrying on of your father's name? It means that to us, Will. (WILL *turns and looks in the fire, saying nothing.*) It's hard for me to talk like this to you.

WILL. I know it is.

MRS. CONNELLY. Listen to me then. (*Catching his hand.*) Write to Virginia, make it up with her. It's not too late.

WILL. No. There's nothing to make up.

MRS. CONNELLY. I wish you would. (*She waits and he says nothing.*) The rest would take care of itself.

WILL. I'll tell you why. Because I'd go on being the same kind of weakling I've always been. It would be her money that did everything, not me. I want to do something.

MRS. CONNELLY. You've not been weak. I've always known you'd make me proud of you.

WILL. I know what I've been.

MRS. CONNELLY. You could do things then, all the great things we dream about. (*Softly.*) And our name will go on.

WILL (*turning and looking at her*). We've thought too much about our name anyway.

MRS. CONNELLY. Will!

WILL. It's true, Mother.

MRS. CONNELLY (*dropping his hand*). Then, excuse me, Will. The plantation and everything will keep on going to pieces. What will the end be? You know—poverty—poverty—to the end.

WILL. Not if I can help it.

MRS. CONNELLY. You can't help it and you know it.

WILL. I can too and I shall.

MRS. CONNELLY. How?

WILL. By starting right here and making things over. It was once the great Connelly plantation and I'll make it so again. (*In excitement.*) I will, Mother.

MRS. CONNELLY. And that's but half of it, even if you could.

WILL. What do you mean?

MRS. CONNELLY. You know very well whom I mean.

WILL (*turning again to the fire*). I don't. (*He picks up the empty glass and tries to drink from it.*)

MRS. CONNELLY. Somebody else will do everything, not you.

WILL. I'll do it myself.

MRS. CONNELLY (*in a soft, cold voice as she watches him*). Can't you see that girl's designs upon you, upon us all?

WILL (*hotly*). You know nothing about it, Mother.

MRS. CONNELLY. Geraldine and Evelyn see it too. She's making use of you to get what she wants.

WILL (*grimly*). I reckon she's not.

MRS. CONNELLY. She's set out in cold blood to become mistress of Connelly Hall and you're helping her to it.

WILL. She's not.

MRS. CONNELLY. You've been spending more time over at her house—your own tenant's house—the last week than you have here. Haven't you any pride?

WILL. We've been working out plans for the farm—(*He stops in embarrassment.*)

MRS. CONNELLY. Of course she—(*She waits awhile and then—suddenly changing her tone of voice*). Well, she loves you?

WILL (*after a moment*). Yes.

MRS. CONNELLY (*smiling*). You don't know a thing about such women as she.

WILL (*defensively, like a boy*). I know she does.

MRS. CONNELLY (*smoothing out her dress*). And how do you know?

WILL (*in a low voice*). I know.

MRS. CONNELLY (*after a moment*). Do you mean what I think—

WILL (*looking at her in shamed triumph*). Well, whatever you think, I know she—loves me.

MRS. CONNELLY (*quietly*). It proves everything I've said if she's gone as far as that.

WILL. It does not.

MRS. CONNELLY. Any honest woman would tell you she's done that to trap you.

WILL. I don't believe it.

MRS. CONNELLY. I'm a woman and I know. (*After a moment, smiling.*) Well, the Connellys are famous for that. You're one of them after all, aren't you? If she wants to play with fire, then let her get burnt. It won't be you, for you're not the woman. (*She looks at him, telling her meaning in her eyes and finally he turns away and looks again in the fire.*)

WILL (*helplessly*). I don't know what to say to you, Mother.

MRS. CONNELLY. Then let's don't talk about it any more. (*In a changed voice.*) After all, I do trust you, Will, you see?

WILL (*abstractedly*). Thank you.

MRS. CONNELLY. Now let's talk over your plans for the farm—

WILL (*dragging forward an answer*). They're not all worked out yet.

MRS. CONNELLY. What was the meeting about?

WILL (*mechanically*). I'm going to put 'em all to work.

MRS. CONNELLY. What did you say to them?

WILL. That.

MRS. CONNELLY (*she waits, but he says nothing more in reply*). We'll go over it all later, then. (*Watching his face.*) Help me out in the sun now, please.

WILL (*turning to her*). Don't you see, Mother—

MRS. CONNELLY (*quietly as he stops*). Yes?

WILL. How you're destroying my confidence in—

MRS. CONNELLY. In what?

WILL. In, well, in myself then.

(UNCLE BOB'*s teasing voice is heard in the kitchen.*)

UNCLE BOB. Good morning, sweet arbutus.

MRS. CONNELLY. I haven't said anything about you, Will.

WILL (*hastily*). All right, all right then. (*Vehemently.*) But it's me—me she cares for, Mother.

MRS. CONNELLY. It's the Connelly land and the Connelly name she wants. (*Turning to him.*) Only selfishness and greed would make a woman violate herself.

WILL. My God!

MRS. CONNELLY (*almost gently*). And Geraldine says Big Sis and Big Sue have heard her scheming in the fields with her father.

WILL. No! No!

(UNCLE BOB *comes in from the kitchen.*)

UNCLE BOB. Another farmer in here wants to see you, Will.

(WILL *makes no answer.*)

MRS. CONNELLY. Help me into the garden, Robert.

UNCLE BOB. Excuse me for interrupting you.

MRS. CONNELLY. We've just finished. (*Sticking her crutch under her arm and climbing up to her feet.*) Go ahead with your plans. We'll talk them over after supper.—Robert.

(*She goes out at the rear leaning on* UNCLE

BOB'*s arm.* WILL *sits looking at the fire a moment, then picks up his notebook from the table, glances at it, and sticks it sharply into his pocket. From the same pocket he pulls out a small bag of tobacco and starts rolling a cigarette. There is a knock at the kitchen door to which he pays no attention.* UNCLE BOB *re-enters at the rear. The knock is repeated.*)

UNCLE BOB. Wake up.

WILL. Come in.

(PATSY TATE *enters, dressed in rough clothes and with a shawl over her shoulders.* WILL *looks up at her, saying nothing, and throws his unfinished cigarette into the fire.*)

UNCLE BOB (*bringing forward a chair for her*). Sit down.

PATSY (*pulling some rolls of paper from under her shawl*). I just brought these plots for you. They're all finished—name, acres, and all.

WILL (*taking them*). Thank you. Sit down.

UNCLE BOB. Let me take off your shoes. Your feet are wet as water.

PATSY (*laughing*). No thanky. (*Sitting down and stretching her feet out to the fire.*) A terrible heavy dew this morning. Same as August. (WILL *turns through the papers.*) Are they all right?

WILL. They look all right.

PATSY. Look at Duffy's plot. I've marked off sixty acres for him.

WILL. He's never farmed more than twenty-five.

PATSY. Him and his crowd ought to tend sixty.

WILL. Yes, that's so. (*He goes on turning through the papers nervously.*)

UNCLE BOB. You oughta been here and heard the speech.

PATSY. Father said it was all right— everything was fine.

UNCLE BOB. Oh yes, lots of applause. Such a change—rejuvenation. Two weeks ago he couldn't have stood up and faced 'em. Now he speaks like an orator. (*He stands watching them with squinting eyes, his lips stuck out in a whistling pucker.* WILL *says nothing and* PATSY *stares at him questioningly once or twice.*)

PATSY. Want me to go over them with you?

WILL. Everything's all right, I reckon.

PATSY. Well, I'll get on back.

UNCLE BOB. What's the hurry? *Abusum non tollit usum.*

WILL (*angrily*). Go to the devil!

UNCLE BOB (*staring at him and then*

waddling across the room). Persona non grata.
(He grins at them and goes out into the kitchen.)

PATSY *(as* WILL *says nothing).* I used to think he was so funny.

WILL. And you don't think so now?

PATSY *(childishly).* There's something deep behind his fun, ain't there?

WILL. Yes, he's deep, like his lust, and that's deep as hell bottom. All the Connellys were like him—ha-ha—deep.

PATSY. What's the matter?

WILL. Not a thing in God's world. What's the matter with you?

PATSY. Nothing.

WILL. We're all well then.

PATSY *(eyeing him).* Won't your mother agree about selling the boxwood bushes?

WILL. We didn't get to that.

PATSY. I don't understand why you're so—like that.

WILL. Don't say I'm too clever for you.

PATSY *(half-angrily).* I won't.

WILL. Sure you wouldn't. *(With sudden over-buoyancy as he springs up from his chair and comes over to her.)* Won't that be a big harvest—cotton, tobacco, corn, peas, potatoes—mountains of crops? *(Patting her on the head.)* Give me a kiss. *(He tries to fondle her.)*

PATSY *(pushing him away).* What did you say to your mother? *(Her face full of pain).* Please, please don't do like that with me.

WILL. Oh, I told her we'd be out of debt by Christmas.

PATSY *(rising from her chair, a half-smile shutting around her lips).* I can guess what she said. Please don't joke with me, Will.

WILL *(looking at her intently).* You're so clever. The poor Connellys are the simple ones.

PATSY *(stammering but never losing her poise as she searches out her reply).* What I've done is not clever. Any woman would tell you that. *(She smiles up at him, now suddenly wistful.)*

WILL *(catching her tightly by the shoulders).* You do love me, don't you?

PATSY *(with turned head).* You already know that.

WILL *(eagerly).* Yes, yes, I do. *(He hugs her to him and kisses her.)*

PATSY *(her head still bowed).* Now don't worry any more. She'll see different later when everything is going fine.

WILL *(in a low voice).* Oh, I'm not worrying.

PATSY *(quickly).* There's nothing to be so sad over. *(Brightly.)* Now you must see after your men and I've got to get to work. You come by later. *(BIG SIS and BIG SUE open the door at the rear and stand unobserved, looking in).*

WILL *(taking up his wine glass again).* Yes, later. *(Like a servant.)* Other orders?

PATSY *(ignoring his manner).* I'll see you this evening then. *(Gazing at the floor.)* There's something I want to talk with you about.

WILL. Well, talk to me now.

PATSY. No, later.

(She rises to go, and then, seeing the two Negro women, starts back. WILL, *noticing her manner, looks up and sees* BIG SIS *and* BIG SUE.)

WILL. What you want?

BIG SUE. Us wanted to borrow a little flour.

WILL. Go around to the kitchen and wait for Miss Geraldine. *(They close the door and go away.)*

PATSY. I don't like the way they follow me.

WILL *(staring at her intently).* Good gracious. *(For a while neither says anything.)*

PATSY. I must go now. *(She starts out at the rear.)*

WILL. Mother's out that way.

PATSY *(softly).* I don't mind.

WILL. I do—Patsy. *(Loudly.)* This way! *(*PATSY *whirls around.)*

PATSY *(her eyes shining suddenly).* Who're you talking to!

WILL *(starting back from her).* You, by God. *(He snatches her arm half-fondly and half-angrily.)*

PATSY. Well, stop it. *(*WILL *turns quickly and goes into the kitchen.* PATSY *starts after him and then stops, standing in the middle of the room as if thinking to herself. Presently she breaks into a low nervous laugh, gazing around at the portraits and half-whispering.)* Oh, you look mighty grand. But you don't scare me a bit, not a bit. *(Clenching her hands.)* All right, me against you, all of you.

*(*GERALDINE *comes suddenly in from the right.)*

GERALDINE *(frigidly).* You wish to see someone?

PATSY *(embarrassed in spite of herself).* No, thanky.

(She looks at GERALDINE *and smiles. Then,*

before her proud haughtiness, the strength seems to go out of her. She pulls the shawl up around her head and leaves through the rear door. GERALDINE *moves about the room setting the chairs to rights.* WILL *comes in still carrying the empty glass in his hand.*)

WILL. Oh—Geraldine—where's— Evelyn?

GERALDINE (*subtly mocking him*). She put her shawl around her face and went out that way.

(*She turns and leaves the room. After a moment* WILL *pulls out his notebook and sits down by the table. Presently he begins rolling another cigarette. The Negro girl,* ESSIE, *comes in with a tray of dishes, which she begins putting away in the corner cupboard. Now and then she looks slyly at him.*)

ESSIE (*snickering*). Sho' is a purty little woman.

WILL. Bring me a glass of whiskey. (*She fetches the whiskey from the sideboard and stands by him as he drinks it.*)

ESSIE. Sho' look at you with them bright eyes.

WILL (*peering at her over the glass—his harassed face gradually breaking into a low, joking grin*). Hah, yes, the way you look at Alec—eh?

ESSIE (*giggling*). Lawd, Mr. Will. (*Scornfully.*) Pshaw, Alec!

WILL. Be married the first thing you know, won't you? How old are you?

ESSIE. 'Bout eighteen or nineteen.

WILL. Yeah, you'll be wearing his ring pretty soon—say, right on that finger there. You want a ring, you know. Yeah, all do. (*He touches her hand lightly and half-disgustedly with his finger.*)

ESSIE. I'd ruther have a lavaliere.

WILL. Be tricky, you'll get that too.

ESSIE. I'd cook a long time for that, Mr. Will. (*With soft cunning.*) It'd make me look a lot prettier too. (*Making a gesture over her abundant bosom.*) Let it hang down there. You buy me one, Mr. Will.

WILL (*suddenly shouting and backing away from her*). Get away from here!

(*He crams his hat on his head and hurries out at the rear.* ESSIE *snickers to herself and begins idly polishing the table, her eyes looking off in a dreamy stare.*)

SCENE TWO

The same—a hot afternoon several months

later. *The Connellys have finished their lunch, and* GERALDINE *and* EVELYN, *now more houseworn and tired than before, are clearing away the dishes.* UNCLE BOB *with a book in his hand is lying on a cot before the screened fireplace, and* MRS. CONNELLY *is sitting in a comfortable chair near the center of the room. They both are languidly fanning themselves with palm-leaf fans.* UNCLE BOB'S *face is more puffy and haggard than ever, and now and then his head sags over the edge of the cot in a doze. Through the open door at the rear the portico can be seen with half-parched vines climbing up it.*)

UNCLE BOB (*rousing himself and reading aloud*).
Regia Solis erat sublimibus alta columnis,
Clara micante auro flammasque imitante
　pyropo;
Cuius ebur nitidum fastigia summa tegebat,
Argenti bifores radiabant lumine valvae.

(*In the fields close by the Negro laborers are heard singing a low work song, their words mingled in a high harmony.*)

LABORERS.
Say, my gal laid her head down,
Laid her head down and cried—
Tears fell on de cold groun',
Can't be satisfied.

EVELYN. The hotter it gets the more they sing about the girl and the gambling man. (*Blowing her breath out in a great sigh.*) Oh, it's so hot!

MRS. CONNELLY. Don't wash the dishes now. It will be cooler in the evening.

GERALDINE. We'll have to cook supper then, Mother.

EVELYN. The thermometer was a hundred in the shade at twelve, Uncle Bob. Excuse me, you are reading your book.

MRS. CONNELLY. It'll have to rain soon.

UNCLE BOB (*mumbling to himself*). Rain! The sky stays like a sheet of glass. (*Sitting up and beating about him with a fan.*) These flies!

GERALDINE. Yes, the screens ought to be mended.

EVELYN (*stopping near the door to the kitchen and scrutinizing a roll of tanglefoot suspended from the wall*). Look, Deenie, we're catching them fast.

(GERALDINE *stands by her with her hands full of dishes. They watch their trap with the eager intent faces of little boys.*)

GERALDINE. There goes another.

(*They go into the kitchen and are heard*

washing the dishes.)

MRS. CONNELLY (*presently*). Why doesn't Will come, Robert? (*Earnestly.*) Why doesn't he come?

UNCLE BOB. He will, Ellen.

MRS. CONNELLY. He's been gone all night. Something might have happened to him.

UNCLE BOB. He's stayed over in town before like this.

MRS. CONNELLY (*quavering for a moment like a childish old woman*). He almost frightens me lately. I don't know him—he's not the same Will any more.

UNCLE BOB. Every man must have his fling.

MRS. CONNELLY. I can't wait up for him much longer.

UNCLE BOB. Yes, you'd better lie down. (*Creeping over to the door at the rear and looking out.*) Yonder's Patsy Tate hoeing away with them niggers in that boiling sun. Done had their dinner and back at it. What a woman! (*As if persecuted.*) Hah, there go the dry whirlwinds traipsing the fields again. (*He twists his head as if in pain, and then stands reading from his book.*)
... *O lux immensi publica mundi,*
Phoebe pater, si das huius mihi nominis usum,
Nec falsa Clymene culpam sub imagine celat—

ESSIE (*outside*). Howdy, Mr. Bob.

UNCLE BOB (*sharply*). Howdy, Essie.

(*At the sound of her voice,* MRS. CONNELLY *stops fanning.* ESSIE *comes in and stands near the door, sniggering and smirking with the faintest touch of familiar spitefulness. She is arrayed in cheap beribboned finery, topped off with a droopy wide-brimmed hat.*)

MRS. CONNELLY. We don't need you any more, Essie.

ESSIE. Lor, I knowed that, Mis' Connelly. I just wanted to drop around again and say good-by.

MRS. CONNELLY. Good-by.

UNCLE BOB. Where you going?

ESSIE. You hadn't no sooner turn't me off this morning, when I seed Alec, and I'm going with him toward Raleigh at a big meeting.

UNCLE BOB. Alec? Why, he can't leave his crops.

ESSIE. Says salvation calling and he got to go. I'll play the orgin for him. (*Swinging nonchalantly over to the kitchen door.*) Good-by, Miss Evelyn. Orter have me to wash them dishes.

GERALDINE (*sharply within*). We don't need you, Essie.

ESSIE (*giggling*). Reckon so. (*Turning back the way she came.*) Well, good-by, you all.

MRS. CONNELLY. Good-by, Essie.

ESSIE (*playing with the ornament around her neck*). Reckon you ain't seen what I got from Sears-Roebuck?

MRS. CONNELLY (*calmly*). Go along, Essie.

UNCLE BOB (*thundering*). Get out o' here, you hussy. (*With a foolish laugh* ESSIE *raises her hand in a queer gesture and goes out.*)

MRS. CONNELLY. Oh, God!

UNCLE BOB. The lowest rung of iniquity has been reached and we hang pendulous there. (*Striking his oratorical attitude but with deep pain in it.*) Yea, to round out the story I should have got me idiot daughters and cried woe.

MRS. CONNELLY (*sharply*). Don't speak like that any more, please.

UNCLE BOB. But always a coward before life and its responsibility. No matter. (*With strained jocularity.*) Evelyn was telling me you'd heard from Virginia this morning.

MRS. CONNELLY (*smiling at him wanly, strangely reminiscent of* WILL's *earlier timidity*). Yes.

UNCLE BOB. She's marrying old Senator Warfield, I hear.

MRS. CONNELLY. Yes.

UNCLE BOB (*with cackling laughter*). Hah-hah-hah—old enough for her father! (*He comes and sits down in a chair near her, and for a long while they say nothing, both nodding now and then in drowsiness.*)

MRS. CONNELLY (*wearily and sleepily*). She'll be entertained a great deal in Washington.

UNCLE BOB. In Washington, in Washington. (*Clearing his throat.*) *Certes ipso facto.* (*Vacuously murmuring.*) When the almond tree shall flourish and fear shall be in the way. At last it's true. We're old. *In nomine Ecclesiastici.*

MRS. CONNELLY (*after a long while—wistfully like a girl, her proud stateliness gone*). It's all so strange now, sometimes it seems it's been a long time and then again just yesterday since— (*Shaking her head and smiling.*) Since we were all so young, you with your hopes, me with mine.

UNCLE BOB (*sharply*). My love and your hopes. (*Twisting in his chair and mopping his face.*) If life were but a dream man might hope to wake from its burden.

(*He stops suddenly and sits staring before him.*)

MRS. CONNELLY (*patting her lace cap*). And now tell me that joke about the Yankee beggar again.

UNCLE BOB (*not replying*). Let the old tree die. (*Looking through the open door at the rear.*) There comes Patsy Tate.

MRS. CONNELLY (*agitated*). I don't wish to see her. (*Raising herself on her crutch.*) Geraldine!

UNCLE BOB (*taking a glass of water from the table and draining it down*). This to him and her, to us all, Ellen.

GERALDINE (*entering*). Yes, Mother.

MRS. CONNELLY. Let me know when Will comes, Robert.

(*She and* GERALDINE *go out. Presently* PATSY TATE *comes up on the porch outside.*)

UNCLE BOB. Come in, Patsy.

(*She enters, dressed in her working clothes, a cotton blouse, apron, and stout shoes. She carries a bonnet and field gloves in her hand, and is harassed and tired.*)

PATSY (*hurriedly*). I want to speak to Will, Mr. Bob.

UNCLE BOB. He's not back from town yet.

PATSY. Not?

UNCLE BOB. Still trying to borrow some money, I reckon. Or spending it. What's the matter?

PATSY. When he comes tell him I want to see him.

UNCLE BOB. Trouble with the tenants again?

PATSY. No, I can manage them.

UNCLE BOB. Come on, tell your Uncle Robert. (*He comes up to her and apparently in self-perversity tries to put his arm around her.*)

PATSY (*stepping away from him*). I've got to see him myself.

UNCLE BOB (*now bitterly and without a shadow of jocularity*). I can still raise that arm to its purpose. Truth remains extant —the entelechy of the shell. Hah-hah. *Eky ho anthropos ten physin apotetelesmenen.*

PATSY. If you'd put your arms in the field with a hoe there'd be a lot more truth, whatever your words mean.

UNCLE BOB. I was saying how perfect is man, how like a god. Me the master-piece of nature. (PATSY *starts out at the rear as* WILL *comes trampling in and almost collides with her. For a moment he stares at her and then goes to the table and sits down. He is dressed in his Sunday clothes, haggard and the* worse for sleeplessness and drink. He has grown stouter and coarser. UNCLE BOB *calls out cuttingly.*) Bless God, the prodigal! Well, here's the calf.

WILL. Had dinner?

UNCLE BOB. We have.

WILL (*shortly*). Morning, Patsy.

PATSY. Good morning.

WILL (*calling*). Essie, bring me some dinner!

UNCLE BOB (*whistling*). Fee-fi-fo-fum—

WILL. And what other bad news has made you happy?

UNCLE BOB. Call her again.

WILL. Essie, bring me something to eat! Where is she?

UNCLE BOB. Lavalieres have cost her her job.

WILL. So. Mother turned her off— anh? Well, we'll see.

(PATSY *with a funny mechanical smile on her face stands gazing at* WILL. *He turns and pours himself some water from the pitcher and drinks glass after glass.*)

UNCLE BOB (*smiling and peering at him over his fan*). Liver afire—hanh?

WILL. Can I do anything for you, Patsy?

UNCLE BOB. And water won't squench it?

PATSY. I don't know.

UNCLE BOB. I'll go tell your mother you're here. (*He starts out.*)

WILL. Your company's welcome, I guess.

UNCLE BOB. She wanted to know when you came.

WILL. How's Mother?

UNCLE BOB. The wayward son has not killed her yet. In time, in time. (*He bows and goes out.*)

WILL (*searching about the room*). How is the chopping?

PATSY. We'll be finished today.

WILL. The old devil must have drunk it all. (*Opening the lower drawer to the cupboard.*) No. (*He takes out a bottle of whiskey and pours himself a full glass, tosses it down and turns to her.*) Well?

PATSY (*gesturing at the glass*). Why do you do that?

WILL. What?

PATSY. Listen, Will, Father's coming to see you.

WILL. Hah, you told him about you and me! I knew you would.

PATSY (*angrily*). No!

WILL. All right, I know I'm low-down.

But who did it?

PATSY. He heard the two nigger women joking out there. He asked me and I said no. I'm afraid something might happen, Will.

WILL. Yes, something will happen.

PATSY. What do you mean by that?

WILL. Whatever you mean. (*They stand eyeing each other, the one as if calculating the strength of the other. At last a faint smile wreathes* PATSY's *lips again.*) I don't understand you.

PATSY. Yes, you do.

WILL. I wish to God I did. It would be easier.

PATSY. You ought to if anybody does.

WILL. Well, I don't.

PATSY. Why not?

WILL (*sneering*). All right! If you've the catechism give me a precept.

PATSY (*her face pale and pinched*). I know what we ought to do. We ought to pull ourselves together and go on the way we planned and not let everything fall to pieces.

WILL. That's what I'm trying to do.

PATSY (*scornfully*). You're not. Everybody in the neighborhood knows you're running around like a fool in town. Do you call that trying? Who has stuck in the fields day after day and tried to keep the tenants at work? Not you.

WILL. You've done it all, haven't you?

PATSY (*with growing feeling*). Yes, I have. Oh, you started out with a great show, making a speech, and saying this and that, and then blow up when your mother won't consent to your marrying me.

WILL (*eyeing her*). And who smiled so sweet and talked about life and was free with kisses? (*Triumphantly.*) And it was all a trap. I'll not be caught with that bait—hah-hah.

PATSY (*her lips trembling*). I'm not begging you. I'm trying to reason with you. If you cared about the farm you'd understand.

WILL. Yes, you love the place and not me.

PATSY. I don't, but why shouldn't I? It's a sight more honest. The land never tricks you. Do your part and she'll do hers. But you—I did my part by you and what did you do? Tried to make a— whore out of me.

WILL (*helplessly*). Ha-ha, you're the wise virgin, clairvoyant like God.

PATSY. I know what we ought to do, I know that. (*She hesitates and turns away.*)

WILL. Go on and say it again—get married—hah?

PATSY. I'd like to see you go on any other way. (WILL *sits down and drums on the table, saying nothing.* PATSY *comes softly up to him.*) You know I'm right, Will. (*Earnestly, her voice shaken.*) I take the blame on myself, but you've got to fight too. I'll help you—I'll do anything to help you. (*Putting her hand gently and now timidly on his shoulder.*) There's no other way in the world for you nor for me.

WILL (*presently*). Don't cry. For God's sake don't cry. I can't stand any more of that. (*He rubs his aching brow with both palms of his hands.*)

PATSY (*looking up, her eyes bright and tearless, full of pain and even fear now*). I know you don't trust me.

WILL. Sometimes I do.

PATSY. And you must understand the person you love, must trust her. I understand you and trust you.

WILL. But you don't love me.

PATSY (*thinking*). Sometimes I do.

WILL. That's not love.

PATSY. How do you know?

WILL. It's not the kind I want.

PATSY (*turning and seizing his hand*). What kind do you want, Will? Tell me, I'll try to give it to you.

WILL. Stop that, Patsy.

PATSY (*with almost a cry*). And what have I done? (*Excitedly*). You didn't do it, I did it. You're right. I set a trap to catch you and it's caught me. (*She clutches his hand with both of hers.*)

WILL. What do you mean?

PATSY. You've got to believe it. All my people have wanted land, wanted land above everything. When we moved here I saw all this great plantation going to ruin. I wanted it, wanted to make something out of it. I loved you because you stood for all I wanted. I had never cared for any man. Never been interested in any man. I saw you liked me and I went on and on with you. (*She claps her hands together, rocking her shoulders like an old peasant woman grieving.*)

WILL (*starting to put his hand on her bowed head*). Patsy—(*But he stops and drops his hand to his side.*)

PATSY. And I went on planning. All that mattered was the land, growing crops, great crops, that's all I could think

of. And so—I went to you—that night—
led you on. (*Shuddering.*) After that I was
different. Something, a feeling for you. I
think about the farm now and what we
can do with it, but always there is something else there, you yourself. I want to
belong to you. Then I think about you,
and there's always the farm, and I want
to rule over everything—make it great
and beautiful! I'm all mixed up inside.
I want to obey you, be your wife, have
your children. I love you now, you yourself, Will. (*Beseechingly.*) You understand
me, don't you? I swear it's the truth. (*She
bows her head over on her knees again, her
shoulders shaking in silent sobs. For a long
while* WILL *says nothing, but stands watching
her in pained uncertainty.*)

WILL (*mechanically*). Please don't, don't
do that.

PATSY. At night I get to thinking and
I'm scared. I feel I've hurt something in
me—(*Struggling for words and for thought.*)
—because I tried to get something my
mind wanted—by—by—(*With heartsick
eagerness.*)—and a woman can't do that,
she must never do that, must she? And
I'm afraid. (*She sits looking up at* WILL *with
tear-stained, feverish eyes. He gazes back at
her in astonishment. Presently he goes over and
gets himself another drink of whiskey.*)

WILL. I don't understand you. (*With
a loud shout.*) Go away and leave me!

(PATSY *stands quickly up, remaining still
by her chair. After a while she turns on him
with the slow dignity of old Tate, mastering
her voice.*)

PATSY. Yes, I'll go and leave you! I
can't stay here any more. I'll let you run
things a while. And you'll see what I've
been doing these months. You've never
had such a crop on this plantation, have
you? Now I'll go away—and I'll wait
till you come for me. You will come,
won't you? I'll go away today.

WILL (*fiercely*). No, you won't!

PATSY. Maybe that's the way for us.
It'll be hard, but in the end it'll be right.
Some day you'll realize how hard it is
for me to leave—you'll come then.

(*She goes out.* WILL *sits there thinking, as
if trying to sense the meaning of words that
mystify him. Once or twice he makes a movement as if to rise and follow her.* UNCLE BOB
comes in.)

UNCLE BOB (*fanning and half-singing, his
eyes glinting with low malice.*)
Drunk last night

And drunk the night before,
And if I ever see tomorrow night
I'm gonna get drunk some more.
Go your way, Will. How much it cost
you last night in town? Stripped you like
the lady in the Bible—unh?

WILL (*flinging out his arms*). Hah, hah,
hah, money? Love, she said.

UNCLE BOB. Lady-killer. These latter
days they all love you, don't they? The
crackling thorns! (*Mocking him.*) Hah,
hah, hah. They know their business.

WILL (*after a moment, raising his harassed
face*). Yes, you're right—dirty, foul,
crooked, all of 'em.

UNCLE BOB. Poor boy—sick. And when
old Tate finishes with you you'll be
sicker than you are. Your mother wants
to see you, Will.

WILL. Let him shoot, I can shoot too.
Let him sue me, I'll pay if that's what he
means.

UNCLE BOB (*earnestly*). Look here, we're
getting into enough trouble and you better fix things up. Throw everything to
the devil and marry Patsy Tate. It's the
thing for us all. You and your mother
are wrong. You do it. (*Looking at him
straight.*) This is the last time I'll ever
give you any advice. You marry that
girl.

WILL. You don't see what she is. (*Half
to himself.*) She's queer. (*Vehemently.*)
She's cunning, full of plans.

UNCLE BOB. That's a lie and you know
it.

WILL. I can't get her out of my mind.
Sometimes I want to catch her by that
pretty throat and kill her.

(*He buries his face in his hands and bows
over the table.* MRS. CONNELLY, *helped along
by* GERALDINE, *comes in. She sits down in her
wide chair as before and begins fanning herself.*)

MRS. CONNELLY (*gently*). Would you
like some dinner, Will?

WILL. No, Mother.

MRS. CONNELLY. I want to talk to you
a moment.

WILL (*springing up*). No, you needn't.
I won't listen to you, Mother.

MRS. CONNELLY (*to those about her*).
Please leave us alone.

(UNCLE BOB *and* GERALDINE *start
out.*)

WILL. Stop! I'll talk to all of you!
(MRS. CONNELLY *raises her hand as if to re-
buke him and then sits still, gripping the arms*

of her chair.) Where's Evelyn? (*Calling.*) Evelyn! (EVELYN *comes in from the kitchen.*) In the kitchen. Will must not have Essie around. Thank God for your help there!

(GERALDINE *stares at him as if he had suddenly gone crazy.*)

EVELYN. Will, what's the matter?

WILL (*with angry triumph*). You all come to condemn me but I'll condemn first. (UNCLE BOB *reaches out for a chair and bends over as if to sit down, but then straightens up again and stands fanning himself.* WILL *goes on with sweeping gestures, and* MRS. CONNELLY *gradually bows her head, saying nothing, as* WILL *fastens his eye upon her.*) I've waked out of my sleep to see it all. (*His voice high and strident.*) I'm down, whipped, beaten, as low as Uncle Bob there. See, two by two they go up the stairs. Let the cross-eyed woman pound on the organ. Rotten, rotten, I know it. Lamb of God, cut my throat and bury me in the garden with the others. No, bury me apart with Uncle Bob.

(UNCLE BOB *puts out a pleading hand.*)

EVELYN (*childishly, as she throws her arms around* GERALDINE). Please, Will.

UNCLE BOB. Go to bed and sleep— (*His tired eyes keep gazing about the room as if seeking a place to rest.*)

WILL (*still eyeing his mother's bowed head*). Follow in the steps of my fathers. (*Gesturing at the portraits on the wall.*) The grand old Connellys—General William Hampton Connelly—(*Raising his glass aloft.*)— in the vanguard of the brave—yea, a nigger wench in every fence-jamb.

GERALDINE (*springing before him, her hands clenched as if to strike him*). Stop! You fool!

WILL (*pushing her back roughly*). Down, down. Sister and brother, cats and dogs. (EVELYN *turns her head away.*) Sisters and brothers? (*As if calling to someone outside the door.*) You Duffy and Harvey and Jenny? All of you come in! Hist, let's set our flesh and blood at the table—a row of mulattoes. "Brother, sister, forgive us." Low? But lower still. And Essie, be seated close at my right. If there's horror we brought it into the world. Who wouldn't vomit and clean out his stomach?

GERALDINE (*bending over* MRS. CONNELLY). Mother, stop him! (*She gets down on her knees, peers up into her mother's face a moment, and then, rising, goes and stands before the fireplace, her back to them.* EVELYN *moves over to her side.*)

MRS. CONNELLY (*in a low voice*). And now?

WILL (*imitating Uncle Bob's thin womanish voice*). As the old family satyr says—
Skip to my Lou, skip to my Lou,
If you can't get a white gal
A nigger'll do.
Give me a torch and I'll burn up the cursed old House of Connelly!

UNCLE BOB. Have some mercy!

WILL. Hah, hah, mercy. I'll cut into this sore. Let innocent Geraldine and Evelyn know the truth.

GERALDINE (*whirling upon him in a wild pleading, her pride and haughtiness gone*). It's a lie, a lie! Say it is, Mother.

MRS. CONNELLY. Let him tell the truth if that's it. (GERALDINE *gazes at her with pale face.*)

GERALDINE (*whispering*). Come on, Evelyn.

WILL. Run away? Can you run away from your body's blood? (*Like a child.*) No, sir, no, sir, you can't. (*Thinking.*) Then I would too. Somewhere I'll start all over again.

UNCLE BOB (*murmuring*). Is that all now?

MRS. CONNELLY. Help me up, Geraldine.

WILL. Not all till you see the niggers thumbing their noses as you pass, you strutting barren peacock!

MRS. CONNELLY (*with an angry cry*). Stop that!

(UNCLE BOB *stands fanning himself mechanically, his face white and dead.*)

WILL. I'm done now. (*Laying his head on the table.*) Patsy's right, we're all— rotten.

(*In the gap of silence the Negroes' harmony outside is carried aloft.*)
I put my little finger ring
On her little hand,
Feel her rolling, tumbling in
my arms,
Loving up her gambling man.

MRS. CONNELLY (*gently as she looks at him*). There's nothing more to say. (*Softly—beggingly.*) Nothing, Robert? No. (*She stretches her hand out to him.* GERALDINE *and* EVELYN *stand with her, their hands dropped at their sides. She catches hold of them and they support her.*) Yes, something—(*Her strong mouth quivering as she struggles for words.*)—of other things, Will —of sacrifice and forgiveness and human love—Your father—your father was a great man. He had a hard struggle, over himself and the world around him. He failed, struggled again, his face set upward—on—(*She sways with weakness and leans heavily on her daughters.*) No whining—no tears—of weakness. Now I'm old—weak—(*Smiling.*) But do I weep? No. (*Sternly.*) Does Uncle Bob? What do you know of his life? (*Softly.*) I know— Go to him, if you are a man, and beg his forgiveness. (*Pleadingly.*) Do it, Will. You've said things too hard for him.

WILL (*in a muffled voice*). No, no, no. Upward! Hah-hah—

MRS. CONNELLY. No? Yes—(*Softly.*)— you will some day—Later we'll talk— I'm tired now. Come to my room.

WILL (*jerking his head up*). I'll not come. It's the truth and you won't face it.

MRS. CONNELLY (*after a moment, quietly, as she sinks back into her seat again—struggling to keep from breaking down.*) I have faced it for forty years, Will. And yet I did my duty to your father.

WILL (*staring at her*). The rottenness, the injustice?

MRS. CONNELLY (*softly with her head bowed*). That, too, if you call it so.

WILL. And Uncle Bob and—Oh God!

MRS. CONNELLY (*whispering*). Please, please—

UNCLE BOB. Ellen, Ellen. It's a lie!

WILL. Hah, hah, a lie! It's God's truth, and she knows it. You and your nigger young'uns!

(UNCLE BOB *bows his head, and* EVELYN *and* GERALDINE *stand gazing speechlessly before them.* MRS. CONNELLY *goes on in a gasping broken voice.*)

MRS. CONNELLY. And now you have your truth, Will. (*With sudden helplessness.*) I don't know what to say to him any more. The shame! The shame!

(GERALDINE *and* EVELYN *help her up and she goes out leaning on them.* WILL *sits bent over the table and* UNCLE BOB *stands wrapped in his own thought, his fan going slower and slower.*)

WILL. She talks to me. The first time in my life. Let that be good-by. (*To* UNCLE BOB.) Go ahead, it's your turn. (*But the old man says nothing for a long while, his fan gradually stopping until he has dropped it. Then as if breaking from a reverie he gives a violent gesture with his hand and begins to fasten up his shirt collar and adjust his tie. His face is set in an empty, desolate look which has appeared on it once or twice before during the scene. He picks up his coat from a chair and puts it on and then goes over to the mirror at the sideboard and stands gazing at himself.* WILL *goes on.*) I stood in the courthouse, a boy, and heard Father sentence poor Purvis, his own son, to—the gallows. You helped prosecute him. (*In a low voice to himself.*) There in the robes of justice he rose up, the power of the law. Why didn't he strip himself and say, "I am the guilty one, judge me"? (*Clenching his fist.*) True! True! There's something right behind all this. (*Triumphantly as if making a discovery.*) But he didn't, the coward, and now I'm a coward. (*Thinking, a note of awe finally coming into his voice.*) There's something to search for—find it—a way to act right and know it's right. Father and Grandfather didn't do it, and we're paying for it. All the old Connellys have doomed us to die. Our character's gone. We're paying for their sins. (*Flinging up his hands.*) Words—words—(*He shakes his head in weariness, his mind growing foggy and losing its short trail. Turning, he pours himself another glass of whiskey and drinks it, and stands looking at* UNCLE BOB.) Dressing for a party? Well, by God, he will have his joke.

UNCLE BOB. Today's the day. Nothing more to be said. She's said it all. My time to speak. Hear her defend me? Forty years she's done so—knowing— knowing what I am—(*His voice breaks off.*)

WILL (*starting up and rubbing the back of his head as if to wipe out an aching there.*) I leave it all to them—to you. I've got enough for my ticket to Texas. Let everything be sold and pay the debts, the rest divided. You're a lawyer, you'll execute. Hah-hah. And tell the pretty girls all hello for me. Tell 'em I'll not be riding out any more. Hah, hah.

UNCLE BOB (*still smoothing his beard and hair*). I will if I see them. And so— good-by.

WILL. I'm not leaving till the morning train.

UNCLE BOB (*surveying himself*). Not much of a garb for a far traveler.

WILL. Where you going? (UNCLE BOB *opens the cupboard drawer and puts a pistol in his pocket.*)

UNCLE BOB. Try another shot at that hawk in the cypress tree.

WILL. You've never hit him and never will.

UNCLE BOB. In my ancient primer Ben Franklin said, "If at first you don't succeed—" (*He stands silent as if trying to recall something to mind. Presently he goes on in the same dulled voice.*) Marry Patsy Tate, Will. (*Murmuring to himself.*) For the proud days are ended. (*He pours himself a drink of whiskey, looks at it a moment, and then raises his glass to the portraits on the wall.*) Ladies, Gentlemen, ave, vos salutamus. (*He touches the glass to his lips and then sets it down without drinking.*) Facilis descensus Averno—quis—quamquam—mea memoria—nemo—mei—mnemisc— I cannot remember.

WILL (*chuckling*). Good, good. An apt joke. A dead language.

UNCLE BOB. Very good and apt. (*As if suddenly full of glee* WILL *pounds on the table.* UNCLE BOB *goes out quietly at the rear.* WILL *watches him out with a scornful questioning smile; then he sits down and takes a roll of bills from his pocket and counts them and marks in a notebook. The single report of a pistol sounds in the garden.* WILL *jerks his thumb in that direction.*)

WILL. Valedictorian, silver-tongued orator, most lately nothing. He shoots at a hawk and away flies—well—ambition. (*He drinks.* BIG SIS *and* BIG SUE *burst in at the rear door, grunting and waving their arms. They throw their aprons over their heads and walk up and down the room moaning.* WILL *goes to the door and looks out—with a shout that dies in his throat.*) Great—

(*Presently* OLD TATE *and* DUFFY *come hurrying up the portico and into the room bearing the body of* UNCLE BOB. WILL *starts back and stands staring at them with open mouth as they lay him on the cot. Then he runs forward to help them.*)

TATE. Have mercy on him! Here, some towels.

(*Spying the open sideboard drawer, he drags out a cloth and stuffs it against* UNCLE BOB'S *side. All the while* WILL *stands speechless.*)

DUFFY (*bobbing his head up and down foolishly*). The pistol was in his hand, Mr. Will. He done it hisself. (*Flinging himself down by the cot and wringing his hands.*) Mr. Bob, I ain't to blame. Don't let the Great Moster hold it against me. Many times I prayed sump'n bad happen to you 'cause you holp hang poor Purvis. Now he done answer me. I repents, I repents. White folks, help me, don't let

it be writ against me in that great Book! Mercy, mercy! Pappy! Pappy! (DUFFY *fumbles around him, gets his hat and runs out of the room.*)

TATE. He's dead. (*He mutters to himself.*)

WILL (*Murmuring as if in a dream*). Dead? (*Mopping his head foolishly.*) He's dead! (*He runs out of the room to the right.*)

TATE (*to the Negro women*). Stay here.

(*He goes out at the rear with his hat in his hand. The Negro women stand by the cot with their aprons still over their heads. Raising their arms and letting them fall, they set up a low melodious moaning.*)

WILL (*in the hall outside*). Come back. Don't go in there.

MRS. CONNELLY. Leave me alone! (*She opens the door and makes her way in on her crutch. Tottering across the room, she stands near the cot, saying nothing.* EVELYN *and* GERALDINE *are seen weeping in the hall.* MRS. CONNELLY *cries out brokenly.*) I failed you. (*With a low convulsive moan that ends in a high shrieking gasp.*) Forgive me!

(*She crumples down on her knees on the floor.* BIG SIS *and* BIG SUE *go on moaning, and far off in the fields the Negroes raise their labor song.*)

WILL. (*loudly*). Geraldine! (*He comes slowly into the room.*)

SCENE THREE

Christmas evening in the Connelly dining room several months later. The fire is burning low on the hearth. BIG SUE *squats hunched over before it, stirring the ashes and blowing on the coals as she mouths and mumbles to herself.*

BIG SUE (*blowing*). Open them eyes, fire-coals, lemme see you. That's right. (*She stares forward, then starts back with a sharp grunt, stretching her mouth in a wide toothless smile.*) Unh-unh!

(*The door at the right opens and* BIG SIS *comes in with two heavily-stuffed and shabby suitcases which she sets down on the floor.*)

BIG SIS. Reading the signs again?

BIG SUE. Yeh, and get the same message. Come here, look. (BIG SIS *goes over and stares down into the fire.*) See?

BIG SIS. Can't see 'em yet.

BIG SUE (*stirring the ashes and blowing*). Look way down in the blue flame.

BIG SIS (*putting her arm around her sister's shoulder*). What's in there, honey?

BIG SUE (*spitting into the fire*). See there.

BIG SIS. Yeh—yeh—do—now—the long black coffin.

BIG SUE. And woe, woe to the transgressor.

BIG SIS (*jubilantly*). And all up above her the wind do mourn—(*In a room far off at the right* EVELYN *is heard sobbing.* SIS *jerks her hand in that direction.*) Poor Miss Evelyn, her little heart done broke in two. (*The Negro women moan and wipe their eyes.*)

BIG SUE. Good-by forever—uhm—

BIG SIS (*sputtering with anger*). Yah, say so. (*Fiercely.*) That gal put a spell on Mr. Will Connelly and run him crazy.

BIG SUE (*sighing*). Poor Mr. Will.

BIG SIS. Poor fool.

BIG SUE. Walking down in the dark valley.

BIG SIS (*scornfully*). Yeh.

BIG SUE. This morning he say the truth done come to him and he gwine follow it.

BIG SIS. The truth wropped up in the shape of a purty woman—all hot and hongry-mouthed. Ah, Lord! (*She throws up her hands.*)

BIG SUE. Eigh Lord, the House of Connelly is fell like the Great Temple.

BIG SIS (*harshly, her lips near her sister's ear*). And only you and me to build it back.

BIG SUE. Done said, yeh, done said.

GERALDINE *and* EVELYN *come in from the right dressed in deep mourning, hats and veils, and with cloaks on their arms which they lay on the table. A few months of grief and change and broken ties have aged the two sisters more than a few months should. The feminine spring and go that once enlivened* EVELYN's *form are almost gone.* GERALDINE's *hair is much grayer and the primness and gentility of her nature have grown more hard and bitter with the disappointments that have been her life. As they enter, the two Negro women stop their moaning and stand quickly up.* BIG SUE *hurries and lights the lamp on the sideboard.*)

BIG SIS (*speaking angrily into the air*). Poor little turkle-doves, you hafter fly from your home.

GERALDINE. Ask Duffy to bring the buggy around to the back drive. Tell him to hurry.

BIG SIS. Yes'm. Go with me out there, Sue.

BIG SUE. That gyarden look skeery—hee-hee?

(*Muttering, they go out at the rear.* GERAL-

DINE *and* EVELYN *stand motionless in the room. And in their words and actions which follow there is a vague indirect hollowness as if something unspeakable and oppressive weighed them down.*)

EVELYN. Wonder what they think of our going, poor things?

GERALDINE (*at the fire*). Come warm yourself. It'll be cold on the way to the station.

EVELYN. What'll Will think?

GERALDINE (*taking the broom and mechanically sweeping the hearth*). He knows he's choosing between us. He chooses her.

EVELYN. But he's never thought we'd leave. I don't believe he has.

GERALDINE. What else could he expect, and he bringing her here as his wife? (*She shudders. With the broom handle she unloops the Confederate flag and lets it drop down, hiding the General's face.*)

EVELYN (*at the sideboard*). Let's drink some wine. (*looking up.*) Why do you do that?

GERALDINE (*smiling*). Just an idea. (*Her words seeming to come only from her lips.*) Grandmother made that flag.

EVELYN. They never do such fancy work these days, do they?

GERALDINE. No. (*In a voice like her mother's.*) The Lord knows we've tried to be good to Will—sympathize with him—talk to him. (EVELYN *pours herself a glass of wine and stands sipping it. They are both silent.* GERALDINE *goes on with a deep, hidden jealousy.*) He has somebody to talk to now. (*She keeps moving about the room as if unable to remain still. At the sideboard her hands take hold of the candlesticks and she wanders with them over to the table.*)

EVELYN. What are you doing?

GERALDINE. Bring the plates.

EVELYN. Are you setting the table for them?

GERALDINE (*as if suddenly realizing what she is doing*). Yes.

EVELYN (*taking the plates in her hands where she stands—with a sob*). I always loved these gold plates. (*Breaking out.*) And to leave all this to her!

GERALDINE. We'll remember it as it's always been.

EVELYN. She'll sell everything and put it in the farm—the boxwoods, the antiques—

GERALDINE. We shan't see it. (*Gazing about the room.*) It will always be this way to me, the way I've known it.

EVELYN (*bursting into tears*). I can't do it. Don't make me go. (*A buggy is heard driving up at the side portico.*)

GERALDINE. I hear the buggy. (*Handing Evelyn her coat.*) Evelyn!

(BIG SIS *and* BIG SUE *re-enter.*)

EVELYN. Yes, yes.

BIG SIS. Duffy's out there waiting.

BIG SUE. And the snow just pouring down.

EVELYN (*putting her coat on, a mournful smile with a touch of joy in it shutting around her lips.*) Remember we wanted it to snow last Christmas—(*She suddenly stops.*)

BIG SIS. And them serenaders is down there at the front already waiting for Mr. Will—and the wedding party.

EVELYN (*running up to the two Negro women*). Good-by!

BIG SIS AND BIG SUE (*covering her hands with kisses*). Don't forget us way where you gwine.

EVELYN AND GERALDINE. No, oh no, we shan't.

BIG SIS. Maybe you be coming back.

BIG SUE. Yeah, maybe you get the message to come back.

EVELYN. Message?

GERALDINE. No, we're never coming back. (*Drawing on her gloves.*) Give Mr. Will our message—we're gone—and stay here till they come. Keep the fire going.

BIG SIS. Oh yes'm, us meet 'em stylish.

BIG SUE. Oh yes'm, us take care of everything for you.

BIG SIS. Till you come again.

EVELYN (*starting out*). Bring the suitcases, Sis. (*Now as if anxious to be going.*) Hurry, Deenie!

(BIG SIS *takes up the suitcases and follows after her.* GERALDINE *gives a long look around the room. She notices the table centerpiece a bit awry and straightens it. Then she follows after* EVELYN. BIG SUE *goes to the fire and stirs it as before. She seems to see something in the fire that pleases her, for she stretches her mouth in a wide toothless grin and cuts a few steps of joy about the room. A moment later the buggy is heard driving away.* BIG SIS *re-enters, drying her eyes with her apron.*)

BIG SIS. Their little hands cold and still like ice.

BIG SUE (*sighing again*). And nobody in the great world to warm 'em. (*Gesturing.*) Can still see it.

BIG SIS (*grinning*). Still read it, right?

BIG SUE. Yah. (*She picks up the gong stick and strikes the gong.*) Ooh!

BIG SIS (*punching the fire and sending the sparks upward*). Make merry for the bride and groom! (*She spies the bottle of wine and in braggadocio takes several gulps and passes it on to* BIG SUE, *who drains it empty. They stand in the middle of the room eyeing each other.*)

BIG SUE. Everything so quiet and still.

BIG SIS (*sighing also*). Hear the snow falling 'gainst the windows.

BIG SUE. And on the houses and fields and trees and on the poor graves.

BIG SIS. And on the grave of Missus, wrapping up this world in its soft blanket.

BIG SUE (*sighing once more*). And the dead rest safe under it in their deep sleep.

BIG SIS. But old Missus lies onrestless there.

BIG SUE. Uhm—

BIG SIS. Uhm—

BIG SUE (*closing her eyes and again spreading her mouth in a wide toothless grimace*). Soon she gwine rest in peace. (*Far down in the garden outside rises the noise of fiddles, horns, and guitars, interrupted now and then with shouts and high cries*).

BIG SIS (*angrily*). White trash make merry 'cause her got him at last.

BIG SUE (*bitterly*). Yeh, she got everything. Got Mr. Will, got the House of Connelly, got all.

BIG SIS. Ain't got you and me.

BIG SUE. You done said. (*Merrily piling wood on the fire.*) Poor little bride her'll be cold.

BIG SIS. Somp'n maybe keep her warm.

BIG SUE. Won't be the hunter neither.

BIG SIS (*winking at her sister*). Hee—hee—

BIG SUE (*winking back*). Hee—hee—

(*They slip away into the kitchen as the door at the right opens and* WILL *and* PATSY *enter dressed up snug against the cold. A light sprinkle of snow covers their shoulders.* WILL *is well dressed in a dark overcoat, dark suit, hat, and gloves. There is something stronger and more manly in his bearing than before, and though his face shows the harassed signs of what he has been through, there is a certain satisfaction in him of one victorious in the struggle with himself. He carries a package in his hand.* PATSY *is dressed in an attractive brown coat-suit with a lace collar showing above it, hat, and gloves. Her cheeks are pink and her eyes bright from the cold.* WILL *puts the package on the table and helps her off with her wraps.*)

..WILL. We are home now.

PATSY (*looking up at him.*) Home.

(WILL *lays their wraps and things on the cot, and turning, puts his hand on her shoulders and stands looking down into her eyes. The serenaders come up under the portico outside, stamping, singing, and ringing their bells. Their shouts and calls are loud and joyous and no longer marked with the teasing and derision of the Christmas before. The musicians begin playing the ballad of "The Brown Girl and Fair Elinor."* WILL *kisses* PATSY, *and then they both go over and open the door.*)

WILL AND PATSY. Howdy, howdy, everybody!

VOICES. There they are!

OTHER VOICES. There's Patsy. Gimme a kiss. Ain't she pretty. Hey, Patsy. Hey, Missus.

(*Several of the serenaders dressed in their outlandish garbs come inside the room, throwing their arms and bodies rhythmically about.*)

MACK LUCAS (*loudly and gravely as he poises his fiddle bow in mid-air*). A speech!

OTHERS. A speech from the bride—no, a kiss from her!

(*The music dies down, and they crowd farther forward into the room, some of them removing their doughfaces and masks to see and hear better.*)

WILL (*a bit uncertainly and hesitating*). I'm glad to see you all having a good time. We thank you for coming over here—and meeting us—(*Stopping.*)—that's about all now. Yes, let today mark a new start for us. I've made mistakes—(*As if with determination he catches* PATSY *by the arm.*)—we both have. But—we're trying to wipe out our mistakes.

A YOUTH (*wearing a bucket over his head with eyes and a mouth cut in it*). That's all right, Mr. Will.

OTHERS. Sure, that's all right.

WILL (*stammering*). We'll all do better now. We're going to build up everything, won't we, Patsy?

PATSY. Yes.

WILL. Let her talk to you. I'm no good at a speech.

A VOICE (*half in mockery*). You're a good speaker, Mr. Will.

VOICES. That he is! (*They clap their hands to applaud him.*)

PATSY (*stepping before them, her eyes bright with high elation*). We both thank you for your welcome. We appreciate it from the bottom of our hearts. Mr. Will wants me to tell you that he knows how hard it's been on you all this last year. Everything's been turned upside down. But it won't be any more. And everything that's been promised you you'll have, won't they, Will?

WILL (*murmuring*). We've had death and trouble, you know. But that's past.

PATSY. And after trouble comes the good things.

VOICES. That's right, that's so. Everything'll be all right. Hooray for Mr. and Mrs. Connelly!

OTHER VOICES. Hooray!

PATSY (*smiling*). I hope you have a grand time serenading the neighborhood tonight. Don't scare Ike Messer too bad.

A BOY. Go with us, Miss Patsy.

ANOTHER BOY. Foolish, they've just got married.

PATSY. I will next time.

WILL (*smiling at them*). Next Christmas we'll have a real party maybe. And now good night to everybody.

(*He steps forward and shakes hands with the serenaders. The idiot boy waddles out, takes his hand, and then runs back among the others.* PATSY *shakes hands with them also, and several of the girls kiss her and whisper, giggling, in her ear. The youth with the bucket takes his headgear off, and giving her a quick kiss, tears laughing and yelling out at the rear.* MACK LUCAS *has already set his fiddle going again and now leads them out. Finally they are all gone, their gay music dying down the lane.* WILL *closes the door and stands abstractedly by the fire.*)

PATSY (*watching him*). They seem so glad about it, Will.

WILL. Yes, they won't go hungry any more with you here.

PATSY (*with strange gentleness and almost in a low whisper as she comes over and leans her head against his shoulder*). I was like a person dead away from the farm and you. Now I am alive again. I knew you'd come some day and I kept working and waiting there in that city factory. But you were so long.

WILL (*after a moment*). It took me a long time to see it the way you said—(*Stopping and staring over her shoulder.*)—and the way Uncle Bob said. It gives me a sort of peace now. We're doing what's right.

PATSY. You'll learn to love me, won't you?

WILL. And you me maybe. (*Gazing at her.*) How beautiful you are.

PATSY. Kiss me. (*He kisses her.*) I do love you, Will. (*After a moment turning about the room in a high burst of spirits.*) Think of all we have to do! (WILL *gives her a fleeting glance and then turns to the fire again, warming himself.*)

WILL. And I'll follow the leader the best I can.

PATSY. It'll be together. (*With humble archfulness.*) Forget your distrust now.

WILL (*smiling*). And you forget it.

PATSY. And the others will forgive and forget, won't they?

WILL. Yes. (*Going to the door at the right and calling.*) Geraldine, Evelyn. (*His voice echoes through the house, and the two stand a while listening.*)

PATSY. They'll come in a minute.

WILL (*glancing over at the package on the table*). I'll give them their Christmas presents then. (*A voice calls beyond the rear door, and* OLD TATE *sticks his head in.*)

PATSY (*in a mixture of pleasure and displeasure*). Father!

WILL. Good evening, Mr. Tate.

TATE (*pulling off his hat*). Good evening. (*Coming up to them and shaking their hands.*) I wanted to come and say bless you and then go away again.

WILL (*kindly*). Thank you, Mr. Tate.

TATE. You've both took the right step and the Lord will prosper you forever. (*In sound good humour.*) Yes, he will.

WILL. Talk to Patsy a moment. I'll be right back.

(*He goes out at the right.* OLD TATE *stands looking around the room. Presently he puts on his hat.*)

TATE. Well, Patsy.

PATSY. Yes.

TATE. Well, be a good girl—yes, be a good wife to him.

PATSY. I will.

TATE (*tapping his hands together*). We'll miss you at home.

PATSY. I thought you'd got used to that. (*The door to the kitchen opens slightly and the roving eyes of* BIG SIS *and* BIG SUE *are seen gleaming in from the darkness beyond.*)

TATE. Come over and cook me some biscuits now and then, won't you?

PATSY (*taking his arm and standing by the table*). Will can sit there at the head. I'll sit here. (*In a low voice.*) You there— (*Pointing.*)—the boys—so—and so. (*She turns and eyes her father in a sort of naïve*

triumph.)

TATE (*looking at her in astonishment*). I'll be plagued!

PATSY. And they'll have rooms of their own to sleep in now.

TATE (*with a prideful glance about him*). Think of that. (*He chuckles, but immediately the stern look returns to his face as he gazes at her.*) I dunno—maybe everything'll be all right. God bless you.

PATSY. And that makes me happier than all the rest. There comes Will now.

TATE. Good night. (*He touches her gruffly on the shoulder and goes out just as* WILL *re-enters.*)

WILL (*calling after* TATE). Good night, Mr. Tate. Thank you for coming.

TATE (*calling back*). A happy Christmas to all.

WILL (*to* PATSY). They're not in their rooms, Patsy.

PATSY (*gazing up at the portrait*). Maybe they're upstairs. I'll get supper and we'll all sit down together.

WILL (*following her glance*). What's happened to that picture? Ah—

PATSY. Maybe the flag fell down.

WILL (*murmuring*). Geraldine! (*He looks from the portrait to the table—then fiercely to himself.*) They'll see it like I've tried to show 'em.

PATSY (*taking the broom handle and pushing the flag back*). Maybe so—yes, that's what happened. It fell down.

(BIG SIS *enters from the kitchen.*)

BIG SIS. Us been waiting here for you all.

(PATSY *looks at her narrowly and goes over to the fire.*)

WILL. Where are Miss Evelyn and Miss Geraldine?

BIG SIS (*rolling her eyes*). Lord, they done gone from here.

WILL (*with a shout*). What!

BIG SIS. They packed their little things and went to the train. Said give Mr. Will the message they wouldn't be coming back no more.

WILL. Great Scott! You hear that, Patsy? You better not joke with me, Sis.

(BIG SUE *enters from the kitchen. She carries a tow sack wadded in her hand.*)

BIG SIS. Tell 'em, Sue.

BIG SUE (*casting up her eyes*). They cried a little bit and wiped their eyes and said good-by to everything. They've gone to Richmond to live with Cousin Vera. (*She looks over at* BIG SIS *who gives a low whickering laugh.*)

WILL (*angrily*). Stop that laughing! When did they go?

BIG SIS. Duffy took 'em over jus' 'fore you all come. They's a letter in the hall for you, they said.

(WILL *hurries out at the right.* PATSY *begins sweeping the hearth. The two Negro women move up softly and stand near her. She glances out at them.*)

BIG SUE. And you the Missus now. (*She massages the sack in her hands.*)

PATSY (*smiling at the two, friendly but firmly*). And I'll try to be a good one too.

BIG SUE. Hear that, sister?

BIG SIS. Can't hear it.

BIG SUE. How come!

BIG SIS. The dead folks cries so loud down in the gyarden.

PATSY (*strongly*). Go build a fire in the kitchen, Sis.

(WILL *comes hurrying in, opening a letter as he enters. He goes to the lamp and reads it. The Negro women remain where they are.*)

WILL (*dropping down in a chair*). I've run them from their own home. (*Springing up excitedly.*) They've got to come back.

(*He starts toward the rear door as if to go after them.* PATSY *runs across the room to him. The two Negro women stand watching them.*)

PATSY (*with almost an angry cry*). No, no, you haven't done it!

WILL (*with half a shout as he stops*). We've both done it, then.

PATSY (*clinging to him*). They know their own minds, Will. Please, please—listen—

WILL (*harshly to himself*). They must have hated me. (*Bursting out and trying to move from* PATSY'S *arms.*) My God, the cruelty of it! (*His voice dies out of him with a gasp, and he stands staring at the floor an instant, his face harassed and torn.*)

BIG SIS (*in a sudden burst of tearful pleading, coming up to him*). Please sir, Mr. Will, git 'em to come back. Ketch up wid 'em, Mr. Will.

BIG SUE (*likewise*). They ain't gone but a little ways.

PATSY (*hugging* WILL *tightly to her as she searches for words to help him*). It is cruel, Will, all this suffering and—

WILL (*with a cry*). And I thought we were done with death and suffering.

PATSY. But we'll stand it, stand it together—whatever pain and suffering there is. (*Vehemently, her words rushing on*

now.) That's the way it has to be, Will. To grow and live and be something in this world, you've got to be cruel—you've got to push other things aside. (*Fiercely.*) The dead and the proud have to give way to us—to us the living. (*Her face close against his, her voice intense and vibrant.*) We have our life to live and we'll fight for it to the end. Nothing shall take that away from us. (*She bows her head against his breast, her shoulders shaking. Then she goes on more quietly but with firm and steadfast voice.*) Right now we have to decide it, Will. Let them go. It's our life or theirs. It can't be both—they knew it. That's why they went away. (*She stops and stands up straight and waiting, looking at* WILL'S *struggling face.*)

BIG SIS. Oh, they moaned at leaving their home and their little hearts are breaking.

BIG SUE. And the salt tears falling from their burning eyes.

BIG SIS. Please'm—Please, suh, Mr. Will.

BIG SUE. Please, suh, Mr. Will.

WILL (*in sudden anger*). This is their home, their home, Patsy! (*Loudly.*) And I'll not run them from it.

(*He flings* PATSY *away from him, grabs up his overcoat, and hurries out at the rear.* PATSY *stands an instant gazing before her, then she goes to the sideboard, sets the package aside, gets out a tablecloth, and begins spreading it over the table.*)

PATSY (*to* SIS). Go build a fire in the stove like I told you.

(*But* SIS *begins piling wood on the fire.*)

BIG SIS (*singing in her deep bass voice*).
They grabble his eye, they work in his head,
Man don't feel 'em three days dead—
(BIG SUE *begins adding her melodious alto.*)
And all up above him the wind do mourn—
Pity poor man ever was born.

PATSY (*staring at them*). That's right, build up the fire, then. Heap it up. They'll be cold.

BIG SIS (*winking at her sister*). Hee-hee, cold. Cold Missus.

PATSY. What's that?

BIG SIS (*speaking into the air*). Gimme some motion, gimme some sound—

BIG SUE. Death gwine take her, church-wedding bound.

BIG SIS. Poor Missus, walking in the gyarden. Her can't sleep, her can't rest in her grave.

BIG SUE. Her done speak and say—a sacrifice. (*Lifting her open tow-bag toward* PATSY.) This here hold many a good sassafras root, honey.

BIG SIS. Yeh, do tell, sweetie pie. (*Singing softly.*)
The sporrer sot with her head in her wing,
The snake crope up and 'gun to sing.

PATSY (*hotly*). You heard what I said! I'm Missus here now and you'll do what I tell you to do. (*She turns suddenly and grabs up the poker from the hearth, but* BIG SIS *is quick as a cat and snatches it from her and throws it out of the way.* PATSY *stares at them, her eyes beginning to widen with a touch of fear.*) You stop that!

BIG SUE (*holding the mouth of the sack open before her*). Look in there, Miss Patsy, us bring you a wedding present.

PATSY (*almost ragingly, as she summons all her strength against the two demonic creatures*). Did you hear me! Go in the kitchen!

BIG SIS (*rocking with laughter*). That's right, that's a wedding present from us, a wedding present in the sack. (*At her gesture the two women fling themselves upon* PATSY.)

PATSY (*crying out*). Wait, wait! Will! Will!—

(*But they crush her down onto the floor and smother her shrieking in the sack. They continue to choke her with their bone-crushing great hands. Her struggles finally stop. Then the two women lay her on the couch and stand looking piteously down at her, their aprons stuffed to their eyes.*)

BIG SUE (*softly*). Purty like a baby—

BIG SIS (*whispering and making her stroking motion in the air*). Flesh soft same like feathers—

BIG SUE. Smooth like a snake—

BIG SIS (*as if about to weep*). Poor little scrushed lily.

BIG SUE (*likewise*). Little Rose of Sharon.

BIG SIS (*suddenly spitting at the still figure*). But they got her safe now, and them snake eyes done shining.

BIG SUE. Got her safe there where Purvis is.

BIG SIS. And with the Old Man and the Missus and Uncle Bob. They all sleep safe now.

BIG SUE. Till the trumpet sound and rise 'em up (*Singing in her man's voice to which Big Sue's rich alto rises again.*)

In the cold earth the sinful clay
Wropped in a sheet is laid away.
Rock to the hills to the trees do mourn,
Pity poor man ever was born.

(*They place the candles on the floor at the dead girl's head and feet and go softly out at the rear, moaning as they go, their aprons to their eyes. The door is left open, and the wind-laden snow blows in from the portico, fluttering the candle flame about. Far across the field the serenaders are heard carrying on their song.*)

THE END

ALTERNATE ENDING

SCENE THREE

Christmas evening in the Connelly dining room several months later. The fire is burning low on the hearth, and for a moment the scene is empty. Then BIG SIS *and* BIG SUE *come in from the right with two suitcases, which they set down, muttering and growling to themselves.*

BIG SIS (*speaking angrily into the air*). Ain't no more use begging, they gwine leave here.

BIG SUE. Yah, poor little turkle-doves, they fly away from their own home. (*They remain silent a moment, wiping their eyes with their aprons.*)

BIG SIS. Poor Miss Evelyn, her little heart done broke in two.

(*In a room far off at the right* EVELYN *is heard sobbing. The Negro women moan and wipe their eyes.*)

BIG SUE. Good-by forever—uhm.

BIG SIS (*sputtering with anger*). Yah, say so. (*Fiercely.*) That Mr. Will Connelly done must gone crazy!

BIG SUE (*sighing*). Poor Mr. Will.

BIG SIS. Poor fool!

BIG SUE. Walking down in the dark valley.

BIG SIS (*scornfully*). Yah!

BIG SUE. This morning he say the truth done come to him and he gwine follow it.

BIG SIS. Patsy Tate the truth he gwine follow! (*Spitting bitterly at the fireplace and half-moaning.*) And this here the end now.

Eigh, Lord, the house of Connelly is fell like the Great Temple.

BIG SUE. Lord, Lord, have mercy!

(GERALDINE *and* EVELYN *come in from the right. They are dressed in deep mourning, hats and veils, and with cloaks on their arms which they lay on the cot. A few months of grief and change and broken ties have aged the two sisters more than a few months should. The feminine spring and go that once enlivened* EVELYN'S *form are almost gone;* GERALDINE'S *hair is much grayer, and the primness and gentility of her nature have grown more hard and bitter with the disappointments that have been her life. As they enter, the two Negro women gradually stop their swaying and moaning.*)

GERALDINE. Ask Duffy to bring the buggy around to the back drive. Tell him to hurry.

BIG SIS. Yes'm. Go with me out there, Sue.

BIG SUE (*bitterly*). That gyarden look skeery—hee-hee?

(*Muttering, they go out at the rear.* GE-RALDINE *and* EVELYN *stand motionless in the room. And in their words and actions which follow, there is a vague, indirect hollowness as if something unspeakable and oppressive weighed them down.*)

EVELYN. Wonder what they think of our going, poor things?

GERALDINE. Warm yourself. It'll be cold on the way.

EVELYN. What'll Will think?

GERALDINE (*taking the broom and mechanically sweeping the hearth*). He knows he's choosing between us. He chooses her.

EVELYN. But he's never thought we'd leave. I don't believe he has.

GERALDINE. What else could he expect and he bringing her here? (*With the broom handle she unloops the Confederate flag and lets it drop down, hiding the General's face.*)

EVELYN (*at the sideboard*). Let's drink some wine. (*Looking up.*) Why do you do that?

GERALDINE (*smiling*). Just an idea. (*Her words seeming to come only from her lips.*) Grandmother made that flag.

EVELYN. They never do such fancy work these days, do they?

GERALDINE. No. (*In a voice like her mother's.*) The Lord knows we've tried to be good to Will—sympathize with him— talk to him. (EVELYN *pours herself a glass of wine and stands sipping it. They are both silent.* GERALDINE *goes on with a deep hidden*

jealousy.) He has somebody to talk to now! (*She keeps moving about the room as if unable to remain still. At the sideboard her hands take hold of the candlesticks and she wanders with them over to the table.*)

EVELYN. What are you doing?

GERALDINE. Bring the plates.

EVELYN. Are you setting the table for them?

GERALDINE (*as if suddenly realizing what she is doing*). Yes.

EVELYN (*taking the plates in her hands where she stands—with a sob*). I always loved these gold plates. (*Breaking out.*) And to leave all this to her!

GERALDINE. We'll remember it as it's always been.

EVELYN. She'll sell everything and put it in the farm—the boxwoods, the antiques—

GERALDINE. We shan't see it. (*Gazing around the room.*) It will always be this way to me, the way I've known it.

EVELYN (*bursting into tears*). I can't do it. Don't make me go!

(*A buggy is heard driving up at the side portico outside, and* BIG SIS *and* BIG SUE *re-enter.*)

GERALDINE (*handing* EVELYN *her coat*). Evelyn.

EVELYN. Yes, yes.

BIG SIS. Duffy's out there waiting.

BIG SUE. And the snow just pouring down.

EVELYN (*pulling on her coat, a mournful smile with a touch of joy in it shutting around her lips*). Remember we wanted it to snow last Christmas—(*She suddenly stops.*)

BIG SIS. And them serenaders is down there at the front already waiting for Mr. Will—and the wedding party.

EVELYN (*running up to the two Negro women*). Good-by!

BIG SIS *and* BIG SUE (*covering her hands with kisses*). Don't forget us way where you gwine.

GERALDINE AND EVELYN. No, oh no, we shan't.

GERALDINE (*drawing on her gloves*). Stay here till they come. Keep the fire going.

BIG SIS. Oh, yes'm, us meet 'em stylish.

EVELYN (*starting out*). Bring the suitcases, Sis. (*Now as if anxious to be gone.*) Hurry, Deenie!

(*The Negro women pick the suitcases up and follow after her.* GERALDINE *gives a long look around the room. She notices the table centerpiece a bit awry and straightens it. Then she follows after* EVELYN. *A moment later the buggy is heard driving away.* BIG SIS *and* BIG SUE *re-enter with their aprons to their eyes.*)

BIG SIS (*presently*). Their little hands cold and still like ice.

BIG SUE (*sighing*). And nobody in this great world to warm 'em. (*They move restlessly about the room.*)

BIG SIS (*punching the fire*). Make merry for the bride and groom!

BIG SUE. Yah! (*She picks up the gong stick and strikes the gong—shuddering.*) Ooh!

(BIG SIS *spies the bottle of wine and in braggadocio freedom takes several gulps and passes it on to* BIG SUE, *who drains it empty. Then they stand in the middle of the room eyeing each other.*)

BIG SIS (*sighing*). Everything so still.

BIG SUE. Hear the snow falling 'gainst the windows.

BIG SIS. And on the houses and the fields and on the poor graves.

BIG SUE (*sighing likewise*). And the dead rest safe under it in their deep sleep.

BIG SIS (*stretching her mouth in a wide bitter grimace*). Poor old Missus lie all restless there.

BIG SUE. Uhm—

BIG SIS. Uhm—

(*From down in the garden outside rises the sound of fiddles, horns and guitars, interrupted now and then with shouts and high cries.*)

BIG SUE (*angrily*). White trash make merry 'cause her got him at last. (*Bitterly.*) Yeh, she got everything—got Mr. Will, got the House of Connelly—got all.

BIG SIS. Ain't got you and me.

BIG SUE. Not yet nohow.

(*They slip away into the kitchen as the door at the right opens and* WILL *and* PATSY *enter, dressed up snug against the cold. A light sprinkle of snow covers their shoulders.* WILL *is well dressed in a dark suit, overcoat, hat, and gloves. There is something stronger and more manly in his bearing than before; and though his face shows the harassed signs of what he has been through, there is a certain satisfaction in him of one victorious in a struggle with himself.* PATSY *is dressed in an attractive brown coat-suit, with a lace collar showing above it, hat, and gloves. Her cheeks are pink and her eyes bright from the cold.*)

WILL (*helping her off with her wraps*). We're home now.

PATSY (*looking up at him*). Home.

(WILL *lays their wraps and things on the cot, and turning, puts his hands on her shoulders and stands looking down into her eyes. The serenaders come up under the portico outside* stamping, singing, and ringing their bells. *Their shouts and calls are loud and joyous and no longer marked with the teasing and derision of the Christmas before.* WILL *kisses* PATSY *and then they both go over and open the door.*)

WILL AND PATSY. Howdy, howdy, everybody!

VOICES. There they are!

OTHER VOICES. There's Patsy! Gimme a kiss! Ain't she pretty? Heigh, Patsy! Heigh, Missus!

(*Several of the serenaders, dressed in their outlandish garbs, come inside the room throwing their arms and bodies rhythmically about.* OLD TATE *comes heavily and shyly in, embraces* PATSY *and shakes hands with* WILL *without a word.*)

MACK LUCAS (*loudly and gravely as he poises his bow in mid-air*). A speech!

OTHERS. A speech from the bride! No, a kiss from her!

(*The music dies down and they crowd further into the room, some of them removing their doughfaces and masks to hear better.*)

WILL (*a bit uncertainly and hesitating*). I'm glad to see you all having a good time. We thank you for coming over here—and meeting us. (*He puts his arm around Patsy.*)

A YOUTH (*wearing a bucket over his head with eyes and a mouth cut in it*). Hooray for Mr. Will!

OTHERS. Hooray!

WILL (*stammering*). Let—let Patsy talk to you. I'm no good at a speech.

A VOICE. You're a good speaker, Mr. Will.

VOICES. That he is. (*They clap their hands and cheer him.*)

PATSY (*stepping before them, her eyes shining*). We both thank you for your welcome. We appreciate it from the bottom of our hearts. Mr. Will wants me to tell you he knows how hard it's been on you all this last year. But it won't be any more. You'll have what's been promised you. Won't they, won't they, Will?

WILL. We've had death and trouble —you know. But that's past, and now—

PATSY (*to all around her*). After trouble comes the good things!

VOICES. That's so. Everything'll be all right. Hooray for Mr. and Mrs. Connelly!

OTHER VOICES. Hooray!

PATSY. I hope you have a grand time serenading the neighborhood tonight. Don't scare Ike Messer too bad.

A BOY. Go with us, Miss Patsy.

ANOTHER BOY. Foolish, they've just got married.

PATSY. I will another time.

WILL (*smiling at them*). Next Christmas we'll have a real party maybe. And now good night to everybody.

(*He steps forward and shakes hands with them. The idiot boy waddles out, takes his hand, and then runs back among the others.* PATSY *shakes hands with them also, and several of the girls kiss her and whisper, giggling, in her ear. The youth with the bucket takes his headgear off, and giving her a quick kiss, tears laughing and yelling out at the rear.* MACK LUCAS *with his fiddle going again now leads them out. Finally they are all gone, their gay music dying down the lane.*)

PATSY (*turning back into the room and closing the door*). They seem so glad about it, Will.

WILL. Yes. They won't go hungry any more with you here.

PATSY (*with strange gentleness and almost in a low whisper as she comes over and leans her head against his shoulder*). I was like a person dead away from the farm and you. Now I am alive again. I knew you'd come some day, and I kept working and waiting. But you were so long.

WILL (*after a moment*). It took me a long time to see it the way you said—(*Stopping and staring off over her shoulder.*)—and the way Uncle Bob said. It gives me a sort of peace now. We're doing what's right.

PATSY. You'll learn to love me, won't you?

WILL. And you me maybe? (*Gazing at her.*) How beautiful you are!

PATSY. Kiss me. (*He kisses her.*) I do love you, Will. (*After a moment turning about the room in a high burst of spirits.*) Think of all we have to do!

WILL (*glancing at her*). Yes. (*Going to the door at the right and calling.*) Evelyn! Geraldine! (*His voice echoes through the house, and they stand listening.*)

PATSY. Maybe they're upstairs. I'll get supper and we'll all sit down together. (*Her gaze sweeps around the room and she stops and stands staring at the General's covered portrait.*)

WILL (*turning back and following her gaze upward—then starting*). What's happened to that picture? Ah—

PATSY. Maybe the flag fell down.

WILL (*murmuring*). Geraldine— (*He looks from the portrait to the table—then*

fiercely to himself.) They'll see it like I've tried to show 'em!

(*He turns and goes hurriedly out at the right.* PATSY *remains still in the middle of the room as if thinking to herself. Far off outside the serenaders are heard singing.*)

PATSY (*as if accepting some hidden challenge*). All right then—

BIG SIS (*coming in from the kitchen, followed by* BIG SUE). Us been waiting heah foh you all.

PATSY (*moving to the sideboard*). Glad you did. (*Now briskly.*) Build a fire in the stove and bring in some wood. (*They eye her with malevolent sassiness.*)

BIG SIS. And you the Missus now?

PATSY (*smiling at them friendly but firmly*). And I'll try to be a good one, too.

BIG SIS. Hear that, sister.

BIG SUE. Naw, can't hear um.

BIG SIS. How come?

BIG SUE. The dead folks cry so loud down in the garden.

BIG SIS (*moaning and watching* PATSY). The old man and the missus and Uncle Bob—all there where Purvis is.

BIG SUE. Till the trumpet sound and rise 'em up.

PATSY (*staring straight at them*). Did you hear me? (*They snicker disrespectfully and move ominously towards her.*) I'm missus here now and you'll do what I say.

BIG SIS (*in sassy and mock alarm*). Uh—uh!

BIG SUE (*likewise*). Uh—uh!

PATSY (*whirling toward the fireplace and snatching up the heavy poker—furiously, her eyes blazing*). You do it or by God I'll—(*She springs at them, the poker uplifted.*)

BIG SIS AND BIG SUE (*their eyes rolling in amazement and fear as they back hurriedly into the kitchen*). Don't Miss Patsy—please'm—yeb'm—yeb'm!

(*The door swings behind them and they are heard clattering at the stove. Presently* PATSY *picks up the broom, and lifts back the flag from the General's face.*)

WILL (*hurrying in*). They're not here. (*Calling.*) Sis!

(*The two Negro women enter again and stand just inside the door.*)

BIG SIS (*meekly*). Yessuh.

WILL. Where are Miss Evelyn and Geraldine?

BIG SIS. Lord, Mr. Will, they done gone from here.

WILL. What!

BIG SIS. They packed their litle things

and went to the train. Said give Mr. Will a message they wouldn't be coming back no more.

WILL. You hear that, Patsy!

BIG SIS. Tell 'em, Sue.

BIG SUE (*casting up her eyes*). They cried a little bit and wiped their eyes and said good-by to everything. They gone to Richmond to live with Cousin Vera.

WILL. Stop that!—When did they go?

BIG SIS. Duffy took 'em over just 'fore you all come.

WILL (*dropping down in a chair*). I've run them from their own home! (*Springing up excitedly.*) They've got to come back! (*He starts toward the rear door as if to go after them.* PATSY *runs across the room to him.*)

PATSY (*with almost an angry cry*). No! No! You haven't done it.

WILL (*with half a shout, as he stops*). We've both done it then.

PATSY (*clinging to him*). They know their own minds, Will. Please—please—listen—

WILL (*fiercely—to himself*). They must have hated me. (*Bursting out and trying to move from* PATSY's *arms.*) My God, the cruelty of it! (*His voice dies out of him with a gasp and he stands staring at the floor, his face harassed and torn.*)

PATSY (*hugging him tightly to her as she searches for words to help him*). It is cruel, Will—all this suffering—and—

WILL (*with a cry*). And I thought we were done with death and suffering.

PATSY. But we'll stand it—stand it together—whatever pain and suffering there is. (*Vehemently, her words rushing on now.*) That's the way it has to be, Will. To grow and live and be something in this world you've got to be cruel—you've got to push other things aside. The dead and the proud have to give way to us—to us the living. (*Her face close against his, her voice fierce and vibrant.*) We have our life to live and we'll fight for it to the end. Nothing shall take that away from us.

(*She bows her head against his breast, her shoulders shaking. Then after a moment she goes on more quietly but with a firm and steadfast voice.*) Right now we have to decide it, Will. It's our life or theirs. It can't be both. They knew it—that's why they went away. (*She stops and stands up straight and waiting, looking at* WILL's *struggling face.*)

WILL (*presently clinging to her, suddenly and almost like a child*). Yes—yes—Help me—ah I need you so, Patsy.

PATSY (*after a moment*). And I'll always be here to help you when you need me.

WILL (*brokenly*). Aye, you will—you will. (*He searches her face with hungry intensity. Suddenly and with loud vehemence.*) Yes, let them go. Let the past die. It's our life now—our house! (*He stands staring out before him as if defiant of the portraits on the wall. The two Negro women who have been looking on bow their heads over their breast in a sort of hopeless resignation.*)

PATSY (*after a moment quietly to* BIG SIS *and* BIG SUE). Go on back to the kitchen. (*But they remain standing where they are, full of a sullen moroseness. Presently* WILL *looks up, his mind echoing* PATSY's *command.*)

WILL. Miss Patsy's my wife now.

BIG SIS AND BIG SUE (*hesitating*). Yessuh.

WILL (*loudly*). Then you do what she tells you!

BIG SIS AND BIG SUE (*as they take each other by the hand and go into the kitchen*). Yessuh, Mr. Will.

WILL (*suddenly sweeping* PATSY *into his arms, his voice grim and eager*). And with you I'll go on—I'll go on!

(*They stand wrapped in each other's embrace. Across the fields the serenaders are heard playing and singing about Fair Elinor.*)

PATSY (*her voice shaking as she tries to keep from breaking down*). Think of it, you've had no supper. (*She gently moves away from his arms and begins lighting the candles.*)

THE END

CHILDREN OF DARKNESS

Edwin Justus Mayer

Children of Darkness was first produced by Kenneth MacGowan and Joseph Verner Reed at the Biltmore Theatre, New York City, on January 1, 1930. The play was staged by Edwin Justus Mayer. The cast was as follows:

MR. SNAP, Under-Sheriff of London and Middlesex .... Walter Kingsford
FIRST BAILIFF .... Albert Bees
MR. CARTWRIGHT .... J. Kerby Hawkes
MR. FIERCE .... Richard Menefee
JONATHAN WILD, THE GREAT .. Charles Dalton

COUNT LA RUSE .... Basil Sydney
LAETITIA .... Mary Ellis
LORD WAINWRIGHT .... Eugene Powers
BAILIFFS ... Joseph Skinner, William Plunket

ACTS ONE, TWO, AND THREE: Room in the house of Mr. Snap, adjoining Newgate Prison, London, in 1725.

Children of Darkness was revived by "Circle in the Square" (Leigh Connell, Theodore Mann, and José Quintero) at the Circle in the Square Theatre, New York City, on February 28, 1958. The play was staged by José Quintero, with settings, costumes, and lighting by David Hays. The cast was as follows:

MR. SNAP, Under-Sheriff of London and Middlesex .... Arthur Malet
FIRST BAILIFF .... Rene Zwick
MR. CARTWRIGHT .... Ben Hayes
MR. FIERCE .... John Lawrence

SECOND BAILIFF .... Tom Noel
JONATHAN WILD, THE GREAT Joseph Barr
COUNT LA RUSE .... Jack Cannon
LAETITIA .... Colleen Dewhurst
LORD WAINWRIGHT ... George C. Scott

Copyright 1927, 1929, by Edwin Justus Mayer.
Copyright 1938, by Samuel French.
Copyright 1954 (in renewal) by Edwin Justus Mayer.
Copyright 1957 (in renewal) by Edwin Justus Mayer.

CAUTION: Professionals and amateurs are hereby warned that *Children of Darkness*, being fully protected under the copyright laws of the United States of America, the British Empire, including the Dominion of Canada, and the other countries of the Copyright Union, is subject to a royalty, and anyone presenting the play without the consent of the owners or their authorized agents will be liable to the penalties by law provided. Do not make any arrangement for the presentation of this play without first securing permission and terms in writing from Samuel French, at 25 West 45th Street, New York City, or at 811 West 7th Street, Los Angeles, Calif.

The author of *Children of Darkness* was, with the exception of Maxwell Anderson, probably the last devoutly romantic American playwright of the Broadway scene. It was appropriate then that Edwin Justus Mayer, born in New York City in 1897, should have first won success with *The Firebrand*, a comedy of romantic bravura revolving around the irrepressible Renaissance artist-adventurer Benvenuto Cellini. The play, which opened in October, 1924, ran on Broadway for 269 performances, was frequently staged thereafter in the non-professional theatre, was filmed under the title of *The Affairs of Benvenuto Cellini* in 1934, and sharing the fate of other successful plays, was in 1945 transformed into a musical comedy, *The Firebrand of Florence*, using a score by Kurt Weill and lyrics by Ira Gershwin, though regrettably without success. It was also appropriate that Mayer's last work on display in New York should have been a revival of *Children of Darkness* two years before his death on September 11, 1960. Although he wrote other plays, they do not display so fine a talent for blending the gay and the grotesque, as well as squalor and splendor. They do not comprise so mature or modern a blending of the heroic and the anti-heroic as this comedy, which was first presented with slight success in January, 1930, but was never forgotten by its small band of admirers.

Mayer, whose love of bravura is perhaps best attested by the fact that in 1923, at the age of twenty-five, he published an autobiography, *A Preface to Life*, plunged into the cultural whirl of the 1920's with considerable volatility and gusto. He became a playwright after an early bout with journalism, chiefly as a reporter for the *Harlem Home News*, the now defunct Socialist *Call* (to which the young O'Neill also contributed), and *The Globe* (also now defunct), an intelligently edited newspaper that favored literature. He then worked as a press agent and subsequently as a caption-writer for the silent movies. Acting also attracted him, and in 1922 he played a small part in the famous John Barrymore production of *Hamlet*. After his success with *The Firebrand*, he was in great demand as a scenarist and spent many profitable years in Hollywood. He is said to have remarked, concerning his sudden success, "It's hard being a Socialist with a $1,500 weekly income," although his affluence did not deter him from helping to establish the Screen Writers Guild. But his first allegiance was to the stage, and he would have devoted himself to it if it had given him sufficient encouragement.

Unfortunately, *Children of Darkness* opened during the depths of the economic depression when long runs were few and far between. Another ill-starred and not particularly engrossing play, *I Am Laughing*, in 1935, failed to reclaim him for Broadway, and his moving Davy Crockett chronicle *Sunrise in My Pocket*, enthusiastically endorsed in a Sunday *Times* article by Brooks Atkinson when it was published by Samuel French, Inc., failed to reach New York. It was staged early in the 1940's by Margo Jones at a Houston, Texas, little theatre. A production at the New School in New York was planned by the German refugee director Erwin Piscator, but abandoned. Less distinguished plays by Mayer were either unsuccessfully produced or not produced at all. When *Children of Darkness* was being revived, Mayer declared, "I never gave up the stage, the stage gave me up. The [moving] pictures gave me a living, and the theatre wouldn't. I see no shame in using your professional weapons to make a living."

Children of Darkness was justly considered a tour de force of poetic and satiric writing, keenly malicious yet, in the end, also curiously moving. It was rightly called a tragicomedy. Mayer's matter is semi-historical even though his manner, despite its literary echoes, is essentially his own.

The play is based on Henry Fielding's satirical pseudo-biography *The History of the Life of the Late Mr. Jonathan Wilde the Great* (1743), founded on the career of a notorious individual who flourished for a time as a receiver of stolen goods at his Office for the Recovery of Lost Property. Other characters in the play had flesh-and-blood counterparts in the Newgate Prison where the action transpires.

A noteworthy revival of the play, prior to the New York revival staged by José Quintero at his Circle in the Square Theatre, was the production by Edward Mangum at the Arena Stage in Washington, D.C., in January, 1951.

ACT ONE

A room on the top floor of Mr. Snap's house, close by Newgate Prison.

There is a barred window, Right Center, at back and another in left wall of hall off Center. The city can be seen lying vaguely away.

At the left rear corner is a fireplace, but as the season is late spring, it is not in use. A fine old tall clock in right rear corner that strikes the hour and the half hour; a sofa under right center window. A door Center. A door at the right front leads into a hall. A door Left.

The room has been designed for living, but latterly someone has been using it as an office; a table at the Left Center, where the clearest light falls, is covered with a disorderly array of ledgers, papers, an ink-pot, quill pens, etc. Chairs Right, Left and back of table; also Right Center and below fireplace.

MR. SNAP, *old and myopic, walks up and down the room. He looks at the clock, then at the* R. *door, as if expecting someone. At length, a* BAILIFF *enters* R.

———

MR. SNAP. Well, well.

BAILIFF. We've brought the boy from the jail, sir.

MR. SNAP. Never mind the boy, knave! Are the gallows prepared for Mr. Wild, sir?

BAILIFF. Aye, sir.

MR. SNAP. Even if Wild don't swing—there will always be a rogue to take his place.

BAILIFF. Aye, sir—so there will.

MR. SNAP. You said you'd brought the boy from the jail. Where is he?

BAILIFF. He's in the hall.

MR. SNAP. Fetch him to me! But wait. You know all the rogues in London. You must know Mr. Fierce.

BAILIFF. Aye, one of Wild's gang. He tumbled me downstairs—when we took Wild.

MR. SNAP. 'Tis your chance to tumble him, for he comes this morning to visit Wild. You will seize him at the door and bring him here—but not before you've put the irons on him, knave. Now let me see the boy. (BAILIFF *goes out* R. MR. SNAP *whistles cheerily.* BAILIFF *returns, with a comrade.* CARTWRIGHT *walks between them; he is young, straight, clear-eyed, but obviously depressed.*) Your servant, Mr. Cartwright. (*Dismisses* BAILIFF.) I am Mr. Snap of the jail.

CARTWRIGHT (*wearily*). Why am I brought here, Mr. Snap?

MR. SNAP. You'll be delighted to hear, Mr. Cartwright. (BAILIFF *goes.*) Sit down, Mr. Cartwright, sit down! (*Crosses to chair* R.C.) That is, if you can on such a morning! I had my walk this morning—I would not have missed my walk on such a morning! (*Crosses back to* C.)

CARTWRIGHT. I would have missed mine gladly. (*Sits* R.C.)

MR. SNAP (*chuckling unpleasantly*).Would you? Would you? Because they walked you to Newgate? You're in the doldrums, Mr. Cartwright. Because you're jailed? At your age I had been jailed a dozen times. Why, 'tis only the effeminate and useless young who keep out of jail completely; the young who have never been in jail are a disgrace to their youth, sir.

CARTWRIGHT. Perhaps. (*Points toward prison, off* L.) But 'tis monstrous that men should treat men so—

MR. SNAP. I guessed at once you were held for debt! It takes a rogue to pay his bills honestly; a gentleman is much too busy accumulating more such, to pay such as he has accumulated.

CARTWRIGHT. I was gulled into signing a paper. But why have you brought me here, Mr. Snap?

MR. SNAP. Why, sir, because I guessed you would far rather be held here than down in the jail.

CARTWRIGHT. But I was consigned to the jail, by writ.

MR. SNAP. Yes, but I've power there, Mr. Cartwright. I'd not have you here were you not a gentleman. I've a daughter, a daughter I prize, a daughter who, I may say, possesses all the domestic virtues! I'd not expose her to the riff-raff—no, not for any sum. You shall be held here, sir.

CARTWRIGHT (*overjoyed*). This is more than kind of you, Mr. Snap.

MR. SNAP. Of course, you have some small fees to disburse through me.

CARTWRIGHT (*dismayed*). Fees!

MR. SNAP. What did you expect, sir? You've said yourself the King's Writ consigned you to Newgate—not to my house!

CARTWRIGHT. I thought you brought me here from kindness—not to be fee'd!

MR. SNAP (*mistakes* CARTWRIGHT's *innocence for impudence*). Do not put me out of temper with such remarks, Mr. Cartwright. What! Must kindness be divorced from profit? I will have you know, Mr. Cartwright, your remark has lowered my spirits—they droop, they droop perceptibly! Perhaps after all you were best returned to the jail.

CARTWRIGHT (*terrified*). Anywhere but there! How much is requisite?

MR. SNAP. For ten guineas you may enjoy the entire privacy of this floor.

CARTWRIGHT. I have but five pounds to my name. (*Takes out money.*)

MR. SNAP. But you can procure five pounds additional? (CARTWRIGHT *shakes his head hopelessly.*) Have you no friend? No mistress?

CARTWRIGHT. No.

MR. SNAP. Pray, what is your means of livelihood, then?

CARTWRIGHT (*defiantly, for he has learned that his proud avowal often brings derision*). I am a poet.

MR. SNAP (*sadly disillusioned*). What, a poet! I thought you were a gentleman. On my word, sir, you have a better air than the vulgarity of your trade allows. But hold—you say you are a poet—and have no mistress?

CARTWRIGHT (*quietly, resentful*). Every poet has the same mistress.

MR. SNAP (*jeeringly*). Is she beautiful, poet?

CARTWRIGHT. So beautiful—that she destroys my own ugliness.

MR. SNAP. Is she rich, poet?

CARTWRIGHT. She owns all seed—all harvests.

MR. SNAP. And yet she cannot provide you with five pounds more! On my word, your fol-de-rol-dol has put me in a mood to do the handsome thing. I will sell you the privacy of the floor for what money you have. (*He takes the money.*)

(*A loud hubbub of blows, cries, and oaths is heard in the hall,* R. MR. FIERCE, *a muscular ruffian, bare-headed, bare-throated and coatless, is dragged in by two bailiffs, to* C. *Although he is manacled, they have a difficult time holding him.*)

MR. FIERCE (*bellowing at* MR. SNAP). Call off your terriers—your male wenches!

MR. SNAP. Mr. Fierce, I believe. I have had the pleasure before, have I not? (*He takes a document from his pocket.*) We have a warrant for your arrest.

MR. FIERCE. Damn your eyes for a lying cuckold!

MR. SNAP (*merrily*). My wife is dead, sir.

MR. FIERCE. She's cuckolding you then in hell!

MR. SNAP (*amiably*). It is my duty to warn you, Mr. Fierce, that anything you say may be used against you. You are charged with the grand larceny of a silver locket from one Lady Margaret Stebbins, since deceased.

MR. FIERCE. Silver locket. (*The words have stunned him; he asks in a curious voice.*) Who swore to the complaint? (MR. SNAP *offers him the warrant. Sullenly:*) I can't read.

MR. SNAP (*reads from the document*). Jonathan Wild made the complaint.

MR. FIERCE (*quivering*). Jonathan Wild!

MR. SNAP. He is witness that you offered him the stolen property, which he declined.

MR. FIERCE. Declined! 'Twas he who told me of the locket—where to filch it—

MR. SNAP. Aye, Mr. Wild usually knows where other people's valuables lie.

MR. FIERCE. And that he'd get rid of it for me! He has it now, for disposal!

MR. SNAP. I doubt if you can prove that. (*He hands the warrant to one of the bailiffs.*) Take him to the jail.

MR. FIERCE (*awakening from his stupor—fighting savagely*). He's here in this house—By God, I'll kill him—the double-cheating bastard—of a French dancing-master—I'll chew him to pieces—I'll bathe in his blood—(*A murderous blow subdues* FIERCE; *he is dragged away out* R.)

CARTWRIGHT. Horrible. Wild has used this unfortunate man and then betrayed him.

MR. SNAP. And betrayed a thousand other tools—and yet he sniffles, prates of his honour and the principle of the thing. Let me warn you against Mr. Wild, and against a precious friend of his, also held here, who calls himself Count La Ruse. Put your faith in me, sir.

CARTWRIGHT. 'Twas published Wild was sentenced to death.

MR. SNAP. He'll swing any day, now. There's no crime so low he hasn't had a hand in it, and here, where his talents are somewhat circumscribed, he robs La Ruse, La Ruse robs him—

CARTWRIGHT. And you rob both of them.

MR. SNAP. I, sir? I, sir! Be more careful, sir.

CARTWRIGHT. Which is my room, Mr. Snap?

MR. SNAP. I will show you. 'Tis in the best of taste. I furnished it myself. (*They exit* L. *And as they do so,* CARTWRIGHT *in the lead,* WILD, *a burly, boisterous man of forty, enters* C.) Ah! Mr. Wild.

JONATHAN. My locket—my silver locket—Have they seized that villain Fierce?

MR. SNAP. We've just jailed him.

JONATHAN. Well, speed his trial, for if they hang me before they hang him, I'll never collect my bounty.

MR. SNAP. Then I'll collect it for you—

(MR. SNAP *exits* R. JONATHAN *looks on table* L.C. *for locket—goes to chimney and peers up it.* LA RUSE, *a polished, cynical, middle-aged man, enters* C.; *watches* JONATHAN *in amusement; takes snuff.*)

LA RUSE. You have missed something, Jonathan?

JONATHAN. My locket's gone.

LA RUSE. You are irritated, what! You should use snuff—there is nothing so good for an irritation as snuff.

JONATHAN (*crossing to table* L.C.). Damn your snuff, sir! You know how I hate it. The thing is not here—it is not to be found—'tis incomprehensible. (*Sits at table, searching.*)

LA RUSE. You have the fault of all great men—you permit yourself to be absorbed by a single business. Yes, greatness is narrowness, preoccupation; second rate men like myself must take refuge in the variation of clouds, images, women.

JONATHAN. A pox on your women! I am sure I made an entry of it.

LA RUSE (*looking into the sky; dreamily*). There are birds in the air, Jonathan, white birds! They are crying something to me which I do not understand. (*Affects to listen to the birds.*) What are you telling me—you free things? (*He is joyful.*) You are crying, one of your kind will soon fly to me—with wings for myself! Wings—wings to bear me far away! Yes, yes. It will be a bird who nests in the sun—a white bird! (*Suddenly.*) What? It will not be a white bird? (*He becomes sorrowful.*) It will be a black bird. (*He shivers.*) My wings will be black.

JONATHAN (*convulsively*). A thousand hells! La Ruse! This is no time for your coloured words.

LA RUSE. Your obedient servant, Jonathan.

JONATHAN (*striking the table for emphasis*). Mr. Fierce, sir, is dishonest.

LA RUSE. This is appalling. You are sure?

JONATHAN. Mr. Fierce had scarcely brought me the locket—I had scarcely entered it on my records, when I missed it again.

LA RUSE. But pray, why should he bring you the locket and then take it away again?

JONATHAN. Because he knew he wouldn't have lived long if he hadn't apparently given it to me. La Ruse, do you know what the rogue did further? While I had left the room for a few moments he obliterated the records, wiped it from my books. I did not credit him with so much wit.

LA RUSE. We have been fooled, then, by a damnable sharper, what! By my honour, I'll call him out—I'll run him through with dispatch—(*Away a little.*)

JONATHAN (*rises*). My dear Count, long before I missed the locket I swore out a warrant against Mr. Fierce.

LA RUSE. A warrant?

JONATHAN. 'Tis the principle of the thing!

LA RUSE. You have delivered him to the hangman?

JONATHAN. Candidly, my dear Count, I thought my delivering him up might favorably affect my fate.

LA RUSE (*bowing*). To me you will always be the great Jonathan, whatever your fate.

JONATHAN. You've heard? They've set the date for my hanging?

LA RUSE. No.

JONATHAN. Bah. What is it to be hanged? 'Tis but a dance—without music. (*Sits on table.*)

LA RUSE. They'll never hang you, Jonathan.

JONATHAN. Yet consider my position, La Ruse. Why should I hang when the Prime Minister is spared? He is the leader of a party, I am the leader of a gang; but both are primarily organized for spoils. And I am to be hanged, not because I differ from those who make and maintain the Law, but because I am too much like them for their own liking. It is declared that I have sacrificed my tools! Can you name me the statesman who has sacrificed his career for a friend? Then why am I to be garroted—rather than received at Court? Because, my fallen aristocratic friend, I was not born an aristocrat. But whatever my fate, your rotten aristocracy will not long survive me. The future belongs to men like my-self—self-made men, if I may coin a phrase—the powers of government will yet pass into the hands of men who know how to build an organization, and make it profitable.

LA RUSE. Yes, yes, you are concentrated; we are diverted. A stray tune—a pretty face—a lyrical line, illusions us. You are not illusioned. Life—(*Up stage.* JONATHAN *crosses* R.)

ME. SNAP (*enters* L). Life! Did you say life, Count? And what could be better than life on such a morning? The air! The balmy air! What! You haven't been out in the balmy air?

LA RUSE. Our spirits have wandered abroad, sir. (*Crosses down* L.)

MR. SNAP. Spirits indeed! Did you say spirits? They've no lungs, sir—you must have lungs for the enjoyment of the air! Why, the streets are packed with knaves. What could have kept you here on such a fragrant morning, gentlemen?

JONATHAN. Do not answer him, Count. He but mocks us. (*Sits* R.C.)

MR. SNAP. Come, sir, let the Count answer for himself.

LA RUSE (*at top chair*). You are easily answered. Our spirits have wandered abroad, but our bodies, detained by locks, bolts, bars and judical process, have necessarily languished where you see them now.

MR. SNAP. Spoken like a scholar, sir. I vow 'tis the very essence of an education to keep you jailed by me. You must pardon my little joke at your expense, but I am in high spirits. I have just jailed a poet.

JONATHAN. Truth to tell, Mr. Snap, I thought your joke in exceeding bad taste—twitting us with our lack of liberty.

MR. SNAP (*visibly incensed*). Bad taste! Did you say bad taste? What! Shall the taste of a jailer be questioned by his felons? What! I am not to have my little joke—simply because you are condemned?

JONATHAN (*starting—ashen-faced*). You have heard—they've set the date for my hanging?

MR. SNAP. I have heard nothing. You have set me out of temper with your impertinence, sir! I am no longer in high spirits. I am in exceeding low spirits—and your fault, Mr. Wild. (JONATHAN *finds the world too much for him.*) What! Does he sniffle!

LA RUSE. He has had a troublous morning, Mr. Snap. (*Sympathetically.*) Jonathan, pray retire to your room.

MR. SNAP. Does he forget that it is only by my grace that he continues to carry on his nefarious business, in jail, as out?

LA RUSE. You accept a certain percentage of the transactions, I believe.

MR. SNAP. I do, I do, and I won't deny it for my soul's sake—except under oath.

LA RUSE. I honour you for owning you are not squeamish, Mr. Snap.

MR. SNAP. I will tell you what, Sir Fop; I am not squeamish—there's not a man in London will say I am squeamish—distinctly, I am not! But as for your friend here—I am squeamish. What! Weeping! Sensitive! This father of bridle-culls — mill-kens — buttocks-and-files — assassins! (JONATHAN *groans.*) This thieving pimp and pimping thief! This fence —who has taught men to steal and then delivered 'em up for the bloody bounty? You may lay to what I have said, sir, as Jack Ketch will presently lay to Mr. Wild.

LA RUSE (*smiling, taking snuff*). You are a gentleman, Mr. Snap—

MR. SNAP (*thumpingly*). I am obliged to you for the notification, sir.

JONATHAN (*leaping to his feet and striding* L.). Sir, as you can see, I can scarcely articulate—I am distraught—a wronged man—but your words shall not go unanswered—my spirit cries out in rebuttal! You are a fool, Mr. Snap—you pervert the truth of my life—which a man of your mean stature must misunderstand. Know, then, sir, that I have an awkward pride in my nature, which is better pleased with being at the head of the lowest class than at the bottom of the highest. (*He pauses for breath.* COUNT LA RUSE *lays his snuffbox on the table and places a strengthening hand on his friend's shoulder.*) Permit me to say, though the idea may be somewhat coarse, I had rather stand on the summit of a dung-hill than at the bottom of a hill in Paradise! (*He collapses into chair* L. *of* L.C. *table.*)

LA RUSE. Your words, Jonathan, are like those pebbles which in the mouth of another Demosthenes turned into jewels. (JONATHAN's *anguished fingers happen on the snuffbox.*) Ah, Mr. Snap, you do not understand Mr. Wild. (JONATHAN *pinches snuffbox.*) I, Count La Ruse, an exile from my country, a stranger in your country, alone understand his true greatness. (*The snuffbox disappears up* JONATHAN'S *capacious sleeve.*)

JONATHAN (*rising unsteadily*). Alone—alone—I ask only to be alone. (*He makes for the* R. *door.*) 'Tis the principle of the thing—

MR. SNAP (*rushing between him and the exit*). Hold! Do you dare complain?

JONATHAN (*piteously*). Let me leave, Mr. Snap. I have every reason to leave immediately.

LA RUSE. Mr. Wild complains of nothing—but that you stand between him and the door.

MR. SNAP (*whirling on him*). Complain, sir! Do you not both eat at my table?

LA RUSE. A man of my position honours your table, Mr. Snap. But do not let us quarrel. Let me admit that I will never forget the way you have treated me—never. (*Crosses up stage a little; works round* R.)

MR. SNAP. That's a better tune than you have been singing, sir.

JONATHAN (*darting by him*). Alone—alone—all things conspire against me. (*He exits* L.)

MR. SNAP (*grumbling*). Ay, twelve good men and true have conspired to hang him by the neck—(JONATHAN *slams door.*) until dead. Bad taste, indeed! (*To* C.) What do you do at the door, sir?

LA RUSE (*shuts door*). A keyhole is like a woman, Mr. Snap; it tells secrets to the world. (*He goes to the fireplace, reaches up the flue, and finds something there; he gives it to* MR. SNAP.) Mr. Wild's silver locket as I promised. He blames its loss on the unfortunate Fierce.

MR. SNAP (*examining it with delight*). Sound, shining silver. By everything holy, a valuable ornament for some fat Duke's slim mistress. (*Crosses slightly* R.)

LA RUSE (*watching* MR. SNAP'S *avarice with a peculiar disdain*). I doubt not such will be its fate. Beauty the world over is born in silence, and dies in carnival.

MR. SNAP. We shall profit by this, never fear. I have yet to see a more desirable trinket.

LA RUSE. I hold there are still more desirable trinkets to be had, sir.

MR. SNAP (*reverently*). And if you can't lay your hands on them, there's no thief in London can.

LA RUSE. Thank you, Mr. Snap. Nothing's so pleasing to the ear of man as flattery. But the things to which I had reference have no pawnable subtance—they lie safely hidden in the silver locket of the spirit.

MR. SNAP. Well, I suppose you must talk so. But it puzzles me why so many of the gentry should be of a melancholic frame of mind. They seem to drink bitterness from their mother's rich breasts. (*Crosses down* R. LAETITIA *appears in the* C. *door. She is twenty-nine, a ravishing woman; vital to the excess of carnality.*) Good morning, daughter. 'Tis Laetitia, Count.

LA RUSE (*with an elaborate gesture*). The enchanting Mistress Laetitia. (*Down* L. *of table.*)

LAETITIA (*with one of her own*). The noble Count Ruse.

MR. SNAP. Daughter, I have business. (*To door* R.) You must cheer the Count—Aye, cheer him, but not to the point where you might lose your maidenly reserve—I would not have that. (*He goes, with a final admonition of his head.*)

LAETITIA (*laughs—throws her arms wide*). Take me, La Ruse.

LA RUSE (*studying the manufacture of a chair*). I am not in a mood.

LAETITIA (*undiscomfited*). I adore you, La Ruse. I do. Show me the lover who knows how to renounce me—ay, and how to denounce me—and he shall be surfeited with my fidelity.

LA RUSE. Liar!

LAETITIA (*approaching him*). I am mad about you, La Ruse. Are you not mad about me?

LA RUSE. I abominate you.

LAETITIA. And yet you make love to me.

LA RUSE. Because I abominate you.

LAETITIA. 'Tis your one drawback as a lover that your reasoning is always original.

LA RUSE. And true. The surrender of a woman one adores is but tepid compared to the subjection of a woman one abominates. Therefore—(*He clasps and kisses her.*)

LAETITIA (*sparkling*). For a prisoner, sir, you take more liberties than a free man dares.

LA RUSE (*coldly, leaving her*). Pray remember, madam, you have granted me greater liberties than any I now implore.

LAETITIA. It is the privilege of a lady to remember, sir, as it is the duty of a gentleman to forget. (LA RUSE *sits* R. *of table.*)

But alas! When a gentleman becomes a lover, he ceases to be a gentleman; the one is killed in the other. Yet I adore you, La Ruse, and would not willingly be without you.

LA RUSE. I shall be free of you yet.

LAETITIA. I shall do my best to hold you here. Yet you are foolish, sir—imagining you can escape me merely by leaving me.

LA RUSE. Out of this jail, and I am out of your life.

LAETITIA. Leave these prison walls, and your days shall be spent in matching your mind against my mind—your nights, (*Sits on his knee*) in matching your strength against my strength—your time, always, in matching your malice against my malice. (*Kisses him.*) You desire me, La Ruse.

LA RUSE. I desire no woman. I have found too many hairs—of too many colours—on my shoulder. (*Surveying her hair; critically.*) Your own is far from the most attractive shade I have found on my shoulder.

LAETITIA. But it is the final shade you will find there. (*Rises.*) You and I can no more escape from each other than from the reflection we must see if we look in the glass, or from the shadow we must see if we walk in the sun.

LA RUSE. But you forget—one may easily walk out of the sun. (*Rises; crosses L., above table.*)

LAETITIA (*lightly*). You will not kill yourself yet, La Ruse.

LA RUSE (*intensely*). Not while there is still a chance I may be free of you. But if the day should come—

LAETITIA. Egoist! Do you think yourself alone in resenting the tie which binds us? Do you never think I have my own moods when I would be free of you?

LA RUSE. Would that they came more often!

LAETITIA. What if I should tell you—I had yielded to such a mood?

LA RUSE. I should be indifferent.

LAETITIA. I have yielded to such a mood.

LA RUSE (*instantly jealous*). You lie.

LAETITIA. No.

LA RUSE. Come here to me, hussy.

LAETITIA (*studying the manufacture of chair R. of table*). I am not in a mood. (*Crosses to chair.*)

LA RUSE. You are simply revengeful.

LAETITIA. And perhaps—I may yield to another such mood!

LA RUSE. Do so, and be damned.

LAETITIA. This is not indifference. This is love!

LA RUSE. Why? And what if it were proved anew what everyone knows: that a woman like yourself has many mouths—all of them lying? (*Sits on table.*)

LAETITIA. Does it mean something to you—that I have been lying?

LA RUSE. Yes. Is it not absurd? I cannot bear the thought of another embracing you with love, although I embrace you with loathing!

LAETITIA. Reassure yourself, La Ruse. I adore you. Yet, what if I had deceived you? 'Twould be no more on my part than the closing of my eyes in an amorous daydream. The dream would pass quickly, my eyes would open—and your enduring image would be still in the glass before me.

LA RUSE. I am unworthy of such chaste fidelity. (*Rises.*) But since you are so sure of me, why do you deny the favour I have petitioned a thousand times?

LAETITIA (*insolently*). To slip the great lock for you? Why should I?

LA RUSE. Because I go mad in my confinement here.

LAETITIA (*amazed. Crosses L.*). But, La Ruse, La Ruse! (*Sits L. of table.*) 'Twas what you said to me when I first saw you in the jail! When I persuaded Papa to bring you here! This is ungracious of you, sir.

LA RUSE. I tell you, minx, I go mad here! Why will you not slip the lock for me? If all you have spoken is true, I shall still be yours while in full flight from you.

LAETITIA. But in an abstraction not wholly satisfactory to the warmth of my nature!

LA RUSE. What if I were to give you my word to return when I had paid the debt which sent me here?

LAETITIA. Poor Papa is fond of observing (*Rises.*) you were well-born. Alas, Count La Ruse! We ladies who were not well-born have learned to our cost that the word of a gentleman is not always sacred when given to a lady of another class.

LA RUSE. You wrong yourself, Laetitia. You do belong to my class.

LAETITIA (*not without a trace of bitterness*). I am a jailer's wench—and past time I was married.

LA RUSE. No matter, you belong to my class: The devil has elevated you to his submerged party. You talk like no jailer's wench; you have been given an infernal gift of tongues. You act like no jailer's wench; you do as you please, and it is your present pleasure to torture me by holding me here.

LAETITIA. I have heard there is no happier state than to be the prisoner of love.

LA RUSE. There is no happier state—when one is the jailer. (*Crosses* R.)

LAETITIA (*clapping her hands*). Was ever a woman so fortunate as myself—to have her lover under lock and key? I vow, sir, half the great love tragedies would have been comedies had the ladies been placed in my position. (*Crosses to* C.)

LA RUSE. This may yet prove more of a comedy than you think, Madam.

LAETITIA. You mean, La Ruse, that you have been tampering with the great lock.

LA RUSE (*casually*). Among others.

LAETITIA. Yes. You have also been tampering with the locks of Papa's arms-chest.

LA RUSE. Nothing is so easily beaten into shape of a key—as a pistol or knife.

LAETITIA. The locks are strong everywhere to hold you. (*Crosses to* L. *of table.*)

LA RUSE (*fiercely*). My spirit is strong everywhere to be free.

LAETITIA. Then our repulsions shall lend an intense piquance to our emotions. We shall spend delicious hours hating one another. You will visit me later, La Ruse?

LA RUSE (*studying the manufacture of* R.C. *chair*). I am not in a mood.

LAETITIA (*dangerously*). Take care, sir! There is always a refuge for a neglected woman! There is always—(*She is interrupted by the entrance of* CARTWRIGHT, L.)

CARTWRIGHT (*very much abashed*). I beg your pardon. I thought—(*He makes a motion to withdraw.*)

LAETITIA (*lyrically*). Stay, young gentleman! (*She flashes a mischievous glance at* LA RUSE). You are a stranger, sir? I do not remember seeing you.

CARTWRIGHT. I was taken only this morning. (*He feels that—somehow—he has spoken too freely, and again attempts to withdraw.*)

LAETITIA (*persuasively*). Do not run away, young gentleman. (*She repeats her mischievous glance at* LA RUSE.)

LA RUSE (*exploding*). Get out, you young fool. (CARTWRIGHT'S *face darkens; he takes a step toward* LA RUSE.)

LAETITIA (*lays a restraining hand on the boy*). You must not mind Count La Ruse. He is not in a mood—or in a mood—I really forget which it is! Devote yourself rather to me.

CARTWRIGHT. I could not help but do that. I did not expect in such a place—

LAETITIA. Yes?

CARTWRIGHT (*colouring*). To find such loveliness.

LAETITIA (*delighted*). For shame, young gentleman! I vow not even the Count vies with you as a gallant.

CARTWRIGHT (*anxiously*). I would not have you think I was being merely a gallant. (LA RUSE *yawns—audibly.*)

LAETITIA. I would not think that, sir, for I hold there's no more pleasing charm than sincerity. (*Sits on table.* LA RUSE *yawns—audibly.*)

CARTWRIGHT (*looks at* LA RUSE). Though they are the fashion of the town, yet I despise these gallants—who make a mask of something better than a mask, a disguise of something real.

LA RUSE (*vigorously*). And I admire those gallants immensely, sir—because I am one myself. (*He goes closer to the couple.*) I perceive from the nature of your eloquence you are hopelessly young.

LAETITIA. Divinely young, La Ruse.

CARTWRIGHT (*smarting at both references*). I was not arrested for the crime of youth, sir. (*Crossing front of chair* L. *of table.*)

LA RUSE. You should have been. At your age every man should be arrested and jailed until thirty. In this way, folly would be ended for all time.

CARTWRIGHT (*lashing back*). There is proverbially no fool like an old fool, sir.

LAETITIA. You mind Count La Ruse without cause; he is by way of being a misanthrope; they say his mistress would be untrue to him.

LA RUSE (*sky-rocketing*). What is your name, sir?

CARTWRIGHT (*steps toward* LA RUSE). Mr. Cartwright.

LAETITIA (*applauding his tone. Rises*). I see you are as valiant as you are quick, Mr. Cartwright. But I pray you, gentlemen, for my sake—let your wits be your weapons.

CARTWRIGHT. Do you think I would fight him? I would not follow his code while I have courage to follow a better code: I have sworn never to lay my hands on a human being, except in love.

LAETITIA (*laughs*). Except in love?—You've been rude, La Ruse.

LA RUSE (*interested by the boy's naïve declaration*). I meant no offense, sir. Last night's wine has left me on edge.

CARTWRIGHT. I regret the words passed. (*They bow to each other.*)

LAETITIA (*vastly entertained by the proceedings. Sits on table*). You were discussing the gallants, gentlemen; it promised to be most edifying to the ignorance of my female ears. (*Offers chair to* CARTWRIGHT.)

CARTWRIGHT. You were defending the beaux, Count La Ruse. (*Sits* L. *of table.*)

LA RUSE. Your servant, Mr. Cartwright. (*Crosses to chair* R. *of table.*) I will prove my case. What is it, sir, to fall in love with a woman? 'Tis a most involuntary gesture; for a woman to be flattered when a man falls in love with her were as if she were to be flattered when a man catches the measles. He can no more help the one than the other. But gallantry, sir—gallantry is the deliberate wisdom of men who do choicely what fools must do willy-nilly; and a woman of perception must always prefer your mature gentleman to your young idiot. I see that you take me amiss, Mr. Cartwright; you must permit me the license of a general remark. It follows, from what I have said, that the very spice of affectation is to appear more sincere than sincerity itself. I must blame my art when people think me insincere—because I so manifestly am.

CARTWRIGHT (*radically*). Count La Ruse: (*Rises; to above chair.*) Your gallants have bravado, without bravery; courtesy, without sacrifice; honour, without a cause to die for.

LAETITIA. I vow, sir, but you talk beyond your years! You must be a collegian. (*Rises.*)

CARTWRIGHT (*proudly*). I was expelled.

LATITIA. Expelled?

LA RUSE. 'Tis a special form of graduation, designed for the more original of the students.

CARTWRIGHT (*with the same self-conscious defiance as when he admitted his talent to* MR. SNAP). I wrote a tract against God.

LAETITIA. That was wicked, sir. I am High Church, and devout. You look as if you were of good family, and sure, one of good family should not be atheistic.

CARTWRIGHT (*the note of the born zealot kindling in his voice*). I am not atheistic. I believe in love.

LAETITIA (*excited*). We shall all be blasted! You are young; you have been led astray by books. You must let me convert you again. (LA RUSE *crosses* R.)

CARTWRIGHT. I must convert you.

LA RUSE. Would you leave me out in the wintry cold? What are the articles of your belief? (*Sits chair* R.C.)

CARTWRIGHT (*with the full note of the zealot*). That the Paradise which men have lost is to be found again on earth. (LAETITIA *sits* R. *of table.*) Is the air given us, only that we may stifle? Is the sea given us, only that we may drown? Are the flowers given us, only that we may faint? No. While we dream of a distant Heaven, Heaven is at hand for us to storm. I believe everything is forbidden by men, yet the wise are passionate; that nothing is forbidden by nature, yet the wise are austere. I believe that fear adds only to fear, hate adds only to hate, but that beauty—beauty adds to everything. (*He has been looking at* LAETITIA.) And you—(*To her.*) you who are so radiant in my eyes, I believe you will take my hand, you will walk with me into shadowy, holy places.

LAETITIA. I know not whether to be flattered—or frightened—or attracted by your presumption! Your talk is strange.

CARTWRIGHT. Truth is strange.

LA RUSE (*extends his hand in the ancient Roman salute*). Hail, Pilate!

LAETITIA (*rises; crosses to* C.). Why do you talk so? Are you a poet?

CARTWRIGHT. Yes.

LAETITIA. Why did you not say as much before? (*To up* C.) 'Tis in his nature, then—such incoherence! (*Recovers her coquetry; as if thrilled.*) A poet! But how charming!

LA RUSE. I am not surprised to find you jailed; the law and the muses have ever played ill together. They are like Mistress Laetitia's spinet—out of tune, the music jars.

LAETITIA (*winningly*). And will you write a poem to me, Mr. Cartwright? Will you dedicate a poem to me?

CARTWRIGHT. My heart is doing so now.

LAETITIA (*away a little*). La Ruse, the pattern of your conceits was never so taking as this. (*Up to sofa.*)

LA RUSE (*bitingly*). Romantic vein! The inspiration of your muse is Mistress Laetitia, daughter of your jailer.

CARTWRIGHT. You are Mr. Snap's daughter?

LAETITIA. Do you hate me, now—since my father is your jailer?

CARTWRIGHT. You have set me free.

LA RUSE (*agonized*). Free! (*Rises.*) Free! Never blaspheme with that word, sir.

CARTWRIGHT. I did not use it as a word, but as a mystery.

LA RUSE (*roughly*). You have another mystery to explain—your bursting in here without a by-your-leave.

CARTWRIGHT. I meant no disrespect. Mr. Snap has sold me the privacy of this floor.

LA RUSE (*warmly*). Oh! Indeed, Mr. Snap has sold me the privacy of this floor. 'Tis not the first time—(*The CLOCK strikes twelve.*)

LAETITIA. Noon! I must look to the cook; we shall be at table directly. I shall persuade Papa to let you sit at table with us, Mr. Cartwright.

CARTWRIGHT. You make me very happy, Mistress Laetitia. (*Bows.*)

LAETITIA. You shall sit by my side.

LA RUSE (*as she passes, aside*). Minx!

CARTWRIGHT. You make me very happy!

LAETITIA. 'Twill be my aim to make you happier while you are lodged here. I must acquaint you afterwards with the more intimate ways of the place. (*Smiles enigmatically at* LA RUSE, *ravishingly at the poet, and exits* C.)

LA RUSE (*sits on sofa. Oblivious of* CARTWRIGHT'S *enchantment*). I must ask you never to degrade the name of freedom by uttering it before that woman—before any woman. Yes, you will find monarchies are ruled by women, republics by men: for liberty bears a fiercer cut than Fashion permits. Mr. Cartwright—I grieve to note you have heard not one of my priceless words.

CARTWRIGHT. I beg your pardon.

LA RUSE. You have heard the sirens' song, and are lost. How old are you, sir?

CARTWRIGHT. Twenty-one.

LA RUSE. Twenty-one! Are people still twenty-one? For what are you held?

CARTWRIGHT. For a debt of two hundred pounds.

LA RUSE. Odd! I am held for the precise amount.

CARTWRIGHT. How long have you been held?

LA RUSE. I was taken the year of the flood. Do you know, I have gambled away as much as fifty thousand pounds at a sitting; I have thrice been held for murder, each time justly—and each time been released within the week; and yet for a beggarly two hundred pounds I have been caged here these three long years?

CARTWRIGHT (*envisioning a like fate*). Three years!

LA RUSE. Two in the jail, and one here. Have you hope for a speedier release?

CARTWRIGHT. None.

LA RUSE. No parents?

CARTWRIGHT. I have an uncle.

LA RUSE. Won't he help you?

CARTWRIGHT. He sent me here.

LA RUSE. You may console yourself with the thought that the malice of a relative is still more endurable than his affection. You borrowed from your uncle?

CARTWRIGHT. No, he sued me for my inheritance.

LA RUSE. And you lost your suit. I myself have several times been defended by eminent counsel, and each time been eminently convicted; for the fame of lawyers appears founded on the number of cases they lose, famously.

CARTWRIGHT. I won my suit.

LA RUSE. My rhetoric has gone astray. Then why are you here?

CARTWRIGHT. My lawyers had me arrested—perceiving as they did I owed them more than the value of the property—which they seized.

LA RUSE. It is not the meek who will inherit the earth: it is the lawyers. Such is the testament of Count La Ruse. (*Rises.*)

CARTWRIGHT. Manifestly, you adopted that as a nom de plume.

LA RUSE. Say rather as a nom de crime. I was born—but no matter. The blood of kings flows in my veins.

CARTWRIGHT (*with pride*). And in mine.

LA RUSE. The Homeric strain: a noble lineage. Beware, sir, lest you cross it with the treason of another Helen.

CARTWRIGHT (*resentfully*). Mistress Laetitia?

LA RUSE. You are acute. Yes, I meant Mistress Laetitia. But did I? (*Crosses* R.) Who knows what anyone means any more? The world threatens to be a garment which has gone out of style, while I still must wear it. This is death, to me, for I long ago took a sense of pleasure in place of my soul. (*Sits chair* R.C.)

CARTWRIGHT. I am sorry for you, Count La Ruse.

LA RUSE. Damn your impudence! Keep your sorrow for yourself; you will need it, here. When you have been detained as long as I have been, you will learn there is only one reality, and a bitter one.

CARTWRIGHT (*crosses to* LA RUSE). There is another reality—and I think I have found it.

LA RUSE (*shrugs his shoulders*). After all, what would it avail you if you desired freedom as passionately as I do?

CARTWRIGHT (*hesitantly*). I should find a way.

LA RUSE (*skeptical. Laughs*). What way, sir?

CARTWRIGHT (*uncertain if he is being wise*). This way. (*He reveals a knife. Rises.*)

LA RUSE (*snatches it from him*). A knife!

CARTWRIGHT (*sure he has not been wise*). I have never carried a blade. A prisoner slipped it to me when we were searched.

LA RUSE (*feeling the blade; with mounting excitement*). Keen—keen! But why am I surprised? Liberty is keen. (*He radiates the knife in the light.*) Bright—bright! But why am I surprised? Freedom is bright. (*His exaltation approaches ecstasy.*) Mouth about your women, you son of Homer! Will they glitter like this? A knife—I have a knife—a knife!

CARTWRIGHT. Let me have the knife back. You grow over-excited.

LA RUSE. Over-excited? You are a poet—and have no more perception? (*Closes his eyes in rapture; runs his fingers over the sharp edge.*) I am calm and at peace with the world at last. Life—my sense of pleasure returns to me; already I am walking the streets, frequenting the tables, dining tête-à-tête with the King's mistress! What hour, think you, will be best?

CARTWRIGHT. Best—

LA RUSE. Midnight—

CARTWRIGHT. For what?

LA RUSE (*impatiently*). Why, when we shall excellently cut the throat of Mr. Snap—seize his keys—and escape.

CARTWRIGHT. Mr. Snap! Laetitia's father!

LA RUSE (*too engrossed by the future to notice the poet's horror*). Hell's father, sir! (*He radiates the blade again.*)

CARTWRIGHT (*snatches vainly*). The knife is mine.

LA RUSE. Yours, sir? You are mistaken. The blade has been in my family for generations, and sentiment forbids me let it go. (*Puts knife in pocket.*)

CARTWRIGHT (*impotently*). I'll not be responsible for the cutting of any throats!

LA RUSE (*dismissing the subject*). You will never make a great poet, for I see you are a moral man.

CARTWRIGHT. I will not harm Mistress Laetitia.

LA RUSE (*solemnly*). She will harm you—

CARTWRIGHT. You have some cause to to be malicious.

LA RUSE. I will tell you, Mr. Cartwright: it would profit you more in Heaven to cut the throat of Mr. Snap—than to kiss the throat of his daughter.

CARTWRIGHT. Doubtless Mistress Laetitia has repelled your advances.

LA RUSE (*sadly*). There is only one possible explanation of this world, Mr. Cartwright: the Gods themselves are stupid. Yes. For that reason it is said we were made in their image. They have had one brilliant idea, sir: snuff. (*He feels for his snuffbox; finds it gone; recalls that he left it on the table, and looks there.*) Gone! My snuffbox gone! Your precious Mr. Snap—or that other damnable rogue— (*Crosses to table.*)

CARTWRIGHT. Jonathan Wild?

LA RUSE (*searching frantically*). The identical villain! I would have parted with my bowels, before that box. It was given me by—a lady! You are new here, Mr. Cartwright; let me warn you against Mr. Wild—and Mr. Snap, two of the consummate thieves of the age. (CARTWRIGHT *crosses to table.*) 'Tis not to be found! Wild was here—Snap was here—is it possible that that minx—? 'Twas while Wild was here—I was comforting him. By God, I'll have it back or I'll demolish the house. (*Crosses to sofa, then down to chair* R.C. CARTWRIGHT *surveys the room. He sees some paper at table, sits back of table and begins writing a lyric. He has scarcely begun, however, when* LAETITIA *en-*

ters C. CARTWRIGHT *to chair* R. *of table.*)

LAETITIA. Oh, La Ruse! Pray, leave the house stand at least for dinner, which is ready.

LA RUSE. Damn dinner! I couldn't digest nectar at the moment!

LAETITIA. What's happened to him?

CARTWRIGHT. He's lost his snuffbox.

LAETITIA. What a pity. If he had it now he might sneeze out his temper.

LA RUSE. If I had it now I wouldn't be in a temper.

LAETITIA. 'Tis the oddest matter (LA RUSE *looks round sofa.*), but one is forever losing things in this charming house.

CARTWRIGHT. For myself I have found much more here than I could ever lose—

LAETITIA. I vow, Mr. Cartwright, you are a sweet young man.

LA RUSE. When you hear that purring —look out for claws, Mr. Cartwright.

LAETITIA. You're in need of food. (WILD *appears* L.) Ah! Mr. Wild—Dinner waits—

LA RUSE (*glares at* WILD). Let it wait, madam. I've been robbed of my appetite by the scoundrel who robbed me of my snuffbox—a treasured piece of mine.

JONATHAN. Sir, you look palpably at me when you say that! Sir, do you dare imply

LA RUSE. Sir, I imply I want my snuffbox back at once!

LAETITIA (*nervously*). Stand aside from them, Mr. Cartwright.

JONATHAN. Sir, I'll not have you talk to me in this manner; 'tis the principle of the thing! (*Coolly.*) Yes. As a principled man, have I asked you for the return of my silver locket?

LA RUSE (*to* JONATHAN). Do you dare imply—

LAETITIA (*firmly*). Enough. We shall have no more of your joint ill-manners! La Ruse, you must look for your box later—and you, Mr. Wild, for your locket. (*Turns upstage.*)

LA RUSE (*fuming*). By Heaven, madam, you may depend that I will! (*Crosses to sofa.*)

MR. SNAP (*bustles in* R.). I am in high spirits again; they bubble over.

LAETITIA. Stop your nonsense, Papa, and come along. (*She takes the poet by the arm.*) I'll show you, as we pass, how the rooms lie, sir. (*Notices* LA RUSE.) Come along, La Ruse.

LA RUSE (*vaguely; to himself*). White birds—

LAETITIA. Awaken La Ruse, Papa. (*Goes out* C. *with* CARTWRIGHT.)

MR. SNAP. Come along, Count. (*Crosses to* C. WILD *disappears off* C.) Wild hangs tomorrow. (*Chuckles.*)

LA RUSE. Tomorrow? You say Wild hangs tomorrow?

LAETITIA'S VOICE (*vexed*). Come along, Papa.

MR. SNAP. Coming, daughter. You are ready, Count? (*Turns toward the* C. *door.*)

LA RUSE (*looks at the knife behind* MR. SNAP'S *back*). Quite ready, dear Mr. Snap.

CURTAIN

ACT TWO

The same, that night. The room is lighted by an adequate number of candles; the window remains open. The papers, etc., have been removed from the table.

LA RUSE *is discovered on sofa, looking out of window, at rise.*

MR. SNAP (*enters* C.). Ah! La Ruse, I'm belching affluently. That was a most excellent supper, Mr. Snap. (*Musing.*) I believe I shall never sup better in your house—never.

MR. SNAP (*sardonic*). Did you say never? You are not thinking of trying to leave us through your window again, Count?

LA RUSE. No. This time I shall leave through your front door. When the clock strikes twelve I shall vanish like the maid with the glass slipper.

MR. SNAP (*pleasantly entertained*). And if you do, sir, Cinderella'll find a coach awaiting her at the door—a police-coach! I am delighted, Count. (*Sits* R. *of table* L.C.) You have recovered your good humour.

LA RUSE. I protest, Mr. Snap. (*Crosses to chair back of table* L.C.) You never saw me in better humour than today at noon.

MR. SNAP. You'll not deny you grew sulky during afternoon.

LA RUSE. I was bored. I was resentful at being left alone.

MR. SNAP. It was plain to see you were in a rage against yourself.

LA RUSE (*with sudden vehemence*). Not against myself.

MR. SNAP (*always prepared to take umbrage*). Against me, sir? Against me? Had you the audacity to resent me at my own table?

LA RUSE (*his anger dying away in soulweariness*). Not against you, Mr. Snap.

MR. SNAP. Then against who—or what, sir?

LA RUSE. Who can tell? (*Sits in chair.*) One has memories, Mr. Snap—or better, one has not. Perhaps I was in a rage against the sun which rises. Perhaps against my first love—or my last. Strange, that one should forget one's last love before one's first!

MR. SNAP. By the bye, while you were vexed with Laetitia's absence this afternoon then, she was in her room.

LA RUSE. Yes. Did you notice Mr. Cartwright at supper? He was singularly animated.

MR. SNAP. He is odd, sir, like all of his kind. He spent the afternoon in his room with his metrical ruminations.

LA RUSE. Yes, I had thundered on his door, without arousing him.

MR. SNAP. Pray, Count, you have said naught of Mr. Wild and his fate.

LA RUSE. You've not told him he hangs tomorrow?

MR. SNAP (*considerate*). It seemed a pity to spoil his supper.

LA RUSE (*unforgiving*). Damn him. He has spoiled my after-supper.

MR. SNAP (*craftily*). I have been thinking of telling him—but I have been thinking more of not telling him.

LA RUSE (*pricks up his ears*). How now? What is in your agile mind?

MR. SNAP. Mr. Wild is a man of wealth.

LA RUSE (*with conviction*). He is certainly the possessor of a valuable snuffbox.

MR. SNAP. He has money.

LA RUSE. Everybody's money.

MR. SNAP. He is about to die.

LA RUSE. Has he relatives?

MR. SNAP. Relatives? Did you say relatives? He has seven wives.

LA RUSE. What do you propose?

MR. SNAP. What if we tell him that a reprieve is possible—if he acts wisely and quickly?

LA RUSE. You would delude him into the belief he could be saved—when he must surely hang in the morning?

MR. SNAP (*his little eyes dancing*). 'Tis the very point, that. He will be on his way to the gallows 'ere he's aware of his duping! 'Twill be choking late then for a hue and a cry over what money we get from him!

LA RUSE. Mr. Snap, forgive me. (*Rises.*) I had failed to perceive the sublime heights of your imagination.

MR. SNAP (*beams*). I'll admit, I think the plot neatly contrived.

LA RUSE. Yes, but why only a reprieve? Why not a full pardon—

MR. SNAP. For that we can easily garner a hundred pounds from the unfeeling villain!

LA RUSE. One hundred pounds. That's but fifty for each of us! Why not more, Mr. Snap?

MR. SNAP. Why, we cannot gouge him of more; he would not pay more, not for his very life, sir!

LA RUSE (*soliloquizes*). The plot is neat —Jonathan is close, he parts unwilling from a bad farthing, but he fears death— how he fears death! (*Sits.*) Mr. Snap, do you fear death?

MR. SNAP (*upset*). Death? Did you say death? 'Tis a word as chilling as a cold sheet.

LA RUSE. There may always be a hot brick for your feet, Mr. Snap.

MR. SNAP. Do not say death, sir! I've no use for the word—no use at all!

LA RUSE (*encouragingly*). You are in good health, Mr. Snap.

MR. SNAP (*brightens*). I've never a day of sickness.

LA RUSE (*thoughtfully*). And still, you can never be sure. Health is no sign we shall not die. Death comes like a thief in the night—like a stab in the dark. Yes, I hear a beating of dark wings, now.

MR. SNAP (*terrified*). If you continue to rave on, I'll leave you! 'Tis my heart you hear beating; you have set shivers like lice running down my spine. Were the wind to blow a candle out, I'd think my life blown out!

LA RUSE (*blows out a candle*). There, sir, 'tis the candle's flame gone out, not yours! (*Rises; lights candle at fireplace.*)

MR. SNAP (*rises*). Be done with your cursed fancies—done, I say!

LA RUSE (*acquiesces*). Think you he could procure the money tonight? (*Crosses to* SNAP.)

MR. SNAP. I don't know. I've tapped

the walls of his room, sounded the floor and all to no effect, yet I could swear he must have coin o' the realm where he could lay his hand on't.

LA RUSE. But why not bell the cat yourself and keep all the profits?

MR. SNAP. I am not enough of an actor for the role, sir. Mr. Wild, being a knave, would see through to my native honesty. (LAETITIA *sings and plays spinet offstage.*) Now, with your refined ability— (*Crosses to door* L. *Voices are heard, passing through the hall.*)

LA RUSE (*listens; becomes intense*). 'Tis Laetitia and her poet. (*The voices are heard in the adjoining room.*)

MR. SNAP. Call him now!

LA RUSE (*looks gloomily toward the voices*). No, later. I have somewhat to say to Laetitia. (*Crosses up to* C.)

MR. SNAP (*authoritative*). No, no, 'tis not Laetitia hangs tomorrow. We must first dispose of Mr. Wild. (*Calling.*) Mr. Wild! Mr. Wild!

JANATHAN (*heard offstage*). Yes, Mr. Snap.

MR. SNAP. He's coming—(*Crosses to door* R.) Remember, one hundred pounds.

JONATHAN (*enters* L.). Yes, Mr. Snap.

MR. SNAP (*as he exits* R.). Count La Ruse has something to say to you, Mr. Wild. (*Exits.*)

JONATHAN. You are disturbed, La Ruse: pray, why? (*Sits* L. *of table.*)

LA RUSE. I am disturbed, sir: I'll not permit myself to be disturbed. What! Shall the stars be obscured by a slut? (*Crosses to door* R.)

JONATHAN. I sympathize with your tender emotion, Count.

LA RUSE. Jonathan! Mr. Snap has asked me to speak to you for him—to give you good news!

JONATHAN (*gasps*). I am not to hang?

LA RUSE. Not quite.

JONATHAN. How, not quite? They will hang me a few feet lower? There's something uncommon in this, La Ruse. Why should you speak for Mr. Snap?

LA RUSE. Mr. Snap feared his inflammable nature—feared that with the best of wills you would come to words again.

JONATHAN. 'Tis still no reason he should not speak for himself.

LA RUSE (*sits* R. *of table*). You are right, Jonathan. 'Tis but the reason he gave me. He asked me to speak, because he

knew me to be your loyal friend—but mostly because he fears to be seen in what must remain, after all, a hanging matter.

JONATHAN. Fears to be seen! Your reasoning grows sounder; Mr. Snap is not the soul of courage.

LA RUSE (*grows animated*). Courage, Jonathan? You have not heard the extent of his cowardice. Not only will he not speak—he'll not accept your money himself! No, sir! It must be passed him through me.

JONATHAN (*upset*). Money? Money for what?

LA RUSE. You know Mr. Snap.

JONATHAN. I know Mr. Snap.

LA RUSE. He has been feeling his way—

JONATHAN. In my room. I have watched him through a crack. There's not a board hasn't felt the soft caress of his fingers.

LA RUSE. Nevertheless, Mr. Snap has been feeling his way towards a full pardon for you, Jonathan. I see you do not believe it.

JONATHAN. Pity is not in Mr. Snap's nature as in yours or mine, Count.

LA RUSE. You forget there are moments when even pity may be combined with profit.

JONATHAN. There's truth in that: it had not struck me before. Mr. Snap would not willingly lose my board, for I am vilely over-charged. There's no tavern in London charges what Mr. Snap charges me for the privilege of being speeded forth some morning on a terrible journey. Though I feign otherwise, Count, I dread that journey of all things.

LA RUSE. You will never make that journey, Jonathan, if you listen well. Of all people, you should be aware that men in office are—men in office.

JONATHAN. Well—to the terms. What am I asked to slip from the halter?

LA RUSE (*dismissing it as a bagatelle*). Three hundred pounds.

JONATHAN (*appalled*). Three hundred pounds!

LA RUSE. There are many to be bribed. If you pay me the money, you may believe me, Mr. Snap will see but little of it. (LAETITIA *is heard singing and playing spinet offstage.*)

JONATHAN. I'll not pay it! What! Pay three hundred pounds to a set of rogues who should be in my place? Let them do it—let it come! By Heaven, they'll not have three hundred pounds from me—not for my life! 'Tis not worth it—

LA RUSE (*shrugs his shoulders*). For myself, I should think a thousand pounds cheap. 'Tis likely, as you choke, you'll wish you'd not been so covetous. (*Turns upstage.*)

JONATHAN. Covetous, sir? 'Tis the principle of the thing!—What shall I do? (*Hopefully.*) They'll take less.

LA RUSE (*decisively*). No. Your reprieve will bring a clamour on their—(MUSIC *stops.*)—heads. You must let them have a fat umbrella for the storm. 'Tis three hundred pounds or your life.

JONATHAN (*groans*). My money or my life! How do I know, sir, if I pay this money I'll get the pardon?

LA RUSE. You must take the chance, Jonathan. I am convinced the offer is authentic. Mr. Snap is not enough of an actor to have deceived me.

JONATHAN. Very well—I'll pay—but after the pardon is signed.

LA RUSE. Do you think you deal with infants, sir? Why, they have made it a point the money be delivered at once—tonight.

JONATHAN (*his suspicions re-awakened*). Tonight? Why so quickly?

LA RUSE. You force me to be unsparing, Jonathan. Those in power say you are such a monstrous villain they are not anxious to do't, not even for the money. You must pin them down at once.

JONATHAN. Three hundred pounds! (LAETITIA *and* CARTWRIGHT *are heard laughing offstage.*) 'Tis Laetitia and Cartwright. They're coming.

LA RUSE (*rising*). Damn Laetitia. I never want to see her again as long as I live. But by God I'll see her once before the night is over when I'm through with you, Mr. Wild—(*They exit* L. LAETITIA *opens the* C. *door and enters with* CARTWRIGHT. *She carries an elegant fan, which she uses well.*)

LAETITIA (*with a shade of disappointment*). I thought I heard voices. (CARTWRIGHT *kisses her.*) La Ruse usually repairs here (*Crosses to light lamps.*) at this time.

CARTWRIGHT. We are fortunate, then.

LAETITIA. Yes, we are fortunate. (*Crosses; lights candles. They cross to the sofa.*) 'Tis more pleasant in this room. Let us sit by the window. (*Taps him with her fan.*) The night is warm for the spring. (*Sits on sofa.*)

CARTWRIGHT. I could not keep my eyes from you, at table. (*Crosses round sofa to her.*) I wished only we were alone together in your room again.

LAETITIA. I noticed you, sir.

CARTWRIGHT. Why would you not meet my glance?

LAETITIA. You were injudicious enough.

CARTWRIGHT. Can love be injudicious?

LAETITIA. Can love be anything else?

CARTWRIGHT. I have had a dream—a dream of spring-madness!

LAETITIA. Madness sufficient to set up a flock of hatter's shops! We were strangers this morning.

CARTWRIGHT. And now—(*Sits on sofa.*) —we are not strangers.

LAETITIA. A single day has sufficed to change the years. I had always known it would be thus—when love at last came into my life—when at last I permitted the sweet and dangerous intimacy of a man! Comfort me, sir, with the assurance I have not yielded to one who took me lightly; let me hear you say, I love you.

CARTWRIGHT. I love you.

LAETITIA. I would believe you did I not know there are three things a man says with equal ease: "I love you—" "I regret, madam, I can see you no more—" "By Gad, sir, she was as pretty a wench as ever I bedded!"

CARTWRIGHT. I love you! (*Kisses hand. Kneels.*)

LAETITIA. My naïve heart would believe you—

CARTWRIGHT. Did I not tell you, this afternoon, I had saved myself for you—as you had saved yourself for me! I was waiting—waiting for someone who would share with me the immense burden of being. Often it seemed to me I was a fool. Spring came tenderly everywhere —so tenderly. Only to me it came like a sword. Laetitia, Laetitia, you have healed my wound of spring! My wound of life!

LAETITIA. I believe that you love me. And you must believe that I love you. (*Kiss.*) Come, sir, let go of me—we shall be seen by the world. (*Rises.*)

CARTWRIGHT. The world will not like us? So much the worse for the world!

LAETITIA. So much the worse for us—nay, for me! Your arm—remove your arm, sir! (*Crosses* L.C.) My good name—'tis nothing to you?

CARTWRIGHT (*upset*). I meant no harm.

LAETITIA. No, only to hold me where we might be discovered! Alas, am I betrayed already? Is this the stuff of your oath, on the threshold of my room?

CARTWRIGHT. Forgive me.

LAETITIA (*to him*). You will remember your promise. You will be discreet.

CARTWRIGHT. I will do always whatever you ask me. (*Away a little* R.)

LAETITIA (*relents further*). Come, sir, you have a face like Mr. Wild at the sight of a rope! My temper is out of me. (*Capriciously kisses him.*) There, sir, you see! World or no world! (*Takes his hands. Kisses hand.*)

CARTWRIGHT (*lifted from the depths*). Laetitia! You are kind.

LAETITIA (*gaily. Lets go hand*). Now you are like Papa—in high spirits!

CARTWRIGHT. In Heaven!

LAETITIA. Where the cherubim sing, like the poets, always of the spring? Tell me why poets must sing always of the spring? (*Turns up* C.)

CARTWRIGHT (*carries the happy mood*). Because they are boys who must run to a fire. April's their fire. They stand too close and catch the flame.

LAETITIA (*sententious*). Wise children soon learn to stand away from the fire. (*Sits on table* L.C.)

CARTWRIGHT (*mystical*). Is it a part of wisdom—to stand away from the fire? (*Crosses to her.*)

LAETITIA. For all that, I do not like your spring as I like my autumn. The skies flame and meadows are cool, but your cool April love is crossed then by some hot wind sweeping back from summer, by an unseasonable heat burning life to a delicious decay. I could gallop, or swoon: the yellow on a leaf has curious power to make me desire. (*Laughs strangely and draws* CARTWRIGHT *close.*) I must teach you the joy of things yellow-tinged, overripe, sir.

CARTWRIGHT (*impulsively*). Let me come to your room again tonight.

LAETITIA. It would be too dangerous. (*Crosses to* C.) I vow you will prove an eager lover. (*Restive, she walks here and there.*) I must warn you, be neither too importunate nor too negligent; for one or t'other is the death of love—(*Crosses to chair* R.C.) I have read. (*Sits.*) Where can La Ruse be, tonight?

CARTWRIGHT (*saddened*). I could al-most believe you wished him with us. I dislike La Ruse.

LAETITIA. Would you be jealous of an impoverished rake? I have as little to do with him as possible—although I will confess he amuses me.

CARTWRIGHT. He is malicious. Why should he amuse you?

LAETITIA. Perhaps because he is malicious. Pray—there was something in your tone—has La Ruse warned you against me?

CARTWRIGHT (*hesitant*). Yes.

LAETITIA (*smiles*). It was like La Ruse. Truth to tell, he made certain advances and found me inaccessible.

CARTWRIGHT (*triumphant*). I guessed as much. (*Crosses to her a little.*) And told him so.

LAETITIA. You shall have a kiss for that—(*He crosses to her.*) presently, Mr. Cartwright.

CARTWRIGHT. Must you still call me Mr. Cartwright? (*Away a little.*)

LAETITIA. More than ever, sir. (*Severely.*) If our intimacy teaches you nothing else, let it teach you this—that discretion is the first talent of a lover. For the last time, I charge you to remember your promise to me—(*Rises.*) Mr. Cartwright.

CARTWRIGHT (*subdued*). I will do always—

LAETITIA. Whatever I ask! Pray, how will you address me before others? Like this: Mistress Laetitia.

CARTWRIGHT (*in her formal accents*). Mistress Laetitia. (*She crosses; sits on table* L.C. *With abrupt animation. He turns round.*) But O! Vile and obscene! We must be formal: we must bow correctly for fear that our pure emotions will be weighed —checked—and found wanting, in the foul balance of the world! Young as I am, Laetitia, I believe love will redeem men when men have redeemed love. (*Up to her.*) Dare with me, Laetitia! Let us cry of the world we are true: we are lovers: our lips have met: our bodies have burned with the clear fire of our spirits: the sky is serene, the wind is tender, because we are lovers! Let us heap flowers under a white heaven on the green earth.

LAETITIA (*gasps*). 'Tis breath-taking to hear you go on! 'Tis a parliamentary wind of words!

CARTWRIGHT (*obsessed*). Will you dare

with me?

LAETITIA. Let me think awhile. Yes, 'tis a pretty picture you have conjured for me! Two lovers, hand in hand, walk desolate ways in defiance of the conventions.

CARTWRIGHT (*prophetic; fierce*). Their desolation shall bloom.

LAETITIA. The fashionable world stands agape and offended—but what of that? They have each other. They are not received—but what of that? They have each other. They are pilloried, they are stoned—but what of that? They have each other. Always and always, each other.

CARTWRIGHT (*exalted*). And love, and victory.

LAETITIA. Always and always, each other. (*Starts from her visionary posture; with sudden dismay.*) Yes—but what then?

CARTWRIGHT (*stupidly*). Then? When?

LAETITIA (*in a torrent*). When they have had each other for an eternity? When he tires of her beauty and she of his oratory? When he cannot abide her friends, and she deceives him with his best friend? When, in short, they have had each other to the point of wishing they had never had each other?

CARTWRIGHT (*stricken*). You have been mocking me.

LAETITIA (*sweetly*). I would not have you think that. I was but measuring your ideal against the reality of things. Come, sir. You must first convert me, as you promised this morning.

CARTWRIGHT (*revived*). The grace of your spirit will make you understand.

LAETITIA. You shall have that promised kiss now. Tell me; how much do you love me?

CARTWRIGHT (*trembles*). Let me tell you in your room tonight.

LAETITIA (*agitated*). No, no—(*Rises; crosses up to sofa.*) 'Twould be too dangerous! And yet—perhaps! Ask me again, sir. Not another word now! (*Sits on sofa.*) I will see—(LA RUSE *enters* L. *She becomes mildly petulant.*) Where have you been, La Ruse? You are later than usual. (CARTWRIGHT *sits* R. *of* L.C. *table.*)

LA RUSE (*coldly*). I doubted not but Mr. Cartwright was capable of amusing you.

LAETITIA. He has been reading me his verses; they are pretty verses. (*Roguishly, to* CARTWRIGHT.) Are they not?

CARTWRIGHT. Pretty?

LA RUSE. If naught else damns you, madam, your choice of adjectives will. I respect your gift, Mr. Cartwright. 'Twas a pity you were not here during the afternoon: the sunlight fell through the windows for a poet! Did I say poet? For more, sir: for lovers. (CARTWRIGHT *starts.*) Yes, 'twas a pity you weren't here.

CARTWRIGHT (*shortly*). I was writing in my room.

LA RUSE (*smiles*). Of love?

CARTWRIGHT (*sullen*). Perhaps.

LA RUSE. Youth, sir—youth is not thus to be served! (*He studies the boy's face.*) Why, sir, because on such a day you should not have written of love—you should have enjoyed love!

CARTWRIGHT. You desire to affront me, La Ruse! (*Rises.* LAETITIA *sends him a frightened glance.*)

LA RUSE. Why should I desire to affront you, Mr. Cartwright? (*Down.*)

CARTWRIGHT. Because you do not like me, and because I do not like you.

LAETITIA (*very uneasy*). Gentlemen, gentlemen! Pray, what causes this sudden heat between you?

LA RUSE. We fight over truth and beauty, madam. Perhaps more beauty than truth, since you are present.

LAETITIA (*angrily*). You are possessed, La Ruse! (*Rises; crosses* L. *to* CARTWRIGHT.) Mr. Cartwright: pray, leave us—you'll find me here when you return!

CARTWRIGHT (*unwilling*). Would you have me withdraw—now?

LAETITIA (*firmly*). Now—now! Until La Ruse is himself again! (LA RUSE *to down* R. CARTWRIGHT *goes out* L.)

LA RUSE. Harlot!

LAETITIA. Your language, La Ruse! I am not in a mood for these profane terms of endearment.

LA RUSE. Where were you this afternoon?

LAETITIA. Pray, if you've nothing better to say than this, say nothing.

LA RUSE. Where were you this afternoon? And where was Cartwright?

LAETITIA. Your silence will at the least be more genteel.

LA RUSE (*to her*). You were both missing, all the afternoon! I cannot believe it possible, minx! Were you really with the boy?

LAETITIA. I was alone this afternoon, but what if I had not been alone, this or any other afternoon? Did you not tell me you should watch such a procedure with magnificent indifference?

LA RUSE (*characterized by the same sudden weariness which overcame him when with* MR. SNAP). I am not concerned for you. (*Crosses* R. *sofa.*)

LAETITIA. Your concern is not for me! La Ruse, you begin to lose your singular force when you are thus obvious: like a common lover, whose jaundiced eyes stain all things yellow, but mostly, those things which are not.

LA RUSE (*rather to himself*). The yellow merges into black; the shadow of a bird I saw. (*Sits sofa.*) I am like an actor whose perfection in a role has forced him to play the part until it has become odious to him. My delight was the comedy of repetition; to say the same word, to make the same gesture, in separate delicate moments. And now—

LAETITIA (*spurs him*). And now, pray?

LA RUSE. I say the word, I make the gesture without the delight. I am resolved Mr. Cartwright shall be saved from a like fate. I discern in the poet's youth a talent more than mere youth. I would not have his quality debased by your merciless instincts. I would protect the shadow of my former self from your attractive ferocity.

LAETITIA. Your name, sir, your name? (*To sofa.*) 'Tis highly improper for me to converse with a gallant whose name is unknown to me—although I perceive he is excellent, virtuous, angelic! One who protects widows, orphans, curates! Your name, your seraphic name, sir!

LA RUSE. Silence, trollop! (*Rises.*)

LAETITIA. La Ruse—you of a thousand crimes, thief, blackguard, ravisher! 'Tis a new penny-whistle you play me! 'Tis a new pamphlet by Mr. DeFoe cried on the streets: The Pope turns Protestant! The King preaches sedition! La Ruse turns evangelist!

LA RUSE (*controls himself*). Yes; the last lock I pick shall be on the gates of Paradise. I shall pick one or two before that, however. (*Crosses* R.C.; *sits.*)

LAETITIA. It seems that the creed of the church is lamentably insufficient. Pray, sir, will you not convert me to your peculiar creed? Your rival—in conversion—is Mr. Cartwright. He has promised to save me: my desolation shall bloom. We are to make love on the high-ways, which I learn is a far more marked virtuous way of making love than in private—

LA RUSE (*catches her up*). Ah! You have been making less virtuous love in private!

LAETITIA. 'Twas a mere figure of speech, such as you use often, and Mr. Cartwright.

LA RUSE (*viciously*). I would have wrung his juvenile neck for him, this afternoon. (*Takes her in his arms.*)

LAETITIA (*trills a few high notes*). I adore you, La Ruse. You were concerned with wringing his neck for him, not with saving his soul from me.

LA RUSE. I could not bear the thought of the cub in your arms. (*Despairingly.*) I could not bear the thought! Yet why? What have I to do with what women do! Who are you—what are you, that your bawdiness causes my blood to choke my brain?

LAETITIA (*impatiently*). 'Tis the moment when your strict grammatical rule requires that you say you do not love me —though you do.

LA RUSE. Yes; in this chemical reality we must kiss evil on the mouth even as our spirits take flight from evil. (*Kisses her. Rises; crosses* C.) Like two wild horses, released by birth, body and soul strain different ways and tear us to pieces. 'Tis your pleasure—(LAETITIA *sits* R.C.) madam, to whip the steeds o' myself until sense careens, but God be praised! your power is but the power of matter lacerating matter in a small confine, and I shall soon be out of that, I promise you. (*Looks at knife.*)

LAETITIA. I have a secret may keep you here longer than you think.

LA RUSE. Mr. Cartwright is no secret, and will not keep me here.

LAETITIA. Perhaps 'tis a new lock, of a special sort, designed to keep you here! I will reveal my secret to you tomorrow —La Ruse.

LA RUSE. Tomorrow? I'll not be the sort of guest who's always leaving tomorrow. I shall make a more graceful exit—who knows—perhaps tonight.

LAETITIA. You talk as if you had some plan.

LA RUSE. Plan?—Never a day or a night goes by but I have some plan—

LAETITIA. You talk now—as if—

LA RUSE. As if? Pray finish your sentence, madam!

LAETITIA (*Rises*). I vow, La Ruse, because I was not to be found—because Mr. Cartwright was not to be found—

LA RUSE (*wryly*). Singular coincidence!

LAETITIA. You indulge in this wild talking of fleeing tonight! When you know 'tis but talk! Do you think the bolts will be weakened by your jealousy? For shame, sir! Would you be jealous of an impoverished poet?

LA RUSE. No—of an amorous daydream.

LAETITIA. Believe whatever you will, I adore you. (LA RUSE *crosses* L.) La Ruse, you will confess that even though you are a Count—

LA RUSE. I am not a Count: I am a Marquis.

LAETITIA (*the snob in her responding*). A Marquis! But La Ruse! You are the strangest of men; you have withheld this from me all the while. Marquis! And one were your wife (*Crosses; sits* R. *of table.*), she would be a Marquise—only to think of that!

LA RUSE. You manage to seem a lady, until your veneration for a trumpery thus reveals you. I lowered my title, madam, when I lowered my standards—an old family custom. My line, which began in a palace, ends in a jail.

LAETITIA. You are still a young man. 'Tis far from impossible—

LA RUSE. Shall I add another mouth to the pack? I have had one child—a bastard. Yes, I have withheld that also. He's a boy of ten by now, and thinks himself the son of an English lord, who is himself deceived, since he was deceived. I shall leave no issue with my name, and for this, much will be forgiven me on high.

LAETITIA (*earnestly*). 'Tis strange, La Ruse, you should talk thus at this juncture—'tis most strange! For 'twas in my thoughts to observe, when you interrupted, that although a Count—a Marquis, you are not much of a match today.

LA RUSE. What do you get at, madam? 'Tis true, mothers with frumpish daughters no longer leer into my face. (*Sits on table.*)

LAETITIA. No, you are not much of a match today. Yet—if you were to ask me to marry you—

LA RUSE. Ask you to marry me!

LAETITIA (*quickly*). I should say yes, and force Papa's consent. (LA RUSE *rises.*) Ah! That was an unmannerly noise, La Ruse.

LA RUSE (*dazed*). Marry you! Marry you! Do you think because you have been my mistress you shall be my familiar? What! Are our bedfellows to answer us back? Monstrous presumption! What is your crest, madam? Does it show bolts and bars against a field of human misery? Marry you! Marry you! Infamous affront to the blood royal in my veins!

LAETITIA (*serenely*). Truth to tell, you have taken the suggestion less violently than I thought you would. (*Rises; crosses* R.)

LA RUSE. There was a sovereign, madam, once offered me the hand of his niece. I refused her, although the refusal must cause my downfall, as it did. I was fastidious: her ankles were confused with her leg. I am still fastidious, madam; if in more elementary respects. Besides—

LAETITIA (*unflinching*). Besides, you think me untrue. (*Crosses* L. *to him.*) I am not, La Ruse, and will prove it. Will you visit me tonight? Is't my fault if you force me to play the man in our courtship? I vow you regard me as something seen late at night in a cemetery!

LA RUSE (*horrified*). This afternoon—

LAETITIA (*exasperated*). This afternoon! I tell you 'twas no different from a thousand afternoons: dishes clattered and were still, the hot sun shone, a drowsiness filled the blue air, and I slept—as I always do.

LA RUSE (*vastly surprised*). As you always do? I thought you never slept, madam! For I have noticed this peculiarity about you—your eyes are always open. You should see an oculist—one with a number of lenses; he will fit you with spectacles made for a wealthy tiger who failed to call back for them. The price is exessive, but the relief cosmological.

LAETITIA (*impatiently*). You are like the Prince in the play you will read me so often, though it bores me: words, words, words! Answer me, La Ruse, one way or t'other.

LA RUSE. Why should you desire me to visit you? I am like the Prince again: I have bad dreams.

LAETITIA (*softening*). I would dispel them.

LA RUSE. Yet 'tis whispered by mothers —you are the mother of nightmares.

LAETITIA (*clipping her words*). I grow weary of your reviling me.

LA RUSE. I have ever thought it strange myself that men should derive their refreshment from the weariness of women.

LAETITIA (*in cold rage*). 'Tis too much! La Ruse, you shall learn I can repay far more than I am loaned!

LA RUSE. Rare creditor! I will have you done in oils and present the portrait to my banker.

LAETITIA. Hearken, La Ruse: you have imagined the poet in my arms; he shall be there. The lips you have tasted, he shall taste; the joy you have known, he shall know! I'll not have you sent back to the prison! I'll keep you here, where you shall see only that which you have cried, "I cannot bear!"—myself in the arms of another.

LA RUSE (*struggles fiercely*). It matters not! My spirit is strong to be free.

LAETITIA (*as the clock strikes the hour*). The torment of the night begins for you!

LA RUSE (*ringingly*). You are late, madam, by the clock which strikes in Heaven! The hour of my deliverance is at hand.

LAETITIA (*malefic*). You are white already, La Ruse; you shall be gray with the gray dawn!

LA RUSE (*exorcises her*). Back to your inferno, devil!

LAETITIA (*throws her fan on the table*). 'Tis you return to the inferno—not I! Enough! You have set my course. (*Exits* c. *rapidly.*)

LA RUSE (*breaking*). Set her course! Fore God she'll do as she swears! Laetitia!

CARTWRIGHT (*enters* L. *To* C. *opening*). What new malice have you inflicted on her? And where is she gone?

LA RUSE (*flicks a spot of dust from his coat*). She has taken a fancy to Pluto, and is over the Styx by now.

CARTWRIGHT. Count La Ruse.

LA RUSE. Mr. Cartwright?

CARTWRIGHT. You are a scoundrel.

LA RUSE. Your opinion has had judicial recognition, sir. (*To table.*)

CARTWRIGHT. You have lied—

LA RUSE. Of Laetitia? To lie of Laetitia is as if one were to speak the truth of another—the same affect is achieved.

CARTWRIGHT (*homicidal*). I'll blood you.

LA RUSE (*sits on table. Laughs*). You have sworn never to lay your hands on a human being, except in love. I would advise you not to lay your hands upon me, Mr. Cartwright. I am much the stronger of the two—and I may be armed.

CARTWRIGHT (*quietly, after a pause*). I never thought I should want to kill a man, but had I had my knife—

LA RUSE. Then I am obliged to the gentleman who took your knife.

CARTWRIGHT. And so am I, Count La Ruse.

LA RUSE. Besides, he has a use for it—tonight.

CARTWRIGHT. What would it profit me to throw myself at you? Mr. Wild is wicked; he can be killed. But you are evil, Count La Ruse, and evil must be killed by itself, or it does not die.

LA RUSE. The young rhetorician to the old rhetorician! (*Suddenly grave.*) I know not why, Mr. Cartwright, but you make me speak not what I feel towards you, but the cutting opposite.

CARTWRIGHT. You are envious of me, sir.

LA RUSE (*sadly*). I am envious of you, not because of a woman, as you think, but because I was myself denied any special gift, and have, perhaps, too high a regard for the gifts of others. In my heart, Mr. Cartwright, I would be your friend.

CARTWRIGHT. Friend!

LA RUSE. Yes. 'Tis a sudden weakness of my past, an outbreak of paternity which ill-becomes my smile, I'll allow. I've a son, somewhere; I speak to you now as I would speak to him, were he your age.

CARTWRIGHT. You speak as a discredited rival.

LA RUSE (*loses his temper*). Rival? *You* my rival? With Laetitia? You! Is the pup in her lap my rival? You are still in your high-chair—pray, tighten your bib, the gruel spills on your flannel!

CARTWRIGHT (*laughs*). 'Tis as you said: you speak as a friend, as father to son.

LA RUSE (*checks himself*). I do, sir, but you goad me damnably. I'd not give much for the young man who succumbs to the ordinary hurt of first love, which is a sort of new teething we must all suffer. But you are in danger of a wound far more perverse, and therefore far more delicate! Heal yourself, before the fester penetrates beyond the heart and becomes permanent in the spirit.

CARTWRIGHT. Is not the very spice of

affectation to appear more sincere than sincerity itself?

LA RUSE. Would you hamstring me on my own idle words? I implore you to heed me, lest you learn to your sorrow that there are women in whom the mother has been completely omitted, and that Laetitia is such a woman.

CARTWRIGHT. I have felt the mother in Laetitia comfort me.

LA RUSE. She could bear a kingdom, and never feel a maternal thrill! Take your light elsewhere, or 'twill go out like my own.

CARTWRIGHT. I have found that my light grows in her radiance, La Ruse.

LA RUSE. Mr. Cartwright: we are all of us defenseless when we love a good woman; how much more so when we love the implacable itself! But 'tis no use. A man, young or old, will as soon admit his secret body-odors as that the perfume of all creation is not in his new mistress! (CARTWRIGHT starts.) You started at the word—damme, but you did! Death-in-Hell! You confirm my suspicions! Is't really so?

CARTWRIGHT. I must know, before I reply, how you speak—as friend, as father to son, or—

LA RUSE. I stepped out of character for your sake, but I speak as the Count La Ruse, lover of Laetitia!

CARTWRIGHT. And you speak to the poet Cartwright, lover of Laetitia!

LA RUSE. Whippersnapper!

CARTWRIGHT. Now I am a blackguard, but I feel better. (Taunting him). La Ruse, she loves me, she loves me, she loves me!

LA RUSE. Add she loves me not; that ends the rhyme always. You elephantine gods! where is your ancient nimbleness? Naught's divine, all's clownish, Mr. Cartwright. You do not believe I have been her lover?

CARTWRIGHT. Were I to believe that, I must believe—

LA RUSE. Laetitia has asked me to visit her tonight.

CARTWRIGHT. Your malice undoes you! She—

LA RUSE. Your silence undoes you: she's hinted you may visit her tonight. Well, I'll offer you this challenge for your soul: that Laetitia loves me, that we mirror each other, are bound to each other; that if I knock on her door tonight, she'll admit me! Do you take my challenge?

CARTWRIGHT. Do you think I would stoop to it?

LA RUSE. She'll admit me, I say, and where will you be? You'll be on the landing, outside her door; you'll be there with cold hands and a burning throat when your knock goes unanswered! Do you take my challenge?

CARTWRIGHT. No!

LA RUSE. I warned you once it would profit you more to cut the throat of Mr. Snap than to kiss the throat of his daughter. Well, poet and sweet-singer, tonight I shall do both! Yes, this shall be my final folly! I will risk my chance of freedom to prove a point of vanity.

CARTWRIGHT. Your point of vanity is my whole faith!

LA RUSE. Vanity or faith, there's a fire abroad which only your tears will put out! Do you take my challenge?

CARTWRIGHT. I take nothing, and I give nothing, but I hold fast to what I know.

LA RUSE. You do take my challenge. It must lie between us as men of honor.

CARTWRIGHT. As blackguards.

LA RUSE. Amen.

LAETITIA (enters C). Ah, gentlemen, conversing most amiably, are you?

LA RUSE. Yes, we've been discussing the astronomical position of Venus tonight.

CARTWRIGHT. And of Lucifer.

LAETITIA. Leave him alone in his dark thoughts.

JONATHAN (enters L). La Ruse! La Ruse!

LA RUSE. Well, Mr. Wild, what's on your mind?

JONATHAN. What's on my mind? Don't you know?

LA RUSE. Of course. You've decided?

JONATHAN. I'll take the risk. (MR. SNAP enters L.) Pay the full three hundred pounds. We'll stop in my room later—three hundred pounds. (Crosses to chair L. of table L.C.)

MR. SNAP. What did he say? (Crosses to LA RUSE.)

LA RUSE. He'll pay the full one hundred pounds. (MR. SNAP crosses to chair back of L.C. table.) Whispering, Mr. Cartwright? (Crosses to sofa.) I don't like whispering.

CARTWRIGHT. Then I'll whisper the whole night through.

LA RUSE. Better go to sleep in your narrow bed.

MR. SNAP. Well, gentlemen—(*Crossing a little to* R.) An amiable round of cards? (JONATHAN *sits chair* L. *of card table.*) Will you join us—(JONATHAN *takes cards.*) Mr. Cartwright?

CARTWRIGHT. Thank you. I don't play.

MR. SNAP (*sits* R. *of card table*). Incredible, La Ruse—he doesn't play.

LAETITIA. My fan—I'm sure I left it on the table before—(CARTWRIGHT *crosses to above card table.*)

LA RUSE. I'll visit you tonight, wench. (*Crossing to card table—sits* R.) Really, Mr. Cartwright, you should have some amusement, and cards are your only chance.

CARTWRIGHT. I might be tricked by the knave in the pack.

MR. SNAP. Oh, come, sir, we are all honest. That was a bad card you threw, La Ruse. I'll wager you hold a bad hand.

LA RUSE. Yes, but I've a wager I hold a better hand before the night is over.

CARTWRIGHT. The cards may not fall as you think, La Ruse. (CARTWRIGHT *crosses up* C. LA RUSE *looks at* LAETITIA, *who is singing lightly.*)

CURTAIN

ACT THREE

SCENE: *The same, next morning.*

MR. SNAP *enters* L. *with* LORD WAINWRIGHT, *a nobleman whose face is a chronic deadly white. His teeth are his most prominent feature; they protrude over his lip. His eyes are his least prominent feature; they are of that peculiar gray which seems to diffuse itself, the better to see. In his bearing, he has the genuine distinction of his class; and his speech is tinged with a hesitancy which is contradicted by the decisiveness of his thoughts.*

MR. SNAP (*cheerily*). Sit down, my lord, sit down! (*Dusting sofa.*) You will stand? As you please. Is't not a fine morning, Lord Wainwright? I had my walk this morning. I wouldn't miss my walk on such a morning, my lord.

LORD WAINWRIGHT. I find myself totally uninterested in your pedestrian habits. (*Feels in his pockets.*) Damn me, if some rascal in the jail hasn't relieved me of my snuffbox! Plague on him! The box was a masterpiece. I shall miss it.

MR. SNAP. 'Tis a pity, your lordship. You are well out of the jail, I'll warrant you. I marked you out of the mob at once —I saw at once you were a gentleman.

LORD WAINWRIGHT (*impatiently*). It is just as obvious that I am a gentleman as that you are not.

MR. SNAP. Your lordship!

LORD WAINWRIGHT. I must insist you abandon the cant of your kind, Mr. Snap. I have had enough of the cant of my own kind, since the day my mother told me a lying story of a stork and a chimney. (*Crosses down* L.) I am here because I finally took extreme measures to stop the flow of unmeaning talk around me. If you will not affect social compliments, but level your conversation to the mean quality of your nature, as 'tis apparent, you will find we will get along a great deal better. (*To fireplace.*) I trust I have made myself plain.

MR. SNAP. Plain, my lord? Plain, did you say? I confess, I do not understand you.

LORD WAINWRIGHT. You found me in the jail; you offered me the privilege of being locked up in your home, instead.

MR. SNAP. Yes, I could not have offered you lodging yesterday, but fortunately Mr. Wild (*coughs.*) vacates his room today.

LORD WAINWRIGHT. As your house could not possibly stink worse than the jail, I accepted your suggestion. Now, sir, what will you gouge me?

MR. SNAP. Gouge you, my lord! Did you say gouge you? You will find, Lord Wainwright, I am not avaricious.

LORD WAINWRIGHT. I see every evidence of avarice in your person. You brought me here to be well paid for your trouble.

MR. SNAP (*smarting*). And why not, my lord? Is't wrong I should be well paid for breaking the law? For chancing my official position? Is't wrong, my lord?

LORD WAINWRIGHT. 'Tis confoundedly right. Why do you not talk thus always? You would find me more amicable. I am well provided with money, Mr. Snap.

MR. SNAP (*a little overcome by his honesty*). My lord!

LORD WAINWRIGHT. What privilege will my money buy for me?

MR. SNAP. For a reasonable sum you may buy the entire privacy of this floor.

LORD WAINWRIGHT. The sum will not be reasonable, and the floor will not be private, but I will buy it. The furnishings here are in the worst of taste; pray, is my bedroom of the same order?

MR. SNAP. 'Tis an exquisite room, your lordship. I furnished it myself, and I am —whatever rogues may say—a man of taste.

LORD WAINWRIGHT. I suspect our tastes differ. I am exceedingly fond of small objects, carved precisely—knickknacks on which the eye may rest with pleasure. There is a want of them in this room, for instance.

MR. SNAP. My lord, we dare not leave them about. We have lodgers here not to be trusted. I should warn you against Mr. Wild, but he leaves (coughs.) this morning. Beware, however, of a scamp calling himself Count La Ruse. As for your knickknacks, sir, chance has put one or two in my way; I hope to interest you in them.

LORD WAINWRIGHT. I'll have a look at them. I'll try to make myself as comfortable as possible until my trial.

MR. SNAP. Pray, my lord, may I inquire for what you are held?

LORD WAINWRIGHT. I thought I heard you inquire of the clerk in the prison?

MR. SNAP. I did, my lord, but I failed to catch his reply.

LORD WAINWRIGHT (indifferently). I poisoned my wife—and a few of her intimate friends.

MR. SNAP (covers the shock with a silly laugh). Dear me! Why did you do that?

LORD WAINWRIGHT. A gentleman does not discuss his family affairs with a vulgar stranger.

MR. SNAP (not quite recovered). Gentleman! 'Tis true—you seem such a gentleman.

LORD WAINWRIGHT. I am a lord, Mr. Snap, and would have you know that all the eminent poisoners were of good family; 'twas a symptom of their subtle breeding. You will do me the justice of not derogating my rank because I rid the world of a few useless people; a fact which, in any competent civilization, would indubitably raise my rank.

MR. SNAP. As for that, my lord, a lord is a lord to me, no matter what he's done. I hope I know the deference due to a man like yourself.

LA RUSE (enters C. and stops short at sight of LORD WAINWRIGHT). Lord Wainwright!

LORD WAINWRIGHT. I am equally astonished. Why, 'tis—

LA RUSE (quickly). Count La Ruse. I have long forgotten I had any other name, and must beg your lordship the favor of forgetting with me.

LORD WAINWRIGHT. Count La Ruse. (Turns to MR. SNAP; in a peculiar tone.) So this is your Count La Ruse! We are old acquaintances—are we not, Count?

MR. SNAP. A happy coincidence! You gentlemen will have the past to discuss. I'll go down below and see if there's a trace of some callers I'm expecting. (Winks at LA RUSE.) Callers for Mr. Wild. (He exits R.)

LORD WAINWRIGHT. Pray, would you loan me your snuff, Count? My box was filched from me in the jail.

LA RUSE. And mine here. I'm starved for the powder. (Crosses to C.) Take heed you leave nothing of value where Mr. Snap can reach it. He's as unprincipled as a fox on the run.

LORD WAINWRIGHT (permits himself a smile). I am obliged for the warning. Mr. Snap has been so good as to tender me a similar warning against yourself. I find myself amused.

LA RUSE (unabashed). I have been derelict in asking—how is your dear lady?

LORD WAINWRIGHT (without emotion). Dead.

LA RUSE (shaken). Dead!

LORD WAINWRIGHT. Quite dead. In fact, will never rise again. Did you think her ladyship would live forever? The expression of your face leads me to think you did.

LA RUSE. The news was unexpected. I remember her ladyship as an example of your fine English beauty, in which health is so much of the beauty. 'Tis hard to think of her dead. I tender you my deepest sympathy, Lord Wainwright.

LORD WAINWRIGHT (passively). Your sympathy is wasted—her ladyship's passing is a blessing, to me.

LA RUSE. I cannot believe you; there were not many like Lady Wainwright. With all respect, I was attached to her.

LORD WAINWRIGHT. You should be consoled by the knowledge, my dear Marquis, she was much attached to you.

LA RUSE. Yes, she did her best to save me from my many follies. May she rest in peace; she was a wise and charming lady.

LORD WAINWRIGHT. To her lovers. At home she was a bitch.

LA RUSE (*flares*). You make too free with your lady's memory!

LORD WAINWRIGHT. On my word, for a mere acquaintance, you are most concerned for my wife's good name! Is't possible you were more than a mere acquaintance of Lady Wainwright?

LA RUSE. I have not been unaware of your insinuations, sir; to answer them would be to dignify them. I have still some of the instincts of my breeding. (*Down to chair* R.C.)

LORD WAINWRIGHT. Cant! We have all the same instincts. Answer what you will, without cant.

LA RUSE. I will say this: you have a son, and when you degrade his mother, you degrade your heir. Sir, the passing of her ladyship may have been a blessing to you, but what a loss it must be to the boy! Do you not think of that? I glimpsed him in the park, not so many years ago: a golden-haired, rollicking boy.

LORD WAINWRIGHT. He will rollick no more.

LA RUSE (*after a pause*). He is dead, also.

LORD WAINWRIGHT. Of the same distemper which removed his mother. (LA RUSE *sits chair* R.C.) By my honor, my dear Count—you have believed my family immortal. A boy dies, and there's such an expression on your face—

LA RUSE. And you—have you no regret for your son's passing?

LORD WAINWRIGHT. None at all. I never believed him to be my son.

LA RUSE. Not your son! But you brought him up.

LORD WAINWRIGHT. I played the father for a while, but the jest wearied me. It became intolerable a bastard should inherit my name and acres. The boy did not resemble me, not in the slighest.

LA RUSE. It scarcely becomes a man to slander his dead wife and her child.

LORD WAINWRIGHT. 'Tis exquisitely fitting I should meet you here and break the news; for a thought had often occurred to me; the boy was altogether of your type; had your head, eyes, mouth, gait, and insufferable habit of talk, talk, talk.

LA RUSE. You knew—(*Rises; crosses to him.*) all the while—You knew—Why are you held, Lord Wainwright? You spoke of a distemper; what was this distemper?

LORD WAINWRIGHT (*brutally*). Arsenic.

LA RUSE. You—O monster!

LORD WAINWRIGHT. And now the jest wearies you. I made little effort to conceal what I had done; to do so would have meant so much more of cant—hypocritical heavings of the breast, streaming tears, and lying eulogies. The funerals delighted me, and I let it be known. (*Crosses* L.)

LA RUSE. You are mad—stark mad, I perceive!

LORD WAINWRIGHT. So my lawyers say, but 'tis they who are mad, or they would not be lawyers. Pray, do me the favor of not intruding overmuch on my privacy here. I've a dislike for your company—always had, but at length can tell you so. (*During speech goes down round table to chair above table.*)

LA RUSE (*mechanically*). I leave this house forever this morning.

LORD WAINWRIGHT. One offense removed from my sight without my going to extremes. (*To fireplace.*)

MR. SNAP (*comes in from the hall* R). What a day! What a day! Life's up and coming gentlemen! You should see the gallants: they're winning the ladies everywhere, with insults; and the children, the happy children, are rollicking in the streets! What a day!

LA RUSE (*stabbed*). Rollicking!

MR. SNAP. I see you've been affected by your recollections with his lordship. There's nothing so pleasant as talking of old times. But you must accompany me now, La Ruse; the crowd gathers below already, and we must discuss, when Mr. Wild discovers—Pray, make yourself at your ease, my lord. (LAETITIA *has entered* C.)

LORD WAINWRIGHT. A wench! A pretty wench!

MR. SNAP. 'Tis my daughter, Laetitia. Daughter, this is Lord Wainwright, a new lodger in the house. His lordship's a real lord, and not one of your nobles born in a deck of cards and glass of whisky.

LAETITIA (*ingratiatingly*). 'Tis most pleasant to have you in the house, my lord. Good morning, La Ruse.

MR. SNAP (*to* LA RUSE). Let us go. The moment arrives, and we've no plan—(*To door* R.)

LAETITIA (*piqued by* LA RUSE'S *silence*). Do you set a new fashion, sir? Do you not say good morning? (*He makes a slight response.*) I vow, if 'tis a good morning, you should admit the fact more graciously, I think.

MR. SNAP. By chance, Laetitia, Lord Wainwright's a great friend of Count La Ruse. (WAINWRIGHT *puts his hands over his ears and walks away.*)

LAETITIA (*gets a fuller view of* LA RUSE). Why what ails you? You seem ill?

LA RUSE (*musters up a little of his usual manner*). Ill, madam? Ill? I am well enough.

LAETITIA. Will you have a glass of spirits?

LA RUSE (*resenting her sympathy*). Thank you. There's no necessity.

MR. SNAP (*has been waiting; irritably*). But there's necessity for haste for both of us, sir! (*At door* R.) Are you rooted in the floor?

LAETITIA. Stay, Papa. I must know—what have you done further with Mr. Cartwright?

MR. SNAP. Further? Did you say further? The young rascal is locked in his room, and 'tis likely still feels the butt of my pistol on his face. In truth, I hope he does.

LAETITIA. 'Tis likely he meant less harm than we thought, Papa. I've forgiven him, this bright morning. I'm sure he's had nought to eat nor drink.

MR. SNAP. 'Twas you cried most: "Whip him! Scourge him! Lock him in his room! Send him back to the jail!"

LAETITIA. The early hour—the noise—the fighting—I was frightened. Since 'twas Love made him act thus, I owe him the duty of kindness.

LA RUSE (*strangely*). He may kill you.

LAETITIA. He's a boy, and easily handled.

MR. SNAP (*peremptorily*). La Ruse! (*Opens* R. *door.*) You've wasted enough time. We must look to Mr. Wild, sir! (WAINWRIGHT *crosses down to chair* L. *of* L.C. *table.* LA RUSE *goes out before him like a blind man who knows the way.* MR. SNAP *whispers to* LAETITIA, *indicating* WAINWRIGHT.) A poisoner! (*Exits* R.)

LAETITIA (*a spring released by the words*). Lord Wainwright! Pray, why is one of your station in such a place as this? (*Bows.*)

LORD WAINWRIGHT. Cant! Your father's whisper had all the discretion of a thunderclap. (*Sits* L. *of table.*) Do you find me repulsive, now?

LAETITIA. 'Twould be presumptuous indeed for me to find one of your station repulsive, my lord. (*Bows.*)

LORD WAINWRIGHT. We have our ugly faces.

LAETITIA. No; far from finding you repulsive, (*crosses to* R. *of table*) I'll confess that for me there's a titillating distinction in the thought you have poisoned people. I am no ordinary woman, my lord; I've lived so long in the atmosphere of a jail that I've come to measure my respect for men by the quality of their misdeeds, and yours would seem to belong in the very aristocracy of crime. Perhaps some day you will excite my ears with the history of your exploits. I should be ravished to hear them.

LORD WAINWRIGHT (*displeased*). For a wench you have a loathsome flow of words.

LAETITIA. I have listened much to the conversation of your friend, Count La Ruse.

LORD WAINWRIGHT. I might have guessed.

LAETITIA. Is he not your friend?

LORD WAINWRIGHT. Certainly not.

LAETITIA. But Papa said—(*Away a little* R.)

LORD WAINWRIGHT. Your father is a knave and a fool.

LAETITIA. You are plain-spoken.

LORD WAINWRIGHT. You will find me increasingly so, wench.

LAETITIA. For myself, I greatly admire Count La Ruse.

LORD WAINWRIGHT. I greatly despise him. A word-monger. I have had the courage to use a vial, and not a phrase.

LAETITIA. He has killed men and done worse with women—Papa has told me.

LORD WAINWRIGHT. He has had his moments—has aspired to be what I am; but there was a flaw in him he could not overcome: a belief in words—in cant! The world knows him as a villain. I know him as a sentimentalist.

LAETITIA. I thought all men were sentimentalists. (*Crosses to chair* R. *of table.*)

LORD WAINWRIGHT. All men but myself. I fight naked. (*Over table.*)

LAETITIA. You are a man with a mind of your own. (*Away* R.) And perhaps will find me a woman with a mind of her own.

LORD WAINWRIGHT. A plague on your mind! Do you think me interested in a woman's mind? I am not twenty, wench.

LAETITIA. Your lordship has called me so a number of times; my name is Laetitia, Mistress Laetitia.

LORD WAINWRIGHT. Your name is Laetitia, and you are still a wench.

LAETITIA. It pleases your lordship to affect an uncouthness which the refinement of your thought denies. (*Bows*.)

LORD WAINWRIGHT. Cant! Nothing but cant! I foresee I must undo the harm La Ruse has done you before I find your presence bearable.

LAETITIA. Your lordship flatters me with your courteous interest.

LORD WAINWRIGHT. My interest is always in myself. (*Casually*.) I propose to enjoy your favors, wench.

LAETITIA (*left breathless*). My Lord! (*Away a little*.)

LORD WAINWRIGHT. Pray, spare me the cant of a lying outburst of your virtue. I can see in your eyes—

LAETITIA (*his gaze forces hers to drop*). Did I ask you to look there, my lord—but not my master?

LORD WAINWRIGHT. It must be as patent to yourself as 'tis to me; you have been placed here for my convenience.

LAETITIA. And you think a woman like myself is to be won thus—(*Crosses to table; sits* R. *of it*.) by being told she is to be a convenience?

LORD WAINWRIGHT. What do you wish of me? Repartee? Shall I speak like the world, of your eyes and the blue skies; your cheeks and the red rose—when all the while, like the world, I am thinking of a bed? I tell you, wench, I would live a celibate all of my days before a word of such cant should pass my lips to a woman.

LAETITIA. Your words have sealed your celibacy here involate, my lord—but not my master!

LORD WAINWRIGHT. I suppose you have some entanglement of a low order with one of the wardens of the prison, or stableboys there.

LAETITIA. Stableboy!

LORD WAINWRIGHT. No? Ah! You greatly admire Count La Ruse. 'Tis he, without a doubt. I'm lucky. He's told me he leaves the house this morning, not to return.

LAETITIA. A favorite notion of La Ruse's—without substance, my lord—but not my master.

LORD WAINWRIGHT. Then we will buy him off. He's threadbare, and will welcome the money.

LAETITIA (*her fingers drumming on the table*). Is this the sum of your courtship?

LORD WAINWRIGHT. No. For yourself —(*Over table*.) I promise you shall have more money than you have ever had.

LAETITIA (*slaps his face*). Filthy beast!

LORD WAINWRIGHT (*wipes his face thoroughly*). I thought you a woman of sense.

LAETITIA. Of too much sense—to sell what can never be bought back.

LORD WAINWRIGHT. Cant! You have nothing to sell of the nature. Where is your room? (*Rises*.) I'll visit you this very night.

LAETITIA (*rising. Passionately*). On the first floor of the moon! Seek it there. You'll not come closer, Lord Wainwright!

LORD WAINWRIGHT. Where is your room, wench? You'll not say? Then I must bribe your father to give me ingress.

LAETITIA. I promise—nay, I swear—if ever you so much as gain ingress over my threshold, I'll recant all I have said; I'll own you for my lord and master.

LORD WAINWRIGHT. A dangerous promise, wench.

LAETITIA. A safe promise. What your crimes could not do, your manners have done. I find you repulsive. I hate you! I hate you!

LORD WAINWRIGHT (*smiles*). Then I have accomplished the beginning of my end. Pray, don't run because of me. I'm content for the moment and will seek my own room. Perhaps you'll tell me where it lies, wench? (*To door* L.)

LAETITIA. I am not your servant.

LORD WAINWRIGHT. You shall be more. (*Flings door open* L.) Adieu, from you lord—and master. (*He exits* L.)

LAETITIA (*her fists clenched*). Turk! Mohammedan! (*Crosses up; sits sofa.* CARTWRIGHT *comes in* L. *There is a large bruise on his forehead, and in his eyes the look of a man who has seen things clear, too suddenly, and is a little strange as a result. He stops short at sight of* LAETITIA, *then bows with exaggerated deference*.)

CARTWRIGHT (*with a peculiar purring softness*). Good morning, Mistress Laetitia. (*To chair* R. *of table*.)

LAETITIA. You! And now you must plague me! It has not been enough—

CARTWRIGHT. It makes me most happy to see you (*crosses to her a little*.), dear lady, charming as always. I trust you slept well?

LAETITIA. Impudence! If I did not sleep well 'twas because of your infant outburst.

CARTWRIGHT (*smoothly*). I greatly regret having incommoded you, Mistress Laetitia. (LAETITIA *rises. Crosses to chair* R.C.) Is it not a delicious day? (*Down a little.*) May I hope, presently, to have your hand in the dance? I've been told your minuet is as irreproachable as my own.

LAETITIA. Pray, what is this nonsense you babble? I am not in a mood for it, I warn you.

CARTWRIGHT. 'Tis not nonsense, but an event of world-shaking importance. I have become a very descreet gentleman; my manners now are exquisite.

LAETITIA. Cant! (*Amazed at her use of the word, and put further out of temper by it.*) And now you have the audacity to make game of me. I'll speak with you, Mr. Cartwright, when you've apologized for your behavior. (*Crosses to* C. CARTWRIGHT *stops her.*)

CARTWRIGHT. I do not make game of you, madam. We play a game together. Pray, would you leave me when the game's just begun?

LAETITIA (*back a little*). You're inexcusably young. I'll humor you. (*Sits sofa.*)

CARTWRIGHT (*to sofa*). The game's called cat-and-mouse; and as you played cat before, you must play mouse now—as is only fair, you'll be the first to admit.

LAETITIA. You played cat enough last night—clawing La Ruse as you did! You—you who swore—"I will do, always, whatever you ask me!"

CARTWRIGHT. And so I will, dear lady. (*Crosses to* L.)

LAETITIA. Pray, were you demented? What was your reason—nay, where was your reason? Falling on La Ruse at three o'clock in the morning—

CARTWRIGHT (*punctilious*). At three-seventeen.

LAETITIA. Falling on him in the hall—

CARTWRIGHT (*more intensely*). As he left your room—

LAETITIA. Causing a hullabaloo—bringing Papa out with a whip and pistol—(*Rises; crosses* L.) When you knocked, I persuaded you to return to your room. Why did you leave it again?

CARTWRIGHT. I did not leave my room. My room left me. (LAETITIA *over* L. *a little.*) Pray, madam, have you ever had the floor drop from under you? The sensation is unique.

LAETITIA. Your talk was always bizarre, but I vow 'tis now altogether lackin in sense, Mr. Cartwright.

CARTWRIGHT. 'Tis sense that your father believes I would have ravished you but for the heroic interference of Count La Ruse. Yes, 'tis sense, but is't not also most bizarre? (*Sits sofa.*)

LAETITIA. Do you think I'm unaware how hard it must be to forgive me for that lie? (*Crosses to sofa and sits.*) But what else could I do?

CARTWRIGHT (*with sudden plaintiveness*). But you cried, "Whip him! Scourge him!" Why did you want me beaten harder than I was beaten?

LAETITIA. I was fearful lest you should cry out—what you knew. Shame and grief consume me—Why should you listen to me now—though I speak the truth at last?

CARTWRIGHT (*impulsively*). Tell me only this: when we were alone together, and I felt your softness—was it true then?

LAETITIA. I'll not deceive you; 'twas partly true. Pray, do not despise me too much. Why should you believe that La Ruse forced his way into my room—That he was never my lover before, and will never be again? Even now, when I speak the truth at last, you are right to put no faith in me.

CARTWRIGHT. I should not have looked into your eyes—

LAETITIA. Have you forgotten so soon —(CARTWRIGHT *rises.*) drawn shades, and open lips? Were you to lie in my arms now, my softness should all be true, and lasting, and still.

CARTWRIGHT. Hearts loud, and life still. (*Bends over her proffered mouth, and bursts into laughter.*) Cat-and-mouse! Who's cat now? Who's mouse? (*Away to down* R.)

LAETITIA (*stupefied*). You'll not kiss me?

CARTWRIGHT. Kiss you! In broad daylight? We might be seen, madam.

LAETITIA. This is witchcraft—(*Rises.*) You speak no longer like yourself, but like La Ruse.

CARTWRIGHT (*cunningly*). Because I'm

no longer a cat. 'Tis said there are no more wolves in England, but most ignorantly, madam; there are no more men; we are all wolves.

LAETITIA. Your eyes burn me, I vow, like a wild animal's! Pray, recollect—I'm a female—your gentility—

CARTWRIGHT. Do you but let down your hair, dear lady, and you'll see me eat it, ravenously.

LAETITIA (*forced to settee*). I'll call for help—(*Crosses to door* R.)

CARTWRIGHT (*laughs. Crosses to her* R. *Pushes her toward sofa*). You will only call in more wolves. (*Prosaically.*) 'Tis strange, dear lady, how lovely you are. I've seen all beasts, clear or striped, but you are the most beautiful beast I have ever seen.

LAETITIA (*has the courage of one at bay*). You'll be whipped for these insults!

CARTWRIGHT (*with melancholy wonder*). Why should your eyes seem different from other eyes? You are loved madly, madam.

LAETITIA. Aye, madly! Think of what you do, Mr. Cartwright—you'll regret later—

CARTWRIGHT. You have brought love to my heart, tears to my eyes, and a great rage to my brain. Where's peace, now? What death must I live—and you die?

LAETITIA. No more—let me pass at once—at once—(LAETITIA *tries to escape.*)

CARTWRIGHT (*pushes her on sofa*). I will do, always, whatever you ask me. (*Strokes her hair.*) Shall I twist this around your throat, tightly—in the charming Italian fashion? I will do, always, whatever you ask me. Will you ask me to whip you, scourge you? Pray, ask me to kill you, madam. I will do, always, whatever you ask me. (*The terrified* LAETITIA *sees* LA RUSE *enter* R.)

LAETITIA (*imploringly*). La Ruse! La Ruse! (CARTWRIGHT *crosses; sits chair* L. *of table* L.C.)

LA RUSE (*hastens*). What's this?

CARTWRIGHT (*turns*). La Ruse?

LAETITIA (*runs by him*). He would have killed me!

CARTWRIGHT (*laughs*). Saved again, by your nocturnal hero!

LAETITIA. He would have killed me!

LA RUSE. Alas! I am punctual only when 'twould have been better never to have arrived.

LAETITIA. I'll have him flayed alive.

LA RUSE. Do you not see, the boy's in travail? (*Takes her hand.*) Hearken to me, madam. You'll not say a word; the boy has suffered enough.

LAETITIA (*in utter caprice, smiles at the poet*). Of course I'll not say a word! Do you know, Mr. Cartwright, I begin to like you. I begin to like you very much, since feeling your violent hand.

LA RUSE. You hear this woman, Mr. Cartwright? Why did you let me distract you? (MR. SNAP *enters* R.)

LAETITIA (*quickly*). No more, now.

MR. SNAP (*jubilant*). 'Tis done, La Ruse! 'Tis well done! 'Tis all prepared, sir!

LAETITIA. What's all prepared, Papa? The money you've promised me for my new bonnet? (*Down* C. *a little.*)

MR. SNAP. She'll have her money; won't she, La Ruse?

LA RUSE. The bailiffs have come for Mr. Wild. He hangs directly. (*Sits sofa.*)

MR. SNAP (*a little over to sofa*). He's left you a legacy, daughter: your new bonnet, and a kerchief or two for myself as well. The payment's over and done with already. (*To* LA RUSE—*then crosses down* R.) They'll seize him as he comes down the hall. (WILD *comes in* L. *The appalled* SNAP *darts behind* LA RUSE'S *back.*)

JONATHAN (*is in a state of perspiring agitation*). Mr. Snap! Mr. Snap! Where's Mr. Snap? (*Crosses* R.)

MR. SNAP (*emerges haltingly*). Your servant, Mr. Wild. What can I do for you? Pray, command me.

JONATHAN. I've been talking with Lord Wainwright—says you said I'm to vacate my room at once—I'm pardoned, am I not? The money's passed and I'm pardoned?

MR. SNAP (*obeys* LA RUSE'S *nod*). Aye, you're pardoned, Mr. Wild.

JONATHAN (*gasps*). Why didn't you tell me?

MR. SNAP. The pardon's but here—I was on the point of rushing to your room—

JONATHAN. Is't a complete pardon?

MR. SNAP. Aye, a complete pardon.

JONATHAN. O, God! They're not going to hang me—they're not going to hang me. They're not going to hang me!

MR. SNAP. Let us adjourn to my office. (CARTWRIGHT *rises; goes upstage.*) Some few minor details of the pardon still must be settled between us.

JONATHAN. Details, sir? Details in your mouth mean money. If 'tis more money you want, you'll not have it—I've paid all that I will pay, and more. (*Crosses to* MR. SNAP.)

MR. SNAP. 'Tis not money, sir. But in a case like your own, there's this and that must be settled before all's concluded according to the law's niceties—

LORD WAINWRIGHT (*enters* L., *carrying fan. Speaks as* MR. SNAP *speaks*). This is not a prison but a bazaar of the arts. I've a gift for you, wench. (*Crosses to her; shows the fan.* WILD *and* MR. SNAP *depart* R.)

LAETITIA (*snatches the fan*). My fan! I missed it last night!

LORD WAINWRIGHT. Mr. Wild sold me the fan for his wife's. I find myself amused! (*Crosses* L. *A horrible cry is heard in the hall* R.—*the cry of a beast who has stumbled into a trap.* MR. SNAP *runs in.*)

MR. SNAP. Lord, he's a bulky fellow, and tussles arrantly! (*The sound of the fight passes from the hall to the adjoining room.*) They don't dare use their pistols on him; he'd rather be shot than hanged.

JONATHAN (*straining against the two bailiffs who hold him, is seen at the* R. *door, where they get him in hand. Wildly*). Gulled! Gulled! Villains! Assassins! Curse you! Curse you! My money! My money! My life! My life!

MR. SNAP (*merrily*). Taste! Did you say I'd no taste, sir? You'll get your walk in the air today, sir!

JONATHAN (*half fainting, as he is led away*). O, God! They're going to hang me—someone stop them—someone help me—O, God! Someone help me. (LAETITIA *exits* C.)

MR. SNAP. Aye, help him for the rogue of rogues! I must attend him to the gallows; 'tis not the hardest duty I've done. (*Exits* R.)

CARTWRIGHT. Wild is an odious man, but I pity him.

LORD WAINWRIGHT. Pray, who is this warmhearted young man? Must I endure his charitable impulses, with all the rest?

LA RUSE. Mr. Cartwright, a poet. Lord Wainwright, a poisoner.

LORD WAINWRIGHT. I detest poets.

CARTWRIGHT. And I detest poisoners. (*Crosses to window and watches. The catcalls of a crowd below rise thickly.*)

LORD WAINWRIGHT. Interminable cant! Well, I've one comfort; I've a snuffbox again. (*Takes a pinch.*)

LA RUSE (*tries to see the box*). A snuffbox again! Pray, my lord, I'm dying for a pinch. (*Crosses to* WAINWRIGHT L. WAINWRIGHT *hands him the box.*) My snuffbox!

LORD WAINWRIGHT. Yours! Am I swindled again?

LA RUSE. Yes. Who sold you the article? Mr. Snap?

LORD WAINWRIGHT. Mr. Wild! You must prove this, sir, for you're as great a thief as the others.

LA RUSE (*traces the lines*). My monogram. You must look close—'tis hidden in the design.

LORD WAINWRIGHT. Cunningly. I never noticed. This fails to amuse me.

CARTWRIGHT (*as another shower of catcalls rises*). He's in the cart now, and the cart starts—

LA RUSE. Godspeed! (*Crosses* L.)

CARTWRIGHT. The mob follows—

LA RUSE. 'Tis a pity they do not follow Wild as far as he goes! I'll paraphrase one of your potentates, sir: "O that the world had but one neck, that I might hang it!"

LORD WAINWRIGHT (*glares at* LA RUSE). One must envy Mr. Wild: he'll soon be stone-deaf! (*Exits* L.)

CARTWRIGHT. Count La Ruse. (*Down to* C.)

LA RUSE. Mr. Cartwright?

CARTWRIGHT. I owe you an apology, sir.

LA RUSE (*surprised*). For what, pray?

CARTWRIGHT. For attacking you.

LA RUSE. You were belabored enough for that.

CARTWRIGHT. And for my behavior in general.

LA RUSE. We must all apologize for that.

CARTWRIGHT. You are generous.

LA RUSE. I am sad—sad at the thought that you must remain here while I have at last found a way to freedom: I leave this morning. Have you no possible means of imitating me soon?

CARTWRIGHT (*looks into the sky*). Can I fly on the wings of those white birds?

LA RUSE. White birds! Do they fly again? Then you are safe. I have discovered they are the true omens of hope.

CARTWRIGHT (*cries out*). Their talons tear me.

LA RUSE. You are torn by your own talons. My friend, my son—more than you guess, my son now—you must not give way. No matter how often we are born, it is always in pain. You have become a man, and must prepare to act as a man.

CARTWRIGHT (*passionately*). Act as a man! I know what you mean, and my heart tells me 'tis a lie. Because I must lean a little awry, be a little dirty, I am a man! Do you think because a woman has smiled or not smiled I'll throw acid on the world? Have I been burned terribly? I'll thrust my hand deeper into the flame.

LA RUSE. I rejoice, for I perceive in you a strength which I lacked.

CARTWRIGHT (*with sudden gloom*). My strength will die, for here the flame is infernal. To be held here—

LA RUSE. Ah, here! Yes—(*Sits on table.*)

CARTWRIGHT. There's a witch in this house; she's sworn to teach me the joy of yellow-tinged things. (*Crosses down* R.)

LA RUSE. You must not permit—

CARTWRIGHT. The inevitable! Do you think, because I am a poet, I am less than a man?

LA RUSE. I think, because you are a poet, you should be more than a man.

CARTWRIGHT. Time and loneliness will make me less—here. I'll shut myself in my room. I'll work. And always I'll hear light feet passing in the hall.

LA RUSE (*excitedly*). I forbid you to hear them.

CARTWRIGHT. I'll hear them, always. One day, or one night, I'll fling my pen aside—I'll run, I'll throw myself into her open arms—

LA RUSE (*anguished*). They'll not release you until you've taken her very mold! You are right: the rest is too awful. 'Tis rankly unfair. Could I but do something for you—

CARTWRIGHT. I am lost for two hundred pounds.

LA RUSE (*starts*). Two hundred pounds! I'll—(*Lays his hands on his pocket and removes it angrily. Down a little.*) Why the devil do you tell me your woes? Because a life is ruined, a talent despoiled, shall I be troubled? Take your own medicine, sir; what's your sickness to do with me? I am well again! Pray, take yourself where I won't pity you for the brief moments I remain: I despise myself for my pity. (*Crosses to* L.)

CARTWRIGHT (*mildly*). I'll trouble you no further. You have tried to be my friend in a friendless place. Will I see you again?

LA RUSE. I'll make it a point. But stay —Yes, I can do something for you. I've a little token of hope you shall have of me now. (*Hands* CARTWRIGHT *his knife.*)

CARTWRIGHT. The knife!

LA RUSE. 'Tis the most I can do for you.

CARTWRIGHT. You have given me a brave testimonial of friendship, and I shall thank you—by using it bravely.

LA RUSE. But not rashly. If the moment comes—when you fling your pen aside— I would have you strike clean. 'Twould be the last honor you could pay to life.

CARTWRIGHT. I will aim for my heart.

LA RUSE. The thought pierces my own, but you will do well. (*The clock strikes the hour.* CARTWRIGHT *puts knife in pocket.*) And now, I must look to my luggage.

CARTWRIGHT. I'll await your call in my room. (*Goes out* L. LA RUSE, *with an effort, puts him from mind; is attracted to the window.*)

LA RUSE (*tenderly*). White birds! I shall fly with you after all.

LAETITIA (*enters* C.). La Ruse. (*Crosses* L.)

LA RUSE. Madam? (*Crosses* L.)

LAETITIA. You've been most ungallant this morning. You'd scarcely greet me, when you should have thanked me.

LA RUSE (*raising his eyebrows*). Thanked you?

LAETITIA. For last night. Of late you have grown obtuse, my lover.

LA RUSE. Of late I have grown wise, madam.

LAETITIA. If weariness is wisdom.

LA RUSE. It may well be.

LAETITIA (*to above table*). I promised you should hear my secret this morning, La Ruse.

LA RUSE (*enjoying himself to the full*). You may keep it forever now. Your business is no longer my business. You'll not scoff when you hear my secret: I've money to pay my debt. You still scoff? Madam, can you count beyond your fingers? (*Shows her the money.*)

LAETITIA (*thunderstruck*). How did you get this money?

LA RUSE. 'Twas like your new bonnet: an unwitting legacy from the lamented Great Jonathan. Two hundred pounds for my debt and fifty for a nest egg. When your father hears this he'll double up with a bellyache, but he can do naught. I have the honor, Mistress Snap, to bid you an eternal farewell.

LAETITIA (*bites her lips*). You can't leave, La Ruse! You must first hear what I say.

LA RUSE. I have given thought to your remarkable words of yesterday, and have guessed your secret, madam. (*They look at each other. She sees that he has.*)

LAETITIA (*sits R. of table*). Have you no feeling? Would you desert me—

LA RUSE. Your secret will speed me on my way.

LAETITIA (*flares*). Not when Papa knows—

LA RUSE. I am down on the books for debt, madam. When that debt is paid, I'll laugh at your papa for the father of a strumpet. I am free of you until the North Star turns south for warmth.

LAETITIA. Cant!

LA RUSE (*struck by this*). Cant! Did you say cant? The monster Wainwright has made an impression. I foresee my successor.

LAETITIA (*shivers*). No, never that horrible man! He terrifies me, La Ruse. I have never met such a man.

LA RUSE. Have you at last met a man who terrifies you? I may yet be revenged.

LAETITIA. Do not say that! The cold passion of that man has made me feel, for the first time in my life, as if I need a protector. I beseech you, La Ruse, do not depart now.

LA RUSE. I am not in a mood—to stay. Good-by, Laetitia.

LAETITIA (*rises*). Go, then! Do you think I'll not be consoled for your loss? There are means at hand—

LA RUSE. Lord Wainwright?

LAETITIA. Do not name him! But the poet—

LA RUSE. He terrified you, also.

LAETITIA. Only for an instant. Do you forget, you once made the same gesture? 'Tis over with him as quickly as 'twas with you. Cartwright is but a doll with your features, and I'm not a woman of my mind if I can't dress him in your clothes—lend him your peculiar charm —paint your smile on his face! Already, he begins babbling like yourself.

LA RUSE (*loses his composure*). Infernal woman!

LAETITIA. Within a week, or a fortnight, I'll think I talk to you when I talk to him. Oh, I can draw your pattern, La Ruse—cut the pretty doll to your elegant vile shape; for 'tis the shape, alas, I adore.

LA RUSE. Infernal woman! If I thought you'd succeed—

LAETITIA. You'll be far away. (*Crosses down L.*) I vow, La Ruse, you haven't told me where you go.

LA RUSE. I go nowhere. When I leave this house—Count La Ruse is no more. I take ship at once for the colonies. There—

LAETITIA. There—you will be what you are here.

LA RUSE (*violently*). No.

LAETITIA (*pityingly*). Do you think you can kill La Ruse in yourself? (*Sits.*) 'Tis late, my lover, for a new marriage of the elements.

LA RUSE. You lie.

LAETITIA. 'Tis to be seen. Take ship for the colonies! What will you do? Work in the Carolina rice-fields with the slaves? But you'll never reach the dock. No. I'll describe your route for you from the prison door. You'll pause at a tavern for a bumper of liberty; 'twill lead to another bumper. A wench will catch your eye; you'll toy with her and have half a mind to do more; you'll have another bumper and you'll do more. This will lead to a bumper of repentance; and as by this time your funds are depleted, you must try your luck at the tables. There you'll be stripped, and as your ship sails you'll be meditating some purse-cutting expedition. From this meditation 'tis but a short step to your return here. Yes, you're old to play a new part; you'll find it easier to don a costume which fits, and speak lines you know.

LA RUSE. Devil, I could almost believe you! What if I should be returned here? What if I should find an echo of myself— where I had left a poet?

LAETITIA. You will, La Ruse, I promise you.

LA RUSE. Infernal woman! You've put thoughts into my head—

LAETITIA. 'Tis palpable someone must.

LA RUSE. Damn you for a lying harlot! (*Crossing to above table.*) I'm off when your father returns.

LAETITIA. You can't leave before, and perhaps not then. I'll downstairs and tell him—what I have to tell him. I'll wager, debt or no debt, he keeps you here. (*Crosses R.*)

LA RUSE (*savagely*). Let him try!

LAETITIA. You're a fool, sir, but I love you—more than the poet who'll sing my praises if you do leave; the poet whom

I'll cut to your pattern! (*She laughs; exits* R.)

LA RUSE (*stares after her*). Cut to my pattern! She'll do't, by God, she'll do't! (*He comes to a dozen decisions in as many moments: he suffers his passion.*) Too old to play a new part! (*His passion grows, and reaches a climax; he accepts his fate, goes to door* L. *and calls.*) Mr. Cartwright! Mr. Cartwright! (CARTWRIGHT *comes in.* LA RUSE *faces him with an air of amazed joy.*)

CARTWRIGHT. You are leaving?

LA RUSE. You are leaving, sir!

CARTWRIGHT (*incredulous*). I am leaving?

LA RUSE. We are both leaving. I've had the most extraordinary communication, within the minute.

CARTWRIGHT. But tell me—

LA RUSE (*pirouettes*). Shout! Laugh! Sing! The world is ours again.

CARTWRIGHT. But tell me—

LA RUSE. True, I must tell you. I've mentioned my son—we've been parted by my escapades. I've just heard from his guardians; they've come to my rescue. Yes, I'm about to be everlastingly reconciled to my son. He's come into a vast and beautiful estate, is rich without measure! And I'm to share in his new wealth. You're held for a beggarly two hundred pounds—here's the sum, and fifty pounds additional for your needs. Now, sir, will you believe at last in white birds?

CARTWRIGHT (*dazed*). 'Tis perhaps the difference to me between life and death, fame and infamy—I'll not be coy over taking the money—

LA RUSE. I was not coy over taking the money myself!

CARTWRIGHT. I rejoice at your own good fortune, Count La Ruse.

LA RUSE. I rejoice at it myself. I would have you have a token of mine for remembrance. Will you accept this snuffbox?

CARTWRIGHT (*overwhelmed*). I've nothing to give in return.

LA RUSE. No? I would like a token. The knife! You'll not need it now, and 'twas yours when first we met; 'twill be a lively memento of our time together. Will you let me have it back? (*Turns back on* C.)

CARTWRIGHT (*gives him knife*). Of course. 'Tis likely I can never repay you; but were I able, where should I reach you?

LA RUSE. Write me—damn me if I know my new address! I've forgotten—'tis a strange one. Write me care of Mr. Snap. I delay to fee him to forward my letters. Run, sir! Joy awaits you.

CARTWRIGHT. And you?

LA RUSE. I am a little too old for joy, but peace will perhaps serve me better.

CARTWRIGHT. You have truly been a father to me, Count La Ruse.

LA RUSE. Would you greatly mind if I give you a father's parting benediction? (*He kisses him.*)

CARTWRIGHT. There are tears in your eyes.

LA RUSE. The tears of reconciliation with my son—and with parting from you. (*Goes* R.) I've grown overly fond of you, sir. And now, like a true father who's never been wise in his own life, I'll instruct you how to be wise. Take no man's advice, love no woman too much. When you come to the shade, as you will, do not disparage it because you have seen the sun: there may be wonders in the darkness. Farewell.

CARTWRIGHT (*rises; crosses* R.; *shakes hands*). Farewell!—If I could say something more—to show my gratitude! I shall write a sonnet to you, if I may. (*Exits* R.)

LA RUSE. Sonnet to me! 'Twill be my fate, 'tis one of his minor works. (*But with this his mask perishes; he walks to the window and stands as he stood a short while before.*) It must be a black bird, after all—

LAETITIA (*enters* R. *Wide-eyed*). O, fool! fool! Given him your money—freed him in your place—O, fool! sentimental fool!

LA RUSE (*walks to the* R. *door heavily*). 'Tis the only wise thing I have ever done. There have been too many hairs on my shoulder—

LAETITIA (*with an evil smile*). Now you belong to me—forever.

LA RUSE. Now I am free forever. (*He goes out* R. LAETITIA *wonders. The thud of a body falling is heard in the hall. She runs, sees, retreats into the room, incapable of an outcry.*)

MR. SNAP (*enters* C. *Chuckling*). 'Twas an expeditious hanging. What is it, daughter? (*She points* R.; *he exits into the hall and returns, awed.*) Stabbed himself—clean through the heart.

LAETITIA (*finds voice; beats hysterically on her father's breast*). I'll strangle his child—I'll strangle his child in my womb—

MR. SNAP (*seizes her hands; looks up at her, a great fear in his face*). His child! (WAINWRIGHT *appears* L. LAETITIA *collapses in her father's arms.*)

WAINWRIGHT (*assists him in picking up her limp form*). Pray, Mr. Snap, show me into her room—I must have ingress into her room.

THE END

BIOGRAPHY
S. N. Behrman

Biography was first presented by the Theatre Guild, Inc., at the Guild Theatre, on December 12, 1932. It was staged by Philip Moeller, with settings by Jo Mielziner. The cast was as follows:

RICHARD KURT .... Earle Larimore
MINNIE, Marion Froude's maid .... Helen Salinger
MELCHIOR FEYDAK, a Viennese composer .... Arnold Korff
MARION FROUDE .... Ina Claire
LEANDER NOLAN .... Jay Fassett
WARWICK WILSON .... Alexander Clark
ORRIN KINNICOTT .... Charles Richman
SLADE KINNICOTT, his daughter .... Mary Arbenz

ACT ONE: About five o'clock of an afternoon in November.

ACT TWO: Afternoon, three weeks later.

ACT THREE: Late afternoon, two weeks later.

The entire action takes place in Marion Froude's studio in New York City. The time is now.

Copyright 1932, 1933, by S. N. Behrman. Reprinted from Four Plays of S. N. Behrman by permission of Random House, Inc.

CAUTION: Professionals and amateurs are hereby warned that Biography, being fully protected under the copyright laws of the United States of America, the British Empire, including the Dominion of Canada, and all other countries of the Copyright Union, is subject to royalty. All rights, including professional, amateur, motion picture, recitation, lecturing, public reading, radio and television broadcasting, and the rights of translation into foreign languages, are strictly reserved. Particular emphasis is laid on the question of readings, permission for which must be secured from the author's agent in writing. All inquiries should be addressed to the author's agent, Harold Freedman, 101 Park Avenue, New York City.

Biography is not only one of the best high comedies written by an American play-wright, but a virtual summation of the ideal of comedy entertained by its author. S. N. Behrman's eminence in the field of comedy has been a hard-won achievement exemplifying a state of tension between faith in comic breadth and detachment on the one hand, and strong personal and social sympathies on the other. It is this tension culminating in conflict that constitutes the central situation of *Biography*.

Born in 1893 of immigrant Jewish parents who settled in Worcester, Massachusetts, Behrman made himself one of the best stylists of our theatre as well as one of the most fluent of our prose writers. He spent two years at Clark University and then took an undergraduate degree from Harvard University in 1916; further studies at Columbia University earned him an M.A. in 1918. Assistant to the editor of the *New York Times Book Review* in 1918, contributor to *Smart Set*, the *New Republic*, the *New Yorker*, and other publications, as well as press agent for a Broadway hit, Behrman came to the theatre with considerable writing experience behind him. But although he subsequently enlarged upon this by writing excellent profiles and reminiscences for the *New Yorker* and publishing such successful books as his biography of Duveen (1952), his autobiography *The Worcester Story*, and his account of the life and wit of Max Beerbohm (1960), Mr. Behrman gave himself primarily to the theatre.

Behrman was discovered as a playwright by the Theatre Guild, which produced his sophisticated high comedy *The Second Man* in 1927, and it was for the Guild that he wrote most of his original plays as well as three successful adaptions: of Jean Giraudoux's *Amphitryon 38* (1937), Ludwig Fulda's *The Pirate* (1942), and Franz Werfel's *Jacobowsky and the Colonel* (1944). *The Second Man* was a brilliant character study of a writer who has attained self-knowledge and is disconcertingly candid about himself. Realizing that there is a second, cynical and pleasure-loving, man in his make-up, Clark Storey renounces the idealizing love of a young girl and returns to a middle-aged mistress who will never trouble his conscience with excessive expectations.

Next Mr. Behrman deserted the Theatre Guild with two plays, an inconsequential collaboration with Kenyon Nicholson and a delightful dramatization, *Serena Blandish* (1929). He also gave the Guild two extremely intelligent plays: *Meteor* (1929), the portrait of a financial wizard who loses his wife and friends in pursuing the phantom of success, and *Brief Moment* (1931), a rueful treatment of the infatuation of a man of wealth and social position with a night-club performer who attracts him because he considers her refreshingly "elemental." Neither play was particularly successful when presented on Broadway, perhaps because neither was particularly lighthearted. But in 1932 Behrman restored trust in his promise as a writer of comedies with *Biography*, chiefly perhaps because he endowed his central heroine, Marion Froude, delightfully impersonated by the distinguished comedienne Ina Claire, with charm, buoyancy, and wit. The contrast he established in introducing into the heroine's life a crusading lover in the person of the earnest journalist Richard Kurt yielded not only a piquant love affair but a provocative conflict between two rights — that of easygoing tolerance and that of unrelenting opposition to evil. The play was, as previously suggested, a veritable expression of the author's own conflict between a desire to commit himself to the social struggles of the day and an inclination to stand apart from events as a dispassionate observer and remain "civilized," rational, or balanced at all costs. And Behrman was himself aware of the dangers of the latter attitude, for his character Kurt, on parting from Marion, remarks that he now knows why evil thrives in the world — people, as they grow older, lose their capacity for indignation and allow themselves to be amused by that which they should hate and crush. *Biography* was Behrman's version of *The Misanthrope*.

By 1934, when Behrman produced *Rain from Heaven*, his somber involvement with the political scene made a comic point of view difficult, if not impossible. In dealing with upper-class intellectuals in the milieu of a cultivated Englishwoman's home, Behrman in this play remained close to the comedy of manners, but the spread of Nazism destroyed the possibility of detachment. The untenability of disengagement was indeed the core of the play, at the conclusion of which a refugee art-critic from Germany, after suffering an insult from an American aviator-hero with Fascist leanings, leaves the English lady's home in order to join the German Underground. The conflict between engagement and disengagement was henceforth to be painted in darker colors by the author of *Biography*.

The American social scene was treated with exemplary lightness and comic flair in Mr. Behrman's next play, *End of Summer*, which the Theatre Guild presented with much success. Ina Claire's attractive and engaging performance as Leonie Frothingham, an idle-rich woman who fears loneliness and therefore escapes the grasp of a designing psychiatrist only to attach herself to a brash young radical, undoubtedly contributed both glamour and humor to *End of Summer*. But this comedy also derived vivacity from the heroine's young daughter and the latter's radical friends, as well as thematic interest. *End of Summer* was a "socialism for millionaires" type of play which, offering the author ample opportunities for comic observation and comment, enabled him to write one more thoroughly realized comedy.

In general, however, the "spirit of the age" depressed Mr. Behrman's comic *élan* or made it share a place in his original plays with sober, if not indeed somber, social and political concerns in the period of social conflict in the United States, Civil War in Spain, and, finally, the outbreak of World War II. His *Wine of Choice* in 1938 was an unsuccessful political comedy; *No Time for Comedy* (1939), presented with Katharine Cornell in the leading role, was a well-written but strained comedy about a writer's efforts to produce serious work when his real flair is for comedy of manners rather than for cumbersome political drama. *The Talley Method* (1941) was too didactic to be buoyant, even if its author managed to score some good points concerning the dangers of dictatorial parental behavior. Another comedy, *Dunnigan's Daughter* (1945), was a good character study but a static play. After the war, his adaptation of a Somerset Maugham story, *Jane*, was brightly written but also rather static, and *The Cold Wind and the Warm*, based on the author's charming autobiographical sketches, also missed success. But Behrman wrote distinctly successful adaptations and show-pieces for Alfred Lunt and Lynn Fontanne, such as *The Pirate* and *I Know My Love* and contributed the book for the profitable musical comedy *Fanny*, based on a well-known trilogy by the French playwright Marcel Pagnol. These professional jobs, along with the author's published volumes, kept Behrman's reputation alive and his coffers filled when his original plays began to falter.

Whatever the subsequent fate of Behrman's dramatic talent, its early triumphs in comedy fill some of the brightest pages in the history of the contemporary American stage. *Biography*, especially, retains its vitality intact; its issue is as provocative today as it was in the third decade of the century.

ACT ONE

SCENE: *The studio-apartment of* MARION FROUDE *in an old-fashioned studio building in West 57th St., New York. A great, cavernous room expressing in its polyglot furnishings the artistic patois of the various landlords who have sublet this apartment to wandering tenants like* MARION FROUDE. *The styles range from medieval Florence to contemporary Grand Rapids; on a movable raised platform in the center is a papal throne chair in red velvet and gold fringes. Not far from it is an ordinary American kitchen chair. The hanging lamp which sheds a mellow light over a French Empire sofa is filigreed copper Byzantine. Another and longer sofa across the room against the grand piano is in soft green velvet and has the gentility of a polite Park Avenue drawing room. Under the stairs, rear, which go up to* MARION'S *bedroom, are stacks of her canvases. There is a quite fine wood carving of a Madonna which seems to be centuries old, and in the wall spaces looking at audience are great, dim canvases—copies by some former tenant left probably in lieu of rent—of Sargent's Lord Ribblesdale and Mme. X.*

Whether it is due to the amenable spirit of the present incumbent or because they are relaxed in the democracy of art, these oddments of the creative spirit do not suggest disharmony. The room is warm, musty, with restful shadows and limpid lights. The enormous leaded window on the right, though some of its members are patched and cracked, gleams in the descending twilight with an opalescent light; even the copper cylinder of the fire extinguisher and its attendant axe, visible in the hall, seem to be not so much implements against calamity as amusing museum-bits cherished from an earlier time. Every school is represented here except the modern. The studio has the mellowness of anachronism.

There is a door upstage Left leading to the kitchen and MINNIE'S *bedroom door, center, under the stairs leads into hallway. A door on the stair landing, Center, leads to* MINNIE'S *bedroom.*

TIME: *About five o'clock of an afternoon in November.*

AT RISE: RICHARD KURT *is finishing a nervous cigarette. He has the essential audacity which comes from having seen the worst happen, from having endured the keenest pain. He has the hardness of one who knows that he can be devastated by pity, the bitterness which comes from having seen, in early youth, justice thwarted and tears unavailing, the self-reliance which comes from having seen everything go in a disordered world save one, stubborn, unyielding core of belief—at everything else he laughs, in this alone he trusts. He has the intensity of the fanatic and the carelessness of the vagabond. He goes to the door from the hall and calls.*

KURT. Say, you, hello there—what's your name?

(MINNIE, *Marion Froude's inseparable maid, a German woman of about fifty, comes in. She is indignant at being thus summarily summoned, and by a stranger.*)

MINNIE (*with dignity*). My name iss Minnie if you please.

KURT. What time did Miss Froude go out?

MINNIE. About two o'clock.

KURT. It's nearly five now. She should be home, shouldn't she?

MINNIE. She said she vas coming home to tea and that iss all I know.

KURT (*grimly*). I know. She invited me to tea. . . . Where did she go to lunch?

MINNIE (*acidly*). That I do not know.

KURT. Did someone call for her or did she go out alone? I have a reason for asking.

MINNIE. She went out alone. Any more questions?

KURT. No. I see there's no point in asking you questions.

MINNIE. Denn vy do you ask dem?

(*The doorbell rings.* MINNIE *throws up her hands in despair. She goes out muttering:* "Ach Gott." KURT *is rather amused at her. He lights another cigarette.*)

(*Sounds of vociferous greeting outside.* "Ach mein lieber Herr Feydak. . . ." MELCHIOR FEYDAK, *the Austrian composer, comes in. He is forty-five, tall, hook-nosed, thinfaced, a humorist with a rather sad face.*)

FEYDAK. Nun, Minnie, und wo ist die Schlechte. . . .? (MINNIE *makes a sign to him not to disclose their freemasonry in the presence of strangers. She is cautious. . . .*) Not home yet, eh Minnie? Where is she? Well—well. How do they say—gallivanting—I love that word—gallivanting as usual. Well, I'll wait. It's humiliating —but I'll wait. Chilly! Brr! I don't mind so much being cold in London or Vienna. I expect it. But I can't stand it in New York. (*He warms himself before fire.*) And who is this young man?

MINNIE (*shortly*). Ich weiss nicht! . . . Er hat alle fünf Minuten gefragt, wo sie ist—. (*She goes out.*)

FEYDAK. You've offended Minnie, I

can see that.

KURT. That's just too bad!

FEYDAK. We all tremble before Minnie. . . . Been waiting long?

KURT. Over half an hour!

FEYDAK. Extraordinary thing—ever since I've known Marion there's always been someone waiting for her. There are two kinds of people in one's life—people whom one keeps waiting—and the people for whom one waits. . . .

KURT. Is that an epigram?

FEYDAK. Do you object to epigrams?

KURT (with some pride). I despise epigrams.

FEYDAK (tolerantly sizing KURT up). Hm! Friend of Miss Froude's?

KURT. Not at all.

FEYDAK. That at least is no cause for pride.

KURT. I just don't happen to be, that's all.

FEYDAK. I commiserate you.

KURT. I despise gallantry also.

FEYDAK (lightly). And I thought Americans were so sentimental. . . .

KURT. And, together with other forms of glibness, I loathe generalization. . . .

FEYDAK (dryly). Young man, we have a great deal in common.

KURT. Also, there is a faint flavor of condescension in the way you say "young man" for which I don't really care. . . .

FEYDAK (delighted and encouraging him to go on). What about me do you like? There must be something.

KURT. If I were that kind your question would embarrass me.

FEYDAK (very pleased). Good for Marion!

KURT. Why do you say that?

FEYDAK. She always had a knack for picking up originals!

KURT. You are under a misapprehension. Miss Froude did not pick me up. I picked her up. (FEYDAK stares at him. This does shock him.) I wrote Miss Froude a letter—a business letter. She answered and gave me an appointment for four-thirty. It is now after five. She has taken a half-hour out of my life. . . .

FEYDAK. I gather that fragment of time has great value. . . .

KURT. She has shortened my life by thirty minutes. God, how I hate Bohemians!

FEYDAK (innocently). Are you by any chance—an Evangelist?

KURT. I am—for the moment—a businessman. I'm not here to hold hands or drink tea. I'm here on business. My presence here is a favor to Miss Froude and likely to bring her a handsome profit. . . .

FEYDAK. Profit! Ah! That accounts for her being late. . . .

KURT (skeptically). You despise profit I suppose! Are you—by any chance—old-world?

FEYDAK. Young man, your technique is entirely wasted on me. . . .

KURT. Technique! What are you talking about?

FEYDAK. When I was a young man—before I achieved any sort of success—I was rude on principle. Deliberately rude and extravagantly bitter in order to make impression. When it is no longer necessary for you to wait around for people in order to do them favors, you'll mellow down I assure you.

KURT (fiercely, he has been touched). You think so, do you! That's where you're mistaken! I'm rude now. When I'm successful I'll be murderous!

FEYDAK (genially). More power to you! But I've never seen it happen yet. Success is the great muffler! Not an epigram I hope. If it is—forgive me.

(A moment's pause. KURT studies him while FEYDAK crosses to stove and warms his hands.)

KURT. I know you from somewhere. It's very tantalizing.

FEYDAK. I don't think so. I have only just arrived in this country. . . .

KURT. Still, I know you I'm sure—I've seen you somewhere. . . .

FEYDAK (understanding the familiarity). Maybe you know Miss Froude's portrait of me. . . .

KURT (doubtfully). Yes—maybe that's it . . . may I ask. . . . ?

FEYDAK. Certainly. My name is Feydak.

KURT. The composer?

FEYDAK (dryly). Yes. . . .

KURT. I thought he was dead. . . .

FEYDAK. That is true. But I hope you won't tell anyone—for I am his ghost. . . .

KURT (putting this down for Continental humor and genuinely contrite). Forgive me. . .

FEYDAK. But why?

KURT. If you really are Feydak the composer—I have the most enormous admiration for you. I worship music above everything.

FEYDAK (Slightly bored). Go on. . . .

KURT. I read in the paper—you're on

your way to Hollywood. . . .

FEYDAK. Yes. I am on my way to Hollywood. . . .

KURT. In the new state men like you won't have to prostitute themselves in Hollywood. . . .

FEYDAK. Ah! A Utopian!

KURT. Yes. You use the word as a term of contempt. Why? Every artist is a Utopian. You must be very tired or you wouldn't be so contemptuous of Utopians.

FEYDAK (*with a charming smile*). I am rather tired. Old-world you would call it.

KURT. You can be anything you like....

FEYDAK (*satirically*). Thank you. . . .

KURT. You've written lovely music—I have a friend who plays every note of it. I didn't see your operetta when it was done here. . . . I didn't have the price . . . it was very badly done though, I heard....

FEYDAK. I must explain to you—you are under a misapprehension. . . .

KURT. It was done here, wasn't it?

FEYDAK. Not about the operetta. You are under a misapprehension—about me. I am a composer—but I didn't write "Danubia." That was my brother, Victor Feydak. You are right. He is dead. You are the first person I have met in New York who even suspected it.

KURT. I'm sorry.

FEYDAK. Not at all. I am flattered. At home our identities were never confused. Is this the well-known American hospitality? It is, in some sort, compensation for his death. . . .

(KURT *is embarrassed and uncomfortable. It is part of his essential insecurity; he is only really at home in protest. He wants to get out.*)

KURT. I'm sorry—I . . .

FEYDAK (*easily*). But why?

KURT. I think I'll leave a note for Miss Froude—get that girl in here, will you?

FEYDAK. Let's have some tea—she's sure to be in any minute. . . .

KURT. No, thanks. And you might tell her for me that if she wants to see me about the matter I wrote her about she can come to my office. . . .

(MARION FROUDE *comes in. She is one of those women, the sight of whom on Fifth Ave., where she has just been walking, causes foreigners to exclaim enthusiastically that American women are the most radiant in the world. She is tall, lithe, indomitably alive. Unlike* KURT, *the tears in things have warmed without scalding her; she floats life like a dancer's scarf in perpetual enjoyment of its colors and contours.*)

MARION (*to* KURT). I'm *so* sorry!

FEYDAK (*coming toward her*). I don't believe a word of it!

(*She is overjoyed at seeing* FEYDAK. *She can't believe for a second that it is he. Then she flies into his arms.*)

MARION. Feydie! Oh, Feydie, I've been trying everywhere to reach you—I can't believe it. . . . Feydie darling!

FEYDAK (*severely*). Is this how you keep a business appointment, Miss Froude?

MARION. How long have you waited? If I'd only known. . . . (*Suddenly conscious that* KURT *had waited too.*) Oh, I'm so sorry, Mr.—Mr.—?

KURT. Kurt. Richard Kurt.

MARION. Oh, of course, Mr. Kurt. I say—could you possibly—would it be too much trouble—could you some back?

FEYDAK (*same tone*). This young man is here on business. It is more important. I can wait. I'll come back.

MARION. No, no, Feydie—no, no. I can't wait for that. I'm sure Mr. Kurt will understand. Mr. Feydak is an old friend whom I haven't seen in ever so long. It isn't as if Mr. Kurt were a regular businessman. . . .

FEYDAK (*amused*). How do you know he isn't?

MARION (*breathless with excitement*). I can tell. He's not a bit like his letter. When I got your letter I was sure you were jowly and you know—(*She makes a gesture.*) convex. I'm sure, Feydie—whatever the business is—(*To* KURT.) you did say you had some, didn't you?—I'm sure it can wait. A half-hour anyway. Can't it wait a half-hour? You see Feydie and I haven't seen each other since . . .

KURT. Vienna!

MARION (*astonished*). Yes. How did you know?

KURT. It's always since Vienna that Bohemians haven't seen each other, isn't it? I'll be back in thirty minutes. (*He goes.*)

MARION. What a singular young man!

FEYDAK. I've been having a very amusing talk with him. Professional rebel I think. Well, my dear—you look marvelous!

(*They take each other in.*)

MARION. Isn't it wonderful . . .

FEYDAK. It *is* nice!

(*They sit on sofa,* MARION *left of* FEYDAK.)

MARION. How long is it?

FEYDAK. Well, it's since . . .

MARION (*firmly*). Since Vicki died.

FEYDAK. That's right. I haven't seen you since.

MARION. Since that day—we walked behind him.

FEYDAK. Yes.

MARION. I felt I couldn't bear to stay on. I left for London that night.

FEYDAK. Yes.

MARION. It's six years, isn't it?

FEYDAK. Yes. Six years last June. (*A pause.*)

MARION. What's happened since then? Nothing. . . .

FEYDAK. How long have you been here?

MARION. Two weeks.

FEYDAK. Busy?

MARION. Not professionally, I'm afraid. People are charming—they ask me to lunch and dinner and they're—"oh, so interested"—but no commissions so far. And God, how I need it. . . .

FEYDAK. I'm surprised. I gathered you'd been very successful.

MARION. It's always sounded like it, hasn't it? The impression, I believe, is due to the extreme notoriety of some of my sitters. Oh, I've managed well enough up to now—if I'd been more provident I dare say I could have put a tidy bit by—but at the moment people don't seem in a mood to have their portraits done. Are they less vain than they used to be? Or just poorer?

FEYDAK. Both, I think.

MARION. Last time I came here I was awfully busy. Had great *réclame* because I'd been in Russia doing leading Communists. Obeying some subtle paradox, the big financiers flocked to me. Pittsburgh manufacturers wanted to be done by the same brush that had tackled Lenin. Now they seem less eager. Must be some reason, Feydie. But what about you? Let me hear about you. How's Kathie?

FEYDAK. Well. She's here with me.

MARION. And Sadye?

FEYDAK. Splendid.

MARION. She must be a big girl now.

FEYDAK. As tall as you are.

MARION. Kathie used to hate me, didn't she? Frightened to death of me. Was afraid I was after Vicki's money.. . .

FEYDAK. Yes. She was afraid you'd marry him and that we should have less from him. When we knew he was dying she was in a panic.

MARION. Poor dear—I could have spared her all that worry if she'd been halfway civil to me.

FEYDAK. Kathie is practical. And she is a good mother. Those are attributes which make women avaricious. . . .

MARION. Did Vicki leave you very much?

FEYDAK. Not very much. Half to you.

MARION. Really? How sweet of him! How dear of him!

FEYDAK. We've spent it. . . .

MARION. Of course you should.

FEYDAK. But I'll soon be in position to repay you your share. I'm on my way to Hollywood.

MARION. Are you really? How wonderful for you, Feydie! I'm so glad. . . .

FEYDAK. You've been there, haven't you?

MARION. Yes. Last time I was in America.

FEYDAK. Did you like it?

MARION. Well, it's the new Eldorado—art on the gold-rush.

FEYDAK (*with a kind of ironic bitterness*). Vicki left me an inheritance subject, it appears, to perpetual renewal.

MARION. How do you mean?

FEYDAK. Things have been going from bad to worse in Vienna—you haven't been there since '25 so you don't know. The theatre's pretty well dead—even the first-rate fellows have had a hard time making their way. I managed to get several scores to do—but they were not—except that they were failures—up to my usual standard.

MARION (*laughing, reproachful*). Oh, Feydie . . . !

FEYDAK. If it weren't for the money Vicki left me—and you!—I don't know how we should have got through at all these six years. About a month ago we reached the end of our rope—we were hopelessly in debt—no means of getting out—when the miracle happened.

(MARION *is excited, touches his knee with her hand.*)

MARION (*murmuring*). I can't bear it. . . .

FEYDAK. It was my dramatic agent on the phone. A great American film magnate was in town and wanted to see me. *Ausgerechnet* me and no other. Even my agent couldn't keep the surprise out of his voice. Why me? I asked. God knows, says the agent. Well, we went around to the Bristol to see the magnate. And as we talked to him, it gradually became apparent. He thought I was Vicki. He didn't know Vicki was dead! He thought I had written "Danubia."

MARION. Did he say so?

FEYDAK. No—not at all. But as we shook hands at the end he said to me: "Any man that can write a tune like this is the kind of man we want." And he whistled, so out of tune that I could hardly recognize it myself, the waltz from Danubia. Do you remember it? (*He starts to hum the waltz and* MARION *joins him. They hum together, then* FEYDAK *continues to talk as* MARION *continues to hum a few more measures.*) He was so innocent, so affable, that I had an impulse to say to him: "Look here, old fellow, you don't want me, you want my brother, and in order to get him you'll have to resurrect him!" But noble impulses are luxury impulses. You have to be well off to gratify them. I kept quiet. We shook hands and here I am. Tonight they're giving me a dinner at the Waldorf Astoria for the press to meet my brother! Irony if you like, eh, Marion?

(*There is a pause.*)

MARION. Feydie . . . (*A moment. He does not answer.*) Feydie—do you mind if I say something to you—very frankly?

FEYDAK. I doubt whether you can say anything to me more penetrating than the remarks I habitually address to myself.

MARION. You know Vicki was very fond of you. He used to say you put too high a valuation on genius.

FEYDAK. Because he had it he could afford to deprecate it.

MARION. Over and over again he used to say to me: "You know, Marion," he would say, "as a human being Feydie's far superior to me, more amiable, more witty, more talented, more patient. . ."

FEYDAK (*shakes his head*). Not true. I simply give the impression of these things.

MARION. You under-rate yourself, Feydie. . . . How this would have amused him—this incident with the Hollywood man!

FEYDAK (*smiling bitterly*). It would, rather.

MARION. Why do you grudge giving him a laugh somewhere? I never had a chance to tell you in Vienna—things were so—so close and terrible—at the end—but he had the greatest tenderness for you. He used to speak of you—I can't tell you how much. "Because of this sixth

sense for making tunes which I have and he hasn't," he said to me one day—not a week before he died—"he thinks himself less than me." He used to tell me that everything he had he owed to you—to the sacrifices you made to send him to the Conservatory when he was a boy. . . . The extent to which he had outstripped you hurt him—hurt him. I felt he would have given anything to dip into the golden bowl of his genius and pour it over you. And do you know what was the terror of his life, the obsessing terror of his life—his fear of your resenting him . . .

FEYDAK (*moved, deeply ashamed*). Marion . . .

MARION. Don't resent him now, Feydie. . . . Why, it's such fun—don't you see? It's such a curious, marginal survival for him—that a badly remembered waltz-tune, five years after his death, should be the means of helping you at a moment when you need it so badly. . . . It's delicious, Feydie. It's such fun! The only awful thing is the possibility that he is unaware of it. It would have pleased him so, Feydie. Must you grudge him it?

FEYDAK. You make me horribly ashamed. . . .

MARION (*brightly*). Nonsense.

FEYDAK. Because I did grudge him it—yes—I won't, though—I see now that it never occurred to me how—(*Bursts out laughing suddenly.*) God, it is funny, isn't it.

MARION (*joining in his laughter*). Of course—it's delightful. . . .

(*They both laugh heartily and long.*)

MARION. And the funny thing is—you'll be much better for them out there than he would have been.

FEYDAK. Surely! They'll be able to whistle *my* tunes!

MARION. Don't you see!

FEYDAK. Oh, Lieber Schatzel, come out there with me.

MARION. Can't!

FEYDAK. I wish, Marion, you would come. I never feel life so warm and good as when you are in the neighborhood.

MARION. Dear Feydie, you're very comforting.

FEYDAK. Is there someone that keeps you here?

MARION. No, there's no one. I'm quite alone.

FEYDAK. Well then . . . !

MARION. No, this isn't the moment for

me, Feydie. Besides, I can't afford the journey. I'm frightfully hard up at the moment.

FEYDAK. Well, look here, I—

MARION. No, that's sweet of you but I couldn't.

FEYDAK. I don't see why—it's too silly . . .

MARION. Vanity. A kind of vanity.

FEYDAK. But I owe it to you!

MARION. I suppose it is foolish in a way—but I've a kind of pride in maneuvering on my own. I always have done it—in that way at least I've been genuinely independent. I'm a little proud of my ingenuity. And do you know, Feydia, no matter how hard up I've been at different times something's always turned up for me. I have a kind of curiosity to know what it will be this time. It would spoil the fun for me to take money from my friends. Nothing—so much as that—would make me doubtful of my own—shall we say—marketability?

FEYDAK. Paradoxical, isn't it?

MARION. Why not? Anyway it's a pet *idée fixe* of mine, so be a darling and let me indulge it, will you, Feydie, and don't offer me money. Anyway, I've a business proposition on. . . .

FEYDAK. Have you?

MARION. That young man who was just here. Do you suppose he'll come back? Now I think of it, we were a bit short with him, weren't we? I was so glad to see you I couldn't be bothered with him! (*Sound of doorbell.*) Ah! You see! (*Calls outside.*) Show him in, Minnie!

(MINNIE *comes in and exits hall door to admit the visitor.*)

FEYDAK. What are you doing for dinner?

MARION. There's a young man who attached himself to me on the boat . . .

FEYDAK. Oh, Marion!

MARION. I seem to attract youth, Feydie. What shall I do about it?

FEYDAK. Where are you dining?

MARION. I don't know. . . . Which speakeasy? Tell me which one and I'll . . .

(MINNIE *ushers in* MR. LEANDER NOLAN. *He is middle-aged, ample, handsome. Looks like the late Warren Gamaliel Harding. Soberly dressed and wears a waistcoat with white piping on it. The façade is impeccable but in* NOLAN'S *eye you may discern, at odd moments, an uncertainty, an almost boyish anxiety to please, to be right, that is rather engaging.*)

(MARION, *who expected the young man, is rather startled.* MR. NOLAN *regards her with satisfaction.*)

NOLAN. Hello, Marion.

MARION (*doubtfully, feels she should remember him*). How do you do? Er—will you excuse me just a second . . . ?

NOLAN (*genially*). Certainly.

(*He moves right.* MARION *walks* FEYDIE *to the hall door.*)

FEYDAK (*under his breath to her*). Looks like a commission.

(*She makes a gesture of silent prayer.*)

MARION (*out loud*). Telephone me in an hour, will you, Feydie, and let me know which speakeasy. . . .

FEYDAK (*once he has her in the hallway out of* NOLAN'S *hearing*). Also, *Du kommst ganz sicher?*

MARION. *Vielleicht später.* Bye, Feydie dear.

(FEYDIE *goes out.* MARION *turns to face* NOLAN, *who is standing with his arms behind his back rather enjoying the surprise he is about to give her.*)

NOLAN. How are you, Marion?

MARION (*delicately*). Er do I know you?

NOLAN. Yes. You know me.

MARION. Oh yes—of course!

NOLAN. About time!

MARION (*brightly insecure*). Lady Winchester's gardenparty at Ascot—two summers ago. . .

NOLAN. Guess again!

MARION. No—I know you perfectly well—it's just that—no, don't tell me. . . (*She covers her eyes with her hand, trying to conjure him out of the past.*)

NOLAN. This is astonishing. If someone had said to me that I could walk into a room in front of Marion Froude and she not know me I'd have told 'em they were crazy!

MARION (*desperate*). I do know you. I know you perfectly well—it's just that . . .

NOLAN. You'll be awful sore at yourself—I warn you . . .

MARION. I can't forgive myself now—I know!

NOLAN. I don't believe it!

MARION. The American Embassy dinner in Rome on the Fourth of July—last year— you sat on my right. . . .

NOLAN. I did not!

MARION (*miserably*). Well, you sat somewhere. Where did you sit?

NOLAN. I wasn't there.

MARION. Well, I think it's very unkind of you to keep me in suspense like this. I can't bear it another second!

NOLAN. I wouldn't have believed it!

MARION. Well, give me some hint, will you?

NOLAN. Think of home—think of Tennessee!

MARION. Oh!

NOLAN. Little Mary Froude. . .

MARION (*a light breaking in on her*). No! Oh, no!

NOLAN. Well, it's about time.

MARION. But . . . ! You were—

NOLAN. Well, so were you!

MARION. But—Bunny—you aren't Bunny Nolan, are you? You're his brother!

NOLAN. I have no brother.

MARION. But Bunny—Bunny dear—how important you've become!

NOLAN. I haven't done badly—no.

MARION. Here, give me your coat and hat— (MARION, *taking his coat and hat, crosses upstage to piano, and leaves them there. Laughing, a little hysterical.*) You should have warned me. It's not fair of you. Bunny! Of all people—I can scarcely believe it. . . . (*A moment's pause. He doesn't quite like her calling him Bunny but he doesn't know how to stop it. She sits on model-stand looking up at him as she says:*) You look wonderful. You look like a—like a—Senator or something monumental like that.

NOLAN (*sits on sofa below piano*). That's a good omen. I'll have to tell Orrin.

MARION. What's a good omen? And who is Orrin?

NOLAN. Your saying I look like a Senator. Because—I don't want to be premature—but in a few months I may be one.

MARION. A Senator!

NOLAN (*smiling*). Senator. Washington. Not Nashville.

MARION. Do you want to be a Senator or can't you help it?

NOLAN (*to whom this point of view is incomprehensible*). What do you mean?

MARION. I'll paint you, Bunny. Toga. Ferrule. Tribune of the people.

NOLAN. Not a bad idea. Not a bad idea at all. I remember now—you were always sketching me. Sketching everything. Say, you've done pretty well yourself, haven't you?

MARION. Not as well as you have,

Bunny. Imagine. Bunny Nolan—a Senator at Washington. Well, well! And tell me—how do I seem to you? You knew me at once, didn't you?

NOLAN. Sure I did. You haven't changed so much—a little perhaps. . .

MARION (*delicately*). Ampler?

NOLAN (*inspecting her*). No . . . not that I can notice.

MARION (*with a sigh of relief*). That's wonderful.

NOLAN. You look just the same. You are just the same.

MARION. Oh, you don't know, Bunny. I'm artful. How long is it since we've seen each other? Twelve years anyway. More than that—fifteen . . .

NOLAN. Just about—hadn't even begun to practice law yet.

MARION. We were just kids . . . children. . . . And now look at you! I can see how successful you are, Bunny.

NOLAN. How?

MARION. White piping on your vest. That suggests directorates to me. Multiple control. Vertical corporations. Are you vertical or horizontal, Bunny?

NOLAN I'm both.

MARION. Good for you! Married?

NOLAN. Not yet . . .

MARION. How did you escape? You're going to be, though.

NOLAN. I'm engaged.

MARION. Who's the lucky girl?

NOLAN. Slade Kinnicott. Daughter of Orrin Kinnicott.

MARION. Orrin Kinnicott. The newspaper publisher?

NOLAN. Yes. He's backing me for the Senate.

MARION. Well, if he's backing you you ought to get in. All that circulation—not very good circulation, is it? Still, one vote's as good as another, I suppose.

NOLAN (*hurt*). In my own state the Kinnicott papers are as good as any.

MARION. Well, I wish you luck. I'm sure you'll have it. My! Senator Nolan!

NOLAN. If get in I'll be the youngest Senator . . .

MARION. And the best-looking too, Bunny . . .

NOLAN (*embarrassed*). Well . . .

MARION. You're fussed! How charming of you! (*She sits beside him.*) Oh, Bunny, I'm very proud of you, really.

NOLAN. You see, Marion, I've been pretty successful in the law. Tremendously successful, I may say. I've organized some of the biggest mergers of recent years. I've made a fortune—a sizeable fortune. Well, one day I woke up and I said to myself: Look here, Nolan, you've got to take stock. You've got to ask yourself where you're heading. I'd been so busy I'd never had a chance to ask myself these fundamental questions before. And I decided to call a halt. You've got enough, more than enough for life, I said to myself. It's time you quit piling up money for yourself and began thinking about your fellow-man. I've always been ambitious, Marion. You know that. You shared all my early dreams . . .

MARION. Of course I did. . . .

NOLAN. Remember I always told you I didn't want money and power for their own sakes—I always wanted to be a big man in a real sense—to do something for my country and my time.

MARION. Yes. Sometimes you sounded like Daniel Webster, darling. I'm not a bit surprised you're going in the Senate.

NOLAN. I never thought—even in my wildest dreams—

MARION. Well, you see you underestimated yourself. You may go even higher—the White House—why not?

NOLAN. I never let myself think of that.

MARION. Why not? It's no more wonderful than what's happened already, is it?

NOLAN (*Napoleon at Saint Helena*). Destiny!

MARION. Exactly. Destiny!

NOLAN (*kind, richly human, patronizing*). And you, my dear!

MARION. As you see. Obscure. Uncertain. Alone. Nowhere at all. Not the remotest chance of my getting into the Senate—unless I marry into it. Oh, Bunny, after you get to Washington will you introduce me to some Senators?

NOLAN. Well, that's premature . . . Naturally if the people should favor me I'd do what I could. I never forget a friend. Whatever faults I may have, disloyalty, I hope, is not one of them.

MARION. Of course it isn't. You're a dear. You always were.

(*A moment's pause.*)

NOLAN. Who was that fellow I found you with when I came in?

MARION. An old friend of mine from Vienna—a composer.

NOLAN. You've been a lot with foreigners, haven't you?

MARION. A good deal . . . .

NOLAN. Funny, I don't understand that.

MARION. Foreigners are people, you know, Bunny. Some of 'em are rather nice.

NOLAN. When I'm abroad a few weeks home begins to look pretty good to me.

MARION. I love New York but I can't say I feel an acute nostalgia for Tennessee.

(*Another pause. He stares at her suddenly—still incredulous that he should be seeing her at all, and that, after all these years and quite without him, she should be radiant still.*)

NOLAN. Little Marion Froude! I can't believe it somehow. . . .

MARION. Oh, Bunny! You're sweet! You're so—ingenuous. That's what I always liked about you.

NOLAN. What do you mean?

MARION. The way you look at me, the incredulity, the surprise. What did you expect to see? A hulk, a remnant, a whitened sepulchre—what?

NOLAN (*uncomfortable at being caught*). Not—not at all.

MARION. Tell me, Bunny, what—? I won't be hurt . . . .

NOLAN (*miserably, stumbling*). Well, naturally, after what I'd heard—

MARION. What have you heard? Oh, do tell me Bunny.

NOLAN. Well, I mean—about your life.

MARION. Racy, Bunny? Racy?

NOLAN. No use going into that. You chose your own way. Everybody has a right to live their own life, I guess.

MARION (*pats his arm*). That's very handsome of you, Bunny. I hope you take that liberal point of view when you reach the Senate.

NOLAN. I came here, Marion, in a perfectly sincere mood to say something to you, something that's been on my mind ever since we parted, but if you're going to be flippant I suppose there's no use my saying anything—I might as well go, in fact. (*But he makes no attempt to do so.*)

MARION (*seriously*). Do forgive me, Bunny. One gets into an idiom that passes for banter, but really I'm not so changed. I'm not flippant. I'm awfully glad to see you, Bunny. (*An undertone of sadness creeps into her voice.*) After all, one makes very few real friends in life—and you are part of my youth—we are part of each other's youth.

NOLAN. You didn't even know me!

MARION. Complete surprise! After all I've been in New York many times during these years and never once—never once have you come near me. You've dropped me all these years. (*With a sigh.*) I'm afraid, Bunny, your career has been too much with you.

NOLAN (*grimly*). So has yours!

MARION. I detect an overtone—faint but unmistakable—of moral censure.

NOLAN (*same tone*). Well, I suppose it's impossible to live one's life in art without being sexually promiscuous! (*He looks at her accusingly.*)

MARION. Oh, dear me, Bunny! What shall I do? Shall I blush? Shall I hang my head in shame? What shall I do? How does one react in the face of an appalling accusation of this sort? I didn't know the news had got around so widely.

NOLAN. Well, so many of your lovers have been famous men.

MARION. Well, you were obscure—But you're famous now, aren't you? I seem to be stimulating if nothing else . . .

NOLAN. If I had then some of the fame I have now you probably wouldn't have walked out on me at the last minute the way you did—

MARION. Dear, dear Bunny, that's not quite—

NOLAN (*irritated beyond control*). I wish you wouldn't call me Bunny. . . .

MARION. Well, I always did. What is your real name?

NOLAN. You know perfectly well—

MARION. I swear I don't. . . .

NOLAN. My name is Leander. . . .

MARION. Bunny, really.

NOLAN. That is my name.

MARION. Really I'd forgotten that. Leander! Who was he—he did something in the Hellespont, didn't he? What did he do in the Hellespont?

NOLAN (*sharply*). Beside the point.

MARION. Sorry! You say you wanted to tell me something—

NOLAN (*grimly*). Yes!

MARION. I love to be told things.

NOLAN. That night you left me—

MARION. We'd quarreled about something, hadn't we?

NOLAN. I realized after you left me how much I'd grown to depend on you—

MARION. Dear Bunny!

NOLAN. I plunged into work. I worked fiercely to forget you. I did forget you—(*he looks away from her.*) And yet—

MARION. And yet—?

NOLAN. The way we'd separated and I never heard from you—it left something bitter in my mind—something—(*He hesitates for a word.*)

MARION (*supplying it*). Unresolved?

NOLAN (*quickly—relieved that she understands so exactly*). Yes. All these years I've wanted to see you, to get it off my mind—

MARION. Did you want the last word, Bunny dear?

NOLAN (*fiercely*). I wanted to see you, to stand before you, to tell myself—"Here she is and—and what of it!"

MARION. Well, can you?

NOLAN (*heatedly, with transparent overemphasis*). Yes! Yes!

MARION. Good for you, Bunny. I know just how you feel—like having a tooth out, isn't it? (*Sincerely.*) In justice to myself—I must tell you this—that the reason I walked out on you in the summary way I did was not as you've just suggested because I doubted your future—it was obvious to me, even then, that you were destined for mighty things—but the reason was that I felt a disparity in our characters not conducive to matrimonial contentment. You see how right I was. I suspected in myself a—a tendency to explore, a spiritual and physical wanderlust—that I knew would horrify you once you found it out. It horrifies you now when we are no longer anything to each other. Imagine, Leander dear, if we were married how much more difficult it would be—If there is any one thing you have to be grateful to me for it is that instant's clear vision I had which made me see, which made me look ahead, which made me tear myself away from you. Why, everything you have now—your future, your prospects,—even your fiancée, Leander dear—you owe to me—no, I won't say to me—to that instinct—to that premonition.

NOLAN (*nostalgic*). We might have done it together.

MARION. I wouldn't have stood for a fiancée, Bunny dear—not even *I* am as promiscuous as that.

NOLAN. Don't use that word!

MARION. But, Leander! It's your own!

NOLAN. Do you think it hasn't been on my conscience ever since, do you think it hasn't tortured me—!

MARION. What, dear?

NOLAN. That thought!

MARION. Which thought?

NOLAN. Every time I heard about you —all the notoriety that's attended you in the American papers—painting pictures of Communist statesmen, running around California with movie comedians!

MARION. I have to practice my profession, Bunny. One must live, you know. Besides, I've done Capitalist statesmen too. And at Geneva—

NOLAN (darkly). You know what I mean!

MARION. You mean . . . (She whispers through her cupped hand.) You mean promiscuous? Has that gotten around, Bunny? Is it whispered in the sewing-circles of Nashville? Will I be burned for a witch if I go back home? Will they have a trial over me? Will you defend me?

NOLAN (quite literally, with sincere and disarming simplicity). I should be forced, as an honest man, to stand before the multitude and say: In condemning this woman you are condemning me who am asking your suffrages to represent you. For it was I with whom this woman first sinned before God. As an honorable man that is what I should have to do.

MARION. And has this worried you— actually!

NOLAN. It's tortured me!

MARION. You're the holy man and I'm Thais! That gives me an idea for the portrait which I hope you will commission me to do. I'll do you in a hair shirt. Savonarola. He was a Senator too, wasn't he? Or was he?

NOLAN (gloomily contemplating her). I can't forget that it was I who—

MARION. Did you think you were the first, Bunny? Was I so unscrupulously coquettish as to lead you to believe that I—oh, I couldn't have been. It's not like me. (She crosses to right of model stand.)

NOLAN (fiercely). Don't lie to me!

MARION (sitting on stand). Bunny, you frighten me!

NOLAN (stands over her almost threateningly). You're lying to me to salve my conscience but I won't have it! I know my guilt and I'm going to bear it!

MARION. Well, I don't want to deprive you of your little pleasures, but—

NOLAN. You're evil, Marion. You haven't the face of evil but you're evil— evil!

MARION. Oh, Bunny darling, now you can't mean that surely. What's come over you? You never were like that—or were you? You know perfectly well I'm not evil. Casual—maybe—but not evil. Good heavens, Bunny, I might as well say you're evil because you're intolerant. These are differences in temperament, that's all—charming differences in temperament.

NOLAN (shakes his head, unconvinced). Sophistry!

MARION. All right, Dean Inge. Sophistry. By the way, I've met the Gloomy Dean and he's not gloomy at all—he's very jolly. (Gets up from stand.) Let's have a cup of tea, shall we? Will your constituents care if you have a cup of tea with a promiscuous woman? Will they have to know?

NOLAN. I'm afraid I can't, Marion. I have to be getting on.

MARION. Oh, stay and have some tea— (Makes him sit down.) What do you have to do that can't wait for a cup of tea? (Calls off.) Minnie—Minnie. . .

MINNIE (appears in doorway). Ja, Fräulein.

MARION. Bitte—Tee.

MINNIE. Ja, Fräulein.

(She goes out. MARION smiles at NOLAN and sits beside him. He is quite uncomfortable.)

NOLAN (slightly embarrassed). About the painting, Marion.

MARION. Oh, I was only joking . . . don't let yourself be bullied into it.

NOLAN. I've never been painted in oils. It might do for campaign purposes. And if I should be elected, it would be very helpful to you in Washington.

MARION. You're awfully kind, Bunny. I must tell you frankly, though, that the dignified Senatorial style isn't exactly my forte. However, I might try. Yes— I'll try . . . (She gives him a long look.) I'll go the limit on you, Bunny—when I get through with you you'll be a symbol of Dignity. Solid man. No nonsense. Safe and sane. Holds the middle course—a slogan in a frock coat. I'll make you look like Warren G. Harding—even handsomer—Get you the women's votes.

NOLAN. Well, that'll be very nice of you. . . .

(MARION *suddenly kisses him.*)

MARION. Thank you, darling!

(*He is very uncomfortable, embarrassed and thrilled.*)

NOLAN. Marion—

MARION. Just a rush of feeling, dear!

NOLAN. You understand that this—this commission—

MARION. Of course. Strictly business. Don't worry. I shan't kiss you again till it's finished.

NOLAN. I don't know whether I told you—I'm going to be married in a month.

MARION. I'll have the portrait ready for your wedding day.

NOLAN. And I am devoted to Slade with every fiber of my being. . . .

MARION. Every fiber—how thorough!

NOLAN. I'm not a Bohemian, you know, Marion.

MARION. Don't tell me! You're a gypsy! (*She continues to study him, poses him, poses his hand.* MINNIE *enters from left with tea tray containing teapot, cups and saucers, spoons, sugar and cream, and a plate of cakes. She puts tray on model stand and exits left.*) Oh, Bunny, what fun it'll be to do you. Thank you, Minnie. Tell me—how do you see yourself?

NOLAN. What do you mean?

MARION. In your heart of hearts—how do you see yourself? Napoleon, Scipio, Mussolini—?

NOLAN. Nonsense! Do you think I'm an actor?

MARION. Of course. Everybody is. Everybody has some secret vision of himself. Do you know what mine is? Do you know how I see myself?

(*The doorbell rings.*)

NOLAN (*ironically*). More visitors!

MARION (*calls to* MINNIE). See who it is, will you, Minnie? . . . Probably the young man I met on the boat coming to take me to dinner.

NOLAN. What's his name?

MARION. I've forgotten. He's just a boy I met on the boat.

NOLAN. How can anybody live the way you live!

MARION. It's a special talent, dear. (*Doorbell rings again.*) Minnie, go to the door. (MINNIE *comes in and exits hallway.*) This is my lucky day, Bunny.

NOLAN. Would you mind, in front of strangers, not to call me Bunny?

MARION. Oh, of course, what is it?

NOLAN (*irritated*). Leander.

MARION (*mnemonic*). Leander—Hellespont—Leander. . . .

(MINNIE *comes downstage a few feet from the door.*)

MINNIE (*just inside the room*). It's the *Junge* who was here before—*er sagt er ist ausgeschifft da*—

MARION. Oh, show him in, Minnie, and bring a cup for him too.

MINNIE (*as she goes*). *Ja.*

NOLAN. And don't use these extravagant terms of endearment—anybody who didn't know you would misunderstand it.

MARION (*very happy*). All right, darling. (MINNIE *ushers in* RICHARD KURT, *goes out, comes back again with more tea.* MARION *comes forward to greet him.*) I'm so glad to see you again, Mr.—

KURT. Kurt.

MARION. Oh.

KURT. With a K.

MARION (*reassured*). Oh—I'll try to remember. This is Senator Nolan—Mr. Kurt.

NOLAN (*glowering*). I am not Senator Nolan.

MARION. But you will be. (*She offers him a cup of tea; he takes it.*) Can't I just call you that—between ourselves? It gives me such a sense of quiet power. And maybe it'll impress my visitor. Do have a cup of tea, Mr. Kurt.

(*She gives him one.*)

KURT (*puts his hat on sofa left*). I am not impressed by politicians. And I didn't come to drink tea. I am here on business. (*Nevertheless he takes a hearty sip.*)

MARION. Well, you can do both. They do in England. American businessmen are so tense.

KURT. I'm not a businessman.

NOLAN. Well, whatever you are, you are very ill-mannered.

KURT (*pleased*). That's true!

MARION (*delighted*). Isn't it nice you agree. For a moment I thought you weren't going to hit it off.

NOLAN. In my day if a boy came in and behaved like this before a lady he'd be horsewhipped.

KURT. Well, when you get into the Senate you can introduce a horsewhipping bill. Probably bring you great kudos.

NOLAN. You talk like a Bolshevik.

KURT. Thank you! You talk like a Senator!

(MARION *wants to laugh but thinks better of it. She looks at* KURT *with a new eye.*)

MARION (*quickly offering him more tea*). Another cup, Mr. Kurt. . . .

KURT (*taking it*). Thank you.

MARION. And one of these cakes— they're very nice . . . Minnie made them —almost as good as *Lebkuchen*. Minnie spoils me.

KURT (*taking it*). Thank you. (*Eats cake.*) Having said, from our respective points of view, the worst thing we could say about each other, having uttered the ultimate insult, there's no reason we can't be friends, Senator. Damn good cake. No lunch as a matter of fact.

MARION. That's what's the matter with him—he was hungry—hungry boy. . . .

NOLAN (*puts teacup on piano*). He probably wants to sell you some insurance.

KURT. Not at all. I'm not here to sell. I'm here to buy.

MARION. A picture!

KURT. Do I look like a picture-buyer!

MARION. As a matter of fact, you don't . . . but I haven't anything to sell except pictures.

KURT (*confidently*). I think you have!

MARION (*to* NOLAN). This young man is very tantalizing.

NOLAN. Well, why don't you ask him to state his proposition and have done with it?

MARION (*turns to* KURT *and repeats mechanically*). State your proposition and have done with it.

KURT (*puts his cup down on table rear of sofa Left*). What a nuisance women are!

NOLAN (*starting toward him*). Why, you insolent young whelp—I've half a mind to—

KURT (*pleasantly*). That's an impulse you'd better control. I wrote to this lady a business letter asking for an appointment. She granted it to me at four o'clock. It is now six. In that interval I've climbed these five flights of stairs three times. I've lost over an hour of my life going away and coming back. An hour in which I might have read a first-class book or made love to a girl or had an idea—an irreparable hour. That's rudeness, if you like. It's unbusinesslike. It's sloppy. (*To* MARION.) Now, will you see me alone or will you keep me here fencing with this inadequate antagonist?

MARION. You are unquestionably the most impossible young man I've ever met. Go away!

KURT. Right! (*He turns to go and means it and she knows that he means it. And she is consumed with curiosity*).(*As he goes.*) So long, Senator! Yours for the Revolution!

MARION (*as he reaches door, goes after him—pleads pitifully*). Young man! Mr. Nolan is an old friend of mine. I should consult him in any case about whatever business you may suggest. Can't you speak in front of him. (*At the same time she shakes her head to him not to go away.*)

KURT. I cannot!

MARION. Please wait a minute.

KURT. All right—one. (*He picks up a magazine and leafs through it negligently.*)

MARION (*to* LEANDER). After all, Leander, I can't afford—it may be something. . . . (*She takes his arm and starts walking him to the door, whispering.*) I'm just curious to hear what he's got to say for himself.

NOLAN. I'm not sure it's safe to leave you alone with a character like that.

MARION. Minnie's in her room . . . with a bow and arrow!

NOLAN (*going up to hall door*). I have to go in any case—I'm late now.

MARION. When will I see you, Bunny? (*She is at door with him.*)

NOLAN (*taking up his hat and coat*). I don't know. I'm very busy. I'll telephone you.

MARION. Do. Telephone me tonight. I'll tell you what he said. It'll probably be funny.

NOLAN (*out loud at* KURT). It pains me, that you are so unprotected that any hooligan—(KURT *turns page of magazine.*) can write you and come to see you in your apartment. However, that is the way you have chosen. Good night.

MARION. Good night, dear. Are you in the book? I'll telephone you—

NOLAN (*hastily*). No—no—you'd better not. I shall communicate with you. Good-by.

KURT. Good-by, Sir Galahad.

(NOLAN *starts to retort, changes his mind and in a very choleric mood, he goes out. There is a pause.*)

MARION. Well, I'm afraid you didn't make a very good impression on him!

KURT (*putting magazine away*). That's just too bad!

MARION. That's no way for a young

man to get on in the world—he's a very important person.

KURT. That's what passes for importance. You're not taken in by him, are you? Stuffed shirt—flatulent and pompous—perfect legislator!

MARION. As a matter of fact, he's a very nice man—simple and kindly.

(*Gets cigarettes and offers one to* KURT, *who takes it and lights it. She takes one too but he forgets to light hers.*)

KURT. I bet he isn't simple and he isn't kindly. I bet he's greedy and vicious. Anyway he's a hypocrite. When a man starts worrying out loud about unprotected women you may know he's a hypocritical sensualist.

MARION. You're a violent young man, aren't you? (*Not getting light from* KURT, *she lights her own, throwing match to floor.*)

KURT. Yes. The world is full of things and people that make me see red. . . . Why do you keep calling me youth and young man? I'm twenty-five.

MARION. Well, you seem to have the lurid and uncorrected imagination of the adolescent.

KURT. Imagination! That's where you're wrong. I may tell you, Miss Froude, that I'm as realistic as anybody you've ever met.

MARION (*sitting on upstage arm of sofa, Right*). Anybody who'd be so unreasonable over a nice fellow like Bunny Nolan . . . if you only knew—if only you'd been present at the interview I had with him just before you came. You'd have seen how wrong you are about him. Why, he was—he was awfully funny—but he was also touching.

KURT. You're one of those tolerant people, aren't you—see the best in people?

MARION. You say that as if tolerance were a crime.

KURT. Your kind is. It's criminal because it encourages dishonesty, incompetence, weakness, and all kinds of knavery. What you call tolerance I call sloppy laziness. You're like those book-reviewers who find something to praise in every mediocre book.

MARION. You are a fanatical young man.

KURT. Having said that, you think you dispose of me. Well, so be it. I'm disposed of. Now, let's get down to business. (*His manner plainly says: "Well, why should I bother to convince you? What impor-*

tance can it possibly have what you think of me?" It is not wasted on MARION.)

MARION. You are also a little patronizing.

KURT (*pleased*). Am I?

MARION. However, I don't mind being patronized. That's where my tolerance comes in. It even amuses me a little bit. (*Crossing to piano seat.*) But as I have to change for dinner perhaps you'd better—

KURT. Exactly.

MARION. Please sit down . . .

(*A moment . . . She sits on piano bench facing him.*)

KURT (*goes to piano and talks to her across it*). I am the editor of a magazine called *Every Week.* Do you know it?

MARION. It seems to me I've seen it on newsstands.

KURT. You've never read it?

MARION. I'm afraid I haven't.

KURT. That is a tribute to your discrimination. We have an immense circulation. Three millions, I believe. With a circulation of that size you may imagine that the average of our readers' intelligence cannot be very high. Yet occasionally we flatter them by printing the highbrows—indiscreet doses we give them, at intervals, Shaw and Wells and Chesterton. So you'll be in good company anyway. . . .

MARION (*amazed*) I will?

KURT. Yes. I want you to write your biography to run serially in *Every Week.* Later of course you can bring it out as a book.

MARION. My biography!

KURT. Yes. The story of your life.

MARION (*with dignity*). I know the meaning of the word.

KURT. The money is pretty good. I am prepared to give you an advance of two thousand dollars.

MARION. Good Heavens, am I as old as that—that people want my biography!

KURT. We proceed on the theory that nothing exciting happens to people after they are forty.

MARION. What a cruel idea!

KURT. Why wait till you're eighty. Your impressions will be dimmed by time. Most autobiographies are written by corpses. Why not do yours while you are still young, vital, in the thick of life?

MARION. But I'm not a writer. I shouldn't know how to begin.

KURT. You were born, weren't you?

Begin with that.

MARION. I write pleasant letters, my friends tell me. . . . But look here, why should you want this story from me—why should anybody be interested?—I'm not a first-rate artist you know—not by far—I'm just clever.

KURT (*bluntly*). It's not you—it's the celebrity of your subjects.

MARION (*amused*). You're a brutal young man—I rather like you . . .

KURT. Well, you've been courageous. You've been forthright. For an American woman you've had a rather extraordinary career—you've done pretty well what you wanted.

MARION. The Woman Who Dared sort-of-thing. . . . Isn't that passé?

KURT. I think your life will make good copy. You might have stayed here and settled down and done *Pictorial Review* covers of mothers hovering fondly over babies. Instead you went to Europe and managed to get the most inaccessible people to sit for you. How did you do it?

MARION. You'd be surprised how accessible some of these inaccessible people are!

KURT. Well, that's just what I want to get from your story. Just that. Tell what happened to you, that's all. The impulse that made you leave home, that made you go, for instance, to Russia before the popular emigration set in, that's made you wander ever since, that's kept you from settling down in any of the places where you had a chance to get established.

MARION (*quite seriously*). But supposing I don't know that. . . .

KURT. Well, that's interesting. That enigma is interesting. Maybe, while writing, you can solve it. It's a form of clarification. The more I talk to you the more I feel there's a great story in you and that you'll have great fun telling it.

MARION. Young man, you make me feel like an institution!

KURT. Should do you a lot of good in your professional career too—we'll reprint the portraits you've made of Lenin, Mussolini, Shaw—anything you like. . . .

(*She begins to laugh, quietly at first, then heartily.*)

MARION. Forgive me—

KURT (*unperturbed*). What's the matter?

MARION. Something I remembered—the funniest thing—isn't it funny how the oddest things pop into your mind?

KURT. What was it?

MARION. Something that happened years ago.

KURT. What?

MARION. Oh, I couldn't possibly tell you. It wouldn't be fair!

KURT. In that case it'll probably be great for the magazine. Save it!

MARION (*frightened*). You won't do anything lurid, will you?

KURT. Just print the story—just as you write it—practically as you write it.

MARION. I'm scared! (*She puts out her cigarette in ashtray on the piano.*)

KURT. Nonsense. Here's your first check. Two thousand dollars. (*He puts the check down on the table in front of her.*)

MARION (*wretched suddenly, picks up check, rises, looks at check*). I can't tell you how old this makes me feel!

KURT. Suppose I asked you to write a novel! That wouldn't make you feel old, would it? Well, I'm simply asking you to write a novel of your life. The only lively reading these days is biography. People are bored with fiction. It's too tame. The fiction-writers haven't the audacity to put down what actually happens to people.

MARION. You may be disappointed, you know. You probably see headlines in your mind. The Woman of a Hundred Affairs, The Last of the Great Adventuresses, The Magda Who Wouldn't Go Home. I promise you—it won't be a bit like that.

KURT. We'll announce it next month—first installment the following month. O.K.?

MARION (*puts down check, paces down Right*). Oh dear! I can't promise a thing like that—I really can't.

KURT. Why not?

MARION. It'll worry me too much.

KURT. Well, don't promise. Just get to work.

MARION (*faces him*). But what'll I do first?

KURT (*getting up*). Well, if I were you I'd sit down. (*She does so helplessly on piano bench.* KURT *then gives her paper, one of his own pencils.*) There now! You're all set!

MARION (*wailing*). How can I go out to dinner—how can I ever do anything—with a chapter to write?

KURT. After all you don't have to make up anything. Just tell what happened to you. (*He lights a fresh cigarette.*)

MARION. Can I use names?

KURT. When they're prominent, yes. The obscure ones you can fake if you want to. Nobody'll know 'em anyway.

MARION (*looks at him*). Oh . . . what's your name?

KURT (*looks at her*). I told you—my name's Kurt.

MARION. I know—with a K—I can't call you Kurt! What's your *name?*

KURT (*sulkily*). Richard.

MARION. That's better. I tell you, Dickie, when I think—when I think—of the funny men I've known . . . they're pretty nearly all brothers under the skin you know, Dickie.

KURT. Well, that, as they say in the office, is an angle.

(*Suddenly her fear vanishes and she is overcome with the marvelous possibilities.*)

MARION (*jumps up and leans toward him as if to kiss him, but quickly thinks better of it*). Dickie, I think it'll be marvelous! It'll be a knockout. And imagine— (*Picking up check.*) I'm going to be paid for it! Dickie, you're an angel!

KURT (*sardonically*). That's me! Angel Kurt! Well, so long. I'll be seeing you. (*Starts upstage toward hall door.*)

MARION (*suddenly panicky*). Oh, don't go!

KURT. You don't think I'm going to sit here and hold your hand while you're remembering your conquests, do you?

MARION. Well, you can't go away and leave me like this—alone with my life.

KURT. Perhaps it's time you got a good, straight, clear-eyed look at it—alone by yourself, without anybody around to hold your hand.

MARION (*suddenly*). No. I don't want to. (*Shrugs her shoulders as if she were cold.*) I think it would worry me. Besides, I feel superstitious about it.

KURT (*following her downstage*). Superstitious!

MARION. Yes. A kind of—ultimate act. After you've written your biography, what else could there possibly be left for you to do?

KURT. Collect material for another!

MARION. What could you do over again —that wouldn't be repetitious? (*Sits right arm of sofa right.*)

KURT. It's repetitious to eat or to make love, isn't it? You keep on doing it.

MARION. You're cynical!

KURT (*almost spits it out*). You're sentimental.

MARION. I am—"Sentimental Journey"—no, that's been used, hasn't it?

KURT. Don't worry about a title—I'll get that from the story after you've finished it.

MARION. There's something about it— I don't know—

KURT. What?

MARION. Vulgar? *Everybody* spouting memoirs. Who cares?

KURT. Well, wrong hunch! Sorry to have taken your valuable time. Good-by.

MARION (*the finality frightens her*). What do you mean?

KURT (*he is withering—crosses to her*). I'm prepared to admit I was mistaken—that's all. In your desire to escape vulgarity you would probably be—thin. You might even achieve refinement. I'm not interested. Padded episodes hovering on the edge of amour—

MARION (*turns on him*). Young man, you're insufferable!

KURT. And you're a false alarm!

MARION (*after a moment*). I congratulate you! You've brought me to the verge of losing my temper! But I tell you this—you're quite mistaken about the character of my life—and about my relations with my friends. My story won't be thin and episodic because my life hasn't been thin and episodic. And I won't have to pad—the problem will be to select. I'm going to write the damn thing just to show you. Come in tomorrow afternoon for a cocktail.

KURT. Whose memoirs are these going to be, yours or mine?

MARION. Well, you're an editor, aren't you? (*She smiles at him.*) Come in and edit.

KURT. All right, I'll come. But if you aren't here I'll go away. I won't wait a minute.

(*He goes out quickly.* MARION *stands looking after him, inclined to laugh, and yet affected. This is a new type even for her.*)

MARION (*she speaks to herself*). What an extraordinary young man! (*In a moment* KURT *comes back in.* MARION *is very glad to see him, greets him as if there had been a long separation.*) Oh, hello!

KURT (*embarrassed*). I forgot my hat! (*He can't see it at once.*)

MARION (*without moving or looking away from him, she indicates the hat on the sofa left.*) There it is! Right next to mine.

KURT (*crosses for it*). Oh yes. (*Picks up*

the hat.) Thanks. (*For a moment he stands uncertainly, hat in hand, looking at* MARION *who has not taken her eyes off him. He is embarrassed.*) Well, so long!

MARION. So long. (KURT *leaves again. She stands as before looking after him. She turns toward the piano—sees the check—picks it up and reads it to make sure it's true. The whole thing has a slightly fantastic quality to her. She is very happy and exited. She waves the check in her hand like a pennant, and humming, she crosses to the piano seat and sits and plays the waltz from "Danubia." She sees the pad and pencil on the piano and stops playing, and picking up the pencil and the pad, she crosses to the small armchair in the upstage end of the window and sits with her feet on the window seat. She repeats the first words of the first chapter aloud to herself as she writes them down.*) I am born . . . (MINNIE *enters from door left to get the tea things she had left on the model stand.* MARION *taps the pencil on the pad as she repeats the words:*) I am born . . . (*The time seems remote to her.*) I am born— I meet Richard Kurt—Well, Minnie, here's the outline—I am born . . . I meet Richard Kurt—now all I have to do is to fill in. . . .

(MINNIE, *used to having irrelevancies addressed to her, takes this program rather stolidly.*)

MINNIE. *Was*, Marion?

MARION (*Trying to get rid of her*). Fix something light, will you, Minnie. . . . I'm not going out.

MINNIE. *Aber der Junge kommt!*

MARION. What *Junge?*

MINNIE. *Der Junge, den Sie* . . .

MARION. Oh, yes! The *Junge* I met on the boat. You'll have to send him away. I can't go out tonight. From now on, Minnie, no more frivolous engagements!

MINNIE (*astonished*). *Sie bleiben den ganzen Abend zu Hause!*

MARION. Yes, Minnie. I'm spending the evening alone with my life . . . (*She remembers* KURT's *words and repeats them as if, after all, they have made a profound impression on her.*) . . . get a good, straight, clear-eyed look at it.

MINNIE (*picks up the tea tray and bustles toward the kitchen, promising delights*). *Eine Fleischbrühe und Pfannkuchen!* (MINNIE *exits door Left.*)

MARION (*already brooding over her past*). I am born. . . .

(*Slowly the* CURTAIN *falls.*)

ACT TWO

SCENE: *The same. About three weeks later. Afternoon.*

AT RISE: MARION *is putting some touches on the full-length portrait of* LEANDER NOLAN *which stands away from the audience. She is wearing her working costume, baggy red corduroy trousers, a sash, and a worn blue smock over a kind of sweater-jacket. She is very happy. . . . On the piano nearby are her writing things. While touching up* LEANDER *she is struck by an idea for her book. Puts down her brush and palette and goes to the piano to jot down some notes. The idea pleases her. She giggles to herself. Then she returns to her easel.* MINNIE *comes in and stands watching her a moment before* MARION *sees her.*

———

MARION (*sees* MINNIE *at last*). Oh yes, Minnie—do you want anything?

MINNIE. You asked me to come right away, Marion.

MARION. Did I?

MINNIE. *Ja.* (*Sitting on sofa Right.*) So! You have left a note on the kitchen I should come in right away I am back from the market.

MARION (*studying the portrait*). Of course I did. That's right, Minnie.

MINNIE. Well, what did you want, Marion?

MARION (*washing paintbrush in turpentine jar*). Did I tell you there'd be two for dinner?

MINNIE. *Ja. Gewiss! Das ist* vy I went to the market.

MARION. Well, I've changed my plans. I'm dining out with Feydie after all.

MINNIE (*rising and looking at picture*). *Ach, Gott!* (*She studies the portrait.*)

MARION (*looks humorously at* MINNIE *and puts her arm about* MINNIE's *shoulders*). *Gut?*

MINNIE. *Ziemlich gut—*

MARION. Do you know who it is?

MINNIE. *Oh, das sieht man ja gleich. Das ist Herr* Nolan!

MARION (*shaking her hand in gratitude*). Thank you, Minnie! (*Doorbell rings.*) See who that is, will you, Minnie?

MINNIE. *Fräulein ist zu Hause?*

MARION. *Ich erwarte Herr* Feydak. *Für ihn bin ich immer zu Hause.*

MINNIE (*agreeing heartily as she crosses to the door*). *Ja, ja, der Herr* Feydak.

(MINNIE *goes out.* MARION *jots down a note on the pad which is on the piano.* FEYDAK *enters.* MINNIE *closes the door and exits Left.*)

MARION (at piano). Hello Feydie! Sit down!

FEYDAK. Well, my dear, which career do I interrupt?

MARION (laughing). I don't know!

FEYDAK. One comes to see you with diffidence nowadays. (FEYDAK removes coat and hat and places them on the upstage end of the sofa Right, and sits on the left side of the sofa.)

MARION. While I'm painting I think of funny things to say, funny phrases. It won't be a serious biography, thank God. I'm dedicating it to Vicki: "To Vicki—the gayest person I have ever known!" By the way, have you got any little snapshots of Vicki—all I've got are formal photographs with his orders. I'd like to get something a little more intimate.

FEYDAK. I'll hunt some up for you.

MARION. Have you heard from the Powers yet, when you are to leave?

FEYDAK. Tomorrow.

MARION (stricken—sits right of him). Feydie!

FEYDAK (fatalistically). Tomorrow. (They sit.) I shall leave you with sorrow, Marion.

MARION. I'll have no one to laugh with.

FEYDAK. For me it's an exile.

MARION. You'll have a wonderful time. I shall miss you terribly.

FEYDAK. Perhaps you'll come out.

MARION. Perhaps I will. I've always wanted to go to China. If I have enough money left from all my labors I'll stop in on you—en route to China.

FEYDAK. That would be marvelous.

MARION. You know, writing one's life has a sobering effect on one—you get it together and you think: "Well! look at the damn thing . . ."

FEYDAK. Do you want to be impressive?

MARION. Well, I don't want to be trivial.

FEYDAK. I think you escape that.

MARION. My friendships haven't been trivial. . . . (She gives his hand a squeeze.)

FEYDAK. Have you seen that bombastic young man?

MARION. Oh, yes. He comes in every once in a while to see how I'm getting on. He's quite insulting. Underneath his arrogance I suspect he's very uncertain.

FEYDAK. Oh, now, don't tell me he has an inferiority complex!

MARION. Well, I think he has!

FEYDAK. The new psychology is very confusing. In my simple day you said:

"That young man is bumptious and insufferable" and you dismissed him. Now you say: "He has an inferiority complex" and you encourage him to be more bumptious and more insufferable. It's very confusing.

MARION. There's a kind of honesty about him that I like.

FEYDAK (instantly putting two and two together). Oh!

MARION. Nothing like that, Feydie! As a matter of fact—I don't mind telling you . . . I like him very much—

FEYDAK. I think he is destined—

MARION. He's not interested. He's some kind of fanatic. Social, I think. I've met that kind in Russia—quite unassailable. But I'm optimistic. . . . (They laugh.) Well, one must never despair, must one. Life is so much more resourceful and resilient than one is oneself. Three weeks ago when you came to see me I felt quite at the end of my rope. I didn't tell you quite but I actually didn't know which way to turn. I felt tired too—which troubled me. Well, now I find myself, quite suddenly, (She indicates portrait.) doing Leander and — (She indicates manuscript on piano.) doing myself. New Vista. Very exciting.

FEYDAK. All this enthusiasm for art alone?

MARION (laughing). Of course!—Feydie, what did you think?

FEYDAK. I don't believe it.

MARION. Come here and have a look at Leander!

FEYDAK (he rises—walks to the canvas on the easel). Hm! Formal!

MARION. It's to hang in the White House.

(She winks at him, he laughs, puts his arm around her shoulder.)

FEYDAK. Marion, you're adorable!

(They walk downstage together, their arms around each other's shoulders, very affectionately.)

MARION. Oh, Feydie, I'm having a wonderful time. Quiet too. Writing enforces silence and solitude on one. I've always lived in such a rush—a kind of interminable scherzo.

FEYDAK. Good title!

MARION. Think so? I'll put it down. . . . (Writes on pad on piano. FEYDAK sits on right arm of sofa left, facing her.) Interminable scherzo. . . . How do you spell it? A little affected. Might do for a hapter heading maybe. . . . (*Returns to im—sitting on model-stand—facing him.*) ut I realize now I haven't in years had me to stop and think. I sit here for ours, Feydie, and nothing comes to me. 'hen, suddenly, the past will come in n me with a rush—odd, remote, semiorgotten things of the past. Are they rue? How much is true? One can never e sure, can one? I remember certain riefs and fears. I remember their existnce without recalling at all their intenity—their special anguish. Why? What vas the matter with me? What made hem so acute? It is like recalling a andscape without color, a kind of colorlindness of the memory. (*Doorbell rings. he calls out to her factotum.*) Minnie!

MINNIE *enters Left and crosses rapidly to all door.* MARION *arranges the model-stand n which stands the papal armchair in red nd gold.*) This is probably the Hon. Nolan. He's due for a sitting. He pretends le doesn't like to have his picture painted, but I know he does.

(MINNIE *enters from hallway. She is lustered and giggly.*)

MINNIE (*very high-pitched voice*). *Herr* Varvick Vilson!

MARION. Tympi Wilson!

MINNIE (*to* FEYDAK). Der *film star!*

FEYDAK. So?

MINNIE (*radiant*). *Ja! Ja!*

MARION. Oh, Feydie, you'll adore this. Ask him in, Minnie.

MINNIE (*as she goes out to admit* WILSON). *Gott, ist er schön!*

MARION. Warwick's public.

FEYDAK. And mine!

MARION (*in a quick whisper*). Whatever you do—outstay him!

(MINNIE *has opened the door and* WARWICK WILSON *enters. He is very handsome, explosively emotional, and given to cosmic generalization. He is in evening clothes.*)

WILSON (*with a red carnation in his buttonhole, crossing to* MARION *and kissing her hand*). Marion!

MARION. Warwick!

WILSON. Darling! How are you?

MARION. I'm splendid. Been up all night?

WILSON. No, no! This is business.

(MINNIE *has crossed to kitchen door Upper Left, never taking her eyes from* WILSON.)

MARION. This is Mr. Feydak. Mr. Warwick Wilson, the famous film star.

WILSON (*crosses to sofa and shakes hands with* FEYDAK—*dramatically*). Feydak! *The* Mr. Feydak?

FEYDAK (*again mistaken for his brother*). *Ja.*

WILSON. I've heard of you indeed!

FEYDAK. Have you? Thanks.

MARION. Mr. Feydak is on his way to Hollywood. He is to write the music for . . .

WILSON (*sits on the model-stand—facing front*). Of course! I am honored, Mr. Feydak—deeply honored. That unforgettable waltz—how does it go? . . . (*He starts to hum with a swaying gesture the waltz from the "Merry Widow."*) Music's my one passion!

MARION. Once you said it was me.

WILSON. A lot of good it did me!

MARION (*to* WILSON). Well, tell me . . . (*She sees* MINNIE, *who is still staring at* WILSON.) Look at Minnie. The mere sight of you has upset her so that she's speechless.

MINNIE. *Aber, Fräulein!*

(WILSON *rises graciously and gives* MINNIE *a friendly wave of the hand. He's no snob.* MINNIE, *speechless with delight, exits left.* WILSON *returns to his position on the model-stand.*)

MARION. All right, Minnie! Warwick, Warwick! You mustn't do things like that to Minnie, at her age!

WILSON (*tragically*). There you are! This face! This cursed face! I should go masked really. One has no private life!

MARION (*sits in throne chair on model-stand*). What would you do with it if you had it, eh, Tympi?

WILSON (*delighted*). That nickname!

MARION. It just rolled off my tongue. Did I call you that?

WILSON. You did! You invented it. No one's called me that since you left Hollywood. And you promised to explain the significance to me, but you ever did.

MARION. Did it have a significance?

FEYDAK. Marion has a knack for nicknames.

MARION. I love 'em. I'd like to do a chapter on nicknames.

WILSON (*highly pleased*). Tympi! Tympi! (*Very patronizing to* FEYDAK.) You are an intuitive person, Mr. Feydak. I can see that. (FEYDAK *ad libs:* "*Danke schön.*") Can you imagine what she meant?

FEYDAK. Her vagaries are beyond me, Mr. Wilson.

WILSON (*leaning back toward* MARION). Speak, Oracle! No! Don't tell me now.

Put it into that book you're writing.

MARION (MARION *and* FEYDAK *exchange glances*). How things get around.

WILSON. It's been in the back of my mind for years, Marion . . . to have you paint me. Now that we're both in town together—

MARION. Well, I'd *love* to . . .

WILSON. In the costume of the Dane. (MARION *and* FEYDAK *exchange a look.* WILSON *strikes a pose.*) I'd like to be done in *his* costume. I hope, Mr. Feydak, that they won't break your spirit in Hollywood as they've almost broken mine!

FEYDAK (*with a smile*). My spirit is indestructible!

WILSON (*rises and crosses to rear of sofa and pats* FEYDAK *on the back*). I'm glad to hear it. (*Returns to left of model-stand and stands with his right foot on it.*) You know, for years I've been begging them to do Shakespeare. (*Gesticulates.*)

MARION (*interrupting him*). Sit down and be comfortable.

WILSON. They simply won't listen. But I'm going to give up acting and produce!

MARION. Oh, good God! Don't do that!

WILSON. Why not?

MARION. What would Minnie do with her night off?

WILSON (*smiles*). My public, eh?

MARION. Yes!

WILSON. Quite so! (*Patronizingly.*) You artists who work in media like painting or literature— (*to* FEYDAK.) Or music, that too is a beautiful art, Mr. Feydak— transcends speech—transcends everything, by saying nothing it says all.

FEYDAK. *Ja!*

(*The doorbell rings.*)

WILSON. You are certainly lucky compared to us poor actors. We— (MINNIE *enters and crosses to halldoor Upper Center.*) Wouldn't it be ironic if all that remained of me after I am gone were your painting of me. That is why I want it perhaps— my poor grasp on immortality.

FEYDAK. You see, Marion, you confer immortality!

MARION. I think immortality is an over-rated commodity. But tell me, Tympi, what are you doing away from Hollywood?

MINNIE (*comes in announcing*). Der Herr Nolan!

(MINNIE *then looks at* WILSON. WILSON *stands—looks at* MINNIE.)

MARION. Show him in. Show him i (*With a lingering look at* WILSON, MINNI goes back. *To others, after watching* MINNI exit.) You see!

FEYDAK. The effect is instantaneou —like music.

(NOLAN *enters.* MINNIE *follows* NOLA in and exits into kitchen, murmuring ecsta ically, "Gott! Ist er schön!" looking WILSON.)

MARION. Hello Bunny! (*Introducin* NOLAN.) You know Mr. Feydak. M Nolan, this is Warwick Wilson, you'v heard of him.

(FEYDAK *bows to* NOLAN, *who returns th bow.*)

WILSON. It's a pleasure, Mr. Nolar I've heard of *you* indeed!

(*They shake hands.*)

MARION. You're late for your sitting Bunny. Will the presence of these gentle men embarrass you? I don't mind if yo don't.

NOLAN (*has entered rather worried an angry. He has a magazine rolled in his hand He now speaks very irritatedly*). As a matte of fact, Marion—

MARION (*putting him in throne chair o model-stand*). Oh, sit down like a goo fellow. The light is getting bad. (NOLA sits. WILSON *sits on the right arm of the sof Left on which* FEYDAK *is sitting.* MARIO gets to work on BUNNY.) How did you fin me, Tympi?

WILSON. I read in a magazine that yo were barging into literature—

NOLAN (*half-rising, showing magazine*) This is true then!

MARION. Don't get up, Bunny . . (*Nevertheless she takes the magazine an looks at it.*) Well, Dickie has gone an spread himself, hasn't he? (*She sits o sofa Left between* WILSON *and* FEYDAK. Look here, Feydie! (*Shows him the full page announcement of her book in magazine*.

FEYDAK (*looking*). Do you think yo can live up to this?

MARION. Why will they write this sor of thing! (*Rises and goes back.*) Makes m out a kind of female Casanova. (*She drop the magazine on the stand at* NOLAN's *feet.* Well, they'll be disappointed.

NOLAN (*bitterly*). Will they?

MARION. Bunny! (*But she thinks nothing of it—merely pushes him into a better light.*

FEYDAK (*tactfully—he senses danger*) May I ask, Mr. Wilson—are you mak ing a picture at the moment?

WILSON. No, I'm in New York making some personal appearances.

MARION. Personal appearances. I love that phrase. Has such an air of magnanimity about it. (*Crosses to painting.*)

WILSON. Pretty boring, I can tell you! I've got writer's cramp signing autograph books. It's a perfect martyrdom, I assure you. It's no fun at all.

(WILSON *crosses to stand—puts his right foot on it, leans on his knee with his right arm and studies* NOLAN, *his face not six inches away from* NOLAN'S. NOLAN *fidgets.*)

MARION. I can imagine! What's the matter, Bunny? You seem under a strain today . . . not relaxed.

NOLAN (*bursting out and glaring at all of them*). It's like being watched while you're taking a bath!

MARION. Oh, I'm so sorry, Bunny!

FEYDAK (*rising*). I quite sympathize with Mr. Nolan.

WILSON (*moves away*). Supposing I were so shy, eh, Mr. Nolan?

FEYDAK (*crosses to* MARION, *who is above her easel, Right*). I'm off, Marion. (*Kisses her hand.*) Auf Wiedersehen!

MARION (*meaningfully*). You'll have to go— (WILSON *sits again on arm of sofa Left*) both of you.

WILSON (*rises*). I was just going myself. My next appearance is at 6:45. (*Speaks to others.*)

FEYDAK (*to help her*). Perhaps I can drop you, Mr. Wilson.

WILSON (*faces* FEYDAK). No, I'll drop you . . . (*Turns to* MARION.) I say, Marion . . .

(FEYDAK, *helpless, goes upstage putting on coat.*)

MARION. Yes, Tympi?

WILSON. If you started my portrait right away and it turns out—I am sure it will turn out—you might put it in your book, mightn't you? I'm frankly sick of just appearing in fan magazines.

MARION. We'll see. Why not?

WILSON. Splendid! *Don't fail to come tonight.* Good-bye, dearest Marion. Good-by again, Mr. Nolan.

(*He starts to shake* NOLAN'S *hand but is interrupted by* MARION, *almost screaming.*)

MARION. No, no, no! Don't do *that*— don't touch him.

WILSON. Most happy! See you later . . .

(*He waves himself off at last*—MARION *returns to her easel.*)

MARION (*to* FEYDAK). Don't forget— I'm dining with you.

FEYDAK (*like the player in Hamlet who burlesques Polonius*). Most happy—see you later. (FEYDAK *leaves.*)

MARION (*with relief*). Now then . . .

NOLAN (*muttering to himself*). Silly ass!

MARION (*working on painting*). That young man is one of the most famous people in the world, do you realize that, Bunny? His profile follows you all over Europe—*and* Asia. Ubiquitous profile. Have you ever seen him?

NOLAN (*unswerved*). He's a silly ass!

MARION. I admit he's somewhat on that side—but that other one—that Feydie—he's the darling of the world!

NOLAN (*very short—bitterly*). Evidently!

MARION (*surprised*). Bunny!

NOLAN (*savage now*). Who isn't a darling! Everyone's a darling as far as I can see! The world's full of darlings. Your world at any rate.

MARION. But, darling—(*She suddenly stops—sits right end of sofa Right.*) Oh, Bunny, I remember now!

NOLAN. You remember what!

MARION. Tympi! Why I nicknamed him Tympi. Don't you see?

NOLAN. No, I don't see.

MARION. For tympanum—a large instrument in the orchestra producing a hollow sound. (*She beats an imaginary drum with her paintbrush.*) Boom! (*Suddenly* NOLAN *quits the pose.*) What is it?

NOLAN. I can't sit today. I'm not in the mood.

MARION. I could tell there was something worrying you.

NOLAN. There is something worrying me!

MARION. Well, what is it?

NOLAN. This confounded story! Are you really writing it?

MARION. Well, yes—I am.

NOLAN. What do you intend to tell?

MARION. Well, that's a rather difficult question to answer—it's like asking me what I've been doing all my life.

NOLAN. When does this biography start?

MARION (*beginning to wonder about this questioning*). With my birth—coincidence, isn't it?

NOLAN. All the time back home— when you were a girl in Knoxville?

MARION. Yes, of course. I've had a wonderful time going back over it all.

NOLAN. Everything?

MARION. Everything I can remember.

NOLAN. Do I come into it?

MARION (*smiling to herself*). You do! You certainly do!

NOLAN. You must leave me out of that story!

MARION. But Bunny, how can I possibly leave you out?

NOLAN. You must, that's all.

MARION. But how can I? You were too important—think of the role you played in my life. By your own confession, Bunny darling, you—you started me. That's a good idea for a chapter-heading, isn't it? "Bunny Starts Me." I must put that down.

NOLAN. This is no joke, Marion. (*With menace.*) I warn you—

MARION. Warn me! Let me understand you. Are you seriously asking me to give up an opportunity like this just because . . .

NOLAN (*rises and gets down from the model-stand. Speaks with brutal command*). Opportunity! Cheap exhibitionism! A chance to flaunt your affairs in a rag like this. (*Indicating magazine on piano.*) I won't be drawn into it. I can tell you that! (*He is in a towering rage.*)

MARION (*after a pause*). I know that by your standards, Bunny, I'm a loose character. But there are other standards, there just are.

NOLAN (*crosses to center—drops magazine on model-stand*). Not in Tennessee!

MARION (*rises*). I'm afraid you're provincial, Bunny.

NOLAN. I'm sorry.

MARION (*takes off her smock, crosses to small table down Right, gets her notes, then crosses to desk Upper Right*). I don't care what the advertisements say about my story—I know what I'm writing . . .

NOLAN. I'm sorry.

MARION. That's all right.

(*But this has gone pretty deep.*)

NOLAN (*after a pause*). If you're doing this for money—(*She turns and watches him.*) I know you've been pretty hard up —I promise you I'll get you commissions enough to more than make up for this story. I was talking about you only the other day to my prospective father-in-law. He's a big man, you know. I am sure I can get him to sit for you.

MARION. The tip isn't big enough.

NOLAN (*scared now that he sees the extent to which he has hurt her*). Marion!

MARION. It amuses me to write my life. I am pleasure-loving—you know that—I will therefore pass up the opportunity of painting your big father-in-law. I will even give up the pleasure of painting you. And we can part friends, then, can't we? (*She reaches out her hand to him.*) Good-by, Bunny.

NOLAN (*devastated*). Marion—you can't do this to me—you can't send me away like this . . .

MARION. I don't think ever in my life that I've had a vulgar quarrel with anyone. This is the nearest I've come to it. I'm a little annoyed with you for that. I think it's better we part now while we can still do so with some—dignity. Shall we?

NOLAN. You don't realize what's involved—or you wouldn't talk like that . . .

MARION. What *is* involved?

NOLAN. My entire career. That's what's involved.

MARION. Oh!

NOLAN. This is the most critical moment of my life. My fiancée's father is the most powerful leader of opinion in my state. Frankly, I depend on him for support. To have this kind of thing bandied about now might cause a permanent rift between him and me— might seriously interfere not only with my candidacy for the Senate, but with my marriage.

MARION. They are interlocking—I quite understand.

NOLAN. A revelation of this kind— coming at this moment—might be fatal.

MARION. Revelation! You make me feel like—I can't tell you what you make me feel like . . . (*She laughs—semi-hysterically.*)

NOLAN (*sepulchral*). You must give this up, Marion.

MARION. I've met distinguished men abroad — politicians, statesmen — a Prime Minister even—and this kind of "revelation"—as you so luridly call it, is no more to them than a theme for after-dinner banter. They take it in their stride. My God, Bunny, you take it so big!

NOLAN. These people I'm depending on to elect me aren't sophisticated like you or me. (MARION *looks at* NOLAN *with some surprise.*) What I means is—they're country people essentially—my future father-in-law is sympathetic to their point of view.

MARION. Tell me—your father-in-law, is he the man with the chest-expansion?

NOLAN. He's a fine sturdy man—as you perhaps know, he makes a fetish of exercise.

MARION (*bubbling again*). You see his pictures in shorts in health magazines.

NOLAN. There's no disgrace in that.

MARION (*sits right arm of sofa Left*). It doesn't shock me, Bunny. I was just identifying him, that's all.

NOLAN. I owe everything to Kinnicott —I wouldn't be running for the Senate right now if not for him. I can't risk offending him.

MARION. What the devil's happened to you anyway? You used to be quite a nice boy—even fun occasionally.

NOLAN (*wistful—turns away*). Maybe— if you had stuck to me—

MARION. Ts! Ts! Ts! Poor Bunny. I'm sorry for you. Really I am! (*She strokes his arm.*)

NOLAN (*suddenly passionate—faces her*). Don't touch me!

MARION (*amazed*). Bunny!

NOLAN. Do you think I'm not human!

MARION. Well, if you aren't the most contradictory—

NOLAN. I realized the moment I came in here the other day—the moment I saw you—

MARION (*interrupting*). But Bunny! You're engaged and you're going to be a Senator.

NOLAN (*walks away from her*). Forget it! Forget I ever said it. . . .

MARION. You bewilder me . . . .

NOLAN (*bitterly*). I'm not surprised I bewilder you. You've spent your life among a lot of foreign counts. It's well known that foreigners are more immoral than we are.

MARION. I'm very touched. I am really. (*She kisses him in a friendly way.*)

NOLAN. Don't do that! I forbid you!

MARION. All right. I'll never attack you again, I promise.

NOLAN. I wish I had never come back into your life—it was a terrible mistake —you'd forgotten me.

MARION (*seriously*). Oh, you're wrong. First love—one doesn't forget that.

NOLAN (*passionately*). But you did! You forgot me! And if you got the chance again, you'd humiliate me again.

MARION. Humiliate! What queer notions you have—Is it a question of pride or vanity between us? We're old friends —friends.

NOLAN (*moves a step right*). Please forget this—I don't know what came over me —I . . .

MARION. Of course. There's nothing to forget. (*Moves a step toward him.*) It's quite all right, dear . . . (*She pats him on his hand.*) . . . Oh, excuse me.

NOLAN. I warn you, Marion—I solemnly warn you—if you persist in this—

MARION. Never in my life have I seen a man vacillate so between passion and threat.

NOLAN. I shall find ways to stop you. Mr. Kinnicott, my future father-in-law, is a powerful man.

MARION. I know. Extraordinary biceps.

NOLAN. I warn you, Marion. This matter is beyond flippancy.

MARION (*sits*). There'll be some very distinguished people in my biography. You needn't be ashamed.

NOLAN. That movie-actor!

MARION. Tympi in Hamlet costume— you in a toga. I'll print your portraits on opposite pages—my two men!

NOLAN. You are malicious!

MARION. I must admit, Bunny, that you provoke in me all my malicious impulses. You come here suddenly and you convey to me what I've missed in not marrying you. (*The back doorbell rings.* MINNIE *crosses to answer it during* MARION'S *speech.*) You dangle before me the inventory of your felicities—a career, a fortune, a fabulous bride—and then, because I get a chance to chronicle my own adventures—you object—you tell me I mustn't! I have a nice nature, Bunny, or I should be angry—I should be indignant.

(KURT *enters.*)

NOLAN (*sharply and with threat*). Now, Marion, I've warned you . . . You'll regret this.

MARION. Hello, Dickie, do talk to Bunny for a minute, will you? (*Crosses to the stairs and starts up them to her bedroom.*) I've simply got to change. (MINNIE *enters up Center and exits Left.*) Feydie's coming to take me out to dinner.

NOLAN. But, Marion . . .

MARION. I couldn't do anything about this in any case, Bunny dear, because

I've promised Dickie. In fact, I signed something, didn't I, Dickie? Don't go away either of you. . . .

(MARION *blows them a kiss and exits into her bedroom. A pause between the two men.* KURT *crosses downstage to above the model-stand. Suddenly* NOLAN *goes to* KURT *and reaches out his hand to him.*)

NOLAN. How do you do, young man?

KURT (*very much surprised*). How do *you* do? (*He looks at him narrowly, his head a little on one side, a terrier appraising a mastiff.*)

NOLAN. I am very glad to see you.

KURT. Isn't that nice.

NOLAN. You may be surprised to learn that on the one occasion when we met you made quite an impression on me.

KURT. Did I?

NOLAN (*sits sofa Right*). You did. Sit down. In fact—I hope you don't mind —if you will allow me as a prerogative of seniority—to ask you a few questions. I have a purpose in mind and not—I trust—an idle purpose.

KURT. Shoot! (*Sits.*) Anything to enlighten the professor! (*He knows he is going to be pumped and has decided to be causal, naïve, and even respectful.*)

NOLAN (*clearing his throat*). Now then —your present position on the magazine you represent—have you been on it long?

KURT. About two years.

NOLAN. And before that?

KURT. Newspaper work.

NOLAN. And before that?

KURT. Tramping around the world. Odd jobs. Quite a variety.

NOLAN. College?

KURT. Believe it or not—Yale—two years . . . worked my way through— washed dishes.

NOLAN. Very interesting preparation . . . very interesting . . . Tell me now— your present work—do you find it interesting? Is the remuneration satisfactory?

KURT. Two hundred smackers a week. That's twice what I've ever earned in my life before.

NOLAN. Now then—to come to the point—no doubt you've heard of my prospective father-in-law, Mr. Orrin Kinnicott?

KURT. Heard of him! We pay him the compliment of imitation. He is our model, our criterion, our guiding star!

NOLAN. As you know, Mr. Kinnicott's interests are varied. He owns some powerful newspapers in my state. The other day I heard him say that he wanted a new man in Washington.

KURT (*playing naïvely excited*). Now that's something to give one's eyeteeth for!

NOLAN (*pleased at the result*). I think it might be possible to swing it—very possible.

KURT. God, what a break!

NOLAN. As it happens, Mr. Kinnicott is at present in town. I shall arrange an appointment for you in the next few days. Naturally, I expect you to keep the matter entirely confidential.

KURT. Naturally! You needn't worry on that score, Senator, I assure you.

NOLAN. Thank you, Mr. Kurt. That is all I ask.

(*A pause.*)

KURT. Mr. Nolan—do you mind if I ask *you* something?

NOLAN. Certainly not . . .

KURT. You won't consider me impertinent?

NOLAN (*with a smile*). I don't object to impertinence, Mr. Kurt. I was often considered impertinent myself when I was your age.

KURT. Why are you making me this offer?

NOLAN. I am not making you an offer. I shall merely attempt to expedite—

KURT. Why? The first time we met we didn't exactly hit it off, now, did we? Why then are you going to all this trouble?

NOLAN. I have discussed you with Miss Froude, who is an old friend of mine and whose opinion I greatly respect. She thinks very highly of you, Mr. Kurt. My own impression—

KURT (*inexorably*). Why? What, as they say, is the pay-off?

NOLAN. I'll tell you. I'll tell you quite frankly. I don't want Miss Froude's autobiography, which you have persuaded her to write, to appear in your magazine. I want it killed!

KURT. Oh! You want it killed?

NOLAN. Exactly.

KURT. Why?

NOLAN. Marion knows why. We needn't go into that.

KURT (*wounded by a sudden and devasting jealousy*). Good God! You! You too!

(MARION *enters from balcony. She is*

wearing a dove-colored evening-dress—the *amine transformed into lady-of-the-world.*)

MARION. Well! How have you two boys been getting on? What do you think?

KURT (*seething. Crosses to foot of stairs*). 'll tell you what I think—

MARION. About the dress, I mean. *She does a turn for them.*)

NOLAN (*without looking up at her or the dress. He is watching* KURT). It's charming.

MARION. Thank you, Bunny. With all his faults Bunny is much more satisfactory than you are, Dickie.

KURT (*at boiling point*). He's chivalrous, he is! His chivalry is so exquisite that he has just been attempting to bribe me to keep your story from being published. His gallantry is so delicate that he's terrified about being mentioned in it.

MARION (*comes down stairs during* KURT'S *speech*). Don't be so worked up about it, Dickie. You're another one who takes it big. It's catching!

KURT (*flaring at her*). You're not very sensitive.

MARION. Why should I be? You misapprehend Bunny. If he doesn't want to be in the same story with me, that's his business. And it's nothing to do with chivalry or gallantry or nonsense like that.

NOLAN. Marion—this young man—

KURT (*taunting him*). What about Washington, Mr. Nolan? Mr. Nolan, a prospective Senator offers to bribe me with a post in Washington controlled by his prospective father-inlaw—

MARION. If it's a good job take it, Dickie, by all means. . . .

KURT. I am afraid, Marion, that your code is more relaxed than mine—

MARION. Code, nonsense! I gave up codes long ago. I'm a big *laissez-faire* girl!

NOLAN. If this young man is an example of the distinguished company you've come to associate with, Marion—

MARION. Don't quarrel children—please. It distresses me.

NOLAN. He's extremely objectionable.

KURT. What about Washington, now, *Senator?* Are you still willing to expedite—!

(KURT *and* NOLAN *stand glaring at each other.* MARION *tries to calm the troubled waters. Crosses to* NOLAN.)

MARION. Really, Dickie, you're very

naughty. Don't mind him, Bunny. He's very young.

KURT. And incorruptible!

NOLAN. Marion, I claim the privilege of a friendship that antedates Mr. Kurt's by some years, to beg you, very solemnly, not to prostitute your talents to his contemptible, sensation-mongering rag.

KURT (*faces them*). There's a Senatorial sentence!

MARION. Hush, Dickie, hush! Bunny darling, it's true that Dickie's magazine isn't the *Edinburgh Review*. On the other hand, your assumption that my story will be vulgar and sensational is a little gratuitous, isn't it?

NOLAN. You *refuse* then?

MARION (*gently but with a serious overtone*). Yes. This—censorship before publication seems to me, shall we say, unfair. It is—even in an old friend—dictatorial.

NOLAN (*with an air of finality*). You leave me, then, no alternative. I am very sorry.

KURT. Don't let him frighten you, Marion. He can't do anything.

NOLAN. I can forgive you anything, Marion, but the fact that you value my wishes below those of this insolent young man.

MARION. But this insolent young man hasn't anything to do with it! Can't you see, Bunny—it's my own wish that is involved.

NOLAN. I have explained to you the special circumstances. If you would consent to delay publication till after election—

(*She turns to* KURT *to ask him to make this concession but can't get a word in. She is wedged between both of them.*)

KURT. She has nothing to do with the publication date. That's my province. Gosh, what a chance for the circulation manager in Tennessee! (*He rubs his palms together in mock anticipation of profits.*)

NOLAN (*Losing his temper at last*). You are tampering with more than you bargain for Mr.— Mr.—

KURT. Kurt.

MARION. With a "K."

NOLAN. There are ways of dealing with a young man like this and you'll soon find out what they are!

KURT. Them's harsh words, Senator!

NOLAN. You wait and see.

MARION. Bunny!

NOLAN. Don't speak to me! I never

want to see you again! (*He goes out.*)

MARION (*really distressed*). This is awful!

KURT (*highly elated*). It's wonderful!

MARION. But I'm very fond of Bunny. Oh dear! I'll telephone him tonight—

KURT (*grimly*). Over my dead body!

MARION. Can it be, Dickie, that I control the election of senators from Tennessee? (*Sits right end of sofa Left.*)

KURT (*after a moment*). How could you ever have loved a stuffed-shirt like that!

MARION. He wasn't a stuffed-shirt. That's the funny part. He was charming. He was a charming boy. Rather thin. Rather reticent. He was much nicer than you, as a matter of fact. . . .

KURT. I'm sure he was!

MARION. He was much less violent!

KURT (*sits*). Hypocritical old buccaneer!

MARION. He used to work hard all day and at night he studied law. We used to walk the country lanes and dream about the future. He was scared—he was wistful. How did he emerge into this successful, ambitious, over-cautious—mediocrity? How do we all emerge into what we are? How did I emerge into what I am? I've dug up some of my old diaries. I was a tremulous young girl. I was eager. I believe I was naïve. Look at me now! Time, Dickie . . . What will you be at forty? A bond-holder and a commuter . . . Oh, Dickie!

KURT (*tensely*). I'll never be forty!

MARION (*laughing*). How will you avoid it?

KURT (*same tone*). I'll use myself up before I'm forty.

MARION. Do you think so? I don't think so. (*Rises.*) I sometimes wake up on certain mornings feeling absolutely—immortal! Indestructible! One is perpetually reborn, I think, Dickie. Everyone should write one's life, I think—but not for publication. For oneself. A kind of spiritual spring-cleaning!

KURT. The Ego preening!

MARION (*sitting right arm of sofa Left*). Well, why not? After all, one's ego is all one really has.

KURT. Reminiscence is easy. So is anticipation. It's the *present* that's difficult, and most people are too lazy or too indifferent to cope with it.

MARION. It's natural for you to say that—at your age one has no past—and no future either, because the intimation of the future comes only with the sense of the past . . .

KURT (*with sudden bitterness*). I see the past as an *evil thing*—to be extirpated.

MARION. How awful! (*Pause.*) Why?

KURT. That's not important.

MARION (*rises*). You freeze up so whenever I try to find out anything about you. I'm not used to that. Usually people open up to me—I'm a born confidante. But not you. . . . I'm interested too, because in an odd way I've become very fond of you.

KURT. My life's very dull, I assure you. *My* past lacks completely what you would call *glamour*.

MARION. No, Dickie. I don't believe that. I don't believe that's true of anybody's life.

KURT. Well, it's true. Moreover, it's true of most peoples' lives. It's easy for anyone who's lived as you have to make romantic generalizations. It's very pleasant for you to believe them. Well, I shan't disillusion you. (*Turns away from her.*) Why should I? It's not important.

(*She is sitting down, smoking a cigarette in a holder, watching him. He becomes conscious that she is studying him.*)

MARION. I had no idea you felt this way about me—you despise me, don't you? (*He doesn't answer.*) Don't you?

KURT. Yes.

MARION. Why?

KURT (*rises. Walks away*). Why did we start this?

MARION. You're annoyed at having even momentarily revealed yourself, aren't you? I'll have your secret, Dickie —I'll pluck out the heart of your mystery.

KURT. Secret! Mystery! More romantic nonsense. I have no secret. Nobody has a secret. There are different kinds of greed, different kinds of ambition—that's all!

MARION. Oh, you simplify too much—really I'm afraid you do. Tell me—why do you disapprove of me? Is it—as Bunny does—on moral grounds?

KURT (*right end of sofa Left—angrily*). You're superficial and casual and irresponsible. You take life, which is a tragic thing, as though it were a trivial bedroom-farce. You're a second-rate artist who's acquired a reputation through vamping celebrities to sit for you.

MARION (*quietly, she continues smoking*).

Go on . . .

KURT. As an unglamorous upstart who has been forced to make my way, I resent parasitism, that's all!

MARION. Isn't there in biology something about benevolent parasites, Dickie? Many great men, I believe, owe a debt of gratitude to their parasites, as many plants do . . . there are varieties. Again, Dickie, you simplify unduly. It is a defect of the radical and the young.

KURT. To return to the Honorable Nolan—

MARION. I return to him with relief.

KURT. He may exert pressure on us, you know.

MARION. How? I'm very interested.

KURT. Well, for one thing, his future father-in-law might get me fired.

MARION. Could he do that?

KURT. He might. He might easily. (MARION *sits upright and looks at him.*) Some form of bribery. He might go to my chief and offer him a bigger job—anything.

MARION. All on account of my poor little biography—it seems incredible that anyone would take all this trouble.

KURT. I'd just like to see them try I'd just like to, that's all.

MARION. What would you do?

KURT. Do? I'd make the Honorable Nolan the laughing-stock of the country, and his athletic father-in-law too. I'd just plaster them, that's what I'd do.

MARION. You sound vindictive.

KURT. Baby, I am vindictive!

MARION. Funny, I'm just amused. . . .

KURT. Well, everything's a spectacle to you! (*Turns away from her.*) God, how I hate detachment!

MARION. Your desire to break up Bunny is quite impersonal then.

KURT. Surgical. Just as impersonal as that.

MARION. You're a funny boy, Dickie.

KURT (*turns away from her*). I'm not funny and I'm not a boy. You've been around with dilettantes so long you don't recognize seriousness when you see it.

MARION. But it's the serious people who are funny, Dickie! Look at Bunny.

KURT (*faces her*). Yes, look at him! An epitome of the brainless muddle of contemporary life, of all the self-seeking second-raters who rise to power and wield power. That's why I'm going to do him in. (*The phone rings—for a moment they pay no attention to it.*) It's the most beautiful

chance anybody ever had, and I'd just like to see them try and stop me.

(*Phone keeps ringing.* MARION *answers it.*)

MARION. Yes . . . yes . . . certainly. (*To* KURT—*a bit surprised.*) It's for you . . . (*She hands him hand-receiver.*)

KURT (*takes phone and talks from rear of sofa*). Yes. Hello . . . sure. Well, what about it? . . . Oh, you want to talk to me about it, do you? . . . I thought you would . . . I'll be around . . . sure . . . so long. (*He hangs up.*) They've begun! (*He is almost gay with the heady scent of battle.*)

MARION. What do you mean?

KURT. That was my chief. He wants to talk to me about your story. Kinnicott's begun to put the screws on him. He's going to ask me to kill it. All right —I'll kill it!

MARION (*faintly*). I can't believe it.

KURT. Neff's had a call from the father-in-law—

MARION. Did he say so?

KURT. No, but you can bet he has!

MARION. I must say this puts my back up.

KURT. I'll make a fight for it to keep my job. But if he's stubborn I'll tell him to go to Hell—and go to a publisher with your manuscript. And if I don't get quick action that way I'll publish it myself— I'll put every penny I've saved into it.

MARION. But why should you? Why does it mean so much to you?

KURT. Do you think I'd miss a chance like this? It'll test the caliber of our magazines, of our press, our Senators, our morality—

MARION. All on account of my poor little story—how Vicki would have laughed!

KURT (*a spasm of jealousy again*). Who's Vicki?

MARION (*aware of it*). An old friend to whom I'm dedicating the biography.

KURT. Yeah! (*Sits beside her, then speaks.*) Where is he now?

MARION. He's dead. (*A pause. She gets up and crosses to Center.*) I've always rather despised these contemporary women who publicize their emotions. (*Another moment. She walks upstage. She is thinking aloud.*) And here I am doing it myself. Too much self-revelation these days. Loud-speakers in the confessional. Why should I add to the noise? I think, as far as this story is concerned, I'll call it a day, Dickie.

KURT. What!

MARION. Let's forget all about it, shall we?

KURT. If you let me down now, I'll hate you.

MARION. Will you? Why won't you take me into your confidence then? Why won't you tell me about yourself? What are you after?

KURT (*after a moment of inhibition decides to reveal his secret dream*). My ambition is to be critic-at-large of things-as-they-are. I want to find out everything there is to know about the intimate structure of things. I want to reduce the whole system to absurdity. I want to laugh the powers that be out of existence in a great winnowing gale of laughter.

MARION. That's an interesting research. Of course it strikes me it's vitiated by one thing—you have a preconceived idea of what you will find. In a research biased like that from the start, you are apt to overlook much that is noble and generous and gentle.

KURT (*challenging and bitter*). Have you found generosity and gentleness and nobility?

MARION. A good deal—yes.

KURT. Well, I haven't!

MARION. I'm sorry for you.

KURT. You needn't be. Reserve your pity for weaklings. I don't need it!

MARION. Are you so strong? (*A pause.* KURT *doesn't answer.*) How old are you, Dickie?

KURT (*Turns away*). What difference does that make?

MARION. Who do you live with?

KURT. I live alone.

MARION. Are you in love with anybody?

KURT. No.

MARION. Where are your parents?

KURT. They're dead.

MARION. Long?

KURT. My mother is. I hardly remember her. Just barely remember her.

MARION. Your father? (*He doesn't answer.*) Do you remember your father?

KURT (*in a strange voice*). Yes. I remember him all right.

MARION. What did your father do?

KURT. He was a coal miner.

MARION. Oh! Won't you tell me about him? I'd like to know.

KURT. I was a kid of fourteen. There was a strike. One day my father took me out for a walk. Sunny spring morning. We stopped to listen to an organizer. My father was a mild little man with kind of faded, tired blue eyes. We stood on the outskirts of the crowd. My father was holding me by the hand. Suddenly somebody shouted: The militia! There was a shot. Everybody scattered. My father was bewildered—he didn't know which way to turn. A second later he crumpled down beside me. He was bleeding. He was still holding my hand. He died like that.... (*A moment. He concludes harshly—coldly—like steel.*) Are there any other glamorous facts of my existence you would like to know?

MARION (*stirred to her heart*). You poor boy ... I knew there was something ... I knew....!

KURT (*hard and ironic*). It's trivial really. People exaggerate the importance of human life. One has to die. (*Turns to her.*) The point is to have fun while you're alive, isn't it? Well, you've managed. I congratulate you!

MARION (*her heart full*). Dickie darling —why are you so bitter against me? Why against me?

KURT. Do you want to know that too? Well, it's because—

(*His voice rises. She suddenly doesn't want him to speak.*)

MARION. Hush, dearest—hush—don't say any more—I understand—not any more ...

(*His defenses vanish suddenly. He sinks to his knees beside her, his arms around her.*)

KURT. Marion, my angel!

MARION (*infinitely compassionate, stroking his hair*). Dickie—Dickie—Dickie ... Why have you been afraid to love me?

THE CURTAIN FALLS

ACT THREE

SCENE: *The same.*

TIME: *Late afternoon. Two weeks later.*

The telephone is ringing as the curtain rises. There is a moment and MINNIE *enters and crosses to rear of the table rear of the sofa Left. She picks up the receiver.*

MINNIE (*speaking into the phone*). Hello—
No, Mr. Kurt, she's not yet back. Vot.
You're not coming home to dinner?—But
I've made the *Pfannkuchen* you like—Vot?
—You're tired of my damn *Pfannkuchen*—
(*She shouts angrily.*) Every night I make
dinner and you and Marion go out!—
I'm *not* yelling— Vot? Vot shall I tell
Marion?—Vot—(*Doorbell rings.*) Wait
—wait a minute—Someone's ringing.

(*She puts the receiver on the table and goes
to the door.* MINNIE *shows in* LEANDER NOLAN,
who is followed by ORRIN KINNICOTT, *who
is a big, well-developed Southerner, about
fifty-five, with a high-pitched voice. He is a
superbly built man with a magnificent chest
development. He is aware that he is a fine
figure of a man, impeccably dressed in formal
afternoon clothes.*)

NOLAN (*to* MINNIE, *who has preceded him
into the room*). Did Miss Froude say she
was expecting us for tea, Minnie?

MINNIE. No, Mr. Nolan. She didn't say
nothing to me.

NOLAN. Not even when she'd be back?

MINNIE (*hangs up coats*). No. She just
went out.

NOLAN. All right, Minnie. We'll wait.

MINNIE. Yes, Mr. Nolan. (*She is about
to go out into kitchen when she remembers that*
KURT *is on the telephone. She picks up the
receiver and says:*) Hello—Mr. Kurt—
you dere?—Good-by! (*She then hangs up
the receiver and exits Left.*)

KINNICOTT (*querulously. Sits sofa Right*).
Did you tell her four o'clock?

NOLAN. Yes. I told her.

(NOLAN's *manner with his father-in-law-
to-be in this scene conveys the beginnings of a
secret irritation, an inner rebellion.*)

KINNICOTT. Does she know I'm a busy
man?

NOLAN (*gloomily*). She's not impressed
much by busy men.

KINNICOTT. I know these fly-by-night
characters. I've dealt with 'em before...
Bad—(*He sniffs the air of the room.*) bad
air. (*Rises—tries to open window, fails, sits
window seat.*) Bet she's under-exercised.

NOLAN. On the contrary—she's radi-
antly healthy!

KINNOCOTT. Cosmetics, I bet! These
fly-by-night characters—

NOLAN (*very irritated*). Why do you keep
calling her a fly-by-night character?
She's nothing of the sort!

KINNICOTT (*crosses to* NOLAN). Look
here, Leander—

NOLAN. Well?

KINNICOTT. Have you been entirely
frank with me, in this matter?

NOLAN. Of course I have.

KINNICOTT (*cryptic*). About the past—
yes. But I refer to the present.

NOLAN. I don't know what you mean.

KINNICOTT. I think you do know what
I mean. Sometimes the way you talk I
suspect—I suspect, Leander—that you
are still in love with this woman.

NOLAN. Nonsense! I simply tell you
that she's not a fly-by-night character.
That doesn't mean I'm in love with her!

KINNICOTT. My daughter feels the same
thing.

NOLAN. Slade! You've discussed this
with Slade!

KINNICOTT. She's discussed it with me.
She's no fool, that girl. She's noticed
things lately.

NOLAN. What things?

KINNICOTT. She says she talks to you
and that you're off somewhere else—
dreaming. I tried to put her on another
scent—but she was positive. She said:
"Come on now, dad—don't stall me—
come clean!" So I told her!

NOLAN. You did!

KINNICOTT. Yes.

NOLAN. When?

KINNICOTT. Yesterday. Told her it happened fifteen years ago, that you were a
naïve young feller didn't know anything
about women, were just naturally taken
in—

NOLAN. That's not true though. I was
not taken in.

KINNICOTT. There you go again—defending the woman that's endangering
your entire career and using up my
energies and yours, when you ought to
be home right now getting together with
folks and thinking how to cinch this here
election. Not going to be a walk-over,
you know. (*Again trying the window.*) How
do you open this thing to get some air?
(*Sits window seat.*)

NOLAN. I don't know. What did Slade
say when you told her?

KINNICOTT. Nothin'. You know Slade's
not the talkin' kind.

NOLAN. Funny she didn't mention it
to me last night.

KINNICOTT. Didn't want to worry yer
probably . . . all wool and a yard wide
that girl is. I warn you, Leander, don't
tamper with the most precious and rare

thing—

NOLAN (*impatient of oratory*). I know— I know. The point is— what are we going to do?

KINNICOTT. Course I can get that young fellow—what's his name?

NOLAN. Kurt.

KINNICOTT. I can get him fired all right. From what you've told me, Leander, he's got something else up his sleeve.

NOLAN. I'm afraid so.

KINNICOTT. That's what I want to find out from your lady friend. And I've got a pretty idea right now what it is.

NOLAN. What do you mean?

KINNICOTT. Money!

NOLAN (*still not understanding*). Money?

KINNICOTT. Blackmail!

NOLAN. You're crazy!

KINNICOTT. You don't know much about women, Leander; when you know the sex as well as I do, you'll know that every woman has blackmail up her sleeve.

NOLAN. Look here, Orrin!

KINNICOTT (*rises, confronts* NOLAN). Now, you listen to me for a moment, son . . . This situation's gone about far enough right now. You'd better make up your mind whether you want this blackmailing female or whether you want my daughter—and you'd better make it up right quick.

NOLAN (*flaring up*). I resent your tone, Orrin, and I won't be ordered around as if I were a high-grade servant!

KINNICOTT. Now son, when you get control of your temper, and cool down a little bit, you'll see that my ordering hasn't been so bad for you. I'll acknowledge you were mighty successful as a lawyer, but in politics, you're nothing but a novice.

NOLAN (*resentful*). Am I!

(*Doorbell.*)

KINNICOTT. Just look back a bit, that's all—I've had to push and bolster you to get you where you are.

NOLAN (*desperately*). I know—I have every reason to be grateful to you— that's the worst of it.

(MINNIE *enters and crosses to hall door. Both* MEN *turn and watch to see who it is that is calling.*)

MINNIE (*speaking to someone at the door*). *Ja, Fräulein?*

SLADE (*offstage*). Is Miss Froude in?

MINNIE. *Nein, Fräulein.*

SLADE (*entering*). Well, I'll just wait. (SLADE KINNICOTT *is a good-looking, dark, high-spirited girl, a rather inspiriting and healthy example of the generation growing up on D. H. Lawrence. To her father and* NOLAN *as she crosses downstage between them.*) Hello.

NOLAN. Slade!

KINNICOTT (*severely*). Daughter! What are you doing here?

SLADE. Came to have my picture painted. What are you?

KINNICOTT. Your coming here at this time is most inopportune, daughter. We are here on business.

SLADE (*mischievously*). I can imagine!

NOLAN. I'm very glad you came, Slade. I want you to meet the woman whom your father has just been accusing of the most reprehensible crimes!

SLADE. I'm pretty anxious to get a load of her myself. (*Looks about the room, taking it in, and then sits on the left end of the sofa below the piano.*) Nice lay-out. Gee, I wish I were artistic. What a lucky gal she is! A paintbrush and an easel and she can set up shop anywhere in the world. That's independence for you! Gosh! (*She looks about, admiring and envious.*)

KINNICOTT. Why must you come here to get your picture painted? We have tolerable good artists in Knoxville.

SLADE. Well, if you *must* know I'm very keen to have a heart-to-heart talk with my fiancé's old girl. Natural, isn't it?

KINNICOTT. No, it isn't natural!

NOLAN (*crosses angrily to window and back toward* KINNICOTT *and sits stool down Right near sofa in which* SLADE *and her father are sitting*). This is what you get for telling her, Orrin.

SLADE. If you think I didn't suspect something was up ever since Froude arrived here, you don't know your little bride. Maybe I haven't been watching the clouds gather on that classic brow! Where is my rival? Don't tell me she's holding up two big shots like you two boys.

KINNICOTT. Slade, this is no time . . . please leave us before she comes.

SLADE. Not I! Just my luck when a story is going to come out which has something in it *I* want to read, you two killjoys are going to suppress it!

NOLAN. This isn't exactly a joke you know, Slade.

SLADE. I mean it.

KINNICOTT (*sadly*). I've spoiled you,

Slade—I've been too easy with you.

SLADE. At least I hope you'll buy the *manuscript*. My God, Father, I'm curious. Can't you understand that? I want to find out what Leander was like before he became ambitious. I've a right to know! This story might hurt you with the voters in Tennessee, Leander, but it's given me a kick out of you I didn't know was there! How did she make you, Leander—that's what I'd like to know. You've been pretty unapproachable to me, but I sort of took it for granted National Figures were like that. Also, I'd gotten to the point when I was going to suggest that we break our engagement, but this little incident revives my interest.

NOLAN (*furious*). Indeed!

SLADE. Yes indeed. Where is this woman? What is that secret? How to Make National Figures—there's a title for you!

KINNICOTT. Slade, you're talking too much! Shut up!

NOLAN (*rises and moves stool toward them a bit*). No, she isn't at all. . . . (*To* SLADE.) If your interest in me requires the artificial stimulus of an episode that happened twenty years ago—

SLADE (*leaning toward him*). It requires something—

NOLAN (*leaning closer toward her. The three heads are now close together*, KINNICOTT's *in the center*). Does it!

SLADE. It does. We were getting so that conversation, when we were alone, was rather difficult.

(NOLAN *starts to argue*.)

KINNICOTT (*pushes them apart*). Children! Children!

NOLAN. We're not children! (*To* SLADE.) If our relationship is so—

SLADE. Tenuous?

NOLAN.—that it requires artificial—

SLADE. Respiration?

NOLAN. If it's as bad as that, then I think perhaps we'd both better—

SLADE. Call it a day? You'll need me in the Senate, Leander, to fill in the gaps when you get hung up in a speech. Consider carefully what you are discarding.

NOLAN. If that is the case, I tell you solemnly we'd better separate now.

SLADE (*mock tragedy*). Father, Leander is giving your daughter the air. Do something!

KINNICOTT. I don't blame him for being irritated. You should not be here. Please go home.

SLADE (*lights cigarette*). Don't worry Dad. I'll get him back.

KINNICOTT. This is a bad mess, Leander. And I must tell you frankly that I don't altogether approve of your attitude—

NOLAN. And I must tell you frankly that I don't approve of *yours*.

KINNICOTT. Is that so!

NOLAN. I don't like your tone in speaking of a woman with whom at one time I had a relation of the tenderest emotion—for whom I still have a high regard.

KINNICOTT. That's evident anyway!

NOLAN. When you apply to such a woman the terms you used before Slade came in, when you impute to her motives so base, you cast an equal reflection on my judgment and my character.

SLADE. And that, Pop, is *lèse-majesté*.

NOLAN. And it may be perfectly true, Slade, that knowing Miss Froude has spoiled me for the flippant modernisms with which you study. . . .

SLADE. I'm dying to ask her one thing: when you made love to her in the old days, did it always sound like a prepared speech on tariff schedules?

KINNICOTT. This is getting us nowhere.

SLADE. Well, Dad, what do you expect? Leander and I have broken our engagement since I came into this room. That's progress, isn't it?

KINNICOTT. Your coming here at this time was most unfortunate.

SLADE. Leander doesn't think so. (*Ironically*.) He's free now to pursue the lady for whom he still has a high regard. (*Rises*.) Are we no longer engaged, Leander?

NOLAN. That's not for me to say.

SLADE (*rises and shakes hands with* NOLAN). Gentleman to the last! And at the very moment—

KINNICOTT (*in despair—speaks as* SLADE *starts to speak*). Slade, if you would only go home!

SLADE (*crosses left*). *Just* at the very moment when I was saying to myself: Well, if a brilliant and beautiful woman who has played footie with royalty in the capitols of the world loved him, maybe there's a secret charm in him that I've overlooked—just when I was saying that and preparing to probe and discover, (*Lightly*.) he gives me the air. (*Sits on sofa Left*.) By God, Orrin, there's life for you. (*Bell rings.*) Ah, that must be my rival!

(NOLAN *gets up and fixes his tie, expecting* MARION. *But it is* KURT *who comes in. He faces them. He is in a white heat of anger.*)

KURT. Well, gentlemen, I'm not surprised to find you here! (*Drops hat on model-stand and comes downstage Left.*)

NOLAN (*about to introduce* KINNICOTT). How do you do Mr. Kurt. This is—

KURT. I can guess who it is. I can guess why you're here. Having failed to intimidate *me*, you are here to intimidate Miss Froude. (SLADE *rises, excited by this tempest.*) Well, I can advise you that you will fail with her too.

NOLAN. This is his usual style, Orrin. Don't mind him.

KURT. I have just come from my office, where I have been informed by Mr. Neff— (SLADE *stands below* KURT—*just behind him—watching him.*) whom *you* doubtless know, Mr. Kinnicott—that I could decide between publishing Miss Froude's story or giving up my job. I invited him to go to Hell. That invitation I now cordially extend to you two gentlemen.

SLADE. Why doesn't somebody introduce me to this interesting young man?

(*She comes toward him.* KURT *is embarrassed, but covers it in a gruff manner. He has actually not been aware of her in the room.*)

KURT. I'm sorry—I—didn't know—

SLADE. Why are you sorry? I'm Slade Kinnicott. (*She gives him her hand. He takes it, limply.*)

KURT. All right—all right. (*He is disarmed and feels, suddenly, rather foolish.*)

SLADE. Leander, why have you kept me apart from this young man?

KURT. I'm sorry—I—

SLADE. Nonsense. What's your name?

KURT. Richard Kurt.

SLADE. Go to it— (*Turns him toward others.*)

KINNICOTT (*impressively—interposing between them*). You're being very foolish, young man.

KURT (*crosses toward them— to right of model-stand*). Possibly.

NOLAN. You can't argue with him. I've tried it. He's a fanatic.

KURT. But if you ask me I think *you're* being very foolish.

KINNICOTT (*who wants to find out what's in* KURT'S *mind*). Are we? How do you

figure that, young man?

SLADE (*parroting—crosses and sits on model-stand. She is having a wonderful time*). Yes, how!

KINNICOTT. Oh, hush your mouth.

KURT. Because I'm going to publish Miss Froude's book myself. And I promise you that it'll be the best-advertised first book that's come out in a long time.

SLADE. Thank God! Will you send me the advance sheets? I'll make it worth your while, Mr. Kurt.

KINNICOTT. I can see you are an extremely impulsive young man. Have you ever inquired, may I ask—

SLADE (*edges a bit closer to* KURT). This is going to be dangerous! Look out, Richard. . . .

(NOLAN *sits on stool, disgusted with* SLADE.)

KINNICOTT (*smoothly*). Have you inquired into the penalties for libel, Mr. Kurt?

KURT. Libel! You're going to sue me for libel, are you!

KINNICOTT (*same voice*). Yes. You and Miss Froude both . . . yes.

KURT. Well, you just go ahead and try it, that's all I can tell you. Go ahead and sue. (*Crosses to above* NOLAN.) It'll put Mr. Nolan in a charming position before those *moral* constituents of his, won't it? (*Includes both* NOLAN *and* KINNICOTT.) Go ahead and sue, both of you—sue your heads off! I promise the two of you I'll give you the fight of your lives!

SLADE (*delighted*). Good for you, Richard!

(MARION *comes in. She wears a long red velvet coat, and a little red cap stuck on the side of her golden head—she looks a little like* PORTIA. *She is at the top of her form.*)

MARION (*beaming with hospitality*). Well! How nice! Minnie!

KURT (*goes upstage to right of* MARION). This chivalrous gentleman has just been proposing to sue you for libel—he considers—

SLADE (*who rises and stands just below the model-stand*). I'm Slade Kinnicott.

MARION (*crosses downstage to her and they shake hands over the model-stand*). How very nice of you to come! (*Turns and faces* KINNICOTT.) Is this Mr. Kinnicott? (*He bows.*) I'm so glad to see you. (*They shake hands.*) I'm so sorry to be late. (*Waves hello to* NOLAN.) Hello, Bunny.

SLADE (*this is too much for her*). Oh, my God—BUNNY! (*She sits, overcome.*)

MARION (*to* NOLAN). I'm so sorry—

NOLAN (*glaring at Slade*). It's all right, Marion!

MARION. Has Minnie given you tea? I'll just . . . Minnie! (MINNIE *enters.*) Tea, Minnie, please. . . . (*To the men.*) Or cocktails—highball?

KINNICOTT. I never drink alcoholic mixtures.

NOLAN (*asserting his independence*). I'll have a highball!

KINNICOTT. I must tell you, Leander, that I do not approve—

NOLAN. I'll have *two* whiskies straight! MARION. Good! Highball for you, Miss Kinnicott?

SLADE. Thanks.

MARION. I'll fix them myself, Minnie. Just bring us some tea, Minnie.

KINNICOTT. Nor do I wish any tea.

KURT (*crosses down Left*). Nor do I.

MARION. Do you mind if I have a cup? Do sit down, Miss Kinnicott. A tiring day. . . . (SLADE *sits on model-stand.* MARION *goes up to rear of piano.*) Minnie, please bring me a cup of tea—

MINNIE. *Ja, Fräulein.* (*Remembering.*) A telegram for you, *Fräulein.*

MARION. Oh, thank you, Minnie. Just put it there on the table. (MINNIE *leaves the telegram on the table rear of the sofa Left and then exits Left.* MARION *removes her coat and hat and crosses to rear of piano and starts to mix the highballs.*) Now then! What is all this nice cheerful talk about a libel suit? That's what they're always having in England, isn't it, on the least provocation. It's when you've circulated a lie about someone—defamed someone—maliciously—isn't it? Bunny! (*She gives* NOLAN *his two drinks. He takes them and returns to his position.* MARION *picks up the other glass and crosses with it to* SLADE.) Now then—whom have I defamed?

KURT. You've defamed the Honorable Mr. Nolan!

MARION (*hands drink to* SLADE). Have I? Oh, I am tired. . . . (*She sits on sofa.*) Sit by me, won't you, Miss Kinnicott?

SLADE (*sauntering over*). Thanks. (*She sits by* MARION *on the sofa.*)

MARION. You're very pretty.

SLADE (*more warmly*). Thanks!

MARION. Bunny, I congratulate you. I've heard so much about you, Miss Kinnicott. And I think it's very gracious of you to come and see me. If Bunny lets me I'd like to paint you— (MINNIE *enters.*) and give you the portrait for a wedding present. (*She rises and crosses to above model-stand to get cup of tea from* MINNIE. MINNIE *exits Left.*) Thank you, Minnie.

SLADE. You're very lovely.

MARION. Thank you, my dear.

SLADE. I can't tell you how curious I've been about you—I—

KINNICOTT. This is all very well—but I'm a busy man—

MARION (*looks at* KINNICOTT *as she crosses and sits right of* SLADE. *A moment, then* MARION *speaks*). It seems so strange to see you with all your clothes on. It seems a pity—as an artist I must say it seems a pity—to conceal that wonderful chest-development that I've admired so often in *The Body Beautiful.*

KINNICOTT. That's neither here nor there.

MARION (*this is almost an aside to* SLADE). It seems to me that it's decidedly *there.*

(MARION *and* SLADE *laugh quietly together.*)

KINNICOTT. Slade, you've upset everything by coming here.

(KURT *comes forward. He has been eaten up with irritation because the superb indignation he felt should have been so dissipated by this cascade of small talk. He can stand it no longer.*)

KURT (*crosses to right of model-stand*). If you understood better what these gentlemen mean to do . . . !

NOLAN (*protests*). It wasn't my idea!

KURT. You wouldn't be quite so friendly, Marion—

MARION. I couldn't possibly be unfriendly to anyone so frank—and—and gladiatorial—as Mr. Kinnicott.

KURT (*furious at her for not letting him launch into it*). A libel suit!

MARION. Oh, yes! A libel suit! It sounds so cozy. Sit down, won't you? (KINNICOTT *sits on stool.*) A libel suit. Now then—what shall it be about?

KURT. The Honorable Nolan is going to sue you for libel.

NOLAN. I'll punch your head if you say that again.

KURT. On the assumption that when you say in your story that you and he were lovers you are lying and defaming his character!

MARION. Dear Bunny, you must want

to be a Senator very very badly!

NOLAN (*in despair*). I never said it, I tell you!

MARION. As a matter of fact, how could I prove it? Come to think of it, are there any letters? Did you ever write to me, Bunny?

NOLAN. I don't remember.

MARION. I don't think you ever did. You see—we were always—during that dim brief period of your youth—we were always so close—letters were hardly necessary, were they? Did I ever send you any letters, Bunny?

NOLAN. I don't remember, I tell you.

MARION. Neither do I. You might look around in old trunks and places and see if you can find some old letters of an affectionate nature—I'd love to read them—they'd probably make wonderful reading now. Why is it that the things one writes when one's young always sounds so foolish afterwards? Has that ever occurred to you, Mr. Kinnicott?

KINNICOTT. I don't admit the fact.

MARION. No.

KINNICOTT. No. I was looking over some old editorials of mine written in the depression of 1907 and they're just as apropos today. I haven't changed my ideas in twenty-five years.

MARION. Haven't you really? How very steadfast. Now if the world were equally changeless, how consistent that would make you. (*To* KURT.) Well, there isn't any documentary evidence.

KURT. It doesn't matter.

KINNICOTT. As I said before, this is getting us nowhere. Don't you think, Miss Froude, that the only way we can settle this is by ourselves? (*She smiles at him.*) I can see you're a sensible woman.

MARION. I am very sensible.

KINNICOTT. And you and I can settle this matter in short order.

KURT. You don't have to talk to him at all if you don't want to.

MARION (*smiling at* KINNICOTT). But I'd love to. I've always wanted to meet Mr. Kinnicott. There are some questions I want very much to ask him. (*To the others.*) You can all wait in my bedroom. It's fairly tidy, I think.

SLADE (*to* KURT— *rises, crosses to him*). Why don't you take me for a walk, Richard?

MARION (*as* KURT *hesitates*). Do that, Dickie. A walk'll do you good.

NOLAN. What'll I do?

MARION (*as if it were another dilemma*). You wait in my bedroom. (*Aware suddenly of the proprieties.*) No—in Minnie's bedroom. It's just next to the kitchen.

NOLAN (*defiantly*). I will! (*He exists into bedroom.*)

KURT (*sulky—he doesn't quite like the turn affairs have taken*). We'll be back in ten minutes.

SLADE (*as they go out*). You can't tell, Richard. (SLADE *and* KURT *exit.*)

(MARION *draws a deep breath. She assumes at once with* KINNICOTT *the air of two equals, mature people talking freely to each other after they've gotten rid of the children.*)

MARION (*they cross to sofa Left*). Now we can talk! It's funny—I feel we've put the children to bed and can have a quiet talk after a lot of chatter.

KINNICOTT. Same here!

MARION. Please sit down.

(*They do.*)

KINNICOTT. I feel sure you and I can come to an understanding.

MARION. I'm sure we can.

KINNICOTT. Now then, about this little matter of the story—You won't mind if I speak very frankly to you?

MARION. Not at all.

KINNICOTT. You see, Miss Froude—

MARION. Oh, call me Marion. Everybody does.

KINNICOTT. Thanks. Call me Orrin.

MARION. All right, I'll try. Not a very usual name. Orrin. Fits you. Strong. Rugged strength.

KINNICOTT. Thank you.

MARION. You're welcome. What were you going to say when I interrupted you? You were going to say something.

KINNICOTT. I was going to say—you're not at all what I expected to meet.

MARION. No? What did you think I'd be like? Tell me—I'd love to know.

KINNICOTT. Well, you're kind of homey—you know—folksy.

MARION. Folksy. (*Smiles.*) After all, there's no reason I shouldn't be, is there? I'm just a small-town girl from Tennessee. I sometimes wonder at myself—how I ever got so far away.

KINNICOTT (*positively*). Metabolism!

MARION. I beg your pardon—

KINNICOTT. I always say—take most of the bad men and most of the loose women—and correct their metabolism and you'll correct them.

MARION. Really?

KINNICOTT (*seriously*). Absolutely. Trouble with our penology experts—so-called—is that they're psychologists—so-called—when they should be physiologists.

MARION. That is very interesting indeed. Have you ever written anything about that?

KINNICOTT. Off and on.

MARION. Any definitive work, I mean?

KINNICOTT. I'm considering doing that right now.

MARION. Oh, I do wish you would! It's extraordinary how little one knows about one's own body, isn't it? I get so impatient of myself sometimes—of my physical limitations. My mind is seething with ideas, but I haven't the physical energy to go on working. I tire so quickly—and often for no apparent reason. Why is that, Mr. Kinnicott?

KINNICOTT. Defective—

(*She speaks at same time with him.*)

MARION—KINNICOTT. Metabolism!

KINNICOTT. Tell me—

MARION. What?

KINNICOTT. Do you eat enough roughage?

MARION. I don't know, offhand.

KINNICOTT (*firmly*). Well, you should know!

MARION. As I say, Orrin—one is so ignorant of these fundamental things.

KINNICOTT (*definitely aware now of* MARION *as a personal possibility*). I can see this, Marion—if you'd met me—instead of Leander—when you were a young girl—you'd have been a different woman.

MARION. I'm sure I would. Imagine—with one's metabolism disciplined early in life—how far one could go.

KINNICOTT (*confidentially offering her hope*). It's not too late!

MARION. Isn't it?

KINNICOTT. Er. . . . (*He drops his voice still lower.*) What are you doing tomorrow evenin'?

MARION. I—I'm free.

KINNICOTT (*same voice*). Will you have dinner with me?

MARION. I'd be delighted.

KINNICOTT. Fine! Then we can go over this little matter of the story and Leander quietly. Leander isn't strong on tact.

MARION. You know, some men aren't.

KINNICOTT. You and I can make a friendly adjustment.

MARION. What fun!

(*They chuckle.*)

KINNICOTT. What time shall we meet? Say seven-thirty?

MARION. Let's say eight . . . do you mind?

KINNICOTT. My apartment?

MARION. If you like.

KINNICOTT. Here's my card with the address. It's a roof apartment. I'm a widower.

MARION. Irresistible combination!

KINNICOTT. By the way—

MARION. What?

KINNICOTT. Don't mention our little date for tomorrow evenin' to Leander.

MARION (*rising*). No, I agree with you. I don't think that would be wise.

KINNICOTT (*nodding trustingly—rises*). Fine! At seven-thirty?

MARION. No—no. Eight.

KINNICOTT. Oh yes . . . eight.

(*A moment's pause. He visibly preens before her, buttoning his beautifully fitting frock-coat across his heroic chest.*)

MARION (*approving*). Wonderful! Wonderful!

KINNICOTT (*going toward bedroom. To her*). Do you mind if I . . . Leander . . .

MARION. Not at all.

KINNICOTT. I'll take the load off his mind.

(*He goes out. She can't believe it. The whole situation is so fantastic. She flings off her little red cap, and shaking with laughter, collapses on the couch.* MINNIE *comes in to clear up the tea things.*)

MARION (*as* MINNIE *enters*). It's too good to be true, Minnie.

MINNIE. Vat is too good to be true?

MARION. I must write some of it down before I forget it . . . (*The bell again.* MARION *gets up to make notes on her script.*) —A widower's penthouse— (*With an irritated sigh* MINNIE *goes out to answer bell.* MARION *sits at desk jotting notes very fast.* SLADE *and* KURT *come in.* KURT *is morose.* MARION *gets up to greet them.*) Well, children?

SLADE. That walk was a total loss.

MARION (*laughing*). What did you expect?

SLADE. Well, a little encouragement—just a soupçon.

MARION. Dickie's very serious.

SLADE. How did you come out with Dad?

MARION. Wonderful! I'm crazy about him!

SLADE. Bet he got you to renege on the story—

MARION. Well, he thinks so. However, we're going to discuss it tomorrow evenin'.

SLADE. Thought he'd date you up—could tell by the way he eyed you.

MARION. He's going to teach me how to live in a state of virtuous metabolism.

SLADE. Oh! Don't you believe it! Dad's an awful old chaser!

MARION (*rather shocked*). Slade!

SLADE (*amused*). Are you shocked?

MARION. You make me feel a little old-fashioned.

(KURT *is intensely irritated by this conversation.*)

KURT. Where are they?

MARION. They're in there sitting on Minnie's bed. Orrin is probably telling Bunny that everything'll be all right.

SLADE (*sits left of* MARION). Marion—

MARION. Yes.

SLADE. What is there about Bunny you can't help liking?

(*Utterly disgusted,* KURT *goes to sofa down Left and sits staring moodily into a gloomily tinted future.*)

MARION. He's a dear—there's something very touching about Bunny—sweet . . .

SLADE. Were you in love with him once?

MARION. Yes.

SLADE. Are you in love with him now?

MARION. No.

SLADE (*in a whisper*). Are you in love with—someone else?

MARION (*a moment's pause*). Yes.

SLADE. I thought you were. He's mad about you—I envy you, Marion.

MARION. Do you? Why?

SLADE. You're independent. You're—yourself. You can do anything you like.

MARION. Yes, I know. But it's possible one can pay too much for independence. I'm adrift. Sometimes—you know what seems to me the most heavenly thing the only thing—for a woman? Marriage, children—the dear boundaries of routine . . .

SLADE. If you had married Bunny he would've given 'em to you. He's still in love with you, but he doesn't quite know it. Shall I tell him?

MARION (*parrying*). What are you talking about?

SLADE. I wish we could change places, Marion. You can with me, but I can't with you.

(KINNICOTT *and* NOLAN *come in from the bedroom.* KINNICOTT *is at his most oleaginous.*)

KINNICOTT (*to* KURT). Well, young man! Over your little temper?

KURT. No, I'm not over it! What makes you think I'm over it?

KINNICOTT. Well, well, well! As far as I'm concerned there are no hard feelings. I'm going to call up your employer myself when I get home and tell him that as far as you are concerned, to let bygones be bygones. Can't do more than that, can I?

KURT. To what do I owe this generosity?

KINNICOTT. To the fact that in Miss Froude you have a most gracious friend and intercepter. (*He gives* MARION *a gallant, old-South bow.*) Miss Froude—this has been a very great pleasure.

MARION (*rises—with an answering bow*). Thank you!

(SLADE *also rises.*)

KINNICOTT (*giving her his hand*). Auf Wiedersehen.

MARION. Auf Wiedersehen. Ich kann es kaum erwarten!

KINNICOTT (*pretending to understand*). Yes, oh, yes, yes, of course! (*To* SLADE) Come, Slade. (*He goes to hall door.*)

SLADE. All right, Dad. (*To* NOLAN.) Coming—Bunny?

NOLAN. Well, yes—I'm coming.

SLADE (*to* NOLAN). You want to stay. Why don't you?

KINNICOTT (*quickly marshaling his little following with a military precision*). I think Leander had better come with us—

SLADE (*to* MARION). Good-by, Marion.

MARION (*to* SLADE). Good-by, Slade. (*They shake hands.*) Come to see me.

SLADE. Thanks, I will.

KINNICOTT (*smiles at* MARION). Miss Froude! (*Bows to* MARION, *who returns his bow*). Come, Daughter. Come, Leander. (*To* KURT). Good-by, young man. No hard feelings. (KURT *glares at him.* KINNICOTT *again bows to* MARION.) Miss Froude! (MARION *is startled into still a third bow. He calls without looking back.*) Come, Slade! Leander! !

SLADE. Bunny! (*As she exits.*)

NOLAN (*lingers an instant, then crosses to*

MARION). I'll be back.

MARION. When?

NOLAN. In a few minutes. All right?

MARION. I'll be in. (*He goes out quickly.* MARION *is in wonderful spirits. She runs to* KURT *and throws her arms around him.*) Oh, Dickie. That Orrin! That Orrin!

KURT. What did you say to him that put him in such good spirits?

MARION. Everything I said put him in good spirits. I can't wait for tomorrow evenin'. I can't wait for that dinner. It'll probably consist entirely of roughage— just imagine! He's the quaintest man I ever met in my life. He's too good to be true. (*Sits right of* KURT.)

KURT. Well, he may be quaint to you, but to me he's a putrescent old hypocrite and I don't see how you can bear to have him come near you, say less go to dinner with him!

MARION (*sobered by his intensity*). You're so merciless in your judgments, Dickie. You quite frighten me sometimes—you do really.

KURT. And so do you me.

MARION. I do! That's absurd!

KURT. You do. It's like thinking a person fastidious and exacting and finding her suddenly . . .

MARION. Gross—indiscriminating?

KURT (*bluntly*). Yes!

MARION. You know, Dickie, I adore you and I'm touched by you and I love you, but I'd hate to live in a country where you were dictator. It would be all right while you loved me but when you stopped—

KURT. It wouldn't make any difference if I stopped—I shouldn't be that kind of a dictator.

MARION (*glances at him. Almost sadly*). I see you've thought of it.

KURT (*inexorably*). What did you say to Kinnicott?

MARION. Your manner is so—inquisitorial. I haven't been able to get used to it.

KURT (*angry and jealous*). I heard you tell Nolan to come back too . . . . How do you think I feel?

MARION. Dickie!

KURT. When Nolan sat there and told me he had been your lover, I felt like socking him. Even when we're alone together, I can't forget that . . . yet you encourage him, and Kinnicott—My God, Marion, you seem to like these people!

MARION. I certainly like Slade.

KURT. Well, I don't. She's conceited and overbearing. Thinks she can have anything she likes because she's Orrin Kinnicott's daughter.

MARION. That's where you're wrong. She's a nice girl—and she's unhappy.

KURT (*bitterly*). Maladjusted, I suppose!

MARION. Dickie, Dickie, Dickie! Studying you, I can see why so many movements against injustice become such absolute—tyrannies.

KURT. That beautiful detachment again! (*He is white with fury. He hates her at this moment.*)

MARION (*with a little laugh*). You hate me, don't you?

KURT. Yes! Temporizing with these . . . ! Yes! I hate you. (*She says nothing, sits there looking at him.*) These people flout you, they insult you in the most flagrant way. God knows I'm not a gentleman, but it horrifies me to think of the insufferable arrogance of their attitude toward you . . . as if the final insult to their pride and their honor could only come from the discovery that this stuffed-shirt Nolan had once been your lover! The blot on the immaculate Tennessee scutcheon! Why, it's the God-damnedest insolence I ever heard of. And yet you flirt and curry favor and bandy with them. And you're amused— always amused!

MARION. Yes. I am amused.

KURT. I can't understand such—

MARION. Of course you can't. That's the difference—one of the differences— between 25 and 35!

KURT. If the time ever comes when I'm amused by what I should hate, I hope somebody shoots me. What did you tell Kinnicott?

MARION. Nothing. Simply nothing. I saw no point in having a scene with him, so I inquired into his favorite subject. He gave me health hints. He thinks tomorrow night he will cajole me— through the exercise of his great personal charm—into giving up my plan to publish.

KURT. Well, why didn't you tell him right out that you wouldn't.

MARION. Because I wanted to avoid a scene.

KURT. You can't always avoid scenes.

That's the trouble with you—you expect to go through life as if it were a beautifully lit drawing-room with modulated voices making polite chatter. Life isn't a drawing-room!

MARION. I have—once or twice—suspected it.

KURT (*rises*). What the devil are you afraid of, anyway? I had a scene today in the office, and I was prepared for one here—until you let me down—

MARION (*lightly*). Prepared? I think you were eager.

KURT. What if I was! It's in your behalf, isn't it?

MARION. Is it? But you forget, Dickie. You're a born martyr. I'm not. I think the most uncomfortable thing about martyrs is that they look down on people who aren't. (*Thinks—looks at him.*) As a matter of fact, Dickie, I don't really understand. Why do you insist so on this story? Why is it so important—now wouldn't it be better to give it up?

KURT. Give it up!

MARION. Yes.

KURT. You'd give it up!

MARION. Why not?

KURT (*Obeying a sudden manic impulse*). After all this—after all I've—Oh, yes, of course! Then you could marry Nolan and live happily forever after. And be amused. Goodby! (*He rushes up Center, grabs his hat from the stand as he passes it, and continues on out the door.*)

MARION (*rises and runs after him*). Dickie!

KURT (*going out the door*). Good-by!

MARION. Dickie! Dickie! (*The door slams.* MARION *walks back into the room. A pause. She stands still for a moment; she shakes her head. . . . She is very distressed and saddened, and a deep unhappiness is gnawing in her heart, an awareness of the vast, uncrossable deserts between the souls of human beings. She makes a little helpless gesture with her hands, murmuring to herself.*) Poor Dickie! Poor boy!

(*In its Italian folder the manuscript of her book is lying on the piano before her. She picks it up—she gives the effect of weighing the script in her hand. Slowly, as if in a trance, she walks with the script to the Franklin stove downstage Left and sits before it on a little stool. She opens the manuscript and then the isinglass door of the stove. The light from behind it glows on her face. She looks again down on her manuscript, at this morsel of her*

recorded past. *She tears out a page or two and puts them into the fire. A moment and she has put the entire script into the stove and she sits there watching its cremation. The doorbell rings. As* MINNIE *comes in to answer it, she shuts the door of the stove quickly.*)

MATION. It's probably Mr. Nolan.

(MINNIE *goes out.* MARION *makes a visible effort to shake herself out of her mood.* NOLAN *comes in, followed by* MINNIE, *who crosses stage and goes in the bedroom Left.* NOLAN *is excited and distrait.*)

NOLAN. Hello, Marion. . . .

MARION. Hello, Bunny dear.

NOLAN (*sparring for time*). Excuse me for rushing in on you like this . . . I—

MARION. I've been expecting you.

NOLAN. That's right! I told you I was coming back, didn't I?

MARION. You did—yes.

NOLAN. I must have known—I must have felt it—what would happen. . . . Marion—

MARION. Bunny dear, you're all worked up. Won't you have a highball?

NOLAN. No, thanks. Marion—

MARION. Yes, Bunny.

NOLAN. I've done it!

MARION. You've done what?

NOLAN. I've broken with Slade. I've broken with Kinnicott. I've broken with all of them.

MARION. You haven't!

NOLAN. Yes! I have!

MARION. Oh—oh Bunny!

NOLAN (*sits*). When Orrin told me what you'd done—that you were going to give up the story—

MARION. But I—

NOLAN. He said he was sure he could get you to do it. It all came over me—your generosity your wonderful generosity.

MARION (*beyond words*). Oh Bunny! (*Sits.*)

(*She is in a sort of laughing despair. He hardly notices her attitude. He rushes on.*)

NOLAN. I realized in that moment that in all this time—since I'd been seeing you—I'd been hoping you wouldn't give up the story, that you would go through with it, that my career would go to smash—

Marion (*faintly*). Bunny. . . .

NOLAN. I saw then that all this—which I'd been telling myself I wanted—Slade, a career, Washington, public life—all of it—that I didn't want it, that

I was sick at the prospect of it—that I wasn't up to it, that I was scared to death of it. I saw all that—and I told her—I told Slade—

MARION. You did!

NOLAN. Yes.

MARION. What did she say?

NOLAN. She said she knew it. She's clever, that girl. She's cleverer than I am. She's cleverer than you are. I'm afraid of her cleverness. I'm uncomfortable with it. Marion, I know I seem stupid and ridiculous to you—just a Babbitt—clumsy—but I love you, Marion. I always have—never anyone else. Let me go with you wherever you go— (*Lest she think it a "proposition"*) I mean—I want to marry you.

MARION. I'm terribly touched by this, Bunny darling, but I can't marry you.

NOLAN. Why not?

MARION. If I married you it would be for the wrong reasons. And it wouldn't be in character really—neither for me—nor for you. Besides that, I think you're wrong about Slade. She's very nice, you know. I like her very much.

NOLAN. I don't understand her. I never will.

MARION. If you did you'd like her. You better have another try. Really, Bunny, I wish you would.

NOLAN. Letting me down easy, aren't you?

MARION. It's Slade's manner that shocks you—her modern—gestures. If you really understood me—as you think you do—I'd really shock you very much, Bunny.

NOLAN. I'll risk it. Marion, my dearest Marion, won't you give me some hope?

MARION (*sees she must tell him*). Besides—I'm in love.

NOLAN (*stunned*). Really! With whom?

MARION. Dickie . . . You see, Bunny . . . (*He can't get over this. There is a considerable pause.*) you see, Bunny . . .

NOLAN (*slowly*). Do you mean that you and he—you don't mean that . . .

MARION. Yes, Bunny.

NOLAN (*dazed*). Are you going to marry him?

MARION. No.

NOLAN (*he passes his hand over his forehead*). This is a shock to me, Marion.

MARION (*gently*). I thought it only fair to tell you.

NOLAN (*in a sudden passion*). You—you.

. . . (*He feels like striking her, controls himself with difficulty.*) Anybody else but him!

MARION. You see, Bunny.

NOLAN (*after a moment—rises*). Sorry! Funny, isn't it? Joke, isn't it?

MARION. I'm terribly fond of you, Bunny. (*Takes his hand.*) I always will be. That kind of tenderness outlasts many things.

NOLAN (*blindly*). I'll go on, I suppose.

MARION. Of course you will! (NOLAN *crosses to model-stand and gets his hat.* KURT *comes in. There is a silence.* NOLAN *forces himself to look at him.* KURT *does not meet his glance.* KURT *is white and shaken—not in the least truculent.*) Goodby, Bunny dear. Bunny!

NOLAN. Yes, Marion.

MARION. Will you do me a favor?

NOLAN. Yes.

MARION. Will you please tell Mr. Kinnicott for me—that as I've been called out of town suddenly—I can't dine with him tomorrow night. You *will* see him, won't you, and you'll tell him?

NOLAN. Yes.

(NOLAN *leaves. A silence again. . . . Suddenly* KURT *goes to her, embraces her with a kind of hopeless intensity.*)

KURT (*in a whisper, like a child*). Please forgive me.

MARION. Yes.

KURT. These moods come over me—I can't control myself—afterwards I hate myself—it's because I love you so much—I can't bear to—

MARION. I know, dear—I know.

KURT. I'm torn up all the time—torn to bits.

MARION. I know, dear.

KURT. When this is all blown over—could we—do you think . . .

MARION. What, dear?

KURT. If we could only go away together, the two of us—somewhere away from people, by ourselves?

MARION. Why not, Dickie? We can go now, if you want to.

KURT. Now? But you're crazy. How can we possibly leave now—with the book—

MARION. Dickie—I must tell you—

KURT. You must tell me what?

MARION. You must be patient—you must hear me out for once—you must try to understand my point of view.

(*She leads him to sofa Left and sits beside him.*)

KURT. What do you mean?

MARION. You know, Dickie, I've been very troubled about you. I've been sad. I've been sad.

KURT. I was angry . . . I didn't mean . . . It was just that . . .

MARION. No, you don't understand—it wasn't your anger that troubled me. It was ourselves—the difference between us—not the years alone but the immutable difference in temperament. Your hates frighten me, Dickie. These people —poor Bunny, that ridiculous fellow Kinnicott—to you these rather ineffectual, blundering people symbolize the forces that have hurt you and you hate them. But I don't hate them. I can't hate them. Without feeling it, I can understand your hate but I can't bring myself to foster it. To you, this book has become a crusade. It couldn't be to me. Do you know, Dickie dear—and this has made me laugh so to myself—that there was nothing in the book about Bunny that would ever have been recognized by anybody. It was an idyllic chapter of first-love—that's all—and there was nothing in it that could remotely have been connected with the Bunny that is now. . . .

KURT. So much the better! Think of the spectacle they'll make of themselves —destroyed by laughter. . . .

MARION. I don't believe in destructive campaigns, Dickie . . . outside of the shocking vulgarity of it all—I couldn't do it—for the distress it would cause.

KURT. You've decided not to publish then. . . .

MARION. I've destroyed the book, Dickie.

KURT. You've destroyed it!

MARION. Yes. I'm sorry.

KURT. You traitor!

MARION. It seemed the simple thing to do—the inevitable thing.

KURT. What about *me?* You might have consulted me—after what I've—

MARION. I'm terribly sorry—but I couldn't possibly have published that book.

KURT (*in a queer voice*). I see now why everything is this way.

MARION. I couldn't . . . !

KURT. Why the injustice and the cruelty go on—year after year—century after century—without change—because—as they grow older—people become—*tolerant!* Things amuse them. I hate you and I hate your tolerance. I always did.

MARION. I know you do. You hate my essential quality—the thing that is me. That's what I was thinking just now, and that's what made me sad.

KURT. Nothing to be said, is there? (*Rises.*) Good-by.

MARION (*rises*). All right! (KURT *starts to go. She calls after him, pitifully.*) Won't you kiss me good-by?

KURT. All right.

(MARION *goes up after him. They kiss each other passionately.*)

MARION (*whispering to him*). I would try to change you. I know I would. And if I changed you I should destroy what makes me love you. Good-by, my darling. Good-by, my dearest. Go quickly. (KURT *goes upstage and exits without a word. He is blinded by pain.*) Dickie. . . . !

(MARION *is left alone. She is trembling a little. She feels cold. She goes to the stove and sits in front of it, her back to it, trying to get warm. She becomes aware that her eyes are full of tears. As* MINNIE *comes in, she brushes them away.*)

MINNIE. Are you worried from anything, Marion?

MARION. No, Minnie, I'm all right.

MINNIE. I think maybe dot telegram bring you bad news.

MARION. Telegram? What telegram?

MINNIE. Dot telegram I bring you.

MARION. Of course—I haven't even —where is it?

MINNIE (*gets telegram from table rear of sofa left and hands it to* MARION). There it is!

MARION. Thank you, Minnie. (*Opens telegram and reads it.*) This is from heaven! Minnie, I want you to pack right away. We're leaving! (*She springs up.*)

MINNIE. Leaving? Ven?

MARION. Right away. Tonight! This is from Feydie! Listen! (*Reads telegram aloud to* MINNIE.) "Can get you commission to paint prize-winners Motion Picture Academy—wire answer at once. Feydie." (*Hysterically grateful for the mercy of having something to do at once, of being busy, of not having time to think.*) Something always turns up for me! Pack everything, Minnie. I want to get out right away. (*She rushes upstage right, picks up her hat and coat, and then runs to the stairs Left.)*

MINNIE. Don't you tink you better vait till tomorrow?

MARION. No, Minnie. Once the temptation to a journey comes into my head, I can't bear it till I'm on my way! This time, Minnie, we'll have a real trip. From Hollywood we'll go to Honolulu and from Honolulu to China. How would you like that, Minnie? *(She starts up the stairs.)*

MINNIE *(for her, enthusiastic)*. Fine, Marion! *(Calls after her as she runs upstairs.)* Dot crazy Kurt, he goes vit us?

MARION *(as she disappears into her bedroom)*. No, Minnie—no one—we travel alone!

QUICK CURTAIN

ON BORROWED TIME

Paul Osborn

(a dramatization of the novel by Lawrence E. Watkin)

On Borrowed Time was produced by Dwight Deere Wiman at the Longacre Theatre in
New York City, beginning February 3, 1938. It was staged by Joshua Logan, with
settings by Jo Mielziner. The cast was as follows:

PUD ..... Peter Holden, Peter Miner, Lawrence Robinson	A BOY .... Dickie Van Patten
JULIAN NORTHRUP (GRAMPS) .... Dudley Digges	WORKMEN .... { Andy Anderson / Elwell Cobb / Nick Dennis
NELLIE (GRANNY) ... Dorothy Stickney	DR. EVANS .... Clyde Franklin
MR. BRINK .... Frank Conroy	MR. PILBEAM .... Richard Sterling
MARCIA GILES ...... Peggy O'Donnell	MR. GRIMES .... Lew Eckels
DEMETRIA RIFFLE .... Jean Adair	SHERIFF .... Al Webster

ACT ONE. *Scene One:* The living-room, afternoon. *Scene Two:* The
living-room, afternoon, a week later. *Scene Three:* Granny's bedroom,
a few minutes later. *Scene Four:* The tree, simultaneously with Scene
Three. *Scene Five:* The tree, nearly dusk, a week later.

ACT TWO. *Scene One:* The tree, two hours later. *Scene Two:* The living-
room, ten o'clock that night. *Scene Three:* The tree, dawn, the next
morning. *Scene Four:* The tree, dusk, the same day. *Scene Five:* The tree,
a few minutes later, the same day. *Scene Six:* The tree, later that night.

From the novel *On Borrowed Time*, Copyright 1937 by Lawrence E. Watkin. Dramatized version, Copyright 1937 by Paul Osborn. Reprinted by permission of the publisher, Alfred A. Knopf, Inc.

CAUTION: Professionals and amateurs are hereby warned that *On Borrowed Time*, being fully protected
under the copyright law of the United States of America, the British Empire, including the Dominion of
Canada, and all other countries of the Copyright Union, is subject to a royalty. All rights, including but
not limited to professional, amateur, motion picture, recitation, lecturing, public reading, radio broadcasting, television, and the rights of translation into foreign languages, are strictly reserved. Particular
emphasis is laid on the question of readings, permission for which must be secured from the author's agent
in writing. All inquiries should be addressed to the author's agent, Harold Freedman, 101 Park Avenue,
New York 17, New York.

Although Paul Osborn first won reputation as a playwright with an original comedy about a woman's effort to recapture memories of an early romance, *The Vinegar Tree* (it ran through the season of 1930-31 with Mary Boland in the leading role), he has been best known as our most dependable adapter of novels. Adapting fiction has proved not only profitable but honorable in his case, for most of the work he has dramatized has added interest and even some importance to the Broadway stage. One of his most gratifying contributions was the homespun fantasy *On Borrowed Time*, which he shaped from the novel by Lawrence Edward Watkins.

Born in Evansville, Indiana, in 1901 and educated at the University of Michigan (B.A., 1923; M.A., 1924), Paul Osborn went on to study playwriting with George Pierce Baker at Yale in 1927, after teaching English at his Alma Mater for a year. His professional career started in 1928 when the Broadway producer Brock Pemberton presented his comedy *Hotbed*. Two other plays, *A Ledge* and *Oliver Oliver*, followed it, but the young author missed success until *The Vinegar Tree* opened in New York in 1930. The movie industry discovered in Mr. Osborn an exceptional talent for adaptation, and the discovery was made even more gratifyingly on Broadway with such work as *On Borrowed Time* in 1937, which was filmed in 1939; *The Innocent Voyage*, based on *A High Wind in Jamaica*, in 1943, in a Theatre Guild production staged by Theresa Helburn with a cast that included Oscar Homolka, Clarence Derwent, Herbert Berghof, and Arvid Paulson; *A Bell For Adano*, adapted in 1944 from the novel by John Hersey, with Frederic March in the leading role of the well-intentioned American officer who tries to help the people of Italy, recently liberated from their Fascist and Nazi oppressors; *Point of No Return* in 1951, based on Marquand's book of the same title, with Henry Fonda as the leading character of this comedy of status-climbing. And *The World of Suzie Wong*, adapted from Richard Mason, proved successful well beyond its worth as a play in the 1958-59 season. (His *Morning's at Seven* follows later in this Supplement.) Mr. Osborn's craftsmanship has placed him at the head of his occupation, and there are many indications indeed that as an artist and a man he stands higher than his profession of adapter would suggest.

On Borrowed Time had a good run during the 1937-38 season in the Broadway production which had the Abbey Theatre and Theatre Guild actor Dudley Digges in the role of Gramps. This role was filled by Victor Moore in the 1953 revival, which had Beulah Bondi playing Granny and Leo G. Carroll Mr. Brink.

ACT ONE

Scene One

The living-room. Late afternoon.

AT RISE: GRAMPS *seated chair right of table, engraving.* PUD *crawls from under chair.*

———

PUD (*crawling out*). You could write Pud on it afterwards.

GRAMPS. Yeh! I could write shikepoke on it too but I ain't goin' to.

PUD. What's shikepoke?

GRAMPS. A shikepoke's a bird.

PUD. Is it what you call the bird?

GRAMPS. Yup.

(*Pause.*)

PUD (*climbs into* GRAMPS' *chair*). If the watch fob belonged to the bird would you write shikepoke on it?

GRAMPS. Birds don't have watch fobs.

PUD. But if it did have one would you write shikepoke on it, Gramps?

GRAMPS. Expect I would.

PUD. Because it's what you call the bird, isn't it, Gramps?

GRAMPS. That's right, sonny.

(PUD *around back of chair. Pause.* GRAMPS *is busy.*)

PUD. Gramps, what do you call me?

GRAMPS. Eh? Oh, I call you all sorts of things—sonny, chummy—

PUD. No, no! What's the *name* you call me?

GRAMPS. Oh, Pud, you mean. Pud. That's what you look like. Pud.

PUD. It's what you call me, isn't it, Gramps?

GRAMPS. That's right, sonny.

PUD (*crosses to chair left*). Then if the watch fob belongs to me and you call me Pud you ought to write Pud on it. If the shikepoke had a fob—

GRAMPS (*pause*). Whoa there! I said I wasn't gonna write Pud on this here fob!

PUD. But Pud's my name.

GRAMPS. Your name is John Gilford Northrup. And that's what I'm gonna engrave on this here fob. John Gilford Northrup.

PUD. I like Pud better.

(*Climbs over chair left.*)

GRAMPS. Pud's too easy, P-U-D. John Gilford Northrup. And don't you forget it.

(*Pause.* GRAMPS *works.* PUD *rises, crosses right to desk.*)

PUD. Where's Mom gone today, Gramps?

GRAMPS. She's gone with your father.

PUD. Where did he go?

GRAMPS. Up to Gainesville to make a call.

PUD (*over chair right*). Is somebody sick?

GRAMPS. Somebody's always sick, sonny.

(*Pause.*)

PUD. I'm going to be a doctor when I grow up.

GRAMPS. You bet you are. You're gonna be as good a doctor as your daddy.

PUD. Maybe better.

(*Crosses to* GRAMPS.)

GRAMPS. That's a stiff order, sonny. Your daddy's a A number one doctor.

PUD. What's A number one? (*Pause.*) What's A number one, Gramps?

GRAMPS. Oh, it's just A number one. There. Now, what do you think of that?

(PUD *looks at fob.*)

PUD. I guess it's all right, Gramps.

GRAMPS. What do you mean you guess it's all right?

PUD (*leans on arm of chair*). Well, that G looks a little more like a C, I think.

GRAMPS. You do? Let's see.

(*Takes fob.*)

PUD. My name is John Gilford Northrup. Not John Cilford Northrup—

GRAMPS. I know that, boy, I know that. Well, guess that G does need a little more of a tail there. Yes sir, I guess it does. Thank you, boy.

(PUD *crosses to collection.*)

PUD. You're welcome, Gramps. Guess we better take a walk out to Milbaur Park one of these days, Gramps. We need some more stones for our collection.

GRAMPS (*reaching in his pocket.* PUD *crosses to* GRAMPS). Oh, here's a bone I found yesterday down by the meat-shop.

PUD. Is it a human bone, Gramps?

GRAMPS (*gives bone to* PUD). Might be—

PUD. Looks pretty human to me, Gramps.

GRAMPS. Might be.

PUD (*crosses left to collection*). It's a very fine specimen, anyway, Gramps. (*Pause.*

PUD *goes over and puts bone in collection and pulls out another object.*) This frog's gettin' kinda old, Gramps.

(*Crosses to table showing* GRAMPS *frog.*)

GRAMPS. Yep. Guess we'll have to throw that old frog out in a few days.

PUD. It's a very fine specimen though, Gramps.

GRAMPS. We'll get another one.

(GRAMPS *gives* PUD *frog.* PUD *crosses to collection. Pause. Puts label on bone.*)

PUD (*suddenly. Singing*):
Aunt Demetria is a pismire.
Aunt Demetria is a pismire.

GRAMPS. Hey, there. Where did you hear that?

PUD. You told Granny she was.

GRAMPS. You mustn't use that word about your Aunt Demetria.

PUD (*pointing at* GRAMPS). *You* said she was a pismire.

GRAMPS. She *is* a pismire! She's the biggest pismire I know. You know what a pismire is, sonny?

PUD. No.

(*Crosses to chair center, kneels on it.*)

GRAMPS. A pismire is one of the meanest of ants there is. And your Aunt Demetria is a pismire. But you mustn't say it. It makes your Granny mad.

PUD. But why is Aunt Demetria so mean, Gramps?

GRAMPS. Born that way.

PUD. Why was she born that way?

GRAMPS. I'll tell you, boy, it's like this. Your other Gramps—

PUD. What, Gramps?

GRAMPS. I say when your other Gramps was alive . . .

PUD. What other Gramps?

GRAMPS. Your mom's father. Pshaw, boy, didn't you know you used to have another Gramps? Everybody has two Gramps.

PUD (*tearfully*). But I don't want any other Gramps, Gramps. (GRAMPS *touches him.*) Did you have another Pud?

GRAMPS. No, 'course I didn't, boy. You're the only Pud I ever had.

PUD (*hits table*). Then you're the only Gramps I ever had.

GRAMPS. All right, boy, all right. That other fellow—we'll call him your grandfather. Is that all right?

PUD. I guess so, Gramps.

GRAMPS. All right, then. So your grandfather had a whole lot of children.

And the first one he had was your Aunt Demetria. That was a long time ago, when your grandfather was a young buck and didn't have no sense at all, so he didn't do a very good job of it. Botched it up all the way round. Then he had a lot more children to practice on and the last one he had was your mother. Now, there he did a real sweet job. Yes, sir, a pretty nigh perfect job.

PUD. But he sure made a mess out of Aunt Demetria.

GRAMPS. That's what I've been trying to tell you, boy.

(GRAMPS *takes bottle from pocket.*)

GRANNY (*off stage*). Juleyun!

GRAMPS. Oh, hell!

PUD. Where is hell, Gramps?

GRAMPS. Where the woodbine twineth. (*He takes sip from bottle.*) Don't you ever touch this, boy.

PUD. Give me some.

GRAMPS. No—

PUD. Just a little taste. . . .

GRAMPS. You wouldn't like 'er, boy!

PUD. Please, Gramps, please.

GRAMPS. Here then, teach yourself.

(*As* PUD *takes a drink* GRANNY *is heard calling again.* PUD *spits it out.*)

GRANNY (*off stage*). Juleyun!

PUD (*wipes mouth*). Peeyew!

GRAMPS. Well, I warned you.

PUD (*gives bottle back*). What do you drink it for, Gramps?

GRAMPS. I drink it for my ches . . . because I li . . . oh, take that damn smelly dog out for a walk.

PUD. But I like the way Betty smells.

GRAMPS. You're welcome to it.

(*Hides bottle as* GRANNY *comes in with dog.*)

GRANNY (*crosses to table*). When you two get together over some gimcrack you're as deaf as a post.

GRAMPS. Was you calling, Miss Nellie? Didn't hear you.

GRANNY (*crosses right center*). None so deaf as those who don't want to hear.

GRAMPS. Well, what d'ye want?

GRANNY. I hollered loud enough to wake the dead. That dog'll get caught short someday.

GRAMPS. Can't she find her own tree yet?

GRANNY. Julian! (*She nods toward* PUD.) Go with your Grandpa, Betty.

GRAMPS (*takes leash*). And I'll thank

you not to claim kin to me with that bitch!

GRANNY. Julian!

(*She points to* PUD.)

GRAMPS (*rises*). Pshaw, that's what she is . . . no more, no less than a bitch.

PUD (*singing, suddenly*). A dog or a bitch, you never know which.

(*They both look at* PUD.)

GRANNY. There you are!

GRAMPS. I never taught him that, Miss Nellie, I swear.

GRANNY (*crossing to desk*). Turning your own grandson into a smutty mouth like yourself.

GRAMPS (*crossing center toward* GRANNY). Honest, I never taught him that, Miss Nellie.

GRANNY. That I should live to see the day . . . .

GRAMPS (*crossing to door*). Oh, come along, Petunia.

GRANNY (*turning toward* GRAMPS). And her name isn't Petunia.

GRAMPS. All right, come along, Sweet Pea.

PUD (*rises, crosses up center to* GRAMPS). I'll take her, Gramps. It's kinda *hot* for you to be out today.

GRAMPS. I guess you're right. It is. Thank you kindly. Go with your uncle, Betty.

(*He gives leash to* PUD.)

PUD. Am I her uncle?

GRAMPS (*looking toward* GRANNY). Seems so.

GRANNY. Just walk her up toward the Browns, darling.

PUD. I know where her twalet is.

(PUD *and dog go off right.*)

GRANNY (*crossing to table left*). That boy's gettin' to be the limit. You're not only making a smutty mouth out of him . . . (*She sits chair left.*) the first thing you know you'll be teaching him to smoke, I suppose. And even drink . . . and goodness knows what all.

GRAMPS (*sitting chair right of table*). It'll be years yet before he can "what all"!

(*He lights pipe.*)

GRANNY. Julian!

GRAMPS. Oh, Miss Nellie.

GRANNY. He mimics everything you do. He hardly has a chance to see his own father. Jim's always so busy. First thing you know, that boy'll grow up and be just like you. Is that what you want?

GRAMPS. Nope. I want him to go further'n I have.

GRANNY. Then you better set him an example. You gotta stop swearin' and smokin' that smelly pipe. You never draw a breath that it ain't full of smokin' and swearin'. You better change your ways, Julian Northrup. If you don't, I'm gonna talk to Jim and Susan about sending Pud away to school.

GRAMPS. Send him away to school? At his age?

GRANNY. It'd be better for him than being around you so much.

GRAMPS. There ain't no school what'd take him. He's too little.

GRANNY. Yes, there is. Demetria knows a school in—

GRAMPS. Demetria! By God, I might have known she was at the bottom of this. (GRANNY *looks at him.*) Old bird-stuffer!

GRANNY. Demetria's a fine, Christian woman and I won't hear a word against her.

GRAMPS. She's a bird-stuffer!

GRANNY. She's no such thing.

GRAMPS. Oh, Miss Nellie—I don't see why you're always sticking up for Demmie. She's a bird-stuffer and you know it.

GRANNY. Demmie may have her faults but she's a God-fearing woman. She's warned Susan time and time again how you're poisoning Pud's mind, and now she's found this nice boarding-school run by a Baptist woman.

GRAMPS. Baptist woman! By God, Pud's not goin' to no school run by a Baptist woman.

GRANNY. Then you better change your ways, Julian Northrup. You are a bad influence on the boy and it's gotta be stopped. It's gotta be. . . . (*She belches sharply.*) There! Now I've got that gas started again. Every time I get excited it starts rumbling and rumbling.

GRAMPS. Well, you'd better not get excited, then.

(*He rises, crosses to window, looking at fob.*)

GRANNY. It won't be long before I'm flat on my back for good now. (*Pause. She looks at* GRAMPS.) What is a bird-stuffer, Julian?

GRAMPS. It's just a bird-stuffer.

GRANNY. But it must *mean* something.

GRAMPS. Nope. It don't. Adam saw a dog and it looked like a dog and he called it a dog. I saw Demmie, she looked like a bird-stuffer and I called her a bird-stuffer, so she is a bird-stuffer.

(*Pause.*)

GRANNY. Sultry today, ain't it?

GRAMPS. Hotter'n a bull mink in matin' season.

GRANNY. That I don't know about. (GRAMPS *laughs. Pause.*) Guess we'll have another shower. Hope it won't spoil Susan's day. She so seldom goes with Jim on a case.

GRAMPS (*crossing to window*). What did she go for today?

GRANNY. For the pleasure of bein' with him. I suppose you can't understand a thing like that. You always used to go off by yourself . . . though like enough there was someone waitin' around the corner.

GRAMPS (*looking out the window*). Here comes someone around the corner now. Umhum!

GRANNY. Who is it?

GRAMPS. The Widow Tritt.

GRANNY (*rises, crosses right to* GRAMPS). That hussy! Demmie says she ought to be run outa town.

GRAMPS. Not a bad-looking woman, considering all she's been through. Five, ain't it?

GRANNY. Demmie says she makes advances to every man she meets.

GRAMPS. Widows always have somethin' about them. She kin put her shoes under my bed anytime she wants to.

GRANNY. Just as well you're eighty-odd. Even then, I don't know. (*She crosses a step or two toward* GRAMPS. *Looks out of window also. He watches her at it.*) Well, don't stand there in the window staring at her. You don't know her, do you?

GRAMPS. Sure wish I did.

GRANNY. Julian!

(*She crosses to chair left.*)

GRAMPS (*singing*).

She remained up in the mountains,
She remained up in the mountains,
Remained up in the mountains all that night.

GRANNY. And I wish you wouldn't sing that lascivious song.

VOICE (*off stage*). Good afternoon, Mr. Northrup.

GRAMPS. Hello there, Mrs. Tritt.

GRANNY. Well, I never.

VOICE. 'Fraid it's goin' to rain.

GRAMPS. Yup, looks like it.

VOICE. I've got to hurry. Mustn't be caught short.

(*Pause.* GRANNY *stands staring at* GRAMPS. *He looks at her sheepishly.*)

GRAMPS. Sure mustn't. (*Pause. He turns and looks at* GRANNY.) Well, what're you standin' there like a hitchin' post for?

GRANNY. And you don't know the Widow Tritt.

GRAMPS (*crossing to* GRANNY). Miss Nellie, I swear to you I never . . .

GRANNY. Never what?

GRAMPS. What you're insinuating. I petted her dog once.

GRANNY. Oh, you petted her dog. . . .

GRAMPS. I didn't even know it was her dog. She was in the grocery store and . . . Oh, you needn't pretend to think I ever had . . .

GRANNY (*crossing center*). Never mind, Julian. And I think I'll go upstairs now.

GRAMPS (*starts to kiss her*). Aw, Miss Nellie!

GRANNY. I'm not jealous. I just don't feel very well.

(*She goes upstairs.*)

GRAMPS (*crossing back of chair right of table*). All right, Miss Nellie. I'll come up and lie down, too, soon as Pud comes in. I'm feeling kind of tired myself. (*He looks after* GRANNY. *Then looks at window. Begins to sing, as he crosses around chair.*)

Her life is beer and skittles
And she is eating fancy vittles
And them West Virginia . . .

(MR. BRINK *appears.* GRAMPS *is stricken with pain. Falls into chair right of table.*)

BRINK. Mr. Julian Northrup, I believe?

GRAMPS. What's that? I didn't catch it.

BRINK (*crossing down center*). Most people don't hear me the first time.

GRAMPS. How in blazes could I hear you if I was asleep?

BRINK. Are you sure you were—asleep?

GRAMPS. Guess I musta drowsed off. Felt kind of tired all of a sudden. Who are you? What d'ye want?

BRINK. I request that you come with me.

GRAMPS. Where yuh goin'?

BRINK. Where the woodbine twineth.

GRAMPS. Where the wood . . . ? *I* just said that. I made it up. It's what yuh say to a child. *I* ain't no child.

BRINK. Aren't you?

GRAMPS. No, I'm not. Say, look here, who the hell are you?

BRINK. You may call me Mr. Brink.

GRAMPS. Well, look here, Mr. Brink, I don't like you. I wouldn't go with you to a rat fight, so now you know.

BRINK. I'm sorry.

GRAMPS. I don't like the way you snuck up here. I don't like the way you talk. (*He leans over to pick up fob and instrument which fell from his hands.*)

BRINK. I'm afraid that will have to be as it may be.

GRAMPS. Oh, you are! Well, you better . . . (*Rises.*) . . . get out of here right awa . . .

(*He becomes suddenly weak and sits, bewildered.*)

BRINK (*crossing closer to him*). You see. It's time for you to come with me.

GRAMPS. No . . . no. . . . It ain't. I ain't goin' nowhere. I'm goin' to stay right here. I'm waitin' for Pud. (*He gets stronger. Rises, waves hands.*) By God, you get the hell out of here! You git off my son's property! You git the hell . . .

(GRANNY's *voice off stage stops him.* BRINK *turns swiftly and leaves.* GRAMPS *turns toward* GRANNY's *voice, then turns back to door.*)

GRANNY (*off stage*). Julian!

GRAMPS (*turning back to door*). You git the . . .

(*He discovers* MR. BRINK *has disappeared and is bewildered.*) Well, I'll be . . .

(*Crosses to chair right of table and sits.*)

GRANNY (*comes down on stairs*). Who you shoutin' at that way?

GRAMPS. Well, I . . . there was a feller here. . . .

GRANNY. Well, where is he?

GRAMPS. He's gone now.

GRANNY. What did he want?

GRAMPS. I don't rightly know, Miss Nellie. I . . .

GRANNY. You better come upstairs out of that hot room, Julian.

(*She goes off.*)

GRAMPS. Yes, I guess I better had.

(PUD *comes in from porch with* BETTY.)

PUD. Gramps, who was that mans?

GRAMPS. You seen him, did you, son?

PUD. Sure. He was coming down the walk. Who was he?

GRAMPS. I don't rightly know who he was.

PUD. What did he want?

GRAMPS. He wanted me to go with him.

PUD. Where?

GRAMPS. Where the woodbine twineth.

PUD. Oh! You mean Hell.

GRAMPS (*rising*). By golly, boy, we better both go upstairs out of this hot room. (*They go upstairs.*)

SCENE TWO

The living-room. Late afternoon. A week later.

AT RISE: PUD *is reading on floor.* GRAMPS *is writing at desk.* GRANNY *is knitting.* MARCIA *is handing* GRANNY *a drink.*

GRANNY (*seated in chair right of table*). Thank you, Marcy. I'll just keep it here till I need it.

(*Wipes eyes with mourning handkerchief.*)

MARCIA. How are you feeling, Mrs. Northrup?

GRANNY. Won't be long before I'm flat on my back for good, now.

MARCIA (*patting* GRANNY's *shoulder*). Oh, you got years and years yet, Mrs. Northrup.

(MARCIA *crosses to bookcase up right and straightens it.*)

GRANNY. Don't know as I want years and years yet.

GRAMPS. Anyways, where the hell's some more ink?

MARCIA (*crossing down to desk*). Here's some, Mr. Northrup.

GRAMPS. Oh, thank ye, Marcy. How did we ever find things before you came to live with us?

(MARCIA *smiles and returns to bookcase. Pause.* GRAMPS *writes.* GRANNY *knits.*)

PUD (*suddenly*). Granny, why do they put dead peoples in coffings?

GRANNY. Oh, Pud!

(*She buries her face in her hands, crying suddenly.*)

GRAMPS. There, there, Miss Nellie! (*Rises and crosses to her.*) Now, don't talk about that any more, boy.

PUD. But why do they, Gramps?

MARCIA (*going down to and kneeling beside* PUD). 'Cause that's the way you take care of 'em. Now, read your story, Pud.

(GRAMPS *looks at* GRANNY. PUD *is quiet.*)

GRAMPS. That's all right, Miss Nellie. That's all right.

GRANNY (*looking up at him*). I don't know—I'm just so tired, Julian.

GRAMPS. 'Course you are. Now, everything's all right, Miss Nellie.

(*He kisses her on the forehead and crosses to desk.*)

PUD. Is it comfable in a coffing?

GRAMPS. Yes, boy, very comfortable in a coffin.

PUD. As comfable as my bed?

GRAMPS (*sitting at desk*). Sure, sure. 'Course it is. As comfortable as your bed. (*Motioning to book on floor.*) Now read your damn story.

(*Pause.* GRANNY *gets hold of herself.*)

GRANNY. It's very comfortable in a coffin, Pud.

PUD (*suddenly. Rises*). My mamma and papa are in coffings. They put them in the ground like this—(*He crosses to* GRANNY *to illustrate.*) You may lower now. Dear Lord, we commend to thy tender—

GRAMPS (*turning quickly*). Don't, Pud. Don't. I told you—

GRANNY (*taking* PUD *in her arms*). That's all right, Julian.—Yes, dear, your mamma and papa are both very comfortable.

PUD. My papa was a brave man, wasn't he?

GRANNY. Yes, he was, dear—very brave.

PUD. He turned his automobile right off the road so he wouldn't hurt a little boy just like me.

GRANNY. That's right, darling.

PUD (*as though repeating a lesson*). But I must never forget that my dear mamma and papa were taken from me and I will never, never have any others. I'm a—orphan.

GRAMPS (*quickly*). Who told you that?

PUD (*turning to* GRAMPS). Aunt Demetria.

GRIMPS (*roaring and pointing to* GRANNY). There! That damned old—!

GRANNY. Julian!

GRAMPS. Telling things like that to the boy! By God, if that God-damned old hellion—

GRANNY. Julian! If you swear any more like that in front of—

GRAMPS. It's enough to make a preacher swear.

PUD. I'm going to swear when I'm nine.

GRAMPS (*shaking his finger*). Ah—Ah—

PUD (*crossing to* GRAMPS). But you said I could, Gramps.

(GRAMPS *motions violently for* PUD *to go back to his book.* PUD *sits.*)

GRANNY (*angrily*). There! Did you tell that boy he could ... Did you tell that boy he could ... (*She belches sharply.*) Whoops, there it goes again! Never know when it's coming. (*She drinks.* GRAMPS *writes. Pause.*) Who you writin' to, anyway, Julian?

GRAMPS. Reverend Murdock. Looked pretty shabby when he was preachin' that funeral sermon. I guess preachin' don't pay what it used to.

(*Pause.* GRAMPS *writes.*)

GRANNY. What are you writin' him for?

GRAMPS. Goin' to send him a check for $50.00. (*Turning to* GRANNY.) Now, that's a good deed, ain't it, even if I do say so myself?

GRANNY. Good deeds and leadin' a Christian life is two different things.

PUD (*rising to his knees, excited*). Oh, Gramps, if you do a good deed, you can make a wish and it'll come true.

GRAMPS (*back at desk*). What's that?

PUD. If you do a good deed, you can make a wish and it'll come true. ·

GRAMPS. That so, boy?

PUD. That's what my book says.

GRAMPS. Must be so then.

PUD (*very excited*). So make a wish, Gramps, make a wish, make a wish.

GRAMPS. All right, boy, soon's I think of a good one. (*Pause. He turns to* GRANNY.) Listen, Miss Nellie, how does this sound?

"Dear Reverend Murdock: Enclosed is a check for $50.00, for which please kindly send me one copy of the sermon you preached at the funeral of my son, James Northrup, M.D., and his wife, Susan. If you don't have it down on paper, maybe you wouldn't mind writing out the gist of the thing which I thought was very good and proper and appropriate to the occasion. I hope the enclosed check will compensate in some part for the trouble this will make you.

Yours truly,
Julian Northrup."

Now, you don't think he'd take offense at that, do you?

GRANNY. I don't think so, Julian.

GRAMPS (*turning back to desk*). No. Don't want to offend the old bastard.

GRANNY (*rising*). Julian!

GRAMPS. Sorry, Miss Nellie. Take it back. Forgot.

(*Pause.*)

PUD (*suddenly rising and unbuttoning pants*). I'm going to the twalet.

GRANNY. What!

PUD. I'm going to the twalet.

GRANNY. Well, you don't have to tell the neighbors about it. When you have to go, just get up quietly and go.

GRAMPS. Just say you have to wash your hands, boy.

PUD (*crossing to* GRAMPS). But I don't have to wash my hands.

GRAMPS. Don't make no difference. That's what you say. Etiquette. (*Pause.*) Matter of fact my hands feels kinda dirty, too, but I guess I'll wait until they're a little dirtier.

GRANNY. Go along, Pud! (PUD *runs upstairs.* GRANNY *puts her knitting on the table and turns back to* GRAMPS, *shaking her head disapprovingly.*) 'Twasn't an accident!

GRAMPS. What's that?

GRANNY. 'Twasn't an accident that killed Jim and Susan.

GRAMPS (*turning to her*). Sure, of course it was, Miss Nellie—they turned over in their car.

GRANNY. God took Jim and Susan, Julian.

GRAMPS. Oh. Oh!

(*Goes back to his writing.*)

GRANNY. As a warnin' to us. Julian, I heard the voice of God at the funeral. I was sittin' there durin' the hymn, askin' myself why this cross had been put upon us. What had we done that was bad? And suddenly it came to me. It was you!

GRAMPS (*turning quickly*). Me?

GRANNY. You and me both, Julian.

GRAMPS. Well, what've we been doin' that's bad, Miss Nellie? I can't think of nothin'. Less you been up to somethin'.

GRANNY. I have, Julian. I've been closing my eyes to the way you've been ruinin' Pud. (*She rises and goes to* GRAMPS *at desk.*) We can't raise a little boy, Julian —all by ourselves—we're too old.

GRAMPS. Why, sure we can, Miss Nellie —same way we raised Jim. I'll keep teaching him to cuss and you'll keep teaching him not to. He'll turn out pretty good, you'll see.

GRANNY (*turning away*). We gotta find some other way to raise that boy.

GRAMPS. Ain't nobody goin' to raise that boy but us!

GRANNY (*turning to him*). Julian, the Lord said . . .

GRAMPS. The Lord be blowed— You heard the voice of Demetria.

GRANNY (*crosses left*). No, it 'twasn't. It was the Lord's!

GRAMPS. It was Demetria's!

GRANNY. Julian Northrup, I guess I know the difference between the Lord's voice and Demetria Riffle's.

(PUD *enters from stairs, trying to fasten his pants.*)

PUD. I've had my fun and now I'm done.

GRANNY. What!

PUD (*coming center*). I've had my fun and now I'm done.

GRANNY. You've had . . . (*Turning toward* GRAMPS.) There you are!

GRAMPS. Never taught him that, Miss Nellie.

GRANNY. Julian.

GRAMPS. I never taught him that.

GRANNY. You're a liar, Julian Northrup.

GRAMPS. Well, maybe I am.

(PUD *goes to* GRAMPS *and backs up toward him.*)

PUD (*pointing to his pants*). Back door's undone.

GRAMPS (*pushes him*). Go to your Granny.

(PUD *crosses to* GRANNY.)

GRANNY (*sits*). Yes, come here, darling. I'll help you. (*Together they fasten the pants.*) Get you all buttoned up nice and tight. (*She tries to kiss him.*) Got a nice kiss for Granny? (PUD *struggles away.*) What's the matter, darling?

PUD. I've had too much ladies' arms around me lately.

GRANNY. Too *many* arms.

PUD (*crosses to* GRAMPS). Too many arms. I'd like to have none arms around me for a while.

GRANNY. Oh, very well.

(*She goes back to her knitting.*)

GRAMPS (*taking hold of* PUD). You hadn't ought to say things like that to your Granny. If she wants to give you a kiss now and then, just let her do it.

PUD. She kisses awful wet.

GRAMPS. What the hell, that don't cut no ice. . . . (PUD *crosses to above desk.*) And I don't want to ever see you smoke or say dirty things . . . and, above all . . . (*Shakes his finger at* PUD.) . . . I don't ever want to hear you swear. . . .

(*Turns and looks triumphantly at* GRANNY.

PUD, *at this point, has turned and is staring out of the window right.*)

PUD. Gramps, Gramps, somebody's stealing the apples again.

GRAMPS. God-damn it to hell. Where is he?

(*Rises.*)

PUD (*getting into chair*). He's up the tree.

GRAMPS (*shouting out the window*). Hey, you damn young shikepoke. I'm comin' out there and get you. You wait right there.

PUD. Hurry, Gramps, he's coming down.

GRAMPS. You stay up there. I'm goin' to give you such a tannin'—

PUD. He's gettin' away, Gramps.

GRAMPS (*crossing closer to window*). Hey, there—wait. . . .

PUD (*turning around from window*). Oh, Gramps, he got away. He didn't wait.

GRAMPS (*snapping fingers*). Oh, hell—

GRANNY (*laughs*). Heh! Heh!

GRAMPS (*coming center*). I swear I wish that anyone who climbed that tree would have to stay up there until I let him down.

PUD (*excitedly crossing to GRAMPS*). Gramps, you made a wish!

GRAMPS. Huh?

PUD. A wish! You wished anyone who climbed that tree would have to stay there until you let him down.

GRAMPS (*crosses to desk, picks up letter*). A lot of good it'll do me.

PUD (*jumps around excitedly*). Gee, I bet we catch one of those bad boys up there and we can keep him up there for a hundred years. Maybe for a million years. Maybe—

(PUD *stops suddenly and becomes very quiet, staring at the door.* DEMETRIA *enters, takes off hat, puts it on hatrack.*)

GRANNY (*following PUD's eyes*). Oh, hello, Demmie.

GRAMPS. Oh, hell.

GRANNY. Come right in.

DEMETRIA (*crossing center, taking PUD in arms*). Poor little lambie, what's the matter? Is he still thinking of his mamma and papa?

GRAMPS. Leave that boy alone, for God's sake!

GRANNY. Julian!

DEMETRIA. Well!

PUD (*struggling*). Let me go!

DEMETRIA. There, there, lambie, your Aunt Demetria understands. (*She ruffles PUD's hair. He straightens it with a defiant gesture*). You must be a brave boy, boy. God has taken . . .

GRAMPS. Leave that boy alone, I say.

DEMETRIA. Would you deny the child Christian comfort, his parents hardly cold in their graves . . . ?

(PUD *runs to* GRAMPS, *crying.*)

GRAMPS (*clasping PUD*). To hell with Christian comfort, you old . . .

DEMETRIA. Come here, Pud.

PUD. I hate you!

GRAMPS. Now you know.

DEMETRIA. Come here to me, Pud.

GRAMPS. Like hell he will!

PUD. Like hell I will!

DEMETRIA (*to* GRANNY). See! See! (*To* GRAMPS). You whited sepulchre!

GRAMPS. What! Whited sepulch . . . You—whore of Babylon! You—

(*He crosses to door center, spluttering.*)

PUD (*following*). You—pismire!

GRAMPS (*taking his hand*). That's right, boy. Come along. Let's get out of this company.

(*They go out by the porch, leaving* DEMETRIA *and* GRANNY *speechless.*)

DEMETRIA. You heard it, Nellie.

GRANNY. I never thought I'd live to—

DEMETRIA (*coming down right*). You heard what he called me! He called me . . .

GRANNY. I know. Revelations 17:5. Don't say it, Demmie.

DEMETRIA (*sitting at desk*). Of course, I know I'm a nobody, Nellie. Maybe I'm no better than some folks say I am. But I'm certainly not a whor—

GRANNY. Of course you're not, Demmie. I don't know what Julian was thinking of.

DEMETRIA. And he said it right in front of that sweet little boy. But, then, of course, it's none of my business.

GRANNY (*sitting in chair left of table*). Of course it's your business.

DEMETRIA. No. I guess I better stay home after this. I'm a downright nuisance.

GRANNY. You're not. You're a dear, sweet, Christian woman and you shouldn't always be runnin' yourself down. You're the only God-fearing woman . . . Well! . . . Maybe that's what the voice of God meant.

DEMETRIA. What?

GRANNY. I wonder if you shouldn't bring Pud up?

DEMETRIA. Me?

GRANNY. Your own sister's child. And you could bring him up the way God wants him to be brought up. Maybe that's what God meant.

DEMETRIA. Well, Nellie, I've thought about it. (*Crossing to chair right of table.*) But I couldn't afford to give Pud all the things he's been used to. That is, unless Jim left a will—or something like that.

GRANNY. Well, he did, Demmie. He left a will.

DEMETRIA (*sits*). Well, think of that. And how m . . . that is . . . well, is the little lambie well taken care of?

GRANNY. Yes, Demmie. Jim left fifty-five thousand dollars.

DEMETRIA. Fifty-five thou . . . ! Dear little lambie. . . . Well, Nellie, maybe you're right.

GRANNY. About what—?

DEMETRIA (*rises, crosses center*). Maybe I should adopt Pud.

GRANNY. Adopt him . . . ?

DEMETRIA. I mean if he has fifty-five thousand dollars, I could give him some of the things he's been used to.

GRANNY. Yes, but adopt him . . . I didn't exactly mean . . . well, you wouldn't really have to adopt him, would you, Demmie? I just thought he'd sort of live over there with you and see Julian in the afternoons maybe and you could kind of . . . No. I guess not, Demmie. . . . I mean, Julian and I better . . .

DEMETRIA. I see. You mean you are going to go on letting Julian bring Pud up like a heathen.

GRANNY. Oh, I don't know what to do, Demmie. I'm so tired.

(MARCIA *enters from hallway, with glass of soda water, crosses down to table.*)

MARCIA. Would you like some more soda, Mrs. Northrup?

GRANNY. Yes, I would, Marcy. Still feel a little rumbly down there.

MARCIA. Good afternoon, Miss Riffle.

DEMETRIA (*crossing right. Coldly*). Good afternoon. (MARCIA *goes out through porch, bewildered.* DEMETRIA *crosses back to table.*) You don't mean to tell me you've got that Marcia Giles in this house.

GRANNY. She came in to help us after the funeral. Why? Good straightforward girl, isn't she?

DEMETRIA. Well, her and that young Bill Murdock, Reverend Murdock's son . . .

GRANNY. Well, yes, Demmie . . . what about them?

DEMETRIA. Carrying on! Just as brazen as you please! (GRAMPS *enters on to porch, carrying dead frog.*) And you're allowing a person like that to be around where Pud is. Nellie Northrup!

GRANNY (*rises*). But I didn't know about it, Demmie.

DEMETRIA. You could've asked me.

(GRAMPS *comes in from porch, whistling.*)

GRAMPS (*coming center to* DEMETRIA). Dead frog! Brand new. Beautiful specimen. Pud just found it.

(*He thrusts frog into* DEMETRIA'S *face. She reacts.* GRAMPS *continues toward collection down right.*)

DEMETRIA. How perfectly disgusting!

GRAMPS (*at collection*). Oh, don't feel that way, Demmie. We're gonna put *you* right up there next to him some day.

GRANNY. Julian!

(GRAMPS *crosses to desk right and picks up mushroom book.*)

GRAMPS. In a hurry, Miss Nellie. Pud's waitin' for me under the barn. He just found a new mushroom. (*He thumbs through the book.*) Think we got a Pleaurotus Ostreatus!

GRANNY (*crossing to right of table*). Julian, be careful. That may be a toadstool!

GRAMPS (*crossing to door and still thumbing through book*). Well, that's what we're gonna find out.

DEMETRIA (*back of table. Whispering to* GRANNY). Marcia!

GRANNY (*moving center*). Julian, wait a minute.

GRAMPS (*going to her*). What is it, Miss Nellie?

GRANNY. It's Marcia. I'm afraid we'll have to get rid of her. It seems she's carrying on with young Bill Murdock.

GRAMPS. Bill Murdock? Good. Nice boy, Bill.

DEMETRIA (*moving around left of table*). And you're willing to have that kind of girl in your own home?

GRAMPS. What do you mean—that kind of a girl?

DEMETRIA. Why, she's nothing more than a common, little—

GRAMPS. You're a God-damned liar!

GRANNY. Don't you talk that way to Demmie, Julian. We don't know anything about Marcia.

GRAMPS. I know about her. Knew she was a nice girl the minute I saw her.

GRANNY. Demmie knows what she's talking about.

GRAMPS (to DEMETRIA). What do you know? Just tell me one thing!

DEMETRIA (crosses to chair right of table). All right. I saw them—right in the park.

GRAMPS. And what were they doin'? Right in the park.

DEMETRIA. Kissin'! Kissin'—like you never saw. Fair make your blood boil. If they carry on like that in public, what must they do when they're alone?

GRANNY. Well, but Demmie—maybe they just kiss.

GRAMPS. Ye Gods—that makes me mad! That makes me so God-damned mad . . .

GRANNY. Julian Northrup, you stop your swearing! You stop your swearing!

GRAMPS. Miss Nellie, if you listen to another word this old hellion says you're just a plain fool!

GRANNY (shakes finger at GRAMPS). Don't you call me a fool, Julian Northrup, don't you call me a fool!

GRAMPS (roaring louder). I'm disappointed in you, Miss Nellie, I'm disappointed in you!

GRANNY (sinks weakly into chair right of table). Oh, dear! Oh, dear.

DEMETRIA. There, now. You've tired yourself all out.

GRANNY (rising). I guess you'd better help me to my room, Demmie. I guess I better lie down, now.

GRAMPS (pushing DEMETRIA). Stand back, you. I'll help you, Miss Nellie.

(DEMETRIA picks up GRANNY's knitting from table).

GRANNY (facing him). No, Julian Northrup, I only want them to help me that knows how to help me.

(DEMETRIA looks at GRAMPS triumphantly as they go out.)

DEMETRIA. I never should have told you about Marcia. It's all my fault.

GRANNY. You did just right, Demmie, you did just right.

(They are out of sight up the stairs. GRAMPS stands watching them off, fuming.)

GRAMPS. Damned old hellion! Even makes me fight with Miss Nellie!

(MARCIA enters from porch.)

MARCIA. Mr. Northrup, Pud's yelling for you— (Starts out.)

GRAMPS (at desk. Shouts at her). Come here. What the devil do you mean by kissing men in the park?

MARCIA (coming to him, frightened). What?

GRAMPS. Don't you know it's a sin for a girl to kiss men in the park?

MARCIA. But—but I didn't—I didn't kiss men in the park! I only kissed one man in the park.

GRAMPS. What'd you kiss him in the park for?

MARCIA (nearly crying). Because we were in the park and . . .

GRAMPS. Well, next time you bring him up here and kiss him!

MARCIA. Wh-what?

GRAMPS. I say, you bring that Bill Murdock up here and kiss him. 'Stime we had a little kissin' in this house again. How the hell's Pud gonna learn about kissin' if he don't never see any of it?

MARCIA. Oh, Mr. Northrup!

(She throws her arms around GRAMPS and begins to cry.)

GRAMPS (softer). There, there, Marcy. You in love with him?

MARCIA. Yes, oh, yes. We've been engaged all summer now.

GRAMPS. Yep. I thought I recognized the symptoms.

MARCIA. Bill's only got one more year at Law School and then we're gonna be married. He took highest honors in his class last year.

GRAMPS. Well, you just tell that to Miss Nellie and everything'll be all right. And the next time you and Bill meet Demetria in the park you make Bill give you a big smacker right in front of her. Just like this.

(He kisses her.)

MARCIA. Oh, did Miss Riffle tell you? That's why she . . .

DEMETRIA (off stage). Marcia!

MARCIA (turning center). Yes, Miss Riffle.

DEMETRIA (off stage). Mrs. Northrup wants you to make her a cup of tea. And she has something to say to you.

MARCIA (looks at GRAMPS). All right, Miss Riffle.

GRAMPS (going to her). You just tell Miss Nellie that you and Bill are engaged and that Bill got highest honors in his class.

MARCIA. All right. (Pause. MARCIA turns.) Mr. Northrup.

GRAMPS. Huh?

MARCIA. Bill only got next to highest honors in his class.

(PUD *enters from porch and stands in doorway.*)

GRAMPS. Tell her he got next to highest honors. Next to highest's good enough—God-damn it. (MARCIA *smiles at him and goes out left.* GRAMPS *stands looking after her, chuckling.*) Real sweet girl, Marcy.

PUD (*looking after* MARCIA). Gee, I wish Granny would knit two bumps on the front of my sweater the way Marcy's got on hers.

GRAMPS (*turns to* PUD). What? Hey there, you! None of that from you, young man. Not that there ain't something in what you say.

(*He drags* PUD *off by ear.*)

CURTAIN

SCENE THREE

GRANNY'S *bedroom, directly above living-room. It is an old-fashioned room, with sloping, attic ceiling. Window right is directly above window in living-room. Door center opens on to hallway. A large, dark closet is left.*

Action is simultaneous with end of Scene Two.

AT RISE: GRANNY *is in bed.* DEMETRIA *is straightening bed covers.*

GRANNY. He can't call me a fool, Demmie. He can't say he's disappointed in me.

DEMETRIA. I don't see why you stand for it, Nellie. (*Hands* GRANNY *her knitting from bed table left.*) Now, here's your knitting. How's your gas?

GRANNY. Feels a little quieter, I guess. 'Course you can't trust it. Sneaks up on you so.

DEMETRIA. Are you going to speak to Marcia?

GRANNY. Well, I don't know—if you just saw them kissin'.

DEMETRIA. Nellie!

GRANNY. All right, Demmie. Call to her. Ask her to make me a cup of tea.

(DEMETRIA *goes to door and calls.* GRANNY *knits.*)

DEMETRIA. Marcia!

MARCIA (*off stage*). Yes, Miss Riffle.

DEMETRIA. Mrs. Northrup wants you to make her a cup of tea and she has something to say to you.

MARCIA (*off stage*). All right, Miss Riffle.

(DEMETRIA *comes back, picks up coverlet from chair left.*)

GRANNY. I hate to do it. She needs the money so bad.

DEMETRIA. There are some things more important than money, Nellie.

GRANNY. Well, maybe you're right. There. I'll just finish this mitten. I was makin' 'em for Jim but Julian can use 'em. And after my cup of tea, think I could drop off for a spell.

DEMETRIA. Just what you should do, Nellie.

(DEMETRIA *crosses right and lights lamp on bed table right.*)

GRANNY. Feel kinda funny. (*Pause.* DEMETRIA *glances out window right; sits in chair right of bed.*) He don't mean all the things he says. He's just a rough-spoken man is all.

DEMETRIA (*ties her shoe*). Who? Julian?

GRANNY. And he ain't a blasphemer either—not exactly. He never sneers at religion. He just don't have no interest in it.

DEMETRIA. Amounts to the same thing.

GRANNY (*reflectively*). Good-looking man too, in his day.

DEMETRIA. Julian?

GRANNY. Umm. I remember him at a party when the old century went out. Handsome as anything. Everybody was after him.

DEMETRIA (*fixing her gloves*). I guess he's had plenty in his day.

GRANNY. Not since we've been married he ain't.

DEMETRIA. Well, I didn't say that, Nellie.

GRANNY. Not any I know about, anyways. Julian's always been a pretty good . . . (*Pause.*) Demmie, will you go down and ask Julian to step up here for a minute? I want to see him.

DEMETRIA. Now, Nellie, you're not goin' to forgive him.

GRANNY. I'm not goin' to exactly forgive him, Demmie. I just want to tell him somethin'.

(GRANNY *gets sleepy and dozes off.*)

DEMETRIA. All right, I'll go in a minute or two. (*Sees* GRANNY *is dozing.*) Nellie dear, do you think I should take Pud's things over with me now?

GRANNY (*sleepily*). Pud's things?

DEMETRIA (*lulling her with her voice*). Yes. And in the morning, I'll go down to Mr. Pilbeam's and have the papers drawn up for you to sign—about the will and the adoption—and all. . . .

GRANNY (*waking with a start*). Now, see here, Demmie—I didn't say anything about your adoptin' Pud. You're trying to put words in my mouth. I don't like the way you're actin', Demmie.

DEMETRIA. Nellie Northrup, you said five minutes ago that I should bring Pud up.

GRANNY. I just wondered about it, Demmie.

DEMETRIA. You said it, Nellie.

GRANNY. If I did, I was wrong. I can see that now. . . . I don't like the way you're actin', Demmie. (*She falls back, weakly.*) Oh, dear.

DEMETRIA (*rises*). There, now, Nellie, don't think about it any more, now.

GRANNY. Ask Julian to come up, Demmie. I want to see him.

DEMETRIA (*pointing down, out of window*). There! There's a boy going up that apple tree!

GRANNY. Apples nice and ripe now.

DEMETRIA. Those nasty brats deserve a good whipping. Stealing other people's property!

GRANNY. Julian never catches 'em. He starts bellowin' to give 'em plenty of time to get away.

DEMETRIA. Well, I bet I can catch 'em! There! He's just gone up the tree. I can just catch him nicely! (*She hurries to the door.*) Nasty little thief. . . . (*Exits.*)

GRANNY. And don't forget to tell Julian to step up a minute. . . .

(DEMETRIA *is already out of the room.* GRANNY *hums, tries to knit, then drowses off. Pause.* MARCIA *enters with tea tray.*)

MARCIA. Here's your tea, Mrs. Northrup.

GRANNY (*faintly*). Oh, just set it down, Marcy.

MARCIA (*frightened*). Is there anything wrong, Mrs. Northrup?

GRANNY. Wrong? No, there's nothing wrong, Marcy. I'm just kind of tired. I'm goin' to go to sleep in a minute. . . . Now, let me see, there was somethin'

I was supposed to talk to you about! Now, what was it? . . . Well, there, I've forgotten. Couldn't have been very important. (*Pause.*) Marcy!

MARCIA. Yes, Mrs. Northrup?

GRANNY (*takes* MARCIA's *hand*). Marcy —you just see that Julian always has his pipe. Will you do that?

MARCIA (*bewildered*). Yes, Mrs. Northrup.

GRANNY. You're a good girl, Marcy. Now, go on back to whatever you're doin'.

(MARCIA *goes out, puzzled.* GRANNY *tries to knit again. Has difficulty in seeing. Drowses off again.* BRINK *appears from closet left.*)

BRINK (*approaching bed*). Don't you think you have done enough?

GRANNY (*waking*). That you, Julian?

BRINK. No, not Julian.

GRANNY. Who is it?

BRINK. It's Mr. Brink. You seem rather tired.

GRANNY. I am kinda tired, Mr. Brink.

BRINK. I thought so. Well, you're to come with me now.

GRANNY (*rousing*). Come with you? Brink? I don't know any . . . (*turns and discovers* BRINK *beside her.*) . . . See here, what call have you to come buttin' into a lady's bedroom!

BRINK. I usually come to bedrooms. It's so much more comfortable.

GRANNY. What is?

BRINK. To come with me.

GRANNY. Why should anyone go with you?

BRINK. It's customary.

GRANNY. Oh? Well, you might as well sit down and wait. Because you needn't think I'll stir a step until I've finished this mitten. (*Confidentially.*) I'm narrowin' off at the top now.

BRINK. Yes. I know you are.

GRANNY (*laughs*). What do you know about knittin'?

BRINK. I don't mean the mitten. I mean you.

GRANNY (*laughs*). What a fool thing to say. Don't you know a lady from a mitten?

BRINK (*turning away*). Yes. I know a lady from a mitten.

GRANNY. Now, don't go 'way. You'll just have to wait. I've got to finish this job for my son, Jim. . . . (*Puzzled for a minute, then nods to affirm statement.*) . . .

When he drives to Gainesville he says there won't anythin' keep his hands warm but a pair of my mittens. (*Laughs.*) Those boughten things you get at the store—they're no good. A doctor has to be out in all kinds of weather, you know.

BRINK (*smiling*). He won't need them this year.

GRANNY (*laughs*). Huh! What do you know about it?

BRINK. Oh, I know many things.

GRANNY. I'll wager I could show you a thing or two about knittin'.

BRINK (*crossing close to bed*). No doubt. Are you ready now?

GRANNY (*breathlessly*). Wait . . . just a minute. . . . I'm almost finished. . . . (*Breaks thread.*) . . . There! That's got it! Don't that red stripe look well with the grey?

BRINK. Excellent, my dear. Excellent. Come now.

(*He leans over and touches her. She smiles and dies.*)

DIM OUT

CURTAIN

SCENE FOUR

Exterior. GRAMPS' *backyard, showing porch down left, with cellar and toolhouse attached, up left. Barn is just behind. Apple tree is up right center, with hill behind, town in distance. Right, is picket fence, showing edge of yard, with practical gate, ajar. Silo and other buildings outside of fence. Hill is practical, with walk down to up left center stage. Garden bench center; garden chair left.*

AT RISE: MARTIN'S BOY *is sitting in tree, tugging at his breeches.* DEMETRIA *enters from porch, goes to tree.*

Action is few minutes later than Scene Three.

DEMETRIA (*crossing to center, shouting*). Come down out of there. I see you.

BOY (*in tree*). I'm not doing anything. I just—

DEMETRIA. You're just a thief, that's what you are.

BOY. I didn't take any apples.

DEMETRIA. You good-for-nothing, you come down from there this minute.

BOY. I can't.

DEMETRIA. You got up all right.

BOY. My pants is caught in behind.

DEMETRIA. Either you come down this minute, or I'll have the law on you.

BOY (*crying*). I'm not doing anything. I didn't take any apples yet. . . .

DEMETRIA (*crosses to* BOY, *pulls his leg*). You come down from there. I'll teach you to trespass.

(GRAMPS *and* PUD *enter from between toolhouse and barn.* GRAMPS *carries a stick.*)

GRAMPS (DEMETRIA *turns*) You'll do what?

DEMETRIA (*defensively*). There's a boy up that tree.

GRAMPS (*crosses left, below bench*). And what were you goin' to teach him?

(PUD *follows* GRAMPS *down to below chair left.*)

DEMETRIA (*coming center*). I should think you'd thank me to catch a trespasser for you.

GRAMPS. And how was you figurin' to teach him not to trespass?

DEMETRIA (*looking at* BOY). I'd give him a good sound whipping, that's what I'd do.

GRAMPS. You would. (*He raises stick*). Thanks for tellin' me, Demmie. Because seein' as how there happens to be two trespassers here, I'll just begin with the one that's handiest. . . .

(*He advances on her.*)

DEMETRIA (*stepping right*). Oh, don't be so silly, Julian.

PUD (*jumping up and down*). Hit her, Gramps. Hit her on the rump!

DEMETRIA (*crossing to* PUD). Why . . . you little brat.

GRAMPS (*waving stick*). You git off my property!

DEMETRIA. All right, Julian Northrup! Maybe you'll find out whose property this is some day!

GRAMPS. You'll find out I can take care of my own.

DEMETRIA. Sometimes the law has something to say about things.

(*She hurries off through gate right.* GRAMPS *stalks her out.* PUD *laughs.* GRAMPS *laughs. Then* BOY *in tree laughs.* GRAMPS *looks up in tree.* BOY *stops laughing suddenly.*)

GRAMPS (*looking in tree*). Whose boy are you?

(*Pud comes above right of bench.*)

BOY. Jud Martin.

GRAMPS. Why're you stealin' my apples?

BOY. I'm hungry.

GRAMPS. Don't your folks give you nothin' to eat?

BOY. Yes, sir.

GRAMPS. So you're apple-hungry?

BOY. Yes, sir.

GRAMPS. Why don't you come down?

BOY. I can't.

GRAMPS. Why can't you?

BOY. My breeches is caught.

GRAMPS. Your breeches is caught.

PUD (*jumping up and down, excitedly*). Gramps, Gramps! Your wish! He can't come down! He can't come down! He can't come down!

GRAMPS (*hushing* PUD). Ssh! (*To* BOY.) Now, you unloosen your breeches. (BOY *tugs again at his breeches, finds they are loose.*) And come down from there as fast as you can.

BOY (*bewildered*). Yes, sir. I'm coming. My breeches is loose now.

PUD (*crossing down left*). Aw, Gramps, you shouldn't have let him unloose his breeches. We could of kept him up there for a million years.

(BOY *comes down from tree,* GRAMPS *collars him.*)

GRAMPS. Now, would that have been nice, son? Now then, I'll teach you to steal. Here. Here. (*He fills* BOY's *pockets with apples.*) The next time you want apples, don't sneak around the back. Walk right up to the front door, ring the bell and ask for some. Will you do that?

BOY. Yes, sir!

PUD. Like hell he will.

(*The boys begin to fight.* BOY *gets* PUD *down on his back.*)

GRAMPS. You fellows stop that! Pud, you lay off that boy. Go along, you.

(GRAMPS *taps* BOY *playfully with stick, chasing him off.*)

BOY. Thanks, Mr. Northrup.

(BOY *goes off right.*)

PUD. Gramps, what'd you stop us for? I had him practical licked.

(PUD *crosses to tree and begins to climb.*)

GRAMPS. Yes, I guess you did. . . . Them apples I gave him'll be pretty bitter, 'cause he didn't steal them.

PUD (*at tree*). Boost me up, Gramps. Boost me up.

GRAMPS (*crosses to* PUD, *helps him*). Boost you up! You don't have to steal. Oh, all

right. By golly, boy, you're a full-time job. . . . Now, you're up!

PUD (*in tree, shakes finger at* GRAMPS). Now, you know I can't get down until you let me.

GRAMPS (*laughs, crosses to bench*). My Lord and Miss Boopydoop, you sure do beat the trolley cars.

PUD. You wished *nobody* could come down until you let them. That was your wish.

GRAMPS (*sits on bench*). That's right, boy. Guess it was.

PUD. So I can't come down either. I hope you won't keep me up here too long, Gramps.

GRAMPS. Liable to keep you up there all week. Maybe a hundred years. Depends on how I feel.

PUD. Oh, no, Gramps.

GRAMPS. Yep. Might leave you there and go down to Milbaur Park and pick up a few new specimens for our collection.

PUD (*starts to climb large branch*). Then I'm coming down, Gramps.

GRAMPS. But you can't. You're under my magic spell. Yep, think I'll go along right now . . . good-by.

(*Rises.*)

PUD. Wait a minute, I'm coming with you. (PUD *comes part way down and hangs.*) Gramps, I can't let loose!

GRAMPS. 'Course you can't. You can't let loose till I tell you.

PUD (*frightened*). But, honest, I can't, Gramps.

GRAMPS (*thundering*). 'Course you can't. You can't go breaking my spells like that!

PUD (*more frightened*). Let me down, Gramps! Let me down! Please! My arms is tired! (GRAMPS *laughs.*) Gramps! Gramps! Let me go, let me go! Gramps! Gramps!

GRAMPS. Come on, then. Let go. Let go, honey. (PUD *falls to the ground with a wail.* GRAMPS *hurries to him.*) What's the matter, boy, what's the matter?

PUD (*wailing*). I couldn't let go!

GRAMPS (*sits beside* PUD). Of course you could.

PUD. No, I couldn't, Gramps. My hands wouldn't move!

(*He stops crying.*)

GRAMPS. I thought we were just foolin'.

PUD. I was foolin' at first and then my hands wouldn't move. The tree was holdin' me.

(*Looks up at tree.*)

GRAMPS. By golly, you do give a person the creeps sometimes. Dog-gone if I don't believe you really thought that tree was holdin' you.

PUD. It was, Gramps, it was.

GRAMPS. Oh, that old apple tree couldn't hold anybody!

PUD (*turning and pointing at* GRAMPS). Yes, it could, Gramps. You wished it could.

(MARCIA *enters from porch.*)

MARCIA (*crying*). Mr. Northrup! Come upstairs! Mrs. Northrup is . . . Mrs. Northrup!

(*She buries her face in her hands.* GRAMPS *and* PUD *continue to look at tree.*)

CURTAIN

SCENE FIVE

Exterior. The tree. A week later. Nearly dusk.

AT RISE: GRAMPS *sits alone on bench. Moody. He is wearing mourning band on arm.* MARCIA *enters from porch.*

MARCIA (*carrying mixing bowl*). Mr. Northrup.

GRAMPS (*looking up*). Oh, hello there, Marcy.

MARCIA. Supper's nearly ready. Time you got washed.

GRAMPS. All right, Marcy.

MARCIA (*coming to bench*). Miss Riffle was just over again.

GRAMPS. Was she?

MARCIA. She's been over every day since the funeral. She keeps asking about your health.

GRAMPS. Damned old hellion. Just waitin' for me to die, ain't she?

MARCIA. Oh, Mr. Northrup. You've got to take care of yourself. If you don't eat any more than you have the last week . . . You've got to keep up your strength, Mr. Northrup.

GRAMPS. All right, Marcy. Thank you.

(*He doesn't move.*)

MARCIA. And Pud seems awfully lonesome lately, too.

GRAMPS. Pud?

MARCIA. He doesn't seem himself at all.

GRAMPS. That so?

MARCIA. When you don't eat, he hardly eats a mouthful either.

GRAMPS. That's what she said. She said "he mimics everything you do."

MARCIA. That's right. He does.

GRAMPS (*suddenly*). If I'd only got there in time, Marcy!

MARCIA (*sits beside* GRAMPS). Oh, don't take it so hard, Mr. Northrup.

GRAMPS. We had words and she died before I could take 'em back and say I was sorry.

MARCIA. She understood!

GRAMPS. She died and she didn't forgive me, she died and she didn't forgive me.

MARCIA. She did, Mr. Northrup. She would have forgiven you for anything. . . . Oh, I almost forgot . . .

(MARCIA *runs off quickly,* ·*through porch.* PUD *runs in through gate right. When he sees* GRAMPS, *he stops short, walks slowly around bench.*)

PUD (*right center*). Gramps!

GRAMPS. Oh, hello there, sonny.

PUD. Shall I sit down here too?

GRAMPS. Sure thing. What makes you think you shouldn't?

PUD. I think I should.

(*Sits right of* GRAMPS.)

GRAMPS. Gonna have supper in a minute.

PUD. I'm not hungry.

GRAMPS. Gotta eat, boy. Hungry or not hungry.

PUD. Why?

GRAMPS. Keep up your strength. (*He suddenly clutches* PUD.) There's only me and you left now. Only me and you. I figure we got to stick together.

PUD. You're damn right.

GRAMPS. Shouldn't cuss, boy.

PUD. Why shouldn't I? *You* say that.

GRAMPS. I shouldn't neither. Your Granny didn't like it. Let's you and me turn over a new leaf, Pud.

PUD. What for?

GRAMPS. So your Aunt Demmie won't keep on saying I'm bad for you and won't keep on trying to get you away from me.

PUD. Aw, we'll kill her.

GRAMPS. By the Lord Harry, I almost wish we could.

PUD (*excited*). We'll kill her; we'll kill her and we'll put her in the ground. We'll lower the coffing and I'll say . . .

GRAMPS. Hush, boy. Hush!

(*He leans down, puts head in hands.*)

PUD (*touching him*). What's the matter, Gramps? Are you sick?

GRAMPS. Growin' pains, I guess.

(MARCIA *comes out of house with* GRAMPS' *pipe.*)

MARCIA (*crossing to bench*). Here's your pipe, Mr. Northrup.

GRAMPS. My pipe, Marcy? Oh, I don't believe I can smoke it, thank you kindly. My throat hurts me a little. Fact is, I don't think I'll ever smoke any more. She didn't like it.

MARCIA. But she did, Mr. Northrup. I know she did.

GRAMPS. Nope. Miss Nellie thought it was a dirty habit. And I guess it is. . . .

MARCIA. She told me I was always to keep your pipe filled.

GRAMPS. Miss Nellie what? When?

MARCIA. Just before she died. I took her up a cup of tea and she caught hold of my hand and said . . . wait, I'll remember her exact words . . . she said: "Marcy . . . Marcy, see that Julian always has his pipe."

GRAMPS. Marcy. . . . You're not just making this up to make me feel good?

MARCIA. No, no, Mr. Northrup. I couldn't do that.

GRAMPS. Give me the pipe.

(*He takes it and tries to light it, but trembles so that* MARCIA *helps him. He smokes.*)

PUD. Does it taste good, Gramps?

GRAMPS. Better'n anything I know, boy.

MARCIA. I'll go finish supper.

(MARCIA *goes off into the house.*)

PUD. Why did your hand wiggle so when you lighted the pipe, Gramps?

GRAMPS. Did it, sonny? Guess I haven't been keepin' up my strength. Do feel kind of shaky. . . .

(BRINK *appears right.*)

BRINK (*crossing to center*). Good evening.

GRAMPS. Oh, it's you, is it? What do you want?

BRINK. You.

GRAMPS. Can't I ever shut my eyes without you buttin' in?

BRINK. I thought perhaps you'd like to come with me now.

GRAMPS (*takes* PUD *over to his left*). Now look here, Mr. Brink. I ain't goin' with you at all. I'm goin' to stay right here with this fellow. And you're about as welcome as a fly on a currant bun, so now you know.

BRINK. Your similitudes are a trifle earthy, but your meaning is clear.

GRAMPS (*turns to* PUD, *laughs*). My similitudes! What kind of talk is that?

PUD. Sure. What kind of talk is that! He sure talks funny, doesn't he, Gramps.

GRAMPS (*rises, crosses to* BRINK). Now go on. Get off my property!

BRINK. Now, let's not be difficult about it. Your wife was so charming to me.

GRAMPS. Miss Nellie? Is she well?

BRINK. Sorry. I can't tell you that. Only that she has changed.

GRAMPS. Miss Nellie changed? That's what you think!

BRINK. Oh, my dear man, let's not argue the point, and this time you can't fight me away. (*Pause.*) Come now.

GRAMPS. No, no—I—

BRINK. Come now. Come.

GRAMPS. No. No.

(GRAMPS *is stricken with pain. Looks at* PUD.)

BRINK. You're being difficult again. It's so easy and so pleasant. Now don't worry. Look at me.

(BRINK *advances to* GRAMPS, *with hand outstretched. Pause.*)

GRAMPS. Just a minute, please, Mr. Brink. I'd like to have one last apple before I go.

BRINK. Oh, all right.

(GRAMPS *starts to climb the tree, fumbles and gropes at tree.*)

GRAMPS. You wouldn't like to get it for me, would you?

BRINK. Curious request. Oh, why not? (BRINK *climbs tree, points to apples.*) This one? Or this one?

GRAMPS (*backs away to front of bench*). I don't want none of them! I got you up that tree and you're gonna stay there until I tell you to come down.

(*Wind shakes tree, as* BRINK *struggles to get free. Is bewildered.*)

PUD (*putting arms around* GRAMPS). You got him, Gramps. You got him!

(GRAMPS *clutches* PUD, *looks at him.*)

GRAMPS. By golly, boy, I believe we have!

CURTAIN

ACT TWO

SCENE ONE

The tree. Two hours later. It is dusk. A fence is being built around the tree.

AT RISE: *Three* WORKMEN *are building fence.* TWO *are stretching barbed-wire.* ONE *is settling post at top of hill, right.* DEMETRIA *enters from house, goes to gate, looks out, goes to* WORKMEN. BRINK *is invisible.*

DEMETRIA (*to* WORKMAN). Here you, come here.

WORKMAN (*crossing down to her*). Yes, ma'am.

DEMETRIA. Has Mr. Northrup told any of you men why he's building this fence?

WORKMAN. Well, not exactly, ma'am. It's to keep people away from the tree.

DEMETRIA. Why?

WORKMAN. He says if we touch the tree we are in danger.

DEMETRIA. Danger of what?

WORKMAN. Well, I'm not sure, ma'am, I thought he said we were in danger of our lives.

DEMETRIA. That's very interesting. That's what he said to me too. (*She motions* WORKMAN *away, as* DR. EVANS *and* MR. PILBEAM *enter through gate right.*) Ah, Doctor Evans, Mr. Pilbeam, how do you do? I'm glad you could come. (EVANS *has crossed to porch.*) Julian is just around the corner burying his dog.

EVANS (*going to her down center*). What does he want us for?

DEMETRIA. He doesn't want you, gentlemen. It was I who asked you to come up. I want you to meet someone.

PILBEAM (*right of* DEMETRIA). Who?

DEMETRIA. A friend of Julian's—a Mr. Brink.

EVANS. I'm rather busy right now, Miss Riffle.

DEMETRIA. I appreciate that, Doctor, but I thought you would like to meet this friend of Julian's.

EVANS. Well, all right, where is he?

DEMETRIA. Well, just at the moment, he's up in the apple tree.

(*Pause. They look at her surprised, then look up into tree.* DEMETRIA *stands watching them in silence.*)

PILBEAM (*back to her*). Er—where did you say he was?

DEMETRIA. Right up in that apple tree. (*They glance up again.*)

EVANS (*crossing up left*). I don't see anyone up there.

(*Crossing down left.*)

DEMETRIA. Oh, no. You can't see him. He's invisible.

PILBEAM. What?

DEMETRIA. He's invisible.—You see, a short while after Julian got Mr. Brink up there, Betty, the old dog, saw him and barked at him. Mr. Brink didn't like that so he became invisible. And right after that, Betty touched her nose to the tree and dropped over dead. Julian and Pud are burying her now.

EVANS. What is this anyway?

PILBEAM. Is this supposed to be a joke, Miss Riffle?

DEMETRIA. What would you say if I told you I believed it was the Gospel truth?

EVANS. 'Fraid I'd say you were crazy.

DEMETRIA. I would be crazy, wouldn't I? And what if I told you that Mr. Brink is a man, just like you, who goes around taking people away with him when it's time for them to die. Now, if I believed that you'd surely say I was crazy, wouldn't you?

EVANS. I'd say you were positively nuts, Miss Riffle.

DEMETRIA. Yes. Well, I don't believe it—but Julian does.

PILBEAM. Come, come, Miss Riffle, what kind of story is this?

DEMETRIA (*sits in chair left*). An hour ago when I happened to be passing, I saw all these pieces of fence being unloaded from a truck. Naturally, I came back to find out what was going on. Julian told me he was building the fence to keep people away from the tree, because anybody who touched the tree would die.

PILBEAM. Die?

DEMETRIA (*rises*). And not only that! Touching that tree is the only way anyone can die. There is no more death in the world, Mr. Pilbeam, until Julian lets Mr. Brink come down.

EVANS (*crosses back of* DEMETRIA *to right center*). See here, Miss Riffle, you don't think Northrup really believes this?

DEMETRIA (*to him*). Julian is an old man and he's been through a great deal lately. I think it's perfectly obvious what has happened. His mind has just suddenly snapped. Julian Northrup is as crazy as a loon.

EVANS. No, no, I saw Northrup only day before yesterday. He was as sane as any man could be. He's just an old joker. I've known him for years. . . .

(*Crosses right.*)

DEMETRIA. You have, Doctor Evans.

And Mr. Pilbeam has been his lawyer for years. That's why I've asked both of you to come up. I'm not asking you to take my word for it. I'm simply asking you to see Julian and convince yourselves that what I'm saying is true.

PILBEAM (*with a look to* EVANS). If Northrup should be insane, you'd have to take Pud, of course, wouldn't you, Miss Riffle?

DEMETRIA. Naturally. I'm next of kin.

EVANS (*crossing upper center right*). Huh!

PILBEAM. That's what I thought.

DEMETRIA. What do you mean? You don't think I'm making this up about Julian?

PILBEAM. I don't know what to think, Miss Riffle.

DEMETRIA (*two steps to* PILBEAM). Ever since Nellie Northrup died, Mr. Pilbeam, you've tried to stop my adopting Pud. Even though I told you that was her dying wish.

PILBEAM. I simply said no court of law would believe you, Miss Riffle.

DEMETRIA. I guess a court of law will feel different about it, if they realize a young boy is being brought up by a maniac? (EVANS *puts bag down by gate, crosses down center.*) I'll be frank with you, Mr. Pilbeam, I intend to get that boy away from this insane man's house before something terrible happens. To-night—if possible! (DEMETRIA *crosses to* EVANS.) There is a way of taking care of such cases immediately, isn't there?

(PILBEAM *crosses up center.*)

EVANS. Well, yes. I'll tell you, I'm not a psychiatrist, Miss Riffle, but if I think Northrup's crazy, I'll talk it over with Grimes. He's the head of the asylum.

DEMETRIA. You will talk it over with him tonight?

EVANS (*crossly*). When a person's insane you don't usually let him run around loose.

DEMETRIA. Thank you, Doctor Evans, I'll just ask the workmen to ... (*She crosses up center to* WORKMEN. GRAMPS *is heard bellowing off stage.*) Just a minute, I think he's coming now.

(PILBEAM *crosses right.*)

GRAMPS (*off stage*). Here you, there. (GRAMPS *enters from top of hill right, followed by* PUD. *They come down the walk.*) What the hell do you mean by gettin' so near to that tree? Didn't I tell you to stay away from that tree on peril of your lives?

PUD (*carries spade*). What the hell's the idea?

GRAMPS (*still to* WORKMEN). Now, you fellows, go on back to that truck and get the rest of that fence unloaded. Get a move on.

PUD (*sits by tree*). Get a move on.

(WORKMEN *exit up hill.*)

GRAMPS (*crosses to* DEMETRIA *center*). Now, what in tarnation are you doin' around here again! I told you ...

DEMETRIA. It's just that I'm so excited about it, Julian.

GRAMPS. And Pilbeam and Evans, eh? By God, you've told them all about it, haven't you? After I told you not to.

DEMETRIA. Why, no, Julian, I haven't told. ...

EVANS (*crosses to* GRAMPS). Yes, she's told us all about it. About the tree, the fence, Mr. Brink ... everything.

GRAMPS (*crosses left*). I might have known it. I might have known it.

EVANS (*follows* GRAMPS *left*). Well, what about it, Northrup? What's the answer?

GRAMP. Well, it's the truth, Evans. It's just as true as I'm standin' here.

PILBEAM (*laughing*). You mean there's somebody sitting up in that tree?

(*He crosses right center.*)

EVANS. And nobody in the world can die any more?

GRAMPS. Nobody can die any more until I say so, unless they touch that tree, or one of them apples, or Mr. Brink himself.

EVANS (*crossing left*). You're not serious about this, Northrup?

DEMETRIA (*crosses down center*). Of course he is, Doctor. He's perfectly serious, aren't you, Julian?

GRAMPS (*crosses center to* DEMETRIA). Hey there, what the hell are you up to anyway?

DEMETRIA. Why, nothing, Julian. I'm just interested. ...

GRAMPS. Well, I don't want you to go telling anybody else about Mr. Brink. I got him up there and now I gotta figure out what the hell I'm gonna do with him.

(*Crosses upper center.*)

DEMETRIA. But you don't think you'll be able to keep a thing like this quiet, Julian.

EVANS. Look here, Northrup. Can you talk to Mr. Brink?

GRAMPS. Sure I can talk to him.

EVANS. Have you talked to him since you got him up there?

GRAMPS. Nope. Haven't had time.

EVANS. I wish you'd talk to him now.

GRAMPS. What for? Just so's you can hear him?

EVANS. I just thought, perhaps if you tried to talk to him—well, you'd find out he isn't up there any more.

GRAMPS. Oh, he's up there, all right.

DEMETRIA. Julian, do try to make him talk. I'd love to hear him.

GRAMPS (crosses to DEMETRIA). Oh, you would. (He turns suddenly and stares at DEMETRIA. Slight pause.) Well, by golly, Demmie, I believe I'll let you. I'll let you all hear him. (DEMETRIA crosses to PILBEAM and EVANS. GRAMPS goes to tree. MARCIA enters from porch.) Mr. Brink, can you hear me if I don't shout?

BRINK. Sir?

GRAMPS. See, he calls me "Sir." . . .

DEMETRIA (to EVANS and PILBEAM). There, he thinks someone's answering.

GRAMPS. Well, Mr. Brink, I'm sorry I haven't had more of a chance to talk to you.

(MARCIA crosses down left.)

BRINK. Perhaps I shouldn't say it but I'm not extremely upset by that.

GRAMPS. You're not mad at me, are you?

BRINK. I think I might justifiably be allowed some slight irritation.

GRAMPS. Well, I wouldn't have put you there without a damn good reason. I got you up there so this old hellion couldn't get Pud and the money his father left him.

BRINK. I appreciate that your motive was probably sincere.

GRAMPS. Now, I got an idea, and it's goin' to settle once and for all this business of her gettin' Pud. (He crosses to DEMETRIA and pulls her center.) Come here, you. Stand out here. (To BRINK.) You see this old battle-ax here—her name is Demetria Riffle. Have you got anything on your schedule about when you are supposed to snuff her out?

BRINK. Riffle? There's no such name that has come to my attention yet.

GRAMPS. Well, Mr. Brink, I'm goin' to keep you up there until it's time for you to exterminate her.

(GRAMPS crosses down right. DEMETRIA crosses left to EVANS and PILBEAM.)

BRINK. My dear man, that may be a

very long time yet. There's no telling how long that woman may hang on.

GRAMPS. Well, that's the way it's goin' to be.

BRINK. But for me to stay here any length of time might be considered by my Superior as a considerable dereliction of duty.

GRAMPS. Can't help it. Them's the terms.

BRINK (with sigh). Ah, well! I was afraid of that. Very well, since you and your tree are so tenacious, I shall have to sit here and wait for Miss Riffle's call.

GRAMPS. Do you think you can hold out that long?

BRINK. My dear man, a human life is like the twinkling of an eye to me.

GRAMPS. Oh, yes, I suppose it is. All right, then, Mr. Brink. (GRAMPS turns back to others.) Well, there you are!

(They all look at him.)

DEMETRIA. Julian, I'm sorry for you. I really am.

GRAMPS. Sorry for me? You heard what Mr. Brink said, didn't you?

DEMETRIA. No—I—didn't hear this thing in the tree say anything.

GRAMPS. You didn't? (Turns to PILBEAM.) You heard Mr. Brink, Pilbeam?

PILBEAM. I'm sorry, Northrup, I didn't.

GRAMPS (to EVANS). Evans!

EVANS (crosses right center). No, Northrup, I didn't. . . .

GRAMPS (frantically). Marcia! (MARCIA turns away. GRAMPS sits in chair left.) Well, I'll be a . . . what the hell's the matter? Am I goin' nuts?

EVANS (crosses to GRAMPS. Motions DEMETRIA, PILBEAM to cross right). It's probably just some sort of a dream or something. Northrup. You'll probably get over it in a few weeks and be all right again.

(Crosses right to others.)

GRAMPS (softly). Didn't no one hear what he said?

(Pause. EVANS stands looking at him sadly.)

PUD (suddenly). He said a human life was like the twinkling of an eye to him.

(He crosses down to right of GRAMPS.)

GRAMPS. Ye Gods, that's just what he said! Just what he said! A dream, eh? What else did he say, Pud?

(MARCIA runs into house.)

PUD. Said he'd have to stay up there 'cause you and the tree was ten . . . ten

. . . it was another funny word, Gramps.

GRAMPS. Tenacious!

DEMETRIA (*to* EVANS *and* PILBEAM). See what he's doing to the boy.

GRAMPS. That's just what he said. (*Rises, crosses right.*) You see where that leaves you.

(*Pause.*)

DEMETRIA. Guess I'm too dull to hear.

GRAMPS. That's it. Must be. Guess you're all too dull to hear.

PILBEAM. Yes, I guess that must be it. (*They are strangely silent.*)

EVANS (*crosses right center*). I want to show you something, Northrup.

GRAMPS. Hey, there, what are you goin' to do?

EVANS (*starting to tree*). I'm going to eat an apple for you.

GRAMPS (*tripping him*). Hey, you Gol-darned fool, after all I've been tellin' you about them apples. (PUD *hands* GRAMPS *the spade.*) You make one more move toward that tree and I'll brain you.

(DEMETRIA *screams.* EVANS *is on ground.*)

EVANS (*quietly*). All right, Northrup. Let me up. I won't go near the tree.

GRAMPS. Gol-darn fool, tryin' to commit suicide!

(PUD *sits in chair left.*)

EVANS (*rises*). All right, Northrup. I just wanted to make sure you weren't joking. (*With look to others.*) Are you going to be home a little later this evening, Northrup?

GRAMPS. 'Course I am.

EVANS. I may be over and—er—talk some more about this.

GRAMPS. All right, Evans.

EVANS. Thanks, well . . .

DEMETRIA. I must go.

PILBEAM. Yes.

(DEMETRIA *and* PILBEAM *ad lib, as they go off.*)

EVANS. Good-by, Northrup.

GRAMPS. Good-by, Evans. Sorry I had to be rough with you.

EVANS (*picking up bag*). That's all right.

GRAMPS. And don't worry about none of your patients dying for a while, yet.

EVANS (*with a look at* GRAMPS). All right. Good-by, Northrup.

(*He goes out right.*)

GRAMPS (*crosses left, places spade against house*). Well, now, back to work, sonny, back to work.

PUD. Why don't they hear Mr.

Brink?

GRAMPS. Don't know, boy, guess they're all too busy.

BRINK (*appears*). Oh, my dear man, that isn't the reason at all.

GRAMPS (*turning to him*). Oh, hello, Mr. Brink. Why is it only Pud and me can hear you, then?

BRINK. I won't go into it now if you don't mind.

GRAMPS. Just as you say, Mr. Brink. One thing I would like to know though.

BRINK. Well?

GRAMPS. You don't think they'll hold it against Pud what I'm doin' to you?

BRINK. I have neither the inclination nor the authorization to dispense information relevant to your inquiry.

PUD (*laughs*). He still talks funny.

GRAMPS. Well, guess I'll have to take that chance. Come on, boy. Say good-by to Mr. Brink.

(*Helps* PUD *up.*)

PUD. 'Bye, Brink.

GRAMPS. Can't you say "Mr. Brink"?

PUD. Good-by, Mr. Brink—excuse me.

BRINK. That's all right—Good-by, Pud.

(GRAMPS *and* PUD *start toward hill.*)

GRAMPS. Well, we gotta get that fence finished tonight, boy.

PUD. We gotta work like hell to do it, though, Gramps.

CURTAIN

SCENE TWO

The living-room. Ten o'clock that night.

AT RISE: GRAMPS *is sleeping in chair right of table, with newspaper over his head.* PUD *is playing with toys on floor, left of* GRAMPS.

PUD (*suddenly*). The King of Massonia wore his crown upon his seat. (*Pause.*) Hey, Gramps.

(*Touches* GRAMPS *on knee.* GRAMPS *pulls paper from his head.*)

GRAMPS. How's that?

PUD. The King of Massonia wore his crown on his seat.

GRAMPS. You don't say. And where did you learn that?

PUD. In Sunday school.

GRAMPS. Don't recall that particular passage myself, sonny. You don't, by any chance, mean the King of Macedonia, do you?

PUD. I guess I mean the King of Massachusetts.

GRAMPS. That's probably it. What did he wear his crown on his seat for?

PUD (*climbing on* GRAMPS' *knee*). He just wanted to sit on it. (*Noise off stage.*) They're doing a pretty good job on that fence, Gramps.

GRAMPS. Yep, they'll finish it before morning. (PUD *is on* GRAMPS' *knee, showing thumb, bound with adhesive tape.*) What on earth did you do to your thumb?

PUD. I hurt it when I was buildin' the fence. But Marcy put a heap o' tape on it, so I guess it's all right.

GRAMPS (*laughs*). A heap o' tape. A heap o' tape. Yes, adhesive tape will fix anythin'.

PUD. Gramps, how long before Doctor Evans is coming over?

GRAMPS. Ought to be along any minute now.

(PUD *leans his head back on* GRAMPS' *shoulder and plays with his hair.*)

PUD. Sinkpea, sinkpea, sinkpea.

GRAMPS. How's that?

PUD. Sinkpea.

GRAMPS. What on earth is that?

PUD. Just sinkpea.

GRAMPS. Where'd you hear that word?

PUD. I thought of it myself. I was thinkin' of a boat sinkin', and of a pea, so I said—sinkpea.

GRAMPS. What more natural!

PUD. Say it, Gramps.

GRAMPS. What would I want to go sayin' a fool thing like that for?

PUD. Please, Gramps. Say it!

GRAMPS (*with a look over his shoulder*). Sinkpea.

PUD. Say it louder.

GRAMPS. Sinkpea! Sinkpea—sinkpea!

(MARCIA *enters from hallway left.*)

MARCIA (*coming left of table*). What's that, Mr. Northrup?

GRAMPS. Sinkpea. . . . Oh, hello, Marcy (*Doorbell rings off stage.* GRAMPS *puts* PUD *off his lap.*) There we are. Now, off to bed with you. Here you are, Marcy. 'Night, boy.

(*Crosses above table to door left. Kisses* PUD *before he goes.*)

PUD (*wiping his mouth*). 'Night, Gramps. I'll see you early in the morning.

(MARCIA *picks up toys from floor.*)

GRAMPS. Sleep tight. I'll let Dr. Evans in, Marcy.

(*Exits left.*)

PUD (*sleepily*). Marcy, I bet I sleep like my top tonight.

MARCIA. Of course you will, darling.

PUD. I should have been in bed hours ago.

(*They go off upstairs.*)

GRAMPS (*off stage*). Come right in, Mr. Grimes. (*He enters followed by* EVANS *and* GRIMES.) I'm glad to make your acquaintance.

(EVANS *comes to chair left of table,* GRIMES *above table right.*)

GRIMES. Yeah.

GRAMPS (*going right*). Well, set down, Evans. Set down, Mr. Grimes. Have a nip?

GRIMES. Haven't got time for that, Northrup. We've got to . . .

EVANS. As a matter of fact, Northrup, I've been telling Mr. Grimes about Mr. Brink and the tree.

GRAMPS (*pulls desk chair around, sits center*). Now, what did you want to go doin' that for?

EVANS. Well, he's very interested.

GRAMPS (*to* GRIMES). Don't suppose you believe he's up there?

GRIMES (*chuckling*). Sure, sure, I believe it. I was just going to ask you to come along with me and talk it over. (*Looks at* EVANS.) Another fellow I'd like to have you meet who wants to hear about it.

GRAMPS. It's this way, Mr. Grimes, I don't want any more people knowin' about this thing until I find out some way of provin' it. This is goin' to be a hard thing to make people believe. 'Tain't everybody that can hear Mr. Brink when he talks. I figger that . . .

GRIMES (*with look to* EVANS). Oh, what the hell's the use? Now try to get this straight, will you? I'm taking you to the state insane asylum!

(*Pause.* GRAMPS *is dazed.*)

GRAMPS (*softly*). You're takin' me . . . ? You're takin' me to the insane . . . (*Rises. Looks at* EVANS, *who shifts uncomfortably.*) Demetria!

EVANS (*rises. Below table*). It's this way, Northrup. . . .

GRAMPS (*softly*). Demmie! . . . Where is Demmie, Evans?

EVANS. Well, she's . . .

GRAMPS. Where is she?

EVANS. Well, she's outside in the car.

GRAMPS. Waitin', eh? Waitin' for Pud.

EVANS. It's just for observation, Northrup. And she'll just keep Pud until you get back.

GRIMES. Sure. Sure. Now, you come along with me and do as you're told and you may get better soon and can come home again.

GRAMPS (*crosses back to chair right*). There ain't nothin' wrong with me, Mr. Grimes.

GRIMES. Then we'll find that out.

GRAMPS. Honest, there ain't nothin' wrong with me.

GRIMES. Now, are you coming along like a good fellow or do I have to put a jacket on you?

(*Pause. They watch him.*)

GRAMPS (*softly*). Sort of looks like I gotta, don't it? (*Moves two steps center, then turns as if to go upstairs.*) Now, I'll just go up and say good-by to Pud.

GRIMES (*blocking his way*). No, no, you'll see him tomorrow. They'll bring him up to the asylum.

EVANS. Better come along, Northrup.

GRAMPS. Yes, maybe it's just as well.

GRIMES (*takes hat off table*). All right. Come on. Let's get goin'.

GRAMPS. Sure. Sure. I'm goin' to go right along with you. Gonna march right up to the bughouse and surprise 'em.

GRIMES (*EVANS crosses to the door left*). That's the way—surprise 'em.

GRAMPS. I guess it will surprise 'em to see how easy I come along.

GRIMES (*crosses to back of table*). Sure it will. That's a good idea.

GRAMPS. All right. Come on. (*Starts left with GRIMES.*) Oh, wait!

GRIMES. What's the matter?

GRAMPS. My badge. I've got to have my badge like I wear in parades. I'm a veteran, you know.

GRIMES. Fine! You couldn't march without your badge, now could you?

GRAMPS (*crosses to desk*). No, siree.

(*As GRAMPS rummages in the desk drawer, GRIMES winks at EVANS. EVANS shakes his head.*)

GRIMES (*crosses to EVANS*). It's all in knowing how to handle 'em. Sometimes the best way is to humor 'em; but sometimes you got to be tough with 'em.

GRAMPS. Here it is. Afraid for a minute it was upstairs. Now then.

(*GRAMPS turns to GRIMES and EVANS, holding gun in hand.*)

EVANS (*rushing down left*). Put that down, Northrup!

GRIMES (*crosses to back of table*). Yeah, put it down now. Put it down.

GRAMPS (*points finger at them*). Ah! Ah! You know you got to humor a crazy person. And since you've both made up your minds that I'm crazy you can understand it would drive me wild, if you didn't humor me.

EVANS. Be careful, Northrup. You're going to get yourself into trouble. This is no way of getting out of it.

GRAMPS. Only way that occurs to me at the minute. Now listen, I ain't goin' to no bughouse!

GRIMES. Listen, Northrup . . .

GRAMPS. I ain't goin' to no bughouse and I ain't goin' to let that old she-cat get Pud. But I see I gotta prove that what I been sayin' in reference to a certain Mr. Brink ain't no poppycock.

EVANS. Now be reasonable, Northrup.

GRIMES. Yeah, you can prove it to us later.

GRAMPS. Wait a minute. (*Slight pause. GRAMPS' eye lights on EVANS' satchel.*) That your medicine kit, Evans?

EVANS. Yes.

GRAMPS. What you got in that kit?

EVANS. Lots of things.

GRAMPS. You got anything in it—poison enough to kill a fly?

EVANS. Of course, but . . .

GRIMES (*advancing*). You can play with all the flies you want when—

GRAMPS. Play! Do you consider it playin' when a man is willin' to risk his freedom on a fly?

EVANS. What's a fly got to do with it?

GRAMPS. I'll make a bargain with you. And you'd best take it, too, because if you don't I'm just liable to go wild as all hell.

(*He wiggles gun at them.*)

GRIMES. Well, what's the bargain?

GRAMPS. You take the worst poison you got in that bag and put some of it in a tumbler. Then you catch a fly and put him in the poison. If that fly dies, I'll give myself up to you, to the police, to anyone, go to the insane asylum, do anythin' you say. (*GRIMES and EVANS look at each other.*) Well?

EVANS. If the fly dies, you'll come along with us without makin' any trouble?

GRAMPS. Yup. I promise. Hope to die. Cross my heart.

EVANS. Well—

GRAMPS (*pointing gun*). It's the easiest way, Mr. Grimes.

GRIMES (*with look to* EVANS). All right.

EVANS. O.K.

GRAMPS. You get the poison. I'll get the glasses and (*Pointing with gun.*) Mr. Grimes, you catch a fly.

(*Crosses to table up right for tumblers.*)

GRIMES (*crosses down left to* EVANS). He's crazy, raving crazy.

EVANS. Looks like it. But don't think he won't use that gun! I know the old boy. . . .

GRIMES. O.K. Let him play with the fly. How do we know he'll keep his word, though?

EVANS. I think he will.

GRIMES. The word of a nut—

EVANS (*sharply*). Well, what do you want to do? Take the gun away from him?

GRIMES (*looking around at gun*). No, no. Let him do it! No hurry.

(GRAMPS *comes back to table. Puts tumblers down on table center.*)

GRAMPS (*coming around right*). Of course, look here, a bet ain't a bet that don't cut both ways. If the fly lives, you gotta swear I'm sane.

GRIMES. Well, I don't know.

EVANS. Don't worry. (*Crosses to back of table.*) I know damn well I can kill a fly.

GRAMPS. No, you can't!

EVANS. If I can't kill a fly, I'll quit medicine. (*With look to* GRIMES.) You'll agree to this, won't you, Grimes?

GRIMES. Oh, all right.

GRAMPS. You swear?

EVANS. Yes, we swear, Northrup.

GRIMES. Sure, sure, that's all right. You don't have to worry about us.

GRAMPS. All right. Where's the fly?

(GRIMES *advances on* GRAMPS. GRAMPS *puts gun behind his back, facing* GRIMES. GRIMES *stops, backs down left.*) Wait a minute. Here's one.

(*He catches one on window screen.*)

EVANS. Got him?

GRAMPS. Yeah. Now, get the tumbler, get the poison. (EVANS *takes poison and tweezers from his bag.*). Don't get so excited, little fly. You'll be buzzin'

around just as good as new pretty soon.

(EVANS *puts tumbler over fly, transfers fly to his hand, then to table.*)

GRIMES. You're the funniest one I've seen, Northrup.

(*Laughs.*)

GRAMPS. Yup. Guess I am.

(*Laughs.*)

EVANS. All right. (*Pouring poison from bottle to other tumbler.*) Here's enough poison to kill a horse. (*In silence,* EVANS *puts the glasses together and drowns the fly, sets the glass down on table.*) And there's your fly!

GRAMPS (*crosses left, looks at fly*). He ain't much of a swimmer, is he? (*Crosses right.*) Leave him there. Let him get his belly full before you take him out. Well, you been practicin' medicine thirty years, ain't you, Evans?

EVANS. About that.

GRAMPS. And you still think you can kill a fly, eh?

EVANS (*gently*). I've always thought I could, Northrup.

GRAMPS. Well, well, you live and learn, Evans, you live and learn.

(GRAMPS *chuckles.* GRIMES *chuckles.*)

EVANS. All right. He's had time enough.

(*They crowd around as* EVANS *takes out the fly with tweezers. He puts him on newspaper and they peer at him.*)

GRAMPS (*crosses to chair right of table, sits*). Looks kinda sick, don't he?

GRIMES. If I ever saw anything deader I don't know what it is.

EVANS. He's dead, Northrup.

(GRAMPS *stirs the fly. Pause. They watch it.*)

GRIMES. Don't tell us we don't know when something's dead.

GRAMPS. Wait a minute. Give this fly a chance. You can't come to yourself all of a sudden.

GRIMES. You're tough all right, Northrup. Tough but crazy. (*Pause. To* EVANS.) Well?

EVANS. He'll come along, I think.

GRIMES. Let's get going then.

(*They look at* GRAMPS. *He seems bewildered and beaten but he stares at the fly.*)

EVANS (*crosses to* GRAMPS). All right, Northrup. A bet's a bet.

GRAMPS. Well, I'll be God-damned. . . .

(*Touches fly with gun.*)

EVANS. Come on now. Put down that gun.

(GRAMPS *suddenly looks up, excited.*)

GRAMPS. Wait a minute . . . wait a minute—he moved. . . .

(*Others look at the paper, quickly.*)

EVANS. Huh?

GRAMPS (*rises*). Look, look! He's drunk as a lord but we didn't say anythin' about that. He's movin' right across that God-damned piece of paper!

(GRAMPS *follows fly around the room.*)

EVANS. I'll be damned! I'll be—

GRIMES. Jesus Christ!

EVANS. What is this, Northrup?

GRIMES. You didn't give him enough poison, Evans.

EVANS. I gave him enough poison to kill a million flies.

GRIMES. Something went wrong.

EVANS. You saw the fly in the poison yourself.

GRAMPS. Well, now will you believe what I've been tellin' you about Mr. Brink?

(*Pause.* GRIMES *turns to him, pulling out handcuffs.*)

GRIMES (*crosses to front of table*). To hell with that! Put down that gun, Northrup.

GRAMPS (*crosses to center*). Hey, wait a minute, you said—

GRIMES. Put it down now! I don't know what kind of a trick this is—

EVANS. You promised him, Grimes.

GRIMES. I came to get him and, by God, I'm going to do it! What's a promise to a lunatic?

GRAMPS. So you don't believe it yet, eh? Even after I proved it to you?

GRIMES (*softly*). You crazy bastard—

EVANS. Look out, Grimes. Wait a minute!

(EVANS *pushes* GRIMES *back left.*)

GRAMPS. And you ain't goin' to keep your word, eh? Well, by God, there's another way of provin' it and it looks like I got to use that way right now.

EVANS (*crosses up center*). For God's sake, Northrup! What—

GRAMPS. I'm goin' to make another experiment and I want you to witness it.

GRIMES (*going toward* EVANS). He's crazy as hell! He's dangerous!

EVANS. What are you going to do, Northrup!

GRAMPS. Evans, at this close range if a man was shot right through the belly, he'd die, wouldn't he?

EVANS. Good God, man!

GRIMES. Look out there, Northrup!

GRAMPS. Wouldn't he?

EVANS. Yes, of course, but—

GRAMPS. That's all I want to know.

(*He fires.* GRIMES *crumples up.* EVANS *rushes to him.*)

GRAMPS. Now, don't worry. He ain't goin' to die.

(EVANS *has been bending over* GRIMES. *He straightens up and looks at* GRAMPS.)

EVANS. You crazy fool! He'll be dead in a hour.

GRAMPS (*at window*). Stay up there, Mr. Brink. If you come down now, by God, I'm in a hell of a fix.

CURTAIN

SCENE THREE

The tree. Dawn.

AT RISE: EVANS *is holding long fishpole through fence. He pulls it out; there is long, gray object on end of it. He kneels beside it, studies it carefully with magnifying glass.* MARCIA *comes out from porch, opens shutters on living-room window. Sees* EVANS.

MARCIA (*startled*). Oh. (EVANS *looks up with a start.*) Oh, good morning, Dr. Evans. I didn't know you were here.

EVANS. Good morning, Marcia.

MARCIA. Did you want to see Mr. Northrup?

EVANS. Why—why, yes, I did. Is he up yet?

MARCIA. Yes. He and Pud are just finishing breakfast. I'll tell him you're here. He'll be right out.

EVANS. Yes, yes, do that.

MARCIA. Is anything the matter?

EVANS. No—I've been up all night.

MARCIA (*pointing*). Is that a mouse, Dr. Evans?

EVANS. Yes, Marcia, that's a mouse.

MARCIA. Oh.

(*She looks at him wonderingly and goes in. Pause.* EVANS *examines mouse again; gets up, puts pole back through fence; stands looking at tree.*)

EVANS. Hello. (*Pause. No answer.*) Hello up there. (*Pause. No answer.*) PILBEAM *enters from gate right, stands looking at him.*) Hello.

PILBEAM. Hello.

(EVANS *turns sharply.*)

EVANS (*crosses center*). Oh, hello, Pilbeam. I was just—er—

PILBEAM (*crosses center*). Feeling all right?

EVANS. Of course. Why?

PILBEAM. I just wondered—well, what do you want to see me about?

EVANS. Thought I might need you.

PILBEAM. Oh. (*Pause.* PILBEAM *watches* EVANS *curiously.*) Hear you didn't lock Northrup up last night.

EVANS. That's right.

PILBEAM. How's that?

EVANS. He isn't crazy.

PILBEAM. What?

EVANS (*louder*). He's not crazy. (*Crosses up left, picks up fishpole.*)

PILBEAM. Oh. (*Pause.*) What you got there?

EVANS. Fishpole.

PILBEAM. Going fishing?

EVANS. Been fishing.

PILBEAM. Catch much? (*Goes left, looks at fishpole, sees mouse.*) Well, that's a mouse.

EVANS (*crosses down left*). Yeah. That's a mouse.

PILBEAM (*crosses down center*). Well, what the hell's the matter with you, Evans?

EVANS. What do you mean—what's the matter?

PILBEAM. You got me out of bed.

EVANS (*crosses center*). Wait a minute, Pilbeam. Now, don't get excited. We got to keep our heads. Because something's happened that'll turn this world upside-down, unless we can stop it. And you gotta help me.

PILBEAM. Uh?

EVANS. Northrup shot Grimes last night, Pilbeam.

PILBEAM. Good God!

EVANS. Shot him right through the belly. He had internal hemorrhages and it was an hour before I could get him to the hospital.

PILBEAM. What did he shoot him for?

EVANS (*looks at tree*). He was experimenting.

PILBEAM. He was—experimenting!

EVANS. Wait a minute, Grimes is all right.

PILBEAM. All right?

EVANS. He's practically well. That's the trouble. According to everything I know about medicine, Grimes should have died last night, Pilbeam. But he didn't. (*Wipes face, crosses to bench center and sits.*) Plenty of things should have died last night. But they didn't. (*He pauses for a second; continues in a confused voice.*) I've been up all night, trying to kill something. (*He rises, crosses to* PILBEAM.) I've experimented on everything I could get my hands on. Insects. Bugs. I've tried to kill every stray cat or dog I could find. I couldn't kill a damned thing. Except that mouse. (PILBEAM *silent.*) And do you know how I killed him? I tied him to the end of this fishpole and touched him to that tree.

PILBEAM. Look here, Evans, you've been up all night—

EVANS. Oh, for Christ . . . (*Crosses to center, by gates of fence.*) Don't see anything up there, do you?

(PILBEAM *has followed him to left of center.*)

PILBEAM. Of course not.

EVANS (*crosses to left center*). Hear anything?

PILBEAM. Not a rustle.

EVANS. Neither do I. But if there is anything up there, by God, it's got to come down. It's got to come down. And you got to help me!

(*They both look back at tree.* GRAMPS *enters, slams screen door. They whirl, startled.*)

GRAMPS. Howdy, Evans. Howdy, Pilbeam.

PILBEAM. Oh, hello, Northrup.

EVANS (*crosses to center*). Hello.

GRAMPS (*crosses down left*). How's Mr. Grimes doin'?

EVANS. Seems to be doing all right.

GRAMPS (*chuckles*). Glad to hear it. Nasty accident. (*Sits in chair left.*) Well, set down. What can I do for you?

(*Pause.* EVANS *crosses to bench, sits.* PILBEAM *crosses to right of center.*)

EVANS. Guess I owe you an apology, Northrup.

GRAMPS. No, you don't. Wouldn't have any respect for you if you believed a thing like this at first. You're a doctor. . . . (*To* PILBEAM.) Kinda interestin', ain't it, Pilbeam?

PILBEAM. Why—er—of course—very interesting.

GRAMPS. Awful nice sort of chap, Mr. Brink is. Real friendly.

BRINK. Thank you very much.

GRAMPS (*rises*). Oh, mornin', Mr. Brink. Didn't know you were up yet.

(EVANS *rises, looks at* GRAMPS, *the tree, then sits.* PILBEAM *looks at* GRAMPS, *then the tree.*)

BRINK. Oh, yes. I've had a lovely morning. I've had a mouse in my face.

GRAMPS (*looks at* EVANS). What! Gol-darn it, what you been up to, Evans? Have you been shovin' a mouse in my friend Brink's face?

PILBEAM (*crosses to center*). Good God, how do you know that?

GRAMPS. Mr. Brink told me, just now.

PILBEAM. Good God, I've got to go! (*He starts rapidly out right.*)

EVANS (*rises, crosses to* PILBEAM). Wait a minute, Pilbeam.

(PILBEAM *hesitates.*)

PILBEAM. I've got a busy day, Jim. I got a lot of work to do—

EVANS (*takes* PILBEAM *by arm, crosses to center,* PILBEAM *crosses down right*). Stick around, Pilbeam.

GRAMPS (*crosses to bench, sits*). Sure, stick around. This is a sort of special occasion. In fact, this is the mornin' Demmie figured I'd be in the nut-house. Yes, sir, I'm feelin' right good this mornin'. Pud's feelin' pretty spry. Mr. Brink sounded pretty pert. Everybody's feelin' fine—'cept Demmie. God bless her!

EVANS. Northrup?

GRAMPS. Yeah.

EVANS (*crosses to right of bench*). There's a man in my hospital who's been suffering for ten years. He's in constant pain.

GRAMPS. I'm real sorry, Evans.

EVANS. Day before yesterday, I decided to operate on him. The operation wasn't successful. He's in more pain now than he ever was.

GRAMPS. Well, Evans, I'm real sorry to hear that.

EVANS. I expected him to die last night. I hoped he would.

GRAMPS. Yeah.

EVANS. There's a nice old lady up in 2C, Mrs. Trenner, remember her?

GRAMPS. The old lady who used to have all the dogs?

EVANS. Yeah.

GRAMPS. By God, I'd forgot all about her.

EVANS. Everybody has. She's been in there for six years, in bed. She hasn't got much left. Only one idea—to die. And this is what's happening in just one small hospital, you know. In a small town. There are two in Gainesville. There are several million in the world, aren't there —full of people just like that.

GRAMPS. I'm sorry for all those people —sorry for all of 'em—but if you're hintin' for me to let Mr. Brink down, you're off on the wrong track.

(EVANS *looks at* GRAMPS *for a moment.*)

EVANS. What do you think is going to happen, Northrup, in the next few days when people find out there's no more death!

PILBEAM. But it isn't true—

EVANS (*crosses to* PILBEAM). No more death. Think about it for a minute. Nobody died last night. Nobody's going to die tonight. Or tomorrow night. Nobody's going to die . . . (*Looks at* GRAMPS.) . . . until Northrup says they can. What do you think about that?

PILBEAM. It's absurd.

EVANS. That's right. It's absurd. (*Facing* GRAMPS.) Five years from today this world will be so overcrowded that it won't be fit to live in . . . think of the disease . . .

GRAMPS. I don't give a damn! I don't care what happens! I've got Mr. Brink up there and he's gonna stay there!

EVANS (*crosses to bench*). He can't, Northrup. You gotta let him down.

GRAMPS. Why should I? I'm looking after Pud and myself.

EVANS. Who the hell are you?

GRAMPS. I'm the feller that got Mr. Brink up that tree and up that tree he's gonna stay until I'm good and ready to let him down.

(*Rises, crosses left and faces house.*)

PILBEAM (*frightened*). Well, I've got to get back to the office. I've got work to do. I've got a hell of a lot of work to do today. 'Bye, Northrup. (*No answer.*) Good-by, Evans. (*No answer. He looks at tree.*) Good-b—

(*Goes out right.*)

GRAMPS (*crosses to bench, sits*). Look here, Evans, 'tain't that I'm afraid to go. I ain't afraid of dyin'. Might be real pleasant to see what's comin' next. But, you see, there's Pud. I just want to stick around in case he needs me.

(*Pause.*)

EVANS. Have you ever seen a man a hundred and ten years old, Northrup?

GRAMPS. Yep. I seen one pretty near that old once. Old Fred Brown's father. Poor old devil—Hey, what the hell are you drivin' at ?

EVANS. I was just thinking—by the time Pud's a young man, you'll be getting about that age yourself.

GRAMPS. No. No. When I saw myself gettin' like that old guy was I'd let Mr. Brink come down and take me.

EVANS. Oh, no, you wouldn't.

GRAMPS. Yes, I would.

EVANS. You wouldn't be able to see yourself getting like that. You'd be too far gone by that time. You might even forget Mr. Brink was up there. (*Pause.* GRAMPS *sits, thinking.*) You gotta let him down, Northrup.

(*Pause.*)

GRAMPS (*softly*). I don't want to be no nuisance to Pud—

EVANS. You've got to let Mr. Brink come down today. I warn you—I'll do everything I can to make you. Better think it over. (*Crosses to tree, picks up bag.*) I'll be back in an hour. (*Starts out, then hesitates.*) Well, thanks for not letting me eat that apple yesterday.

GRAMPS. You kin have one now, if you want it.

EVANS. No, thanks. Well—good-by, Northrup.

GRAMPS. Good-by.

EVANS. I'm—I'm sorry.

GRAMPS. Yeah. (EVANS *goes out, leaving* GRAMPS *sitting and thinking.*) Mr. Brink, if I let you come down, you're bound and determined you're gonna take me, ain't you?

BRINK. You will be the first.

GRAMPS. That's what I thought. . . . No way of getting out of that, is there?

BRINK. None.

GRAMPS. No, I didn't think so.

BRINK. It would seem to me that you had got out of a great deal already.

GRAMPS. I just wondered. I just wondered. Don't get upset. . . . (*Rises and crosses to tree.*) . . . Mr. Brink, do you think Evans is right about me and Pud? Think maybe I might become a nuisance to the boy?

BRINK. My dear man, there's no doubt about it.

GRAMPS (*turns and faces upstage*). Hmmn. (PUD *comes out of the house acting like an engine.*)

PUD (*in the house*). Here comes Casey down the track . . . bingety, bingety, bing. . . . (*Enters.*) . . . Here comes Casey down the track . . . bingety, bingety, bing . . . (*Down around chair left.*) . . . choo, choo, choo . . . (*Across stage to down stage right.*) . . . choo, choo, choo. . . . (*Stops.*) Say, God, you are standing there in the middle of my track. Get out of the way, God; get off my railroad track or I'll run over you. . . . I guess I'll have to strike you dead, Casey. . . . BOOM ! . . . Now, look what you did, God, you wrecked my train all to splinters. Now I have to get a new engine. . . . All right, Casey, here's a new engine. . . . (GRAMPS *walks slowly down to left of bench, watching* PUD.) . . . Thanks, God. Get on and I'll give you a ride. Here we go . . . choo, choo, choo . . . ding, ding. . . . Get out of the way, everybody. Get out of the way. Here comes God and Casey Jones. . . . Toot, toot! (*He stops and sees* GRAMPS. *Continues till he bumps into him.*) Toot, toot, choo, choo. . . . (*Hugs* GRAMPS.) I love you, Gramps, I love you more'n my engine!

CURTAIN

SCENE FOUR

The tree. Toward close of same day.

AT RISE: GRAMPS *stands behind bench center, with* PUD *to his right.* SHERIFF BURLINGHAME, DEMETRIA *and* EVANS *are moving across stage, from left to right.* MARCIA *is just coming out on porch, stands left.*

GRAMPS. Just read the last part of that document again, Sheriff. Where Dr. Evans signed. . . .

SHERIFF (*down right*). All right, Northrup. "Dr. James Evans, having testified that the said Julian Northrup is incapable of managing himself and his property, it is the order of this Court that he be committed to the Gainesville Institution for the Insane, according to the Laws of this State, and it is further ordered that the custody of the child, John Gilford Northrup, be awarded to his aunt, Demetria Riffle."

GRAMPS. Thank you, Sheriff. (*Turns to* EVANS.) You've kinda fixed me up good and proper, ain't you?

EVANS. I warned you I'd do anything I could.

GRAMPS (*to* SHERIFF). So, Evans has told you I'm crazy, ain't he?

SHERIFF. I guess there's no doubt about that, Northrup.

DEMETRIA (*crosses to center*). I'll be good to the boy while you're in the asylum, Julian. I really will. ... Come, Pud, you're to come home with me now.

PUD (*clutching* GRAMPS). Gramps!

SHERIFF (*moving up right*). Come along, Northrup.

GRAMPS. Wait a minute. (*They all stop.*) I'd like to speak to Pud a minute first.

(EVANS *and* SHERIFF *look at each other.*)

EVANS (*motions* SHERIFF *and* DEMETRIA *to go out*). You two, wait outside a moment. (*Crosses right center.*) I'm sorry, Northrup, but I've given you all day to make up your mind. I can't wait any longer. So you're going to the insane asylum.

GRAMPS. You're pretty smart, ain't you, Evans? You figger I won't go to the nut-house. You figger I'll let Mr. Brink down instead.

EVANS. I'm hoping you will.

GRAMPS. You figger long as I lost the boy, I don't much care what happens to me.

EVANS. That's what I figure, Northrup.

GRAMPS. All right. You're a pretty smart feller.

(*He motions* EVANS *away.* EVANS *joins the others.*)

PUD. What's the matter with Dr. Evans, Gramps?

GRAMPS. Guess he's kinda sorry, boy. (*Crosses to front of bench, sits right.*)

PUD. What's he sorry for?

GRAMPS (MARCIA *crosses upstage*). Come here a minute.

PUD (*sits left of* GRAMPS). O.K.

GRAMPS (*looks at* PUD, *turns away to get up his courage*). I'm goin' away, boy.

PUD. Where, Gramps?

GRAMPS. Where the woodbine twineth.

PUD. You goin' with Mr. Brink?

GRAMPS. Yep, I'm goin' with Mr. Brink. You see, your Gramps is gettin' to be a pretty old man. And when you get to be a pretty old man you begin to get kinda tired.

PUD. Are you tired?

GRAMPS. Right at this minute, I'm pretty dog-gone tired.

PUD. Let's lie down and rest.

GRAMPS. That's just what I'm gonna do. But the only way an old man can really lie down and rest is to go with Mr. Brink.

PUD. I'll go with you, Gramps.

GRAMPS. No, you can't go with me, boy. You've got your whole life ahead of you.

PUD. Don't want my whole life ahead of me. I want to go with you. I love you, Gramps. (*Puts arms around* GRAMPS.)

GRAMPS. Shouldn't love me that much, boy. You see, Pud, I been thinkin' things over. Maybe it ain't such a good thing for you to be livin' with me any more. And, you know, maybe your Aunt Demetria ain't as much of a pismire as we thought she was.

(PUD *rises and backs down center.*)

PUD. Gramps!

GRAMPS. No, sir, maybe she ain't. Maybe it'd be better if you was to go over to your Aunt Demetria's house and live with her. (PUD *backs further away.*) What's the matter, boy?

PUD. Don't you love me any more, Gramps?

GRAMPS. Pshaw, boy, I'm just tryin' to make you understand—

PUD. Gramps, you don't love me any more.

GRAMPS. Of course I do. It's just that I gotta go away.

PUD (*crosses to bench, sits*). But I'll go with you, Gramps.

GRAMPS. But you can't, boy, you can't.

PUD. Please, Gramps, please!

GRAMPS. No.

PUD. Then I don't love you any more either. ... I don't love you any more either. ...

(*He turns and runs into house, crying.*)

GRAMPS. Wait a minute, boy, wait a minute.

BRINK. That's the better way.

GRAMPS. Maybe so.

BRINK. He will forget.

GRAMPS. Maybe so.

(SHERIFF, DEMETRIA *and* EVANS *come back.*)

SHERIFF. What about it, Northrup?

GRAMPS. Oh, I ain't goin' with you. I'm goin' with Mr. Brink. Didn't Evans tell you about Mr. Brink?

SHERIFF. Oh, yeah. He did. Well, get it over with. We haven't got all night.

EVANS. Take it easy, Sheriff. ... Northrup, would you rather we left you alone?

GRAMPS. No. As a matter of fact, I'd like to have somebody around.

(EVANS *turns upstage.* DEMETRIA *crosses to* GRAMPS. SHERIFF *reads document.*)

DEMETRIA (*going to him*). Well, Julian . . .

GRAMPS. Demmie, honest to God, will you be good to Pud?

DEMETRIA. I'll be good to him, Julian.

GRAMPS. Will you see he gets some fun out of life?

DEMETRIA. I will.

GRAMPS. Will you not keep huggin' him all the time like you do?

DEMETRIA. I'll be good to Pud, Julian. You don't have to worry. I have wonderful plans for him already.

GRAMPS. What plans you got for him?

DEMETRIA. Well, I'm going to start right in getting him ready to go to school next year.

GRAMPS. How d'ye mean, gettin' him ready?

DEMETRIA. I'm gonna start teaching him things myself, Julian. So that when he gets to school, he'll be way ahead of any of the others.

GRAMPS. Ain't you gonna let him play any?

DEMETRIA. Of course, Julian. He'll have his play period. But now he'll have education too. I'll begin to form his mind. . . .

GRAMPS. His mind's formin' all right as it is.

DEMETRIA. And I'll teach him little poems to recite.

GRAMPS. Oh, my God!

DEMETRIA. I'll teach him how to behave nicely, Julian. How to say "Yes, sir" and "No, sir" and how to curtsey when older people—

GRAMPS. Curtsey! Pud!

DEMETRIA. And by the time Miss Ramsdell's school opens in the Fall . . .

GRAMPS. Miss Ramsdall's school is a girls' school!

DEMETRIA. Not any more, Julian. They're going to have three little boys in it next year.

GRAMPS. You're gonna make Pud into a sissy! By God, you are still a pismire! I'm gonna change my mind. I ain't goin' with Mr. Brink. I'm gonna stay right here and take care of Pud.

EVANS (*sharply*). Northrup! How can you take care of Pud if you're in the asylum?

GRAMPS. Oh.

EVANS. Because that's where you'll be.

GRAMPS. Yeah. Well, what the hell am I gonna do? (*Slight pause.*) Well, no use stretchin' it out. 'Bye, Marcy.

MARCIA. Oh, Mr. Northrup.

EVANS (*crossing to* GRAMPS). I realize what I'm asking you to do, Northrup. (*Crosses left.*)

GRAMPS. Yeah. . . . Well, Mr. Brink, looks kinda like the time has come.

(GRAMPS *crosses to gates.*)

BRINK. Yes, the time has come now.

GRAMPS. I expect you're all ready.

BRINK. All ready as soon as you say the word.

GRAMPS. Well, I'll just open the gates, then, so's you don't have to climb this here fence.

BRINK. That will be more convenient. I've had quite enough climbing for a while.

(MARCIA *down left to chair.* GRAMPS *opens gates.*)

GRAMPS. I hope you ain't goin' to hold nothin' against me, Mr. Brink.

BRINK. We'll see. We'll see.

GRAMPS. Remember the only reason I got you up there was to keep Demmie from gettin' the boy.

BRINK. I've taken that into consideration.

GRAMPS. I wasn't cheatin'. I was gonna let you down as soon as you had word you was to take her.

BRINK. I know. I know.

(DEMETRIA *laughs.*)

GRAMPS (*looking at* DEMETRIA). Don't suppose by any chance you've had any word about takin' her yet.

BRINK. No, there's been no call for Miss Riffle. There probably won't be for years.

GRAMPS (*suddenly*). What's that? You say you were supposed to take her an hour ago?

BRINK. No, no. I said I probably wouldn't take her for years.

GRAMPS. My God, why didn't you tell me, Mr. Brink? Why, if you're supposed to take Demmie too—

BRINK. But I am *not* supposed to take her!

EVANS (*crosses to end of bench left*). Northrup, did he really say that?

GRAMPS. Yep. Says he was supposed to take Demmie an hour ago. This changes everything. Come on, Demmie!

(*He drags* DEMETRIA *to tree.*)

DEMETRIA (*breaking away from him*). No—No, Julian. This is absurd! This is—! Dr. Evans.

EVANS. I'm sorry, Miss Riffle. But when a person's time comes . . .

DEMETRIA. But—there isn't really anyone up in that tree— This is all so—so silly.

GRAMPS. Thank you, Mr. Brink, for takin' Demmie. I wonder if you'd do one more thing. I wonder if after you've taken Demmie, you'd just slip the Sheriff in for good measure.

SHERIFF. Hey—what th' hell—

GRAMPS. The old stiff's tryin' to take me to the nut-house—

EVANS (*crosses to* GRAMPS). Good God, Northrup! Do you know what you're doing? This is practically murder!

DEMETRIA. M-m-murder! D-d-doctor! M-m-murder!

EVANS. Listen you, all of you, Northrup's as sane as any one here.

SHERIFF. What's that? Hey, what is this, anyway?

EVANS. Northrup's not insane. You realize what he's going to do? Death is up in that tree. Northrup's talking to him. If he lets him down you're as good as dead, both of you.

DEMETRIA. What! What? I don't believe it—

BRINK. This is—

GRAMPS. Ssh! Ssh!

BRINK. This is the wildest absurdity I ever heard. You know perfectly well I have no authorization to take any of these people. It is utterly out of the question.

GRAMPS. What's that? You say you'll take the Sheriff too? Thank you, Mr. Brink. I appreciate that a great deal.

DEMETRIA (*crosses left center. Hysterically*). I don't believe it—! You can't frighten me! I didn't hear anything up in that tree! I didn't hear a blessed thing!

MARCIA (*crosses right to* GRAMPS. *Suddenly*). I did! I heard him!

GRAMPS (*crosses down center*). Eh? What's that?

MARCIA. I heard him! I heard Mr. Brink!

GRAMPS. You did— Now look here, Marcy!

DEMETRIA. You d-didn't—

MARCIA. I did! I did! I heard him just as plain as I hear you.

(DEMETRIA *looks at* EVANS.)

GRAMPS. But, Marcy—

MARCIA (*quiets him with gesture*). And he said that if he could just come down he would take anyone Mr. Northrup asked him to.

(GRAMPS *turns right, hiding laughter with his hand.*)

DEMETRIA. He didn't! He didn't say he was going to take me?

MARCIA. Oh, yes, he did, Miss Riffle. He said he was going to take you—first!

(DEMETRIA *sits on bench.*)

BRINK. That girl—

GRAMPS. Ssh! Ssh!

BRINK. That girl cannot hear a word I say. She is the most inordinate liar I ever met.

GRAMPS. Hear him then, Marcy?

MARCIA. Yes.

GRAMPS. What did he say? Now, be careful.

MARCIA. He said to please hurry and let him down. He's getting nervous and can't stand it another minute.

(*Crosses left.*)

GRAMPS. Yup. That's just what he said. So I better get started. Don't want to make him any angrier.

BRINK. That would be impossible. You let me down!

GRAMPS. Well, good-by, everybody. But then I'll be seein' you two in a second. Now I'm gonna start the magic words. (*Takes* DEMETRIA *and* SHERIFF *by hand.*) Come on, Demmie. Sheriff. Line up. Here we go. Off to glory!

(*He starts mumbling.* SHERIFF, DEMETRIA *and* GRAMPS *walk around in circle.*)

BRINK. Stop that monkey-business and let me down.

EVANS. Stop it, Northrup!

DEMETRIA. Stop him! Stop him, somebody! Stop him.

SHERIFF. Hold on there, Northrup. Hold on!

EVANS (*grabbing* GRAMPS). Stop it, Northrup! Stop it! We'll do anything you want us to.

SHERIFF (*tears up adoption paper*). Look, Northrup, look.

GRAMPS. All right! . . . Now, you keep your hands off my boy, Demmie.

DEMETRIA (*crosses upper right*). I will, Julian, I will.

GRAMPS. And you keep the hell away from me, too.

DEMETRIA. I will, Julian. I'll keep the hell away from you, too.

GRAMPS (*turns to tree*). All right. Mr. Brink, from now on, anybody who tries to make me let you down you gotta take them too.

BRINK. I will not! I will not!

GRAMPS. Thank you very much. . . . Now, you get out of here. All of you. I'm gonna stay right here and take care of Pud. I don't care if the whole damn world goes to hell. Git out of here. Git off my property. Go on. Go on! If you ask me you got off pretty lucky. (*They all go off right.* MARCIA *crosses to bench, crying, sits.*) Marcy, I love yuh. (*Crosses to bench, sits.*) By God, I love yuh. And there ain't nothin' in this world can stop us now. Just you and me and Pud. Nothin' in the world can stop us, now.

BRINK (*appears*). Which world do you mean?

GRAMPS. What's that, Mr. Brink?

BRINK. Which world do you mean?

GRAMPS. Why—I don't understand, Mr. Brink.

BRINK. Of course you don't. My poor man!

MARCIA. What did he say, Mr. Northrup?

GRAMPS. He said: "My poor man." And I didn't like the way he said it, Marcy. I didn't like the way he said it.

CURTAIN

SCENE FIVE

The tree. Few minutes later. It is dark.
AT RISE: GRAMPS *and* MARCIA *enter from house, looking for* PUD.

GRAMPS. Pud! Pud!

MARCIA. Where are you, Pud?

GRAMPS. We got to find him, Marcy. We got to find him. I got to explain to him.—Hey, boy, where are you?

MARCIA. Pud!

GRAMPS. You didn't see nothin' of him at all?

MARCIA. Not a thing. Maybe he went over to see Jimmy.

GRAMPS. You run over and see, Marcy. Don't think he'd stay over there this late. You go on.

MARCIA. I'll be right back, Mr. Northrup.
(*Exits right.*)

GRAMPS. Pud! Hey, Pud! Where are you, boy? Time to come home now. Hey, boy, where are you? Pud! Pud!

(GRAMPS *goes off right, calling for* PUD. PUD *comes out of cellar up left. He is sniffling. He walks down to chair left center.* MR. BRINK *appears.* PUD *carries some belongings in a handkerchief.*)

BRINK. Pud!

PUD (*tearfully*). Hello there, Mr. Brink.

BRINK. What's the matter, Pud?

PUD. My Gramps doesn't love me any more.

BRINK. He doesn't?

PUD. No. Didn't you follow the conversation?

BRINK. Yes, what are you going to do, Pud?

PUD. I'm going to run away. Then he'll be sorry.

BRINK. What have you got there?

PUD (*showing them*). These are some cookies I got. . . . And this is my watch fob Gramps wrote on for me. . . . And a couple of specimens.

BRINK. And you're really going to run away?

PUD. 'Course I am.

BRINK. I wouldn't if I were you.

PUD. You would too.

BRINK. They'll only find you and bring you back. You're not big enough to run away, my little man.

PUD. I am so! And I'm not your little man! I'm not a little man at all. I'll spit in your eye.

BRINK. You might find that difficult.

PUD. Why?

BRINK. I'm afraid you couldn't reach me.

PUD. I could too.

BRINK. You would be afraid.

PUD. I'm not afraid of the biggest giant on earth.

BRINK. How do you know I'm not the biggest giant on earth?

PUD. Because you're in the littlest tree.

BRINK. There is a certain logic in that. Your mind is taking shape. That's too bad that has to happen.

PUD. Why?

BRINK. Because man's logic is the most pitiful thing about him. It stands in his way. It confuses him, so that he can't quite see the giants. You won't be able to see them much longer.

PUD. Aw, I will too.

BRINK. No, you will not. Not until you

are as old as your grandfather. Then you will be able to see them again.

PUD. Nuts.

BRINK. You're not very polite.

PUD. I'm politer than you, you big squashapussoshapuss.

BRINK. I'm afraid I never heard that word before.

PUD. Neither did I.

BRINK. You can make up words?

PUD. Sure, I can do anything.

BRINK. No, you can't. You can't even climb a tree.

PUD. I can too. I climbed that tree before you got up it and I climbed down again. That's more than you can do.

BRINK. You're right about that. But you couldn't do it now. Why, you can't even climb that fence.

PUD. I could do it with one hand.

BRINK. Let's see you.

PUD (crosses to fence left). All right.
(He goes to fence and tries and fails.)

BRINK. You'll never get up on that side. Better come over to this side. It's much easier.
(PUD does better but still slides back.)

PUD. Ouch, that hurts my hand. Guess I'll have to get myself a heap o' tape.
(Turns and crosses to screen door, quickly.)

BRINK. Baby calf! Baby calf!

PUD (turns to BRINK). Who's a baby calf!
(He crosses to fence determinedly. He climbs and slowly approaches the cross beam.)

BRINK. That's right. I never thought you could do it. I guess you must be stronger than I thought. Come on now. Just a little more. Go along the edge there. Get one leg over. There! That's it. Now you're here. Splendid! I guess you can do everything.

PUD. Golly, I can see far up here.

BRINK. Can you see me now?

PUD. Yes. Gee, why do you make your voice so whispery, Mr. Brink?

BRINK. Don't you like it?

PUD. Yes.

BRINK. Good. Can you see me?

PUD. Yes, I can see you. I'm up as high as you are now.

BRINK. Look at me!

PUD. Gee, you've got funny eyes, Mr. Brink. They make me dizzy. You've got ghost eyes.
(Slowly PUD stands up, gripping the post.)

BRINK. Look at me again. (PUD does so.) That's right. Keep on looking at me.

Give me your hand. Lean forward.
PUD suddenly loses his balance and falls.)

PUD (in terror). Gramps! Gramps! Gramps!

CURTAIN

SCENE SIX

The tree. Later that night. Moonlight.
AT RISE: GRAMPS *is holding* PUD *in his arms. Walks toward tree.* BRINK *is visible.*

PUD. Gramps, I want a heap o' tape, my back hurts, my back.

GRAMPS. Hush, boy, hush for a minute. . . . Mr. Brink?

BRINK. Yes?

GRAMPS. Pud's in terrible pain. Doctor Evans just left and says he'll never be able to walk again. Why did you let him do it, Mr. Brink?

BRINK. My dear man, I didn't mean to hurt the boy. I just meant to take him. It was the only way out. I even waited a day to let the others force you. But you were too clever for them.

GRAMPS. But you could have found some other way than to pick on the boy.

BRINK. It is only through the boy that I have any hope of getting down from here. He is the only reason that you won't let me come down. What if I should tell you that I'm bound to stay out the time to which you sentenced me? Until Miss Riffle dies?

GRAMPS. You're not, are you? You're not. You don't have to stay up there, do you?

BRINK. No. But I want you to understand how much it means to you, to your whole world, to deny me. Already the world is beginning to feel the pain and sorrow and bewilderment in keeping me here. It is getting worse every hour.

GRAMPS. I guess I tried to bite off more'n I could chew.

BRINK. Much more.

GRAMPS. Will you come down, please, and take us both?

BRINK. Gladly.

GRAMPS. Please come then. Quickly.

PUD. Gramps—

GRAMPS. Yes, boy.

PUD. A heap o' tape. My back hurts

so awful—

GRAMPS. Yes, boy. There, there, boy. Just a minute—just a minute.

(BRINK *is down.* GRAMPS *holds out* PUD.)

BRINK. No, you are first. (*He touches* GRAMPS' *brow.* GRAMPS *suddenly straightens up.*) Ah, that's better, isn't it?

GRAMPS. Well, well. He was quite a load before. He's light as a feather now. Here, here.

(BRINK *bends over and touches* PUD. GRAMPS *lets* PUD *down.* BRINK *and* GRAMPS *bend down to him.*)

PUD (*rousing*). Hello, Mr. Brink.

BRINK. Hello, Pud.

PUD. Are we deaded, Gramps?

GRAMPS. Must be. I feel like a two-year-old. How do you feel?

PUD. I feel like a two-year-old, too, Gramps.

GRAMPS. Mr. Brink, why didn't you tell me it was goin' to be like this?

BRINK. My dear man, I've been trying to tell you how pleasant it is to go with me, but you wouldn't listen.

PUD. You talk so funny, Mr. Brink.

BRINK. Well, never mind me— Come on. Come along!

PUD (*crosses center,* GRAMPS *follows*).

But, where we goin', Gramps?

GRAMPS (*stops*). Oh, yes—by golly, that's important. Where are we goin', Mr. Brink?

BRINK. You'll find out.

PUD (*looks at* BRINK). How long will we be there?

BRINK. For eternity.

PUD (*looks at* GRAMPS). How long is eternity, Gramps?

GRAMPS. Right smart piece of time, boy.

PUD. Anyway, we'll be there together, won't we, Gramps?

GRAMPS (*shaking hands with* PUD). You're damn right we will be! You're damn right!

GRANNY (*off stage*). Juleyun! Juleyun, do you have to use such language in front of the boy?

(*They all look up.*)

GRAMPS. Oh, hell, I thought you said she'd changed! (BRINK *shakes his head disapprovingly.* GRAMPS *throws* GRANNY *a kiss.* GRAMPS *and* PUD *march hand in hand through the gates and up the ramps.*)

CURTAIN

MORNING'S AT SEVEN

Paul Osborn

Morning's at Seven was produced by Dwight Deere Wiman at the Longacre Theatre in New York City on November 20, 1939. The play was directed by Joshua Logan, the setting was designed by Jo Mielziner, and the cast was as follows:

In the house at the left:		*Others:*	
THEODORE SWANSON	.Thomas Chalmers	MYRTLE BROWN	Enid Markey
CORA SWANSON	Jean Adair	ESTHER CRAMPTON	Effie Shannon
AARONETTA GIBBS	Dorothy Gish	DAVID CRAMPTON	Herbert Yost

(Cora, Aaronetta, Ida, and Esther are sisters)

In the house at the right:

IDA BOLTON .... Kate McComb
CARL BOLTON .... Russell Collins
HOMER BOLTON ...... John Alexander

SCENE: Two backyards in an American town. TIME: The present.

ACT ONE: Late afternoon in early fall.
ACT TWO: Early the next morning.
ACT THREE: An hour later.

Morning's at Seven was revived by Proscenium Productions at the Cherry Lane Theatre in Greenwich Village, New York City, on June 22, 1955. It was staged by Warren Enters with scenery by John Cornell. The cast was as follows:

In the house at your right:		*In the house at your left:*	
THEODORE SWANSON	Walter Klavun	IDA BOLTON	Mary Loane
CORA SWANSON	Martha Morton	CARL BOLTON	Harrison Dowd
AARONETTA GIBBS	Kate Harrington	HOMER BOLTON	Tom Bosley

Others

MYRTLE BROWN .... Gubi Mann
ESTHER CRAMPTON ..... Dorrit Kelton
DAVID CRAMPTON .... Richard Bowler

Copyright 1939, by Paul Osborn (under the title *Summer Solstice*).
Copyright 1940, by Paul Osborn.

CAUTION: Professionals and amateurs are hereby warned that *Morning's at Seven*, being fully protected under the copyright law of the United States of America, the British Empire, including the Dominion of Canada, and all other countries of the Copyright Union, is subject to a royalty. All rights, including but not limited to professional, amateur, motion picture, recitation, lecturing, public reading, radio broadcasting, television, and the rights of translation into foreign languages, are strictly reserved. Particular emphasis is laid on the question of readings, permission for which must be secured from the author's agent in writing.

All inquiries concerning rights (other than amateur rights for the United States and Canada) should be addressed to the author's agent, Harold Freedman, Brandt & Brandt Dramatic Department, Inc., 101 Park Avenue, New York 17, New York, without whose permission in writing no performance of the play may be made.

The amateur acting rights of *Morning's at Seven* are controlled exclusively by Samuel French, Inc., 25 West 45th Street, New York 36, New York, without whose permission in writing no amateur performance of the play may be made.

Robert Browning's Pippa sings a familiar message as she passes:

> The year's at the spring
> And day's at the morn;
> Morning's at seven;
> The hill-side's dew-pearled;
> The lark's on the wing;
> The snail's on the thorn;
> God's in His heaven—
> All's right with the world!

And that is just what we shall get out of Paul Osborn's play, provided we bring to it an irony the good Victorian poet did not intend and are willing to accept the diminution of background, characters, and issue that Paul Osborn did intend. In this, one of his few entirely original plays on Broadway, he aimed at achieving folksy realistic comedy.

Morning's at Seven, however, was not a conventional choice for Broadway production. The Theatre Guild found it difficult to keep the play running beyond its subscription season. Neither the folk-comedy quality nor the semi-rustic life of the characters was sufficiently attractive to metropolitan playgoers. When the play was revived on June 22, 1955 in an off-Broadway production at the downtown Cherry Lane Theatre, well staged by Warren Enters with attractive scenery by John Cornell, it was still possible to find Broadway and *Morning's at Seven* somewhat at odds with each other. Brooks Atkinson posed the inevitable question next day in the *New York Times* when he wrote: "Why did it fail when it was first put on in 1939? Because it doesn't have a yak in every line? Because it has the temerity to discuss the problems of people who are old? Not being machine-made, it does not pop out a laugh every time an actor opens his mouth."

But it was evident both from the original production and the off-Broadway one that Paul Osborn had written one of the few American comedies that are rooted in non-metropolitan life and yet free from the rude rusticity of amateur theatricals. It may be surmised that the playwright, a former student and devoted friend of Robert Frost, found a stimulus in the latter's wry idyls, and like the New England poet knew "what to make of a diminished thing." The absurd complications that tangle the lives of the characters and bring a measure of excitement into their hitherto more or less placid way of life belong to the trivial dilemmas of the world's "little people." An old man leaving home in order to get to know himself or, rather, to find out "where he stands" in the twilight of his life; a wife who wants to acquire a new house in order to rid herself of the sister she cannot bring herself to oust from her present home; two naïve young people timidly betrothed for the past five years who discover that they are about to become parents—out of these and similar complications Paul Osborn extracted endearing folly and ultimate assurance. For most of the characters, who are either middle-aged or elderly, the year is *not* at the spring; but God remains in His heaven and at least some things are all right with the world—including the play that Mr. Osborn wrote about his restive *dramatis personae*. It was worth sacrificing wit in this play for the sake of its humor, especially since the humor sagged but rarely and was rescued by irony from the saccharinity usual in such instances. Frequently presented in our little theatres, most recently by the Rochester Community Players (February 11-20, 1960), *Morning's at Seven* has become a staple of the American stage.*

---

* For biographical details concerning the author, the reader should turn to the preface to *On Borrowed Time*.

ACT ONE

SCENE: *The back porches and back yards of two houses in a Middle Western town.*

On the stage right is a neatly kept lawn with a few trees and under them a wicker chair. At back is seen the rear of the house, with windows on two levels. There are steps leading up to the porch. The lawn is bordered at extreme right by a hedge. This house and lawn take up four-fifths of the stage on the right.

Stage center is a path which extends back, separating the two lawns and the two houses and leading to the street beyond.

On stage left is practically a duplication of stage right except that the house is not in as good repair, the grass is not as neatly clipped, and there are more trees and bushes, giving it a somewhat wilder appearance. It is bordered at extreme left by a hedge.

Exits and entrances can be made from either house through the back doors, from the drive between the houses and through the hedges extreme right and left.

TIME: *Present.*

Although it is not yet dusk it is evidently toward the close of a summer's day. Before the act is over it is dark. AT RISE: As the curtain rises, THOR, CORA, and ARRY are discovered sitting in the back yard of the house at stage right. THOR is sitting on the tree stump center, smoking. CORA sits on the porch ledge by the steps. Apart from them on the porch near the drive center sits ARRY. She is looking down the drive between the houses toward the street beyond. She seldom takes her eyes from the street.

THOR. Then he listened to my heart. With one of those ear things. Listened quite a while. Didn't say a word. Scared me to death. Then he began to thump me. Chest, sides, back—all over. Still didn't say a word. Took my blood pressure. Wound a little sack around my arm, pumped a little machine, watched a needle—oh, he did everything you could think of! Examination lasted over an hour. Then you know what he said?

CORA. What?

THOR. He says, "Mr. Swanson, there's not a thing in the world the matter with you. You've got a good heart, sound lungs, fine stomach—I don't know when I've seen a man of your age as well off as you are." Now what do you know about that? He's just a lousy doctor, that's all.

CORA. Did you tell him about your neck?

THOR. Of course I did! Said it wasn't anything to worry about! By God, I don't know how a doctor like that gets the reputation he has! Didn't even say I had to give up smoking!

CORA. Well, that's silly. Everybody knows you ought to give up smoking.

THOR (*disgusted*). Of course they do! I smoke much too much. Look at that. (*Refers to his cigarette.*) It stands to reason when a man gets along in his late sixties he's got to cut down on things like that! Well, I'll see old Doc Brooks tomorrow. He may be old but I bet he knows enough to tell me to quit smoking.

CORA. You didn't say anything to the doctor about my side, did you?

THOR. By God, Cora, I didn't! I forgot all about it.

CORA. It doesn't matter.

THOR. I was so damned mad. I'll speak to Doc Brooks about it tomorrow. Does it hurt you? (*He rises—crosses to* CORA.)

CORA. Just when I lean over.

THOR. Want me to rub it for you?

CORA. It'll be all right.

THOR. Well, you want to watch those things. Can't be too careful. (*He crosses to chair down right—sits.*)

CORA (*whispering*). Thanks for asking to rub it, though.

ARRY (*from up on porch*). What's that? What did you say?

THOR. Nothing!

ARRY. Cora did. I heard her. She was whispering.

THOR. Well, she told me she didn't want me to rub her back for her.

ARRY. I don't see what there is to whisper about. When your own sister talks behind your back—

THOR (*after slight pause*). See anything yet, Arry? Aaronetta?

ARRY (*still looking down the street*). What?

THOR. See anything yet?

ARRY. The Davies just drove by.

THOR. Which way they going?

ARRY. Toward town.

(CORA *produces a banana and begins to strip it.*)

THOR. Going to have supper down there and going to a movie—No sign of Homer and Myrtle?

ARRY. Not yet. (*Rises and comes to head of porch steps.*) Dear, I wonder why they don't come. Wouldn't it be awful if he didn't bring her after all?

CORA. Maybe her train's late.

ARRY. My, I bet Ida's excited! (*Crosses down and takes a piece of banana just as* CORA *is about to eat it.*) I wonder if I shouldn't go over there and see if there's anything I can do. (*Starts cross center.*)

CORA. No, you stay away from there. Ida's got that Allen girl in to help her. If she wants us for anything she'll call us.

ARRY. Do you think we'll meet her? Myrtle, I mean? (*Crosses to* THOR.)

THOR. Meet her? I guess Homer won't be bringing any girl of his home without introducing her to his old aunts and uncle.

ARRY. Well, there's something awful funny about it, if you ask me. How long has Homer been engaged to Myrtle now, Cora?

CORA. It must be nearly seven years. Of course they were going together four or five years before that.

ARRY. Well, don't you think it's funny, Homer's going with a girl for twelve years and none of us has ever seen her? Not even his own mother?

THOR. Well, Homer's shy. He can't be rushed into anything. Anyway, he's bringing her home now.

ARRY. Well, that's just because of that movie Ida saw the other day about the old bachelor. She said she felt so sorry for that old bachelor she came right home and gave Homer a terrible talking to. Said if he didn't bring Myrtle home she'd make him eat his dinners downtown for a whole month.

CORA. Oh, she didn't either, Arry!

ARRY (*to* CORA). She told me she did! (*To* THOR.) She said she wasn't going to have any son of hers end up the way that old bachelor in the movie did.

THOR. Why? How'd he end up?

ARRY. He shot himself. (*They all giggle.* ARRY *crosses center and takes last piece of banana as she goes.*) Anyway, Ida's right about that old bachelor business. Homer's forty years old his last birthday, remember. If he's going to marry Myrtle he'd better do it pretty soon. (*Sits stump.*)

THOR. Well, I don't think Ida ought to rush him. You got to let a man work out those things for himself.

CORA. Homer likes his *home*. He likes it here with his mother.

ARRY. Well, I just wonder what Myrtle thinks. I see myself waiting twelve years for any man.

THOR. You been waiting sixty-five years for one! (*He laughs heartily.*)

ARRY (*flaring up—rises*). Don't you worry, Theodore Swanson! I could have had plenty of men if I'd wanted them!

THOR (*suddenly placating*). Sure you could, Arry.

ARRY. And they're plenty I could have right now too! Don't fool yourself about that!

THOR. Sure there are.

ARRY. Don't think I don't see the way men look at me on the street. I know what they're thinking. I could have a home of my own in two minutes if I wanted one. (*Crosses to* THOR.)

THOR. Don't doubt it for a second, Arry.

ARRY. I was the prettiest of all us four sisters, wasn't I, Cora?

CORA. No. You weren't as pretty as Esty.

ARRY. Well, I was prettier than you or Ida. And look at what Esty got. Do you think I'd be married to a man like David?

THOR. Of course you wouldn't, Arry.

ARRY (*crosses to porch steps*). Trouble with me is I never saw a man who was worth the powder to blow him up with. Pretty poor specimens on the whole. (*She is now halfway up the steps. Puts her hand out for banana and finds it gone.*) Where'd that banana go? (CORA *holds up the empty skins.* ARRY *giggles.*) For goodness' sakes, did I eat all that?

CORA. No, I had a bite.

ARRY. Want me to get you another one?

CORA. No, I've had enough.

(ARRY *returns to her post on the porch.*)

THOR. You know what I hate most about this Myrtle-Homer situation?

CORA. What?

THOR. That nice house up there on Sycamore Drive that his father built for them.

(CORA *sits up.*)

CORA. You certainly do like that house, don't you, Thor?

THOR. Five years that house's been standing there empty. All nicely furnished. I said to Carl just the other day, "Why don't you rent that house until Homer's ready for it, Carl?"

CORA. You did! What'd he say?

THOR. He says "No, Thor, no. That's

Homer's house. I want it to be all new and ready for him any time he wants to move in." By God, if I was a young fellow I'd get married just to live in that nice house!

(*Pause.* ARRY *rises and comes to top step. In a confidential tone.*)

ARRY. Thor, you know what I've been wondering about Homer and Myrtle?

THOR. What?

ARRY. I wonder if there isn't something going on there.

CORA (*sitting up*). Oh, Arry!

ARRY. Oh, you can be as innocent as you like but I know what men are. Something could be going on there every night for all we know.

THOR. Nope! Couldn't be going on every night! She lives in North Lyons. They don't see each other every night.

CORA. Well, I think that's a terrible thought to have about your own nephew!

ARRY. Well, it certainly could be true, couldn't it, Thor?

THOR (*expanding*). Well, it's hard to say. If it was anybody but Homer I'd be inclined to say it could be. But Homer —I don't know.

CORA. Well, I know it isn't! Homer has never spent a night away from his home in his whole life as far as I know. He's always here in the mornings.

ARRY. Well, my goodness, he wouldn't have to spend the whole night, would he?

(*Suddenly the door of the house at left is thrown open and* IDA *comes out hurriedly onto the porch and motions to* CORA.)

IDA. Cora! Cora!

CORA (*rising and starting toward her on a run*). What's the matter, Ida?

IDA. Come here a minute.

(CORA *hurries to her and the two step inside the screen door and stand there whispering excitedly.* IDA'*s sudden burst out of the door has brought* THOR *and* ARRY *out of their lethargy.* THOR *leans forward in his chair, and* ARRY *crosses center. They both watch with curiosity and excitement. Pause. The whispering goes on.* ARRY *can stand it no longer.*)

ARRY (*suddenly*). Yap, yap, yap, yap, yap! When those two get together they're like a couple of old hens.

THOR. What's the matter with her?

ARRY. How do I know? Does anybody ever tell *me* anything?

THOR (*rising*). Gee, Ida seems excited.

ARRY. It's "Cora, Cora, Cora" all the time! They just like to keep me out of things. She's probably burned her roast and I hope she has! (*She crosses back to* THOR *and speaks in a low voice.*) And another thing, Theodore Swanson, the next time Cora starts any more of this business about me getting a man and having a home of my own like she did this morning—

THOR (*uncomfortable—sits*). Oh, Arry, Cora didn't mean anything.

ARRY. Well, I don't know. Cora's made a couple of awful funny remarks lately about me living by myself. She's got some bee in her bonnet. She's up to something.

THOR. Oh, she isn't either.

ARRY. Well, she hadn't better be, that's all I say.

THOR. Now your home's right here with us, Arry. Just as long as you want it.

ARRY. Well, don't you forget it either. I guess I'm entitled to some consideration around here.

(CORA *starts back.*)

THOR. All right. All right. Now keep still. Here comes Cora.

(IDA *has gone back into house.* CORA *joins* ARRY *and* THOR.)

ARRY. Well, did you have your little conference?

CORA. Oh, my goodness, it's Carl! Ida says he's acting funny.

ARRY (*quickly*). He's not going to have a spell, is he?

CORA. That's what she's afraid of. He's got his forehead leaned up against the kitchen wall and he won't move. Everybody's having to walk around him.

ARRY (*crossing center*). Oh, that's it, all right! No doubt about it!

CORA. That poor Allen girl doesn't know what's the matter. She's scared stiff. And Ida's nearly frantic. With Homer and Myrtle coming—

ARRY (*crossing back to* THOR). And that's just what brought it on! Myrtle! Don't you see? He can't face her. That's the way it always used to be. Any new person he wanted to make an impression on— Oh, I bet he's going to have a terrible spell! I'd better go over and see what I can do. (*She starts over.*)

CORA (*grabbing her*). You do no such thing!

ARRY. Oh, my goodness!

CORA. You stay right where you are!

(*At this point* ARRY *is looking up the drive. She turns suddenly and calls in a hoarse voice.*)

ARRY. Thor!

THOR (*jumping*). Huh? What?

ARRY (*running up on the porch*—THOR *and* CORA *following*). They're here! They're here! (CORA *and* THOR *are back*—ARRY *way out in view.*) Oh, my goodness, he really brought her! Look! Look! (*She dances in excitement.*)

CORA (*pulling her back out of view*). Now be careful, Arry. Go up closer to the house.

(*They station themselves right in front of the door, and all huddle together, looking down the drive toward the front of the house opposite.* ARRY *is nearest the corner,* THOR *behind her,* CORA *behind him.*)

ARRY. Look! Look! They're getting out! That's her! That's Myrtle! Oh, Lord, he's helping her out of the car!

THOR. Yes sir, by God, he certainly is!

ARRY. Look! He's got hold of her arm!

THOR. By God, he has! Imagine that!

ARRY. You don't think she's a cripple or something?

CORA. Oh, Arry, he's just helping her.

ARRY. Well, he's certainly doing a good job of it—My goodness, look how he's got hold of her arm! You can't tell me there isn't something going on there!

CORA. We'd better go in. We can see better from the dining room anyway.

(CARL *enters from the other house.* THOR *sees him, but* ARRY *and* CORA *don't.* THOR *tries to draw* ARRY's *attention by nudging her.*)

ARRY. Look! Look! Stop pushing, Thor. There they go—Stop it, Thor.

THOR (*taking the bull by the horns*). Good afternoon, Carl.

(ARRY *and* CORA *look up guiltily and look over at* CARL *with a mixture of curiosity and embarrassment. They start moving away nonchalantly from their posts.*)

CARL (*quietly*). Good afternoon, Thor.

CORA (*crossing to head of porch steps and down*). Oh, good afternoon, Carl.

CARL (*crossing center a bit*). Good afternoon, Cora.

ARRY (*at the head of steps. With an embarrassed laugh*). Well, I see you've got company.

CARL. Yes. Homer brought Myrtle for over Sunday.

ARRY. Oh, is that it? Isn't that nice.

(*Pause.* CARL *stands there quietly. The others don't know what to do.* THOR *crosses center*—ARRY *comes down the steps.*)

THOR (*heartily*). Well, begins to look as if you're going to have that house oc-cupied pretty soon, Carl. Up there on Sycamore Drive.

CARL (*trying to force a laugh*). Yes. Yes, it does, doesn't it?

THOR (*encouraged*). Well, I'll be glad to see it happen. I always say all you have to do is to leave young people alone and pretty soon things will take care of themselves. Guess that's about the size of it.

(*Pause.* CARL *hasn't been listening. He has been staring past them. Now he looks up quickly, noticing the silence.*)

CARL. What's that?

THOR (*lamely*). I say I guess that's about the size of it.

CARL. Oh!

(*He crosses to tree down left and puts his hand against it and then leans his head on his hand. Pause.* CORA, ARRY *and* THOR *all stand watching him a minute.*)

THOR (*in an awed whisper*). By God, he's having a spell all right!

CORA. Poor Ida! I'd better telephone her he's out of the kitchen. (*She goes in house right.*)

ARRY (*following up the steps*). I think we ought to 'phone Esty about it all, too. It's only fair. Goodness knows she doesn't have much in her life any more. Come on, Thor. (*She stands with screen door open.*)

THOR. All right. I kind of hate to leave Carl. (*Phone rings.*) There! There's Cora talking to her now.

(*They exit into house.* CARL *is still leaning against the tree.* IDA *enters—doesn't see* CARL.)

IDA. Carl! (*He makes no sign.*) Carl! (*Still makes no sign. She sees him. Crosses to him.*) Carl! What *is* the matter? You're not really going to have a spell, are you? Answer me, Carl! (*She shakes his arm.*) Now you've got to stop this. Right away! Before it gets hold of you! You've got to shake it off and come right into the house with me and see Myrtle and Homer. They want you to come in.

CARL. They don't want to see me.

IDA. They do, Carl! They do! Myrtle asked for you especially. She wants to meet you.

CARL. Why should she want to meet me?

IDA. Stop talking that way, Carl!

CARL. Why should anybody want to meet a failure like me!

IDA. Oh, Carl, you're just giving in to it! Now stop it! Myrtle is here. You've got to help entertain her. You know how hard it is for Homer to talk in front of strangers. You're the host, Carl. You just *can't* have a spell now!

CARL (*straightens up—faces front*). I never asked much out of life! Never made many demands! All I wanted to be was just a dentist!

IDA. Oh, my goodness! Never mind about that now, Carl!

CARL. That's not so much to ask! Just to be a dentist. Charlie Watson went on and became a dentist! But I wasn't up to it!

IDA. Of course you were, Carl! It just didn't work out that way.

CARL. I had a lofty ideal but I never achieved it.

IDA. You're just as good as anybody else, Carl.

CARL. I failed!

(*He leans on the tree again.* HOMER *and* MYRTLE *come out onto the porch at door stage left center.* HOMER *speaks.*)

HOMER. This's the back yard.

IDA (*pushing* CARL *off left—they both exit*). Oh, my goodness! They're coming out! Carl! Carl!

MYRTLE (*crosses to center opening on porch*). The back yard! Oh, isn't it lovely!

HOMER (*at head of steps—points stage left*). That's the garage.

MYRTLE. Oh, yes! Isn't it nice!

HOMER (*crosses down—then center*). That one's my father's and mine and that one's Uncle Thor's. My father built them both.

MYRTLE. He must be terribly clever.

HOMER. He's a good builder. (*Pause—* HOMER *points right.*) That's the hedge.

MYRTLE (*following down*). Oh, yes.

HOMER. That's where Aunt Cora thinks she heard a man hilding a couple of times.

MYRTLE. Oh, that's right. I remember.

HOMER. She says she heard him cough once just about dark.

MYRTLE. Well, does she think it's somebody watching the house?

HOMER. I guess so. Guess she just imagined it though.

MYRTLE. Oh!

HOMER. Uncle Thor says it's probably just one of Aunt Arry's men hanging around to check up on her.

MYRTLE. Oh, maybe that's it.

HOMER. No, that's a joke.

MYRTLE. Oh, I see. (*She laughs at the joke, nervously. Sees* IDA *who is backing on stage left—looking off after* CARL. MYRTLE *steps toward her.*) Oh, there you are! Did you find Mr. Bolton?

IDA (*a bit flustered*). I—I guess he must have gone for a little walk.

MYRTLE (*looking off left*). Oh, dear. I do so want to meet him.

IDA (*blanking her view*). Oh, he'll be back in time for supper. He often takes a little walk about this time.

MYRTLE (*in her best social manner*). I love your back yard, Mrs. Bolton. It looks so cool. It's simply heavenly.

IDA. Yes, we like it very much.

MYRTLE. All the trees and everything. I bet you sit out here all the time.

IDA. We sit out here a good deal of the time.

MYRTLE. Well, I should think you would. It's simply heavenly. I don't know when I've seen a more attractive back yard.

IDA. Yes, we're very fond of it.

MYRTLE. Well, I should think so. It's so nice and wild, too. Like being in a forest.

IDA. I'm glad you like it.

MYRTLE. Well, I certainly do. It's simply—heavenly, that's all there is to it.

IDA. Well, it's nice of you to say so.

MYRTLE. Well, I mean it.

(*Pause. Conversation comes to an end abruptly—* HOMER *steps forward.*)

HOMER (*suddenly*). Have mosquitoes sometimes.

IDA. Yes, there are mosquitoes sometimes.

MYRTLE. How dreadful!

IDA. But I don't think we've had quite so many this year as usual. Have you noticed that, Homer?

HOMER (*in a loud voice*). Not so many. That's right.

MYRTLE. Isn't it interesting the way those things go? (*To* HOMER.) One year you'll have a lot of mosquitoes and the next year not so many mosquitoes. (*To* IDA.) Or a lot of caterpillars one year and the next year not so many caterpillars. I wonder why that is.

IDA. I don't know why that is. Do you, Homer?

HOMER. No. I don't know why it is.

MYRTLE. It's very interesting, isn't it? Anyway I suppose the mosquitoes and caterpillars and all those things have some purpose. They wouldn't have been put here if they hadn't.

IDA. No, I don't suppose they would have.

HOMER. Don't suppose so.

MYRTLE. It's all a part of some big plan. Some big—plan of some kind.

(*Pause. Conversation ends abruptly.*)

HOMER (*suddenly*). Want to sit down?

MYRTLE. All right. (*Crosses to stump.*) I'll take this cozy little place over here. Won't you sit down too, Mrs. Bolton?

IDA (*starting up steps*). No, I really should be about supper.

MYRTLE. Oh, do sit down for just a minute.

IDA (*reluctantly sits chair left center*). Well, for just a minute then. (*In silence they sit.* HOMER *squats down and starts cutting weeds with his pen knife.* MYRTLE *and* IDA *smile at each other.* IDA *on the edge of her chair. Short pause.* IDA *rises.*) And now I really must go in. (*Crosses to head of steps.* HOMER *rises.*) I'll leave you two youngsters out here by yourselves. I guess you can attend to yourselves all right.

MYRTLE (*rises—giggling, embarrassed*). Well—maybe we can.

IDA. You probably have a lot to talk over.

HOMER. We haven't got anything to talk over.

IDA. Of course you have! I know! I'll come out again as soon as I can—If you should see your father tell him I want to see him, Homer.

HOMER. All right, Mother. (*She goes into house left.*)

MYRTLE (*sits on stump*). Oh, I think your mother's too wonderful!

HOMER. She's pretty nice, all right.

MYRTLE. She's so *friendly!* She's just what a mother should be!

HOMER. She's pretty nice. (*He sits in chair left center.*)

MYRTLE. Oh, she's more than that. She's so—*human!* (*Pause.* HOMER *sits staring before him.* MYRTLE *rises—croses up of stump—looks at the house right.*) And that's where your Uncle Thor and Aunt Cora live.

HOMER. And Aunt Arry.

MYRTLE. Oh, yes. She's the maiden aunt, isn't she?

HOMER. She's the old maid.

(MYRTLE *gives a little nervous laugh.*)

MYRTLE. How long has she been living with them?

HOMER. About forty-five to fifty years.

MYRTLE. My goodness, that must be pretty hard on your Aunt Cora.

HOMER. Why? They're sisters.

MYRTLE (*sits on stump*). Yes, but wouldn't you think a woman would want to live alone—I mean just alone with her husband.

HOMER. Aunt Arry didn't have any other place to go when her mother died so Aunt Cora took her in.

MYRTLE. Aunt Cora must be pretty nice, I think, to share her home like that.

HOMER. Aunt Cora's nice. Not as nice as mother.

MYRTLE. Oh, of course not! Of course not. My goodness—Anyway it must be awfully pleasant for all of them to live so close together now that they're getting older. They must be a lot of company for each other.

HOMER. Then there's Aunt Esther, too.

MYRTLE. Oh, yes, Aunt Esther.

HOMER (*indicating with his finger*). She lives up the street about a block and a half.

MYRTLE. And she's married to—?

HOMER. Uncle David.

MYRTLE. That's right. He's the one who studies all the time.

HOMER. He's a very highly educated man. He doesn't like us.

MYRTLE. Why not?

HOMER. He thinks we're morons.

MYRTLE. Morons? Why does he think that?

HOMER. I don't know. He says we don't think about important enough things.

MYRTLE. Does he think about important things?

HOMER. Practically all of the time.

MYRTLE. What does he do?

HOMER. Doesn't do anything now. He used to be a college professor. But he couldn't get along with the President.

MYRTLE. Oh.

HOMER. He said the President was a moron too!

MYRTLE. Well, he doesn't think *you're* a moron, Homer?

HOMER. He thinks we all are except my father.

MYRTLE. Why, what's the matter with your father?

HOMER. He says my father has something more than the rest of us. Something that makes him question life sometimes.

MYRTLE. Oh, I see.

HOMER. But the rest of us are all morons. That's why he never comes down here and never lets any of us come up there.

MYRTLE. He sounds awfully odd to me.

HOMER. He doesn't let Aunt Esther come down either. He's afraid we'll pull her down to our level.

MYRTLE. So she never comes down.

HOMER. Just when he doesn't know it. She hasn't been down now for over a week though.

MYRTLE (*rises—crosses left—takes off hat and leaves it on porch*). I'm afraid I wouldn't like your Uncle David very well.

HOMER. Oh, I think you would. He's awfully nice. I've always sort of liked Uncle David.

(*Pause.* MYRTLE *turns to* HOMER.)

MYRTLE. Homer—do you think your mother liked me?

HOMER. She didn't say anything—I guess so though.

MYRTLE. Dear, I hope she did. I tried to make a good impression on her. I liked her so much.

HOMER. She's pretty nice all right.

MYRTLE. It was terribly sweet of her to ask me to come. (*Pause. She takes a quick look at him. Steps toward him.*) Of course I couldn't help but wonder why it just happened that this time you decided to bring me. Because she has asked you to before, hasn't she?

HOMER (*uncomfortable*). Uh-huh.

(*Pause.*)

MYRTLE. I mean I wondered if anything happened to change your mind about bringing me.

(*Slight pause.*)

HOMER (*suddenly*). My mother saw a movie.

MYRTLE. A movie?

HOMER. Uh-huh.

MYRTLE. Oh! (*Pause.*) I guess she wouldn't think very much of me if she knew about us, would she?

HOMER. Well, there's no reason for her to know.

MYRTLE. She'd think I wasn't very nice.

HOMER. Older people don't understand things like that very well, Myrtle. Maybe we'd better not talk about it here.

MYRTLE (*sits on ledge of porch steps*). Oh, all right. Of course your mother must think it's rather funny about you and me though. Being engaged so long. (*Pause.*) Hasn't she ever asked you anything about it? About when we're going to get married, I mean?

HOMER. Uh-huh.

MYRTLE. What did you say to her?

HOMER. I told her you had a job.

MYRTLE. Oh!—Well, I was thinking about my job the other day. I was wondering whether I oughtn't to give it up.

HOMER. I thought you liked it.

MYRTLE. Oh, I do! It's a good job. But—well, I get awfully sick of it sometimes. And after all, I am thirty-nine years old, you know.

(*Pause.* MYRTLE *stares at* HOMER. *Nervously, he looks off left.*)

HOMER (*pointing off left*). My father set out most of these trees himself. Transplanted some of them. That one there I remember when it was just a twig he brought over from a house he was building on Maple Street. It must have been fifteen years ago.

MYRTLE. My, you wouldn't think it would get that big in fifteen years.

HOMER. They grow awfully fast.

(*Pause.* HOMER *is staring before him.* MYRTLE *looks at him, nervously.*)

MYRTLE. There isn't anything the matter, is there, Homer?

HOMER (*shaking his head*). Un-uh—

MYRTLE. You're not mad at me about anything, are you?

HOMER. No.

MYRTLE. You act so funny here. Are you sorry you brought me after all?

HOMER. No, I guess not.

(MYRTLE *smiles at him and suddenly takes his arm and snuggles to him.*)

MYRTLE. You silly!

HOMER (*pulling away*). They'll see you from the other house, Myrtle.

MYRTLE. Oh! (*She drops his arm. Pause. Then she rises and moves over by the trees left— stands looking off.*) I get awfully lonesome sometimes about this time of day. Or maybe a little later. I guess it's really not so bad at the office. I'm usually pretty busy. But when I get through and have to go to my room—And then when it starts getting dark—(*Turns to* HOMER.) Often when I know you're not going to be coming down I don't bother to get myself any supper. I just go right to bed. (*They laugh—embarrassed. Pause.*) Sometimes I wonder how I ever happened to get stuck with that job. It doesn't seem natural. I guess when you come right down to it what a woman really wants is a home of her own.

(*Pause.* HOMER *makes no answer.* ARRY *wanders out from the porch at right, casually, as though she were not aware of the others. They watch her for a time without speaking. She fans herself energetically.*)

HOMER. That's Aunt Arry. (*Pause as* ARRY *looks off right.*) She knows we're here.

MYRTLE. Oh!

(*They watch her as she wanders down center pretending not to notice them. Sees a weed and makes a great fuss over picking it up. Then notices* HOMER *and* MYRTLE, *with much surprise.*)

ARRY. Oh! Oh, hello, Homer.

HOMER. Hello, Aunt Arry.

ARRY (*throwing the weed over the hedge*). When did you get home?

HOMER. Little while ago.

ARRY. Well! (*Pause.* ARRY *waits expectantly. As there is no move toward an introduction she bows politely to* MYRTLE.) How do you do?

MYRTLE. How do you do?

ARRY. It has been a pleasant day, hasn't it?

MYRTLE. Hasn't it?

(*Pause. Nothing more to say.*)

HOMER (*suddenly—rising*).This's Myrtle Brown.

ARRY.Oh!Oh,how do you do,Myrtle?

MYRTLE. How do you do?

ARRY. I'm Homer's aunt.

MYRTLE. Well, I guess I know that. You're Aunt Arry. You're the one that sent me that handsome linen luncheon set for my hope chest.

ARRY (*confused*). Oh, my goodness, that wasn't anything.

MYRTLE (*crossing center*). Well, I just guess it *was* something! That's about the most handsome linen luncheon set I've ever seen.

ARRY (*laughs, embarrassed*). Did you really like it?

MYRTLE. I certainly did. You'd be surprised how often I take that luncheon set out and look at it. Sometimes those flowers on the napkins seem to me to be absolutely real.

ARRY (*flattered—turns away a bit, laughs*). They're appliquéd, you know.

MYRTLE. I know they are. You must have used your eyes altogether too much doing that.

ARRY. Oh, my goodness! I don't have very much to do. I'm working on a quilt.

It's appliquéd, too. Perhaps you'd like to see it while you're here.

MYRTLE. I'd simply love to.

HOMER (*suddenly*). Myrtle knits.

(CORA *is seen passing the screen door, house right.*)

ARRY (*bowing pleasantly*). Oh?—Haven't seen your father yet, have you, Homer?

(CORA *listens in door.*)

HOMER. No.

ARRY (*crossing to steps*). Dear, I hope he's going to be all right.

(HOMER *looks up suddenly, startled. At the same moment* CORA *sticks her head out of the door.*)

CORA (*hissing*). Arry!

ARRY (*crossing to* CORA). Oh, all right, Cora. (*Sweetly to others as she starts in.*) I guess I have to help with supper. I just came out for a breath of air.

HOMER (*rising abruptly*). Where is Father?

ARRY (*crossing down the steps again*). I don't know, Homer. He and Ida were out there in the yard when you came out. I just happened to notice them from the house. He must have gone off through the hedge.

(HOMER *turns suddenly and goes off to the house.* MYRTLE *watches him, startled.*)

MYRTLE (*crossing after him a bit*). Well, Homer, what—?

HOMER (*at the door*). Mother!

(MYRTLE *turns back to* ARRY, *who is nearly in the house again.*)

MYRTLE. Mr. Bolton isn't ill, is he?

ARRY (*crossing center on porch. Confidentially.*) Well, no, he isn't ill exactly, but you see sometimes he has these awful sp——

(*This time* CORA *comes right out onto the back porch.*)

CORA. Arry!

ARRY. Oh, my goodness!

CORA. It's time to set table.

ARRY (*giving* CORA *a cross look—turns back to* MYRTLE *sweetly*). Well, I'm very glad to have met you, Myrtle. Perhaps we'll see you after supper.

MYRTLE. I hope so.

(ARRY *bows politely to* MYRTLE *and starts in door.*)

ARRY (*in an undertone to* CORA). I wasn't going to tell her a thing!

(*She exits—*CORA *has been staring curiously at* MYRTLE.)

CORA (*stepping forward—embarrassed*).

How do you do, Myrtle?

MYRTLE. How do you do?

CORA. I expect we'll meet each other after supper.

MYRTLE. I expect so.

CORA. Well, excuse me. I've got to go in now. (*Starts in.*)

MYRTLE. All right.

(CORA *turns back.*)

CORA. I'm Aunt Cora.

MYRTLE. Yes, I know. (CORA *bows politely and goes in quickly.* IDA *and* HOMER *come out of house left, and start down the steps.* HOMER *acts very moody.*) Is there anything wrong with Mr. Bolton?

IDA (*crossing down to chair*). No, no, he just had a little headache is all. He'll walk it off and be all right when he gets back.

MYRTLE (*sits stump*). Oh!

IDA. And I guess I can sit down for a little while now. Supper's nearly ready.

(*Sits chair*—HOMER *sits on porch step by* IDA.)

MYRTLE. It is? I had no idea it was so late. (*Rises—crosses to porch left.*) I think I'd better go in and wash up then.

IDA. Oh, all right. Just ask the Allen girl in there and she'll show you where to go. The little towel with the escalloped border is for you.

MYRTLE. Oh, all right, thank you. I won't be long.

(MYRTLE *exits.* HOMER *rises—crosses center.*)

IDA. Now, Homer!

HOMER (*center*). I don't care, Mother! If he started talking about going back to the fork again.

IDA. But I tell you he didn't. He didn't say anything about the fork at all.

HOMER. Are you sure?

IDA. It hadn't got to that.

HOMER. Well, it hadn't better! If he starts talking about going back to the fork again—

IDA. Well, he didn't. I felt kind of sorry for him this time. It was one of those dentist spells. Now stop acting up and sit down. I want to tell you how much I like Myrtle. I think she's just as nice as she can be.

(HOMER *sits stump.*)

HOMER. Well, I wish you wouldn't leave me alone with her all the time.

IDA. Now Homer—!

HOMER. I don't care, it's embarrassing. I don't know what to say to her.

IDA. Well, aren't you the limit. What do you say to her when you go down to visit her in North Lyons?

HOMER. That's different.

IDA. You are a goose, aren't you?

HOMER. Well, I just wish you wouldn't leave us alone. She keeps hinting things when you're not with us.

IDA. What things?

HOMER. Oh, she wants to know why I brought her home.

IDA. Well, I should think she'd know that. When a man brings a girl home to meet his mother—

HOMER. Now, Mother, you know I haven't made up my mind about anything yet!

IDA. Now Homer—!

HOMER (*shaking his head obstinately*). Haven't made up my mind.

IDA. Well, when are you going to?

HOMER. Well, I like it living here at home.

IDA. But that's no excuse. And it isn't as though you'd be going way off somewhere. After all, Sycamore Drive is only half a mile away. You can come down here every night if you want to at first.

HOMER. It wouldn't be the same.

IDA. You'll be surprised how quickly you'll feel at home in that new house, Homer.

HOMER. But I've got all my things here and everything.

IDA. Well, I just wish you'd seen that movie I saw, Homer. That movie actor even looked a little like you.

HOMER. Who was it?

IDA. Oh, nobody important.

HOMER. Oh!

IDA. But he certainly gave you a very clear picture of just how lonely an old bachelor can be.

(*Pause.*)

HOMER (*turns to* IDA). You'd be awfully lonesome.

IDA (*turning away from him*). Oh, I don't say it's going to be easy for me either.

HOMER. Of course it isn't.

IDA. It'll seem strange not to have you coming home after your day's work. But I've had you a long time. Longer than most mothers.

HOMER. I don't know what you'd do with my little room up there.

IDA. I've thought of that too. I think I'll keep it just as it is. And you'll know that it'll be ready for you any time you want it. Perhaps you'll want to spend a night down here sometime—you and Myrtle.

HOMER (*gloomily*). My room's too small for two people.

IDA. We might move in a double bed.

HOMER (*embarrassed*). Oh, Mother! (*Pause. They are both rather embarrassed.* HOMER *rises and crosses left. It starts to grow dark.* HOMER *turns back to face his mother.*) And Myrtle gets so personal sometimes.

IDA. What do you mean?

HOMER. Oh, she wants to know all sorts of things. The other day she asked me what size underwear I wore.

IDA. She did? What for?

HOMER. I guess she wanted to buy me some.

IDA. Well, that does seem odd.

HOMER. She wrote it down in a little book she's got.

(*Pause. They are both depressed.*)

IDA. Of course after you're married she'll be buying your underwear.

(*Pause.*)

HOMER. There's something awful nice about Myrtle though.

IDA. Of course there is.

HOMER. She's awfully good-hearted and she does nice little things for you all the time.

IDA. Does she?

HOMER. She's awfully lonesome down there in North Lyons too. It isn't that I'm not awfully fond of her, Mother.

IDA. Do you love her, Homer?

HOMER. Well, I wouldn't want never to see her again. (*Pause.*) Mother.

IDA. Yes, Homer?

HOMER. If I was to marry Myrtle do you think I'd—get used to it?

IDA (*faintly*). I guess so—

HOMER. I don't know. Maybe I would. And you want me to do it so bad—(IDA *is crying.*) Mother, what's the matter! (HOMER *crosses to* IDA.)

IDA. Never mind me, Homer!

HOMER. Mother, you're crying!

IDA. I never thought of that! That she'd be buying your underwear! (*She has a fresh burst of crying and gets up and starts toward the house.*)

HOMER. Mother—

IDA (*as she exits into house left*). Never mind me, Homer. I'll be all right. I'm just a silly old goose!

(HOMER *pushes the chair back. Kicks the ground, disgusted with himself for upsetting*

his mother. *He wanders down to the tree left and leans against it much as his father did. It has become quite dark.* THOR *comes out of the door at right and stands on the porch. Suddenly he sees* HOMER *and stares at him in amazement.*)

THOR (*softly*). By God! (*He puts his head into the door.*) Arry! Cora! Come here! (HOMER *starts up guiltily, having heard* THOR. THOR *comes back out and looks over at* HOMER. *He sees that* HOMER *has heard him. Casually.*) Oh, that you, Homer?

HOMER. Yes.

(CORA *and* ARRY *rush out of the house and stop abruptly at a signal from* THOR. *They stare at* HOMER.)

THOR. What you doing out there all by yourself?

HOMER. Nothing—I—I was just going in. (*He starts up the steps left.*)

THOR (*crossing center*). Anything the matter with you?

HOMER. No—no(*He goes into the house, hurriedly.*)

ARRY (*crossing down with* CORA). What is it? What's the matter?

THOR. Homer, by God! He was having a spell! I damn near thought it was Carl!

CORA (*excited*). What do you mean, Thor?

THOR. Had his head leaned up on that tree just like Carl does!

CORA. No!

THOR. Yes!

ARRY. Heredity!

THOR. By God, it is! It's heredity!

(ESTHER *is seen hurrying down between the houses.*)

CORA. No, no, it can't be!

THOR. He was standing just like this! (*He turns suddenly and leans his forehead against the back of the house, his rear facing the audience.*)

ARRY. That's it! That's it! Just the way Carl does!

(ESTHER *appears.*)

CORA. Here's Esty!

ESTHER. Good gracious! What's happened to Thor?

ARRY. Esty! Esty! Now Homer's got 'em!

ESTHER. Got what?

ARRY. Spells! Like Carl's!

ESTHER (*pointing to* THOR). You mean Thor!

THOR (*disgusted*). Naw, naw. Homer!

ARRY. Thor saw him standing right against that tree over there. (ESTHER *laughs suddenly.*) Well, I don't see what there is to laugh at!

ESTHER (*sitting on the stump*). Now, Arry, you don't really think Homer's going to have spells too?

ARRY. I certainly do!

ESTHER. Well, I don't! I don't think Homer's got the gumption to have a spell. He's too lazy.

CORA (*giggling*). Of course he is.

(ESTHER *laughs with her.*)

ARRY. Of course you two smarties would know it all! And Thor saw him with his own eyes! Didn't you, Thor?

THOR. Well, you know it was kind of dark—I just thought for a minute it looked funny—

ARRY (*angry*). Well, Theodore Swanson! How can you back down like that?

THOR. You know how it is, Arry—I got kind of excited—

ARRY. You mean to stand there and say Homer's not going to have spells? After bringing us all the way out here?

THOR (*apologetically*). No, I guess not, Arry—Maybe he was just kind of resting.

ARRY (*crossing up the stairs*). Well, if I couldn't live up to my convictions better than that—Men have no more courage than—(*Exits into house.*)

THOR. Oh, Arry! (*He starts after her.*) I'll just go in and—I guess I shouldn't have said anything about it at all.

CORA. Oh, let her alone, Thor. Don't pamper her so!

THOR. No, I don't want her to be mad at me. Poor Arry! She's all alone in the world.

(*He goes in.* ESTHER *rises and crosses to porch steps by* CORA.)

CORA (*disgusted*). All alone in the world! The way Arry can always take Thor in—(*Turns to* ESTY—*they smile at each other*—*both sit on porch steps.*) It's good to see you, Esty. You don't have to get right back, do you?

ESTHER. David'll be back from his walk in a little while. I want to be there before he is. Carl hasn't come back yet, has he?

CORA. Not yet.

ESTHER. Ida phoned me. She wants me to talk to him if he's acting bad.

CORA. Oh, I think he'll be all right. It's just one of those dentist spells.

ESTHER. Well, I've seen those dentist spells when they got pretty bad sometimes. It's only one step from a dentist

spell to a "Where am I" spell, you know.

CORA. Now, Esty! Carl's not going to have a "Where am I" spell!

ESTHER. I certainly hope not.

CORA. Why, he hasn't had one of those in years and years.

ESTHER. Well, we can't do anything until he gets back. I'll talk to him. Maybe if he isn't too far gone it might help some—Now tell me. Have you met Myrtle yet?

CORA. I haven't really met her. I just talked to her a second.

ESTHER (*controlling a giggle*). What's she like?

CORA (*giggling nervously*). Now, Esty! She's very nice! Not the way we imagined at all!

ESTHER. She has got teeth like this though, hasn't she?

CORA. Now, Esty, she has no such thing!

ESTHER. And she talks like this to Homer.

(*They both giggle.*)

CORA. She doesn't either! She's perfectly all right! And we shouldn't sit here and giggle about it!

ESTHER. I can't help it! Somehow the idea of Homer's having a girl—

CORA. You know what Arry thinks? Well, Arry thinks that maybe everything isn't as straight there as it might be.

ESTHER. Well, maybe it isn't. Wonderful things can happen.

CORA. Esty!

(*This sends them into a mild case of hysterics.*)

ESTHER (*she wipes her eyes*). My goodness, I haven't laughed so much for a long time.

CORA. That's right. How *is* David behaving?

ESTHER. Oh, I don't know, Cora. This last week I've hardly been out of the house.

CORA. I think it's a shame.

ESTHER. He made me promise I'd never come down again without his permission.

CORA. You didn't promise him—?

ESTHER. Well—I—I really had to. He said—(*She gives a nervous giggle.*) He said if I ever came down again I'd—I'd have to live on the second floor the rest of my life.

CORA. Live on the second floor?

ESTHER. Upstairs. And he'd live downstairs.

CORA. But that's silly, Esty! You couldn't live on the second floor.

ESTHER. I guess I'd have to. The house divided, you know.

CORA. How would you get your meals?

ESTHER. He says I can come down the back stairs and use the kitchen when I want it.

CORA. If that isn't just like David! Why doesn't *he* live on the second floor?

ESTHER. He thought it would be easier for me on account of the bathroom.

CORA. Oh! Well, what would *he* do for a bathroom?

ESTHER. He'd have another put in. In that little closet off the kitchen.

CORA. But that would cost money, Esty!

ESTHER. I know it would. That's the one thing that worries me. Of course he'd only put in a seat and a basin. He says maybe I'd let him use the bath now and then.

CORA (*sharply*). Well, *I* wouldn't!

ESTHER. Oh, I'd have to. He says he'll put up a bell that will ring when he wants to use it. So we wouldn't bump into each other.

CORA. And you wouldn't see each other at all?

ESTHER. I guess not. He says if we're going to be independent we might as well be independent. Of course if we should meet in the hall we'd bow to each other, like two acquaintances.

CORA. Well, he's just trying to scare you, Esty. And I think you ought to take a stand against him! You ought to be able to come down here any time you want to. David's just jealous!

ESTHER. I know it, Cora. He gets more so all the time. If he'd only stop talking about his Crystal Fortress.

CORA. You know, Esty, I always thought that Crystal Fortress was rather a lovely idea.

ESTHER. You wouldn't if you'd lived in it fifty-five years.

CORA. No, I think it's lovely. Your friends or anybody can come up to the fortress and look in through the door—and you can see them and talk to them and everything—but no one can ever really come into it except just the two of you. Just you two all alone there by yourselves. It must be nice sometimes to be all alone with—the person you live

with. (*Pause.* ESTHER *sits watching* CORA. *Suddenly* CORA *turns on her and says with surprising viciousness.*) Esty! I hope Homer doesn't marry Myrtle!

ESTHER. What!

CORA. Oh, I know it's selfish of me! But I hope he doesn't!

ESTHER. But why, Cora?

CORA. Because if he doesn't, Carl has promised to let me have that house up on Sycamore Drive, to lease it to me for as long as I want.

ESTHER. But what would you want with that house?

CORA. I want to live in it! I want for Thor and me to live in it! All by ourselves.

ESTHER. And this house?

CORA. Arry can have it! She can have everything that's in it!

ESTHER. I see.

CORA. Wouldn't it be wonderful, Esty?

ESTHER. Yes, I suppose it would, Cora.

CORA (*pause.* CORA *feels* ESTHER *staring at her*). Of course, I suppose it would make Arry good and mad.

ESTHER. Do you think Thor will do it?

CORA. Well, I—I don't know. I haven't asked him yet, of course.

ESTHER. When is Carl going to let you know?

CORA. Well, Carl says that if Homer doesn't say definitely that he's going to get married while Myrtle's here—that is, set an actual date and all—well, Carl thinks Homer never will marry her and then I can have the house. I've got the lease all drawn up, right here. All he's got to do is sign it.

(*She shows the lease in front of her waist.* ESTHER *looks at her sharply.*)

ESTHER (*rising*). Well, I just hope it goes through without making any trouble for anyone.

CORA (*rising—suspicious*). What do you mean? Who could it make any trouble for?

ESTHER. Oh, I didn't mean anybody in particular—I just meant—

CORA. I don't understand, Esty—

ESTHER. Shhh—!

CORA. What is it?

ESTHER. Carl.

CORA. Dear, I hope he's all right. How does he look to you?

ESTHER. I can't tell yet. Let's see what he'll do.

(CARL *has entered from stage left. The lights*

have gone on in the house and he stops in the patch of light from the window. Puts foot on step, and then decides not to go in. Stands there.)

CORA (*in a whisper*). Dear, he looks kind of sad standing there, doesn't he?

ESTHER. Yes, he does.

CORA. He's afraid to go in.

ESTHER. I guess I'd better go over.

CORA. You're not scared, are you?

ESTHER. No, I guess not.

CORA. I'll be in the kitchen watching if you want me.

ESTHER. All right. (CORA *exits into house right.* ESTHER *starts across to* CARL. *He is so absorbed staring at the house he doesn't hear* ESTHER *until she is on him*). Good evening, Carl.

(CARL *turns on her quickly and stands staring at her. Pause.*)

CARL. Oh!

ESTHER. It's Esty.

CARL. Oh, yes—

ESTHER. I'm sorry I startled you.

CARL (*confused*). Well, that's—that's all right, Esty—I was just—standing here—(*He becomes self-conscious and ashamed and, to cover it, very jovial.*) Well, well, how are you, Esty? How are you?

ESTHER. I'm all right, Carl.

CARL. Well, it's nice to see you. Haven't seen you for several days.

ESTHER. No, I've been pretty busy with my garden.

CARL (*pulling chair up by porch steps*). Well, come and sit down. How's David?

ESTHER (*she sits—*CARL *sits by her on steps*). David's fine.

CARL. Glad to hear it! Glad to hear it! Wonderful man, David. Wonderful man.

ESTHER. Yes, there's some fine things about David.

CARL. Fine things? No! He's a wonderful man, Esty! (CARL *suddenly realizes* ESTHER *has been staring at him. Pause. He becomes self-conscious and embarrassed.*) Well—er—Myrtle's here.

ESTHER. Yes, I know.

CARL. Haven't met her yet. Guess I will at supper.

ESTHER. I want to meet her too.

CARL (*eagerly*). You do? Well now, see here, Esty, you can go right in with me and we'll meet her together. (*He rubs his hands happily.*) Yes, sir, that's just what we'll do!

ESTHER. All right, Carl. Come on. Let's go in. (*She starts to rise.*)

CARL (*quickly stopping her*). No, no. Not just yet. Let's wait a minute. (*Pause. He is ashamed.*) Fact is, I sort of had one of my old—spells come on me, Esty.

ESTHER. Yes, Ida told me.

CARL. Guess I'm all right now.

ESTHER. Yes, you seem all right, Carl...

CARL. Yes. All right now. (*Pause—he suddenly drops his pose of joviality and turns on* ESTHER *intensely.*) It's just that—! Just that—! I'm not a stupid man, Esty!

ESTHER. I know you're not, Carl.

CARL. I'm not an educated man like David, but I'm not a stupid one!

ESTHER. Of course you're not.

CARL (*rising*). Then WHERE AM I, Esty? WHERE AM I?

ESTHER (*rising—sharply*). Now, Carl!

CARL (*excited*). That's what I say, "Where am I in life." I'm caught, Esty!

ESTHER. Now listen to me, Carl—

CARL. I'm not where I should be at all! There's some other place in life where I should be! I'm *Carl Bolton*, Esty!

ESTHER. Yes, yes, now be quiet—

CARL. The same Carl Bolton I was when I was a boy!

ESTHER. Yes, Carl, but—

CARL. But now I'm sixty-eight years old and WHERE AM I?

ESTHER. Now stop this, Carl!

CARL. Maybe I'm not Carl Bolton any more at all!

ESTHER. Well, maybe you're not!

(*Sudden pause.* CARL *stares at her slowly.*)

CARL. What's that, Esty?

ESTHER. I say maybe you're not Carl Bolton any more.

CARL. I don't understand. How could that be?

(ESTY *pats his arm reassuringly.*)

ESTHER. Carl, you don't think you're the only one who feels this way about things, do you?

CARL. Why—I don't know, Esty—

ESTHER. Well, I think lots of people feel exactly the same way as you do, only they don't go around having spells about it. You know, Carl, I don't think it's been any harder on you than on any of the others. Just think of all that Cora's been through. Never having a real home of her own . . . And Thor—Arry having the whip hand over him all these years... I bet sometimes he wishes he were somewhere else in life, too.

CARL. Yes, that's true, Esty, but—

ESTHER. Even if it only meant living alone with Cora in another house.

(*Pause.* CARL *looks up.*)

CARL. Did Cora tell you about that?

ESTHER. Yes. She said you might lease her the house.

CARL. Well, I—I did promise her, Esty. She kept at me so about it—I guess I shouldn't have, though—

ESTHER. Why not? If Homer isn't going to use it there's no reason to just go on keeping it empty.

CARL (*after slight pause*). But there's another thing about letting Cora have the house, though, you know, Esty—I mean—well, what do you think?

ESTHER. You mean—Arry?

CARL (*nods*). What do you think? Do you think Arry would—let Thor go?

ESTHER. Well, we've never been sure about Arry and Thor, Carl.

CARL. You girls have always been pretty sure. Gee, Esty, I'd hate for Arry to start anything.

ESTHER. I know. I thought of that when Cora was telling me. But I think you ought to do it, Carl. I think you ought to do it.

(*Pause.* CARL *watches* ESTY *for a minute*).

CARL. All right, Esty. (*Pause.*) I wonder if Cora ever knew about Arry and Thor?

ESTHER. If she did she's kept it to herself pretty well—Oh, well, I think Arry really loved Thor. I think she probably still does. Anyway, it's the closest thing to a husband she'll ever know. Come to think of it, Carl, I guess Arry doesn't quite know where she is either. (*Pause.*)

CARL. Well, things get tangled up, don't they, Esty?

ESTHER. Don't they, though.

CARL. For everybody, I guess. (*Pause.*) I feel better. Lots better.

ESTHER. That's good. Shall we go in and see Myrtle then?

CARL. All right. (*They start toward the house.*) I always feel better talking to you, Esty.

ESTHER. Well, I'm the oldest.

(*They exit into house left. The stage is empty for a minute. A* MAN *is seen to come from behind the hedge at right and approach the house at left, cautiously. He goes up to it and stands peering through the lighted window.* CORA *comes into dining room of house right and starts to set table. Sees* MAN *and calls* THOR *and* ARRY.)

CORA (*in an excited whisper. All three come out on the porch*). There he is! See! I knew it was someone!

THOR (*calling*). What do you want?

(*He switches on the porch light. Then crosses down.* MAN *turns—there is a sudden shocked pause—then a frenzied fear seizes them all. They all speak at once.*)

CORA. It's David! My goodness, it's David! (*She crosses down.*)

ARRY (*yelling frantically*). Esty! Esty!

THOR (*in a loud voice*). Now look here, David! Esty's not here!

ARRY (*yelling*). Get out the front door, Esty!

CORA. Arry!

ARRY (*coming to head of steps—crossing down*). Well, he was looking in the window! He must have seen her.

THOR. I've been in the house, David. She might have slipped in when—

CORA. She was only going to stay a second, David. She was just going home—

(ESTHER *comes out of the house at left, hurriedly. The others freeze.* DAVID *stands center, watching* ESTHER. *She comes down left center, followed by* IDA *and* CARL. HOMER *and* MYRTLE *stay on the porch left.*)

ESTHER (*nervously*). Why, David, what are you doing here? I was just coming home. I really was. Myrtle is here, you see, and I just ran down to—

IDA. She's only been here a minute—

ESTHER. You see, Ida phoned me Carl was having a spell—

CARL. That's right, David. I had a spell.

ESTHER. But I'm all ready to go now. Come on, let's—

(DAVID *has not moved.* ESTHER *stops suddenly and watches him. He is looking at her. The others watch in silence. Suddenly he looks at the group containing* THOR, CORA *and* ARRY. *They shrink back as he eyes them. He looks them over slowly, from head to foot, giving each a thorough inspection. Then he looks at the other group. He gives them the same individual, critical inspection. He stands a moment, throwing his head back in a puzzled way. He speaks to himself as though he were trying to reason something out.*)

DAVID (*softly*). "And God created man in his own image; male and female created he them." (*After a moment's thought, he gives a sudden shrug, as though the entire problem were beyond him. He turns suddenly to* THOR, *as though seeing him for the first time.*) Good evening, Theodore.

THOR (*taken aback*). Good—evening, David—

DAVID (*bowing pleasantly*). Cora—Aaronetta—

CORA (*as* DAVID *turns to the others*). Good —evening, David—

DAVID (*more genuine*). Good evening, Carl.

CARL (*eagerly*). Good evening, David.

DAVID. Ida—Homer—(*He hesitates before* MYRTLE.)

HOMER. This's Myrtle Brown.

DAVID. Ah! This is Myrtle Brown. Good evening, Myrtle.

MYRTLE. Good evening. I'm very pleased to—

(*He turns to* ESTHER. *Formally as to the others.*)

DAVID. Good evening, Esther.

ESTHER (*bewildered*). Good evening, David—

(*He bows to her formally and then surveys them all, smiling.*)

DAVID. Well, well, here we all are together again. Our own little circle. I must say, you all seem to me very much the same as you always did.

(*He beams on them. There is a rustling in the groups. They look at one another, bewildered.*)

CORA. That's—very nice of you, David.

DAVID. Yes, just about the same. A little older, perhaps. Grayer. Pulses all a trifle slower, probably. But I can still see the same bright, intelligent expressions on your faces that I remember so well. (*Slight pause as he beams on them.*) And now before I leave you there is just one thing more. You have all been in my home at one time or another. You all know how the entry hall leads into the living room and so is the entrance to the lower floor. And from the entry hall the staircase leads to the second floor. Well, now since Esther has decided it will be better for us to live apart from each other—

ESTHER (*steps toward him*). David—

DAVID. From now on, I will be living on the lower floor, Esther on the second.

ARRY. What's he mean, Esty?

ESTHER (*crossing to her*). Why, you know David. He didn't mean—

IDA (*following* ESTY). What's he mean?

CORA. He told Esty if she came down here again she'd have to live on the second floor.

ARRY. He what? He did not.

IDA. I don't believe it.

CORA. S'fact.

} *Ad lib.*

THOR. By God, what d'ye know about that!

DAVID (*raising his hand for silence*). Esther is a free agent now. She has a perfect right to come and go as she pleases and to have anyone she wishes visit her. Doubtless you will be there a great deal. Now none of you would come into the lower floor, of course. But may I suggest that as you pass through the entry hall and on up the stairs to be as— silent as possible?

(*Pause.*)

ESTHER. But David, you don't really mean it?

DAVID (*surprised*). That was our understanding, was it not, Esther? It seems to me it was.

ESTHER. But, David, these are my *sisters!* They're all I have! I've got to have something in my life!

DAVID. And now you have your sisters. Who am I to deprive you of that?

ARRY. That's what I say! Who are you to—

CORA. Arry!

ARRY. I don't care! He hasn't got any right to treat Esty like that!

IDA. I don't think he has either!

ARRY. Esty ought to be able to come down and see us any time she wants to.

CORA. After all, we are her sisters, David. It's only natural.

ESTHER (*encouraged*). We don't do any harm, David. We just talk. I have a good time with my sisters. I don't care how ignorant they are!

ARRY. Of course she don't. Give it to him, Esty!

IDA. We're behind you, Esty.

ESTHER. I want to be able to come down here any time I want to!

ARRY. That's the ticket, Esty!

ESTHER. And I don't want to live on the second floor either!

IDA. 'Course she don't!

ARRY. Good for you, Esty!

CORA. She's got to have something in her life!

ARRY. Give it to him, Esty!

} *Ad lib.*

(*They are all clustered around* ESTHER, *facing* DAVID, *excited and angry. Sudden pause.*)

DAVID (*bowing courteously*). Good night, Cora.

CORA (*taken aback*). Well—good night —David—

DAVID (*bowing*). Theodore—Ida—Aaronetta—

THOR. Good night, David—

(*They all watch him, bewildered. He turns to* CARL.)

DAVID. Good night, Carl—By the way, Carl, in the houses you have built you have also installed the plumbing, haven't you?

CARL (*crossing to* DAVID). Why, yes, I have, David.

DAVID. I am turning the little closet near my kitchen into a bathroom. Do you suppose you could do it?

CARL. Why, I guess so—

DAVID. Would it be much of an undertaking?

CARL. That all depends on the bathroom upstairs. Is it right over the closet?

DAVID. Ah, that I'm afraid I wouldn't know.

CARL. If it is it would be easy.

DAVID. Perhaps you would come up and look at it in the morning.

CARL. Well, I'd be glad to, David.

DAVID. Thank you, Carl. Good night, Carl—Homer—Myrtle—

MYRTLE. Good night. I'm delighted to have—

(DAVID *has started out. He stops, turns.*)

DAVID (*gently*). You won't forget my little reminder, will you? About being quiet when you visit Esther? I say it out of the utmost kindness. You know, of course, without my telling you, how much you all depress me? (*He looks from one to another, smiling.*) Yes—Well, good night, then. Good night. (*He bows and exits between houses.*)

THOR. By God! David can be awful nice when he wants to be. (*Crosses to chair right—sits.*)

ESTHER (*crossing to the edge of porch—sitting*). Oh, dear. I never should have come down here. It's all my fault.

ARRY (*crossing up center*). It's not your fault at all! David's an old fool, if you want my opinion.

CARL (*suddenly*). David's no fool! (*Quick silence. They all look at* CARL, *sharply.*) David lives straight ahead the way he was meant to. *He* knows where he is. *He* didn't branch off.

IDA (*crossing to him*). Oh, my goodness!

HOMER (*pushing* MYRTLE *in house*). Come in to supper, Myrtle.

IDA. It's time to come in to supper, Carl. Come along.

CORA. Go in to supper, Carl.

HOMER. Come in to supper, Father.

CARL. David thought it all out way back there at the crossroads. Then he went straight ahead.

IDA. Now stop it, Carl. Homer!

HOMER (*joining them*). I'm coming, Mother.

CARL. He lived his life just the way he planned it. But *I* branched off.

IDA (*taking his arm*). Come on now, Carl.

CARL (*to* IDA). Don't you see? I took the wrong turn. I got lost.

HOMER. Now get hold of yourself, Father.

CARL (*suddenly*). I've got to go back to the fork!

IDA (*distressed*). Oh, Carl, Carl! Don't say that!

CARL. I've got to take the other way.

HOMER (*trying to shake him*). Father!

CARL. I've got to go back to the fork.

IDA (*her hands over her ears*). Don't say that, Carl.

HOMER. Father, stop it! You're hurting my mother. You stop it now.

(*He shakes him.* CARL *stops suddenly. They have all been watching, breathless. Suddenly* CARL *seems to come to himself. He sees* HOMER's *attitude, sees all the others watching, sees* IDA *crying, sees* MYRTLE *staring in amazement.*)

CARL (*trying to explain*). I—I—I didn't mean—(*Starts left—speaks to* MYRTLE *on porch steps.*) I didn't mean—(*Turns to all of them.*) I just meant that I got to go back to the fork.(*Exits through hedge left.*) I've got to take the other way. I've got to—

IDA (*taking a step toward him*). Carl.

HOMER (*his arms around her*). Never mind, Mother.

IDA. Carl!

HOMER (*comforting her*). Come in the house, Mother.

(IDA *drops her head on* HOMER's *shoulder.*)

IDA (*sobbing*). It came so quick—

HOMER. I knew it would. I knew he was working up to it.

IDA. And he's always going back to that fork—I never know what that means.

HOMER. That's all right, Mother. I'll be here. I won't leave you, Mother.

IDA. Oh, Homer, Homer—

HOMER. Come in the house, Mother. Don't you worry. I'll take care of you. There, there, Mother, there, there.

(*As he leads the sobbing* IDA *into the house left,* MYRTLE *crosses down left from the steps and watches them bewildered. The others have been watching and after* HOMER *and* IDA *have gone in, all eyes center on* MYRTLE. MYRTLE *eyes them, helplessly. She gives a nervous laugh and falteringly walks up the steps. Again she gives a little laugh.* HOMER *has switched porch light off.*)

MYRTLE. I guess I better—

ARRY (*deeply touched, takes a few steps toward her, wanting to do something but not knowing what*). I—I—Myrtle?

MYRTLE (*stopping*). Yes?

ARRY. I—I've just been thinking—I wondered—Well, if supper isn't quite ready I thought maybe—maybe you'd have time to see that quilt I'm making—

MYRTLE (*grateful, relieved—crosses down to* ARRY). I'd *love* to see it.

ARRY (*taking her arm and leading her toward the house right*). It isn't finished, you know—There's more to be done on it—

MYRTLE. I'm sure it's beautiful—

ARRY. I hope you think so. You see—I didn't mean to tell you—But I'm making it for you—To go with the luncheon set—

MYRTLE. Oh, no!

ARRY. Yes, it's the same pattern.

MYRTLE. Oh, but, I couldn't accept it. A *quilt!*

ARRY (*they are going up the steps*). You won't have to take it if you don't like it.

MYRTLE. I know I'll like it but—

ARRY (*they are inside now*). Well, it's yours then. My goodness, I certainly wouldn't have any use for it.

(*They exit out of sight. Pause.* CORA *has been watching where* HOMER *and* IDA *left.*)

CORA. Esty, Homer will never marry Myrtle now, will he?

ESTHER. Looks pretty bad.

THOR. Damn shame. Myrtle's a nice girl, too.

CORA. Well—(*Light goes on in* ARRY'S *room.*) Esty, you just stay down here with us tonight and David'll come to his senses by morning. You can have the bedroom downstairs.

ESTHER (*rising*). I'm tired.

CORA. Of course you are.

ESTHER. It takes it out of you.

(*They start up the porch steps and around center.*)

CORA. You're not as young as you were, Esty.

ESTHER. I guess that's it.

CORA. Besides, it's been a busy day.

ESTHER. Busy! It's been the busiest day I've had for a long time!

(*They exit into side porch door. Pause.* ARRY *comes out and looks around, suspicious.*)

ARRY. Where's Cora and Esty?

THOR. Just went in.

ARRY (*crossing to porch edge, sitting*). Oh! —Myrtle's lying down in my room. I think she wanted to be alone.

THOR. Uh-huh.

ARRY. She's real nice, Myrtle.

THOR. Yup.

ARRY. Well, guess we better go in. (*Rises—switches porch light off.*)

THOR (*rising—crossing to porch step*). Yup.

ARRY (*moving back to front of porch. Stands looking at the sky a minute*). 'S going to be a nice night, Thor.

THOR (*turns and looks*). Yup.

(*Pause.*)

ARRY (*dreamily*). Remember how bright it was that night we took the boat to—

THOR (*quickly*). Shh! Arry! (*He glances over shoulder toward the house.*)

ARRY (*resigned*). All right! (*Suddenly bursting out.*) I get awful sick of having to keep still all the time! Sometimes I wish Cora would die!

THOR (*shocked*). Arry!

ARRY (*suddenly frightened*). I didn't mean that, Thor! I didn't mean that!

THOR. I should hope not! (*Crosses up to porch.*)

ARRY. I really didn't, Thor!

THOR. I don't like that, Arry.

(THOR *goes in abruptly.* ARRY *stands a moment, alone, frightened. She looks up at the sky.*)

ARRY (*frightened*). I didn't mean that! Honest! (*She hurries into the house.*)

CURTAIN

ACT TWO

SCENE: *The same. Seven-fifteen the next morning. Bright sun.* THOR *comes out of the house at right. Is eating an apple, contentedly. Suddenly throws it from him.*

THOR. God, how I hate apples! (*He moves down to his chair and sits.*) Cora! I wonder where the hell she's got to? Arry!

ESTHER (*enters from the center porch door. Crosses down steps.*) Good morning, Thor.

THOR. Oh, morning, Esty.

ESTHER. What time is it?

THOR. About quarter past seven.

ESTHER. My goodness, isn't that awful. I never stay in bed that late. Is everybody else up?

THOR (*sleepily*—ESTY *sits porch ledge*). Dunno, Esty. Haven't seen anybody. Just got up myself—Still, Cora must be up. She wasn't in bed—By God, the way she kicked around last night—you'd thought she had the measles or something.

ESTHER. Thor, what happened last night after I went to bed? Ida came over, didn't she?

THOR. Yes, she did, Esty.

ESTHER. What did she say?

THOR. Well, seems Homer broke off with Myrtle.

ESTHER. Oh, my goodness, I was afraid that was it.

THOR. Yup. Told her it was all off. Couldn't leave his mother now that Carl was having spells again.

ESTHER (*furious*). Oh, that makes me so mad! I was afraid that would happen. Did Myrtle go back to North Lyons?

THOR. Nope. Can't get a train till this afternoon.

ESTHER. Oh, poor girl. Where is she?

THOR. Over at Ida's in bed, probably.

ESTHER. Poor thing. What an awful position for her to be in. (ARRY *comes out of* IDA'S *house—crosses center.*) Oh, there's Arry: Good morning, Arry.

ARRY. Good morning, Esty. (*To* THOR.) Where's Cora?

THOR. I haven't seen her, Arry.

ARRY. Well, she isn't at Ida's and she isn't in bed.

THOR. Did you look on the roof?

ARRY. What would Cora be doing on the roof?

THOR. Dunno. She just might suddenly have gone crazy or something. (*He chuckles.*)

ARRY (*peeved*). All right, you're so smart, listen to this. Carl didn't come home last night.

ESTHER. What?

ARRY. He didn't come home last night, and he hasn't been home this morning.

THOR. The hell you say!

ESTHER. How do you know?

ARRY (*impatiently*). How do you think I know? Ida just told me. She's nearly frantic. She wants to get out the Boy Scouts, but Homer won't let her.

ESTHER. Why won't he?

ARRY. Oh, you know how Homer is. He says it's embarrassing. It might get around.

THOR. It's a hell of a time for Homer to get embarrassed.

ESTHER. Hasn't Ida any idea where he is?

ARRY. Of course she hasn't. He's probably wandering around the streets having a spell with everyone he meets.

THOR (*getting up*). By God, we ought to do something.

ARRY. And another thing. Cora's gone, too.

THOR. What do you mean, "gone"?

ARRY. Well, where is she?

THOR. I don't know, but—(*Suddenly accusing—crosses to* ARRY.) Now, look here, Arry, Cora hasn't got anything to do with Carl being gone. Cora was right in that bed with me all night—

ARRY. I didn't say anything about—

THOR. She kicked me every five minutes—

ARRY (*shouting*). I didn't say Cora had gone with Carl—

THOR. Well, don't go making any cracks about Cora—(*Crosses right—sits chair.*)

ARRY. I'm not making any cracks about her. But Cora went over to Ida's to talk to Carl. She was all excited about something. Said she had to see him right away. And when she found out Carl hadn't been home she ran out without saying a word. That was twenty minutes ago and she hasn't been seen or heard of since.

THOR (*uneasily*). What did she want to talk to Carl about?

ARRY. That's what I'd like to know. Cora's up to something, you mark my words. Last night when she found out Homer wasn't going to marry Myrtle she got as nervous as a monkey. She's got some bee in her bonnet and if it's what I think it is—(ESTHER *suddenly puts her hand up to her mouth.* ARRY *catches her and eyes her, sharply.*) What do *you* think she wants to see Carl about, Esty?

ESTHER (*innocently*). Me?

ARRY (*imitating her*). Yes, me!

ESTHER. How would I know, Arry?

ARRY. Oh, you make me sick. But I'll tell you one thing! If Cora is up to something—and if it's what I think it is—

well, some people around here had just better watch out, that's all I say.

(*She looks significantly at* THOR, *who squirms uneasily.* IDA *comes out of house at left.*)

IDA (*mournfully crossing down steps—sits ledge left*). Esty, Esty, have you heard—?

ESTHER (*crossing to her*). Yes, Ida—

IDA. Poor Carl!

ESTHER. Now nothing's happened to him, Ida.

IDA. If we could only drag the river or something—

(ARRY *crosses center.*)

ESTHER. Now, Ida, there's no river anywhere round here.

IDA. He was always such a good husband to me. Never a cross word. (*Calling to* THOR.) Have you heard about Carl, Thor?

THOR (*calling back*). Yeah! Terrible thing, Ida.

IDA. He was such a good man.

THOR. By God, he was, Ida! That's a fact!

IDA. What do you think I ought to do?

THOR. Well, if it was me, I think I'd begin to look around a little—

IDA. That's what I think. But Homer says we don't want the whole neighborhood to know.

THOR (*rises—crosses center*). Tell you what I'll do. I know a fellow down at the police station—Jim—

IDA (*horrified—rises and crosses center.* ESTY *follows*). Police!

THOR. Sure. They're the ones to handle things like this. I could call Jim up sort of casually—not giving anything away—you know, and ask him what you're supposed to do in a case like this.

ESTHER. That's just the thing to do, Ida.

IDA (*hesitantly*). But Homer says if anything had happened we'd have heard—

ARRY. Not necessarily. (*Crosses to* IDA.) Just suppose Carl took it into his head last night to walk up on Randall's hill where he goes. And suppose he fell off that bad drop there. He was having a spell, remember. And suppose he knocked himself unconscious on one of those rocks —or even just broke a leg—why, he could lie there for weeks before—

ESTHER. Oh, Carl wouldn't fall off that drop!

ARRY (*crosses to her*). In the dark he wouldn't?

ESTHER. No, he wouldn't. Carl's no fool.

(IDA *sits stump.*)

ARRY. Esty, sometimes you are the most exasperating woman I ever knew!

THOR (*to* IDA). What do you say, Ida? I won't give away a thing. I'll just say, "Hello, Jim. How are you? How're the kids?"

ESTHER. You might mention something about Carl.

THOR. Sure, I'll sneak Carl in.

IDA. Well, all right. But if it comes out all over the paper tomorrow—?

ARRY (*crosses right—starts in*). Come on, Ida. It's not going to get in the paper.

IDA (*rises—follows* THOR *up steps*). Well, all right. But you be careful what you say, Thor.

THOR. By God, Ida, if Jim gets any idea of what I called him for I'll eat my hat.

(THOR *and* IDA *go in house right.* ARRY *is still on the porch—*ESTHER *sits stump.*)

ARRY. All over the paper! Anybody'd think Carl was running for mayor or something—(*Notices that* ESTY *has sat down.*) Aren't you coming in, Esty?

ESTHER. I don't think so. They don't need me.

ARRY (*hesitantly*). I don't suppose they *need me* either but—(*She takes one step down.*) You're not angry, are you?

ESTHER (*surprised*). Why should I be angry?

ARRY. Well, I thought maybe I— spoke to you kind of sharp. (*Crosses down stairs.*)

ESTHER (*smiling*). Oh! Oh, that's all right, Arry.

ARRY. I didn't mean to be—You know how I talk sometimes.

ESTHER. Yes, I know.

ARRY. I've just been all on edge the last few days.

ESTHER. Really? Why?

ARRY. Well, I don't know exactly. But there's something going on around here I don't know about. And if there's one thing I hate it's to have things going on behind my back.

ESTHER. Yes, you always hated that, Arry.

ARRY. For one thing it isn't polite. I like people to be open and aboveboard. When people start to sneak and—(CORA *enters hurriedly from between the houses. She is excited.* ARRY *turns on her sharply.*) Well, it's about time! Where have you been?

CORA (*anxiously*). Has Carl come back?

ARRY. What do you want to know for?

ESTHER. No, he hasn't, Cora.

CORA. Nobody's heard anything?

ESTHER. Not a thing.

ARRY (*who has been eyeing her*). What are you so excited about it for?

CORA (*flustered*). Who wouldn't be excited about it?

ARRY. And where have you been?

(*Pause.* CORA *gets over being flustered. She becomes rather superior, as though possessed of some secret knowledge.*)

CORA. Well, I'll tell you, Arry. I've been for a little walk.

ARRY. You haven't either. You've been looking for Carl.

CORA. Well, my goodness, we've all got to do everything we can. I went over to Ida's—

ARRY. That's right. To see Carl.

CORA. Yes. And when I found he wasn't there I thought he might have gone up to Homer's house. But when I got up there, there wasn't any sign of him.

ARRY. But what did you want to see him for?

CORA (*suddenly impatient*). Oh, Arry, if I wanted to tell you that I would.

ARRY (*suddenly very dignified*). Oh! Well, I certainly crave your pardon, Cora. I assure you I had no intentions of prying. (*She starts toward the house.*)

CORA (*sorry*). Oh, it—it isn't anything, Arry—Don't get hurt.

ARRY. Please, Cora. I certainly wouldn't want you to tell me anything you didn't want to. I'll just go in and you can tell it to Esther. (ARRY *goes in.*)

CORA. Oh, dear, now Arry's angry—Well, I can't help it! (*She turns to* ESTHER, *excited.*) Oh, Esty, I'm so upset I don't know what to do! The first thing this morning I go over to see Carl—the lease all ready to sign—and he's gone. (*She takes the lease from her blouse.*) I've put in here forty-five dollars a month. Twenty-year lease. I think he'll agree to that, don't you, Esty?

ESTHER. That seems fair enough.

CORA. Oh, Esty, isn't it wonderful?

ESTHER. It isn't wonderful yet. Thor hasn't agreed to it yet, you know.

CORA (*crossing to steps right—sitting*). Oh, he *will!* He's *got* to! He loves that house! Oh, Esty, I've never been so happy in my whole life as I am right this minute!

ESTHER (*rises—crosses to* CORA—*hesitantly*). Thor may not take this just the way you think, you know. (*Hurriedly.*) I mean—Well, remember it isn't so easy to pick up and leave a house you've lived in so long—leave all the furniture and everything you're used to—So you know what I think?

CORA. What?

ESTHER. I think it might be a good idea to talk it over first with—Arry.

(*Quick pause.* CORA *draws back.*)

CORA. Arry! (*She looks suspiciously at* ESTY.)

ESTHER. Yes.

CORA (*in a hard voice*). Why? What business is it of hers?

ESTHER. It is her business in a way.

CORA. I don't see how.

ESTHER. Well, she's always lived with you. You're the only home she's ever known. You can't say she's not concerned.

CORA. I don't care if she is concerned. Thor is *my* husband, Esty.

ESTHER. Of course, Cora—I just thought—

CORA (*with a slight sneer*). You just thought nothing—(*She crosses center.*)

ESTHER. But, Cora—

(THOR *comes out, followed by* IDA *and* ARRY. CORA *hurriedly slips the lease into her waist although a small part of it shows.*)

IDA. But what's the next step for us to take, Thor?

THOR (*coming down the steps, followed by* IDA. ARRY *stays on the porch.*) By God, Ida, you got me. If you won't let me tell the police who Carl is—They can't very well start looking for somebody they don't know.

(ESTY *sits stump.*)

ESTHER. What did they tell you, Thor?

THOR. They said to give a description of him.

ESTHER. I should think you could do that.

THOR. Ida says I can't.

IDA (*nervously—crosses to* ESTY). Well, Esty, Homer says—

CORA (*up right center—sweetly*). Good morning, Thor.

THOR. What've you been up to this morning?

CORA. Me? Nothing at all.

IDA. Did you see anything of Carl?

CORA. Not a thing, Ida.

THOR. What'd you want to see Carl in such a hurry about?

CORA. I just wanted to find him for Ida.

ARRY (*on porch just above* CORA—*laughing*).That's very funny. Very funny. (*She changes to a matter-of-fact voice.*) And what's this sticking out of your waist? (*Pulls the lease.*)

CORA (*slapping her hand*). You keep your hands to yourself.

ARRY. Well, what is it?

CORA. None of your business.

ARRY. Hoity-toity!

(ARRY *moves up on the porch—but during the following scene eyes* CORA *intently.*)

IDA. Maybe if we just gave a description without giving his name—

THOR. Sure! No use giving his name. Just his description. Sixty-six years old—

IDA. Sixty-eight, Thor.

THOR. Sixty-*eight?* Are you sure?

IDA. Well, I—I thought I was. Sixty-eight, isn't it, Esty?

ESTHER. Let's see. I'm seventy-two. And Cora's two years younger than I—

CORA. That's right. And Ida's four years younger than me.

IDA. Sixty-six, that's right. And Carl's two years older—

ESTHER. Sixty-eight.

THOR. Well, what the hell do you know about that! I wouldn't have said Carl was a day over sixty-six. By God, we're certainly getting along, this crowd. (*Hearty laugh.*)

IDA (*crosses porch ledge, left—sits*). Yes, sir, we certainly are.

THOR. We're certainly not getting any younger. And by God, I'm glad we're not. When I think how I used to go to that office every day at eight o'clock—

CORA. You never used to mind that so much, Thor.

THOR. Well, I'd mind it now.

ESTHER. Still, if you were getting younger you'd get back to the age where you wouldn't mind it.

THOR. What's that, Esty?

ESTHER. I say if you were forty again you wouldn't mind going to the office.

THOR. I'm not forty though.

ESTHER. But if you were getting younger you'd get back to forty.

THOR (*looking at her*). What the hell are you talking about, Esty?

ESTHER. Never mind—Anyway, blue eyes.

(ARRY *gets down off the porch and starts slowly toward* CORA.)

IDA. What's that, Esty?

ESTHER. Carl.

IDA. Oh, yes, Carl.

ESTHER. He's got blue eyes.

IDA. Oh!—Yes, that's right. Blue eyes.

THOR. Bald. (*Slight pause. He looks up at* IDA, *puzzled.*) Carl's bald, isn't he?

IDA. He's got kind of a fringe.

THOR. You sure? I would have said Carl was pretty damn near completely bald.

CORA. No, he had quite a bit of hair in back, Thor.

THOR. Really? Well, that just goes to show. You look at a thing and you look at it and still you don't see it. I'm going to get a good square at Carl the next time I see him.

IDA (*tearfully*). If you ever have a chance to see him.

THOR. Oh, by God, Ida, I'm sorry, I forgot.

(ARRY *has been circling closer and closer. At this point she is near enough to* CORA *to make a quick dive for the paper. She gets it and starts racing across the lawn as fast as she can go.* CORA *is on her feet in an instant and after her, shrieking.* THOR *sits up, startled.*)

CORA. Arry! You give that back! You come back here with that paper. Arry! (*A race ensues in which* ARRY, *running as hard as she can, tries to get the paper out of the envelope and read it.*) Catch her, Ida! Hurry! Head her off that way!

(IDA *heads her off from going in the house.*)

ESTHER. Give her back that paper, Arry!

THOR. What the hell's going on here?

CORA. You dare read that paper and I'll fix you, Aaronetta Gibbs!

ESTHER. You stop, Arry! Stop!

IDA (*suddenly entering into the spirit of the thing*). Look out, Arry, Cora's gaining on you.

THOR. What are they doing?

IDA (*laughing*). I don't know. Arry's got something of Cora's (*Shouting.*) Look out, Arry.

(*They are all shrieking, ad lib.* ARRY *races right and gets cornered by* IDA *right—*ESTY *center—and* CORA *coming after her from the left. They are at the height of their shrieking and pulling at each other as* DAVID *enters left. The noise subsides. Even* ARRY *quiets down, and with a final jerk* CORA *gets the paper.* ESTHER, *in utter confusion, faces* DAVID, *weakly.* DAVID *surveys them, smiling.*)

DAVID (*pleasantly*). Playing tag?

ESTHER. No, no—We were just—

DAVID. But don't apologize, Esther. You are a free agent now. You can amuse yourself any way you wish.

ESTHER. But you don't understand, David—

DAVID. Please go on with the game. Don't let me interrupt you—

ESTHER. But we weren't playing a game. We were—

DAVID (*calling off left*). I'll go in and wait for you in your room, Carl. (*Starts up steps of house left.*)

CARL (*off stage*). All right, David.

EVERYBODY. Carl!

ESTHER. David!

(*She follows him into house.* CARL, *loaded down with tools, enters left.* IDA *crosses to him.*)

IDA. Carl!

CARL (*puts down bags*). Oh, Ida—I hope you haven't been worried, Ida.

IDA. Worried! My goodness, Carl, I've been nearly frantic! Where have you been? What's the matter? Are you all right? Are you hurt?

CARL (*surprised*). Hurt?

IDA. But where have you been, Carl? You stayed out all night. I've been nearly frantic. We even called the police.

CARL. Police?

IDA. We thought you might be dead!

CARL. Dead? No.

IDA. You didn't come home all night. I've been nearly frantic. Where have you been, Carl?

CARL (*surprised she doesn't know*). Why, I've been up at David's.

IDA. But where did you sleep?

CARL. Well, we didn't sleep, Ida—We talked. David's going to help me find out where I am. We're right in the middle of it now. We just stopped long enough to come down and get my tools and pack my clothes—

IDA. Pack your clothes?

CARL. Yes, I—(*Realizes she doesn't understand.*) Oh! You see, I'm moving, Ida.

IDA. What do you mean?

CARL. Well, David has invited me to live with him. He wants me to.

IDA. Live with David?

CARL (*crossing left center*). Yes. You see, we're going to live on the lower floor. We're going to put in a real bath instead of just a seat and a basin and we're going to use the side entrance and—

IDA. What are you talking about, Carl?

CARL (*turns to her—as to a child*). I'm going to live with David for a while.

IDA. But what about *me?*

CARL (*blankly*). You?

IDA. Yes, *me*, Carl.

CARL. Oh, that's right. Well, you can live here just the way you do now.

IDA. You don't mean you're going to leave me, Carl?

CARL. But I've lived here a long time, Ida. I want to live somewhere else for a while. You'll be all right. You've got Homer.

IDA. I just don't understand—

CARL (*crossing to pick up tools*). I'll explain it to you sometime, Ida. I'll come down and see you—

(DAVID *calls from inside house.*)

DAVID. We're wasting valuable time, Carl.

CARL (*briskly—going in*). Be right there, David. Be right there.

IDA. Carl! I've got to talk to you, Carl—

(*Follows him*—ARRY, THOR, *and* CORA *are watching.*)

THOR. Well, what the hell do you know about that.

ARRY. I always knew that marriage wouldn't last—Anyway, Carl *has* got hair on the back of his head. Quite a bit of it.

THOR. There you are! Damn it all, I forgot to look again! (*Crosses back to chair right—sits.*)

CORA (*starting left*). Well, I've got to run over and see him.

ARRY (*suddenly pulling* CORA *around*). Oh, you do, eh! What for?

(*Sudden pause. They revert to their old tension.*)

CORA. If you ask me that again, Arry, I'll—

THOR. That's right. What the hell's the matter with you two?

ARRY. What's in the paper, is what I want to know.

THOR. Whose paper is it?

ARRY. Cora's. She's been hiding it.

THOR. What business is it of yours then?

ARRY. Cora's up to something and I know it.

COEA (*hard*). You want to know what's in this paper, Arry?

ARRY. Yes, I do!

(*Pause.* CORA *glares at* ARRY. *She hands her the paper.*)

CORA (*in a hard voice*). All right, look for

yourself.

(*She gives* ARRY *the paper.* ARRY *reads it and looks up slowly. They eye each other in silence.*)

THOR (*impatiently*). Well, what is it? (CORA *takes the paper and gives it to* THOR. *He reads it as* ARRY *watches* CORA, *trying to figure out exactly what it means.* THOR *looks up, puzzled.*) This here's a twenty-year lease on Homer's house.

CORA (*steadily*). Yes.

THOR. It's made out to you.

CORA. Yes.

THOR. What's it for?

ARRY. That's what I want to know.

THOR. Look here, Cora, what's the big idea?

CORA (*after a moment*). I'm going to rent it for us, Thor.

THOR. Us? What do we want with it?

CORA. You like that house, don't you, Thor?

THOR. Of course I like it but—

CORA. You like it better than this one, don't you?

THOR. What if I do? That's no reason to rent it.

CORA. Listen, Thor. We haven't got many years left ahead of us, have we?

THOR. What's that got to do with it?

CORA. Everything. I want for the rest of the years we *have* got for you and me to move up there and live together in that nice house. Have a real home of our own.

THOR (*frightened*). Now, look here, Cora, I don't know what you're getting at.

ARRY. I know what she's getting at.

CORA. There's no reason in the world that I can see why we can't do it. Carl has promised to sign the lease. We can afford it. And we'd love it. Just you and me—alone.

THOR (*rises*). Good Lord, Cora, now look here—

CORA (*steadily*). I've thought it all out, Thor. We can give this house to Arry. We can make out some kind of transfer and she can own it in her own name. She won't be lonesome with Ida and Esty here. And we can have what's left of the years together—alone—as we should always have had them in the past.

THOR (*horrified*). Cora! (*Slight pause.* ARRY *turns quickly and runs into the house.*) Arry—(*He takes a step toward her and then turns back.* CORA *is watching him.*) By God, Cora, how could you say a thing like that?

CORA (*crosses center a step—steadily*). It's the truth, isn't it?

THOR. But right in front of Arry.

CORA. She had it coming to her.

THOR. But think how she must feel.

CORA. I know how she feels—Well, what about it, Thor? Shall we do it?

THOR (*uneasily*). But we can't do a thing like that—

CORA. Why not?

THOR. We just couldn't. It wouldn't be fair to Arry. Poor Arry, she's all alone in the world.

CORA. So am I. You can be alone a lot of different ways, Thor.

THOR. And Carl isn't going to rent that house—

CORA. If he doesn't then we can't do it. But if he does, are you willing?

THOR. But Cora—

CORA. You're not afraid, are you, Thor?

THOR. Afraid? Afraid of what?

CORA. Of anything.

THOR (*uneasily*). I don't know what you mean.

CORA. All right. Then you think it over, Thor, will you?

THOR (*same*). I guess—I can think it over—

CORA (*crossing left to* IDA's *house*). Thank you—Now I'm going over to Ida's and talk to Carl. I think we can get that house, Thor.

THOR (*crossing center—afraid*). Don't do it now, Cora. Wait till we talk it over.

CORA (*on steps*). No, Carl may get away again. We don't want to take any chances. (*She exits into house.*)

THOR (*desperate*). But—(ARRY *enters from house right.* THOR *turns.*) Gee, Arry, I'm so sorry about that. Cora didn't mean anything—

ARRY. She meant it all right.

THOR. She was just mad. I'm sorry as I can be.

ARRY. No use being sorry. The point is what are you going to do about it? If Cora gets that house are you going to move up there?

THOR (*at stump*). Of course not, Arry—

ARRY. How will you get out of it?

THOR. I'll talk to Cora and—

ARRY. What will you tell her?

THOR (*sits stump*). I'll fix it up someway.

ARRY. She's over seeing Carl now. Why didn't you stop her?

THOR. I couldn't just then—

ARRY. You listened to Cora. Now you listen to me, Thor. Cora can talk about having what's left of her life alone with you. Well, what about me? How many years do you think I've got left?

THOR. I know, Arry, I know—

ARRY. And whose fault is it that *I* haven't got a home of my own?

THOR. All right, Arry. Now your home's right here with us—

ARRY. I've got just as much right here as Cora.

THOR. Now be quiet, Arry. I'll think of something.

ARRY. You'd better. Because I'm not going to spend the rest of my life alone. After all I've given up.

THOR. I don't think Carl'll give her the house anyway.

ARRY. Well, if he does, and you leave me now, Thor, don't think I won't tell what's happened. I'm not ashamed. I'd *like* to have Cora know.

THOR (*sharply*). Now keep still, Arry.

ARRY. All right. But don't think Cora's going to make it easy for you. You'd better think up something pretty good, Thor. (*She starts in—stops on top step.*) You didn't have much breakfast this morning, did you?

THOR (*abused*). I had an apple.

ARRY. Well, come in. I'll fix you something.

(*She goes in.* THOR *starts in, gloomily.*)

THOR. Doggone it all! (*As he starts in,* HOMER *comes out of house left, furious—he slams porch door—starts around center on porch—then sees* THOR. THOR *speaks gloomily.*) 'Morning, Homer.

HOMER (*stops pacing*). 'Morning, Uncle Thor. (*Continues pacing—suddenly stops and looks up, furious.*) Aunt Cora got my house away from me!

THOR (*quickly*). What's that?

HOMER. While I was shaving!

THOR. What do you mean, Homer?

HOMER. I was upstairs shaving and when I came down my father had rented my house to Aunt Cora.

THOR. You mean he signed the lease?

HOMER. Just as I was coming downstairs.

THOR. Oh, my God!

(THOR *exits into house right—*IDA *comes out of house left—follows* HOMER *down center.*)

IDA. Homer—Oh, Homer, I'm so sorry about it!

HOMER (*moving away*). I don't want to talk about it, Mother. I've got to think.

IDA. Do you feel awfully bad?

HOMER. How do you think I feel? How would you feel if you suddenly found out you didn't have a house any more? That was *my* house. Myrtle's and mine. (*Crosses to chair left center.*)

IDA. Yes, it was, Homer, but—

HOMER (*sits*). And now it's not my house any more. Now Myrtle and I haven't got a house any more.

IDA. I don't suppose Carl thought you'd care—You and Myrtle weren't going to use it—

HOMER. We go up and look at it, don't we? We talk to each other about it. Now what are we going to talk about?

IDA. But you said you weren't going to get married and—

HOMER. I didn't say we weren't engaged.

IDA. Oh, dear, I'd do anything to get it back for you. I've never seen Cora so stubborn about anything. She won't even talk about it. She's calling up the electric company right now to have the lights turned on.

HOMER. What I'm going to say to Myrtle when she gets up, I don't know. It'll just about break her heart. She makes plans about that house all the time. She's told all her friends down in North Lyons about her beautiful house. Well, now she hasn't got one any more. We just took it away from her. Pretty small business, I must say! Invite a girl to stay over night and then take her house away from her when she's asleep. Pretty small business! *I* don't know what the world's coming to.

IDA. Well, I'll talk to Carl about it just as soon as I can. He and David have locked themselves in the bedroom until they're finished packing and won't talk to us, but as soon as they come out I'll—

HOMER. That won't do any good. He can't do anything. No, my house is gone, Mother. It's just gone.

IDA (*distressed—sits stump*). Oh, Homer, I'm so sorry—

HOMER (*suddenly—rising*). What's it all about, that's what I ask myself!

IDA. What's what all about, Homer?

HOMER (*turning to* IDA). All of it. Why hasn't Myrtle a home and been living up there in my house all this time? What's it all about that I'm forty years old and still living here and not having a home of my own?

IDA. But that's what you've always wanted, Homer.

HOMER (*accusingly*). Why have I wanted it? I'm a man.

IDA. Of course, Homer.

HOMER. Then what's it all about? Myrtle cried half the night last night. I heard her. And then my father leaves home. And then they take our beautifull house away from us. So what's it all about?

IDA (*rising*). I'm so sorry, Homer.

HOMER (*crossing to left exit*). I've got to think these things out. That's what I've got to do. I've got to think these things out. (*Exits.*)

IDA (*following—and off*). Oh, dear. Oh, dear—(DAVID *and* CARL *come out of house left. They are loaded with suitcases, tools, etc.* CARL *eagerly listens to* DAVID.)

CARL. Of course, it's just a supposition, David.

DAVID. That's right, Carl, just a supposition. (*Puts bags down left center—*CARL *does same.*) Let us suppose that right now, at this moment, you *are* a dentist. Let's assume that.

CARL (*eagerly*). All right, David, all right.

DAVID. You have your office. All your instruments, your chair, your tools—

CARL. X-ray machine.

DAVID. X-ray machine. Everything. And you're working on a patient. And suddenly do you know what you're going to say to yourself?

CARL. What?

DAVID. WHERE AM I? What am I doing here? I'm caught! I'm *Carl Bolton!* Where am I? Just as you do now—And how are you going to answer yourself? You can't say: Where am I? I'm a dentist. *What* am I, yes. But that's not what you ask yourself, Carl. You ask yourself: *Where* am I? Where am I in *life?* What's the meaning of it? And that's a very natural question, Carl. It's a question that a man like you must inevitably ask himself. The only reason that you think it strange, that anyone thinks it's strange, is because the people you have been in contact with have never let that problem worry them. They are content to answer the question: "Where am I?" by: "I'm a dentist." And why shouldn't they? After all, it

doesn't much matter where they are, does it?

CARL (*eagerly*). But the answer, David. What's the answer?

DAVID. Ah, that's another thing. That's what we must find out.

CAR. If I could only find out that answer—

DAVID. We'll talk about it, Carl. We'll talk about it. Well, shall we get loaded?

(IDA *enters left—*ESTHER *comes out of house and down steps.*)

CARL. Yes, yes.

(*They start to load each other with the bags and tools.*)

IDA (*tearfully*). Carl, I've always been a good wife to you. I've always been faithful and—(*Turning to* ESTY.) Esty, what are we going to do?

ESTHER (*crossing down steps—sitting porch ledge*). I don't know what *you're* going to do, Ida. But I know what *I'm* going to do.

IDA. What?

ESTHER. I'm going to sit right here and sort of bask in the sun.

(DAVID *looks up, surprised.*)

IDA. But they're going to leave us, Esty.

ESTHER. Well, let them! For heaven's sakes let them go and find out where they are once and for all. If they get to be as old as they are without knowing, the Lord knows it's high time for them to find out.

DAVID. You see, Carl, as I was saying, there are some people who never ask themselves the question: Where am I?

ESTHER. There're some people who don't have to. I *know* where *I* am. I'm on the second floor. And to tell the truth, I'm beginning to like the idea pretty well.

DAVID. Well, I'm glad if the arrangement pleases you, Esther.

ESTHER. It does. I've had more fun last night and today than I've had for a long time.

DAVID. Ah, yes. Your games and so forth—

ESTHER. That's right. I like games. With lots of people on both sides.

DAVID. Ah, yes. Well, you're a free agent now, Esther.

ESTHER. I know I am. When I sat outside that locked door a few minutes ago waiting for you two to come out, I suddenly said to myself: "There's no fool like an old fool," and I was thinking of you and Carl. And then I said it again and it suddenly meant *me*. For fifty years I've washed and cooked and brought up children and now suddenly I've got a chance to be free. I can come down here any time I want to, can go to the movies with the girls—do anything. (*She stretches*.) It's nice!

(*Pause.* DAVID *stands looking at her. Suddenly he turns to* CARL.)

DAVID. Well, Carl, we'd better get back to the bathroom.

CARL (*picking up tools*). All right, David. I'll come down and see you, Ida. (*Starts up center*.)

IDA (*following*). I never thought you'd leave me, Carl.

CARL. I never thought I would either, Ida, but—

(*They exit up center*.)

DAVID (*starts out—then turns back to* ESTHER). You'll be occupying the second tonight?

ESTHER. I haven't decided yet. I may stay down here. Thor says I can stay as long as I like.

DAVID. Ah!

ESTHER. But I'll be quiet if I come in late.

(*He stands looking at her for a second*.)

DAVID. Well, pleasant dreams, Esther.

ESTHER. Thank you.

(*He starts out—stops and turns*.)

DAVID. I meant to say, if you prefer the lower floor to the upper—

ESTHER. No, I think I prefer the upper.

DAVID. I thought perhaps the stairs—

ESTHER. The stairs won't bother me any.

DAVID. That's fine. (*He hesitates a minute*.) If there is any rearrangement of furniture you wish done, Carl and I will be glad to help you.

ESTHER. Thank you, David.

DAVID. There's no use straining yourself.

ESTHER. No.

DAVID. Well, good morning, Esther.

ESTHER. Good morning, David. (DAVID *exits up path.* ESTHER *watches him go, amused. Suddenly she starts to sing softly*.) Oh, sole mio—Ti-di-di-di-di— Ti-di-di-di-di—

(CORA *comes out of* IDA's *house. She crosses down the steps and walks center to the path, waving the lease at* ESTY *as she goes*.)

CORA. Hello, Esty. All signed!

ESTHER. Where are you going?

CORA (*stopping*). I'm going down the street to see Harold Blake. To see if we can use his truck. Maybe he can move us up there after work tomorrow or the next day. (*Slightly malicious*.) You see, Esty, I've decided you're right. It *is* hard to go away and leave a house you've lived in so long—all the furniture and all—. So I've decided to take some furniture along. Just Thor's chair so he won't be lonesome—and a couple of pieces out of the bedroom—Arry won't miss those. My goodness, Arry's got the whole house to live in. Isn't that right, Esty? (ESTHER *has been looking at her steadily. She doesn't reply*.) Well, good-by, Esty, and if anybody wants to make trouble, they can. (*She starts out between the houses —airily—and meets* IDA *coming in. She greets her effusively*.) Hello, Ida.

(*She exits—* IDA *crosses to* ESTY.)

IDA. Well, I must say you didn't do much to—

ESTHER (*rises—grabs* IDA *tensely*). Ida!

IDA. What's the matter, Esty?

ESTHER. Cora! I'm kind of scared. She's going through with this house thing, Ida. Cora means business.

IDA. Do you really think so?

ESTHER. Yes, I do. And you know what's going to happen, don't you?

IDA (*uneasily*). Oh, I don't think if it comes right down to it Arry will really stir up anything.

ESTHER. You don't, eh? Well, I do! (*Crossing right*.) Arry's mad enough to do anything. She'll tell all there is to tell and more too.

IDA. Well, what can we do about it?

ESTHER. What do you suppose Arry would do if we told her we knew about her and Thor?

IDA (*shocked*). We couldn't do that!

ESTHER. Now, wait a minute, Ida. The only thing that Arry's got over Thor is that she thinks none of us know about it.

IDA. She's hinted it in front of us often enough.

ESTHER. I know, but she hasn't any idea we ever caught on. She thought she was so smart about it. So if we tell her that all of us—even Cora—have known all along—Well, there wouldn't be much point in her telling. Anyway, it would take some wind out of her sails, wouldn't it?

IDA. It would be awfully hard on Arry.

ESTHER. Not as hard as it will be on everybody if she starts to make trouble. (*Suddenly.*) Let's go in and talk to Arry before Cora gets back. (*She starts drawing* IDA *toward the house.*)

IDA. But Thor's in there.

ESTHER. We'll get her out here then. We'll get her out if we have to drag her out.

IDA. All right—Oh, dear! It never rains but it pours.

(*They start in.* MYRTLE *comes out house left.*)

MYRTLE. Oh, good morning, Mrs. Bolton.

IDA (*stops—comes down steps*). Oh! Oh, good morning, Myrtle. Are you up?

MYRTLE. Yes, I am.

ESTHER. Good morning, Myrtle.

MYRTLE. Good morning. Isn't it lovely out?

ESTHER. Yes, isn't it? (*To* IDA.) I'll go in. Come in as soon as you can.

IDA. All right. (ESTHER *goes in.*) Well, you had a pretty good sleep, didn't you?

MYRTLE. I guess you think I'm a dreadful laggard, staying in bed so long?

IDA. Not at all. I'm glad you did.

MYRTLE. I don't always do it!

IDA. I bet you don't. And I'll bet you're good and hungry, too.

MYRTLE. No. I helped myself to some coffe and a little toast.

IDA. But you'll want more than that.

MYRTLE. I couldn't, really. That was just what I wanted.

IDA. Are you sure?

MYRTLE. Yes, really.

IDA. Well, if you're sure. (IDA *makes a move to start in.*)

MYRTLE. Oh, is Homer—around?

IDA. Why, I wonder where he got to—Homer?

(HOMER *enters stage left.*)

HOMER. Here I am.

IDA. Oh! I thought you'd gone in.

MYRTLE. Good morning, Homer.

HOMER. Good morning, Myrtle.

MYRTLE. Isn't it a lovely day?

HOMER. Sure is.

MYRTLE. My, you can feel the sun on you as warm as toast. I thought maybe you'd like to take a little walk?

HOMER. I'd like to.

MYRTLE. That's the first thing I thought of when I woke this morning, and saw the sunshine. I thought, Homer and I will take a nice walk this morning, till train time. Maybe we'll go up and look at our new house even.

(*Embarrassed pause.*)

HOMER. Well—

MYRTLE. Of course if you don't want to—

HOMER (*stepping toward her*). No, it isn't that. I—All right.

IDA. That's right. Now you take a nice walk and be back for lunch. Now I've got to run over to Cora's for a minute if you'll excuse me.

MYRTLE. Oh, of course.

IDA. You're sure you don't want any more breakfast?

MYRTLE (*brightly*). Honest Injun! (IDA *enters house right—Pause.* HOMER *waits awkwardly.* MYRTLE *turns to him with a bright smile.*) Hello.

HOMER. Hello.

MYRTLE. Did you have a good sleep?

HOMER. Not very.

MYRTLE. Oh, what a shame. I slept ever so nicely.

HOMER. Did you?

MYRTLE. That's the softest bed I think I ever slept on.

HOMER. I thought about things all night.

MYRTLE. Now you shouldn't have done that. I told you when you went to bed that you were to go right to sleep and not think about anything.

HOMER (*turns away*). I couldn't help it.

MYRTLE. That was bad of you.

HOMER (*turns toward her*). Myrtle.

MYRTLE (*stopping him*). Now don't you feel bad about anything, Homer. I thought it all out last night. I see just what you mean about not leaving your mother. And I think it's nice of you. We can go on just the way we have been. It's been wonderful this way and—

HOMER. No, it's not that. It's something else.

MYRTLE. What?

HOMER. It's—something I've got to tell you before we go. It wouldn't be fair not to.

MYRTLE. What is it?

(*She waits—*HOMER *hesitates.*)

HOMER. It's not very nice.

MYRTLE. My goodness, it can't be so very bad. Now out with it.

HOMER. It's about our house.

MYRTLE (*suddenly alarmed*). Nothing's happened to it, Homer! It hasn't burned down or anything—?

HOMER. No, it's—all right.

MYRTLE (*her hand to her heart*). My goodness, you scared me. You shouldn't say things like that.

HOMER. It's just that—It isn't our house any more.

(*Pause.* MYRTLE *looks at him, puzzled.*)

MYRTLE. Our house—isn't our house any more?

HOMER. My father just rented it to Aunt Cora. She's got a twenty-year lease on it.

MYRTLE. On *our* house?

HOMER. Uh-huh. I guess he thought we weren't going to be using it. (MYRTLE, *bewildered, puts her hand to her head. She turns away slightly, too stunned to understand it yet.* HOMER *watches her. Anguished.*) Gee, Myrtle, I'm so sorry!

MYRTLE (*in a dazed voice*). It's all right. Of course, it's all right—It really wasn't our house, was it? Not really. It was your father's house. You couldn't expect him to just keep it empty until—He has kept it empty for five years—You couldn't expect—(*She turns away from him—trying to reason it out—and to keep back the tears.*)

HOMER (*stepping toward her*). I'll build you one myself, Myrtle. I'll build you a house that'll make that house look like a garage.

MYRTLE. Don't be silly! (*She moves over by stump.*)

HOMER (*crossing to chair left—sitting*). Myrtle—I've been thinking things out.

MYRTLE (*wearily*). Yes, you said you had. (*Sits stump.*)

HOMER. Not just last night. Today, too. I ought to have got married and had a home of my own a long time ago. I ought to have done it.

MYRTLE (*faintly*). Why didn't you, Homer?

HOMER. I got caught. Somehow or other I got caught. But I'd do it now, Myrtle. I'd do it now except—(*Rises. Crosses center.*)

MYRTLE. Except what?

HOMER. Except now I really have to stay with my mother.

MYRTLE. What do you mean?

HOMER. My father's going away. He said to my mother, "You'll be all right. You've got Homer."

MYRTLE. What did he mean?

HOMER. He meant she had me to take care of her. She didn't need him.

MYRTLE (*slightly bitter*). She's always depended on you, Homer. You told me that last night.

HOMER. Yes, that's what I mean. She's always had me to take care of her. Maybe that's the trouble. (*Sits chair left.*)

MYRTLE (*pause—then suddenly turns to him*). Homer! Do you mean you really want to marry me now—? (*Rising and crossing to him—rapidly.*) Because if you do—if you really want to—it doesn't matter about our house—and you could be with your mother too. I could come and live here with you in this house. And we could have your little room. It's a darling little room. I looked at it on the way down. And we could all be together. (HOMER *turns to her—She pauses.*) That is, if you *wanted* to, of course.

HOMER. You mean, you'd live here—with everybody?

MYRTLE. Of course I would. I'd just love it.

HOMER. You always said a woman wanted a home of her own.

MYRTLE. Well, I'd be having it. It'd be even nicer in one way than being up there on Sycamore Drive. We'd never be lonesome here.

(*Pause.* HOMER *rises.*)

HOMER (*suddenly*). I'm awfully fond of you, Myrtle.

MYRTLE. Are you, Homer?

HOMER. I'm fonder of you than anything I could think of. (*Pause, he stands looking at her.*) I think you're wonderful.

(*They stand looking at each other a minute.*)

MYRTLE. Thank you, Homer. (MYRTLE *looks away a minute—starts to say something —then changes her mind—looks back.*) Shall we take our walk?

(HOMER *comes to her. He starts to put his arm around her. Hesitates. Looks over at the other house. Puts his arm around her anyway. They exit up center.—The door of the house at right opens and* ESTHER *comes out. She has hold of* ARRY'S *hand and is pulling her.* ARRY *is drawing back.*)

ARRY. What do you want to talk to me about?

ESTHER. Oh, come on, Arry. We're not going to hurt you.

ARRY (*drawing back*). I don't trust you, Esty. When you start talking—(*She suddenly comes out with a rush.* IDA, *who has given her a push, appears in the door behind her—steps to the right of her.*) Hey! Quit that! What'd you push me for?

IDA. I didn't push you.

ARRY. You did too.

IDA. I just wanted to come out and you were blocking the way.

ARRY. What's going on here anyway? (*They are at each side of her—she looks from one to the other.*) I'm going back in.

(*She starts to duck into the house.* IDA *grabs one arm*—ESTHER *the other.*)

ESTHER. Oh, no, you're not.

IDA. You're coming right along with us.

ARRY (*struggling*). You let go of me. Let go of me!

ESTHER. Oh, be quiet, Arry.

ARRY. Let go of me! (*Screaming.*) Let go of me!

ESTHER. Oh, my goodness. Let go of her, Ida.

(*They let go of* ARRY.)

ARRY. Thank you. Thank you so much. (*She starts up steps.*)

ESTHER. Go on back in. If you don't want to hear what we have to say, you don't need to.

ARRY (*stops—turns slowly*). I didn't say I wouldn't like to hear what you had to say, Esty, but when one person wishes to talk to another, there are certain rules of nice behavior they try to observe.

ESTHER (*trying not to giggle*). I'm sorry, Arry.

ARRY. I doubt very much whether in the best society you would find one person approaching the back of another person and pushing them from behind.

IDA. I'm sorry. Arry. We just wanted to have a little talk with you. Of course, if you don't care to—

ARRY. I'd be very glad to. (*She walks over to the stump, sits. Faces* ESTHER *and* IDA.) Well, Esther!

ESTHER. Well, Arry, I'll tell you. It's about Thor and Cora moving up to Homer's house—

(ARRY *jumps up and starts to run in.*)

ARRY. Oh, no, you don't! I know you, Esty!

ESTHER (*as she and* IDA *stop* ARRY). Now wait a minute, Arry.

ARRY (*between them*). I don't want to talk about it.

IDA. You *got* to talk about it.

ARRY. I knew I shouldn't have trusted you—

ESTHER. Why? What do you think we're going to say?

ARRY. You're going to say Thor and Cora ought to move up there.

ESTHER. Well, don't you think they should?

ARRY. No, I don't.

IDA. Why not?

ARRY. Just because I don't, that's all.

ESTHER. But if Cora wants to—and Thor wants to—

ARRY. Thor doesn't want to.

IDA. How do you know?

ARRY (*hesitating*). Well, I—I don't think he does.

ESTHER. Why, have you talked to him?

ARRY. Well, I—Not much.

ESTHER. Then you're not sure, are you?

ARRY. No, I'm not sure—

IDA. Then if he does want to and Cora wants to—why, it would be pretty nice for them, don't you think?

(ARRY, *trapped, moves back to the stump. They watch her.*)

ARRY (*sullenly—sits*). I don't know what business it is of yours anyway.

ESTHER. Strictly speaking, I don't suppose it is. But after all, we're sisters. And it means so much to Cora. . . . I'm just thinking of her happiness.

ARRY. And what about *my* happiness?

ESTHER. Well, in this case, certainly Cora's happiness is the one to consider.

ARRY. I don't see why.

ESTHER. Don't you? Cora wants to live alone with Thor, Arry.

ARRY (*suddenly vicious*). Well, she's not going to!

IDA. Oh, isn't she?

ARRY. Over my dead body she is. If they try anything there's a few things I can tell—

IDA. You've made that threat a lot of times, Arry—

ARRY. I mean it.

ESTHER. What could you tell, Arry?

ARRY. Plenty.

ESTHER. What could you tell that all of us don't already know? That we haven't all known for years?

(*Sudden pause.* ARRY *looks up at* ESTHER, *startled.*)

ARRY (*softly*). What do you mean, Esty? (*She looks at* IDA, *frightened, and back at* ESTHER. *In a whisper.*) What do you mean?

IDA. Do you think we're all blind, Arry?

ESTHER. Don't you think all of us know by this time about you and Thor?

(*Pause.*)

ARRY (*frightened*). No—no—Esty—

IDA. We've all known for years. All of us.

ARRY. No—no—

ESTHER. But we've all kept our mouths shut for Cora's sake. If you want a nasty business out of it go on and do it. But it won't get you anywhere, Arry. And you won't look so nice, carrying on for years with the husband of your own sister right under her very nose—

ARRY (*shocked—rises*). Esty! Esty, what do you mean? You don't think—Ida, you don't think—that Thor and me—all this time—Oh, my God!

(*She buries her face in her hands.* IDA *and* ESTHER *watch uneasily.*)

IDA. What do you mean, Arry?

ARRY (*moaning—sits stump*). Oh, my God! Oh, my God!

ESTHER (*uneasily*). But you've always hinted in front of everyone, Arry—

ARRY. You've all thought that Thor and me—all these years—Does Cora think that?

ESTHER. I don't know, Arry. Nobody's ever said anything to Cora. I guess Cora doesn't think anything.

ARRY (*suddenly she turns toward the house. Rises, and yells with a sudden frenzied frightenedness*). Thor! Thor! Thor!

ESTHER (*she and* IDA *move down right*). Arry—Wait—

ARRY. Thor! Thor!

THOR (*hurries out of the house right*). What's the matter? What's the matter, Arry?

ARRY. They say that—They think that—

(CORA *has entered between the houses. She stops, frozen, watching the scene.*)

CORA. Why, Arry, what's the matter?

(ARRY *hesitates a minute—looks at* CORA —*then suddenly runs into the house, weeping.*)

THOR. What's the matter with her?

ESTHER (*starting into house*). I don't quite know. I'll find out.

THOR. What did you say to her, Esty?

CORA (*hard*). Yes. What did you say to her?

ESTHER (*looking at* CORA). We just had a little fuss, Cora.

CORA. About what?

(*Pause.* ESTY *looks at* CORA.)

ESTHER. I'll tell you later. (*She exits.*)

CORA. Thor! (*He turns and sees her watching him.*) I wonder what she could

have said to Arry?

THOR. I don't know, Cora. Maybe she said something Arry didn't like so much.

CORA. Yes, she must have. I wonder what it could have been?

THOR. I don't know, Cora.

(*Pause.* CORA *turns to* IDA *brightly.*)

CORA. Ida, has Carl still got those packing cases he used to have in his garage?

IDA (*mystified*). Why—I don't know, Cora—

CORA. Harold Blake hasn't got any. He says he can move Thor and me up day after tomorrow, but he just hasn't got any packing cases.

(THOR *looks at her startled.*)

THOR (*hesitantly*). Day after tomorrow?

CORA. Uh-huh! (*To* IDA.) Can we go over and see if they're still there? (*She has started off left.*)

IDA (*following*). Yes—of course—

THOR. But Cora—But Cora—(*They go off left—*THOR *watches them. He sits on ledge—depressed.*) The day after tomorrow! Good God!

(HOMER *and* MYRTLE *enter from between the houses. They see* THOR *but he doesn't see them.* MYRTLE *goes quickly into* IDA's *house and* HOMER *crosses to* THOR.)

HOMER. Uncle Thor.

THOR (*startled*). Oh, hello, Homer.

HOMER. I've got to talk to you, Uncle Thor.

THOR. Well, go ahead, Homer.

HOMER. It's about my house. I've got to have it back.

THOR. Well, by God, Homer, nobody wishes you had it back more than I do.

HOMER. But I've *got* to have it back.

THOR. Well, there's no use talking to me about it. You'll have to talk to your Aunt Cora.

HOMER. No, I've got to talk to you about it. You see, last night when I thought my father was going to start having spells again—I felt I shouldn't leave my mother—and I told that to Myrtle and—

THOR. Yeah, I see the predicament, Homer, but—

HOMER. But this morning Myrtle said we could get married and live here with my mother and—

THOR. I know, Homer. That's kinda tough but—

HOMER. It isn't that so much but, you see—Myrtle just told me. She's going to have a—baby.

(Pause. There is a complete, dead silence. THOR *looks at* HOMER *in complete and utter bewilderment.)*

THOR *(in a ghostly whisper).* What?

HOMER. Uh-huh.

THOR. A—baby—?

HOMER. Uh-huh.

THOR. You mean—a—*(He gestures with his hands.)*—baby—

HOMER. Uh-huh.

THOR *(in a whisper, slowly looking* HOMER *over).* Well, for God's sakes! *(He rises and walks around* HOMER, *staring at him from all angles.* HOMER *stands, head down in embarrassment.)* Well, what the hell do you know about that! *(*HOMER's *head sinks lower.)* Well, I'll be God damned! *(Suddenly* THOR's *face lights up with a great glow. He beams at* HOMER. *He shouts—)* Well! Well! *(He rubs his hands together, beaming at* HOMER.*)* Well, well! Well, well! What the hell do you know about that! *(Slaps* HOMER *on the back.)* That's a pretty good one! Yes sir, by God, you certainly had your old Uncle Thor fooled!

HOMER *(suddenly smiling, modestly).* Just one of those things, you know.

THOR. Sure, sure!

HOMER. Don't really know how it happened.

THOR. By God, ain't it the truth.

HOMER. Kinda lose your head sometimes—

THOR *(clapping him on the back).* Ain't it the truth. By God! Well, what the hell do you know about that!

CURTAIN

ACT THREE

SCENE: *The same. A short time later.*

As the curtain rises, CORA *is eagerly watching the expression on* ESTHER's *face, which is one of sheer blankness. Both are seated, on steps house right, and chair left of steps.*

ESTHER. Homer?

CORA. That's what he told Thor.

ESTHER. But it's not possible, Cora.

CORA. Seems it is.

ESTHER. A baby!

CORA *(nervously).* Shh! For goodness' sakes, Esty, don't keep saying it. If Arry ever got hold of it Ida would find out in a minute.

ESTHER. But I just don't understand. How did it happen?

CORA. How does it usually happen?

ESTHER. But Homer must have—must have—

CORA. Of course he must have. That's the point.

ESTHER. Must have been all this time—

CORA. Seven years—

ESTHER. Well, I give up. I've seen a lot of things in my time, Cora. First the telephone. Everybody said it wouldn't work.

CORA *(giggling).* Now stop it, Esty! Somebody'll hear you. Besides, it's an awful thing.

ESTHER. Of course it's an awful thing.

CORA. If Arry should ever find out—

ESTHER. What are they going to do about it?

CORA. Well, they're going to get married—

ESTHER. I know, but even so—

CORA. Oh, they'll take a trip somewhere when the time comes. There's no hurry. Now for goodness' sakes, you mustn't let on to Thor that I told you. I promised him I wouldn't.

ESTHER. Does Homer know you know?

CORA. *Nobody* knows, Esty! *Nobody!* Thor promised Homer he wouldn't breathe it to a soul.

ESTHER. But why *did* Homer tell Thor?

CORA. Well—*(She rises—crosses down right—hesitates. Suddenly she reverts to the grim attitude she had in the previous act.)* He wants his house back.

ESTHER *(looking at her quickly).* Oh! I see.

CORA. I've just had a talk with Thor. He says I've got to let them have it.

ESTHER. Well, I suppose he feels if they're going to have a baby—

CORA *(turns to* ESTY*).* That's not the reason Thor wants me to give it back. Is it, Esty?

ESTHER. What do you mean, Cora?

CORA. You know what I mean. Thor's afraid to move up there with me.

ESTHER *(rises—crosses to* CORA*).* Cora, I'd like to ask you something.

CORA. What?

ESTHER. Have you ever doubted that Thor loved you?

*(*CORA *is not prepared for this. She is rather surprised. She thinks it over.)*

CORA. Why—no—

ESTHER. Have you ever doubted that

you came first—always—with Thor?

CORA (*after a moment*). No—I've never doubted that—

ESTHER. And you know you always will come first?

CORA. Yes—

ESTHER. Well, that's something to be able to say after fifty years of marriage, isn't it?

CORA (*slowly*). Yes, it's something. It's a *lot*. If that's all you can get. (*She turns away.* ESTHER *watches her.*) Well, I better go in. Now for goodness' sakes, Esty, don't let on to Thor.

ESTHER. Let on what? Oh, about the baby!

CORA (*motioning her to be quiet*). Esty! Esty!

ESTHER (*in a whisper—sitting*). All right. All right.

(CORA *stands quietly a moment.*)

CORA. Anyway, it'll be nice to have a baby in the family again, won't it?

ESTHER. Real nice.

(CORA *starts in as* THOR *comes out of the house at left, followed by* IDA, MYRTLE *and* HOMER. ESTHER *and* CORA *watch* MYRTLE.)

THOR (*as he comes down the steps*). What you want to do, Homer, is to take a nice long honeymoon. To hell with these picky little two-, three-week affairs. Months, I say, even if you have to wait a few months before you can get away.

HOMER. That sounds like a good idea, Uncle Thor.

THOR. You bet it's a good idea. Pick some nice quiet place and just settle down and live there awhile. Get to know each other. Come on, we'll dig up that atlas and have a look—Oop! Watch out there! Take it easy! (*He catches* MYRTLE *by the arm and helps her down the steps.*)

MYRTLE. Oh, thank you.

THOR (*carefully walking her center*). Bad step there—Well, Esty, old girl, have you heard the news?

ESTHER (*startled*). Why—I—I thought it was a se—(*She glances at* CORA.)

CORA (*quickly*). Homer and Myrtle are going to be married.

THOR (*chuckling — standing between* HOMER *and* MYRTLE). Yes, sir, gonna tie them up tighter'n a drumstick.

ESTHER. Congratulations, Homer.

HOMER. Thank you, Aunt Esther.

ESTHER (THOR *has crossed center right*). I'm sure you'll be very happy, Myrtle.

MYRTLE. Well, I just guess I will be. My goodness, I'm about as happy right now as a girl has any right to be. Everybody's being so nice it just—hurts.

THOR. Well, they better be nice! Aren't you going to congratulate them, Cora?

CORA (*who has been absorbed looking over* MYRTLE *for evidence*). Of course I am. Congratulations, Homer.

(*There is a slight pause.* HOMER *looks at her suddenly. Then turns away.*)

HOMER (*gruffly*). Thank you.

(CORA *is disturbed. The others watch her.*)

CORA (*flustered—after pause*). Well, well, I know you're going to be very happy, Myrtle.

MYRTLE. Well, I do, too. I just guess I will be. My goodness, I'm almost as happy right this minute as any girl—It isn't every day a girl gets a proposal of marriage. I just guess we'll be happy, won't we, Homer?

HOMER. Might be happy if we had a house to live in.

(*There is a dead pause. All eyes are focused on* CORA. *She becomes very flustered and turns away.*)

MYRTLE. Now you stop talking about that, Homer. My goodness, we can get along without that house. We'll be so happy right here in this house that you're going to be astounded.

HOMER. I don't want to live in this house.

MYRTLE. Well, we're going to. Now you stop striking discordant notes, Homer. We're just going to change the subject and not revert to it again. We'll just change the subject—er—(*Pause. They all wait for her to do it.*) Did you hear what Mother Ida said? (*She crosses to stump.*)

ESTHER. No. What did Mother Ida say?

MYRTLE. She said she didn't feel so much as if she was losing a son but more like she was gaining a daughter.

ESTHER. Did she say that!

MYRTLE. Yes, she did. (*Sits stump.*)

IDA (*sadly*). It isn't going to be so easy though—

HOMER (*firmly*). Now, Mother, none of that. I've made up my mind.

IDA (*timidly*). Oh, I know you have, Homer. And I'm so glad. I just meant if you shouldn't live here it isn't going to be so easy—with your father gone—

HOMER. I'll speak to my father, but it isn't going to influence me. I've made up my mind. Myrtle and I are going to be married and we're going to live alone. If we can find some old house. Just us two.

THOR. By God, that's all right for a while, Homer, but you can't keep a marriage down to two forever, you know.

MYRTLE (*giggling nervously*). Oh, you!

IDA. Well, there's plenty of time to think of that later.

THOR (*roaring*). By God, that's a fact, Ida. Plenty of time for that later. (*He nudges* HOMER *and gives him a knowing wink.*)

MYRTLE. Well, my goodness, we're certainly crossing our bridges—

HOMER (*firmly*). If I should ever have a son I won't let him stay around the house after he's nineteen.

IDA. Homer!

HOMER. I won't, Mother. There's no use arguing. At nineteen he gets out.

MYRTLE. Homer!

HOMER. Animals, too. You don't see an animal hanging around home after it's grown up, do you?

THOR. No sir, you don't, Homer. That's a fact.

HOMER (*to* ESTHER). Did you ever hear of a grown male dog who wouldn't leave his mother?

ESTHER. I don't think I ever did, Homer.

HOMER (*to* IDA). Did you ever hear of *any* animal that wouldn't get out when he grew up?

IDA. I—I don't know, Homer—

HOMER. Even pigs. The mother pushes them out right away. And that's the way it ought to be.

MYRTLE (*to them all*). It's very interesting, isn't it?

IDA (*tearfully*). I'm sure I never tried to do anything to hold Homer—

MYRTLE (*crossing to her quickly*). Well, I should just guess you didn't either—

IDA. I always tried to push him out—

MYRTLE. Of course you did. Now we won't have any more talk like this! Don't you say anything more, Homer. My goodness, I guess I can realize how your mother feels!

HOMER. Well, every animal *I* ever heard of—

MYRTLE. Homer!

IDA (*tearfully*). Oh! (*She runs into house left.*)

MYRTLE. Oh, Mother Ida—He didn't mean—(*She turns to* HOMER.) My goodness, Homer, I just don't know what's got into you! You used to always be so nice to your mother. You just seem to be striking discordant notes all the time. Pigs, indeed! You're getting just terrible, Homer!

THOR (*crossing right*). Well, come on. Let's get this honeymoon figured out. Where do you suppose that atlas is, Cora?

(*They all look at* CORA.)

CORA (*crossing center—strangely grim*). I don't know.

THOR (*uneasily*). Well, come on. We'll find it. (*As they start in* ARRY *comes out. They all stop suddenly and look at her.* CORA *watches her. Tentatively.*) Hello, Arry. Headache gone?

ARRY. I want to talk to you a minute, Thor.

THOR (*uneasily*). Well, we were just going in and—

ARRY. I guess you can spare a few minutes.

(*Slight pause.* THOR *is uneasy.* ARRY *starts down the steps.*)

THOR. Well, all right, Arry.

ARRY. Thank you. (*She crosses down to* ESTY.)

THOR. Look in the bottom of the victrola, Homer. I think the atlas's in there. I'll be in in a minute.

(MYRTLE *and* HOMER *exit.* ARRY *reaches* ESTHER. *There is a feeling of tension.* ARRY *hands* ESTHER *a letter.*)

ARRY. I want you to read this sometime, Esty.

ESTHER. What is it?

ARRY. You'll find out.

ESTHER. All right, Arry. (*She eyes her a moment sharply.*) Is your head better?

ARRY. My head's all right.

ESTHER. Good.

(ARRY *turns to* CORA, *who has been watching her.*)

ARRY (*suddenly*). Don't you worry, You won't have to bother with me any more. Just don't you worry.

(*A moment's pause. They stand looking at each other.*)

CORA (*after a moment, quietly*). Arry wants to talk to Thor, Esty. Would you take a little walk with me?

ESTHER *and* CORA *go out between the houses in silence.* THOR *looks after them a moment, uneasily, and then he goes to* ARRY *who has seated herself and sits looking quietly into space.*)

THOR (*uneasily*). You oughtn't to say things like that to Cora, Arry. No use getting her any madder than she is. (*He looks at her. She is paying no attention.*) And what did you mean by she won't have to bother with you any more? (*She doesn't answer.* THOR *looks at her, uneasy. With fake cheerfulness.*) Anyway, I think everything's going to turn out fine. (*He sits by her on the lower step—Pause.* ARRY *has not moved—*THOR *still uneasy.*) All of us got a little excited—but, hell, what's the difference. Nobody meant what they said. (*Pause. He eyes her.*) Anything the matter, Arry?

ARRY (*after a moment*). What does it mean to you to grow old, Thor?

(THOR *looks at her in surprise.*)

THOR. What do you mean, Arry?

ARRY. Doesn't getting old mean that —well, that things don't trouble you so much any more? That everything's more peaceful and quiet—

THOR. Peaceful and quiet! I guess that must be when you get *real* old, Arry. Say in your late eighties.

ARRY. I always thought of getting old sort of like going to bed when you're nice and drowsy—and yet you know you won't fall to sleep for a little while yet —and you just lie there sort of comfortably —and enjoy it—But it isn't that way at all.

THOR. I don't know what you're getting at, Arry.

ARRY. Well, I've been lying down thinking. (*She turns to him suddenly.*) You've been real good to me, Thor. You're a real good man.

THOR (*embarrassed*). Oh, hell, Arry.

ARRY. I mean it. Cora too. I want you to know I appreciate the way you've had me in your home all these years.

THOR. It was your home too, Arry.

ARRY. Nope. That's what I found out. It wasn't ever my home. I haven't got a home. That's what I mean about getting old. I guess it's nice and peaceful if you got a home. If you got a husband. If you got somebody to get old with—But I haven't. So you know what I'm going to do, Thor?

THOR. What, Arry?

ARRY. I'm going to go away.

THOR. What do you mean?

ARRY. I'm leaving. I'm leaving you and Cora to have a home together.

THOR. But Arry—

ARRY. No, Thor, I'm going to do it. I should have done it years ago, but I didn't. I'm going to try to forget you, Thor.

THOR. Gee, Arry, I don't know what to say.

ARRY. There's nothing to say. (ARRY *rises and crosses to steps.*) Thor.

THOR. Yeah?

ARRY. When I die—you know what I want on my stone?

THOR. What?

ARRY. "Home is the sailor, home from the sea

And the hunter, home from the hill."

THOR. All right, Arry.

ARRY. Mama used to say that. . . . Now I'll go in and pack. (*Goes up stairs— at top—turns.*) Thor. (*He turns.*) I'm not sorry about anything.

THOR. All right, Arry.

ARRY. Not sorry at all.

(*She exits.* THOR *looks after her, sadly.*)

THOR (*rising—going up steps*). Poor Arry! All alone in the world.

(THOR *stands looking after her a moment. He stops as* DAVID *and* CARL *enter, loaded down with* CARL's *luggage and tools as they were when they left.* THOR, *unnoticed, watches them.* DAVID *puts bags on the porch—*CARL *leaves his down left.*)

DAVID. For example, if you were taken blindfolded to some part of the city and the blindfold were taken off, how would you find out where you were?

CARL. I'd look to see what street I was on.

DAVID. Exactly. Now say there wasn't any sign—or say you were lost in a woods. At night. How would you find out where you were?

(THOR *shakes his head, and exits.*)

CARL. Well, I know the North Star. And I could wander around until I found some landmark I knew and get my location that way—

DAVID. All right. Now to find your location in life, Carl, you do the same thing. Just wander around until you find a few landmarks. A man like you has got to make it his business to find his own location among the concepts that we know. He has got to search himself, search all the knowledge that he has, all the knowledge that others have, until the last blade of grass in that lawn or the last pebble in that road bears some relation to him, takes on some meaning, becomes a landmark so he knows just where he is. Only then is a man like you safe; when you can say, "I am eight miles north of water; I am three thoughts under love; I am ten beats past despair," then you'll know where you are, Carl. (DAVID *pauses and looks at* CARL.) Do you understand what I mean, Carl?

CARL. Well—I don't *quite* understand. David.

DAVID (*thoughtfully—crossing left*).Well, there's an *idea* there, Carl.

CARL (*eagerly*). I know there is, David.

DAVID (*turning to* CARL). Yes, there's an idea there *somewhere*, if we can pin it down. Well, let's pin it down, Carl. Let's pin it down.

CARL. All right, David. Let's!

(ESTHER *comes in between the houses center to stump—* DAVID *breaks off.*)

DAVID. Ah, Esther.

ESTHER. I thought it was you, David.

DAVID. Yes, Esther, it is I.

CARL. We're—we're bringing my things back.

ESTHER. Yes, I see. There's nothing wrong, is there?

CARL. Well, it's that little closet we were going to make into a bath. It's not very well located. It's not under the upstairs bathroom.

ESTHER. Yes, I could have told you that.

CARL. Well, it would cost nearly three hundred dollars to put it in shape.

EATHER. As much as that? Oh, dear, dear!

CARL. We'd practically have to tear the whole house down.

ESTHER. I see. I see.

CARL. And as David says you haven't the three hundred dollars—the idea doesn't seem very practical.

ESTHER. Well, no, it certainly doesn't, does it?

CARL. And so—we're bringing my things back. (*Embarrassed pause.*) Well, I'll just take these out.

(*He exits left with tools.* ESTHER *stands warching* DAVID.)

ESTHER. Poor Carl. He seems upset.

DAVID. Upset? No. . . . Fundamentally I should say Carl's a very sound person, Esther.

ESTHER (*smiling*). Really?

DAVID. Yes. He thinks things out very clearly—very logically. (*Pause. She stands regarding him, smiling. He is embarrassed. Starts to pick up bags.*) Well—

ESTHER (*sits*). David, I'd like to read you something.

DAVID (*hesitating with bags in hand*). Well, Esty, I—

ESTHER. You know what we've all suspected about Arry and Thor all these years, don't you, David?

DAVID (*turning*). Oh, I've heard the talk, Esther. I never paid much attention to it.

ESTHER. Arry just gave me this letter. (*Shows the letter.* DAVID *puts down bags and crosses to stump and sits.*) Do you remember —oh, it must have been all of forty years ago—after Arry had been living with them about a year—Cora had to go to the hospital for a couple of weeks?

DAVID. I think I do—vaguely—

ESTHER. Thor and Arry were alone. She was about seventeen. She didn't know much about anything. Right off the farm. She was pretty, full of life. You remember how Arry was. And—(*She reads.*) ". . . and I don't know how it happened, Esty. I just don't. I loved Thor so much. I didn't realize it. I should have gone away but I couldn't. We were both so miserable and scared. We didn't know what to do. But never after that time, Esty. Never. If Cora should ever know I'd just die." (ESTHER *puts the letter down. They both sit thinking a moment.*) And so she just went on—living with them—because there wasn't any other place for her to go after that. (*Pause.*) Well, I feel kind of sorry for Arry. I guess she feels her life hasn't been to much purpose. (*She reads.*) "When you and Ida told me what all of you had been thinking all this time—it seems to me I'd never be able to hold up my head again. It doesn't much matter about the years ahead—but it suddenly seemed as if all the years I've already lived didn't make much sense. I might just as well not have lived them." (*Pause. She puts the letter down.*)

DAVID (*rises—moves up left*). In the eyes of the world—I'm a failure—but we've kept our lives clear, Esther, and intelligent.

ESTHER. Yes, David, we have, haven't we?

DAVID. We've never let that other third element ever come in. We've kept ourselves to ourselves.

ESTHER (*smiling*). Yes, I know what

you mean by a Crystal Fortress, David. (*He turns away. There is a moment's pause.* ESTHER *watches him, smiling.*)

DAVID. It's a tragic line Aaronetta says about the years behind her, "I might just as well not have lived them."

ESTHER. Yes.

DAVID (*he turns to her, hesitating*). Did you ever feel like that, Esther?

ESTHER. No, David.

DAVID (*eagerly*). That's good.

ESTHER. But, you see, I always had you, David.

(DAVID *is touched, embarrassed.*)

DAVID. Thank you, Esther. (*He turns to her with a smile and a short bow.*) Thank you. I'll take these in.

(DAVID *goes in house left with bags.* ESTHER *rises and puts letter away as she sees* CORA *come down the path.* CORA *stops at the stump and stands looking ahead of her in silence.*)

ESTHER. Well, Cora?

CORA (*quietly*). I'm going to give Homer back his house.

ESTHER (*surprised*). You are?

CORA. Yes. I've just been looking at it. I walked up there after you left me. It's a beautiful house and Thor loves it—But as I stood there looking at it I suddenly realized something. Living up there alone with Thor is not what I'm after. *That's* not the important thing. But there *is* something that's important and I'm going to have it. (*She turns away.*) I hate Arry!

ESTHER. No, Cora.

CORA. I hate her. But she can go on living with us. There's no other place for her. But she's not going on living with us the way she has been. Because I'm going to find out where I stand, Esty. And I'm going to live alone with Thor in that very house—even with Arry there. (*After a moment.*) You remember that poem Papa used to say about us girls, Esty?

  "Esty's smartest,
  Arry's wildest,
  Ida's slowest,
  Cora's mildest."

And then he always used to look at me and say, "Poor Cora." You remember that?

ESTHER. Yes.

CORA (*tensely*). Well, I'm not "Poor Cora" any more! There's such a thing as being too mild!

(CARL *enters from the house left. Comes down porch steps.*)

CARL (*hesitantly*). Oh, Cora! I sort of hate to say anything to you about it, but—

CORA. I'm giving Homer back his house, Carl.

CARL (*relieved*). You are? Well, now that's awfully nice of you, Cora. (*Crosses left center.*) Somehow I just knew you would.

(THOR, MYRTLE *and* HOMER *come out from the house at right.* CORA *watches them.* ESTHER *watches* CORA.)

THOR (*crossing down steps*). By God, that's just the place for you. Now why the hell do you suppose I didn't think of that sooner?

MYRTLE. My goodness, it sounds simply heavenly.

THOR. You wait till you see that water coming down. And there's a little boat that goes right out under the falls. Cora and I spent a whole week there once.

(DAVID *and* IDA *enter from house left.*)

HOMER. What do you think, Myrtle?

MYRTLE. I think it sounds simply—divine!

HOMER. Then that settles it. That's where we'll go.

THOR. Hello, David. Heard the news?

DAVID. Ah, yes. My congratulations, Homer.

(IDA *crosses down.*)

HOMER. Thank you, Uncle David.

DAVID. I hope you're not being too impetuous. (*Bowing to* MYRTLE.) Myrtle, I hope—

MYRTLE (*crossing down*). My goodness, I just guess I will be. I'm just about as happy this minute as any girl has a right to be—

CARL. Homer.

HOMER. Yes, Father?

CARL. Aunt Cora is giving you your house back.

HOMER. What?

MYRTLE. Our house!

(*They both look at* CORA.)

CORA (*flustered*). Yes, I—Of course, I guess I meant all along for you to have it back. I—

MYRTLE (*crossing center left*). Oh, I just think you are all the nicest people I ever met. I just have never met so many nice people before. Aren't you going to say anything, Homer?

HOMER (*crossing to* CORA—*kissing her*). Well, thank you, Aunt Cora. Thank you ever so much.

CORA. Well—that's all right, Homer—

MYRTLE. I just feel like crying—

(ARRY *comes out with hatbox and suitcase. She has on a large picture hat and looks very pretty. They all look at her. She poses at the top of steps for them. You see* CORA *stiffen and turn away.* ESTHER *watches her.*)

THOR. By God, don't you look pretty, Arry.

ARRY (*the great lady*). Thank you, Thor. (ESTY *rises.*)

IDA. Where are you going, Arry?

(*Pause.* ARRY *comes down a step.*)

ARRY. I'm moving out. (*She looks around at them all.*)

IDA. Moving?

ESTHER. Where are you going?

CARL. What do you mean, Arry?

MYRTLE. Why, Aunt Arry—?

ARRY. Yes, I'm leaving. I should have left years ago, of course, but I didn't realize all the things I know now—(*Starts center.*)

ESTHER. Now, look here, Arry—

ARRY. Don't try to stop me, Esty. Please. It's a little upsetting, of course, when you get to be my age to suddenly find out you're not wanted any more.

THOR (*sorry*). Ah, Arry—!

CORA (*evenly*). Let her finish, Thor.

ARRY. That all the years you thought you were a part of a home you were really just sort of a—servant in it—and you could be dismissed when your services were no longer needed—(*Cross center.*)

THOR. By God, don't say that, Arry. You don't have to go anywhere.

(*As* ARRY *goes on* ESTY *moves nearer* CORA.)

ARRY (*with a little smile*). But, Thor, I'm not wanted here.

THOR. You are, too. By God, this is your home, Arry. Isn't that so, Cora?

ARRY. Oh, don't ask Cora, Thor. Cora wants to live alone—She doesn't want any sister of hers—

CORA (*starting toward* ARRY, *furious*). All right, Arry—I've stood—

ESTHER (*grabbing* CORA). Wait a minute, Cora.

CORA. Arry—!

ESTHER. Cora!

(CORA *turns and* ESTHER *hands her* ARRY'S *letter and motions for her to read it.* CORA *does so during the following scene.* ARRY *turns to* MYRTLE.)

ARRY. I haven't had the opportunity to felicitate you on your approaching nuptials, Myrtle. I know you'll be very happy.

MYRTLE. Thank you, Aunt Arry.

ARRY. Homer too, of course.

HOMER. Thank you, Aunt Arry.

ARRY. But when you come right down to it, it's the woman that ought to be the happiest.

MYRTLE. I just guess that's the truth.

ARRY. She's the one who makes the home and looks after things and keeps it together.

MYRTLE. That's just the woman's function, I should think.

(CORA *has finished half the letter. She turns swiftly to* ESTHER—ESTY *motions her to finish the letter*—CORA *moves to* THOR'S *chair—sits.*)

ARRY. And marriage gives a woman dignity, Myrtle. It gives her dignity and companionship and a place to be when she gets old. I know you'll be very happy, Myrtle.

MYRTLE. I know I will be.

ARRY. That's right. (*She turns.* CORA *has finished the letter and you see it has softened her.* ARRY *and she look at each other.* ARRY *is terrified and looks accusingly at* ESTY.) Esty!

(ESTY *nods admission that she gave* CORA *the letter. A moment's pause.* CORA *rises slowly. Crumples the letter and goes to* ARRY.)

CORA. You're going away, Arry.

ARRY. Yes, Cora.

CORA (*touched*). I'll—I'll miss you, Arry—

(ARRY *looks at her slowly.*)

THOR. By God, you don't have to go, Arry.

ARRY. Yes, Thor, I must go. We'll see each other now and then, but I'm not going to live here any more.

THOR. But where are you going to go?

ARRY. Well, I'm going to move over to Ida's. Ida told me years ago if I ever wanted to move over to her I could. Didn't you, Ida?

IDA. Of course, Arry.

CARL. Anytime you want to, Arry.

ARRY (*crossing between* IDA *and* CARL). Well, now I want to. I want to spend the rest of the years with you.

(*Pause.*)

HOMER. Well, if we're going to see our house we'd better go.

MYRTLE. Our house! My goodness! I've just never had so many people so nice to me all at once—

THOR. By God, Myrtle, if anybody isn't nice to you just come to your old Uncle Thor.

MYRTLE (*crossing to* THOR). Well, I certainly will. I'll just look on you as— well, as my—protector.

(*They laugh together.*)

HOMER (*taking hold of* MYRTLE, *gruffly*). All right. That's enough. We better go now.

MYRTLE. Yes, Homer.

(*They exit up center between houses.* ARRY *hands* CARL *her bags and starts toward* IDA'S *house as—* CURTAIN

ETHAN FROME

Owen Davis and Donald Davis

(a dramatization of Edith Wharton's novel, suggested by a dramatiza-
by Lowell Barrington)

Ethan Frome was first produced by Max Gordon at the National Theatre, New York
City, on January 21, 1936. It was staged by Guthrie McClintic and the sets were by
Jo Mielziner. The cast was as follows:

HARMON GOW	John Winthrop	JOTHAM	Francis Pierlot
A YOUNG MAN	Oliver Barbor	ED VARNUM	Charles Henderson
ETHAN FROME	Raymond Massey	NED HALE	W. Dana Hardwick
ZENOBIA FROME	Pauline Lord	RUTH VARNUM	Sylvia Weld
DENIS EADY	Tom Ewell	MRS. HALE	Marie Falls
MATTIE SILVER	Ruth Gordon	Citizens of Starkfield, etc.	

SYNOPSIS OF SCENES

PROLOGUE: The exterior of the Frome farmhouse in Northern New
England.

ACT ONE. *Scene One:* Spring—twenty years earlier. The kitchen.
Scene Two: Outside the doorway of the vestry of the Starkfield Congregational Church—the following winter. Evening. *Scene Three:*
The crest of a hill above Starkfield—a few minutes later—the same
night. *Scene Four:* The exterior of the Frome farmhouse—a few minutes
later.

ACT TWO. *Scene One:* The Frome bedroom—five-thirty the following
morning. *Scene Two:* The kitchen—immediately following preceding
scene. *Scene Three:* The kitchen—that evening.

ACT THREE. *Scene One:* The bedroom—the next evening. *Scene Two:*
The kitchen—the following afternoon. *Scene Three:* The crest of the
hill—half an hour later.

EPILOGUE: The kitchen—twenty years later. The action follows that
of the Prologue.

Dramatization, copyright 1935 Owen and Donald Davis.
Copyright 1936 Charles Scribner's Sons. Reprinted with the permission of Charles Scribner's Sons.
Original text of story, copyright 1911 Charles Scribner's Sons; renewal copyright 1939 Frederic R. King
and Leroy King.

CAUTION: Professionals and amateurs are hereby warned that *Ethan Frome*, being fully protected under
the Copyright Laws of the United States of America, the British Empire, including the Dominion of
Canada, and all other countries of the Copyright Union, is subject to royalty. All rights, including
professional, amateur, motion picture, recitation, lecturing, public reading, radio broadcasting, and the
rights of translation into foreign languages, are strictly reserved. Particular emphasis is laid on the
question of readings, permission for which must be secured from the publisher in writing. All inquiries
should be addressed to Charles Scribner's Sons, 597 Fifth Avenue, New York City.

The best things that can be said about the dramatization of Edith Wharton's short novel *Ethan Frome* were all said by the aged novelist in her foreword to the play. Upon reading the dramatization made by Owen and Donald Davis, she wrote from France, "I found myself thinking at every page: 'Here at last is a new lease of life for Ethan! And the discovery moved me more than I can say." She added that she believed "few have had the luck to see the characters they had imagined in fiction transported to the stage without loss or alteration of any sort, without even that grimacing enlargement of gesture and language supposed to be necessary to 'carry' over the footlights."

With its superb cast, the production of *Ethan Frome* was also one of the most appealing offerings of the Broadway stage of the 1930's, a period that abounded in sympathetic presentations of the common man in tragic and near-tragic situations. On hearing about the excellence of the production, Edith Wharton wrote from St. Claire le Château, Hyères, in 1936, that she was gratified that "my poor little groups of hungry lonely New England villagers will live again for a while on their stormy hillside before finally joining their forebears under the village headstones." She was glad this good fortune might be theirs, she wrote, since "their strained starved faces" were still near to her.

An unusual amount of competence went into the making of this adaptation by Owen Davis and his son. Mere dramaturgic skill could be supplied readily by the senior partner of the collaboration, about whom Burns Mantle wrote as long ago as 1938, "No one knows just how many plays Owen Davis has written, not even Owen Davis." Starting with *Through the Breakers* in 1898, he wrote over 300 plays, mostly melodramas in the extravagant thriller tradition, such as *The Gambler's Daughter* and *Driftwood*. He became known as the pre-modern theatre's ablest and most successful fabricator. In the 1920's, however, Owen Davis applied his well-tried skill to modern subject matter, and proved himself especially attuned to New England themes of frustration and failure. Working in this vein, he was able to build a second and less debatable reputation with such original plays as *The Detour* (1921) and *Icebound*, which won the Pulitzer Prize in 1923 as the best production of the 1922-23 season. Not unexpectedly, he also applied his craftsmanship successfully to the dramatization of modern fiction, and *Ethan Frome*, in 1936, was the climax of his career.

In dramatizing Edith Wharton's celebrated book, originally published in 1911, Owen Davis collaborated with his eldest son Donald, who had worked with him on the adaptation of Pearl Buck's novel *The Good Earth* in 1932, and had established a career as a Hollywood scenarist after training for the sea, drifting about for two years as an able seaman, and then studying somewhat desultorily at Cornell and at New York University. Father and son were assigned the job of adapting the Wharton opus by the Broadway producer Max Gordon, after the waning of his interest in a prior version by Lowell Barrington, upon which they drew to some extent — which explains the credit line on the title page.

Owen Davis, who published an entertaining autobiography, *I'd Like to Do It Again*, in 1931, died in 1956.

PROLOGUE

Exterior of the Frome farmhouse, near Starkfield in Northern New England.

Dusk—a winter evening.

The section of the house which is visible extends from off D. R. *to a point* R. *of* C. *The house is flimsy with age, a sadly cold and stark, unpainted clapboard structure. The snow-covered ground rises from a point in front of the house to the crest of a hill at back* L. *where presumably the ground falls away toward the valley below. At back* L., *on the crest of the rise, a corner of the Frome burial ground is visible—silhouetted weirdly against the gray sky, the old granite slabs project through the snow. A pale yellow glow from the oil lamp in the kitchen outlines the closed front door of the house. There is a moment of silence, the bleak exterior of the house is deserted. After a moment* HARMON GOW, *a man of about fifty, and a* YOUNG MAN *enter along the path at* L.

HARMON (*down* C.). This is Frome's place. (THE YOUNG MAN *has stopped up* C. L. *and is staring at the bleak house, and cold landscape.*) C'mon, I'll ask Ethan 'bout drivin' you over . . . you won't never get to Corbury standin' there. (THE YOUNG MAN *has not moved.*) You ain't changed your mind about wantin' to go?

THE YOUNG MAN (*moves forward* C., *now murmuring*). No, no . . . of course not. I've got to get over to Corbury tonight . . . somehow. (HARMON *moves toward the house.*) Do you think he'll want to take me?

HARMON (*with some surprise*). Ethan? (THE YOUNG MAN *nods.*) Well, I guess he won't be sorry to earn a dollar. (*He hesitates.*) Don't be surprised if Ethan don't ask you in. He don't's a rule. (*Defensively.*) He don't mean anythin' by it. It's just his way. Things ain't gone any too well with them in there, you know—an' I guess Ethan likes to keep his troubles pretty well to himself. (HARMON *moves toward door, murmuring.*) As far's that goes, I'd just as soon we talked to him out here. (*He knocks at door, moves back, and stands beside* THE YOUNG MAN. *A bolt is shot back—the door opens jerkily and* ETHAN *stands in the partly opened doorway, leaning upon the door for support.* . . . HARMON *speaks quickly.*) How do, Ethan!

ETHAN. Harmon?

HARMON. A-yeah. Like a word with you, Ethan . . . if you've got a minute. (ETHAN *steps outside, closing the door after him. Neither* HARMON *nor* THE YOUNG MAN *has moved and they stand waiting a few feet from the door.* ETHAN *is not much over fifty . . . the ruin of a once powerful man, though still a striking figure. His face is scarred, there is a huge deep gash across his forehead, and his right side is so warped that each step he takes costs him a visible effort. There is something terribly bleak and unapproachable in his face . . . and he is so stiffened and grizzled that he might easily be taken for a much older man. He moves away from the doorway, his lameness checking each step he takes.* ETHAN *nods to* HARMON . . . *glances at* THE YOUNG MAN.)

THE YOUNG MAN (*quickly*). How do you do, Mr. Frome. I saw you yesterday—when you were getting your mail over at the post office.

ETHAN (*shortly*). A-yeah.

HARMON. He's a newcomer, Ethan . . . stayin' over to Mrs. Ned Hale's place . . . tells me he come up to do a job of work on that new power plant't they're buildin' over to Corbury. . . . (ETHAN *makes no comment and* HARMON *continues abruptly.*) He claims he's just got to get over there for a few minutes tonight an' again in the mornin', Ethan.

THE YOUNG MAN. We thought we'd ask if you could drive me over.

ETHAN. If I was you . . . I'd've asked at Eady's livery stable.

HARMON. Eady claims his horses is all laid up with the epidemic.

ETHAN. A-yeah.

HARMON. I happened to remember that old bay of yours is still on his feet.

ETHAN. A-yeah.

THE YOUNG MAN. I'd be very grateful if you could do it, Mr. Frome.

HARMON (*seeing* ETHAN's *hesitation*). 'Course I know't you don't usually go drivin' folks around, Ethan.

ETHAN. No . . . I don't.

THE YOUNG MAN. It's just that you'd be doing me the biggest kind of a favor!

ETHAN (*abruptly*). Why'd you think I'd want to do it, Harmon?

HARMON. Well, I don't know . . . if I had a rig . . . 'course I'd be more'n glad to do the job myself. He's willin' to pay, Ethan.

ETHAN (*with sudden interest*). Oh.

HARMON. I told him it'd be 'bout a dollar for the round trip.

ETHAN (*thoughtfully*). A-yeah. (*Then to* THE YOUNG MAN.) When'd you want to go?

THE YOUNG MAN. As soon as possible . . . but of course if you think it's too much of a trip for you . . .

ETHAN (*sharply*). I'll see't you get there. (*He turns and limps toward the door.*)

HARMON (*quickly*). You c'd be back before bedtime, Ethan.

ETHAN. I'll get my coat. (*Reluctantly.*) You c'n come in a minute . . . if you want.

HARMON (*quickly*). No . . . that's all right, Ethan . . . we'll just wait for you down to the barn. (ETHAN *glances at* HARMON. *Opens door and exits into the house, closing the door after him.* THE YOUNG MAN *stares at the closed door.*)

THE YOUNG MAN. I hate to make that man drag himself out on a night like this and drive me all the way over there and back.

HARMON. He won't mind, not's long's as he gets the dollar. (HARMON *moves forward and* THE YOUNG MAN *follows.*) This place never was wuth much . . . but before anythin' happened to Ethan he kind've choked a livin' out of it somehow . . . I don't just see how he gets along now.

THE YOUNG MAN. But he looks as though he must have been a strong man once.

HARMON. Ethan? Yes, he was! Yessir!

THE YOUNG MAN (*with great interest*). But whatever happened to him?

HARMON (*shortly*). Don't know much about it.

THE YOUNG MAN. After I had seen him yesterday I asked people around the post office—everybody knew who he was all right, but nobody would tell me anything about it.

HARMON. A-yeah . . . well, it was more'n twenty years ago.

THE YOUNG MAN. Well, whatever it was . . . how did it happen? Don't you even know that?

HARMON. Well! I remember old Mrs. Hale trying to find out about it at the time from Zeena—but she didn't get very far, and Zeena's Ethan's wife. An' Ethan . . . well . . . he knows all right . . . But I wouldn't never ask him . . . an' from that day to this he ain't's much's mentioned it.

THE YOUNG MAN (*in amazement*). Why not?

HARMON (*as they move off* R., *toward the path*). Well . . . I don't know . . . some folks say one thing . . . some another. (*Both cross* R.) C'mon, we can be hitching up the sleigh for him. (*They exit* R. *It is growing darker now. After a moment* ETHAN *opens the door and steps outside. As he moves slowly away from the door, it is bolted again from the inside.* ETHAN, *wearing his hat and coat, and carrying a lighted lantern. He limps slowly and haltingly. His forlorn figure is silhouetted against the bleak snowy landscape. He exits* R. *The lights dim out slowly.*)

CURTAIN

ACT ONE

SCENE ONE

The drab kitchen of the Frome farmhouse. Early spring—twenty years before the time of the Prologue. Door R. *opens to reveal steep stairway to the attic floor above. Door at* C. *back to outside. Window up* L. *looks out upon the bleak landscape. Sink beneath window with hand pump. Door* L. *to unused parlor. Open cupboard up* R. *with shelves to ceiling. On the kitchen table* C. *is a basin of clear water, three pieces of fancy bric-a-brac, cream pitcher and sugar bowl. On the chair* L. *is a Sears Roebuck catalogue. A rocking chair stands* R., *and by it a handstove. On the cookstove* C. *are a pot of stew and ladle, a coffeepot, two flatirons and pads for the handles, and a kettle full of hot water.* L. *is a shelf with a clock, candlesticks, and a sewing basket.* R. *of the stove is a wood-bin, with a hatchet by it.*

ZEENA *enters from the stairs* R. *She wears a shapeless nondescript calico dress, high black shoes, brown stockings and a thick knitted shawl drawn close about her shoulders. She could obviously never have been anything but a rather drab, humorless woman, but long years of many indescribable maladies, or of chronic hypochondria (ZEENA herself would be the last one in the world to know which) . . . or possibly both, and we find* ZEENA *tired, sickly, and seemingly ageless at 32. She carries a bucket of water and cleaning rag. Carries them to sink* L., *wipes drain and board around the sink, washes cloth out at pump, exits* C., *and hangs rag on nail outside door. Returns and goes to sink, empties pail of water and puts pail under sink.* ETHAN *enters from outside* C. *with an armful of small logs. He is about 28 years old. He is a slim, powerfully built New Englander . . . a drab part of the poverty-stricken farm which is his life, and like it, severe and hard and cold. He dumps the logs upon the floor close to the woodbin. Tosses two pieces into the bin. When* ZEENA *puts pail under sink,* ETHAN *turns from wood bin, goes to table, pushes china aside, and starts to sit down on chair* R. *of table.*

ZEENA (*crosses to table*). Ethan, don't, you might break them! (ETHAN *gets up, goes back to woodbin at* C. *and stacks the kindling.* ZEENA *stands at table admiring her china.*) I've been hanging on to these for I don't know how long. Of course I've given up hopin' we'll ever get a place where there'd be any use of havin' nice things. (*Stands on chair which she has dragged to cupboard and puts china away on top shelf of cupboard. Gets teapot, shows it to him; he does not look.*) This is real pretty, ain't it? But I always say, what's the use of it without I have cups and saucers to match. (*Finishes with things on shelf. Gets down and replaces chair by table.*) Where did you put my Sears Roebuck catalogue?

ETHAN. I never touched it.

ZEENA. (*Picks up catalogue from chair* L. *of table, and sits at table.*) Here it is. I got the place marked. Did you fix the window in the spare room?

ETHAN. I fixed it yesterday like you asked me. Why did you *want* it fixed?

ZEENA (*reading*). Energex Vibrator . . . New Type . . . tones up the system—beneficial in the treatment of inflammatory conditions—and all deep-seated complaints—$22.95. I wish you'd get me one of them Energex Vibrators—you could get it all right, Ethan, if you were a mind to.

ETHAN. How'd I pay for it?

ZEENA. We could sell a cow. (*He looks at her.*) To Ed Varnum and get the Energex. (*Pause, he turns away.*) We might get as much as thirty, or forty dollars. You ain't been listening.

ETHAN. No, I ain't. WHY did you want that window fixed in the spare room?

ZEENA. Lets in the cold, don't it?

ETHAN. A-yeah.

ZEENA. It's freezin' in here right now. The doctor asked me again, did you see

about gettin' somebody here to help me with the housework. You don't never answer anythin' I say.

ETHAN. You don't never say anythin' I can answer.

ZEENA. Dr. Harmon says to me, he says, "Mrs. Frome, you see't Etan gets you a hired girl!"

ETHAN. What did you send Jotham over to the Flats for?

ZEENA. If you'd listen you'd know.

ETHAN. What did you send him over to the station for—did you send him over to fetch some more medicine or some other foolishness't you bought?

ZEENA (*imitating him*). How'd I pay for it? (*Rises. Crosses to rocker chair* R., *sits and looks at him.*) Mattie Silver's comin'.

ETHAN. No, she ain't. Nó, she ain't! If I told you once—I told you fifty times I won't have her here—I won't have nobody here! And I—(*Crosses down* R. *facing her.*) won't have you whinin' and moanin' for doctorin' and Energex Vibrators and hired girls with my cattle out there starvin' to death!

ZEENA (*innocently—wrapping shawl about her shoulders*). She's only comin' to try and help me out.

ETHAN (*desperately*). I got cows in that barn starvin' because I can't buy feed—I ain't paid Jotham in months—we ain't had enough to feed ourselves—Zeena, there ain't no use talkin'—we can't do it—we just can't have no hired girl!

ZEENA (*patiently*). Now, Ethan—Mattie ain't a hired girl—she's my cousin—She's comin' all the way up here just to help me out. (*She sighs pathetically.*) Besides, the poor girl ain't got any place else to go—you can't turn her out, Ethan, my own flesh and blood. . . . (*Practically.*) And bein' my cousin—'course we won't have to pay her wages.

ETHAN (*turns away to* L.). I can't do it and I won't!

ZEENA (*shortly*). Well—she's comin' just the same, Ethan! (*We hear the sound of a horse and cart approaching rapidly.* ZEENA *crosses* C. *to* L.)

DENIS (*off stage*). Whoa! Whoa! (ETHAN *strides to window; his eye follows as he watches through window* L.)

ZEENA. I guess that's Jotham— bringin' her now!

ETHAN (*with a certain triumph*). No, t'ain't! It's Denis Easy!

ZEENA (*nods with satisfaction*). I guess

Jotham got Denis to bring Mattie's trunk along in his grocery wagon. (ETHAN *up to* C. *door, opens it, and steps out to* L.)

DENIS (*calls from just outside* L.). Ethan! Got a trunk here for you!

ETHAN (*calls vehemently*). You might's well take that trunk right on back where it come from, Denis!

DENIS. Can't do that, Ethan! (DENIS *enters the room* C. *He is the son of the Starkfield grocer and therefore comparatively prosperously dressed. He is, in fact, what is known in the village as a "snappy dresser":* DENIS *is about* 20, *in a few years he won't be unlike* ETHAN. *He has a tinge of the same cold, curt manner, but he is too young to be completely frozen.* DENIS *sets the trunk down on the floor* L. C. *and straightens up, greeting* ZEENA *with a nod.*) Zenobia.

ZEENA. Much obliged, Denis.

DENIS. Ain't seen neither of you around since along last summer—How're you feelin' these days, Zenobia?

ZEENA. I ain't any better.

DENIS. That so? You'd ought to get into Starkfield more. Mother was sayin' only the other day . . . "Too bad the Fromes don't come in to the church sociables once in a while."

ZEENA (*sighs sadly*). I ain't even hopin' for stren'th enough to do that any more. . . .

DENIS (*embarrassedly*). A-yeah—well—that's the way it goes, I guess.

ETHAN. You ain't goin' right back to the station, are you, Denis?

DENIS. No, I ain't!

ETHAN. I'd be obliged, if you'd take that trunk right back where it come from!

DENIS. Well, I'd like to oblige you, Ethan, but I couldn't do it for nothin' . . . (*That finishes that subject,* ETHAN *realizes it, and turns away, crossing up* R. ZEENA *smiles a little.*)

ZEENA. You won't have a cup of coffee, Denis?

DENIS (*stiffened by* ETHAN'S *manner*). No, I won't.

ZEENA (*with eager interest*). D'you see my cousin over to the Flats?

DENIS (*nods*). I seen her standin' on the platform while I was helpin' Jotham get her trunk down off the train. Didn't take much notice though. (*He exits* C., *nodding shortly.*) Zenobia. Ethan.

ZEENA (*crosses up to door*). Obliged, Denis. Remember me to your mother.

DENIS (*from outside*). A-yeah. (ETHAN *closes door. We hear the horse and cart move off.*)

ETHAN (*turns on* ZEENA. *Furiously and determinedly*). You been writing . . .

ZEENA (*she speaks pointedly to quell his rebellion, turns her back on him—crosses to rocker*). Ain't no use sayin' a word, Ethan. She's comin' anyhow. You just got to let her stay.

ETHAN (*crosses down to* R. C. *facing her*). All this time you ain't said a word about her comin' here—you been writin' Aunt Prudence down to Bettsbridge—plannin' and arrangin' and most likely sending my money so's to get that girl here—knowin' as well as I do I ain't even able to feed her!

ZEENA (*sits in rocker—tucks blanket around her legs*). Ethan, the doctor says I just got to have somebody here. (ETHAN *turns away abruptly. She sighs sadly, having decided to be pathetic.* ETHAN *sits* R. *of table.*) All right, Ethan, but it won't cost you nothing, I don't cost you anything, I ain't got a stitch to my name but that old blue merino I was married in. You promised me then you'd sell the farm so's we could try our luck in some town! You promised me that, didn't you?

ETHAN. I tried . . . didn't I?

ZEENA. It just seems as if the good Lord's decided that you and me and the Fromes before us . . . them layin' out there . . . just ain't ordained to ever get away from here, living or dead. Sometimes I think I'll be losin' my mind like your mother did if I don't get someone here to talk to. Ethan, you can let Mattie stay, without it costin' you anythin'! . . . Just the spare rom'n three meals a day. Well, the way I'm feelin' now . . . I can't eat anythin' myself to speak of . . . so what she gets'll be the same as my share if I was able to eat proper! (ETHAN *rises, crosses to sink.*) Mattie's a real bargain, Ethan. The last letter I got from Aunt Prudence says Mattie's willin' enough; but none of the family'll give her anythin' but advice, since her father died an' left his drug store bankrupt . . . so she ain't much use to herself or anybody else . . .

ETHAN (*shortly*). Sounds promisin'! (*He stands at window. A horse and cart are heard approaching slowly.*)

ZEENA. That them?

ETHAN. A-yeah.

ZEENA. What's she look like?

ETHAN. She don't look much to me! (*Turns on her.*) You been plannin' this for weeks and never so much as said a word to me about it! (*Knock at door* C.)

ZEENA. Well, Ethan, why don't you open the door for her? (ETHAN *goes to door, opens it, and* MATTIE SILVER *enters. He stops; she stands in doorway looking at* ETHAN. MATTIE *is twenty. To an urban eye she is a rather drab-looking small-town girl, pretty, but certainly not beautiful, nondescript except for her youthful exuberance which has not been dulled by a rather hopeless existence. She wears a drab coat and a dress that is shabby enough but is gay and even perhaps a bit too dressy. She carries a battered straw suitcase, and a package wrapped in newspaper is under her arm.* MATTIE *brings an eagerness into the room.*)

MATTIE (*looks from one to the other, addresses* ETHAN *first because he is the nearer; she speaks gladly*). You must be Ethan!

ETHAN (*hesitates a second, speaking shortly*). A-yeah! (*He passes her, calling to* JOTHAM. *Exits* C., *closes door—he is heard offstage.*) Jotham! You go along home when you get the sorrel put up! (MATTIE *moves towards* ZEENA.)

ZEENA. So you're Mattie!

MATTIE. How are you, Zeena? (ZEENA *draws shawl close about her shoulders.* MATTIE *refuses to be upset. She looks around the room eagerly, and out window, and says gaily.*) My thk ... my, it's real pleasant here, ain't it? (*She turns back and crosses above table to* R. C.) How'd you say you was feelin', Zeena?

ZEENA. How do I look like I was feelin'?

MATTIE (*innocently and cheerfully, crosses* R. C.) Well, of course I don't know how you're used to lookin', Zeena! And from the way you went on about it in your letters, well ... (*Laughs.*) I just don't know what all I expected! (*She smiles brightly.*) So I guess you ain't's bad off's you might be! (*Then remembering, takes small package wrapped in newspaper from under her arm.*) Look ... I brought you somethin'. (ZEENA *seizes package, starts unwrapping it.*) I made it myself ... it's molasses candy. ... (ZEENA *puts wrappings on floor.* ZEENA *puts package aside upstage without comment,* MATTIE *laughs.*) I guess it ain't so very good.

ZEENA (*looks up at* MATTIE, *speculatively*). Well ... Mattie ...

MATTIE. Well, I'm just awful glad to see you, Zeena.

ZEENA. Me too! You look sort of foolish hangin' on to that suitcase.

MATTIE (*laughs*). Don't I just! (*She chuckles.*) You know I was in the ladies' waitin' room down to Worcester where I changed to the branch line, and I got one look at myself ... and I thought I'd die laughin'.... (ZEENA *looks at her without comment.* MATTIE *goes on after a second, not to be disheartened.*) And I says to myself ... I says ... Mattie Silver ... you look awful foolish standin' there holdin' on to that. ... (*Sets suitcase down abruptly, upstage, murmuring.*) That ain't where to put it, is it, Zeena?

ZEENA. No ... it ain't! (MATTIE *looks around for the proper place.*) Never mind it now, Mattie ... you can take it upstairs after supper. (ETHAN *and* JOTHAM, *the occasionally hired man, enter* C. JOTHAM *is a dour-faced old fellow.* MATTIE *undoes her coat.* ZEENA *continues to* MATTIE *as* ETHAN *and* JOTHAM *pause in doorway.*) You'll have to start right in, Mattie. I'm so tired I won't be able to help you much this evenin'.

MATTIE (*goes to look room over.* JOTHAM *crosses down*). Oh, I ain't a bit tired!

ZEENA. Jotham, you see't that trunk gets upstairs, to the spare room if you ain't too helpless. Ethan might help you, stead of standing there. (*Then to* MATTIE.) You can put supper right on, soon's it's ready, Mattie.

ETHAN (*as he and* JOTHAM *cross the room; carrying trunk between them,* ETHAN *addresses* MATTIE, *who is standing with her coat on, at stove*). If I was you ... I'd take my coat off first.

MATTIE (*smiling*). I forgot! I've been in it so long ... I forgot I had it on! (*She slips out of her coat, drops it on chair* L. ETHAN *and* JOTHAM *start upstairs* R. *with trunk.*)

ETHAN (*dryly*). There's pegs to hang it up on.

ZEENA. You'll have to learn not to clutter up the whole place with your things, Mattie. (MATTIE *puts coat on peg, back of door* L. C.)

ETHAN (*to* JOTHAM, *who is chuckling*). What's so funny?

JOTHAM (*laughing as he and* ETHAN *exit up the stairs* R.). Nothin'.

MATTIE. I like him! (*Crosses to* C.)

ZEENA. Ethan?

MATTIE. No—Jotham! (*She adds quick-*

ly.) Oh, I like Ethan too. (*Eagerly.*) But Jotham's so . . . I don't know . . . nice . . . he's been laughin' all the way over from the Flats!

ZEENA. I don't know's he's got much to laugh about.

MATTIE (*opens* C. *door. Has stepped outside, looks around eagerly*). It's real nice here. (*She steps back into the room.*)

ZEENA (*irritably*). Don't they never close doors down to Willamantic?

MATTIE (*closing door quickly*). I'm awful sorry . . . I thought maybe you'd want it open.

ZEENA. What'd I want it open for?

MATTIE (*crosses down* R.). It's spring out!

ZEENA. It's cold! (ZEENA *watches her critically.*) What's that you got on—a dress? Looks kind of like a pair of "porteers."

MATTIE (*crosses down* R. C.). Well, it's my one and only—I kind of like the trimmin's—don't you?

ZEENA. No, I don't!

MATTIE. Say now, that's too bad, ain't it? I only wish't I had somethin' else now. I got that dress I planned to work in, and then I had one of them calico wrappers when I was working in the pulp mill . . . but when I got sick I got fired and they wouldn't let me keep it 'cause I'd only been workin' there three months. (*Laughs.*) I didn't like it anyhow, and I told the foreman so—I says "all right" . . . (JOTHAM *and* ETHAN *return down the steps* R., ETHAN *first,* JOTHAM *next.* ETHAN *crosses to* L. C., *sits at table.* JOTHAM C. *to stove.*) "if that's the way you feel, Mr. Jenson," I says, "you keep it and see if I care!"

ZEENA. Jotham, you put the sorrel up and go 'long home!

JOTHAM. Don't I get anythin' to eat for goin' way over to the Flats and back?

(ETHAN *sits in his chair by table.*)

ZEENA. Not tonight — there ain't enough.

JOTHAM (*gleefully, apparently delighted at worrying* ZEENA). Seein's believin'. (*Grins at* ZEENA.) Let's see now—(*Peering into pots and pans.*) What would you say that is there, Mattie?

MATTIE (*lightly, crosses up to stove*). I don't know! Stew, I guess!

ETHAN (*quickly*). If Zeena says there ain't enough, that settles it!

JOTHAM (*dryly*). I ain't denyin' that!

(*Turns up to door.* JOTHAM *stops at* C. *door, gleefully to* MATTIE.) Remember, steppin' off the train over to the Flats? Remember what you said? (*Then to* ETHAN.) She says to me she just can't wait to get here! (*Laughs.*) Have to laugh every time I think of it! (*He and* MATTIE *laugh.* JOTHAM *exits* C.)

ZEENA. You're forgettin' I'm a very sick woman; you'll have to learn 'bout holdin' your tongue!

MATTIE (*crosses down to* ZENA R. C.). I'm terribly sorry, Zeena.

ZEENA. Well, we'll see how you get along, but you might's well know you come here to work. Of course we can't afford to pay you anythin' but seein's you're my blood cousin, we'll treat you right an' I'll see't Ethan takes and fetches you from the church sociables once a month.

MATTIE. I'm beholdin' to you, Zeena. . . . I want you should tell me just everythin' you want me to do!

ETHAN (*impatiently*). You might get supper!

MATTIE (*goes up to stove, stares helplessly into pot, not knowing what to do next*). It looks all right. (*Adds hastily.*) I mean, I think the stew's about done all right, ain't it?

ETHAN. It was all right last night. (*Pause.*)

ZEENA. Mattie, you know how to get it into a plate, don't you?

MATTIE (*laughs*). Well, I guess—so! (*She looks around helplessly, unable to find the dishes.*)

ETHAN (*shortly*). Never mind, I'll do it! (*He rises, crosses below table to cupboard up* R. *Puts 3 cups and saucers on table.*)

MATTIE. No, I'll do it! (ETHAN *gets 3 plates from shelf at cupboard, puts two of them down, holds one out to her. She takes it from him, starts to put it on table.*)

ZEENA. If you'd just show her where things are once, Ethan, 'stead of scaring the poor girl to death . . . she might do all right.

ETHAN. Here!

MATTIE (*turns and sees him holding out a ladle full of stew from simmering pot*). Oh! (*She laughs nervously.*) Guess I'm not much help.

ETHAN (*as he fills plate*). I guess not! (MATTIE *puts plate upon table at* ETHAN'S *place. He has refilled ladle and is waiting for another plate.*)

MATTIE (*lightly*). I guess about all I'm good for is to make molasses candy. (*Crosses up at stove, laughs, and adds.*) And I can play "The Lost Chord" on the piano!

ZEENA (*as* MATTIE *carries second plate over the* R. *end of table*). Mattie, you know I ain't up to movin' about much, but I would like somethin'.

MATTIE (*puzzled, then realizing* ZEENA *is going to stay where she is*). Oh . . . I thought you'd be coming to the table, Zeena. I'm awful sorry. (*Gives* ZEENA *fork and plate of stew.*)

ZEENA (*whispers to* MATTIE). Ethan's waiting.

ETHAN (*as* MATTIE *turns back to table— he is still standing by stove with another ladle full of stew, waiting for 3rd plate*). I'm a mite hungry myself.

MATTIE. I'm coming! (*She hurries over to stove with third plate.*)

ZEENA. Now, Ethan, she ain't doing so bad, considerin' . . . (*Looking at* MAT-TIE, *speculatively,* ETHAN *brings coffeepot to table.*)

MATTIE. I'll be all right, when I kind of get the hang of things a bit. Honest I will, Zeena!

ZEENA (*thoughtfully*). 'Course, Ethan, I guess we can't look a gift horse in the face. (*MATTIE giggles gaily.* ETHAN *looks at her.*)

ETHAN. Fresh, ain't you!

MATTIE. I didn't mean to be! I just laughed a little. (*She giggles slightly again and then stops herself.*) I'm terribly sorry! I want you should be pleased with me, Zeena. . . . You see I got to stay. (*She looks at* ZEENA, *then at* ETHAN *frightenedly.*) You just don't know—I just got to have a place to stay, Zeena!

ETHAN (*hesitates, glances at* MATTIE. *He thaws a little, for the first time, and smiles very slightly, and then concedes:*) Well, she ain't a fretter, anyhow! (*MATTIE smiles gratefully and sits down.*)

CURTAIN

SCENE TWO

The following winter. Evening.
The church sociable. Outside the vestry door of the white wooden Starkfield Congregational Church. *The vestry door is in the "L" which juts out from the side of the otherwise box-shaped building. The set is small and merely suggests the Colonial form of a church extending off at an angle* R. *There is a storm door, a small projecting shelter, built out from the vestry door, which opens into the vestry, known locally as the village "social hall."* L. *of the door, broad bands of yellow light flow out through snow-banked windows upon the frosty darkness. Within the hall the shadows of the rapidly swirling dancers are elongated upon the windows. The snow is banked high about the projecting storm door and along the cleared paths which lead off* R. *and* L. *The sounds of a fiddle and harmonium increase in volume and tempo, and the shadows of the dancers move faster and faster, nearing the end of a square dance.* ETHAN *enters from* L., *avoids the revealing rays about the doorway and, hugging the deep still shadows, edges his way to a position outside the nearest window, through which he glimpses the room. A moment later the music stops, the shadows of the dancing couples cling together for an instant; then they are blurred into one surging black mass. As the dancers break apart and move away from the* C. *of the room, several of the elder Villagers come out . . . pausing in the shelter of the vestibule between the vestry door and the storm door, to bundle coats and woolen scarfs closely about themselves. In spite of these precautions, which are automatic and habitual, each of them submerges deep into the shelter of an upturned coat collar as he steps out into the still cold of the night.* ETHAN *draws back into the seclusion of the side wall, of the projecting doorway— in spite of which his presence is immediately detected by the departing people . . . almost as though they habitually expected to find him waiting there. The First Man out thrusts his mittened hands deep into the pockets of his mackinaw, moves down the path* L., *passing* ETHAN *without looking at him.*)

1ST MAN (*curtly*). Ethan . . . (*He moves off down the path off* L. *without pausing. Music is heard.*)

ETHAN (*in the same tone, without turning to the man as the man exits*). Samuel. (*A* WOMAN *and a* MAN *step out into the night from the comparative shelter and warmth of the storm vestibule. The* WOMAN *pauses to greet* ETHAN.)

THE WOMAN. Well . . . Ethan.

ETHAN (*nods, abruptly, to the* WOMAN). Ethel . . . (*A nod to the* Man.) George . . .

THE WOMAN (*conversationally*). Cold

enough for you, Ethan?

THE MAN (GEORGE) (*to save* ETHAN *the bother of replying denies her statement cheerfully.*) 'Tain't cold at all. It's been a fine open winter . . . week after week . . . just hoverin' 'round zero. (*Turns to go, adding shortly.*) 'Night, Ethan!

THE WOMAN (*hesitates*). How's Zeenie?

ETHAN. 'Bout the same, thanks.

THE MAN (*starts off down the path* L., *turns back, grabs the* WOMAN *by the arm, starts her off with him this time*). She'd gab all night if I'd let her!

THE WOMAN (*as she is led off down the path* L). 'Night, Ethan!

ETHAN (*as the* MAN *and* WOMAN *exit*). 'Night! (*He turns back to his post by the window as chattering voices are heard from within, and a burst of laughter breaks for a moment and then dies down again.* ED VARNUM, *one of the more formidable citizens of Starkfield, enters from* R., *goes to storm door, pauses there as he sees* ETHAN *with his face glued to window to the* L. *of the doorway.*)

ED (*jovially*). Playin' "hide and seek," Ethan?

ETHAN (*turns quickly, then nods*). 'Evenin', Ed. (*He is rather embarrassed for a second. Laughs a little awkwardly and then explains.*) Waiting to fetch Mattie Silver home . . . (*Adds.*) For Zenobia.

ED (*non-committally*). A-yeah!

ETHAN. Come to fetch your daughter?

ED. A-yeah. (*He moves toward* ETHAN.) Say, Ethan, got any more cows like that one you sold me?

ETHAN. No, I haven't, Ed.

ED. Good milker, now she's fed up a little.

ETHAN. A-yeah. 'Bout the best milker around—when she's fit. (*Then with great difficulty.*) I was wonderin' . . . (ED *laughs and shakes his head, but* ETHAN *persists.*) I'm a little short of cash right now . . . Zenobia went and bought herself one of them Energex Vibrators, you know. . . .

ED (*grins*). A-yeah.

ETHAN (*terribly earnestly*). But I got some mighty fine spruce—if you'd take some of it, Ed—I'd like to buy that cow back from you.

ED (*heading for storm door*). Don't need any spruce, Ethan—and a deal's a deal. . . . (ED *gets to door.*) Comin' in? (*He hesitates a second.*) Whyn't you come in and warm up a bit, Ethan?

ETHAN (*embarrassedly*). Me! No, no, I wouldn't go in, Ed—I'll just wait here.

(ED *exits through inner door of the vestibule.* ETHAN *is left alone for a moment. He is bitterly disappointed—he watches* ED *go. He turns and moves to the seclusion of the shadow beneath the window. A moment later the inner door opens and a Villager enters the vestibule—pausing there to bundle up—conquers the impulse to recoil from the cold, then out into the night.*)

1ST MAN. B-r-r-r! (*He ducks his head down into the depths of his upturned coat collar, mumbling.*) Why don't you wait inside, Ethan? (MAN *hurries on* L. *without waiting for a reply.*)

A WOMAN (*moving off in opposite direction* C.). She's dancin' one more, Ethan—better step inside and wait!

2ND MAN (*with the* WOMAN, *he turns around and walks backward against the cold moving away from* ETHAN *and calling back to him*). She's dancin' with Denis Eady, no use hangin' around—waitin'—he'll bring her home all right!

A WOMAN (*to the* MAN, *they are moving off* C. *to* R.). If you ask me, Mattie's got a crush on Denis. (*This couple moves off* R., *the* MAN *backing, the* WOMAN *bent over to shield herself from cold.*)

2ND WOMAN (*stepping out of vestibule as* MATTIE *comes into the vestibule from inner door*). Ain't you riding home, Mattie?

MATTIE (*calls as the* WOMAN *moves off* R. *and she steps outside, drawing her "fascinator" close about her throat*). Not yet! I'm just looking for someone—

ETHAN (*crosses down. Moves forward toward* MATTIE *as* DENIS EADY *comes out quickly toward* MATTIE). Mattie!

MATTIE. Oh—I didn't see you right off, Ethan!

DENIS (*moves up beside* MATTIE *quickly*). We was wonderin' if you'd mind waitin' one more dance, Ethan, you know how 'tis—you was young once yourself—wasn't you, Ethe?

MATTIE. You c'n come inside and wait—if you want. The dancin's just—oh, my!

DENIS. Sure—it's cold out here—come on in, Ethan—no point freezin' yourself!

(*A* MAN *with a fiddle in his hand comes to the inner door and calls impatiently.*)

FIDDLER (*in doorway*). Hurry up, there, Mattie, we're awaitin' on you!

MATTIE. Denis an' me—we're supposed to lead the square dance, Ethan.

DENIS (*quickly, to* ETHAN). You don't mind, come on in—

MATTIE (*sensing* ETHAN's *discomfort—*

she laughs nervously). Well—'course if you say so—I'll come right off.

DENIS (*quickly to* MATTIE). You ain't goin' back on me, Mattie—you promised me one more!

FIDDLER. Come on there, Mattie—we're all waitin'! (*Exits into church.*)

DENIS (*takes her arm and draws her toward door*). Come on in, Ethan—or if you don't want to wait, I'll see 't she gets home all right. (*The* FIDDLER *starts fiddling.* DENIS *whirls* MATTIE *through the vestibule.*)

MATTIE (*calls as she is drawn in through doorway*). Wait for me, Ethan! (ETHAN *turns away, moves back to the seclusion of the shadow, stands watching the dance through the window. The door opens quickly, a* YOUNG MAN *hurries out, pauses as he hurriedly bundles his coat about him. Another* YOUNG MAN *opens the inner door and calls.*)

YOUNG MAN (*enters* C. *Calling surreptitiously as* NED HALE, *the other youngster, starts out quickly*). Say, Ned! Ruthie's father's in there lookin' fer her so Ruthie just skinned out the back way! (*The* YOUNG MAN *closes door quickly, disappearing inside.*)

NED. I know! (*Crosses up, looks, hurries to corner of "L" at* L. ETHAN *has stepped back into the shadow.* NED *glances around the corner, turns, hurries* R. *to the other corner as* RUTH VARNUM *comes from* R. *Crosses down* R. C. *and meets him.*) Ruthie! Did you see your father lookin' for you?

RUTH (*crosses down* R.). Sure—that's why I went out the back way! He makes me sick always followin' us around—watchin' us like a hawk—it ain't as if we wasn't goin' to be married! (NED *laughs, catches her close, kisses her quickly. As he releases her she sees* ETHAN *standing in the shadow. She whispers.*) Who's that?

NED (R.). It's only Ethan—(*He calls.*) Hello there, Ethan!

RUTH. Hello, Ethan!

ETHAN. Hello, Ruth—Ned!

NED (*as* RUTH *and he move toward* ETHAN). Why ain't you dancin', Ethe?

RUTH. Oh, Ethan don't dance—he always waits out here like he wasn't wanted, or somethin'—don't you, Ethan?

NED. Want me to tell Mattie you're here?

RUTH. She'll be along presently. She's dancin' with Denis Eady! I guess that's the last one. (*The dance ends in a loud crescendo.*)

NED (*quickly*). Yeah and your old

man'll be comin' out, too.

RUTH (*crosses* L.) All right, Ned. 'Night, Ethe! If you see the old man, don't tell him you seen us!

NED. He won't! He knows how it is! Don't you, Ethe! So long! (*Starts off with* RUTH. ETHAN *watches them, smiling a little, pleased by their warm youthful familiarity with him. Suddenly* NED *leaves* RUTH'S *side, darts back to* ETHAN, *tags him boyishly and cries:*) Last touch! (NED *jumps aside—out of* ETHAN'S *reach.* ETHAN *smiles but doesn't offer to give chase.* RUTH *has moved around behind him. Suddenly she darts forward, tags* ETHAN *as she passes him.*)

RUTH (*shouts*). Last touch! (*She joins* NED. *He takes her hand and they run, expecting* ETHAN *to follow.*)

RUTH and NED. 'Night!

ETHAN (*calls after them as they start off arm in arm down path* L.) 'Night.... (RUTH *and* NED *exit. Then the door opens and the departing dancers pour out into the vestibule.*) Better run! (ETHAN *remains in his position beneath the window, avoiding contact with the crowd. However, the people who hurry off in his direction from the door greet him with a nod or a short "Ethan." He acknowledges them.*) Josh. (*To a woman who passes with a brief "Ethan."*) Abigail. (*To a man.*) Harmon. (*And to the woman with this man.*) Temperance! (MATTIE *and* DENIS *enter the vestibule from inner door.* MATTIE *pauses to fix her coat.* DENIS *emerges from the group in the vestibule—the last of the dancers to leave. He hurries to where* ETHAN *stands waiting.*)

DENIS (*crosses to* ETHAN.) Say, Ethe, would you mind if I was to take Mattie home?

ETHAN (*shortly*). Yes, I would.

DENIS. I got the old man's cutter waitin' down there. I thought maybe she c'd take a little ride. We won't be long.

ETHAN (*shortly*). Nope!

DENIS. I'll see 't she gets home safe.

ETHAN. Nope.

DENIS. Well, maybe you c'd come along with us—save you walkin'.

ETHAN. Don't mind walkin'! (*Two girls ad lib.* MATTIE *comes out of the vestibule now, hurrying toward them.*)

DENIS (*calling to* MATTIE). Say, Mattie, see if you can't make Ethan come along with us for a little ride in the old man's cutter! (MATTIE *crosses to* ETHAN.)

ETHAN (*firmly*). It's gettin' kind of late, Mattie. (*He starts to turn from her, then says:*) You comin' with me? 'Course if you want to stay and go with him, I guess I can't stop you.

DENIS. Come on, Mattie—I'll take you home. . . . Ethan won't mind, will you, Ethan?

ETHAN (*shortly*). Yes—I will—but it's up to her!

DENIS. Aw, come on, Ethe . . . be a sport! Can't you? You was young once yourself!

ETHAN (*irritably*). You goin' with him, Mattie?

MATTIE. G'bye, Denis! . . . Hope you have a lovely ride!

DENIS (*starts to move away, then hesitates*). The colt's all hitched up and ra'rin' to to go—how 'bout changin' your mind? (*She shakes her head.*) All right—maybe next time, huh? (*He turns back, tags her, jumps out of reach.*) Last touch! (*He steps out of reach, calls.*) 'Night, Ethan—so long, Mattie! (*Exits* R. ETHAN *and* MATTIE *are left alone, standing some distance apart,* ETHAN *is looking at her embarrassedly.*)

MATTIE (C.). If I'd knowed you was goin' to be put out about it, I wouldn't never've waited for that last dance, Ethan.

ETHAN (*irritably*). I ain't put out. (*He turns from her abruptly, and starts to cross up* L.) Come on, if you're comin'! (*She goes three or four steps. Sees that he has started the other way—stops and turns and calls.*)

MATTIE. Let's go this way, Ethan, it's easier walkin'. . . . (*Crosses* C.)

ETHAN (*stops and turns, but stays where he is.*) I'm goin' this way, it's shorter.

MATTIE. You're as stubborn's a mule, Ethan—

ETHAN (*furiously*). I ain't near's stubborn's you are. (*Two steps toward* C. *to her. They stand looking at each other for a second, then he turns on his heel and starts moving off up* L.) This way—if you're goin' with me!

MATTIE. Oh, Ethan, come on this way, huh? (*Crosses up to him.*) *They stand still for a second; then suddenly she darts to him, touches his sleeve, and darts away, calling:*) Last touch! (*She turns quickly and runs off* D. L. ETHAN *watches her, then turns without a word and walks off up the path* U. L.)

CURTAIN

SCENE THREE

A few minutes later.

The crest of a hill above Starkfield and on the way to the Frome farm. The snow-covered ground slopes up toward the back and suggests a sheer steep drop into the valley below. At C. *the snow has been packed down around a V-like indentation which is the starting place for the village bobsled slide. A small sled with wooden runners lies half-buried in the snow at* L. *A log is downstage, slightly* L. *of* C. *At back* R. *there is a path—and at* R. *front another path—these meet, and at the head of the bobsled slide a less-used path leads from there off* L. ETHAN *enters along path* R., *advances* C. *slowly.*

MATTIE (*calling from off* D. R.). Ethan, oh, Ethan! (ETHAN *stops. She enters on path* R.)

ETHAN (*over* R., *almost formally*). Hello, Matt.

MATTIE (*she is quite embarrassed, crosses* C., *looks at him for a moment, then says:*) It's an awful nice night . . . don't let's be stubborn.

ETHAN (*crosses* C. *matter-of-factly*). I won't, if you won't. (*Then generously.*) I guess you got a right to go home with him, if you want.

MATTIE (R. C., *irritably*). That's what makes me so mad!

ETHAN (C., *blankly*). Well—you have.

MATTIE. You thinkin' I'd want to walk home with him! Don't you suppose I know that walkin' two miles in to Starkfield and back ain't much fun for you after a day's work around the farm . . . and you wouldn't walk it anyways, if Zeena didn't make you do it!

ETHAN (*it's hard for him to give an inch*). I might.

MATTIE (*eagerly*). Would you?

ETHAN (*pauses, thinks, then speaks very honestly*). I don't mind the walk.

MATTIE (*quickly*). Don't you, Ethan?

ETHAN. Nope . . . lately I been gettin' so I kind of like it.

MATTIE. So do I! I like it an awful lot!

ETHAN. It gets kind of lonesome out to the farm.

MATTIE (*eagerly, grasping for his understanding*). Don't it, though!

ETHAN (*hesitates, then says with unusual volubility*). Sometimes I kind of like getting away awhile.

MATTIE. It's real nice all right, ain't it?

ETHAN (*impulsively*). Zeena ain't a whole lot of company when she's feelin' low.

MATTIE (*honestly*). No, she ain't.

ETHAN (*hastily*). Not that I blame her!

MATTIE. Oh, no, Ethan! (*He cannot think of anything at all to say and he looks at her helplessly—after a moment she helps him.*) I ain't a mite cold . . . are you, Ethan?

ETHAN. Me? No!

MATTIE. I was thinkin' . . . I don't know as there'd be any harm in settin' awhile!

ETHAN (*sits on log*). Don't know as there would. (*She sits, eagerly, beside him on the log. There is a pause.*)

MATTIE (*at last, eagerly*). It ain't often we get a chance to say much around the house, and you know when you get started talkin' sometimes, like take now, it's real interestin'.

ETHAN (*warming up*). Yes—'tis! (*Pause.*) I ain't talked so much since before I was married! (*They laugh.*)

MATTIE. Well, you ain't bad's you was . . . and that's a fact, Ethan! (*She looks at him and smiles encouragingly.*) I was awful glad when I seen you waitin' outside the social hall there tonight. I thought maybe you couldn't come back for me.

ETHAN. Couldn't! Why, who'd ever stop me?

MATTIE. Oh, I don't know! (*Thoughtfully.*) I knew she wasn't feelin' any too good today. I figured maybe you might have to stay and do for her till I got back.

ETHAN. No, no, she's in bed long ago.

MATTIE. I had an awful funny dream last night. You know what I dreamed? I dreamed Zeena come downstairs sayin' she was feelin' better and for a while this mornin' I didn't know if it was a dream or not . . . till I heard her!

ETHAN. Feelin' better! (*Pause.*) Well, that's one thing I ain't never heard her complainin' about! (*They are silent, sitting side by side on the log, close to the sheer drop at back. After a moment, MATTIE peers down over the edge of the crest of the hill.*)

MATTIE (*they rise*). Awful steep down there, ain't it?

ETHAN. A-yeah. (*MATTIE laughs nervously.*)

MATTIE. There was a lot of them out here coastin' tonight before the moon set. (*He crosses up to edge—she crosses up stage.*)

ETHAN (*interestedly*). There was?

MATTIE (*nods*). Oh, an awful lot of them. (*She glances down incline off* R.) I never been coastin' . . . even once in my life!

ETHAN (*after a moment*). Would you like to go sometime?

MATTIE. Would I? You just ask me!

ETHAN (*shortly*). We could go sometime.

MATTIE. Could we really?

ETHAN (*with difficulty*). We could go tomorrow night maybe—if there's a moon.

MATTIE. I was watchin' them tonight —but my—I never thought I'd get a chance to go myself!

ETHAN (*determinedly*). We'll go tomorrow night!

MATTIE (*joyously*). Oh, Ethan . . . Say! (*She moves close to him and says excitedly.*) You know . . . Ned Hale . . . and Ruth Varnum . . . they went down together and we was all watchin' and all of a sudden! . . . (*She stops abruptly, looks at him, frightenedly, then adds quickly:*) You should've seen . . . why, they come just as close to runnin' right plumb into a big tree . . . and gettin' theirselves killed . . . (*Glances down over the hillside.*) I guess it was that big black elm down there at the bend . . . see it? (*She draws back from edge of the hillside.*) Wouldn't it have been just too awful for anythin'!

ETHAN (*close to her*). A-yeah—well, Ned ain't so much on steerin', but . . . I guess't I could take you down all right.

MATTIE. Could you, Ethan? (*She peers down over the edge of the hill.*) Right past the big elm? . . . It's awful dangerous-lookin' . . .

ETHAN (*positively*). I guess you wouldn't have to be afraid with me.

MATTIE. No . . . I don't guess I would!

ETHAN. Say, Matt . . . that's Sam Colt's sled settin' over there and he don't never use it, and you know there ain't no reason in the world why we couldn't borrow it.

MATTIE (*looking up at him, daring to hope for a second*). You mean right now?

ETHAN (*suddenly doubtful*). Well . . .

MATTIE. I guess maybe it is kind of late go go down tonight. . . . (*Crosses down* L.) Maybe we could go tomorrow night.

ETHAN. Yeah. (*MATTIE crosses down. After a moment he thinks of something to say, looking up* R.) There's lots of stars out tonight, though, ain't there?

MATTIE (*coming down*). Ain't there just! (*She stands beside him, looking up.*) Did you ever try to count 'em all? ... Oh, my! Don't it seem like there's most a million of them?

ETHAN. A-yeah. (*Authoritatively.*) There's more'n that.

MATTIE (*amazed at his knowledge*). What do you know!

ETHAN (*eagerly, as he points*). See that one, that big fellow there—see? (*She nods.*) I think they call him Aldebaran— or some such.

MATTIE (*incredulously*). They do!

ETHAN (*rapidly*). And that bright one ... that's Orion. And that bunch of little ones ... no, over there—see? Swarming about there?

MATTIE (*crosses to* R. C.). I see! Ain't they though ... just like a little flock of bees! (*She glances at him, and then up at the sky and murmurs.*) Oh, my! Don't it look like it was all just painted!

ETHAN (*practically*). They call them the Pleiades.

MATTIE. They do! Well! Thk! (*Turns, looks at him admiringly.*) Gorry, you know an awful lot, don't you, Ethan? How'd you ever find it all out? (ETHAN *looks at her.*)

ETHAN (*with pardonable pride*). Had pretty near a year in Worcester ... down there to the technological college.

MATTIE. You did!

ETHAN. A-yeah. But then the old man died and I had to come back and take care of the farm. So I didn't get to learn much to speak of, just enough to get me wonderin' about things once in a while.

MATTIE. You know, I get to wonderin' once in a while myself ... about things, and places. Nice, warm places mostly, like take down South!

ETHAN. Ever seen any pictures of them palm trees they have down there? (*She nods eagerly.*) Mighty pretty.

MATTIE. I can just imagine!

ETHAN (*dryly*). A-yeah. Well, for a good while there I could call up the sight of them pictures easy ... but these last couple of winters the recollection's been gettin' kind of snowed under!

MATTIE (*sighs*). Oh, my ... it must be real nice to travel places. ...

ETHAN. A-yeah.

MATTIE. I got's far down as Hartford once. ... (*She sighs.*) Guess that's 'bout's far's I ever will get.

ETHAN. Hartford's quite a ways at that. ...

MATTIE. Yes ... 'tis.

ETHAN. Most to New York.

MATTIE. Can you picture it! And I didn't get tired travelin' at all. ... I could've kept right on goin' an' goin' an' goin' ... (*She sighs longingly.*) Oh, dear!

ETHAN. Glad you didn't.

MATTIE. It's awful interestin' to talk about things like that though, ain't it! I still ain't a mite cold ... are you?

ETHAN. Me? No ... 'course not!

MATTIE. I was thinkin' we might set awhile longer. (*She sits. He follows. She considers for a moment.*) Ain't it funny the way things go now when you just stop to think about 'em? Just supposin' my father hadn't of married Zeena's cousin ... why, I most probably wouldn't've been born at all! (*Then thoughtfully.*) Still 'n' all ... I don't know's I'd mind that!

ETHAN. Some people might!

MATTIE. Well ... anyhow ... bein' me, I'm glad he did.

ETHAN. A-yeah. ... Well ... I'm kind of glad myself ... bein's that's why you're here.

MATTIE. Ain't it just the luckiest thing! Why, I'm just so glad to be here ... 'stead of down there in them big towns! You know, I never did take to workin' in the mills ... first off I ain't got the stren'th ... and then them foremen used to get me so flustered ... why, the harder I tried the more flustered I'd get and the sooner I'd get fired ... and then first thing you know ... I got fired so much ... there wasn't any more jobs. ... (*She sighs contentedly.*) An' my health's better here an' everything, and I don't have to fuss about a place to sleep and somethin' to eat ...! Oh, my, yes, bein' here's been real pleasant.

ETHAN (*after a moment, reluctantly*). A-yeah ... still ... I presume what folks says is only natural. ...

MATTIE. Why, what is folks sayin', Ethan?

ETHAN (*very reluctantly*). They say— that sooner or later—you'll be leavin' us.

MATTIE (*rises, worriedly*). Why, what do you mean, Ethan?

ETHAN. Well ... I don't know.

MATTIE. Why—(*Looks at him and then is suddenly terrified.*) You mean it's Zeena, you mean she ain't suited? Oh, Ethan, has she said anything? (*She stares it him.*) I know I ain't near as smart as I ought to be, and Zeena says there's lots of things around the house want doin', that a regular hired girl . . . she c'd do them all right, but I ain't got the stren'th in my arms! (*Then sits.*) Oh, Ethan . . . if Zeena sends me away I don't know wherever I'd go or whatever I'd do . . . if she'd only tell me what I don't do right . . . but she don't hardly say a word for days . . . and sometimes I can see she ain't suited . . . yet, still 'n' all, I don't know why! (*With an impetuous gesture toward him she says indignantly:*) You'd ought to tell me what to do, Ethan Frome. You'd ought to tell me yourself. (*She stares at him for a second.*) Unless you want me to go too!

ETHAN. Now don't fret, Matt . . . don't fret . . . if you don't want to go of your own accord . . .

MATTIE. Where'd I go?

ETHAN. Well . . . all I was *tryin'* to say was . . . folks is sayin' that sooner or later . . . you might be wantin to leave us to get married.

MATTIE (*with great relief and amazement*). Married! (*She laughs nervously.*) Why, whoever'd want to go and marry me!

ETHAN. Well, now . . . folks do marry . . . no gettin' away from that. So if you was to marry some fellow . . . why, it'd be only natural you'd be leavin' us!

MATTIE. If! That's a mighty big "if." Ethan! (*Rises, faces R.* ETHAN *rises.*)

ETHAN. Say, Matt, you ain't cryin'?

MATTIE. 'Course I ain't! (*Turns to him.*)

ETHAN. Why, Matt, lots of folks'd want to marry you. . . .

MATTIE. I ain't noticed any great rush so far.

ETHAN (*as she moves away*). Well . . . take now . . . I would . . . if I could.

MATTIE (*stops abruptly, turns, and looks at him*). That's interestin', ain't it? (*She shrugs.*) Oh, well—Maybe you would, Ethan . . . but nobody else . . . anyhow you couldn't.

ETHAN. No, I don't guess I could . . . but I mean, if I could . . . I would. (*Crosses to R. She follows, taking his arm.*)

MATTIE. Oh, well, sayin' that don't mean anythin'! (*As they exit she looks up at him and smiles.*) Still 'n' all . . . it's real nice of you to say it!

CURTAIN

SCENE FOUR

A few moments later.

Exterior of the Frome farmhouse. (*This scene is same as the Prologue.*) *It is quite dark, and the set is but dimly seen except at certain spots where the snow-covered ground faintly reflects an eerie starlight.*

MATTIE *and* ETHAN *are heard approaching from off* R. *above the house. They enter together.*

MATTIE (*looking up at the sky, she points off* L.). Where? That big one, there?

ETHAN (*up stage pointing off* L.). No, no, no, look. See the dipper?

MATTIE. I guess so. Ethan, will you look where we are already!

ETHAN. A-yeah.

MATTIE. Show me again, Ethan.

ETHAN. See the pourin' side of the dipper?

MATTIE (*doubtfully*). Hhm . . . hhm . . .

ETHAN (*pointing* L.). Now follow them two stars right out . . . away over here to a little one . . .

MATTIE (*crosses below him to* R. *With the utmost contempt*). Is that the North Star? That little thing?

ETHAN. It's as big as the world, maybe bigger.

MATTIE. Well, it don't look it.

ETHAN. That's because it's so far away. (*A pause. Confronted by the* FROME *burial ground, she stares at the slanting slabs a moment.*)

MATTIE. Is that all the Fromes they ever was?

ETHAN (*joins her*). Most of them.

MATTIE (*looks at him*). Ethan, didn't you ever want to get away from here? (ETHAN *nods emphatically.*) This one's got your name on it—Ethan Frome!

ETHAN. That's from away back.

MATTIE. Look, Ethan, you can make out what it says! (*She gets close beside the old tombstone, and peers at it.*)

ETHAN. I know.

MATTIE (*reads, slowly*). "Sacred to . . . the memory . . . of Ethan Frome . . . and Endurance . . . his wife . . . who . . . dwelled together . . . in peace . . . for fifty years." (*Looking at him.*) Fifty years, Ethan!

ETHAN. That's an awful long time.

MATTIE (*after a moment, innocently, rises*). How long've you and Zeena been married, Ethan?

ETHAN. Seven years.

MATTIE. Ever since your mother died?

ETHAN (*nods*). Zeena always was a great hand for sickness and doctorin'. . . . She come over from the next valley to nurse her, when my mother went, the way she did from bein' so lonely here, the long winter after my father died . . .

MATTIE. But you was here that winter —wasn't you—with your mother?

ETHAN (*nods again*). She seldom talked. Sometimes when I couldn't stand it any longer, I used to ask mother why she didn't never say anything! And she'd just sit there and say, "I'm listening" . . . and then if I spoke to her she'd say, "They're talkin' so loud out there . . . I can't hear you!" (*After a moment he explains.*) It gets pretty lonesome sometimes in the winter.

MATTIE. Yes, it does, Ethan! (*After a moment.*) Was that the same winter you got married?

ETHAN. Right after the funeral. . . . Zeena was packin' to go along back home . . . but I got to thinkin' . . . if I didn't get somebody around here to talk to . . . I might go the way my mother did, so I asked Zeena to stay and marry me and she did, that's all. (*They are silent for quite a while. Then he adds:*) Sometimes I think . . . I might never have done it . . . if mother'd died in the spring . . . instead of winter! (*There is a long pause.*)

MATTIE (*quietly*). If I stay, will I be here too, some day?

ETHAN. I guess so, Matt . . . right beside me . . . and Zeena.

MATTIE. Do you think it'll be . . . fifty years?

ETHAN (*honestly*). I hope not!

MATTIE (*turns front*). It ain't right we should talk like this, Ethan. . . . It's awful interestin' though. (*Sound of a dog howling off* R. MATTIE *listens, is momentarily frightened.*) What's that?

ETHAN (*reassuringly*). Nothin'.

MATTIE. Was it a fox?

ETHAN. No. It was just a dog howling.

MATTIE. A dog! That means death, don't it? (*She says it without fear of the word.*) I ain't superstitious but—

ETHAN. Then it don't mean nothin'. (*But she is really frightened, so he adds:*) Besides, you have to hear a dog howl twice and even then it ain't sure.

MATTIE (*laughs a little nervously*). Maybe it won't be fifty years, Ethan! (*Turns to house. They move toward house. Suddenly she stops and exclaims with great surprise.*) Ethan. . . . Look! The house is dark!!

ETHAN (*stops too. A step to* L. C. *He has noticed it for the first time*). I didn't take notice. . . . That's funny . . . Zeena always left a light before!

MATTIE (*suddenly*). Oh, Ethan, you don't suppose . . . !

ETHAN (*looks toward house*). No, no!

MATTIE (*reassured*). I guess she just forgot. (ETHAN *chuckles.*)

ETHAN. Ain't we foolish . . . bein' ascared like that!

MATTIE (*not entirely reassured*). Ain't we just!

ETHAN (*crosses to house*). I'll get the key. (*He crosses porch, looks in box on wall. Finds nothing. Then he straightens up and whispers worriedly.*) It's gone!

MATTIE (*in a loud whisper, frightenedly*). Ethan! (*They stare at each other for a second; then she adds more normally.*) It can't be! Ethan, it just can't be! (*Crosses to him, searches frantically.*) Ethan . . . it *is* gone!

ETHAN. She's always put it there. (*They search again.*)

MATTIE (*whispers*). Maybe she was afraid to leave it.

ETHAN. It ain't like her.

MATTIE (*tensely*). She always left a light! Every other time!

ETHAN. It's awful late!

MATTIE. Ain't it though. It must be . . . just terrible late!

ETHAN. Wait! I'll light a match. (*Rises, gets match out of his pocket.*) The key must be here somewhere! (*He lights a match. They bend over together and search about in the flickering glare on the ground, until the match burns out. He whispers:*) That's the last match I had! (*Rises, crosses* C.)

MATTIE (*whispers with tense fright*). Oh, Ethan! (*Rises.*) It's so late. Ethan, we shouldn't have! . . . (*Crosses to him.*)

ETHAN (*as a vague, eerie light appears suddenly shining through the cracks of the house, he stops* MATTIE *suddenly*). Shush! (*They wait tensely, as the light grows stronger, approaching the inside of the door. Suddenly the door opens and* ZEENA *stands there in the doorway against the black background of the kitchen, one hand drawing a quilted counterpane about her shoulders, the other holding a flickering oil lamp. The light deepens fantastically the hollows and the boniness of her drawn, severe white face.* ETHAN *and* MATTIE *face* ZEENA *guiltily and in frightened silence for a moment. Then they move forward slowly and reluctantly, through the doorway into the kitchen, without a word.* ZEENA *closes the door. Iron bolt is shot into place. Dog howls.*

CURTAIN DESCENDS

ACT TWO

SCENE ONE

Five-thirty the following morning.

ETHAN'S *and* ZEENA'S *bedroom. A small bleak room cramped close under the slanting eaves of the roof. There is a tiny snow-encrusted window at* R. *and a door at back* C. *The room is attic-like and bare. A string stretched across* R. *corner of the room, from which a faded curtain is suspended, marks the space in which the Frome clothing is kept. Between the closet space and the window at* R. *is a plain washstand supporting a cracked pitcher and bowl. The bed, which is cramped under the slanting roof at* L., *is rickety but apt to be (from an urban point of view) a quite good Colonial bed. It faces the audience. There is a small table beside the bed ... the top of which is littered with bottles and pharmaceutical boxes and stained tumblers with spoons in them and various other patented medical supplies. Excepting 3 straight-back chairs, there is very little else in the room. A commode up* C.

It is still quite dark at 5:30 of a New England winter morning. But a pale, wan light is beginning to fight its way through the tightly closed, heavily frosted window, the cracks of which are stuffed with newspaper. ETHAN, *already dressed except for his shirt, stands in front of the washstand* R., *shaving with an old-fashioned straight razor—aided more or less by a small piece of broken mirror nailed to the wall. He wears corduroy trousers thrust into the tops of high laced boots, as usual, and a heavy, fleecy woolen undershirt.* ZEENA *(her flannel wrapper is on hook* L.*) sits in bed—the blankets drawn up over her body. She takes her stocking, puts it under the covers, draws it on her leg—she gets it on, then sits there, shuddering with the cold.* ETHAN *is in a generous, voluble mood this morning, suffused with the memory of his talk with* MATTIE. *As he scrapes away at his chin*

he hums a tune he heard at the church sociable last night.

———

ZEENA. Gettin' a bit light-headed lately, ain't you, Ethan? *(He is scraping away at his chin. She glares at him for another moment. Looks at* ETHAN *accusingly.)* That's the third time't you've shaved this week!

ETHAN *(good-naturedly, but absorbed in screwing up one side of his face to give a smooth surface to the other).* A-yeah. Sort of nippy, ain't it? *(Sets razor down on washstand.)* A-yeah ... mighty sharp, this mornin'. You know what, Zeenie ... I'd stay right under them blankets today ... if I was you! I wouldn't get up out of bed at all!

ZEENA *(pettishly).* If I had someone to take care of things proper, maybe I could stay in bed.

ETHAN. Well, Mattie'll do for you all right.

ZEENA *(scornfully).* Mattie!

ETHAN. You just tell her anythin' you want she sh'd do ... and she'll do it for you right off—you know that, Zeenie!

ZEENA *(whiningly).* That's what's ailin' me ... followin' her around ... showin' her ... watchin' over her ...

ETHAN *(cleans razor, puts it away on table).* Well—Mattie's willin' enough ... that's one sure thing!

ZEENA *(continues in same tone, as though he hadn't interrupted).* I'm beginnin' to wonder if she's wuth it! She can't cook. She can't scrub—

ETHAN. You wanted company!

ZEENA. She don't talk to me none.

ETHAN *(has finished shaving and now he plunges his face into water).* Oh, you're just frettin' yourself, Zeenie! *(Straightens up from washbowl—reaches out blindly for a towel. There is a pause as he finds a towel, rubs his face briskly.* ZEENA *watches him.)*

ZEENA. Well ... I won't be sorry to see her go. ... *(*ETHAN *stops abruptly.* ZEENA *glances at him.)* 'Course she will go ... sooner or later ... I wouldn't want it said't I'd stood in her way. *(*ETHAN *starts getting into his shirt.)* ... a poor girl like Mattie Silver ... it wouldn't be right to stop her leavin' ... if she got a chance to get married.

ETHAN *(easily).* Well, 'tain't very likely!

ZEENA. Don't you go and be too sure now, Ethan! *(He looks at her. She adds, just empatically enough to be significant:*) Anyway—whatever happens—I ain't goin' to be left alone!

ETHAN. What's got into you this morning, Zeena! You must be gone queer in the head!

ZEENA (*violently*). No, I ain't! And don't you never say a thing like that to me again! You hear!

MATTIE (*calls from kitchen below, heartily*). Ethan! Ethan!

ZEENA (*whines*). You never talked that way to me before . . . never . . . why, you never said anythin' like that. . . . (*She is whining.*) I don't know how I c'n go on like this. (*He gets finished with shirt; she takes spoonful of liquid medicine from bottle.*) With you bein' so cruel . . . and me sufferin' and doin' for that girl . . . when she'd ought to be doin' for me! (MATTIE *is heard running quickly upstairs. She knocks lightly at door* L. *upper.*)

ETHAN (*quickly*). Come in, Matt!

MATTIE (*enters quickly, crosses* C., *moving blithefully into room. She is eager and quite gay this morning*). Why, Ethan Frome, do you know it's most 6 o'clock! Breakfast's been ready for hours! (*Then to* ZEENA *pleasantly.*) 'Mornin', Zeena! (ZEENA *looks at her without replying.*)

ETHAN (*hastily*). Say, Matt!—fill up that hot-water bottle there—(*She turns to get it from commode up* C.) Zeenie's gone and got herself a terrible chill this mornin'.

ZEENA. I got my chill last night—goin' down them drafty stairs to open that door in the middle of the night! (MATTIE *glances at* ETHAN *quickly and then at* ZEENA.)

MATTIE. Oh, now, ain't that a shame! Just you wait one second . . . Zeena . . . I got water boilin' on the stove . . . and I'll be back before you know it! (*She takes hot-water bottle, exits hurriedly, out* L. *Slight pause.*)

ETHAN (*as soon as* MATTIE *is gone, puts on sweater and says casually*). Guess that was my fault, Zeenie. . . . I got gabbin' with Ed Varnum about business . . . and first thing you know . . . I was late gettin' to the sociable to fetch Mattie. (*He glances at* ZEENA, *a bit self-consciously reaches for his coat and murmurs:*) Now, Zeenie, don't you go frettin' yourself . . . Mattie's all right, she's doin' fine. . . . (*Smoothly.*) 'Course I know she ain't the housekeep-er't you are! . . . But you can't expect

that. (*Pointedly as he struggles into sweater.*) One thing I know . . . Mattie ain't leavin's long's she's needed. (*Gets his coat on and buttons it up.*) Well, Jotham's comin' and we're loadin' spruce and startin' to haul over to Andrew Hale's place today. (*Puts coat on.*) I guess't I'm a little late gettin' started.

ZEENA. I guess't you're always late . . . now't you shave every mornin'. (*The implication stops* ETHAN.)

MATTIE (*enters with the hot-water bottle and a breakfast tray*). Here you are, Zeena! (MATTIE *hurries to bed with hot-water bottle,* ZEENA *shifts about petulantly.*)

ZEENA (*grabs hot-water bottle from* MATTIE). I'll do for myself!

MATTIE (*sets tray on chair*). I'm terribly sorry about last night . . . we was just awful late, wasn't we, Zeenie? (ETHAN *is standing stock-still . . . nervous and embarrassed, and alarmed at what* MATTIE *is about to say.*) Well . . . it was all my fault, every bit. . . . I went and promised Denis Eady the last dance and he just wouldn't let me go . . . and there was poor Ethan waitin' out in the cold. . . . (ZEENA *glances from one to other of them, smiles slightly.* ETHAN *is overwhelmed with embarrassment.*)

ZEENA. Ethan, I thought you was late gettin' about your business.

ETHAN. A-yeah, well, I'll get there. You see't everythin' gets done, Mattie . . . so's Zeena c'n rest easy. . . . I'll be back in time to give you a hand around the house later on. (*Crosses to door* L. MATTIE *gets tray from chair.*)

ZEENA. Ethan! (*He stops.*) You 'tend to the haulin'—we'll see to the house-work! (*He exits.* MATTIE *sets the tray on* ZEENA's *lap,* ZEENA *is watching her steadily, which increases* MATTIE's *uneasiness.* ZEENA *looks at the tray full of food.*) All them things . . . just goin' to waste . . . thk, thk, thk. . . .

MATTIE (*cheerfully*). You always say that, Zeena. Well . . . (*Crosses up to door* L.)

ZEENA (*sharply*). Mattie! (MATTIE *turns quickly.* ZEENA *composes herself.*) Oh, I didn't mean to be cross. You know, I didn't sleep much last night. (*Takes sip of coffee, looks up at* MATTIE.) You been leadin' quite a lot of dances with Denis Eady—lately, ain't you?

MATTIE (*relieved at the turn of the conversation*). Oh, well—I don't know—I guess he dances a lot with most every-body.

ZEENA (*significantly*). His father owns the Starkfield grocery.

MATTIE (*innocently*). I know—an' folks say they're real well off, too.

ZEENA. Denis is quite a catch for some girl.

MATTIE (C.). My , I should say!

ZEENA (*pleasantly*). If you was to get goin' steady with him—you c'd ask him over to the house Wednesday evenin's. Denis is a mighty fine boy, and I wouldn't stand in your way if he was ever to propose to you.

MATTIE (*laughs*). Oh, my—why, he wouldn't never do that!

ZEENA. He might . . . if you was to give him the chance.

MATTIE (C.). Why—gorry—whatever put that into your head, Zeena? And I never thought of him that way at all! I don't like *him*!

ZEENA. Paupers can't be choosey. (*Drinks coffee.*)

MATTIE (*quickly*). Oh, I'm not choosey . . . Zeena . . . honest', I'm not. Like I was saying to Ethan only last night . . . I says nobody ain't never asked me yet, I said, and he said, if he wasn't married he might ask me himself . . . so 'course I said, "Sayin' that don't mean anythin'. . . . But still an' all," I says, "it's real nice of you to say it" . . . and it was, too, wasn't it? (*She beams.*) And that's about's near to proposin's anybody ever—got— (ZEENA *is sitting rigidly bolt-upright in the bed, and is staring at* MATTIE *fixedly.*)

ZEENA (*indicates tray*). You c'n take this . . . if you're a mind to.

MATTIE (*hastily and frightenedly*). Yes, Zeena. (MATTIE *goes to lift the tray.* ZEENA *lurches away from* MATTIE. MATTIE *upsets the coffee cup on the tray and the coffee spills out over the blankets.* ZEENA *sits rigidly motionless, staring at the rapidly spreading stain.* MATTIE *is terrified. She suddenly darts forward, sets the cup upright upon the tray.*) Oh, Zeena! Oh, my! . . . if I'd only been thinkin' what I was doin' . . . oh, them blankets is just ruint, simply ruint! (*Puts tray on chest up* C., *stops, straightens up, glances at* ZEENA *helplessly, and then after a moment, unable to bear* ZEENA's *steady gaze of terrific hatred, she mumbles faster and faster:*) I don't know what I'm going to do! (*She sighs, unconsciously adopting* ZEENA's *perpetually worried manner.*) I got

an awful lot needs tendin' to up here today . . . them floors to scrub and the windows want washin' real bad . . . an' them blankets'll have to be washed out and I don't know how I'll ever get things to dry this weather! (*Picks up blankets from bed.* ZEENA *gets up, goes to closet, searches frantically.* MATTIE, *with blankets, crosses* C.) Don't you want I sh'd help, Zeena! I'll get whatever you're looking for! (*She reaches out to help* ZEENA.)

ZEENA (*fiercely*). I ain't askin' any favors from you. (*Grabs dress from* MATTIE.) You leave that be! That's my wedding dress. Don't you never touch none of my things! You keep you hands off my things! An' don't forget that as long as you live! (MATTIE *hesitates.* ZEENA *raises her head, smiles wanly, murmurs quietly:*) Get along downstairs now, Mattie! (MATTIE *bolts for the hallway, exits* L. ZEENA, *her pains forgotten, stares at the dress. Suddenly she buries her face in the dress and sobs.*)

CURTAIN

SCENE TWO

The kitchen. Immediately following the action of the preceding scene. Three tin pots of flowers are on the sink and a pot of geraniums stands on sink table.

ETHAN *is seated* R. *of the table eating his breakfast. It is rapidly growing lighter outside.* MATTIE *comes quickly down the stairs* R. *Her arms are laden with the coffee-stained blankets, and she is visibly frightened and distraught.*

ETHAN. Why, what is it, Mattie? What you doing with them blankets?

MATTIE (*puts blankets on chair* L., *glances at him and murmurs frightenedly:*) Oh, Ethan—Ethan—I went and spilled coffee all over everythin'!

ETHAN (*rises, closes stair door,* C. *back of table*). What's she said to you, Matt? (MATTIE *puts wood in stove.*) Why are you frettin' so much? The blankets ain't no crime!

MATTIE (*shakes her head, murmurs in terror*). They're ruint—simply ruint—oh, I don't know what to do. I got to wash 'em out right off—and the fire's low and the water won't boil, I know it won't never boil with the fire so low. Oh, Ethan, how'm I ever goin' to get things to dry this weather! (*Crosses, gets tub from under table up* L.)

ETHAN (*follows her*). Whatever's she said to you? (*Abruptly, as he moves to sink. Takes tub from her.*) Let me at that for a minute, Mattie! You're trembling, Matt. What is it? It can't be only them blankets. Why won't you tell me, Matt, why . . .?

MATTIE. It's nothing, Ethan, nothing!

ETHAN. There is something wrong, Matt. Was it about our being so late last night, was it?

MATTIE. Oh, Ethan! (ZEENA *enters down the stairs* R. MATTIE *and* ETHAN *turn quickly toward stairway.* ZEENA *is wearing her best blue merino dress and her bonnet. She is carrying her coat and an old battered suitcase.*)

ETHAN (*as* ZEENA *enters the room and he gazes at her, amazed and bewildered*). Why —where're you goin', Zeena? (ZEENA *makes no reply. She lays her coat meticulously over chair* R. . . . *puts suitcase down at chair* R. *of table, goes to stove—lifts the cover on one of the pots, goes to* C. *place at the table, sits down.*)

ZEENA. I guess't I might try one of them potatoes . . . if you don't mind, Mattie. (MATTIE *hurries to stove, scoops a boiled potato from the pot onto a plate.*)

ETHAN. Why—Zeena—I thought you was stayin' in bed up there!

ZEENA (*as* MATTIE *sets the plate in front of her,* ZEENA *spears the potato with her fork—she continues to* MATTIE—*ignoring* ETHAN'S *interruption.*)—and some of that coffee too. (MATTIE *pours coffee* R. *of table.* ZEENA *glances up at* MATTIE *and smiles pleasantly.*) ! didn't get very much coffee this mornin'—you know, Mattie. (*She takes a bite of potato—then glances at* ETHAN.) Ain't you got a lot of spruce to haul today?

ETHAN (*apprehensively*). Zeena, I asked you, where you going?

ZEENA (*she puts milk and sugar in coffee*). While I'm gone, Ethan, if you c'n spare a minute from all that there haulin't you're doin' today . . . you'd better be sure't this girl gets tham blankets washed out and dried before night, or you'll have to sleep down here in the kitchen. (*Takes gulp of coffee.*) Go out to the barn there, Mattie . . . like a good girl . . . and find Jotham right off . . . and tell him't I said he sh'd hitch up the sorrel. . . . (MATTIE

has stood motionless, watching ZEENA. *She glances at* ETHAN *questioningly.* ZEENA *sees the look between them.*) Mattie, do like I say an' don't stand there gazin' at Ethan, neither! (MATTIE *hesitates a second, crosses back of table. Exits* C. ZEENA *glances at* ETHAN.) I don't suppose't you've got anythin' to say against Jotham hitchin' up the sorrel?

ETHAN (*down* L.). Jotham's got the sorrel hooked onto the sledge . . . waitin' to haul the spruce on over to Andrew Hale's place.

ZEENA (*pleasantly*). Well, Ethan, 'course I ain't got a lot of stren'th to go plowin' through all that snow, but I'll try walkin' as far's Starkfield—sooner'n put you out any.

ETHAN. Why'd you want to go to Starkfield?

ZEENA. If I got that far—'course I c'd ask Denis Eady to drive me on over to the Flats.

ETHAN. What're you goin' to the Flats for, Zeena?

ZEENA. I'm takin' the train to Bettsbridge!

ETHAN. But why—what'd you want to go to Bettsbridge for?

ZEENA. To see that new doctor—that's what for! (*Eats.*)

ETHAN (*looks at her, aware that she has some sinister motive*). But you can't do that, Zeena! You know we just ain't got the money to lay out for any new doctors any more'n we had for that new-fangled vibratin' machine there—that you don't even know what it's for!

ZEENA (*sighs*). I know! (*She stares at him.*) I know I'm just a burden to you!

ETHAN. Zeena, why're you goin' to Bettsbridge all of a sudden?

ZEENA (*calmly*). I told you once . . . to see that new doctor.

ETHAN. How're we ever goin' to pay a new doctor?

ZEENA (*easily*). Well . . . I got what's left of the cow money . . . 'taint much . . . but it'll have to do, I s'pose!

ETHAN. You can't take that money, Zeena, you just can't!

ZEENA. Nonsense! Why, 'course I can, Ethan . . . you ain't that mean!

ETHAN. I don't aim to be mean.

ZEENA. As I was saying . . . I hate to put you out any, but I just ain't got the stren'th to walk . . . somebody'll have to drive me over's far's the Flats. (*Rises, takes coat.*)

ETHAN. I can't drive you over to the Flats. I just ain't got the time. I got to see Andrew Hale and try an' get cash— (*She stops putting coat on.*) enough out of him to buy feed for the stock . . .

ZEENA (*shrewdly*). I thought Andrew Hale didn't pay under three months!

ETHAN. He don't's a rule . . . but I need it bad. . . . I got to get enough for the feed anyhow!

ZEENA. If he does pay cash down for all that spruce—that'd pay for the feed and some to spare. . . . (*Then thoughtfully.*) There's an awful lot of medicines I been needin' real bad.

ETHAN (*desperately*). I said I ain't got no reason to s'pose he will pay cash! He ain't never done it before!

ZEENA (*her coat is on now, she is getting it buttoned*). I know! That's just what I was thinkin'! (*She sighs.*) Well . . . it's all right, Ethan . . . if you don't want to bother to drive me over . . . Jotham will. . . . I wouldn't want to trouble you none. . . . (MATTIE *enters* C.) Did you tell Jotham to hitch up? (MATTIE *nods.* ZEENA *turns to the cupboard—selects a bottle thoughtfully. It is nearly empty. Crosses to table* C.) It ain't never done me a speck of good. . . . But I guess't I might's well use it up. (*She empties the bottle over the glass to get the last drop. Gulps down the medicine.*) I'm gettin' so's I c'n tell right off—(*Smacks lips.*) that ain't goin' to help any. (*Holds out empty bottle.*) Here . . . (ZEENA *gives* MATTIE *bottle.*) If you c'n get the taste out of it—it'll do for pickles. (*Puts on her gloves.*) There's only the one train up from Bettsbridge—so I don't figure't I'll be back before tomorrow evenin'—if then. I'll spend the night with Aunt Martha Pierce. . . . (*She picks up satchel.*) Not't I'll be missed. (*Crosses to door up* C.) I guess't you c'n get along fine without me. (*Exits* C.)

ETHAN. She don't say so much as a word for days and days—an' all the time them little things that don't amount to a hill a beans keep poisonin' her till sooner or later she's just got to bust loose. Well, I'll be down to the wood lot most of the day. Got to see Andrew Hale, and try and get some money for the feed— them critters'll never live another month if I don't. (*Sleigh bells offstage.*)

MATTIE (*frightened*). Oh, Ethan, Ethan, what's she goin' to do? (ETHAN *pauses at door.*) Oh, Ethan, I'm scared! Why can't she never say what she's goin' to do? Why can't she never say it right out!

ETHAN. Don't be too sure she's going to do anythin'. She got herself a chill last night, and she's going to Bettsbridge to see a new doctor. That's what she said just now. (*He gets his coat from nail on door* C.)

MATTIE (*crosses to pump*). Oh—well . . . I guess't there's no use frettin' about it, now is there?

ETHAN (*after a moment awkwardly*). No. Well . . . I'll be gettin' along. . . . (*He goes out* C. *quickly, embarrassed and worried, and ill at ease. She turns to the pump.*)

CURTAIN

Scene Three

Dusk—the same day. The kitchen. It is rapidly growing dark. (Handstove has been removed to parlor offstage R.)

MATTIE *is eagerly and excitedly preparing supper and setting the table, and though she is not yet by any means domestically efficient, she has succeeded in giving the table a faintly festive appearance. She is wearing her "other" dress, over which she wears an apron. She is humming to herself as she critically examines the table* C., *goes* L. *Lights table lamp at sink, carries it to bracket on* R. *wall. Lights come up. Crosses to* C. *table, looks at it, gets tin can plant from sink, puts it on* C. *table, gets pickles in jar, puts on* C. *table, decides to get a fancy dish for them, studies the top shelf of the cupboard, gets chair, reaches to top shelf, brings down red pickle dish—washes it carefully, takes to* C. *table.*

ETHAN (*calling from upstairs*). Say, Matt! Ain't that supper ready yet? . . . I'm starvin'!

MATTIE. Just a minute, Ethan!

ETHAN (*calling*). What you doin' down there, Mattie?

MATTIE (MATTIE *glances toward stairway and calls quickly*). Never you mind! (*Puts pickles into dish, puts empty pickle jar on sink.*) All right, Ethan . . . supper's 'most ready now! (*Takes apron off. Replaces* C. *chair. Outside door* C. *opens and* JOTHAM *enters and quickly closes door after him. He sets jug on the floor near door.*)

JOTHAM. 'Evenin'.

MATTIE (*hanging up apron at the window hook*). Oh, hello, you!

JOTHAM (*heading toward stove, stands over it, warming his hands*). If I ain't in your way, Mattie, I'll just thaw a bit before I start on down home.

ETHAN (*calling suddenly from the head of stairs*). Is that Jotham? (*He is heard starting downstairs.*)

MATTIE (*at sink*). Yes.

ETHAN (*with obvious relief*). Oh! (*He enters quickly and eagerly downstairs* R.) Say, Jotham, did you bring in that thing?

JOTHAM. A-yeah, Ethan. She's settin' by the door there. (*He is sniffing about under pot covers and peering at the cooking supper.* ETHAN *hurries to the* C. *door, picks up jug, turns to* MATTIE.)

ETHAN. Brought you somethin', Matt!

MATTIE (*crosses to* R. *of table*). Why, whatever? (*He pulls cork out of the top of the jug, holds out the jug for her to smell.*)

ETHAN (*at end of table*). Mrs. Andrew Hale give it to me.

MATTIE (C.). Why—my sakes—that's apple cider, ain't it? (*Then suspiciously, goes up to cupboard for glasses, brings two to table.*) It ain't gone hard or nothin?

ETHAN. Nope, Jotham and me—we seen that there same juice come oozin' through the press, didn't we, Jotham?

JOTHAM (*absorbed in things on the stove*). A-yeah— (*He is ostensibly warming his hands, examining the supper critically.*) Well, I'll be goin' along now.... (ETHAN *crosses to* R., *puts jug on floor at table.*) Irritatin' havin' me snoopin' around— gettin' under your feet ... when you got a big supper to handle, ain't it, Mattie?

MATTIE (*goes up* C., *gets dishes for* JOTHAM, *brings them to* C. *of table. Moves towards stove, busily*). You'd be out of my way more, Jotham, if you was to sit right up to the table there.

JOTHAM. A-yeah—guess so—I'll be movin' along in a minute—(*He gets to the table.* ETHAN *stands watching him, grinning. He sits* L. *end of table.*) Sure I ain't in the way here?

ETHAN (R. *of table*). Catch your death sittin' around with that coat on, Jotham!

JOTHAM (*looks up at him blankly, then nods*). A-yeah—(*He gets up, peels off his coat, puts coat on hook at* C. *door.*)

MATTIE (*as she comes back to table with plate full of stew*). Just dig right in,

Jotham, and you too, Ethan. . . .

JOTHAM (*crosses down, as* MATTIE *sets a steaming plate of stew in front of him*). You ain't askin' me to stay to supper!

MATTIE (*laughs, brings down second stew*). Why, I fixed everythin' special!

JOTHAM (*eats rapidly for a moment—then pauses—with a mouthful, looks at them questioningly.* MATTIE *and* ETHAN *look at him and laugh*). A-yeah—well, long's you're sure I'm wanted, I'll go when I ain't. (MATTIE *puts third stew down.*)

MATTIE (*standing at table, turns and looks at* ETHAN, *who has crossed to stove. A broad grin upon his face.*) Why, whatever's come over you, Ethan?

ETHAN (*bursting with news*). You ain't asked me how did I make out today!

MATTIE (*eagerly*). Oh, Ethan, how did you make out?

ETHAN. All right!

MATTIE. Oh, Ethan—really!

ETHAN. A-yeah!

MATTIE. Oh, I bet anythin' you got the cash from Andrew Hale!

ETHAN. Well, no—not exactly!

MATTIE (*disappointedly*). Oh . . . !

JOTHAM (*is the only one at the table, and he is eating heartily. He looks up, mumbles with mouth full*). Well—you as good's got cash, Eth!

ETHAN (*very pleased*). A-yeah—guess I did, at that!

JOTHAM. Same thing, ain't it?

ETHAN. A-yeah!

MATTIE (*bursting with curiosity*). Oh, Ethan, tell me!

ETHAN (*proudly*). Made him give me twenty dollars' wuth of feed right off for the livestock! It's out there to the barn now!

MATTIE. Oh, Ethan—Ethan!

ETHAN. A-yeah.

MATTIE. Why, ain't that fine though— now them cattle's got feed to last straight up to pasturin' time!

ETHAN. A-yeah!

MATTIE (*so happy she is bursting*). Well, set yourself right down, Ethan—oh, now say—(*Pours coffee for* ETHAN, *then* JOTHAM, *then herself.*) Ain't I glad I fixed supper special . . .! (ETHAN *goes to table, sits.*)

JOTHAM. 'Taint a bad supper, neither! (*Sugar and cream in coffffee.*)

MATTIE. And you know what? I fixed more'n enough coffee for three cups apiece! (ETHAN *and* JOTHAM *are both eating away eagerly.* MATTIE *watches them content-*

edly as she eats. Then her eye falls upon the red glass dish and she picks it up cautiously, in front of ETHAN's *eyes. They all pour cream and take sugar.*) Pickles?

ETHAN (*helps himself to pickles*). A-yeah! (*Then passes dish to* JOTHAM.) Pickles, Jotham?

JOTHAM (*seizing dish eagerly*). Don't mind if I do!

ETHAN (*looking at dish*). Say, where'd you get that there dish, Mattie?

MATTIE (*innocently*). Oh—up there! (*Nods towards top of cupboard.*)

ETHAN. Never seen it before.

MATTIE. It ain't never been used before. (*She helps herself, puts dish down again and says "Ah," relieved it is still intact.*)

JOTHAM (*to* ETHAN). Don't she like pickles? S'pose that new doctorin'll do her any good, Ethan? (ETHAN *does not reply.* JOTHAM *adds dryly.*) Hope so. . . . Them pains of hers has been gettin' a mite tryin'. (ETHAN *looks at* MATTIE.) Stew's all right, at that.

MATTIE. Oh, you think so, Jotham?

JOTHAM. A-yeah.

ETHAN. I guess you more'n earned that all right, Jotham, drivin' away over to the Flats.

JOTHAM (*dryly*). Well, you can just bet your boots I did! (*He sits there thoughtfully for a second.*) A-yeah—train was late—'count of snow up the line—'course Zeena got the notion it was my fault or somethin'. . . . I ain't figured out yet how that could be. All's I know is . . . we sat an' waited 'bout an hour and a half . . . and she was still goin' strong. . . . (*He sits there remembering painfully; then he sighs, and shakes his head.*) Guess I'd ought to be glad it wasn't longer. (*Looks around* L. *at window. Cleans his plate. Sits back, sighs contentedly, glancing out window, remarks good-naturedly.*) Snowin' again!

MATTIE. More stew?

JOTHAM. Nope.

MATTIE. Ethan?

ETHAN (*a bit absently*). Hhm?

MATTIE (*slightly flustered because he is looking at her so closely*). Stew?

ETHAN. Nope.

MATTIE (ETHAN *is looking at* MATTIE *intently. She glances away, looks in stew pot which is on table, laughs.*) Ain't that lucky! You know what, there ain't any more! (*Puts her dish and* JOTHAM's *in sink. Gets dessert out of oven.*)

ETHAN. Guess't we've had enough stew to last a lifetime!

JOTHAM (*thoughtfully*). Well, stew ain't bad though!

MATTIE. No, it ain't!

ETHAN. Nope, 'taint bad at all when you're hungry. ·

MATTIE (*she takes* ETHAN's *plate to sink*). Anyhow, we got puddin'! (*Brings pudding to* JOTHAM *and* ETHAN.)

ETHAN (*amazed*). Why, how'd you ever make a puddin', Matt?

MATTIE (*modestly*). Oh . . . prunes! (*Gets dessert for* ETHAN. *Gets her own dessert, goes to table.*)

JOTHAM. Don't look so bad.

ETHAN. No . . . it's all right!

MATTIE (*eagerly*). Oh, Ethan, do you really think so? (ETHAN *nods thoughtfully, and goes on eating.*) You know, puddin' don't come a bit natural! (*Sits.*)

ETHAN. It ain't bad though.

JOTHAM. A-yeah—it's all right, considerin' . . . Blamed if I can see why she's always kickin' about you, Mattie! (*For the first time the thought of* ZEENA, *and why she is complaining about* MATTIE *constrains them.* ETHAN *glances at* MATTIE *and is acutely conscious of her tension.*)

ETHAN (*he murmers elaborately*). Snow's driftin'.

JOTHAM (*completely unaware of their embarrassment, he sits back*). A-yeah, s'pose it'll interfere any with her gettin' back tomorrow?

ETHAN (*with a great effort to be casual*). You never can tell this time of year.

JOTHAM. Drifts bad on them Flats . . . don't it? Just as like as not—this'll tie them trains up for fair!

MATTIE (*quickly*). Anythin' more, Jotham?

JOTHAM. Well . . . I don't know's I'd mind a swallow of that there sweet cider!

MATTIE. Oh, ain't I crazy. I went and forgot all about it! (*Holds* JOTHAM's *glass.* ETHAN *pours three glasses.*)

JOTHAM. If you're sure I ain't stayin' too long . . . (ETHAN *is filling their glasses. Nobody replies.* JOTHAM *adds:*) Guess't I'd ought to be startin' down home pretty quick now. (*He gulps down his cider, smacks his lips.*) Hhm! Mighty fine that!

MATTIE (*tasting the cider*). Ain't it though!

ETHAN. A-yeah!

JOTHAM (*looks at his empty glass*). A-yeah! (ETHAN *and* MATTIE *are looking at each other, a little self-consciously.* JOTHAM *suddenly drains his already empty glass, gets up from table.*) Well . . . goin' home now.

ETHAN. Sit down, Jotham, pour yourself another cider! (*Puts jug on table, toward* JOTHAM.)

JOTHAM. Nope—goin' home! (*He goes over to door, gets his coat and hat down from the peg.*) Don't want to be in the way any. (*He is struggling into coat.* MATTIE *is clearing table.*) Don't never like to wear out a welcome . . .

MATTIE. Oh, you ain't wearin' out nothin', Jotham . . . help yourself to the apple cider!

JOTHAM (*shortly*). Nope—goin' now. (MATTIE *crosses below table for dishes.* JOTHAM *buttoning his coat now at window.*) Tough haulin' tomorrow, Ethan—if this keeps up.

ETHAN. A-yeah . . . well . . . we'll get an early start. . . .

JOTHAM (*still at the window*). Comin' down plenty now, all right. (*He turns away.*) Cozy in here tonight—if I was you two—I'd just sit right up into that there "Fancy Hero" stove. . . . (*He nods toward the cookstove* C. *He gets to the outside door* C. . . . *and without pausing, murmurs as he opens it and exits quickly:*) 'Night—obliged to you both.

ETHAN (*calls quickly*). 'Night!

MATTIE (*simultaneously she calls*). 'Night, Jotham! (*They are left alone, glancing at each other, both terribly self-conscious.* ETHAN *is sitting at the table, finishing his coffee.* MATTIE *crosses down for apron at window, crosses up for kettle, takes water to sink, kettle back to stove.* ETHAN *stares out window a moment, then glances at her. She is busy* C. *back of table.* MATTIE *takes bread to cupboard* R.)

ETHAN (*still seated, glances at her*). Well . . . ! (*She looks up at him and smiles eagerly. There is a pause.*) Mighty fine supper, Matt!

MATTIE (*puts on apron, chortling with pleasure and pride*). Oh, I guess 't it wasn't so much—I c'd do even better'n that another time! (ETHAN *exits to parlor* R.) Do you want a lamp in the parlor, Ethan?

ETHAN. Nope—just fetchin' the handstove. (*He returns with stove—sets it by chair. Sits, looks at the window, then glances at her.*) Say, Matt!

MATTIE (*she has started to wash the dishes, back of table*). Hhm?

ETHAN. Bet you don't never see snow like this down there to Willimantic!

MATTIE (*glancing out window*). No, sir, I ain't never seen nothin' like . . . nowheres near!

ETHAN (*gazing out at the flurries of snow, against the blackness of the night. He speaks suddenly and with a note of great surprise*). By jiminy, you know, it's kind of pretty at that! (*There is a pause. She glances up from her work, smiles slightly, then goes on. He looks out at the snow.*) A-yeah—don't seem to mind it at all tonight! (*He glances about, conscious of the warm glow of the room.*) Stove's drawin' like a house a-fire. (*After a time.*) Say . . . ain't this the night we was goin' coastin'!

MATTIE. I guess you must've forgot all about it, Ethan. (*Takes napkin to cupboard* R.)

ETHAN. No, no, I didn't exactly forget, Mattie. . . . (*He stretches luxuriously, glances around the room and at her.*) Only thing is . . . (*He hesitates, looks around for an excuse, murmurs:*) I guess it's . . . sort of dark out. (*He sits there basking in the warmth of the room.*)

MATTIE (*moves over to window*). Let's see . . . (*Nods solemnly.*) Oh, my, yes . . . isn't it though! (*Pause.*) My goodness! It's dark as Egypt out! (*She stacks dishes.*)

ETHAN (*after a moment, a bit reluctantly*). 'Course if you really want to go . . .

MATTIE (*turns to him*). Do you?

ETHAN (*doubtfully*). Well . . . it's kind of dark, but . . . I'll go . . . if you say so. . . . (*Another pause.*) Nice and warm in here tonight, ain't it?

MATTIE. Maybe it is too dark, huh, Ethan!

ETHAN (*with relief*). A-yeah. Maybe it is . . . we c'd wait an' go tomorrow if there's a moon.

MATTIE (*just as relieved, and now eager*). Oh, that'd be just wonderful!

ETHAN. A-yeah. Well, we'll go tomorrow. . . . I'd be afraid to go down that Corbury road tonight!

MATTIE (*laughs at him, starts to wash silver*). Yes, you would! (*She chuckles, as she goes back to work washing dishes.*) Still 'n' all, it would be awful dangerous, bein' it's so dark out and all!

ETHAN. A-yeah.

MATTIE. I guess we're well enough here tonight, Ethan!

ETHAN. A-yeah. (*Sits back, relaxing. He murmurs:*) Couldn't ask no better. (*Stretches out his feet toward the glow of the*

"Fancy Hero," watches her.) Say, Matt, I c'd give you a hand there, with them dishes, if you say so!

MATTIE (*glances at him, sees him stretched out comfortably. She chuckles*). You just set, Ethan!

ETHAN (*lazily*). A-yeah—it's all right!

MATTIE. Hhm? (ETHAN *does not answer. He is comfortably watching her.*) What's all right, Ethan?

ETHAN (*chuckles*). Sittin'.

MATTIE (*laughs, washes dishes*). I'll just bet! (*She goes on working.*)

ETHAN (*after a moment, he yawns, starts to speak*). You know . . . (*His speech is lost in the luxurious yawn.*)

MATTIE (*after a moment, she glances over her shoulder at him*). What was you just too lazy to say, Ethan?

ETHAN (*finishes his yawn, gazes at her blankly, murmurs*). Oh . . . I don't know. . . . (*She goes back to work. After a moment, he speaks.*) Mighty peaceful tonight, ain't it, Mattie?

MATTIE. Ain't it though!

ETHAN. A-yeah. (MATTIE *has finished washing the dishes, she hangs up the dish towel.*) Hurry up and set, Matt. . . .

MATTIE. Soon's I put the dishes away!

ETHAN (*gets up and crosses to her at sink*). I'll give you a hand there. . . .

MATTIE (*equally conscious of his nearness, murmurs.*) No . . . no . . . you . . . (*They reach out simultaneously for the stack of dishes, and knock the red-glass pickle dish to the floor. It crashes and breaks. . . .* MATTIE *stares down at it.*) Ethan! (*Then she looks up at him, frightenedly.*) Oh, Ethan! It's broke . . . it's all to pieces. . . .

ETHAN. But you couldn't help it! (*He bends over and starts to pick up the pieces of the dish.*)

MATTIE. Ethan, whatever'll she say! She never meant it was to be used even, not ever . . . and I had to reach it down from the top shelf there . . . and she'll want to know why I did it . . .! Oh, Ethan, what'll I say?

ETHAN (*quickly*). Don't say anything, Matt. . . . I'll get another one just like it over to Starkfield tomorrow.

MATTIE (*frantically*). Oh, you can't . . . you can't . . . (*She looks up at him, now deeply frightened.*) Oh, Ethan, she hates me so! And she told me never to even touch anythin' of hers . . .! She hates me, Ethan . . . and I'm so scared of her!

ETHAN. Don't, Matt . . . don't . . . don't

now . . .! Wait, Matt. (*He carries the pieces in his cupped hands to the cupboard, climbs up on chair, raises both arms, to top shelf.*) Matt, was it here?

MATTIE (*cries impatiently*). What good's that goin' to do, Ethan?

ETHAN (*moves his hands along shelf*). Look, Matt, she'll never see it. I put it way back. (*She doesn't answer. He carefully arranges the segments of broken glass, fitting them together so that from below the damage is not immediately apparent. Then he stands back.*) Well, she'll never know it now. (*He jumps down off the chair and goes to her.*) Look, Matt, she'll never see it from here.

MATTIE. Oh, what's the use, Ethan? She'll find out anyhow!

ETHAN (*rapidly*). No—she won't now. . . . First thing in the mornin' I'll get some glue at the Widow Homan's and stick them pieces together, and before spring cleanin' time, I'll match that dish over to Shadd's Falls or Bettsbridge or some place. Don't be too sure she'll take any notice. . . .

MATTIE (*sits L. of table*). Oh, Ethan . . . she don't never miss a thing!

ETHAN (*reluctantly*). Well . . . no . . . no . . . she don't miss much. That's a fact. (*Sits R. of table. There is a pause.*)

MATTIE (*very practically, seeing his admission of defeat*). Still 'n' all it don't look half bad from here, Ethan, an' bein's she won't be back till tomorrow and we can get it fixed by then—why, I guess there ain't no use worryin' tonight!

ETHAN (*quickly turns back to her*). No, I guess there ain't!

MATTIE. All right, Ethan. (*Rises.*) Let's don't think about it any more now! (*Crosses back of table, gets sewing basket out of cupboard.*)

ETHAN (*with great difficulty*). Let's don't, Matt. . . . I been lookin' forward a lot . . . all day, I ain't been thinkin' about a thing . . . but this evenin' . . . (*Stops abruptly, embarrassed by this comparatively voluble confession.*)

MATTIE (*a little self-consciously*). Me neither, Ethan. . . . (*She looks at him and smiles. Crosses to back of table with basket.*) I been most of the day fixin' my "one and only"! (*She indicates her dress.*) Them dewdabs was all comin' off! . . . My . . . what'd I ever do if they did! (*She looks at him again.*) It don't look so bad now, does it, Ethan? I mean . . . considerin'. (*She sits. He is gazing at her intently. He shakes his head.*) Oh, Ethan, what'd she say to you up there this mornin' before I came up?

ETHAN (*impatiently*). We wasn't goin' to talk about it! (*Rises.*) This time tomorrow night she'll be back here, raging and complainin' . . .

MATTIE. Ethan . . . I promise . . . I ain't goin' to even think about it once more tonight!

ETHAN (*crosses to window, stands looking out window . . . his back to her*). I wish to God that mornin' train'd be buried in fifty feet of snow!

MATTIE (*quickly*). Oh, Ethan! That's awful . . . it ain't right you sh'd talk like that! (*Resignedly, then after a moment, thoughtfully.*) Still 'n' all . . . (*Intrigued with her thought.*) I bet some of them drifts over there to the Flats is 50 feet easy! (*He is still restless, she calls—eager to divert him.*) Ain't it funny, Ethan . . . how all the things you ain't 'sposed to talk about, is way by far the most fascinatin'? (*She goes on speaking, anxious to reawaken his peace and tranquility.*) Like now take when I was workin' in the shoe factory . . . (*He starts to cross R. back of table.*) till I got fired . . . all I did all day long was no more'n I got the leathers I'd paint 'em with plain water and pass 'em on to the next girl and grab another leather an' paint it with a brush and water till I thought I'd bust and one day I says to the foreman, I says . . . "Why do I paint them leathers with plain water?" . . . and he says, "You know what's the matter with you?" he says, "You talk too much!"

ETHAN (*sits R. of table C. Relaxed now*). That was to make 'em easier to glaze, I guess.

MATTIE. It was? (ETHAN *nods.*) That's interestin' to know all right. (*He watches her contentedly.*) Do you think I talk too much?

ETHAN (*fervently*). Oh, no, Matt. . . . No, I don't think so!

(*But he has no more words. They are silent for a time . . . until she looks up and sees him gazing at her intently. She glances away toward the window.*)

MATTIE. My—it's still snowin', ain't it?

ETHAN (*eagerly*). A-yeah.

MATTIE. Oh, my! (*He gazes at her, content and warm and pleased. After a time she glances toward the kitchen clock.*) Ethan!

ETHAN (*murmurs contentedly*). Hhm?

MATTIE. You know what! (*He shakes his head.*) It's most nine o'clock!

ETHAN (*turns in direction of the clock*). Oh . . . no! No, Matt . . . it ain't! It can't be already!

MATTIE. Well . . . 'tis—look! (*She sighs.*) Oh, my! Don't it just go to show . . . (*She rises, puts sewing away in cupboard, gets two candles from cupboard, brings to table C., also bringing box of matches.*) how the time flies!

ETHAN. You ain't goin' to bed, Matt!

MATTIE. Well, my! I guess it's time all right! (*Lights candles. She sees his terrific disappointment.*) 'Course I ain't a mite sleepy, are you? (*He shakes his head.*) Well . . . I s'pose I ought to be goin' up now. . . .

ETHAN. Don't go, Matt! Don't go right away!

MATTIE (*stops immediately, turns to him, says eagerly*). No . . . I won't go right away, Ethan. . . . (*Takes apron off, leaves it on C. chair. Sits C. back of table. She looks up at him, waits. He cannot say anything. She smiles slightly.*) It's so nice and warm down here, I guess I ain't hankerin' to go right up anyway!

ETHAN. Mattie . . . (*He stops, looks at her helplessly. Rises, crosses R. to move handstove a little to R. After a moment he murmurs helplessly:*) Mattie . . . !

MATTIE. I guess I'd better see . . . is the fire all right.

ETHAN (*eagerly, glad of this duty to perform*). I'll see . . . wait, Matt, and I'll see! (*Hurries to the stove, glances at the fire, closes the lower damper, opens the upper . . . turns to her . . . and he is suddenly aware of his inability to go on.*) Matt . . . I . . . I forgot what I was goin' to say.

MATTIE (*rises, takes candle. At last . . .*). Well . . . (*She is forced to start to go again.*) Ethan, it's been a real wonderful evenin' . . . (*He nods quickly but cannot reply. . . . She waits, then smiles at him . . . understandingly. Crosses R. with candle to stairs, opens door.*)

ETHAN. Matt . . .

MATTIE (*stops on first step*). What, Ethan?

ETHAN (*almost inaudibly*). Good night, Matt!

MATTIE (*turns at bottom of the stairs, smiles*). Good night, Ethan! (*She goes on upstairs—he stands motionless watching her, until flicker of lighted candle she carries disappears after her.*)

CURTAIN

ACT THREE

Scene One

ETHAN and ZEENA's *bedroom. (Same as Scene One, Act Two.) Dusk the following evening.*

It is rapidly growing dark outside, and the meager furnishings within the small room cramped close under the eaves are already obscured in the winter twilight, though there is still a short ray of cold, gray light, forcing its way through the small frosted window.

The room is deserted. Door closed. We hear ETHAN *coming upstairs.*

ETHAN (*heard calling eagerly*). Matt! (*Enters* C. *Crosses to* R. *He appears in the doorway, and calls again.*) Hello, Matt!

MATTIE (*calling from off* L.) Hello, Ethan!

ETHAN (*flings off his coat. Rolls up his shirt sleeves. Pours water into basin*). Supper ready?

MATTIE (*calls*). 'Most! (*Then she enters and crosses to* C.) Oh, Ethan, did you get the glue to mend the pickle dish?

ETHAN. Hmmm?

MATTIE (*worriedly*). Oh, now . . . you didn't go and forget about the pickle dish?

ETHAN (R. *lightly*). A-yeah.

MATTIE. Oh, Ethan!

ETHAN (*as he pulls a small paper-wrapped parcel out of his pocket and gives it to her*). Scared you, huh?

MATTIE. Oh, Ethan . . . if you'd forgot that glue . . . I'd just've died! (ETHAN *has poured himself a bowlful of water . . . he plunges his hands into the water . . . and starts washing.* MATTIE *moves closer to him.*) Are you sure you c'n fix it all right? (*He nods.*) So't it won't show?

ETHAN (R. C. *he is washing hands.*) I'm sure goin' to try, Matt!

MATTIE (C.). Let's fix it right off, Ethan . . . before supper!

ETHAN. Soon's I wash up. Open it, Matt . . . so's we'll be all ready! (MATTIE *quickly opens the package . . . and stares down at a pin cushion.*)

MATTIE (*glances up at him and stammers*). Oh! Oh, Ethan!

ETHAN (*straightens up and looks at her. Dries hands.*) It's for pins. (*She nods and is speechless, as he continues proudly.*) I seen it over to the widow Homan's place when I was buyin' the glue . . . and I told Mrs. Homan she c'd wrap it right up and put it on the bill with the rest of it. (*Finished drying hands.*)

MATTIE (*holds it up . . . looks at it this way and that . . . and murmurs.*) Oh, my, Ethan, my, it's pretty, ain't it? (*Then she looks at him and says modestly.*) I'm most obliged, Ethan. (*She turns abruptly and goes out of the room.*)

ETHAN. It looks as if we'll have one more evening. (*Returns to the job of washing up and calls meanwhile.*) See how it looks there, Matt. . . . We'll mend that dish right off, first thing . . . after we have supper. (*The sound of a horse and sleigh is heard approaching in the distance.* MATTIE *comes back to the doorway of the bedroom . . . a frightened look upon her face.*)

MATTIE (*crosses into room* C.). Oh, Ethan—Zeena's come! (*The smile evaporates from his face . . . he stares at her blankly for a moment . . . the sleigh is heard stopping just below. . . .* MATTIE *adds with quick fright:*) I seen her and Jotham from my window just now . . . as they was makin' the turn in. (ZEENA *is heard in the kitchen below. . . .* MATTIE's *eyes dart around the room worriedly . . . she sees the package containing the glue on the table and cries quickly.*) Ethan, the glue! (*Gives him bottle —he puts it in his pocket.*) What'll we do?

ETHAN. Don't fret, Matt!

MATTIE (*whispers*). We ain't fixed the dish yet!

ETHAN (*in a whisper*). I'll go down in the night and fix it so's she'll never know the difference.

MATTIE (*vaguely*). I oughtn't be here, Ethan. . . . I'd better go down. (*Crosses to* L. *toward door.*)

ETHAN (*whispers hurriedly*). No, no, Matt—don't leave now! (*She makes a futile move away.* ZEENA *appears in the hallway, wearing her coat open and beneath it her best merino dress and the bonnet high upon her head. She pauses in the doorway, puffing heavily, and looking from one to the other. After a moment, she moves forward without bothering to remove coat, sits down. The room is rapidly growing darker.* ETHAN, *embarrassed and ill at ease.*) Well, Zeena, I . . . (ETHAN *leaves his sentence unfinished. He and* MATTIE *exchange a quick look.* JOTHAM *follows* ZEENA *in. He is carrying* ZEENA's *suitcase.* JOTHAM *sets it down near the bed.* L. ETHAN, *with perhaps too much anxiety. Over* R.) You might's well stay for a bite of supper, Jotham!

JOTHAM (*has already glanced toward* ZEENA's *rigid figure and his reply is positive*). Obliged, Ethan. . . . I'll run along down home.

ETHAN (*stops him at the door*). Better draw up close to the stove and dry off.

JOTHAM. Not tonight, Ethan. (*He sighs.*) I just ain't up to it! (*He exits down the stairs.*)

MATTIE (L. *a bit timidly*). Supper's ready, Zeena.

ZEENA (C.). Well . . . I ain't.

MATTIE (*a step to* ZEENA). I mean, if you are.

ZEENA (*takes off arctics*). I ain't comin' down.

MATTIE. I'm sorry, Zeena, if you ain't well . . . (*Pauses awkwardly, then says pleasantly:*) I'll bring you up a bite. (MATTIE *glances at* ETHAN *embarrassedly, then turns abruptly and exits down the stairs.*)

ETHAN (*ventures at last*). I presume you're a mite tired after your long trip.

ZEENA. You should have heard what Aunt Martha said—

ETHAN. What did you go and tell her?

ZEENA. Nothing.

ETHAN. So you didn't just go to see that new doctor?

ZEENA. But I did see him and he says I'm a good deal sicker than you think—

ETHAN. Zeena, I hope that's not so.

ZEENA. Well, it is so. An' I want you should know it right off so's you won't set yourself against me.

ETHAN. I don't aim to set myself against you.

ZEENA. See't you don't.

ETHAN (*referring of course to the "complications" and treating them in a low, awed tone*). Sicker—is that what the new doctor told you?

ZEENA (*with infinite satisfaction*). That's what he said.

ETHAN. Well . . . he may be wrong . . . what do you know about this doctor, anyhow? I never even so much's heard of him.

ZEENA. You never heard of him. 'Course everybody else knows he only comes over to Bettsbridge once a fortnight for consultations. Everybody else knows he has a office in Worcester . . . right on the main street!

ETHAN. That don't say he ain't wrong. (*Rises—crosses* C. *to* L.) What did he say you should do? (*Sits on bed.*)

ZEENA (*slowly, calmly, and deliberately*).

First off—he says I oughtn't to do a single thing around the house . . . why, he can't understand how I've stood it's long's I have.

ETHAN. Stood what?

ZEENA. Worrying the way I have.

ETHAN. Worrying!

ZEENA. Worrying. He says it's got to stop right off . . . that is unless you want I should die.

ETHAN. Of course I don't want you should die.

ZEENA (*firmly*). He wants I should have a hired girl.

ETHAN (*suddenly trapped and frightened and puzzled*). He does, huh?

ZEENA (*calmly. Rises, takes coat off*). So, I got Aunt Martha Pierce to find me one right off!

ETHAN (*frenziedly. Rises*). Zeena—seems to me you're daft on havin' yourself a regular hired girl!

ZEENA (*throws coat on* C. *commode. Raises her voice for the first time. . . .*). I told you . . . don't you never say that to me again! (*She stares at him fiercely for a moment . . . her frenzy subsides with the growing knowledge of her power . . . she says then . . . firmly, but quietly.*) Don't you set yourself against me, Ethan. (*Having given him fair warning, she turns her head away again and goes on pleasantly. Sits on* C. *again.*) Everybody down to Bettsbridge said I was awful lucky to get a girl to come away out here . . . and I agreed to give her a dollar extry—just to make sure . . . she'll be over on the Bettsbridge local tomorrow.

ETHAN (*furiously*). You had a right to tell me if you was goin' to go and hire a girl! You had a right to talk to me about it first.

ZEENA. How could I tell you before I started?

ETHAN. Was that what you went for—to get a new girl?

ZEENA. No, it wasn't. No, it wasn't. How'd I know what Doctor Buck was goin' to say?

ETHAN (*scornfully*). Doctor Buck! (*Then, his fury mounting.*) Did Doctor Buck say how I was to pay her wages?

ZEENA. No, he didn't!

ETHAN. Well, I can't!

ZEENA (*simultaneously, without waiting to hear him*). For I'd 'a' been ashamed to tell him you grudged me the money to get back my health when you know I lost it nursin' your mother!

ETHAN (*angrily*). You lost your health nursin' my mother!

ZEENA (*her voice rising above his now*). Yes, I did . . . and my folks all told me at the time . . . you couldn't do no less than to marry me after . . .

ETHAN (*screams at her*). Zeena!

ZEENA (*simultaneously, though less violently*). I went and lost my health nursin' your mother . . . and the good Lord knows she was nothin' to me. . . .

ETHAN. Zeena! (*Crosses R. He stops his violence and savagely moves toward her . . . stands glaring at her for a moment, then turns abruptly away. The room is in darkness now, and he strikes a match and lights a candle in the tin holder upon the table R.*)

ZEENA (*calls sharply*). Mattie!

MATTIE (*calling from hallway*). I'm comin', Zeena.

ZEENA. I thought you was goin' to bring me a bite. . . .

MATTIE (*is heard coming up the stairs. She speaks through* ZEENA's *speech . . . replying timorously*). I am, Zeena . . . ! I'm bringin' it now! . . .

ZEENA (*simultaneously and without pausing*). Stead of standing halfway up them stairs listenin' to what's none of your business! (ETHAN *crosses to bed* L.)

MATTIE (*enters the room carrying a tray upon which she has set* ZEENA's *supper. Places tray on chair* R). I wasn't listenin', Zeena. . . . (*Puts chair up near* ZEENA.)

ZEENA. 'Course you was listenin'.

MATTIE (*lightly, but in denial nevertheless*). No, I wasn't! (*Then quickly, as* ZEENA *seizes the tray and sets it on her lap.*) 'Course I couldn't help hearin' voices! Why, you was both talkin' just ever so loud!

ETHAN (*hurriedly*). You go along down and eat your supper, Matt . . . Zeena's just a mite upset.

ZEENA (*calmly*). I ain't upset.

MATTIE (*crosses* C.). All right, Ethan . . . I'll wait for you. (*She tries to smile at him reassuringly.* ZEENA *sighs and shakes her head.* ETHAN *closes the door . . . leans back against it with his hand on the knob . . . remains there motionless . . . staring at* ZEENA. *She commences eating eagerly.*)

ETHAN (*determinedly*). I guess we've talked about this more'n enough . . . so's you know . . . no matter what you say . . . I can't afford a hired girl. (*Her silence in-*

furiates him.*) I said . . . I ain't got the money to pay a hired girl!

ZEENA. I thought you said you was goin' to get cash down from Andrew Hale.

ETHAN (*evasively*). Andrew Hale never pays under three months, Zeena . . . and you know it.

ZEENA (*goes back to her eating. She nods*). I know it . . . but you told me . . . yesterday . . . you said you was goin' to get cash from him and that's why you couldn't drive me over to the Flats.

ETHAN (*weakening*). I guess that was a mistake.

ZEENA. Meanin' you didn't get the cash?

ETHAN. Meanin' I ain't got a cent.

ZEENA. And you ain't goin' to get it?

ETHAN. No—I ain't.

ZEENA (*self-righteously*). Well . . . I couldn't know that when I hired the girl . . . could I!

ETHAN (*honestly*). No. (*Then firmly.*) But you know it now.

ZEENA. I knowed yesterday, you just said it to me so's you wouldn't have to drive me over to the Flats. (*Pokes at food —her back to* ETHAN.)

ETHAN. I asked him for it! Like I said I would, and I got twenty dollars' wuth of feed for the livestock. But I didn't get any cash. (*Then suddenly with a certain triumph.*) So . . . seein's I ain't got a cent in the world . . . and ain't goin' to see a cent for three months anyhow and nothin' then to speak of . . . I guess you'll just have to do without the hired girl. You're a poor man's wife all right, Zeena. . . . I'd like to do what I can for you . . . but I guess you'll have to send that there new girl right back where she's comin' from. (*Crosses down* L. *below bed.*)

ZEENA (*pushes back the empty plate. . . .*). Oh, I figured I wouldn't take no chances countin' on you . . . so 'stead of buyin' myself a lot of medicines I been needing real bad . . . I paid the girl a half a month in advance out of the cow money and give her a dollar extry like I said.

ETHAN (*furiously. Crosses up to* ZEENA L. C.). You get that money back from her . . . and send her packin' just as soon's she comes! I can't afford it.

ZEENA. Oh, I guess we'll make out all right. There'll be Mattie's board less anyhow. (ZEENA *pushes chair away. Crosses to closet to get shawl. She turns, facing him, putting on shawl.*) Why, Ethan Frome . . . you didn't suppose I wanted you should keep two hired girls . . . did you! (*She laughs.*) No wonder you was so upset about the expense!

ETHAN (*after a moment . . . bewilderedly*). Mattie Silver ain't a hired girl . . . *you* said that—she's your own blood relation.

ZEENA (*casually*). Oh, she ain't nothin' to me . . . 'cept a pauper like her no-good father before her . . . and just 'cause she can't take care of herself's no reason we should keep her . . . it's somebody else's turn now.

ETHAN. You know there ain't anybody else!

ZEENA. That ain't my fault!

ETHAN. You ain't goin' to do it, Zeena. . . . (*Crosses up to her.*) You ain't goin' to send Mattie away! I ain't goin' to let you do it! (*He stops abruptly. They are both acutely aware that his passionate words and tone have betrayed him. With sudden determination he tries to reason with her.*) You can't do it, Zeena . . . where'd she go if you send her away . . . Why, even if she could get a job down there to Willimantic . . . she couldn't keep it . . . what with the work bein' too heavy and all. . . . (*He hesitates.*) She's got no place to go, Zeena! (*ZEENA stares at him complacently. He adopts a friendly, reasonable tone.*) Why, think what'd happen if you was ever to drive Mattie away . . . think what Emma and Abigail Varnum and Mrs. Hale and even your own Aunt Martha Pierce— think what they'd go and say of you!

ZEENA. I know too well what they're sayin' now . . . of my havin' kep' her here's long's I have! (*ETHAN turns from her down* L. *Sits on edge of bed.*) Mattie! (*ZEENA turns to* ETHAN, *and says in a low voice for his ears only and with an air of mutual conspiracy.*) The new girl'll be over tomorrow, and I presume she'll have to have somewhere's to sleep. (*She deliberately waits until* MATTIE *arrives. Then* ZEENA'S *manner changes completely.*) Oh, Mattie! You can get the dishes together now. (MATTIE *crosses* R. *to chair, puts it back where it was over* R.) That pie of yours was a mite heavy! I've a good mind to go down and hunt up them stomach powders . . . the ones I got sent up from Springfield last summer. . . . I ain't tried them in quite a spell . . . and maybe they'll help some.

MATTIE (*uneasily*). You want I should get them for you, Zeena?

ZEENA. Oh, no! I c'd get 'em for myself if I was a mind to, but I guess I'll hold out's long's I can. (*She beams at them both pleasantly.*) Oh, well, I guess't I got to go down anyhow an' see't things is straightened out proper. Ethan's got somethin' to say to you. (ZEENA *exits to the hall.*)

MATTIE (R. C. *After a moment*). I hope Zeena ain't really sick.

ETHAN (*dully and without significance*). I don't know . . .

MATTIE. Your supper's down there gettin' ever so cold. . . . (*She stops and adds.*) Ethan, you must be just starved! (ETHAN *is unable to reply.*) Still 'n' all, if you ain't really hungry . . . (*She stops again, makes one more vain effort to avoid the issue.*) Why, I guess then there ain't no reason to eat. (MATTIE *crosses to* C. *He turns to her but can't speak.*) I knew there was somethin' wrong . . . I just knew there was! (*He cannot bring himself to answer her. . . .*) Ethan, what is it? Oh, I knew there was somethin' wrong!

ETHAN (*stares at her helplessly, and mumbles rapidly*). You see this here new doctor, he's got her so scared about herself . . . you know how she is . . . believes everything they tell her . . . and he says . . . (*Suddenly.*) I can't let you go, Matt! I don't care what she says . . . I can't let you go now!

MATTIE (*in a low, scarcely audible voice, slowly*). Must—I—go?

ZEENA (*heard calling from* L.). Mattie!

MATTIE (*in a low voice*). Ethan . . . must I go?

ETHAN. Well . . . that's what she says tonight.

MATTIE (*very practically*). If she says it tonight . . . she'll say it tomorrow. (*They are both aware of the undeniable truth of this.*)

ZEENA (*calls again, more sharply*). Mattie . . . I been calling you!

MATTIE. Ethan—don't trouble—(*Crosses* R., *picks up tray, crosses* C. *She exits; he stands there helpless.*)

CURTAIN

SCENE TWO

The next afternoon.

The kitchen. Late afternoon. Geranium on sink at window. MATTIE'S *suitcase and trunk off* R. *Three pieces glass in cupboard.* C. *table cleared.*

MATTIE *is at the window. She wears her "other dress," which marks the moment as an occasion. She is ready to go away. After a moment we hear someone just outside the* C. *door.* . . . MATTIE *turns eagerly and quickly and starts excitedly across the room toward the door as it opens and* JOTHAM *enters* C. MATTIE *stops abruptly and is visibly disappointed.* JOTHAM *enters briskly, moves over to the stove automatically. He rubs his hands together vigorously, over the stove.*

MATTIE. Oh, Jotham!

JOTHAM. Warmin' up a bit!

MATTIE (*crosses to him*). Didn't Ethan come with you?

JOTHAM. Nope!

MATTIE. But he didn't even come for his dinner at noontime!—He ain't been home all day!

JOTHAM (*casually*). Went to town, I guess.

MATTIE (*at stove. Bewilderedly*). Didn't he say anythin' . . . not to wait dinner or anythin' like that?

JOTHAM. A-yeah . . . think he said he'd be late . . . he had business or somethin' over to Starkfield. (MATTIE *turns away to window.* JOTHAM *glances at her as he goes across toward stairway.*) Well, I'll be gettin' that trunk on down. (*He pauses.*) Don't blame you a bit for leavin'. (MATTIE *stands at the window.*) I'd clear out myself, but I guess I ain't as souple as I was. (*He pauses.*) That trunk closed? (*She turns to him and shakes her head.*) I recall the lock was broke. . . . I'll tie it up for you. (*He starts to stairs* R.) A-yeah . . . it's just about the smartest thing you c'd do. (*He goes on up the stairway.* MATTIE *moves slowly to the window, bewildered and terribly alone. After a moment* ETHAN *enters from door* C. MATTIE *moves toward him.*)

MATTIE. Oh, Ethan! I thought I wasn't never goin' to see you again!

ETHAN. Matt! What'd ever'd make you go and think that!

MATTIE (*still a little breathless*). You wasn't here for breakfast . . . and I was scared . . . and then when Jotham come and told me you said you was goin' to town and we wasn't to wait dinner for you . . . Oh, Ethan . . . I thought for sure . . .

ETHAN. Oh, no, Matt! (*Puts hat and coat up on hook* C. *at door.*)

MATTIE (*worriedly*). Oh, Ethan . . . you must be just froze and starved . . . you was down here all night, wasn't you?

ETHAN (*turns down to her*). How'd you ever know that, Matt?

MATTIE. I heard you go downstairs again after I went to bed and I lay there listenin' all night . . . and you didn't never come back up. . . . (ETHAN *crosses* L. *to sink. She goes to him.*) Don't be too sorry, Ethan . . . I don't want you should trouble!

ETHAN (*looking out window*). I don't want you should trouble either.

MATTIE (*in a low voice*). Well, I ain't troublin'. (*A little too highly.*) I ain't troublin' a bit!

ETHAN (*intensely*). Matt! (*He nods toward the stairway.*) She said anythin' more? (MATTIE *shakes her head.*)

MATTIE. She ain't said anythin' at all! I ain't so much's seen her. She's upstairs there and ain't been out of her room all day. . . . I knocked on the door there onc't and said to her, I said . . . "Zeena, what should I do—should I try and get my trunk down or what?" And she said she had them inside pains again and didn't want to be troubled.

ETHAN (*dryly*). She don't trouble easy.

MATTIE (*quickly*). No, she don't and that's a fact, Ethan . . . not when she ain't a mind to.

ETHAN. Things might straighten out— all night and all day I been figurin' and plannin' . . . You wait an' see. I'm going to speak to her and she's bound to see things different today. (JOTHAM *has come slowly down the stairs with the trunk on his back.* ETHAN *breaks and* MATTIE *turns and looks at the trunk.* JOTHAM *gets into the room* C. . . . *lowers trunk to the floor* . . . *sighs.*)

JOTHAM. Well . . . here she is!

ETHAN (*crosses* C. *Curtly*). I ain't said anythin' 'bout takin' that trunk down. (MATTIE *crosses to sink.*)

JOTHAM. A-yeah—well—Denis Eady's drivin' Mis' Andrew Hale over to Corbury to the Eastern Star meetin' this evenin' . . . I spoke to him 'bout it and he said he c'd take the trunk along's far's the Flats and make it easier pullin' for the sorrel when I take Mattie on over in the sleigh.

ETHAN (*astonished and dismayed at the thoroughness of the plans that have been made*). Why'd you want to speak to him 'bout it?

JOTHAM. Mis' Frome said the new girl'd be at the Flats at five and I was to take Mattie over then so's she can ketch the six o'clock for Willimantic . . . or wherever she's goin'.

ETHAN (*crosses up behind table*). Well, it ain't so sure about Mattie's goin'!

JOTHAM. That so? Well, considerin' all Mis' Frome said . . .

ETHAN (*furiously*). Supposin' I say somethin' else again!

ZEENA (*has been slowly clumping down the stairs; she enters the room now*). Jotham, 'round what time'd you say Denis Eady was takin' Mis' Hale over to the Eastern Star?

JOTHAM. 'Round about now.

ZEENA (*has crossed to the window*). Mattie . . . Denis Eady's been kind enough to say he'd stop around to take your trunk over to the Flats for you.

MATTIE. I'm obliged, I'm sure, Zeena.

ZEENA. There's quite a few things you want to do, you know . . . and you ain't got a lot of time.

ETHAN. What'd she want to do?

ZEENA. My room ain't been touched yet. . . . (MATTIE *completely submissive. Crosses R. via above table.* ZEENA *is at the window . . . picking faded leaves off the geranium plant . . . she sighs.*) Just look! (MATTIE *stops.* ZEENA *sighs again.*) Aunt Martha's geranium ain't got so much's a single faded leaf onto it. . . . (*She sighs.*) But just look at this!

MATTIE (*has been growing more and more angry. For some unaccountable reason this implication is too unjust and she says with quick temper*). One thing I done, Zeena . . . if I do say it myself . . . I nursed that there geranium plant like it was my own!

ZEENA. Well . . . just look at it! (*She sighs.*)

MATTIE (*furiously, and with the ready tears suddenly welling up*). I don't care, Zeena . . . I don't care . . . what you say else about me . . . that geranium I been tendin' every day regular's clockwork . . . and you can't say different 'cause it ain't so! (MATTIE *turns suddenly and exits up the stairs* R.)

JOTHAM. Well . . . I guess we might's

well be bumpin' that trunk out's far's the porch there, Ethan.

ETHAN (*opens door.* JOTHAM *crosses to door*). Jotham, you leave that trunk be.

ZEENA (*warningly*). I don't want you to set yourself against me today, Ethan. I'm warnin' you. . . . (ETHAN *makes no move . . . he stands his ground determinedly.*)

JOTHAM (*heading toward the door* C.— *says to* ETHAN, *at door*). If you c'n handle this—(*Indicates* ZEENA's *objections.*) I figure you c'n handle the trunk all right. (*He exits.* ETHAN *closes door.* ZEENA *crosses* C. *below table.*)

ETHAN (*suddenly and passionately. Crosses* R.) Zeena . . . Mattie's always done her level best for you, and you know it! (ZEENA *stops* C.)

ZEENA. Well—'taint enough. (*Crosses* L. *of table.*)

ETHAN (*crosses* R. *of table*). But she's tried . . . you know that . . . she's tried awful hard and you can't go and drive her out of the house like she's a thief!

ZEENA. Fiddlesticks! (*crosses* L. *of table* C.)

ETHAN (*crosses front of table*). She's got no place to go, Zeena . . . what'll she do? . . . You can't drive her out!

ZEENA (*with grim pleasure and complete confidence.* L. *of table* C.) Rubbish! First you deviled me and nagged because you wouldn't have her here . . . and now . . . If she can't take care of herself like you say . . . how's she goin' to take care of this house!

ETHAN. Zeena . . . you won't have to raise a hand in this house . . . you won't have to do a stick of work around here . . . I promise you . . . I'll do it all myself . . . I'll do every bit of it!

ZEENA (*sits* L. *of table*). A-yeah! I been noticin' how you been neglectin' the farm lately . . . hangin' around here helpin' Mattie sweepin' and scrubbin' floors . . . gettin' to be a regular old woman . . . ain't you, Ethan? Hm? (*He turns up* R. C.) Well . . . I only hope't you'll get a little work done once the new girl gets settled. (ETHAN *suddenly sees the uselessness of his pleas . . . and that there is one last course open to him. He closes stair door. Sits* R. *of table.*)

ETHAN. It just ain't no use, Zeena . . . for seven years now I done all I could for you . . . and it just ain't no use, and I want you to listen to me now! I ain't blamin' you at all, Zeena, but I got to do somethin'. (*He stops . . . her apparent indifference increases his desperation . . . he pleads frantically now.*) I been tied hand and foot to this farm all my life, I been wearin' out my years one right after t'other . . . and what's it got either of us? Zeena, I can't go on! (*He stops, leans across table.*) I ain't never had a chance here. . . . I mean like now take the opportunities they is out there in the West. If ever I c'd get out there . . . I'd be sure of pickin' up work. Why, that year I put in down to the technological school in Worcester—the same year my father died . . . Well, now I ain't sayin' I learned much to speak of—but maybe—it was enough so's if ever I got the chance I might be able to make's much of my life's the next fellow! I want a chance to make a fresh start—I want to get away and go out West an' make a fresh start, Zeena!

ZEENA. What'd I do?

ETHAN (*quickly and eagerly*). I'll give you the farm and the mill! For your own—I'll make 'em right over to you!

ZEENA. What'd I do with 'em?

ETHAN (*with less certainty*). If you couldn't get somebody like now Jotham, he's a good man . . . or somebody to run 'em and make 'em pay—you could sell them . . . (*And he adds emphatically.*) and keep the money! You c'd sell 'em both and keep the money, Zeena . . . all for yourself!

ZEENA. Who'd I sell 'em to? (*He stops abruptly. This is the answer—he knows it as well as she does.*)

ETHAN. Well—maybe you couldn't sell 'em right off—I guess I got to admit I been tryin' hard enough—but you c'd try—(*He sees her glance of contempt and hastens to add:*) Well—I'd pay for your board as soon's I could . . . don't you see maybe it'd more'n pay you in the end, Zeena . . . why, if you c'd see your way clear to lettin' me go an' get myself a fresh start out there somewheres in the West—why, I'd send you money all right and you might be's well off as Mis' Hale or any of them one day!

ZEENA (*shortly*). And how'd I eat till then?

ETHAN. I'll try an' raise some money for you! (*Then, not so certainly.*) Some way. I'll borrow or somethin' somehow. I know it ain't easy, but—well—now Andrew Hale—he still owes me some-

thin' on the spruce—he might pay up a little.

ZEENA. You seen him yesterday—what'd he say?

ETHAN. He give me the feed all right.

ZEENA. A-yeah.

ETHAN. Well, if I was to tell him we need it bad . . . right off, for the doctor . . . If I was to put it up to him like that . . . he's a kind man and a good friend and he might pay maybe a little cash.

ZEENA. And if you did! Hm! Well—I guess't Mr. Hale ain't's big a fool's you think he is. D'you suppose he's ever goin' to go and help you desert me? Andrew Hale, a deacon in the church and I don't know what all! Now would he do a thing like that? Would he, Ethan? I must say't I'm a mite surprised't you'd go to a good friend like Andrew Hale and tell him a lot of nonsense . . . just to get a few dollars. (*She sighs.*) You an' him been doin' business off'n on—how long? Why, Ethan Frome—if you was in your right senses—you couldn't no more go an' take advantage of Andrew Hale bein' a good kind man—could you, Ethan? Hm? (*He glances at her and away again—he couldn't and he knows it and he is being completely annihilated.*) If you got any sense at all—you'll buckle down and tend to your business and stop all this stuff'n nonsense! (*Sleigh bells are heard offstage.* ZEENA *calls.*) Mattie!

MATTIE (*calling from upstairs.*) Was you callin', Zeena?

ZEENA. 'Bout ready?

MATTIE. Yes!

DENIS (*calling off.*) Zenobia!

ZEENA (*rises*). Better be gettin' that trunk on out, Ethan . . . there's Denis now and Mis' Hale won't want to be late to the Eastern Star. (ZEENA *crosses up to porch door* C. *and opens it—goes out.* ETHAN *sits motionless at the table. . . .* MATTIE *starts down stairs.* ZEENA *can be seen just outside.*)

DENIS (*calls from outside*). Tell Ethan to bring that trunk right on out, Zenobia.

ZEENA. Ethan—Ethan—they're waiting on the trunk. (ETHAN *rises, gets trunk.* MATTIE *enters from stairs* R.)

MIS' HALE (*offstage. A large, pleasant voice, calls to* ZEENA *from just outside.*) Howdy, Zenobia . . . Denis was just now tellin' me you was over to Bettsbridge

. . . How're all the folks and what's that new doctor like? (ETHAN *exits* C. *door with trunk.* MATTIE *puts towel on* C. *table—looks about room. Holding her suitcase.*) How-do-Ethan—Awful glad you been able to get Zenobia a new hired girl like the doctor said. My, I only wish't Andrew c'd afford to get me one. Well, I always said I don't know what poor Zeena'd a done without she had you to take care of her all these years . . . Well, g'bye, Ethan . . . Zenobia! (*The sleigh is heard starting off.*)

ZEENA (*smiles*). Obliged to you, Denis! Mis' Hale! (*She turns back into the room—faces* MATTIE *with her very best social smile still on her face.*) Well—Mattie! (*Crosses* C. ETHAN *enters from the porch.* JOTHAM *is following him.*)

MATTIE. Well—!

JOTHAM (*in doorway*). 'Bout ready, Mattie?

MATTIE (*bewilderedly*). Well—I guess so, Jotham. (*Then to* ZEENA). Is it time?

JOTHAM. The sorrel's all hitched and waitin'.

ETHAN (*with sudden and indisputable authority*). You c'n go along home now, Jotham . . . I'm goin' to drive her over myself.

ZEENA (*determinedly*). I want you should stay here this afternoon, Ethan . . . Jotham can drive Mattie over.

ETHAN (*firmly*). I'm goin' to drive her over myself!

ZEENA (C *at stove*). I want you should stay here! You wait in the barn, Jotham. Mattie'll be right out. (*Puts* JOTHAM *out* C. *and closes door.*)

ETHAN. I'll drive you over, Mattie. (*Gets hat and coat from hook on door.*)

ZEENA. I ain't goin' to let you drive her, do you hear me? I want you should stay here, Ethan.

ETHAN. I'm goin' just the same.

ZEENA. I told you I don't want you should set yourself against me today, Ethan. I want you should stay here this afternoon. Mattie, I won't let him go with you . . . I won't . . . (*She gasps and clutches at her side.*)

MATTIE (*over* R. *Frightened*). Don't trouble about me, Ethan!

ETHAN. It ain't no trouble—I guess it's little enough I'm driving you over's far as the Flats, Mattie, and there ain't nobody going to stop me!

ZEENA (*leans back against cupboard and gasps.*) I can't breathe, I can't breathe. My medicine! My medi . . .

MATTIE (*quickly*). You want I should get you something, Zeena?

ZEENA (*ignores* MATTIE. *She clambers up onto the chair at the cupboard.* ETHAN *and* MATTIE *exchange a look of great alarm as they see* ZEENA *reach up and fumble about on the top shelf. She stops suddenly, as her fumbling hand strikes one of the broken fragments of the pickle dish which* ETHAN *has set back on that shelf. It falls to the floor. She stares at it blankly. Then suddenly she reaches up to the shelf again with both hands, lowers the other pieces . . . stands staring down at the broken pickle dish held in cupped hands. Then, her manner completely changed, she turns to* ETHAN *and* MATTIE, *the heartburn forgotten.*) I want to know who done this! (*Neither* ETHAN *nor* MATTIE *replies. She climbs down from the chair, holding the pieces reverently in her hands, looks first at* MATTIE, *then at* ETHAN.) I want to know who done this! (*They stand facing her . . . riveted to the spot. Suddenly her eye is caught by the glitter of the fragments of red glass. She stares at them fascinatedly, then looks up at* ETHAN.) Why, Ethan . . . I had it away up there—on the top shelf where I keep all the things I set most store by . . . just so's folks shan't meddle with them. (*Now more bewildered than angry.*) Why, you seen where I was . . . it took me the kitchen chair and a good long reach. I put it up there o' purpose when we was married . . . so's it shouldn't never get broke . . . (*She stops . . . looks at* ETHAN *and cries.*) I want to know who could've done it!

ETHAN. I ain't interested.

ZEENA. You ain't interested.

ETHAN. That's what I said.

MATTIE. It's my fault, Zeena. (*Quickly realizing* ZEENA's *growing hysteria.*) I got it down from the top shelf and I'm the only one to blame for its getting broke.

ZEENA (*staring down at the broken bits of glass in her hand, she says dully*). I don't see why you done it . . . I don't see how anybody c'd of went and done a mean thing like that . . .

MATTIE. I wanted to make the table look pretty.

ZEENA. You never wanted to make the table look pretty when I was here. If I'd a only listened to what folks is sayin' . . . you'd a gone long before now . . . (*Unable to go on until the sight of the broken pieces of glass held reverently in her cupped hands . . . arouses her fury again.*) You're a no-good girl, Mattie Silver, and I've always knowed it. . . . I was warned against you when I took you in here and . . . (*She stops for a second.*) . . . and now you've went and broke the one thing I cared for most of all! (*She turns away abruptly . . . goes slowly to the stairs R., carrying the bits of pickle dish. She exits up the stairs. . . .* ETHAN *and* MATTIE *stand watching her. Then abruptly* ETHAN *stoops over . . . picks up* MATTIE'S *suitcase and strides to the porch door* C. MATTIE *is following slowly . . . looking around. She quickens her pace and exits after him.*)

CURTAIN

SCENE THREE

Half an hour later. At the crest of the hill. It is dusk. The delicate blue shadows on the snow-covered hillside are rapidly turning black, and the reflection of the cold, red winter sun mingles with the rising blur of the night. The hillside is deserted . . . the tinkling sound of sleigh bells is heard approaching . . . the sound stops abruptly with a last jingle as the sleigh stops off R.

ETHAN *enters first . . . walking slowly . . . to the crest of the hill at back . . .* MATTIE *enters and stops at* R. *They stand there for a moment . . . listening tensely to the stillness.*

———

MATTIE (*after a moment, in a low voice*). We'd ought to go.

ETHAN (*doesn't answer her immediately . . . then suddenly he says in a low voice, tense with tingling nervousness.*) I feel dizzy . . . like I'd stopped in at the saloon down to Starkfield for a drink.

MATTIE (*after a time, nervously*). We mustn't stay here any longer, Ethan!

ETHAN (*turns to her. Almost impatiently*). I just wanted't we sh'd stand here a minute, Mattie. (*She crosses* C. *to him . . . they stand looking out across the valley below for a moment. Then he says dully:*) Remember bein' here the other night . . .!

MATTIE (*in a low, dull voice*). It seems like it was years ago . . . don't it?

ETHAN (*after a moment, pointing down over the slope at back to* R.) Over there's where we sat at the church picnic last summer. (*She nods.*) I remember findin'

your locket for you when you'd went and lost it . . .

MATTIE. I never knowed anyone for such sharp eyes. . . .

ETHAN (*thoughtfully*). You know . . . you was awful pretty in that pink hat.

MATTIE (*very gratefully*). Aw—I wouldn't go's far's that—I guess it was just the hat. (*They are looking at each other intently . . . suddenly she crosses* C. *a step.*)

ETHAN (*vaguely as he watches her*). There's plenty of time. (*He follows her, and says abruptly and tensely:*) Matt . . . where'll you go . . . what'll you do!

MATTIE (*looks up at him*). Oh well . . . maybe I'll get a place in the mills.

ETHAN. You know you can't . . . and if you did . . . the standin' and heavy liftin' . . . nearly done for you before!

MATTIE. Well . . . I'm a whole lot stronger'n I was though . . .

ETHAN. And now you're just goin' to go and throw away all the good bein' here's done you! (*There isn't any answer to this. After a moment he says hopefully:*) Ain't there any of your father's folks'd help you?

MATTIE (*with sudden fierceness and bitterness*). There ain't any of them I'd ask!

ETHAN (*C. moves closer to her*). Matt . . . you know there's nothin' I wouldn't do for you . . . if I could! (*He is silent for a moment . . . then:*) Oh, Matt . . . if I only could'a gone with you now . . . I'd a done it!

MATTIE (*quickly,* C. *Faces* R.). I know!

ETHAN. Matt . . . if I coulda done it . . . gone somewheres with you . . . (*He hesitates*). Would you've gone with me?

MATTIE (*with quick tears*). Oh Ethan . . . Ethan . . . what's the use!

ETHAN. Tell me, Matt! Tell me!

MATTIE. I used to think of it sometimes, summer nights when the moon was shinin' in my window so bright't I couldn't sleep . . .

ETHAN (*in amazement*). As long ago as that!

MATTIE (*nods very honestly*). The first time was . . . at the picnic in the beginning of summer . . . (*She sees his look of strange wonder and smiles a little.*) Still 'n' all . . . I guess we didn't get to be what you might call friends for a long while after that . . . did we?

ETHAN. I guess I was thinkin' a lot about you . . . right from the first, Matt.

MATTIE. You was! My you'd never've

knowed it!

ETHAN (*with great difficulty*). I guess I didn't get to know it myself . . . right up till we was here . . . the other night . . . (*He stands looking at her intently for a moment and then says abruptly and tensely:*) I'm tied hand and foot, Matt . . . there just ain't anythin' I c'n do!

MATTIE. You c'n write me sometimes . . .

ETHAN. What good'll writin' do! I want to do for you and care for you like you need! I want to put out my hand and touch you . . . I want to be there if you're sick and when you're lonesome!

MATTIE (*urgently, trying hard to convince him*). Oh you mustn't think but what I'll be all right, Ethan! (*Then suddenly.*) Oh, I wish't I was dead! I wish't I was!

ETHAN. Matt! Don't you say it!

MATTIE (*more frantically and frightenedly*). Why shouldn't I when it's true? I been thinkin' it all night and all day!

ETHAN. Matt!

MATTIE. It's so, it's so, and I want to be dead!

ETHAN (*simultaneously*). You be quiet, Matt, and don't you even think of it!

MATTIE. There's nobody been good to me but you!

ETHAN (*sharply*). Don't go and say that neither, 'cause I can't so much's lift my hand for you!

MATTIE. But it's true all the same! (*The cries of the children playing on the opposite slope of the hill reach them faintly*). Listen . . . the kids is coastin' . . . over on the other slope!

ETHAN (*off up* R. *Stands watching for a moment, then says bitterly*). We was goin' coastin' tonight . . . remember? (*She nods quickly. The children's voices fade out.*) I ain't even took you coastin' . . . (*Looks at her for a moment and then says determinedly:*) You know what? We'll go now! (*Crosses up* L.).

MATTIE (*quickly and nervously, as he turns from her and crosses up* L. *to the sled.*) Oh no, Ethan, we can't . . . we can't! (*Follows up* L.)

ETHAN (*almost angrily*). Yes we can too . . . I guess we can do that all right . . . you wait now! (*Gets sled put in place on runners.*)

MATTIE (*crosses up to him. Really frightened now*). I don't want to go, Ethan! And anyhow, the new girl'll be waitin' at the station. Her train gets in more'n an hour before mine and she'll be waitin'!

ETHAN. Let her wait . . . you'd have to . . . if she didn't.

MATTIE. No, Ethan, it's away too dark. . . .

ETHAN. Come on, Matt—(*But she shakes her head and turns away from him.*) It's the last chance we'll get! You ain't a-scared, are you?

MATTIE (*turns on him fiercely*). I told you onc't I ain't the kind to be a-scared! (*She looks up at him as he comes toward her.*) Oh, Ethan . . . Ethan! (*He has drawn close to her and she moves closer to him . . . until their bodies are touching and her head is buried in his coat. He stands there looking down at her . . . she looks up at him and then suddenly throws her arms around his neck, draws his face down to hers, and kisses him. He holds her tightly to him, and kisses her with fierce passion.* MATTIE *murmurs:*) Good-by . . . good-by, Ethan! (*She kisses him again and then releases herself from his hold.*)

ETHAN. I can't let you go now! I can't!

MATTIE. Oh, I can't go either! (*The clock strikes in the distant valley below—five chimes.*)

ETHAN (*murmuring vaguely*). What'll we do . . . what'll we do!

MATTIE. Oh, Ethan, it's time!

ETHAN. I'm not goin' to leave you!

MATTIE. If I miss my train . . . where'll I go?

ETHAN. Where'll you go . . . if you catch it! (*They are silent for a moment.*) And what's the use of either of us goin' any place now without the other one.

MATTIE (*breathlessly*). Ethan, Ethan, we're goin'!

ETHAN (*bewilderedly*). But where . . . Matt?

MATTIE. I want you sh'd take me down with you!

ETHAN. Down where?

MATTIE. Down the coast right off! (*Without waiting for him, she whispers faster and more urgently and breathlessly.*) Down that coast so't we'll never, never come up again . . . never!

ETHAN. What do you mean?

MATTIE. Right into that big elm down there . . . you c'd do it . . . you c'd, Ethan . . . so't we'd never have to leave each other any more!

ETHAN. What're you sayin' . . . what're you sayin' . . . Oh Matt . . . Matt . . .

MATTIE (*still more rapidly and breath-*

lessly and sweeping him along with her). Ethan, where'll I go if I leave you . . . I don't know however I'd get along alone . . . you said so yourself . . . you said I couldn't never do it . . . an' I don't want to.

ETHAN (*in her breathless, hurried tone*). I can't go back there . . . I can't go back to that place never again!

MATTIE (*is now drawing him with her to the sled*). Hurry, Ethan . . . hurry . . . let's go now . . . (*She seats herself on the front of the sled quickly.*)

ETHAN (*suddenly*). Get up!

MATTIE. No!

ETHAN (*vehemently*). Get up! (*Picks her up.*) We're goin' down head first and together . . . holdin' each other tight! (*Without waiting for her to reply . . . he seizes her roughly.*) I want to feel you holdin' me!

MATTIE (*a murmur*). Is it goin' to hurt, Ethan?

ETHAN. Don't be a-scared, Matt . . . it ain't goin' to hurt . . . it ain't goin' to hurt at all . . . we're goin' to fetch that elm so hard we won't feel anything at all . . . exceptin' only each other! (*Both on sled. He stretches out at her side and their arms go around each other. He murmurs:*) Matt . . . Matt . . .

MATTIE. Hold me . . . hold me tight, Ethan!

(*The sled is heard in the darkness . . . bounding faster and faster down the lope.*)

EPILOGUE

During the brief moment of darkness before the curtain rises, the sled is heard bounding down the hill with increasing speed.

The kitchen. Winter. Twenty years later. The action takes place later, the same evening as that of the Prologue. The room is even more drab and bare than it was twenty years ago. It is night and the room is almost in darkness. There is a faint glow from the dying embers of the wood fire in the stove.

ZEENA *is aged fifty-five now. Her hair is thin and gray and she wears a slatternly and shapeless calico dress. And though she is still acutely aware of her aching bones and various maladies, she has, through sheer necessity, developed a certain subtle comparative domestic competence. She sits dozing in her rocker* C., *a shawl over her shoulders.*

A sleigh is heard approaching. The sound arouses ZEENA. *She sits there for a moment longer, huddling the shawl closer about her shoulders. The sound of the sleigh bells stops abruptly as the sleigh is driven into the barn.* ZEENA *is now fully awake. She gets up, shivering slightly with the cold, contemplates the fire in the stove thoughtfully for a moment, turns away, puts wood in* C. *stove.*

The glow from a lighted lantern has become faintly visible through the frosted window. The light approaches slowly. ZEENA *goes to the door, unbolts it. After a moment a halting step is heard outside. The door opens and* ETHAN *enters the room slowly, his lameness checking each step.*

He is wearing the clothes he wore in the Prologue and he carries a magazine and the lighted lantern, which he sets down on C. *table.* ZEENA *helps him off with coat and hat.*

ZEENA. What's that, Ethan?

ETHAN. Engineering magazine that young feller give me. (*Puts it on table* C.)

ZEENA. Did you get that dollar?

ETHAN (*as he limps slowly to his chair* L. *of table*). That's what I went for. (*Sits at table.*)

ZEENA. Well . . . a dollar's a dollar . . . but it ain't a whole lot for drivin' all the ways over there to Corbury an' back this weather . . . I don't know's I'd do it again in the mornin'. (*She hangs his coat on peg at door.*)

ETHAN. Another dollar'll come handy, won't it?

ZEENA. I was just wonderin' how much Eady's Livery'd get out of that young fellow.

MATTIE (*calling from off* R.). Zeena— Zeenie! (ZEENA *crosses to door* R., *goes out.* ZEENA *enters with* MATTIE *in wheelchair, closes door.* MATTIE'S *hair is thin and gray, and her face is drawn. She is partly paralyzed and never moves except for an occasional surge of petulant vitality.* MATTIE, *as she enters, petulantly whining:*) Zeenie, you hurt, Zeena . . . You done that on purpose. (ZEENA *goes to stove—gets cup of milk— feeds* MATTIE.)

ZEENA. Don't say that! You can't say that when I been doin' what I can for you for twenty years. (*Goes back to stove with cup.*)

MATTIE. Why didn't you let me die there that night when they brought Ethan and me in here? (*She is silent for a moment—then she whines:*) Zeenie, I'm cold!

ZEENA. Give her the blanket, Ethan. (ETHAN *rises, takes blanket off back of his chair, gives it to* ZEENA. *He sits as* MATTIE *speaks.*)

MATTIE. No, don't let him touch me— Zeenie, you do it! He's so clumsy—he always hurts me.

ZEENA (*tucks blanket around* MATTIE'S *knees*). Sh-h-h-h! You're worse'n a baby, Mattie!

MATTIE. Zeena, you'll carry me down in the morning, won't you? I can't stand to have him touch me. Ain't you never goin' to die, Ethan Frome!

ETHAN. The Fromes're tough, I guess. The doctor was sayin' to me only the other day . . . "Frome," he says, "you'll likely touch a hundred."

CURTAIN

MEN IN WHITE

Sidney Kingsley

Men in White was first produced by the Group Theatre and Sidney Harmon & James R. Ullman at the Broadhurst Theatre, New York City, on September 26, 1933. The play was staged by Lee Strasberg, with settings by Mordecai Gorelik. The cast was as follows:

DR. GORDON, Attending in
  Medicine . . . . Luther Adler
DR. HOCHBERG, Attending Chief of
  Surgical Staff . J. Edward Bromberg
DR. MICHAELSON,
  Interne . . . . William Challee
DR. VITALE, young practi-
  tioner . Herbert Ratner (Elia Kazan)
DR. MC CABE, retired
  surgeon . . . . Grover Burgess
DR. FERGUSON, Interne—House
  Surgeon . . . . . . Alexander Kirkland
DR. WREN, Attending in
  Medicine . . . . Sanford Meisner
DR. OTIS (SHORTY), Interne . . Bob Lewis
DR. LEVINE, in General
  Practice . . . . Morris Carnovsky
DR. BRADLEY (PETE),
  Interne . . Walter Coy (Alan Baxter)
DR. CRAWFORD (MAC),
  Interne . . . . Alan Baxter
NURSE JAMISON . . . . . . Eunice Stoddard
MR. HUDSON, a wealthy
  patient . . . . Art Smith
JAMES MOONEY, his business
  associate . . . . Gerrit Kraber

LAURA HUDSON, his
  daughter . . . . Margaret Barker
DOROTHY SMITH, a young
  patient . . . . Mab Maynard
MR. SMITH, her father . Sanford Meisner
MRS. SMITH, her mother . . Ruth Nelson
BARBARA DENNIN, student
  nurse . . . . Phoebe Brand
DR. CUNNINGHAM, a "courtesy"
  physician at
  St. George's . . . . Russell Collins
FIRST NURSE . . . . Paula Miller
NURSE MARY RYAN . . . . Dorothy Patten
ORDERLY . . . . Elia Kazan
MR. HOUGHTON, a trustee of the
  hospital . . . Clifford Odets (Roman
  Bohnen)
MR. SPENCER, a trustee of the
  hospital . . . . Lewis Leverett
MR. RUMMOND, a trustee of the
  hospital . . . . Gerrit Kraber
MRS. D'ANDREA, the mother of a
  patient . . . . . Mary Virginia Farmer
SECOND NURSE . . . . Elena Karam

The entire action takes place within the walls of St. George's Hospital. Three months elapse between Acts One and Two.

Copyright 1933, by Sidney Kingsley.
Reprinted by permission of Crown Publishers, Inc.
This play in its printed form is designed for the reading public only. All dramatic rights in it are fully protected by copyrights, both in the United States and Great Britain, and no private performance—professional or amateur—may be given without the written permission of the producers and the payment of royalty. As the courts have also ruled that the public reading of a play for pay or where tickets have been sold constitutes a performance, no such reading may be given except under the conditions above stated. Anyone disregarding the author's rights renders himself liable to prosecution. Communications should be sent to Brandt & Brandt, 101 Park Avenue, New York City.

Sidney Kingsley, the son of a physician, born in New York City on October 22, 1906, appears to have been headed for a successful career from boyhood on, when he was admitted to Townsend Harris Hall, a public high school reserved for the brightest pupils. Next he won a New York State scholarship to Cornell University, where he distinguished himself from 1924 to 1928 with his talents in forensic and dramatic art, winning a variety of awards. Following graduation, a stint of acting with a Bronx stock company and in a bit part on Broadway, he just naturally continued to collect honors, once he was properly launched as a playwright. He won the Pulitzer Prize in 1934 for *Men in White;* the Theatre Club medal in 1934, 1936, and 1943; the New York Drama Critics Circle Award in 1943 and 1951, and a variety of other prizes and citations. He also has the distinction of having provided the pioneering Group Theatre, which became pre-eminent in the 1930's and indirectly still exerts an influence on the American stage, with its first Broadway success. Without *Men in White*, it is possible that the Group Theatre would have folded up early in its career.

After his success in 1933 with this medical play, first called *Crisis* and held by several producers before the Group Theatre produced it in association with James Ullman (now better known as author), Kingsley turned his attention to a variety of social facts and tensions. Slum life provided him with the material for his next successful contribution to the theatre of realism, *Dead End*, in 1935. Senator Robert Wagner credited this long-running play, stunningly produced and designed by the late Norman Bel Geddes, with helping to facilitate slum-clearance legislation under the New Deal. With *Ten Million Ghosts* in 1936, Mr. Kingsley was less successful in treating a social theme—profiteering in munitions and war-making, and he found only moderate support in 1939 for *The World We Make*, his moving dramatization of a Millen Brand novel. Both plays, however, added to his prestige as a thoughtful dramatist, and more reputation accrued to him from the 1943 production of his Drama Critics Award drama *The Patriots*, dealing with the rivalry of Jefferson and Hamilton during the early years of the Republic. He won a second Drama Critics Award with *Darkness at Noon*, his dramatization of Arthur Koestler's novel of the same name, which appeared on Broadway during the season of 1950–51, and his play *Detective Story* (opening in March, 1949), with Ralph Bellamy in the leading part as a victim of self-righteousness, was even more successful though less remarkable. Having acquired the golden touch, Mr. Kingsley scored a considerable success with a distinctly secondary effort, the comedy *Lunatics and Lovers*, which opened in December, 1954, with Dennis King in the leading role.

Men in White, the play with which this lucrative career began, commended itself to the public both with a slice-of-life view of a city hospital and a presentation of conflicts of principle and self-interest within its walls. This son of a New York physician, in his first effort to establish himself as an authoritative realist, found a subject and sustained a viewpoint that came naturally to him. No doubt it was also fortunate that the Group Theatre, with its hard-won mastery of realistic performance after its struggle as a new producing company, was in a financial position to give *Men in White* as full a production as it needed. In the young Lee Strasberg, co-founder and brilliant mentor of the Group, moreover, Kingsley's drama had a stage director who combined theatrical imagination with a genuine feeling for reality of character as well as of background. The same happy combination of "theatre" and "reality" was abundantly evident in the stage settings of the gifted designer Mordecai Gorelik, and in virtually the entire cast headed by Alexander Kirkland, Morris Carnovsky, J. Edward Bromberg, and Margaret Barker. One part of the play, the operation scene, was indeed a "complete pantomime."

"After two years of real hardship," wrote Brooks Atkinson in the *New York Times*, "the Group Theatre is not only still in existence, but still determined to keep the theatre in its high estate. This time they have a play worthy of their ambition, and they have adorned it with the most beguiling acting the town affords. It is a good brave play and it is just the play to summon all the latent idealism from the young players of the Group Theatre." And writing in *The Nation*, Joseph Wood Krutch called *Men in White* "a work of art." Some Group Theatre actors were less happy with the result because they distrusted financial success and because the play, in their opinion, had less "social significance" than a work performed by them should have. It was certainly remote from proletarian propaganda drama, and its direct involvement with the problems of individual character, or with psychology, seemed too conservative. But even recalcitrant members of the company could agree with Harold Clurman's retrospective estimate in *The Fervent Years* (1945): "It was our most finished production. Strasberg had given it a dignity, a distinction all his own. For a fusion of all the elements of the theatre this no doubt was his masterpiece. The settings were another example of Gorelik's unusual talent for combining the discoveries of certain abstractionists with the uses of a functional and expressive stage design."

Postscript:

In publishing the play, which the author dedicated to "the men in medicine who dedicate themselves, with quiet heroism, to Man," Mr. Kingsley included the following excerpts from the Hippocratic oath:

> I swear by Apollo, the physician, and Aesculapius, and Hygieia, and Panacea and all the gods and all the godesses—and make them my judges—that this mine oath and this my written engagement I will fulfill as far as power and discernment shall be mine.
>
> I will carry out regimen for the benefit of the sick, and I will keep them from harm and wrong. To none will I give a deadly drug even if solicited, nor offer counsel to such an end; but guiltless and hallowed will I keep my life and mine art.
>
> Into whatsoever houses I shall enter I will work for the benefit of the sick, holding aloof from all voluntary wrong and corruption. Whatsoever in my practice, or not in my practice, I shall see or hear amid the lives of men which ought not to be noised abroad—as to this I will keep silent, holding such things unfitting to be spoken.
>
> And now, if I shall fulfill this oath and break it not, may the fruits of art and life be mine, may I be honored of all men for all time; the opposite if I transgress and be foresworn."

ACT ONE

Scene One

The library of St. George's Hospital. The staff of the hospital gather here to read, to smoke, and to discuss many things—primarily Medicine.

This is a large, comfortable room flanked on the left by tall windows, on the right by ceiling-high bookcases crammed with heavy tomes. There is a bulletin-board in one corner, on which various notices, announcements, advertisements, schedules, etc., are tacked; there is a long table, an abandon of professional magazines and pamphlets strewn upon it; there are many plump leather club chairs, some of which are occupied at the moment by members of the staff. In a series of stalls against the back wall are a number of phones.

Niched high in the wall is a marble bust of Hippocrates,[1] the father of Medicine, his kindly, brooding spirit looking down upon the scene. At the base of the bust is engraved a quotation from his Precepts: *"Where the love of man is, there also is the love of the art of healing."*

A number of the staff are smoking and chatting in small groups, the nucleus of each group being an older man in civilian clothes— an attending physician; the young men, internes, recognizable by their white short-sleeved summer uniforms, are doing most of the listening, the older ones most of the talking, the hush of the room on their voices.

One elderly white-haired physician, seated well to the right, is straining his eyes over a thick medical volume. A number of other books and pamphlets are on a stool beside him. A middle-aged physician, his back to us, is searching the bookcase for a desired volume. A younger practitioner is standing by the window, looking out into the street.

Through a wide, glass-paneled, double door, set in the rear wall, we see a section of the corridor alive with its steady cavalcade of nurses, internes, etc., all hurrying by to their separate tasks. The quick activity of the hospital outside contrasts noticeably with the classical repose of the library.

The loud speaker at the head of the corridor calls: "Dr. Ramsey! Dr. Ramsey! Dr. Ramsey!"

[1] *Hippocrates* (460 to 359 B.C.): ancient Greek physician whose figure is revered by all medical men as that of the ideal physician. He has left a group of writings known as the "Hippocratic Collection," and an oath which is the beacon for all ages of the incorruptibility of medicine.

Phone rings. An interne crosses to the phones, picks one up, talks in low tones.

Enter DR. HOCHBERG, *a short, vital man, whose large head is crowned by a shock of graying hair. He carries himself with quiet, simple dignity. There is strength in the set of his jaw; but the predominating quality expressed in his face is a sweet compassion—a simple goodness.[1] That he is a man of importance is at once apparent in the respectful attention bestowed on him by the others.*

———

DR. GORDON (*the middle-aged physician, who has just found his book; sees Hochberg*). Ah, Doctor Hochberg! I've been waiting for you. (*He quickly replaces the volume and goes to Hochberg.*)

(*The young practitioner by the window wheels round at the mention of Hochberg's name.*)

DR. GORDON. There's a patient I want you to see.

DR. HOCHBERG. Certainly, Josh. We'll look at him in a minute. I just—(*His eye sweeps the room.*) George Ferguson isn't here, is he?

MICHAELSON (*one of the internes seated; looks up from his reading*). No, Dr. Hochberg. Shall I call him?

HOCHBERG (*nods*). Please.

(MICHAELSON *rises and goes to a telephone.*)

DR. VITALE (*the young practitioner, leaves the window and approaches* HOCHBERG). Er . . . Dr. Hochberg—

HOCHBERG. Good morning, doctor.

VITALE. I sent a patient of mine to your clinic yesterday. Did you have a chance to . . . ?

HOCHBERG (*recollecting*). Oh—yes, yes. (*Reassuringly, knowing that this is perhaps* VITALE's *first private patient, and most likely a relative at that.*) No rush to operate there. You try to cure him medically first.

VITALE (*relieved*). I see. All right, Doctor. Thank you. Thank you.

HOCHBERG. Not at all. Keep in touch with me. Let me know what progress you make.

VITALE. I will.

HOCHBERG. If we have to, we'll operate. But I think if we wait on nature this case will respond to expectant treatment.

VITALE. Right! (*He goes.*)

GORDON (*shakes his head, kidding* HOCH-

[1] "All knowledge attains its ethical value and its human significance only by the human sense in which it is employed. Only a good man can be a great physician."—Nothnagel.

BERG). Fine surgeon you are—advising against operation!

HOCHBERG (*smiles and shrugs his shoulders*). Why not give the patient the benefit of the doubt? You can always operate! That's easy, Josh.

MICHAELSON (*returning from the phone*). Dr. Ferguson'll be right down, sir.

HOCHBERG. Thanks.

GORDON. I hear you've some interesting cases at your clinic.

HOCHBERG.Yes, yes—er—suppose you have dinner with me tonight. We'll talk, hm? I discovered a little place on Eighty-fourth Street where they serve the most delicious schnitzel and a glass of beer (*measuring it with his hands.*)—that high! . . . But beer!

GORDON. Sounds good. I'll just phone my wife and—

HOCHBERG. It won't upset her plans?

GORDON.Oh, no! (*He crosses to the phone.*)

HOCHBERG (*approaches the white-haired physician and places a hand gently on his shoulder*). And how is Dr. McCabe today?

MC CABE. My eyes are bothering me! (*He indicates the pyramid of books beside his chair.*) Trying to read all of this new medical literature. It certainly keeps piling up! (*He shakes his head.*) Has me worried!

HOCHBERG. But, why?

MC CABE (*nods toward internes*). These young men today—how can they ever catch up with all this?[1]

HOCHBERG. These young men are all right. They're serious—hard-working boys. I've a lot of faith in them.

MC CABE. But there's so much. (*He shakes his head.*) We've gone so far since I was a boy.[2] In those days appendicitis

[1] "The amount of human labor and ingenuity that is now being thrown into the investigation of Nature is almost incredible even to men of science. Some conception of the enormous and unreadable bulk of scientific literature may be gained by a glance at the *International Catalogue of Scientific Literature*. This gives the *titles alone* of original articles in the various departments of physical science. These titles for the year 1914 alone occupied seventeen closely printed volumes! The rate of publication has accelerated considerably since then. There are very few departments of science which do not have some bearing on Medicine. It is evident that no human mind can possibly compass even a year's output of this material."—Charles Singer in *A Short History of Medicine*.

[2] Medicine has advanced farther in the last fifty years than in the preceding fifty centuries.

Without anaesthesia, and X-ray, all of which were developed during the last half-century, major surgery would have remained an impossible dream.

was a fatal disease. Today it's nothing. These youngsters take all that for granted. They don't know the men who dreamed and sweated—to give them anaesthesia and sterilization and surgery, and X-ray. All in my lifetime. I worked with Spencer Wells in London,[1] and Murphy at Mercy Hospital.[2] Great men. None of these youngsters will equal them. They can't. There's too much! I'm afraid it will all end in confusion.

HOCHBERG. Where the sciences *in general* are going to end, with their mass of detail—nobody knows. But, good men in medicine . . . we'll always have. Don't worry, Dr. McCabe . . . one or two of these boys may surprise you yet, and turn out another Murphy or another Spencer Wells.

MC CABE (*shaking his head*). Not a Spencer Wells! No! Not a Spencer Wells! (HOCHBERG *helps him rise.*) Chilly in here, isn't it? (*He walks slowly to the door.*) I'm always cold these days. (*He shakes his head.*) Bad circulation!

(GORDON *finishes his phone call, hangs up and crosses to* HOCHBERG.)

HOCHBERG. All right for dinner, Josh?

GORDON. Oh, of course. Certainly!

(*An interne,* GEORGE FERGUSON, *and an attending physician,* DR. WREN, *come up the corridor engaged in discussion. The interne stops outside the door to give some instructions to a passing nurse, who hastens to obey them. He pauses in the doorway of the library, still talking to* DR. WREN.

(GEORGE FERGUSON *is about twenty-eight; handsome in an angular, manly fashion, tall, wiry, broad-shouldered, slightly stooped from bending over books and patients; a fine sensitive face, a bit tightened by strain, eager eyes, an engaging earnestness and a ready boyish grin.*)

FERGUSON. If we used Dakin tubes[3] it might help. . . .

DR. WREN. They're worth a trial!

FERGUSON. And, this afternoon, first

[1] Thomas Spencer Wells (1818-1897): pioneer in abdominal surgery—noted for his simple and effective methods.

[2] J. B. Murphy (1857-1916): outstanding among the men who developed the technique of abdominal surgery.

[3] Dakin tubes: arrangement of tubes invented during the world war by Dr. H. D. Dakin to provide constant flushing of deep and gangrenous wounds with an effective antiseptic (Dakin's solution) also devised by him.

chance I have, I'll take him up to the O.R.¹ and debride all that dead tissue.

WREN. Good idea! (*And he marches on down the corridor.*)

(DR. MC CABE *reaches the door.* FERGUSON *holds it open for him.* MC CABE *returns* FERGUSON'S *smile and nod.* MC CABE *goes on.* FERGUSON *enters and approaches* HOCHBERG.)

MICHAELSON. They've been ringing you here, George.

FERGUSON. Thanks, Mike! (*To* DR. HOCHBERG.) Good morning, Doctor Hochberg.

HOCHBERG. Good morning, George.

FERGUSON. I was down in the record room this morning. (*He takes a pack of index cards out of his pocket.*) The first forty-five cases seem to bear you out. . . .

HOCHBERG (*smiles*). Uh, hm! . . .

FERGUSON. Some three hundred more charts to go through yet, but . . .

GORDON. What's this?

HOCHBERG. Oh, Ferguson and I are doing a little research. I have some crazy notions about modern surgical technique. Ferguson, here, is writing a paper to prove that I'm right!

FERGUSON. As a matter of fact, Dr. Hochberg is writing the paper. I'm just helping collect the data and arrange it.

HOCHBERG. Ah! You're doing all the hard work! How's 217?

FERGUSON. Pretty restless during the night, but her temperature's down to normal now.

HOCHBERG. Good! And Ward B—bed three?

FERGUSON. Fine! Asked for a drink of whiskey.

HOCHBERG (*smiles*). He'll be all right.

FERGUSON. He is all right! (*He grins.*) I gave him the drink.

HOCHBERG (*laughs*). Won't hurt him. . . .

FERGUSON (*becomes serious, turns to* DR. GORDON). I wish you'd have another look at 401, Doctor.

GORDON. Any worse today?

FERGUSON. I'm afraid so. He's putting up a fight, though. He may pull through.

GORDON (*shaking his head dubiously*). Mm, I don't know.

FERGUSON. I hope so. He's a fine fellow. He's planning great things for himself—when he gets out of here.

GORDON (*significantly*). When he gets out.

(*The phone rings. A short interne crosses to phones and picks one up.*)

HOCHBERG. Oh, by the way, George, we're sending Mr. Hudson home Tuesday.

FERGUSON (*suddenly excited*). Tuesday? Great! Does Laura know, yet?

HOCHBERG (*nods*). I phoned her this morning.

FERGUSON. She happy?

HOCHBERG. Naturally!

FERGUSON. I wish you had let me tell her.

HOCHBERG (*twinkling*). Ah—I should have thought of that!

SHORTY (*at phone*). One second. (*Calls.*) Ferguson! For you.

HOCHBERG. Go on! Call for you. (FERGUSON *goes to phone.* HOCHBERG *beams at* GORDON.) Good boy! Lots of ability! We're going to be proud of him some day.

(*Enter a lean, shabby man who at first glance appears out of place here. His coat is rusty, and rough weather has left its stain on the hat he carries so deferentially. Tucked under one arm is a large envelope of the type used for X-ray pictures. He has a timid, beaten manner. He is a fairly young man, but worry has lined his forehead, and prematurely grayed his hair, making him seem years older. He hesitates at* DR. HOCHBERG'S *elbow, and finally ventures to touch it.*)

HOCHBERG (*turns, looks at him. Politely, as to a stranger*). Yes? (*Suddenly he recognizes the man.*) Why . . . Levine! (*He grips* LEVINE'S *arms with both hands, almost in an embrace.*) My dear Levine! . . . I didn't recognize you. . . .

LEVINE (*nods and smiles sadly*). I know.

HOCHBERG. Dr. Gordon! You remember Dr. Levine?

GORDON (*hesitates a moment*). Why, of course. (*They shake hands.*)

HOCHBERG. Such a stranger! Where have you been hiding all this time? Why it must be . . . five years since—

LEVINE. Six!

HOCHBERG. Six? My! Mm. . . . (*To* GORDON.) We're getting old. (*Then affectionately.*) Ah! It's good to see you again.

LEVINE. It's nice to get back, but . . . (*He looks around.*) Things here seem pretty much the same. New faces—that's all.

GORDON. Nothing much changes in a hospital.

LEVINE. Only people! We change . . . get old . . . break up so quickly. (*The*

¹ O.R.: hospital jargon for operating-room.

tragic quality in his voice affects the others. Pause.)

GORDON. Well. . . . (*To* HOCHBERG.) I'm going up to look at that boy in 401. (HOCHBERG *nods.* GORDON *turns to* LEVINE.) I'm glad to have seen you again. (*Exit* GORDON.)

HOCHBERG. Tell me . . . how are things with you?

LEVINE. Oh. . . . (*He shrugs his shoulders.*) Just about getting along.

HOCHBERG. And how is Katherine?

LEVINE (*his brow wrinkles*). Not so well.

HOCHBERG (*concerned*). What seems to be the trouble?

LEVINE. Her lungs. . . . She has a slight persistent cough! Some X-rays[1] here. . . . (*He opens the large envelope he is carrying and from it takes two X-ray plates.* HOCHBERG *holds up the plates to the window and examines them.*)

(FERGUSON *hangs up and returns to* HOCHBERG.)

HOCHBERG (*holds the plates so that* FERGUSON *can see them*). George . . . ?

FERGUSON. That shadow there! The right apex.

LEVINE. Yes—I was afraid of—

HOCHBERG. Now, don't be an alarmist! (*Sees something.*) Mm! (*Squints at the plate, and asks, gravely.*) Have you examined the sputum? (*Pause.*)

LEVINE. I brought a specimen. (*He takes out a bottle, wrapped in paper, and explains apologetically:*) My microscope is broken.

HOCHBERG. We'll look at it here!

FERGUSON. Certainly! (*He takes the bottle.*) I'll have the path lab[2] check up on this. Is it anything important?

LEVINE. My wife.

FERGUSON. Oh.

HOCHBERG. Er . . . Dr. Ferguson, Dr. Levine! (*They shake hands and exchange greetings.*)

FERGUSON. I'll tend to this at once, Doctor.

LEVINE. Thanks. Do you think if I came back this evening—?

FERGUSON. Oh, yes, the report will be ready then. Drop into my room—106.

LEVINE. 106? (*He turns to* HOCHBERG.

With nostalgia.) My old room.

FERGUSON. You interned here? Are you the—Oh, of course. Bellevue, aren't you?

LEVINE (*nods*). '23!

FERGUSON. Professor Dury mentions you quite often.

LEVINE. Dury? (*To* HOCHBERG.) He still remembers me. . . .

FERGUSON. He thinks a great deal of you.

HOCHBERG. George, here, is one of his prize pupils, too.

LEVINE. And does he want you to study abroad?

FERGUSON. Yes. I planned to go with Sauerbruch, but he has been forced to leave Germany.[1] So, instead of that, I'm going to study under Von Eiselsberg[2] in Vienna.

HOCHBERG. Hm! I remember when I was a student in Berlin, one of my classmates came to an examination in military uniform . . . sabre and all. Virchow looked at him, and said, "You! What are you doing here in that monkey suit? Your business is with death! Ours is with life!" Virchow was a man of science. He knew.[3] (*He shakes his head.*) I wonder what he would say to our beloved Germany today.

[1] "In the physician's professional relations, though divided by national lines, there remains the feeling that he belongs to a Guild that owes no local allegiance, which has neither king nor country, but whose work is in the world."—Sir William Osler, in *Counsels and Ideals.*

Attempting to make the physician deny this, his fundamental creed, Hitler's Reich has merely succeeded in halting the progress of modern German medicine. Nazi intolerance forced not only all the prominent Jewish figures in medicine, but also non-Jews like Ernst Ferdinand Sauerbruch, greatest living German surgeon, to close their clinics and leave Germany in despair. Not satisfied with expatriating their finest surgeons, the Nazis, with peculiar compassion, enforced anti-vivisection laws restricting their young surgeons from practicing . . . except on human subjects! Surgery, which is a fine art requiring, in addition to other things, the digital sensitivity of a pianist, demands incessant practice. Germany will see no more Sauerbruchs till she learn to respect the autonomy, the humanity, and the tolerance which are the spirit of medicine, and without it cannot exist.

[2] Anton von Eiselsberg: the foremost living Viennese surgeon.

[3] Rudolf Virchow, pathologist and anthropologist (1821-1902) made many important contributions to modern medicine.

Though I have taken some liberties in the telling, this anecdote has its basis in fact and was recounted to me with relish by an old pupil of the great Virchow.

[1] X-ray: discovered by Wilhelm Konrad Röntgen (1845-1922). It has since become so important an accessory that today a good physician would not set a broken finger without it.

[2] Path lab: hospital jargon for pathology laboratory.

LEVINE. Yes. . . .

FERGUSON (*to* HOCHBERG). Well, Laura prefers Vienna, anyway, so . . . (*To* LEVINE.) I'm going on my honeymoon too, you see.

LEVINE. You'll find it difficult mixing the two. I know Von Eiselsberg.

HOCHBERG. It's going to be very difficult. You don't know Laura.

FERGUSON. After a year in Vienna I'm working with Dr. Hochberg. So the real labor won't begin till I come back from Europe.

HOCHBERG. Oh, I'll drive you, George! With a whip, eh?

LEVINE. Lucky! (*Retrospectively.*) Yes... I once looked forward to all that. (*He sighs.*)

HOCHBERG. Well, come, Levine. We'll go down to X-ray and read these pictures properly.

FERGUSON (*holds up bottle*). And don't worry about this.

LEVINE. Thank you . . . thank you. (*Exit* HOCHBERG. LEVINE *turns to* FERGUSON.) Remember, there's only one Hochberg. Every minute with him is precious.

FERGUSON. I won't miss a second of it.

(LEVINE *goes.* FERGUSON *crosses to a long table at which* MICHAELSON *and* SHORTY *are seated.*)

MICHAELSON (*who has been watching* LEVINE *and* FERGUSON). He's telling *you,* huh? (FERGUSON *nods, smiles, and looks for a particular book in the shelves.*) Say, there's a damned interesting article on Hochberg in this week's A.M.A.[1]

FERGUSON. I know. (*He finds the magazine and hands it over to* SHORTY, *a small, chubby, good-natured, irresponsible, wise-cracking fellow, who takes life in his stride.*) Here it is. You want to read this, Shorty.

(SHORTY *sits down to read it.*)

MICHAELSON. Yep. I wish I could get in with him for a year. . . .

FERGUSON (*to* SHORTY). What do you think of that first case? The way he handled it? Beautiful job, isn't it? Beautiful!

PETE (*interne, a tall, gawky lad, slow-moving and casual about everything but food,*

enters, *fixing his stethoscope. He drawls*). Say, George . . .

SHORTY. Pete! Sweetheart! You're just the man I've been looking for.

PETE (*dryly*). The answer is no.

SHORTY. Will you lend me your white tux vest for tonight? I've got—

PETE (*abruptly*). The answer is still no. (*He turns to* FERGUSON.) That little—

SHORTY (*sits down again*). Thanks!

PETE. You're welcome. (*To* FERGUSON *again.*) The little girl we just operated on is coming out of her ether nicely. I was kind of worried about that preop[1] Insulin.[2]

FERGUSON. Why? How much did you give her?

PETE. Forty units.

FERGUSON. Twenty would have been enough.

PETE. I know.

FERGUSON. Then why the hell did you give her forty? You might have hurt the kid.

PETE. Dr. Cunningham ordered it.

SHORTY. That dope—Cunningham!

FERGUSON. You should have told me before you gave it to her. I'm not going to have any patient go into shock on the operating table![3] Understand?

PETE. O.K.

FERGUSON (*good-naturedly, slapping* PETE *on the head with a pamphlet*). If this happens again, Pete, you get your behind kicked in . . . and not by Cunningham!

PETE. O.K.

(*A Nurse, passing by, carrying a tray of medication, halts in the doorway, looks in and calls.*)

NURSE. Oh, Dr. Ferguson, that drink worked wonders. Bed three is sitting up and taking notice.

FERGUSON (*laughs*). A new school of therapy!

SHORTY. Say, Jamison, you're not looking so hot. You ought to stay home one night and get some sleep.

JAMISON. Oh, I'm doing all right. (*She*

[1] Preop: hospital jargon meaning "before operation."

[2] Insulin: an extract from the pancreas used in the treatment of diabetes.
The patient referred to has diabetes, and hence special preoperative treatment is required.

[3] Insulin shock: In diabetes, insulin is used to enable the body to utilize the abnormal amounts of sugar in the blood. Too much insulin, however, will reduce the sugar content of the blood below normal and throw the patient into a condition of shock.

[1] A.M.A.: the journal of the American Medical Association. The most widely read medical publication in the United States; published with the purpose of welding the medical profession into an efficient, competent body to guard against quackery and to preserve the highest standards of ethics and education.

laughs and goes.)

SHORTY. Yeah? I'll bet you are.
(*The loud-speaker starts calling, "Dr. Bradley! Dr. Bradley!"*)

PETE. Say, I'm hungry! Somebody got something to eat?

SHORTY. What, again? (PETE *looks at him with scorn.*) Lend me your white vest for tonight, will you, Pete? I'll fix up a date for you with that redhead.
(*Phone rings.*)

PETE (*nodding at* FERGUSON). Fix him up.
(FERGUSON *laughs.*)

SHORTY. It'd do him good. That's the trouble with love—it kills your sex-life. . . (*Indicates the phone.*) Pete! Phone!

PETE. I was once in love myself. (*He starts for phone.*) But when it began to interfere with my appetite . . . Hell! No woman's worth that!
(*They laugh.*)

FERGUSON. Thing I like about you, Pete, is your romantic nature.

PETE (*on phone*). Dr. Bradley! O.K. I'll be right up! (*He hangs up.*) Yep. At heart I'm just a dreamer.

SHORTY. At heart you're just a stinker!

PETE. Thanks!

SHORTY (*quickly*). You're welcome!
(PETE *goes toward the door.*)

FERGUSON. Going upstairs, Pete?

PETE. Yep.

FERGUSON (*gives him the bottle of sputum*). Will you take this to the path lab? Ask Finn to examine it and draw up a report.

PETE. O.K.
(*Enter* DR. GORDON.)

FERGUSON. Tell him to give it special attention! It's a friend of Hochberg's.

SHORTY (*follows* PETE *to door*). I take back what I said, Pete. You're a great guy, and I like you. Now, if you'll only lend me that white vest—

PETE. No!

SHORTY. Stinker! (*They exit.*)
(GORDON *comes over to* FERGUSON.)

GORDON (*his face grave*). Well . . . I just saw 401. He's a mighty sick boy. He may need another transfusion.

FERGUSON. We'll have to go pretty deep to find a good vein.

GORDON. That's what I'm worried about. If it comes up tonight I want you to be here to do it.

FERGUSON. Tonight?

GORDON. There are three donors on call.

FERGUSON. This is my night out. . . . My fiancée has made arrangements. . . . So I'm afraid I won't be here.

GORDON. I'm sorry, Ferguson. When the House needs you . . .

FERGUSON. I'd like to, Doctor, but the same thing happened last week. I can't disappoint my fiancée again . . . or . . . (*He smiles.*) . . . I won't have any.

MICHAELSON. Er—Dr. Gordon, couldn't I do that transfusion?

GORDON. I'm afraid not—the superficial veins are all thrombosed.[1] Ferguson has followed the case from the start; he knows the veins we've used.

FERGUSON. Laidlaw knows the veins....

GORDON. Frankly, I don't trust any of the other men on this case. I know I'm imposing, but I want this boy to have every possible chance . . . (*Pause.*) He's a sick boy, Ferguson. What do you say?

FERGUSON. All right! I'll stay.

GORDON. Thanks! (*He starts to go—turns back.*) And if your sweetheart kicks up a fuss send her around to me. I'll tell her about my wife. Up at four-thirty this morning to answer the phone. Somebody had a bellyache. . . . (*He laughs, nods, and goes.* FERGUSON *remains, dejected.*)

FERGUSON. Damn it! I wanted to be with Laura, tonight.

MICHAELSON. That's tough, George. I'm sorry I couldn't help you out.
(*The loud-speaker starts calling: "Dr. Manning! Dr. Manning!"*)

FERGUSON (*rises and walks about*). Laura's going to be hurt. You'd think they'd have a little—

NURSE (*comes quickly down the corridor, looks in, and calls, a bit breathless*). Dr. Ferguson? (*She sees him.*) Dr. Ferguson, a woman just came in on emergency with a lacerated throat. She's bleeding terribly! Dr. Crane told me to tell you he can't stop it.

FERGUSON. Get her up to the operating-room. (*He snaps his fingers.*) Stat.[2] (*She hurries off. He turns to* MAC.) Drop that, Mac, and order the O.R.! Come on! (MAC *goes to a phone. To* MICHAELSON.) Call an anaesthetist, will you? And locate Dr. Hochberg! Try the X-ray room!

MICHAELSON. Right! (*He jumps to a phone. Exit* FERGUSON.)

---

[1] Thrombosed vein: a plugged or occluded vein.
[2] Stat: hospital jargon for immediately.

MAC. Operating-room!....
Emergency B!... Quick!...
O.R.? . . . Set up the O.
R. right away! Lacerated
throat! Dr. Ferguson! Yes!
MICHAELSON. Find Dr.
Hochberg! Right away!
Emergency! . . . (*The loud-
speaker, which has been calling,*
"Dr. Manning!" *changes to a
louder and more persistent,* "Dr.
Hochberg! Dr. Hochberg,
Dr. Hochberg!") Well, try
the X-ray room!.... And lo-
cate the staff anaesthetist!

*(On
phones,
simulta-
neously.)*

(*In the back corridor we catch a glimpse of an
orderly hurriedly pushing a rolling-stretcher on
which the emergency patient is lying, crying
hysterically. An interne on one side, and the
nurse at the other are holding pads to her throat
and trying to calm her.*)

FADE OUT

SCENE TWO

*The largest and the most expensive private
room in the hospital. It is luxuriously furnished
in the best of taste and tries hard to drive all
clinical atmosphere out into the corridor. What
the room can't eliminate, it attempts to disguise;
not, however, with complete success. For there,
behind a large, flowered screen, the foot of a
hospital "gatch" bed peeps out, and in the
corner we see a table with bottles of medication
on it.*

MR. HUDSON, *a large man, haunched,
paunched and jowled, clad in pajamas and a
lounging robe, is sitting up on a divan being
shaved by the hospital barber.*[1] *He is talking
to one of his business associates, a* MR.
MOONEY, *who is a smaller, nattier, less impressive, and, at the moment, highly nervous
edition of* HUDSON.

HUDSON (*through a face full of lather*).

---

[1] The barber of mediaeval days is the great-
granddaddy of the modern surgeon. He let blood,
cupped, leeched, gave enemas, extracted teeth and
treated wounds.
This particular barber would be delighted to
learn the honorable antecedence of his profession,
for, with the help of his white jacket, he tries, like
many of his brethren, to resemble an interne, and
is delighted when occasionally some near-sighted
visitor does call him "Doctor."

We'll get that property, Mooney! And
we'll get it now . . . on our own terms.
MOONEY (*marching impatiently to and fro*).
How are you going to break that Clinton
Street boom?
HUDSON. You get in touch with the real
estate editor of every paper in town. Tell
them we've decided to change the location of Hudson City from Clinton to . . .
say Third Street. Map out a territory!
Make it convincing!
(*A nurse enters with a bowl of flowers,
places it on a small table, arranges the flowers,
and departs.*)
MOONEY (*hesitantly*). Think they'll be-
lieve it?
HUDSON. Sure. . . . Got a cigar?
MOONEY (*produces one, then hesitates*).
You're not supposed to smoke, you know.
HUDSON. I'm all right! Can't think
without a cigar! (*He takes it. The barber
gives him a light. He puffs once or twice with
huge relish.*) Start negotiations with every
realty owner in the new territory. Buy
options! They'll believe that!
(*The barber finishes, starts to powder*
HUDSON's *face, but is waved away.*)
MOONEY. Oh yes. . . .
HUDSON. In the meantime sell ten of
our houses on Clinton Street—including
corners. Sell low!
MOONEY. Hey! We want that stuff!
HUDSON. Get Henderson! Form two
dummy corporations—and sell to them.
MOONEY. Oh! . . . Yes, I think it'll
work . . . that ought to bring down those
prices.
(*The barber packs his shaving kit, and
exits.*)
HUDSON. We'll wait till they're ready
to take nickels . . . then our dummy
corporations can grab all that property.
. . . Mooney, we'll be excavating this
spring, yet.
(*Enter* DR. HOCHBERG. *He sees* HUDSON
*smoking, frowns, goes to him, takes the cigar
out of his mouth, and throws it away.*)
HOCHBERG. Didn't Dr. Whitman say
no more cigars?
HUDSON (*startled, his first impulse one of
extreme annoyance*). Hochberg, please. . . .
(*He controls himself, turns to* MOONEY.)
MOONEY (*glances at* HOCHBERG, *picks up
his coat and hat*). Well, I'll be going now.
HUDSON (*helps him into his coat*). Phone
me!
MOONEY. I will. . . . Don't worry!
(*Shakes* HUDSON's *hand.*) Take care of

yourself! (*To* HOCHBERG.) Good-by, Doctor! (HOCHBERG *nods. Exit* MOONEY.)

(HOCHBERG *watches* MOONEY *go, then turns to* HUDSON *and shakes his head.*)

HUDSON. Whitman's sending me home Tuesday, isn't he? What do you want to do? Make an invalid of me? (*He goes to the phone.*) Operator! Get me Vanderbilt 2-34——(*He gasps, an expression of pain crosses his face, his free hand goes to his breast.*)

HOCHBERG (*nods grimly*). Uh, huh! (HUDSON *glances at* HOCHBERG *guiltily, controls himself, continues on the phone.*)

HUDSON. 3471!

HOCHBERG (*goes to him, takes the phone out of his hand, puts it down, with an abrupt nod of the head toward the bed*). You better lie down!

HUDSON. It's nothing. Just a. . .

HOCHBERG (*softly*). I know. Get into bed.

(HUDSON *shakes his head and smiles to himself at* HOCHBERG'S *persistence. Then he goes to the bed and lies down.* HOCHBERG *feels his pulse.*)

HUDSON. I tell you, I'm all right!

HOCHBERG. I don't understand people like you, John. Whitman is the best cardiac man in the country, but he can't give you a new heart! Don't you know that? Are you such a fool?

(*Enter* LAURA, *a spirited, chic young lady; lithe, fresh, quick, modern, a trifle spoiled perhaps, but withal eminently warm, lovable, and human.*)

LAURA. What's he done now, Hocky?

HUDSON. Hello, honey!

HOCHBERG. Laura!

LAURA (*kissing* HUDSON). How's my dad, today?

HUDSON. I'm fine, dear, just fine.

LAURA (*takes* HOCHBERG'S *hand*). And Hocky, wie gehts?

HOCHBERG. Laura, my dear, can't you do anything with him?

LAURA. Why? . . . Smoking again?

HOCHBERG. Yes.

LAURA. Oh, Dad!

HUDSON. Now, don't you start, Laura!

LAURA. But it's so foolish.

HUDSON. I have an important deal on, honey. Besides I'm all right. Whitman's sending me home Tuesday.

LAURA. I know, dear, and that's great! But it isn't going to do any good if you act this way. Can't you forget the office? Close it up! I mean that.

HOCHBERG. She's right, John— absolutely.

LAURA. What good is your money, damn it! if you can't enjoy it?

HUDSON. Well, it can still buy my little girl a honeymoon.

LAURA. I could spend my honeymoon right here! And have a swell time. As long as it's with George. . . . (*To* HOCHBERG.) Where is that man?

HOCHBERG. Upstairs—busy!

LAURA. Oh! (*To her father.*) So, are you going to behave yourself, Dad?

HUDSON (*smiles and pinches her cheek*). Don't worry about me! I'm all right. . . . I'll live. (*Deliberately changing the subject.*) How was Doris' party last night?

LAURA. Noisy.

HUDSON. Not much fun, eh?

LAURA. Not much.

HUDSON. Too bad George couldn't be there.

LAURA. I spent most of the time upstairs with Doris' baby. It woke and wanted some attention. Babies are awfully human that way, aren't they? Do you know that Doris was going to let him cry himself to sleep? Can you imagine? ! . . . Believe me, when I have my baby, it's going to get all the care and love and attention it can use.

DR. HOCHBERG (*chuckles*). You have the right instincts, Laura.

LAURA. Have I? (*Rises.*) I haven't had a real kiss in days. . . . Can I get George on the phone, Hocky?

HOCHBERG. He'll be down soon.

LAURA (*goes to phone*). I want to see that man! (*She picks up the phone.*)

HOCHBERG (*brusquely*). Better wait! (LAURA *looks at him, a bit resentfully.*) He's in the operating-room.

LAURA. Oh!

HUDSON. Er . . . while you're there, Laura, will you call the office like a good girl, and ask Henderson if . . .

LAURA. No! (*She hangs up sharply.*)

HUDSON. But this is on my mind.

HOCHBERG. Again? John, you're a madman!

LAURA (*quickly, with a tinge of bitterness*). And he's not the only one, Doctor Hochberg.

HUDSON (*looks up at her quizzically, sees what's eating her, then turns to* HOCHBERG). God, they make a slave of that boy. And he doesn't get a dime! I can't see it.

HOCHBERG (*smiles at that one*). He's not here for the money! He's here to learn.

The harder he works the more he learns. If he wanted to make money he wouldn't have chosen medicine in the first place. You know, when he comes with me, his pay is only going to be $20 a week, but there's a chance to work. The man who's there with me now works from 16 to 18 hours a day. He even has a cot rigged up in one of the laboratories, where he sleeps sometimes.[1]

HUDSON. For $20 a week?

HOCHBERG (*nods vigorously*). Yes, yes. . . . (*He turns to* LAURA.) George is a fine boy with great promise. The next five years are crucial years in that boy's life. They're going to tell whether he becomes an important man or not.[2]

LAURA. George is an important man right now, Hocky, to me.

HOCHBERG. To *you*. . . .

LAURA. Well . . . I don't count?

HOCHBERG. Of course you do, dear!

LAURA (*controls herself, turns to her father, abruptly changing the conversation*). What time shall I call for you Tuesday?

HUDSON (*to* HOCHBERG). When can I get out of here?

HOCHBERG. In the morning. Eight—nine o'clock.

HUDSON. Good! (*To* LAURA.) Have Martha prepare a big juicy steak—they've been starving me here.

HOCHBERG. No big steaks!

(HUDSON *groans*.)

(FERGUSON *enters, tired and upset*.)

LAURA. George! (*She goes to him*.)

FERGUSON. Hello, darling! (*He kisses her*.)

LAURA. Why so glum, dear—toothache?

FERGUSON (*grins—looks at her hat*). Where did you get that hat?

LAURA. Don't you like it?

FERGUSON. Looks like a sailboat! (LAURA *wrinkles her face, pretending to be on the verge of tears*.) No, it's becoming! You look beautiful . . . doesn't she, Dr. Hochberg?

HOCHBERG (*disparagingly*). Hm—she

<hr>

[1] Following the eminent example of Sir William Osler.

[2] "The education of most people ends upon graduation; that of the physician means a lifetime of incessant study."—Marx in Garrison's *History of Medicine.*
How much truer this is, then, for a man in medicine who wishes to extend himself in special fields above and beyond those normally trodden by his colleagues!

looks all right.

LAURA (*laughs*). I'll kill that man.

HOCHBERG. You should have seen the brat when I delivered her. (*The recollection is too much for him. He looks at* LAURA, *shakes his head, and chuckles*.)

FERGUSON (*goes to the bedside*). And Dad—I guess we're going to lose our best patient Tuesday.

LAURA. Isn't it marvelous?

FERGUSON. Did you ever see him look so healthy?

HUDSON. I feel fine, George! Good enough to eat a big steak!

HOCHBERG (*grunts*). Mm!

HUDSON. Oh, by the way, George, my secretary's tending to the wedding invitations. Better get your list in to him. And see him about your visas, too. He'll tend to all that.

FERGUSON (*to* LAURA). You know—I still can't believe it's going to happen! I mean just happen!

LAURA. Neither can I.

FERGUSON. Vienna's going to be lots of fun.

LAURA. Fun? You don't know. Wait till you've seen the Prater. It's Coney Island with a lift! Lights all over . . . and those lovely people all laughing and happy . . . and the whole place just tinkling with music.

FERGUSON. I've always had a yen to hear Strauss on his home grounds.

HOCHBERG (*softly*). When I visited Von Eiselsberg his students spent all their time working—with an occasional glass of beer for relaxation. That's what George's Vienna is going to be, Laura.

(GEORGE *and* LAURA *are brought up sharp. Enter a nurse with a wheelchair*.)

NURSE. Time for your sun bath, sir.

HUDSON. Oh—go away!

HOCHBERG. Come on, Mr. Hudson, no nonsense.

HUDSON. Aw, hell, I can walk, I'm no cripple!

LAURA. Sit down, dad.

HUDSON (*sits in the chair. The nurse tucks a blanket around him.* HUDSON *grumbles to himself*). Treat me like a God-damned baby! . . . (*To nurse*.) Get me that report, will you?

HOCHBERG. John . . .

HUDSON. I can read, can't I? There's nothing the matter with my eyes. . . . For God's sake . . . (*He turns to* GEORGE *and* LAURA.) Don't you listen to that old fogey! You kids enjoy yourselves. You're only young once.

(*The nurse wheels him out.* HOCHBERG *watches him go and nods.*)

HOCHBERG. Yes, that's true enough! (*He looks at* FERGUSON *and* LAURA, *a twinkle in his eyes, and sits down as if he were there to stay.*)

FERGUSON. You don't need me yet, Dr. Hochberg, do you?

HOCHBERG. Why not?

LAURA (*threateningly*). Hocky!

HOCHBERG (*rises, grinning like a little boy who's had his joke*). All right! (*To* FERGUSON.) I'll call you when I want you. (*He goes.*)

LAURA (*softly*). Sweetheart! (*She holds out her hands to him.*)

FERGUSON (*taking them*). Darling! (*He draws her up out of the chair to him.*)

LAURA. How's my boy?

FERGUSON (*stares at her in adoration. He almost whispers*). You're lovely. . . . Lovely, Laura.

(*Big hug.*)

LAURA. If you knew how I've been aching for this. (*Silence for a moment, as she clings to him.*) Three months! (*She sighs deeply.*) I don't know how I can live till then.

FERGUSON (*tenderly*). Sweet! They're going to be long—those three months—terribly.

LAURA. Yes, I know—I hate to think of them! (*She takes his hand, leads him to a huge easy-chair.*) Come here and—

FERGUSON. Ah!

LAURA. Sit down! (*She pushes him down into the chair and curls up on his lap. Then she takes his head in her hands and scrutinizes his face.*) Let me look at you. (*She shakes her head.*) You're getting thin, young man! And your eyes are tired.

FERGUSON. I didn't have much sleep last night. It was a pretty sick house.

LAURA. You're overworked. . . . (*Pulls his head over on her shoulder.* And I don't like it one bit. (*Pause.*) You know, you've spoiled everything for me. (FERGUSON *raises his head,* LAURA *pushes his head back.*) I was thinking last night, all the music and noise and fun . . . didn't mean a thing without you. I don't seem to get a kick out of life any more, unless you're around. (*She pauses.*) And that's not very often, is it?

FERGUSON. Darling, we'll make up for it all . . . later on. Honestly.

LAURA. I don't know if we can, George. Last night, for instance. If you had been there—perfect! Now's it's—gone. You see, dearest, the way I feel, if I had you every minute from now on, it wouldn't be enough. (FERGUSON *starts to speak, she puts her hands over his lips.*) I wish I'd lived all my life with you. I wish I'd been born in the same room with you, and played in the same streets.

FERGUSON (*smiles*). I'm glad you missed them. They were ordinary and gloomy. They might have touched you . . . changed you. . . . (*He cups her face in his hands and looks at her.*) About seven months ago there was a boy here who'd been blind from birth. We operated on him—successfully. One night I showed him the stars—for the first time. He looked at them a moment and began to cry like a baby, because, he said, they were so lovely, and—he might never have seen them. When I look at you, Laura, I get something of that feeling. I . . . I can't tell you how large a part of me you've become, Laura! You're . . . (*The loud-speaker is heard calling.*) "Dr. Ferguson! Dr. Ferguson." Oh, damn it! . . .

LAURA. Don't move! (*She clutches him tightly.*)

FERGUSON. It's no use, Laura! That's my call! Let me up!

LAURA. No!

FERGUSON. Come on! (*He rises, lifting her in his arms, kisses her, sets her on her feet.*)

LAURA. Oh! You spoiled it.

(*He goes to the phone, picks up the receiver.* LAURA *finds her vanity case—powder and lipstick.*)

FERGUSON. Dr. Ferguson! . . . Yes! . . . Oh! Yes, sir! . . . Yes, Doctor! I'll be ready. . . . I'll tend to all that. Right! (*He hangs up—turns to* LAURA.)

LAURA. All right, go on—go to work!

FERGUSON. I won't be needed for half an hour yet.

LAURA. Well, I have to go to my hairdresser's and make myself beautiful for tonight.

FERGUSON. Laura, dear, I . . .

LAURA. And what a night we're to going to have! Doris asked us over there, but I want you to myself. I want to go to that cute little roadhouse where the food and the music were so good—then a long drive up the Hudson—and, darling, there's a full moon, tonight!

FERGUSON. Laura, I've some bad news. You won't be upset, will you?

LAURA. Why?

FERGUSON. I can't make it tonight. I have to stay in . . .

LAURA (*almost in tears*). Again?

FERGUSON. I'm so sorry, dear. I tried to duck out of it, but I couldn't. There's a transfusion I have to do.

LAURA. What time? I'll wait.

FERGUSON. Better not! It depends on the patient. I've just got to be around and ready!

LAURA. Are you the only one here who can do that transfusion?

FERGUSON. Dr. Gordon seems to think so!

LAURA. George! They're overworking you. It's not fair . . .

FERGUSON. I don't mind it so much for myself . . . only . . .

LAURA (*dully*). No? Well I do. (*Pause. Then* LAURA *continues in a low voice, suddenly hoarse.*) I was planning so much on tonight.

FERGUSON. Don't you think I was, Laura? All week I've been looking forward to it.

LAURA. Sure. I know.

FERGUSON. You're not sure?

LAURA. It's not your fault. I don't imagine it's much fun for you, either—

FERGUSON. Fun! If you knew how fed up I can be with this place sometimes. . . .

LAURA. George, I'm so low—I've been this way for weeks.

FERGUSON. Damn Gordon! Laidlaw could have done that transfusion.

LAURA. Oh, George, what's our life going to be like?

FERGUSON (*gently*). Pretty grand, I should say.

LAURA. How can it be? How can it?

FERGUSON. Dear . . . we'll go out tomorrow instead. Mac promised to take my floor. And we'll have a swell time. Saturday's more fun anyway.

LAURA. It's not just tonight! It's all the nights.

FERGUSON. Darling! You're exaggerating! You're . . .

LAURA. No, I'm not.

FERGUSON. What do you expect me to do? I want to get out . . . I want to enjoy myself . . . but I can't, that's all. I can't.

LAURA. George, I know this is important to you . . . and if it's going to help you . . . I can go on like this for another three months . . . for another year and three months; but when we come back to New York, let's arrange our lives like human beings. You can open up an office and have regular hours . . . specialize!

FERGUSON. If I work with Hochberg, darling, I won't have the time to go into practice.

LAURA. That's just it. I know Hocky. I'll never see you then, George.

FERGUSON. But, Laura . . . (*He laughs nervously.*) I've plugged all my life just in the hope that someday I'd have a chance to work with a man like Hochberg. . . . Why . . .

LAURA. I couldn't go on this way. I just couldn't. . . . I'd rather break off now, and try to forget you. . . .

FERGUSON. Laura! Don't ever say a thing like that!

LAURA. I mean it—it would kill me. But I'd rather die quickly than by slow torture. I can't . . . (*The loud-speaker is calling him.* FERGUSON *and* LAURA *stand there both in anguish.*) They're calling you.

FERGUSON. I know. (*He hesitates a moment . . . goes to the phone.*) Dr. Ferguson! Yes . . . who? South 218 . . . yes? . . . well, call Dr. Cunningham. It's his case . . . let him. (*Suddenly his voice becomes brittle.*) When? What's her temperature? . . . Pulse? . . . Is she pale? . . . Perspiring? . . . Did she ask for food before she became unconscious? . . . No! No more insulin! Absolutely. I'll be right down. (*He hangs up.*) I have to go now, Laura. And please—please don't worry. (*He bends down to kiss her. She turns her face away. He straightens up and regards her with a worried expression.*)

FERGUSON. As bad as that?

LAURA (*in a low voice—a bit husky with emotion*). Yes.

FERGUSON (*forcing a smile*). Things will straighten themselves out.

LAURA. No, they won't.

(*Pause.* FERGUSON *pulls himself together, looks towards the door.*)

FERGUSON. I'll see you tomorrow night dear? Right?

LAURA. Yes. (*She puts on her hat.*) Think it over, George! We'll have to come to some decision!

FERGUSON. Oh Laura, will you please . . .

LAURA. I mean it! Absolutely!

FERGUSON (*pauses for a moment in the doorway*). All right . . . all right!

(FERGUSON goes. LAURA stands there a moment, the picture of frustration and woe, then she walks in a little circle, crying quietly.)

BLACK OUT

SCENE THREE

A bed, screened off from the others, in a corner of the children's ward. The entire wall, separating ward from corridor, is framed in glass panels, so that the nurse on duty out there can always keep a watchful eye over the youngsters.

A little girl of ten is lying back, eyes closed, skin pale and clammy. Her father stands at the foot of the bed, gazing fearfully at his little daughter. He is wan and unkempt, his hair disheveled, his eyes sunken, his collar open, tie awry—the picture of despair. His wife is standing beside the child, weeping.

At the phone is a young student-nurse, BARBARA DENNIN. She is speaking rapidly into the phone.

NURSE. South 218! . . . Calling Dr. Ferguson! At once!

MRS. SMITH. She's so pale, Barney. . . . She's so pale!

MR. SMITH. Where's Cunningham? . . . Why isn't he here? *(To the nurse.)* Miss Dennin! Can't you do something?

NURSE. Dr. Ferguson will right here, sir!

(Enter DR. CUNNINGHAM, a dignified, impressive-looking gentleman, immaculately attired, goatee, pince-nez, throaty voice—just a bit too much of the "professional manner," arrived at in this instance by a certain false philosophy which one occasionally finds in the profession. CUNNINGHAM believes that nine patients out of ten will be cured by nature anyway, and the tenth will die no matter what the physician does for him. This system of logic concludes that impressing the patient and assuaging his fears are more important than keeping up with medical journals and the march of treatment. The sad part of it is that CUNNINGHAM is a successful practitioner—successful, that is, in terms of bank account. True, most of his colleagues look down on him with scorn, but he has a magnificent Park Avenue office, with all the impressive equipment wealthy patients, and political influence—which, although he is not a member of the staff,

has gained him the "courtesy" of the hospital—meaning that he may bring his patients here for hospitalization.)

NURSE. Dr. Cunningham! Thank God you're here!

MRS. SMITH. Dr. Cunningham! My baby! She's fainted! She's . . .

CUNNINGHAM. Now please . . . please, Mrs. Smith! *(He takes off his coat, turns to BARBARA.)* What's happened here?

NURSE. Complete collapse . . . about two minutes ago. . . .

CUNNINGHAM. Let's see the chart! *(She hands him the chart. He looks at it, frowns, shakes his head.)* Hm! This is bad! *(He takes DOT's wrist and feels the pulse, closing his eyes.)*

NURSE. Pulse is barely . . .

CUNNINGHAM. Sh! Quiet, please! . . . *(Silence.)* Hm! . . . Let me have my stethoscope! *(She takes his stethoscope out of his bag and hands it to him. He listens to DOT's heart. His frown deepens.)* Diabetic coma!

MRS. SMITH. Doctor—you've got to save her!

MR. SMITH. Rose . . . come here!

CUNNINGHAM. Miss Dennin—*(He indicates MRS. SMITH with a gesture of the head.)*

NURSE *(takes MRS. SMITH's arm)*. You'll have to wait outside . . . just a moment

MRS. SMITH. Oh, my God!

(BARBARA leads them out, then returns.)

CUNNINGHAM. Prepare some insulin! At once . . . forty units . . . with fifty grams of glucose.

BARBARA. But, sir, Dr. Ferguson advised against insulin. . . .

CUNNINGHAM. Ferguson? You please take your orders from me . . . forty units! Quick!

BARBARA. Yes, sir.

(FERGUSON enters the room. DR. CUNNINGHAM glances at him, nods curtly, and turns to BARBARA.)

CUNNINGHAM. Please, hurry that!

FERGUSON *(looks at the patient, shakes his head)*. I was afraid of shock!

CUNNINGHAM. This isn't shock! It's diabetic coma!

FERGUSON *(his brow wrinkled, looks at the patient again)*. Her temperature's subnormal?

CUNNINGHAM *(impatiently)*. Yes! *(To BARBARA.)* Is that insulin ready yet?

FERGUSON. I beg your pardon, Doctor, but isn't insulin contra-indicated here?

CUNNINGHAM. No. It's our last chance.

(FERGUSON bites his lips to restrain him-

self. CUNNINGHAM *takes the hypo from* BAR-BARA *and presses out the air bubbles.*)

FERGUSON. Doctor, I mean no offense, but I've studied this case history, and it looks like shock . . . not coma!

CUNNINGHAM (*pauses—looks at the patient, shakes his head*). No . . . no. . . .

FERGUSON. But, the clinical picture is so clear-cut. . . . Look at the patient! She's pale, cold, clammy, temperature subnormal. She's complained of hunger! Sudden onset!

CUNNINGHAM (*angrily*). Suppose you let me handle this case, young man. (*To* BARBARA.) Prepare that arm!

(BARBARA *swabs the arm.* CUNNINGHAM *leans over the patient.* FERGUSON *hesitates a moment, then goes to* CUNNINGHAM, *puts his hand on* CUNNINGHAM'S *arm.*)

FERGUSON. Please, doctor! Call in one of the other men! . . . Ask them! Anybody!

CUNNINGHAM. There's no time! Take your hand off!

FERGUSON. That insulin's going to prove fatal.

CUNNINGHAM (*wavers a moment, uncertain, hesitant, then he turns on* FERGUSON). Get out of here, will you? I don't want any interruption while I'm treating my patient! (*He shakes* FERGUSON'S *arm off. . . . Bends to administer the hypo, hesitates a moment, then straightens up . . . confused and worried.* FERGUSON, *with sudden resolve, takes the hypo from* CUNNINGHAM'S *fingers and squirts out the insulin.*) Here! What are you . . . Why did you do that, you fool?

FERGUSON (*ignores him, turns to* BAR-BARA, *his voice crisp and cool*). Shock position! (BARBARA *goes to the foot of the bed, turns the ratchet that elevates the foot of the bed.* FERGUSON *dashes to the door, looks out, calls down the corridor.*) Nurse! Nurse!

A NURSE (*answers from down the corridor*). Yes, sir?

FERGUSON. Sterile glucose! Quick! And a thirty c.c. syringe.

BARBARA. Some glucose here, sir, all ready!

FERGUSON. How much?

BARBARA. Fifty grams!

FERGUSON. Good! Half of that will do! Apply a tourniquet . . . right arm!

BARBARA. Yes, sir.

FERGUSON (*calls down the corridor*). Never mind the glucose—a hypo of adrenalin!

(*The nurse's voice answers:* Yes, sir.)

FERGUSON (*turns up the corridor*). Nurse, nurse! Some hot packs . . . and blankets! Quick . . . come on . . . hurry! (*He starts to return to the patient, but* DR. CUNNINGHAM, *who has sufficiently recovered from his shock, blocks* FERGUSON'S *path.*)

CUNNINGHAM. What do you think you're doing? I'll have you brought up before the medical board. . . . I'll have you thrown out of this hospital . . . you can't . . .

FERGUSON. All right! Have me thrown out! I don't give a damn! I don't care! I really don't . . . pardon me! (*He brushes* CUNNINGHAM *aside and hurries to patient.*)

CUNNINGHAM (*flustered and impotent*). I never heard of such a thing . . . why. . . .

FERGUSON. Ready?

BARBARA. Yes, sir!

FERGUSON (*quickly*). Let's have that glucose. (BARBARA *gives it to him.*) Swab that arm! Never mind the iodine! Just the alcohol! (BARBARA *swabs the arm.*) Thank God! A good vein! (*He administers the hypo.*)

CUNNINGHAM. You'll pay for this, young man! . . . That patient's life is on your hands. . . .

(*A nurse enters with blankets and hot packs.*)

NURSE. Blankets and hot packs, Doctor!

FERGUSON. Yes . . . (*He and* BARBARA *place the hot packs on* DOT, *then* BARBARA *covers her with the blankets.*)

(*Enter another nurse.*)

SECOND NURSE. A hypo of adrenalin!

FERGUSON. Here! (*He takes it from her, administers it. Then straightens up, sighs, turns to two nurses.*) That's all. Thank you! (*They go.* FERGUSON, BARBARA *and* CUN-NINGHAM *watch the patient intently. There is no change in her condition.*)

FERGUSON. That's about all we can do!

CUNNINGHAM. You report downstairs . . . at once!

(*They watch the patient, strained, tense. After a long moment* DOT'S *arm, which has been hanging limp over the bedside, moves. She raises her hand to her forehead, opens her eyes. She looks at* FERGUSON.)

DOROTHY (*faintly*). Dr. George . . .

FERGUSON. Yes, baby?

DOROTHY. I'm thirsty . . . I want a drink. . . .

FERGUSON. You bet, sweetheart. (*To* BARBARA.) Water!

(BARBARA *gives the child a glass of water,* DOT *sits up and sips it, still rubbing her eyes sleepily.*)

DOROTHY. I feel so funny . . . Dr. George! Dizzylike. . . .

FERGUSON. Drink that!

DOROTHY. What happened?

FERGUSON. Nothing! You just fell asleep, that's all. (DOT *has stopped sipping her water to stare at* FERGUSON *with huge blue eyes, wide open now. He grins at her and points to the glass.*) Come on! Bottoms up! (*She smiles back at him, and drains the glass.*) Atta girl!

(BARBARA *lowers foot and raises head of bed.*)

DOROTHY. Barbara!

BARBARA. Yes, dear?

DOROTHY. I want mother. Where's mother?

BARBARA. She's just outside, dear.

DOROTHY. I want mother. . . .

BARBARA. I'm bringing her right in.

(FERGUSON *meanwhile has turned to face* CUNNINGHAM *who is nervously fidgeting with his pince-nez.*)

DOROTHY. Dr. George . . . my operation hurts me here. . . .

FERGUSON (*sympathetically*). Oh! We'll fix that up in a minute! (*To* CUNNINGHAM.) An opium suppository, Doctor?

CUNNINGHAM. No! (*To* BARBARA.) Morphine! A twelfth!

BARBARA. Yes, sir. (*She goes.*)

CUNNINGHAM (*turns his glance on* FERGUSON). I ought to report you, of course! You're a damned, meddling young puppy. . . . (*He hesitates a moment.*) However . . . under the circumstances, I guess I can afford to be lenient . . . this time. But if you ever dare interfere again in any of my cases . . . !

(MR. *and* MRS. SMITH *enter. They rush to the bedside.*)

MRS. SMITH (*crying and laughing*). Dorothy, my darling.

MR. SMITH. Dots! Dots!

MRS. SMITH. Are you all right, my baby? (*She kisses* DOT.) My baby!

DOROTHY. Oh! . . . my operation, mother. . . .

CUNNINGHAM. Careful, Mrs. Smith. . . .

MR. SMITH. Careful, Rose!

MRS. SMITH. Yes . . . yes . . . of course. Did I hurt my darling?

CUNNINGHAM. Now, the child's been through quite an ordeal. You mustn't excite her. I want her to have some rest . . . you'd better . . . (*Indicating the door with his hand.*)

MR. SMITH. Yes, come, Rose. . . . She's weak. . . . (*To* DOT:) Go to sleep, darling.

MRS. SMITH. Good-by, dear! (*She kisses her.*) Is there anything mother can bring you, darling?

DOROTHY (*sleepily*). No, mama. . . .

(MR. SMITH *kisses the child, takes his wife's arm and leads her away.*)

CUNNINGHAM (*turns to* FERGUSON). Order a blood sugar! If there are any new developments phone my secretary at once!

MRS. SMITH (*to* CUNNINGHAM). She'll be all right, Doctor?

CUNNINGHAM. Yes . . . yes . . . You call me tonight!

(DR. CUNNINGHAM, MR. *and* MRS. SMITH *starts to go.*)

MRS. SMITH (*as they exit, to* CUNNINGHAM). Doctor, how can I ever thank you enough for this?

FERGUSON (*goes to* DOROTHY). Well, young lady, how about getting some sleep?

DOROTHY. O.K., Dr. George!

FERGUSON. Close your eyes!

DOROTHY. But don't go away!

FERGUSON (*sits on bedside*). No. . . . I'll sit right here! Come on! (DOROTHY *takes his hand, shuts her eyes, and dozes off. Enter* BARBARA *with hypo.* FERGUSON *whispers.*) She won't need that!

BARBARA. Did Dr. Cunningham say anything to you?

FERGUSON. No. (*He stares down at* DOROTHY.) Pretty kid, isn't she?

BARBARA. I was scared we were going to lose her.

FERGUSON (*touches the sleeping child's hair, and murmurs.*) She has hair like Laura's.

BARBARA. What, Doctor?

FERGUSON. Nothing. . . . Nothing. . . .

BARBARA. I think it was wonderful of you to stand up against Dr. Cunningham that way—

FERGUSON (*annoyed, turns to hypo, etc., and says a bit curtly*). Better clean up that mess.

BARBARA. Yes, sir. (*She puts hypos, etc., on trays. Suddenly her trembling fingers drop the hypo. It splinters with a crash.*)

FERGUSON (*angrily*). Here! (*Glances over at the sleeping child.*) What's the matter with you?

BARBARA. I'm sorry. I was just . . . nervous, I guess. . . .

FERGUSON (*looks at her a moment. She is a soft, feminine girl. Her jet-black hair and serious, large brown eyes are set off to pretty advantage by the blue-and-white student-nurse uniform. She has a simple, naïve quality that lends her an air of appealing wistfulness. He sees how genuinely nervous she is . . . and smiles to reassure her).* Has Cunningham been treating you too?

BARBARA (*smiles*). No, sir. This is my first case with a sick child and I got to like her an awful lot. I guess that was . . .

FERGUSON. I see. What's your name?

BARBARA. Barbara Dennin.

FERGUSON. You're going to be a swell nurse, Barbara!

BARBARA. Thanks!

FERGUSON. Now, take my advice! I know just how you feel—nerves all tied up in a knot . . . want to yell! Feel the same way myself. . . . You get as far away from here as you can, tonight. Have a good time! Relax! Forget hospital! Tomorrow you'll be all right.

BARBARA. I . . . I can't. I have an exam in Materia Medica tomorrow.

FERGUSON. Materia Medica? . . . Hm! . . . I think I have some notes that may help you. . . . I'll leave them with the orderly on the first floor, and you can get them on your way down.

BARBARA. Thanks.

FERGUSON. May help you a bit. You won't have to cram all night, anyway. (*The loud-speaker is calling "Dr. Ferguson." MARY, another and much older nurse, enters with a basin, etc.*)

MARY. Your call, Doctor Ferguson?

FERGUSON (*listening*). Yes. Are you on duty here now?

MARY. Yes, sir.

FERGUSON. If she wakes with any pain, give her an opium suppository! If her temperature goes below normal, call me! I'll be in.

MARY. Tonight, too?

FERGUSON (*almost savagely*). Yes, tonight, too! (*His name is called louder, more insistent. He turns to the door, mutters to the 'oud-speaker.*) All right! All right! I'm coming! (*He goes.* MARY *turns to stare after him, her eyebrows raised in surprise.*)

MARY. Gee! Ain't he snappy today? (BARBARA *simply stares after him.*)

BLACK OUT

SCENE FOUR

A tiny, sombre, austere, cell-like room, with hardly enough space for its simple furnishings—a cot-bed, a bureau, a desk, a chair, a small bookcase and a washbasin. On the bureau is a small radio—the one luxury in the room. On the walls are two framed diplomas—the sole decorations. The room is untidy—as all internes' rooms are; the bed is messed, it being customary for internes to use it as a lounge; the books are piled irregularly on the book-shelves, on the desk, on the bureau, and on the floor.

A moonlit night filters in through a single square window.

FERGUSON, *wearing spectacles, is at his desk reading, by the light of a desk lamp, a ponderous medical tome. Occasionally he jots down a note.*

———

(*A knock at the door.*)

FERGUSON (*without looking up, in a tired voice*). Come in!

(*Enter* SHORTY *in a stiff-bosom shirt, collar, white vest.*)

SHORTY (*triumphantly*). Well, I got the vest. . . .

FERGUSON. That's good.

SHORTY. Can you lend me a tie, George? Mine is—er—

(FERGUSON *rises and wearily goes to his dresser, finds a tux bow tie, hands it to* SHORTY.)

FERGUSON. Here you are, Shorty. (*He sits down again to his book.*)

SHORTY. Thanks! Say, do you mind making a bow for me? I can never get these things straight.

FERGUSON. Come here! I'll try. (*He starts to tie* SHORTY'S *bow.*)

SHORTY. Drink in my room . . . if you want one.

FERGUSON. I don't think so, Shorty!

SHORTY. Good drink! . . . Ginger ale, sugar, and alcohol . . . out of the large jar in the path lab. . . .

FERGUSON. Stand still, will you? (*After fumbling nervously with the tie, he makes a bad job of it.*) Oh, hell! I can't do it! Sorry! (*He undoes the tie.*) Ask Laidlaw!

SHORTY (*looks askance at* FERGUSON). Nerves, young fellow! . . . Better see a doctor about that!

PETE (*pokes in his head*). Anything to eat in here?

FERGUSON. Some chocolate!

PETE. Good! (*Enters—comes up to desk.*)

FERGUSON. Here! (*Gives him a chunk.* SHORTY *starts to go.*) Have a good time, Shorty!

SHORTY (*confidently*). I will.

PETE (*stands there, eating chocolate*). Hope she gives in without a struggle.

SHORTY. No fun, you dope—without a struggle. (*Exits.*)

PETE. Oh yeah? (*Calls after him.*) Well, take off my vest before you start. I don't want any stains on it. (*He returns to the desk and points to the chocolate.*) Now can I have some of that myself! (*He reaches over and breaks off a piece of chocolate.*)

FERGUSON (*smiles*). Who was the first piece for?

PETE. Oh, that? That was for my tapeworm. (*He holds up the chocolate.*) This is for me. (*Pops it into his mouth.* FERGUSON *laughs a tired laugh, and hands him the rest of the large bar, anxious to get rid of him.*)

FERGUSON. Here, take it all, Pete!

PETE. Thanks! What a lousy dinner we had tonight! Fish! . . . Oh, how I hate fish!

FERGUSON. Friday night.

PETE. Yeah! Say! What are *you* doing in?

FERGUSON. 341 may need a transfusion. . . .

PETE. A lot of good that'll do him! (*Stuffs his mouth with chocolate.*) For Christ's sake . . . he passed out. . . .

FERGUSON. No?

PETE. About ten minutes ago.

FERGUSON (*slowly*). Gee, that's too bad!

PETE (*jamming in a huge chunk of chocolate*). Yeah! Say, I'm hungry. . . . I'm going to run out to Fleischer's and grab a sandwich. Will you keep an eye on my floor till I get back?

FERGUSON. All right! Hurry it, will you? . . . I may be going out myself.

PETE. Be right back! (*Exits.*)

(FERGUSON *sits there a moment, staring blankly at the wall. Finally he sighs, wearily closes the book, pushes it away, takes off his spectacles, puts them in a case, and reaches for the phone.*)

FERGUSON. Outside wire, please! . . . Atwater 9-0032. . . . Yes. . . . Hello! Hello! Is Miss Hudson there? Dr. Ferguson calling. . . . Yes. . . . Hello, Laura! . . . How are you dear? . . . Feeling better? . . . Oh! . . . Well, look dear, I can make it tonight, after all. What? . . . Oh, don't be silly! . . . But darling . . . we'll work that out! We'll find some . . . It's

so far away, yet. . . . Why talk about . . . ? Listen Laura! That chance to work with Hochberg is one of the best breaks I've ever had! You don't expect me to throw it over, like that, at a moment's notice, simply because you have some crazy idea that . . . No, no! I don't want to even talk about it, tonight. I'm tired, Laura. It's been a hell of a day! Three operations and . . . I can't think! I can't make an important decision tonight . . . in a minute! Oh, Laura! What the hell are you doing? Punishing me? . . . All right, Laura. (*A knock at the door.*) All right. . . . I'll see you tomorrow night! . . . Yes . . . yes . . . good-by! (*He hangs up, somewhat sharply, then wearily goes to the door, opens it.* DR. LEVINE *is standing there.*)

LEVINE. I'm sorry if I . . .

FERGUSON. Oh, no! Come on in, Dr. Levine!

(DR. LEVINE *murmurs a hardly audible thanks and enters. He looks about, touches the desk, smiles, nods, and murmurs almost to himself:*) Yes. . . . Yes . . . it certainly is nice! Six years . . . like yesterday. (*Looks at his watch:*) Think that report is ready?

FERGUSON. I'll see. (*Takes phone.*)

LEVINE. Oh, don't trouble!

FERGUSON. That's . . . (*Into phone.*) Hello! Path-lab, please! (*To* DR. LEVINE.) What did Dr. Hochberg find?

LEVINE. He left it for the X-ray man to read.

FERGUSON (*into phone*). Hello! . . . Dr. Finn? . . . Ferguson! What about that sputum? . . . Oh! (*To* DR. LEVINE.) Under the microscope, now. (*Into phone.*) Fine! Hurry that through, will you? . . . And send it down to my room! . . . Yes. Thanks! (*He hangs up.*) A few minutes . . . I hope it's nothing. . . .

LEVINE (*nods*). Poor Katherine! She's had so much. Things were so different when I was here . . . before I married.

FERGUSON. Yes . . . Professor Dury told me.

LEVINE. Dury? I know just what he says: Levine—the fool!—wealthy mother—chance to work with Hochberg—to be somebody. Threw it all away . . . for a pretty face. (*He laughs to himself, sadly.*) Hm . . . Dury!

FERGUSON. Your mother? Hasn't she . . . ? (DR. LEVINE *shakes his hand.*) Not yet? . . . Well, she'll come around to your way.

LEVINE (*shakes his head again*). No.

When I married Katherine, a gentile, and my mother disowned me . . . it must have broken her heart. But still, she was doing the right thing from her point of view. . . . (*He sighs.*) Poor Katherine! I didn't count on that! East side! Tenements! Fifty-cent patients! Poverty! Dirt! Struggle! (*He shakes his head.*) I don't know. Maybe it would have been better for her the other way . . . maybe. (*He smiles sadly at* FERGUSON.) Burnt offerings! Jehovah and Aesculapius![1] They both demand their human sacrifice. . . . (*Pauses.*) Medicine! Why do we kill ourselves for it?

FERGUSON. I don't know. I often wonder, myself, whether it was worth the grind of working my way through college and med school. . . .

LEVINE. Med school, too?

FERGUSON. Yes.

LEVINE. I don't see how you kept up with classes.

FERGUSON. I managed.

LEVINE. Terrific grind!

FERGUSON. It wasn't much fun . . . but, still . . . I guess it's the only thing I really want to do. . . . (*Pause.*) My dad used to say, "Above all is humanity!" He was a fine man—my dad. A small-town physician—upstate. When I was about thirteen, he came to my room one night and apologized because he was going to die. His heart had gone bad on him. He knew if he gave up medicine and took it easy he could live for twenty years. But he wanted to go right on, wanted to die in harness. . . . And he did. (*Pause.*) Above all else is humanity—that's a big thought. So big that alongside of it you and I don't really matter very much. That's why we do it, I guess.

LEVINE. You're right of course! Ah . . . it's not good—too much suffering! Kills things in you. . . . A doctor shouldn't have to worry about money! That's one disease he's not trained to fight. It either corrupts him . . . or it destroys him. (*He sighs.*) Well . . . maybe someday the State will take over medicine. . . .

FERGUSON. Before we let the State control medicine, we'd have to put every politician on the operating table, and cut out his acquisitive instincts.

LEVINE (*laughs*). That, I'm afraid, would be a major operation!

FERGUSON (*smiles*). Yes. . . . (*Then he becomes serious again, working himself up, thinking of* LAURA.) But, it *is* a danger! We can't allow outside forces, or things . . . or people to interfere with us. . . . We can't! And, if they do, we've got to bar them out . . . even if we have to tear out our hearts to do it. . . . (LEVINE *looks puzzled. He can't quite follow this.* FERGUSON *suddenly realizes the personal turn his thoughts have taken, sees* LEVINE's *bewilderment, and stops short. He laughs, a bit self-conscious.*) I'm sorry. I guess that's a bit off the track . . . just something personal.

LEVINE (*smiles*). Oh! Yes. . . .

(*A knock at the door.* FERGUSON *goes to the door. An orderly is there.*)

ORDERLY. Dr. Ferguson?

FERGUSON. Yes?

ORDERLY. Dr. Finn sent this down! (*He hands* FERGUSON *a printed report.*)

FERGUSON. Oh, yes, thanks! (*Orderly goes.* FERGUSON *is about to hand it to* LEVINE.) Doctor . . . (FERGUSON *glances at it and suddenly stiffens.*) One second!

LEVINE (*suddenly becomes tense, too*). Dr. Ferguson! Is that . . . ?

FERGUSON (*in a strained, brittle voice*). Wait! (*He goes to the phone.*) Path Lab!

LEVINE. Is that for me?

(FERGUSON *doesn't answer him.*)

FERGUSON. Path Lab? . . . Dr. Finn? . . . Ferguson! That report you just sent me . . . are you positive? . . . Make sure! Look again. . . .

LEVINE. Is that the finding on my . . .

FERGUSON (*over the phone*). Yes . . . Yes . . . Clear as that? (*Slowly.*) I'm afraid you're right. (*He hangs up slowly, turns to* LEVINE, *hands him the card in silence.*)

LEVINE (*takes it. He droops. His fingers tremble, the card falls to the ground. After a moment's silence he wets his lips and murmurs, almost inaudibly.*) I knew it . . . I knew it. . . .

FERGUSON. Gee, I wish I could tell you how sorry I . . .

LEVINE. Tuberculosis! Oh, my poor Katherine! (*He sits down on the bed and stares vacantly ahead.*) What are we going to do, now?

FERGUSON (*goes to the bed, sits down next to him, tenderly puts a hand on his shoulder.*) She'll come through, all right! You'll see. (*A silence.* DR. LEVINE *pulls himself together.*) Perhaps if you took her to a drier climate . . .

[1] Aesculapius: Greek God of Medicine.

LEVINE. Maybe . . . maybe! (*He rises.*) That means . . . giving up the little practice I have . . . means starting all over again. I don't know if we can do it. We're not young, any longer. I don't know . . .

(DR. LEVINE *turns toward the door.*)

FERGUSON. Is there anything I can do?

LEVINE. No, thanks! Thanks! (*Exit* DR. LEVINE.)

(FERGUSON *stands there a moment, staring after him. Enter* PETE.)

PETE (*sucking his teeth with great gusto*). Boy, what a roast-beef sandwich I had! Mm! (*He sucks his teeth louder.*) Have you got a . . . oh, yeah! (*He reaches over, and takes a tongue-depresser out of* FERGUSON'S *breast pocket.* PETE *splits the depresser, and using one of the splinters as a tooth-pick, continues to make even a greater noise with his lips.* FERGUSON, *pretty near the cracking point, turns his back on* PETE. PETE *goes to the radio, and tunes in on a loud jazz number. He flops down onto the bed—sucks his teeth.*) Going out?

FERGUSON. No!

PETE. Change your mind?

FERGUSON. Yes.

PETE. Boy, you know that Miss Simpson down in the X-ray lab—She was over at Fleischer's. Next table to mine. Say— she's swell all dressed up in street clothes. I looked at her for ten minutes without recognizing her. I guess maybe it was because I wasn't looking at her face. (*Sucks his teeth.*) Luscious! She had one of those tight black silk dresses . . . absolutely nothing else on underneath—you could see that. And a pair of mammaries! Mm!

FERGUSON (*tensely*). Pete! I want to do some reading. Will you get the hell out?

PETE (*sits up, looks at* FERGUSON, *rises quickly*). Sure!

(*With a puzzled, backward glance at* FERGUSON, *he goes.* FERGUSON *switches off the radio; walks up and down the room, almost frantic, then throws himself face down, on the bed. There is a timid little knock at the door.*)

FERGUSON. Come in! (*The knock is repeated.* FERGUSON *rises, calling impatiently.*) Come in. Come in! (BARBARA *opens the door and slips in, breathless with the adventure.*) What . . . er?

BARBARA. I came down for those notes . . .

FERGUSON. Oh! Of course. I forgot . . . stupid of me. Let's see—what was it? Materia Medica?

BARBARA. Yes.

FERGUSON (*looks through drawer in his desk*). I had them here some place.

BARBARA. I suppose I oughtn't to have come in.

FERGUSON (*assorting notes*). Pathology, Histology—no—no.

BARBARA. I hope nobody saw me.

FERGUSON. Materia Medica. Here! *He takes a notebook out of the drawer, glances through it, hands it to her.*) There you are!

BARBARA. Thanks!

FERGUSON. Not at all! . . . Hope they're some help. (*He goes to the window, looks out —dismissing her. Still in his old mood.*)

BARBARA (*stands there a moment, waiting. Finally she asks timidly*). Is there . . . anything wrong?

FERGUSON. What?

BARBARA. Anything wrong?

FERGUSON. Oh! No! No! (*He turns to the window again.* BARBARA *hesitates a moment —sees that he has already forgotten her in the intensity of his mood. She slowly turns, opens the door, looks out, and suddenly shuts it with an exclamation of fright.*) What—

BARBARA (*breathless . . . frightened*). Head-nurse! Outside!

FERGUSON. See you? Wait a minute! She'll be gone! Better sit down!

BARBARA. Thanks! (*She watches him a moment.*) Are you sure Doctor Cunningham didn't—(FERGUSON *shakes his head.*) Because . . . if it would mean anything . . . I'd go right down and tell them all— everybody—just what happened. . . .

FERGUSON. No, it's not Cunningham—

BARBARA. What is it, then?

FERGUSON. It's just—(*With an effort he shakes off his mood.*) Don't mind me, to-night.

BARBARA. You work very hard, don't you?

FERGUSON (*almost savagely*). Work? Sure! What else is there but *work*—and work! (*He suddenly realizes* BARBARA *is staring at him. He pulls himself together.*) Let's see those notes! (*She brings them to him. He places the book on the desk, leans over it, and turns the pages.*) There! (BARBARA *is next to him, leaning over the notes, her head near his.*) These pages synopsize the whole business. Read through the notes carefully; memorize these pages—and you've got it! I think you'll find it lots easier that way.

BARBARA (*pointing to a word*). What's this?

FERGUSON. Calomel!

BARBARA (*her head almost touching his*). Oh, of course! It's a C.

FERGUSON (*hands her the book*). Clear?

BARBARA. Yes. (*As she reaches for the book, her hand meets his, and she clings to it.*) You know, when I thought Dots was going to die ... I got the feeling like I ... I ... God! ... I can't put it into words!

FERGUSON. I know. I know that feeling. ...

BARBARA. You, too?

FERGUSON. Me, too? (*Clutching his throat.*) Up to here, Barbara! Right now! Christ! I'm tired of work, and blood and sweat and pain! And the chap in 341 is dead! And Levine's wife is going to die ... and one begins to wonder where in Heaven's God, and what in Hell's it all about, and why on earth does anything make any difference.

BARBARA (*clutches his arm with her hand*). Yes, that's the feeling ... and you get so lonely ... and you feel ... tomorrow it's me ... and the only thing that matters is just being alive ... just being alive. Now! ... Isn't it? (*She is very close to* GEORGE *now, clutching his arm with her hand.*)

FERGUSON (*looks at her sympathetically*). You kids have a pretty tough time of it, don't you? Grind all day and lights out at ten o'clock.

BARBARA. And only one night out till twelve-thirty ... and I haven't taken mine in two months. There's just nobody. ... (*They are very close, now. She almost whispers the last words to him.*)

FERGUSON. You're a sweet girl, Barbara. (*Suddenly he takes her in his arms and kisses her. She clings to him for a moment. Then they separate. He is confused and upset.*) I'm sorry, Barbara ... I ... (*He goes to the notes, opens them—after a pause.*) These diagrams here go with this page. Aside from that, I guess they'll be pretty clear. (*He gives the book to her ... grips her shoulder.*) Please don't feel that I ... just ...

BARBARA. Oh! No! No!

FERGUSON. Thanks. (*Goes to the door ... opens it ... looks out.*) I'm going up to Ward C, to look around for a few seconds. The coast is clear—you'd better go now. (*Exit* FERGUSON.)

BARBARA *takes up the notes ... walks slowly to the door ... hesitates there a moment ... is about to go out, suddenly stops ... decides to stay. For a moment she leans against the*

door, breathless, then she goes back into the room, slowly drops the notes on the table, goes to the bed, sits down, takes off her cap, throws it on the bed and sits there ... waiting.

CURTAIN

ACT TWO

SCENE ONE

A softly lit room, the main feature of which is a long table. Seated about it are the members of the Joint Committee—three laymen representing the Lay board, and four doctors representing the Medical board. Beyond them, we see mahogany panels, a huge fireplace and an oil portrait hanging over it, dark plush portières drawn to conceal windows and doors —in effect, a rich board-room of the same general conspiratorial appearance as the board-room of a railroad, a steel, oil, banking or other big business institution.

AT RISE:

MR. HOUGHTON, *short, stodgy, aggressive ... the economist, has just finished reading a report.*

———

MR. HOUGHTON. ... 28,000—19,000—33,500 which adds up to a total deficit of 163,000 dollars so far, Doctors. (*He shakes his head.*) You'll have to cut down those expenses, Doctors.

DR. GORDON. How?

DR. WREN. We're to the bone, already. We've cut—

MR. SPENCER (*presiding, gray-templed, sure, suave, six generations of Harvard! He gives* DR. WREN *the floor*). Dr. Wren!

DR. WREN (*rises*). Everything—our staff, nurses, technicians, salaries, meals —telephones even! Our internes are allowed only two outside calls. ...

DR. HOCHBERG. An absurd economy!

MR. HOUGHTON (*taking some papers out of his briefcase*). Mm! ... It seems to me we've a lot of people in our laboratories. Couldn't we reduce—

DR. HOCHBERG. No, no—(*To the chairman.*) Mr. Spencer!

MR. SPENCER (*giving* HOCHBERG *the floor*). Dr. Hochberg.

DR. HOCHBERG (*rises, and explains, very patiently*). Those laboratories, Mr. Houghton, *are* the hospital. Most of our real work is done in them. (*He smiles and shakes his head.*) Without that pathology lab and the chemistry lab and the X-ray lab we're helpless.

MR. RUMMOND (*rather old and dim-witted, trying very hard to be a constructive part of this business, but not quite able to grasp it*). You are? . . . Really?

DR. HOCHBERG. Absolutely.

MR. RUMMOND. Hm. Interesting. I didn't realize they were that important.

DR. HOCHBERG. Oh, yes.

DR. GORDON. I should say so.

MR. HOUGHTON. Well, then . . . (*He looks at his papers, and shakes his head.*) I don't know—163,000 dollars—these days! The Board of Trustees is—

MR. SPENCER. Er . . . we'll come back to that later, Mr. Houghton. I want to clear away all . . . er . . . Dr. Gordon! Any reports from the Medical Board to this joint committee?

DR. GORDON. Appointments! Two-year interneships, gentlemen—recommended on the basis of competitive examinations. (*Starts looking through some papers for the list.*) Internes. . . . Ah yes. (*Finds his list and reads from it.*) Aubert, Dickinson, Flickers, Frankey, Gordon, Kern, Monroe! The Medical Board awaits your approval of these men.

MR. HOUGHTON (*quickly*). Where's Ten Eyck?

MR. SPENCER. You still can't do anything for Ten Eyck?

DR. GORDON. Ten Eyck? (*He glances over his lists, murmuring.*) Ten Eyck, Ten Eyck, Ten Eyck. Oh, yes—here it is. Gentlemen! Charles Arthur Ten Eyck finished fourth from the bottom—on a list of three hundred men examined.

MR. HOUGHTON. Senator Ten Eyck's going to be sore as hell. . . .

DR. LARROW (*pompous pedant, cut pretty much from the same pattern as* DR. CUNNINGHAM). I met the boy. Seems well-bred. Good family . . .

DR. WREN. He doesn't *know* anything. I gave him his oral in medicine. An ignoramus.

DR. LARROW. Examinations! Bah! He graduated at an approved medical school, didn't he?

DR. WREN. How he managed it is a mystery to me.

DR. GORDON. We gave him special consideration, Mr. Spencer. But he just won't do.

} (*Together.*)

MR. SPENCER. Well—his uncle's kicking up a fuss, but if the boy's that bad . . . After all you know best. The appointments are in your hands. Which brings me to the real purpose of this special meeting. (*He organizes his papers, clears his throat, and looks at them a moment. Then portentously.*) Mr. Houghton has just . . . er . . . read the bad news.

DR. WREN. We usually run up a much larger deficit.

MR. SPENCER (*smiles at this naïveté, so typical of the doctor in business*). Yes . . . but these are unusual times, Doctor. As you, no doubt, have heard, there has been a depression.

DR. GORDON. *Has* been? I like that. You try and collect some of my bills.

DR. LARROW. Yes. People are too poor to get sick these days.

DR. HOCHBERG. That's something no matter how poor a man is he can always get—sick!

(GORDON *and* WREN *enjoy a laugh at* LARROW's *discomfiture.*)

MR. SPENCER. Er . . . Doctors! Please! This is a very important matter! (*They quiet down, and lean forward. There is no escaping the note of impending ill news in* SPENCER's *manner.*) Two of our Trustees are very shaky, and may not be able to meet their usual subscription at all. They've already spoken to me about resigning. (*The doctors look at each other. This* IS *bad.*) And so, I've been looking around carefully for a new Trustee—and believe me, Doctors, it was a mighty hard search. But, finally—(*He smiles.*) I found someone to underwrite our deficit. (*Sighs of relief and approval from the doctors.*) A man well known for his philanthropies, his generous soul, his civic and social services—John Hudson—the real estate Hudson. (HOCHBERG *grunts.*) A friend of yours, I believe, Doctor!

DR. HOCHBERG. Yes. But I didn't recognize him by the description. (MR. SPENCER *laughs.*) He'll be useful. The only real estate man I heard of who's made money the last few years. Good business head. He'll put St. George's on a paying basis.

MR. SPENCER (*laughs*). If he can do that, he's a wizard. Mr. Houghton will resign in favor of him tomorrow.

MR. HOUGHTON. With pleasure.

MR. SPENCER. I've talked the matter

over with him, and he's definitely interested.

(*Chorus of approval from the Committee.*)

MR. HOUGHTON. If we can get him to subscribe for . . .

MR. SPENCER. Mr. Houghton! Please!

MR. HOUGHTON. Sorry!

MR. SPENCER. Now, it happens that one of our internes is marrying John Hudson's daughter—in a few weeks, I believe. Of course, Doctors, appointments lie completely in your hands, but we feel here is an opportunity. We suggest the medical-board offer Dr. Ferguson an associateship. . . .

DR. HOCHBERG. What? Impossible!

MR. SPENCER. Impossible? A serious student, capable, going to study a year abroad under a well-known man—why impossible?

DR. HOCHBERG. He won't be *ready* for the job!

MR. SPENCER. Have you any personal prejudice against the boy?

DR. HOCHBERG (*annoyed*). No . . . no! (*He rises.*) As a matter of fact I'm very fond of that boy. I think he has promise of becoming a good surgeon, someday. But not over night. He has years of intensive study ahead of him. I don't care what strength of character is native to a man—he will not work for something he can get for nothing—and Ferguson's no exception. An associateship here now simply means he'll go into practice and drop his studies.

DR. LARROW. And why shouldn't he? He's marrying well. . . . With his wife's connections, he ought to . . . er . . . do very nicely.

DR. HOCHBERG. If he doesn't continue his studies, he'll never be worth a damn as far as medicine goes.

MR. SPENCER. After all, Dr. Hochberg, that's *his* concern, not ours.

DR. LARROW. Oh! (*Dubiously.*) He's all right. . . . But (*With conviction.*) he's no infant Cushing[1] by any any means.

MR. SPENCER. We must think of the hospital, Doctors! That's our job.

} (*Together.*)

DR. HOCHBERG (*losing his temper. To*

DR. LARROW). You're wrong, Doctor. That boy has *unusual* ability. Yes, yes—another Cushing, perhaps! (*Controls himself—to* MR. SPENCER *quietly.*) Exactly, Mr. Spencer! The hospital! Do you realize the responsibility in precious human life that lies in an associate's hands? Ferguson doesn't know enough, yet; he's apt to make mistakes that will hurt not only himself, but the integrity of St. George's Hospital.

MR. SPENCER. Oh, come now, Dr. Hochberg!

MR. HOUGHTON. Oh, for Christ's sake . . .

RUMMOND. Nothing to be thrown away so lightly!

} (*Together.*)

MR. SPENCER. What do you think, Dr. Wren?

DR. WREN (*slowly*). Well . . . he won't be ready for it, of course, but—er—we could see to it that he'd always be covered by an older man!

DR. HOCHBERG. And give him nothing to do! Make a figurehead of him. Fine! That's fine!

MR. HOUGHTON. What of it?

DR. GORDON. Of course, we don't exactly approve of the appointment, however—

MR. HOUGHTON (*exploding*). Approve! Approve!

MR. SPENCER (*irritably*). Mr. Houghton! Please! (HOUGHTON *subsides with a grunt.*) Dr. Gordon! Go on!

DR. GORDON. Of course, we don't exactly approve the appointment for such a young man; however, we do need Hudson. And Ferguson's not a fool, by any means.

MR. SPENCER. Exactly, Dr. Gordon.

DR. HOCHBERG. But, Josh, don't you see—?

DR. GORDON. Leo, we've got to face the facts. There's hardly a hospital in this city that hasn't shut down on its charity wards. I know a dozen that have completely closed off entire floors and wings! If we have to economize any more, our wealthy patients will take care of themselves, but who's going to take care of all your charity cases? The wards upstairs are full, right now.

MR. HOUGHTON. It takes money to run a hospital, Doctor!

DR. HOCHBERG (*to* GORDON). You're right, Josh

} (*Together.*)

[1] Harvey Cushing (1869-   ): professor of surgery at the John Hopkins and Harvard Universities—the most eminent brain surgeon in the world.

... you're ... (*To* HOUGHTON). I know, Mr. Houghton, I know. And, believe me, we're deeply grateful to you gentlemen for your help.

MR. RUMMOND. A good cause. } (*Together.*)

MR. SPENCER. I only wish I could subscribe more, Doctor! I would.

DR. HOCHBERG. Yes. Deeply grateful. ... Although, it's a social crime, gentlemen, that hospitals should depend on the charity of a few individuals.

(*The Trustees look at each other, not quite sure whether they've been attacked or flattered.*)

DR. LARROW. The fact remains that we can't afford to refuse Hudson's help.

DR. HOCHBERG. I don't say that.

DR. LARROW. We need him.

DR. HOCHBERG. We do. And till hospitals are subsidized by the community and run by men in medicine, we'll continue to need our wealthy friends. I realize that. I say by all means make Hudson a Trustee. Take all the help he can give. And promise Ferguson an associateship as soon as he's *ready* to go into practice.

SPENCER. And that'll be—when?

DR. HOCHBERG. In five or six years.

MR. HOUGHTON. Oh, for Christ's sake! You're dealing with a business man there, not a child!

MR. RUMMOND. You can't expect the man to— } (*Together.*)

MR. SPENCER (*smiling wryly*). I'm very much afraid Hudson will tell us to come around ourselves in five or six years.

HOCHBERG (*to* SPENCER). How do you know?

MR. SPENCER. He wants the boy to open an office and settle down.

DR. HOCHBERG. He does? That's nice. Well, Ferguson won't be ready.

MR. SPENCER. If we don't appoint the boy we can't expect Hudson to be interested.

DR. WREN. There you are right, probably.

MR. SPENCER. Well, that's—er—the important thing, after all, isn't it? Hudson's interest.

MR. HOUGHTON. I should say it was his *capital!* (HOUGHTON *roars with laughter at his own quip.*)

MR. SPENCER. Then you'll submit our recommendation to the medical board?

DR. WREN. Yes. And they'll O.K. it, too. I'm pretty sure it'll go through.

(DR. HOCHBERG *throws up his hands.*)

MR. SPENCER. Fine! Fine! After all, Dr. Hochberg, as you say, we're here in a common cause—the hospital. (*He smiles. Looks over his papers.*) Mm! ... guess that's about all! (*He glances around.*) Anything else, gentlemen? Mr. Houghton? (HOUGHTON *gathers his papers, shakes his head "No," puts papers in portfolio.*) Dr. Wren?

DR. WREN (*looks at his watch*). No. Nothing!

MR. RUMMOND. What time have you there? (*Compares watches, nods, rises, and gets his coat.*)

MR. SPENCER. Anybody? Then the meeting is—

DR. GORDON. One second, Mr. Spencer! Since you're discussing this with Mr. Hudson, I think it would be a fine thing if we could extend our X-ray therapy department.

MR. SPENCER. First give him the associateship, then we'll talk about equipment

DR. HOCHBERG (*rises*). Don't count your chickens, Josh!

DR. GORDON. Oh, he'll get the appointment!

DR. HOCHBERG. Yes. But he won't accept it.

MR. SPENCER (*smiles*). What makes you say that?

DR. HOCHBERG. I know the boy! He's too honest, too wise, to sacrifice his career for a nice office and an easy practice. Besides he won't have the time. He's going to work with me! And ... er ... well. ... (*He laughs.*) It was perhaps a bit foolish to waste so much energy arguing the matter. (*He starts for the door.*)

MR. SPENCER (*laughs*). As a matter of fact—I had dinner last night at the Hudsons' and I spoke to Ferguson about the appointment. He's delighted with the idea. ...

DR. HOCHBERG (*stops—returns—incredulous*). He said that?

MR. SPENCER. Certainly! And, why not? It's a fine opportunity for him. (*Looks around.*) Nothing else, gentlemen? No? ... (*Bangs his mallet on the table.*) Meeting is adjourned!

(*All except* HOCHBERG *move toward the*

door. He stands there, stock-still, palpably hit.)

BLACK OUT

SCENE TWO

The library.

DR. MC CABE *is sitting in armchair reading.* MICHAELSON *is seated at the long table. Nearby* SHORTY *is swinging an imaginary golf club.*

SHORTY. My stance was all wrong, see? That's one reason I sliced so much. (MC CABE *looks up, grunts, and goes back to his book.*)

MICHAELSON. I wouldn't even know how to hold a club any more.

SHORTY. You'd be surprised. A couple of games, and you're right back in form. Look at Ferguson! He hasn't played tennis in years—since high school, I think he said—and yet, last week he beat Laura two sets in a row. And that girl swings a mean racquet.

PETE (*enters, sour-faced*). That patient in 310! Boy, I'd like to give him two dozen spinal taps and bite the point off the needle to make sure he feels them.

MICHAELSON. Whoa! (*Laughs.*) Your gall-bladder needs draining, Pete!

PETE. Ah! The smart alec! He invited me to share this special lunch with him. When I heard *lunch*, I accepted (*he snaps his fingers.*) like that! (*Then, morosely.*) Smart alek!

SHORTY. Well, what's the matter with that?

PETE. Do you know what 310's here for? (*Shrilly.*) Rectal feeding!

(*The others laugh.*)

MC CABE (*looks up, annoyed*). Sh! Sh! Quiet!

(*They glance over at him and quiet down. He goes back to his books. They kid* PETE *in an undertone, muffling their laughter.*)

CUNNINGHAM (*enters—looks around irritably*). Where's Ferguson?

SHORTY. Not here, Doctor.

CUNNINGHAM. I've been trying to find him since twelve o'clock. What kind of house-service is this? Where is he?

MICHAELSON. Why, you see, Doctor —Ferguson's being married next week,

and he's at a ceremony rehearsal or something.

CUNNINGHAM. I told him not to let 327's bladder become distended.

MICHAELSON. 327? Ferguson catheterized him this morning.

CUNNINGHAM. Well, he needs another.

SHORTY. I'll get one of the juniors to do it, right away.

CUNNINGHAM. Never mind! I'll do it myself. (*He goes to the door, grumbling.*) Fine house-service you get around here. 327 is full of urine.

PETE. And so are you.

MC CABE (*looks up*). What's that?

PETE. I'm sorry, Doctor.

MC CABE. What for? You're quite right. He is. (*The internes grin.* MC CABE *looks at them quizzically. He turns to* SHORTY.) Young man! How would you treat the different forms of acute pancreatitis?[1]

SHORTY (*a study in blankness*). Er ... acute pancrea ... mm ... Why, the same way. I'd—

MC CABE. Wrong! (*Pause; he shakes his head at* SHORTY.) You play golf, huh? (*He tosses a pamphlet to* SHORTY.) Read that, and find out something about pancreatitis. (*He suddenly draws his shoulders together and looks over at the windows.*) There's a—(*He turns to* MICHAELSON.) Will you see if that window's open? There's a draught in here, some place. (MICHAELSON *crosses to the window.*)

(*Through the glass-paned door, we see* FERGUSON *in civilian clothes, and* LAURA *coming up the corridor. They are in high spirits, joking and laughing.* FERGUSON *starts to enter the library, but* LAURA *hesitates in the doorway.*)

PETE. How was it?

FERGUSON (*grinning*). Terrible.

MICHAELSON (*to* FERGUSON *and* LAURA). Ho' there! (*To* MC CABE.) They're all closed, Doctor.

FERGUSON (*to* LAURA). Come on in!

LAURA. Well—is it all right for me to—?

(*The Internes assure her in chorus that it's quite all right.* FERGUSON *takes her arm and pulls her into the room.*)

FERGUSON. Sure. Come on! (*To others.*) Any calls for me?

MICHAELSON. Yes. Quite a few, George.

LAURA. You should have seen my

---

[1] Pancreatitis: inflammation of the pancreas.

hero! He was scared to death.

FERGUSON. Who wouldn't be?

SHORTY. What was it like?

FERGUSON. Every step a major operation. Next time I take spinal anaesthesia first. (SHORTY *sings a funereal wedding march.*) Exactly, Shorty! The last mile. (*They laugh.* MC CABE *looks up very much annoyed. He snorts, shuts his book with a bang. The others stop laughing and glance at him.* MC CABE *reaches for his cane, rises rustily, and goes out mumbling.*)

LAURA (*watches him go, then turns to the others, who grin*). Perhaps I shouldn't have come in here.

SHORTY. Nonsense!

MAC. It's perfectly O.K.

PETE. Don't mind old Doc McCabe! He thinks the world ended in 1917 when he retired.

LAURA. Retired!

FERGUSON. Yes, but he still comes around to talk, read, watch operations. Gives us hell for not knowing anything. Medicine's not just his profession—it's his life. (*He shakes his head admiringly.*) Great guy! If I live to be eighty, that's the way I want to grow old!

LAURA. Not I. When I'm too old to enjoy life first hand I want to lie down, and say "Laura, it was good while it lasted. Now, *fini!*"

SHORTY. My idea exactly. Why sit around and listen to your arteries hardening?

PETE. Don't worry, sweetheart! The chances are none of us will live to grow that old. (*To* LAURA.) Most doctors die pretty young, you know.

(LAURA *looks pained.*)

MICHAELSON. That's right. The strain gets them around forty-five. Heart goes bad.

LAURA (*glances at* FERGUSON *and grimaces*). There's a pleasant thought.

FERGUSON (*laughs*). Cheerful bunch!

PETE. So I say—eat, drink and be merry—for tomorrow you . . . (*With a gesture.*) Pht!

MICHAELSON. George! Better phone in! Cunningham's been looking for you!

FERGUSON. What's he want now?

SHORTY. His shoes shined, or something. I don't know.

PETE. 327 catheterized!

FERGUSON. Again? He'll wind up by— (*Goes to phone.*)—giving that patient a urethritis.[1] (*Picks up the phone.*) Dr. Ferguson! I just came in. Any calls for me? Find him, will you? Library!

PETE. He's certainly been giving you all the dirty work lately.

MICHAELSON. Yes!

SHORTY. What'd you do? Kick his mother?

FERGUSON. What's the difference? Four more days and I'll be *aus* interne.

LAURA. Who is this charming fellow?

FERGUSON. He doesn't matter, darling! Nothing matters, now—except Vienna!

MICHAELSON. I bet you'll have a swell time over there.

FERGUSON. You bet right! (*The phone rings.* FERGUSON *goes to it. On phone.*) Yes, Dr. Cunningham? . . . Yes, Dr. Cunningham! . . . Yes. . . . Oh, you're quite right! . . . Yes. . . . Yes. . . . (*He winks at the boys, who smile and shake their heads.*) Uh, huh! . . . Yes . . . yes. . . . All right, Doctor! Sure.

MAC. Will you have lunch with us, Laura?

PETE. A lousy lunch.

LAURA (*laughs*). Just had one, thanks! George and I dropped into Rumpelmayer's after the rehearsal!

SHORTY. Rumpelmayer? At the St. Moritz?

LAURA. Yes.

PETE (*hungrily*). How was the food? Good?

LAURA. Delicious!

PETE. Oh? (*Sighs enviously, then in a resigned tone.*) Well—guess I'll go down and eat slop.

MAC. Sure we can't coax you?

LAURA. I'm full up to here! Thanks!

MAC. Sorry. So long.

(MAC, SHORTY *and* PETE *go.*)

FERGUSON (*still on the phone*). Yes. . . . Absolutely right, Doctor. I'll tend to it. (*He hangs up, wrings the phone as if it were* CUNNINGHAM's *neck and grins at* LAURA.)

LAURA. Can I smoke in here?

FERGUSON. Sure.

LAURA (*puts a cigarette in her mouth and waits for a light*). Well?

FERGUSON. What? (*She points to her cigarette.*) Oh! (*He laughs, fishes out a packet of matches and lights her cigarette.*)

LAURA. Darling! You're marvelous this way. I've never seen you so high.

FERGUSON. I've never been so high!

---

[1] Urethritis: inflammation of the urethra.

You know, dear, I love this old place, and yet, my God, I can't wait to get out of here.

LAURA. I was worried last night, after Mr. Spencer spoke to you—you looked so glum. I was afraid you might change your mind.

FERGUSON. Not a chance!

LAURA. Not bothered about that appointment?

FERGUSON. No. That'll be all right— if I get it.

LAURA. You'll get it.

FERGUSON. What do you know about it?

LAURA. I know you, you fish!

FERGUSON (*grins, then suddenly becomes serious*). I wonder if . . . Mr. Spencer spoke to the committee, yet?

LAURA. If he did, it's quick work.

FERGUSON. I hope he hasn't yet.

LAURA. Why?

FERGUSON. Well, I—want to talk to Dr. Hochberg first.

LAURA (*laughs*). Why are you so afraid of Hocky? He won't bite you! Or, do you think by delaying it, you can change my mind—and work with Hocky when we come back?

FERGUSON. No, that's not it.

LAURA. Because if you do, I'm warning you! I'll just drop out of the picture, George. Even if we're married—you'll come home one day, and I just won't be there.

FERGUSON (*takes her in his arms. Tenderly*). Shut up, will you? It's just that I don't want to seem ungrateful.

LAURA. Oh, he'll probably find somebody else.

FERGUSON. Of course he will. (*Smiles, somewhat wistfully.*) There isn't a man I know who wouldn't give a right eye for the chance to work with Dr. Hochberg. You don't realize it, dear, he's an important man. He . . .

LAURA (*impatiently*). The important man, George, is the man who knows how to live. I love Hocky, I think an awful lot of him. But, he's like my father. They have no outside interests at all. They're flat—they're colorless. They're not men —they're caricatures! Oh, don't become like them, George! Don't be an important man and crack up at forty-five. I want our lives together to be full and rich and beautiful! I want it so much.

FERGUSON (*fervently*). Oh, my dear, so

do I . . . And believe me, that's the way it's going to be. (*He looks at her fondly.*) And I once thought I could live without you.

LAURA. What? When?

FERGUSON. Never! (*He kisses her.* NURSE JAMISON *enters, smiles, embarrassed.* FERGUSON *turns around, sees her, grins.*) Yes?

NURSE. Mrs. D'Andrea—the mother of that boy—the automobile accident that came in this morning—she's outside, raising an awful rumpus. Wants to see you.

FERGUSON. Take her to Michaelson!

NURSE. I did! She wants to see you!

FERGUSON. There's nothing I can tell her now.

NURSE. I know, Doctor, but she insists on seeing you.

FERGUSON. What for? We won't know till tomorrow whether he'll live or die. (*The Italian woman tries to enter.* NURSE JAMISON *restrains her.*) All right! Let her in, Jamison! Let her in!

ITALIAN WOMAN. Dottori . . . Dottori. . . . Heeza all right? Yes? Heeza all right?

FERGUSON. I'm sorry! There's nothing I can tell you now.

ITALIAN WOMAN. Heeza gonna . . . live? Dottori?

FERGUSON. Tomorrow! Tomorrow! You come back tomorrow! We'll know then—tomorrow.

ITALIAN WOMAN. Tomorrow?

FERGUSON. Yes.

ITALIAN WOMAN. Mamma mia! Tomorrow! . . . Oh, Dottori! Pleeza! Pleeza! Don't let my boy die! Pleeza! . . .

FERGUSON. I'll do everything I can, mother. And you, try not to worry too much.

NURSE. Come! You'd better . . .

ITALIAN WOMAN (*to* NURSE). Oh, lady, heeza my boy. . . . (*To* LAURA.) Heeza my boy! Heeza besta boy I got. Heeza besta boy in the world. If he's gonna die I'm gonna die, to. . . . (*She prays in Italian.*)

NURSE. Come! Come! (*She leads out Italian woman.*)

(*As they go to the door,* DR. HOCHBERG *enters, passing them. He pauses to watch them go, then turns to* FERGUSON.)

LAURA. Hello, Hocky!

DR. HOCHBERG. Hello, Laura! (*To* FERGUSON.) Who was that?

FERGUSON. Mrs. D'Andrea, mother of

that case . . . automobile accident . . . this morning.

DR. HOCHBERG. Oh, yes, yes, yes, I know—you gave him a shot of tetanus anti-toxin?

FERGUSON. Doctor Michaelson took care of that.

DR. HOCHBERG. He did? Good! (*Glances at his watch.*) Where have you been since twelve o'clock?

FERGUSON. I was gone a little longer than I expected to be.

LAURA. It was awfully important, Hocky.

DR. HOCHBERG. It must have been.

FERGUSON. I left Michaelson in charge to cover me. I only meant to be gone half an hour. . . .

DR. HOCHBERG. In the meantime it was two.

FERGUSON. Sorry, Doctor! This won't happen again.

DR. HOCHBERG. I hope not. (*He relaxes —becomes the old familiar again.*) Watch it! A few more days to go. Your record is clean. Keep it that way! (*There is a pause.* HOCHBERG *looks at* GEORGE, *steadily for a moment.* GEORGE *becomes self-conscious and uneasy. Finally* DR. HOCHBERG *speaks.*) George . . . I heard something this morning—I didn't know quite what to make of it. (*Pause.*) You still want to accomplish something in medicine?

FERGUSON. Certainly.

DR. HOCHBERG. You mean that?

FERGUSON. Yes.

DR. HOCHBERG (*to* LAURA). You love George, don't you, Laura?

LAURA. You know I do.

HOCHBERG. Of course you do and you want to help him—but that's not the way, Laura. Believe me, nobody can help George but himself—and hard work! He cannot buy this; he must earn it. (*To* FERGUSON.) That appointment they talked to you about, George . . . you won't be ready for it. . . .

FERGUSON. After a year with Von Eiselsberg, I thought. . . .

HOCHBERG. One year? (*He shakes his head.*)

FERGUSON. It's not as if I were going to drop my studies. I intend to keep on.

(HOCHBERG *shakes his head.*)

LAURA. I don't see why not!

HOCHBERG (*to* LAURA). My dear child . . .

LAURA. After all, George has worked so terribly hard till now, Hocky. If it's going to make things easier . . .

HOCHBERG. There are no easy roads in medicine.

FERGUSON. I didn't expect it to be easy. I counted on work. Hard work!

DR. HOCHBERG. Ten years of it! Then . . . yes.

LAURA. I can't see how it's going to hurt George.

DR. HOCHBERG. There are a great many things you can't see, Laura.

LAURA. If he goes into practice, we'll have some time for ourselves, Hocky.

DR. HOCHBERG. Time? How? There are only twenty-four hours in a day. He's working with me and if—(*He suddenly stops short as the truth strikes him.*) Or is he—? (*To* FERGUSON.) Are you?

FERGUSON. Dr. Hochberg, I haven't loafed yet, and I don't intend to start now. But Laura and I are young, we love each other. I want little *more* out of life than just my work. I don't think that's asking too much.

DR. HOCHBERG. I see. I see. (*Pause.*) So, you've decided not to come with me next year.

(*There's a long silence. Finally* LAURA *answers apologetically.*)

LAURA. After all, Hocky, we feel that we'll be happier that way—and . . .

DR. HOCHBERG. Of course, Laura. It's George's life and yours. You've a right to decide for yourselves—what you're going to do with it. I didn't mean to meddle. . . .

LAURA. Oh, Hocky, you know we don't feel that way about you.

DR. HOCHBERG. I'm glad you don't. . . . (*Pause. Trying to hide his hurt, he continues.*) How's papa?

LAURA. So-so. . . . He still has an occasional attack.

DR. HOCHBERG. Still smokes, I suppose.

LAURA (*nods*). When I'm not around. He's building again.

DR. HOCHBERG. Well—don't let him work too hard!

LAURA. As if I have anything to say about that! You know dad! He usually has his way.

DR. HOCHBERG (*glances at* FERGUSON, *then nods significantly*). Yes. . . . (DR. HOCHBERG *turns to* GEORGE *and says gently.*) You'd better get into your uniform,

George. We may have to operate shortly. A new case just came in on the surgical service. One of our own nurses. What's her name—? That nice little girl up in pediatrics? Oh yes—Dennin! Barbara Dennin! You remember her? Pediatrics.

FERGUSON (*embarrassed*). Oh, yes, yes. I remember her—an excellent nurse.

DR. HOCHBERG. Poor child! Such a nice little girl, too. . . . Sepsis![1]

FERGUSON (*sympathetically*). Oh! That's awful! She bad?

DR. HOCHBERG. Temperature 105, blood count way up.

FERGUSON. Tch! What was it—ruptured appendix?

DR. HOCHBERG (*shakes his head*). Septic abortion!

FERGUSON. Abortion?

DR. HOCHBERG. Yes. Poor girl—it's a shame. Well, we'll see what we can do. Meet me up there.

(*He starts towards the door.* FERGUSON *stands there, his brow wrinkling.*)

MICHAELSON (*entering*). That D'Andrea fellow is still unconscious. Seems to be something the matter with his lower jaw. . . .

DR. HOCHBERG. What!

MICHAELSON. Protruding—somewhat rigid. Thought it might be tetanus.

DR. HOCHBERG. No! Not so soon! Anyway, you gave him anti-toxin, didn't you?

MICHAELSON. Why—er . . . (*He shoots a quick glance at* FERGUSON.) No!

DR. HOCHBERG. What? (*Angrily.*) Don't you know yet that T.A.T.[2] is routine in this hospital?

MICHAELSON. Yes, sir. . . . But I thought —(*To* FERGUSON.) You didn't tell me. I thought you gave it!

DR. HOCHBERG (*to* FERGUSON). Dr. Ferguson!

FERGUSON. I intended to . . . mention it to him. I guess—I—forgot. . . .

DR. HOCHBERG. Forgot? Is that a thing to forget? You should have given the anti-toxin yourself!

LAURA. It's my fault, Hocky, I dragged him away—we were late.

DR. HOCHBERG. That's no excuse. He's not supposed to leave the house at all! And a very sick house, too. You know that, Dr. Ferguson!

FERGUSON. Yes, sir.

LAURA. Oh, Hocky—it was important! Terribly important! It was a rehearsal of our wedding.

DR. HOCHBERG. A rehearsal? Yes, Laura, that's nice. A rehearsal of your wedding. But, do you realize, upstairs, there is a boy all smashed to bits. There'll be no wedding for him, if he develops tetanus. (*To* FERGUSON.) Dr. Ferguson! Inject that anti-toxin at once!

FERGUSON. Yes, sir! (*He goes.*)

DR. HOCHBERG (*turns to* LAURA, *looks at her a moment, then shakes his head and speaks slowly*). Laura, you deserve to be spanked! (LAURA's *face becomes angry and defiant. Her jaw tightens, but she says nothing.*) Don't you realize what that boy's work means?

LAURA. Of course I do, Hocky.

DR. HOCHBERG (*very softly, almost to himself*). No . . . no, you don't! (*Then, louder.*) Would you like to see perhaps?

LAURA. Yes . . . why not? . . .

DR. HOCHBERG (*glances toward the corridor where* MICHAELSON *is standing, talking to a nurse*). Dr. Michaelson! (MICHAELSON *enters.*) Take Miss Hudson here upstairs, see that she gets a cap and gown, and have her in the operating room in about . . . (*With a sharp jerk of his arm he bares his wrist watch and looks at it.*) twenty minutes! (*Without so much as another glance at* LAURA, *he marches briskly out of the library.*)

BLACK OUT

---

[1] *Sepsis:* septic poisoning—the presence of various pathogenic organisms or their toxins in the blood or tissues.

[2] T.A.T.: Hospital jargon for tetanus-antitoxin. Tetanus, the disease commonly known as "lockjaw," follows the contamination of a wound with dirt, which frequently contains tetanus bacilli. Antitoxin given shortly after such contamination is capable of preventing the disease. In most hospitals this antitoxin is administered routinely to all patients who sustain lacerations in automobile accidents, etc., where there is a chance of dirt gaining entrance into the wound.

SCENE THREE

The end of the corridor. In the corner are the night-desk and a medicine cabinet. To the left of them is a room, numbered 401.

To the right are the elevator doors. A woman and a boy are waiting for the elevator.

A nurse carrying a basin, some towels, etc., enters from the left. MARY *comes out of 401, crosses to the night desk—takes a hypodermic needle and some bottles from the chest.* THE NURSE *with the basin enters 401. The elevator whirs, and the doors open with a clang. An aged couple step out first, then* FERGUSON. *The woman and the boy enter the elevator. The door clangs shut, and the elevator whirs. The aged couple cross to the left and disappear off.* FERGUSON *starts to go into 401, stops, turns to* MARY. MARY, *who has been eyeing him, looks away.*

———

FERGUSON. How is she? (MARY *shakes her head. She is pale, grim, restrained.*) Temperature?

MARY. 106.

FERGUSON. 106?

MARY. Yeah!

FERGUSON. Delirious?

MARY. She was—before—(*Pause, as she lights a small alcohol lamp, and sterilizes a hypodermic needle by boiling it in a spoon held over the flame.*) She kept calling—for you.

FERGUSON (*suddenly rigid*). For me?

MARY. Yeah!

FERGUSON (*stunned*). Oh! (*He turns to enter the room.*)

MARY. Better wait! Doctor Hochberg's in there. She's quiet, now. If you went in she might start talking again.

(THE NURSE *with the basin and towels comes out of the room, sees* FERGUSON, *smiles at him, and as she crosses left, throws a cheery hello to him over her shoulder. He doesn't answer.* NURSE, *puzzled, exits left.*)

FERGUSON. God! I never dreamed this would happen.

MARY. Men don't—usually. . . .

FERGUSON. Why didn't she come to me? Why didn't she tell me? Why did she keep away?

MARY. I guess that was my fault. Long time ago I saw she was falling for you. I told her you were in love with someone else, and engaged to be married—and to keep away from you. I didn't know, then, she already . . .

FERGUSON. I see! I see! That's why she—I thought after that night . . . she'd just realized how crazy we'd both been. . . . Crazy! I thought she at least knew

how to take care of herself. But when this happened . . . she should have told me! You should have told me! Why did you let her do this?

MARY. I didn't know . . . till last night. It was . . . too late, then! She was just a green kid! Didn't realize what it was all about!

FERGUSON. God! I wouldn't have let this happen! I wouldn't have let this happen . . .

MARY. I suppose you'd have helped her—

FERGUSON. Yes! Yes! Yes . . . rather than this. . . .

DR. HOCHBERG (*pokes his head out the door of 401*). Where's that hypo?

MARY. In a second, Doctor!

HOCHBERG (*to* HOCHBERG). Did you tend to D'Andrea?

FERGUSON. Yes, sir! Gave him the T.A.T. He's conscious, now.

HOCHBERG. That business with his jaw—?

FERGUSON (*mechanically*). Slight dislocation. Put it back into place. Bandaged it! No further evidence of internal injury. . . . Although there may be a slight fracture of the tibia or the fibula of the left leg. I'll have some X-ray pictures taken this afternoon!

HOCHBERG. Uh huh! Pain?

FERGUSON. Complained of slight pain . . . general.

HOCHBERG. Did you give him some morphine?

FERGUSON. No, sir. . . .

HOCHBERG. Why not?

FERGUSON. Accident case! Didn't want to mask any possible internal injuries.

HOCHBERG. Ah! Yes. Very good, very good. (*To* MARY.) Er . . . tell me . . . was this Miss Dennin a friend of yours?

MARY. Yeah . . . in a way. I sort a . . . liked her.

HOCHBERG. Well, she's a mighty sick girl. You'd better notify her relatives. . . .

MARY. Ain't none . . . that would be interested.

HOCHBERG. No? Her friends, then? (MARY *shakes her head.*) My . . . my! (*To* FERGUSON.) What a pity! Tch, tch! (*He turns back into the room.*) Oh, Wren, I want you to—(*He disappears into the room.*)

MARY. Nobody! Nobody to turn to!

FERGUSON. Her folks? Her people? At home! Surely there's—

MARY. Yeah!—a stepfather! And to top it all, she's going to be kicked out of here!

FERGUSON. They wouldn't do that!

MARY. Wouldn't they, though? Ask Miss Hackett! And she won't get into any other hospital, either. They'll see to that!

FERGUSON. Poor kid!

MARY. It might be a lucky break for her if she just passed out!

FERGUSON. What are you talking about? She can't die! She's got to pull through! She's got to!

MARY. And then, what? . . . She hasn't got a dime to her name.

(HOCHBERG *and* WREN *come out of the room.*)

DR. HOCHBERG. Tch! Poor girl! . . . Why do they go to butchers like that?

DR. WREN. Well . . . she couldn't have come to us.

DR. HOCHBERG. No . . . that's the shame! Ah, Wren, some of our laws belong to the Dark Ages! Why can't we help the poor and the ignorant? The others will always help themselves—law or no law.[1]

FERGUSON. What are your findings on the case, Doctor?

HOCHBERG. Definite evidence of sepsis. . . . Better order the operating room, at once! A hysterectomy![2]

FERGUSON. Don't you think operation is contra-indicated?

HOCHBERG. Not in this case.

FERGUSON. If we put her in Fowler's position and. . . .

HOCHBERG. You see, the infection is localized in the uterus . . . and it's been my experience in cases like this . . . the only way to save the patient is to remove the focus of infection.[1] Otherwise she hasn't a chance. . . .

FERGUSON. The girl was up in the children's ward. She asked to be put there, because she loves them. It seems a terrible shame to deprive her of the chance of ever having any of her own.

HOCHBERG. It is. It is terrible shame —yes. But, it's future life or her life. We'll save hers . . . if we can. Order the operating-room!

FERGUSON. Yes, sir.

HOCHBERG (*to* MARY). And the man who—was responsible—(FERGUSON *stiffens.*) Does he realize what's happened?

MARY. I suppose so.

HOCHBERG. Mmm, hmm! . . . Who is the man?

MARY. I don't know!

HOCHBERG. Well—if you can find out he should be notified, at least. (*To* FERGUSON.) What are you waiting for? Order the operating-room!

FERGUSON. Yes, sir. (*He goes to the phone.*) Operating-room! . . . Hello! . . . How soon can you have the O.R. ready for a hysterectomy? Dr. Hochberg! Yes. . . . (*Turns to* HOCHBERG.) Ready now.

HOCHBERG. Good! (*To* MARY.) Patient prepared?

MARY. Yes!

HOCHBERG. Fine! Er—give her that hypo!

MARY. Yes, sir! (*Goes into* BARBARA'S *room.*)

HOCHBERG (*to* FERGUSON). Have her brought up at once.

FERGUSON (*into phone*). Patient ready! Send a rolling stretcher down to 401, at once! (*He hangs up.*)

HOCHBERG. Call the staff anaesthetist!

WREN. I'll give the anaesthesia, if you want me to, Hochberg.

HOCHBERG. There's no one I'd rather have.

WREN. General?

HOCHBERG. No—no. I'm afraid to give her ether. . . . We can work better under spinal anaesthesia.[2]

---

[1] Dr. Rongey, former president of the A.M.A., estimates that there are more illegal abortions every year in New York and Chicago than there are children actually born in those cities. Most of these operations are performed on otherwise respectable, law-abiding, married women. Proof enough that here is another social problem that can't be eliminated by legislation. No one wants to encourage the indiscriminate use of this grim practice. However, the lash of the law, instead of correcting the evil, only whips it into dark corners, creating a vicious class of criminal practitioner—bootleg doctors and ignorant midwives who work in dark, back-room apartments. A saner, healthier attitude is that adopted by the Soviet government, which is fostering birth control education, and instituting legal abortion clinics in a spirit best expressed by the motto inscribed over the door of one such clinic: "You are welcome this time, but we hope you will never have to come here again".

[2] Hysterectomy: removal of the uterus.

[1] Those who question this surgical procedure, see: Robinson, M. R.—Revaluation of the prevailing theories and principles of Puerperal Infection —*Am. Jour. of Surg.* 20:131:1933.

[2] Anaesthesia: Ethyl ether and nitrous oxide, both intoxicants, were to the early part of the nine-

WREN. Spinal?—Good!

HOCHBERG. Come! I'd like to take a quick look at that D'Andrea boy.

WREN. I want to prepare my—

HOCHBERG. A second! Come. (*To* FERGUSON.) You can start scrubbing, now. (*Exit* HOCHBERG *and* WREN.)

(FERGUSON *stands there a moment.* MARY *comes out. She puts the alcohol and iodine back on the emergency shelf.*)

MARY. Well, that's—

(*The elevator begins to whine.* MARY *and* FERGUSON *glance over at the indicator dial over the elevator door. It slowly comes round from O.R. to 3, where it stops. The door opens with a clang. An Orderly steps out, backward, pulling a rolling stretcher after him. He turns to* MARY *and grins.*)

ORDERLY. Well, here I am, sweetheart!

MARY (*suddenly bursts into tears*). Who the hell are you calling sweetheart? (*She hurries into the room.*)

ORDERLY (*puzzled*). What the— (*He looks at* FERGUSON, *embarrassed, smiles, and shakes his head in bewilderment. Then he wheels the stretcher into the room.*)

THE ELEVATOR MAN (*who has kept the elevator-door open, calls to* FERGUSON *in a monotone*). Going down?

FERGUSON (*slowly enters the elevator, then, in a low, harsh voice*). Up! Operating-room! (*The door clangs shut, the elevator whines siren-like, rising to a crescendo, as the indicator dial goes up.*

BLACK OUT

---

teenth century what rye, scotch and gin are to the twentieth. No hectic party was complete without an "ether frolic." An American dentist, noticing the numbness and insensitivity to pain produced by "ether jag," applied the principle to the extraction of teeth. In 1846 he successfully demonstrated the simplicity and safety of ether in this type of minor operation. Before the year was up, ether was being used for many kinds of operation. "Shock" was now minimized, and speed became less important than good, neat, complete surgery. Then, for superficial operations, Halsted and Cushing, American surgeons, developed anaesthesia of a partial area by injecting solutions of cocaine into the tissue around that area. Another surgeon, J. L. Corning, introduced "spinal anaesthesia" by injecting cocaine derivatives into the spinal canal. This process gives the patient complete insensitivity to pain below the site of injection, without rendering him unconscious. The technique of spinal anaesthesia has been developed to a high degree and is now used by many hospitals in preference to "general anaesthesia".

SCENE FOUR

The Operating-Room. A feeling of sharp, white gleaming cleanliness! Back center, the huge, hanging, kettle-drum lamp, with its hundreds of reflecting mirrors, throws a brilliant, shadowless light on the chromium operating table. All the nooks and corners of the room are rounded off to facilitate cleansing, and to prevent the accumulation of dust.

To the right is the sterilizing room with its polished nickel autoclaves, bubbling and steaming.

To the left is a long north skylight, double paned.

There is one sterile nurse, wearing cap and gown, mask and long rubber gloves; there are two unsterile nurses, similarly clothed but wearing no gloves. They move to and fro like so many pistons, efficiently, quickly, quietly—ghost-like automata.

In the right-hand corner nearest us, stands a row of half a dozen sinks, the faucets in them turned on and off by means of knee-stirrups attached underneath. Above, a shelf holds cans of sterile brushes, pans of liquid soap, and eight-minute glasses—one to each sink. Well apart from these sinks, and to the right, are two basins in a white-enamel stand; one contains blue bichloride, the other alcohol. Beyond them again stands a foot-pedal gown drum, scarred from its purifying baths of steam.

To the left is a long glove table, on which are the gloves wrapped in canvas "books," sterile powder can, and towels covered by a sterile sheet.

WREN, *in cap and mask, is dipping his hands in the bichloride pan;* PETE, *at the washbasin, is cleaning his nails with an orange-stick, and* MICHAELSON *is scrubbing his hands with long, easy rhythmic strokes of the brush. They are chatting quietly.*

The sterile nurse goes to the glove table and folds over the sheet, uncovering the glove books, etc.

A nurse comes from the sterilizing-room, carrying a steaming tray of instruments to the instrument table at the foot of the operating-table. The sterile nurse returns to the instrument table and there is a clink of instruments as she arranges them.

WREN *holds up his hands so that the bichloride rolls down the forearm and off the elbow; he repeats this once more in the bichloride, and twice in the alcohol pan, then walks away, holding his dripping hands high and away from him.*

A sterile nurse gives him a sterile towel. He dries his hands, using the separate sides and ends of the towel for each hand, then he tosses the towel to the floor, and crosses to the glove table.

An unsterile nurse quickly crosses, picks up the towel, and takes it away. WREN *powders his hands, opens a glove book, gingerly plucks out a glove, handling it by the cuff, careful not to touch the outside of the glove, as that might still soil it (since the hands themselves can never be completely sterilized) and slips it on. The second glove he slips on, careful not to touch his wrist with his already gloved hand. He then snaps the gloves over the cuffs of his jacket, wraps a sterile towel about his hands and walks over to the operating table.*

PETE *finishes scrubbing, goes to the bichloride basin, and dips his hands, using the same technique as* WREN. *When he is through with the alcohol, however, he turns to the gown "drum." The sterile nurse crosses to the drum, steps on the pedal which raises the lid, and deftly extracts a folded gown, without touching the drum itself. She releases her foot, and the lid clunks back. She hands the folded gown to him; he takes a corner of it, unrolls it, and slips into it. An unsterile nurse comes up behind, careful not to touch him, and ties the gown for him.*[1]

[1] Behind the fascinating ritual of this "sterile" or "aseptic" technique, which has the beat and the rhythm of some mechanical dance composition, lies the whole story of modern surgery and, indeed, the modern hospital.

Less than eighty years ago, hospitals were festering death-houses. It was far safer to be operated on in a private home than in a hospital, where the slightest surgical cases almost inevitably developed infection. So high was the fatality that surgeons began to discuss seriously the demolition of all hospitals.

Medicine pondered, "Where did infection spring from; and, how to combat it?" Dr. Oliver Wendell Holmes, appalled at the devastating mortality in childbirth, was one of the first to suggest that the physician himself might be the carrier of infection. Semmelweis, a Hungarian doctor, cleaned up his assistants' hands, and lo!— he transformed a Viennese delivery ward from a chamber of almost certain death to one of birth and hope. Then the Frenchman, Pasteur, looked through a microscope, and the whole course of medicine was changed. He saw the vast, invisible armies of microbes that ride the dust of the air, and realized they were the cause of decay and fermentation. But the great name in this story is that of Lister, the British surgeon, who took the torch from Pasteur and led surgery out of darkness into light. Realizing that infection of a wound was nothing more than a fermentation caused by Pasteur's tiny creatures, he sought about for a means of destroying these agents of destruction.

The whole effect is that of a smooth, well-oiled machine, a routine so studied that the people in the operating room can afford to be casual—as they are.

One of the unsterile nurses enters with LAURA, *whom she has just helped into a cap and gown.*

———

NURSE. All right?

LAURA. Yes.

MICHAELSON (*to* LAURA). Well, you're all set, now!

LAURA (*smiles nervously*). Yes—thanks!

MICHAELSON. Not at all! A pleasure!

LAURA (*doubtfully*). Oh! The pleasure's all mine!

MICHAELSON (*laughs*). I'll bet it is.

LAURA. This gown seems awfully wrinkled.

NURSE. They're never pressed. That would unsterilize them.

LAURA. Oh! I see. (*Enter* DR. HOCHBERG *and* FERGUSON *in operating pajamas. They are putting on their masks.*) Hello!

HOCHBERG. Oh, hello! (*To* FERGUSON.) We have a guest! (*He turns over the eight-minute glass and begins to scrub up.*)

FERGUSON (*stands stock-still for a moment*). Laura! What . . .

LAURA. Surprise! (*She starts to go toward* GEORGE.)

HOCHBERG (*warning her back with a quick gesture*). Uh, uh! (*She stops.*) Stand over there—in the corner! Don't come near us! We're getting clean! You're full of contamination.

LAURA. Oh—am I?

(FERGUSON *begins to scrub up.*)

HOCHBERG. Yes. (*A long pause while they scrub.* HOCHBERG, *still scrubbing, turns to* LAURA.) Well—how do you feel?

LAURA (*trying to bluff off her nervousness*). Great!

HOCHBERG. Mm, hm!

LAURA. How do I look? (*She holds out her gown at both sides.*)

HOCHBERG. Very becoming!

He found a powerful weapon in carbolic acid. This was the beginning of "antisepsis" and a new epoch in surgery.

Gradually the "antiseptic" method was replaced by another which grew out of it. A technique evolved whereby instruments, dressings, gowns, gloves, etc., all steam-sterilized, precluded the necessity for powerful antiseptics, which often destroy human tissue as well as the enemy germs. No living bacteria are allowed near the wound. This gentler, if more elaborate, technique is the "sterile" or "aseptic" one in use today.

LAURA. Think so, George?

FERGUSON. Yes—very!

HOCHBERG. You can look around, but keep out of the way! Don't touch anything! Put your hands behind your back! (*A long silence, broken only by the rasping sound of scrubbing brushes.* LAURA *stares, fascinated.*)

HOCHBERG. Oh, nurse. (*A nurse comes over.*) See that Miss Hudson here gets a mask before she goes in. Find a stool for her—and put it near the operating table! I don't want her to miss anything!

LAURA (*wryly*). Thanks, Hocky!

HOCHBERG. Don't mention it, Laura!

(DR. HOCHBERG *finishes scrubbing, and goes through the same routine as the others. When he gets his gown he disappears to a corner of the operating-room, hidden by the basins.* FERGUSON, *also, goes through the routine of gown and gloves, etc.*)

WREN. Orderly! Orderly!

ORDERLY (*enters from anaesthesia-room*). Yes, sir?

WREN. Bring the patient in!

(BARBARA *is wheeled in by the orderly. As she enters,* WREN *bends over to look at her.* FERGUSON *comes over.*)

FERGUSON. How is she, Doctor?

BARBARA. George!

FERGUSON. Yes?

BARBARA. What are they going to do to me?

FERGUSON. There's nothing to be afraid of, Barbara!

BARBARA. You won't let them hurt me?

FERGUSON. No, of course not.

BARBARA. Will you be there? George, darling, please be there!

FERGUSON. I'll be there.

BARBARA. Thanks, dear. . . . I loved you . . . I don't care . . . (*Her head goes back.*)

WREN (*looks at* FERGUSON, *who is rigid. Then at* LAURA, *who is equally rigid. He turns to* ORDERLY *and speaks sharply*). Come on! Come on!

(*The* ORDERLY *wheels* BARBARA *to the operating table.* WREN *follows. The patient is transferred to the operating table.*)

LAURA. What was that all about?

FERGUSON. Laura, I'm sorry as hell—I wish I . . .

LAURA. George! Is it—? (*She clutches his arm.*)

FERGUSON (*recoiling from her touch*). Don't! You mustn't! Stand away! Over there! You've unsterilized the gown! (*He tears off his gown and gloves, throws them on the floor, and calls into the sterilizing-room.*) Nurse! Nurse! Sterile gown, gloves, towels! Quick! (*He turns to* LAURA, *explains apologetically.*) We've got to be very careful. . . . You know . . . germs . . .

(*A nurse enters, picks up the gown and gloves. He dips his hands into the bichloride pan, and then the alcohol pan. A sterile nurse brings him a sterile gown, he unfolds it and slides into it. And the sterile nurse, behind him, ties it. In the meantime another nurse returns with a sterile towel. He dries his hands, and throws the towel on the floor. The unsterile nurse picks it up and takes it away. The sterile nurse powders his hands, brings him a sterile glove book and opens it. He plucks out a glove, and puts it on, the nurse helping him, in approved aseptic technique, by thrusting her fingers under the cuff, and pushing home the glove. In the meantime the patient, concealed by the people around her, has been anaesthetized, and is being draped. All the time* LAURA *has been staring at* FERGUSON. FERGUSON, *working the fingers of the gloves, looks at* LAURA. *Exit the orderly with the rolling stretcher.*)

LAURA. Did you . . . did you have an affair with that girl—or what?

FERGUSON (*almost inaudibly*). Yes . . .

LAURA. Oh! (*A bitter little laugh.*) That's a funny one!

DR. HOCHBERG (*on a footstool, bends over the patient—calls*). Dr. Ferguson! (*The call is taken up by a number of voices. A nurse crosses to* FERGUSON.)

NURSE. Dr. Ferguson! The patient is draped and ready!

FERGUSON. All right! I'm coming! (*He goes to the operating table.*)

NURSE (*to* LAURA). If you want to watch—you'd better go over. I'll get a stool for you—mask!

LAURA. No, thanks . . . I've had enough . . .! I've had enough!

2ND NURSE (*enters*). Here! Here! Get busy! (*Notices* LAURA.) You! What's the matter? You look so . . . Feel ill, dear? (*To* 1ST NURSE.) Take her out! Near a window! Give her some water!

LAURA. No . . .! No . . .! I'm . . . I'm fine . . .! Thanks! (*She tears off the tight cap, begins to sob, and exits.*

(*The nurses look at each other and grin.*)

1ST NURSE. Med-student?

2ND NURSE. Of course! First time! What else?

1ST NURSE. She's got a long way to go,

yet! (*They laugh.*)

(NURSE *and* DOCTORS *about the table turn and say, "Sh! Sh!"* THE NURSES *immediately hush.*)

HOCHBERG. Ready, Dr. Wren?

WREN. All set!

HOCHBERG. Ready, Dr. Ferguson?

FERGUSON. Ready!

HOCHBERG (*reaching out his hand, without looking up*). Scalpel!

(*The operating nurse hands over the scalpel, cutting a gleaming arc through the air, then she clumps it into* DR. HOCHBERG's *hand. He bends over the patient. There is a sudden burst of activity and gleam of clamps about the table.*

The unsterile nurses, hands behind their backs, stand on tiptoes, and crane their necks to see over the shoulders of the assistant.

All lights dim down, except the operating light, which bathes the tableau in a fierce, merciless, white brilliance.)

CURTAIN

ACT THREE

SCENE ONE

FERGUSON's *room. The next morning. The The shade is drawn, the room dark, except for the small lamp at the bed.* FERGUSON *is sitting on the bed, his head in his hands. His clothes are wrinkled—he hasn't changed them all night. His hair is mussed, his eyes red.*

A knock at the door.

FERGUSON *doesn't stir. The knock is repeated.* FERGUSON *still remains motionless. The door slowly opens.* HOCHBERG *enters.*

––––––––––

HOCHBERG. Good morning, George.

FERGUSON. Oh. Good morning. (HOCHBERG *pulls up the shade. A great burst of sunlight streams in, blinding* GEORGE. *He turns his face away, rubs his eyes.*) What time? (*He picks up the clock.*) Oh—I didn't know it was so late.

HOCHBERG. Lovely out, isn't it?

FERGUSON. Yes. . . . (*He rises wearily, goes to the washbasin, washes himself, and combs his hair.*)

HOCHBERG (*examining a brain in a jar on the desk*). Hm. . . . That's a fine specimen. Ah . . . yes . . . you've been doing some study on brain surgery?

FERGUSON. Yes. . . .

HOCHBERG. Fascinating work. Miss Dennin's temperature is down this morning. . . .

FERGUSON. I know.

HOCHBERG. The nurse tells me you watched the case all last night. That's very nice. . . . Hm. Excellent book—this. You should read all of Cushing's reports. How is er—D'Andrea?

FERGUSON. Examined those pictures. He did have a fracture of the tibia of the left leg. No further evidence of internal injury. He'll be all right, I guess.

HOCHBERG. Good. Good. He's a lucky boy. He looked badly hurt.

FERGUSON. Dr. Hochberg. There's something I've got to tell you—

HOCHBERG (*quickly*). I know. Wren told me. (*Pause.* HOCHBERG *looks at the specimen.*) Great field—brain surgery—for a young man.

FERGUSON. You must think it was pretty low of me.

HOCHBERG. George . . . George!

FERGUSON. I didn't know anything about it till yesterday. I wouldn't have let her . . . I swear I wouldn't have . . .

HOCHBERG. It was a bad job . . .

FERGUSON. Oh, that poor kid. God, I ought to be shot.

HOCHBERG. Did you force her to have an affair with you, or did she come to you of her own free will? Then why do you blame yourself so?

FERGUSON. That has nothing to do with it.

HOCHBERG. That has everything to do with it!

FERGUSON. Dr. Hochberg, you don't know what she's up against.

HOCHBERG. I know.

FERGUSON. It's not as if she were just a tramp. . . . She's a fine, sensitive girl! God. What a mess I've gotten her into! She can't bear any children. Thrown out of the hospital—nowheres to go—no one to turn to. What's she going to do?

HOCHBERG. Don't worry. We'll find something for her.

FERGUSON. Just giving her a job—isn't going to help her very much. There's only one decent thing . . . I'm going to . . . marry her . . . if she'll have me.

HOCHBERG. George! Stop talking like an idiot! Pull yourself together! What about Laura?

FERGUSON. She's through with me, Dr. Hochberg.

HOCHBERG. She knows?

FERGUSON. Yes. I kept phoning her all day yesterday—all last night. She wouldn't come to the phone . . . wouldn't even talk to me, Dr. Hochberg.

HOCHBERG. Hm . . . that's too bad. Yet you know, George, in a way—that's not the worst that could have happened to you. . . .

FERGUSON. No! Don't say that!

HOCHBERG. Well, now there's work, my boy. Remember that's the master word—work.

FERGUSON. I'm going to marry that girl.

HOCHBERG. What for?

FERGUSON. I have to take care of her, don't I?

HOCHBERG. I see. You've saved some money then?

FERGUSON. Out of what?

HOCHBERG. Then how are you going to help her? How are you going to take care of her?

FERGUSON. I'm going into practice . . .

HOCHBERG. Mid-Victorian idealism won't solve this problem, George. . . .

FERGUSON. That girl is human, isn't she? She needs me.

HOCHBERG. If you think you can provide for both of you by first starting practice—then you just don't know. . . .

FERGUSON. I'll manage somehow. I'm not afraid of that.

HOCHBERG. Remember Levine? I got a letter from him yesterday. Colorado. He's trying to build up a practice. . . . (The loud-speaker in the corridor starts calling DR. HOCHBERG.) They're starving, George. He begs me to lend him twenty dollars.

FERGUSON. I don't see what that has to do with me.

HOCHBERG. You didn't know him six years ago. He wouldn't let me help him, then. He was sure! So confident! And, better equipped for practice than you are.

FERGUSON. Possibly!

HOCHBERG. I won't answer for Levine . . . at least he loved Katherine. But you don't love this girl. It was an accident and for that you want to ruin yourself—the rest of your life—destroy your ambition, your ideals—fill yourself with bitterness, live day and night with a woman who will grow to despise you. . . .

FERGUSON. Dr. Hochberg. Please—it's no use. I've thought of all that! It doesn't make any difference. There's only one decent thing to do—and I'm going to do it.

HOCHBERG (picks up the phone). Yes? . . . Dr. Hochberg. . . . Yes, hello. . . . That's all right. Wait for me down in the—no . . . come up here to 106. Yes. Is the man there at the desk? Yes. Hello, Arthur. Please ask one of the orderlies to show this young lady up to 106. Yes, thank you.

FERGUSON. Is that Laura?

HOCHBERG. Yes.

FERGUSON. I can't see her now! I can't talk to her.

HOCHBERG. Don't be a child! You've got to see her and have this out. (Pause.)

FERGUSON. Dr. Hochberg, I want you to know that . . . I appreciate all you've done for me.

HOCHBERG. What have I done?

FERGUSON. I mean yesterday. I . . . I must have seemed very ungrateful. But it's just because there are so many other things that I thought I wanted.

HOCHBERG. I know. It's our instinct to live, to enjoy ourselves. All of us.

FERGUSON. I love Laura so much. She's so full of life and fun, and all the things I've missed for so many years. I just didn't have the guts to give them up. I kidded myself that I could have that, and still go on. And last night, I realized I kidded myself out of the most important thing that ever happened to me, a chance to work with you. . . .

HOCHBERG. Do you still want to? You can, if you do.

FERGUSON. No—not now.

HOCHBERG. But why? If you realize, now, what you really want . . .

FERGUSON. I'm going into practice, I told you. . . .

HOCHBERG. Now, George, calm down. Give yourself a chance to think it over.

FERGUSON. I've thought it over.

HOCHBERG. I warn you, George. You'll be sorry.

FERGUSON. I can't just ignore this!

HOCHBERG. In that case, you're through—you're finished—you're—

FERGUSON. All right! Then I am. Why not? What good's a profession that can't give you bread and butter after you've sweated out ten years of your life on it? And if I can't make a go of practice, I'll find a job at something else—and to hell with medicine! I won't starve. I'll always make a living. . . .

(LAURA *appears in the doorway accompanied by an orderly.*)

ORDERLY. Right here, Miss.

FERGUSON. Good morning, Laura.

(LAURA *deliberately ignoring* GEORGE, *looking only at* HOCHBERG, *clipping every word*). Hello, Hocky. . . . Did you want me up here?

HOCHBERG. Yes. Come in, Laura.

LAURA. Sorry to call you so early, but . . .

HOCHBERG. It isn't early for me, Laura. . . . (*She's still standing in the doorway, tense and hard. Impatiently.*) Come in, come in. . . . (*She wavers a moment, then enters.*) Sit down.

LAURA. No. I'm in a hurry, Hocky. I just wanted to see you for a minute . . . alone.

HOCHBERG. Sit down, Laura.

LAURA. I suppose you wondered why I disappeared, yesterday.

HOCHBERG. No . . . I heard all about it. . . .

LAURA. Oh, you did? A laugh, isn't it?

HOCHBERG. Not particularly.

LAURA. Well, you spanked me all right.

HOCHBERG. Harder than I meant, Laura. . . . Forgive me.

LAURA. Oh, that's all right. Better now than later, Hocky.

HOCHBERG. Will you please sit down, Laura? (LAURA, *suddenly limp, sits down.* HOCHBERG, *scrutinizing her face closely.*) Sleep much last night?

LAURA. Sure. Why not? (*She puts a cigarette into her mouth, searches for a match.* GEORGE'S *hand automatically goes to his pocket, to find a match for her.*) Light, Hocky? (HOCHBERG *gives her a light. She exhales a huge puff of smoke.*) I'm washed up with the whole business, Hocky.

HOCHBERG. Yes, of course you are . . . of course.

FERGUSON. I'm sorry you feel so bitter about it, Laura. . . .

LAURA. How did you expect me to feel?

FERGUSON. I don't blame you. I . . .

LAURA. Thanks. That's sweet of you.

HOCHBERG. Neither do I blame him, Laura.

LAURA. There's no excuse for a thing like that—you know it, Hocky. None at all. . . .

HOCHBERG. I know nothing—except

the human body, a little. And I haven't met the wise man or woman, Laura, whom impulse couldn't make a fool of. . . .

LAURA. If you want to reason that way, there isn't anything you couldn't justify.

HOCHBERG. I'm not trying to, Laura. It's so far beyond that. . . . (FERGUSON *starts for the door.*) Where are you going?

FERGUSON. Upstairs.

HOCHBERG. Wait, George! Wait a minute!

FERGUSON. There's nothing more to be said, Dr. Hochberg. Laura's perfectly right.

LAURA (*rises*). Don't leave on my account. I've got to go now, anyway. I've got to pack. I'm sailing on the Olympic, tonight. Going to get as far away from all this as I can. (*She laughs.*) Humph! I was making plans. I was worried all the time. . . . God! What a fool I was. . . .

HOCHBERG. Do you think he's having such an easy time of it?

LAURA. Oh, he'll take care of himself.

HOCHBERG. Maybe you'd better go home now, Laura.

LAURA. I think it was a pretty rotten trick.

HOCHBERG. Stop it! Laura, stop it!

LAURA. He had no time for me—he was too busy for me—but he did find time to . . . That's what hurts, Hocky! Hurts like the devil!

HOCHBERG. Don't you think I know how you feel, Laura?

(*The loud-speaker is calling* DR. HOCHBERG.)

LAURA. You think I still care? Well, I don't!

HOCHBERG. That's fine! Then it doesn't make any difference to you that right now he's throwing his life away. (*Goes to the phone, picks it up, speaks into it.*) Yes? Dr. Hochberg! (*To* LAURA.) He's going to marry her, Laura.

LAURA. No?

FERGUSON. Dr. Hochberg! Please!

HOCHBERG. Yes. And go into practice, and starve and give up his studies and maybe get out of medicine altogether. The thing he's meant for! And worked so hard for. (*Into the phone, suddenly tense.*) Yes! What! Prepare a hypo of caffeine, and adrenalin, long needle! At once! (*He hangs up and hurries to the door.*)

FERGUSON. Do you want me—?

HOCHBERG. No . . . no . . . no. . . . You

stay here! (*He hurries out.* LAURA *stands there a moment looking at* GEORGE, *then starts to go.*)

FERGUSON. Laura!

LAURA. What?

FERGUSON. I don't want you to go away feeling like this. . . .

LAURA. What difference does it make how I feel?

FERGUSON. A great deal . . . to me.

LAURA (*pause*). You love her, don't you?

FERGUSON. I love you, Laura.

LAURA (*laughs bitterly*). Yes, I'm sure you do.

FERGUSON (*grasps both of* LAURA'S *arms tightly*). I don't care whether you believe it or not, Laura, it just happens that I do.

LAURA. Let go—let go my arm! You're . . .

FERGUSON. Sorry! (*He turns from her and sinks down despondently on the bed.*)

LAURA (*after a pause*). Then how? I don't quite understand . . . I didn't sleep a wink last night, George. I was trying to figure this out. But it doesn't make sense . . . except that . . . I don't know. If you cared for me how could you do that?

FERGUSON. I don't know myself, Laura. Everything had gone wrong that day. Six long operations. I had a battle with Cunningham, I lost a patient. . . . Things sort of kept piling up till I thought I'd bust . . . this kid came to my room for some notes . . . she was sympathetic and lonely herself, and . . . well. . . . But after that I didn't see her around, and . . . I just forgot about it. You'd think she'd come to me when this happened. But, she didn't. I know I should have looked her up. I know I was pretty small and rotten. I thought . . . I thought it didn't mean very much to her. But it did, Laura! Now she's up against it, and. . .

LAURA. If we meant anything at all to each other, you'd have come to me. I don't give a damn about ceremony! But the point is you didn't really care about me, George. Not for a minute.

FERGUSON. I wanted you more than anything else in the world that night, Laura. But we'd quarreled and—you wouldn't even go out with me.

LAURA. It was that night?

FERGUSON. Yes.

LAURA. Oh!

FERGUSON. I didn't want to give up Hocky . . . and I didn't want to give you up . . . and I was fighting you . . . and. . .

LAURA. Through her?

FERGUSON. Yes. . . .

LAURA (*laughs bitterly*). And you say you loved me!

FERGUSON. If I hadn't, I'd have called quits then and there, Laura. I'd have gone to Vienna and worked my way through. That's what I was planning to do . . . before I met you. Alone in Vienna I'd really accomplish something. . . .

LAURA. Well, why don't you go on? Go on and do it, now. If it's so important to you. I won't be around to distract you! Go on! . . . But you're not, you see. You're going to marry a girl you say you don't care for. You're going to let a casual incident rob you of all the things you say are important.

FERGUSON. It's not a casual incident, any more, Laura.

LAURA. All right, make your beautiful gestures. Marry her!

FERGUSON. I'm going to.

LAURA. Go ahead! And inside of a year you'll be hating the sight of each other.

FERGUSON. That's a chance I'll have to take.

LAURA. You think you're being brave and strong, I suppose. But you're not. You're a coward. You're doing it because it's the easiest way out. Because you're afraid people'll say things about you. You have no backbone.

FERGUSON. Yes, Laura. You're right. I had no backbone when I let myself be talked out of a chance to work with Hocky. And maybe to do something fine some day. But right now I have no choice. I'm not doing this because I give a good God damn what anybody says or thinks; I'm doing it because that girl's life is smashed, and I'm responsible, and I want to try and help her pick up the pieces and put them together again. (*He stops short.* LAURA *is weeping quietly.*) Oh, Laura . . .! Don't!

LAURA. I knew how you felt about Hocky and I shouldn't have . . . insisted. I've been selfish, but it was only because I loved you so much. And . . . I still do. That's the way I am, George. I can't help it. . .

(*Enter* HOCHBERG, *slowly, his face drawn and grave, something tragic written on it. He looks at* FERGUSON.)

FERGUSON (*sensing* HOCHBERG's *look*). What is it, Doctor?

HOCHBERG. Miss Dennin died.

FERGUSON (*dazed*). What . . . ?

LAURA. Oh, God!

HOCHBERG. A few minutes ago.

(FERGUSON *looks blankly at* DR. HOCHBERG, *glances, as if for corroboration, at* LAURA, *and suddenly starts for the door.* HOCHBERG *catches his arm and holds it tightly.*)

HOCHBERG (*softly*). There's nothing you can do, George. Embolism! Went into collapse! Died instantly.

FERGUSON (*almost inaudibly*). Oh! (*He sinks down on the bed, his back to them.*)

HOCHBERG. George!

LAURA. Darling!

FERGUSON. Only a few hours ago . . . she was pleading with me for a chance to live. . . . She was so young. She didn't want to die. . . .

LAURA. Stop it, George! Stop torturing yourself. Please! These things happen. It might have happened to anybody.

FERGUSON. Couldn't you do anything, Dr. Hochberg?

HOCHBERG. I tried . . . everything. Caffein intravenously. Adrenalin directly into the heart. Useless! That little blood-clot in the lung . . . and we're helpless. Forty years I've spent in medicine . . . and I couldn't help her.

FERGUSON. Then what's the use? What good is it all? Why go on? It takes everything from you and when you need it most it leaves you helpless. We don't know anything. . . . We're only guessing.

HOCHBERG. We've been doing a little work on embolism . . . getting some results. It's slow, though . . . slow. Maybe, someday, George. . .

FERGUSON. Someday . . . ?

HOCHBERG. There isn't a man in medicine who hasn't said what you've said and meant it for a minute—all of us, George. And you're right. We are groping. We are guessing. But, at least our guesses today are closer than they were twenty years ago. And twenty years from now, they'll be still closer. That's what we're here for. Mm . . . there's so much to be done. And so little time in which to do it . . . that one life is never long enough. . . . (*He sighs.*) It's not easy for any of us. But in the end our reward is something richer than simply living. Maybe it's a kind of success that the world out there can't measure . . . maybe it's a kind of glory, George. (*Pause.*) Yes, question as much as we will—when the test comes we know—don't we, George?

FERGUSON. Yes. . . .

HOCHBERG (*goes slowly to the door, pauses there*). Er . . . we'll reduce that fracture at ten. Schedule the appendix at three . . . the gastric-ulcer immediately afterwards.

FERGUSON. Yes, sir.

(HOCHBERG *goes.* LAURA *turns to* FERGUSON.)

LAURA. Oh, darling! I'm so sorry! (*Pause.*) George, let's get away from here. Let's go some place where we can talk this thing over quietly and sanely.

FERGUSON. No, Laura. This is where I belong!

LAURA. Yes. . . . (*Pause.*)

FERGUSON. You see. . .

LAURA. I understand. . . . (*Pause.*) Well . . . when you come back from Vienna, if Hocky'll let you off for a night give me a ring! I'll be around. And, maybe someday we'll get together, anyway.

(*The loud-speaker is heard calling:* Dr. Ferguson!)

LAURA (*smiles wryly*). They're calling you.

FERGUSON. Yes.

LAURA. Work hard.

FERGUSON. So long, Laura. (LAURA *tears herself away, and hurries out.* FERGUSON *stares after her till she disappears. The loud-speaker calls him back. He goes to the phone, slowly, a bit stunned. He picks up the phone.*) Yes? Dr. Ferguson! . . . Who? . . . Oh, Mrs. D'Andrea? Sure! Your boy's all right! Yes. Now, you mustn't cry, mother! You mustn't! He's all right! (*With his free hand he is brushing the tears from his own eyes and nose, for he is beginning to weep himself. But you could never tell it by his voice, which is strong with professional reassurance.*) We'll fix his leg this morning, and he'll be home in a week. Yes . . . he's going to live . . . don't cry!

(*He is still reassuring her as the curtain descends.*)

CURTAIN

YELLOW JACK*

Sidney Howard, in collaboration with Paul de Kruif

Yellow Jack was first produced by Guthrie McClintic at the Martin Beck Theatre, New York City, on March 6, 1934. It was staged by Guthrie McClintic, with settings by Jo Mielziner. The cast was as follows:

STACKPOOLE . . . . Geoffrey Kerr	ORDERLIES . . . . . . { Clyde Walters / Frank Stringfellow
AN OFFICIAL OF THE KENYA COLONY GOVERNMENT . . . . Colin Hunter	WALTER REED . . . . John Miltern
A MAJOR OF THE ROYAL AIR FORCE . . . . Francis Compton	JAMES CARROLL . . . . . Barton MacLane
LABORATORY ASSIST- . . . { Bernard Jukes / Lloyd Gough	ARISTIDES AGRAMONTE . . . . Eduard Ciannelli
ANTS	JESSIE W. LAZEAR . . . . . . Robert Keith
KIM . . . . Kim	COLONEL TORY . . . . Richie Ling
HARKNESS . . . . Robert Shayne	WILLIAM CRAWFORD GORGAS . . . . George Nash
KRAEMER . . . . Wylie Adams	MAJOR CARTWRIGHT . . . Robert Shayne
ADRIAN STOKES . . . . Charles Gerard	ROGER P. AMES . . . . Harold Moffat
O'HARA . . . . James Stewart	DR. CARLOS FINLAY . . . . Whitford Kane
CHAMBANG . . . . Jack Carr	WILLIAM H. DEAN . . . . Millard Mitchell
MC CLELLAND . . . . Edward Acuff	AN ARMY CHAPLAIN . . . . . Lloyd Gough
BUSCH . . . . Samuel Levene	A COMMISSARY SER-
BRINKERHOF . . . . . Myron McCormick	GEANT . . . . Wylie Adams
MISS BLAKE . . . . Katherine Wilson	

*An historical play which deals with events of recent times may well give offense to those characters in the play who are still alive. It is out of consideration for the survivors, therefore, that the authors have invented names for the characters still living.

But since the play is in part concerned with the deeds of four American soldiers whose heroism should not go unrecorded, the true names of these soldiers are here given. They are: John J. Moran, John Kissenger, Warren Gladsden Jernegan, and Levi E. Folk.

Yellow Jack celebrates what these men did without attempting to portray them as they were.

THE SETTING:

This play is written to be produced without conventional scenery upon a modern approximation of the Elizabethan stage. To facilitate the reader's understanding of the text, a description follows of the sculptural and noble setting designed by Jo Mielziner for the play's original production at the Martin Beck Theatre in New York.

The stage is divided into two levels, the upper lifted five feet above the floor of the stage and approached from below by twin flights of steps. These steps curve on either side of the central element of the upper level, a round bay which remains Reed's laboratory throughout the play. When the action does not utilize the laboratory, the bare equipment of which is arranged upon this central element, concealment is furnished by a semicircular wooden screen of lattice design to suggest a protection against the glare of tropic sunlight. This screen, of six leaves, divides in the center and rolls back on a circular track, so that when it is opened for the scenes in the laboratory, it serves the actors as background. Properties or equipment for other laboratories, hospital beds, tents, and other essentials, are mounted on low platforms which are pushed on at stage level through curtained arches to either side. A simple, flat arch masks the sky backdrop. The whole of the setting, including arch and floor, is covered with an unpainted khaki tan material.

The production uses nothing of realism beyond the properties which are absolutely essential to the action. Changes of locale are indicated only by alteration in the lighting. The action being continuous, the play flows in a constantly shifting rhythm of light.

NOTE ON THE TEXT:

The stage directions throughout the text refer to the original New York production. But the directors should realize that it has been possible to stage the play in other ways. A production staged by Donald R. Tavers at the Lawrenceville School (Lawrenceville, New Jersey) yielded suggestions included in the Dramatists Play Service acting edition (Dramatists Play Service, Inc., 14 East 38th Street, New York 16, N.Y.) One suggestion concerns the use of two levels; the second should be 5½ feet high and about 12 feet deep. Steps in the center of the stage and a cyclorama are recommended. A screen in front of the laboratory is not indispensable; it should be omitted unless it can be solidly built and placed on rollers, since changes in the set would have to be made in the dark. It would be well, too, to "skeletonize" the tents and place both the tents and the cots in them on rollers.

Characters whose names appear in italics are inventions of the author to serve as substitutes for living participants in this story.

London: January, 1929

Stackpoole.
A Major of the Royal Air Force.
An Official of the Kenya Colony Government.
Two Laboratory Assistants.

West Africa: June, 1927

ADRIAN STOKES, of Guy's Hospital, London, attached to the West African Yellow Fever Commission, the Rockefeller Foundation.
Harkness, of the Rockefeller Commission.
Kraemer, of the same.
Chambang.

Cuba: Summer and Fall of 1900

WALTER REED, Major, M.C., U.S.A.
O'Hara ⎫
Brinkerhof ⎪   Privates,
McClelland ⎬   M.C., U.S.A.
Busch ⎭

Miss Blake, special nurse in charge of the Yellow Fever Ward.
Two Orderlies.

ARISTIDES AGRAMONTE	Assistant Surgeons, M.C., Members
JESSE W. LAZEAR	of the American Yellow Fever
JAMES CARROLL	Commission in Cuba.

WILLIAM CRAWFORD GORGAS, Major, M.C., U.S.A.
Colonel Tory, of the Marine Hospital Corps.
MAJOR CARTWRIGHT.
ROGER P. AMES, Assistant Surgeon, M.C., U.S.A.
CARLOS J. FINLAY, M.D.
WILLIAM H. DEAN, Private, U.S.A.
An Army Chaplain.
A Commissary Sergeant.
Soldiers.
Three Buglers.

West Africa, September, 1927

Harkness, of the West African Yellow Fever Commission, Rockefeller
Foundation.

London: September, 1929

Stackpoole.

From *Yellow Jack* by Sidney Howard, in collaboration with Paul de Kruif.
Copyright 1933, 1934, by Sidney Howard. By permission of Harcourt Brace and Company, Inc.

CAUTION: Professionals and amateurs are hereby warned that *Yellow Jack*, being fully protected under the copyright laws of the United States of America, the British Empire, including the Dominion of Canada, and all other countries of the Copyright Union, is subject to royalty. All rights, including professional, amateur, motion picture, recitation, lecturing, public reading, radio and television broadcasting, and the rights of translation into foreign languages, are strictly reserved. Particular emphasis is laid on the question of readings, permission for which must be secured from the author's agent in writing. All inquiries except in connection with the amateur rights, should be addressed to the author's agent, Harold Freedman, 101 Park Avenue, New York City.

The amateur acting rights of *Yellow Jack* are controlled exclusively by the Dramatists Play Service, Inc., 14 East 38th Street, New York 16, N.Y. No amateur performance of the play may be given without obtaining in advance the written permission of the Dramatists Play Service, Inc., and paying the requisite fee.

In order to produce an effective play, Sidney Howard's craftsmanship needed only a situation and a point of view favorable to his realistic bias in art and congenial to his liberal sympathies. In *Yellow Jack* both conditions were met. The subject was an important episode in the history of man's struggle against disease, and the story provided by Dr. Paul de Kruif in his book *Microbe Hunters* combined data from the history of science with an account of the common man's contribution to the effort to wipe out yellow fever. That contribution, moreover, involved realistically observed characters in natural rather than glamorous situations and gave Howard an opportunity to indulge his interest in colloquial speech. Without wholly escaping the perils of composing a chronicle and providing a kaleidoscopic view of events, Howard went as far as he could in the direction of an objective drama of fact rather than fiction.

It was, no doubt, a logical step in the development of consistent realism in a country oriented toward pragmatic democratic life and devoted to the amelioration of man's lot by means of applied science. Interestingly enough, moreover, the same concern that carried Sidney Howard *toward* realism also carried him *beyond* it. The impulse to compose a documentary drama compelled this intelligent playwright to break down the constricting walls of the well-built play of realistic dramaturgy. The play structure that consists of a single concentrated action had to be displaced by a wide-ranging multi-scened drama consisting of numerous separate vignettes. In short, with *Yellow Jack*, Howard moved in the direction of so-called *epic theatre* best represented after World War I in Europe by the work of the German playwright Bertolt Brecht and in the United States, during the decade of the 1930's and the New Deal, by the "living newspapers" presented by the Federal Theatre.

Sidney Howard was born in Oakland, California, in 1891. He was graduated from the University of California in 1915 (he also had a year's study in Switzerland and a course with George Pierce Baker). Howard came to the theatre after serving in World War I, first as an ambulance driver and then as an Air Force officer. His experiences left a deep impression and undoubtedly were his incentive in the writing of such anti-war plays as *The Ghost of Yankee Doodle* (1937) and the dramatization *The Paths of Glory* (1935). He also brought to the stage an interest in the cause of the common man and the sociological bent that led to his study of the activities of the I.W.W., the International Workers of the World, a syndicalist union of migratory workers constantly in conflict with the authorities in the West, somewhat given to violence but itself the victim of violence. The result of this interest was his book *The Labor Spy*, a work of some importance in the early 1920's, since it dealt with the use of spies and *agents provocateurs* by employers.

Howard's early effort at playwriting was a romantic melodrama indeed, *Swords* (1921), revolving around jealousy, rape, and murder in Renaissance Italy. But this costume play is inferior to the rest of his work and atypical. Typical was his first successful production *They Knew What They Wanted*, presented by the Theatre Guild in 1924 with the appealing actress Pauline Lord in the leading part. A comedy as noteworthy for its folk flavor, drawn from observation of the winegrowing Italian farmers of California, as for its compassion, *They Knew What They Wanted* won the Pulitzer Prize for its author. A large factor in the success of the play was its realism— not merely descriptive but thematic, since the action consisted of a middle-aged husband's willingness to keep his wife and her illegitimate child, begotten in a moment of desperation when she spent her wedding night with his handsome foreman, memorably played by Glenn Anders. Typical, too, of Howard's realism were his pictures of life in other sections of the country, such as *Ned McCobb's Daughter* (1926), set in Maine, and *Alien Corn* (1933), a study of an artist's frustration in a stodgy Midwestern academic community. These were closely constructed plays, but in *Lucky Sam McCarver* (1925) Howard employed a looser structure in relating the rise of an untutored son of the poor to Wall Street respectability after an interlude as the owner of a nightclub selling liquor illegally. The relative failure of this vivid character study and picture of social conflict did not dampen Howard's interest in social contrasts, and he won great success with his dramatization of the Sinclair Lewis novel *Dodsworth* (1934), dealing with the confusions of an American matron exposed to European society. His partiality for simple, common people, combined with his penchant for regional flavor, resulted in *The Late Christopher Bean* (1932), a delightful comedy adapted from a French comedy (René Fauchois' *Prenez garde à la peinture*) and given a small-town American setting. And of social as well as psychological interest was his single venture into psychological drama, *The Silver Cord* (1926), an exposé of possessive motherhood and the cult of "momism" in middle-class American life.

With these plays and sundry other adaptations of foreign plays, Sidney Howard was giving the American theatre a good deal of interest and vitality when a freak accident caused his untimely death in 1939. He left behind a socially rooted fantasy, *Madam, Will You Walk?* (1939), which was the first production of the experimental Phoenix Theatre in New York in the 1950's. Of all his plays, however, his reputation continued to rest on *They Knew What They Wanted*, revived on Broadway in the 1940's with Paul Muni in the leading male role, and in 1956 turned into the musical *The Most Happy Fella* by Frank Loesser, and *Yellow Jack*, revived in the 1940's, filmed, and also frequently performed in the country's little theatres.

*The scene is London—Stackpoole's labora-
tory; the time, January, 1929, and the sky is a
London sky, a near sky, friendly for all its
wintry grayness.*

*A young laboratory assistant, slightly Cock-
ney and George by name, sits above on a stool at
a bacteriological workbench in a bacteriological
laboratory. He faces the audience over a line of
flasks. He is at work on a combination of the
liver of a monkey—lately dead of yellow fever
—and sterile saline solution. His object is to
transfer a minute amount of this commodity
from the mortar in which he has prepared it to
the Erlenmeyer flask in which, as he proposes,
it will take its next step toward some desired
result. Stackpoole, British, keen, aloof, distinguished and thirty-five, a Major of the
Royal Air Force, and an Official of the Kenya
Colony government are grouped around the
table watching George perform the experiment.
The Major is portly and florid in the British
imperial manner. The Official is an elderly
and easily mannered gentleman and has a fine
tropical sunburn.*

———

STACKPOOLE. That stuff he's grinding
in the mortar is the pulp of a monkey's
liver. A monkey that died this morning
of yellow fever. Of course, the hope is
that the liver's loaded with virus. The
tricky thing about these monkeys,
though—particularly with yellow fever
—is the way the amount of virus in them
varies. And the idea now is to test the
degree of deadliness in this one.

MAJOR. I suppose that's a useful thing
to know?

STACKPOOLE. When you're trying to
get at a vaccine? Oh, yes, Major. Very.

OFFICIAL. How can you test the deadliness?

STACKPOOLE. That's simple enough.
George is making a suspension of pulp in
that first flask there. Then he'll dilute
the suspension out weaker and weaker in
each of those other flasks till he's arrived
at the weakest dilution that will still be
fatal. (*He points to the fifth flask in the row.*)
We have done the trick with as weak as
one to a hundred thousand. But that was
from a very high type of liver!

MAJOR. The trick? What trick, Dr.
Stackpoole?

STACKPOOLE. Of killing another monkey! But this must seem very dry to you,
gentlemen. You didn't come all this way
to London to . . . Suppose we go down
and get to your business. Any problem

of the Colonial Airways interests me,
Major. We won't disturb you, George?
(STACKPOOLE, *the* MAJOR, *and the* OFFICIAL
come down the stair.)

GEORGE. No, sir.

STACKPOOLE. Sit down. Well, Major,
so you don't like our quarantine regulations for air travel?

MAJOR (*pulling himself together*). The
men who built the British Empire
weren't stopped by a tropical fever here
and there! It's my job to develop new
aviation projects. That's my notion of
holding the Empire together. And you
doctors and your confounded League of
Nations are blocking me!

STACKPOOLE (*smiling*). As bad as that?

MAJOR. Good God, I'm required to set
up medical and pathological plants and
maintain mosquito squads on every field
I organize!

STACKPOOLE. Only in Africa!

MAJOR. I'm required to quarantine
passengers for six days!

STACKPOOLE. Only passengers from
the West Coast!

MAJOR. Do you expect passengers from
anywhere to stand for that?

STACKPOOLE (*indicating* OFFICIAL). Is
my friend from Kenya Colony in sympathy with your protest?

OFFICIAL. I'm in favor of anything
that keeps West Coast yellow fever on the
West Coast where it belongs and away
from the comparatively healthy people
in my district.

MAJOR. Life's full of reasonable risks!

STACKPOOLE. Your planes are making
yellow fever a bit too risky.

MAJOR. Rot, Dr. Stackpoole! I insist
my . . .

STACKPOOLE. We're not in London,
Major. We're on one of your African
landing fields. (MAJOR *is puzzled.* STACK-
POOLE *includes* OFFICIAL.) In Kenya
Colony, say, in my old friend's district . . .
(*Back to* MAJOR.) . . . where they haven't
had yellow fever yet. And I'm just stepping out of one of your planes. A plane
that's just brought me across from the
West Coast, where I've caught the disease. The merest beginnings of a case,
you know. Might be malaria, might be a
cold, might even be air pockets on the
way. Well, I land, and a certain female
mosquito bites me. Plenty of mosquitoes
in Kenya Colony. Plenty of this particular mosquito. We'll call her the yellow

fever mosquito, because she's especially equipped by an all-wise Providence to carry yellow fever from man to man. (*His tone becomes downright confidential.*) After she's bitten me—a few days after— she bites you. Or, perhaps, some fast traveling passenger bound north for the Sudan or south to Tanganyika or the Cape. Where plenty more of her agreeable species are waiting for their first meal of yellow fever blood. Has my fable answered your objections, Major?

MAJOR (*uncomfortably*). There's always danger!

STACKPOOLE. You, with the British Empire on your mind! Think of India!

MAJOR. All right! I'm a good imperialist! I'll think of India!

STACKPOOLE. This mosquito's very much at home in India. Those steaming millions are still waiting for yellow fever. There's another point about India, too. The only animal ever found to be susceptible to the disease—except man, of course—is the common Indian monkey Stokes gave it to. Do you get the full beauty of the Indian picture? Monkeys and men both stricken together! Death in the village! Death falling from the treetops! And only one yellow fever passenger required to start the whole thing going! And every year your planes make the leap to India swifter and easier. It's a race between plague and science, isn't it? With your planes helping the plague to win. (*At this moment GEORGE in the eagerness of his work tips his stool too far forward and loses his balance. In doing this he breaks the pipette with which he is working.* STACKPOOLE *hears the noise and looks around.*) What is it, George?

GEORGE. Pipette broke! Cut through the glove!

STACKPOOLE. Let's see. (GEORGE *comes down to him.*) Get it off! (GEORGE *removes glove.*) Yes, by Jove!

GEORGE (*panic*). I'll get it, Doctor. I'll get it!

STACKPOOLE. There's no use carrying on about it. Sit down and take hold of yourself.

OFFICIAL. An accident?

MAJOR. Serious?

STACKPOOLE. He's cut himself on a pipette full of yellow fever virus. It's only a pinprick, but . . . (*He calls.*) Mullins! (MULLINS, *another laboratory assistant, enters.*) Clean up!

MULLINS. Crickey!

STACKPOOLE. Sit down, George.

MAJOR. Will he get yellow fever from that?

OFFICIAL. I say, the poor devil!

(*Together.*)

STACKPOOLE. If you don't mind, gentlemen! (*To* GEORGE, *in good-humored irritability.*) Damn you, George. (*To* MULLINS.) Mullins!

MULLINS. Yes, sir?

STACKPOOLE. Get rubber tubing! (*He is rolling up his sleeve as* MULLINS *comes down to obey.*) Get a twenty c.c. syringe and alcohol. Draw up one c.c. of citrate salt solution. (*To* GEORGE.) Lend a hand, George. (GEORGE *fetches tubing and knots it around* STACKPOOLE'S *extended arm as* MULLINS *offers the syringe on a towel.*) Sterile?

MULLINS. Oh, yes, Doctor. (STACKPOOLE *sits at desk, offering his arm to* MULLINS.)

STACKPOOLE. Well, go ahead! There's the vein. What are you waiting for? (MULLINS, *after proper swabbing with alcohol, inserts the needle into the vein.*) Fill her right up. (*To* GEORGE.) Take off your coat. (*Back to* MULLINS.) Right.

MULLINS. Centrifuge, Doctor?

STACKPOOLE. Quicker we get it into him the better. (*Indicating* GEORGE.) Pull up his shirt. (MULLINS *pulls* GEORGE'S *shirt out of his trousers, baring his back.*) Right. (*He makes injection.* GEORGE *winces.* MAJOR *and* OFFICIAL *turn aside.*) No good worrying, George. We've done what we could. (*To* MULLINS.) Better take him home.

GEORGE. I can carry on, sir.

STACKPOOLE. Take him out of here. Buy him a drink. (*The two assistants go,* STACKPOOLE *watching them as he restores his shirt-sleeve to order. He puts on his coat and rubs alcohol on his hands, then smiles at his guests in apologetic explanation.*) Sorry, gentlemen. When we take a glass rod and rub a drop of that virus on a monkey's belly, on the unbroken skin, the monkey dies. So you see, an actual cut . . .

OFFICIAL. Will he be all right?

STACKPOOLE. If he were a monkey he would. . . . I don't know that that's ever been done before . . . to a man.

MAJOR. Blood transfusion?

STACKPOOLE (*amused*). No, Major. I'm lending him some of my immunity, that's all. I hope it serves. He's a good assistant.

OFFICIAL. Have you had yellow fever? (STACKPOOLE *nods casually.*)

MAJOR. In Africa?

STACKPOOLE. No. I caught it right here in the lab.

MAJOR. I think I'll sit down again. I feel a bit unsteady. (*He sits.*)

STACKPOOLE. Drink?

MAJOR. No, thanks.

STACKPOOLE. We'll all sit down and go on where we left off. (*He motions* OFFICIAL *to a chair.*)

MAJOR. I'm not sure I can get back to the subject.

OFFICIAL. The Major's here in London working out the new flight schedule to India. Cutting the time considerably, you know. . . . (*A glance at* MAJOR.) With stop-overs in Cairo to connect with yellow fever.

STACKPOOLE (*stern*). How long will you take from the West Coast of Africa to India? Don't cut that down too much.

MAJOR. We can't hold progress back for you science fellows! (*The scene becomes angry.*)

STACKPOOLE. Don't think we're not doing what we can! In West Africa, in Brazil, in New York and Boston! I've been at it here for the past . . .

MAJOR. What's holding you back?

STACKPOOLE. It isn't easy to work with a microbe you can't see!

MAJOR. But with your microscopes . . .

STACKPOOLE. Not with any microscope ever made!

MAJOR. Ah, but you can't see small-pox, either! And if you can vaccinate against that . . .

STACKPOOLE. I'm working on a vaccine for this.

MAJOR. Use it!

STACKPOOLE. I don't dare yet. What protects a monkey might kill a man.

MAJOR. Get after your mosquito then!

STACKPOOLE. Will you pay for the oil to cover equatorial Africa?

MAJOR. Well, for God's sake, get your vaccine in time!

STACKPOOLE. In time, Major! Knowledge won't be hurried! They'd been working a hundred and some years at this when that solid American citizen, Walter Reed, found the yellow fever mosquito in Havana. In 1900 that was. Had to experiment on human beings to find it. Didn't have any laboratory animal then that would take the disease.

Quite a yarn that. Should have gone quickly on to a general festival of vaccination! But for eighteen years Germans and Frenchmen, Britishers and Brazilians sweated in tropical jungles and fever towns to finish Reed's work and got nowhere, till the little Jap Noguchi announced he'd discovered the microbe in Ecuador. Only Noguchi turned out to be wrong. That's a yarn, too. And the thing stuck there, still for want of a laboratory animal. Human beings aren't practical for experiment. Men of Reed's "thoroughness" don't happen often. That may be just as well. Then in the summer of 1927 Stokes succeeded at last in giving the disease to his Indian monkey. Gave us an animal we could experiment on. Put the thing in our labs where we could get at it! Started us after a vaccine in earnest! But the disease turned on us workers then. Killed Stokes in his laboratory in West Africa. Killed Noguchi. Killed and will kill plenty more of us. The whole thing's a yarn, looking back on it. A thirty-year-long detective serial. And the best any of us can hope for is to get his own installment written and fitted in. How many more installments? I wish I knew! I'm afraid you'll have to stick to your quarantines, Major. (*A pause.* MAJOR *rises, disgruntled.*)

MAJOR. I can't say you've helped my problem, Dr. Stackpoole. Nor increased my respect for medical science, either.

STACKPOOLE (*laughing*). Now, don't despair of science, Major! We never do! Never wake up in the morning without saying: "Today may be the day for the lucky accident!"

MAJOR. I shall have to blunder on as best I can. (MAJOR *is going.*)

STACKPOOLE. Come back in a year! We might have something to show you!

OFFICIAL. You did say just what I wanted of you. I hope we haven't taken too much of your time. (*They shake hands.*)

STACKPOOLE. Not at all! Not at all! Good-by. (OFFICIAL *goes.* STACKPOOLE *stands thoughtful for a moment, glances at his calendar, then, solo.*) The twelfth. Four days. If George gets through the sixteenth all right . . . (*He shrugs, glances at his watch, and calls.*) Mullins!

MULLINS (*Offstage*). Yes, sir?

STACKPOOLE. Is Kim ready?

MULLINS (*Offstage*). Ready, sir. (*He enters, carrying under his arm a small Scottish terrier pup.*)

STACKPOOLE. How's George feeling?

MULLINS. Oh, he's all right, sir. A bit shaky, you know.

STACKPOOLE. I'm that myself. I shall walk Kim over.

MULLINS. If anyone asks for you, sir?

STACKPOOLE. I'm only going to Dr. Laidlaw's. I shan't be long. (*Then, to the dog.*) Are you ready, Kim? (*Kim is ready.*) Good. Yellow fever may have us stumped, but we *can* vaccinate you against distemper. (*He stops in his tracks. Then, so absently.*) Think you could put your finger on those notes Laidlaw and Dunkin sent over? About their vaccine for dog distemper?

MULLINS (*extracting typed papers from the desk drawer*). Right here, sir.

STACKPOOLE. Thanks. Take Kim, George! (MULLINS *takes the pup.* GEORGE *enters.* STACKPOOLE *drops papers on desk and stands looking down on them.*) "Dogs of known susceptibility to distemper are taken and a small but certainly infective dose of living *virus* is injected into each. This is followed by an appropriate injection of immune blood serum. The results of this *combined* dosage of *both* living virus and immune serum have been in every case highly satisfactory and *solid immunity* to later doses of living virus has been demonstrated in every animal." (*He looks up.*) More or less what just happened to you, George. Virus plus a shot of immune blood. Only we'll have to be neater about things than you were. At least control the amount of virus. Still, if you pull through . . . (*He looks down at Kim.*) The principle does seem to work for Kim. . . . (*Then, very low.*) Why shouldn't it work for . . . (*He stops embarrassed. Then:*) Thanks, Kim. (*He leans over to pat Kim's head.*) Thanks for the suggestion. (*To* MULLINS.) You walk Kim over. He's earned a walk and I'm not going out. (*His whole manner sharpens as* MULLINS *leads Kim out.*) Any other monkeys die last night, George?

GEORGE. There's one that's pretty near gone, Dr. Stackpoole.

STACKPOOLE (*very deliberate*). We'll get the living virus out of him and the immune blood serum out of me and if Laidlaw's principle can be applied . . .

GEORGE (*kindling*). Yes, sir! Right, sir!

STACKPOOLE. I'll want four healthy monkeys. Stokes's Indian monkeys. You

pick 'em out for me, George.

GEORGE. Trust me, sir.

STACKPOOLE. We'll vaccinate one pair with Laidlaw's combination and shoot living virus into the others straight. They'll die, that second pair, but the first pair . . . (*He sits at his desk making notes.*)

GEORGE. They'll be all right, sir! They'll be as well as . . .

STACKPOOLE. Go slow, George! Been fooled so many times! It would be a step in the right direction, though.

GEORGE. Yes, sir. (*He goes.*)

STACKPOOLE. What's the date? (*A glance at calendar.*) January 12th, 1929. (*He is writing. Slowly the light concentrates upon him until only his head and shoulders are visible.*) Reasonable hope . . . experiments initiated herewith . . . establish at least principle of vaccination against yellow fever . . . Following the discovery made eighteen months ago in West Africa . . . (*In the distance a tom-tom is faintly audible.*) by the late Dr. Adrian Stokes . . . of the susceptibility of the Indian Rhesus monkey . . . (HARKNESS's *voice interrupts from the darkness.*)

HARKNESS. "This recommendation is based upon a record of failure . . ." (*The click of a portable typewriter is audible through the beat of the tom-tom, then light shows another laboratory workbench, far less complete in equipment than its predecessors. It displays little more than the microscope, the typewriter itself and a bottle of whiskey with syphon and glasses.* HARKNESS, *a young American adventurer in medical science, sits on a stool. He is clad in soiled summer linen slacks and shirtsleeves and his mood is sour as he operates the typewriter to transcribe from a longhand draft which he has to hand.*) ". . . . a failure so consistent . . . as to offer no encouragement to continuing the present research here in West Africa." (*He mops his brow.*) "The animals which we have attempted to infect with yellow fever blood include . . . rabbits, white mice, African and South American monkeys . . . puppies, kittens, goats . . . and over a thousand European and American guinea pigs." (*Another swallow of his drink.*) "In no instance during the entire nine months has any animal shown the least reaction to the disease. Nor does the enthusiasm of Dr. Stokes hold any promise of . . ." (KRAEMER *enters above. He is another young American similarly dressed except that he wears a pith helmet. He carries a wire basket container filled with cotton-plugged test tubes and packed with small pieces of ice.*)

KRAEMER. You still up, Harkness?

HARKNESS. Where did you come from?

KRAEMER. Those native villages up behind Suhum. Waited for dark to drive in. Thought it might be cooler. It wasn't.

HARKNESS. New cases?

KRAEMER. Plenty. (*He sets wire basket on table.* HARKNESS *turns to sweeten his drink.*)

HARKNESS. What's that?

KRAEMER. Didn't hear anything.

HARKNESS. Sounded like somebody whooping.

KRAEMER. Natives.

HARKNESS. Didn't sound like natives.

KRAEMER. Not Stokes!

HARKNESS. What would Stokes have to whoop about?

KRAEMER. Can't imagine. Can't tell about the Irish, though.

HARKNESS. Don't hear anything now.

KRAEMER. You're cracking up.

HARKNESS. Just two white men going to hell in the tropics. (*A sip of his drink.*) Better make yourself one.

KRAEMER. I've got a day's work to do tomorrow. . . . So have you. (*The scene becomes quick with stubborn anger.*)

HARKNESS. I don't need to be reminded of that, Kraemer.

KRAEMER. Where do you want these bloods?

HARKNESS. Don't leave 'em there. The damn ice will melt and mess everything up.

KRAEMER. Aren't you going to inject the animals?

HARKNESS. Why should I?

KRAEMER. I drove eighty miles and got stuck twice and changed a flat in this heat to get those bloods here.

HARKNESS. Put 'em in the icebox. I'll go through the motions in the morning. I'm turning in now.

KRAEMER. They won't be fresh in the morning.

HARKNESS. What difference will that make?

KRAEMER. All right! I'll go down and inject 'em myself!

HARKNESS. Go ahead. (*He is gathering up coat, cigarettes, and whiskey bottle.*) There's a whole new generation of guinea pigs and you can help yourself to Stokes's imported monkeys. I'm fed up.

If you don't know we're wasting time here you're a bloody fool.

KRAEMER (*low*). I'm not wasting time!

HARKNESS. On a disease you can't give to any animal but man?

KRAEMER. I don't believe that yet.

HARKNESS. How can we get anywhere with no animal to experiment on!

KRAEMER. We may find one yet.

HARKNESS (*turning savagely*). Want to know where to look for your animal? I'll tell you the only place! Go down to the village and shanghai some natives. You'll get nowhere with this any other way.

KRAEMER. Oh, Harkness, for the love of . . .

HARKNESS. What the hell! Reed and his gang did that in Cuba! (*The idea fascinates him.*) I walked through the village this afternoon and saw 'em. If these planes turn out the menace people say . . .

KRAEMER. Don't talk like a fool! (*He sits wearily.*)

HARKNESS. I'm sorry, Kraemer. I'll go down and inject the animals, of course. You go to bed. (*He is picking up container.*)

KRAEMER (*peacemaker*). We'll get out of here sometime, Harkness. Where we won't have to shoot quinine every day. It's hard to believe, but we will. (ADRIAN STOKES *enters quickly above. He is an Irishman, aged forty. At the moment his hair is tousled and he wears thoroughly mussed pajamas. He carries four microscope slides on a board. He is followed by* CHAMBANG, *a stalwart African negro in shorts, shoes, and nothing else.* CHAMBANG *carries two glass dishes in which some bloody mess is dimly visible.*) Hello there, Stokes! (STOKES *has come down to workbench and set himself to the adjustment of the microscope.* CHAMBANG *places glass dishes before him and stands easily at attention.* STOKES *works in intense concentration, his eyes shining.* KRAEMER *has decided on a drink after all and is reaching for the bottle as he continues easily.*) What got you out of bed? Harkness thought he heard you whooping a while back.

STOKES. Likely he did.

HARKNESS. Just lying in bed whooping himself to sleep.

STOKES. I wasn't in bed.

HARKNESS. Where were you?

STOKES. I was down in the monkey house. (*The slightest pause.*)

KRAEMER. What for?

CHAMBANG (*grinning*). Number Eleven. He is dead, Dr. Kraemer.

HARKNESS. Dead? Number Eleven?

CHAMBANG. Surely not unexpected, Dr. Harkness, in view of fever this afternoon.

HARKNESS. He was all over his cage before supper!

STOKES (*indicating dishes in turn*). If it's evidence of his death you want, that's liver there and those are his kidneys.

KRAEMER (*breathless*). My God, have you cut him up already? (*And he is on his knees to examine the liver dish.*)

STOKES. He wasn't wearing his liver around his neck.

HARKNESS. Don't get too cocky, Stokes. Monkeys do die of all kinds of things besides yellow fever.

STOKES. Have I made any assertion? I say only this: that monk was injected with yellow fever blood eight days ago. Blood from Christian Otumanko, black, and Kwasi Danso, even blacker. Mild native cases, up and about already. But the monkey's dead, Harkness! Fever this afternoon! Dead as a mackerel now! Dead, Holy God Almighty! (*Even* HARKNESS *is shaken with the impact of this, but* KRAEMER *looks up from liver at which he has been peering*).

KRAEMER. Hey! Look!

(HARKNESS *looks.*)

HARKNESS. Well, something certainly hit that liver!

KRAEMER. I haven't seen a liver like that since . . .

HARKNESS. Since that dead Syrian we had last March at Lagos!

KRAEMER. The rug man!

HARKNESS. Right!

STOKES. The eyes were a disappointment to me, showing little or no yellow at all. But the kidneys are a beautiful color. (HARKNESS *turns to look at kidneys.* STOKES's *slide is prepared.*) Shall we look at the liver section now? (KRAEMER *springs to his feet and* HARKNESS, *too, moves suddenly, but they both remember in the nick of time that this is primarily* STOKES's *moment.*)

KRAEMER (*a gulp, then:*). Go ahead. (*In the distance the tom-tom resumes its throb.* STOKES *looks long and carefully while* KRAEMER *watches, holding his breath. Then he rises and motions to* KRAEMER *to take his place. He stands back, his chest swelling, his*

smile *broadening.* HARKNESS *looks up as* KRAEMER *sits and looks.* KRAEMER *surrenders his place to* HARKNESS, *who looks in turn quickly, then lifts his head.*)

HARKNESS. My God! (*He gets to his feet and moves giddily away from the miracle, and* STOKES *is quickly back in his place for a second look.* HARKNESS *can hardly speak for his excitement.*) I'm sold. Those liver cells are enough for me. (*Then, with good-humored irritability:*) Damn you, Stokes!

KRAEMER. Yes, and you only just off the boat from London!

HARKNESS. And we wasting months trying every monk in Africa! And here you come with your damn Indian monk . . .

KRAEMER. That's where Stokes was smarter than . . .

HARKNESS. You've done it, Stokes! By God, I hand it to you! A disease that's been a closed book all these years! A disease we've known only from its human victims! And here you've found us an animal at last! And put the thing where we . . .

KRAEMER (*wild*). Twenty-five, twenty-seven years they've all been looking! Ever since Reed's experiments on the soldiers!

HARKNESS. Longer than that! Do you think Reed didn't look before he . . .

KRAEMER. No more human experiment now that Stokes has done it! (STOKES *sits smiling but quite calm as he examines the other three slides on his board.*)

STOKES. Done it, you say?

KRAEMER. Yes, that's what I said.

STOKES. But we haven't even started.

HARKNESS. I'm satisfied. We can get after the vaccine now!

STOKES (*working*). I'm not satisfied. Chambang, fetch me another monk.

HARKNESS. Wait a minute, Chambang! (*To* STOKES.) What for?

STOKES (*working*). The first thing's to keep this strain alive and going from monkey to monkey till . . .

KRAEMER. We've only got three monks left.

STOKES. This one took eight days dying. At that rate three more should allow us twenty-four days to get others from Hamburg. Kraemer, send Karl Hagenbeck a cable! Tell him you want all the Rhesus monkeys he's got on hand! And he'd better get more from India!

HARKNESS. Monkeys cost money!

STOKES. Five hundred monkeys are cheaper than one man! Can we begin to think of a vaccine till we've seen dozens of monks die as this one's died? Till we've exhausted every possible test? We'll have the whole world firing questions at us?

KRAEMER. Questions?

HARKNESS (at the same time). After this?

STOKES (scorn). This? What is this? A monk's dead of a fever out of a black man's blood! A fever mild among African natives. Will they agree out there that this is the real old murdering yellow jack? Do we know that it is?

CHAMBANG (quietly, from above). Black man little fever. White man big fever. White man die.

STOKES. Chambang's said it! I'll not be satisfied till I've seen dead white man and dead monk side by side on the autopsy table!

HARKNESS. Jesus!

STOKES. Fetch me another monk, Chambang! (CHAMBANG goes above.) There's an epic of work for us to be doing now, for I'll believe nothing till I can't help myself! (He is back at his work again.)

KRAEMER (quiet and smiling). Well, it may be years, but it must come now.

HARKNESS. Walter Reed once said those very words!

STOKES. Walter Reed!

KRAEMER. Wonder what they'll say in New York tomorrow?

STOKES. I'd rather think of what Walter Reed would have said . . . (In the distance a QUARTET is heard singing very faintly.)

QUARTET. "When you hear dem bells go ding-a-ling . . ."

BASS. "Boom. Boom. Boom."

STOKES (continuing over the singing). And of what Lazear and Carroll would have said . . .

QUARTET (a little louder). "All join round and a-sweetly you must sing . . ."

BASS. "And when the . . ."

STOKES (over the singing). Yes, and the soldiers back there in Havana in 1900. What would they say to . . . (Darkness.)

QUARTET (full volume).
"Verse am over, in the chorus all join in: There'll be a hot time in the old town
tonight!"

BASS. "My baby . . ."

(Through the darkness QUARTET repeats full volume. Then the scene is Columbia Barracks at Quemado, near Havana, Cuba. The time is late July, 1900. A line of American soldiers is crossing the stage. It walks through shadow, in tragic single file, each pair of soldiers carrying a stretcher. On each stretcher is a dummy corpse covered with an army blanket. The refrain is repeated as the scene is revealed.)

QUARTET. (Continuing.)
"Good-bye, Dolly, I must leave you,
    Though it breaks my heart to go;
Something tells me I am wanted
    At the front, to fight the foe,
See, the soldier boys are marching
    And I can no longer stay,
Hark, I hear the bugles calling,
    Good-bye, Dolly Gray!"
(And then continuing from "Dolly Gray.")
"Good-bye, my Blue Bell,
    Farewell to you!
One last fond look into
    Your eyes of blue.
'Mid campfires' gleaming
    'Mid shot and shell,
I will be dreaming
    Of my own Blue Bell!"

(Then, as the last stretcher passes, "There'll Be a Hot Time in the Old Town Tonight" is repeated diminuendo. Four American soldiers, all of whom wear the Medical Corps insignia, are fixedly watching the passage of the stretchers. These four are, by name, O'HARA, BRINKERHOF, MCCLELLAND, and BUSCH. O'HARA is a husky young Irishman of spirit and intelligence, his speech still stiff with the brogue of Galway. BRINKERHOF is an Ohio Valley boy, gentle, serious, and soft-spoken. BUSCH is a city chap of Jewish extraction and intensity. MCCLELLAND, a Southerner, is the sturdy and commonplace member of the group. All four are still in their earliest twenties, and because they are all dressed alike should be cast with due consideration for variety of personal type. The singing comes to a halt. The last of the stretchers passes. O'HARA makes the sign of the cross.)

O'HARA. Pray God that may be the last of them for this day!

MCCLELLAND (shuddering). This medical corps's a bad disappointment to me! Drill and tote stretchers! Swab out the ambulance! Swab out the latrine! I don't like the smell of chlorine and carbolic! Sickness and dying ain't congenial to my nature! And all the time waiting for my turn to go out feet first!

The war's over! Why don't they send us home?

BUSCH (*indignant*). Ain't you heard how they're making the Caribbean an American lake? Uncle Sam's going to keep us right here in Cuba till the natives have all learned to call him daddy! Or anyway till they quit calling him a thief! We're pawns, that's all, in the game of imperialism! I get my ideas out of reading Karl Marx.

BRINKERHOF (*blandly*). One man's meat is another man's poison, as the saying goes. I think Cuba's a real Paradise on earth. It don't matter how hot the days get, there's always a cool breeze at night. I got to admit yellow jack's a drawback. But even so, this life's a lot better than what I used to have in Liberty Mills, Indiana, where I come from.

O'HARA (*blarney*). 'Tis a fine, easy land, as John Brinkerhof says, and the tropical climate offers advantages over the rainy coast of Ireland where I was born. As to yellow jack, such afflictions are questions of fate, and it behooves us to be philosophers where fate is concerned—which the Irish are, so long as their fate remains agreeable.

MC CLELLAND. I'd sooner be home than here, raising a family and living a normal life.

BUSCH. And me! I'd sooner be back in Chicago where I belong, furthering the interests of the radical movement.

BRINKERHOF. I'll bide my time here till I get my sergeancy.

O'HARA. A future of noble medical ambition stretches out before Johnny O'Hara like a green meadow ablossom with the sufferings of his fellow men. I'll never be satisfied till I'm Dr. O'Hara! (MISS BLAKE *enters. She is a trained nurse, Southern, lean, and in her thirties.*)

MISS BLAKE. Will you tell the Major, please, Mr. Brinkerhof, that the patient he was interested in has just died? (*Extreme solemnity descends on the four soldiers.*)

O'HARA. Died, is it?

MC CLELLAND. One of our boys?

BUSCH. Was it yellow jack?

BRINKERHOF. Major Reed's right here in his laboratory, Miss Blake, waiting for Dr. Carroll to come back from Pinar del Rio.

MISS BLAKE. Then I'll go tell him myself. (*But* TWO ORDERLIES *enter carrying a stretcher covered with a blanket. They pass below the soldiers, who look on hypnotized as* MISS BLAKE *goes toward where light grows on the laboratory of the American Yellow Fever Commission in Cuba. The laboratory furnishings consist of a workbench upon which the now antiquated brass microscopes stand amidst a litter of slides, slide boxes, and notebooks. Stools and some shelves filled with culture flasks, bottles of stain, and other specimens of laboratory glassware complete the equipment.* WALTER REED, *Major M.C.—slim, distinguished, Virginian, fifty—sits at the workbench in the meanwhile.*)

1ST ORDERLY. Go easy, there!

2ND ORDERLY. Let me get hold!

1ST ORDERLY. Hands slipping?

2ND ORDERLY. Jesus, it's hot! I'm sweating. (*The stretcher is set down while he mops his brow*). Hope they get the door of that autopsy room unlocked and don't keep us waiting where everybody can see. (*The stretcher resumes its course.*)

1ST ORDERLY. Straight ahead. (*They are going. Reed looks up from the papers* MISS BLAKE *has handed him.*)

REED. Name: John Davies. Age: twenty-two. He wasn't married. That's always some consolation. I must write to his mother.

MISS BLAKE. Yes, doctor.

BRINKERHOF. I knew that boy. He come from Indiana near where I come from. I was pitching horseshoes with him last Friday. (*He turns sorrowfully apart.*) Now he's dead.

REED (*calling*). Brinkerhof! (BRINKERHOF *goes up into laboratory and salutes.*)

MC CLELLAND. This Cuba's a hell of a place to spend the summer.

REED (*to* BRINKERHOF). Get word to Dr. Agramonte that there's a subject for him in the autopsy room. Say I'll join him there. (BRINKERHOF *salutes and goes.* REED *buries his head in his hands.*) That's all, Miss Blake. (MISS BLAKE *hesitates an instant, then turns out of laboratory and comes down towards the soldiers. In the meanwhile:*)

BUSCH (*a fearful whisper to* O'HARA.) O'Hara!

O'HARA. What?

BUSCH. Will they cut him up now?

O'HARA. In the lofty hope of finding a microbe in him!

MC CLELLAND (*sickened*). Will you lay off that medical talk!

O'HARA. If I had the disease myself I'd

take comfort in offering my remains to the service of science and not waste them buried whole beneath grass or marble!

BUSCH. Why couldn't these lousy docs of cured him?

MISS BLAKE. That's no way to speak of the doctors, Mr. Busch!

BUSCH. What kind of doctors are they? Do they think us boys enlisted and come down here so they can cut us up and squint at our insides?

MC CLELLAND. The doctors kind of give me a pain, too. And in front of you, Miss Blake, I wouldn't say where.

BUSCH (to MISS BLAKE). You know yellow jack when you see it, don't you?

MISS BLAKE. I ought to by this time.

BUSCH. You don't think any of us got it? You don't think I got it? I bet I got it!

MC CLELLAND. He looks yellow to me!

MISS BLAKE. That's not funny!

BUSCH. No, it ain't! All this week I been feeling terrible and my food don't set right and I can't keep my mind on Karl Marx!

MC CLELLAND. That's what give it to him! Karl Marx give it to him!

O'HARA. The way sitting on a cold stone gives a man piles!

MISS BLAKE. Be quiet, you two!

BUSCH. I can't eat! By rights I ought to eat to keep up my strength! I can't get no strength out of my food! It don't stay with me long enough!

MISS BLAKE. Put out your tongue. (He obeys. O'HARA and MC CLELLAND strain to watch the examination, grinning.) How long did you say you'd been feeling badly?

BUSCH. Oh, God, I have got it! (O'HARA and MC CLELLAND recoil. BRINKERHOF looks up.)

MISS BLAKE. Castor oil will cure any yellow fever you've got.

BUSCH. Oh, no, Miss Blake! Things is bad enough with me that way already! I bet I got it! I bet I'm a stiff before I know it!

O'HARA. Oh, he's as good as on the autopsy table already!

MISS BLAKE. Are you trying to scare the boy to death?

BUSCH. He don't have to try! I ain't ashamed I'm scared of this! I'll take on any man twice my weight! I may be Jewish but I got guts! Would I be a radical if I didn't have? Put me up against anything and I'll show you! (Then he adds:) Only it's got to be something I can see.

MISS BLAKE. A disease like this wants a special courage, Mr. Busch.

O'HARA. It wants the noble variety that's in us medical men the way we can live in the midst of a dreadful plague with no effect on the gayety of our spirits! When I see Major Reed and his men of science how they expose themselves to the perils of this, worrying after the unknown truth of it like a bevy of bulldogs, glory be to God, I . . . (During these remarks REED has risen wearily and come out of the laboratory just in time to hear his name. MC CLELLAND sees him.)

MC CLELLAND. 'TenSHUN!

BUSCH (under his breath). Jesus!

(The four boys are statues. A low exclamation of dismay from MISS BLAKE, then:)

REED. Hadn't you better get back to your ward, Miss Blake?

MISS BLAKE. Yes, Doctor. Perhaps I had. (She goes. Agramonte enters above carrying a dish, presumably of tissue from the autopsy just performed. He proceeds at once to prepare his slide for microscopic examination. In the meanwhile REED has turned to BUSCH.)

REED. What's your name?

BUSCH. Busch. Levi P., sir. Private, Quartermaster Department.

(REED turns inquiringly to MC CLELLAND.)

REED. And yours?

MC CLELLAND. McClelland. Warren G., sir. Private, Transportation Unit.

(REED turns to O'HARA.)

O'HARA. O'Hara. John J., sir. Acting sergeant in charge of the operating room, sir.

REED. Oh, you're the one who wants to be a doctor!

O'HARA. I am that, sir, and progressing nicely thanks to the doctors the way they allow me opportunities to observe surgery and even administer the anesthetic, as I have done on three separate occasions due to my natural aptitude for the healing arts. (REED smiles.)

REED. I think you've kissed the Blarney stone in your day.

O'HARA. I was born where the eloquent tongue is native, sir.

("Retreat" is sounding.)

REED. You'll do well to be less eloquent about doctors, Mr. O'Hara. You'll all do well to talk less about this epidemic. (BRINKERHOF returns carrying an official document of some five or six pages.) Epidemics are best not talked about.

There's "Retreat." (*The three soldiers salute and go.* REED *has turned to* BRINKERHOF.) Yes, Mr. Brinkerhof? (BRINKERHOF *proffers the document.*)

BRINKERHOF. From General Wood's headquarters. For you, sir.

REED. What is it?

BRINKERHOF. The army death list brought up to date, sir.

REED (*wincing as he takes document*). Thank you, Mr. Brinkerhof. (*He turns and goes somberly up into laboratory, studying document as he goes. The sky is reddening with sunset. He is surprised to find* AGRAMONTE *working at microscope.* BRINKERHOF *goes.*) I didn't know you'd come in, Agramonte.

AGRAMONTE (*not looking up*). Just now, Doctor. To examine this.

REED. Is it . . . is it from the dead boy you've just had down there?

AGRAMONTE (*as before*). You didn't join me.

REED (*turning distressfully away*). I was waiting for Carroll to get back from Pinar. I didn't feel up to another autopsy today.

AGRAMONTE (*as before*). I can understand that.

REED. Still nothing?

AGRAMONTE. Did you expect anything? After two months of this? And how many boys cut up? Did you still expect anything? We've made a record for thoroughness at any rate, Doctor.

REED (*shaken*). I can't stand much more of this, Agramonte. Have you looked over the army death list lately? They're our boys!

AGRAMONTE. Yes, Doctor.

REED. And I look out there over the sea and watch our transports steaming home and I daren't think what they may be carrying! And we've taken Cuba on! Taken it on with this awful thing smoldering in it! Smoldering and waiting for fresh fuel. For fresh American fuel now, Agramonte! Waiting its chance to jump over home to us! As it's been doing for over a hundred years! To Philadelphia and New Orleans and . . . And to know we've had it under our microscopes a thousand times and never seen it! And men will die and go on dying for all . . .

AGRAMONTE. It is not an agreeable condition from my point of view either, Doctor. I am Cuban born.

REED. I didn't mean to offend you, Agramonte. It isn't easy to admit one's failed. It shakes one's nerve. (*He sits smiling.*) I've said to myself all this afternoon: "If Carroll brings me back anything from Pinar, anything that even looks like a new lead . . ." (CARROLL *has entered through the gathering dusk outside.*) Carroll!

CARROLL. Well, I did get here.

REED. What news from the camp at Pinar?

CARROLL. There's no doubt about your diagnosis. Pernicious malaria my eye! It's yellow jack and going great guns, too! Christ! They're dropping like flies! (REED *turns away.*)

AGRAMONTE. Is that all you have to tell us?

CARROLL. I can't tell you a damned thing that we don't know already! There's nothing to do but wait and see how bad it gets.

AGRAMONTE. And I'm told General Wood's lost a third of his staff in the past month!

REED. At his mess they've been drinking toasts to the last to go. Now they've begun drinking to the next.

CARROLL (*nodding*). And Wood knows it was yellow jack, not Rough Riders, that licked the Spaniards here. And it will lick us if we don't lick it first.

AGRAMONTE. There's no doubt about that.

REED. And our commission—you, Agramonte, and you, Carroll, and Lazear and I—we were sent down here to stop this horror! To isolate a microbe and find a cure! And we've failed! It isn't easy to admit that.

CARROLL. It's better than pretending you're getting somewhere.

REED. If I could only think of some fresh angle. . . .

CARROLL. We've tried every angle! Give it up, Chief! It's no use!

REED. I'm calling the Commission to disband it tonight. It won't be a long session. Then we'll go home.

CARROLL. Thank God! I hate wasting time! I've got to have something I can *see* and *get* at! Like that typhoid job before we came down here! Those flies traveled straight as an arrow from backhouse to mess hall! That was a job you could get some enjoyment out of! Let's go home and get on to something else!

Only you'd keep me with you, wouldn't you, Chief? Hell, you know I'm a one-man dog. Christ! I know how you feel, though! (*An affectionate gesture from* REED *to* CARROLL.)

AGRAMONTE. The most we could do would be to keep on working. We have at least discredited everyone else.

REED (*desperate*). And we're quitting. We're breaking the chain! Have we the right?

CARROLL. I can see I've stayed away from you too long.

REED. We know so little, Carroll. We know so little!

CARROLL. I ran into one puzzler out there at Pinar.

REED. I've heard enough puzzlers I can't solve.

CARROLL. This is a funny one. Case of a soldier. Sick July 12th. Died on the 18th.

REED. You reported him?

CARROLL. Didn't know he hadn't been near the disease for over a month before he took sick.

REED (*looking up*). How was that?

CARROLL. They had him locked up in the guardhouse!

AGRAMONTE. Sure of that, Carroll?

CARROLL. And there he lay in that guardhouse for three days after, with eight other prisoners and they didn't catch it. Not even the one who slept in his blankets after he'd died.

(*"Mess Call" sounds.*)

REED (*sharply*). How about contaminated food or water?

CARROLL. The whole outfit ate and drank the same.

REED. The other eight may have been immunes.

CARROLL. Records don't show it. One came from Iowa, one from Maine, two from Wisconsin . . .

REED. The man may have been extra susceptible.

CARROLL. That might explain it. If *we* could explain why we don't catch it. (*But* REED, *caught in sudden thought, holds up his hand for silence.*) What?

REED. Nothing. I'll see you tonight. (AGRAMONTE *and* CARROLL *exchange a glance, but decide against asking questions.*)

CARROLL. After supper. All right.

AGRAMONTE. We'll go clean up.

REED. Eight-thirty, gentlemen. (AGRAMONTE *and* CARROLL *go out into the dusk, leaving* REED *alone. "Mess Call" sounds again, nearer and louder. The light concentrates upon the tensely thoughtful* REED *until only his figure remains of the entire scene. A pause, then, solo.*) What was it crawled or jumped or flew through that guardhouse window, bit that one prisoner and went back where it came from?

(*The scene goes into complete darkness. "Tattoo" sounds. Then the sky freezes to the green of tropic night and light shows* CARROLL, AGRAMONTE, GORGAS *and* TORY *talking easily on one of the flights of steps.* REED *stands apart on the edge of the shadow and* LAZEAR *lounges in the shadow above.* GORGAS, *aged forty-six, is friendly, keen, and humorous.* LAZEAR, *thirty-four, is imaginative and wildly alive. Again the summer uniforms of officers of the Medical Corps.* TORY, *Colonel of the Marine Hospital Corps, is sixty, pompous, and objectionable.*)

TORY (*as the last notes of "Tattoo" die away*). If you really have reached the end of your tether, Major Reed, my advice to you and to the members of your Commission is to call it a day. Go home. Give out a salty personal interview. Say your accomplishment here has been too technical for popular consumption. You will thus preserve the atmosphere of success which we all require for our reputations and to safeguard our service of our glorious mistress, Science! You will then feel free to move on to pastures new, as the farmers say, and, as my friend, Major Gorgas, can assure you, you will be leaving this epidemic in worthy hands. The Marine Hospital Corps with which I have the honor to be connected . . . (LAZEAR *stirs irritably.* CARROLL *sits nodding approval.* REED *steps forward. But* GORGAS *interrupts.*)

GORGAS. Aren't you rather missing the point of this conference, Colonel Tory? It isn't General Wood's idea for anyone to go home. Wood wants us all working together on this. Wood's getting anxious for action. He watches me scrubbing and you fumigating and they tell him Reed's busy with microscopes. But he doesn't see any results. And it isn't only Cuba he's got on his mind. It's this whole Caribbean and Central American part of the world that we're getting involved in. It's Panama! How can we talk about a Panama Canal with yellow jack rampaging all over the place? This is the toughest problem Wood's governor-generalship has to grapple with and he's not going to let anyone quit. And neither am I, if I can help it! I'm the one Wood gets after and I'm tired of taking all the blame alone!

REED. I called the Commission to disband it tonight. Three hours ago I was certain we should disband. I hesitate now to propose continuing. The only course which remains open to us leads so far afield, seems so blocked with difficulty and beset with danger that I stand appalled before it. .

GORGAS. You're being damn mysterious!

TORY. What is the course?

REED. To set our microscopes aside.

CARROLL. Say!

REED. And concentrate on new methods for prevention.

AGRAMONTE. How?

REED. By turning our minds to how yellow fever spreads, Agramonte. From man to man and village to village and even across the sea.

GORGAS. I should like to know something about that!

CARROLL. Not me. It's not my line. I'm a microscope man. I don't give a hoot in hell how it spreads. I'll work on cause or nothing.

TORY. I admire determination in men of science and if the Marine Hospital Corps hadn't covered the ground . . .

AGRAMONTE. Yes, doctor. What more can this commission add?

REED (to AGRAMONTE). I've come to suspect a middleman here. An infection carrier. In all likelihood an insect. Which we might hope to identify and which you, Gorgas, might subsequently wipe out.

AGRAMONTE. What kind of insect?

REED. Present evidence seems to point to a mosquito.

LAZEAR (coming forward). Did you say mosquito?

GORGAS (a weary smile). You're not going off on that tangent, are you, Reed?

TORY. You can't be serious!

REED. I couldn't possibly be more so.

LAZEAR. And why not, Colonel Tory? If we find that a mosquito is the carrier of yellow fever and stop that, won't we have done our job? And what a job finding it's going to be! The kind that comes once in a lifetime! God bless you, Reed! Mosquitoes are meat and drink to me. (General laughter except from TORY.)

TORY. These fads are the curse of modern medicine!

LAZEAR. Fads? What fads?

TORY. Is medical science going insect mad?

LAZEAR. Where have you been at? Never hear of Smith's Texas fever tick? How about Bruce and the tsetse fly in Africa? Haven't Ross and Grassi just nailed malaria to a mosquito? I confirmed that myself! This fits in! This belongs! Insect mad! That's a hell of a thing to say these days, Colonel!

REED. Easy, Lazear.

TORY. Your junior colleague is a modern, Major. We have the dignity of science to consider!

LAZEAR. That girl! Holding a torch, standing in a niche!

TORY. We have enough theories about this already!

LAZEAR. There's still room for one that works!

TORY. We must draw some line against these radicals!

LAZEAR. Not so long since they called Pasteur a radical!

TORY. And so he was!

LAZEAR. May be! But he was right!

REED (smiling). Easy, Lazear! I want to hear what Gorgas has to say.

GORGAS (also smiling). Why the mosquito? Why not the flea, the louse or the homely bedbug?

LAZEAR. Let me answer that, Reed! (To GORGAS.) Because yellow jack's not confined to the louse and bedbug belt! The cleanest parts of town may be deadliest! You find fleas in the best families everywhere, but you don't find yellow jack outside mosquito districts! And it's worse in summer, which is mosquito season! You see, I've got all the answers, Major Gorgas! If you want more, read Carter on the epidemic in Alabama! He came so near this!

GORGAS. You've silenced me, Lazear! You've silenced me!

TORY (rising angrily). He has not silenced me! I fail to see why the Marine Hospital Corps with its long record in tropical epidemics should waste its time on inexperienced and untrained amateurs who . . .

GORGAS. This is no time for jealousies, Colonel Tory!

TORY. The Marine Hospital Corps, Major, does not stoop to . . .

LAZEAR. Aren't you the boys who diagnosed malaria at Pinar? Haven't you been fumigating Havana for three years? Who are you to talk!

REED. That isn't the subject in hand, Lazear!

LAZEAR. All right. One thing more and I'll shut up. We're not going home! We're not going to say: "Humanity and knowledge can both go hang, because we haven't got the guts to exceed instructions!" The hell with instructions! The hell with cause and cure! Reed's right and I'll go it alone if I have to! Only I won't have to work alone! There's a crazy old troglodyte here in this town! An old Scotchman with spectacles and side whiskers. Finlay, his name is. . . . (*Sensation.*)

TORY (*horrified*). Finlay!

GORGAS. You don't mean old Finlay!

AGRAMONTE. Carlos Finlay?

LAZEAR. So you Cubans call him. . . .

TORY. You don't propose going to him for . . .

LAZEAR. Why not? He broke this mosquito idea years ago! He's got his particular guilty mosquito all picked out. I'm on my way to Dr. Finlay tomorrow morning and I'm going to say . . .

REED. I was just coming to Dr. Finlay, Lazear.

LAZEAR. We'll go see him together!

REED. I was just about to propose . . .

TORY. Do you *know* Finlay?

REED. I hope to know him before I'm many days older.

CARROLL. I never heard of him.

AGRAMONTE. I know him, of course. We Cubans revere and love him as a patriot. He did nobly throughout our revolution. As a scientist, however, I am afraid . . .

GORGAS. I know him, too. He was almost the first friend I made when I came here. He's a dear old fellow and a first-rate physician. But he'll talk your ear off about that mosquito and if there'd been anything in the idea, Reed, wouldn't nineteen years have brought it out?

TORY. Finlay's a crank. No more. A harmless crank.

REED. He may be, Colonel. He may be completely mad. If he is, though, he has a brave kind of madness. The jumping forward kind that's always too risky for the completely sane. You have your convictions. I have only my curiosity.

AGRAMONTE. I can think of nothing better to suggest.

CARROLL. This isn't my line. But go ahead anyway.

LAZEAR (*through his teeth*). Finlay's got to be tried! There's no doubt about it!

TORY (*slyly*). There is very grave doubt, if you'll allow me, Doctor. The scheme isn't even possible.

LAZEAR. Why isn't it?

TORY. Could you draw any conclusion regarding mosquitoes without producing real cases of yellow fever from their bites?

LAZEAR. Did I say we could?

TORY. Aren't you forgetting that yellow fever's unlike other diseases? You can't give it to guinea pigs or monkeys or mice. You can't give it to any animal except man.

LAZEAR. I hadn't thought of that!

TORY. Think of it now and tell me how you could hope to test Dr. Finlay's mosquitoes by any conceivable experiment.

REED (*quietly*). We haven't yet tried experimenting on men.

(*A general gasp.* TORY *rises, astounded.*)

CARROLL. For Christ's sake, Reed!

LAZEAR. By God! Get the mosquitoes! Feed 'em on sick men! Let 'em bite healthy men! See what happens!

TORY (*stammering*). You don't propose using human guinea pigs!

REED. I hadn't thought of calling them by that name.

TORY. I can't believe my ears! Doctors, you call yourselves! Do you realize this is human vivisection! And might be manslaughter! Or even murder!

(*More or less together.*)

GORGAS. He's got you there, Reed!

CARROLL. You *are* going it pretty strong!

AGRAMONTE. Yes, I admit I hadn't thought of . . .

TORY. If Finlay were right and one of your victims died!

REED. If we fail at this, our victims, as you call them, will be none the worse for a few harmless mosquito bites. If we succeed, we shall have risked a few dozen lives to save countless thousands.

TORY. No! No! You've got to be stopped!

LAZEAR. We haven't started yet!

TORY. You're not going to start! Wait until General Wood hears of this!

REED. I'll take my chances, Colonel,

with Leonard Wood, and if the members of this Commission . . .

AGRAMONTE. You can count on me, Doctor!

CARROLL. We stand by, of course, Reed!

LAZEAR. This is an independent Commission, Colonel!

TORY. It isn't independent of Washington!

LAZEAR. Even Washington will think twice before it . . .

TORY (*shouting him down*). American public opinion won't think twice! The American press and pulpit won't think twice! You know how they stand on animal vivisection! I'll go to them before I let you disgrace science and the army with this monstrous . . .

LAZEAR. Do you mean you'd run to yellow journals! Obstructing the very thing you pretend to . . . (MISS BLAKE *has entered below carrying a lantern.*)

MISS BLAKE. Dr. Agramonte?

AGRAMONTE. Yes, Miss Blake?

MISS BLAKE. Please overlook my interrupting. There's a case just come in and Dr. Ames very much wants Major Gorgas's opinion before they take him over to my ward. (TWO ORDERLIES *enter carrying* MAJOR CARTWRIGHT, *sick unto death on a stretcher.* DR. AMES, *a vigorous Southerner in his forties, follows them in.* GORGAS *goes down to meet them. The others come down gradually.*) It's a Major Cartwright. I knew him in Matanzas before I came here. His papers show he had yellow fever two years ago.

AGRAMONTE. Dr. Ames is the physician in charge of our yellow fever ward, Major Gorgas. (GORGAS *nods to* AMES *and bends over stretcher.*)

AMES. If he hasn't got it now, what has he got?

GORGAS (*to the sick man*). Major Cartwright?

CARTWRIGHT. They're trying to tell me I've got yellow jack, Major! You can't have it twice!

GORGAS (*examining*). Never heard of anyone having it twice.

CARTWRIGHT. Well, I had it two years ago behind Santiago.

GORGAS. Yes, it was bad in Santiago two years ago.

CARTWRIGHT. I had a bad case, too. And just turning a little yellow doesn't mean . . .

GORGAS. It needn't mean a thing. (*He straightens up, nodding to* AGRAMONTE.)

CARTWRIGHT. That's why I didn't come over four days ago.

AGRAMONTE. It's a pity you didn't come four days ago. You might be more comfortable now. Your ward, Miss Blake. (MISS BLAKE *starts, then nods to the* ORDERLIES, *who carry* CARTWRIGHT *out.*)

CARTWRIGHT (*as they go*). I knew I couldn't have yellow jack! (*To* AMES, *who is following him.*) You ought to know better than to scare a man half to death! Nobody ever gets yellow jack twice! Lord, but I'm sick, though! (*He is gone, an attack of vomiting audible off stage. The light has gone from the sky. As before, only the foreground group is lighted.*)

CARROLL. They've been calling yellow jack malaria at Pinar. Wonder what he had that they called yellow jack two years ago.

TORY. You don't mean he's got it?

GORGAS (*flatly*). He'll be dead tomorrow. (REED's *face sets.*)

TORY. And you'd have done that to men in cold blood! (*He can say no more, except:*) If you're ready, Major Gorgas, I'll bid these gentlemen a very good evening.

REED (*steadily*). Good evening, Colonel. (*But the Colonel is already on his way.*)

GORGAS (*To* REED, *somewhat apologetic*). Well, it turned out livelier than most medical meetings. Sorry I couldn't give you more support. It wouldn't have panned out, though. I'm right about Finlay.

REED. You may be.

GORGAS. That poor devil Cartwright certainly cut the discussion short! Just what was needed to drive the point home!

REED. Good night, Gorgas.

(*Ad lib. good nights as "Call to Quarters" sounds.* GORGAS *goes, turns up into the laboratory,* LAZEAR *following, letting out the full hurt of his disappointment. The others in their turn follow into laboratory.*)

LAZEAR. Reed, if you had this in the back of your head why didn't you just tell us? Why did you have to let them in on it? We could have tackled it alone!

CARROLL. If you ask me, it's just as well!

LAZEAR (*hotly*). I don't agree! We might have made history!

CARROLL. Yes. Or made damn fools

of ourselves!

LAZEAR. Don't be so sure of that!

REED (*quietly*). Did you think I'd be stopped by anything they said? After that poor devil "drove the point home"?

LAZEAR. Reed!

CARROLL. Now listen, Reed! You know what Tory can do to you!

REED (*strong because imperturbable*). There's no doubt of what Colonel Tory can do; I see no reason, though, why he or anyone should know what we're up to from now on.

(*Pause, then:*)

AGRAMONTE (*low*). But, Doctor, would it be possible to experiment on men in secret?

LAZEAR (*quick and low*). It's got to be!

CARROLL. Men, though!

(*Offstage* THE QUARTET *begins singing very softly.*)

QUARTET.
"Oh, the moonlight's fair tonight along
                    the Wabash,
From the fields there comes the breath
                    of new-mown hay;
Through the sycamores the candle lights
                    are gleaming,
On the banks of the Wabash, far
                    away."

CARROLL. Men, God Almighty!

LAZEAR (*quickly*). That's got to be, too!

REED (*low but stern*). I'm afraid so. I'm afraid so.

CARROLL (*a whisper*). Men . . . (*The light dies on the laboratory as the screen closes. At the same time light shows two tents on either side of the stage. On the R.* O'HARA *sits on his cot studying Gray's "Anatomy" while* BRINKERHOF, *seated on the cot opposite, undresses for his night's rest. On the L.,* BUSCH *and* MC CLELLAND *sit on their cots drinking beer.* MC CLELLAND *is dozing.* BUSCH *also has a book.* O'HARA *looks up from his book.*)

O'HARA. Will you listen to this, now, John? (*He reads.*) "A thorough study of human physiology is in itself an education. Like the Atlantic between the Old and New Worlds, its waves wash the shores of the two worlds of matter and of mind. Through its waters, as yet unfurrowed by the keel of any Columbus, lies the road from one to the other." (BRINKERHOF *is impressed but baffled.*)

BUSCH. Get this, Mac. (*He reads.*) "You were horrified at our intending to do away with private property, but in our existing society private property is already done away with for nine-tenths of the population. In other words, you reproach us with intending to do away with your property. Precisely so; this is just what we intend." (*He looks up.*) Let 'em answer that! (*He sees that* MC CLELLAND, *due to unconsciousness, is not interested. He resumes reading.* QUARTET *carries on with "Good-bye, Dolly Gray."*)

BRINKERHOF (*to* O'HARA, *with the morbid fascination of a small boy*). Let's see the picture of the unborn baby.

O'HARA (*learnedly*). The embryo, it's called. (*He shows the picture.*)

BRINKERHOF. Do you mean to say I once looked like that?

O'HARA. It's hard for me to believe I ever did!

BRINKERHOF (*a shudder*). Guess I'll go brush my teeth. (*He finds his toothbrush and goes.* O'HARA *resumes reading.* MC CLELLAND *has roused himself.*)

MC CLELLAND. You read too much. It ain't good for a man to have so much on his mind.

BUSCH (*bitterly*). Dough! You can't even be a good radical without dough! That's what gets me! If I had three hundred dollars . . . (O'HARA *closes his book disconsolately and sits staring before him in abject self-pity.*) I'd go back to my printing trade like I'm always saying. In my own shop like my old man had before me that the cops smashed up in Chicago when I was a kid. And I'd get out a paper that'd tell the workers the truth. I know a printing shop in Newark, New Jersey, I could buy in on if I had three hundred dollars. And the other partners all radicals like me.

MC CLELLAND. I wouldn't waste any three hundred on no workers. Not me! I'd buy me a little home back in Savannah and get me a wife and quit whoring around. I want to get back to Savannah and take my girl walking around the Plaza evenings.

BUSCH (*violently*). And me! Do you think I don't want to get home to Chicago? And ride on the "El" and smell that old coal smoke again!

QUARTET (*carrying on from "Dolly Gray."*)
"Just tell them that you saw me,
    She said, they'll know the rest.
Just tell them I was looking well, you
                    know.

Just whisper if you get a chance
To mother dear, and say,
    I love her as I did long years ago."
(MC CLELLAND *and* BUSCH *are submerged in homesickness.* BRINKERHOF *has returned to* O'HARA.)

BRINKERHOF. You'll ruin your eyesight reading.

O'HARA. I wasn't reading.

BRINKERHOF. What were you doing?

O'HARA. Thinking that when God gives a man a call to a profession he should provide the wherewithal to answer. (*He proceeds morosely to undress.*)

BRINKERHOF. Now you mustn't get discouraged, John.

O'HARA. What is discouragement but submission to fate? (BRINKERHOF *gets into bed.*)

MC CLELLAND. That's a beautiful song. I can't stand songs about mothers. I'm an orphan and I ain't thought of my mother in years and years.

BUSCH. I'm an orphan, too. But I'm a Jewish orphan.

MC CLELLAND. Drink some more beer.

BUSCH (*as* MC CLELLAND *fills his glass*). If that beer was rum I could drink it neat and never show it! That's how I am when I think about my ambitions.

MC CLELLAND. Me, too, when I get homesick. (*They drink up morosely.* QUARTET *carries on with* "Good-bye, My Blue Bell!" O'HARA *has paused in his undressing, lost in melancholy and none too soon for the sake of decency.*)

O'HARA. To them that ask little, what they ask may be given. You'll get the stripes and satisfaction of your sergeancy. And Mac will get his girl to marry and the satisfaction of her. And Busch may find the three hundred he's wanting to buy him his revolutionary printing press and spread death and destruction over all the land. For even that's little compared with the vision of service in my mind's eye, and the passionate conviction of my gifts for the same in my heart, and the need of a costly training before me and the wage of a private soldier in my pocket! (*He gets into his cot.*)

QUARTET (*softly, off-stage*).
"When you hear dem bells go ding-a-
                                        ling . . .
Boom. Boom. Boom. . . ."

BRINKERHOF. We all got to watch for our opportunities, John.

MC CLELLAND. We just got to wait for our chances, Chicago.

QUARTET. (*A little louder.*)
"All join round and a-sweetly you must
                                        sing,
And when the . . .'"
(*Light begins to grow slowly upon the laboratory.*)

BUSCH. When'll they come and where'll they come from, Mac?

BRINKERHOF. I'm a great believer in opportunities, John.

O'HARA. Thanks for the comfort and good night to you, John. (*The light dims upon both pairs of soldiers at the same time. Now the laboratory, its shelves, glassware, and microscopes, shines with unearthly effulgence, as from within itself, and the four members of the Commission still seated there seem prophetically to answer the soldiers' needs out of night and the future.*)

CARROLL (*a whisper*). Men, God Almighty! Men!

QUARTET. (*Crescendo to full volume.*)
"Verse am over and the chorus all join in,
There'll be a hot time in the old town
                                        tonight."

(*Darkness, then:*)

AGRAMONTE. I have the honor, Major Reed, to present my colleague, Dr. Finlay, for these many years a distinguished leader of our profession here in Havana. Dr. Finlay, this is Dr. Lazear and this, Dr. Carroll. (*Then bright sunlight and* DR. FINLAY *stands above, gravely and formally shaking hands with the four members of the Commission.* FINLAY *is an elderly and bewhiskered little Scotchman. The ceremony of introduction completed,* FINLAY *leads his guests down to the foreground.*)

FINLAY. We shall sit here in the patio if you don't mind, gentlemen. My office is dark. I see your faces more clearly here in the sun. Make yourselves as comfortable as you can. (*They sit,* FINLAY *composing himself last.*)

REED. Shall we omit the preliminaries? Dr. Finlay can guess what our errand is.

FINLAY (*With a wary smile*). Men come to my house on many errands, Major. Bibliophiles to examine my Latin manuscripts. Revolutionists to discuss politics. My fellow scientists don't honor me so often.

REED. We come to join you, doctor, in the war you have waged these many years alone. We offer you our co-operation and ask your assistance.

FINLAY (*on his guard*). One thing at a time. We can discuss your co-operation later. What form of assistance had you expected of me?

REED. Your knowledge of your yellow fever mosquito.

AGRAMONTE. And, specifically, Doctor, the mosquito herself. As many specimens as you can spare.

FINLAY. Did you think I should have them flying about my house? Or in bird cages like canary birds?

AGRAMONTE. The eggs will do.

REED. You have the eggs, I think? (*But* FINLAY *draws back.*)

FINLAY. For nineteen years science has laughed at me, Major. At the cracked old Finlay and his mosquitoes. And nowhere more cruelly than through American army doctors. Now you come running to me to save your faces! I might enjoy laughing myself now. I have a sardonic sense of humor. Will you be surprised if I have no impulse to share my secret?

REED. We shall be deeply disappointed, Dr. Finlay.

AGRAMONTE. We shall hope to persuade you.

FINLAY. I wonder you have not come to me before.

AGRAMONTE. We were committed to a particular line of investigation.

FINLAY. At which you have failed.

AGRAMONTE. At which we certainly have not succeeded.

FINLAY. I could have told you you would be wasting time! The microbe of yellow fever is not to be found by any technique yet developed.

AGRAMONTE. The four of us have reached that conclusion.

FINLAY. The disease could have been conquered long since, however, had it not been for the stupidity of men of science . . . so-called!

CARROLL. Can't say that to us, Doctor! We're likely to prove your case for you if you've got a . . .

FINLAY (*offended at once*). Prove my case? You mean you doubt my discovery?

CARROLL. There isn't anything I doubt! Till I'm shown!

FINLAY. For thirty years I've battled with this disease and seen all other observable conditions change and only this one mosquito remain constant. The truth I gave out nineteen years ago, Dr. Carroll, was founded on observation . . .

CARROLL. That isn't proof.

FINLAY. Will any proof convince the fools who've doubted me?

CARROLL. Fools have to be convinced, Dr. Finlay. That's what they're for!

FINLAY. If this is your attitude, let me say forthwith that I have no interest in your co-operation. (*The members of the Commission are dismayed.*)

LAZEAR. This is what might be called unexpected!

AGRAMONTE (*breaking in*). If you'll pause to consider, Dr. Finlay, that . . .

REED (*breaking in*). Dr. Finlay can hardly include us among . . .

CARROLL (*breaking in*). Get me right, Dr. Finlay! This isn't my line. But Reed . . . (*His manner becomes solemn.*) Walter Reed's a great man, Doctor!

REED. Better leave that part to me, Carroll!

CARROLL. Well, God damn it, you are and I know what I'm talking about! (*Back to* FINLAY.) I ought to! It's his training made a scientist of me! Christ! I was a lousy lumberjack when he took me on! You're getting Walter Reed on this! And that's something you don't want to turn down!

FINLAY (*cold*). I am not unmindful of Major Reed's reputation.

REED. I can't say as much for myself as Carroll's said, Doctor. But I *am* a worker, a careful and thorough worker. And I shall go after this with all there is in me.

FINLAY. I have my own reputation to think of, Major!

CARROLL (*angry*). Well, if you think that's going to suffer from . . .

FINLAY (*fairly shaking with indignation*). I have cherished my great discovery for nineteen years! Do you expect me to give it up to you? To make use of it and get glory from it when I . . .

LAZEAR (*breaking in*). Glory isn't the idea, Dr. Finlay!

AGRAMONTE (*breaking in*). Not give it up, Doctor! Share it!

FINLAY (*finally*). No, gentlemen! No! I appreciate your disappointment, but . . . No.

CARROLL. Well, if he doesn't want to work with us . . .

LAZEAR. Go easy, Carroll. (*His own wild smile.*) Whether Dr. Finlay wants us or not we want him! To see his discovery through to a finish with us!

FINLAY (*somewhat cheered*). You believe in my discovery, Dr. Lazear?

LAZEAR (*shining enthusiasm*). Yes, I believe in it!

CARROLL. Now *you* go easy!

LAZEAR (*riding him down*). It's simple! It fits into the scheme of things! It's got to be right!

FINLAY. It is!

LAZEAR (*ablaze*). We know how many truths have to bide their time and wait for the world to catch up with 'em! We know how many go down unrecognized! We're what you've been waiting for, Dr. Finlay! We're going to save your discovery for you and pull the whole tribe of science into line!

FINLAY (*enchanted*). An admirable young man! And the look of the seeker in the eyes!

LAZEAR. All you need is one bang-up demonstration!

FINLAY (*drawing back*). Doubt again! Proof again!

LAZEAR. Thank God for both of 'em and the stiffer we make 'em the better! Doubt and more doubt till there's no escaping proof! Then we'll set your discovery where it belongs! Where folks can see it! Up there! In the constellation of established fact!

FINLAY. You almost persuade me!

LAZEAR. Come along with us, Doctor! You belong with us!

FINLAY. Why didn't you come nineteen years ago?

REED. I'm no stranger to waiting, Dr. Finlay. All my life long my prayer has been that I might in some way alleviate human suffering. I think this may be my chance as well as yours.

FINLAY (*desperate*). What can you do more than I have done already?

CARROLL. No one man can do all of any job.

FINLAY. But the proof you demand lies beyond any man's power!

REED. We don't feel that!

FINLAY (*full blast*). You show your ignorance, Major! Look at you! A gentle, kindly man! No better fitted for this than I was myself! This wants the courage to be ruthless! You cannot test my mosquito without risking life!

LAZEAR. We know that, but . . . (*But nineteen years of bitterness breaks out in FINLAY.*)

FINLAY. There is no "but"! That is the bitter fact! Do you think I have not dreamed that dream myself! What if we do risk a few lives, I've said, to save countless generations for the future! How many times I've said it! It cannot be! Are you asking me to believe you will be allowed to experiment on your soldiers!

CARROLL. I don't like the idea myself!

REED. Since there's no other way. And since the need . . .

LAZEAR. What the hell! An army of occupation! Nothing to think about but rum and women! We've only to call for volunteers!

FINLAY. And then? What then?

AGRAMONTE. Why, then the demonstration!

FINLAY (*scornful*). You live in your own little world of professionals. You forget that other world outside, where the humane and kind-hearted and Christian live and love their fellow men! They may send their sons off to be butchered in battle, but let one of you lift one finger in this war and they will engulf you! You will be destroyed! There will arise such power of public fury . . .

LAZEAR (*in a whisper of suppressed excitement*). All right, Dr. Finlay! Let the soldiers wait! They'll keep! They'll be there any time we need 'em! We'll start this off ourselves!

FINLAY. You, gentlemen!

REED (*kindling*). The four of us!

LAZEAR. No. Only three. Agramonte's had yellow fever.

AGRAMONTE (*regretful*). Yes.

CARROLL. Am I in on this?

LAZEAR. Don't you want to be?

CARROLL. I like to be considered before I . . .

LAZEAR. I'll try it first. You can follow me.

CARROLL. I can follow you, can I?

LAZEAR (*nodding*). You've got five kids.

CARROLL. You've got a kid yourself.

LAZEAR. That's four less than you. We'll hold Reed back to see that we don't bungle and . . .

REED. Why didn't we think of this before?

LAZEAR. What a job it's turning out to be!

FINLAY (*his vocal powers only just restored*). But I can't have it, gentlemen!

You must put this idea out of your minds at once!

LAZEAR (*laughing*). Thought you wanted us to be ruthless!

FINLAY. But this is carrying things too far!

CARROLL. After all, there may not be any risk.

FINLAY. There is, Doctor! Believe me, there is!

REED. Then the three of us should make easy marks!

CARROLL. If you're right!

LAZEAR. And your mosquitoes aren't too fastidious!

FINLAY. No! You are men of science! Your lives are valuable!

REED. Is any man's life worth more than the cause he risks it on?

(*Pause, then:*)

FINLAY (*deeply stirred*). You must let me thank you. Major Reed. My friends, all of you. You come to me after nineteen years. Strangers. You fill my life with hope as sudden music fills our Cuban nights. I concede your skepticism and revere your courage. I am honored. Tell me how I may serve you.

AGRAMONTE (*suavely covering the embarrassment of the others.*) Let them have the eggs, doctor. I think you had better let them have the eggs.

FINLAY. When I give them into your hands I give you nineteen years of my life. Well, I do it gladly. (*He goes out. The four members of the Commission eye each other in the most intense excitement, but each one in his own mood,* AGRAMONTE *worried,* CARROLL *amused,* REED *solemn,* LAZEAR *white hot.* FINLAY *returns carrying a porcelain dish covered with a gauze. He sets it down on the table to uncover it, the four members of the Commission leaning eagerly forward. The light begins imperceptibly to fade until only the five faces are visible, the old Scotchman's lit with a religious fervor as he describes his great discovery.*) You have only to raise the water in that dish and those eggs will hatch the criminal. Beware of her. She isn't one of your wild marsh mosquitoes. She's your domestic pet. Shares your home with you, takes her siesta underneath your eaves, raises her family in your patio fountain and rewards your hospitality with death. How do I know? I know! I have a mystic's faith in this mosquito! You hold the key to yellow fever in your hands. I pray for your sake

and all humanity's that you may turn the lock I failed to turn.

REED. Curious. Very curious.

CARROLL. They look like little black cigars.

LAZEAR (*a dry whisper*). Come on! Let's get going! (*Darkness. Then* THE QUARTET *is singing again.*)

QUARTET.

"After the din of the battle's roar,
   Just at the close of day,
Wounded and bleeding upon the field,
   Two dying soldiers lay.
One held a ringlet of thin gray hair,
   One held a lock of brown,
Bidding each other a last farewell,
   Just as the sun went down."

(AMES *is standing, below, between two cots in which soldiers lie sick of yellow fever, and* MISS BLAKE *looks on as he speaks over the singing.*)

AMES. I don't know any more about it than you do, boys. I'm only a doctor. These lab experiments are 'way over my head. I get my orders to let 'em bring their mosquitoes in here to the ward to suck a few yellow fever germs out of your blood. You've got plenty to spare, so there's nothing for you to get excited about. My God, one little mosquito bite won't make you feel any worse than you do already. (AGRAMONTE *enters above and comes quickly down the stair. He carries a wire basket filled with test tubes, the mouths of which are covered with tightly stretched gauze*). You back again so soon?

AGRAMONTE. Don't tell me I'm wearing out my welcome.

AMES. Oh, no! I was just preparing these new arrivals, that's all.

AGRAMONTE (*hesitant*). I don't like to trouble them, but if you've explained ...

AMES. Go ahead. They're too sick to mind. Skeeters hungry?

AGRAMONTE. They've been crying like babies. (*Then, to* MISS BLAKE.) If you'll turn back the blankets so I can get at him, Miss Blake ...

MISS BLAKE (*as she turns blankets back from first cot.*) Don't be afraid. Doctor isn't going to hurt you. (AGRAMONTE *selects a test tube from the basket and deftly inverts it, applying its mouth to the patient's abdomen. He taps the end lightly to jar the mosquito down towards the flesh.*)

AGRAMONTE. Tap. Tap. There! Don't move. They itch less afterwards if you let 'em finish.

AMES (*looking on*). You're getting neat at that. Who taught you?

AGRAMONTE. Lazear.

AMES. Where did he learn?

AGRAMONTE. Malaria. (*Then to the patient, as he removes test tube.*) There, that's all. That wasn't so bad, was it? Insect No. 47, Miss Blake.

MISS BLAKE (*noting it down on her pad*). Insect 47. Infected from a severe case. Second day of illness. (*Then as she applies alcohol to the bite.*) Just a little medication to soothe the itching. (AGRAMONTE *returns first test tube to basket and selects a second.*)

AMES. Once you get your skeeters filled up with yellow jack blood, though . . .

AGRAMONTE (*wry*). Yes, Ames?

AMES. What do you do with 'em back there in that lab of yours?

(*Pause, then:*)

AGRAMONTE (*evasive*). Oh, various things. (*Then:*) Why?

AMES. I was wondering. There are some pretty brutal rumors going around.

AGRAMONTE. You mustn't believe everything you hear, Ames. (*Then, to* MISS BLAKE.) Next. (*Business as before*).

MISS BLAKE. Don't be afraid. Doctor isn't going to hurt you.

AGRAMONTE. Tap. Tap.

QUARTET.
"One thought of mother at home, alone,
Feeble and old and gray,
One of the sweetheart he left in town,
Happy and young and gay.
One kissed a ringlet of thin gray hair,
One kissed a lock of brown,
Bidding farewell to the Stars and Stripes,
Just as the sun went down."
(*Darkness, under cover of which the cots vanish. Then light again as* O'HARA, BUSCH, *and* MC CLELLAND *enter above and come sauntering down the stairs.*)

O'HARA (*speaking over the music.*) Go on, Mac. Don't stop. I crave all information of a medical nature.

MC CLELLAND. He keeps the mosquitoes each one in a kind of a bottle and he starts at one end and goes straight through the place till every boy there's got a bite in the belly.

BUSCH. I wouldn't know what to make of a thing like that. I wouldn't believe it unless I seen it.

MC CLELLAND. I hope to tell you I ain't never seen it! And I hope to God I don't

never see it! I got no wish to go inside that place!

O'HARA. Major Reed! There's a man for thinking up bright ideas!

BUSCH. I think it's a hell of an idea! It's just one more lousy trick they thought up to put over on us! My God, ain't sick boys got enough on their minds without scratching bites! They wouldn't stand for it only they ain't class-conscious. (O'HARA *and* MC CLELLAND *lift their hands in protest.*) There can't be nothing in the idea at that! How could a little harmless bug like a mosquito carry a terrible disease like yellow jack?

O'HARA. The insect may be small, Chicago, but germs are smaller and it's a question of relative size and capacity.

BUSCH. You give me a pain with your medical information. Mosquitoes ain't insects. Insects is things that crawl and jump and bite.

MC CLELLAND. Lions do that and lions ain't insects. (*"Call to Quarters" sounds.*) There's "Quarters."

O'HARA (*as they go*). There's more here than meets the eye, Chicago. And only the few of us are privileged to grasp the mysteries of medical science. (*At the same time light grows on the laboratory and the screen, opening, shows* REED *seated at his desk facing the audience, deep in troubled thought.*)

REED. Brinkerhof! (BRINKERHOF *enters laboratory*). Did you see the transport people?

BRINKERHOF. They're holding a stateroom for you, sir.

REED. What time does the transport sail?

BRINKERHOF. Six in the morning, sir. But you can go aboard tonight.

REED. Thank you.

BRINKERHOF. I'm sorry to hear you're thinking of leaving us, sir.

REED. It isn't my idea, Mr. Brinkerhof. I've been ordered home. (*Then:*) You haven't mentioned it to anyone?

BRINKERHOF. Not a soul, sir.

REED. Ask Major Gorgas to come in. Then see if you can locate Dr. Lazear and round up the other members of the Commission. (BRINKERHOF *salutes and goes.* REED *draws a long envelope from his pocket and extracts an official paper from it. He unfolds this, studies it, and suddenly, with a gesture of desperate rage, begins pacing to and fro.* GORGAS *enters.*) Sit down, Gorgas! Well?

GORGAS (*pointing to paper*). Are those the orders?

REED. To Washington by the first available transportation. (*And he throws paper angrily on desk.*)

GORGAS. Thought I'd find you all raging about it together.

REED. I haven't broken the news to the others yet. I waited for you.

GORGAS (*humorously distressed for him*). Don't know what I can do for you, Reed. General Wood couldn't tell me any more than we know already. The orders came through, that's all. You'll find out when you get to Washington.

REED. I can't leave Cuba now! I can't let go of this job now! I'm too deep into it to get out now!

GORGAS. Your leaving needn't hold things up. Lazear and Carroll are both good men.

REED. I can't desert Lazear and Carroll now!

GORGAS (*curious*). Sounds interesting.

REED. It's the confounded stupidity of it, Gorgas! And when you begin fitting things together and see what's behind these orders!

GORGAS. Oh, Reed! Reed! We've been in the army too long for that! They've forgotten what they sent you here to do or they've found something else for you or they've just got tired of waiting.

REED. I know that's possible. (*Pause, then:*) But I think we owe this to your friend Tory!

GORGAS (*surprised*). Tory? (*Then:*) Why Tory? (REED *decides on making a clean breast of things.*)

REED. You were out here with him that night a month ago. You heard him that night. He's been out here since. Seeing what he can see. Making inquiries. (*Then, with suppressed fury.*) Even asking questions of soldiers!

GORGAS (*incredulous*). Have you started on that?

REED. With Lazear. So you see I've more than my own disappointment to think of.

GORGAS (*awed*). Results?

REED. You never know when. (GORGAS *smiles, but* REED *continues with the deepest possible feeling.*) I've infected Lazear. I might be at sea and not know. And Carroll comes next. I might be in Washing-

ton with both of them down. I'd never forgive myself! Right now, Gorgas, this moment, Lazear's watching his temperature, waiting for the first sign . . . (*Then:*) I am deeply fond of Lazear. I know you don't believe in this, but you'll admit it's possible I'm right.

GORGAS. At any rate, I understand how you feel.

REED. Can't you do something to keep me here?

(*A pause,* GORGAS *moving about. Then he speaks with sudden decision.*)

GORGAS. Sure you want to stay?

REED. Gorgas!

GORGAS. No, I mean it! If Tory's responsible for these orders and you do want Lazear and Carroll to keep going, they may need your influence in Washington more than they need you here. (REED *is impressed.*)

REED. If I do go and anything should happen?

GORGAS. I'll do what's expected of me. (*Then:*)

REED. I'll go. Thanks for giving me a reason.

GORGAS. If that's all I can give you . . .

REED. Won't you wish me luck?

GORGAS. At bringing Lazear and Carroll down with yellow fever? I'm afraid I can't go that far with you, Reed.

REED. Well, don't talk about it and . . .

(LAZEAR *enters.*)

LAZEAR. How are you, Major Gorgas?

GORGAS. The important question is: how you are, Dr. Lazear?

(LAZEAR *turns, surprised, to* REED.)

REED. He had to be told.

LAZEAR (*to* GORGAS). I'm very well. (*He laughs.*) Seems a pity, doesn't it?

GORGAS. Does it? (*He gives up.*) The laboratory mind is beyond me! Good night, Reed.

REED. Good night, Gorgas.

(GORGAS *goes.*)

LAZEAR (*quick and anxious*). Was it wise to tell him?

REED. It couldn't be avoided.

LAZEAR. Why not?

REED. There were reasons.

LAZEAR. Has anything gone wrong?

(*For answer* REED *grasps the younger man's shoulders with sudden intensity.*)

REED. You want to keep on with this, don't you, Lazear?

LAZEAR (*horrified*). You're not thinking of stopping me yet?

REED. I'm thinking of you!

LAZEAR (*relieved*). Is that all?

REED. That's all. (*Then his own feeling embarrasses him and he draws back.*) Still no sign?

LAZEAR. Normal as hell. (*He offers a clinical thermometer.*)

REED (*examining it*). How long since?

LAZEAR. Just now. (REED *smiles, returning thermometer.*)

REED. Not even a headache?

LAZEAR. Without any temperature?

REED. That would be a good deal to ask! (*He backs off.*) No feeling here? (*His hands press his own groins.*)

LAZEAR (*repeating action*). Don't think so.

REED. You'd know. All over your body. Let's look at Agramonte's record. (*He sits at his desk, pulling notebook toward him.* CARROLL *and* AGRAMONTE *enter, buttoning their tunics.*)

AGRAMONTE. You sent for us, Doctor?

CARROLL. We were right in the midst of a card game. What's the idea?

REED. I'll tell you in a minute.

AGRAMONTE. Not Lazear! Lazear, it hasn't happened!

CARROLL (*to* LAZEAR). Don't tell us the skeeters have got you!

LAZEAR. No.

REED (*to* LAZEAR). How many days is it since . . .

LAZEAR. Since the last bite I took? Six.

REED. I should think you'd have shown something in six days.

(CARROLL *relaxes as usual.*)

CARROLL. Well, you can't keep on feeling fit indefinitely and not cast some shadow over this mosquito business.

LAZEAR. Did you expect things to be easy? They never are!

CARROLL. What do you say we give up mosquitoes and try seagulls!

LAZEAR. Go to hell!

CARROLL. I'd rather go home. I'm sick of this show.

REED (*deep in his notebooks*). Sit down, Carroll. I'll come to you. (CARROLL *sits, well pleased with himself.*)

LAZEAR (*stubborn*). If only our facts would keep up with our hunches what a cinch things would be! What if my first three bites haven't come off? What odds will you give me on my thirty-seventh? You can't let go once you're caught in a thing like this! There's always the chance of the lucky accident! There are plenty more combinations to try yet!

REED (*grim*). Plenty.

LAZEAR. I can tell you one trick we've overlooked! (*He is walking about in his excitement.*) And it's the same Ross struck on with malaria. (REED *looks up.*) You can feed *those* mosquitoes *full* of malaria blood and they can't hurt a baby for two weeks afterwards! They've got to have a good two weeks to ripen! We haven't given our skeeters any time!

REED (*to* AGRAMONTE). How long has your oldest mosquito had to digest her meal of yellow fever blood?

AGRAMONTE. Twelve days. There are still three left from the first lot we infected. No. Two. One died yesterday.

REED. Both infected from good strong cases?

AGRAMONTE. One case five days along. The other six. Both cases fatal.

LAZEAR. They're the next combination! Come on, Agramonte! We'll try both!

REED. Both, by all means. (*To* AGRAMONTE.) Understand, Agramonte? (AGRAMONTE *nods.*) Lazear starts again with two ripe ones day after tomorrow. If they take. (*To* LAZEAR.) Use Carroll to confirm you.

CARROLL. They won't take.

(LAZEAR *turns angrily, but* REED *cuts him off.*)

REED (*to* CARROLL). If Lazear still shows nothing by a week from Wednesday, Carroll, we'll start with you.

CARROLL. But, Chief, if Lazear still shows nothing in ten days, why do I have to . . .

REED. I'm giving orders.

CARROLL. All right, Chief. All right.

LAZEAR (*low*). Call yourself a scientist!

CARROLL. What the hell!

REED. Can you keep this pair in order, Agramonte?

AGRAMONTE. The experiment itself should do that, Doctor.

CARROLL. My heart may not be in this, but . . .

REED. You'll control your heart. If you were less pig-headed, Carroll, and you less hot-headed, Lazear, I should feel far more comfortable about . . .

LAZEAR. About what?

REED. I'll come to that. If either of you falls ill, let Gorgas know.

CARROLL. Gorgas! (REED *holds up his hand for silence.*)

REED. Ames is a good man, but I shall want Gorgas on hand, too. Your illness will mean the success of this, but you both mean a great deal to me.

CARROLL. Aren't you looking pretty far ahead, Chief?

REED (*riding him down*). Whether this succeeds or fails, however, I demand unimpeachable workmanship, because nothing less will . . .

LAZEAR. Why are you going into all this, Reed?

REED. Do you think you can handle this alone?

AGRAMONTE. Alone?

REED. I'm putting it up to you. (*He hands* LAZEAR *the orders identified earlier by* GORGAS. LAZEAR *glances and stares blankly back.*)

LAZEAR. Called home!

CARROLL. Who?

AGRAMONTE. Not Reed!

LAZEAR. Yes, Reed.

CARROLL (*voiceless*). My God! Let's see! (*He takes paper.*)

AGRAMONTE (*stammering*). But you can't go, Doctor! We can't go on without . . .

CARROLL (*pleading*). Now, listen, Chief! You've got to stick with this! It isn't fair to . . .

LAZEAR. You certainly are putting it up to us! (*The light concentrates upon* REED *alone.*)

REED. We were four in this. Now you'll be only three. God bring you safely through, Carroll . . . and Lazear.

(*Darkness. Then "Reveille" is sounded by the assembled field music. Then "Assembly" sounds. Then bright daylight shows the laboratory, its equipment augmented, now, by a considerable addition of glassware consisting of racks of the same gauze-covered test tubes which* AGRAMONTE *carried earlier to the yellow fever ward and of larger gauze-covered beakers.* CARROLL, *at his microscope, is deeply engrossed in the examination of a series of slides,* AGRAMONTE, *at the workbench, is entering infected mosquitoes in his record book. Behind the laboratory, back and forth against the sky,* LAZEAR *paces, restless and distraught. Sometimes he comes to the head of the stair on one side or the other. Soldiers are crossing the forestage,* O'HARA, BRINKERHOF, MC CLELLAND, *and* BUSCH *included, buttoning their tunics as they go and grumbling.*)

MC CLELLAND. Drill and tote stretchers. Then stand inspection and drill some more.

BRINKERHOF. There ain't nothing for armies to do in times of peace *but* drill!

O'HARA. And the sweat oozing out of our armpits with the heat and the brains oozing out of our skulls with the monotony!

BUSCH. Militarism! Capitalism! Imperialism! (*They are gone.*)

COMMAND (*offstage*). Company, fall IN! (*Two or three late-comers hurry across the stage.* AGRAMONTE *looks up.*) Company, attenSHUN! . . . Right DRESS! . . . FRONT! . . . Call the roll!

(*The roll is called and answered diminuendo as the scene progresses.*)

AGRAMONTE (*a smile, then, solo*). Camp goes on and so do we, God help us! (*Then, solo, as he works.*) Insect Number Two Hundred and Fifty-three. Infected from a moderate case. Fifth day in hospital. (*He makes the entry.*)

CARROLL. They've got measles over in the enlisted men's barracks. I made 'em give me some bloods to play around with. You can't see a thing in measles bloods either, but they're a change from these damned mosquitoes.

COMMAND. (*offstage*). Company, attenSHUN! . . . Squads RIGHT! . . . Forward MARCH! . . . (*Offstage the sound of marching feet diminuendo as* LAZEAR *reappears outside the laboratory.*)

LAZEAR. Ten days, Reed said! Ten days! Why in God's name did Reed have to go home and leave us? He'd know where we've gone wrong! He'd know! (*He goes.* CARROLL *has risen and gone to stand over* AGRAMONTE.)

AGRAMONTE (*solo as before*). Insect Number Two-Fifty-four . . .

CARROLL. My God, will you never get enough of those?

AGRAMONTE. Could we get enough to satisfy Lazear? (CARROLL *laughs.*)

CARROLL. This epidemic's petering out on him. Only had four new cases here since Sunday. That must be pretty disappointing to you boys.

AGRAMONTE. You look on matters too practically, Carroll. Are you blind to the artistry of science? (*A gesture takes in the laboratory.*) Each one in her own little glass house. Each one with her own ticket and number. It's nature in the raw reduced to method. Results or not, Carroll, look at it! (LAZEAR *is on the stairs.* CARROLL *points to him.*)

CARROLL. Look at him!

AGRAMONTE. He's disappointed.

CARROLL. He's bughouse.

AGRAMONTE (*as before*). Insect Number Two Fifty-five . . . (LAZEAR *has turned suddenly into the laboratory, stripping off his coat. He snatches up a rack of test tubes, selects one, and makes an annotation in a notebook.*)

LAZEAR. Number Ninety-eight. Infected from severe case on the day of death.

CARROLL. What? Again?

LAZEAR. Never say die, Carroll! Never say die! (*He is about to apply the mouth of the test tube to his arm.*)

AGRAMONTE (*stopping him*). No, Lazear.

LAZEAR. Why not?

AGRAMONTE. You have had your turn. Even your second turn according to Reed's instructions, and . . .

LAZEAR. Even so . . .

AGRAMONTE. And the ten days since are passed without results.

LAZEAR. But we've got to keep on trying, Agramonte!

AGRAMONTE. Is there any good wasting any more time?

(*A pause, then:*)

LAZEAR (*sober*). No. (*And he returns the test tube to rack.*) None.

CARROLL. My God, have you boys really come to your senses?

(LAZEAR *turns angrily but* AGRAMONTE *cuts him off.*)

AGRAMONTE. Perhaps not according to your lights, Carroll!

CARROLL. No good wasting any more time, you said! I say: Pack up! Let the skeeters loose! Go home and . . .

AGRAMONTE. It was to be your turn after Lazear.

CARROLL. My turn!

AGRAMONTE. Those were Reed's orders.

LAZEAR (*steady*). I'm stepping out. This is your show now.

CARROLL. Thanks.

LAZEAR. I hope you mean that. Because there's nothing wrong here except with me.

CARROLL. I can see there's plenty wrong with you.

LAZEAR. You needn't sneer. I may be a natural immune. Some men are. You'll give us the real test. If it fails with you, I'll begin to worry. Not before.

CARROLL. Ever hear the word "monomaniac"?

LAZEAR (*smiling*). It fits me like a glove. (*He offers* CARROLL *the test tube just now rejected.*) Here's Number Ninety-eight waiting for you. Are you ready?

CARROLL. Don't point that thing at me!

AGRAMONTE. Forgive me, Lazear, for interfering again, but in my opinion he is not quite ready.

LAZEAR. Why isn't he? I was!

AGRAMONTE. I should like to see more precise preparation than we have made thus far. I should like to see . . .

CARROLL. I won't be rushed into this!

LAZEAR. Who's rushing you?

AGRAMONTE. You are, Lazear! He's right . . .

LAZEAR (*wild again*). Either you go through or you don't! But if you're going, for God's sake, go! And pray for the lucky accident! That's all science amounts to, anyway!

AGRAMONTE. Not quite, Lazear! If you will permit me to say one word . . .

LAZEAR. What is there to say? He promised Reed!

CARROLL. I don't care if I did! Reed knows I've got no damned use for this! Grown men coaxing a bottled mosquito to bite 'em! Sucking thermometers for days afterwards, my God! Can't you see that's funny?

LAZEAR. What's funny about it?

CARROLL. You are! You're a scream! Sunk one minute and crazy wild the next! I can't keep up with you! I can't be bothered with you! I happen to be gifted with horse sense!

LAZEAR. Well, if that isn't a liability!

AGRAMONTE. Please!

CARROLL. Call yourself a scientist!

LAZEAR. Hell, I don't care whether you go through or not!

AGRAMONTE. Much better not go through unless you can do it properly.

LAZEAR. If you're trying to help him welch on this . . .

AGRAMONTE. I have not said that.

CARROLL. Who says I'm welching? I'm going through. But only to humor you, Lazear! (*Quick with hope,* LAZEAR *again offers test tube.*)

AGRAMONTE. I have tried to say that if we cannot do this properly we had much better not do it at all.

LAZEAR. For God's sake, quit butting in! (*He shoves entire rack of test tubes towards* CARROLL.)

CARROLL. I don't want any of those!

LAZEAR. These happen to be from the deadliest cases, Carroll.

CARROLL (*grinning*). I don't like their expression. (*An exclamation of disgust from* AGRAMONTE.)

LAZEAR. I believe you're scared.

CARROLL. I wouldn't feel so damn foolish if I were! (*He finds a single tube in a basket set apart.*) What's this one all alone by herself?

LAZEAR (*looking*). Number Forty-six. (*Then, to* AGRAMONTE.) It's the one we fed on that boy two weeks ago. The boy they'd just brought into the ward that day.

AGRAMONTE. That case hadn't even begun to develop, Carroll.

CARROLL (*grinning*). Are you letting the poor thing starve because she . . .

AGRAMONTE. I had set her aside to infect her properly!

LAZEAR. Why do you have to waste time on that measly thing! I took mine from fatal cases! Why can't you?

CARROLL. A mosquito's a mosquito!

LAZEAR. Why can't you stick to routine?

CARROLL. Will you, for Christ's sake, let me have my fun with this God-damn nonsense? (*He has stripped off his coat and is rolling up his sleeve.*)

AGRAMONTE. I warn you, you are being both slovenly and frivolous about this!

CARROLL (*grinning delightedly back*). Come on, Black Beauty! (AGRAMONTE *turns angrily out of the laboratory. But* LAZEAR *watches fascinated as* CARROLL *applies the mouth of the test tube to his forearm.*) Bite me!

COMMAND (*through the darkness*). Port ARMS! . . . Order ARMS! . . . Right shoulder ARMS! . . . Port ARMS! . . . Order ARMS! . . . Parade REST!

(*Then, as light shows the laboratory again.*)

AGRAMONTE (*angry*). I have come to the end of my patience, now! (*And the three are discovered as before except that they now wear their laboratory work coats and that* AGRAMONTE *now dominates the scene.*) I have worked for you as your clerk! I have kept your records! Now I shall tell you both what I think of you! And I ask you: Is this a scientific experiment or . . .

LAZEAR (*hotly*). You're damn right it is!

AGRAMONTE. It does not have that appearance for me! (*He swings on* CARROLL.)

You! Are you not supposed to be testing infection by mosquito? Yet you went to the autopsy room this morning! You performed an autopsy on a man just dead of yellow fever! When you are testing one source of infection you deliberately expose yourself to another! If you *were* to become infected by the mosquito, how would you know, I ask you, how would you know which source of infection to hold responsible?

CARROLL (*his temper also lost*). Do you expect me to chuck my real work to test an idea he's already exploded?

AGRAMONTE (*topping him*). I protest for more than this one idea! I protest for all scientific workmanship! Unimpeachable workmanship Reed demanded of you! And from the very day you offered to prove Dr. Finlay's case, I have warned you against rushing into things without preparation! Without thought or precaution!

CARROLL. Will you, for God's sake, quit yapping at me!

AGRAMONTE. I yap at Lazear, too!

LAZEAR. What can I do? Look what I'm up against! Has he even watched his temperature these last four days?

CARROLL. Go to it, boys! Then maybe I'll get some peace!

AGRAMONTE. When you were letting mosquitoes bite you in dozens! Were you not then exposing yourself in a hundred ways? If you had become infected then, could you have proven any more than Carroll?

LAZEAR. I'd have been so happy I wouldn't have cared!

AGRAMONTE. Is that workmanship?

LAZEAR. I'd have known what gave it to me!

AGRAMONTE. Is that science?

LAZEAR. It's the way I am!

CARROLL. Why in hell are you making this row now? If either one of us had come down you might have some kick. But we haven't come down and all this adds up to is theology!

AGRAMONTE (*quiet but stern*). A time comes, Carroll, when a man must turn and speak out for his standards. I have made workmanship my religion. You will laugh and tell me I have a Latin mind. I have made my protest.

LAZEAR (*resolved but sober*). No hard feelings. You're right. Workmanship now. Discipline. (*He turns to* CARROLL.)

We're in earnest now. We won't count your playful attempt the other day. We'll pick out your next ourselves. No more rushing things, though. This time you go into isolation before we let any mosquito touch you.

CARROLL. *Do* I!

LAZEAR. Where nothing gets at you for a good two weeks.

CARROLL. All by myself?

LAZEAR. Then if you come down we'll know why.

CARROLL. I'll be God-damned if you put any more over on me! I'm through! I'm putting what I just got out of that dead spiggoty under the microscope for one last look. Then I hop a boat for home and kiss yellow jack good-by!

LAZEAR (*to* AGRAMONTE). Now do you see what I'm up against? (AGRAMONTE *clutches his head in despair.*)

CARROLL (*fortissimo*). Coop me up for two weeks!

LAZEAR (*topping him*). All right, you bloody, pig-headed clown! You can explain to Reed, though!

CARROLL. Sure I can! Think Reed would expect me to let you put this one over! Think Reed doesn't know me better than that! Coop me up? I couldn't stand it! I'm an active man. I've got to use my mind! This damn thing's got me crazy as it is! It's got me all off my feed! That's a fact! It has! (AGRAMONTE *pricks up his ears.* CARROLL *sits again, pleading with* LAZEAR.) I'm sorry, Lazear. But you can't keep on day after day getting nowhere at something you've got no use for and not feel the effects! It wears you out! It gets you all run down! I woke up this morning feeling . . .

AGRAMONTE (*low but sharp*). How?

CARROLL. Like hell. And I made up my mind then . . .

AGRAMONTE (*rising and circling him for a closer look*). How like hell?

CARROLL. How would a man of my type feel after a month of this?

AGRAMONTE. Headache?

CARROLL. Head's felt like a dog's breakfast all morning! Shouldn't wonder if I've picked up some malaria. Once you get run down, you know, anything . . .

AGRAMONTE. Have you examined your blood for malaria?

CARROLL (*indicating microscope*). Just now. Didn't find anything but . . .

AGRAMONTE. Feverish?

CARROLL. Not particularly. No.

AGRAMONTE (*very distinct*). Blood negative and no fever. Somehow I doubt it's being malaria, Carroll. (LAZEAR *looks up, a wild light in his eye.*)

LAZEAR. Carroll, you lousy bum!

CARROLL. What?

LAZEAR. You've got yellow jack!

AGRAMONTE. Yes, I was going to say . . .

CARROLL (*incredulous indignation*). I have not got . . .

LAZEAR. He's got it, Agramonte! I know he's got it!

CARROLL (*to* AGRAMONTE). Will you listen to this maniac wishing yellow jack on me!

LAZEAR. You ought to be wishing it on yourself! What have we all been sweating over here! Isn't it four days since you took your bite? Four days may be schedule! We don't know that it isn't!

AGRAMONTE. From *that* mosquito?

LAZEAR. She may have had something in her after all! We don't know! We don't know! (*He shouts.*) Brinkerhof!

AGRAMONTE. What do you want with . . .

LAZEAR. I want Ames here!

CARROLL. You'll turn into a mosquito yourself if you don't watch out! (BRINKERHOF *enters.*)

LAZEAR (*to* BRINKERHOF). Fetch Dr. Ames.

CARROLL. Do nothing of the sort!

LAZEAR. Go on! (BRINKERHOF *runs out.*)

CARROLL. I'm damned if I see Ames! When I want a doctor . . . What in hell are you laughing at?

LAZEAR (*splitting with laughter*). Only humoring me! Went into the autopsy room and exposed yourself this morning! Won't it be the God-damnedest joke on you if you have got yellow jack and die of it!

CARROLL. Joke!

LAZEAR. Yes, joke! (*To* AGRAMONTE.) Look at him! He's getting scared I'm right!

CARROLL (*frightened in spite of himself*). You're a son of a bitch, Lazear!

LAZEAR (*choking*). The laugh's on you, Carroll, you bungling . . . (*But* AGRAMONTE *turns to shake* LAZEAR.)

AGRAMONTE. Stop it, Lazear! That's too horrible! (LAZEAR *is sobered as* AMES *enters.*) Here's Ames now.

AMES. Did you want me for something?

CARROLL. No. Lazear did. The damn fool's trying to tell me I've got . . . (*On his feet, however, he totters and* AGRAMONTE *catches his elbow.*) Take your hands off me! (*But his own hand goes to his dizzy brow.*) Come over to my quarters, Ames. There's nothing wrong with me. All I need is a little quinine and a headache powder and I'll be . . . (*He is gone,* AMES *following bewildered.*)

LAZEAR. Agramonte!

AGRAMONTE. What?

LAZEAR. I'm scared to death.

AGRAMONTE. What of? That Carroll's got yellow jack or that he hasn't?

LAZEAR. Both.

(*Darkness. "Drill—First Call" again. Then again light on the laboratory and* LAZEAR *sits in his shirtsleeves at the microscope, while* AGRAMONTE, *now in uniform, paces to and fro evidently under a severe strain.* FINLAY *enters to them in a tremolo of mingled delight and awe.*)

FINLAY. I have seen Dr. Carroll! Whatever doubts you may have had yesterday, there can be no question now! First I was sorry for him! Then I remembered to thank God!

LAZEAR (*looking up in excitement from microscope*). There's not a trace of malaria in the blood! Malaria would have shown itself by this! (*He is on his feet.*) Let's celebrate, Dr. Finlay! Let's get drunk!

AGRAMONTE (*full force at both of them*). What you and Dr. Finlay may or may not believe is not evidence, and you cannot deceive yourselves that it is! (*The pair fairly scream back at him.*)

FINLAY. A man has been bitten by my mosquito!

LAZEAR. And has got yellow jack as a result!

AGRAMONTE. Not necessarily as a result!

FINLAY. What he did, where he went yesterday, is of no importance!

AGRAMONTE. It is of the most disastrous importance!

LAZEAR. He came through three months of exposure before he was bitten!

AGRAMONTE. That is not proof!

FINLAY. It was my mosquito that infected him!

AGRAMONTE. We don't know that!

LAZEAR. You're splitting hairs!

AGRAMONTE. I'm talking science! You know that we have bungled Carroll's sickness! You know his life will be wasted if he dies!

LAZEAR. There's no good looking on

the dark side, is there?

AGRAMONTE. You know that is what you must report to Reed!

LAZEAR. Reed will know that we've got this! Here! Under our fingers!

AGRAMONTE. Where?

LAZEAR. We *have* got it! This *must* be the mosquito!

AGRAMONTE. You *want* to believe that!

LAZEAR. I've *got* to believe it! Carroll may die!

AGRAMONTE. All right! Tell me why that one mosquito should succeed with Carroll when fifty failed with you and *I* will believe! But I must know why, Lazear, before I can!

(*Pause, then:*)

LAZEAR (*defeated*). Damn your bloody logic, Agramonte!

FINLAY. Yes. When you know that you will know everything.

LAZEAR. Yes. *When.*

FINLAY. Oh, I realize it may be difficult to determine. You must produce another case! That *will* be proof and confirm Dr. Carroll! So that his life need not be wasted if he dies. So that my mosquito may come into her own!

LAZEAR. How?

FINLAY. I leave that to you.

LAZEAR. Thanks. (*A pause; then desperately he turns to the shelves.*) Which one was Carroll's?

AGRAMONTE (*very steady*). Dated the twenty-seventh.

LAZEAR (*reading off the labels*). The twelfth. Mine. No good. Fourteenth. Sixteenth. Eighteenth. Mine. All mine. (*He finds it.*) Here. Carroll. The twenty-seventh. (*He picks tube out of rack.*) Read me the record.

AGRAMONTE (*glancing down upon the page of an open notebook*). "Insect infected from case in second day of disease. Symptoms not definite but subsequently well developed." (LAZEAR *holds up his hand for silence.*)

LAZEAR (*strangely absorbed*). Second day! How many others did we feed on patients that early in the disease?

AGRAMONTE. I don't know. A few.

LAZEAR. You've got 'em in the record, haven't you?

AGRAMONTE. Certainly. (*He runs his finger down page.*) Here's another from a case in the second day. Here's a third day. Here's a first.

LAZEAR. And I was too smart to try

any of those!

AGRAMONTE. You didn't want to waste time on them.

LAZEAR. Waste time! (*Then:*) Christ! Oh, Christ!

AGRAMONTE. What is it?

FINLAY. Dr. Lazear! (*He rises.*)

LAZEAR (*very deliberate*). Suppose— mind, I'm only thinking aloud—but here's this microbe no one has ever seen. Suppose it's in the blood only the first few days. Before you really know what's wrong with you . . .

FINLAY. What could become of it afterwards?

LAZEAR. I don't know!

AGRAMONTE (*low*). Do you mean that it might go somewhere else? Out of the blood?

FINLAY (*low*). Or change? Or die after the first few days?

LAZEAR (*his throat painfully dry*). I don't know. I don't know. If there were anything in the idea, though, we've been wasting time feeding our skeeters on advanced cases. There wouldn't have been any microbes left in them. And that would explain why I couldn't . . .

AGRAMONTE (*an awed whisper*). And Carroll could!

FINLAY (*an awed whisper*). Have you found it at last? (*But* LAZEAR *can only smile weakly.*)

LAZEAR. It's too easy. Things can't be that simple.

FINLAY. Truth can.

AGRAMONTE. I wish that Reed were here.

LAZEAR. Yes. So do I. (*Dazed, he holds out test tube to* AGRAMONTE.) Put all your early birds in a special rack. (*He turns to* FINLAY, *as* AGRAMONTE *proceeds to obey.*) If this *is* the trick, I never ran any risk at all. And I may be as susceptible as any man. And I could be the case to confirm Carroll.

AGRAMONTE (*firmly*). Only you'd have to be isolated for two weeks first.

FINLAY. And in two weeks Dr. Carroll will be well or dead.

LAZEAR (*wild again*). We can't leave him lying there if he's done this! We can't let him die without knowing what he's done! God, why can't we come out in the open now and commandeer a whole regiment to experiment on? (*"Recall" sounds.*)

FINLAY. You'll come to it! I told you in the beginning!

COMMAND. (*offstage*). Company, dis-MISSED!

LAZEAR (*insane*). God send me one pure, unsuspecting human guinea pig! One I can't bungle! One I can cram down the whole world's throat! All wool! A yard wide! Fireproof! Watertight! (*Soldiers cross stage, returning to their barracks from drill,* O'HARA, BRINKERHOF, BUSCH, *and* MC CLELLAND *among them. They mop their brows and their guns are slung idly, any way, for comfort. Some of them are singing as they cross.*)

SOLDIERS.
"Well, I guess I'll have to telegraph
                    my baby,
I needs some money bad, indeed I do!
My Lucy is a very generous lady,
And I can always touch her for a few.
I find the Western Union a convenience,
No matter where I roam,
So I'll telegraph my baby,
She'll send ten or twenty maybe,
And I won't have to walk back home."
(FINLAY *is leaning out of the laboratory.*)

FINLAY. Dr. Lazear!

LAZEAR. What?

FINLAY. Have you never heard of a prayer being answered?

LAZEAR. No, Doctor. Those are our Medical Corps boys. They know too much.

FINLAY. All of them? All? Can't you find one? (*The soldiers have cleared away, leaving one—*PRIVATE DEAN, *a nondescript, hick American—looking up at laboratory.*)

LAZEAR. Do you know that cavalryman out there, Agramonte?

AGRAMONTE. No, I don't think so. (*Then he understands.*) No, Lazear! Not that! (LAZEAR *is on his way out of laboratory.*)

LAZEAR. Why not?

AGRAMONTE (*stopping him*). Will your conscience let you?

LAZEAR. What's conscience got to do with it? (*He has broken away and runs down steps to* DEAN.)

AGRAMONTE (*to* FINLAY). Stop him, Dr. Finlay!

FINLAY. And let Dr. Carroll die without confirmation? (*He follows* LAZEAR *down. Offstage* THE QUARTET *strikes into "Good-bye, Dolly Gray."*)

LAZEAR (*to* DEAN). Good morning.

DEAN (*saluting lamely*). Good morning, sir.

LAZEAR. I don't think I've seen your face before.

DEAN. I'm what might be called a stranger over this way, sir.

LAZEAR. Were you looking for someone?

DEAN. No, sir. Just looking around.

LAZEAR (*a deep breath and a glance at* FINLAY, *then:*) Would you like to come in?

DEAN. In where, sir?

LAZEAR. Into the laboratory.

AGRAMONTE (*low*). No!

FINLAY. Come in, young man! Come in! (*He bows* DEAN *up the stair.*)

DEAN. I wouldn't mind. This the place where you got all the mosquitoes? (*He looks about. Turning to* LAZEAR.) I've been hearing quite a lot about your mosquitoes, sir.

LAZEAR. Oh? What have you heard?

DEAN. Well, you know how the boys talk.

FINLAY. What do they say? Tell us. We don't mind.

DEAN. They say you're raising 'em for pets.

LAZEAR. That's not far wrong.

DEAN. You sure got plenty of 'em. I seen a flea circus once. Can these do tricks?

FINLAY. We have one here who has just learned a fine trick.

LAZEAR. That is, we hope she has!

DEAN. She? A lady, is it?

LAZEAR. We don't bother with anything else.

FINLAY. Except when one of them needs a husband.

LAZEAR. We keep the husbands all together in that jar there.

DEAN (*examining*). In that jar? Are those the husbands?

FINLAY. For breeding purposes.

DEAN. Oh, yes, I know about breeding! I was raised on a farm. Do mosquitoes . . . ? (*He seeks for the word, but cannot find it.*) Do they?

LAZEAR. Oh, yes.

DEAN. I'm interested in natural history. (*He turns to examine others.*)

LAZEAR. Where have you been keeping yourself the last few weeks?

DEAN. The last two weeks I been in hospital here. Before that I was stationed at . . .

LAZEAR (*to* FINLAY). Two weeks in hospital!

FINLAY (*to* DEAN). What was the trouble?

DEAN. Well, I . . . The fact is . . . Kind of got poisoned . . . (*Embarrassment.*)

FINLAY. Young men haven't changed. (*To* LAZEAR.) I don't think that presents any obstacle? After all, two weeks in hospital . . .

LAZEAR. You haven't been near the contagious wards, I hope?

DEAN. Oh, nothing like that! All I had was a . . .

LAZEAR. Haven't been near anyone sick with yellow fever?

DEAN. Jesus, I hope not! I mean I hope not, sir.

FINLAY. How much longer are they keeping you in hospital?

DEAN. They just let me out. Just now.

LAZEAR. Oh! Where will you go?

DEAN. My outfit's sailing home in a week.

LAZEAR (*a prick of conscience*). Home!

DEAN. Got to be done some day.

FINLAY. You're not pleased to be going home?

DEAN. You don't know my home, sir.

FINLAY. No.

DEAN. It ain't worth while. I wish they'd kept me here a few days longer. Enough for the outfit to get off without me.

LAZEAR. What's your name?

DEAN. Dean. William H. Troop A. Seventh Cavalry.

FINLAY. Married, Mr. Dean?

DEAN. I was going to be but I give it up.

LAZEAR. That doesn't count.

DEAN (*agreeing*). That ain't worth while either.

FINLAY. Well, now, that all depends on how you look at it, Mr. Dean. (*General laughter and so disarming that* LAZEAR *seems not to notice what he is doing when he picks up the fateful test tube.*)

LAZEAR. How would you like to give Black Beauty her lunch?

DEAN. Black Beauty?

FINLAY. That trick mosquito I told you about.

DEAN. You mean for her to bite me?

LAZEAR. That's all. Roll up your sleeve.

DEAN (*drawing back*). No. No, I don't think I'd care to do that, Doctor. Just something about it don't strike me.

FINLAY. You're bitten by mosquitoes

every day!

DEAN. That ain't the same as giving 'em lunch off you!

LAZEAR. Come on, now, Mr. Dean! Roll up your sleeve!

DEAN (*beginning very unwillingly to comply*). It ain't natural, Doctor!

FINLAY. Young man, he's offering you a great honor!

DEAN. I don't get this!

(LAZEAR *applies mouth of tube to* DEAN's *forearm, tapping the end precisely as* AGRA-MONTE *did previously but with even more deftness.*)

LAZEAR (*to* DEAN). Don't move!

DEAN. Makes me feel kind of funny!

FINLAY (*closing in on him*). Look the other way, Mr. Dean.

LAZEAR. We've got a few more here that are hungry, too. You wouldn't mind giving them a meal while you're at it?

FINLAY. Certainly not!

LAZEAR. Then, Agramonte, if you'll just push that special basket over here where I can reach it? (AGRAMONTE *obeys mechanically.*)

FINLAY. We may have something of real interest to tell Dr. Carroll in a few days' time.

(LAZEAR *has removed test tube. But he does not relinquish his grip on* DEAN's *wrist.*)

LAZEAR. That's the idea, Doctor. (*He selects another test tube.*) Now, Mr. Dean . . . (*Darkness.*)

MISS BLAKE (*through the darkness*). Quiet now, Dr. Carroll. Save your strength. You'll feel much more comfortable if you just relax. (*The bleak light of early morning slowly reveals* CARROLL *sick unto death on a hospital cot attended by* AMES *and* MISS BLAKE. LAZEAR *sits morosely apart.* AMES *is listening to the sick man's heart with his stethoscope. The scene is played below, the laboratory screen being closed.*)

CARROLL (*feeble, but in the best of good humor*). If you can keep that heart of mine going, Ames, you're a better man than I think. (LAZEAR *turns wretchedly.*)

AMES. I can't even hear your heart till you quit talking!

CARROLL. Helps me to talk. Keeps me from going out.

AMES. Go out if you want to. Won't hurt you any.

CARROLL. Going out's not so bad. Coming back's getting harder. (AMES *folds stethoscope and goes to* MISS BLAKE.)

AMES. What time did you give that last injection?

LAZEAR. I gave it at three this morning.

AMES (*to* MISS BLAKE). Get another ready. (LAZEAR *rises.*) She'll do it. (LAZEAR *sits again heavily.* MISS BLAKE *goes out.* AMES *turns to* CARROLL. *Then:*) He's out again. Think you can keep your eyes open a few minutes longer?

LAZEAR (*rising*). What do you want me to do?

AMES. Just sit here. It's seven-thirty. I ought to go look over the morning sick list.

LAZEAR. Go ahead. (AMES *is going, but* LAZEAR *stops him.*) If you find any new customers in the yellow jack ward, I'd like to know.

(AMES *eyes him curiously, then:*)

AMES. I don't expect I will find any.

LAZEAR. You might. (*But* AMES *is gone. Then* LAZEAR *goes groggily to look down on* CARROLL. *Then, solo.*) For God's sake, get a move on, Private Dean! (*Then:*)

CARROLL. That you, Lazear?

LAZEAR. You back with us again?

CARROLL. I come and go. It's very interesting. Ames and that damn nurse gone? I hate nurses.

LAZEAR. Ames doesn't want you talking.

CARROLL. The hell with Ames. I want you to know the irony of this isn't wasted on me.

LAZEAR. Think it's wasted on me?

CARROLL. Took me quite a while to get around to it. I've got to die to appreciate it completely.

LAZEAR. You don't have to die if you fight.

CARROLL. You said it would be a joke on me. That was your idea.

LAZEAR. For God's sake, Carroll!

CARROLL. I don't mind that part. You're a better man than I thought, too, and I might have died anyway. Only I'd be making history now instead of a mess if I hadn't been so damn smart.

LAZEAR. You and me both, Carroll! Damn us both for a pair of incompetent bunglers! When I think of the waste of this! (*But* CARROLL *is laughing.*)

CARROLL. You know I was the first. That's some satisfaction. You can't curse me out of that.

LAZEAR. I didn't mean to curse you.

CARROLL. Someday, when you get a second to back me up and break out in print, find room for me in a footnote, will you? (AGRAMONTE *enters*.)

AGRAMONTE. Lazear . . . (LAZEAR *turns and fairly runs to him*.)

LAZEAR. News?

AGRAMONTE (*holding out a paper*). His name's on the sick list.

LAZEAR (*examining*). Oh, God bless you, Private Dean! (*He turns back in great exultation*.) Carroll, you're set! We've got your confirmation! (*But* CARROLL *has gone out again*.) Oh . . .

AGRAMONTE. What?

LAZEAR. No. He comes and goes like that. (*Then:*) He was just asking me to . . . (*He stops to control himself. Then:*) I guess I'm tired. (*He sits again*.) Time like this you forget what it's all about. What was it all about? The chase of the carrier of yellow fever. That was it, wasn't it? The chase. (*He smiles*.) I might remember to ask how Dean is.

AGRAMONTE. I don't know.

LAZEAR. You don't know?

AGRAMONTE. I haven't seen him! He isn't in the yellow fever ward. I expect they don't know what's the matter with him.

LAZEAR. If you haven't seen him we don't know ourselves!

AGRAMONTE. Can't we guess?

LAZEAR. I've got to *know!* I can't tell Carroll till I do know!

AGRAMONTE. Can't you show him the sick list with Dean's name on it?

LAZEAR. Carroll wants confirmation!

AGRAMONTE. Tell him you've seen Dean then, and there's no doubt . . .

LAZEAR. I don't want to lie to him if I can help it! Find Dean! He's in this hospital somewhere! Ask where they've put him!

AGRAMONTE. And give the whole show away?

LAZEAR. Who cares what happens now? You've got to see Dean with your own eyes! (AMES *returns carrying, in his hand, the hypodermic needle for* CARROLL'S *injection. He goes to the bed*. LAZEAR *follows. Then:*) Didn't you find any new yellow jack cases?

AMES. No.

LAZEAR. Nor hear of any?

AMES (*surprised*). No!

LAZEAR. Go on, Agramonte! (AGRAMONTE *goes, troubled*.) Can I help you?

AMES. Alcohol. (LAZEAR *applies alcohol to* CARROLL'S *arm*.) Hold it. (LAZEAR *holds the arm while* AMES *makes injection*.) Here. (LAZEAR *takes needle and sets it aside*. AMES *listens with his stethoscope again*. LAZEAR *comes back to bedside*. AMES *looks up. Pause, then:*)

LAZEAR. How long do you give him?

AMES. I don't know. If we could make him fight . . . (MISS BLAKE *has entered*.)

MISS BLAKE. Dr. Ames.

AMES. Yes?

MISS BLAKE. Can you get away to look at a new case? (LAZEAR'S *head comes up*.) It's a soldier they . . .

LAZEAR (*almost fainting*). What's the soldier's name?

MISS BLAKE (*consulting a scrap of paper*). Dean. William H. Troop A. Seventh Cavalry. (LAZEAR'S *eyes close as she continues to* AMES.) And everybody's upset because he insists he hasn't been out of camp for weeks and they're afraid of its breaking out here again and . . .

AMES (*to* LAZEAR). Good God!

LAZEAR (*low*). Hadn't you better take a look at him? (AMES *hands* LAZEAR *his stethoscope*.)

AMES. You watch that heart. (*He goes,* MISS BLAKE *following*.)

MISS BLAKE. I'm afraid there's no doubt but it *is* yellow . . .

(*They are gone.* LAZEAR *turns towards* CARROLL.)

LAZEAR (*behind his voice that grim pressure which doctors employ to reach through unconsciousness*). I'll make you fight now, you bloody bonehead! (*He kneels beside bed. His tone is low but shaken with all the force in him*.) You did it after all . . . in spite of yourself . . .

CARROLL (*as he comes to somewhat*). I was the first. Remember that . . . I was the first . . .

LAZEAR (*the pressure increasing as the tone drops in pitch*). Damn right you were! And nobody's ever going to forget it! . . . We've got your second now! . . . We know now, Carroll! We know! Do you get that! We know! (*Darkness, but not before we have seen the smile on the sick man's face. Then:*)

MISS BLAKE (*calling frantically through the darkness*). Dr. Ames! Dr. Ames! (*Light strikes her from behind* AMES *as he enters*.)

AMES. What are you doing up at this time of night?

MISS BLAKE. It's Dr. Lazear . . .

AMES. What's wrong with him?

MISS BLAKE. I don't know! I'm afraid!

I went in just now. To make my report on what fine progress Dr. Carroll's making. And he ... (*Her voice chokes with tears.*) He's very sick, Dr. Ames ...

AMES. Lazear, too! (*They cross through the darkness, the light increasing to show* LAZEAR *seated at laboratory workbench, haggard and ill, notebooks and sheets of paper scattered before him. The sky remains dead and unlighted.*)

LAZEAR (*pushing the words out as he writes*). I don't deny I bungled Carroll's case, though Dean does seem to have confirmed him. Now they're both out of the woods, I have to confess to you about myself. I can't account for it, but I'm beginning to be afraid ... (MISS BLAKE *and* AMES *have entered to him.*) Go away. I'm busy.

AMES. She tells me you're under the weather.

LAZEAR. I'd have told you myself if I'd wanted you to know!

AMES. You don't have to tell me. I can see.

LAZEAR. I've got a touch of malaria.

AMES. Sure it isn't the same malaria Carroll had?

LAZEAR (*low and stubborn*). Carroll got yellow jack from our mosquitoes. I haven't taken a bite myself for weeks. Whatever this is, it can't be yellow jack!

AMES (*eyeing him sharply*). The fact remains ...

MISS BLAKE. Oh, if doctors would only take care of themselves!

(AGRAMONTE *has entered.*)

AGRAMONTE. What's this about Lazear?

AMES. Looks to me very much like ...

LAZEAR. Don't pay any attention to him, Agramonte!

AGRAMONTE (*as he sees* LAZEAR). My God! Have you been trying this again on yourself? You gave me your word ...

(LAZEAR *turns away.*)

LAZEAR. No.

AMES. He's caught it from Carroll, then!

LAZEAR. Don't say that!

AGRAMONTE (*decisively to* AMES). No, you get it from a mosquito or not at all!

LAZEAR. That's true! I believe that! I've proved that!

(*He has got to his feet in his excitement, but giddiness sits him down again. A pause while* AGRAMONTE *lays an anxious palm on* LAZEAR's *brow. Then:*)

AGRAMONTE. I don't want to tire you, Lazear. Think back over the last four or five days, though. Hasn't there been one single mosquito that might account ... I don't mean experimentally. I mean, just in the course of things ... out of doors ... ?

LAZEAR. Wouldn't I have noticed?

AGRAMONTE. I hope so! That's why I'm asking you.

LAZEAR. There was one. Yes.

AGRAMONTE. Aha!

LAZEAR. Four or five days back. I was in the wards infecting our mosquitoes and a little stranger 'lighted on my hand. (*Then quickly.*) But it wasn't one of the yellow fever brand!

AGRAMONTE. Are you sure of that?

LAZEAR. Think I don't know these stegomyias by now? It was an ordinary brown one!

AGRAMONTE. You're positive there haven't been any others?

LAZEAR. Positive!

AGRAMONTE (*again decisive to* AMES). Then this can't very well be yellow jack.

AMES. Just the same I wish we could get him to bed.

LAZEAR. I've got work to do. Notes to get up. For Reed when he gets back. (*A pause, then:*)

AMES. He's not getting back tomorrow.

LAZEAR. I know that.

AMES. What's the hurry then?

LAZEAR. Get to hell out of here and leave me alone!

(MISS BLAKE *gasps.*)

AMES (*topping him*). All I ask is a chance to take care of you!

(*Another pause.* LAZEAR *gives up the struggle.*)

LAZEAR. Give me two minutes with Agramonte, you can take all the care you like. (AMES *and* MISS BLAKE *move out of laboratory.* LAZEAR *turns piteously to* AGRAMONTE.) I've done the best I could with these notes. I was just writing Reed a letter. I was going to write my wife. This pair came in. You're the only one of us left on the job now. Will you finish my letter to Reed?

AGRAMONTE. Go to bed now!

LAZEAR. I haven't told you what to tell Reed yet. (*His voice drops.*) Warn him to keep Dean's name in the dark. I've called him Private X. Y. in the notes. The truth of that mustn't ever get out.

It would bring 'em down like a band of Cossacks.

AGRAMONTE. Is that all?

LAZEAR. No. But I'm not up to thinking of anything more.

AGRAMONTE. What am I to tell Reed about you?

LAZEAR. That's a very neat question! It's a great thing, the scientific life! More ups and downs in it than they know about! But you keep working at it and sooner or later things click into place. The good job well done. It's damn well got to be the good job well done! (*He buries his head in his arms.*)

AGRAMONTE. Ames! (AMES *and* MISS BLAKE *return to laboratory.*) He's worn out. You must get him to bed. (LAZEAR *rises.*)

LAZEAR. All right. I'll go. (*He turns, smiling, to* AGRAMONTE.) And do you want to know what you can do then, Agramonte? You can take all those notes and all those reports and all those mosquitoes and tell Reed to shove 'em up!

AGRAMONTE. Lazear! What . . . !

LAZEAR. There's nothing in 'em! There's not a damn thing in 'em.

AGRAMONTE. You can't mean that!

LAZEAR. Want to hear a joke? A better joke than the one we had on Carroll?

AGRAMONTE (*horrified as he guesses*). Oh, no, Lazear!

LAZEAR. You've guessed it! I've wrecked our great demonstration, Agramonte! I've shot the whole God-damn works to hell! I've gone and got yellow jack without our mosquito!

AGRAMONTE. It isn't possible! How could you!

LAZEAR (*again laughing uncontrollably*). I don't know! I've got it, though! I had it yesterday and I've got it today and my head . . . Oh, my God, my head! (*He collapses forward among the notes and glassware. The two doctors look at him horrorstruck.* MISS BLAKE *takes command.*)

MISS BLAKE. We can get him to bed now.

(*Darkness upon a roll of drums. Then the sky takes on the most serene beauty of the light before dawn and light grows where* CARROLL *sits, wasted with recent illness, and* FINLAY *and* GORGAS *stand over him.*)

GORGAS. You must think how easily this might have happened to you. Men can't go against death and not risk death themselves. Pasteur sent Thuillier to Alexandria for the cholera there. Thuil-lier didn't come back. Lazear won't be the last.

FINLAY. Humanity won't have done asking this sacrifice of his kind for a long time yet. Science won't have done.

CARROLL. His wife's just had another baby. He won't ever see it.

(*Light grows on the screened bed on which* LAZEAR *lies dying.* MISS BLAKE *attends him.* AMES *is just leaving him to approach the other doctors.*)

AMES. Make Carroll go back to bed, Major Gorgas.

CARROLL. How much sleep did he get the nights you thought I was a goner?

GORGAS. He hadn't just been sick. You have.

CARROLL. Lazear's dying! For a lot of God-forsaken halfwits of men and women! Will they ever appreciate what he's done for them? Will they even hear of him?

FINLAY. Neither death nor what he's dying for belong in words.

CARROLL. I haven't got your philosophy, Dr. Finlay. Lazear's the best fellow I've ever known.

GORGAS. And his death is so much waste.

LAZEAR (*faintly from behind the screen*). Waste! Waste!

CARROLL (*on his feet*). He heard you! He understood! Lazear!

AMES. Keep your shirt on, Carroll! He's beyond understanding now.

CARROLL. Christ!

GORGAS. Won't you go back to bed?

CARROLL. No. (AGRAMONTE *enters.*)

AGRAMONTE. Is there any change?

AMES. There won't be before morning. (*He goes behind screen.*)

FINLAY. An admirable young man. There was doom in the look he had. One sees that sometimes. A single task, and at the end, fulfillment.

AGRAMONTE. Fulfillment! Dr. Finlay, don't make this harder to bear than it is already!

CARROLL. I'm with you, Dr. Finlay! I've come around! It was your mosquito that hooked me! There's no other way of explaining me!

FINLAY. This is a time for faith!

AGRAMONTE. Faith in what?

FINLAY. In the search at any rate.

AGRAMONTE. What's Reed going to say?

FINLAY. There are worse things than to

die seeking. Major Reed will know that.

LAZEAR (*as before*). Where's Walter Reed?

CARROLL (*on his way to* LAZEAR's *bedside*). I've got to try once more! I've got to reach him! (CARROLL *goes to* LAZEAR.)

MISS BLAKE. It won't do any good!

CARROLL. It can't do any harm!

AMES. Well, if it's any comfort to you!

CARROLL. It is. (*He bends over foot of cot, speaking at the sick man with that awful clarity doctors use to reach those who are beyond reach.*) Listen, Lazear . . . It's Carroll. . . . Make an effort to get what I'm telling you. . . . Reed's coming back. . . . Do you get that? We've had a cable. . . . He says . . . Tell—Lazear—to—hold out. . . . Did you hear me? . . . Can you make some sign? . . .

LAZEAR. Waste! Waste!

AGRAMONTE. Good God! (LAZEAR *moves suddenly.*)

LAZEAR (*his voice rising*). Waste!

MISS BLAKE. Dr. Ames!

AMES. Stand by!

LAZEAR (*struggling to sit up*). Waste! Waste!! Waste!!! (*He is overcome by* AMES *and* MISS BLAKE.)

AMES. That's better.

GORGAS. He's getting weaker now.

FINLAY. No, Major Gorgas! The stuff of courage doesn't grow weaker! It grows stronger. Stronger and brighter! Until it blinds us! But we do see its flaming sword cut through the veil!

GORGAS. What veil?

FINLAY (*pointing*). Out there, where knowledge hides!

(*In the distance the Bugler blows "Reveille."*)

AGRAMONTE. There's "Reveille"!

MISS BLAKE. It's morning already.

LAZEAR. Where's Walter Reed?

(*The characters stand immobile as stage and sky dim to darkness. Then lurid light strikes* BUSCH, MC CLELLAND, O'HARA, *and* BRINKERHOF, *huddled together. They speak in hushed whispers.*)

MC CLELLAND. He was still alive at sundown.

O'HARA. When was it he went?

BRINKERHOF. Just now it must have been.

BUSCH. I seen 'em coming back when it was over. Walking and looking at the ground.

O'HARA. A young man and a great one!

BUSCH. I never met him.

BRINKERHOF. I won't forget him but I wish I had something to remember him by.

MC CLELLAND. It's a tough thing to die. It's a tough thing to die like that.

O'HARA. Us medical men have no regrets dying for science.

BRINKERHOF. And for humanity, John.

BUSCH. Humanity. Yeah. That's what us revolutionaries die for.

BRINKERHOF. He died useful just like he lived. It must be a grand thing to be useful.

O'HARA. There's no end to the glory of sacrifice for science!

(*Black-out as light strikes* AGRAMONTE *with the* POST CHAPLAIN.)

AGRAMONTE (*in intense agitation*). You call yourself chaplain of this post!

CHAPLAIN. We usually omit the service in such cases.

AGRAMONTE. You're afraid to bury him!

CHAPLAIN. You might find some local clergyman who's had yellow fever.

AGRAMONTE. But I tell you you couldn't catch it from him now!

CHAPLAIN. Can you prove that?

(*Black-out as light of the same quality strikes* CARROLL *in violent argument with a* COMMISSARY SERGEANT.)

CARROLL. And you refuse to give us . . .

SERGEANT. I can't issue no post flag for no such purpose!

CARROLL. We've got to have a flag to cover him!

SERGEANT. I'm held responsible for these here stores. I can't issue no flag that's got to be burned after it's used.

CARROLL. I tell you there's no danger!

SERGEANT. I been told different. I can give you a flag to fly over him, but I can't give you no . . .

(*Black-out. Light strikes an American flag floating against darkness.*)

COMMAND (*offstage in the darkness*). Firing squad, atten-SHUN! READY! AIM! FIRE! (*A volley is fired. As the flag is slowly lowered to half-mast the bugle sounds the thin, solemn strains of "Taps." On the last note* REED's *voice is heard barking sharply through the darkness.*)

REED. Didn't I warn both you and Lazear the night I left you! Unimpeachable workmanship I demanded! And what have you given me?

(*Bright daylight shows that the flag has disappeared and that* REED *is striding to and*

fro in the laboratory, while CARROLL, AGRA-
MONTE, *and* GORGAS *sit morosely apart.*)
You at death's door for no purpose and
he dead for less!

CARROLL. Be fair, Reed!

REED. I'm not unfair! God honor both
of you for gallant men!

GORGAS. Reed! You've done enough!
The summer's over and the epidemic
with it!

REED. There'll be other summers and
worse epidemics! There's knowledge
and this fact's not yet established!

GORGAS. It's got away from you!

AGRAMONTE. I'm afraid it has.

CARROLL. The hell it has!

REED. Gorgas, I can't let go!

AGRAMONTE. What have you to hang
on to?

CARROLL. Let Agramonte go back on
this if he wants to, Reed! I'm convinced!

AGRAMONTE. I cannot be romantic
about this, Carroll! Scientifically, we
have no evidence that Finlay's mosquito
played any part either in Lazear's death
or in your sickness! And I must agree
with Major Gorgas that . . . (*But* BRIN-
KERHOF *has entered.*)

BRINKERHOF. Colonel Tory is here asking for you, Major.

(TORY *enters. The entire company rises.*
BRINKERHOF *goes.*)

TORY. I welcome your return to Cuba,
Major. All my sympathy for your young
colleague's death. I call on you to serve
a notice on you. The American Public
Health Association will hold its annual
conference next month. My staff in the
Marine Hospital Corps has been invited
to report on yellow fever. Since we shall
criticize your experiment and you, it
seems only fair that you should read
what we have to say. (*He proffers a manuscript with a smile of triumph.*) So you may
prepare your defense. If you have one.

REED. The usual course would have
been to wait for us to make some public
assertion. (*He indicates paper.*) This may
prevent the continuance of our work.

TORY. I venture to hope it will.

REED. Death has given tragic testi-
mony in our behalf.

TORY. More tragic than conclusive.

REED. I can say no more.

TORY. Major.

REED. Colonel. (*Salutes.* TORY *goes.*
REED *turns desperately to* GORGAS.) I need
your support desperately now, Gorgas!

GORGAS. Wouldn't you have it if I
could give it, Reed? But Lazear did catch
yellow fever without your mosquito and
you can't keep on in the face of that!

CARROLL. I'm damned if Lazear's
death puts a stop to this! (*To* GORGAS.)
Lazear was exposed to special dangers,
Major! Dangers that don't exist outside
of labs! We don't know what he was up
to here in our lab! Dissecting mosquitoes!
Looking into 'em! And every one of 'em
loaded with deadly virus! Any one of a
hundred accidents might have happened! A pinprick would have been
enough!

GORGAS. You've got to do better than
that, Carroll!

CARROLL. What's wrong with that?
I believe that! I got yellow jack from a
mosquito! You can't account for my case
any other way!

REED. There's another case I can't account for either, except . . .

AGRAMONTE (*alarmed*). Careful, Doctor!

REED. We've got to play the ace now,
Agramonte. Have you got your Private
X. Y. Dean handy? Call him in. Let's
see him. I want Major Gorgas to hear me
talk to him! (AGRAMONTE *goes to door of
laboratory and beckons offstage.* DEAN *enters
and salutes.*) Are you Mr. Dean?

DEAN. Dean. William H. Troop A.
Seventh Cavalry.

REED. At ease. You've recently had an
attack of yellow fever.

DEAN. I sure have, sir.

REED. We're anxious to learn how you
contracted it.

DEAN. I wouldn't mind knowing about
that myself!

REED. I have a few questions for you to
answer. We'll begin with dates. (*He
consults notes.*) We'll begin with the second
of September. On that day you were discharged from treatment for a previous
illness in the hospital here. And you happened into this laboratory where, at Dr.
Lazear's request, you permitted some
mosquitoes to bite your arm. (GORGAS
starts. REED *holds up his hand for silence.*)

DEAN. That's right, sir.

REED. When did you last go into
Havana before that?

DEAN. Over the fourth, sir.

REED. August fourth?

DEAN. The Glorious Fourth, sir.

REED. That's two months before you

came down with yellow fever. (*A sharp look at* GORGAS.) You can't claim that he caught it that far ahead!

DEAN. What I did catch then was just about as bad.

REED (*dryly*). I've seen your record. When did you go into hospital for that?

DEAN. August fifteenth, sir.

REED. How many times did you leave camp between July fourth and the fifteenth of August?

DEAN. Just once, sir.

REED. In six weeks, only once?

DEAN. Me and four others rode five horses a mile and a half down to the beach and back.

REED. And you stayed in hospital till the day in the laboratory. September second.

DEAN. That's right, sir.

REED. Now it was four days later that you reported sick with yellow fever. (*Full blast.*) How about those four days?

DEAN. They had me working around camp, sir.

REED (*another glance at* GORGAS, *then he produces a ten-dollar bill from his pocketbook*). Mr. Dean, I'll give you ten dollars if you'll admit that you went some place where you might have been exposed to yellow fever during those four days.

DEAN. I tell you I never left camp, Major! I couldn't get leave!

REED. You went without leave, Mr. Dean.

DEAN. Major, I swear to God!

REED. You needn't be afraid of my telling on you. I give you my word I won't. Now, didn't you leave camp once during those four days? If only for an hour, didn't you? You could use ten dollars.

DEAN. No, sir. I didn't! So I can't take the money!

REED. Thank you, Mr. Dean. That's all I need to know.

DEAN. You asked me a lot of questions about me having yellow jack. How about finding the guy that give it to me? (*An embarrassed pause, then:*)

REED. Here! (*He produces another bill.*) Here's twenty dolars. That's twice as good as ten. There are no strings tied to it.

DEAN (*taking it*). Say! Gee! Thanks! (*He remembers himself.*) Thank you, Major!

REED. Thank you, Mr. Dean. (*He turns triumphantly to* GORGAS.)

GORGAS. May I put one question to Mr. Dean?

REED. Discretion, please!

GORGAS. I understand. (*To* DEAN.) Who was present in this laboratory on the day you let those mosquitoes bite you?

DEAN (*pointing to* AGRAMONTE). That gentleman there, and him that died— Dr. Lazear—and an elderly gentleman.

AGRAMONTE. Dr. Finlay.

GORGAS. Thank you. (*To* REED.) That's all.

REED. We won't detain you any longer, Mr. Dean. (*Salutes.* DEAN *goes.*)

GORGAS (*embarrassment*). I know what it is to hope, Reed, but I can't accept a soldier's word in lieu of demonstration.

REED (*frantic*). Surely that story of his indicates something!

GORGAS. If you could substantiate every word he said you'd still have to admit he was in this lab that day with three doctors any one of whom might have carried the infection from Carroll's bedside! If he's all the defense you have against Tory, I'm sorry for you!

AGRAMONTE. He's perfectly right. We haven't any defense.

CARROLL. Do we sit tight, then, and let Tory do his worst?

REED. No! I believe our mosquitoes have the real deadly stuff in 'em! I believe Lazear really did find the catch before he died! In spite of his death and Gorgas's doubt I believe it!

GORGAS. You've all gone off your heads over this!

REED. I can see I'm in no shape to convince you, Gorgas! But, by God, we *have* got enough to take to Leonard Wood! (*Both* CARROLL *and* AGRAMONTE *are on their feet in great excitement.*)

CARROLL. Wood!

REED. He's our last chance, Carroll!

AGRAMONTE. What can Wood do for us?

REED. I can't tell you that! I can only tell you what I shall ask him for!

GORGAS. And what will that be?

REED (*full blast*). Facilities for a foolproof demonstration of this mosquito! The full power of his governor-generalship behind us! Ten thousand dollars for operating expenses! An isolation camp where we can experiment under ideal conditions! And his leave to call for volunteers to experiment on! I think the time has come for that at last! (*Sensation.*)

QUARTET (*softly in the distance*).

"You're in the army now!
You're not behind the plow!
You son of a bitch,
You'll never get rich,
You're in the army now!"

CARROLL. So we fall back on the army after all!

REED. As soldiers should, Carroll! As soldiers should!

(*The light dims, concentrating on the four officers.*)

GORGAS. Do you think Wood will even consider that?

REED. I don't know, Gorgas. All I know is: Lazear and Carroll showed the way! And I know this will give the army a new kind of hero! Do you think Leonard Wood won't see that?

(*Darkness*, THE QUARTET *swelling. At the same time light strikes* AMES, *where he is talking to a sergeant.*)

AMES. Understand now, Sergeant, General Wood doesn't want any pressure brought. Just let it leak out. Keep it going all over camp. I don't know why any healthy kid should volunteer, but three hundred's a lot of money to a soldier.

(*Then night sky and* THE QUARTET *is singing "There'll Be a Hot Time in the Old Town Tonight" and soldiers in a seemingly interminable line of silhouettes are trooping along the horizon. They are all talking and gesticulating excitedly.*)

SOLDIERS. Now, what was that again? . . . Just what I heard. Three hundred dollars' compensation for volunteers . . . Volunteers to catch yellow jack and die of it? . . . I'm telling you what I heard . . . They got a nerve! . . . It's the God-damnedest thing I ever heard of! . . . I *don't* think! . . . *I'm* not crazy! . . . Three hundred dollars! . . . I'm only telling you what they told me! . . . How did you hear about it? . . . General Wood fixed it up with Major Reed . . . He told Dr. Carroll, who told Dr. Ames . . . I heard him telling one of our sergeants . . . Ain't you boys heard how the Major . . . You're crazy! . . . I'm only telling you what they told me! . . . Would you take a chance on it? . . . For three hundred dollars? It's a pile of money! . . . Not for me! Not for mine! . . . Three hundred dollars! I wouldn't for three thousand! . . . No, I've been lucky enough to come through this far! . . . I ain't taking no more

chances neither . . . I'll keep my health, if the Major's got no objection! . . . What do they take soldiers for anyway! . . . What do they think they're doing! . . . Catch yellow jack . . . Die of yellow jack! . . . What for? . . . Three hundred dollars! . . . To advance science! . . . And benefit humanity! . . . Good God Almighty! . . . Ain't soldiers humanity! . . .

(*Four soldiers have drifted down from the line of passing silhouettes, and now as light grows upon the steps we see that they are* BUSCH, MC CLELLAND, O'HARA, *and* BRINKERHOF *and that* MISS BLAKE *is seated in the midst of them.*)

MISS BLAKE. You can't say it hasn't given camp something to talk about!

MC CLELLAND. Well, as long as they don't do nothing but talk!

BRINKERHOF. Are you sure talking's all there is to do?

MC CLELLAND. It's all for any man with any sense.

BUSCH. I wouldn't be so sure of that, Mac.

O'HARA. I'm tempted! Holy God, I'm tempted!

MC CLELLAND. Still, three hundred dollars is a lot of money.

BRINKERHOF. A man couldn't do a thing like this for money.

MC CLELLAND. What would you do it for?

BRINKERHOF. There's patriotism.

MC CLELLAND. That's what landed us in the army!

BRINKERHOF. I ain't said I'd do it. For argument, though, and not committing myself, if Dr. Lazear was still alive, I'd consider doing it for him on personal grounds.

MC CLELLAND. I wouldn't do it on personal grounds for God Almighty!

O'HARA. Are you on personal grounds with God Almighty?

BRINKERHOF. Never bring religion into an argument.

BUSCH. It's the very sum of money I been praying for! Jesus, maybe it's a hunk of muzal!

MISS BLAKE. The Major said: "Tell the boys this gives them a real chance to advance medical science and benefit humanity."

BRINKERHOF. Medical science and humanity ain't bad reasons.

MC CLELLAND. What's medical science ever done for me?

BRINKERHOF. You been to the dentist, ain't you? That was medical science.

MCCLELLAND. Am I supposed to catch yellow jack for dentists?

BRINKERHOF. Well, don't ask me what humanity's done for you or I'll ask you where you'd be without it!

BUSCH. It's an awful way to earn money, but I could use it!

MCCLELLAND. I got nothing against the financial offer. All my objections are to the yellow jack.

BUSCH. It's an awful risk. I wonder if it's worth it!

MCCLELLAND. There's an old army rule I wouldn't forget. Keep your mouth shut and your bowels open and never volunteer.

BUSCH. If this was economics I could make up my mind, but it ain't, and I can't get no guidance out of Karl Marx!

MISS BLAKE. "Tell them they'll be giving the army a new kind of hero," the Major said.

O'HARA. Glory be to God, 'tis the heroic side appeals to the Irish always, as I said to myself when I made up my mind I'd do it!

MISS BLAKE. You did make up your mind?

O'HARA. Would you think a man of my type could resist volunteering?

MISS BLAKE. I knew they'd get one of you!

O'HARA. You should have known it'ud be me, Miss Blake! And I'm with John Brinkerhof! I'll only do it free, I said!

MISS BLAKE. That's beautiful!

O'HARA. But that height of nobility, naturally as I come by it, is not practical. As I soon realized when I thought how well I could use this sum of money for my medical training which, as you well know, is my life's ambition. So I made up my mind I'd accept the payment.

MISS BLAKE. And why not?

O'HARA. Would you believe it, the heroic side got in my way and stopped me! What a noble start I'd be getting in my profession, I thought, if I can say later: "Yes, I am that same John O'Hara who gave his life that mankind might be preserved from yellow fever!" There was an uplifting notion for you! With that in my mind I went running to the Major.

MISS BLAKE. I knew he'd get one of you!

O'HARA. Oh, no man could have held me back if I hadn't thought still another thought in the nick of time. "If I do give my life," I said to myself, "it may be noble, but will it be a start?"

BUSCH. It's a thing any radical could go into and not be ashamed of, only I got to have more time on it.

MISS BLAKE. Won't the Major get a single volunteer?

BRINKERHOF. I wouldn't know.

MISS BLAKE. I want him to get one.

O'HARA. Don't be using your sex to shame us into this!

MISS BLAKE. I'm talking to Mr. Brinkerhof now. To Mr. Brinkerhof, who wants to stay on in the army. Drill. Ten, maybe twenty years of drill. Then another war. And more lives thrown away. Then drill again. Then a pension and the old soldiers' home. If that's all being a soldier comes to!

BRINKERHOF. It ain't much.

MISS BLAKE. Now, maybe for the first time since armies began, soldiers are given a chance to do good, not harm. To make the world better, not worse, as a place to live in. (*They listen hypnotized,* O'HARA *rising slowly to his feet.*) You'd get well! We'd take care of you! Don't be afraid!

BRINKERHOF. But I *am* afraid.

MISS BLAKE. That makes it all the braver!

BRINKERHOF. I wouldn't do it for money!

MISS BLAKE. For your sergeancy then!

BRINKERHOF. That'd be just as bad.

MISS BLAKE. For science and humanity!

BRINKERHOF. Oh, I'd never be up to anything like that!

MISS BLAKE. Choose your own reason!

BRINKERHOF. There'd be a lot of satisfaction in it.

MISS BLAKE. Indeed there would!

BRINKERHOF. No! Just to me, I mean!

MISS BLAKE. But that's enough!

BRINKERHOF. I ain't committed myself! I only said, for the sake of argument . . .

MISS BLAKE. "If one, only one, of our boys will step forward," the Major said, "he'll make this reach and touch the heart of the world and the world will weep and have faith in this!"

O'HARA. By God, I'll do it for the hell of it! (*A glad cry from* MISS BLAKE. *"Call to Quarters" sounds.*)

MC CLELLAND. For Christ's sake, O'-Hara!

O'HARA. Will you come with me, John?

BUSCH. Don't be in a hurry, Brinkie!

O'HARA. Will you come with me!

BRINKERHOF. Where?

O'HARA. To the Major!

BRINKERHOF. Now?

O'HARA. Before I have time to change my mind again!

BUSCH. It's a God-damn gallery play! All he wants is to be a hero!

BRINKERHOF. I don't know that I'm cut out for a hero, John!

O'HARA. Will the Major know that? Would any man with the sense of science in him look a gift hero in the teeth!

MC CLELLAND. You're crazy, O'Hara!

O'HARA. I am not crazy! This is the better side of my nature rising up, as it's sure to do in the end with the Irish! (*To* BRINKERHOF.) Are you coming or do I have to drag you!

BRINKERHOF. Oh, I'm coming, John! I'm coming!

BUSCH. Stop him!

MC CLELLAND (*to* MISS BLAKE). You talked him into this!

MISS BLAKE. Thank God if I did!

MC CLELLAND. You're responsible if they . . .

MISS BLAKE. I can't help that! I can't help wanting them to . . .

(*But* O'HARA *has already pulled* BRINKERHOF *to his feet, turned him about, and dragged him over below where* REED *is waiting in the upper shadow alone.* REED *sees them, and while the others look on breathless, comes down to them and returns their salutes.*)

REED. Did you want something, Mr. O'Hara?

O'HARA. We've come to volunteer, sir.

BRINKERHOF. The both of us, sir. For the experiment.

(BUSCH *makes as though to follow them, then draws back to* MC CLELLAND, *and the pair stand together frightened.* MISS BLAKE *remains motionless in her exultation.* REED *smiles, then a deep breath, and:*)

REED. You know the risk?

O'HARA. Yes, sir, we know, all right.

REED. You've heard what the compensation is?

BRINKERHOF. Yes, sir, we've heard. Only . . . (*He catches* O'HARA'S *eye.*)

O'HARA (*drawing himself up in the manner of a schoolboy speaking a valedictory oration*). We're volunteering in the interests of science, sir.

BRINKERHOF (*same manner*). And for the benefit of humanity.

O'HARA. And the only condition on which we volunteer . . .

BRINKERHOF. Is that we receive no compensation, sir. (*Pause.*)

REED. Gentlemen, I salute you.

(*He does.* O'HARA *and* BRINKERHOF *are covered with confusion. Darkness, but immediately the regimental band bursts full blast into "The Stars and Stripes Forever" and* CARROLL *is standing in light in front of the laboratory screen, a carnival barker selling it to the universe.*)

CARROLL. Did you hear that, folks! Did you see it! We're off and nobody can stop us now! We've got heroes to answer 'em with now! And Wood's given us everything else we needed! Backing, dough, isolation camp! This is it, folks! Camp Lazear we call it! Ideal conditions! No mosquitoes here we don't bring with us in test tubes! And we're going to show you the God-damnedest demonstration that's ever been! (*Light strikes the tent below, where* BRINKERHOF *and* O'HARA *sit solemnly on their bunks, stripped to the waist.*) O'Hara and Brinkerhof are in that tent this minute! Two weeks they've been there, where not a thing could get at 'em! So you couldn't ask for more perfect subjects than they'll be when they step out to take their bites today! And they'll get yellow jack, no fear of that! But they're only the half of this show! (*Light strikes a crude windowless wooden shack above.*) Do you see that shack? Reed isn't satisfied just to nail the mosquito and stop there! Not Reed! He's going to show 'em that nature's got things fixed so you can't catch yellow jack any way *but* from the mosquito! Never you mind how Lazear caught it! This is what happens in nature, not in labs! And Reed's thought up the God-damnedest scheme! (*Daylight begins slowly to spread over the stage and what has been a bustle in the darkness is now seen to be caused by a horde of American soldiers.*) He calls that shack "the dirty house"! And it's dirty, all right! He's packed it full of every stinking by-product of this disease that ought to spread it around if anything could and he's got two more soldiers . . . (*A particularly bright light picks out* BUSCH *and* MC CLELLAND *standing close together, frightened and wishing they had not come.*) . . . to sleep nights in there for three weeks! They're going to sleep in the un-aired, undisinfected and unwashed bedding and night shirts men have died in, on pillows and mattresses soaked with fever sweat and black vomit! And wouldn't it take a God-fearing son of a bitch of a workman like Reed to do a thing like that to a couple of kids? But if we keep the mosquitoes out of that shack, the chances are good—and they're damned good, folks!—that this second pair doesn't catch yellow jack! And that ought to show our fellow doctors and scientists they've been wrong in everything they ever thought about this! By God, if this job doesn't make medical history . . .

BUSCH. I wonder if we were right about volunteering.

MC CLELLAND. Why?

BUSCH. Once you get in you don't get out.

MC CLELLAND. I thought of that, too. (*He calls.*) O'Hara! (O'HARA *emerges from tent.*)

O'HARA. Come out, John, and see what's putting itself forward where it's not wanted. (BRINKERHOF *follows him out.*)

MC CLELLAND. Who says we're not wanted and who don't want us?

O'HARA. Too many heroes leave none outstanding, which is not in agreement with the Irish ideal!

BRINKERHOF. I'm sure the Major wants all that'll come, John.

O'HARA. Will you think before you speak, John, or not speak at all? (*To* MC-CLELLAND.) What brings you here, whom I last heard scorning the very idea, and did you refuse compensation like the two of us or are you selling your bodies like a couple of whores?

MC CLELLAND. We're taking all the compensation we can get on account we got no use for gallery plays!

BUSCH. And me doing this for the wherewithal to further the radical movement puts me above any bourgeois hero, and what's heroes amount to and who wants to be one?

O'HARA. Heroes amount to the inspiration of mankind! And the difference between compensation and none leaves John and me our superiority!

(*The Band concludes the Sousa march.* REED *has entered above, followed by* AGRA-MONTE, *who carries the mosquitoes in the usual gauze-capped tubes.*)

A SERGEANT. AttenSHUN!

AGRAMONTE. Are you ready, Reed? (*Complete silence, then:*)

REED. I'm ready. Carroll, call the roll.

CARROLL. O'Hara. Brinkerhof. Busch. Mc Clelland. (*Each soldier answers up.*)

REED. Now, then, Mr. Busch and Mr. Mc Clelland, you'll take up your residence in the dirty house. (BUSCH *and* MC-CLELLAND *move slowly up toward the shack. They open door and spring back in horror.*)

MC CLELLAND. Christ Almighty! (BUSCH *turns to* REED *with a sickly grin.*)

BUSCH. I never knew anything could stink like that!

MC CLELLAND (*The same state of mind.*) Me neither. But it's too late to back down now.

(BUSCH *replies with a little Jewish gesture of resignation which sums up two thousand years of making the best of things.*)

BUSCH. I'll pull the blankets out. You make up the bunks. (*He goes into the shack.*)

MC CLELLAND. They just closed the Paris Exposition! I read about it in the papers. You won't never read about this. Nobody could write how this smells! Take a good look, heroes! (*He goes into the house.*)

REED. Sergeant, close the door. (SER-GEANT *closes and padlocks door.* REED *turns to* O'HARA *and* BRINKERHOF.) Are you ready, Brinkerhof and O'Hara?

BRINKERHOF. We had a good sleep, a good breakfast, and a sterile bath. I don't know what more we got coming to us.

O'HARA. Unless somebody would be after taking our pictures?

BRINKERHOF. Why would you want your picture taken, John?

O'HARA. I like a bit of a send-off, John, but it doesn't matter.

REED. I'll give you a send-off. (*He turns to* AGRAMONTE.) Will you give me the mosquitoes, Agramonte?

(AGRAMONTE *steps toward* REED *with the test tubes. A longer roll of drums offstage. Darkness. Then light grows within the lower tent and the sky is tropical night once more.* BUSCH *and* MC CLELLAND *sit smoking in front of the wooden shack.* O'HARA *lounges in the opening of the lower tent, within which* BRIN-KERHOF *sits on a cot in the act of taking his temperature. A* SERGEANT *stands apart.*)

SERGEANT. Five minutes more, boys. Then recess is over.

BUSCH. Ain't the Major coming to tell us good night?

SERGEANT. Don't he always come to tell you good night?

BUSCH. He don't pay no attention to the two of us. (*Indicating* BRINKERHOF *and* O'HARA.) He ain't interested only in those two guys.

(SERGEANT *goes. A pause.*)

O'HARA. Being a hero should be quickly over and on to the glory that comes after.

MC CLELLAND. Will you listen to all that quiet!

BUSCH. I heard it before and I didn't like it. They'd ought to have give us a bugler out here.

MC CLELLAND. I never expected this to be this way. This was a hell of a Thanksgiving Day!

BUSCH. I ain't complaining. I'm putting on weight living in that stink.

O'HARA (*to* BRINKERHOF). Will you take that thermometer out of your mouth, John!

BRINKERHOF. I'm hot.

O'HARA. It's a cold night with a wintry dampness in it the way you could see your breath if you troubled to blow it!

MC CLELLAND. O'Hara!

O'HARA. What is it?

MC CLELLAND. How are you feeling?

O'HARA. I'm feeling fine.

BUSCH. How's Brinkerhof feeling?

O'HARA. He feels better than me.

BRINKERHOF. I don't feel well, John! I got vertigo.

O'HARA. If you don't feel right it's your willful imagination! If you felt bad I'd feel worse than you! Do you think it's friendly to try stealing a march on me? We started on this together and we'll finish together or not finish at all!

BRINKERHOF. This is the night of the fourth day. The Major said things ought to begin to happen the fourth day.

O'HARA. For the last time I tell you, if you've got a fever you're no friend of mine!

MC CLELLAND. Quit scrapping, O'-Hara!

BUSCH. We'll all be scrapping before we get out of this.

(*A pause, then:*)

O'HARA. Likely there'll nothing come of this in the end. Likely we'll wait here for two days or three, then go back to be the laughing stock of the barracks.

MC CLELLAND. That has one drawback you ain't thought of, O'Hara. If nothing don't come of this for neither of you, then the Major's mosquitoes ain't as dangerous as he thought. And if they ain't, the stink inside there may not be so safe!

BUSCH. For God's sake, don't say that!

O'HARA. Are you afraid?

MC CLELLAND. Why wouldn't he be? We been sitting inside there all afternoon. Waiting to hear the ambulance take one or both of you off to the hospital! When they let us out to eat supper, there both of you was as big as life and twice as healthy! Can you imagine how that made us feel! Looks like Busch and me may be the heroes who catch yellow jack!

O'HARA. The cowardice of those remarks sounds highly suitable on your tongue, McClelland, and it coated with the biliousness of beer!

BUSCH. It's only half-wits ain't afraid of danger.

MC CLELLAND. I hope that's some consolation to you.

(*General irritability.* BRINKERHOF *has risen to close the tent flap.*)

O'HARA. What are you after doing with that tent flap?

BRINKERHOF. I'm cold.

O'HARA. Two minutes ago the fever was burning you up!

BRINKERHOF. I got a chill now. My ears is roaring and my teeth is chattering and my head . . .

O'HARA. You'll not give yourself yellow jack ahead of me, sucking thermometers one minute and chattering your jaws together the next! This was agreed to be both of us or neither! (*The* SERGEANT *returns.*)

SERGEANT. Pipe down! (*Silence, then he continues to* O'HARA.) Major ordered the ambulance to stand by on the chance that either you or Brinkerhof might need it.

O'HARA. You can tell the ambulance to go to bed.

SERGEANT. All right. Lights out.

BUSCH (*rises and goes to shack*). Either the stink inside is weakening or we're getting used to it. (*Opening door of shack, he stops on the threshold.*)

MC CLELLAND. No, she ain't weakened much.

BUSCH. The fresh air makes her seem worse than she is!

MC CLELLAND. Take a deep breath outside. (*He goes in.*)

BUSCH (*to* O'HARA *and* BRINKERHOF). We'll feel safer if the both of you die before morning. (*He fills his lungs and follows* MC CLELLAND *into shack, closing the door. The* SERGEANT *padlocks door on outside and goes. In the meanwhile:*)

BRINKERHOF. You been hard on me, John. You know I wouldn't take no advantage of you if I could help it. (*Removing his shoes, he shudders again as with a chill and looks up.*) You wouldn't like to speak some Shakespeare for me? You usually like to when there's no one around. If you said your favorite lines from Julius Caesar, they might put heart in me. (*Another shudder of chill comes over him He looks uneasily towards* O'HARA, *then reaches stealthily for the thermometer, shakes it, sticks it back in his mouth and turns away so that he will not be observed. In the meanwhile:*)

O'HARA.
"Cowards die many times before their death;
The valiant never taste of death but once.
Of all the wonders that I yet have heard,
It seems most strange to me that men should fear,
Seeing that death, a necessary end,
Will come when it will come."

BRINKERHOF (*his diction obstructed by thermometer*). Thank you, John. (O'HARA *turns furious.*)

O'HARA. Are you at that thing again! Give it to me! I'll smash it to atoms!

BRINKERHOF (*defending it*). No, John, don't break it.

O'HARA. I want no more of your treachery! (*He secures thermometer.*)

BRINKERHOF. Don't break it, John! Look for yourself! See if I ain't got something wrong with me! (O'HARA *looks scornfully. Then bends to look more closely under the lamp. Then:*)

O'HARA. Holy God! (*He hands thermometer back to* BRINKERHOF, *who reads it. They look at one another,* BRINKERHOF *nodding with a sickly smile.*)

BRINKERHOF. It'd go higher if I gave it time.

O'HARA. And me as fit as a fiddler's bitch in heat. (*He feels his brows, his pulse, and strikes his chest despairingly.*) What ails you, O'Hara, that you let others get ahead of you? Here, give me that thing back! (*He snatches thermometer from* BRIN-KERHOF'S *mouth and puts it into his own.*)

BRINKERHOF. Could I ask you to go down to the ambulance and tell them? (*Pause, as* O'HARA *takes thermometer out of his mouth, is disappointed, puts it back to suck it harder than ever.*) Could I ask you, John? (*Staring uncomprehendingly,* O'HARA *again removes thermometer from his mouth. Then he turns suddenly and runs out, shouting as he goes:*)

O'HARA. Ambulance! Ambulance! Ambulance!

MC CLELLAND (*from within shack*). What the hell! What are you yelling about out there?

BUSCH. They got it, Mac! They got it!

MC CLELLAND. Which one of 'em's got it? (*Door of shack is rattled from within as they beat upon it.*) Is it you, Brinkerhof?

BUSCH. For God's sake!

MC CLELLAND. Answer up!

BUSCH. Let us out of here! Let us out! (*The turmoil continues, with* BRINKERHOF *on his feet, frightened and swaying dizzily. Then darkness and immediately upon it the* QUARTET *is singing "Good-bye, My Blue Bell." The chorus through once and daylight strikes* BRINKERHOF *in bed.* FINLAY *and* GORGAS *bend over him, subjecting him to an intense and meticulous examination.* MISS BLAKE *stands apart to one side,* REED *to the other. The examination continues in pantomime over the music. Apart and somewhat above on the side opposite* BRINKERHOF'S *bed,* CARROLL *and* AGRAMONTE *are waiting,* AGRAMONTE *pacing restlessly to and fro.*)

AGRAMONTE (*after a pause*). Will they never finish their examination?

CARROLL. You're taking this harder than Reed is.

AGRAMONTE. I feel for Reed. This is Reed's moment. Everything hangs on what Gorgas says.

CARROLL. Whatever Gorgas says, that's a real case of genuine yellow jack.

AGRAMONTE. But the world will listen to what Gorgas says. (FINLAY *straightens and turns to* GORGAS.)

FINLAY. Well, Major Gorgas?

GORGAS. I'll give my opinion when I've seen the records.

REED. Miss Blake has the records for you. Suppose you take them aside to look them over. I don't want you to tire the boy out. (GORGAS *and* FINLAY *see* REED'S *point and go to* MISS BLAKE.)

GORGAS. Yes, I expect we were being a bit inhuman.

FINLAY. That's one of the drawbacks of experiment, Major Gorgas. (*They have crossed to* MISS BLAKE, *who hands them each a file of the record. They sit to study them in silence while she looks on and* CARROLL *and* AGRAMONTE *watch from above.* REED *has gone to* BRINKERHOF's *bedside and stands looking down on him.*)

REED. That was part of the game, Brinkerhof. An essential part from my point of view. I hope you didn't mind it too much.

BRINKERHOF. I wouldn't feel up to minding anything, Doctor.

REED. It's a bad sickness, I know that. We got your case at the beginning, though, so you're going to be all right. Don't worry.

BRINKERHOF. I wouldn't feel up to worrying, either.

(REED's *hand is on the boy's forehead.*)

REED. They tell me you didn't drink the champagne I sent you.

BRINKERHOF. Do I have to drink it, sir?

REED. It might make you feel less sick at your stomach.

BRINKERHOF. I ain't used to it and I didn't care for it.

(REED *smiles, then:*)

REED. My wife's just sent me a fine fruit cake. I'm saving it for you. For your Christmas dinner. We'll try to have you on your feet by then. So you can get sick all over again. Not for science, though. Just for the fun of it. Nothing else we can do for you now?

(*A pause.* BRINKERHOF *manages to lift his head a little. Then:*)

BRINKERHOF. Why was it, sir, yellow jack took me and give O'Hara the go-by?

REED (*surprised*). I don't know, Brinkerhof. Some men seem to be born immune to some diseases.

BRINKERHOF. Could a man be immune one time and catch it another?

REED. It's possible. We don't know much about immunity.

BRINKERHOF. John O'Hara he's quite a friend of mine, sir. You just asked me what more you could do for me. John set his heart on getting this disease for the start it'd give him practicing medicine. It's likely the only start he'll ever get. Would you give John another chance at it, sir?

REED. It's hard for me to say no to you, Brinkerhof. I'm afraid O'Hara's a waste

of time for my purposes. I can't afford to break our record of success. I'll do what I can to help him with his medical studies. But I wish you'd ask me for something else now. (BRINKERHOF *sinks back.*)

BRINKERHOF. Give John my best. Ask him not to be angry with me if he can help it.

REED. I'll do that much.

(*But* GORGAS, *going through file, has come to the fever chart.*)

GORGAS (*low and quick*). A hundred and three and six tenths last night. Dropped again, though, at six this morning and again at eight.

FINLAY. You've noticed the granular casts in the urine, I hope?

(REED *goes toward them.*)

GORGAS. Oh, yes.

FINLAY. The eyes were beautifully jaundiced today, too.

GORGAS (*to* MISS BLAKE). How about the gums?

MISS BLAKE. A little bleeding.

FINLAY. Headache and nausea still troublesome, though?

MISS BLAKE. He's very uncomfortable.

FINLAY. Splendid! I should defer to the Major's diagnosis, but I can't think of a symptom the boy's omitted! It's beautiful! Beautiful! The fourth day of his sickness, too! (*Then, to* REED.) And how long did you say between the bite and the first symptom?

REED. Three days, nine and a half hours.

FINLAY. Nineteen years for me! Three days, nine and a half hours for Major Reed! (*He is pumping* REED's *hand.*) I conceived a truth! You delivered it into life! Together we have added to the world's arsenal of knowledge!

GORGAS. You promised you'd make me eat my doubts, Reed. Didn't know eating doubts could be such a pleasure! Damned if this isn't an impressive moment! I'm going out after this mosquito now. And after that, Panama! You've made the Panama Canal possible now! May I? (*He holds out his hand.*)

REED (*sternly*). If that boy's convinced you, Gorgas, that he did get the infection from the mosquito and if those other two, healthy as ever in the filth of that dirty house, have shown you the disease cannot in nature be contracted except from the mosquito, then you may! But if you have any shadow of reservation on either point . . . (AMES *has entered hastily to second cot.*)

AMES. You certainly are knocking 'em over out at that camp, Major! Will you fix up this cot, Miss Blake?

(MISS BLAKE *goes to prepare cot.*)

CARROLL. What do you mean?

AGRAMONTE. You haven't got another case from out there!

REED. Not Busch or McClelland!

(*Together.*)

AGRAMONTE. They couldn't have caught it in the dirty house!

REED. There hasn't been a mosquito near that pair . . .

CARROLL. That'd wreck things worse than Lazear's death did, my God!

FINLAY. Oh, no, no, no! Not just at the moment when we . . .

GORGAS. Good Lord! Well, it goes to show you never . . .

(*All talking together in their dismay, the three members of the Commission have left* FINLAY *and* GORGAS *and hurried towards* AMES. *Before they can reach him, however,* TWO STRETCHER BEARERS *have carried a stretcher in and the recumbent form upon it belongs to* O'HARA.)

REED (*climax*). O'Hara!

O'HARA (*feeble but triumphant*). Good afternoon to you, Doctor.

REED. But this man hasn't got yellow fever, Ames!

AMES. Oh, yes, he has!

CARROLL (*to* O'HARA). But, God damn it, you should have come down four days ago!

REED. That's true. O'Hara! How . . . ?

O'HARA. Have you never heard, Major, how it's the human element that still baffles you men of science?

AGRAMONTE. That is no answer!

REED (*shaking with excitement*). Do you know how you got it?

O'HARA. You weren't out at camp the day after they took Brinkerhof away.

REED. No.

O'HARA. You should have left those mosquitoes of yours locked up! (*Sensation.* MISS BLAKE *is shocked,* REED *stunned.*)

BRINKERHOF (*feeble, but delighted*). Hooray!

(*The light focuses sharply down upon* O'HARA.)

O'HARA. Now science and humanity become one in the person of Johnny O'Hara! And no shadow of gain for him but his own satisfaction, and only the hell and vanity of that!

(*Darkness, and the* QUARTET *strikes into "The Old Folks at Home." Then the sky is night once more and the foreground bare and dark and the only illumination of the setting is within the laboratory, where* REED, CARROLL, *and* AGRAMONTE *are dimly visible.* REED *comes out of laboratory, the other two following.*)

REED. Well, Carroll, the job's done and the doubts and discouragements are memories now. And the last microscope's packed and we've closed the door of our Cuban laboratory. And our dirty house has made us a fine bonfire and grass can grow once more where Brinkerhof and O'Hara pitched their tent. And none of the boys seem much the worse for wear and we're going home. I could wish we were taking Lazear home with us. I could wish that you were coming, Agramonte.

AGRAMONTE. No, Doctor. I am Cuban born. I must stay in Cuba.

(BRINKERHOF *enters and salutes.*)

REED. Yes, Mr. Brinkerhof?

BRINKERHOF. The rig you ordered to take you down to the transport's ready, sir, whenever you are.

REED. Are you and O'Hara ready to sail with us?

BRINKERHOF. Yes, sir. We're ready, sir. O'Hara he's still a bit weak in the knees. He's resting down there on the pile of baggage.

(REED *turns smiling up the stair, but* CARROLL *is after him.*)

CARROLL. Let's not go, Chief! Let's stay and finish things! It can't be far from here to vaccine and cure! Are you with me, Chief?

REED. No, Carroll, I'm not with you. A man does what he has to do and is tired. (*They are all four silhouettes now against the sky.*) I see the struggles and tragedies ahead.

(*In the distance the African tom-tom begins to throb faintly.*)

AGRAMONTE. Yes, Carroll. For the men who will follow after us and carry on the chase in the years to come. In Ecuador and Mexico and Brazil. And in that vast reservoir of African jungle whence this thing came, where it will persist . . .

(*The tom-tom swells suddenly and* REED *lifts his hand as though to silence* AGRAMONTE *so that he may listen to the future, and the four, motionless, recede into the past. At the same time, indeed already through* AGRAMONTE'S *last words,* STACKPOOLE *has entered below to a faint glow of light, thoughtful and detached, and is standing motionless. Simultaneously* HARKNESS *has entered to a brighter light on the other side below.*)

HARKNESS. Lagos, West Africa. September 19th, 1927. Dr. Adrian Stokes died here of yellow fever this afternoon after an illness of three days and a few hours. We cannot say how he contracted the disease. It is certain that no infected mosquito had bitten him. In that, his death recalls the death of Dr. Lazear in Havana, in 1900. It would appear that yellow fever laboratories are filled with dangers hitherto unrealized. Stokes continued directing our work from his bed, insisting that his blood be taken for injection into monkeys and that mosquitos be fed on him for infection. His work ceased only as he sank into the final coma. Due to the mildness of yellow fever among African natives, Stokes felt that we should never be able positively to demonstrate that we had given his monkeys the real thing until we had seen white man and monkey both dead of the same infection and side by side on the autopsy table. . . . (*The light on* HARKNESS *dies to a glow, leaving him as motionless as* REED *and his group above and behind. Simultaneously it increases on the waiting* STACKPOOLE.) We have seen that now in the autopsy just performed on Stokes himself.

STACKPOOLE. London. September 23rd, 1929. Conclusion of experiment on monkeys one hundred and seventeen and one hundred and fifty-five. Summary of record. These two monkeys were vaccinated on January 12th last, according to the principle established for dog distemper by Laidlaw and Dunkin, namely, a combination of immune blood with active virus. Being still in good health on April 12th following, the animals were on that date injected with a fatal dose of active virus, to which they showed no reaction. No conclusion was drawn from this single success, however, and both animals were held, still in good health, until September 12th, when one hundred thousand fatal doses of virus were administered to each. The fact that the health of these animals remains good on this, the tenth day following so severe a test, indicates . . . (*He corrects himself.*) . . . would indicate . . . (*He corrects himself again.*) No, damn it, *does* indicate the establishment of at least a principle of vaccination against yellow fever. Reed took the disease from mosquito to man. Stokes took it from man to monkey. Now we shall be taking it from monkey back to man.

(*The Chorus strikes full force and full volume into the refrain of "There'll Be a Hot Time in the Old Town Tonight" and there is a distant sound of soldiers marching and the light goes into darkness and the play is ended.*)

CURTAIN

AWAKE AND SING

Clifford Odets

Awake and Sing was first presented by the Group Theatre at the Belasco Theatre on February 19, 1935, directed by Harold Clurman, with settings by Boris Aronson, with the following members of the Group Theatre Acting Company:

MYRON BERGER . . . . Art Smith
BESSIE BERGER . . . . Stella Adler
JACOB . . . . Morris Carnovsky
HENNIE BERGER . . . . Phoebe Brand
RALPH BERGER . . . . Jules Garfield
SCHLOSSER . . . . Roman Bohnen
MOE AXELROD . . . . Luther Adler
UNCLE MORTY . . . . J. E. Bromberg
SAM FEINSCHREIBER . . Sanford Meisner

The entire action takes place in an apartment in the Bronx, New York City.

Copyright 1935, by Clifford Odets.
Reprinted from *Six Plays of Clifford Odets* by permission of Random House, Inc.

CAUTION: Professionals and amateurs are hereby warned that *Awake and Sing*, being fully protected under the copyright laws of the United States of America, the British Empire, including the Dominion of Canada, and all other countries of the copyright union, is subject to royalty. All rights, including professional, amateur, motion picture, recitation, lecturing, public reading, radio and television broadcasting, and the rights of translation into foreign languages, are strictly reserved. Particular emphasis is laid on the question of readings, permission for which must be secured from the author's agent in writing. All inquiries should be addressed to the author's agent, Harold Freedman, 101 Park Avenue, New York City.

The original, unproduced, version of *Awake and Sing!* was called *I've Got the Blues.* "When I read it first," Harold Clurman recalls in *The Fervent Years,* "I could not see the woods for the trees." Neither could the author's associates, the other directors and the actors of the Group Theatre, which Odets had joined as an actor when this splinter group of the Theatre Guild started on its own in 1930. Somewhat earlier, he had written another inchoate play about unhappy young people under the title of *910 Eden Street,* and Mr. Clurman, to whom he had shown it, remembers that he "hardly thought of it as a play, or of its author as a playright."

At the summer camp called Green Mansions, in Warrensburg, New York, the Group devoted two evenings to a reading of the second act of *I've Got the Blues,* the new play Odets had started in 1932 and completed in 1933. The reading convinced Mr. Clurman that the young Group Theatre actor had talent. But he was still put off by a clutter of "rather gross Jewish humor and a kind of messy kitchen realism" in the first act and an "almost masochistically pessimistic" third act. Others were troubled by lapses of taste in the early versions. Nevertheless, confidence in the work grew after it was revised and retitled *Awake and Sing!,* and confidence in its author also rose after he caused a sensation in the theatre with his long one-act strike play, *Waiting for Lefty.* It had won a New Theatre League prize in 1935, and was given a memorable, rather impromptu, Sunday night production by a pro-labor group on January 5, 1935, at Eva Le Gallienne's abandoned Civic Repertory Theatre in downtown New York. Following this baptism on the left, *Waiting for Lefty* had well over a hundred amateur productions in the United States and other countries, as well as a Broadway production by the Group Theatre in March, 1935, along with another Odets one-actor, *Till the Day I Die,* an exciting drama about the early anti-Nazi Underground in Germany. The Group Theatre production of *Awake and Sing!* in the same year (the play had been in rehearsal for about ten days when *Waiting for Lefty* was first presented to the scrutiny of the press) climaxed a determined struggle for recognition by its intense young author.

Born in Philadelphia of middle-class Jewish parents on July 18, 1906, brought to New York in his childhood, and educated in a Bronx high school from 1921 to 1923, Odets first sought a career as an actor, and played some juvenile roles in Theatre Guild productions. He joined the Group Theatre as a founding member and filled minor roles in its early productions, including Kingsley's *Men in White.* Once launched on his playwriting career by *Waiting for Lefty* and *Awake and Sing!,* however, Mr. Odets devoted all his professional energies to writing until he also began to direct his plays and Hollywood scenarios in the 1940's.

In 1936, the Group Theatre presented his second and for a long time favorite full-length play, *Paradise Lost,* written while *I've Got the Blues* was gathering dust on the Group's shelves. This play amplified the subject of middle-class decay Odets had already treated in *Awake and Sing!* but did so with such thoroughness and suggestiveness that the new work seemed phantasmagoric. Its symbolic realism met with apathy and disapproval in most quarters. Clifton Fadiman and the present editor were probably the only reviewers in New York to be strongly affected by the play, chiefly (in my case) by its apocalyptic atmosphere and its attitude of desolation and desperate affirmation. (As a matter of fact, I am still haunted by the mood of the play and by the performances of Morris Carnovsky, Luther Adler, and other Group actors in Harold Clurman's vibrant production.) *Paradise Lost* was a failure on Broadway, but Odets' next work, *Golden Boy,* produced by the Group Theatre in 1938, was an unqualified success. Once more Odets displayed a wealth of piquant characterization which Carnovsky, Roman Bohnen, and Luther Adler, who had the leading role, re-created with vivid color and noteworthy vitality. Its subject, the deterioration and death of a young violinist who turns into a prize-fighter under the pressure of the times, was familiar to the playgoing public. But the semi-allegorical treatment—the implied conflict between creativity expressed by the "fiddle" and commercialized destructiveness represented by the "fist"—lent significance to the otherwise commonplace situations.

The plays that followed *Golden Boy* on the Broadway stage met with a lukewarm reception, although *Rocket to the Moon*, in 1938, an original treatment of love and marriage in a troubled world, deserved more appreciation than it received. In *Night Music*, in 1940, Odets blended romance and economics more imaginatively but also to considerably less effect. It suffered equally from tenuous symbolism and diffuse realism, though without indeed missing intensity of compassion and protest. *Clash by Night*, in 1941, treated the familiar theme of adultery with more depth than it was given credit for, in a production starring Tallulah Bankhead. Odets conceived the play as a study in humiliation; and relating love and economics once more, as well as making timely references to fascism, he apparently hoped *Clash by Night* would be understood as a warning against pushing the world's "little men" too far. Neither on the realistic nor the symbolic plane did the play prove absorbing enough to the reviewers, and once more Odets' high purpose and brooding talent were frustrated on Broadway.

Material success came to the author in Hollywood, for which he wrote, produced, and directed successfully; and at least one of his films, *None but the Lonely Heart*, starring Ethel Barrymore and Cary Grant, had considerable distinction. But discontent with the Hollywood milieu brought Odets back to Broadway in 1949 with a melodramatic exposé, *The Big Knife*, which was later filmed despite its animadversions on the movie industry. Two other Odets plays, suggesting a widening of his subject matter, reached Broadway in the 1950's, in addition to a revival of *Golden Boy*, excitingly staged by the author although at some sacrifice of its original poetic quality. The first play was *The Country Girl*, a strong character-drama set in the theatre and concerned with the triangular conflicts of a jittery alcoholic actor, his greatly tried wife (a role superbly played by that fine actress Uta Hagen), and a young admirer of the actor who supervises the latter's return to the stage. The absence of the visionary passion of the author's early plays, however, made this thoroughly sound work an uncharacteristic success which Odet's early admirers could not regard with any enthusiasm. The other play, *The Flowering Peach*, was a retelling of the biblical story of the Deluge in a folksy spirit of sympathetic humor. Only moderately successful on Broadway, in spite of the presence of the superb "Second Avenue" comedian Menasha Skulnik in the lovable role of Noah, *The Flowering Peach* was not regarded by its author as a finished work. Odets has endeavored to revise it while returning to his work in films, for which he evinces an aptitude not always, apparently, approved by his conscience.

To return to *Awake and Sing!* is to return to the youthful Odets whose as yet untried and unsubdued talent was compounded of anguish and rebellion and seemed all afire with evangelical fervor. Although not entirely free of callow sentiment, which Harold Clurman's masterly production minimized, the play showed a true artist's sensitivity, and nearly half a dozen fully dimensioned characterizations enriched it. Along with its author's quasi-lyrical rebelliousness and a wry yet lively sense of humor, *Awake and Sing!* also carried the weight of true compassion, and this last-mentioned quality also produced one of the most genuine and appealing characterizations seen on the American stage—the grandfather, Jacob, played by Morris Carnovsky. It seemed unlikely that anyone who saw the Carnovsky performance in 1935, or when the play was successfully revived by the Group in 1939, would ever forget it. Written colloquially, the play also impressed its public with a style that was both realistic and poetic, authentic and elliptical. Odets' characters possessed angularity and authenticity in equal measures. They seemed somewhat bizarre but intimately real characters, felt and remembered by the author yet also re-created by his keen temperament. It is little wonder that in 1937 he was referred to in the press as O'Neill's successor and as "the white hope of the American theatre." The cliché stuck to Odets until the end of the decade, when it was briefly transferred to William Saroyan on the strength of *My Heart's in the Highlands* and *The Time of Your Life*.

After a lapse of many years, one may single out as perhaps most relevant Joseph Wood Krutch's comments on *Awake and Sing!* and its author. "What Mr. Odets has done is to achieve a paradoxical combination of detachment and participation," Mr. Krutch wrote. "Emotionally he is still close to the people he is writing about and he understands them from the inside out. His is another generation and it has formulated a new philosophy, but he holds his convictions and pursues his aims with the intensity of his fathers." (*The American Drama Since 1918*, 1939). And Mr. Krutch rightly praised, above all, the presence of not "one specific protest and rebellion but the persistent and many-sided rebellion of human nature against anything that thwarts it." Each character "knows what it is to want something with agonizing intensity and to nurse that want day in and day out without a moment's remission."

At the same time that these comments are gratefully accepted, it should be noted that *Awake and Sing!* excelled in two other respects so far as Odets' career is concerned. First, the play contains his most authentic yet specially charged dialogue. It belongs both to the characters and the young Odets. Also, this is the one play, with the exception of *Golden Boy*, in which Odets found a completely satisfactory form for his distinctive talent; that talent was insufficiently served in other plays whether his intent was realistic or allegorical, or both. There was always in the other plays a gap between the realistic matter and an implied social and moral frame of reference; the work was marred or blurred by an incomplete fusion of the photograph and the idea, the small reality and the large shadowy symbol. For one thing is certain— Odets has not been by nature and intention a reporter, a descriptive realist, or a propagandist as much as he has been a poet in the theatre. In March, 1961, Odets was given a special award for drama by the American Academy of Arts and Sciences.

THE CHARACTERS OF THE PLAY

All of the characters in Awake and Sing! *share a fundamental activity: a struggle for life amidst petty conditions.*

BESSIE BERGER, *as she herself states, is not only the mother in this home but also the father. She is constantly arranging and taking care of her family. She loves life, likes to laugh, has great resourcefulness and enjoys living from day to day. A high degree of energy accounts for her quick exasperation at ineptitude. She is a shrewd judge of realistic qualities in people in the sense of being able to gauge quickly their effectiveness. In her eyes all of the people in the house are equal. She is naïve and quick in emotional response. She is afraid of utter poverty. She is proper according to her own standards, which are fairly close to those of most middle-class families. She knows that when one lives in the jungle one must look out for the wild life.*

MYRON, *her husband, is a born follower. He would like to be a leader. He would like to make a million dollars. He is not sad or ever depressed. Life is an even sweet event to him, but the "old days" were sweeter yet. He has a dignified sense of himself. He likes people. He likes everything. But he is heartbroken without being aware of it.*

HENNIE *is a girl who has had few friends, male or female. She is proud of her body. She won't ask favors. She travels alone. She is fatalistic about being trapped, but will escape if possible. She is self-reliant in the best sense. Till the day she dies she will be faithful to a loved man. She inherits her mother's sense of humor and energy.*

RALPH *is a boy with a clean spirit. He wants to know, wants to learn. He is ardent, he is romantic, he is sensitive. He is naïve too. He is trying to find why so much dirt must be cleared away before it is possible to "get to first base."*

JACOB, *too, is trying to find a right path for himself and the others. He is aware of justice, of dignity. He is an observer of the others, compares their activities with his real and ideal sense of life. This produces a reflective nature. In this home he is a constant boarder. He is a sentimental idealist with no power to turn ideal to action.*

With physical facts—such as housework—he putters. But as a barber he demonstrates the flair of an artist. He is an old Jew with living eyes in his tired face.

UNCLE MORTY *is a successful American business man with five good senses. Something sinister comes out of the fact that the lives of others seldom touch him deeply. He holds to his own line of life. When he is generous he wants others to be aware of it. He is pleased by attention—a rich relative to the BERGER family. He is a shrewd judge of material values. He will die unmarried. Two and two make four, never five with him. He can blink in the sun for hours, a fat tomcat. Tickle him, he laughs. He lives in a penthouse with a real Japanese butler to serve him. He sleeps with dress models, but not from his own showrooms. He plays cards for hours on end. He smokes expensive cigars. He sees every Mickey Mouse cartoon that appears. He is a 32-degree Mason. He is really deeply intolerant finally.*

MOE AXELROD *lost a leg in the war. He seldom forgets that fact. He has killed two men in extra-martial activity. He is mordant, bitter. Life has taught him a disbelief in everything, but he will fight his way through. He seldom shows his feelings: fights against his own sensitivity. He has been everywhere and seen everything. All he wants is* HENNIE. *He is very proud. He scorns the inability of others to make their way in life, but he likes people for whatever good qualities they possess. His passionate outbursts come from a strong but contained emotional mechanism.*

SAM FEINSCHREIBER *wants to find a home. He is lonely man, a foreigner in a strange land, hypersensitive about this fact, conditioned by the humiliation of not making his way alone. He has a sense of others laughing at him. At night he gets up and sits alone in the dark. He hears acutely all the small sounds of life. He might have been a poet in another time and place. He approaches his wife as if he were always offering her a delicate flower. Life is a high chill wind weaving itself around his head.*

SCHLOSSER, *the janitor, is an overworked German whose wife ran away with another man and left him with a young daughter who in turn ran away and joined a burlesque show as chorus girl. The man suffers rheumatic pains. He has lost his identity twenty years before.*

THE SCENE

Exposed on the stage are the dining room and adjoining front room of the BERGER *apartment. These two rooms are typically furnished. There is a curtain between them. A small door off the front room leads to* JACOB'S *room. When his door is open one sees a picture of* SACCO *and* VANZETTI *on the wall and several shelves of books. Stage left of this door presents the entrance to the foyer hall of the apartment. The two other bedrooms of the apartment are off this hall, but not necessarily shown.*

Stage left of the dining room presents a swinging door which opens on the kitchen.

Awake and sing, ye that dwell in dust:
ISAIAH—26:19

ACT ONE

TIME: The present; the family finishing supper.

PLACE: An apartment in the Bronx, New York City.

RALPH. Where's advancement down the place? Work like crazy! Think they see it? You'd drop dead first.

MYRON. Never mind, son, merit never goes unrewarded. Teddy Roosevelt used to say—

HENNIE. It rewarded you—thirty years a haberdashery clerk!

(JACOB *laughs.*)

RALPH. All I want's a chance to get to first base!

HENNIE. That's all?

RALPH. Stuck down in that joint on Fourth Avenue—a stock clerk in a silk house! Just look at Eddie. I'm as good as he is—pulling in two-fifty a week for forty-eight minutes a day. A headliner, his name in all the papers.

JACOB. That's what you want, Ralphie? Your name in the paper?

RALPH. I wanna make up my own mind about things . . . be something! Didn't I want to take up tap dancing, too?

BESSIE. So take lessons. Who stopped you?

RALPH. On what?

BESSIE. On what? Save money.

RALPH. Sure, five dollars a week for expenses and the rest in the house. I can't save even for shoelaces.

BESSIE. You mean we shouldn't have food in the house, but you'll make a jig on the street corner?

RALPH. I mean something.

BESSIE. You also mean something when you studied on the drum, Mr. Smartie!

RALPH. I don't know. . . . Every other day to sit around with the blues and mud in your mouth.

MYRON. That's how it is—life is like that—a cakewalk.

RALPH. What's it get you?

HENNIE. A four-car funeral.

RALPH. What's it for?

JACOB. What's it for? If this life leads to a revolution it's a good life. Otherwise it's for nothing.

BESSIE. Never mind, Pop! Pass me the salt.

RALPH. It's crazy—all my life I want a pair of black and white shoes and can't get them. It's crazy!

BESSIE. In a minute I'll get up from the table. I can't take a bite in my mouth no more.

MYRON (*restraining her*). Now, Momma, just don't excite yourself—

BESSIE. I'm so nervous I can't hold a knife in my hand.

MYRON. Is that a way to talk, Ralphie? Don't Momma work hard enough all day? (BESSIE *allows herself to be reseated.*)

BESSIE. On my feet twenty-four hours?

MYRON. On her feet—

RALPH (*jumps up*). What do I do—go to night clubs with Greta Garbo? Then when I come home can't even have my own room? Sleep on a day bed in the front room! (*Choked, he exits to front room.*)

BESSIE. He's starting up that stuff again. (*Shouts to him*). When Hennie here marries you'll have her room—I should only live to see the day.

HENNIE. Me, too. (*They settle down to serious eating.*)

MYRON. This morning the sink was full of ants. Where they come from I just don't know. I thought it was coffee grounds . . . and then they began moving.

BESSIE. You gave the dog eat?

JACOB. I gave the dog eat.

(HENNIE *drops a knife and picks it up again.*)

BESSIE. You got dropsy tonight.

HENNIE. Company's coming.

MYRON. You can buy a ticket for fifty cents and win fortunes. A man came in the store—it's the Irish Sweepstakes.

BESSIE. What?

MYRON. Like a raffle, only different. A man came in—

BESSIE. Who spends fifty-cent pieces for Irish raffles? They threw out a family on Dawson Street today. All the furniture on the sidewalk. A fine old woman with gray hair.

JACOB. Come eat, Ralph.

MYRON. A butcher on Beck Street won eighty thousand dollars.

BESSIE. Eighty thousand dollars! You'll excuse my expression, you're bughouse!

MYRON. I seen it in the paper—on one ticket—765 Beck Street.

BESSIE. Impossible!

MYRON. He did . . . yes he did. He says he'll take his old mother to Europe . . . an Austrian—

HENNIE. Europe . . .

MYRON. Six per cent on eighty thousand—forty-eight hundred a year.

BESSIE. I'll give you money. Buy a ticket in Hennie's name. Say, you can't tell—lightning never struck us yet. If they win on Beck Street we could win on Longwood Avenue.

JACOB (ironically). If it rained pearls—who would work?

BESSIE. Another county heard from.

(RALPH enters and silently seats himself.)

MYRON. I forgot, Beauty—Sam Feinschreiber sent you a present. Since I brought him for supper he just can't stop talking about you.

HENNIE. What's that "mockie" bothering about? Who need him?

MYRON. He's a very lonely boy.

HENNIE. So I'll sit down and bust out crying "'cause he's lonely."

BESSIE (opening candy). He'd marry you one-two-three.

HENNIE. Too bad about him.

BESSIE (naïvely delighted). Chocolate peanuts.

HENNIE. Loft's week-end special, two for thirty-nine.

BESSIE. You could think about it. It wouldn't hurt.

HENNIE (laughing). To quote Moe Axelrod, "Don't make me laugh."

BESSIE. Never mind laughing. It's time you already had in your head a serious

thought. A girl twenty-six don't grow younger. When I was your age it was already a big family with responsibilities.

HENNIE (laughing). Maybe that's what ails you, Mom.

BESSIE. Don't you feel well?

HENNIE. 'Cause I'm laughing? I feel fine. It's just funny—that poor guy sending me presents 'cause he loves me.

BESSIE. I think it's very, very nice.

HENNIE. Sure . . . swell!

BESSIE. Mrs. Marcus' Rose is engaged to a Brooklyn boy, a dentist. He came in his car today. A little dope should get such a boy.

(Finished with the meal, BESSIE, MYRON, and JACOB rise. Both HENNIE and RALPH sit silently at the table, he eating. Suddenly she rises.)

HENNIE. Tell you what, Mom. I saved for a new dress, but I'll take you and Pop to the Franklin. Don't need a dress. From now on I'm planning to stay in nights. Hold everything!

BESSIE. What's the matter—a bedbug bit you suddenly?

HENNIE. It's a good bill—Belle Baker. Maybe she'll sing "Eli, Eli."

BESSIE. We was going to a movie.

HENNIE. Forget it. Let's go.

MYRON. I see in the papers (As he picks his teeth.) Sophie Tucker took off twenty-six pounds. Fearful business with Japan.

HENNIE. Write a book, Pop! Come on, we'll go early for good seats.

MYRON. Moe said you had a date with him for tonight.

BESSIE. Axelrod?

HENNIE. I told him no, but he don't believe it. I'll tell him no for the next hundred years, too.

MYRON. Don't break appointments, Beauty, and hurt people's feelings.

(BESSIE exits.)

HENNIE. His hands got free-wheeling. (She exits.)

MYRON. I don't know . . . people ain't the same. N-O- The whole world's changing right under our eyes. Presto! No manners. Like the great Italian lover in the movies. What was his name? The Sheik. . . . No one remembers? (Exits, shaking his head.)

RALPH (unmoving at the table). Jake . . .

JACOB. Noo?

RALPH. I can't stand it.

JACOB. There's an expression—"strong as iron you must be."

RALPH. It's a cock-eyed world.

JACOB. Boys like you could fix it some day. Look on the world, not on yourself so much. Every country with starving millions, no? In Germany and Poland a Jew couldn't walk in the street. Everybody hates, nobody loves.

RALPH. I don't get all that.

JACOB. For years, I watched you grow up. Wait! You'll graduate from my university.

(*The others enter, dressed.*)

MYRON (*lighting*). Good cigars now for a nickel.

BESSIE (*to* JACOB). After take Tootsie on the roof. (*To* RALPH.) What'll you do?

RALPH. Don't know.

BESSIE. You'll see the boys around the block?

RALPH. I'll stay home every night!

MYRON. Momma don't mean for you—

RALPH. I'm flying to Hollywood by plane, that's what I'm doing.

(*Doorbell rings.* MYRON *answers it.*)

BESSIE. I don't like my boy to be seen with those tramps on the corner.

MYRON (*without*). Schlosser's here, Momma, with the garbage can.

BESSIE. Come in here, Schlosser. (*Sotto voce.*) Wait, I'll give him a piece of my mind. (MYRON *ushers in* SCHLOSSER, *who carries a garbage can in each hand.*) What's the matter the dumb-waiter's broken again?

SCHLOSSER. Mr. Wimmer sends new ropes next week. I got a sore arm.

BESSIE. He should live so long your Mr. Wimmer. For seven years already he's sending new ropes. No dumb-waiter, no hot water, no steam—In a respectable house, they don't allow such conditions.

SCHLOSSER. In a decent house dogs are not running to make dirty the hallway.

BESSIE. Tootsie's making dirty? Our Tootsie's making dirty in the hall?

SCHLOSSER (*to* JACOB). I tell you yesterday again. You must not leave her—

BESSIE (*indignantly*). Excuse me! Please don't yell on an old man. He's got more brains in his finger than you got—I don't know where. Did you ever see—he should talk to you an old man?

MYRON. Awful.

BESSIE. From now on we don't walk up the stairs no more. You keep it so clean we'll fly in the windows.

SCHLOSSER. I speak to Mr. Wimmer.

BESSIE. Speak! Speak. Tootsie walks behind me like a lady any time, any place. So good-by ... good-by, Mr. Schlosser.

SCHLOSSER. I tell you dot—I verk verry hard here. My arms is. . . . (*Exits in confusion.*)

BESSIE. Tootsie should lay all day in the kitchen maybe. Give him back if he yells on you. What's funny?

JACOB (*laughing*). Nothing.

BESSIE. Come. (*Exits.*)

JACOB. Hennie, take care. . . .

HENNIE. Sure.

JACOB. Bye-bye.

(HENNIE *exits.* MYRON *pops head back in door.*)

MYRON. Valentino! That's the one! (*He exits.*)

RALPH. I never in my life even had a birthday party. Every time I went and cried in the toilet when my birthday came.

JACOB (*seeing* RALPH *remove his tie*). You're going to bed?

RALPH. No, I'm putting on a clean shirt.

JACOB. Why?

RALPH. I got a girl. . . . Don't laugh!

JACOB. Who laughs? Since when?

RALPH. Three weeks. She lives in Yorkville with an aunt and uncle. A bunch of relatives, but no parents.

JACOB. An orphan girl—tch, tch.

RALPH. But she's got me! Boy, I'm telling you I could sing! Jake, she's like stars. She's so beautiful you look at her and cry! She's like French words! We went to the park the other night. Heard the last band concert.

JACOB. Music. . . .

RALPH (*stuffing shirt in trousers*). It got cold and I gave her my coat to wear. We just walked along like that, see, without a word, see. I never was so happy in all my life. It got late ... we just sat there. She looked at me—you know what I mean, how a girl looks at you—right in the eyes? "I love you," she says, "Ralph." I took her home. . . . I wanted to cry. That's how I felt!

JACOB. It's a beautiful feeling.

RALPH. You said a mouthful!

JACOB. Her name is—

RALPH. Blanche.

JACOB. A fine name. Bring her sometimes here.

RALPH. She's scared to meet Mom.

JACOB. Why?

RALPH. You know Mom's not letting my sixteen bucks out of the house if she can help it. She'd take one look at Blanche and insult her in a minute—a kid who's got nothing.

JACOB. Boychick!

RALPH. What's the diff?

JACOB. It's no difference—a plain bourgeois prejudice—but when they find out a poor girl—it ain't so kosher.

RALPH. They don't have to know I've got a girl.

JACOB. What's in the end?

RALPH. Out I go! I don't mean maybe!

JACOB. And then what?

RALPH. Life begins.

JACOB. What life?

RALPH. Life with my girl. Boy, I could sing when I think about it! Her and me together—that's a new life!

JACOB. Don't make a mistake! A new death!

RALPH. What's the idea?

JACOB. Me, I'm the idea! Once I had in *my* heart a dream, a vision, but came marriage and then you forget. Children come and you forget because—

RALPH. Don't worry, Jake.

JACOB. Remember, a woman insults a man's soul like no other thing in the whole world!

RALPH. Why get so excited? No one—

JACOB. Boychick, wake up! Be something! Make your life something good. For the love of an old man who sees in your young days his new life, for such love take the world in your two hands and make it like new. Go out and fight so life shouldn't be printed on dollar bills. A woman waits.

RALPH. Say, I'm no fool!

JACOB. From my heart I hope not. In the meantime—

(*Bell rings.*)

RALPH. See who it is, will you? (*Stands off.*) Don't want Mom to catch me with a clean shirt.

JACOB (*calls*). Come in. (*Sotto voce.*) Moe Axelrod.

(MOE *enters.*)

MOE. Hello girls, how's your whiskers? (*To* RALPH.) All dolled up. What's it, the weekly visit to the cat house?

RALPH. Please mind your business.

MOE. Okay, sweetheart.

RALPH (*taking a hidden dollar from a book*). If Mom asks where I went—

JACOB. I know. Enjoy yourself.

RALPH. Bye-bye. (*He exits.*)

JACOB. Bye-bye.

MOE. Who's home?

JACOB. Me.

MOE. Good. I'll stick around a few minutes. Where's Hennie?

JACOB. She went with Bessie and Myron to a show.

MOE. She what!

JACOB. You had a date?

MOE (*hiding his feelings*). Here—I brought you some halavah.

JACOB. Halavah? Thanks. I'll eat a piece after.

MOE. So Ralph's got a dame? Hot stuff—a kid can't even play a card game.

JACOB. Moe, you're a no-good, a bum of the first water. To your dying day you won't change.

MOE. Where'd you get that stuff, a no-good?

JACOB. But I like you.

MOE. Didn't I go fight in France for democracy? Didn't I get my goddam leg shot off in that war the day before the armistice? Uncle Sam give me the Order of the Purple Heart, didn't he? What'd you mean, a no-good?

JACOB. Excuse me.

MOE. If you got an orange I'll eat an orange.

JACOB. No orange. An apple.

MOE. No oranges, huh? What a dump!

JACOB. Bessie hears you once talking like this she'll knock your head off.

MOE. Hennie went with, huh? She wantsa see me squirm, only I don't squirm for dames.

JACOB. You came to see her?

MOE. What for? I got a present for our boy friend, Myron. He'll drop dead when I tell him his gentle horse galloped in fifteen to one. He'll die.

JACOB. It really won? The first time I remember.

MOE. Where'd they go?

JACOB. A vaudeville by the Franklin.

MOE. What's special tonight?

JACOB. Someone tells a few jokes . . . and they forget the street is filled with starving beggars.

MOE. What'll they do—start a war?

JACOB. I don't know.

MOE. You oughta know. What the hell you got all the books for?

JACOB. It needs a new world.

MOE. That's why they had the big war —to make a new world, they said—safe for democracy. Sure, every big general laying up in a Paris hotel with a half-dozen broads pinned on his mustache. Democracy! I learned a lesson.

JACOB. An imperial war. You know what this means?

MOE. Sure, I know everything!

JACOB. By money men the interests must be protected. Who gave you such a rotten haircut? Please (*Fishing in his vest pocket.*) give me for a cent a cigarette. I didn't have since yesterday—

MOE (*giving one*). Don't make me laugh. (*A cent passes back and forth between them,* MOE *finally throwing it over his shoulder.*) Don't look so tired all the time. You're a wow—always sore about something.

JACOB. And you?

MOE. You got one thing—you can play pinochle. I'll take you over in a game. Then you'll have something to be sore on.

JACOB. Who'll wash dishes?

(MOE *takes deck from buffet drawer.*)

MOE. Do 'em after. Ten cents a deal.

JACOB. Who's got ten cents?

MOE. I got ten cents. I'll lend it to you.

JACOB. Commence.

MOE (*shaking cards*). The first time I had my hands on a pack in two days. Lemme shake up these cards. I'll make 'em talk.

(JACOB *goes to his room, where he puts on a Caruso record.*)

JACOB. You should live so long.

MOE. Ever see oranges grow? I know a certain place— One summer I laid under a tree and let them fall right in my mouth.

JACOB (*off, the music is playing; the card game begins*). From *L'Africana* . . . a big explorer comes on a new land—"O Paradiso." From act four this piece. Caruso stands on the ship and looks on a Utopia. You hear? "Oh paradise! Oh paradise on earth! Oh blue sky, oh fragrant air—"

MOE. Ask him does he see any oranges?

(BESSIE, MYRON, *and* HENNIE *enter.*)

JACOB. You came back so soon?

BESSIE. Hennie got sick on the way.

MYRON. Hello, Moe. . . .

(MOE *puts cards back in pocket.*)

BESSIE. Take off the phonograph, Pop. (*To* HENNIE.) Lay down . . . I'll call the doctor. You should see how she got sick on Prospect Avenue. Two weeks already she don't feel right.

MYRON. Moe . . . ?

BESSIE. Go to bed, Hennie.

HENNIE. I'll sit here.

BESSIE. Such a girl I never saw! Now you'll be stubborn?

MYRON. It's for your own good, Beauty. Influenza—

HENNIE. I'll sit here.

BESSIE. You ever seen a girl should say no to everything. She can't stand on her feet, so—

HENNIE. Don't yell in my ears. I hear. Nothing's wrong. I ate tuna fish for lunch.

MYRON. Canned goods.

BESSIE. Last week you also ate tuna fish?

HENNIE. Yeah, I'm funny for tuna fish. Go to the show—have a good time.

BESSIE. I don't understand what I did to God He blessed me with such children. From the whole world—

MOE (*coming to aid of* HENNIE). For Chris' sake, don't kibitz so much!

BESSIE. You don't like it?

MOE (*aping*). No, I don't like it.

BESSIE. That's too bad, Axelrod. Maybe it's better by your cigar-store friends. Here we're different people.

MOE. Don't gimme that cigar-store line, Bessie. I walked up five flights—

BESSIE. To take out Hennie. But my daughter ain't in your class Axelrod.

MOE. To see Myron.

MYRON. Did he, did he, Moe?

MOE. Did he what?

MYRON. "Sky Rocket"?

BESSIE. You bet on a horse!

MOE. Paid twelve and a half to one.

MYRON. There! You hear that, Momma? Our horse came in. You see, it happens, and twelve and a half to one. Just look at that!

MOE. What the hell, a sure thing. I told you.

BESSIE. If Moe said a sure thing, you couldn't bet a few dollars instead of fifty cents?

JACOB (*laughs*). "Aie, aie, aie."

MOE (*at his wallet*). I'm carrying six hundred "plunks" in big denominations.

BESSIE. A banker!

MOE. Uncle Sam sends me ninety a month.

BESSIE. So you save it?

MOE. Run it up, Run-it-up-Axelrod, that's me.

BESSIE. The police should know how.

MOE (*shutting her up*). All right, all right —Change twenty, sweetheart.

MYRON. Can you make change?

BESSIE. Don't be crazy.

MOE. I'll meet a guy in Goldman's restaurant. I'll meet 'im and come back with change.

MYRON (*figuring on paper*). You can give it to me tomorrow in the store.

BESSIE (*acquisitive*). He'll come back, he'll come back!

MOE. Lucky I bet some bucks myself. (*In derision to* HENNIE.) Let's step out tomorrow night, Par-a-dise. (*Thumbs his nose at her, laughs mordantly, and exits.*)

MYRON. Oh, that's big percentage. If I picked a winner every day—

BESSIE. Poppa, did you take Tootsie on the roof?

JACOB. All right.

MYRON. Just look at that—a cakewalk. We can make—

BESSIE. It's enough talk. I got a splitting headache. Hennie, go in bed. I'll call Dr. Cantor.

HENNIE. I'll sit here . . . and don't call that old Ignatz 'cause I won't see him.

MYRON. If you get sick Momma can't nurse you. You don't want to go to a hospital.

JACOB. She don't look sick, Bessie, it's a fact.

BESSIE. She's got fever. I see in her eyes, so he tells me no. Myron, call Dr. Cantor.

(MYRON *picks up phone, but* HENNIE *grabs it from him.*)

HENNIE. I don't want any doctor. I ain't sick. Leave me alone.

MYRON. Beauty, it's for your own sake.

HENNIE. Day in and day out pestering. Why are you always right and no one else can say a word?

BESSIE. When you have your own children—

HENNIE. I'm not sick! Hear what I say? I'm not sick! Nothing's the matter with me! I don't want a doctor.

(BESSIE *is watching her with slow, progressive understanding.*)

BESSIE. What's the matter?

HENNIE. Nothing, I told you!

BESSIE. You told me, but— (*A long pause of examination follows.*)

HENNIE. See much?

BESSIE. Myron, put down the . . . the . . . (*He slowly puts the phone down.*) Tell me what happened.

HENNIE. Brooklyn Bridge fell down.

BESSIE (*approaching*). I'm asking a question.

MYRON. What's happened, Momma?

BESSIE. Listen to me!

HENNIE. What the hell are you talking?

BESSIE. Poppa—take Tootsie on the roof.

HENNIE (*holding* JACOB *back*). If he wants he can stay here.

MYRON. What's wrong, Momma?

BESSIE (*her voice quivering slightly*). Myron, your fine Beauty's in trouble. Our society lady—

MYRON. Trouble? I don't under—is it—?

BESSIE. Look in her face. (*He looks, understands, and slowly sits in a chair, utterly crushed.*) Who's the man?

HENNIE. The Prince of Wales.

BESSIE. My gall is busting in me. In two seconds—

HENNIE (*in a violent outburst*). Shut up! Shut up! I'll jump out the window in a minute! Shut up! (*Finally she gains control of herself, says in a low, hard voice:*) You don't know him.

JACOB. Bessie . . .

BESSIE. He's a Bronx boy?

HENNIE. From out of town.

BESSIE. What do you mean?

HENNIE. From out of town!!

BESSIE. A long time you know him? You were sleeping by a girl from the office Saturday nights? You slept good, my lovely lady. You'll go to him . . . he'll marry you.

HENNIE. That's what you say.

BESSIE. That's what I say! He'll do it, take *my* word he'll do it!

HENNIE. Where? (*To* JACOB.) Give her the letter.

(JACOB *does so.*)

BESSIE. What? (*Reads.*) "Dear sir: In reply to your request of the 14th inst., we can state that no Mr. Ben Grossman has ever been connected with out organization . . ." You don't know where he is?

HENNIE. No.

BESSIE (*walks back and forth*). Stop crying like a baby, Myron.

MYRON. It's like a play on the stage.

BESSIE. To a mother you couldn't say

something before. I'm old-fashioned—like your friends I'm not smart—I don't eat chop suey and run around Coney Island with tramps. (*She walks reflectively to buffet, picks up a box of candy, puts it down, says to* MYRON:) Tomorrow night bring Sam Feinschreiber for supper.

HENNIE. I won't do it.

BESSIE. You'll do it, my fine beauty, you'll do it!

HENNIE. I'm not marrying a poor foreigner like him. Can't even speak an English word. Not me! I'll go to my grave without a husband.

BESSIE. You don't say! We'll find for you somewhere a millionaire with a pleasure boat. He's going to night school, Sam. For a boy only three years in the country he speaks very nice. In three years he put enough in the bank, a good living.

JACOB. This is serious?

BESSIE. What then? I'm talking for my health? He'll come tomorrow night for supper. By Saturday they're engaged.

JACOB. Such a thing you can't do.

BESSIE. Who asked your advice?

JACOB. Such a thing—

BESSIE. Never mind!

JACOB. The lowest from the low!

BESSIE. Don't talk! I'm warning you! A man who don't believe in God—with crazy ideas—

JACOB. So bad I never imagined you could be.

BESSIE. Maybe if you didn't talk so much it wouldn't happen like this. You with your ideas—I'm a mother. I raise a family they should have respect.

JACOB. Respect? (*Spits.*) Respect! For the neighbors' opinion! You insult me, Bessie!

BESSIE. Go in your room, Papa. Every job he ever had he lost because he's got a big mouth. He opens his mouth and the whole Bronx could fall in. Everybody said it—

MYRON. Momma, they'll hear you down the dumb-waiter.

BESSIE. A good barber not to hold a job a week. Maybe you never heard charity starts at home. You never heard it, Pop?

JACOB. All you know, I heard, and more yet. But Ralph you don't make like you. Before you do it, I'll die first. He'll find a girl. He'll go in a fresh world with her. This is a house? Marx said it—

abolish such families.

BESSIE. Go in your room, Papa.

JACOB. Ralph you don't make like you!

BESSIE. Go lay in your room with Caruso and the books together.

JACOB. All right!

BESSIE. Go in the room!

JACOB. Some day I'll come out I'll— (*Unable to continue, he turns, looks at* HENNIE, *goes to his door, and there says with an attempt at humor:*) Bessie, some day you'll talk to me so fresh ... I'll leave the house for good! (*He exits.*)

BESSIE (*crying*). You ever in your life seen it? He should dare! He should just dare say in the house another word. Your gall could bust from such a man. (*Bell rings,* MYRON *goes.*) Go to sleep now. It won't hurt.

HENNIE. Yeah?

(MOE *enters, a box in his hand.* MYRON *follows and sits down.*)

MOE (*looks around first—putting box on table*). Cake. (*About to give* MYRON *the money, he turns instead to* BESSIE.) Six fifty, four bits change ... come on, hand over half a buck. (*She does so. Of* MYRON.) Who bit him?

BESSIE. We're soon losing our Hennie, Moe.

MOE. Why? What's the matter?

BESSIE. She made her engagement.

MOE. Zat so?

BESSIE. Today it happened ... he asked her.

MOE. Did he? Who? Who's the corpse?

BESSIE. It's a secret.

MOE. In the bag, huh?

HENNIE. Yeah. . . .

BESSIE. When a mother gives away an only daughter it's no joke. Wait, when you'll get married you'll know.

MOE (*bitterly*). Don't make me laugh—when I get married! What I think a women? Take 'em all, cut 'em in little pieces like a herring in Greek salad. A guy in France had the right idea—dropped his wife in a bathtub fulla acid. (*Whistles.*) Sss, down the pipe! Pfft—not even a corset button left!

MYRON. Corsets don't have buttons.

MOE (*to* HENNIE). What's the great idea? Gone big time, Paradise? Christ, it's suicide! Sure, kids you'll have, gold teeth, get fat, big in the tangerines—

HENNIE. Shut your face!

MOE. Who's it—some dope pullin'

down twenty bucks a week? Cut your throat, sweetheart. Save time.

BESSIE. Never mind your two cents, Axelrod.

MOE. I say what I think—that's me!

HENNIE. That's you—a lousy four-flusher who'd steal the glasses off a blind man.

MOE. Get hot!

HENNIE. My God, do I need it—to listen to this mutt shoot his mouth off?

MYRON. Please—

MOE. Now wait a minute, sweetheart, wait a minute. I don't have to take that from you.

BESSIE. Don't yell at her!

HENNIE. For two cents I'd spit in your eye.

MOE (*throwing coin to table*). Here's two bits.

(HENNIE *looks at him and then starts across the room.*)

BESSIE. Where are you going?

HENNIE (*crying*). For my beauty nap, Mussolini. Wake me up when it's apple blossom time in Normandy. (*Exits.*)

MOE. Pretty, pretty—a sweet gal, your Hennie. See the look in her eyes?

BESSIE. She don't feel well.

MYRON. Canned goods—

BESSIE. So don't start with her.

MOE. Like a battleship she's got it. Not like other dames—shove 'em and they lay. Not her. I got a yen for her and I don't mean a Chinee coin.

BESSIE. Listen, Axelrod, in my house you don't talk this way. Either have respect or get out.

MOE. When I think about it . . . maybe I'd marry her myself.

BESSIE (*suddenly aware of* MOE). You could—What do you mean, Moe?

MOE. You ain't sunburnt—you heard me.

BESSIE. Why don't you, Moe? An old friend of the family like you. It would be a blessing on all of us.

MOE. You said she's engaged.

BESSIE. But maybe she don't know her own mind. Say, it's—

MOE. I need a wife like a hole in the head. . . . What's to know about women, I know. Even if I asked her. She won't do it! A guy with one leg—it gives her the heebie-jeebies. I know what she's looking for. An Arrow-collar guy, a hero, but with a wad of jack. Only the two don't go together. But I got what it

takes . . . plenty, and more where it comes from. . . . (*Breaks off, snorts, and rubs his knee. A pause. In his room* JACOB *puts on Caruso singing the lament from "The Pearl Fishers.*")

BESSIE. It's right—she wants a millionaire with a mansion on Riverside Drive. So go fight City Hall. Cake?

MOE. Cake.

BESSIE. I'll make tea. But one thing—she's got a fine boy with a business brain. Caruso! (*Exits into the front room and stands in the dark, at the window.*)

MOE. No wet smack . . . a fine girl. . . . She'll burn that guy out in a month.

(MOE *retrieves the quarter and spins it on the table.*)

MYRON. I remember that song . . . beautiful. Nora Bayes sang it at the old Proctor's Twenty-third Street—"When It's Apple Blossom Time in Normandy."

MOE. She wantsa see me crawl—my head on a plate she wants! A snowball in hell's got a better chance. (*Out of sheer fury he spins the quarter in his fingers.*)

MYRON (*as his eyes slowly fill with tears*). Beautiful . . .

MOE. Match you for a quarter. Match you for any goddam thing you got. (*Spins the coin viciously.*) What the hell kind of house is this it ain't got an orange!!

SLOW CURTAIN

ACT TWO

SCENE ONE

One year later, a Sunday afternoon. The front room. JACOB *is giving his son* MORDE-CAI (UNCLE MORTY) *a haircut, newspapers spread around the base of the chair.* MOE *is reading a newspaper, leg propped on a chair.* RALPH, *in another chair, is spasmodically reading a paper.* UNCLE MORTY *reads colored jokes. Silence, then* BESSIE *enters.*

BESSIE. Dinner's in half an hour, Morty.

MORTY (*still reading jokes*). I got time.

BESSIE. A duck. Don't get hair on the rug, Pop. (*Goes to window and pulls down shade.*) What's the matter the shade's up to the ceiling?

JACOB (*pulling it up again*). Since when do I give a haircut in the dark? (*He mimics her tone.*)

BESSIE. When you're finished, pull it down. I like my house to look respectable. Ralphie, bring up two bottles seltzer from Weiss.

RALPH. I'm reading the paper.

BESSIE. Uncle Morty likes a little seltzer.

RALPH. I'm expecting a phone call.

BESSIE. Noo, if it comes you'll be back. What's the matter? (*Gives him money from apron pocket.*) Take down the old bottles.

RALPH (*to* JACOB). Get that call if it comes. Say I'll be right back. (JACOB *nods assent.*)

MORTY (*giving change from vest*). Get grandpa some cigarettes.

RALPH. Okay. (*Exits.*)

JACOB. What's new in the paper, Moe?

MOE. Still jumping off the high buildings like flies—the big shots who lost all their cocoanuts. Pfft!

JACOB. Suicides?

MOE. Plenty can't take it—good in the break, but can't take the whip in the stretch.

MORTY (*without looking up*). I saw it happen Monday in my building. My hair stood up how they shoveled him together—like a pancake—a bankrupt manufacturer.

MOE. No brains.

MORTY. Enough . . . all over the sidewalk.

JACOB. If someone said five-ten years ago I couldn't make for myself a living, I wouldn't believe—

MORTY. Duck for dinner?

BESSIE. The best Long Island duck.

MORTY. I like goose.

BESSIE. A duck is just like a goose, only better.

MORTY. I like a goose.

BESSIE. The next time you'll be for Sunday dinner I'll make a goose.

MORTY (*sniffs deeply*). Smells good. I'm a great boy for smells.

BESSIE. Ain't you ashamed? Once in a blue moon he should come to an only sister's house.

MORTY. Bessie, leave me live.

BESSIE. You should be ashamed!

MORTY. Quack quack!

BESSIE. No, better to lay around Mecca Temple playing cards with the Masons.

MORTY (*with good nature*). Bessie, don't you see Pop's giving me a haircut?

BESSIE. You don't need no haircut. Look, two hairs he took off.

MORTY. Pop likes to give me a haircut. If I said no he don't forget for a year, do you, Pop? An old man's like that.

JACOB. I still do an A-1 job.

MORTY (*winking*). Pop cuts hair to fit the face, don't you, Pop?

JACOB. For sure, Morty. To each face a different haircut. Custom built, no ready made. A round face needs special—

BESSIE (*cutting him short*). A graduate from the B.M.T. (*Going.*) Don't forget the shade. (*The phone rings. She beats* JACOB *to it.*) Hello? Who is it, please? . . . Who is it please? . . . Miss Hirsch? No, he ain't here. . . . No, I couldn't say when. (*Hangs up sharply.*)

JACOB. For Ralph?

BESSIE. A wrong number.

(JACOB *looks at her and goes back to his job.*)

JACOB. Excuse me!

BESSIE (*to* MORTY). Ralphie took another cut down the place yesterday.

MORTY. Business is bad. I saw his boss Harry Glicksman Thursday. I bought some velvets . . . they're coming in again.

BESSIE. Do something for Ralphie down there.

MORTY. What can I do? I mentioned it to Glicksman. He told me they squeezed out half the people.

(MYRON *enters dressed in apron.*)

BESSIE. What's gonna be the end? Myron's working only three days a week now.

MYRON. It's conditions.

BESSIE. Hennie's married with a baby . ∴ . money just don't come in. I never saw conditions should be so bad.

MORTY. Times'll change.

MOE. The only thing'll change is my underwear.

MORTY. These last few years I got my share of gray hairs. (*Still reading jokes without having looked up once.*) Ha, ha, ha —Popey the sailor ate spinach and knocked out four bums.

MYRON. I'll tell you the way I see it. The country needs a great man now—a regular Teddy Roosevelt.

MOE. What this country needs is a good five-cent earthquake.

JACOB. So long labor lives it should increase private gain—

BESSIE (*to* JACOB). Listen, Poppa, go talk on the street corner. The government'll give you free board the rest of your life.

MORTY. I'm surprised. Don't I send a five-dollar check for Pop every week?

BESSIE. You could afford a couple more and not miss it.

MORTY. Tell me jokes. Business is so rotten I could just as soon lay all day in the Turkish bath.

MYRON. Why'd I come in here? (*Puzzled, he exits.*)

MORTY (*to* MOE). I hear the bootleggers still do business, Moe.

MOE. Wake up! I kissed bootlegging bye-bye two years back.

MORTY. For a fact? What kind of racket is it now?

MOE. If I told you, you'd know something.

(HENNIE *comes from bedroom.*)

HENNIE. Where's Sam?

BESSIE. Sam? In the kitchen.

HENNIE (*calls*). Sam. Come take the diaper.

MORTY. How's the Mickey Louse? Ha, ha, ha . . .

HENNIE. Sleeping.

MORTY. Ah, that's life to a baby. He sleeps—gets it in the mouth—sleeps some more. To raise a family nowadays you must be a damn fool.

BESSIE. Never mind, never mind, a woman who don't raise a family—a girl —should jump overboard. What's she good for? (*To* MOE—*to change the subject.*) Your leg bothers you bad?

MOE. It's okay, sweetheart.

BESSIE (*to* MORTY). It hurts him every time it's cold out. He's got four legs in the closet.

MORTY. Four wooden legs?

MOE. Three.

MORTY. What's the big idea?

MOE. Why not? Uncle Sam gives them out free.

MORTY. Say, maybe if Uncle Sam gave out less legs we could balance the budget.

JACOB. Or not have a war so they wouldn't have to give out legs.

MORTY. Shame on you, Pop. Everybody knows war is necessary.

MOE. Don't make me laugh. Ask me— the first time you pick up a dead one in the trench—then you learn war ain't so damn necessary.

MORTY. Say, you should kick. The rest of your life Uncle Sam pays you ninety a month. Look, not a worry in the world.

MOE. Don't make me laugh. Uncle Sam can take his *seventy* bucks and— (*Finishes with a gesture.*) Nothing good hurts. (*He rubs his stump.*)

HENNIE. Use a crutch, Axelrod. Give the stump a rest.

MOE. Mind your business, Feinschreiber.

BESSIE. It's a sensible idea.

MOE. Who asked you?

BESSIE. Look, he's ashamed.

MOE. So's your Aunt Fanny.

BESSIE (*naïvely*). Who's got an Aunt Fanny? (*She cleans a rubber plant's leaves with her apron.*)

MORTY. It's a joke!

MOE. I don't want my paper creased before I read it. I want it fresh. Fifty times I said that.

BESSIE. Don't get so excited for a five-cent paper—our star boarder.

MOE. And I don't want no one using my razor either. Get it straight. I'm not buying ten blades a week for the Berger family. (*Furious, he limps out.*)

BESSIE. Maybe I'm using his razor too.

HENNIE. Proud!

BESSIE. You need luck with plants. I didn't clean off the leaves in a month.

MORTY. You keep the house like a pin and I like your cooking. Any time Myron fires you, come to me, Bessie. I'll let the butler go and you'll be my housekeeper. I don't like Japs so much—sneaky.

BESSIE. Say, you can't tell. Maybe any day I'm coming to stay.

(HENNIE *exits.*)

JACOB. Finished.

MORTY. How much, Ed. Pinaud? (*Disengages self from chair.*)

JACOB. Five cents.

MORTY. Still five cents for a haircut to fit the face?

JACOB. Prices don't change by me. (*Takes a dollar.*) I can't change—

MORTY. Keep it. Buy yourself a Packard. Ha, ha, ha.

JACOB (*taking large envelope from pocket*). Please, you'll keep this for me. Put it away.

MORTY. What is it?

JACOB. My insurance policy. I don't like it should lay around where something could happen.

MORTY. What could happen?

JACOB. Who knows—robbers, fire . . . they took next door. Fifty dollars from O'Reilly.

MORTY. Say, lucky a Berger didn't lose it.

JACOB. Put it downtown in the safe. Bessie don't have to know.

MORTY. It's made out to Bessie?

JACOB. No, to Ralph.

MORTY. To Ralph?

JACOB. He don't know. Some day he'll get three thousand.

MORTY. You got good years ahead.

JACOB. Behind.

(RALPH enters.)

RALPH. Cigarettes. Did a call come?

JACOB. A few minutes. She don't let me answer it.

RALPH. Did Mom say I was coming back?

JACOB. No.

(MORTY is back at new jokes.)

RALPH. She starting that stuff again? (BESSIE enters.) A call come for me?

BESSIE (waters pot from milk bottle). A wrong number.

JACOB. Don't say a lie, Bessie.

RALPH. Blanche said she'd call me at two—was it her?

BESSIE. I said a wrong number.

RALPH. Please, Mom, if it was her tell me.

BESSIE. You call me a liar next. You got no shame—to start a scene in front of Uncle Morty. Once in a blue moon he comes—

RALPH. What's the shame? If my girl calls I wanna know it.

BESSIE. You made enough mish mosh with her until now.

MORTY. I'm surprised, Bessie. For the love of Mike tell him yes or no.

BESSIE. I didn't tell him? No!

MORTY (to RALPH). No!

(RALPH goes to a window and looks out.)

BESSIE. Morty, I didn't say before—he runs around steady with a girl.

MORTY. Terrible. Should he run around with a foxie-woxie?

BESSIE. A girl with no parents.

MORTY. An orphan?

BESSIE. I could die from shame. A year already he runs around with her. He brought her once for supper. Believe me, she didn't come again, no!

RALPH. Don't think I didn't ask her.

BESSIE. You hear? You raise them and what's in the end for all your trouble?

JACOB. When you'll lay in a grave, no more trouble. (Exits.)

MORTY. Quack quack!

BESSIE. A girl like that he wants to marry. A skinny consumptive-looking . . . six months already she's not working—taking charity from an aunt. You should see her. In a year she's dead on his hands.

RALPH. You'd cut her throat if you could.

BESSIE. That's right! Before she'd ruin a nice boy's life I would first go to prison. Miss Nobody should step in the picture and I'll stand by with my mouth shut.

RALPH. Miss Nobody! Who am I? Al Jolson?

BESSIE. Fix your tie!

RALPH. I'll take care of my own life.

BESSIE. You'll take care? Excuse my expression, you can't even wipe your nose yet! He'll take care!

MORTY (to BESSIE). I'm surprised. Don't worry so much, Bessie. When it's time to settle down he won't marry a poor girl, will you? In the long run common sense is thicker than love. I'm a great boy for live and let live.

BESSIE. Sure, it's easy to say. In the meantime he eats out my heart. You know I'm not strong.

MORTY. I know . . . a pussy cat . . . ha, ha, ha.

BESSIE. You got money and money talks. But without the dollar who sleeps at night?

RALPH. I been working for years, bringing in money here—putting it in your hand like a kid. All right, I can't get my teeth fixed. All right, that a new suit's like trying to buy the Chrysler Building. You never in your life bought me a pair of skates even—things I died for when I was a kid. I don't care about that stuff, see. Only just remember I pay some of the bills around here, just a few . . . and if my girl calls me on the phone I'll talk to her any time I please. (He exits. HENNIE applauds.)

BESSIE. Don't be so smart, Miss America! (To MORTY:) He didn't have skates! But when he got sick, a twelve-year-old boy, who called a big specialist for the last $25 in the house? Skates!

JACOB (just in. Adjusts window shade). It looks like snow today.

MORTY. It's about time—winter.

BESSIE. Poppa here could talk like

Samuel Webster, too, but it's just talk. He should try to buy a two-cent pickle in the Burland Market without money.

MORTY. I'm getting an appetite.

BESSIE. Right away we'll eat. I made chopped liver for you.

MORTY. My specialty!

BESSIE. Ralph should only be a success like you, Morty. I should only live to see the day when he rides up to the door in a big car with a chauffeur and a radio. I could die happy, believe me.

MORTY. Success she says. She should see how we spend thousands of dollars making up a winter line and winter don't come—summer in January. Can you beat it?

JACOB. Don't live, just make success.

MORTY. Chopped liver—ha!

JACOB. Ha! (*Exits.*)

MORTY. When they start arguing, I don't hear. Suddenly I'm deaf. I'm a great boy for the practical side. (*He looks over to* HENNIE *who sits rubbing her hands with lotion.*)

HENNIE. Hands like a raw potato.

MORTY. What's the matter? You don't look so well . . . no pep.

HENNIE. I'm swell.

MORTY. You used to be such a pretty girl.

HENNIE. Maybe I got the blues. You can't tell.

MORTY. You could stand a new dress.

HENNIE. That's not all I could stand.

MORTY. Come down to the place tomorrow and pick out a couple from the "eleven-eighty" line. Only don't sing me the blues.

HENNIE. Thanks. I need some new clothes.

MORTY. I got two thousand pieces of merchandise waiting in the stock room for winter.

HENNIE. I never had anything from life. Sam don't help.

MORTY. He's crazy about the kid.

HENNIE. Crazy is right. Twenty-one a week he brings in—a nigger don't have it so hard. I wore my fingers off on an Underwood for six years. For what? Now I wash baby diapers. Sure, I'm crazy about the kid too. But half the night the kid's up. Try to sleep. You don't know how it is, Uncle Morty.

MORTY. No, I don't know. I was born yesterday. Ha, ha, ha. Some day I'll leave you a little nest egg. You like

eggs? Ha?

HENNIE. When? When I'm dead and buried?

MORTY. No, when *I'm* dead and buried. Ha, ha, ha.

HENNIE. You should know what I'm thinking.

MORTY. Ha, ha, ha, I know.

(MYRON *enters.*)

MYRON. I never take a drink. I'm just surprised at myself, I—

MORTY. I got a pain. Maybe I'm hungry.

MYRON. Come inside, Morty. Bessie's got some schnapps.

MORTY. I'll take a drink. Yesterday I missed the Turkish bath.

MYRON. I get so bitter when I take a drink, it just surprises me.

MORTY. Look how fat. Say, you live once. . . . Quack, quack.

(*Both exit.* MOE *stands silently in the doorway.*)

SAM (*entering*). I'll make Leon's bottle now!

HENNIE. No, let him sleep, Sam. Take away the diaper.

(*He does. Exits.*)

MOE (*advancing into the room*). That your husband?

HENNIE. Don't you know?

MOE. Maybe he's a nurse you hired for the kid—it looks it—how he tends it. A guy comes howling to your old lady every time you look cock-eyed. Does he sleep with you?

HENNIE. Don't be so wise!

MOE (*indicating newspaper*). Here's a dame strangled her hubby with wire. Claimed she didn't like him. Why don't you brain Sam with an axe some night?

HENNIE. Why don't you lay an egg, Axelrod?

MOE. I laid a few in my day, Feinschreiber. Hard-boiled ones too.

HENNIE. Yeah?

MOE. Yeah. You wanna know what I see when I look in your eyes?

HENNIE. No.

MOE. Ted Lewis playing the clarinet —some of those high crazy notes! Christ, you coulda had a guy with some guts instead of a cluck stands around boilin' baby nipples.

HENNIE. Meaning you?

MOE. Meaning me, sweetheart.

HENNIE. Think you're pretty good.

MOE. You'd know if I slept with you again.

HENNIE. I'll smack your face in a minute.

MOE. You do and I'll break your arm. (*Holds up paper.*) Take a look. (*Reads:*) "Ten-day luxury cruise to Havana." That's the stuff you coulda had. Put up at ritzy hotels, Frenchie soap, champagne. Now you're tied down to "Snake-Eye" here. What for? What's it get you? . . . a 2 x 4 flat on 108th Street . . . a pain in the bustle it gets you.

HENNIE. What's it to you?

MOE. I know you from the old days. How you like to spend it! What I mean! Lizard-skin shoes, perfume behind the ears. . . . You're in a mess, Paradise! Paradise—that's a hot one—yah, crazy to eat a knish at your own wedding.

HENNIE. I get it—you're jealous. You can't get me.

MOE. Don't make me laugh.

HENNIE. Kid Jailbird's been trying to make me for years. You'd give your other leg. I'm hooked? Maybe, but you're in the same boat. Only it's worse for you. I don't give a damn no more, but you gotta yen makes you—

MOE. Don't make me laugh.

HENNIE. Compared to you I'm sittin' on top of the world.

MOE. You're losing your looks. A dame don't stay young forever.

HENNIE. You're a liar. I'm only twenty-four.

MOE. When you comin' home to stay?

HENNIE. Wouldn't you like to know?

MOE. I'll get you again.

HENNIE. Think so?

MOE. Sure, whatever goes up comes down. You're easy—you remember—two for a nickel—a pushover! (*Suddenly she slaps him. They both seem stunned.*) What's the idea?

HENNIE. Go on . . . break my arm.

MOE (*as if saying "I love you"*). Listen, lousy.

HENNIE. Go on, do something!

MOE. Listen—

HENNIE. You're so damn tough!

MOE. You like me. (*He takes her.*)

HENNIE. Take your hand off! (*Pushes him away.*) Come around when it's a flood again and they put you in the ark with the animals. Not even then—if you was the last man!

MOE. Baby, if you had a dog I'd love the dog.

HENNIE. Gorilla! (*Exits.* RALPH *enters.*)

RALPH. Were you here before?

MOE (*sits*). What?

RALPH. When the call came for me?

MOE. What?

RALPH. The call came.

(JACOB *enters.*)

MOE (*rubbing his leg*). No.

JACOB. Don't worry, Ralphie, she'll call back.

RALPH. Maybe not. I think somethin's the matter.

JACOB. What?

RALPH. I don't know. I took her home from the movie last night. She asked me what I'd think if she went away.

JACOB. Don't worry, she'll call again.

RALPH. Maybe not, if Mom insulted her. She gets it on both ends, the poor kid. Lived in an orphan asylum most of her life. They shove her around like an empty freight train.

JACOB. After dinner go see her.

RALPH. Twice they kicked me down the stairs.

JACOB. Life should have some dignity.

RALPH. Every time I go near the place I get heart failure. The uncle drives a bus. You oughta see him—like Babe Ruth.

MOE. Use your brains. Stop acting like a kid who still wets the bed. Hire a room somewhere—a club room for two members.

RALPH. Not that kind of proposition, Moe.

MOE. Don't be a bush leaguer all your life.

RALPH. Cut it out!

MOE (*on a sudden upsurge of emotion*). Ever sleep with one? Look at 'im blush.

RALPH. You don't know her.

MOE. I seen her—the kind no one sees undressed till the undertaker works on her.

RALPH. Why give me the needles all the time? What'd I ever do to you?

MOE. Not a thing. You're a nice kid. But grow up! In life there's two kinds—the men that's sure of themselves and the ones who ain't! It's time you quit being a selling-plater and got in the first class.

JACOB. And you, Axelrod?

MOE (*to* JACOB). Scratch your whiskers!

(*To* RALPH.) Get independent. Get what-it-takes and be yourself. Do what you like.

RALPH. Got a suggestion?

(MORTY *enters*, eating.)

MOE. Sure, pick out a racket. Shake down the cocoanuts. See what that does.

MORTY. We know what it does—puts a pudding on your nose! Sing Sing! Easy money's against the law. Against the law don't win. A racket is illegitimate, no?

MOE. It's all a racket—from horse racing down. Marriage, politics, big business—everybody plays cops and robbers. You, you're a racketeer yourself.

MORTY. Who? Me? Personally I manufacture dresses.

MOE. Horse feathers!

MORTY (*seriously*). Don't make such remarks to me without proof. I'm a great one for proof. That's why I made a success in business. Proof—put up or shut up, like a game of cards. I heard this remark before—a rich man's a crook who steals from the poor. Personally, I don't like it. It's a big lie!

MOE. If you don't like it, buy yourself a fife and drum—and go fight your own war.

MORTY. Sweatshop talk. Every Jew and Wop in the shop eats my bread and behind my back says, "A sonofabitch." I started from a poor boy who worked on an ice wagon for two dollars a week. Pop's right here—he'll tell you. I made it honest. In the whole industry nobody's got a better name.

JACOB. It's an exception, such success.

MORTY. Ralph can't do the same thing?

JACOB. No, Morty, I don't think. In a house like this he don't realize even the possibilities of life. Economics comes down like a ton of coal on the head.

MOE. Red rover, red rover, let Jacob come over!

JACOB. In my day the propaganda was for God. Now it's for success. A boy don't turn around without having shoved in him he should make success.

MORTY. Pop, you're a comedian, a regular Charlie Chaplin.

JACOB. He dreams all night of fortunes. Why not? Don't it say in the movies he should have a personal steamship, pajamas for fifty dollars a pair, and a toilet like a monument? But in the morning he wakes up and for ten dollars he can't fix the teeth. And millions more worse off in the mills of the South—starvation wages. The blood from the worker's heart. (MORTY *laughs loud and long.*) Laugh, laugh . . . tomorrow not.

MORTY. A real, a real Boob McNutt you're getting to be.

JACOB. Laugh, my son.

MORTY. Here is the North, Pop.

JACOB. North, south, it's one country.

MORTY. The country's all right. A duck quacks in every pot!

JACOB. You never heard how they shoot down men and women which ask a better wage? Kentucky 1932?

MORTY. That's a pile of chopped liver, Pop.

(BESSIE *and others enter.*)

JACOB. Pittsburgh, Passaic, Illionis—slavery—it begins where success begins in a competitive system.

(MORTY *howls with delight.*)

MORTY. Oh Pop, what are you bothering? Why? Tell me why? Ha ha ha. I bought you a phonograph . . . stick to Caruso.

BESSIE. He's starting up again.

MORTY. Don't bother with Kentucky. It's full of moonshiners.

JACOB. Sure, sure—

MORTY. You don't know practical affairs. Stay home and cut hair to fit the face.

JACOB. It says in the Bible how the Red Sea opened and the Egyptians went in and the sea rolled over them. (*Quotes two lines of Hebrew.*) In this boy's life a Red Sea will happen again. I see it!

MORTY. I'm getting sore, Pop, with all this sweatshop talk.

BESSIE. He don't stop a minute. The whole day, like a phonograph.

MORTY. I'm surprised. Without a rich man you don't have a roof over your head. You don't know it?

MYRON. Now you can't bite the hand that feeds you.

RALPH. Let him alone—he's right!

BESSIE. Another county heard from.

RALPH. It's the truth. It's—

MORTY. Keep quiet, snotnose!

JACOB. For sure, charity, a bone for

an old dog. But in Russia an old man don't take charity so his eyes turn black in his head. In Russia they got Marx.

MORTY (*scoffingly*). Who's Marx?

MOE. An outfielder for the Yanks.

(MORTY *howls with delight.*)

MORTY. Ha ha ha, it's better than the jokes. I'm telling you. This is Uncle Sam's country. Put it in your pipe and smoke it.

BESSIE. Russia, he says! Read the papers.

SAM. Here is opportunity.

MYRON. People can't believe in God in Russia. The papers tell the truth, they do.

JACOB. So you believe in God . . . you got something for it? You! You worked for all the capitalists. You harvested the fruit from your labor? You got God! But the past comforts you? The present smiles on you, yes? It promises you the future something? Did you found a piece of earth where you could live like a human being and die with the sun on your face? Tell me, yes, tell me. I would like to know myself. But on these questions, on this theme—the struggle for existence—you can't make an answer. The answer I see in your face . . . the answer is your mouth can't talk. In this dark corner you sit and you die. But abolish private property!

BESSIE (*setting the issue*). Noo, go fight City Hall!

MORTY. He's drunk!

JACOB. I'm studying from books a whole lifetime.

MORTY. That's what it is—he's drunk. What the hell does all that mean?

JACOB. If you don't know, why should I tell you.

MORTY (*triumphant at last*). You see? Hear him? Like all those nuts, don't know what they're saying.

JACOB. I know, I know.

MORTY. Like Boob McNutt you know! Don't go in the park, Pop—the squirrels'll get you. Ha, ha, ha. . .

BESSIE. Save your appetite, Morty. (*To* MYRON.) Don't drop the duck.

MYRON. We're ready to eat, Momma.

MORTY (*to* JACOB). Shame on you. It's your second childhood.

(*Now they file out.* MYRON *first with the duck, the others behind him.*)

BESSIE. Come eat. We had enough for one day. (*Exits.*)

MORTY. Ha, ha, ha. Quack, quack. (*Exits.*)

(JACOB *sits there trembling and deeply humiliated.* MOE *approaches him and thumbs the old man's nose in the direction of the dining room.*)

MOE. Give 'em five. (*Takes his hand away.*) They got you pasted on the wall like a picture, Jake. (*He limps out to seat himself at the table in the next room.*)

JACOB. Go eat, boychick. (RALPH *comes to him.*) He gives me eat, so I'll climb in a needle. One time I saw an old horse in summer . . . he wore a straw hat . . . the ears stuck out on top. An old horse for hire. Give me back my young days . . . give me fresh blood . . . arms . . . give me—

(*The telephone rings. Quickly* RALPH *goes to it.* JACOB *pulls the curtains and stands there, a sentry on guard.*)

RALPH. Hello? . . . Yeah, I went to the store and came right back, right after you called. (*Looks at* JACOB.)

JACOB. Speak, speak. Don't be afraid they'll hear.

RALPH. I'm sorry if Mom said something. You know how excitable Mom is . . . Sure! What? . . . Sure, I'm listening. . . Put on the radio, Jake. (JACOB *does so. Music comes in and up, a tango, grating with an insistent nostalgic pulse. Under the cover of the music* RALPH *speaks more freely.*) Yes . . . yes . . . What's the matter? Why're you crying? What happened? (*To* JACOB.) She's putting her uncle on. Yes? . . . Listen, Mr. Hirsch, what're you trying to do? What's the big idea? Honest to God. I'm in no mood for joking! Lemme talk to her! Gimme Blanche! (*Waits.*) Blanche? What's this? Is this a joke? Is that true? I'm coming right down! I know, but— You wanna do that? . . . I know, but— I'm coming down . . . tonight! Nine o'clock . . . sure . . . sure . . . sure . . . (*Hangs up.*)

JACOB. What happened?

MORTY (*enters*). Listen, Pop. I'm surprised you didn't— (*He howls, shakes his head in mock despair, exits.*)

JACOB. Boychick, what?

RALPH. I don't get it straight. (*To* JACOB.) She's leaving—

JACOB. Where?

RALPH. Out West— to Cleveland.

JACOB. Cleveland?

RALPH. In a week or two. Can you

picture it? It's a put-up job. But they can't get away with that.

JACOB. We'll find something.

RALPH. Sure, the angels of heaven'll come down on her uncle's cab and whisper in his ear.

JACOB. Come eat. . . . We'll find something.

RALPH. I'm meeting her tonight, but I know—

(BESSIE throws open the curtain between the two rooms and enters.)

BESSIE. Maybe we'll serve for you a special blue plate supper in the garden?

JACOB. All right, all right.

(BESSIE goes over to the window, levels the shade, and on her way out, clicks off the radio.)

MORTY (within). Leave the music, Bessie. (She clicks it on again, looks at them, exits.)

RALPH. I know . . .

JACOB. Don't cry, boychick. (Goes over to RALPH.) Why should you make like this? Tell me why you should cry, just tell me. . . . (JACOB takes RALPH in his arms and both, trying to keep back the tears, trying fearfully not to be heard by the others in the dining room, begin crying.) You mustn't cry. . . .

(The tango twists on. Inside the clatter of dishes and the clash of cutlery sound. MORTY begins to howl with laughter.)

CURTAIN

SCENE TWO

That night. The dark dining room.

AT RISE, JACOB is heard in his lighted room, reading from a sheet, declaiming aloud as if to an audience.

JACOB. They are there to remind us of the horrors—under those crosses lie hundreds of thousands of workers and farmers who murdered each other in uniform for the greater glory of capitalism. (Comes out of his room.) The new imperialist war will send millions to their death, will bring prosperity to the pockets of the capitalist—aie, Morty—and will bring only greater hunger and misery to the masses of workers and farmers. The memories of the last world slaughter are still vivid in our minds.

(Hearing a noise, he quickly retreats to his room. RALPH comes in from the street. He sits with hat and coat on. JACOB tentatively opens door and asks.) Ralphie?

RALPH. It's getting pretty cold out.

JACOB (enters room fully, cleaning hair clippers). We should have steam till twelve instead of ten. Go complain to the Board of Health.

RALPH. It might snow.

JACOB. It don't hurt . . . extra work for men.

RALPH. When I was a kid I laid awake at nights and heard the sounds of trains . . . faraway lonesome sounds . . . boats going up and down the river. I used to think of all kinds of things I wanted to do. What was it, Jake? Just a bunch of noise in my head?

JACOB (waiting for news of the girl). You wanted to make for yourself a certain kind of world.

RALPH. I guess I didn't. I'm feeling pretty, pretty low.

JACOB. You're a young boy, and for you life is all in front like a big mountain. You got feet to climb.

RALPH. I don't know how.

JACOB. So you'll find out. Never a young man had such opportunity like today. He could make history.

RALPH. Ten P.M. and all is well. Where's everybody?

JACOB. They went.

RALPH. Uncle Morty too?

JACOB. Hennie and Sam he drove down.

RALPH. I saw her.

JACOB (alert and eager). Yes, yes, tell me.

RALPH. I waited in Mount Morris Park till she came out. So cold I did a buck'n wing to keep warm. She's scared to death.

JACOB. They made her?

RALPH. Sure. She wants to go. They keep yelling at her—they want her to marry a millionaire, too.

JACOB. You told her you love her?

RALPH. Sure. "Marry me," I said. "Marry me tomorrow." On sixteen bucks a week. On top of that I had to admit Mom'd have Uncle Morty get me fired in a second. . . . Two can starve as cheap as one!

JACOB. So what happened?

RALPH. I made her promise to meet me tomorrow.

JACOB. Now she'll go in the West?

RALPH. I'd fight the whole goddam world with her, but not her. No guts. The hell with her. If she wantsa go—all right—I'll get along.

JACOB. For sure, there's more important things than girls.

RALPH. You said a mouthful . . . and maybe I don't see it. She'll see what I can do. No one stops me when I get going. (*Near to tears, he has to stop.* JACOB *examines his clippers very closely.*)

JACOB. Electric clippers never do a job like by hand.

RALPH. Why won't Mom let us live here?

JACOB. Why? Why? Because in a society like this today people don't love. Hate!

RALPH. Gee, I'm no bum who hangs around pool parlors. I got the stuff to go ahead. I don't know what to do.

JACOB. Look on me and learn what to do, boychick. Here sits an old man polishing tools. You think maybe I'll use them again! Look on this failure and see for seventy years he talked with good ideas, but only in the head. It's enough for me now I should see your happiness. This is why I tell you—DO! Do what is in your heart and you carry in yourself a revolution. But you should act. Not like me. A man who had golden opportunities but drank instead a glass tea. No. (*A pause of silence.*)

RALPH (*listening*). Hear it? The Boston airmail plane. Ten minutes late. I get a kick the way it cuts across the Bronx every night.

(*The bell rings:* SAM, *excited, disheveled, enters.*)

JACOB. You came back so soon?

SAM. Where's Mom?

JACOB. Mom? Look on the chandelier.

SAM. Nobody's home?

JACOB. Sit down. Right away they're coming. You went in the street without a tie?

SAM. Maybe it's a crime.

JACOB. Excuse me.

RALPH. You had a fight with Hennie again?

SAM. She'll fight once . . . some day. . . . (*Lapses into silence.*)

JACOB. In my day the daughter came home. Now comes the son-in-law.

SAM. Once too often she'll fight with me, Hennie. I mean it. I mean it like anything. I'm a person with a bad heart. I sit quiet, but inside I got a—

RALPH. What happened?

SAM. I'll talk to Mom. I'll see Mom.

JACOB. Take an apple.

SAM. Please . . . he tells me apples.

RALPH. Why hop around like a billiard ball?

SAM. Even in a joke she should dare say it.

JACOB. My grandchild said something?

SAM. To my father in the old country they did a joke . . . I'll tell you: One day in Odessa he talked to another Jew on the street. They didn't like it, they jumped on him like a wild wolf.

RALPH. Who?

SAM. Cossacks. They cut off his beard. A Jew without a beard! He came home —I remember like yesterday how he came home and went in bed for two days. He put like this the cover on his face. No one should see. The third morning he died.

RALPH. From what?

SAM. From a broken heart. . . . Some people are like this. Me too. I could die like this from shame.

JACOB. Hennie told you something?

SAM. Straight out she said it—like a lightning from the sky. The baby ain't mine. She said it.

RALPH. Don't be a dope.

JACOB. For sure, a joke.

RALPH. She's kidding you.

SAM. She should kid a policeman, not Sam Feinschreiber. Please . . . you don't know her like me. I wake up in the night-time and she sits watching me like I don't know what. I make a nice living from the store. But it's no use—she looks for a star in the sky. I'm afraid like anything. You could go crazy from less even. What I shall do I'll ask Mom.

JACOB. "Go home and sleep," she'll say. "It's a bad dream."

SAM. It don't satisfy me more, such remarks, when Hennie could kill in the bed. (JACOB *laughs.*) Don't laugh. I'm so nervous—look, two times I weighed myself on the subway station. (*Throws small cards to table.*)

JACOB (*examining one*). One hundred and thirty-eight—also a fortune. (*Turns it and reads:*) "You are inclined to deep thinking, and have a high admiration for intellectual excellence and inclined to be very exclusive in the selection of friends." Correct! I think maybe you got mixed up in the wrong family, Sam.

(MYRON *and* BESSIE *now enter.*)

BESSIE. Look, a guest! What's the matter? Something wrong with the baby? (*Waits.*)

SAM. No.

BESSIE. Noo?

SAM (*in a burst*). I wash my hands from everything.

BESSIE. Take off your coat and hat. Have a seat. Excitement don't help. Myron, make tea. You'll have a glass tea. We'll talk like civilized people. (MYRON *goes.*) What is it, Ralph, you're all dressed up for a party? (*He looks at her silently and exits. To* SAM.) We saw a very good movie, with Wallace Beery. He acts like life, very good.

MYRON (*within*). Polly Moran too.

BESSIE. Polly Moran too—a woman with a nose from here to Hunts Point, but a fine player. Poppa, take away the tools and the books.

JACOB. All right. (*Exits to his room.*)

BESSIE. Noo, Sam, why do you look like a funeral?

SAM. I can't stand it.

BESSIE. Wait. (*Yells:*) You took up Tootsie on the roof.

JACOB (*within*). In a minute.

BESSIE. What can't you stand?

SAM. She said I'm a second fiddle in my own house.

BESSIE. Who?

SAM. Hennie. In the second place, it ain't my baby, she said.

BESSIE. What? What are you talking?

(MYRON *enters with dishes.*)

SAM. From her own mouth. It went like a knife in my heart.

BESSIE. Sam, what're you saying?

SAM. Please, I'm making a story? I fell in the chair like a dead.

BESSIE. Such a story you believe?

SAM. I don't know.

BESSIE. How you don't know?

SAM. She told me even the man.

BESSIE. Impossible!

SAM. I can't believe myself. But she said it. I'm a second fiddle, she said. She made such a yell everybody heard for ten miles.

BESSIE. Such a thing Hennie should say—impossible!

SAM. What should I do? With my bad heart such a remark kills.

MYRON. Hennie don't feel well, Sam. You see, she—

BESSIE. What then?—a sick girl. Believe me, a mother knows. Nerves. Our Hennie's got a bad temper. You'll let her she says anything. She takes after me—nervous. (*To* MYRON.) You ever heard such a remark in all your life? She should make such a statement! Bughouse.

MYRON. The little one's been sick all these months. Hennie needs a rest. No doubt.

BESSIE. Sam don't think she means it—

MYRON. Oh, I know he don't, of course—

BESSIE. I'll say the truth, Sam. We didn't half the time understand her ourselves. A girl with her own mind. When she makes it up, wild horses wouldn't change her.

SAM. She don't love me.

BESSIE. This is sensible, Sam?

SAM. Not for a nickel.

BESSIE. What do you think? She married you for your money? For your looks? You ain't no John Barrymore, Sam. No, she liked you.

SAM. Please, not for a nickel.

(JACOB *stands in the doorway.*)

BESSIE. We stood right here the first time she said it. "Sam Feinschreiber's a nice boy," she said it, "a boy he's got good common sense, with a business head." Right here she said it, in this room. You sent her two boxes of candy together, you remember?

MYRON. Loft's candy.

BESSIE. This is when she said it. What do you think?

MYRON. You were just the only boy she cared for.

BESSIE. So she married you. Such a world . . . plenty of boy friends she had, believe me!

JACOB. A popular girl . . .

MYRON. Y-e-s.

BESSIE. I'll say it plain out—Moe Axelrod offered her plenty—a servant, a house . . . she don't have to pick up a hand.

MYRON. Oh, Moe? Just wild about her . . .

SAM. Moe Axelrod? He wanted to—

BESSIE. But she didn't care. A girl like Hennie you don't buy. I should never live to see another day if I'm telling a lie.

SAM. She was kidding me.

BESSIE. What then? You shouldn't be foolish.

SAM. The baby looks like my family. He's got Feinschreiber eyes.

BESSIE. A blind man could see it.

JACOB. Sure . . . sure . . .

SAM. The baby looks like me. Yes.

BESSIE. You could believe me.

JACOB. Any day. . . .

SAM. But she tells me the man. She made up his name too?

BESSIE. Sam, Sam, look in the phone book—a million names.

MYRON. Tom, Dick, and Harry.

(JACOB *laughs quietly, soberly.*)

BESSIE. Don't stand around, Poppa. Take Tootsie on the roof. And you don't let her go under the water tank.

JACOB. *Schmah Yisroeal.* Behold! (*Quietly laughing, he goes back into his room, closing the door behind him.*)

SAM. I won't stand he should make insults. A man eats out his—

BESSIE. No, no, he's an old man—a second childhood. Myron, bring in the tea. Open a jar of raspberry jelly.

(MYRON *exits.*)

SAM. Mom, you think—?

BESSIE. I'll talk to Hennie. It's all right.

SAM. Tomorrow I'll take her by the doctor.

(RALPH *enters.*)

BESSIE. Stay for a little tea.

SAM. No, I'll go home. I'm tired. Already I caught a cold in such weather. (*Blows his nose.*)

MYRON (*entering with stuffs*). Going home?

SAM. I'll go in bed. I caught a cold.

MYRON. Teddy Roosevelt used to say, "When you have a problem, sleep on it."

BESSIE. My Sam is no problem.

MYRON. I don't mean . . . I mean he said—

BESSIE. Call me tomorrow, Sam.

SAM. I'll phone suppertime. Sometime I think there's something funny about me.

(MYRON *sees him out. In the following pause Caruso is heard singing within.*)

BESSIE. A bargain! Second fiddle. By me he don't even play in the orchestra— a man like a mouse. Maybe she'll lay down and die 'cause he makes a living?

RALPH. Can I talk to you about something?

BESSIE. What's the matter—I'm biting you?

RALPH. It's something about Blanche.

BESSIE. Don't tell me.

RALPH. Listen now—

BESSIE. I don't wanna know.

RALPH. She's got no place to go.

BESSIE. I don't want to know.

RALPH. Mom, I love this girl.

BESSIE. So go knock your head against the wall.

RALPH. I want her to come here. Listen, Mom, I want you to let her live here for a while.

BESSIE. You got funny ideas, my son.

RALPH. I'm as good as anyone else. Don't I have some rights in the world? Listen, Mom, if I don't do something, she's going away. Why don't you do it? Why don't you let her stay here for a few weeks? Things'll pick up. Then we can—

BESSIE. Sure, sure. I'll keep her fresh on ice for a wedding day. That's what you want?

RALPH. No, I mean you should—

BESSIE. Or maybe you'll sleep here in the same bed without marriage.

(JACOB *stands in his doorway, dressed.*)

RALPH. Don't say that, Mom. I only mean—

BESSIE. What you mean, I know . . . and what I mean I also know. Make up your mind. For your own good, Ralphie. If she dropped in the ocean I don't lift a finger.

RALPH. That's all, I suppose.

BESSIE. With me it's one thing—a boy should have respect for his own future. Go to sleep, you look tired. In the morning you'll forget.

JACOB. "Awake and sing, ye that dwell in dust, and the earth shall cast out the dead." It's cold out?

MYRON. Oh, yes.

JACOB. I'll take up Tootsie now.

MYRON (*eating bread and jam*). He come on us like the wild man of Borneo, Sam. I don't think Hennie was fool enough to tell him the truth like that.

BESSIE. Myron!

(*A deep pause.*)

RALPH. What did he say?

BESSIE. Never mind.

RALPH. I heard him. I heard him. You don't needa tell me.

BESSIE. Never mind.

RALPH. You trapped that guy.

BESSIE. Don't say another word.

RALPH. Just have respect? That's the idea?

BESSIE. Don't say another word. I'm boiling over ten times inside.

RALPH. You won't let Blanche here, huh. I'm not sure I want her. You put one over on that little shrimp. The cat's whiskers, Mom?

BESSIE. I'm telling you something!

RALPH. I got the whole idea. I get it so quick my head's swimming. Boy, what a laugh! I suppose you know about this, Jake?

JACOB. Yes.

RALPH. Why didn't you do something?

JACOB. I'm an old man.

RALPH. What's that got to do with the price of bonds? Sits around and lets a thing like that happen! You make me sick too.

MYRON (after a pause). Let me say something, son.

RALPH. Take your hand away! Sit in a corner and wag your tail. Keep on boasting you went to law school for two years.

MYRON. I want to tell you—

RALPH. You never in your life had a thing to tell me.

BESSIE (bitterly). Don't say a word. Let him, let him run and tell Sam. Publish in the papers, give a broadcast on the radio. To him it don't matter nothing his family sits with tears pouring from the eyes. (To JACOB.) What are you waiting for? I didn't tell you twice already about the dog? You'll stand around with Caruso and make a bughouse. It ain't enough all day long. Fifty times I told you I'll break every record in the house. (She brushes past him, breaks the records, comes out.) The next time I say something you'll maybe believe me. Now maybe you learned a lesson. (Pause.)

JACOB (quietly). Bessie, new lessons . . . not for an old dog.

(MOE enters.)

MYRON. You didn't have to do it, Momma.

BESSIE. Talk better to your son, Mr. Berger! Me, I don't lay down and die for him and Poppa no more. I'll work like a nigger? For what? Wait, the day comes when you'll be punished. When it's too late you'll remember how you sucked away a mother's life. Talk to him, tell him how I don't sleep at night. (Bursts into tears and exits.)

MOE (sings). "Good-by to all your

sorrows. You never hear them talk about the war, in the land of Yama Yama . . ."

MYRON. Yes, Momma's a sick woman, Ralphie.

RALPH. Yeah?

MOE. We'll be out of the trenches by Christmas. Putt, putt, putt . . . here, stinker . . . (Picks up Tootsie, a small, white poodle that just then enters from the hall.) If there's reincarnation in the next life I wanna be a dog and lay in a fat lady's lap. Barrage over? How 'bout a little pinochle, Pop?

JACOB. Nnno.

RALPH (taking dog). I'll take her up. (Conciliatory.)

JACOB. No, I'll do it. (Takes dog.)

RALPH (ashamed). It's cold out.

JACOB. I was cold before in my life. A man sixty-seven—(Strokes the dog.) Tootsie is my favorite lady in the house. (He slowly passes across the room and exits. A settling pause.)

MYRON. She cried all last night—Tootsie—I heard her in the kitchen like a young girl.

MOE. Tonight I could do something. I got a yen . . . I don't know.

MYRON (rubbing his head). My scalp is impoverished.

RALPH. Mom bust all his records.

MYRON. She didn't have to do it.

MOE. Tough tit! Now I can sleep in the morning. Who the hell wantsa hear a Wop air his tonsils all day long!

RALPH (handling the fragment of a record). "O Paradiso!"

MOE (gets cards). It's snowing out, girls.

MYRON. There's no more big snows like in the old days. I think the whole world's changing. I see it, right under our very eyes. No one hardly remembers any more when we used to have gaslight and all the dishes had little fishes on them.

MOE. It's the system, girls.

MYRON. I was a little boy when it happened—the Great Blizzard. It snowed three days without a stop that time. Yes, and the horse cars stopped. A silence of death was on the city and little babies got no milk . . . they say a lot of people died that year.

MOE (singing as he deals himself cards). "Lights are blinking while you're

drinking,
That's the place where the good fellows
go.

Good-by to all your sorrows,

You never hear them talk about the war,
In the land of Yama Yama
Funicalee, funicala, funicalo. . . ."

MYRON. What can I say to you, Big Boy?

RALPH. Not a damn word.

MOE (*goes "ta ra ta ra" throughout*).

MYRON. I know how you feel about all those things, I know.

RALPH. Forget it.

MYRON. And your girl—

RALPH. Don't soft-soap me all of a sudden.

MYRON. I'm not foreign born. I'm an American, and yet I never got close to you. It's an American father's duty to be his son's friend.

RALPH. Who said that—Teddy R.?

MOE (*dealing cards*). You're breaking his heart, "Litvak."

MYRON. It just happened the other day. The moment I began losing my hair I just knew I was destined to be a failure in life . . . and when I grew bald I was. Now isn't that funny, Big Boy?

MOE. It's a pisscutter!

MYRON. I believe in Destiny.

MOE. You get what-it-takes. Then they don't catch you with your pants down. (*Sings out:*) Eight of clubs . . .

MYRON. I really don't know. I sold jewelry on the road before I married. It's one thing to—Now here's a thing the druggist gave me. (*Reads:*) "The Marvel Cosmetic Girl of Hollywood is going on the air. Give this charming little radio singer a name and win five thousand dollars. If you will send—"

MOE. Your old man still believes in Santa Claus.

MYRON. Someone's got to win. The government isn't gonna allow everything to be a fake.

MOE. It's a fake. There ain't no prizes. It's a fake.

MYRON. It says—

RALPH (*snatching it*). For Christ's sake, Pop, forget it. Grow up. Jake's right—everybody's crazy. It's like a zoo in this house. I'm going to bed.

MOE. In the land of Yama Yama . . . (*Goes on with ta ra.*)

MYRON. Don't think life's easy with Momma. No, but she means for your good all the time. I tell you she does, she—

RALPH. Maybe, but I'm going to bed. (*Downstairs doorbell rings violently.*)

MOE (*ring*). Enemy barrage begins on sector eight seventy-five.

RALPH. That's downstairs.

MYRON. We ain't expecting anyone this hour of the night.

MOE. "Lights are blinking while you're drinking, that's the place where the good fellows go. Good-by to ta ra tara ra," etc.

RALPH. I better see who it is.

MYRON. I'll tick the button.

(*As he starts, the apartment doorbell begins ringing, followed by large knocking. MYRON goes out.*)

RALPH. Who's ever ringing means it. (*A loud excited voice outside.*)

MOE. "In the land of Yama Yama, Funicalee, funicalo, funic—"

(*MYRON enters, followed by SCHLOSSER, the janitor. BESSIE cuts in from the other side.*)

BESSIE. Who's ringing like a lunatic?

RALPH. What's the matter?

MYRON. Momma . . .

BESSIE. Noo, what's the matter?

(*Downstairs bell continues.*)

RALPH. What's the matter?

BESSIE. Well, well?

MYRON. Poppa . . .

BESSIE. What happened?

SCHLOSSER. He shlipped maybe in de snow.

RALPH. Who?

SCHLOSSER (*to BESSIE*). Your fadder fall off de roof. . . . *Ja.*

(*A dead pause. RALPH then runs out.*)

BESSIE (*dazed*). Myron . . . Call Morty on the phone . . . call him. (*MYRON starts for phone.*) No. I'll do it myself. I'll . . . do it. (*MYRON exits.*)

SCHLOSSER (*standing stupidly*). Since I was in dis country . . . I was pudding out de ash can . . . The snow is vet . . .

MOE (*to SCHLOSSER*). Scram.

(*SCHLOSSER exits.*)

(*BESSIE goes blindly to the phone, fumbles, and gets it. MOE sits quietly, slowly turning cards over, but watching her.*)

BESSIE. He slipped . . .

MOE (*deeply moved*). Slipped?

BESSIE. I can't see the numbers. Make it, Moe, make it . . .

MOE. Make it yourself. (*He looks at her and slowly goes back to his game of cards with shaking hands.*)

BESSIE. Riverside 7—(*Unable to talk, she dials slowly. The dial whizzes on.*)

MOE. Don't . . . make me laugh. . . . (*He turns over cards.*)

CURTAIN

ACT THREE

A week later in the dining room. MORTY, BESSIE, *and* MYRON *eating. Sitting in the front room is* MOE *marking a "dope sheet," but really listening to the others.*

BESSIE. You're sure he'll come tonight —the insurance man?

MORTY. Why not? I shtupped him a ten-dollar bill. Everything's hot delicatessen.

BESSIE. Why must he come so soon?

MORTY. Because you had a big expense. You'll settle once and for all. I'm a great boy for making hay while the sun shines.

BESSIE. Stay till he'll come, Morty. . . .

MORTY. No, I got a strike downtown. Business don't stop for personal life. Two times already in the past week those bastards threw stink bombs in the showroom. Wait! We'll give them strikes—in the kishkas we'll give them. . . .

BESSIE. I'm a woman. I don't know about policies. Stay till he comes.

MORTY. Bessie—sweetheart, leave me live.

BESSIE. I'm afraid, Morty.

MORTY. Be practical. They made an investigation. Everybody knows Pop had an accident. Now we'll collect.

MYRON. Ralphie don't know Papa left the insurance in his name.

MORTY. It's not his business. And I'll tell him.

BESSIE. The way he feels. (*Enter* RALPH *into front room.*) He'll do something crazy. He thinks Poppa jumped off the roof.

MORTY. Be practical, Bessie. Ralphie will sign when I tell him. Everything is peaches and cream.

BESSIE. Wait for a few minutes.

MORTY. Look, I'll show you in black on white what the policy says. *For God's sake, leave me live!* (*Angrily exits to kitchen. In parlor,* MOE *speaks to* RALPH, *who is reading a letter.*)

MOE. What's the letter say?

RALPH. Blanche won't see me no more, she says. I couldn't care very much, she says. If I didn't come like I said. . . . She'll phone before she leaves.

MOE. She don't know about Pop?

RALPH. She won't ever forget me she says. Look what she sends me . . . a little locket on a chain . . . if she calls I'm out.

MOE. You mean it?

RALPH. For a week I'm trying to go in his room. I guess he'd like me to have it, but I can't.

MOE. Wait a minute! (*Crosses over.*) They're trying to rook you—a freeze-out.

RALPH. Who?

MOE. That bunch stuffin' their gut with hot pastrami. Morty in particular. Jake left the insurance—three thousand dollars—for you.

RALPH. For me?

MOE. Now you got wings, kid. Pop figured you could use it. That's why . . .

RALPH. That's why what?

MOE. It ain't the only reason he done it.

RALPH. He done it?

MOE. You think a breeze blew him off? (HENNIE *enters and sits.*)

RALPH. I'm not sure what I think.

MOE. The insurance guy's coming tonight. Morty 'shtupped" him.

RALPH. Yeah?

MOE. I'll back you up. You're dead on your feet. Grab a sleep for yourself.

RALPH. No!

MOE. Go on! (*Pushes boy into room.*)

SAM (*whom* MORTY *has sent in for the paper*). Morty wants the paper.

HENNIE. So?

SAM. You're sitting on it. (*Gets paper.*) We could go home now, Hennie! Leon is alone by Mrs. Strasberg a whole day.

HENNIE. Go on home if you're so anxious. A full tub of diapers is waiting.

SAM. Why should you act this way?

HENNIE. 'Cause there's no bones in ice cream. Don't touch me.

SAM. Please, what's the matter . . .

MOE. She don't like you. Plain as the face on your nose.

SAM. To me, my friend, you talk a foreign language.

MOE. A quarter you're lousy. (SAM *exits.*) Gimme a buck, I'll run it up to ten.

HENNIE. Don't do me no favors.

MOE. Take a chance. (*Stopping her as she crosses to doorway.*)

HENNIE. I'm a pushover.

MOE. I say lotsa things. You don't know me.

HENNIE. I know you—when you knock 'em down you're through.

MOE (*sadly*). You still don't know me.

HENNIE. I know what goes in your wise-guy head.

MOE. Don't run away. . . . I ain't got hydrophobia. Wait. I want to tell you. . . . I'm leaving.

HENNIE. Leaving?

MOE. Tonight. Already packed.

HENNIE. Where?

MORTY (*as he enters followed by the others*). My car goes through snow like a dose of salts.

BESSIE. Hennie, go eat.

MORTY. Where's Ralphie?

MOE. In his new room. (*Moves into dining room.*)

MORTY. I didn't have a piece of hot pastrami in my mouth for years.

BESSIE. Take a sandwich, Hennie. You didn't eat all day. . . . (*At window.*) A whole week it rained cats and dogs.

MYRON. Rain, rain, go away. Come again some other day. (*Puts shawl on her.*)

MORTY. Where's my gloves?

SAM (*sits on stool*). I'm sorry the old man lays in the rain.

MORTY. Personally, Pop was a fine man. But I'm a great boy for an honest opinion. He had enough crazy ideas for a regiment.

MYRON. Poppa never had a doctor in his whole life.

(*Enter* RALPH.)

MORTY. He had Caruso. Who's got more from life?

BESSIE. Who's got more?

MYRON. And Marx he had.

(MYRON *and* BESSIE *sit on sofa.*)

MORTY. Marx! Some say Marx is the new God today. Maybe I'm wrong. Ha ha ha. . . . Personally, I counted my ten million last night. I'm sixteen cents short. So tomorrow I'll go to Union Square and yell no equality in the country! Ah, it's a new generation.

RALPH. You said it!

MORTY. What's the matter, Ralphie? What are you looking funny?

RALPH. I hear I'm left insurance and the man's coming tonight.

MORTY. Poppa didn't leave no insurance for you.

RALPH. What?

MORTY. In your name he left it—but not for you.

RALPH. It's my name on the paper.

MORTY. Who said so?

RALPH (*to his mother*). The insurance man's coming tonight?

MORTY. What's the matter?

RALPH. I'm not talking to you. (*To his mother.*) Why?

BESSIE. I don't know why.

RALPH. He don't come in this house tonight.

MORTY. That's what *you* say.

RALPH. I'm not talking to you, Uncle Morty, but I'll tell you, too, he don't come here tonight when there's still mud on a grave. (*To his mother.*) Couldn't you give the house a chance to cool off?

MORTY. Is this a way to talk to your mother?

RALPH. Was that a way to talk to your father?

MORTY. Don't be so smart with me, Mr. Ralph Berger!

RALPH. Don't be so smart with *me*.

MORTY. What'll you do? I say he's coming tonight. Who says no?

MOE (*suddenly, from the background*). Me.

MORTY. Take a back seat, Axelrod. When you're in the family—

MOE. I got a little document here. (*Produces paper.*) I found it under his pillow that night. A guy who slips off a roof don't leave a note before he does it.

MORTY (*starting for* MOE *after a horrified silence*). Let me see this note.

BESSIE. Morty, don't touch it!

MOE. Not if you crawled.

MORTY. It's a fake. Poppa wouldn't—

MOE. Get the insurance guy here and we'll see how— (*The bell rings.*) Speak of the devil—Answer it, see what happens. (MORTY *starts for the ticker.*)

BESSIE. Morty, don't!

MORTY (*stopping*). Be practical, Bessie.

MOE. Sometimes you don't collect on suicides if they know about it.

MORTY. You should let—You should let him—

(*A pause in which* ALL *seem dazed. Bell rings insistently.*)

MOE. Well, we're waiting.

MORTY. Give me the note.

MOE. I'll give you the head off your shoulders.

MORTY. Bessie, you'll stand for this? (*Points to* RALPH.) Pull down his pants and give him with a strap.

RALPH (*as bell rings again*). How about it?

BESSIE. Don't be crazy. It's not my fault. Morty said he should come tonight. It's not nice so soon. I didn't—

MORTY. I said it? Me?

BESSIE. Who then?

MORTY. You didn't sing a song in my

ear a whole week to settle quick?

BESSIE. I'm surprised. Morty, you're a big liar.

MYRON. Momma's telling the truth, she is!

MORTY. Lissen. In two shakes of a lamb's tail, we'll start a real fight and then nobody won't like nobody. Where's my fur gloves? I'm going downtown. (*To* SAM.) You coming? I'll drive you down.

HENNIE (*to* SAM, *who looks questioningly at her*). Don't look at me. Go home if you want.

SAM. If you're coming soon, I'll wait.

HENNIE. Don't do me any favors. Night and day he pesters me.

MORTY. You made a cushion—sleep!

SAM. I'll go home. I know . . . to my worst enemy I don't wish such a life—

HENNIE. Sam, keep quiet.

SAM (*quietly; sadly*). No more free speech in America? (*Gets his hat and coat.*) I'm a lonely person. Nobody likes me.

MYRON. I like you, Sam.

HENNIE (*going to him gently; sensing the end*). Please go home, Sam. I'll sleep here. . . . I'm tired and nervous. To-morrow I'll come home. I love you . . . I mean it. (*She kisses him with real feeling.*)

SAM. I would die for you. . . . (SAM *looks at her. Tries to say something, but his voice chokes up with a mingled feeling. He turns and leaves the room.*)

MORTY. A bird in the hand is worth two in the bush. Remember I said it. Good night. (*Exits after* SAM.)

(HENNIE *sits depressed.* BESSIE *goes up and looks at the picture calendar again.* MYRON *finally breaks the silence.*)

MYRON. Yesterday a man wanted to sell me a saxophone with pearl buttons. But I—

BESSIE. It's a beautiful picture. In this land, nobody works. . . . Nobody wor-ries. . . . Come to bed, Myron. (*Stops at the door, and says to* RALPH.) Please don't have foolish ideas about the money.

RALPH. Let's call it a day.

BESSIE. It belongs for the whole family. You'll get your teeth fixed—

RALPH. And a pair of black and white shoes?

BESSIE. Hennie needs a vacation. She'll take two weeks in the mountains and I'll mind the baby.

RALPH. I'll take care of my own affairs.

BESSIE. A family needs for a rainy day. Times is getting worse. Prospect Avenue, Dawson, Beck Street—every day furni-ture's on the sidewalk.

RALPH. Forget it, Mom.

BESSIE. Ralphie, I worked too hard all my years to be treated like dirt. It's no law we should be stuck together like Siamese twins. Summer shoes you didn't have, skates you never had, but I bought a new dress every week. A lover I kept—Mr. Gigolo! Did I ever play a game of cards like Mrs. Marcus? Or was Bessie Berger's children always the cleanest on the block?! Here I'm not only the mother, but also the father. The first two years I worked in a stocking factory for six dollars while Myron Berger went to law school. If I didn't worry about the family who would? On the calendar it's a different place, but here without a dollar you don't look the world in the eye. Talk from now to next year—this is life in America.

RALPH. Then it's wrong. It don't make sense. If life made you this way, then it's wrong!

BESSIE. Maybe you wanted me to give up twenty years ago. Where would you be now? You'll excuse my expression—bum in the park!

RALPH. I'm not blaming you, Mom. Sink or swim—I see it. But it can't stay like this.

BESSIE. My foolish boy . . .

RALPH. No, I see every house lousy with lies and hate. He said it, Grandpa—Brooklyn hates the Bronx. Smacked on the nose twice a day. But boys and girls can get ahead like that, Mom. We don't want life printed on dollar bills, Mom!

BESSIE. So go out and change the world if you don't like it.

RALPH. I will! And why? 'Cause life's different in my head. Gimme the earth in two hands. I'm strong. There . . . hear him? The airmail off to Boston. Day or night, he flies away, a job to do. That's us and it's no time to die.

(*The airplane sound fades off as* MYRON *gives alarm clock to* BESSIE, *which she begins to wind.*)

BESSIE. "Mom, what does she know? She's old-fashioned!" But I'll tell you a big secret: My whole life I wanted to go away too, but with children a woman stays home. A fire burned in *my* heart too, but now it's too late. I'm no spring chicken. The clock goes and Bessie goes. Only my machinery can't be fixed. (*She lifts a button: the alarm rings on the clock; she stops it, says "Good night," and exits.*)

MYRON. I guess I'm no prize bag.

BESSIE (*from within*). Come to bed, Myron.

MYRON (*tears page off calendar*). Hmmm . . . (*Exits to her.*)

RALPH. Look at him, draggin' after her like an old shoe.

MOE. Punch drunk. (*Phone rings.*) That's for me. (*At phone.*) Yeah? . . . Just a minute. (*To* RALPH.) Your girl . . .

RALPH. Jeez, I don't know what to say to her.

MOE. Hang up?

(RALPH *slowly takes phone.*)

RALPH. Hello. . . . Blanche, I wish . . . I don't know what to say . . . Yes . . . Hello? . . . (*Puts phone down.*) She hung up on me. . . .

MOE. Sorry?

RALPH. No girl means anything to me until—

MOE. Till when?

RALPH. Till I can take care of her. Till we don't look out on an airshaft. Till we can take the world in two hands and polish off the dirt.

MOE. That's a big order.

RALPH. Once upon a time I thought I'd drown to death in bolts of silk and velour. But I grew up these last few weeks. Jake said a lot.

MOE. Your memory's okay?

RALPH. But take a look at this. (*Brings armful of books from* JACOB's *room—dumps them on table.*) His books, I got them too —the pages ain't cut in half of them.

MOE. Perfect.

RALPH. Does it prove something? Damm tootin'! A ten-cent nailfile cuts them. Uptown, I'll read them on the way. Get a big lamp over the bed. (*Picks up phone.*) My eyes are good. (*Puts book in pocket.*) Sure, inventory tomorrow. Coletti to Driscoll to Berger—that's how we work. It's a team down the warehouse. Driscoll's a show-off, a wise guy, and Joe talks pigeons day and night. But they're like me, looking for a chance to get to first base too. Joe razzed me about my girl. But he don't know why. I'll tell him. Hell, he might tell me something I don't know. Get teams together all over. Spit on your hands and get to work. And with enough teams together maybe we'll get steam in the warehouse so our fingers don't freeze off. Maybe we'll fix it so life won't be printed on dollar bills.

MOE. Graduation Day.

RALPH (*starts for door of his room, stops*). Can I have . . . Grandpa's note?

MOE. Sure you want it?

RALPH. Please— (MOE *gives it.*) It's blank!

MOE (*taking note back and tearing it up*). That's right.

RALPH. Thanks! (*Exits.*)

MOE. The kid's a fighter! (*To* HENNIE.) Why are you crying?

HENNIE. I never cried in my life. (*She is now.*)

MOE (*starts for door. Stops*). You told Sam you love him . . .

HENNIE. If I'm sore on life, why take it out on him?

MOE. You won't forget me to your dyin' day—I was the first guy. Part of your insides. You won't forget. I wrote my name on you—indelible ink!

HENNIE. One thing I won't forget— how you left me crying on the bed like I was two for a cent!

MOE. Listen, do you think—

HENNIE. Sure. Waits till the family goes to the open air movie. He brings me perfume—He grabs my arms—

MOE. You won't forget me!

HENNIE. How you left the next week?

MOE. So I made a mistake. For Chris' sake, don't act like the Queen of Roumania!

HENNIE. Don't make me laugh!

MOE. What the hell do you want, my head on a plate?! Was my life so happy? Chris', my old man was a bum. I supported the whole damn family—five kids and Mom. When they grew up they beat it the hell away like rabbits. Mom died. I went to the war; got clapped down like a bedbug; woke up in a room without a leg. What the hell do you think, anyone's got it better than you? I never had a home either. I'm lookin' too!

HENNIE. So what?!

MOE. So you're it—you're home for me, a place to live! That's the whole parade, sickness, eating out your heart! Sometimes you meet a girl—she stops it—that's love. . . . So take a chance! Be with me, Paradise. What's to lose?

HENNIE. My pride!

MOE (*grabbing her*). What do you want? Say the word—I'll tango on a dime. Don't gimme ice when your heart's on fire!

HENNIE. Let me go!

(*He stops her.*)

MOE. WHERE?

HENNIE. What do you want, Moe, what do you want?

MOE. You!

HENNIE. You'll be sorry you ever started—

MOE. You!

HENNIE. Moe, lemme go— (*Trying to leave.*) I'm getting up early—lemme go.

MOE. No! . . . I got enough fever to blow the whole damn town to hell. (*He suddenly releases her and half-stumbles backward. Forces himself to quiet down.*) You wanna go back to him? Say the word. I'll know what to do. . . .

HENNIE (*helplessly*). Moe, I don't know what to say.

MOE. Listen to me.

HENNIE. What?

MOE. Come away. A certain place where it's moonlight and roses. We'll lay down, count stars. Hear the big ocean making noise. You lay under the trees. Champagne flows like—(*Phone rings. MOE finally answers the telephone.*) Hello? . . . Just a minute. (*Looks at HENNIE.*)

HENNIE. Who is it?

MOE. Sam.

HENNIE (*starts for phone, but changes her mind*). I'm sleeping.

MOE (*in phone*). She's sleeping. . . . (*Hangs up. Watches HENNIE, who slowly sits.*) He wants you to know he got home O.K. . . . What's on your mind?

HENNIE. Nothing.

MOE. Sam?

HENNIE. They say it's a palace on those Havana boats.

MOE. What's on your mind?

HENNIE (*trying to escape*). Moe, I don't care for Sam—I never loved him—

MOE. But your kid—?

HENNIE. All my life I waited for this minute.

MOE (*holding her*). Me too. Made believe I was talkin' just bedroom golf, but you and me forever was what I meant! Christ, baby, there's one life to live! Live it!

HENNIE. Leave the baby?

MOE. Yeah!

HENNIE. I can't—

MOE. You can!

HENNIE. No.

MOE. But you're not sure!

HENNIE. I don't know.

MOE. Make a break or spend the rest of your life in a coffin.

HENNIE. Oh God, I don't know where I stand.

MOE. Don't look up there. Paradise, you're on a big boat headed south. No more pins and needles in your heart, no snake juice squirted in your arm. The whole world's green grass, and when you cry it's because you're happy.

HENNIE. Moe, I don't know. . . .

MOE. Nobody knows, but you do it and find out. When you're scared the answer's zero.

HENNIE. You're hurting my arm.

MOE. The doctor said it—cut off your leg to save your life! And they done it— one thing to get another.

(*Enter RALPH.*)

RALPH. I didn't hear a word, but do it, Hennie, do it!

MOE. Mom can mind the kid. She'll go on forever, Mom. We'll send money back, and Easter eggs.

RALPH. I'll be here.

MOE. Get your coat . . . get it.

HENNIE. Moe!

MOE. I know . . . but get your coat and hat and kiss the house good-by.

HENNIE. The man I love. . . . (*MYRON entering.*) I left my coat in Mom's room. (*Exits.*)

MYRON. Don't wake her up, Beauty. Momma fell asleep as soon as her head hit the pillow. I can't sleep. It was a long day. Hmmm. (*Examines his tongue in buffet mirror.*) I was reading the other day a person with a thick tongue is feeble-minded. I can do anything with my tongue. Make it thick, flat. No fruit in the house lately. Just a lone apple. (*He gets apple and paring knife and starts paring.*) Must be something wrong with me—I say I won't eat but I eat. (*HENNIE enters, dressed to go out.*) Where you going, little Red Riding Hood?

HENNIE. Nobody knows, Peter Rabbit.

MYRON. You're looking very pretty tonight. You were a beautiful baby too. 1910, that was the year you was born. The same year Teddy Roosevelt come back from Africa.

HENNIE. Gee, Pop, you're such a funny guy.

MYRON. He was a boisterous man, Teddy. Good night. (*He exits, paring apple.*)

RALPH. When I look at him, I'm sad. Let me die like a dog, if I can't get more from life.

HENNIE. Where?

RALPH. Right here in the house! My days won't be for nothing. Let Mom have the dough. I'm twenty-two and kickin'! I'll get along. Did Jake die for us to fight about nickels? No! "Awake and sing," he said. Right here he stood and said it. The night he died, I saw it like a thunderbolt! I saw he was dead and I was born! I swear to God, I'm one week old! I want the whole city to hear it—fresh blood, arms. We got 'em. We're glad we're living.

MOE. I wouldn't trade you for two pitchers and an outfielder. Hold the fort!

RALPH. So long.

MOE. So long.

(*They go and* RALPH *stands full and strong in the doorway seeing them off as the curtain slowly falls.*)

CURTAIN

HERE COME THE CLOWNS
Philip Barry

Here Come the Clowns was first presented by Eddie Dowling at the Booth Theatre in New York City on December 5, 1938. It was directed by Robert Milton, and the setting was designed by John Koenig.

WALTER	James Hagan	DAN CLANCY	Eddie Dowling
MAJOR ARMSTRONG	Jerry Austin	JIM MARBLE	Frank Gaby
JOHN DICKINSON	Russell Collins	GERT MARBLE	Hortense Alden
MA SPEEDY	Ralph Bunker	MAX PABST	Leo Chalzel
CONNIE RYAN	Madge Evans	FREDDIE BALLANTINE	A. H. Van Buren
NORA CLANCY	Doris Dudley	LEW COOPER	Thomas Palmer
VAL GURNEY	Bertram Thorn	FAY FARREL	Eve March

The play takes place in an American city on a Saturday night in late March, several years ago. The action is continuous, beginning at about eleven o'clock in the Back Room of Ma Speedy's Café des Artistes, where it concludes two hours later. In the intervals between acts no time is presumed to have elapsed.

Copyright 1937 by Philip Barry and Ellen S. Barry. Published by Coward-McCann, Inc. Used by permission.

CAUTION: Professionals and amateurs are hereby warned that *Here Come the Clowns*, being fully protected under the copyright law of the United States of America, the British Empire, including the Dominion of Canada, and all other countries of the Copyright Union, is subject to royalty. All rights, including professional, amateur, motion picture, recitation, lecturing, public reading, radio broadcasting, and the rights of translation into foreign languages, are strictly reserved. Particular emphasis is laid on the question of readings, permission for which must be secured from the author's agent in writing. All inquiries should be addressed to the author's agent, Harold Freedman, 101 Park Avenue, New York City.

In previous volumes of the *Best American Plays* series, it was my pleasure to present the bright and genial side of Philip Barry's playwriting career. No American playwright has excelled Barry as a cultivated humorist and mild satirist since he made his Broadway debut in 1923 with the production of the light comedy *You and I*. With *Paris Bound, Holiday, The Animal Kingdom*, and *The Philadelphia Story*, plays produced with considerable success between the years 1927 and 1939, Barry won an honorable place in the professional theatre. But it became increasingly apparent that he was not content to be considered as a contriver of clever comedies. He had serious matters close to his heart and tried to express them in *Hotel Universe* (1930), a play concerned with contemporary neuroticism and disorientation, as well as in several minor plays such as *John* and *The Joyous Season*. The place of evil and suffering in a world ruled by the Christian God agitated this author of sophisticated and modish plays up to the time of his death in 1949.

Here Come the Clowns is without question Philip Barry's masterpiece in the serious vein he tried to cultivate virtually from the beginning of his career as a specialist in the comedy of manners. In it he managed to maintain a necessary balance between *mystique* and realism, morality and milieu, allegorical abstraction and individualization. If *Here Come the Clowns* is a morality play in representing the familiar conflict between good and evil, it is also imaginative drama. One half of its premise is distinctively original in the theatre, consisting of the mordant speculation that God may have lost the war in heaven (*War in Heaven* is the title of the novel by Barry that contains the groundwork for the play) and that ever since then the shrewd Devil has been masquerading as God in order to confuse and betray mankind. The second and less original half of the premise is that it is up to Man to surmount misfortune or evil with his good will and courage. But more absorbing in the theatre is the actual working out of the action, especially the deviltry of the illusionist Max Pabst.

The nihilism of the author, which is more dramatically impressive than his optimistic idealism, produces varieties of conflict and revelation unusual in the American theatre. If the abstract statements in the last act fail to yield gratification in direct proportion to the author's ambition to attain to positive faith (the achievement, I believe, declines into cloudy affirmations and cliché), it cannot be said that the play as a whole is abstract. Applying the term allegory to the play scarcely does justice to the complexity that accompanies the author's simplification of the issue.

Philip Barry died on December 2, 1949, at the age of fifty-three, leaving behind a reflective comedy *Second Threshold*, which was completed and revised by his close friend Robert Sherwood. Presented on Broadway with moderate success in 1951, it represented both sides of his temperament and productivity, the comic and the serious. This graceful writer, an alumnus of Yale, from which he was graduated in 1919, a student in George Pierce Baker's Workshop 47 at Harvard (1921-22), an aspirant to the diplomatic service, and altogether a gentleman to the manner born, would have been most gratified if he had succeeded as a philosophical playwright. He had the mind, the mood, and the need for realizing himself in the somber vein. He nearly did so in *Hotel Universe* and in *Here Come the Clowns*, to which the New York reviewers brought so much good will that they came twice to the 1938 Eddie Dowling production and revised their opinion upward after a second viewing of the play.

Many years later, first in 1954 and then in 1960, they again brought respect to the play and derived a special satisfaction, albeit not an unqualified one, when it was given off-Broadway productions. Brooks Atkinson in 1960 could qualify his regard for the work with penetrating sentences: "The symbolism is intricate and elusive. Or perhaps the questions Mr. Barry asks are unanswerable, at least in terms of the workaday world. They need larger frames of reference than the personal experiences of the rather commonplace characters in this play." But " it does look

deep into the human heart, and the things it sees there are pitiful and moving,"
Mr. Atkinson added. Although time had not improved the play for him, he felt
that "of the theatre's lost causes, this is one of the most endearing." But two revivals
in New York and numerous little theatre productions throughout the country do
not constitute an entirely "lost" cause.

ACT ONE

MA SPEEDY'S CAFÉ DES ARTISTES *is a long, narrow building extending from the corner of Front Street and Vine halfway down the block to the stage-alley of James Concannon's Globe Theater, of which it is a structurally integral part.*

The Back Room is MA SPEEDY'S *special and secret pride. There is a miniature stage set into the back wall, flanked on either side by a small booth, on the same level. Red curtains, which pull from the side, now partially cover the stage. The booths can be used as dressing rooms when occasion demands, also by pulling curtains across them. The artists are given to trying out new acts here in the presence of their critical fellows and sometimes, when the spirit moves, spontaneous entertainments take place. From the booth at left a small, steep staircase mounts to a narrow balcony which stretches the length of that side of the room and leads into the dance hall which occupies the upstairs front of the building. In addition to the tables in the booths, there are two other tables set on ground level in each corner of the room, and one in the center, facing the stage.*

In the left wall there are two doors, the large one giving access to the restaurant, the smaller swinging one leading directly to pantry and kitchen. Opposite them is the private entrance from the alley, available only to the sacred and special few. It is after the show on a Saturday night in late March and the little lamps on the tables are lighted and the gas log on the alley-side aglow, making the room quite cozy and inviting. In the booth at the right sits MAJOR ARMSTRONG, *a copy of the then current "Billboard" propped up before his face. This, and the long, checkered tablecloth almost completely hide him from view. Certainly no one not knowing him could be aware of the cushion upon which he sits.* JOHN DICKINSON, *also alone, occupies the opposite booth. A siphon and glass stand upon the table before him and his head is down upon his folded arms.*

The door from the alley has been cautiously opened not more than six inches. WALTER, *the waiter, stands there looking out, one hand securely grasping the door knob, the other flat on his flank, holding his apron down against the wind which blows up the alley on March nights such as this one. He speaks quietly to the two dim figures who stand in the half-light beyond the door.*

WALTER. I'm sorry, ladies. You'll have to go to the front entrance. This is private.

(*A woman's voice, husky, pleasing, replies from outside the door.*)

CONNIE. I know—but it was Mr. Gurney who sent us. He said just to mention his name.

WALTER. I'm sorry, ladies, but Mr. Gurney would have to be with you.

(*Another woman's voice, frail, lighter, is heard.*)

NORA. You know me—I've been here lots of times.

WALTER. All the same, he'd have to be with you.

CONNIE. He'll be along in a minute. He and Mr. Ballantine are just finishing counting up.

WALTER. I'm sorry, but it's the rules. You'll have to wait for him in the front.

NORA. Come along, Connie. I'm all right.

CONNIE. Like fun you are. You need something and you need it quick. (*Then again to the waiter.*) Look, whatever your name is, it's raining. Please, will you?

WALTER. You'll have to go around to the front. Just back down the alley and around. This room is strictly reserved for the artists from the Globe.

CONNIE. But I tell you it was Val Gurney himself, who—

WALTER. No one can come in without their private key or else accompanied.

NORA. Come along, Connie.

CONNIE. But she's sick, I tell you! She's had a shock. She's all in. She needs something. She needs something right away.

WALTER. You must of made a mistake. This is no Speak. We don't serve a thing here. This is Ma Speedy's Café des Artistes, and strictly within the—

CONNIE. Listen! Tell Ma Speedy for me that Connie Ryan, head usher at the Globe, is here with her sister who's had a shock!

WALTER. I'm sorry, ladies. The proprietor is in the front. You'll have to ask there.—And *strictly* within the law. (*He closes the door and waits a moment, his hand still on the knob, until he is sure they have gone. Then he moves to the booth nearest him and inquires cheerfully:*) What'll it be, Major Armstrong?

(*The voice that replies from behind "The Billboard" has its own peculiar quality.*)

THE MAJOR. A bottle of the Canadian ale, if you please.

WALTER. The Molson's?

THE MAJOR. The Molson's.

(WALTER *scratches upon his pad and moves toward the kitchen door. He is about to pass the second booth when the figure within it stirs and speaks.*)

DICKINSON. Wait. (WALTER *stops and turns.* DICKINSON *slowly raises his head and drops both hands upon the table from the elbows. Then he lifts his face, smiling slightly, all like a machine capable of but one motion at a time. There are forty years in the face, every one of them, every day, every minute.*) What's the prodigious rush?

WALTER. No rush, Mr. Dickinson, no rush at all.

DICKINSON. Another double rye.

(WALTER *hesitates an instant.*)

WALTER. Are you sure?

DICKINSON. Certainly I'm sure.

THE MAJOR. Also a small sandwich. Any kind.

(*He lowers the paper from before his face, and the great head with its thin crest of white hair is for the first time visible.*)

WALTER. You know Ma don't want us serving food in here, Major.

(*So far as he can,* THE MAJOR *draws himself erect upon his bench. The patient eyes grow larger under their shaggy brushes. The fine, bony beak of a nose widens slightly with the intake of breath.*)

THE MAJOR. And you know I can't go in there and be stared at. Tell Ma who it's for.

WALTER. If you say so, Major.

THE MAJOR. Any kind but cheese.

WALTER. I'll see what they have on hand.

DICKINSON. And don't be so damned officious.

WALTER. Ma expects us to exercise discretion, in the cases of—

DICKINSON. Exercise it outside.

(WALTER *lowers his head, crosses and pivots through the swinging door. For a moment the two men sit staring out in front of them from their opposite cubicles, without speech. Finally, without turning his head,* THE MAJOR *addresses* DICKINSON.)

THE MAJOR. That must have been Clancy's wife at the alley door.

DICKINSON. So I gathered.

THE MAJOR. Then she must have been in the theater when it happened.

DICKINSON. Ask me the three worst

weeks in show-business—

THE MAJOR. Three—let me see. Are there three?

DICKINSON. Yes: the week before Christmas, Holy Week, and Naomi and her Violin.

THE MAJOR. Very good. Very good indeed.

DICKINSON.—So they combine two of them and wonder what happens to business. They run in a number like Naomi and then tell me I don't know how to handle the publicity. Will you tell me how to get space for a female frog with a fiddle?

THE MAJOR. Will you tell me what we can do about Clancy?

DICKINSON. I wonder what it was that hit that crazy stagehand?

THE MAJOR. Clancy's not crazy, John.

DICKINSON. He gave a good imitation of it, stopping the show that way.

THE MAJOR. It was the last number—and it was only Cooper and Farrel.

DICKINSON. A swell world. A swell job all around.

THE MAJOR. Poor Clancy.

DICKINSON.—But the nerve of the guy, disappearing for a year, nobody knows where the hell to or at, then coming back out of the blue and right on stage in the middle of a turn and asking for someone!—Who, for God's sake?

THE MAJOR. His wife, maybe.

DICKINSON. No—he said "Sir."—*I* thought maybe Gurney.

THE MAJOR. He could have gone straight to the box-office.

DICKINSON. The house-manager?

THE MAJOR. He saw Ballantine coming through from the front and never blinked, even.

DICKINSON. Damned if I know, then.

THE MAJOR. All those misfortunes, one after the other: I guess things just got to happening too fast for him.

DICKINSON. He was a good mascot for the Globe, but he was a bum one for himself, all right.

THE MAJOR. He was always very religious: I hope it helps him.

DICKINSON. The poor dope—the poor, bewildered dope. I was there backstage a year ago when the baby-spot came loose and caught him in the eye. It wasn't a week since his kid died. And then, as if that wasn't enough, that prize of a wife of his—well, as I say, it's a fine, pretty world.

THE MAJOR. I'll never forget his white face tonight, staring out over those foot-lights.

DICKINSON. What I'll never forget is what that whoozis—that swine of an illusionist—what he did afterwards.

THE MAJOR. "Max" something—Max Pabst.

DICKINSON. Pabst—that's it. He looked familiar somehow.

THE MAJOR. I was so surprised when he appeared that way.

DICKINSON. I could have killed him. I could have blown him right out of his upper box. (*He half-rises, leans forward upon his table, assumes a bland expression and mimics the voice of a man speaking with a Middle European accent.*) "I wonder—I wonder could it be me—simple Max Pabst—for whom that poor, unfortunate stagehand was just now looking?" (*And sinks back into his chair again.*) God! Anything for a cheap effect these days.

THE MAJOR. It seems so, doesn't it?

(*The door from the restaurant opens and a short, stout, pink-and-white man comes in, carrying two vases of white carnations. He wears a dinner-coat, which drapes gracefully over his curves. He has very small feet and rotates upon them a trifle as he walks. His face is genial and kindly under its crown of wavy, unconvincingly reddish hair, and for all the fact that his features are now somewhat blurred by fat, one can see that he has once been handsome in his way. This is* MA SPEEDY *and he is in an expansive mood. He cries out in his musical voice:*)

SPEEDY. Good evening, John! Good evening, Major!

THE MAJOR. Good evening, Ma.

DICKINSON. Hello, Ma.

(WALTER *comes in with the drinks.* SPEEDY *places the carnations on the tables and stands off to view the effect.*)

SPEEDY. Everything all right?

DICKINSON. Oh, just hunky-dory.

(WALTER *sets a glass, a bottle, and a small sandwich before* THE MAJOR.)

SPEEDY. I wanted to see who was here. A couple of ladies just came in the front, and—do you remember our old friend Clancy, the stagehand?

DICKINSON. We certainly do.

SPEEDY. Well, it seems that one of them's his wife. Women and their nerves! I gather he's turned up again—I mean Clancy.

DICKINSON. He certainly has.

SPEEDY. The dance team, Cooper and Farrel—they just told me as they were going upstairs. I've never heard the like. Who do you suppose it is that he's after? Why wouldn't he at least say the name? You don't suppose he'll come wandering in here, do you?

DICKINSON. I doubt it.

SPEEDY. His wife needs a little refresh-ment, her sister says. Shock.—And I wondered if you'd mind them coming in here for a moment?

DICKINSON. Not me. I'll move in with The Major. (*He moves from his booth to* THE MAJOR'S.)

SPEEDY. I know they won't be long.

DICKINSON. For all me, they can both get stewed to the eyes.

THE MAJOR. Give us the cribbage set, Walter.

WALTER. Cribbage.

DICKINSON. A dollar says I'm going to beat the little pants off you.

THE MAJOR. We'll see about that.

(WALTER *returns with the game.*)

DICKINSON. Privacy, Walter.

(WALTER *draws a red curtain partially around the booth, making* THE MAJOR *and* DICKINSON *invisible from the table near the restaurant door, through which* SPEEDY *now calls:*) This way, ladies! Right in here, please! (*He glances about him.*)—Cozy. Where will one find a cozier nook?

(NORA CLANCY *and* CONNIE RYAN *come in from the restaurant.* NORA *is slight and frail, somewhere in her pretty, middle twenties.* CONNIE *is two years older, without* NORA'S *cheap refinement of feature, but curiously vital and attractive. Her half-open coat reveals the blue uniform of a Globe usher. Her low, husky voice is full of strength and self-confidence.*)

CONNIE. Thanks, Mr. Speedy.

NORA. Yes—thanks, I'm sure.

(SPEEDY *draws out chairs for them, flutters over them.*)

SPEEDY. Just sit yourselves doon and order what you like, only no food, please. Food in the front, sandwiches to write home about, a grilled chicken that would break your heart. (NORA *and* CONNIE *seat themselves.* SPEEDY *claps his hands together.*) Walter!—Ask the ladies what they will have, Walter.

WALTER. Yes, ladies?

CONNIE. A beer for me and a double brandy for her.

WALTER. With seltzer?

CONNIE. With plain water.

SPEEDY. Perfect. A perfect prescription for the nerves.—The really good brandy, Walter. (*He looks knowingly at* WALTER, *who marks on his pad, tucks his pencil behind his ear, and goes out into the pantry.*) We'll soon get the roses back into those pretty cheeks again!

NORA. Thanks. I guess I could use a couple.

SPEEDY. If anyone who comes in speaks to you, please don't mind. We're all just one big family here.

CONNIE. We won't mind. Come one, come all.

SPEEDY. It's really like a little club, you know—Ma Speedy's little nook for members of the N.V.A.—Artistes for Artistes, you know!

(*He purses his little mouth into an O and goes out again into the restaurant, whistling happily.* CONNIE *scrutinizes* NORA *intently.*)

CONNIE. Stop shaking.

NORA. I'm not shaking.

CONNIE. You are and you're a fool, Nora.

NORA. I—I can't help it.

CONNIE. Clancy couldn't have seen you way up there in the balcony. He couldn't possibly have.

NORA. It wasn't that.

CONNIE. Then what was it?

NORA. His voice. He—he acted so crazy.

CONNIE. You think it's Val that he's after, don't you?

NORA. I'm scared, Connie. I'm so scared.

CONNIE. You know he's gentle as a baby. You know he wouldn't lift a finger to you.

NORA. But Val—if he goes after Val—

CONNIE. He doesn't even know it was for Val you walked out on him! He doesn't know it was for anyone, the poor innocent.

NORA. He might of found out some way.

CONNIE. How could he have? He left town two days after. And that was months ago.

NORA. Someone might of wised him up—some busybody.

CONNIE. Go on—it's nothing but your own guilty conscience.

NORA. It was only while I was with him I had a guilty conscience.

CONNIE (*after a moment*). There are times I just don't get you at all.

NORA. We're different, that's all. We always have been.

CONNIE. I'll say we have.—But don't kid yourself that if Clancy's gone off his head it wasn't you who did it, because it was.

NORA. It was not! It was not!

CONNIE. All right, all right—calm yourself!—Anyway, I don't believe for a minute that he has.

NORA. He was always half nuts—half the time he didn't make sense at all.

CONNIE. You mean the kind of sense *you* could understand. You never had his imagination.

NORA. Oh my God—"imagination"!

CONNIE. You heard me.

NORA. I know I did. And I know how you've always stuck up for him, regardless.

CONNIE. Why shouldn't I have?—If ever a guy got a dirty deal from life *and* his wife—

NORA.—Why? Lots of people have accidents and lose their jobs and have a kid die on them and—

CONNIE.—*And* his wife, I said.

NORA. Maybe you should of married him instead.

CONNIE. Wha-at? (*She laughs shortly.*) Me marry Clancy? That's a good one. I should've sailed right up to him, I suppose. I should've said, "Mr. Clancy, I know you've got an eye for a pretty face, but I'm the girl for you, Mr. Clancy. Plain Connie Ryan, good and dependable."—Yes: I wouldn't've married him if he'd offered himself on a silver platter. Not if he'd come to me on his knees, I wouldn't've. Me married to Clancy! That really *is* to laugh.

NORA. Maybe yes, maybe no. At least you could of plowed through all those foolish books with him and talked big talk till two in the morning on one glass of beer about God knows what. And of course *you'd* never of wanted to go to dances and things.

CONNIE. Listen: I like dances just as much as you do! Clancy likes them too—if he goes with someone who sticks to him and doesn't roll her eyes around like a couple of hoops.

NORA. Tell me one thing: how'd you like to be married to someone who made

540 PHILIP BARRY

you feel mean all the time?

CONNIE. Nobody could me.

NORA.—When all you wanted was a little fun every other year or so.

CONNIE. Show me somebody funnier than Dan Clancy when he wanted to be.

NORA. I guess he just didn't want to be, with me: I guess that was it.

CONNIE. *I* never had to wait around for the laughs with him.

NORA. It's just what I'm telling you: *you're* the one who should of—

CONNIE. Here's your drink. (WALTER *swings in from the pantry and up to them with their orders.* CONNIE *fingers her purse.*) How much, Old Willie the Watchdog?

WALTER. Sixty and twenty-five: eighty-five.

CONNIE. He can count.

NORA. Val will settle for them when he comes.

CONNIE (*to* WALTER). Mr. Gurney is doing the honors. Is that all right?

WALTER. Sure thing. Why not?

(*He moves to the other table and wipes it off, around the vase of white carnations that stands upon it.* NORA *takes a swallow of her drink.*)

NORA. It's strong.

CONNIE. You surprise me.

NORA.—If only I could get him to hate me. If I could just simply get him to hate me.

CONNIE. There's none of it in him— not for anyone.

(NORA *finishes her glass, then sits staring down into it, turning it in her fingers.*)

NORA. I don't know why a fellow like Clancy—a stagehand who never made more than forty-eight a week at the most—I don't know why *he* should be so important, anyway.

(CONNIE *looks at her over her beer.*)

CONNIE. I don't know either. I wonder why he is?

(WALTER *has glanced up with sudden interest at the mention of* CLANCY's *name.*)

WALTER. Is Clancy back?

CONNIE. He's back.

WALTER. How is he?

CONNIE. Fine. They call him Lucky Dan he gets so many of the breaks.

(*A key is turned in the alley-door and* VAL GURNEY *comes in—a jaunty, tricked-out, sharp-featured little man of thirty. He sails his natty hat onto a hook on the wall, adjusts his cuffs, and makes directly for the table where* CONNIE *and* NORA *sit, and bends over* NORA, *who brightens at his approach.*)

GURNEY. Well, well. Well, well, well! —I see you're taking your tonic, Baby.

NORA. Hello, Val.

CONNIE. I thought you were so well known here.

GURNEY. You seem to have got in all right.

CONNIE. Just like a couple of pianos through a transom.

GURNEY. Exclusive, is what Ma's is. (*He seats himself with them, takes one of* NORA's *hands in his, and calls across his shoulder to the waiter:*) Make mine a Scotch highball, Walter m'boy!

(WALTER *continues his polishing.*)

WALTER. One Scotch.

GURNEY (*to* NORA). Now don't you worry, sweetheart. Nothing's going to happen to you.

NORA. I'm all right now.

GURNEY. There's no way Clancy could've got onto the fact that we've been friends, that I can see.

CONNIE. "Friends"!

GURNEY. Now sister! Don't put your oar in again. Fingers out of other people's pies, sister. Little girls get burned.

CONNIE. You're disgusting. You're just plain disgusting.

GURNEY. And don't try to insult me. I been insulted by experts. (*Then, to* NORA.) You get upset too easy, dearie. It couldn't've been me he was looking for. Not old Val—not me. He'd've come right to my little cage in the lobby. Wouldn't he? Wouldn't he of?

NORA. I guess so—yes, I guess so.

CONNIE. And suppose he had?

GURNEY. Suppose not, sister, lest ye be supposed.

CONNIE (*to* NORA). How you can stand him!

NORA. If you don't like it, you know what you can do.

CONNIE. You said it. (*She pushes her glass away and rises from the table.*)

GURNEY (*to* NORA).—Clancy don't know a thing, not one thing. Take my word for it. Walter m'boy—another for the lady!

WALTER. One Scotch, one brandy.

(CONNIE *has crossed to the alley-door.*)

CONNIE. I suppose it's all right to go out this way?

WALTER. Absolutely, lady, absolutely.

CONNIE. Funny, the difference between two sides of a door.

(WALTER *moves toward the pantry.* CON-
NIE *opens the door. Halfway through it, she
stops and listens up the alley, then re-enters,
closing the door behind her, and moves swiftly
back to the table.* GURNEY *is reassuring*
NORA.)

GURNEY. Baby—Baby!

NORA. I'm all right, Val—I'm all
right. The only thing that worries me is
—oh, to hell with it.

(GURNEY *glances up at* CONNIE.)

GURNEY. What's up? Who asked for
an encore?

CONNIE. Get out. Get in there—
quick! Get into the front!

NORA. Oh my God, Val.

(NORA *rises,* GURNEY *after her.*)

GURNEY. We'll take our drinks in the
front, Walter.

WALTER (*going out*).—Isn't allowed.

CONNIE. Go *on*!

NORA. I got to have another drink.

GURNEY (*to* CONNIE). Will you keep
him here?

CONNIE. I don't guarantee anything.

NORA.—I just simply got to.

(GURNEY *pilots* NORA *toward the restaurant door.*)

GURNEY. Listen, Honey, don't worry:
there's something on the old hip. And
we'll just sit ourselves right down and
get outside of a nice welsh rabbit, or
what would the lady like?

NORA. No, no—I don't want anything
to eat! All I want is—you keep him here,
Connie—you hear me?

GURNEY.—Now look, Honey: nobody's going to bust up Val Gurney's
Saturday night snack with his own girl,
believe you me—Clancy or nobody else.
Who does he think he is, anyhow?

(*They go out into the restaurant.* CONNIE
*reseats herself at the table with her back to the
alley-door and pulls her glass toward her.
Again a key turns in the lock and a boyish,
discontented-looking young woman,* GERT
MARBLE, *enters, followed by* JIM MARBLE, *a
lanky individual of about forty, and* DAN
CLANCY. CLANCY *is probably somewhere in
his middle thirties, but with such lines of
fatigue in his face, such anxiety in his fearsome
eyes, as to make any conjecture as to his actual
age irrelevant and beside the point. One of*
MARBLE'S *arms is about his shoulders as they
enter, and in the crook of the other he carries a
bulky object in a large canvas bag, like a
duffle-bag.* MARBLE *is talking very fast.*

MARBLE.—And Frank's got the mak-
ings of a great dramatic artist, see? And
he's a personal friend of mine, but what
he don't know about business would fill
a book, see? And they're trying to sign
him for a series of twenty short subjects,
so I go to the Grossett office with him,
see? (MARBLE *puts the bag on the piano
bench.* GERT *lights a cigarette and looks about
her, distastefully.* MARBLE *continues to talk
without pause.* CLANCY *sits staring out in
front of him, barely listening.*)—And Jack
Grossett himself, he starts to roll it out.—
And—

GERT. *This* dump. Why do we do it?

MARBLE.—And I say, "Talking pictures my eye. Who wants to hear
shadows talk?" And he pounds the
table and shouts, "They want sound.
The public's crying for sound!"
"Wrong," I say. "They don't know
what they want till we give 'em it."
"Just what I say," he says. "And we're
going to give 'em sound." (GERT *rises
from the table. He turns to her.*)—Where
you going, Gert?

GERT. Give me some chips.

MARBLE. What for?

GERT. Food. I'm empty as a drum.

(MARBLE *takes two bills from a roll and
gives them to her.*)

MARBLE. Don't be long.

GERT. You bet. (*She passes* CLANCY,
prods him affectionately.) You're all right,
Clancy.

MARBLE (*to* CLANCY).—Where was I?

CLANCY. What?

MARBLE. I say, where was I?

CLANCY. You were talking.

(GERT *goes out into restaurant.* MARBLE
settles back again.)

MARBLE. I remember!—"We are
not interested in your opinions, Mr.
Marble," he says. "But in the case of
your friend Frank here—" "So long as
I'm taking care of him," I say, "he's
going to stay in vaudeville." "Then he'd
better get a new nurse," he says, "because vaudeville is not long for this
world."—Can you beat it?

CLANCY. Can you beat it? (*He shifts
his position slightly and looks around him.
His eyes fix upon* CONNIE'S *back at the table
opposite him.* MARBLE *undoes the strings of
the black bag and draws* THE DUMMY *out of
it; he folds the bag into a cushion for* THE
DUMMY *and places it on the piano bench.*)

MARBLE.—There you are, Frank, my

friend. Now mind you behave yourself.

(THE DUMMY's *grotesque mouth flaps open and shut*.)

THE DUMMY. God, how you love to hear yourself talk!

(MARBLE *pushes him in the face*.)

MARBLE. Insect!

(THE DUMMY *collapses face-down upon the piano bench*. CLANCY *pronounces the name slowly, directly at* CONNIE's *back*.)

CLANCY. Connie Ryan.

(CONNIE *raises her head, without turning it*.)

CONNIE. Hello, Dan Clancy. (*Then she turns and eyes him evenly*.) You don't seem too glad to see me.

(CLANCY's *accent has not breadth enough for a brogue. It is only through a faintly musical intonation and an occasional odd locution that his Irish reveals itself*.)

CLANCY. I'm glad to see you.

CONNIE. You look thin.

CLANCY. You ought to see me sideways. How's Nora?

CONNIE. She's all right.

CLANCY. What's she living by? Is she working again?

CONNIE. She is.

CLANCY. There wasn't much she could do.

CONNIE. How have you been?

CLANCY.—She's flighty, you know. Nora's flighty.

CONNIE. You're telling me—who brought her up from a baby?

(THE DUMMY *makes a snoring sound*.)

MARBLE.—Disagreeable little mutt. When will you learn manners?

THE DUMMY. Shut up and let me sleep.

CONNIE (*to* CLANCY).—Tell me, how's it been going with yourself? I got to wondering about you once or twice, when I had a spare minute or two.

CLANCY. I've been all over the place.

CONNIE. So I heard tell, from the stage of the Globe tonight.

CLANCY. That was a bad thing I did.

CONNIE. Only for Cooper and Farrel— and they're young.

CLANCY. All the same, it was bad and ill-mannered, interrupting the show that way. But I was almost out of my senses, Connie.

CONNIE. And where are you now, would you say?

CLANCY. The sight of you brings me back into 'em. You're the real foul-weather friend, Connie.

CONNIE. You'll turn my head with your compliments.

CLANCY. I'm a queer duck, and there's no denying it.

CONNIE. Who is it you're after, Dan? Who've you been looking for? (CLANCY *looks away*.)—I only thought I might maybe give you a steer.

CLANCY. No, there's no one can do that.

CONNIE. You certainly got all the bum breaks there were.

CLANCY. You have to take what comes.

CONNIE.—What they call "resignation."

CLANCY. They do, and they call it well.

CONNIE. If I were you, I'd get good and sore, believe me I would.

(*Suddenly* CLANCY *flares up*.)

CLANCY. Why should I? God damn it, it's the will of God! (WALTER *comes swinging in from the pantry*. CLANCY *glances at him*.) Hello, Walter.

WALTER. I heard you were back. I'm that glad to see you.

CLANCY. It's good to be back.

WALTER. What'll it be?

MARBLE. Whisky for Clancy, whisky for me.

CLANCY. Thanks, Jim, I don't want it.

MARBLE. How do you know till you've tried?—Who's in the booth there, Walter? Anyone thirsty?

WALTER. It's Mr. Dickinson and The Major.

(MARBLE *sets his mouth and the next instant from the inside of the booth, the yapping of a small dog is heard. The curtain is pulled roughly aside and* DICKINSON *is seen peering under the table*. MARBLE *laughs*.

MARBLE. Look out—he bites!

(DICKINSON *looks out at him*.)

DICKINSON. Why, you low-life clown. You dirty low-life clown. (*He comes down from the booth*.)—And who's this guy with you, with a face like the Coast of Kerry?

CLANCY. Hello, John. (*He takes* DICKINSON's *hand*.) How are you?

DICKINSON. Drunk—and mean to get drunker. How's it with you?

CLANCY. I'm fine. Why shouldn't I be?

DICKINSON. Well, don't get tough about it. Who's the mystery-man you're trailing around theaters and such?

CLANCY. If I told you, you still wouldn't know.

(THE MAJOR *calls from his booth.*)

THE MAJOR. Welcome home to you, Clancy!

CLANCY. Thank you, Major. Welcome to yourself.

DICKINSON. Drinks all around. This is a celebration.

THE MAJOR. Ale for me, if you don't mind.

MARBLE. Two. Gert likes ale.

CONNIE. Three—one for me. That is, if I'm included.

(WALTER *goes out into the pantry.*)

WALTER.—Got 'em.

CLANCY. You are all of you acquainted with Connie Ryan, my wife's sister?

MARBLE. The fair Connie? I know her well. (*Again he bends over* THE DUMMY.) And surely you remember my unpleasant little friend, Frank Frenzy?—Manners, Insect!

(THE DUMMY *sits bolt upright, grinning.*)

THE DUMMY. Hello, Connie! How's tricks?

CONNIE. Hello, Frank! Fine!—How's with you?

THE DUMMY. Couldn't be better. (*He winks broadly.*)—So long as I get my liquor.

(*Again* MARBLE *pushes him in the face but this time he remains upright.*)

CLANCY.—And John Dickinson.

DICKINSON. How are you, Connie?

CONNIE. How-de-do, Mr. Dickinson.

DICKINSON. Wearing the usher's uniform to bed these nights, are you?

CONNIE. I—I came out in a sort of a hurry.

(CLANCY *gestures toward the booth.*)

CLANCY.—Major Armstrong, Miss Connie Ryan.

CONNIE. Very pleased to meet you, I'm sure, Major.

(THE MAJOR *lets himself down from his cushion upon the bench, is lost to view for a moment as he comes under the table, and then emerges again from behind the tablecloth, the cushion under his arm. His tiny form—for now it is seen that* THE MAJOR *is a dwarf— negotiates the two steps to the floor-level, and stumps with dignity up to* CONNIE *and offers her a hand.*)

THE MAJOR. The pleasure is mine, Miss Ryan.

CONNIE. I and the rest of the girls've enjoyed your act so much this week.

THE MAJOR. I am sincerely glad.

MARBLE.—Always a favorite with the ladies, eh, Major? Tom Thumb the Second.

THE MAJOR. Do you know, they had General Tom Thumb in wax in Madame Tussaud's Museum in London for many years?

MARBLE. You don't say!

CLANCY. Did they, now!

THE MAJOR. He stood there among other world notables, such as Napoleon and Nelson, and was the object of much interested comment.

(DICKINSON *takes the cushion from him and puts it upon a chair.*)

DICKINSON. Let's all sit. (*He lifts* THE MAJOR *from the floor and places him upon the cushion.*) For God's sake, let us sit upon our bums and tell sad stories of the death of kings.

(*All, with the exception of* CLANCY, *seat themselves, all friends together, a new liveliness in their talk.*)

THE MAJOR. Don't misquote The Bard, John. That's not allowed even to scholars like you.

DICKINSON. Scholars and scholarliness be damned together. Where are the drinks?

MARBLE. You drink too much, see?

DICKINSON. Or not enough—I was never sure. Clancy, I see in your eye that at last you agree with me it's one louse of a world.

CLANCY. It can bite, can't it, John?

THE MAJOR.—"The Best of All Possible Worlds," a book I know says.

DICKINSON. For what? For whom?

MARBLE. I guess we all of us have our troubles.

CLANCY. That's right—and must be resigned to 'em.

DICKINSON. A beautiful virtue, resignation.

CLANCY. That's right.

DICKINSON. Horse feathers.

THE MAJOR.—Of course, the main thing is how we take them. That's where philosophy comes in.

DICKINSON. Where philosophy comes in, is where I go out.

CLANCY. If you were as hard as you think you are, John, they'd have split you up long since, and used you for coffin-wood.

DICKINSON. I wish they had. It must be the rat-holes.

CONNIE. This is a real gay party. This is certainly an evening out. When do the

Australian Wood Choppers come on?

(*Again* MARBLE *sets his lips and from above them a falsetto voice is heard singing:*)

THE VOICE. "O dry those tears, O calm those fears. Life was not made for sorrow."

(THE DUMMY *twists his head around and looks up.* CONNIE *exclaims admiringly.*)

CONNIE. It's wonderful the way you do that, Mr. Marble.

MARBLE. I'm a very wonderful fellow.

(CLANCY *glances toward the balcony.*)

CLANCY. What's that other sound I hear, like an orchestra?

(*He moves toward the restaurant.* CONNIE *follows him swiftly.*)

CONNIE. Don't go in there! (*He stops. She explains:*)—They've had music upstairs since the first of the year. They dance there, eleven to one.

(CLANCY *speaks without interest.*)

CLANCY. Do they, now.

CONNIE (*after a moment*). Dan—

CLANCY. What?

CONNIE. Do something for me?

CLANCY. What?

CONNIE. Will you promise to do it?

CLANCY. I will if I can.

CONNIE. You'll really promise?

CLANCY. If I—

CONNIE. No "ifs"!

CLANCY. Then I will.

CONNIE. Come up to the hall and dance a dance with me!

CLANCY. Oh no, Connie—what are you talking about?

CONNIE. You promised.

CLANCY. But I've forgotten how. My feet wouldn't—

CONNIE. You've not! It's not a thing, once known, you forget. It's like swimming or riding a bike—it stays with you. (*She holds out both hands to him.*) Come on —one dance, like in the old days.

CLANCY. God help me, I'll try.

(*She snatches a white carnation from the vase on the table, breaks the stem, and fixes the flower in his lapel.*)

CONNIE. There! Now you look more like your old jaunty self!

(CLANCY *gazes down at the flower.*)

CLANCY. That's an odd thing. *He* always used to wear one, didn't he?

CONNIE. Who did?

CLANCY. A man I know. (*Then his eyes look off into the far distance, across years, across waters.*) Carnations—my father used to raise them in the gardens of Roche's Hotel in Glengariff, where he worked. And my mother told me once the white one was the flower of God, God bless her. And we had a lemon tree, too. They grow there, you know. There's a warm current passes the coast. Figs, as well—even a palm now and then. My, how that lemon tree used to smell of a morning! It was glorious. It was like heaven. (*He stops and passes his hand over his face.*)—And still I was always wanting to go to Connemara. I never got there, I don't know why. The good Lord willed it otherwise, I suppose.

THE MAJOR. It was your father who wore the carnations?

CLANCY. No. Never him. They were too dear, and must be kept for the table. But a man I know did—and you know him, too.

(*A moment's silence. Then* CONNIE *laughs lightly and slips her arm through his.*)

CONNIE. You and your lemon tree and carnations! Come along—you're daydreaming! (*She leads him to the stairway.*) Just remember one thing, dancing— they don't whirl about as they did. (*They mount the stairs.*)

CLANCY. What is it they do, then?

CONNIE. You'll see! It always came natural to you, Dan! Once on the floor, you were like a man inspired.

CLANCY. Me grandfather claimed he introduced the waltz into Ireland.

(*They are moving along the balcony now.*)

CONNIE. (*mocking him*).—Me grandmother claimed she introduced Irish to your grandfather.

CLANCY. The language or the whisky?

CONNIE. Both!—Will you promise to whirl me, Dan?

CLANCY. That I will—like a top on a table!

(*There is a burst of music as they pass through the door and into the dance hall.* MARBLE *glances up, then takes a deep breath, and settles down into his chair again. He replaces* THE DUMMY *in the bag and sets the bag upon the floor at his feet.*)

MARBLE. Well, I guess if he can dance—

DICKINSON.—And if he can whistle very loud in the dark.

MARBLE. He's like a man that's been hit over the head, isn't he?

DICKINSON. Well, so he has—and I'd hate to count the times.

(*Unnoticed by them the door on the balcony*

again opens and a FIGURE *appears there: a stoutish man of uncertain age, wearing a dark suit of foreign cut. His face is bland, and, in repose, curiously benevolent. What hair he has, is cropped short. He comes to the railing and stands there, looking out thoughtfully.* THE MAJOR *reflects:*)

THE MAJOR. It's true: *he* always did wear one.

DICKINSON. Who wore what?

THE MAJOR. I think I know now who it is Clancy wants to see—

DICKINSON. Who?

THE MAJOR. The Old Gentleman himself—the owner of the Globe, James Concannon.

MARBLE. Go on—nobody ever sees Concannon any more.

DICKINSON.—And very few in the past, did they?

THE MAJOR. Clancy did now and then. So did I. I think it's to him he would naturally turn. In fact, I don't believe I've ever known one human being to reverence another as Clancy does James Concannon.

DICKINSON. Concannon, my foot. (*He rises and moves to the little stage.*) I'll bet the dust is deep on that private staircase of his, the old fake. Let's have a look. I even doubt if he's here at all any more.

(*He opens the stage curtains wide.* MARBLE *calls after him:*)

MARBLE. Well, if he isn't, where is he?

DICKINSON. Ask Jack Grossett down in New York—he might tell you. Sure—just go right up to the door of Grossett Enterprises and say, "How come we don't see Mr. Concannon, since your Mr. Jack went out to get him?" (*He draws aside the spangled curtain which masks the brick wall at the back of the stage, and discloses a small door marked "*MR. CONCANNON. PRIVATE.*"*)—Locked tight. I thought so. Where *is* the old fake? I'd really like to know. Who runs things now, anyway? Don't tell me Ballantine!

THE MAJOR. Mr. Concannon is not a fake, John.—And I think Clancy came back tonight believing he'd be—

(THE FIGURE *on the balcony leans out and inquires in a low, precise voice with a Middle European accent.*)

THE FIGURE.—Or I wonder—I wonder could it be me, simple Max Pabst, for whom that poor, unfortunate fellow has been looking?

(DICKINSON *turns quickly and stares up at him.*)

DICKINSON. The great illusionist again, is it?—Listen: old bag of tricks, say that once more, and I'll—!

THE FIGURE.—So sorry to disturb.

MARBLE. Sit down, John.

(DICKINSON *reseats himself, muttering:*)

DICKINSON. What's he doing here tonight anyway? What's the point of arriving in town two days ahead of time? He doesn't go on until Monday, does he? Who ever heard of an Act blowing in on a Saturday? Anyhow, I swear to God I've seen him some place.

(THE FIGURE *on the balcony comes quietly along it to the stairs.* SPEEDY *re-enters from the restaurant, calling back after him.*)

SPEEDY. This way, gentlemen! Right in here, Professor Pabst! (MARBLE *brings a loose deck of cards from his pocket and shows them to* THE MAJOR *who nods. They go to the table in the booth at right of the little stage and begin to deal out cold hands.* DICKINSON *hunches his chair nearer to his table and picks up his drink again.* FREDDIE BALLANTINE *enters, a dapper little middle-aged man in a dinner coat, carrying an umbrella.* SPEEDY *cries out in surprise:*) But where's the Professor?

(BALLANTINE *turns and looks back into the restaurant.* THE FIGURE *coming down the stairs speaks very softly:*)

THE FIGURE. Here I am.

SPEEDY. Gracious! You're just everywhere at once, *you* are!

PABST. A little tour: I like to see things for myself. (*He looks around him.*) Pleasant—how pleasant—a charming setting. Anything could happen here—no?

SPEEDY.—This little nook is my pet, Professor!—*This* is the true Café des Artistes—isn't it, Freddie?

BALLANTINE. Absolutely.

PABST.—And a stage, also?

BALLANTINE. We've absolutely even rehearsed here at times.

(WALTER *re-enters.*)

SPEEDY. But it's chiefly for little informal entertainments—you know—just among ourselves, when the spirit moves us.

(WALTER *places drinks before the card-players.*)

DICKINSON. Thanks. It's about time.

SPEEDY (*to* PABST). Don't you think it's cozy?

PABST. Very.—Full of what-you-call-it—*gemütlichkeit.*

SPEEDY. Oh, I love that word! It's just the word for it!

PABST. Take it—take it for your own.

SPEEDY. "*Gemütlichkeit.*"

(*Ballantine draws out chairs at the other table.*)

BALLANTINE. His liquor's all right. I'll grant him that.

SPEEDY. Bring a bottle of the "Perfection," Walter. (*He explains.*) We're serving "Perfection" now. It's really quite good. (*He calls to the other table.*) Hello, fellows!—Got every little thing you want?

MARBLE. Sure thing.

THE MAJOR. Yes, indeed.

DICKINSON. And a couple we don't.

(WALTER *goes out.* SPEEDY *seats himself with* BALLANTINE *and* PABST.)

BALLANTINE. What a night! I never made such a long speech in my life.

PABST. But an explanation to the audience was indicated, was it not?

BALLANTINE. Just let Clancy try something like that again. Just once more.

SPEEDY. Poor Cooper and Farrel. I never heard of such a thing happening. (*He ponders a moment.*) Except once, I remember, at Keith's in Washington, a cat walked on stage right in the middle of my act. It was one of the worst ordeals I've ever gone through. I was in the middle of the Prayer from *La Tosca* and, you know, the House threatened to get quite out of hand.

PABST. I have no doubt.

SPEEDY. Well, sir, you know what I did? I held the top note as long as I could—(*He arches the fingers of one hand upon his bosom and elevates the other hand like a chalice. He throws back his head and in a shrill falsetto sings a line from the aria.*)—I can't get up there any more. Then I let —quite unexpectedly, you know—I let out a long "meaow" (*He demonstrates, and finds his lower register again.*) Well, sir, they loved it! They laughed with me, not at me. They were absolutely mine.

PABST. An inspiration—a most happy inspiration.

SPEEDY. Those were the days. Three years running, I was held over a second week at The Palace. I had a special curtain and drop of my own—a living mass of sequins. Harry Collins made my gowns. I traveled with six trunks and had thirty-two changes. All New York

was mad about me. I had a cigar named after me.

PABST. Those must, indeed, have been the days.

BALLANTINE. You should have stuck it out a little longer, Ma.

SPEEDY. I couldn't, Freddie. I simply couldn't. (*To* PABST.)—I don't know about in Europe, but here, in some way, the War changed the audience's attitude toward my kind of art. Well, sir, I saw the handwriting on the wall, as they say—so I just bought this little nest and settled down in it. In a way it was a relief: I could eat all I wanted to at last and see all my old friends as they came through and just sit back and let my figure go—and don't you think it's cute?—My little set-up here, I mean.

PABST. *Gemütlich.*

SPEEDY. *Ja—ganz gemütlich.* (WALTER *re-enters with drinks from the pantry, and* GERT *from the restaurant.*) That's right, Walter.—Good evening, Gert.

GERT. Hello, Ma.

(*She proceeds to the table in the booth and seats herself with* MARBLE *and* MAJOR *as* WALTER *places drinks before* SPEEDY, BALLANTINE, *and* PABST.)

SPEEDY.—The wife of the ventriloquist you saw tonight. She assists.

PABST. He was very good.

MARBLE (*to* GERT). Where've you been all this time?

GERT. I got to talking.—You know the kid I got the fan note from yesterday?

MARBLE. What about her?

GERT. She was in the Front—and guess what.

MARBLE. What?

GERT. She's spending next week in Syracuse too—with friends.

(MARBLE *slams down his cards.*)

MARBLE. The hell she is!

GERT. Why? What's the matter?

MARBLE. I'll show you what's the matter. I'll show her, too! See?

GERT. Is he drunk?

THE MAJOR. Would you like a hand?

GERT. Sure. All aces, please. (*She glances contemptuously at* MARBLE. *He picks up his cards again, still watching her under his eyelids. She murmurs:*) Try not to be more of a fool than God made you.

(*The game proceeds.* BALLANTINE *turns to* PABST, *who has been listening attentively to the altercation at the other table.*)

BALLANTINE. You haven't said how

you liked the rest of the bill.

PABST. On the whole, very much. Well selected and well arranged. I was particularly interested in the performance of the Irishman who afforded me such a what-you-call-it—good build-up—

BALLANTINE. Clancy. — Yes — some performance! Absolutely!

(DICKINSON *turns in his chair.*)

PABST. I think he is a natural comic.

DICKINSON. Horse feathers.

PABST. I beg your pardon?

DICKINSON. A comic, eh?—That's most discerning of you, I'm sure.

BALLANTINE. Come on over.—I want you to meet the Professor. (DICKINSON *makes his way to them a little too steadily.*) —Professor Max Pabst—Dickinson, our press man.

(PABST *rises and bows stiffly.*)

DICKINSON. How do you do, I'm sure.

BALLANTINE. He'll absolutely want to ask you a few questions for the Monday press.—Sit down, John.

(DICKINSON *and* PABST *seat themselves.* DICKINSON's *manner is definitely antagonistic.*)

DICKINSON. I must have caught your Act somewhere.

PABST. You have traveled much in Europe?

DICKINSON. No. Not any.

PABST. Then it is not possible.

DICKINSON. But you look familiar.

PABST. That is an impression I often give. It is part of my what-you-call—stock in trade.

DICKINSON.—Got the usual advance stuff with you, I suppose.

PABST. Unhappily no.

BALLANTINE. He came on in such a hurry. When La Paloma took sick in Detroit—

DICKINSON.—We were stuck for an Easter Week headliner, sure. But how'd we happen to get such a break as the Professor?

PABST. I was in the Grossett Offices in New York when the telegram came about the sudden illness of the Thinking Horse.

DICKINSON.—So you leaped right into La Paloma's shoes, eh?

PABST. On an impulse, I offered myself as substitute.

DICKINSON. There's something phoney about this. Maybe Jack Grossett did push Concannon out, back there when he thought he'd run vaudeville, north and south, east and west—himself, single-handed. Maybe he's had you here all along. Maybe, in fact, you're the present Concannon.

PABST. An amusing idea, but no.

DICKINSON. You and Ballantine aren't in cahoots, of course?

BALLANTINE. Cahoots! Me?

PABST. "Cahoots"—what is that?

DICKINSON. It's cahoots. Anyhow there's an idea around that it's Concannon our friend Clancy was looking for tonight.

PABST. Really? How very interestin'. I met the old gentleman once or twice in years past. He was most impressive. —He seemed to me a very lonely man—but then who, of any importance, is not?

(BALLANTINE *thrusts a piece of paper at* DICKINSON.)

BALLANTINE. Here's the change in the program copy. You'll absolutely have to check it.

(DICKINSON *takes it and looks it over. At the next table,* MARBLE *leans to* GERT, *speaking lowly.*)

MARBLE. You'll have to head her off. See?

GERT. Who?

MARBLE. Your new Little Number.

GERT. God, what a mug you can be.

(MARBLE's *hand falls on her arm.*)

MARBLE. You heard me. It's bad enough having to play a split-week like Syracuse, without any of that going on.

GERT. I don't know what you mean.

MARBLE. You heard me!

(SPEEDY *glances at them.* PABST *has already been listening intently,* SPEEDY *calls gaily:*)

SPEEDY. Now, now! No domestic strife, please!

MARBLE. Out! This is a private conversation.

(THE MAJOR *inquires mildly over his cards:*)

THE MAJOR. Are we playing?

GERT (*to* MARBLE). Behave yourself, you!

(MARBLE *removes his hand and stares at his cards, swearing softly under his breath.*)

MARBLE. What a load I've taken on. God! Will it never end?

GERT. If you can't take it, you know what to do.

THE MAJOR. Please. I can't think.

SPEEDY (*to* PABST). And they're really

the most devoted couple, you know.

PABST. Very interestin', very—

(DICKINSON *puts the paper in his pocket*.)

DICKINSON. This ought to be all right, *mutatis mutandis*. Just the usual crap.

PABST. You seem a trifle—shall we say, unfriendly?

DICKINSON. I guess the fact is I've never cared much for magicians.

PABST. But I am not a magician.

DICKINSON. Then what are you?

PABST. An illusionist.

DICKINSON. What's the difference?

PABST. There is a great one. Magicians are interested primarily in deception. I am interested only in truth.—But truth is so often an illusion I must, you see, in truth call myself an illusionist.

DICKINSON.—A new slant on the same old tricks: crap and double crap.

PABST. Not "tricks," I beg of you. I am not interested in tricks. I have a modest gift for eliciting the truth, that is all.—For instance, you carry a gun. Is that not the truth?

DICKINSON (*after a moment*). Yes. Very clever. How did you know?

PABST. That is not interestin'. What is interestin', is the purpose for which you carry it.

DICKINSON.—And what might that be?

PABST. Yourself. (DICKINSON *stares at him*.)—But I wouldn't, if I were you. It would help nothing.

DICKINSON. Thanks for the advice.

PABST.—Merely the truth. Amusing to audiences because one sees and hears so little of it—particularly about oneself, you know. (*He turns to* BALLANTINE.) Tell me more of your man Clancy. I find him most interestin' also. I should like to see more of him.

DICKINSON. You won't have to wait long: he's upstairs now.

SPEEDY. Here? You don't mean it!

DICKINSON. Upstairs, I said. Dancing.

PABST. So? I must have missed him.

BALLANTINE. Dancing! Absolutely!

DICKINSON. You know how they do— on volcanoes?

SPEEDY. Oh dear—I don't like this at all!

PABST. He is a natural comic. I hope I may be able to do something for him —something, perhaps, to help him forget his troubles.

DICKINSON. I'm sure he'd appreciate that no end.

PABST. Such a curious search of his— for whom—for what?

DICKINSON. You tell us, Professor.

(PABST *gazes at him for a moment. Then speaks in a brisk, matter-of-fact voice to* SPEEDY:)

PABST. I hope my bag of effects will be safe in the coatroom?

SPEEDY. Don't you worry. No one's ever lost even a hat at Ma Speedy's.

PABST. And that was his wife in the Front, with her lover?

SPEEDY. Well, they do say she and Gurney are—of course *he* doesn't *dream*—

(CLANCY's *voice is heard from the balcony above*.)

CLANCY. This way, Lew! Come along, Fay!

PABST. Shh! *Jetzt kommt er. Er ist punkt.* (*He looks up at the balcony from which a brief blare of music is heard as the door from the dance hall is opened, admitting* CONNIE *and* CLANCY, *who stand there, waiting for their companions*. PABST *smiles in anticipation. He speaks softly:*) Yes, we must see— we must certainly see what we can do for this unfortunate clown.

(CONNIE *and* CLANCY *still wait, and* PABST *watches*.)

CURTAIN

ACT TWO

The Same.

The positions are the same as at the end of Act One. The time is immediately after it. The action is continuous.

CONNIE *and* CLANCY *are joined on the balcony by the dance team,* LEW COOPER *and* FAY FARREL, *a slim, youthful, and engaging pair, who enter from the dancehall and precede them along the balcony toward the stairs.*

FAY. Honest, I never had such a whirl in my life!

(*All are laughing and seem very merry as they come down the stairway*.)

CLANCY.—And the night at the Beach, when we danced in the marathon—you remember, Lew? Fay, do you remember?

FAY. My feet hurt yet, when I think of it.

CONNIE. I've still got the doll we won.

CLANCY. Have you, now!—It was a big doll.

CONNIE. It still is. The fact is, it's grown three or four inches.

LEW. Connie, I could fall for you!

(*And without warning he falls down the last half-dozen steps and lies prone on the floor at the bottom.* MA SPEEDY *springs up with an exclamation, then sits down again as* FAY *walks calmly over* LEW.)

SPEEDY.—Now *that's* why I like this place!

(CLANCY *looks down admiringly.*)

CLANCY. I'd give my left arm to be able to do that, Lew.

CONNIE. Only you couldn't without it.

(FAY *moves up to the empty table at the left.*)

SPEEDY. They're song-and-dance: Cooper and Farrel.—And that's Clancy.

PABST. I know.

(CONNIE *and* CLANCY *step over* LEW's *still prostrate form.*)

CONNIE. Oh that music, that music!

CLANCY. Wasn't it grand? It went right to my feet.

MARBLE (*to* THE MAJOR). The boy's better.

THE MAJOR. Much.

(LEW *picks himself up and follows the others to the table, calling to the waiter.*)

LEW. Beer all around, Walter.

WALTER. Four beers—count 'em—four. (*He goes out again into the pantry.*)

FAY. How long ago was it we all went to the Beach together?

CONNIE. Three years Decoration Day.

CLANCY. Where was Nora that night?

CONNIE. She was laid up with a cold—don't you remember?

CLANCY. That's right.

CONNIE. I named the doll after you, Clancy.

CLANCY. Did you, now?

FAY. Fay Jack of the Jack Sisters, I was named after.

LEW. I was named after nobody.

FAY. *You* don't mind, though!

LEW. The hell I don't.—How'd you like to be called something the top dame in an orphan asylum made up for you?

FAY. I wouldn't mind. (*She mocks him, singing:*) "No foolin', who do you love? Who are you thinking of, no foolin'?"

(*At the other table,* DICKINSON *lets his arms down wearily.*)

DICKINSON. If we had numbers for names, someone would try to make 7 stand out over 4.

BALLANTINE. Absolutely!

DICKINSON. 7 grows a beard, and 4 goes to night-school.

PABST. Quiet! Quiet, and listen! This is most interestin'.

LEW. You'd more or less like to know who you are though, wouldn't you?

FAY. "No foolin', who do you miss, when it's time to kiss, no foolin'?" (*She stops singing, and replies:*) I wouldn't care! Really I wouldn't. (*She cocks her head gaily up at him.*) Are names the reason you won't marry me?

LEW. They might be.—And that ugly mug, of course.

FAY. This guy has been crazy for me for five years, nearly. Ever since we teamed up and developed our act, he has. And still he won't marry me. He won't even sleep with me.

LEW. Nary a wink, so lay off. (*He leaves the table and moves to the piano bench.*)

CLANCY. He's the deep one, Lew is. You need a long line with Lew.

(LEW *begins to play* FAY's *song softly upon the piano.* CONNIE *has been shaping her napkin into a cone. She sets it up before her upon the table.*)

CONNIE. Night and day he stands up there on my dresser like this, that doll does. "Dan Clancy," I say to him, "you keep out of trouble. You're always getting into trouble."

CLANCY. *I* must have been named after Daniel in the Lion's Den.

CONNIE. "If you were troubled with lions," said the King, "you must have brought them youself."

CLANCY. If my little Angela had been a boy, I was going to name *her* after Michael the Archangel.

FAY. Who? What circuit does he play?

CONNIE. Listen to her!

CLANCY. The Universal! Up the heavens and down again. He's captain of the selfsame troops that defended the throne of God against the assault and battery of the Old Nick, that time there was the trouble.

DICKINSON. "And there was War in Heaven!"

CLANCY. There was that all right—and what a war! My mother told me all about it, over and over. Three hundred years it went on. Of course, their time is not like ours.

CONNIE. Three days, most likely—or else three minutes.

DICKINSON. "Michael and his angels fought against the Dragon. And the great Dragon was cast out into the Earth." (*to* PABST.) I thought you looked familiar.

PABST. You are so amusing.

CLANCY. Anyhow, Michael's the fine old bird, and without him God knows where we'd be now.

DICKINSON. And where are we?

CONNIE. And don't be so irreverent, calling him an "old bird."

CLANCY. I'm not. I know The Captain well.—Once in the army—the time I got conked—I thought I saw him. (*He salutes*.)—Maybe I did.

CONNIE. Oh, sure.

FAY. I'll tell you what, Clancy: if Lew ever marries me and we have any kids I'll name the first one "Michael Daniel," after you both.

CLANCY. You can leave out the "Daniel"—or call the next one it.

(*Abruptly* LEW *stops his playing*.)

LEW. Oh, lay off this marrying-and-kids stuff! It's enough to drive a guy crazy!

FAY. Why, Lew—

LEW.—Just lay off it! Talk sense!

FAY. He's been this way all week—some chip on his shoulder for everything and nothing.

LEW. Well, it's been one hell of a week—playing to empty houses—and on the same bill with a flock of midgets. Midgets—God!

(CONNIE *glances in the direction of* THE MAJOR.)

CONNIE. Hush, Lew—

LEW. I don't care. I hate 'em. I hate the sight of 'em. (WALTER *re-enters*.) Hey, come on! Come on with those drinks, will you? I want a drink!

(PABST *leans confidentially toward* DICKINSON *and murmurs*:)

PABST. He does not know who he is, he will not marry—and he dislikes midgets.—Isn't it interestin'?

DICKINSON. No.

(MAJOR ARMSTRONG *lays down his hand*.)

THE MAJOR. I think this is mine.

GERT. You think wrong. Look!

(*She lays down hers*. MARBLE *examines both hands and pushes* GERT's *back to her impatiently*.)

MARBLE. Your mind's wandering.

GERT. But with three jacks and a pair of—

MARBLE.—And wandering where?

(WALTER *comes up to them and puts a folded note on the table before* GERT.)

WALTER. A young lady in the Front asked would I bring this note to you.

(GERT *is about to pick up the note but* MARBLE's *quick hand reaches it first*.)

GERT. You give that here!

(MARBLE *opens it and reads it, then crumples it up and flings it upon the floor*.)

MARBLE. God! it's sickening. God, it makes me want to vomit.

GERT. Get down on your knees and pick it up and give it to me.

MARBLE. What am I to do with you? How can I keep you off it, you filthy, underhanded little—

(SPEEDY *rises and calls*.)

SPEEDY. Jim—Jim Marble!

MARBLE. What do you want?

(SPEEDY *smiles and shakes his finger at him*.)

SPEEDY.—Please, Jim, for the sake of the rest of us.

(MARBLE *gestures him away*. GERT *rises, finds the note and reads it*. MARBLE *mutters*.)

MARBLE. How is a man supposed to stand it? Tell me, someone—tell me, will you?

(GERT *tucks the note into her bosom, returns to the table and begins unconcernedly to deal out another hand*. PABST *smiles to himself and murmurs*:)

PABST. Perfection. (SPEEDY *slides the bottle toward him, but that is not what he means. He repeats*:) Simple perfection.

BALLANTINE. What?

PABST.—As fine a collection of wretched, unhappy human beings as ever it has been my privilege to behold.

DICKINSON. So what?

PABST. Oh, nothing—nothing at all. The world in miniature—the variety-show *par excellence*—we cannot but regard it with pity. We must not be too amused.

(BALLANTINE *half rises*.)

BALLANTINE. Let's go.

PABST. Oh no—no, I beg of you! I am learning so much.

BALLANTINE. One more drink, then.

SPEEDY. Oh yes—at least! (*He claps his hands together*.) Walter! (WALTER *turns to him*.) Freshen us up, Walter.

BALLANTINE. One—and one only.

(WALTER *nods and goes out into the pan-*

try. PABST *has turned and is gazing intently at the other table. Finally he calls very softly:*)

PABST. Mr. Clancy? Oh—Mr. Clancy!

CLANCY. Me?

PABST. Yes—yes. (*He beckons him to them.*) Come—join us for a moment.

CLANCY. Thank you—but it's—it's my friends I'm among here.

PABST. A moment—only for a moment. Come—

(*Reluctantly* CLANCY *rises and moves to the table.*)

DICKINSON. He thinks you're wonderful, Clancy. He wants to marry you.

PABST (*to* BALLANTINE). Introduce us, please.

BALLANTINE. Dan Clancy—former chief stagehand—meet the great Professor—world-famous illusionist—fresh from European triumphs—next week's headliner in place of La Paloma, who has the heaves in Detroit.—And maybe you'll tell me what you meant by coming on stage and ruining our show tonight?

CLANCY. Good evening to you, Professor.—I'm sorry about it, Mr. Ballantine. It was impolite and unthinking of me.

BALLANTINE. Haven't we absolutely done everything that could have been for you?

CLANCY. Mr. Concannon has always been very kind.

BALLANTINE. Mr. Concannon was away. It was me who slipped those extra bills in your envelope.

CLANCY. You were very kind.—And is he returned, as yet?

BALLANTINE. No—at least, I don't think so.

(SPEEDY *glances toward the stage.*)

SPEEDY. That stairway of his hasn't been used since I don't know when. I know, for I looked. I picked the lock.

DICKINSON. There's a rumor around it's the Old Man himself you came back to see, Clancy.

(*At the next table* THE MAJOR *folds his cards into a book and listens. In fact, by now they are all listening.* CLANCY *shakes his head.*)

CLANCY. No, it was not. (*He thinks a moment.*) Mr. Concannon is a great and a noble man and always was. I've never in my life known a better or finer, but— (*And another moment. Then thoughtfully, to himself:*)—And to be sure, he might take

that form as well as another, I suppose. But—

PABST. "Form"?

DICKINSON. Who might?

CLANCY. I don't like to say. It's a personal matter between me and him.

MARBLE. What is this?

(*There is a silence. At last* PABST *leans toward* CLANCY *and speaks very softly:*)

PABST. Mr. Clancy—(CLANCY *turns to him.*)—Unhappy and luckless Mr. Clancy—is it possible, by some curious chance, that he for whom you have been searching is no less a personage than—

CLANCY. Stop where you are!

PABST.—Than God Himself?

(*Another silence. Then* CLANCY *raises his head proudly.*)

CLANCY. It is!—And what's there curious about it?

CONNIE. Dan! What are you talking about?

SPEEDY. Good gracious!

DICKINSON.—A still hunt for the Almighty! It's marvelous.—Clancy, you certainly fly high.

(CLANCY *wheels on him and demands:*)

CLANCY. And why not? Isn't He everywhere? Is there a nook or a corner where He's not? What's there so strange in going out to find Him? Others have done it, and others will again! (*Once more his head sinks and his wild eyes stare blankly at the floor. He goes on, half to himself:*) I have to find Him! 'Tis a necessary thing to me. I have some things to ask Him which nobody else can answer. I know it is His will that things happen as they do, but I've come to a place where I have to know the reason for certain of them.—And know I will!

PABST. Of course, of course—

MARBLE. It's the damnedest thing—

THE MAJOR. Why, Jim?

BALLANTINE. But in a Vaudeville House—on a Saturday night! Absolutely!

SPEEDY. Yes—that takes the cake, it certainly takes the—

MARBLE. Why, of all places, did you think He'd pick the Globe for a personal appearance?

CLANCY. I don't know.—I was in Cleveland. I'd been many other places among the poor and the lowly, where they say it's easiest to—where they say He spends much of His time—but nor hide nor hair of Him. I was out walkin' by myself when all of a crack it came over me, like a cat jumped down on my back from a wall: "Tomorrow night at James Concannon's Globe—Holy Saturday night—hurry, me boy, hurry!"— So I came as quick as I could. I don't know how I got here. I don't even remember the—the train, it must have been. It wasn't till near curtain-time did I arrive. The sweat was pouring from me, for fear of missing Him—(*His voice rises.*) But I can't have! I can't! I know in my bones He was there!

(*Swiftly* CONNIE *moves to his side.*)

CONNIE. Come along now, Dan. Come along with Connie.

(CLANCY *pulls away from her.*)

CLANCY. Don't treat me as if I was bereft of my senses! I'm not!—I'm sane as the next one, maybe more so. I could be a bit off on my reckoning, of course.— Maybe it was tomorrow night—no, tomorrow's Sunday and the House will be locked fast, and dark.—Or maybe it was somewhere not precisely *in* the Globe, but roundabouts. Maybe it was even— even—(*He glances about him.*)—No, Connie—the night's not over yet.

CONNIE. Will you please to come along, please?

CLANCY. And maybe miss Him entirely?—After all this time render me search null and void?

(PABST *rises and touches his elbow and gently steers him into a chair at the table, then turns and calmly surveys the incredulous faces about him.*)

PABST. This seems not at all as strange to me as it appears to seem to you. A man searches for the Truth and calls it "God"—Why not? It has many names, and as many faces.

CLANCY.—It has one: and that's the name and the face of God!

DICKINSON (*to* PABST). Maybe you can scare Him up for the poor guy, Professor. Maybe *you* can evoke Him.

PABST. The Truth, I can evoke.

DICKINSON. Who says?

PABST. You do not believe me.

DICKINSON. No.

PABST. You would like a demonstration, perhaps?

(*There is a silence. Then:*)

DICKINSON. Yes. Strut your stuff.

MARBLE.—And be sure you make it good.

PABST. Very well.—But you must promise not to interfere.—Agreed?

(DICKINSON *gestures assent.* PABST *moves swiftly to the little stage and mounts it.*)

SPEEDY. An entertainment! Oh, good! I did hope there'd be! (*He rises to view the stage. Suddenly he cries out angrily:*) Those drapes! Who touched those drapes?

DICKINSON. I did.

SPEEDY. Well—you shouldn't have!

(PABST *tries the private door, finds it fast, then carefully draws the spangled curtains together again over it.*)

PABST.—And surely if He should choose to reveal Himself, Truth would prepare the way for Him, would it not?

(*He arranges a chair and table at the center of the little stage.* BALLANTINE *rises and picks up his hat and umbrella.*)

BALLANTINE. I've had enough for one week. Good night, all. (*He moves toward the alley-door.*) Me, I take Sundays off. I absolutely do my theater-going on week-days.

(BALLANTINE *goes out.* PABST *comes forward upon the stage and inquires:*)

PABST. Shall we begin?

FAY. Look, Lew—he's going to do his Act!

(*She moves to the piano bench and seats herself beside* LEW.)

PABST. Act?—I have no Act. It is you who have the Acts. (*He descends the steps and turns to* MARBLE.) Mr. Marble— please—

SPEEDY. But—but aren't *you* going to do *something*?

(PABST *smiles his slow, intolerable smile and levels his palms.*)

PABST. I? Oh no—*I* shall merely be master of ceremonies. (*He turns again to* MARBLE.) You are a ventriloquist, I understand.

MARBLE. That's the old rumor about me.

PABST. And this is your wife with you?

MARBLE. Yes, you might call her that.

GERT. Don't turn my head, will you?

PABST.—And you have your little man there in the black bag.

(*A muffled voice is heard from the bag:*)

THE DUMMY. Let me out! Let me out!

PABST. At once, little man. (*To* MARBLE.) Your wife assists you?

MARBLE. In black tights: she has a fine figure, they say.

GERT.—And don't fail to tell us everything.

PABST. You will not need an assistant tonight. Take your place on the stage, please.

MARBLE. Listen, Professor: I've played twelve performances this week and I'm weary, see? I'm throatsore and weary.

THE DUMMY (*from the bag*). Me too! Me too!

PABST (*without accent*). This will refresh you both.

DICKINSON. At times your English is better than at others.

PABST. *Danke.* Thank you very much. —Well, Mr. Marble?

(MARBLE *rises, draws* THE DUMMY *from the bag and makes his way toward the stage.* SPEEDY *follows him, turns a switch at the side of the stage and lights a spotlight which casts a brilliant circle of light directly upon stage-center.* DICKINSON *drags himself to his feet and stands swaying, bracing himself against the table.*)

DICKINSON. Marble's too good for Number One on any bill. I'll do the opener: it's a recitation, very short and to the point. Listen, Clancy—this is for you—(MARBLE *mounts the little stage and arranges himself there on the chair in the circle of light, a whisky glass, a package of cigarettes and an ash-tray upon the table beside him, as* DICKINSON *proceeds:*) Once there was a little man like you in County Kerry—and he led a little life—and one day he began to pack a little bag. And *They* said, "Where are you off to? Where are you going?" And *he* said, "I'm packing my bag and I'm going to Connemara." And They said, "You mean, you're going to Connemara, God willing." And he said, "I mean I'm going to Connemara."—So God changed him into a frog and put him in a frog-pond and kept him there for seven years.

(CONNIE *laughs.*)

CONNIE. What kind of a God would do that to a little man?

DICKINSON. Oh—Clancy's—and yours —and other people's generally.—And then God changed him back again—and what did the little man do? He began at once to pack his little bag.—And They said, "Where are you off to? Where are you going?" And he said, "I'm going to Connemara." And They said, "You *mean,* you're going to Connemara, *God willing.*" And he said, "I mean I'm going to Connemara, or back to the frog-pond!"

(*He gestures drunkenly toward* CLANCY *and reseats himself.*)

CLANCY. I see what you mean.

DICKINSON.—When you arrive there, send me a postcard.

CLANCY. A postcard?

DICKINSON. A postcard—with the answer.

PABST. Apt—but we must have no more interruptions. (*He turns to* MARBLE, *who now has* THE DUMMY *astride his knee.*) Shall we begin?

MARBLE. Come now, Frank! Speak nicely to the gentleman.

(THE DUMMY *turns to* PABST.)

THE DUMMY. Good evening, Professor.

PABST. Good evening, Frank.

(*He seats himself upon the bench at the foot of the little stage.* THE DUMMY *barks at him:*)

THE DUMMY. "*Mr.* Frenzy" to you, please!

PABST. A thousand pardons.

THE DUMMY.—Make it two thousand.

PABST. Two thousand, then.

THE DUMMY. I'll take it! (THE DUMMY *blinks its eyes and turns its empty face up to* MARBLE.) You seem depressed, Jim. What's the matter?

MARBLE. Me? Depressed?

THE DUMMY. Yeh—down in the mouth. What for?—Has the little witch been acting up again?

MARBLE. The little— ?—I don't know who you mean, Frank.

THE DUMMY. W-i-t-c-h—"w" as in "butter." She certainly runs you ragged. I don't see how you stand it.

MARBLE. If it's my wife you are referring to—

THE DUMMY. Of course it's your wife! Who else would it be?

MARBLE. I don't care to discuss my domestic affairs.

THE DUMMY. You're going to whether you care to or not.

(GERT *stirs in her chair.*)

GERT. Oh, lay off.

(THE DUMMY'S *head swings in her direction.*)

THE DUMMY. Out! This is a private conversation—What a woman! Just a chippie off the old block, eh, Jim?

MARBLE. To what block do you refer, Frank?

THE DUMMY. Tenth Avenue, between Fourteenth and—

MARBLE.—That's enough!

THE DUMMY. It ought to be.

MARBLE. You'd better learn not to be so outspoken, my friend.

THE DUMMY. Hooey! The trouble with you is you never speak out. You let her get away with murder.

GERT. Oh, he does, does he?—Look out, or there'll be a real one.

MARBLE. I can't allow you to talk this way, Frank.

THE DUMMY. Try and stop me.

MARBLE. What are your views on politics? Do you think the Democrats—?

(*He takes a swallow of his drink.* THE DUMMY *talks through it:*)

THE DUMMY. I don't give a damn about politics! What worries me is the ride that dame's taking you on.

(MARBLE *puts down his glass.*)

MARBLE. My wife and I are very happy together, see?

THE DUMMY. Like fun you are.

MARBLE. She is the soul of loyalty—kind, generous, sweet-tempered—

THE DUMMY. Don't make me laugh.

MARBLE.—Loving and economical. In fact, the perfect help-meet.

THE DUMMY. "Hell-cat," did you say?

GERT. Thanks. That'll be about all!

MARBLE. "Help-meet" is what I said.

THE DUMMY. Hooey.

MARBLE. I beg your pardon?

THE DUMMY. Hooey! Hooey!

MARBLE. Quiet, Frank—people will hear you.

THE DUMMY. So they'd ought! All this secrecy—that's how she gets away with it. If everyone knew the way she—

(MARBLE *claps a hand over the mouth.*)

MARBLE. Insect!—Quiet, I say!

THE DUMMY. Okay! Okay!

MARBLE. Promise?

THE DUMMY. Hope to die.

(MARBLE *removes his hand.* THE DUMMY *gasps, coughs once, and is quiet for a moment.*)

GERT. Very funny. In fact, a howl. I'll book you.

(MARBLE *lights a cigarette, keeping it in his mouth.*)

MARBLE. You know, Frank, sometimes you're almost as dumb as a man.

THE DUMMY. Yep—and two women.

(MARBLE *offers the cigarette.*)

MARBLE. Would you like a smoke?

THE DUMMY. No thanks. It gets in my eyes.

MARBLE. Too bad.

THE DUMMY. Yep—both of 'em.

MARBLE. Do you care for bridge?

THE DUMMY. Nope.

MARBLE. Why not?

THE DUMMY. I get tired of all the time being the dummy.

SPEEDY. Marvelous! He's as good as Marshall Montgomery.

PABST.—But this is extraneous. I feel the Truth struggling to come through. Something is holding it back—No?

(MARBLE *removes the cigarette from his mouth and puts it out, turning his head to one side with great deliberation as* THE DUMMY *turns in the opposite direction and gazes blankly into a space, attempting a whistle that does not quite come off. Finally it inquires disinterestedly:*)

THE DUMMY. Why are you such a liar, Jim?

MARBLE. A liar? Me?

THE DUMMY. Yes.—Why not out with the truth once in a while? It would do you good—her, too.

MARBLE. Truth is pretty dangerous medicine, old boy.

PABST.—But effective—very often effective. (THE DUMMY'S *head swings around toward him.*)—I beg your pardon.

THE DUMMY. I grant your grace. I hope the cat will spit in your face.

PABST. But are we not again departing from our subject?

MARBLE. What subject is he referring to, Frank?

THE DUMMY. You know: that little b-i-t—that little bit of a wife of yours.

(GERT *half rises.*)

GERT. I won't stand it!

THE DUMMY. Then sit it!

MARBLE. I'm afraid I'll have to ask you to mend your language, my friend.

THE DUMMY. She's got her claws in you and she won't let go, will she?

MARBLE. As a matter of fact, she's often told me I can leave any time I like.

GERT. And I tell you again!

THE DUMMY. Then why don't you?

MARBLE. Why—I guess I just don't want to.

THE DUMMY. More hooey—you mean you're too soft-hearted to. You know if you don't watch her like a hawk she'll go straight to hell in a hack—well, why not let her?

MARBLE (*after a moment*). She was a sweet kid, once.

(*Then* MARBLE'S *face changes, and* THE DUMMY *barks:*)

THE DUMMY.—You mean before the girls came around.

MARBLE. The what?

THE DUMMY. The girls! The girls! The girls!

(GERT *springs up*.)

GERT. What do you mean, you—!

(*The head swings around on her*.)

THE DUMMY. You heard me!—The girls!—The little ones—the soft ones—the frilly ones—the girly-girls—

(GERT *advances threateningly*.)

GERT. I'll kill you, you damned little—

THE DUMMY. And what do you call yourself?—What could sink a man lower than to have to live with a woman who—

GERT. I won't stand it! I—I'll—(*She seizes* THE DUMMY *and shakes it violently*.) You—you foul little, lying little—(*She flings it down and makes her way blindly to the restaurant door*.) You'll never see me again! Never in this world—you hear me?

(*She is gone, the door banging closed after her*. MARBLE *picks up the sprawling* DUMMY, *replaces it in its black bag, pulls the strings together, hunches it into the crook of his arm and moves in the direction taken by* GERT. PABST *follows him*.)

PABST. Where are you going?

MARBLE. After her. She'll just sit in there till I come.

PABST. I would not, if I were you.

MARBLE. Why not?

PABST. Is that not just what she wants? Is that not just what you always have done?

CONNIE. But the poor misguided creature—who else is she to turn to?

SPEEDY. She's got a right to her own life!

DICKINSON. Who says?

(MARBLE *stares at* PABST, *hesitates*. CLANCY *cries out*.)

CLANCY. Go on, Jim! Go on, man!

(MARBLE *turns and gazes at him. Finally he speaks:*)

MARBLE. No.

(*He sinks into a chair at the table, the black bag dropping at his feet*.)

CLANCY.—But she's your own wife!—And she might do some harm to herself.

MARBLE. Let her! Who gives a damn?

CLANCY. That's no thing to say!

PABST. Wise—at last he grows wise.

CLANCY. Wise, me foot! Who's to help her but him?

PABST. Never mind her. The truth has set *him* free!

DICKINSON. The hell it has. It's only moved him into another kind of prison.

MARBLE. Shut up, the lot of you!

THE MAJOR. You shouldn't have done it, Jim.

(PABST *turns blandly to* THE MAJOR.)

PABST. You, also, did not care for the performance?

THE MAJOR. No, I did not.

PABST. Perhaps you and I might give a better one—you think?

(THE MAJOR *stares at him*.)

THE MAJOR. How do you mean?

PABST. You could be *my* little man—no?

THE MAJOR. I don't understand you.

PABST. Would you be so kind as to come on stage with me, please?

THE MAJOR. No. No, thank you.

(PABST *moves closer to him, stands over him*.)

PABST. But I must insist! It is very important to a friend of yours—(*He glances at* CLANCY.)—It is, in fact, essential.

SPEEDY. Oh go on, Major—it's all in fun. Gracious!

THE MAJOR. But I don't see how—

(PABST *holds a hand out to him*.)

PABST. Come—you will soon find out how. It is really as simple as what-you-say—a-b-c.

(*Reluctantly* THE MAJOR *takes the proffered hand and together they move to the rear of the room, mount the shallow steps and are upon the stage*.)

SPEEDY. The long and the short of it! Isn't it sweet?

(PABST *seats himself upon the chair that* MARBLE *had occupied, swings* THE MAJOR *around to him, lifts him up and sets him upon his knee*.)

DICKINSON. Do you see what I see?

SPEEDY. Shh! No comments from the audience.

PABST. Now then! Attention, please—everyone attention!—Good evening, Major.

THE MAJOR. Well, what is it you want to know from me?

PABST. Just a few little things.—Like our friend Clancy, there are small things that puzzle me.

THE MAJOR. Well, what are they?

PABST. We are a little world in ourselves, we vaudeville artists, are we not?

THE MAJOR. In a way, yes.—Yes, I expect we are.

PABST. Our lives are so concentrated: twice a day, six days a week, we must give our all in the brief space of ten minutes.

THE MAJOR. *My* act runs twenty.

PABST. Twenty for the headliners—true. But we are not all headliners. Take our friend Clancy—he is hardly one of us at all—and yet, he, too, is a kind of essence. Wouldn't you say?

THE MAJOR. Yes. Yes, I would. Very much of a one.

PABST. And at present seems to believe that he represents, in his small self, all the essential troubles of the world.

CLANCY. I never said—!

PABST. Move nearer, Mr. Clancy. (*With a downward, sweeping motion of his arm he invites him to them.*) Sit here at our feet, that you may be even more one of us.

(CLANCY *comes forward and seats himself upon the second step of the stage-steps.*)

CLANCY. I don't know at all what it is that you're after—

PABST. Only the Truth, Mr. Clancy. The ways there, alas, are not always straight ways. (*He turns again to the* MAJOR, *urging him.*) Tell me about this Clancy. Acquaint me briefly with the facts of his decline and his fall.

CLANCY. That might be private.

PABST. Quiet, please.

(THE MAJOR *speaks woodenly.*)

THE MAJOR. From the beginning, his life has been a hard one. As a boy he knew cold and hunger, and he has known them since.—He never asked for much, and much was never given him.

CLANCY. Don't make me out sorry for myself now—for I'm not!

THE MAJOR.—In fact, the little that he had, at last was taken from him. He lost his little home and he lost his little savings. He lost the sight of one eye.

CLANCY. Well, I never did any crying over myself with either of them. It's not such things alone—

THE MAJOR.—He lost his job—his young brother and his little daughter. That was the worst. He was left with only his beloved wife to mourn all these things that had been so dear to him. Then he woke one fine morning and found that she was gone too.

PABST. His wife? Where to? With whom—a lover?

(CLANCY *springs up.*)

CLANCY. Put up your dukes! You get a poke in the nose for that!

(PABST *holds his hands out to him.*)

PABST. Forgive me—

CLANCY. Then why did you say such a thing?

PABST. I was in error: forgive me.

CLANCY. The poor child left me because she thought she was bad luck for me. She said it to me once: "I bring you bad luck, Dan," she said.

PABST. Of course—of course—

CLANCY.—"Of course" no such thing! She only thought it!

PABST. I understand.

CLANCY. See that you do!—And in the future, mind your tongue.

(PABST *bows his head.* CLANCY *reseats himself.* PABST *turns again to* THE MAJOR.)

PABST.—And his little girl—how old was she?

THE MAJOR. I don't know precisely. Two—three—

CLANCY. Three years, four months, two days.

PABST. They are sweet at that age.

CLANCY. *She* was!—And she was good, too, and pretty as a picture and full of jokes and laughing. Never a tear out of her, except now and then when her little insides hurt her, with the wind or the like—or when she grew aware of the vast world about her and felt too small in it and needed comforting.

PABST.—A bitter blow to lose her.

CLANCY. . It was, that. How it happened, I don't know—or why it ever did. She was always well and strong, for all that she was a seven months' baby. It started with no more than a little cold—the same as any child might have in changing weather. But it grew and it grew until it was all the way through her and then the doctor could only shake his head and sit and watch her, fighting for breath, beating her little fists in the air.

PABST. What could be sadder?

CLANCY. There's little that could be.—I don't know of anything could, now I think of it.—Angela was all that was ever all my own. My job could be taken any time—the eye is a delicate organ, subject to accidents—my house was never fully paid for—young Timmy, my brother, drank—and my Nora was my wife only so long as she was willing to put up with me. But Angela was all my own.

PABST. Still, all such deprivations mean something—don't you agree, Major? They all have some purpose in the scheme of life.

DICKINSON. Oh, sure, sure—they add zest.

CLANCY. But mean *what*? That's what I want to know! The purpose of 'em!—And I want to know other things!

PABST. Would you wish to have had a child, too, Major?

(THE MAJOR's *face sets.*)

THE MAJOR. I had one.

(PABST *seems surprised.*)

PABST. Indeed.

THE MAJOR. Yes, I had a son.

PABST. That was long ago—

THE MAJOR. Yes—that was long ago.

PABST (*after a moment*). And where is he now?

THE MAJOR. I can't say. I don't know.

PABST. Tell us a little, Major. Speak out to us. It will do you good.

(*There is a brief silence. Then* THE MAJOR's *voice begins, toneless and flat, as if reading faded print aloud:*)

THE MAJOR. Anna and I had wanted a child for years, but we had been afraid. We—

(*He stops again.* PABST *helps him:*)

PABST. She was small, too, I take it.

THE MAJOR.—Smaller even than me. She could walk under my arm. That's the way she came on stage with me: it made a—it made a very good entrance. She was the only grown-up I have ever known that I was bigger than. She was a true midget, not a dwarf like me—fine in every part—hands, feet, little wrists and ankles, all perfectly proportioned. She had the bluest eyes ever there were—my, they were blue! She was a treat to see. A reviewer in Savannah once referred to her as "the Vest-pocket Venus" and other papers took it up. Finally we used it in our billing: "Major Armstrong and His Vest-pocket Venus."

PABST. Charming.—And the child?

THE MAJOR. We—we thought that having one would be like shouting from the housetops, "Look! See how these small people have loved! Love is not denied the small in stature if their souls, if their spirits be—" (*Again he stops and swallows. Then he goes on:*)—He was born as Caesar was, and the medical men in attendance were very interested and very pleased with themselves. He was—all right in every way—like Anna's grandmother—like my father.

SPEEDY. Who'd ever believe such a thing! Gracious!

PABST. But were you not gratified?

THE MAJOR. At first, yes—we were even proud of it. But finally, as he kept growing, it got so that we couldn't sleep at night, wondering, planning, fearing. At four he was as tall as his mother was. At five, he came to here on me. We were—we were like three children together.—But when he was seven, we sent him away.

PABST.—For his own good. An unselfish and noble act.

THE MAJOR.—All I know is, that try as she might my Anna could not endure a world without him. Month by month she dwindled away to nothing and one night she just turned on her pillow and died.

PABST. Dear, dear, how dreadful.

THE MAJOR. It was here, in the Sims' Hotel. I would have followed her, but Mr. Concannon gave me the courage to wait.

PABST. James Concannon?

THE MAJOR. Is there another?

PABST.—And what became of the boy?

THE MAJOR. The people he was with were not good people—they couldn't have been, because he ran away from them. I've never been able to find out where—or anything about him—though I've tried very hard to. (*He looks away.*) He'd be a grown man now. I—I daresay he'd make a dozen of me.

(*He waits an instant, then looks up at* PABST.)—And now may I get down, please?

PABST. One moment. (*He turns to* CLANCY.) Well, Mr. Clancy—?

(CLANCY *looks up. His eyes are dazed again.*)

CLANCY. Who—? Where—? What did you say?

(PABST *turns to the others.*)

PABST.—It appears that our saddened friend does not yet realize that others among us also have our burdens to bear.

CLANCY. Ah, that I do! I do indeed! But what help is that to anyone? (*He turns to* THE MAJOR.) My heart is knotted up into a fist for you, Major.

THE MAJOR. Thank you, Clancy.

(PABST *frowns down upon* CLANCY.)

PABST. Which is the worse—to have the Almighty take a child, or to have to give it away to strangers? To have it safe in heaven—or to have it roam the world, nameless and alone?

CLANCY. The cases are not the same —nor the circumstances! But both are bad, both!

PABST. Which is the better—to have one's wife die, wracked to the bone with grief—or to have her leave one, and live on?

CLANCY. It's not the same—there's no similarity!

(*There is a pause.* PABST *ponders, then turns and speaks suddenly:*)

PABST. You, there—Cooper and Farrel—(*They start in surprise. He adds, softly:*) Would you come a little nearer, please? (LEW *and* FAY *look at each other uncertainly, then rise.*) You, Miss—another step forward—one, two, three! (*Deliberately* FAY *advances three steps, and three only.*) Now, then, little song-and-dance lady—hearing what you have heard, do you still wish to marry?

(FAY *replies stoutly:*)

FAY. Yes. I do.

PABST. And have a child—children?

FAY. Yes. I do!

LEW. Look: what's the idea?

PABST. So young, so brave, so unafraid. Is it not interestin', Major? Is it not interestin', Mr. Clancy? (*They do not reply. He turns to* FAY *again, smiling his smile.*) Pretty as you are, it should be so simple—just to take him by the hand and lead him to the altar—no?

FAY. Maybe it should be, but it's not.

PABST. And why, pray?

FAY. He won't come.

PABST. He must have his reasons.

FAY. I suppose he has. But he keeps them to himself.

PABST. Dear, dear.—Are you quite sure he loves you?

FAY. Yes. Yes, I am.

LEW. What *is* this? Why should you have to tell this old goat what you—

PABST. "Old goat"? That is not nice. That is not nice at all.

LEW (*advancing*). Oh, can it! What right have you got to mix in, anyway?

PABST. That's it—closer. Come a little closer.

(LEW *stops abruptly.*)

LEW. I'll stay where I am, thanks.

PABST. But this is impolite of you. It is not in the interests of a varied entertainment. (*He coaxes and smiles, gesturing:*) Come, young man—come—come—

LEW. That'll be all right!

PABST. He is stubborn, little Major. It appears *we* must go to *him.* (*With* THE MAJOR *perched awkwardly against his shoulder he proceeds down the stage steps, advances to* LEW *and stands directly facing him.*) Look at him, little Major. Gaze upon this strange contradiction: a young man in love who will not marry. Talented, well-off, sound in limb and in sinew, and still he will not marry.

LEW. That's my business, isn't it?

PABST. Ah yes—deeply so. Look at him, Major—you are a wise little man —perhaps you can account for this perverse attitude. All that we know of him is that he is a foundling, that he is in love and that he will not marry.—Ah, yes! And one thing more—

LEW. Shut up. Shut up, you!

PABST.—Just one—a certain unaccountable distaste for very small people, like yourself. Look at him closer—consider the brow, the elevated cheek-bones. And the eyes—did you ever see eyes so blue in a man's head? Where have you ever seen their like before? (LEW *begins to tremble. His hands close and unclose spasmodically.*) He seems to grow nervous— I wonder why? Of what can he be afraid? (*His voice lowers.*) Little Major— does it not grow more apparent why he will not marry? (*A sudden cry is wrung from* THE MAJOR *and he turns his gaze sharply from the dancer's face. But* PABST *goes on:*) Is it not now somewhat more evident who he is?

(THE MAJOR *struggles in* PABST'S *arms.*)

LEW. You—you fishy, fat-headed slob, you—what the hell do you think you're trying to pull off?

THE MAJOR. Let me go! Let me go!

PABST.—But certainly.

(*He sets him carefully down upon his feet.* THE MAJOR *totters toward the stage, sinks down upon the lowest step and sits there, his head in his hands, his narrow shoulders shaking.* FAY *looks wonderingly from him to* LEW, *then back again.*)

FAY. Oh Lew—

(*Suddenly* LEW *shouts:*)

LEW. He lies! He's not!

(PABST *inquires mildly:*)

PABST. Who is not what? Have I said anything?

LEW. Plenty! But it's not true I'm his—he's my—!—And you know damn well it's not!

PABST. Of course, of course—

LEW. Then why do you make it seem that it is? You, with your oily round-about way of—your cheap, ten-twenty-thirty trick of piling it up, and then making it sound like it was the McCoy—!

(*He flounders and stops.*)

FAY. Lew—listen, Lew—

LEW. I tell you it's just his rotten idea of being funny! It's a stinking lie, the whole thing, cooked-up out ot nothing! I'll be damned if I'll hang around and take any more of it! To hell with the lot of you—

(*He storms out into the alley.* CLANCY *drops down upon the step and throws one arm protectingly about* THE MAJOR. FAY *moves to the alley-door, where she turns and faces* PABST.)

FAY. I think—I think you're a living horror. God damn you to hell.

(*She goes out.* PABST *sighs, lowers his head and clasps his hands across his front.*)

PABST. Dear, dear. It seems that even the semblance of Truth is not popular.

CLANCY. The "semblance," is it? Then you're admitting yourself it's not so!

PABST. We always have coincidence to contend with.

CONNIE.—And "coincidence," too—it's a grand time to be saying that!

PABST. I regret I have not your command of the language.

CONNIE. And don't be coming at us with that kind of five-act talk! Even if it was a fact, facts aren't the truth always.

PABST. Now there—*there* you have me. That is very astute of you.

DICKINSON. Why should we take all this from you, anyhow?

PABST. Shall I stop where I am, perhaps?

DICKINSON. Hell, no. We've seen nothing yet that any small-time ham couldn't pull off as well or better.

(PABST *looks at him oddly.*)

PABST. Thank you. Then I shall proceed.

DICKINSON. In the interests of accuracy, it just happens that *I* know who Lew's father is—and where he is.

CLANCY. Then tell him, man, tell him!

DICKINSON. I'd sooner draw and quarter him.

SPEEDY. Is it that bad?

DICKINSON. It's worse.

(PABST *is looking at* DICKINSON *with new interest. He crooks his finger at him and murmurs mockingly.*)

PABST. Ah-ha!

(DICKINSON *gestures him away.*)

CLANCY (*after a moment*). Anyhow, Major, now you know it's not so, not a bit of it.

THE MAJOR. All I know is that if ever I did find him, it might—it might be like that.

(CLANCY *glances angrily at* PABST.)

CLANCY. You tricky old wretch, you. Lew and Fay were better off as they were —and so was the Major.

PABST.—But advise me seriously, Mr. Clancy—would you not rather your daughter were dead than that she had ever grown up to deny you?

CLANCY. She never would have!

CONNIE. Why should she have? Where's the girl ever had a better man for a father?

CLANCY. And I say again, you shouldn't have done this to the Major. You've not done him good, you've done him ill!

PABST. A matter of opinion.—Would you rather it had been done to you?

CLANCY. There's nothing can be done to me any more! All that could be, has been.

PABST. Are you sure?

CLANCY. I am.

PABST. That must console you.

CLANCY. I have other consolations.

PABST. Ah? Such as—

CLANCY. I had a wife who loved me once, and still does maybe. I had a good job to occupy my mind. I had my health and I had a small house with a flower-bed behind it. And for a time I had a little girl who was all my own. I had everything!

PABST. Brave memories.

CLANCY. There'll never be braver! They're of a nature to comfort any man alive!—But as for you, I can't for the life of me figure you out. What are you up to with all these cooney tricks, anyhow? Why do you do what you do?

PABST. Perhaps at heart I am a humanitarian.

CONNIE. At what?—I doubt if you've

got one.—Come along, Dan, you can sleep at Mrs. Carlson's. She's got an empty bed.

CLANCY. Yes—I'll come—(*He turns again to* PABST.) Good night to you, old sly-boots, and small thanks, if any.

PABST. So—you give up your great search so easily.

CLANCY. You can leave that to me!

PABST.—You hug you "consolations" to you, and settle for a penny in the pound. Most interestin', most.

(DICKINSON *thumps upon the table.*)

DICKINSON. Connemara—to Connemara!

(CLANCY *glances at him, then back to* PABST.)

PABST. No—it is too difficult. The Irish are a soft race, really. The bravery is all in front.

CLANCY. Who says it is?

CONNIE. Dan—here we go, Dan—

CLANCY. No. Wait a bit. (*To* PABST.) Who says they are?

PABST.—An Irishman without a cause —is there a sadder sight in the world?

CLANCY. If my cause is a lost one, it's none the less my own, you old crock!

PABST.—One moment, please. (*In the center of the room he deftly arranges two chairs, facing each other. Then he moves quickly to* SPEEDY, *bends and whispers something to him.* SPEEDY *looks at him blankly. Now* PABST *speaks aloud to him:*) Please not to make difficulties. Tell her it is only for a moment. Tell her he has gone—

(SPEEDY *hesitates briefly, then goes to the restaurant door and out.* CLANCY *seats himself stubbornly in the chair with its back to the door.* CONNIE *advances to him.*)

CONNIE. Well, are you coming or aren't you?

CLANCY. Sit down a bit, Connie.

CONNIE. I will not.

(PABST *approaches them.*)

CLANCY. Why not? Just one little minute, till—

CONNIE. Because that's what he wants us to do! And I'll tell him nothing!

PABST. What is there to tell?

CONNIE. You heard me, didn't you?—Nothing!

PABST. No?—Not one little word to the one man in the whole world you—

CONNIE.—That isn't so! I don't! I don't at all!

PABST.—Don't what? What have I said?

CONNIE. Never mind!—Come on, Dan. I don't like it here. I don't like it a bit. I've got a queer feeling it's—well, what are you looking at me so funny for? (*He is gazing at her, his eyes again dazed, as if he had found something gravely amiss.*) Are you coming or are you not?

CLANCY. What's different about your face, Connie? What's wrong with it?

CONNIE. Nothing that hasn't always been. You don't have to look at it!

CLANCY. *I* know!—Where are your earrings?

CONNIE. I never had earrings.

CLANCY. You did so. Your grandmother pierced your ears with a hot needle when you were small and she set little round gold earrings in them and said you'd never get the rheumatism.

CONNIE. She did no such thing!

CLANCY. You told me she did.

CONNIE. You're thinking of Nora.

(*A moment, then* CLANCY'S *head droops and he murmurs.*)

CLANCY. So I am. So I am.

CONNIE. *I* wouldn't have them on a bet.

CLANCY. They're pretty things.

CONNIE.—Not if I had to die for the lack of them, I wouldn't.

CLANCY. You were always the stubborn one, Connie.

CONNIE. Be that as it may, I—! (*She stops suddenly and gazes in alarm beyond him to the opposite side of the room where* NORA *stands in the doorway,* SPEEDY *behind her.* CONNIE *speaks softly:*)—Take it easy, Dan. You're in for it now, all right.

CURTAIN

ACT THREE

The Same.

The positions are the same as at the end of Act Two. The time is immediately after it. The action is continuous.

SPEEDY *is urging* NORA *into the room.*

SPEEDY. Just a little informal entertainment, that's all.

NORA. But why should I be the stooge for a trick-man, for God's sake? The gentleman I'm with steps into the washroom for a minute, and—

(CLANCY *straightens abruptly at the sound of her voice, but does not turn.* PABST *holds the chair opposite him out for* NORA.)

PABST.—This way, Madam, if you will be so good.

(*She moves uncertainly past* CLANCY *to the chair.*)

NORA. But what's the point? My friend won't know where I've— (*She turns, sees* CLANCY, *and gasps:*) You! (*She grasps the back of the chair.*) Speedy said you'd gone. He said—

CLANCY. Nora — (*Then suddenly he springs up, crying out joyously:*) Ah, Nora, Nora—you've come back!

(*And moves swiftly toward her.* NORA *draws herself erect against the chair.*)

NORA. I have not! And you stay where you are—keep your distance away from me! (CLANCY *stops in his tracks and gazes at her.*) Go back where you were. (*He does not move.*) I mean it!—Don't you know yet that I mean what I say? (*Dumbly* CLANCY *returns to his chair.* NORA *turns and meets* CONNIE's *accusing eyes, with dark resentment in her own.*) I suppose it's you I've got to thank for this.

CONNIE. I'd nothing to do with it. I'd've done wonders to keep it off.

(NORA *seats herself with deliberation, faces* CLANCY *squarely and demands:*)

NORA. Well—what do you want?

(CLANCY *can only stare.* DICKINSON *waits a moment, then speaks.*)

DICKINSON. I suppose we just might have the decency to clear out and leave them.

MARBLE. I was thinking that.

THE MAJOR. Yes.

NORA. What for? This is a free-for-all. The more the merrier. (*She turns again to* CLANCY.) Well—get it out, can't you? I left a good plate of eggs for this.

CLANCY. You're changed.

NORA. Only to you, I imagine.

CLANCY. You were never like this.

NORA. I was always like this.

CLANCY. No—you've got hard.

NORA. I was born hard, hard as nails.

CLANCY. I never saw it.

NORA. You weren't let: I took good care of that.

(CLANCY *frowns at her, puzzled.*)

CLANCY. What is it you're saying? What is it you mean?

NORA. You had such a sweet little idea of me, I thought I'd live up to it, that's all.

CLANCY. I don't believe it.

NORA. You never believe anything but what you want to.

CLANCY. And that's not so, either.

NORA. It is, and everything I'll be telling you will be! That's why I'm willing to sit here, to put you straight once and for all—so you'll never trouble me again, ever.

CLANCY. "Trouble" you, did you say?

NORA. That's what I said. You're a blight on me, Dan Clancy, and you always have been.

CLANCY. This can't be you, Nora. Surely it can't.

NORA. But it is.

CLANCY. You who were so good and gentle and loving—

NORA. I know!—I ought to of gone on the stage.

CLANCY. Something's just suddenly come over you. Tell me, so I can—

NORA. Oh, tie it outside! You're a worse fool than I thought you.

(CLANCY *half rises.*)

CLANCY. You mind your tongue, Miss!

NORA.—Irish.—It doesn't scare me. It never did. I was raised on it.

(CLANCY *turns in bewilderment to* CONNIE.)

CLANCY. What's the matter with her, Connie? What is it?

CONNIE. She's had a drink or two, I guess. Dutch courage, I guess.

NORA. You keep your oar out!

CLANCY. But she never touched anything.

NORA. Oh didn't I? And didn't I used to have a fine laugh at you, for not catching on!

CLANCY. You've been bewitched.

(*She leans toward him, elbow on knee, chin on hand, exasperated.*)

NORA. Listen—will you never learn?

CLANCY. Why did you run away from me with never a word? Was it because of all the misfortune that had suddenly come on us—and you thinking you'd brought it?

NORA. That's what you told yourself, is it?

CLANCY. I'm asking you, Nora—and what's more, you're to tell me.

NORA. That was part of it, yes.

CLANCY. What else?

NORA. Because I couldn't stand you! (*He looks at her aghast.*)

CLANCY. You don't mean that all at

once there was no more love in your heart for me—

NORA. I mean there never was any!

(CLANCY *frowns, still unable to comprehend. Again he turns to* CONNIE.)

CLANCY. She's joking.—You hear her, Connie: she's trying to make some kind of a joke.

NORA. Joke, my eye! I'm saying what I mean now, for once—and I mean just that—never ever—never a scrap of love!

(*He looks at her from under his brows.*)

CLANCY. For nearly four years we were man and wife—

NORA. You don't need to tell *me* that!

CLANCY.—You can't fool me, Nora. I have too good a memory.

(*She sees what he means, and laughs shortly.*)

NORA. Oh, I liked that part of it all right. I got round heels, you know.

(CLANCY's *face seets and his now angered eyes travel her from head to foot and back again. Finally he speaks very softly.*)

CLANCY.—From a dear and a loving and warm-hearted girl, full of grace and delight, something or someone has turned you in no time at all into a cheap, dirty-mouthed little piece. Someone has put a spell on you—who is it?

NORA. So there has to be someone *else*, does there? Listen, you—

CLANCY. Who is it? Tell me who it is. Because I'll render him null and void, so I will!

NORA. Don't be a fool. No one's anything to me but myself, and never has been.

CONNIE. That's nice of you. It's right sweet of you to leave him something.

(CLANCY *looks from one to the other, then rises and goes to* NORA, *stands over her, searching the impudent pretty face for something he wants desperately to find there. At last he speaks.*)

CLANCY. It's not that I don't love and cherish you as I always have, but you anger me. Your unwomanly talk and your vast impertinences and the silly, hollowed-out sound of a laugh that used to be sweet like a string-orchestra—it makes me angry.

NORA. So what?

CLANCY. I don't know yet, but you must be made to unlearn your new tricks.

NORA. Oh? By who?

CLANCY. By me!—You fresh, brassy little jape, sitting there on your hard seat with that new chippie look in your shoe-button eyes and that two-for-a-dollar smile round your mouth, you were once my wife, you still are. And I'll have no wife of mine abroad on such behavior, and you can make book on it!

NORA. So what do you plan to do?

CLANCY. You know what I'd like to do this minute?—I'd like to give you one with the flat of me hand that'd send you spinning down the Ages.

NORA.—Only you won't.

CLANCY. Don't be so sure, Miss.

NORA. You haven't it in you to. You're the original Mister Softheart, and your hands were made for love-pats. (*She rises.*) Well—save 'em for someone else. I'm not taking any. (*She drops a step or two back from him, opens her handbag, peers into a mirror in it, puts powder on her nose, snaps the bag shut and addresses him with a fine air of finality.*) Anything more?—If not, I'll be getting along now.

CLANCY. You will, will you?

NORA. Yes I will.

CLANCY. You'll stay directly where you are! You'll not move a step till I've found out another thing or two.

NORA. You're the thorough one, aren't you? Just a real good housecleaning.

CLANCY. There's many the dirty chimney I'd like to send the goose down tonight, I can tell you that!

(*She turns to* SPEEDY *with a great show of dignity.*)

NORA. Mr. Speedy, is it customary for ladies to be detained in your place against their wish?

SPEEDY. I never come between husband and wife. I've learned enough for—

(*He stops as the door from the restaurant is opened and* GURNEY *comes in. He is lighting a cigarette and kicks the door io after him.*)

GURNEY. Hello, everybody. How about a round on me? (*Silence greets him. He looks up, puzzled, and snaps his cigarette lighter shut with a flourish as* CLANCY *turns slowly and regards him. He tosses the lighter into the air, catches it again, pockets it and casually advances into the room.*) How are you, Clancy, old man? We've missed you round the Globe. It hasn't been the same place without your daily Specialty. How about a small one on me, to celebrate the homecoming?

CLANCY. No thank you.

GURNEY. No?—Then how about—er

—your good lady?

CLANCY. She neither.

PABST.—Isn't it interestin'?

GURNEY.Your eye looks fine—damned if I'd know it was any different from the other.

CLANCY. Never mind my eye!

GURNEY. Oh, come on! What's all the gloom about? Lent's over!

CLANCY. I wish you would go.

GURNEY. Thanks for the buggy-ride, only I'm staying.

CLANCY. I wish you would kindly leave now.

GURNEY. You're kidding. You know I'm a permanent attraction here. (*He seats himself at* DICKINSON's *table and slaps his hand down upon it.*) Come on—fill 'em up! (*He fills a glass from the whisky bottle and looks about him.*) What! No music? Where's Piano Mary?

(CLANCY *leans back against the table. Again his eyes have the dazed look in them.*)

CLANCY. Maybe I'm hungry. I don't know when I ate last.

(CONNIE *rises.*)

CONNIE. I'll bring something in for you from the Front.

(CLANCY *straightens.*)

CLANCY. No. I don't want it. (*Again he turns and addresses* GURNEY.) I ask you please to move along out of here. I'm talking with my wife.

(GURNEY *squints through his glass at the others.*)

GURNEY. I see: just a private run-through with all the boxes full. Why pick on me?

CLANCY. I don't like you, Val Gurney, and I never did. All I ever owed you was that it was through you that I first met up with Nora. But since she's left me I owe you no more.

GURNEY. Why, Clancy, you surprise me. I thought we were old friends. What's the trouble between you and the Missus?

(CLANCY *looks at* NORA.)

CLANCY. It turns out it was a stray cat I brought home. I buttered her paws, but she stayed only to lick them off, and then strayed again.

GURNEY. You don't say. And I thought you'd be the perfect match.

CLANCY. I remember you said so. (*Suddenly he advances to* NORA *and seizes her wrist.*) Only where did you stray *to*?

NORA. Let go!

CLANCY. I never thought—but I'm thinking now! Who was it?

CONNIE. Go easy, Dan.

NORA. You let me go!

CLANCY. Tell me his name! I'll—!

(NORA *cries out for help.*)

NORA. Val! Val!

(CLANCY *drags her up to him and stares into her face, then thrusts her aside and gazes incredulously at* GURNEY. PABST *whispers something to* SPEEDY, *and unnoticed by the others, they move to the restaurant door and go out.* GURNEY *puts out his cigarette and rises uncertainly.*)

GURNEY. Look here, old man—no need for any rough stuff, you know.

CLANCY.—So it was you.

GURNEY. Never mind about that. The point now is—

CLANCY. Never mind about it?

GURNEY. What I mean is, we can settle everything peacefully, with no hard feelings.

CLANCY. Settle a man's wife running off from him to another man—and one the likes of you?

GURNEY. Let's not get personal, now.

MARBLE. What would you like him to get?

DICKINSON. Yes—*you* tell us, will you?

GURNEY. Keep out, the lot of you! This is between Clancy and me. Am I right, Dan?

CLANCY. It is, that. It is surely.

GURNEY. It could happen to any of us, you know. What a man wants with a woman he can't hold, I could never see anyway.

CLANCY. Couldn't you?

GURNEY. No, frankly I couldn't.

CLANCY. And why?

GURNEY. Well, it's—you know—just bad box-office. It's bound to flop sooner or later.

CONNIE. Oh, the worm!

(CLANCY *advances.*)

GURNEY. Keep away!—If you so much as touch me, I'll—(*But* CLANCY's *hand is at the back of his neck now, and has begun to shake him slowly, like a sack.* GURNEY *struggles to free himself from the grasp, gasping:*) Let go, you fool! What do you think you're doing?

NORA. Stop it! Stop!

(*But the shaking goes on.*)

GURNEY. You, Speedy—call somebody! What kind of a joint is this?

NORA. Oh, stop it! Stop! Stop!

CONNIE. He had it coming. You both of you had.

(*With one twist of his arm,* CLANCY *sends* GURNEY *crashing against the base of the little stage, where he lies for a moment before he finds his feet again. Finally he rises, pulls himself together, brushes himself off, eyeing* CLANCY *with a look half fear, half hatred. He makes his way to the alley-door. His hand fumbles behind him for the door knob, finds it, turns it and holds on to it. Then he spits out his words:*)

GURNEY. You scum. You half-witted moron. Come around and ask me some more questions sometime. Ask me about your kid, for instance. She came pretty quick, didn't she?—Seven months, my foot—six was nearer it! Why else do you think Nora married you, you poor, dumb—

CONNIE. No, no!

(NORA *breaks in frantically:*)

NORA. Don't listen to him! (CLANCY *strides toward* GURNEY *but he is out the door before he can reach him.* NORA *stands shaking with rage, muttering to herself:*) He's lying. He's—

(CLANCY *comes up behind her.*)

CLANCY. Then why did you marry me —and not him? (*He swings her around to him.*) Tell me!

CONNIE. Don't hurt her, Dan!

CLANCY. She'll tell me!—Why?

NORA. He—he wouldn't. However much I asked—however much I—

CLANCY. It was him introduced us, him that brought us together. And from the first sight of you, you knew it was all up with me. And you took me straight off—

NORA. He made me! He kept after me till I—

CLANCY.—You put your head on my shoulder and said, "Let's not wait, Dan. Let's not wait a week even." Do you remember you did?

NORA. You don't know—you don't know—

CLANCY. That was in April—and less than seven months after—on the second day of November—though we'd not looked for it till the first of the year, if that soon—and the doctor said often at seven months if the mother was not as strong as she might be—(*Suddenly his voice catches and he stops. His head drops upon his breast. He murmurs to himself:*)—And I told myself there was no more ill could

happen to me! (*He raises his head, his face working. He touches her once, twice, lightly upon the shoulder with two fingers, speaking very gently.*)—You can go along now, Nora. (*He takes her coat from the chair and lays it upon her shoulders, pulling it awkwardly into place.*) There now—there we are. (*The pressure of his hand directs her to the door. He holds it open for her.*) Good-by now. When I think of the frets and the worries you've had, my heart aches for you, you bad girl, you.—Good-by, now. Good-by, Nora—(*She turns and looks at him. Finally she speaks.*)

NORA. Don't hate me, Dan.

CLANCY. No, Nora—no. (*She goes out and he closes the door after her. He stands there for a moment, then squares his shoulders, comes up to the table where* THE MAJOR *and* DICKINSON *sit and takes the chair left by* MA SPEEDY. I think I'll have a small drink now, if that's agreeable. (DICKINSON *fills a glass and sets it before him. He drains it at a gulp, puts it down and draws the back of his hand across his mouth.*)—That's what I needed.—"There comes a time," as they say.

DICKINSON. Oh yes, it's a swell world. God's in His Heaven, all right—and He's going to stay there.

(*This time* CLANCY *makes no attempt to refute him. He stares down at the table and his fingers begin to drum on it.* CONNIE *slips into the chair beside him, catches at the hand and holds it flat between her two own, rubbing it back and forth, as if to draw the blood back into it.*)

CONNIE. She was yours, little Angela was. She was all your own. Never have I known a baby to go so for any man. You were the one bright star in her little life. She was just a little fool for you, Dan—no one else even counted with her.

(*He swings around, frees his hand and joyously opens and shuts it between his face and* CONNIE'S. *His eyes are bright with tears, though he is half-laughing. He demands of her:*)

CLANCY. D'you remember—? How she used to—? The way she would—?— When I'd come in before supper and she heard my tread on the stairs, how she'd—?

(*He cannot finish.* CONNIE'S *arm goes around his shoulders, contracts briefly and is withdrawn.*)

CONNIE. She was all yours. She was all your own.

(CLANCY *shakes his head slowly.*)

CLANCY. She was not—and Nora never was neither. And all my fine consolations are no more than a heap of angel-droppings, as my young brother Tim used to say.

CONNIE. Hush, Dan—

(*Suddenly he strikes his fist upon the table.*)

CLANCY. I'll not! There's too much hushing done! We hush when we should be—! (*He throws back his head and shouts:*) —You up there, why do You send such blank confusion upon the world? What's the earthly good of half the things that happen?—Things that on the face of them are blundering injustices with no sense nor purpose—what's the reason for them? (*He drags himself to his feet and half-circles the room.*) Have You not said You'd come when we called You? Then where are You keeping Yourself?— What have You to lose by passing a moment or two with a man of Your own making in such unholy need of You? (*His arm lashes through the air in a peremptory gesture and his voice thunders the command:*) Can You not hear me? Then come to me! Come!

(*There is an expectant moment, as if the others half-believed the command would be obeyed. Then* DICKINSON's *glass upon the table shatters the silence.*)

DICKINSON. Knock, and it shall be knocked in your face. Seek, and you'll go on seeking.

CLANCY. Don't say it. Never say such a thing.

MARBLE. It's a sell, Dan, see?—All we can do is to make the best of it.

THE MAJOR.—That's what I say—the best of it.

CONNIE. It's—it's a long way up to heaven, you know—and it's a long way down.

CLANCY. It's a long time here—that I know, I know that.

DICKINSON.—*Now* do you believe in Him?

CLANCY. I don't know where He keeps Himself.

DICKINSON. Because your only hope is not to, Clancy. Anyone's is.

(CONNIE *goes to* CLANCY *and takes his hand in hers.*)

CONNIE. Don't mind him. Don't mind anything. Come along, now. It's sleep you need, Dan.

CLANCY. It is, it is that.

CONNIE.—And maybe it's a better day tomorrow, you know.

CLANCY. Yesterday was the good day —yesterday a long time ago. (*He stands for a moment, staring dully at the floor, then kicks at it once, as if to remove a worthless object from his path.*) What good is the Truth when you don't know what to do with it?

DICKINSON. Don't tell me it hasn't set *you* free, either.

(CLANCY *moves toward the alley with* CONNIE, *mumbling:*)

CLANCY. Free for what? Free for what?

(*Suddenly, through the spangled curtains at the back of the little stage a light is seen.* CLANCY *stops at the sight of it. Then the curtains are opened quietly, and from the now open private doorway there emerges the figure of an old man in a gray suit. He wears a soft white shirt with a flowing black tie. He has a gray mustache and his head is crowned with a great shock of white hair. He wears spectacles, and although his features are somewhat blurred against the strong light from the staircase behind him, it can be seen that his face is kindly, even benevolent. There is a white carnation in his buttonhole. He comes a few steps forward upon the stage and stands looking down over it, into the room.* THE MAJOR *looks up with a start and catches his breath.*)

THE MAJOR. It's—it's—it's Mr.—! (*All follow his eyes. When* THE FIGURE *speaks, it is in a thin, musical Irish voice, the accent much broader than* CLANCY's.)

THE FIGURE. Dan Clancy—(CLANCY *turns slowly.* THE FIGURE *smiles down at him, his face growing suddenly almost youthful with the smile.*)—Don't be in such a hurry, Clancy.

CLANCY. Mr. Concannon! — Look, Connie—it's Mr. Concannon!

CONNIE. I—I see it is. (THE MAJOR *slips down from his chair and stands stiffly erect. The venerable* FIGURE *comes forward a little further upon the stage.* CLANCY *exclaims joyfully:*)

CLANCY. Well now, well now—this is more like it! Welcome back to you, Sir!

MR. CONCANNON. Thank you, thank you! (*He turns to* THE MAJOR.)—Major Armstrong, good evening.

THE MAJOR. How—how do you do, Sir?

MR. CONCANNON. Much the same, thank you—much the same! And how are you, Clancy?

CLANCY. I'm fine, Sir—just fine! (MR.

CONCANNON *seats himself and indicates the step at his feet.*)

MR. CONCANNON. Sit where I can see you. (CLANCY *seats himself, looking up at him.* SPEEDY *re-enters quietly from the restaurant, resumes his place at the table and watches them with his hand over his mouth, cunning and privy.* MR. CONCANNON *smiles down upon* CLANCY.) What's been the trouble, my boy?

CLANCY. Trouble? (*Then, apologetically.*) I'm sorry, Sir, but things in general haven't been going quite as well as they might for me.

MR. CONCANNON. Things in general rarely do for anyone, it seems.

(CONNIE *seats herself with* THE MAJOR *at the other table.*)

CLANCY. They've just about got me down, I'm ashamed to admit.

MR. CONCANNON: You?—I don't believe you, Clancy. We all of us have our bad times, you know. Even I have had mine.

CLANCY.—That devil Jack Grossett— I recollect well. But he couldn't down *you.* Why, you look younger even than when I first saw you, though you must have stretched sixty then.

MR. CONCANNON. Sixty—was I ever that young?

CLANCY. Anyway, it's a real treat to have a sight of you again. Where is it you've been, Sir, if I may ask?

MR. CONCANNON. Oh—to and fro— up and down—all over, you know.

CLANCY. That was me own itinerary, too! And when did you get back, if I may also ask?

MR. CONCANNON. Just tonight.

CLANCY. This very night—and didn't I do the same! (*A moment, then.*) And were you at the Globe by any chance, Sir?

MR. CONCANNON. I was there.

CLANCY. I regret deeply I had to make such a holy display of myself.

MR. CONCANNON. You were deeply troubled: I understood that.

CLANCY. I guess there's not much you don't understand.

MR. CONCANNON. I have lived a long time.

(CLANCY *ponders a moment before going on.*)

CLANCY. It's a fair marvel that you happened to come back just tonight. It's a matter of—of vast encouragement to me. (*Then, carefully.*) Was there—? Did

somebody—? Don't take me amiss, Sir, but was there something special that brought you?—Just precisely on this very night, you know—

(MR. CONCANNON's *smile comes and goes. Finally, with a little gesture toward* CLANCY, *he speaks:*)

MR. CONCANNON. It's hard to explain. Somehow, I felt impelled to come.

CLANCY. Was it—was it as if—as if a cat jumped down on your back from a wall, maybe?

MR. CONCANNON. Why yes—yes, that expresses it perfectly.

CLANCY. Like me in Cleveland! Then you were—you must have been—! (*He checks himself.*)—And how long will you be staying, if I may ask?

MR. CONCANNON. That depends on you, Dan Clancy. How long do you think you will need me?

(*Suddenly* CLANCY *bounds to his feet with a joyous shout.*)

CLANCY. Oh Glory be, it's the truth then!

MR. CONCANNON. What, my boy?

CLANCY. Mr. Concannon, you're the noblest, godliest man ever I've—

MR. CONCANNON. Oh, come now!

CLANCY.—And the fact is, that all unbeknownst to yourself, you've been sent to answer my questions for me.

CONNIE. Dan—!

MARBLE. Well, for the love of—!

DICKINSON. Oh, let him get it off his chest.

CLANCY. I regret the inconvenience, but surely it's so.

MR. CONCANNON. Questions, you say?

CLANCY. I'm near to bursting with 'em!

MR. CONCANNON. What are they, Clancy?

CLANCY. Well—now I'm put to it I can hardly—(*He pauses.*) Well, you see, I—there've been a number of things— (*And pauses again.*)—But I mustn't speak of myself alone. There are plenty worse off than me. (*And again.*)—Maybe *you* can tell me, Sir—maybe you can tell me why, for all its pretty scenery, the whole earth is full of human misery, of death and tyranny and torture? Wherever I've been, for one contented individual I've found a dozen who suffered and sweat and strained—for what?—To get their backs broken and the hope put out of their eyes. (*In his excitement he rises and, still talking, paces up and down in front of the little stage.*) Even the rich I've seen, leading the life of Riley, have no great look of enjoying it—on the contrary! And even the luckiest ones must die in the end.

MR. CONCANNON. You are afraid of death?

CLANCY. I don't savor the thought of it. Not while I've yet to find the meaning of life—and find it, I can't for the life of me. For from what I can make out, it's an old, old story: the ancients being as full of corruption in their time as the Sixth Ward along River Street is today.

MR. CONCANNON. What else have you to ask?

CLANCY. Well, Sir, to come straight out with it, if it's Good that rules over us, why is it Evil that always seems to have the upper hand?

MR. CONCANNON. Things are not always what they seem.

CLANCY. Begging your pardon, Sir—but that's hardly an answer. I'm well aware that misfortune sometimes makes better men of us, but just as often—in fact, oftener—we're made the worse by it. So what's a man to think?

MR. CONCANNON. The problem of Good and Evil is a difficult one, Clancy. I expect we shall all know the answer one day.

CLANCY. But I'd like to know now—for I'm tough, and the hereafter looks a long way away to me.

MR. CONCANNON (*after a moment*). There must be the occasions for sin, must there not—that Virtue may hold her lovely head aloft? There must be persecution, must there not—to fortify man's faith in heaven? There must be slavery, must there not—that he may know the priceless boon of freedom?

CLANCY. Maybe there must be, but why must we *stand* 'em? Why can't we fight 'em off the face of the earth?

MR. CONCANNON. Submission: it is the Will of God. All must be left to the Almighty Will.

CLANCY. The same old—

(CONNIE *rises and demands.*)

CONNIE. Why? Why should we be leaving everything to Him, when long ages ago He left it all to us?

(CLANCY *turns and frowns at her.*)

CLANCY. How do you mean He did?

CONNIE. He gave us a will of our own, didn't He? It showed too much faith in us, maybe—but give it He did. How'd you like it taken back again? A man of your build—never able so much as to think or choose for himself—how'd you like that?

CLANCY. I wouldn't.

CONNIE. Well, then!

(CLANCY *swings around slowly and looks at* MR. CONCANNON, *distrust and suspicion growing in his eyes.* MARBLE *speaks to* DICKINSON.)

MARBLE. It seems to me life's nothing but a sleeper-jump to death. Why can't we have more wars, and get the whole job over with?

DICKINSON. Wars, yes! And rapes and lynchings—plagues and purges!

SPEEDY. Life's all right. It all depends on how you live it.

(THE MAJOR *looks at him, then stumps up beside* CLANCY *and addresses* MR. CONCANNON *in a shaky, earnest voice.*)

THE MAJOR. Tell me if you will, Sir—tell me His reason for—for creating things like—like me and Ma Speedy. Why are—why are freaks?

(MR. CONCANNON *smiles, not so benevolently this time.*)

MR. CONCANNON. Would you deny Him a sense of humor?

(THE MAJOR *starts back as if struck.*)

THE MAJOR. Oh, don't—please don't—

(CLANCY *springs up angrily.*)

CLANCY. That's no thing to say! What kind of a thing is that to be saying? And every question I've asked you, you've turned off with one of your own. You're not the James Concannon *I* know! Who are you, you old devil?—(*Suddenly he advances up the steps and upon the stage.*) Maybe the old war in Heaven came out the other way—maybe Michael the Archangel lost the fight after all—and to a crafty old rat too smart to let on that he'd won.—So we'd take *his* will as the will of God, eh? (*He plucks the carnation from* MR. CONCANNON's *buttonhole and flings it away.*) That would explain a lot of things, eh? Holy God, what wouldn't it! (*Deliberately the old gentleman takes off his wig, mustache and glasses, and a familiar face smiles mockingly at* CLANCY. CLANCY *steps back.*) You—?

(SPEEDY *crows delightedly.*)

SPEEDY. The Professor! Isn't he marvelous? He had his little kit in the coatroom and did the whole change in less than—Gentlemen, the Professor!

MARBLE. The Professor, my foot! That was an act, too. Who is it? Is it Jack Grossett himself maybe—here all along?

DICKINSON. Why not? *He* knows this town. He knows it's the Big Time's last stand, or damn near it—and why? James Concannon! Like hell they'd come to *his* Globe, or anyone else's. They'd follow the rest to the picture houses—*he* knows!

CLANCY (*to* PABST). Me life long I've thought it was Good ruled the world, but from the way you've ruled us here this night—

PABST. How dared you interfere with a show in my theater? How dared you interrupt as smooth a bill as tonight's?

(DICKINSON *rises*.)

DICKINSON. Clancy, you're right. The Devil is God now.

(*He draws his revolver.* SPEEDY *springs up.*

SPEEDY. Stop that! What do you think you're doing?

DICKINSON (*to* PABST). Oh you beauty, you beauty, you.—All right, Professor—relax, your act's over. It stank, Professor.

SPEEDY. Stop it, I say!

DICKINSON. Sit down. The guy who doubles God has got to be good. Otherwise—

(PABST *glances at* CLANCY, *smiles, and beckons to* DICKINSON.)

PABST. Come to the Globe Easter Monday.

DICKINSON. You don't open on Monday. You're canceled—booked out!

(DICKINSON *advances*.)

MARBLE. Easy there, boy.

DICKINSON. I hate the evil bastard. The world'll be better for—

PABST. Closer—come closer—

CONNIE. No, no! Look at him—it's what he wants!

DICKINSON.—And gets.

(*The beckoning hand is still a safe distance from the pistol. Once more* PABST *glances at* CLANCY, *then beckons again.*)

PABST. Closer—closer—a little closer—

DICKINSON.—Sweetheart.

(*He levels the pistol. Suddenly* PABST *cries out:*)

PABST. Help me, Clancy!

CONNIE. Watch out, Dan!

(*But* CLANCY *springs down from the stage toward* DICKINSON *just as the double discharge is heard. He buckles once, straightens again, and stands there, his eyes round with astonishment.*)

CLANCY. Well now, well now—

CONNIE. It was another trick! Dan—are you all right?

CLANCY. For a second I felt as if something hit me, but I feel nothing now. (*He bears down upon* DICKINSON *and knocks the pistol from his hand.*) You!—That's no way to be doing it!

DICKINSON. I tell you the Devil is God! Pabst is Grossett and Grossett, Concannon. And the Devil is God and we do his will!

CLANCY. No—that's as wrong as the other! Oh, I see now it's no will of God things are as they are—no, nor Devil's will neither! It's the will of all them like himself, the world over—men bad by their own choice—and the woods full of 'em!

(*He moves toward the table, sways and braces himself against it,* CONNIE *follows him.*)

CONNIE. Dan! What is it?

CLANCY. Answer? *You* gave me it!—the proud will of Man is my answer! The free will of Man, turned the wrong way. By the grace of God, free to think and choose for himself, was he?—Free to make his own world, eh? The fine job he's made of it! (*He comes around the table laughing joylessly.*)—With pride at the top and despair at the bottom and all manner of misery in the between—turning lies into truth and truth into lies until nobody knows the one from the other—

(*He gropes for a chair and sinks into it.* CONNIE *stands over him anxiously.*)

CONNIE. Dan—what's the matter with you?

(CLANCY's *face sets and his hand strikes the table.*)

CLANCY. But know we will, know we *will*!—For it's a fine instrument, the free will of man is, and can as easy be turned to Good as to Bad.—Ah, it's the grand thing, is man's will! Whatever it's sunk to, it can rise again. It can rise over anything, anything!

(PABST *is watching him intently.*)

PABST. Except one: Death, my poor clown.

CLANCY. Even that! By the stars, it can live and die and resurrect itself!

PABST. An appropriate sentiment for the day.

(CONNIE *cries out to* PABST.)

CONNIE. "Death"! What do you mean

by that!

PABST. Look at him.

(DICKINSON *and* MARBLE *move toward* CLANCY.)

DICKINSON. Clancy, for Christ's sake—

MARBLE. You, Speedy—get some one, quick!

CONNIE. Hurry—hurry!

CLANCY. No! Let me be! This is me own affair.

(*But* SPEEDY *has hastened out.* CLANCY'S *head sinks.*)

DICKINSON. Clancy!

(CLANCY *turns his head and smiles sideways at him.*)

CLANCY. Poor John — so glorious drunk, you thought you could rid the world of evil in a blow.

PABST. He is fantastic. He is incredible. (*He moves toward the restaurant door.* MARBLE *moves to stop him.* PABST *gestures peremptorily.*) One side!

(CLANCY *looks up.*)

CLANCY. Let him go. There are bigger birds than him.

(MARBLE *stands aside.* PABST *addresses them all.*)

PABST. I think we may view this as an accident.—That is, unless the change at the Globe is made public. Then I am afraid we shall have to hang Dickinson.

(*He goes out.* CLANCY'S *head lowers again.*)

CONNIE. Dan!

CLANCY. Come here, girl—

(*She comes to the table, drops down into a chair beside him.*)

CONNIE. But *are* you hurt? Tell me!

CLANCY. Just give me a look at you.

CONNIE. But tell me!

CLANCY. Do you know something?

CONNIE. What?

CLANCY. I like it better without.

CONNIE. It?

CLANCY. Your face.

CONNIE. Without what?

CLANCY. The little gold earrings.

CONNIE. But what's that got to do with—? (*Then in spite of herself, she cries out happily:*) Oh, do you, Dan?

CLANCY. I do—and that's the truth— and me last word on the subject.

(*For a moment they gaze at each other, saying nothing.* DICKINSON *begins softly:*)

DICKINSON. Once there was a little man in Country Kerry and he began to pack his little bag—

(CLANCY *turns to him. There is a broad smile upon his face, and his eyes are merry.*)

CLANCY. I'll send you the postcard.

(*He makes a half gesture toward* CONNIE, *then slumps forward upon the table.*)

CONNIE. Dan!

(*He does not reply.* THE MAJOR *murmurs:*)

THE MAJOR. The things that happen. Is—is he going to die?

(CLANCY *raises his head once more.*)

CLANCY. Who is not going to?

DICKINSON.—Those who live and die like you, Dan Clancy.

CLANCY. Thank you, John. (*His eyes half close. He draws a deep and satisfied breath.*) I smell the lemon tree. The air's full of it. Good-by to you all, now.

(*His head sinks slowly.* CONNIE *seizes his hand, clings to it desperately.*)

CONNIE. No, no! I won't let you!— Dear God, don't let him!

CLANCY. Hush, girl. I go of me own will, where I go.

(*His head settles down upon his breast and he is still.*)

CURTAIN

HARVEY
Mary Chase

Harvey was produced by Brock Pemberton at the Forty-Eighth Street Theatre, New York City, on November 1, 1944. It was directed by Antoinette Perry, with settings by John Root. The cast was as follows:

MYRTLE MAE SIMMONS . . Jane Van Duser
VETA LOUISE SIMMONS . . . Josephine Hull
ELWOOD P. DOWD . . . . Frank Fay
MISS JOHNSON . . . . Eloise Sheldon
MRS. ETHEL CHAUVENET Frederica Going
RUTH KELLY, R.N. . . . . Janet Tyler
DUANE WILSON . . . . Jesse White

LYMAN SANDERSON, M.D. . . . Tom Seidel
WILLIAM R. CHUMLEY, M.D.
                    Fred Irving Lewis
BETTY CHUMLEY . . . . Dora Clement
JUDGE OMAR GAFFNEY . . . . John Kirk
E. J. LOFGREN . . . . Robert Gist

The action of the play takes place in a city in the Far West in the library of the old Dowd family mansion and the reception room of Chumley's Rest. Time is the present.

ACT ONE. *Scene One:* The library, late afternoon. *Scene Two:* Chumley's Rest, an hour later.

ACT TWO. *Scene One:* The library, an hour later. *Scene Two:* Chumley's Rest, four hours later.

ACT THREE: Chumley's Rest, a few minutes later.

Copyright 1953, by Mary Chase.
Copyright 1943, by Mary Chase (under the title *The White Rabbit*).
Copyright 1944, by Mary Chase (under the title *Harvey*).

CAUTION: Professionals and amateurs are hereby warned that *Harvey*, being fully protected under the copyright laws of the United States of America, the British Empire, including the Dominion of Canada, and all other countries of the Copyright Union, is subject to a royalty. All rights, including but not limited to professional, amateur, motion picture, recitation, lecturing, public reading, radio broadcasting, television, and the rights of translation into foreign languages, are strictly reserved. Particular emphasis is laid on the question of readings, permission for which must be secured from the author's agent in writing.

All inquiries concerning rights (other than amateur rights for the United States and Canada) should be addressed to the author's agent, Harold Freedman, Brandt & Brandt Dramatic Department, Inc., 101 Park Avenue, New York 17, without whose permission in writing no performance of the play may be made.

The amateur acting rights of *Harvey* are controlled exclusively by the Dramatists Play Service, Inc., 14 East 38th Street, New York 16, without whose permission in writing no amateur performance of the play may be made.

The author of *Harvey*, Mary Coyle Chase, has followed a busy career, and although an assiduous writer, has led a full rich life. Perhaps the well appreciated humor she has lavished on *Mrs. McThing* and *Bernardine* as well as *Harvey* is something she developed as wife and mother in her native Denver, high above the oppressive valleys and considerably removed from the frantic show-place of Broadway.

Born on February 25, 1907 in Denver, Colorado, Mary Coyle was educated in that city's public schools and for three years (1921-23) at the University of Denver, after which she spent a year at the University of Colorado, at Boulder. She married the Denver journalist Robert Lamont Chase in 1928 and became the mother of three sons. In 1924, she became a newspaper reporter, and worked regularly for the *Rocky Mountain News* in Denver from 1928 to 1931. Following this stint, she worked as a free-lance correspondent for the International News Service and the United Press from 1932 to 1936. Subsequently she became a publicity director and served the local Teamsters' Union in that capacity from 1942 to 1944.

She wrote her first play, *Now You've Done It*, in 1937, and had another play called *Sorority House* produced as a motion picture in 1938. In 1938 she also wrote another work for the stage, *Too Much Business*. But she attained success as a playwright late, in 1944, with the Brock Pemberton production of *Harvey*, following which she succeeded on Broadway twice again, in 1952, with the fantasy *Mrs. McThing*, in which Helen Hayes delighted the public with a bizarre characterization, and in the same year with *Bernardine*, which commended itself to playgoers with a fresh treatment of adolescence, about which it is to be presumed the mother of three children would know a thing or two.

Mrs. Chase is reported to have worked for two years on her *chef d'oeuvre*; she wrote eighteen versions of *Harvey* before getting this delicately poised play, which blends comedy of character with fantasy, ready for the stage. Even then, she and her producer, Brock Pemberton, faced a problem—what to do with an eight-foot rubber rabbit made specially for the production. The problem was solved when *The Pooka*, as the play was then called, had its tryout in Boston. One look at the rabbit crossing the stage during the dress rehearsal, and both the author and the producer decided to do away with the pixilated Elwood P. Dowd's synthetic companion! Another problem, whom to cast as the lovable lush, was fortunately solved earlier when Pemberton chose the former vaudevillian Frank Fay. The success of the play was assured by the presence of Frank Fay and the absence of his furry companion—and, let us not forget, the assistance of the delightful Josephine Hull in the chief supporting role. No small portion of credit goes, of course, to Mrs. Chase herself. Plays have come and plays have gone since 1945, but New York playgoers have yet to see a more endearing comic fantasy.

ACT ONE

SCENE ONE

TIME: *Mid-afternoon of a spring day. The present.*

SCENE: *The library of the old Dowd family mansion—a room lined with books and set with heavy, old-fashioned furniture of a faded grandeur. The most conspicuous item in the room is an oil painting over a black marble Victorian mantelpiece at the lower part of the wall at stage* L. *This is the portrait of a lantern-jawed older woman. There are double doors at* R. *These doors, now pulled apart, lead to the hallway and across to the parlor, which is not seen. Telephone is on small table* L. *This afternoon there is a festive look to the room—silver bowls with spring flowers set about. From the parlor* R. *comes the sound of a bad female voice singing, "I'm Called Little Buttercup."*

AT RISE: MYRTLE MAE *is discovered coming through door* R. *and as telephone rings, she goes to it.*

———

MYRTLE. Mrs. Simmons? Mrs. Simmons is my mother, but she has guests this afternoon. Who wants her? (*Respectful change in tone after she hears who it is.*) Oh—wait just a minute. Hang on just a minute. (*Goes to doorway* R. *and calls.*) Psst—Mother! (*Cranes her neck more.*) Psst —Mother! (*Crooks her finger insistently several times. Singing continues.*)

VETA (*enters* R., *humming "Buttercup"*). Yes, dear?

MYRTLE. Telephone.

VETA (*turning to go out again*). Oh, no, dear. Not with all of them in there. Say I'm busy.

MYRTLE. But, Mother. It's the Society Editor of the Evening News Bee—

VETA (*turning*). Oh—the Society Editor. She's very important. (*She fixes her hair and goes to phone. Her voice is very sweet. She throws out chest and assumes dignified pose.*) Good afternoon, Miss Ellerbe. This is Veta Simmons. Yes—a tea and reception for the members of the Wednesday Forum. You might say—program tea. My mother, you know—(*Waves hand toward portrait.*) the late Marcella Pinney Dowd, pioneer cultural leader—she came here by ox-team as a child and she founded the Wednesday Forum. (MYR-

TLE *is watching out door.*) Myrtle—how many would you say?

MYRTLE. Seventy-five, at least. Say a hundred.

VETA (*on phone*). Seventy-five. Miss Tewksbury is the soloist, accompanied by Wilda McCurdy, accompanist.

MYRTLE. Come on! Miss Tewksbury is almost finished with her number.

VETA. She'll do an encore.

MYRTLE. What if they don't give her a lot of applause?

VETA. I've known her for years. She'll do an encore. (MYRTLE *again starts to leave.*) You might say that I am entertaining, assisted by my daughter, Miss Myrtle Mae Simmons. (*To Myrtle—indicates her dress.* MYRTLE MAE *crosses to* C.) What color would you call that?

MYRTLE. Rancho Rose, they told me.

VETA (*into phone*). Miss Myrtle Mae Simmons looked charming in a modish Rancho Rose toned crepe, picked up at the girdle with a touch of magenta on emerald. I wish you could see her, Miss Ellerbe.

MYRTLE (*crossing up* R. *Looks through door*). Mother—please—she's almost finished and where's the cateress?

VETA (*to Myrtle*). Everything's ready. The minute she's finished singing we open the dining-room doors and we begin pouring. (*Into phone.*) The parlors and halls are festooned with smilax. Yes, festooned. (*Makes motion in air with finger.*) That's right. Yes, Miss Ellerbe, this is the first party we've had in years. There's a reason but I don't want it in the papers. We all have our troubles, Miss Ellerbe. The guest list? Oh, yes—

MYRTLE. Mother—come.

VETA. If you'll excuse me now, Miss Ellerbe. I'll call you later. (*Hangs up.*)

MYRTLE. Mother—Mrs. Chauvenet just came in!

VETA (*arranging flowers on phone table*). Mrs. Eugene Chauvenet Senior! Her father was a scout with Buffalo Bill.

MYRTLE. So that's where she got that hat!

VETA (*as she and* MYRTLE *start to exit*). Myrtle, you must be nice to Mrs. Chauvenet. She has a grandson about your age.

MYRTLE. But what difference will it make, with Uncle Elwood?—Mae!

VETA. Myrtle—remember! We agreed not to talk about that this afternoon. The point of this whole party is to get you started. We work through those older women to the younger group.

MYRTLE. We can't have anyone here in the evenings, and that's when men come to see you—in the evenings. The only reason we can even have a party this afternoon is because Uncle Elwood is playing pinochle at the Fourth Avenue Firehouse. Thank God for the firehouse!

VETA. I know—but they'll just have to invite you out and it won't hurt them one bit. Oh, Myrtle—you've got so much to offer. I don't care what anyone says, there's something sweet about every girl. And a man takes that sweetness, and look what he does with it! (*Crosses to mantel with flowers.*) But you've got to meet somebody, Myrtle. That's all there is to it.

MYRTLE. If I do they say, That's Myrtle Mae Simmons! Her uncle is Elwood P. Dowd—the biggest screwball in town. Elwood P. Dowd and his pal—

VETA (*puts hand on her mouth*). You promised.

MYRTLE (*crossing above table, sighs*). All right—let's get them into the dining-room.

VETA. Now when the members come in here and you make your little welcome speech on behalf of your grandmother— be sure to do this. (*Gestures toward portrait on mantel.*)

MYRTLE (*in fine disgust*). And then after that, I mention my Uncle Elwood and say a few words about his pal Harvey. Damn Harvey! (*In front of table, as she squats.*)

VETA (*the effect on her is electric. She runs over and closes doors. Crosses behind table to* C). Myrtle Mae—that's right! Let everybody in the Wednesday Forum hear you. You said that name. You promised you wouldn't say that name and you said it.

MYRTLE (*rising, starting to cross* L.). I'm sorry, Mother. But how do you know Uncle Elwood won't come in and introduce Harvey to everybody? (*To mantel. Places flowers on it.*)

VETA. This is unkind of you, Myrtle Mae. Elwood is the biggest heartache I have. Even if people do call him peculiar he's still my brother, and he won't be home this afternoon.

MYRTLE. Are you sure?

VETA. Of course I'm sure.

MYRTLE. But Mother, why can't we live like other people?

VETA. Must I remind you again? Elwood is not living with us—we are living with him.

MYRTLE. Living with him and Harvey! Did Grandmother know about Harvey?

VETA. I've wondered and wondered about that. She never wrote me if she did.

MYRTLE. Why did she have to leave all her property to Uncle Elwood?

VETA. Well, I suppose it was because she died in his arms. People are sentimental about things like that.

MYRTLE. You always say that and it doesn't make sense. She couldn't make out her will after she died, could she?

VETA. Don't be didactic, Myrtle Mae. It's not becoming in a young girl, and men loathe it. Now don't forget to wave your hand.

MYRTLE. I'll do my best. (*Opens door.*)

VETA. Oh, dear—Miss Tewksbury's voice is certainly fading!

MYRTLE. But not fast enough. (*She exits.*)

VETA (*exits through door, clapping hands, pulling down girdle*). Lovely, Miss Tewksbury—perfectly lovely. I loved it.

(*Through door* U.L. *enters* ELWOOD P. DOWD. *He is a man about 47 years old with a dignified bearing, and yet a dreamy expression in his eyes. His expression is benign, yet serious to the point of gravity. He wears an overcoat and a battered old hat. This hat, reminiscent of the Joe College era, sits on the top of his head. Over his arm he carries another hat and coat. As he enters, although he is alone, he seems to be ushering and bowing someone else in with him. He bows the invisible person over to a chair. His step is light, his movements quiet and his voice low-pitched*).

ELWOOD (*to invisible person*). Excuse me a moment. I have to answer the phone. Make yourself comfortable, Harvey. (*Phone rings.*) Hello. Oh, you've got the wrong number. But how are you, anyway? This is Elwood P. Dowd speaking. I'll do? Well, thank you. And what is your name, my dear? Miss Elsie Greenawalt? (*To chair.*) Harvey, it's a Miss Elsie Greenawalt. How are you today, Miss Greenawalt? That's fine. Yes, my dear. I would be happy to join your club. I belong to several clubs now —the University Club, the Country Club and the Pinochle Club at the

Fourth Avenue Firehouse. I spend a good deal of my time there, or at Charlie's Place, or over at Eddie's Bar. And what is your club, Miss Greenawalt? (*He listens—then turns to empty chair.*) Harvey, I get the Ladies Home Journal, Good Housekeeping and the Open Road for Boys for two years for six twenty-five. (*Back to phone.*) It sounds fine to me. I'll join it. (*To chair.*) How does it sound to you, Harvey? (*Back to phone.*) Harvey says it sounds fine to him also, Miss Greenawalt. He says he will join, too. Yes— two subscriptions. Mail everything to this address. . . . I hope I will have the pleasure of meeting you some time, my dear. Harvey, she says she would like to meet me. When? When would you like to meet me, Miss Greenawalt? Why not right now? My sister seems to be having a few friends in and we would consider it an honor if you would come and join us. My sister will be delighted. 343 Temple Drive—I hope to see you in a very few minutes. Good-by, my dear. (*Hangs up.*) She's coming right over. (*Moves C. to* HARVEY.) Harvey, don't you think we'd better freshen up? Yes, so do I. (*He takes up hats and coats and exits* L.)

VERA (*enters, followed by* MAID). I can't seem to remember where I put that guest list. I must read it to Miss Ellerbe. . . . Have you seen it, Miss Johnson?

MAID. No, I haven't, Mrs. Simmons.

VETA. Look on my dresser. (MAID *exits* L.)

MYRTLE (*enters* R.). Mother—Mrs. Chauvenet—she's asking for you. (*Turning—speaking in oh-so-sweet tone to someone in hall.*) Here's Mother, Mrs. Chauvenet. Here she is. (*Enter* MRS. CHAUVENET. *She is a woman of about 65—heavy, dressed with the casual sumptuousness of a wealthy Western society woman—in silvery gold and plush, and mink scarf even though it is a spring day. She rushes over to* VETA.)

MRS. CHAUVENET. Veta Louise Simmons! I thought you were dead. (*Gets to her and takes hold of her.*)

VETA (*rushing to her, they kiss*). Aunt Ethel! (*Motioning to* MYRTLE *to come forward and meet the great lady.*) Oh, no— I'm very much alive—thank you—

MRS. CHAUVENET (*turning to* MYRTLE).— and this full-grown girl is your daughter —I've known you since you were a baby.

MYRTLE. I know.

MRS. CHAUVENET. What's your name,

dear?

VETA (*proudly*). This is Myrtle—Aunt Ethel. Myrtle Mae—for the two sisters of her father. He's dead. That's what confused you.

MRS. CHAUVENET. Where's Elwood?

VETA (*with a nervous glance at* MYRTLE MAE). He couldn't be here, Aunt Ethel — now let me get you some tea. (*Cross to* R. *of table* R.)

MRS. CHAUVENET. Elwood isn't here?

VETA. No—

MRS. CHAUVENET. Oh, shame on him. That was the main reason I came. (*Takes off scarf—puts it on chair* L. *of table.*) I want to see Elwood.

VETA. Come—there are loads of people anxious to speak to you.

MRS. CHAUVENET. Do you realize, Veta, it's been years since I've seen Elwood?

VETA. No—where does the time go?

MRS. CHAUVENET. But I don't understand it. I was saying to Mr. Chauvenet only the other night—what on earth do you suppose has happened to Elwood Dowd? He never comes to the club dances any more. I haven't seen him at a horse show in years. Does Elwood see anybody these days?

VETA (*and* MYRTLE *glance at each other*). Oh, yes—Aunt Ethel. Elwood sees somebody.

MYRTLE. Oh, yes.

MRS. CHAUVENET (*to* MYRTLE). Your Uncle Elwood, child, is one of my favorite people. (VETA *rises and crosses around chair* R. *of table.*) Always has been.

VETA. Yes, I remember.

MRS. CHAUVENET. Is Elwood happy, Veta?

VETA. Elwood's very happy, Aunt Ethel. You don't need to worry about Elwood——(*Looks through* R. *doorway. She is anxious to get the subject on something else.*) Why, there's Mrs. Frank Cummings— just came in. Don't you want to speak to her?

MRS. CHAUVENET (*crosses above chair to peer out* R). My—but she looks ghastly! Hasn't she failed though?

VETA. If you think she looks badly— you should see him!

MRS. CHAUVENET. Is that so? I must have them over. (*Looks again.*) She looks frightful. I thought she was dead.

VETA. Oh, no.

MRS. CHAUVENET. Now—what about tea, Veta?

VETA. Certainly—(*Starts forward to lead the way.*) If you will forgive me, I will precede you——(ELWOOD *enters.* MRS. CHAUVENET *turns back to pick up her scarf from chair, and sees him.*)

MRS. CHAUVENET (*rushing forward*). Elwood! Elwood Dowd! Bless your heart.

ELWOOD (*coming forward and bowing as he takes her hand*). Aunt Ethel! What a pleasure to come in and find a beautiful woman waiting for me!

MRS. CHAUVENET (*looking at him fondly*). Elwood—you haven't changed.

VETA (*moves forward quickly, takes hold of her*). Come along, Aunt Ethel—you mustn't miss the party.

MYRTLE. There's punch if you don't like tea.

MRS. CHAUVENET. But I do like tea. Stop pulling at me, you two. Elwood, what night next week can you come to dinner?

ELWOOD. Any night. Any night at all, Aunt Ethel—I would be delighted.

VETA. Elwood, there's some mail for you today. I took it up to your room.

ELWOOD. Did you, Veta? That was nice of you. Aunt Ethel—I want you to meet Harvey. As you can see he's a Pooka. (*Turns toward air beside him.*) Harvey, you've heard me speak of Mrs. Chauvenet? We always called her Aunt Ethel. She is one of my oldest and dearest friends. (*Inclines head toward space and goes* "Hmm!" *and then listens as though not hearing first time. Nods as though having heard someone next to him speak.*) Yes—yes—that's right. She's the one. This is the one. (*To* MRS. CHAUVENET.) He says he would have known you anywhere. (*Then as a confused, bewildered look comes over* MRS. CHAUVENET'S *face and as she looks to* L. *and* R. *of* ELWOOD *and cranes her neck to see behind him—*ELWOOD, *not seeing her expression, crosses her toward* VETA *and* MYRTLE MAE.) You both look lovely. (*Turns to the air next to him.*) Come in with me, Harvey—We must say hello to all of our friends—— (*Bows to* MRS. CHAUVENET.) I beg your pardon, Aunt Ethel. If you'll excuse me for one moment—(*Puts his hand gently on her arm, trying to turn her.*)

MRS. CHAUVENET. What?

ELWOOD. You are standing in his way —(SHE *gives a little—her eyes wide on him.*) Come along, Harvey. (HE *watches the invisible Harvey cross to door, then stops him.*) Uh-uh! (ELWOOD *goes over to door. He turns and pantomimes as he arranges the tie and brushes off the head of the invisible Harvey. Then he does the same thing to his own tie. They are* ALL *watching him,* MRS. CHAUVENET *in horrified fascination. The heads of* VETA *and* MYRTLE, *bowed in agony.*) Go right on in, Harvey. I'll join you in a minute. (*He pantomimes as though slapping him on the back, and ushers him out. Then turns and comes back to* MRS. CHAUVENET.) Aunt Ethel, I can see you are disturbed about Harvey. Please don't be. He stares like that at everybody. It's his way. But he liked you. I could tell. He liked you very much. (*Pats her arm reassuringly, smiles at her, then calmly and confidently goes on out at* R. *After his exit,* MRS. CHAUVENET, MYRTLE *and* VETA *are silent. Finally* VETA—*with a resigned tone—clears her throat.*)

VETA (*looking at* MRS. CHAUVENET). Some tea—perhaps—?

MRS. CHAUVENET. Why, I—not right now—I—well—I think I'll be running along. (*Crosses back of table.*)

MYRTLE. But—

VETA (*putting a hand over hers to quiet her*). I'm so sorry—

MRS. CHAUVENET. I'll—I'll be talking to you soon. Good-by—good-by—(*She exits quickly out* L. VETA *stands stiffly—her anger paralyzing her.* MYRTLE *finally tiptoes over and closes one side of door—peeking over, but keeping herself out of sight.*)

MYRTLE. Oh, God—(*Starts to run for doorway.*) Oh, my God!

VETA. Myrtle—where are you going?

MYRTLE. Up to my room. He's introducing Harvey to everybody. I can't face those people now. I wish I were dead.

VETA. Come back here. Stay with me. We'll get him out of there and upstairs to his room.

MYRTLE. I won't do it. I can't. I can't.

VETA. Myrtle Mae! (MYRTLE *stops.* VETA *goes over to her and pulls her down* C., *where they are directly in line with doorway.*) Now—pretend I'm fixing your corsage.

MYRTLE (*covering her face with her hands in shame*). Oh, Mother!

VETA. We've got to. Pretend we're having a gay little chat. Keep looking. When you catch his eye, tell me. He always comes when I call him. Now, then—do you see him yet?

MYRTLE. No—not yet. How do you do, Mrs. Cummings.

VETA. Smile, can't you? Have you no pride? I'm smiling— (*Waves off* R. *and laughs.*) and he's my own brother!

MYRTLE. Oh, Mother—people get run over by trucks every day. Why can't something like that happen to Uncle Elwood?

VETA. Myrtle Mae Simmons, I'm ashamed of you. This thing is not your uncle's fault. (*Phone rings.*)

MYRTLE. Ouch! You're sticking me with that pin!

VETA. That's Miss Ellerbe. Keep looking. Keep smiling. (*She goes to phone.*)

MYRTLE. Mrs. Cummings is leaving. Uncle Elwood must have told her what Harvey is. Oh, God!

VETA (*on phone*). Hello—this is Mrs. Simmons. Should you come in the clothes you have on—What have you on? Who is this? But I don't know any Miss Greenawalt. Should you what?—May I ask who invited you? Mr. Dowd! Thank you just the same, but I believe there has been a mistake.—Well, I never!

MYRTLE. Never what?

VETA. One of your Uncle Elwood's friends. She asked me if she should bring a quart of gin to the Wednesday Forum!

MYRTLE. There he is—he's talking to Mrs. Halsey.

VETA. Is Harvey with him?

MYRTLE. What a thing to ask! How can I tell? How can anybody tell but Uncle Elwood?

VETA (*calls*). Oh, Elwood, could I see you a moment, dear? (*To Myrtle.*) I promise you your Uncle Elwood has disgraced us for the last time in this house. I'm going to do something I've never done before.

MYRTLE. What did you mean just now when you said this was not Uncle Elwood's fault? If it's not his fault, whose fault is it?

VETA. Never you mind. I know whose fault it is. Now lift up your head and smile and go back in as though nothing had happened.

MYRTLE. You're no match for Uncle Elwood.

VETA. You'll see. (ELWOOD *is coming.*)

MYRTLE (*as THEY pass at door*). Mother's waiting for you. (*She exits.*)

VETA. Elwood! Could I see you for a moment, dear?

ELWOOD. Yes, sister. Excuse me, Harvey. (VETA *steps quickly over and pulls double doors together.*)

VETA. Elwood, would you mind sitting down in here and waiting for me until the party is over? I want to talk to you. It's very important.

ELWOOD (*crossing* C). Of course, sister. I happen to have a little free time right now and you're welcome to all of it, Veta. Do you want Harvey to wait too?

VETA (*To* R. *of* ELWOOD. *Quite seriously —not in a pampering, humoring tone at all*). Yes, Elwood. I certainly do. (*She steals out—watching him as she crosses through* R. *door. After she has gone out we see doors being pulled together from the outside and hear the click of a lock.* ELWOOD *goes calmly over to bookcase, peruses it carefully, and then when he has found the book he wants, takes it out and from behind it pulls a half-filled pint bottle of liquor.*)

ELWOOD (*looking at book he holds in one hand*). Ah—Jane Austen. (*He gets one chair, pulls it down, facing front. Gets chair* L. *and pulls it right alongside. Sits down, sets bottle on floor between chairs.*) Sit down, Harvey. Veta wants to talk to us. She said it was important. I think she wants to congratulate us on the impression we made at her party. (*Reads. Turns to Harvey. Inclines head and listens, then looks at back of book and answers as though Harvey had asked what edition it is, who published it and what are those names on the fly leaf; turning head toward empty chair each time and twice saying "Hmm?"*) Jane Austen—De Luxe Edition—Limited—Grosset and Dunlap— The usual acknowledgements. Chapter One—

AND THE CURTAIN FALLS

ACT ONE

SCENE TWO

SCENE: *The office in the main building of Chumley's Rest—a sanitarium for mental patients. The wall at back is half plaster and half glass. There is a door* U.C. *Through this we can see the corridor of the sanitarium itself. In the wall lower* R. *is a door which is lettered "Dr. Chumley." Above on* R. *wall is a bookcase, a small filing-case on top of it. Across the room at upper* L. *is another door lettered "Dr. Sanderson." Down* L. *is the door leading from the outside. There is a big desk* L.C. *at right angles with footlights, with chair either side of desk. At* R. *is a table with chairs on either side. One small chair upstage* C.

TIME: *An hour after the curtain of Scene One.*

AT RISE: MISS RUTH KELLY, *head nurse at Chumley's Rest, is seated* L. *of desk, taking notes as she talks to* VETA SIMMONS, *who stands* C. MISS KELLY *is a very pretty young woman of about twenty-four. She is wearing a starched white uniform and cap. As she talks to Veta she writes on a slip of paper with a pencil.*

KELLY (*writing*). Mrs. O. R. Simmons, 343 Temple Drive, is that right?

VETA (*nodding, taking handkerchief from handbag*). We were born and raised there. It's old but we love it. It's our home. (*Crosses to table* R., *puts down handbag.*)

KELLY. And you wish to enter your brother here at the sanitarium for treatment. Your brother's name?

VERA (*coming back to desk—raising handkerchief to eyes and dabbing*). It's—oh—

KELLY. Mrs. Simmons, what is your brother's name?

VETA. I'm sorry. Life is not easy for any of us. I'll have to hold my head up and go on just the same. That's what I keep telling Myrtle and that's what Myrtle Mae keeps telling me. She's heart-broken about her Uncle Elwood—Elwood P. Dowd. That's it. (*Sits chair* R. *of desk.*)

KELLY (*writing*). Elwood P. Dowd. His age?

VETA. Forty-seven the 24th of last April. He's Taurus—Taurus—the bull. I'm Leo, and Myrtle is on a cusp.

KELLY. Forty-seven. Is he married?

VETA. No, Elwood has never married. He stayed with Mother. He was always a great home boy. He loved his home.

KELLY. You have him with you now?

VETA. He's in a taxicab down in the driveway. (KELLY *rings buzzer.*) I gave the driver a dollar to watch him, but I didn't tell the man why. You can't tell these things to perfect strangers. (*Enter* WILSON, C. *He is the sanitarium strongarm. He is a big burly attendant, black-browed, about* 28. KELLY *crosses in front of desk toward bookcase.*)

KELLY. Mr. Wilson, would you step down to a taxi in the driveway and ask a Mr. Dowd if he would be good enough to step up to Room number 24—South Wing G?

WILSON (*glaring at* L. *upper corner of desk*). Ask him?——

KELLY (*above table* R., *with a warning glance toward Veta*). This is his sister, Mrs. Simmons. (KELLY *crosses to cabinet* R. *for card.*)

WILSON (*with a feeble grin*). How do—why, certainly—be glad to *escort* him. (*Exits down* L.)

VETA. Thank you.

KELLY (*coming* C. *to* R. *of Veta—handing her printed slip*). The rates here, Mrs. Simmons—you'll find them printed on this card.

VETA (*waving it away*). That will all be taken care of by my mother's estate. The late Marcella Pinney Dowd. Judge Gaffney is our attorney.

KELLY. Now I'll see if Dr. Sanderson can see you. (*Starts toward office* L.)

VETA. Dr. Sanderson? I want to see Dr. Chumley himself.

KELLY (*backs down* C). Oh, Mrs. Simmons, Dr. Sanderson is the one who sees everybody. Dr. Chumley sees no one.

VETA. He's still head of this institution, isn't he? He's still a psychiatrist, isn't he?

KELLY (*shocked at such heresy*). Still a psychiatrist! Dr. Chumley is more than that. He is a psychiatrist with a national reputation. Whenever people have mental breakdowns they at once think of Dr. Chumley.

VETA (*pointing*). That's his office, isn't it? Well, you march right in and tell him I want to see him. If he knows who's in here he'll come out here.

KELLY. I wouldn't dare disturb him, Mrs. Simmons. I would be discharged if I did.

VETA. Well, I don't like to be pushed off onto any second fiddle.

KELLY. Dr. Sanderson is nobody's second fiddle. (*Crosses to back of desk, her eyes aglow.*) He's young, of course, and he hasn't been out of medical school very long, but Dr. Chumley tried out twelve and kept Dr. Sanderson. He's really wonderful—(*Catches herself.*) to the patients.

VETA. Very well. Tell him I'm here.

KELLY (*straightens her cap. As she exits into door* L., *primps*). Right away. (VETA *rises, takes off coat—puts it on back of chair* R. *of desk, sighs.*) Oh dear—oh dear (*and crosses to table* R. WILSON *and* ELWOOD *appear in corridor.* ELWOOD *pulls over a little from* WILSON *and sees* VETA.)

ELWOOD. Veta—isn't this wonderful! (WILSON *takes him forcefully off upstairs.* VETA *is still jumpy and nervous from the surprise, and her back is to door* U.L. *as* DR.

SANDERSON *enters.* LYMAN SANDERSON *is a good-looking man of 27 or 28. He is wearing a starched white coat over dark trousers. His eyes follow* MISS KELLY, *who has walked out before him and gone out* C., *closing* C. *doors. Then he sees* VETA, *pulls down his jacket, and gets a professional bearing.* VETA *has not heard him come in. She is busy with her compact.*)

SANDERSON (*looking at slip in his hand. Crosses to* C). Mrs. Simmons?

VETA (*startled—she jumps*). Oh—oh dear—I didn't hear you come in. You startled me. You're Dr. Sanderson?

SANDERSON (*he nods*). Yes. Will you be seated, please?

VETA (*sits chair* L. *of table* R). Thank you. I hope you don't think I'm jumpy like that all the time, but I—

SANDERSON (*crossing in front of table to chair* R). Of course not. Miss Kelly tells me you are concerned about your brother. Dowd, is it? Elwood P. Dowd?

VETA. Yes, Doctor—he's—this isn't easy for me, Doctor.

SANDERSON (*kindly*). Naturally these things aren't easy for the families of patients. I understand.

VETA (*twisting her handkerchief nervously*). It's what Elwood's doing to himself, Doctor—that's the thing. Myrtle Mae has a right to nice friends. She's young and her whole life is before her. That's my daughter.

SANDERSON (*sits* R. *of table*). Your daughter. How long has it been since you began to notice any peculiarity in your brother's actions?

VETA. I noticed it right away when Mother died, and Myrtle Mae and I came back home from Des Moines to live with Elwood. I could see that he—that he— (*Twists handkerchief—looks pleadingly at Sanderson.*)

SANDERSON. That he—what? Take your time, Mrs. Simmons. Don't strain. Let it come. I'll wait for it.

VETA. Doctor—everything I say to you is confidential? Isn't it?

SANDERSON. That's understood.

VETA. Because it's a slap in the face to everything we've stood for in this community the way Elwood is acting now.

SANDERSON. I am not a gossip, Mrs. Simmons. I am a psychiatrist.

VETA. Well—for one thing—he drinks.

SANDERSON. To excess?

VETA. To excess? Well—don't you call it excess when a man never lets a day go by without stepping into one of those cheap taverns, sitting around with riff-raff and people you never heard of? Inviting them to the house—playing cards with them—giving them food and money. And here I am trying to get Myrtle Mae started with a nice group of young people. If that isn't excess I'm sure I don't know what excess is.

SANDERSON. I didn't doubt your statement, Mrs. Simmons. I merely asked if your brother drinks.

VETA. Well, yes, I say definitely Elwood drinks and I want him committed out here permanently, because I cannot stand another day of that Harvey. Myrtle and I have to set a place at the table for Harvey. We have to move over on the sofa and make room for Harvey. We have to answer the telephone when Elwood calls and asks to speak to Harvey. Then at the party this afternoon with Mrs. Chauvenet there—We didn't even know anything about Harvey until we came back here. Doctor, don't you think it would have been a little bit kinder of Mother to have written and told me about Harvey? Be honest, now—don't you?

SANDERSON. I really couldn't answer that question, because I——

VETA. I can. Yes—it certainly would have.

SANDERSON. This person you call Harvey—who is he?

VETA. He's a rabbit.

SANDERSON. Perhaps—but just who is he? Some companion—someone your brother has picked up in these bars, of whom you disapprove?

VETA (*patiently*). Doctor—I've been telling you. Harvey is a rabbit—a big white rabbit—six feet high—or is it six feet and a half? Heaven knows I ought to know. He's been around the house long enough.

SANDERSON (*regarding her narrowly*). Now, Mrs. Simmons, let me understand this—you say—

VETA (*impatient*). Doctor—do I have to keep repeating myself? My brother insists that his closest friend is this big white rabbit. This rabbit is named Harvey. Harvey lives at our house. Don't you understand? He and Elwood go every place together. Elwood buys railroad tickets, theater tickets, for both of them. As I told Myrtle Mae—if your uncle was so lonesome he had to bring something home—why couldn't he bring home something human? He has me, doesn't he? He has Myrtle Mae, doesn't he? (*She leans forward.*) Doctor—(*She rises to him.* HE *inclines toward her.*) I'm going to tell you something I've never told anybody in the world before. (*Puts her hand on his shoulder.*) Every once in a while I see that big white rabbit myself. Now isn't that terrible? I've never even told that to Myrtle Mae.

SANDERSON (*now convinced. Starts to rise*). Mrs. Simmons—

VETA (*straightening*). And what's more —he's every bit as big as Elwood says he is. Now don't ever tell that to anybody, Doctor. I'm ashamed of it. (*Crosses to* C., *to chair* R. *of desk.*)

SANDERSON (*crosses to* VETA). I can see that you have been under a great nervous strain recently.

VETA. Well—I certainly have.

SANDERSON. Grief over your mother's death depressed you considerably?

VETA (*sits chair* R. *of desk*). Nobody knows how much.

SANDERSON. Been losing sleep?

VETA. How could anybody sleep with that going on?

SANDERSON (*crosses to back of desk*). Short-tempered over trifles?

VETA. You just try living with those two and see how your temper holds up.

SANDERSON (*presses buzzer*). Loss of appetite?

VETA. No one could eat at a table with my brother and a big white rabbit. Well, I'm finished with it. I'll sell the house— be appointed conservator of Elwood's estate, and Myrtle Mae and I will be able to entertain our friends in peace. It's too much, Doctor. I just can't stand it.

SANDERSON (*has been repeatedly pressing a buzzer on his desk. He looks with annoyance toward hall door. His answer now to* VETA *is gentle*). Of course, Mrs. Simmons. Of course it is. You're tired.

VETA (*she nods*). Oh, yes I am.

SANDERSON. You've been worrying a great deal.

VETA (*nods*). Yes, I have. I can't help it.

SANDERSON. And now I'm going to help you.

VETA. Oh, Doctor . . .

SANDERSON (*goes cautiously to door— watching her*). Just sit there quietly, Mrs. Simmons. I'll be right back. (*He exits* C.)

VETA (*sighing with relief, rises and calls out as she takes coat*). I'll just go down to the cab and get Elwood's things. (*She exits out down* L. SANDERSON, KELLY, *and* WILSON *come from* C.)

SANDERSON. Why didn't someone answer the buzzer?

KELLY. I didn't hear you, Doctor—

SANDERSON. I rang and rang. (*Looks into his office. It is empty.*) Mrs. Simmons— (*Looks out door* L., *shuts it, comes back.*) Sound the gong, Wilson. That poor woman must not leave the grounds.

WILSON. She's made with a getaway, huh, Doc? (WILSON *presses a button on the wall and we hear a loud gong sounding.*)

SANDERSON. Her condition is serious. Go after her. (WILSON *exits* C.)

KELLY. I can't believe it. (*Above chair* R. *of desk.* SANDERSON *sits* L. *of desk and picks up phone.*)

SANDERSON. Main gate. Henry, Dr. Sanderson. Allow no one out of the main gate. We're looking for a patient. (*Hangs up.*) I shouldn't have left her alone, but no one answered the buzzer.

KELLY. Wilson was in South, Doctor.

SANDERSON (*making out papers*). What have we available, Miss Kelly?

KELLY. Number 13, upper West R., is ready, Doctor.

SANDERSON. Have her taken there immediately, and I will prescribe preliminary treatment. I must contact her brother. Dowd is the name. Elwood P. Dowd. Get him on the telephone for me, will you please, Miss Kelly?

KELLY. But Doctor—I didn't know it was the woman who needed the treatment. She said it was for her brother.

SANDERSON. Of course she did. It's the oldest dodge in the world—always used by a cunning type of psychopath. She apparently knew her brother was about to commit her, so she came out to discredit him. Get him on the telephone, please.

KELLY. But, Doctor—I thought the woman was all right, so I had Wilson take the brother up to No. 24 South Wing G. He's there now.

SANDERSON (*staring at her with horror*). You had Wilson take the brother in? No gags, please, Kelly. You're not serious, are you?

KELLY. Oh, I did, Doctor. I did. Oh, Doctor, I'm terribly sorry.

SANDERSON. Oh, well then, if you're sorry, that fixes everything. (*He starts to pick up house phone and finishes the curse under his breath.*) Oh—no! (*Buries his head in his hands.*)

KELLY. I'll do it, Doctor. I'll do it. (*She takes phone.*) Miss Dunphy—will you please unlock the door to Number 24—and give Mr. Dowd his clothes and——? (*Looks at Sanderson for direction.*)

SANDERSON. Ask him to step down to the office right away.

KELLY (*into phone*). Ask him to step down to the office right away. There's been a terrible mistake and Dr. Sanderson wants to explain—

SANDERSON (*crosses below table to* C). Explain? Apologize!

KELLY (*hanging up*). Thank heaven they hadn't put him in a hydro tub yet. She'll let him out.

SANDERSON (*staring at her*). Beautiful—and dumb, too. It's almost too good to be true.

KELLY (*crosses to* L. *of Sanderson*). Doctor—I feel terrible. I didn't know. Judge Gaffney called and said Mrs. Simmons and her brother would be out here, and when she came in here—you don't have to be sarcastic.

SANDERSON. Oh, don't I? Stop worrying. We'll squirm out of it some way. (*Thinking—starts toward* R.)

KELLY. Where are you going?

SANDERSON. I've got to tell the chief about it, Kelly. He may want to handle this himself.

KELLY. He'll be furious. I know he will. He'll die. And then he'll terminate me.

SANDERSON (*below table, catches her shoulders*). The responsibility is all mine, Kelly.

KELLY. Oh, no—tell him it was all my fault, Doctor.

SANDERSON. I never mention your name. (*Crossing to door* R.) Except in my sleep.

KELLY. But this man Dowd——(*Kneels on chair* R.)

SANDERSON. Don't let him get away. I'll be right back.

KELLY (*crosses to* L. *of chair* R. *of table*). But what shall I say to him? What shall I do? He'll be furious.

SANDERSON. Look, Kelly—he'll probably be fit to be tied—but he's a man, isn't he?

KELLY. I guess so—his name is Mister. (*Off chair.*)

SANDERSON (*across chair from her*). Go into your old routine—you know—the eyes—the swish—the works. I'm immune—but I've seen it work with some people—some of the patients out here. Keep him here, Kelly—if you have to do a strip tease. (*He exits* R.)

KELLY (*very angry. Speaks to closed door*). Well, of all the—oh—you're wonderful, Dr. Sanderson! You're just about the most wonderful person I ever met in my life. (*Kicks chair.*)

WILSON (*has entered from* C. *in time to hear last sentence*). Yeah—but how about giving me a lift here just the same?

KELLY. What?

WILSON. That Simmons dame.

KELLY (*crosses to Wilson*). Did you catch her?

WILSON. Slick as a whistle. She was comin' along the path hummin' a little tune. I jumped out at her from behind a tree. I says "Sister—there's a man wants to see you." Shoulda heard her yell! She's whacky, all right.

KELLY. Take her to No. 13 upper West R. (*Crosses* WILSON *to back of desk.*)

WILSON. She's there now. Brought her in through the diet kitchen. She's screamin' and kickin' like hell. I'll hold her if you'll come and undress her.

KELLY. Just a second, Wilson. Dr. Sanderson told me to stay here till her brother comes down—(*Round back of desk.*)

WILSON. Make it snappy—(*Goes out* C. ELWOOD *enters* C. KELLY *rises*).

KELLY. You're Mr. Dowd?

ELWOOD (*carrying another hat and coat over his arm. He bows*). Elwood P.

KELLY. I'm Miss Kelly.

ELWOOD. Let me give you one of my cards. (*Fishes in vest pocket—pulls out card.*) If you should want to call me—call me at this number. Don't call me at that one.

KELLY. Thank you.

ELWOOD. Perfectly all right, and if you lose it—don't worry, my dear. I have plenty more.

KELLY. Won't you have a chair, please, Mr. Dowd?

ELWOOD. Thank you. I'll have two. Allow me. (*He brings another chair down from* U.C. *to* L. *of table. Puts extra hat and coat on table* C. *Motions Harvey to sit in chair* L. *of table. He stands waiting.*)

KELLY. Dr. Sanderson is very anxious

to talk to you. He'll be here in a minute. Please be seated.

ELWOOD (*waving her toward chair* R. *of desk*). After you, my dear.

KELLY. Oh, I really can't, thank you. I'm in and out all the time. But you mustn't mind me. Please sit down.

ELWOOD (*bowing*). After you.

KELLY (*she sits chair* R. *of desk. He sits on chair he has just put in place*). Could I get you a magazine to look at?

ELWOOD. I would much rather look at you, Miss Kelly, if you don't mind. You really are very lovely.

KELLY. Oh—well. Thank you. Some people don't seem to think so.

ELWOOD. Some people are blind. That is often brought to my attention. And now, Miss Kelly—I would like to have you meet—(*Enter* SANDERSON *from* R. MISS KELLY *rises and backs up to below desk.* ELWOOD *rises when she does, and he makes a motion to the invisible Harvey to rise, too.*)

SANDERSON (*going to him, extending hand*). Mr. Dowd?

ELWOOD. Elwood P. Let me give you one of my cards. If you should want—

SANDERSON (*crossing to* C). Mr. Dowd—I am Dr. Lyman Sanderson, Dr. Chumley's assistant out here.

ELWOOD. Well, good for you! I'm happy to know you. How are you, Doctor?

SANDERSON. That's going to depend on you, I'm afraid. Please sit down. You've met Miss Kelly, Mr. Dowd?

ELWOOD. I have had that pleasure, and I want both of you to meet a very dear friend of mine—

SANDERSON. Later on—be glad to. Won't you be seated, because first I want to say—

ELWOOD. After Miss Kelly—

SANDERSON. Sit down, Kelly—(SHE *sits* L. *of desk, as does* ELWOOD—*who indicates to Harvey to sit also.*) Is that chair quite comfortable, Mr. Dowd?

ELWOOD. Yes, thank you. Would you care to try it? (*He takes out a cigarette.*)

SANDERSON. No, thank you. How about an ash tray there? Could we give Mr. Dowd an ash tray? (KELLY *gets up—gets it from wall* L. ELWOOD *and Harvey rise also.* ELWOOD *beams as he turns and watches her.* KELLY *puts ash tray by* DOWD, *who moves it to share with Harvey.*) Is it too warm in here for you, Mr. Dowd? Would you like me to open a window? (ELWOOD

hasn't heard. He is watching Miss Kelly.)

KELLY (*turning, smiling at him*). Mr. Dowd—Dr. Sanderson wants to know if he should open a window?

ELWOOD. That's entirely up to him. I wouldn't presume to live his life for him. (*During this dialogue* SANDERSON *is near window.* KELLY *has her eyes on his face.* ELWOOD *smiles at Harvey fondly.* KELLY *sits at* L. *of desk.*)

SANDERSON. Now then, Mr. Dowd, I can see that you're not the type of person to be taken in by any high-flown phrases or beating about the bush. (*Sits on lower* R. *corner of desk.*)

ELWOOD (*politely*). Is that so, Doctor?

SANDERSON. You have us at a disadvantage here. You know it. We know it. Let's lay the cards on the table.

ELWOOD. That certainly appeals to me, Doctor.

SANDERSON. Best way in the long run. People are people, no matter where you go.

ELWOOD. That is very often the case.

SANDERSON. And being human are therefore liable to mistakes. Miss Kelly and I have made a mistake here this afternoon, Mr. Dowd, and we'd like to explain it to you.

KELLY. It wasn't Doctor Sanderson's fault, Mr. Dowd. It was mine.

SANDERSON. A human failing—as I said.

ELWOOD. I find it very interesting, nevertheless. You and Miss Kelly here? (THEY *nod.*) This afternoon—you say? (THEY *nod.* ELWOOD *gives Harvey a knowing look.*)

KELLY. We do hope you'll understand, Mr. Dowd.

ELWOOD. Oh, yes. Yes. These things are often the basis of a long and warm friendship.

SANDERSON. And the responsibility is, of course, not hers—but mine.

ELWOOD. Your attitude may be old-fashioned, Doctor—but I like it.

SANDERSON. Now, if I had seen your sister first—that would have been an entirely different story.

ELWOOD. Now there you surprise me. I think the world and all of Veta—but I had supposed she had seen her day. (KELLY *sits chair* R. *of desk.*)

SANDERSON. You must not attach any blame to her. She is a very sick woman. Came in here insisting you were in need of treatment. That's perfectly ridiculous.

ELWOOD. Veta shouldn't be upset about me. I get along fine.

SANDERSON. Exactly but your sister had already talked to Miss Kelly, and there had been a call from your family lawyer, Judge Gaffney

ELWOOD. Oh, yes, I know him. Know his wife, too. Nice people. (*He turns to Harvey takes cigarette; he needs a match.*)

SANDERSON. Is there something I can get for you, Mr. Dowd?

ELWOOD. What did you have in mind?

SANDERSON. A light—here—let me give you a light. (*Crosses to* DOWD, *lights his cigarette.* ELWOOD *brushes smoke away from the rabbit*). Your sister was extremely nervous and plunged right away into a heated tirade on your drinking. (*Crosses back to sit on chair* R. *of desk.*)

ELWOOD. That was Veta.

SANDERSON. She became hysterical.

ELWOOD. I tell Veta not to worry about that. I'll take care of that.

SANDERSON. Exactly. Oh, I suppose you take a drink now and then—the same as the rest of us?

ELWOOD. Yes, I do. As a matter of fact, I would like one right now.

SANDERSON. Matter of fact, so would I, but your sister's reaction to the whole matter of drinking was entirely too intense. Does your sister drink, Mr. Dowd?

ELWOOD. Oh, no, Doctor. No. I don't believe Veta has ever taken a drink.

SANDERSON. Well, I'm going to surprise you. I think she has and does—constantly.

ELWOOD. I am certainly surprised.

SANDERSON. But it's not her alcoholism that's going to be the basis for my diagnosis of her case. It's much more serious than that. It was when she began talking so emotionally about this big white rabbit—Harvey—yes, I believe she called him Harvey—

ELWOOD (*nodding*). Harvey is his name.

SANDERSON. She claimed you were persecuting her with this Harvey.

ELWOOD. I haven't been persecuting her with Harvey. Veta shouldn't feel that way. And now, Doctor, before we go any further I must insist you let me introduce—(*He starts to rise.*)

SANDERSON. Let me make my point first, Mr. Dowd. This trouble of your sister's didn't spring up overnight. Her condition stems from trauma.

ELWOOD (*sits down again*). From what?

SANDERSON. From trauma spelled T-R-A-U-M-A. It means shock. Nothing unusual about it. There is the birth trauma. The shock to the act of being born.

ELWOOD (*nodding*). That's the one we never get over—

SANDERSON. You have a nice sense of humor, Dowd—hasn't he, Miss Kelly?

KELLY. Oh, yes, Doctor.

ELWOOD. May I say the same about both of you?

SANDERSON. To sum it all up—your sister's condition is serious, but I can help her. She must however remain out here temporarily.

ELWOOD. I've always wanted Veta to have everything she needs.

SANDERSON. Exactly.

ELWOOD. But I wouldn't want Veta to stay out here unless she liked it out here and wanted to stay here.

SANDERSON. Of course. (*To Kelly.*) Did Wilson get what he went after? (KELLY *nods.*)

KELLY. Yes, Doctor. (*She rises.*)

SANDERSON. What was Mrs. Simmons' attitude, Miss Kelly?

KELLY (*crosses above desk to file cabinet* R). Not unusual, Doctor.

SANDERSON (*rising*). Mr. Dowd, if this were an ordinary delusion—something reflected on the memory picture—in other words, if she were seeing something she had seen once—that would be one thing. But this is more serious. It stands to reason nobody has ever seen a white rabbit six feet high.

ELWOOD (*smiles at Harvey*). Not very often, Doctor.

SANDERSON. I like you, Dowd.

ELWOOD. I like you, too, Doctor. And Miss Kelly here. (*Looks for* MISS KELLY, *who is just crossing in front of window seat.* ELWOOD *springs to his feet.* KELLY *sits quickly.* ELWOOD *motions Harvey down and sits, himself.*) I like her, too.

SANDERSON. So she must be committed here temporarily. Under these circumstances I would commit my own grandmother. (*Goes to* L. *of desk.*)

ELWOOD. Does your grandmother drink, too?

SANDERSON. It's just an expression. (*Leans over desk.*) Now will you sign these temporary commitment papers as next-of-kin—just a formality?

ELWOOD (*rises, crosses to* R. *of desk*). You'd better have Veta do that, Doctor. She always does all the signing and managing for the family. She's good at it. (*Pushes chair* R. *of desk under desk.*)

SANDERSON. We can't disturb her now. (*Sits* L. *of desk.*)

ELWOOD. Perhaps I'd better talk it over with Judge Gaffney?

SANDERSON. You can explain it all to him later. Tell him I advised it. And it isn't as if you couldn't drop in here any time and make inquiries. Glad to have you. I'll make out a full visitor's pass for you. When would you like to come back? Wednesday, say? Friday, say?

ELWOOD. You and Miss Kelly have been so pleasant I can come back right after dinner. About an hour.

SANDERSON (*taken aback*). Well—we're pretty busy around here, but I guess that's all right.

ELWOOD. I don't really have to go now. I'm not very hungry.

SANDERSON. Delighted to have you stay—but Miss Kelly and I have to get on upstairs now. Plenty of work to do. But I tell you what you might like to do.

ELWOOD. What might I like to do?

SANDERSON. We don't usually do this— but just to make sure in your mind that your sister is in good hands why don't you look around here? If you go through that door—(*Rises—points beyond stairway.*) and turn right just beyond the stairway you'll find the occupational therapy room down the hall, and beyond that the conservatory, the library, and the diet kitchen.

ELWOOD. For Veta's sake I believe I'd better do that, Doctor.

SANDERSON. Very well, then. (*He is now anxious to terminate the interview. Rises, shakes hands.*) It's been a great pleasure to have this little talk with you, Mr. Dowd. (*Gives him pass.*)

ELWOOD (*walking toward her*). I've enjoyed it too, Doctor—meeting you and Miss Kelly.

SANDERSON. And I will say that for a layman you show an unusually acute perception into psychiatric problems.

ELWOOD. Is that a fact? I never thought I knew anything about it. Nobody does, do you think?

SANDERSON. Well—the good psychiatrist is not found under every bush.

ELWOOD. You have to pick the right bush. Since we all seem to have enjoyed this so much, let us keep right on. I would like to invite you to come with me now down to Charlie's Place and have a drink. When I enjoy people I like to stay right with them.

SANDERSON. Sorry—we're on duty now. Give us a rain check. Some other time be glad to.

ELWOOD. When?

SANDERSON. Oh—can't say right now. Miss Kelly and I don't go off duty till ten o'clock at night.

ELWOOD. Let us go to Charlie's at ten o'clock tonight.

SANDERSON. Well—

ELWOOD. And you, Miss Kelly?

KELLY. I—(*Looks at Sanderson.*)

SANDERSON. Dr. Chumley doesn't approve of members of the staff fraternizing, but since you've been so understanding perhaps we could manage it.

ELWOOD. I'll pick you up out here in a cab at ten o'clock tonight and the four of us will spend a happy evening. I want you both to become friends with a very dear friend of mine. You said later on— so later on it will be. Good-by, now. (*Motions good-by to Harvey. Tips hat, exits* C.)

KELLY (*places chair and ash tray against back wall*). Whew—now I can breathe again!

SANDERSON. Boy, that was a close shave all right, but he seemed to be a pretty reasonable sort of fellow. That man is proud—what he has to be proud of I don't know. I played up to that pride. You can get to almost anybody if you want to. Now I must look in on that Simmons woman. (*Crosses below desk toward* C.)

KELLY (*at* R. C.). Dr. Sanderson—! (SANDERSON *turns.*) You say you can get to anybody if you want to. How can you do that?

SANDERSON. Takes study, Kelly. Years of specialized training. There's only one thing I don't like about this Dowd business.

KELLY. What's that?

SANDERSON. Having to make that date with him. Of course the man has left here as a good friend and booster of this sanitarium—so I guess I'll have to go with him tonight—but you don't have to go.

KELLY. Oh! (*Back of chair* L. *of table.*)

SANDERSON. No point in it. I'll have a drink with him, pat him on the back and leave. I've got a date tonight, anyway.

KELLY (*freezing*). Oh, yes—by all means. I didn't intend to go, anyway. The idea bored me stiff. I wouldn't go if I never went anywhere again. I wouldn't go if my life depended on it.

SANDERSON (*stepping back to her*). What's the matter with you, Kelly? What are you getting so emotional about?

KELLY. He may be a peculiar man with funny clothes, but he knows how to act. His manners were perfect.

SANDERSON. I saw you giving him the doll-puss stare. I didn't miss that.

KELLY. He wouldn't sit down till I sat down. He told me I was lovely and he called me dear. I'd go to have a drink with him if you weren't going.

SANDERSON. Sure you would. And look at him! All he does is hang around bars. He doesn't work. All that corny bowing and getting up out of his chair every time a woman makes a move. Why, he's as outdated as a cast-iron deer. But you'd sit with him in a bar and let him flatter you—You're a wonderful girl, Kelly.

KELLY. Now let me tell you something—you—(*Enter from down* R. *the great* DR. WILLIAM CHUMLEY. DR. CHUMLEY *is a large, handsome man of about 57. He has gray hair and wears rimless glasses, which he removes now and then to tap on his hand for emphasis. He is smartly dressed. His manner is confident, pompous, and lordly. He is good and he knows it*).

CHUMLEY (*enters with book*). Dr. Sanderson! Miss Kelly! (THEY *break apart and jump to attention like two buck privates before a C.O.*)

KELLY AND SANDERSON. Yes, Doctor?

CHUMLEY. Tell the gardener to prune more carefully around my prize dahlias along the fence by the main road. They'll be ready for cutting next week. (*At upper corner of bookcase.*) The difficulty of the woman who has the big white rabbit— has it been smoothed over?

SANDERSON. Yes, Doctor. I spoke to her brother and he was quite reasonable.

CHUMLEY. While I have had many patients out here who saw animals, I have never before had a patient with an animal that large. (*Puts book in bookcase.*)

SANDERSON. Yes, Doctor. She called him Harvey.

CHUMLEY. Harvey. Unusual name for an animal of any kind. Harvey is a man's name. I have known several men in my day named Harvey, but I have never heard of any type of animal whatsoever with that name. The case has an interesting phase, Doctor. (*Finishes straightening books.*)

SANDERSON. Yes, Doctor.

CHUMLEY. I will now go upstairs with you and look in on this woman. It may be that we can use my formula 977 on her. I will give you my advice in prescribing the treatment, Doctor. (*Crosses to below table.*)

SANDERSON. Thank you, Doctor.

CHUMLEY. (*Starts to move across stage toward* C. *and stops, draws himself up sternly.*) And now—may I ask—what is that hat and coat doing on that table? Whose is it?

SANDERSON. I don't know. Do you know, Miss Kelly? Was it Dowd's?

KELLY (*above table, picking up hat and coat*). He had his hat on, Doctor. Perhaps it belongs to a relative of one of the patients.

CHUMLEY (*crosses to* C.). Hand me the hat. (KELLY *hands it. Looking inside:*) There may be some kind of identification— Here—what's this—what's this? (*Pushes two fingers up through the holes.*) Two holes cut in the crown of this hat. See!

KELLY. That's strange!

CHUMLEY. Some new fad—put them away. Hang them up—get them out of here. (KELLY *takes them into upper* L. *office.* CHUMLEY *starts crossing to table.* KELLY *has come out of* L. WILSON *comes in through* C.)

WILSON (*very impressed with Dr. Chumley and very fond of him.*) Hello, Dr. Chumley.

CHUMLEY. Oh, there you are.

WILSON. How is every little old thing? (DR. CHUMLEY *picks up pad of notes from* R. *of desk;* R. *of table, looking at notes.* KELLY *re-enters from upper left.*)

CHUMLEY. Fair, thank you, Wilson, fair.

WILSON (*top of desk*). Look—somebody's gonna have to give me a hand with this Simmons dame—order a restraining jacket or something. She's terrible. (*To Kelly.*) Forgot me, didn't you? Well, I got her corset off all by myself.

CHUMLEY. We're going up to see this patient right now, Wilson.

WILSON. She's in a hydro tub now— my God—I left the water running on her! (*Runs off* C. *upstairs, followed by*

KELLY.) (BETTY CHUMLEY, *the Doctor's wife, enters down* L. *She is a good-natured, gay, bustling woman of about 55.*)

BETTY. Willie—remember your promise—Hello, Dr. Sanderson. Willie, you haven't forgotten Dr. McClure's cocktail party? We promised them faithfully. (*Sits* L. *of table* R.)

CHUMLEY. That's right. I have to go upstairs now and look in on a patient. Be down shortly—(*Exits* C. *upstairs.*)

BETTY (*calling after him; as she crosses down to chair* L. *of table, she sits, fixes her shoe*). Give a little quick diagnosis, Willie—we don't want to be late to the party. I'm dying to see the inside of that house. (*Enter* ELWOOD *from* C. *He doesn't see Betty at first. He looks around the room carefully.*) Good evening.

ELWOOD (*removing his hat and bowing*). Good evening. (*Puts hat on desk. Walks over to her.*)

BETTY. I am Mrs. Chumley. Doctor Chumley's wife.

ELWOOD. I'm happy to know that. Dowd is my name. Elwood P. Let me give you one of my cards. (*Gives her one.*) If you should want to call me—call me at this one. Don't call me at that one, because that's—(*Points at card.*) the old one. (*Starts one step. Looking.*)

BETTY. Thank you. Is there something I can do for you?

ELWOOD (*turns to her*). What did you have in mind?

BETTY. You seem to be looking for someone.

ELWOOD (*walking*). Yes, I am. I'm looking for Harvey. I went off without him.

BETTY. Harvey? Is he a patient here?

ELWOOD (*turns*). Oh, no. Nothing like that. (*Cross to door down* L.)

BETTY. Does he work here?

ELWOOD (*looking out down* L. *door*). Oh, no. He is what you might call my best friend. He is also a pooka. He came out here with me and Veta this afternoon.

BETTY. Where was he when you last saw him?

ELWOOD (*behind chair* L. *of desk*). In that chair there—with his hat and coat on the table.

BETTY. There doesn't seem to be any hat and coat around here now. Perhaps he left?

ELWOOD. Apparently. I don't see him anywhere. (*Looks in* SANDERSON's *office.*)

BETTY. What was that word you just said—pooka?

ELWOOD (*crosses* C. *He is looking in hallway* C.) Yes—that's it.

BETTY. Is that something new? (*Looks in hallway.*)

ELWOOD (*coming down*). Oh, no. As I understand it, that's something very old.

BETTY. Oh, really? I had never happened to hear it before.

ELWOOD. I'm not too surprised at that. I hadn't myself, until I met him. I do hope you get an opportunity to meet him. I'm sure he would be quite taken with you. (*Down* C. *on a line with Betty.*)

BETTY. Oh, really? Well, that's very nice of you to say so, I'm sure.

ELWOOD. Not at all. If Harvey happens to take a liking to people he expresses himself quite definitely. If he's not particularly interested, he sits there like an empty chair or an empty space on the floor. Harvey takes his time making his mind up about people. Choosey, you see. (*Crosses above table to door* R.)

BETTY. That's not such a bad way to be in this day and age.

ELWOOD. Harvey is fond of my sister, Veta. That's because he is fond of me, and Veta and I come from the same family. Now you'd think that feeling would be mutual, wouldn't you? (*Looks in office* R. *Crosses to chair* R. *of table.*) But Veta doesn't seem to care for Harvey. Don't you think that's rather too bad, Mrs. Chumley?

BETTY. Oh, I don't know, Mr. Dowd. I gave up a long time ago expecting my family to like my friends. It's useless.

ELWOOD. But we must keep on trying. (*Sits chair* R. *of table.*)

BETTY. Well, there's no harm in trying, I suppose.

ELWOOD. Because if Harvey has said to me once he has said a million times— "Mr. Dowd, I would do anything for you." Mrs. Chumley—

BETTY. Yes—

ELWOOD. Did you know that Mrs. McElhinney's Aunt Rose is going to drop in on her unexpectedly tonight from Cleveland?

BETTY. Why, no I didn't—

ELWOOD. Neither does she. That puts you both in the same boat, doesn't it?

BETTY. Well, I don't know anybody named—Mrs.—

ELWOOD. Mrs. McElhinney? Lives next door to us. She is a wonderful woman. Harvey told me about her Aunt Rose. That's an interesting little news item, and you are perfectly free to pass it around.

BETTY. Well, I——

ELWOOD. Would you care to come downtown with me now, my dear? I would be glad to buy you a drink.

BETTY. Thank you very much, but I am waiting for Dr. Chumley and if he came down and found me gone he would be liable to raise—he would be irritated!

ELWOOD. We wouldn't want that, would we? Some other time, maybe? (*He rises.*)

BETTY. I'll tell you what I'll do, however.

ELWOOD. What will you do, however? I'm interested.

BETTY. If your friend comes in while I'm here I'd be glad to give him a message for you.

ELWOOD (*gratefully*). Would you do that? I'd certainly appreciate that. (*Goes up* C. *to top of desk for his hat.*)

BETTY. No trouble at all. I'll write it down on the back of this. (*Holds up card. Takes pencil from purse.*) What would you like me to tell him if he comes in while I'm still here?

ELWOOD. Ask him to meet me downtown—if he has no other plans.

BETTY (*writing*). Meet Mr. Dowd downtown. Any particular place downtown?

ELWOOD. He knows where. Harvey knows this town like a book.

BETTY (*writing*). Harvey—you know where. Harvey what?

ELWOOD. Just Harvey.

BETTY (*rises—crosses to desk*). I'll tell you what.

ELWOOD. What?

BETTY (*swings chair* R. *of desk in position*). Doctor and I are going right downtown—to 12th and Montview. Dr. McClure is having a cocktail party.

ELWOOD (*at* L. *of desk; he writes that down on pad on desk*). A cocktail party at 12th and Montview.

BETTY. We're driving there in a few minutes. We could give your friend a lift into town.

ELWOOD. I hate to impose on you—but I would certainly appreciate that.

BETTY. No trouble at all. Dr. McClure is having this party for his sister from Wichita.

ELWOOD. I didn't know Dr. McClure had a sister in Wichita.

BETTY. Oh—you *know* Dr. McClure?

ELWOOD. No.

BETTY (*puts Elwood's card down on desk*). But——(*Sits chair* R. *of desk.*)

ELWOOD. You're quite sure you haven't time to come into town with me and have a drink?

BETTY. I really couldn't—but thank you just the same.

ELWOOD. Some other time, perhaps?

BETTY. Thank you.

ELWOOD. It's been very pleasant to meet you, and I hope to see you again.

BETTY. Yes, so do I.

ELWOOD. Good-night, my dear. (*Tips hat—bows—goes to door, turns.*) You can't miss Harvey. He's very tall—(*Shows with hands.*) Like that—(*Exits down* L. *From back* C. *now comes* CHUMLEY, *followed by* SANDERSON *and* KELLY. CHUMLEY *goes to chair* R. *of desk.* KELLY *crosses above table to* R. C. *office for Chumley's hat and coat.* SANDERSON *goes to top of desk.*)

CHUMLEY (*working with pen on desk-pad*). That Simmons woman is unco-operative, Doctor. She refused to admit to me that she has this big rabbit. Insists it's her brother. Give her two of these at nine—another at ten—if she continues to be so restless. Another trip to the hydro-room at eight, and one in the morning at seven. Then we'll see if she won't co-operate tomorrow, won't we, Doctor?

SANDERSON. Yes, Doctor.

CHUMLEY (*putting pen away*). You know where to call me if you need me. Ready, pet?

BETTY. Yes, Willie—and oh, Willie—

CHUMLEY. Yes—

BETTY. There was a man in here—a man named—let me see—(*picks up card from desk.*) Oh, here is his card—Dowd—Elwood P. Dowd. KELLY *enters from* R. *to below table—she has Dr. Chumley's hat.*)

SANDERSON. That's Mrs. Simmons' brother, Doctor. I told him he could look around, and I gave him full visiting privileges.

CHUMLEY. She mustn't see anyone tonight. Not anyone at all. Tell him that.

SANDERSON. Yes, Doctor.

BETTY. He didn't ask to see her. He was looking for someone—some friend of his.

CHUMLEY. Who could that be, Dr. Sanderson?

SANDERSON. I don't know, Doctor.

BETTY. He said it was someone he came out here with this afternoon.

SANDERSON. Was there anyone with Dowd when you saw him, Miss Kelly?

KELLY (R. C. *giving hat to* SANDERSON). No, Doctor—not when I saw him.

BETTY. Well, he said there was. He said he last saw his friend sitting right in that chair there with his hat and coat. He seemed quite disappointed.

KELLY (*at top of table—a funny look is crossing her face*). Dr. Sanderson—

BETTY. I told him if we located his friend we'd give him a lift into town. He could ride in the back seat. Was that all right, Willie?

CHUMLEY. Of course—of course—

BETTY. Oh here it is. I wrote it down on the back of this card. His friend's name was Harvey.

KELLY. Harvey!

BETTY. He didn't give me his last name. He mentioned something else about him—pooka—but I didn't quite get what that was.

SANDERSON AND CHUMLEY. Harvey!

BETTY (*rises*). He said his friend was very tall—Well, why are you looking like that, Willie? This man was a very nice, polite man, and he merely asked that we give his friend a lift into town, and if we can't do a favor for someone, why are we living? (*Back to down* R.)

SANDERSON (*gasping*). Where—where did he go, Mrs. Chumley? How long ago was he in here?

CHUMLEY (*thundering*). Get me that hat! By George, we'll find out about this! (KELLY *goes out upper* L. *to get it.* BETTY *crosses* R. *to chair* R. *of table.* CHUMLEY *and* SANDERSON *sit at* R. *of desk.*)

BETTY. I don't know where he went. Just a second ago. (SANDERSON, *his face drawn, sits at* L. *of desk and picks up house phone.* CHUMLEY, *with a terrible look on his face, has started to thumb through phone book.*)

SANDERSON (*on house phone*). Main gate —Henry—Dr. Sanderson—

CHUMLEY (*thumbing through book*). Gaffney—Judge Gaffney——

SANDERSON. Henry—did a man in a brown suit go out through the gate a minute ago? He did? He's gone? (*Hangs up and looks stricken.* KELLY *enters from* L.

with hat, comes C.)

CHUMLEY (*has been dialing*). Judge Gaffney—this is Dr. William Chumley —the psychiatrist. I'm making a routine checkup on the spelling of a name before entering it into our records. Judge—you telephoned out here this afternoon about having a client of yours committed? How is that name spelled? With a W, not a U—Mr. Elwood P. Dowd. Thank you, Judge—(*Hangs up—rises—pushes chair in to desk—takes hat from* KELLY. *Stands silently for a moment, contemplating* SANDERSON.) Dr. Sanderson—I believe your name is Sanderson?

SANDERSON. Yes, Doctor.

CHUMLEY. You know that much, do you? You went to medical school—you specialized in the study of psychiatry? You graduated—you went forth. (*Holds up hat and runs two fingers up through holes in it.*) Perhaps they neglected to tell you that a rabbit has large pointed ears! That a hat for a rabbit would have to be perforated to make room for those ears?

SANDERSON. Dowd seemed reasonable enough this afternoon, Doctor.

CHUMLEY. Doctor—the function of a psychiatrist is to tell the difference between those who are reasonable, and those who merely talk and act reasonably. (*Presses buzzer. Flings hat on desk.*) Do you realize what you have done to me? You don't answer. I'll tell you. You have permitted a psycopathic case to walk off these grounds and roam around with an overgrown white rabbit. You have subjected me—a psychiatrist—to the humiliation of having to call—of all things—a lawyer to find out who came out here to be committed—and who came out here to commit! (WILSON *enters.*)

SANDERSON. Dr. Chumley—I—

CHUMLEY. Just a minute, Wilson—I want you. (*Back to* SANDERSON.) I will now have to do something I haven't done in fifteen years. I will have to go out after this patient, Elwood P. Dowd, and I will have to bring him back, and when I do bring him back, your connection with this institution is ended—as of that moment! (*Turns to* WILSON—OTHERS *are standing frightened.*) Wilson, get the car. (*To* BETTY.) Pet, call the McClures and say we can't make it. Miss Kelly— come upstairs with me and we'll get that woman out of the tub—(*Starts upstairs on the run.*)

KELLY (*follows him upstairs*). Yes—
Doctor—

(SANDERSON *turns on his heel, goes into his office.* WILSON *is getting into a coat in hall.*)

BETTY (*at bookcase* R.) I'll have to tell the cook we'll be home for dinner. She'll be furious. (*She turns.*) Wilson—

WILSON. Yes, ma'am.

BETTY. What is a pooka?

WILSON. A what?

BETTY. A pooka.

WILSON. You can search me, Mrs. Chumley.

BETTY. I wonder if it would be in the Encyclopedia here? (*Goes to bookcase and takes out book.*) They have everything here. I wonder if it is a lodge, or what it is! (*Starts to look in it, then puts it on table open.*) Oh, I don't dare to stop to do this now. Dr. Chumley won't want to find me still here when he comes down. (*Starts to cross to lower* L. *door very fast.*) He'll raise —I mean—oh, dear! (*She exits down* L.)

WILSON (*goes above tables, picks up book, looks in it. Runs forefinger under words.*) P-o-o-k-a. "Pooka. From old Celtic mythology. A fairy spirit in animal form. Always very large. The pooka appears here and there, now and then, to this one and that one at his own caprice. A wise but mischievous creature. Very fond of rum-pots, crackpots," and how are you, Mr. Wilson. (*Looks at book startled—looks at* C. *doorway fearfully— then back to book.*) How are you, Mr. Wilson? (*Shakes book, looks at it in surprise.*) Who in the encyclopedia wants to know? (*Looks at book again, drops it on table.*) Oh— to hell with it! (*He exits quickly out down* L.)

CURTAIN

ACT TWO

Scene One

SCENE: *The Dowd library again.*

TIME: *About an hour after the curtain of Act One.*

AT RISE: *Doorbell is ringing and* MYRTLE *enters from door up* L. *She calls behind her.*

MYRTLE (*calling*). That's right. The stairs at the end of the hall. It goes to the third floor. Go right up. I'll be with you in a minute. (*Crosses to chair* L. *of table.* JUDGE OMAR GAFFNEY *enters* R., *an elderly white-haired man. He looks displeased.*)

JUDGE (*entering and looking around*). Well, where is she? (*Back of table.*)

MYRTLE. Where is who? Whom do you mean, Judge Gaffney? Sit down, won't you?

JUDGE. I mean your mother. Where's Veta Louise? (*Crosses in front of chair.*)

MYRTLE. Why Judge Gaffney! You know where she is. She took Uncle Elwood out to the sanitarium.

JUDGE. I know that. But why was I called at the club with a lot of hysteria? Couldn't even get what she was talking about. Carrying on something fierce. (*Sits chair* R. *of table* R.)

MYRTLE. Mother carrying on! What about? (*Crosses down to chair* L. *of table* R.)

JUDGE. I don't know. She was hysterical.

MYRTLE. That's strange! She took Uncle Elwood out to the sanitarium. All she had to do was put him in. (*Goes back* R., *opens door and looks through, calling.*) Did you find it? I'll be right up. (*Waits. Turns to him.*) They found it.

JUDGE. Who? Found what? What are you talking about?

MYRTLE. When Mother left the house with Uncle Elwood I went over to the real estate office to put the house on the market. And what do you think I found there? (*She sits.*)

JUDGE. I'm not a quiz kid.

MYRTLE. Well, I found a man there who was looking for an old house just like this to cut up into buffet apartments. He's going through it now.

JUDGE. Now see here, Myrtle Mae. This house doesn't belong to you. It belongs to your Uncle Elwood.

MYRTLE. But now that Elwood is locked up, mother controls the property, doesn't she?

JUDGE. Where is your mother? Where is Veta Louise?

MYRTLE. Judge, she went out to Chumley's Rest to tell them about Harvey and put Uncle Elwood in.

JUDGE. Why did she call me at the club when I was in the middle of a game, and scream at me to meet her here about something important?

MYRTLE. I don't know. I simply don't know. Have you got the deed to this house?

JUDGE. Certainly, it's in my safe. Myrtle, I feel pretty bad about this thing of locking Elwood up.

MYRTLE. Mother and I will be able to take a long trip now—out to Pasadena.

JUDGE. I always liked that boy. He could have done anything—been anything—made a place for himself in this community.

MYRTLE. And all he did was get a big rabbit.

JUDGE. He had everything. Brains, personality, friends. Men liked him. Women liked him. I liked him.

MYRTLE. Are you telling me that once Uncle Elwood was like other men—that women actually liked him—I mean in that way?

JUDGE. Oh, not since he started running around with this big rabbit. But they did once. Once that mailbox of your grandmother's was full of those little blue-scented envelopes for Elwood.

MYRTLE. I can't believe it.

JUDGE. Of course there was always something different about Elwood.

MYRTLE. I don't doubt that.

JUDGE. Yes—he was always so calm about any sudden change in plans. I used to admire it. I should have been suspicious. Take your average man looking up and seeing a big white rabbit. He'd do something about it. But not Elwood. He took that calmly, too. And look where it got him!

MYRTLE. You don't dream how far overboard he's gone on this rabbit.

JUDGE. Oh, yes I do. He's had that rabbit in my office many's the time. I'm old but I don't miss much. (*Noise from upstairs.*) What's that noise?

MYRTLE. The prospective buyer on the third floor. (*Looks up.* VETA *is standing in doorway, looking like something the cat dragged in. Shakes her head sadly; looks into the room and sighs; her hat is crooked.* MYRTLE *jumps up.*) Mother! Look, Judge—

JUDGE (*rising*). Veta Louise—what's wrong, girl?

VETA (*shaking her head*). I never thought I'd see either of you again. (MYRTLE *and* JUDGE *take* VETA *to chair* L. *of table* R.)

MYRTLE. Take hold of her, Judge. She looks like she's going to faint. (JUDGE *gets hold of her on one side and* MYRTLE *on the other. They start to bring her into the room.*) Now, Mother—you're all right. You're going to be perfectly all right.

JUDGE. Steady—steady, girl, steady.

VETA. Please—not so fast.

JUDGE. Don't rush her, Myrtle—Ease her in.

VETA. Let me sit down. Only get me some place where I can sit down.

JUDGE (*guiding her to a big chair*). Here you are, girl. Easy, Myrtle—easy. (VETA *is about to lower herself into chair. She sighs. But before she can complete the lowering,* MYRTLE MAE *lets out a yelp and* VETA *straightens up quickly.*)

MYRTLE. Oh—(*She picks up envelope off chair. Holds it up.*) The gas bill.

VETA (*hand at head*). Oh—oh, my—(*Sits.*)

JUDGE. Get her some tea, Myrtle. Do you want some tea, Veta?

MYRTLE. I'll get you some tea, Mother. Get her coat off, Judge.

JUDGE. Let Myrtle get your coat off, Veta. Get her coat off, Myrtle.

VETA. Leave me alone. Let me sit here. Let me get my breath.

MYRTLE. Let her get her breath, Judge.

VETA. Let me sit here a minute and then let me get upstairs to my own bed where I can let go.

MYRTLE. What happened to you, Mother?

VETA. Omar, I want you to sue them. They put me in and let Elwood out.

JUDGE. What's this?

MYRTLE. Mother!

VETA (*taking off hat*). Just look at my hair.

MYRTLE. But why? What did you say? What did you do? (*Kneels at* VETA'*s feet.*) You must have done something.

VETA. I didn't do one thing. I simply told them about Elwood and Harvey.

JUDGE. Then how could it happen to you? I don't understand it. (*Sits chair* R.)

VETA. I told them about Elwood, and then I went down to the cab to get his things. As I was walking along the path —this awful man stepped out. He was a white slaver. I know he was. He had on one of those white suits. That's how they advertise.

MYRTLE. A man—what did he do, Mother?

VETA. What did he do? He took hold of me and took me in there and then he—(*Bows her head.* MYRTLE *and* JUDGE *exchange a look.*)

JUDGE (*softly*). Go on, Veta Louise. Go on, girl.

MYRTLE (*goes over, takes her hand*). Poor Mother—Was he a young man?

JUDGE. Myrtle Mae—perhaps you'd better leave the room.

MYRTLE. Now? I should say not! Go on, Mother.

JUDGE (*edging closer*). What did he do, Veta?

VETA. He took me upstairs and tore my clothes off.

MYRTLE (*shrieking*). Oh—did you hear that, Judge! Go on, Mother. (*She is all ears.*)

JUDGE. By God—I'll sue them for this!

VETA. And then he sat me down in a tub of water.

MYRTLE (*disappointed*). Oh! For heaven's sake! (*Rises.*)

VETA. I always thought that what you were, showed on your face. Don't you believe it, Judge! Don't you believe it, Myrtle. This man took hold of me like I was a woman of the streets—but I fought. I always said if a man jumped at me—I'd fight. Haven't I always said that, Myrtle?

MYRTLE. She's always said that, Judge. That's what Mother always told me to do.

VETA. And then he hustled me into that sanitarium and set me down in that tub of water and began treating me like I was a—

MYRTLE. A what—?

VETA. A crazy woman—but he did that just for spite.

JUDGE. Well, I'll be damned!

VETA. And those doctors came upstairs and asked me a lot of questions— all about sex-urges—and all that filthy stuff. That place ought to be cleaned up, Omar. You better get the authorities to clean it up. Myrtle, don't you ever go out there. You hear me?

JUDGE. This stinks to high heaven, Veta. By God, it stinks!

VETA. You've got to do something about it, Judge. You've got to sue them.

JUDGE. I will, girl. By God, I will! If Chumley thinks he can run an unsavory place like this on the outskirts of town he'll be publicly chastised. By God, I'll run him out of the state!

VETA. Tell me, Judge. Is that all those doctors do at places like that—think

about sex?

JUDGE. I don't know.

VETA. Because if it is they ought to be ashamed—of themselves. It's all in their head anyway. Why don't they get out and go for long walks in the fresh air? (*To* MYRTLE.) Judge Gaffney walked everywhere for years—didn't you, Judge?

JUDGE. Now let me take some notes on this. (MYRTLE *goes to back of table.*) You said—these doctors came up to talk to you—Dr. Chumley and—What was the other doctor's name?

VETA. Sanderson—(*Sits up straight, glances covertly at them, and becomes very alert.*) But, Judge, don't you pay any attention to anything he tells you. He's a liar. Close-set eyes. They're always liars. Besides—I told him something in strictest confidence and he blabbed it.

MYRTLE. What did you tell him, Mother? (*She is back of table.*)

VETA. Oh, what difference does it make? Let's forget. I don't even want to talk about it. (*Rises—crosses to back of chair.*) You can't trust anybody.

JUDGE. Anything you told this Dr. Sanderson you can tell us, Veta Louise. This is your daughter and I am your lawyer.

VETA. I know which is which. I don't want to talk about it. I want to sue them and I want to get in my own bed. (JUDGE *rises.*)

MYRTLE. But, Mother—this is the important thing, anyway. Where is Uncle Elwood?

VETA (*to herself*). I should have known better than to try to do anything about him. Something protects him—that awful Pooka—

MYRTLE. Where is Uncle Elwood? Answer me.

VETA (*trying to be casual*). How should I know? They let him go. (*Crosses to door* R.) They're not interested in men at places like that. Don't act so naïve, Myrtle Mae. (*Noise from upstairs.*) What's that noise?

MYRTLE. I've found a buyer for the house.

VETA. What?

MYRTLE. Listen, Mother, we've got to find Uncle Elwood—no matter who jumped at you, we've still got to lock up Uncle Elwood.

VETA. I don't know where he is. The next time *you* take him, Judge. Wait until Elwood hears what they did to me. He won't stand for it. Don't forget to sue them, Judge—Myrtle Mae, all I hope is that never, never as long as you live a man pulls the clothes off you and dumps you down into a tub of water. (*She exits* R.)

MYRTLE (*turning to* JUDGE. *Behind chair* L). Now, see—Mother muffed everything. No matter what happened out there—Uncle Elwood's still wandering around with Harvey.

JUDGE (*pondering*). The thing for me to do is take some more notes.

MYRTLE. It's all Uncle Elwood's fault. He found out what she was up to—and he had her put in. Then he ran.

JUDGE. Oh, no—don't talk like that. (*Crosses up to back of chair*.) Your uncle thinks the world and all of your mother. Ever since he was a little boy he always wanted to share everything he had with her.

MYRTLE. I'm not giving up. We'll get detectives. We'll find him. And, besides—you'd better save some of that sympathy for me and Mother—you don't realize what we have to put up with. Wait till I show you something he brought home about six months ago, and we hid it out in the garage. You just wait—

JUDGE. I'm going up to talk to Veta. There's more in this than she's telling. I sense that.

MYRTLE (*as she exits* L). Wait till I show you, Judge.

JUDGE. All right. I'll wait. (WILSON *enters from* R.)

WILSON (*crosses to table* R). Okay—is he here?

JUDGE (*crosses to chair* R. *of table* R). What? What's this?

WILSON. That crackpot with the rabbit. Is he here?

JUDGE. No—and who, may I ask, are you?

WILSON (*stepping into hallway, calling*). Not here, Doctor—okay—(*To* JUDGE.) Doctor Chumley's comin' in, anyway. What's your name?

JUDGE. Chumley—well, well, well—I've got something to say to him! (*Sits*.)

WILSON. What's your name? Let's have it.

JUDGE. I am Judge Gaffney—where is Chumley?

WILSON. The reason I asked your name is the Doctor always likes to know who he's talkin' to. (*Enter* CHUMLEY.) This guy says his name is Judge Gaffney, Doctor.

JUDGE. Well, well, Chumley—

CHUMLEY. Good evening, Judge. Let's not waste time. Has he been here? (*Crosses to* L. *of table*.)

JUDGE. Who? Elwood—no—but see here, Doctor—

WILSON. Sure he ain't been here? He's wise now. He's hidin'. It'll be an awful job to smoke him out.

CHUMLEY. It will be more difficult, but I'll do it. They're sly. They're cunning. But I get them. I always get them. Have you got the list of the places we've been, Wilson? (*Crosses to* WILSON.)

WILSON (*pulling paper out of his pocket*). Right here, Doctor.

CHUMLEY (*sits*). Read it.

WILSON (*crosses to* CHUMLEY). We've been to seventeen bars, Eddie's Place, Charlie's Place, Bessie's Barn-dance, the Fourth Avenue Firehouse, the Tenth and Twelfth and Ninth Avenue firehouses, just to make sure. The Union Station, the grain elevator—say, why does this guy go down to a grain elevator?

JUDGE. The foreman is a friend of his. He has many friends—many places.

CHUMLEY. I have stopped by here to ask Mrs. Simmons if she has any other suggestions as to where we might look for him.

JUDGE. Doctor Chumley, I have to inform you that Mrs. Simmons has retained me to file suit against you—

DR. CHUMLEY. What?

JUDGE. —for what happened to her at the sanitarium this afternoon . . .

CHUMLEY. A suit!

JUDGE. And while we're on that subject—

WILSON (*crosses to back of table*). That's pretty, ain't it, Doctor? After us draggin' your tail all over town trying to find that guy.

CHUMLEY. What happened this afternoon was an unfortunate mistake. I've discharged my assistant who made it. And I am prepared to take charge of this man's case personally. It interests me. And my interest in a case is something no amount of money can buy. You can ask any of them.

JUDGE. But this business this afternoon, Doctor—

CHUMLEY. Water under the dam. This is how I see this thing. I see it this way—(MYRTLE *has come into the room. She is carrying a big flat parcel, wrapped in brown paper.*

Stands it up against wall and listens, by chair L.) The important item now is to get this man and take him out to the sanitarium where he belongs.

MYRTLE (*coming forward*). That's right, Judge—that's just what I think—

JUDGE. Let me introduce Miss Myrtle Mae Simmons, Mr. Dowd's niece, Mrs. Simmon's daughter. (CHUMLEY *rises*.)

MYRTLE. How do you do, Dr. Chumley.

CHUMLEY (*giving her the careful scrutiny he gives all women*). How do you do, Miss Simmons.

WILSON. Hello, Myrtle—

MYRTLE (*now seeing him and looking at him with a mixture of horror and intense curiosity*). What? Oh—

CHUMLEY. Now, then let me talk to Mrs. Simmons.

MYRTLE. Mother won't come down, Doctor. I know she won't. (*To Judge.*) You try to get Mother to talk to him, Judge. (*Puts package down.*)

JUDGE. But, see here—your mother was manhandled. She was—God knows what she was—the man's approach to her was not professional, it was personal. (*Looks at Wilson.*)

CHUMLEY. Wilson—this is a serious charge.

WILSON. Dr. Chumley, I've been with you for ten years. Are you gonna believe —what's your name again?

JUDGE. Gaffney. Judge Omar Gaffney.

WILSON. Thanks. You take the word of this old blister Gaffney—

CHUMLEY. Wilson!

WILSON. Me! Me and a dame who sees a rabbit!

JUDGE. It's not Mrs. Simmons who sees a rabbit. It's her brother.

MYRTLE. Yes, it's Uncle Elwood.

JUDGE. If you'll come with me, Doctor—

CHUMLEY. Very well, Judge. Wilson, I have a situation here. Wait for me. (HE *and* JUDGE *exit* R.)

WILSON. OK, Doctor. (MYRTLE MAE *is fascinated by* WILSON. *She lingers and looks at him.* HE *comes over to her, grinning.*)

WILSON. So your name's Myrtle Mae?

MYRTLE. What? Oh—yes—(*She backs up.* HE *follows.*)

WILSON. If we grab your uncle you're liable to be comin' out to the sanitarium on visiting days?

MYRTLE. Oh, I don't really know—I—

WILSON. Well, if you do, I'll be there.

MYRTLE. You will? Oh—

WILSON. And if you don't see me right away—don't give up. Stick around. I'll show up.

MYRTLE. You will—? Oh—

WILSON. Sure. (*He is still following her.*) You heard Dr. Chumley tell me to wait?

MYRTLE. Yeah—

WILSON. Tell you what—while I'm waiting I sure could use a sandwich and a cup of coffee.

MYRTLE. Certainly. If you'll forgive me I'll precede you into the kitchen. (*She tries to go.* HE *traps her.*)

WILSON. Yessir—you're all right, Myrtle.

MYRTLE. What?

WILSON. Doctor Chumley noticed it right away. He don't miss a trick. (*Crowds closer; raises finger and pokes her arm for emphasis.*) Tell you somethin' else, Myrtle—

MYRTLE. What?

WILSON. You not only got a nice build —but, kid, you got something else, too.

MYRTLE. What?

WILSON. You got the screwiest uncle that ever stuck his puss inside our nuthouse. (MYRTLE *starts to exit in a huff, and* WILSON *raises hand to give her a spank, but she turns and so he puts up raised hand to his hair. They exit. The stage is empty for a half-second, and then through* R. *comes* ELWOOD. HE *comes in, goes to phone, dials a number.*)

ELWOOD. Hello, Chumley's Rest? Is Doctor Chumley there? Oh—it's Mrs. Chumley! This is Elwood P. Dowd speaking. How are you tonight? Tell me, Mrs. Chumley, were you able to locate Harvey?—Don't worry about it. I'll find him. I'm sorry I missed you at the McClure cocktail party. The people were all charming and I was able to leave quite a few of my cards. I waited until you phoned and said you couldn't come because a patient had escaped. Where am I? I'm here. But I'm leaving right away. I must find Harvey. Well, good-by, Mrs. Chumley. My regards to you and anybody else you happen to run into. Good-by. (*Hangs up, then he sees the big flat parcel against wall. He gets an "Ah, there it is!" expression on his face, goes over, and takes off paper. We see revealed a very strange thing. It is an oil painting of Elwood seated on a chair while behind him stands a large white rabbit, in a blue polka-dot collar and red necktie.* ELWOOD *holds it away from him and surveys it proudly. Then looks around for a place to put it. Takes it over and sets it on mantel. It obscures the picture of Marcella Pinney Dowd completely. He gathers up wrapping paper, admires the rabbit again, tips his hat to it, and exits* R. *Phone rings and* VETA *enters* L., *followed by* DR. CHUMLEY.)

VETA. Doctor, you might as well go home and wait. I'm suing you for fifty thousand dollars and that's final. (*Crosses to phone—her back is to mantel, she hasn't looked up.*)

CHUMLEY (*follows her to chair* L). Mrs. Simmons—

VETA (*into phone*). Yes—Well, all right.

CHUMLEY. This picture over your mantel.

VETA. That portrait happens to be the pride of this house.

CHUMLEY (*looking at her*). Who painted it?

VETA. Oh, some man. I forget his name. He was around here for the sittings, and then we paid him and he went away. Hello—yes—No. This is Dexter 1567. (*Hangs up.*)

CHUMLEY. I suppose if you have the money to pay people, you can persuade them to do anything.

VETA. Well, Dr. Chumley—(*Walks over and faces him.*) When you helped me out of that tub at your place, what did I say to you?

CHUMLEY. You expressed yourself. I don't remember the words.

VETA. I said, "Dr. Chumley, this is a belated civility." Isn't that what I said?

CHUMLEY. You said something of the sort—

VETA. You brought this up; you may as well learn something quick. I took a course in art this last winter. The difference between a fine oil painting and a mechanical thing like a photograph is simply this: a photograph shows only the reality; a painting shows not only the reality but the dream behind it—It's our dreams that keep us going. That separate us from the beasts. I wouldn't even want to live if I thought it was all just eating and sleeping and taking off my clothes. Well—putting them on again—(*Turns—sees picture—screams—totters—falls back.*) Oh—Doctor—oh—hold me—oh—

CHUMLEY (*taking hold of her*). Steady now—steady—don't get excited. Everything's all right. (*Seats her in chair* L.) Now—what's the matter?

VETA (*pointing*). Doctor—that is *not* my mother!

CHUMLEY. I'm glad to hear that.

VETA. Oh, Doctor. Elwood's been here. He's been here.

CHUMLEY. Better be quiet. (*Phone rings.*) I'll take it. (*He answers it.*) Hello. Yes, yes—who's calling? (*Drops his hands over mouthpiece quickly.*) Here he is. Mrs. Simmons, it's your brother!

VETA (*getting up. Weak no longer*). Oh—let me talk to him!

CHUMLEY. Don't tell him I'm here. Be casual.

VETA. Hello, Elwood—(*Laughs.*) Where are you? What? Oh—just a minute. (*Covers phone.*) He won't say where he is. He wants to know if Harvey is here.

CHUMLEY. Tell him Harvey *is* here.

VETA. But he isn't.

CHUMLEY. Tell him. That will bring him here, perhaps. Humor him. We have to humor them.

VETA. Yes—Elwood. Yes, dear. Harvey is here. Why don't you come home? Oh, oh, oh—well—all right. (*Looks around uncomfortably. Covers phone again.*) It won't work. He says for me to call Harvey to the telephone.

CHUMLEY. Say Harvey is here, but can't come to the telephone. Say—he—say—he's in the bathtub.

VETA. Bathtub?

CHUMLEY. Say he's in the bathtub, and you'll send him over there. That way we'll find out where he is.

VETA. Oh, Doctor!

CHUMLEY. Now, you've got to do it, Mrs. Simmons.

VETA. Hello, Elwood. Yes, dear. Harvey is here but he can't come to the telephone, he's in the bathtub. I'll send him over as soon as he's dry. Where are you? Elwood? (*Bangs phone.*)

CHUMLEY. Did he hang up?

VETA. Harvey just walked in the door! He told me to look in the bathtub—it must be a stranger. But I know where he is. He's at Charlie's Place. That's a bar over at 12th and Main.

CHUMLEY (*picking up his hat from table* R). 12th and Main. That's two blocks down and one over, isn't it?

VETA. Doctor—where are you going?

CHUMLEY. I'm going over there to get your brother and take him out to the sanitarium, where he belongs.

VETA. Oh, Dr. Chumley—don't do that. Send one of your attendants. I'm warning you.

CHUMLEY. But, Mrs. Simmons, if I am to help your brother—

VETA. He can't be helped. (*Looks at picture.*) There is no help for him. He must be ·picked up and locked up and left.

CHUMLEY. You consider your brother a dangerous man?

VETA. Dangerous!

CHUMLEY. Why?

VETA. I won't tell you why, but if I didn't, why would I be asking for a permanent commitment for him?

CHUMLEY. Then I must observe this man. I must watch the expression on his face as he talks to this rabbit. He does talk to the rabbit, you say?

VETA. They tell each other everything.

CHUMLEY. What's that?

VETA. I said, of course he talks to him. But don't go after him, Doctor. You'll regret it if you do.

CHUMLEY. Nonsense—(*He is going toward* R.) You underestimate me, Mrs. Simmons.

VETA. Oh, no, Doctor. You underestimate my brother.

CHUMLEY. Not at all. Don't worry now. I can handle him! (*He exits* R.)

VETA (*after he has gone*). You can handle him? That's what you think! (*Calls up* L.) Myrtle Mae! See who's in the bathtub. OH!

CURTAIN

ACT TWO

SCENE TWO

SCENE: *The main office at* CHUMLEY'S REST *again.*

TIME: *Four hours after the curtain of Scene One, Act Two.*

AT RISE: KELLY *is on the phone.* WILSON *is helping* SANDERSON *carry boxes of books out of his office up* L. *and onto table* C.

KELLY. Thank you. I may call later. (*Hangs up.*)

WILSON (L. *of table* R). How about the stuff in your room, Doctor—upstairs?

SANDERSON (*to table, puts box on it*). All packed—thanks Wilson.

WILSON. Tough your gettin' bounced.

I had you pegged for the one who'd make the grade.

SANDERSON. Those are the breaks.

WILSON. When you takin' off?

SANDERSON. As soon as Dr. Chumley gets back.

WILSON (*to* KELLY). Did you get a report back yet from the desk sergeant in the police accident bureau?

KELLY. Not yet. I just talked to the downtown dispensary. They haven't seen him.

WILSON. It's beginning to smell awful funny to me. Four hours he's been gone and not a word from him. (*Goes to* SANDERSON—*extends hand.*) I may not see you again, Doctor, so I want to say I wish you a lot of luck and I'm mighty sorry you got a kick in the atpray.

SANDERSON. Thanks, Wilson—good luck to you, too—

WILSON (*starts to exit, but stops at door back* C., *turns toward* KELLY.) Look, Kelly, let me know when you hear from the desk sergeant again. If there's no sign of the doctor, I'm goin' into town and look for him. He should know better'n to go after a psycho without me. (*Starts up* C.)

SANDERSON. I'd like to help look for the doctor, too, Wilson.

WILSON. That's swell of you, Doctor, right after he give you the brush.

SANDERSON. I've no resentment against Dr. Chumley. He was right. I was wrong. (*He rises.*) Chumley is the biggest man in his field. It's my loss not to be able to work with him. (*Crosses up to bookcase.*)

WILSON. You're not so small yourself, Doctor—

SANDERSON. Thanks, Wilson.

WILSON. Don't mention it. (*Exits* U.C.)

KELLY (*taking deep breath and standing above desk*). Dr. Sanderson—

SANDERSON (*without looking up*). Yes—

KELLY (*plunging in*). Well, Doctor— (*Takes another deep breath.*) I'd like to say that *I* wish you a lot of luck, too, and I'm sorry to see you leave.

SANDERSON (*going on with his work*). Are you sure you can spare these good wishes, Miss Kelly?

KELLY (*she flushes*). On second thought —I guess I can't. Forget it. (*Starts for below desk.*)

SANDERSON (*now looking up*). Miss Kelly —(*To back of table.*) This is for nothing— just a little advice. I'd be a little careful if I were you about the kind of company I kept.

KELLY. I beg you pardon, Doctor?

SANDERSON (*crosses* C). You don't have to. I told you it was free. I saw you Saturday night—dancing with that drip in the Rose Room down at the Frontier Hotel.

KELLY (*putting books on desk*). Oh, did you? I didn't notice you.

SANDERSON. I'd be a little careful of him, Kelly. He looked to me like a schizophrenic all the way across the floor.

KELLY. You really shouldn't have given him a thought, Doctor. He was my date—not yours. (*Hands book to* SANDERSON.)

SANDERSON. That was his mentality. The rest of him—well—(*Puts book in box front of table.*)

KELLY. But she was beautiful, though—

SANDERSON. Who?

KELLY. That girl you were with—

SANDERSON. I thought you didn't notice?

KELLY. You bumped into us twice. How could I help it?

SANDERSON. Not that it makes any difference to you, but that girl is a charming little lady. *She* has a sweet kind disposition and *she* knows how to conduct herself.

KELLY. Funny she couldn't rate a better date on a Saturday night!

SANDERSON. And she has an excellent mind.

KELLY. Why doesn't she use it?

SANDERSON (*crossing toward* KELLY). Oh, I don't suppose you're to be censured for the flippant hard shell you have. You're probably compensating for something.

KELLY. I am not, and don't you use any of your psychiatry on me.

SANDERSON. Oh—if I could try something else on you—just once! Just to see if you'd melt under any circumstances. I doubt it.

KELLY. You'll never know, Doctor.

SANDERSON. Because you interest me as a case history—that's all. I'd like to know where you get that inflated ego—(*Goes back of desk.*)

KELLY (*now close to tears*). If you aren't the meanest person—inflated ego—case history! (*Turns and starts out* C.)

SANDERSON. Don't run away. Let's finish it. (PHONE *rings.*)

KELLY. Oh, leave me alone. (*Goes to answer it.*)

SANDERSON. Gladly. (*Exits.*)

KELLY (*in angry, loud voice*). Chumley's Rest. Yes—Sergeant. No accident report on him either in town or the suburbs. Look, Sergeant—maybe we better—(*Looks up as door down* L. *opens and* ELWOOD *enters. He is carrying a bouquet of dahlias.*) Oh, never mind, Sergeant. They're here now. (*Hangs up. Goes toward* ELWOOD.) Mr. Dowd!

ELWOOD (*crosses to* C. *Handing her flowers*). Good evening, my dear. These are for you.

KELLY (*crosses to* C). For me—oh, thank you!

ELWOOD. They're quite fresh, too. I just picked them outside.

KELLY. I hope Dr. Chumley didn't see you. They're his prize dahlias. Did he go upstairs? (*Backing up.*)

ELWOOD. Not knowing, I cannot state. Those colors are lovely against your hair.

KELLY. I've never worn burnt orange. It's such a trying color.

ELWOOD. You would improve any color, my dear.

KELLY. Thank you. Did Dr. Chumley go over to his house?

ELWOOD. I don't know. Where is Dr. Sanderson?

KELLY. In his office there—I think. (*Crosses back to desk.*)

ELWOOD (*going over to door and knocking*). Thank you.

SANDERSON (*enters*). Dowd! There you are!

ELWOOD. I have a cab outside, if it's possible for you and Miss Kelly to get away now.

SANDERSON. Where is Dr. Chumley?

ELWOOD. Is he coming with us? That's nice.

KELLY (*answering question on* SANDERSON's *face*). I don't know, Doctor.

ELWOOD. I must apologize for being a few seconds late. I thought Miss Kelly should have some flowers. (*Crosses to table.*) After what happened out here this afternoon, the flowers really should be from you, Doctor. As you grow older and pretty women pass you by, you will think with deep gratitude of these generous girls of your youth. Shall we go now? (KELLY *exits.*)

SANDERSON (*pressing buzzer*). Just a moment, Dowd—(*Starts* R.) The situation has changed since we met this afternoon. But I urge you to have no resentments.

Dr. Chumley is your friend. He only wants to help you.

ELWOOD. That's very nice of him. I would like to help him, too. (*At table.*)

SANDERSON. If you'll begin by taking a co-operative attitude—that's half the battle. We all have to face reality, Dowd —sooner or later.

ELWOOD. Doctor, I wrestled with reality for forty years, and I am happy to state that I finally won out over it. (KELLY *enters.*) Won't you and Miss Kelly join me—down at Charlie's? (*Enter* WILSON *from* C.)

WILSON. Here you are! (*Goes over to* ELWOOD.) Upstairs, buddy—we're going upstairs. Is the doctor O.K.? (*He asks* SANDERSON *this.*)

ELWOOD. There must be some mistake. Miss Kelly and Dr. Sanderson and I are going downtown for a drink. I'd be glad to have you come with us, Mr.——

WILSON. Wilson.

ELWOOD. —Wilson. They have a wonderful floor show.

WILSON. Yeah? Well—wait'll you see the floor show we've got—Upstairs, buddy!

SANDERSON. Just a minute, Wilson. Where did you say Dr. Chumley went, Dowd?

ELWOOD. As I said, he did not confide his plans in me.

WILSON. You mean the doctor ain't showed up yet? (*Crosses to desk.*)

KELLY. Not yet.

WILSON. Where is he?

SANDERSON. That's what we're trying to find out.

KELLY. Mr. Dowd walked in here by himself.

WILSON. Oh, he did, eh? Listen, you— talk fast or I'm workin' you over!

ELWOOD. I'd rather you didn't do that, and I'd rather you didn't even mention such a thing in the presence of a lovely young lady like Miss Kelly —

SANDERSON. Mr. Dowd, Dr. Chumley went into town to pick you up. That was four hours ago.

ELWOOD. Where has the evening gone to?

WILSON. Listen to that! Smart, eh?

SANDERSON. Just a minute, Wilson. Did you see Dr. Chumley tonight, Dowd?

ELWOOD. Yes, I did. He came into Charlie's Place at dinnertime. It is a cozy spot. Let's all go there and talk it over

with a tall one.

WILSON. We're going no place—(*Crosses between* ELWOOD *and* SANDERSON.) Now I'm askin' you a question, and if you don't button up your lip and give me some straight answers I'm gonna beat it out of you!

ELWOOD. What you suggest is impossible.

WILSON. What's that?

ELWOOD. You suggest that I button up my lip and give you some straight answers. It can't be done. (*Sits chair* L. *of table.*)

SANDERSON. Let me handle this, Wilson. (*Puts* WILSON *to* L.)

WILSON. Well, handle it, then. But find out where the doctor is. (*Back of desk.*)

SANDERSON. Dr. Chumley *did* come into Charlie's Place, you say?

ELWOOD. He did, and I was very glad to see him.

WILSON. Go on—

ELWOOD. He had asked for me, and naturally the proprietor brought him over and left him. We exchanged the conventional greetings. I said, "How do you do, Dr. Chumley," and he said, "How do you do, Mr. Dowd." I believe we said that at least once.

WILSON. Okay—okay—

ELWOOD. I am trying to be factual. I then introduced him to Harvey.

WILSON. To who?

KELLY. A white rabbit. Six feet tall.

WILSON. Six feet!

ELWOOD. Six feet one and a half!

WILSON. Okay—fool around with him, and the doctor is probably some place bleedin' to death in a ditch.

ELWOOD. If those were his plans for the evening he did not tell me.

SANDERSON. Go on, Dowd.

ELWOOD. Dr. Chumley sat down in the booth with us. I was sitting on the outside like this. (*Shows.*) Harvey was on the inside near the wall, and Dr. Chumley was seated directly across from Harvey where he could look at him.

WILSON (*crosses a step* R). That's right. Spend all night on the seatin' arrangements!

ELWOOD. Harvey then suggested that I buy him a drink. Knowing that he does not like to drink alone, I suggested to Dr. Chumley that we join him.

WILSON. And so?

ELWOOD. We joined him.

WILSON. Go on—go on.

ELWOOD. We joined him again.

WILSON. Then what?

ELWOOD. We kept right on joining him.

WILSON. Oh, skip all the joining!

ELWOOD. You are asking me to skip a large portion of the evening—

WILSON. Tell us what happened—come on—please—

ELWOOD. Dr. Chumley and Harvey got into a conversation—quietly at first. Later it became rather heated and Dr. Chumley raised his voice.

WILSON. Yeah—why?

ELWOOD. Harvey seemed to feel that Dr. Chumley should assume part of the financial responsibility of the joining, but Dr. Chumley didn't seem to want to do that.

KELLY (*it breaks out from her*). I can believe *that* part of it!

WILSON. Let him talk. See how far he'll go. This guy's got guts.

ELWOOD. I agreed to take the whole thing because I did not want any trouble. We go down to Charlie's quite often —Harvey and I—and the proprietor is a fine man with an interesting approach to life. Then the other matter came up.

WILSON. Cut the damned double-talk and get on with it!

ELWOOD. Mr. Wilson, you are a sincere type of person, but I must ask you not to use that language in the presence of Miss Kelly. (*He makes a short bow to her.*)

SANDERSON. You're right, Dowd, and we're sorry. You say—the other matter came up?

ELWOOD. There was a beautiful blonde woman—a Mrs. Smethills—and her escort seated in the booth across from us. Dr. Chumley went over to sit next to her, explaining to her that they had once met. In Chicago. Her escort escorted Dr. Chumley back to me and Harvey and tried to point out that it would be better for Dr. Chumley to mind his own affairs. Does he have any?

WILSON. Does he have any what?

ELWOOD. Does he have any affairs?

WILSON. How would I know?

KELLY. Please hurry, Mr. Dowd—we're all so worried.

ELWOOD. Dr. Chumley then urged Harvey to go with him over to Blondie's Chicken Inn. Harvey wanted to go to Eddie's instead. While they were arguing about it I went to the bar to order another drink, and when I came back they were gone.

WILSON. Where did they go? I mean where did the doctor go?

ELWOOD. I don't know—I had a date out here with Dr. Sanderson and Miss Kelly, and I came out to pick them up—hoping that later on we might run into Harvey and the doctor and make a party of it.

WILSON. So you satisfied? You got his story—(*Goes over to* ELWOOD, *fists clenched.*) O.K. You're lyin' and we know it!

ELWOOD. I never lie, Mr. Wilson.

WILSON. You've done somethin' with the doctor and I'm findin' out what it is—

SANDERSON (*moving after* him). Don't touch him, Wilson—

KELLY. Maybe he isn't lying, Wilson—

WILSON (*turning on them. Furiously*). That's all this guy is, a bunch of lies! You two don't believe this story he tells about the doctor sittin' there talkin' to a big white rabbit, do you?

KELLY. Maybe Dr. Chumley *did* go to Charlie's Place.

WILSON. And saw a big rabbit, I suppose.

ELWOOD. And why not? Harvey was there. At first the doctor seemed a little frightened of Harvey, but that gave way to admiration as the evening wore on— The evening wore on! That's a nice expression. With your permission I'll say it again. The evening wore on.

WILSON (*lunging at him*). With your permission I'm gonna knock your teeth down your throat!

ELWOOD (*not moving an inch*). Mr. Wilson—haven't you some old friends you can go play with? (SANDERSON *has grabbed* WILSON *and is struggling with him.*)

WILSON (*he is being held. Glares fiercely at* ELWOOD. KELLY *dials phone*). The nerve of this guy! He couldn't come out here with an ordinary case of D.T.'s. No. He has to come out with a six-foot rabbit.

ELWOOD (*rises—goes toward desk* L). Stimulating as all this is, I really must be getting downtown.

KELLY (*on phone*). Charlie's Place? Is Dr. Chumley anywhere around there?

He was there with Mr. Dowd earlier in the evening. What? Well, don't bite my head off! (*Hangs up.*) My, that man was mad. He said Mr. Dowd was welcome any time, but his friend was not.

ELWOOD. That's Mr. McNulty the bartender. He thinks a lot of me. Now let's all go down and have a drink.

WILSON. Wait a minute—

KELLY. Mr. Dowd—(*Goes over to him.*)

ELWOOD. Yes, my dear—may I hold your hand?

KELLY. Yes—if you want to. (ELWOOD *does.*) Poor Mrs. Chumley is so worried. Something must have happened to the doctor. Won't you please try and remember something—something else that might help her? Please—

ELWOOD. For you I would do anything. I would almost be willing to live my life over again. Almost. But I've told it all.

KELLY. You're sure?

ELWOOD. Quite sure—but ask me again, anyway, won't you? I liked that warm tone you had in your voice just then.

SANDERSON (*without realizing he is saying it*). So did I. (*Looks at* KELLY.)

WILSON. Oh, nuts!

ELWOOD. What?

WILSON. Nuts!

ELWOOD. Oh! I must be going. I have things to do.

KELLY. Mr. Dowd, what is it you do?

ELWOOD (*sits, as* KELLY *sits* R. *of desk*). Harvey and I sit in the bars and we have a drink or two and play the jukebox. Soon the faces of the other people turn toward mine and smile. They are saying: "We don't know your name, Mister, but you're a lovely fellow." Harvey and I warm ourselves in all these golden moments. We have entered as strangers —soon we have friends. They come over. They sit with us. They drink with us. They talk to us. They tell about the big terrible things they have done. The big wonderful things they *will* do. Their hopes, their regrets, their loves, their hates. All very large because nobody ever brings anything small into a bar. Then I introduce them to Harvey. And he is bigger and grander than anything they offer me. When they leave, they leave impressed. The same people seldom come back—but that's envy, my dear. There's a little bit of envy in the best of us—too bad, isn't it?

SANDERSON (*leaning forward*). How did you happen to call him Harvey?

ELWOOD. Harvey is his name.

SANDERSON. How do you know that?

ELWOOD. That was rather an interesting coincidence, Doctor. One night several years ago I was walking early in the evening along Fairfax Street— between 18th and 19th. You know that block?

SANDERSON. Yes, yes.

ELWOOD. I had just helped Ed Hickey into a taxi. Ed had been mixing his rye with his gin, and I felt he needed conveying. I started to walk down the street when I heard a voice saying: "Good evening, Mr. Dowd." I turned, and there was this great white rabbit leaning against a lamp-post. Well, I thought nothing of that, because when you have lived in a town as long as I have lived in this one, you get used to the fact that everybody knows your name. Naturally, I went over to chat with him. He said to me: "Ed Hickey is a little spiffed this evening, or could I be mistaken?" Well, of course he was not mistaken. I think the world and all of Ed, but he was spiffed. Well, anyway, we stood there and talked, and finally I said—"You have the advantage of me. You know my name and I don't know yours." Right back at me he said: "What name do you like?" Well, I didn't even have to think a minute: Harvey has always been my favorite name. So I said, "Harvey," and this is the interesting part of the whole thing. He said— "What a coincidence! My name happens to be Harvey."

SANDERSON (*crossing above desk*). What was your father's name, Dowd?

ELWOOD. John. John Frederick.

SANDERSON. Dowd, when you were a child you had a playmate, didn't you? Someone you were very fond of—with whom you spent many happy, carefree hours?

ELWOOD. Oh, yes, Doctor. Didn't you?

SANDERSON. What was his name?

ELWOOD. Verne. Verne McElhinney. Did you ever know the McElhinneys, Doctor?

SANDERSON. No.

ELWOOD. Too bad. There were a lot of them, and they circulated. Wonderful people.

SANDERSON. Think carefully, Dowd. Wasn't there someone, somewhere, sometime, whom you knew—by the name of Harvey? Didn't you ever know anybody by that name?

ELWOOD. No, Doctor. No one. Maybe that's why I always had such hopes for it.

SANDERSON. Come on, Wilson, we'll take Mr. Dowd upstairs now.

WILSON. I'm taking him nowhere. You've made this your show—now run it. Lettin' him sit here—forgettin' all about Dr. Chumley! O.K. It's your show—you run it.

SANDERSON. Come on, Dowd— (*Pause. Putting out his hand.*) Come on, Elwood—

ELWOOD (*rises*). Very well, Lyman. (SANDERSON *and* KELLY *take him to door.*) But I'm afraid I won't be able to visit with you for long. I have promised Harvey I will take him to the floor-show. (THEY *exit* U.C. WILSON *is alone. Sits at desk, looks at his watch.*)

WILSON. Oh, boy! (*Puts head in arms on desk.* DR. CHUMLEY *enters* L. WILSON *does not see him until he gets almost* C. *stage.*)

WILSON (*jumping up, going to him*). Dr. Chumley—Are you all right?

CHUMLEY. All right? Of course I'm all right. I'm being followed. Lock that door.

WILSON (*goes to door* L., *locks it.*) Who's following you?

CHUMLEY. None of your business. (*Exits into office* R., *locks door behind him.*) (WILSON *stands a moment perplexed, then shrugs shoulders, turns off lights and exits* U.C. *The stage is dimly lit. Then from door* L. *comes the rattle of the doorknob. Door opens and shuts, and we hear locks opening and closing, and see light from hall on stage. The invisible Harvey has come in. There is a count of eight while he crosses the stage, then door of* CHUMLEY'S *office opens and closes, with sound of locks clicking. Harvey has gone in—and then—*

CURTAIN

ACT THREE

SCENE: *The sanitarium office at Chumley's Rest.*

TIME: *A few minutes after the curtain of Act Two.*

AT RISE: *Lights are still dim as at preceding curtain. There is a loud knocking at* L. *and the sound of* CHUMLEY'S *voice calling,* "Wilson! Wilson!"

WILSON (*enters from* C., *opens door* L. CHUMLEY *enters, whitefaced*). How didja get out here, Doctor? I just saw you go in there.

CHUMLEY. I went out through my window. Wilson—don't leave me!

WILSON. No, Doctor.

CHUMLEY. Get that man Dowd out of here.

WILSON. Yes, Doctor. (*Starts to exit* C.)

CHUMLEY. No—don't leave me!

WILSON (*turning back—confused*). But you said—

CHUMLEY. Dumphy—on the telephone.

WILSON. Yes, Doctor. (*Crosses to phone.*) Dumphy—give that guy Dowd his clothes and get him down here right away. (*A knock on the door.*)

CHUMLEY. Don't leave me!

WILSON. Just a minute, Doctor. (*Crosses up and turns on lights. Crosses down and opens door* L.) Judge Gaffney.

JUDGE. I want to see Dr. Chumley. (*Enter* JUDGE *and* MYRTLE MAE.)

WILSON. Hiya, Myrtle.

MYRTLE. Hello.

JUDGE. Chumley, we've got to talk to you. This thing is serious.

MYRTLE. It certainly is.

GAFFNEY. More serious than you suspect. Where can we go to talk? (*Moves toward Chumley's office.*)

CHUMLEY (*blocking door*). Not in there.

WILSON. The doctor doesn't want you in his office.

CHUMLEY. No, sir.

JUDGE. Then sit down, Dr. Chumley. Sit down, Myrtle Mae.

CHUMLEY (*dazed*). Sit down, Dr. Chumley. Sit down, Myrtle Mae. Don't go, Wilson. Don't leave me.

JUDGE. Now, Chumley, here are my notes—the facts. Can anybody hear me?

WILSON. Yeah, we can all hear you. Is that good?

JUDGE (*gives Wilson a look of reproof*). Now, Chumley, has it ever occurred to you that possibly there might *be* something like this rabbit Harvey?

MYRTLE. Of course there isn't. And

anybody who thinks so is crazy. (CHUMLEY *stares at her.*) Well, don't look at me like that. There's nothing funny about me. I'm like my father's family they're all dead.

JUDGE. Now, then, my client, the plaintiff, Mrs. Veta Louise Simmons, under oath, swears that on the morning of November second while standing in the kitchen of her home, hearing her name called, she turned and saw this great white rabbit, Harvey. He was staring at her. Resenting the intrusion, the plaintiff made certain remarks and drove the creature from the room. He went.

CHUMLEY. What did she say to him?

JUDGE. She was emphatic. The remarks are not important.

CHUMLEY. I want to know how she got this creature out of her sanitarium— I mean—her home.

MYRTLE. I hate to have you tell him, Judge. It isn't a bit like Mother.

WILSON. Quit stalling. Let's have it.

GAFFNEY. She looked him right in the eye and exclaimed in the heat of anger — "To hell with you!"

CHUMLEY (*looking at door*). "To hell with you!" He left?

JUDGE. Yes, he left. But that's beside the point. The point is—is it perjury or is it something we can cope with? I ask for your opinion. (KELLY *enters from stairs* U.C. SANDERSON *comes from* U.C. *diet kitchen.*)

SANDERSON. Ruthie! I've been looking all over for you.

CHUMLEY. Dr. Sanderson, disregard what I said this afternoon. I want you on my staff. You are a very astute young man.

KELLY. Oh, Lyman! Did you hear?

SANDERSON. Oh, baby!

KELLY. See you later. (*Exits* U.C., *blowing him a kiss.* SANDERSON *exits into his office.*)

MYRTLE. You've just got to keep Uncle Elwood out here, Doctor. (JUDGE *crosses to desk.*)

CHUMLEY. No. I want this sanitarium the way it was before that man came out here this afternoon.

MYRTLE. I know what you mean.

CHUMLEY. You do?

MYRTLE. Well, it certainly gets on anyone's nerves the way Uncle Elwood knows what's going to happen before it

happens. This morning, for instance, he told us that Harvey told him Mrs. McElhinney's Aunt Rose would drop in on her unexpectedly tonight from Cleveland.

CHUMLEY. And did she?

MYRTLE. Did she what?

CHUMLEY. Aunt Rose—did she come just as Harvey said she would?

MYRTLE. Oh, yes. Those things always turn out the way Uncle Elwood says they will—but what of it? What do we care about the McElhinneys?

CHUMLEY. You say this sort of thing happens often?

MYRTLE. Yes, and isn't it silly? Uncle Elwood says Harvey tells him everything. Harvey knows everything. How could he when there is no such thing as Harvey?

CHUMLEY (*goes over, tries lock at door* R). Fly-specks. I've been spending my life among fly-specks while miracles have been leaning on lamp-posts on 18th and Fairfax.

VETA (*enters down* L. *Looks around cautiously. Sighs with relief*). Good. Nobody here but people.

MYRTLE. Oh, Mother! You promised you wouldn't come out here.

VETA. Well, good evening. Now, Myrtle Mae, I brought Elwood's bathrobe. Well, why are you all just sitting here? I thought you'd be committing him.

JUDGE. Sit down there, girl. (*Motioning to chair near Wilson.*)

VETA. I will not sit down there. (*Sits chair* R. *of desk.*)

WILSON. How about you and me stepping out Saturday night, Myrtle Mae?

VETA. Certainly not. Myrtle Mae, come here.

MYRTLE. I'm sorry. (*Goes down to* VETA.)

VETA. Is everything settled?

CHUMLEY. It will be.

SANDERSON (*enters from his office*). Doctor, may I give an opinion?

CHUMLEY. Yes, do. By all means.

VETA (*sniffing*). His opinion! Omar— he's the doctor I told you about. The eyes!

SANDERSON. It's my opinion that Elwood P. Dowd is suffering from a third-degree hallucination and the—(*Pointing at Veta's back.*) other party concerned is the victim of autosuggestion. I recommend shock formula number 977 for him and bed-rest at home for—(*Points again.*)

CHUMLEY. You do?

SANDERSON. That's my diagnosis, Doctor. (*To Veta.*) Mr. Dowd will not see this rabbit any more after this injection. We've used it in hundreds of psychopathic cases.

VETA. Don't you call my brother a psychopathic case! There's never been anything like that in our family.

MYRTLE. If you didn't think Uncle Elwood was psychopathic, why did you bring him out here?

VETA. Where else could I take him? I couldn't take him to jail, could I? Besides, this is not your uncle's fault. Why did Harvey have to speak to him in the first place? With the town full of people, why did he have to bother Elwood?

JUDGE. Stop putting your oar in. Keep your oar out. If this shock formula brings people back to reality, give it to him. That's where we want Elwood.

CHUMLEY. I'm not sure that it would work in a case of this kind, Doctor.

SANDERSON. It always has.

VETA. Harvey always follows Elwood home.

CHUMLEY. He does?

VETA. Yes. But if you give him the formula and Elwood doesn't see Harvey, he won't let him in. Then when he comes to the door, I'll deal with him.

MYRTLE. Mother, won't you stop talking about Harvey as if there was such a thing?

VETA. Myrtle Mae, you've got a lot to learn and I hope you never learn it. (*She starts up toward* Wilson.)

(ELWOOD *is heard offstage, humming.*)

JUDGE. Sh! Here he is.

ELWOOD (*enters* C). Good evening, everybody.

(ALL *nod.*)

VETA. Good evening, Elwood. I've brought you your bathrobe.

ELWOOD. Thank you, Veta.

JUDGE. Well, Chumley, what do we do? We've got to do something.

VETA. Oh, yes, we must.

MYRTLE. I should say so.

CHUMLEY (*looking at door*). Yes, it's imperative.

ELWOOD. Well, while you're making up your minds, why don't we all go down to Charlie's and have a drink?

VETA. You're not going anywhere, Elwood. You're staying here.

MYRTLE. Yes, Uncle Elwood.

JUDGE. Stay here, son.

ELWOOD. I plan to leave. You want me to stay. An element of conflict in any discussion is a good thing. It means everybody is taking part and nobody is left out. I like that. Oh—how did you get along with Harvey, Doctor?

CHUMLEY. Sh-h!

JUDGE. We're waiting for your answer, Doctor.

CHUMLEY. What?

JUDGE. What is your decision?

CHUMLEY. I must be alone with this man. Will you all step into the other room? (MYRTLE *exits* U.L.) I'll have my diagnosis in a moment.

VETA. Do hurry, Doctor.

CHUMLEY. I will.

VETA. You stay here, Elwood. (*She and* JUDGE GAFFNEY *exit* U.L.)

CHUMLEY. Here, Mr. Dowd. Let me give you this chair. (*Indicates chair* L. *of table* R.) Let me give you a cigar. (*Does so.*) Is there anything else I can get you?

ELWOOD (*seated in chair*). What did you have in mind?

CHUMLEY. Mr. Dowd (*Lowers voice, looks toward office.*) What kind of a man are you? Where do you come from?

ELWOOD (*getting out card*). Didn't I give you one of my cards?

CHUMLEY. And where on the face of this tired old earth did you find a thing like him?

ELWOOD. Harvey the Pooka?

CHUMLEY (*sits chair* R. *of table*). Is it true that he has a function—that he—

ELWOOD. Gets advance notice? I'm happy to say it is. Harvey is versatile. Harvey can stop clocks.

DR. CHUMLEY. What?

ELWOOD. You've heard that expression, "His face would stop a clock"?

CHUMLEY. Yes. But why? To what purpose?

ELWOOD. Harvey says that he can look at your clock and stop it and you can go away as long as you like with whomever you like and go as far as you like. And when you come back not one minute will have ticked by.

CHUMLEY. You mean that he actually — (*Looks toward office.*)

ELWOOD. Einstein has overcome time

and space. Harvey has overcome not only time and space—but any objections.

CHUMLEY. And does he do this for you?

ELWOOD. He is willing to at any time, but so far I've never been able to think of any place I'd rather be. I always have a wonderful time just where I am, whomever I'm with. I'm having a fine time right now with you, Doctor. (*Holds up cigar.*) Corona-Corona.

CHUMLEY. I know where I'd go.

ELWOOD. Where?

CHUMLEY. I'd go to Akron.

ELWOOD. Akron?

CHUMLEY. There's a cottage camp outside Akron in a grove of maple trees, cool, green, beautiful.

ELWOOD. My favorite tree.

CHUMLEY. I would go there with a pretty young woman, a strange woman, a quiet woman.

ELWOOD. Under a tree?

CHUMLEY. I wouldn't even want to know her name. I would be—just Mr. Brown.

ELWOOD. Why wouldn't you want to know her name? You might be acquainted with the same people.

CHUMLEY. I would send out for cold beer. I would talk to her. I would tell her things I have never told anyone—things that are locked in here. (*Beats his breast.* ELWOOD *looks over at his chest with interest.*) And then I would send out for more cold beer.

ELWOOD. No whiskey?

CHUMLEY. Beer is better.

ELWOOD. Maybe under a tree. But she might like a highball.

CHUMLEY. I wouldn't let her talk to me, but as I talked I would want her to reach out a soft white hand and stroke my head and say, "Poor thing! Oh, you poor, poor thing!"

ELWOOD. How long would you like that to go on?

CHUMLEY. Two weeks.

ELWOOD. Wouldn't that get monotonous? Just Akron, beer, and "poor, poor thing" for two weeks?

CHUMLEY. No. No, it would not. It would be wonderful.

ELWOOD. I can't help but feel you're making a mistake in not allowing that woman to talk. If she gets around at all, she may have picked up some very interesting little news items. And I'm sure you're making a mistake with all that beer and no whiskey. But it's your two weeks.

CHUMLEY (*dreamily*). Cold beer at Akron and one last fling! God, man!

ELWOOD. Do you think you'd like to lie down for awhile?

CHUMLEY. No. No. Tell me Mr. Dowd, could he—would he do this for me?

ELWOOD. He could and he might. I have never heard Harvey say a word against Akron. By the way, Doctor, where is Harvey?

CHUMLEY (*rising. Very cautiously*). Why, don't you know?

ELWOOD. The last time I saw him he was with you.

CHUMLEY. Ah!

ELWOOD. Oh! He's probably waiting for me down at Charlie's

CHUMLEY (*with a look of cunning toward his office*). That's it! He's down at Charlie's.

ELWOOD. Excuse me, Doctor. (*Rises, starts upstage.*)

CHUMLEY (*going* U.L. *of table*). No, no, Mr. Dowd. Not in there.

ELWOOD. I couldn't leave without saying good-night to my friend, Dr. Sanderson.

CHUMLEY. Mr. Dowd, Dr. Sanderson is not your friend. None of those people are your friends. *I* am your friend.

ELWOOD. Thank you, Doctor. And I'm yours.

CHUMLEY. And this sister of yours—she is at the bottom of this conspiracy against you. She's trying to persuade me to lock you up. Today she had commitment papers drawn up. She's got your power of attorney and the key to your safety box. She brought you out here

ELWOOD. My sister did all that in one afternoon? Veta is certainly a whirlwind.

CHUMLEY (*moving down below desk*). God, man, haven't you any righteous indignation?

ELWOOD. Dr. Chumley, my mother used to say to me, "In this world, Elwood"—she always called me Elwood —she'd say, "In this world, Elwood, you must be oh, so smart or oh, so pleasant." For years I was smart. I recommend pleasant. You may quote me.

CHUMLEY. Just the same, I will protect you if I have to commit her. Would you like me to do that?

ELWOOD. No, Doctor, not unless Veta wanted it that way. Oh, not that you don't have a nice place out here, but I think Veta would be happier at home with me and Harvey and Myrtle Mae. (KELLY *enters from* C. *with flower in hair, goes to put magazines on table* R. ELWOOD *turns to her.*) Miss Kelly! "Diviner grace has never brightened this enchanting face!" (*To Chumley.*) Ovid's Fifth Elegy. (*To Miss Kelly.*) My dear, you will never look lovelier!

KELLY. I'll never feel happier, Mr. Dowd. I know it. (*Kisses him.*)

CHUMLEY. Well!

KELLY. Yes, Doctor. (*Exits up stairs* C.) (WILSON *enters hall in time to see the kiss.*)

ELWOOD. I wonder if I would be able to remember any more of that poem?

WILSON. Say, maybe this rabbit gag is a good one. Kelly never kissed me.

ELWOOD (*looking at Wilson*). Ovid has always been my favorite poet.

WILSON. O.K., pal — You're discharged. This way out—(*Takes him by arm downstage.*)

CHUMLEY. Wilson! Take your hands off that man!

WILSON. (R. *of desk*). What?

CHUMLEY. Apologize to Mr. Dowd.

WILSON. Apologize to him—this guy with the rabbit? (*He is below desk.*)

CHUMLEY (*looking toward his office*). Apologize! Apologize—

WILSON. I apologize. This is the door.

ELWOOD. If I leave, I'll remember. (WILSON *exits* D.L.)

CHUMLEY. Wait a minute, Dowd. Do women often come up to you and kiss you like Miss Kelly did just now?

ELWOOD. Every once in a while.

CHUMLEY. Yes?

ELWOOD. I encourage it, too.

CHUMLEY (*to himself*). To hell with decency! I've got to have that rabbit! Go ahead and knock. (ELWOOD *starts for Sanderson's door just as* SANDERSON *comes out.*)

ELWOOD. Dr. Sanderson, I couldn't leave without—

SANDERSON. Just a minute, Dowd— (*To Chumley.*) Doctor, do you agree with my diagnosis?

CHUMLEY. Yes, yes! Call them all in.

SANDERSON. Thank you, Doctor. Mrs. Simmons—Judge Gaffney—will you

step in here for a minute, please?

VETA (*enters*). Is it settled? (MYRTLE *and* JUDGE *enter.*)

CHUMLEY. I find I concur with Dr. Sanderson!

SANDERSON. Thank you, Doctor.

MYRTLE. Oh, that's wonderful! What a relief!

JUDGE. Good boy!

ELWOOD. Well, let's celebrate—(*Takes little book out of his pocket.*) I've got some new bars listed in the back of this book.

CHUMLEY (*speaking to others in low tone*). This injection carries a violent reaction. We can't give it to him without his consent. Will he give it?

VETA. Of course he will, if I ask him.

CHUMLEY. To give up this rabbit—I doubt it.

MYRTLE. Don't ask him. Just give it to him.

ELWOOD. "Bessie's Barn Dance. Blondie's Chicken Inn. Better Late Than Never—Bennie's Drive In"—

VETA. Elwood!

ELWOOD. We'll go to Bennie's Drive In—We should telephone for a table. How many of us will there be, Veta?

VETA (*starting to count, then catching herself*). Oh—Elwood!

CHUMLEY. Mr. Dowd, I have a formula—977—that will be good for you. Will you take it?

JUDGE. Elwood, you won't see this rabbit any more.

SANDERSON. But you will see your responsibilities, your duties—

ELWOOD. I'm sure if you thought of it, Doctor, it must be a very fine thing. And if I happen to run into anyone who needs it, I'll be glad to recommend it. For myself, I wouldn't care for it.

VETA. Hear that, Judge! Hear that, Doctor! That's what we have to put up with.

ELWOOD (*turning to look at her*). Veta, do you want me to take this?

VETA. Elwood, I'm only thinking of you. You're my brother and I've known you for years. I'd do anything for you. That Harvey wouldn't do anything for you. He's making a fool out of you, Elwood. Don't be a fool.

ELWOOD. Oh, I won't.

VETA. Why, you could amount to something. You could be sitting on the Western Slope Water Board right now if you'd only go over and ask them.

ELWOOD. All right, Veta. If that's what you want, Harvey and I will go over and ask them tomorrow.

VETA. Tomorrow! I never want to see another tomorrow. Not if Myrtle Mae and I have to live in the house with that rabbit. Our friends never come to see us—we have no social life; we have no life at all. We're both miserable. I wish I were dead—but maybe you don't care!

ELWOOD (slowly). I've always felt that Veta should have everything she wants. Veta, are you sure? (VETA nods.) I'll take it. Where do I go, Doctor?

CHUMLEY. In Dr. Sanderson's office, Dowd.

ELWOOD. Say good-by to the old fellow for me, won't you? (Exits U.L. CHUMLEY exits C.)

JUDGE. How long will this take, Doctor?

SANDERSON. Only a few minutes. Why don't you wait? (Exits.)

JUDGE. We'll wait. (Sits L. of desk.)

VETA (sighs). Dr. Sanderson said it wouldn't take long.

MYRTLE. Now, Mother, don't fidget.

VETA. Oh, how can I help it?

MYRTLE (picks up edge of draperies). How stunning! Mother, could you see me in a housecoat of this material?

VETA (to Myrtle—first looking at draperies. Sighs again). Yes, dear, but let me get a good night's sleep first. (Loud knocking at door.)

JUDGE. Come in. (Enter CAB DRIVER.)

JUDGE. What do you want?

CAB DRIVER. I'm lookin' for a little, short—(Seeing Veta.) Oh, there you are! Lady, you jumped outta the cab without payin' me.

VETA. Oh, yes. I forgot. How much is it?

CAB DRIVER. All the way out here from town? $2.75.

VETA (looking in purse). $2.75! I could have sworn I brought my coin purse—where is it? (Gets up, goes to table, turns pocketbook upside down, in full view of audience. Nothing comes out of it but a compact and a handkerchief.) Myrtle, do you have any money?

MYRTLE. I spent that money Uncle Elwood gave me for my new hair-do for the party.

VETA. Judge, do you have $2.75 I could give this man?

JUDGE. Sorry. Nothing but a check.

CAB DRIVER. We don't take checks.

JUDGE. I know.

VETA. Dr. Chumley, do you happen to have $2.75 I could borrow to pay this cab driver?

CHUMLEY (He has just entered C., now wearing white starched jacket). Haven't got my wallet. No time to get it now. Have to get on with this injection. Sorry. (Exits L.)

VETA. Well, I'll get it for you from my brother, but I can't get it right now. He's in there to get an injection. It won't be long. You'll have to wait.

CAB DRIVER. You're gonna get my money from your brother and he's in there to get some of that stuff they shoot out here?

VETA. Yes, it won't be but a few minutes.

CAB DRIVER. Lady, I want my money now.

VETA. But I told you it would only be a few minutes. I want you to drive us back to town, anyway.

CAB DRIVER. And I told you I want my money now or I'm nosin' the cab back to town, and you can wait for the bus—at six in the morning.

VETA. Well, of all the pig-headed, stubborn things!

MYRTLE. I should say so.

JUDGE. What's the matter with you?

CAB DRIVER. Nothin' that $2.75 won't fix. You heard me. Take it or leave it.

VETA (getting up, going L). I never heard of anything so unreasonable in my life. (Knocks.) Dr. Chumley, will you let Elwood step out here a minute. This cab driver won't wait.

CHUMLEY (off L). Don't be too long. (Enter ELWOOD. CHUMLEY follows.)

VETA. Elwood, I came off without my coin purse. Will you give this man $2.75? But don't give him any more. He's been very rude.

ELWOOD (extending his hand). How do you do? Dowd is my name. Elwood P.

CAB DRIVER. Lofgren's mine. E. J.

ELWOOD. I'm glad to meet you, Mr. Lofgren. This is my sister, Mrs. Simmons. My charming little niece, Myrtle Mae Simmons. Judge Gaffney and Dr. Chumley. (ALL bow coldly.)

CAB DRIVER. Hi—

ELWOOD. Have you lived around here long, Mr. Lofgren?

CAB DRIVER. Yeah, I've lived around here all my life.

ELWOOD. Do you enjoy your work?

CAB DRIVER. It's O.K. I been with the Apex Cabs fifteen years and my brother Joe's been drivin' for Brown Cabs pretty near twelve.

ELWOOD. You drive for Apex and your brother Joe for Brown's? That's interesting, isn't it, Veta? (VETA *reacts with a sniff.*) Mr. Lofgren—let me give you one of my cards. (*Gives him one.*)

CHUMLEY. Better get on with this, Mr. Dowd.

ELWOOD. Certainly. One minute. My sister and my charming little niece live here with me at this address. Won't you and your brother come and have dinner with us some time?

CABBY. Sure—be glad to.

ELWOOD. When—when would you be glad to?

CABBY. I couldn't come any night but Tuesday. I'm on duty all the rest of the week.

ELWOOD. You must come on Tuesday, then. We'll expect you and be delighted to see you, won't we, Veta?

VETA. Oh, Elwood, I'm sure this man has friends of his own.

ELWOOD. Veta, one can't have too many friends.

VETA. Elwood, don't keep Dr. Chumley waiting—that's rude.

ELWOOD. Of course. (*Gives him bill.*) Here you are—keep the change. I'm glad to have met you and I'll expect you Tuesday with your brother. Will you excuse me now?

LOFGREN. Sure. (ELWOOD *exits* U.L. CHUMLEY *follows.*)

CAB DRIVER. A sweet guy.

VETA. Certainly. You could just as well have waited.

CAB DRIVER. Oh, no. Listen, lady. I've been drivin' this route fifteen years. I've brought 'em out here to get that stuff and drove 'em back after they had it. It changes 'em. (*Crosses to desk.*)

VETA. Well, I certainly hope so.

CAB DRIVER. And you ain't kiddin'. On the way out here they sit back and enjoy the ride. They talk to me. Sometimes we stop and watch the sunsets and look at the birds flyin'. Sometimes we stop and watch the birds when there ain't no birds and look at the sunsets when it's rainin'. We have a swell time and I always get a big tip. But afterward—oh—oh—(*Starts to exit again.*)

VETA. Afterwards—oh—oh! What do you mean afterwards—oh—oh?

CAB DRIVER. They crab, crab, crab. They yell at me to watch the lights, watch the brakes, watch the intersections. They scream at me to hurry. They got no faith—in me or my buggy—yet it's the same cab—the same driver—and we're goin' back over the very same road. It's no fun—and no tips—(*Turns to door.*)

VETA. But my brother would have tipped you, anyway. He's very generous. Always has been.

CAB DRIVER. Not after this he won't be. Lady, after this, he'll be a perfectly normal human being and you know what bastards they are! Glad I met you. I'll wait. (*Exits* L.)

VETA (*starts to run for door* U.L.). Oh, Judge Gaffney—Myrtle Mae! Stop it —stop it—don't give it to him! Elwood, come out of there.

JUDGE. You can't do that. Dr. Chumley is giving the injection.

MYRTLE. Mother—stop this—

VETA (*pounding on door*). I don't want Elwood to have it! I don't want Elwood that way. I don't like people like that.

MYRTLE. Do something with her, Judge Mother, stop it—

VETA (*turning on her*). You shut up! I've lived longer than you have. I remember my father. I remember your father. I remember—

CHUMLEY (*opens door*). What's this? What's all this commotion?

WILSON (*enters* U.C.). What's the trouble, Doctor? She soundin' off again?

JUDGE. She wants to stop the injection.

VETA. You haven't—you haven't already given it to him, have you?

CHUMLEY. No, but we're ready. Take Mrs. Simmons away, Wilson.

VETA. Leave me alone. Take your hands off me, you whiteslaver!

JUDGE. You don't know what you want. You didn't want that rabbit, either.

VETA. And what's wrong with Harvey? If Elwood and Myrtle Mae and I want to live with Harvey it's nothing to you! You don't even have to come around. It's our business. Elwood—

Elwood! (ELWOOD *enters from* U.L. SHE *throws herself weepingly into his arms.* HE *pats her shoulder.*)

ELWOOD. There, there, Veta. (*To others.*) Veta is all tired out. She's done a lot today.

JUDGE. Have it your own way. I'm not giving up my game at the club again, no matter how big the animal is. (*He exits down* L.)

VETA (*crossing Elwood to desk*). Come on, Elwood—let's get out of here. I hate this place. I wish I'd never seen it!

CHUMLEY. But—see—here—

ELWOOD. It's whatever Veta says, Doctor.

VETA. Why, look at this! That's funny. (*It's her coin purse.*) It must have been there all the time. I could have paid that cab driver myself. Harvey!

VETA. Come on, Myrtle Mae. Come on, Elwood. Hurry up. (*She exits down left.* MYRTLE *follows.*)

ELWOOD. Good night, Doctor Chumley. Good night, Mr. Wilson.

VETA (*offstage*). Come along, Elwood.

ELWOOD. Doctor, for years I've known what my family thinks of Harvey. But I've often wondered what Harvey's family thinks of me. (*He looks beyond* CHUMLEY *to the door of his office* R.) Oh—there you are! Doctor—do you mind? (*Gestures for him to step back.*) You're standing in his way. (*There is the sound of a lock clicking open and the door of* CHUMLEY's *office opens wide. The invisible Harvey crosses to him and as they exit together:*) Where've you been? I've been looking all over for you—

CURTAIN

THE TEAHOUSE
OF THE AUGUST MOON

John Patrick

(adapted from the novel by Vern Sneider)

The Teahouse of the August Moon opened at the Martin Beck Theatre in New York City on October 15, 1953. It was produced by Maurice ¯vans in association with George Schaefer and was directed by Robert Lewis. The production was designed by Peter Larkin with costumes by Noel Taylor. The cast, in order of appearance, was as follows:

SAKINI . . . . David Wayne
SERGEANT GREGOVICH   Harry Jackson
COL. WAINWRIGHT PURDY III   Paul Ford
CAPTAIN FISBY . . . . John Forsythe
OLD WOMAN . . . . Naoe Kondo
OLD WOMAN'S DAUGHTER . . Mara Kim
THE DAUGHTER'S CHILDREN . . . . . Moy Moy Thom, Joyce Chen and Kenneth Wong
LADY ASTOR . . . . Saki
ANCIENT MAN . . . . Kame Ishikawa
MR. HOKAIDA . . . . Chuck Morgan
MR. OMURA . . . . Kuraji Seida
MR. SUMATA . . . . Kaie Deei

MR. SUMATA'S FATHER Kikuo Hiromura
MR. SEIKO . . . . Haim Winant
MISS HIGA JIGA . . . . Shizu Moriya
MR. KEORA . . . . Yuki Shimoda
MR. OSHIRA . . . . William Hansen
VILLAGERS . . . Jerry Fujikawa, Frank Ogawa, Richard Akagi, Laurence Kim and Norman Chi
LADIES' LEAGUE FOR DEMOCRATIC ACTION Vivian Thom, Naoe Kondo, Mary Ann Reeve and Mara Kim
LOTUS BLOSSOM . . . . Mariko Niki
CAPTAIN MC LEAN . . . . Larry Gates

ACT ONE. *Scene One:* Okinawa. Colonel Purdy's Office, GHQ. *Scene Two:* Outside Captain Fisby's Quarters, GHQ. *Scene Three:* Tobiki Village.

ACT TWO. *Scene One:* Tobiki Village. *Scene Two:* Colonel Purdy's Office, GHQ. *Scene Three:* Captain Fisby's Office, Tobiki. *Scene Four:* Tobiki Village.

ACT THREE. *Scene One:* The Teahouse of the August Moon. *Scene Two:* Captain Fisby's Office, Tobiki. *Scene Three:* The Teahouse of the August Moon.

Copyright 1952, by John Patrick.

The Teahouse of the August Moon is the sole property of the author and is fully protected by copyright. It may not be acted either by professionals or by amateurs without written consent. Public readings and radio or television broadcasts are likewise forbidden. All inquiries concerning rights including stock and amateur rights should be addressed to the author's agent, Miss Miriam Howell, 579 Fifth Avenue, New York 17, N. Y.

(Words from the song "Deep in the Heart of Texas" by June Hershey and Don Swander are reprinted by permission of Melody Lane Publications, Inc. The selection is owned and controlled for the territory of Australasia by Allan & Co. Pty. Ltd., Melbourne, Australia. Copyright, 1941.)

The topicality of *The Teahouse of the August Moon* was both an advantage and a disadvantage. It was a factor in the popularity of the play in New York and elsewhere. But since the political situation after World War II was everywhere unstable, the amity of the Okinawans and the American government of occupation celebrated in the play (and in the novel by Vern Sneider upon which it is based) was subjected to severe strain. Political rumblings began to shake Okinawa a few years after the play was successfully produced on Broadway, where it harvested such plums of critical approval as the New York Drama Critics award and the Pulitzer Prize in 1954. Discontent with the American occupation of Okinawa and the other Ryukyu Islands and agitation for their return to Japan had been expressed for some time before President Eisenhower's visit to the island. But his arrival there in 1960 created a particularly embarrassing climax in the history of our foreign good-will policy. Despite the elaborate precautions against violence taken by the native authorities, the President of the United States was greeted with hostile demonstrations. "When the President reached the center of town," reads the *New York Times* report of June 20, 1960, "he was confronted with about 1500 snake-dancing, shouting demonstrators. They chanted 'Go home, go home!' in English and other slogans in Japanese." The *Times* called the demonstrations only a small index of widespread disaffection among the natives and their desire to return to Japanese control, which would, it was alleged, reduce taxes, finance public improvements,* and secure social benefits for the inhabitants. Under these circumstances, it would be difficult to return to *The Teahouse of the August Moon* with the optimism that greeted the original production. It is fortunate, therefore, that the charm and liveliness of Mr. Patrick do not depend upon the unreliable international situation. The New York reviewers who called it an enchanting and amusing stage piece did not have an eye on diplomatic relations. Brooks Atkinson of the *Times* was especially sagacious in his review of the Broadway opening. Although he called the play "completely captivating," he described it as "a piece of exotic make-believe in a style as intimate as fairy-story." Mr. Atkinson declared that what the dramatist said was "interesting" but "how he says it is imaginative and original." This was certainly a just comment in so far as it pertained to the beautifully staged and designed New York production, which had David Wayne in the principal role.

John Patrick, born in 1907, a native of Carmel, California, had already won distinction as a playwright and a screenwriter when he undertook to dramatize Vern Sneider's book. Educated at Columbia and Harvard and subsequently a successful writer of radio plays for Helen Hayes, he became a "produced playwright" in 1935 with *Hell Freezes Over*, and the author of a greatly admired, if not particularly popular, drama, *The Willow and I*, in 1942. World War II, in which he participated as a captain in the American Field Service, inspired his next play, *The Hasty Heart* (1945), which was a warm and understanding character-drama as well as an admirable group picture of soldiers hospitalized behind the front lines. This play was followed by a distinctly moving historical drama, *The Story of Mary Surratt*, in which Mr. Patrick vindicated Mrs. Surratt, who was hanged for her alleged part in the assassination of Abraham Lincoln. Mr. Patrick then supplied the not altogether grateful New York public with two light comedies. *The Curious Savage* (1950) revolved

---

* In fairness to the United States, I would call attention to the following paragraphs from a March 19, 1961, *New York Times* report:

"In spite of Japan's growing economic interest in the Ryukyus, the United States contributes most of the aid given to the island. Aid given by the United States last year was estimated at $3,000,000.

"United States projects in 1960 included construction of a new electric plant, establishment of a free-trade zone, organization of unions for Ryukyu military employees, development of water systems, roads, sea walls and a port on Ishigaki Island, in the southern Ryukyus, and land reclamation.

"The United States aid also built cultural centers in different areas, a sixth radio station and a third television station on Okinawa."

around an eccentric widow, played by Lillian Gish, who invests her wealth in a so-called Happiness Fund intended to help people do the foolish things they have always wanted to do. *Lo and Behold* was a fantastic play concerning a Nobel Prize winner who dies of willful overeating and finds himself comically harassed by an odd collection of ghosts in the other world. If *The Teahouse of the August Moon* is expertly written, the credit belongs equally to the dramatist's genial sympathies and buoyant craftsmanship.

Scene One

Directly behind the house curtain is a second curtain consisting of four panels of split bamboo. Each of these sections can be raised and lowered individually.

AT RISE: *As the house lights dim, the Oriental strains from a stringed instrument can be heard playing softly in the background. A pool of light picks up* SAKINI *standing framed against the bamboo backing. He wears a pair of tattered shorts and a native shirt. His shoes, the gift of a G.I., are several sizes too large. His socks are also too large and hang in wrinkles over his ankles. He is an Okinawan who might be any age between thirty and sixty. In repose his face betrays age, but the illusion is shattered quickly by his smile of childlike candor.*

With hands together in prayer-like supplication, he walks down to the footlights and bows to the audience center in solemn ritual. Then he bows from the waist—to the left and to the right.

Straightening up, he examines the audience seated before him with open curiosity. The music ceases. As it ceases, SAKINI *begins to work his jaws vigorously.*

———

SAKINI
Tootie-fruitie.
   (*He takes the gum from his mouth and, wrapping it carefully in a piece of paper, puts it in a matchbox and restores it to a pocket in his shirt.*)
Most generous gift of American sergeant.
   (*He resumes his original posture of dignity.*)
Lovely ladies, kind gentlemen:
Please to introduce myself.
Sakini by name.
Interpreter by profession.
Education by ancient dictionary.
Okinawan by whim of gods.
History of Okinawa reveal distinguished record of conquerors.
We have honor to be subjugated in fourteenth century by Chinese pirates.
In sixteenth century by English missionaries.
In eighteenth century by Japanese war lords.
And in twentieth century by American Marines.
Okinawa very fortunate.
Culture brought to us. . . . Not have to leave home for it.
Learn many things.
Most important that rest of world not like Okinawa.
World filled with delightful variation.
Illustration.
In Okinawa . . . no locks on doors.
Bad manners not to trust neighbors.
In America . . . lock and key big industry.
Conclusion?
Bad manners good business.
In Okinawa . . . wash self in public bath with nude lady quite proper.
Picture of nude lady in private home . . . quite improper.
In America . . . statue of nude lady in park win prize.
But nude lady in flesh in park win penalty.
Conclusion?
Pornography question of geography.
But Okinawans most eager to be educated by conquerors.
Deep desire to improve friction.
Not easy to learn.
Sometimes painful.
But pain makes man think.
Thought makes man wise.
Wisdom makes life endurable.
So . . .
   (*He crosses back to the left of the first of the panels.*)
We tell little story to demonstrate splendid example of benevolent assimilation of democracy by Okinawa.
   (*He claps his hands, signaling the stagehand to raise the first of the four panels. Flush against the curtain is revealed a sign nailed onto a denuded palm stump. It points toward the other side of the stage and reads:* COL. WAINRIGHT PURDY III.)
Boss by name of Colonel Purdy—Three.
Number three after name indicate he is a son of a son of a son.
   (*He steps to the next panel and claps again. The screen rolls up revealing a laundry line tied to a second denuded stump. As these panels are raised the background is revealed in sections. It includes a jeep parked against a pile of empty gasoline drums, trees ripped of foliage by recent gunfire—all creating an impression of general destruction. There are several articles of wearing apparel hanging on the laundry line, foremost of which is a pair of khaki pants size forty.*)
Colonel Purdy, Three, displays splendid example of cleanliness for native population to follow. But native population cannot follow. Native not *have* two pairs of pants.

(He then claps for the next screen to rise, revealing more of the laundry. To the extreme right is seen the outside of Colonel Purdy's Quonset office. Nailed on the post holding the other end of the line is a sign reading: OFFICERS' LAUNDRY ONLY.*)*

Colonel Purdy put up many signs. This exceedingly civilized. Make it very easy for uncivilized to know what *not* to do. Here laundry of officer not to fraternize with laundry of enlisted man.

*(*SAKINI *now signals for the last panel to be raised, revealing the inside of the hut. Colonel Purdy's vacant desk is beside the door. A sign denotes his proprietorship. Another sign admonishes the visitor to* THINK! *The office is small and sparse. A bulletin board for "Daily Orders" hangs on the upstage wall. Against this wall is the desk of Sergeant Gregovich. Behind a sign denoting his rating sits the* SERGEANT. *His posture is frozen—as if awaiting a signal to come to life.* SAKINI *crosses down center to explain to his audience.)*

This gentleman honorable Sergeant Gregovich—assistant to Colonel Purdy. Not son of a son of a son.

(He turns toward the SERGEANT.*)*

Play has begun, Sergeant.

*(*GREGOVICH *now comes to life. He begins to chew his gum vigorously and to look about the office. He rises and crosses down to Colonel Purdy's desk. He gets down on his hands and knees in front of the desk and reaches under it.)*

Oh, you know what he is doing? Explanation. Colonel Purdy great student of history. Every month wife of Colonel Purdy send him magazine called *Adventure Magazine.* Cover has picture of pirate with black patch over eye. Everybody try to steal magazine. Colonel hide under desk so he can read first.

*(*GREGOVICH *rises triumphantly with the magazine.)*

But Sergeant always find. Smart mouse.

*(*GREGOVICH *returns to his desk and buries himself behind the pages of the magazine. At this point* COLONEL PURDY *himself enters from the left. As his laundry has indicated, he is a man of proportions. The worries of the world in general and the Army of Occupation in particular weigh heavily on his shoulders. He stops to glance at the nearest official sign. He takes out a small notebook to make an entry. Sakini's presence is not recognized until indicated.)*

This gentleman exalted boss—Colonel Purdy, Three. Subject of sovereign American city of Pottawattamie, Michigan.

*(*COLONEL PURDY *hiccups and taps his chest.)*

Also subject to indignity of indigestion. Colonel Purdy explain this by saying—

PURDY *(clears his throat and says to himself).* An occupational disorder of the Army of Occupation. *(He taps his chest again and puts the notebook away.)*

SAKINI. Colonel Purdy very wise man. Always hit nail on head. Every morning, look at sky—(COLONEL PURDY *puts his hands on his hips and glances skyward.)* And make prophecy.

PURDY. It's not going to rain today.

SAKINI. And you know what? Not rain. Of course, not rain here this time of year in whole history of Okinawa. But Colonel not make mistake. (COLONEL PURDY *goes down the laundry line and stops to button the top of a pair of shorts.)* Colonel Purdy gentleman of propriety. (PURDY *goes back to count articles of clothing.)* And precision. Always count laundry.

PURDY *(counts aloud).* Un—deux—trois.

SAKINI. Explanation. Army teach Colonel French for invasion of Europe. Then send to Okinawa instead.

PURDY. . . . quatre—cinq—six—sept. *(He beams with satisfaction.)*

SAKINI. Very good. Colonel count in French and not notice one pair shorts missing in Okinawa.

PURDY *(his expression quickly changes).* What? *(He goes down the line and counts again in English.)* One, two, three, four, five, six, seven! *(He inhales deeply for an explosion.)*

SAKINI *(rushes down to the footlights).* Oh—ladies please close ears unless want to hear unladylike oath. *(He puts his hands over his own ears.)*

PURDY *(explodes).* Damitohell! Damitohell! Damitohell!

SAKINI. Now Colonel yell loud for Sakini. But Sakini hide. Pretend to be asleep. *(He promptly curls up on the ground beside the office, with his back to the* COLONEL.*)*

PURDY. Sakini! (SAKINI *snores.* PURDY *strides over to tower above him.)* Sakini!

SAKINI *(rises quickly).* Oh—oh. Good

morning, boss. You sure surprise me.

PURDY. *Where* is the boy that does my laundry!

SAKINI. Bring laundry back and go home to sleep, boss.

PURDY. I want you to find out why my laundry comes back every week with one piece missing!

SAKINI. Gets lost, boss.

PURDY. I *know* it gets lost. What I want to find out is *how* it gets lost.

SAKINI. Very simple. Boy takes laundry to top of mountain stream and throws in water. Then runs down hill fast as dickens to catch laundry at bottom. Sometimes not run fast enough.

PURDY (*heaves a martyr's sigh*). No wonder you people were subjugated by the Japanese. If you're not sleeping you're running away from work. Where is your "get-up-and-go"?

SAKINI. Guess "get-up-and-go" went. (SAKINI *starts to sit on the ground.*)

PURDY. Well, get up and go over to the mess and see if Captain Fisby has arrived. If he has, tell him to report to me at once. Hurry! (*As* SAKINI *starts across the stage* PURDY *looks with annoyance at the G.I. socks that hang down over Sakini's ankles.*) Sakini!

SAKINI (*Stops*). Yes, boss?

PURDY. You're a civilian employee in the pay of the United States Army. And should dress accordingly. *Pull Your Socks Up!*

SAKINI. Yes, boss. (*He leans over and pulls up his socks—not a great improvement.*) Anything else, boss?

PURDY. That will be all. (SAKINI *ambles across the stage so slowly that the* COLONEL *explodes in exasperation.*) Is that as *fast* as you can walk!

SAKINI. Oh no, boss. But if walk any faster—socks fall down. (*As* SAKINI *exits,* COLONEL PURDY *closes his eyes and counts to ten in vehement French.* PURDY *remains arrested in this position.* SAKINI *re-enters downstage. He signals the closing of the panels left, shutting out the* COLONEL.)

SAKINI. Introduction now over. Kindly direct attention to office. (*He leans out toward the footlights and calls across stage.*) Oh, Honorable Sergeant—ready now to continue. (SERGEANT GREGOVICH *again comes to life. He glances out the office door and quickly hides the* Adventure Magazine. *He stands at attention as* COLONEL PURDY *enters.* SAKINI *exits into the wings.*)

GREGOVICH. Good morning, sir.

PURDY. At ease. (COLONEL PURDY *sits down behind his desk and begins searching through the papers on it.*) I'm thinking of getting rid of that interpreter. He doesn't set a good example.

GREGOVICH. We've got to have someone around that speaks the language, sir.

PURDY. You're quite right, Sergeant. You're quite right. It isn't often I make a mistake, but when I do—

GREGOVICH. It's a beaut?

PURDY (*stiffly*). I wasn't going to say that. I was going to say—I admit it.

GREGOVICH. Sorry, sir.

PURDY. We've got a new officer reporting this morning. He's been transferred to us from "Psychological Warfare." (*Benevolently*) I don't suppose you happen to know who *they* are?

GREGOVICH. Aren't they something at the rear of the Rear Echelon?

PURDY. They're just the cream of the Army's geniuses. They're just the brains behind the fighting heart. Every man jack of them has a mind like a steel trap. And we are lucky to be getting one of their officers.

GREGOVICH. I'll watch my step, sir.

PURDY. While we're waiting for Captain Fisby, I want you to make a note of some new signs I want painted.

GREGOVICH (*takes up a pad*). The painter hasn't finished the ones you ordered yesterday, sir.

PURDY. There's only one answer to that. Put on another sign painter. Now. I noticed the men were dancing with each other in the canteen the other night.

GREGOVICH. Yes, sir. (*He writes on his pad.*) "No dancing allowed."

PURDY (*annoyed*). I didn't say that, Gregovich! I don't object to the men dancing. I want them to enjoy themselves. But it doesn't set a good example for the natives to see noncoms dancing with enlisted men. So have a sign posted saying, "Sergeants Are Forbidden to Dance with Privates."

GREGOVICH. Yes, sir.

PURDY. Have another sign put up beside that clear pool of water just below the falls—"For Officers Only."

GREGOVICH. Where will the men bathe, sir?

PURDY. There is another pool just below it they can use.

GREGOVICH. If you'll pardon me, sir—they're not going to like that. They'll be bathing in water the officers have already bathed in.

PURDY: That's a valid objection, Gregovich. We don't want to do anything unreasonable. (*He concentrates for a moment.*) How far is the second pool below the first?

GREGOVICH. About three hundred yards.

PURDY (*satisfied*). Then it's quite all right. Water purifies itself every two hundred feet.

GREGOVICH. Do you think that will satisfy the men, sir?

PURDY. I don't see why it shouldn't. It satisfies science. Well, you might as well take those memos to the sign painter now.

GREGOVICH. Yes, sir.

(*He goes out. As soon as he is gone,* COLONEL PURDY *moves around to the front of his desk and feels under it for his* Adventure Magazine. *When he fails to find it, he kneels down on all fours to peer under the desk.* SAKINI *enters and looks around. He steps over and taps the nearest part of Colonel Purdy—his ample rear end.*)

SAKINI. Sakini here, boss.

PURDY (*glances around indignantly*). Don't *ever* put your finger on an officer!

SAKINI. Not right, boss?

PURDY. No! If you want to announce your presence—knock! (*He peers under the desk again.*) Can't you natives learn anything about custom? (SAKINI *stands unhappily a moment, then leans forward and knocks gently on the* COLONEL. PURDY *rises in wrath.*) What do you think you're doing?

SAKINI. Not know, boss. Do what you ask.

PURDY (*moves behind his desk*). Everything in this Godforsaken country conspires to annoy me. (*He turns to* SAKINI.) Well, where is Captain Fisby?

SAKINI (*points out the door*). He come now. I run ahead. (*He points to his ankles.*) Socks fall down.

(*He then steps back to allow* CAPTAIN FISBY *to enter.* CAPTAIN FISBY *is in his late twenties, nice-looking and rather on the earnest side. He is nervous and eager to make a good impression. He salutes smartly.*)

CAPTAIN FISBY. Captain Fisby reporting, sir.

PURDY (*returns the salute*). Welcome to Team 147, Captain. (*He puts out his hand.*)

FISBY (*shakes hands*). Thank you, sir.

PURDY. I can't tell you how glad I am to have you, Captain. Frankly, we're so desperate for officer personnel I'd be glad to see you even if you had two heads. (SAKINI *breaks into gales of laughter.* PURDY *turns to him icily.*) That will be all, Sakini. You can wait outside.

SAKINI (*bows*). I sit by door. Not sleep! (*He exits.*)

PURDY. Sit down, Captain, sit down. (FISBY *sits facing* PURDY.) Have you unpacked?

FISBY (*proudly*). Yes *sir!* I got in last night and unpacked at once.

PURDY. Well, that's too bad, because you'll have to pack again. I'm sending you to Tobiki at once. We need a man of your caliber up there right away. (*He laughs with forced heartiness.*)

FISBY (*forces a laugh in return*). Thank you.

PURDY. I'm informed, Captain, that you requested this transfer from "Psychological Warfare" to *my* outfit. May I say that I am honored.

FISBY. Well—in all fairness, sir—I think I should tell you . . . the information is only partly true.

PURDY (*pauses*). You *didn't* request this transfer to me?

FISBY. I was *requested* to request it, sir.

PURDY. Oh. (*He blinks to aid his digestion of this information.*) May I ask why?

FISBY. Well, my propaganda to undermine enemy morale always seemed to undermine the staff's morale instead, sir.

PURDY. *How* did you get into "Psychological Warfare" in the *first* place?

FISBY. I had been requested to request a transfer.

PURDY. From what?

FISBY. Paymaster General's office.

PURDY. What was your duty there?

FISBY. I was in charge of the payroll computation machine until—until—(*He flounders unhappily.*)

PURDY. Until *what?*

FISBY. Well, sir, machines have always been my mortal enemies. I don't think they're inanimate at all. I think they're full of malice and ill will. They—

PURDY. I *asked* you what happened, Captain.

FISBY. Well, this computation machine made a mistake of a quarter of a million dollars on the payroll. Unfortunately, the men were paid *before* the mistake was discovered.

PURDY. What did they do to you?

FISBY. For a while I was given a job licking envelopes.

PURDY. Then you asked for a transfer?

FISBY. No, sir, I developed an allergy to glue.

PURDY. How many outfits in this man's army have you been in, Captain?

FISBY. How many are there, sir?

PURDY. Never mind. I admit disappointment but not defeat. I'd thought you were given to me in recognition of my work here. Frankly, I expect to be made a general soon, and I want that star for my wife's crown. Naturally, that's very hush-hush.

FISBY (*nods*). Naturally. Maybe I just wasn't cut out to be a soldier.

PURDY. Captain, none of us was cut out to be a soldier. But we do the job. We adjust. We adapt. We roll with the punch and bring victory home in our teeth. Do you know what *I* was before the war?

FISBY (*hesitates unhappily*). A football coach?

PURDY. I was the Purdy Paper Box Company of Pottawattamie. What did I know about foreigners? But my job is to teach these natives the meaning of democracy, and they're going to learn democracy if I have to shoot every one of them.

FISBY. I'm sure your wife wouldn't want her star that way, sir.

PURDY. What did you do before the war?

FISBY. I was an associate professor at Muncie.

PURDY. What did you teach?

FISBY. The humanities.

PURDY. Captain, you are finally getting a job you're qualified by training to handle—teaching these natives how to act human.

FISBY. The humanities isn't quite that, sir.

PURDY. If you can teach one thing you can teach another. Your job at Tobiki will be to teach the natives democracy and make them self-supporting. Establish some sort of industry up there.

FISBY. Is there a general plan?

PURDY. There is a specific plan. (*He extends a document the size of a telephone book.*) Washington has drawn up full instructions pertaining to the welfare and recovery of these native villages. *This* is Plan B. Consider it your *Bible*, Captain.

FISBY. I'll study it carefully, sir. There might be some questions I'd like to ask you.

PURDY (*points to Plan B*). Washington has anticipated all your questions.

FISBY. But I was thinking—

PURDY. You don't even have to think, Captain. This document relieves you of that responsibility.

FISBY. But in dealing with the natives, sir—

PURDY (*interrupts*). It's all covered in Section Four: "Orienting the Oriental." How is your Luchuan?

FISBY. I don't know, sir. What is it?

PURDY. It's the native dialect. Well, I can see you'll need an interpreter. (*His eyes light up and he slaps his desk.*) I have just the man for you! (*He turns and calls out the door.*) Sakini!

FISBY. I could study the dialect, sir.

PURDY. No need. We won the war. I'll give you my own interpreter.

FISBY. Oh, I wouldn't want to deprive you of—

PURDY. I insist.

(SAKINI *enters. He bows—and then remembers. He leans forward and politely knocks on the desk.*)

SAKINI. Sakini present. Socks up. Not sleeping.

PURDY. Sakini, this is Captain Fisby.

FISBY. Hello, Sakini.

SAKINI (*bows, then turns to* PURDY). We meet already. (*He smiles in comradeship.*) You forget, boss?

PURDY (*covers his face, counts to ten, then looks up*). I am assigning you to Captain Fisby. He's going to take charge of a village at the top of Okinawa—a village called Tobiki.

SAKINI. Oh! Tobiki very nice place, boss. But not at top of Okinawa. At bottom.

PURDY. Don't tell me where the villages under my command are located. I happen to have looked at the map.

SAKINI. So sorry, boss. But I happen to get born in Tobiki. Is at bottom.

PURDY (*whips a map out of his desk*). Then it's time you learned where you were born. I also happen to give a course in map reading.

SAKINI (*looks at map*). So sorry, boss. But map upside down.

FISBY (*looks at map*). He's right.

PURDY (*looks at map—turns it around*). Why in hell doesn't the Army learn how to draw a map properly! (*Turns to* SAKINI.) That will be all, Sakini. Find Sergeant Gregovich and have him assign a jeep to Captain Fisby. Then load supplies and the captain's gear in the jeep. You will be leaving at once. I'll send rice rations later.

SAKINI (*takes the colonel's hand and pumps it*). Oh, thank you, boss. You very kind to send me home. I mention you in prayer to gods. (*He turns to* FISBY.) I wait at jeep for you, Captain. (*He starts to run, then slows down quickly.*) Very happy, sir. Socks up. (*He goes out.* PURDY *turns wearily to* FISBY.)

PURDY. I sometimes think we Occupation Teams have it tougher than combat troops. (*He quickly holds up a protesting hand.*) Granted they have it rough for a while. But we have the killing daily grind, with no glory in it.

FISBY. Yes, sir, I know what you mean. Life itself is a battlefield with its own obscure heroes.

PURDY (*looks at* FISBY *with surprise*). I consider that poetry, Captain.

FISBY. I'm afraid it's just prose, sir. And it isn't mine, it's Victor Hugo's.

PURDY (*corrected*). Oh, yes. Victor Hugo! How I loved *Tale of Two Cities*.

FISBY. Isn't that Dickens, sir?

PURDY. I guess I was thinking of the movie. Well! To get back to Tobiki. Your first job when you get there will be to establish a municipal government and build a school.

FISBY. A school?

PURDY. It's all in Plan B. I'll see that cement and lumber are sent down to you. Plan B calls for the schoolhouse to be pentagon-shaped.

FISBY. If you say so, sir.

PURDY. When the school is built, you will organize a Ladies' League for Democratic Action. You will deliver a series of lectures on democracy as outlined in the outline. Captain, this is a chance for you to make a name for yourself.

FISBY. I will, sir. You see, I feel that I've personally delayed victory at least a year, and I have to vindicate myself.

PURDY. That's the kind of talk I like to hear from my officers. Well, I won't detain you then. (*He rises.*) My only order to you is: Put that village on the map.

FISBY. Yes, sir.

PURDY. Send me a bimonthly Progress Report—in triplicate.

FISBY. Yes, sir.

PURDY. Don't duplicate your work.

FISBY. No, sir.

PURDY. Fire those natives with the Spirit of Occupation.

FISBY. Yes, sir.

PURDY. And remember—that the eyes of Washington are on our Occupation Teams. And the eyes of the world are on Washington.

FISBY. I'll keep the eyes in mind, sir.

PURDY. Good-bye, Captain. (FISBY *salutes smartly and goes out.* PURDY *stands for a moment, moved by the vastness of the canvas. Then he turns to his desk.*) Where the hell is my *Adventure Magazine!*

THE SCENE BLACKS OUT QUICKLY

SCENE TWO

SCENE: *Outside Captain Fisby's quarters.*
TIME: *A few minutes later.*
AT RISE: CAPTAIN FISBY *and* SAKINI *enter from left and cross before the panels, all of which are now down.*

SAKINI Everything all ready, boss. We go to Lobiki now?

FISBY. I guess so. Well, wish me luck, Sakini. I'm going out to spread the gospel of Plan B.

SAKINI. You already lucky, boss. You got me.

FISBY (*smiles*). Thanks . . . do you know the road?

SAKINI. No road, boss—just path for wagon cart and goat.

FISBY. Will a jeep make it?

SAKINI. We find out, boss.

FISBY. Naturally. How long will it take us?

SAKINI. Oh—not know until we arrive, boss.

FISBY. Naturally. Well, we might as well get started. I'll drive and you give directions.

SAKINI. Oh, very happy to go home.

FISBY. Where is the jeep?

SAKINI. Right here, boss.

(*He turns and claps his hands. The panels go up. The laundry line has been removed and the jeep pulled down center. The jeep is piled with Fisby's belongings. Perched high on the top of this pyramid sits a very old and very wrinkled* NATIVE WOMAN. SAKINI *pays no attention to her as he goes around the jeep test-kicking the tires. And the* OLD WOMAN *sits disinterested and aloof from what goes on below her.*)

FISBY. Hey, wait a minute! What's she doing up there? (*He points to her. The* OLD WOMAN *sits with hands folded serenely, looking straight ahead.*)

SAKINI. She nice old lady hear we go to Tobiki village. She think she go along to visit grandson.

FISBY. Oh, she does. Well, you explain that I'm very sorry but she'll have to take a bus.

SAKINI. No buses to Tobiki. People very poor—can only travel on generosity.

FISBY. I'm sorry, but it's against regulations.

SAKINI. She not fall off, boss. She tied on.

FISBY. Well, untie her and get her down. She'll just have to find some other way to visit her grandson.

SAKINI. Her grandson mayor of Tobiki village. You make him lose face if you kick old grandmother off jeep.

FISBY. She's the mayor's grandmother?

SAKINI. Oh yes, boss.

FISBY. Well, since she's already tied on, I guess we can take her. (*He looks at the bundles.*) Are all those *mine?*

SAKINI. Oh, no. Most of bundles belong to old lady. She think she visit three or four months so she bring own bed and cooking pots.

FISBY. Well, tell her to yell out if she sees any low branches coming. (*He starts to get in.*) Let's get started.

SAKINI. Oh, can't go yet, boss.

FISBY. Why not?

SAKINI. Old lady's daughter not here.

FISBY (*glances at watch*). We can't wait for a lot of good-byes, Sakini!

SAKINI (*looking behind* FISBY). Oh, she come now—right on dot you bet.

(CAPTAIN FISBY *turns to witness a squat young* NATIVE WOMAN *come on pushing a wheelbarrow loaded with bundles. She stops long enough to bow low to* FISBY—*then begins to tie bundles onto the jeep.*)

FISBY. Sakini, can't the old lady leave some of that stuff behind?

SAKINI. Not her things, boss. Belong to daughter.

FISBY. Wait a minute. Is the daughter planning on going with us, too?

SAKINI. Old lady very old. Who take

care of her on trip?

FISBY. Well, I— (THE DAUGHTER *takes the wheelbarrow and hurries off.*) Hey—you come back! Sakini—tell her to come back. We can't carry any more bundles.

SAKINI (*calmly*). Oh, she not go to get bundles, boss. She go to get children.

FISBY. Come here, Sakini. Now look—this sort of thing is always happening to me and I have to put a stop to it some place. This time I'm determined to succeed. It's not that I don't *want* to take them. But you can see for yourself, *there's no room left for kids!*

SAKINI. But daughter not go without children and old lady not go without daughter. And if old lady not go, mayor of Tobiki be mad at you.

(*Turns to see the* DAUGHTER *hurry back with three children in tow. They all bow politely to* FISBY. *Their mother then piles them on the hood of the jeep.*)

FISBY. For Pete's sake, Sakini, how does she expect me to see how to drive!

SAKINI. Old lady got very good eyesight. She sit on top and tell us when to turn.

(*At this point one of the* CHILDREN *climbs off the hood and points offstage.*)

CHILD. A! Wasureta!

DAUGHTER. Wasureta? Nanisa?

CHILD. Fija dayo.

(*The* CHILD *dashes offstage.*)

FISBY. Now, where's *he* going?

SAKINI (*to* DAUGHTER). Doshtano?

DAUGHTER. Fija turete kurendes!

SAKINI (*to* FISBY). He go to get goat.

FISBY. A goat!

SAKINI. Can't go and leave poor goat behind.

DAUGHTER (*waves gaily to the* OLD WOMAN *on top of the jeep*). Okasan daijobu! (*She climbs the pyramid of bundles to settle beside her.*)

FISBY. Well, right here is where we start seeing who's going to lose face. No goat is going to travel on this jeep.

SAKINI. You not like goats, boss?

FISBY. It has nothing to do with whether I like goats or not. I'm positive the colonel wouldn't like it.

SAKINI. But children not go without goat, mother not go without children, old lady not go without daughter—

FISBY (*repeats with* SAKINI). —and if old lady not go, the mayor of Tobiki be mad at you! (FISBY *sees the goat being led on by the* SMALL BOY.) Oh, no!

SAKINI. Everybody here, boss. Goat not got children. Goat unmarried lady goat.

FISBY. All right, all right. Put it on the hood with the kids. (*The goat is placed on the hood and held by the* CHILDREN.) We've got to get started or we'll never get off the ground.

SAKINI. All ready to go, boss. You get in now. Nobody else going.

(*But before* FISBY *can climb in an* OLD MAN *comes hurrying in and, without looking to the right or left, climbs on the back of the jeep and settles down.*)

FISBY. Now who the hell is he?

SAKINI (*looks at* OLD MAN). Now who the hell is he? (*Back to* FISBY.) Not know, boss, never see before.

FISBY. Is he a relation of theirs?

SAKINI (*to the woman on top of the jeep*). Kore dare?

MOTHER. Mitakoto nai hito desu.

SAKINI. She say she never see him before, boss.

FISBY. Well, ask him what he's doing here!

SAKINI (*goes to the* OLD MAN). Ojisan, doshtano?

OLD MAN. Washimo notte ikuyo.

SAKINI. He say he see people going somewhere on trip and he think maybe he like to go somewhere, too.

FISBY. Tell him to get off and get off quick!

SAKINI. Dame dayo, ojisan, orina, orina!

OLD MAN (*angrily*). Fija noserunnera washimo noruyo!

SAKINI. He say why not take him? You take goat. He say maybe you think he not as good as goat?

FISBY. Look, Sakini, explain to him that the eyes of the world are on Washington and the eyes of Washington are on me. I can't be responsible for—

(*But before this can be translated,* COLONEL PURDY *stalks on and comes to an abrupt halt.*)

PURDY. Captain Fisby!

FISBY. Yes, sir.

PURDY. What in the name of Occupation do you think you're doing!

FISBY. It's hard to explain, sir. . . . I, ah . . . ah . . .

(*As he founders, the* OLD LADY *on top of the bundles comes to life. She looks down and screams shrilly.*)

OLD LADY. Yakamashii oyajijana, hayo iko, iko!

PURDY. What is *she* saying?

SAKINI. She say . . . tell fat old man to shut up so we can get started! (*As* COLONEL PURDY's *jaw drops, the panels drop also.*)

BLACKOUT

SCENE THREE

SCENE: *Tobiki village.*
TIME: *Ten days later.*
AT RISE: *All the bamboo panels are down.*
SAKINI *walks in front of them to the center of the stage from the wings.*

———

SAKINI
    (*Bows*)
Distance from Headquarters to Tobiki village by map . . . two inches.
By horse . . . three days.
By foot . . . four days.
By jeep . . . ten days.
Explanation:
Captain want to go to Tobiki.
Children want to go ocean. Never see ocean.
We see ocean.
Captain want to go to Tobiki.
Old lady's daughter want to visit Awasi.
We go Awasi.
Old lady make second mistake.
Captain demand we go Tobiki.
Ancient man have cousin in Yatoda.
We go Yatoda.
Damn fool old lady not know one road from another.
Now we arrive Tobiki.
Tobiki welcome rice and democracy.
    (*He claps his hands for the panels to be raised, then walks into the scene. The destitute village of Tobiki is revealed with its sagging huts and its ragged villagers grouped in the square just outside of Captain Fisby's office. This is a small bamboo structure with a thatched roof. It has a makeshift desk and field telephone. There is a cot crowded against the upper wall.* FISBY, *his glasses on, sits studying Plan B. He puts the document down, and, taking off his glasses, calls to* SAKINI.)

FISBY. Sakini!

SAKINI. Right here, boss. Not asleep, boss.

FISBY. Good. According to Plan B, my first job here is to hold a public meeting.

SAKINI. Public waiting in public square . . . eager to meet new boss, boss.

FISBY. Good. Now, Plan B calls for a lecture on the ABC's of democracy. (*He turns to* SAKINI.) Make sure they understand that I come as a friend of the people. That we intend to lift the yoke of oppression from their shoulders.

SAKINI. Oh, they like that, boss. This their favorite speech.

FISBY. What do you mean, their favorite speech?

SAKINI. Oh, Japanese say same things when they come, boss. Then take everything.

FISBY. Well, we're not here to *take* anything.

SAKINI. They got nothing left to take away, boss.

FISBY (*annoyed*). Well, if they *did* have, we wouldn't take it. We're here to *give* them something.

SAKINI. Oh, not get angry, boss. We not mind. After eight centuries we get used to it. When friends come now, we hide things quick as the dickens.

FISBY (*rises, a little upset*). Well, I guess it's up to me to convince them we really are friends. Let's meet the villagers. (*He picks up his papers.*) And let them meet Plan B.

(*As they step out the door to the office, the villagers rise and bow respectfully in unison.* FISBY *surveys them.*)

SAKINI (*introducing* FISBY). Amerikano Taisho-san, Captain Fisby.

FISBY (*bows in return*). Well, we might as well get started, Sakini. (*He finds a box and stands on it. He glances into Plan B and clears his throat.*) Citizens of Tobiki village. I—

SAKINI (*interrupts him*). Sorry, boss. Can't begin lecture yet.

FISBY. Why not?

SAKINI. Not good manners. People bring you gifts. You must accept gifts first.

FISBY. But I'm here to bring gifts from my government to them.

SAKINI. Very rude to make people feel poor, boss.

FISBY. I don't want to make anyone feel poor, but—

SAKINI. You make them lose face if you refuse, boss. They not accept democracy from you.

FISBY. All right. All right, then. Say to them that I'll accept their gifts in the name of the United States Occupation Forces.

SAKINI (*turns to the* VILLAGERS). Soreja moratte okuyo!

(MR. HOKAIDA, *an enormous villager in tattered peasant clothes, steps forward.*)

MR. HOKAIDA (*bows diffidently and offers his present to* FISBY). Amerika-san, korewo dozo.

SAKINI. This Mr. Hokaida, boss. He give you fine present.

FISBY. Thank you. Thank you very much. (*He takes it and turns to* SAKINI *puzzled.*) What is it?

SAKINI. You not know?

FISBY. No.

SAKINI. Oh, where you been all your life, boss?

FISBY. Living without one of these, I guess.

SAKINI. Is very splendid cricket cage, boss.

FISBY. What's it used for?

SAKINI. Keep cricket in.

FISBY. Why?

SAKINI. So Fortune smile on you. Cricket very good luck.

FISBY. But there's no cricket in it.

SAKINI. Bad luck to give cricket. You must catch your own fortune. No one can get it for you.

FISBY (*considers this*). Thank him and tell him I'll keep my eye out for a cricket.

SAKINI. Ya, arigato. (MR. HOKAIDA *bows away as an* ANCIENT NATIVE *steps forward and bows.*) This Mr. Omura. He bring you gift of chopsticks.

MR. OMURA. Korede mainichi gochiso wo, dozo.

SAKINI. He say: May only food of gods touch your lips.

(*As* FISBY *bows,* MR. SUMATA, *a nervous citizen in a torn straw hat, pushes his way toward* SAKINI.)

MR. SUMATA. Sugu modotte kuruyo!

SAKINI. Doshtandes?

MR. SUMATA. Ima sugu presento motte kuruyo. (*He turns and runs hurriedly off stage right.*)

FISBY. What was that?

SAKINI. That Mr. Sumata. He have present at home for you. He say not go away until he get.

(*A rather handsome young Tobikian,* MR. SEIKO, *now steps forward and extends a pair of wooden sandals.*)

MR. SEIKO. Dozo korewo chakini.

SAKINI. This Mr. Seiko. He brings you geta.

FISBY. Geta?

SAKINI. Wooden sandals. Very comfortable for tired feet. He say: May you walk in prosperity.

FISBY. Tell him I shall walk in the—the cool—meadow—of—of pleasant memories. Is that all right?

SAKINI. Oh, that's very pretty, boss. (*He turns to* MR. SEIKO.) Ya, arigato, Seikosan.

MR. SEIKO (*beams, bows, and backs away*). Iya, kosi no itari desu.

SAKINI. He say you do him honor. (*Here a chunky, flat-faced, aggressive* YOUNG WOMAN *with heavy glasses pushes forward with her present.*) Oh, this Miss Higa Jiga—unmarried lady. She bring you three eggs.

FISBY. Tell her I shall eat them for breakfast. (*He bows to her.*)

SAKINI. Captain-san, daisuki desu.

MISS HIGA JIGA. Kame no tamago desu. (*She bows away.*)

SAKINI. She say she hope you enjoy turtle eggs.

FISBY (*grins and bows to her*). She'll never know.

SAKINI. You very big success. They sure like you already. (*Another* VILLAGER *steps forward and offers a gift.*) This Mr. Keora. He bring you another cricket cage. Minus cricket.

FISBY. Say to him—that my prospects of good fortune are doubled. (*He looks rather pleased with himself.*)

SAKINI. Kagowa futatsu de, un wa bai!

MR. KEORA. Hoho! Naka naka shiteki desna! (*He bows away.*)

SAKINI. He say you are inspired poet.

FISBY (*modestly*). It's all in getting the hang of it.

SAKINI (*introducing the next citizen, a very* OLD MAN *leaning on a stick*). This old man Mr. Oshira. He bring you fine lacquered cup he make himself.

FISBY. Tell him I'm forever in his debt for such a beautiful gift.

OSHIRA. You are most welcome, Captain.

FISBY (*turns to him in surprise*). You speak English!

SAKINI. Mr. Oshira teach me English when I am little boy in Tobiki.

OSHIRA. In my youth I work in Manila. How is Mr. McKinley?

FISBY (*puzzled for a moment*). Who? Oh—President McKinley. I'm afraid someone shot him.

OSHIRA. I am sad.

FISBY. It was a long time ago.

OSHIRA. Yes, a long time. (*He indicates the cup.*) May August moon fill your cup.

FISBY. May I ask, why an August moon?

OSHIRA. All moons good, but August moon little older, little wiser.

FISBY. Did Sakini say you made this cup yourself?

OSHIRA. Oh, yes. I learned from my father before me who learned from his father before him. Is our heritage.

SAKINI. Look, boss, this cup thin as paper, carved from one block of wood. Then painted many times with red lacquer.

FISBY. And did you paint the gold fish inside?

OSHIRA (*nods*). It is imperfect.

SAKINI. When Mr. Oshira little boy, he work ten years to learn how to paint gold fish exactly like his papa paint.

FISBY. It's just beautiful! Can you still make things like this?

OSHIRA. One does not forget.

FISBY. Sakini, here's an industry we can start right away. This is a lost art. (*Turns to* OSHIRA.) Is there any way we could mass-produce these?

OSHIRA. Mass-produce?

FISBY. You know—set up machines and turn them out by the gross.

OSHIRA (*shakes his head*). I take pride in making one cup at time, Captain. How can I take pride in work of machine?

FISBY. How many of these could you turn out in a day?

OSHIRA. If I work hard, maybe one or two a week.

FISBY (*disappointed*). Well, it's a start. Make as many as you can. We'll send them up to the American Post Exchange and sell them as fast as you can turn them out.

OSHIRA. I shall do my best. The swiftness of my youth has deserted me, sir. (*He bows and moves back.*) But I shall make fewer mistakes.

FISBY (*excitedly*). Sakini, tell Mr. Omura to make up a batch of chopsticks. Have everybody get to work making cricket cages, wooden sandals and— (*Pointing.*)—these straw hats. We'll put this village in the souvenir business.

SAKINI. We all make money, boss?

FISBY. If they can turn out enough of these things, I guarantee the recovery of Tobiki village. Tell them.

SAKINI. Kore dondon tskuru yoni . . .

(*There is a general exchange of chatter and approval.*) They say they make everything, fast as the dickens, boss.

FISBY. Good. We're in business. Now ask them if they'd mind postponing the rest of the gifts until later. I'd like to tell them what *we're* planning for *them*.

SAKINI. Sa, sono hanashi shiyo.

CITIZENS. No agerumono naiyo! Hanashi wo kiko.

SAKINI. They say sure. They got no more presents anyhow.

FISBY. Good. First I want to tell them about the school we're going to build for their children. All set to translate?

SAKINI. All set.

FISBY. All right. (*He consults Plan B.*) Plan B says the direct approach is most effective. This is it. (*He steps back up on a box and looks forcefully at his listeners. Then he points a dramatic finger at them.*) Do you want to be ignorant?

SAKINI (*also points a finger*). Issho bakaja dame daro?

(*The* CITIZENS *make a noise that sounds like* "*Hai.*")

FISBY What did they say?

SAKINI. They say "Yes."

FISBY. What do you mean, "yes"? They *want* to be ignorant?

SAKINI. No, boss. But in Luchuan "yes" means "no." They say "yes," they *not* want to be ignorant.

FISBY. Oh. (*He turns back to his rapt audience and assumes his forensic posture.*) Do you want your *children* to be ignorant?

SAKINI. Issho kodomotachi mo bakaja dame daro?

(*The* VILLAGERS *respond quickly with a noise that sounds like* "*Iie.*")

FISBY. What did they say then?

SAKINI. They say "No."

FISBY. "No" they do, or "No" they don't?

SAKINI. Yes, they not want no ignorant children.

FISBY. Good. (*He turns back to the* VILLAGERS.) Then this is what my government is planning to do for you. First there will be daily issues of rice for everyone.

SAKINI. Mazu kome no hykyu!

(*The* VILLAGERS *cheer.*)

FISBY. We will build a fine new school here for your children. (*Then recalling Colonel Purdy's dictum.*) Pentagon-shaped.

SAKINI. Gakko taterundayo katachi wa—(*He flounders.*) Ah—Pentagon.

(*The* CITIZENS *look at each other, puzzled.*)

MISS HIGA JIGA. Nandesutte?

SAKINI. Pentagon.

MISS HIGA JIGA. Sore wa nandesuka?

SAKINI. They say what is Pentagon? Never hear before.

FISBY. Never heard of the *Pentagon!*

SAKINI. No, boss.

FISBY. Well, they certainly do need a school here. The Pentagon is—is— (*He looks down at their eager faces.*) Well, it really means five-sided.

SAKINI. Kabega itsutsusa, ii, ni, san, yon, go. (*Holds up five fingers. There is a burst of laughter from the* CITIZENS.)

MISS HIGA JIGA (*giggling*). Ara, goka-kuno kodomo nante arimasenyo.

SAKINI. They say no children in Tobiki got five sides.

FISBY. The *school* will be five-sided—like a building in Washington.

SAKINI (*explains*). Chigauyo, chigauyo, onaji mono arundes yo, Washington ni. (*There is a decided reaction of approval.* SAKINI *turns back to* FISBY.) They very impressed.

FISBY (*continuing*). Everyone will learn about democracy.

SAKINI. Mazu minshu shugi bera-bera bera-bera.

MISS HIGA JIGA. Minshu shugi bera-bera bera-bera?

SAKINI. They say: Explain what is democracy. They know what rice is.

FISBY. Oh. (*He scratches his head.*) Well, it's a system of self-determination. It's—it's the right to make the wrong choice.

SAKINI. Machigattemo iindayo.

(*They look up blankly, silently.*)

FISBY. I don't think we're getting the point over. Explain that if I don't like the way Uncle Sam treats me, I can write the President himself and tell him so.

SAKINI. Daitoryo ni tegami kaitemo iinosa.

(*The* VILLAGERS *all laugh heartily.*)

MISS HIGA JIGA. Masaka soonakoto!

SAKINI (*triumphantly*). They say: But do you *send* the letters?

FISBY. Let's get on with the lecture. (*He turns back to the citizens and reads from Plan B.*) Tell them hereafter all men will be free and equal. . . .

SAKINI. Subete, jiyuu, to byodo, de ar, de ar.

FISBY (*increases his tempo and volume*). Without discrimination . . .

SAKINI (*taking* FISBY's *tone*). Sabetsu, taigu—haishi de ar.

FISBY. The will of the majority will rule!

SAKINI. Subete minna de kime, de ar!

FISBY (*finishing with a flourish*). And Tobiki village will take its place in the brotherhood of democratic peoples the world over!

SAKINI (*rising to new demagogic heights*). Koshite, Tobiki, jiyuu, Okinawa, byodo sabetsu, taigu—haishi, jiyuu, byodo de ar, de ar. (*A great burst of applause greets Sakini's performance. He turns to* FISBY.) We going over big, boss.

FISBY (*agrees with a nod*). Now to get this village organized. Is the mayor here?

SAKINI (*points*). Mr. Omura is mayor, boss. (MR. OMURA *steps forward.*) He only one in Tobiki with white coat.

FISBY (*glances at the worn, ragged coat*). It looks to me as if you'll have to get a new coat or a new mayor soon.

SAKINI. Better keep mayor, boss. Impossible to get white coat.

FISBY. Well, since we've got a mayor, we only have to find a Chief of Agriculture and a Chief of Police. That's going to present a problem.

SAKINI. No problem, boss. You just look over gifts and see who give you best gift. Then you give him best job.

FISBY. Sakini, that is *not* the democratic way. The people themselves must choose the man best qualified. Tell them they are to elect their own Chief of Agriculture.

SAKINI. Sah! Senkyo desu. Mazu Chief of Agriculture.

WOMEN VILLAGERS (*push* MR. SIEKO *forward shouting*). Seiko-san, Seiko-san ga ii, Seiko-san!

SAKINI. They say they elect Mr. Seiko. He best qualified for agriculture.

FISBY. He's an experienced farmer?

SAKINI. No, boss. He's artist. He draw lovely picture of golden wheat stalk with pretty green butterfly.

FISBY. Drawing pictures of wheat doesn't make him a wheat expert.

SAKINI. Wheat not grow here anyhow, boss. Only sweet potatoes.

FISBY. All right, all right! If he's their choice.

SEIKO. Ano! Watashimo shiroi koto wo.

SAKINI. He say do he get white coat like the mayor?

FISBY. Tell him I'll get him a helmet that says "Chief of Agriculture" on it.

SAKINI. Yoshi, yoshi, kammuri ageru-yo. (SEIKO *bows and backs away.*)

FISBY. Next we want to elect a Chief of Police.

SAKINI. Kondowa Chief of Police!

VILLAGERS (*clamor and push the fat* MR. HOKAIDA *forward*). Hokaida-san. Soda, soda. Hokaida-san.

FISBY. What are *his* qualifications for office?

SAKINI. People afraid of him. He champion wrestler.

(MR. HOKAIDA *flexes his muscles.*)

FISBY. Well, no one can say this isn't self-determination.

MR. HOKAIDA. Washime ano kammuri wo.

SAKINI. He say do he get helmet too?

FISBY (*nods*). I'll requisition another helmet.

SAKINI. Agemasuyo.

MR. HOKAIDA (*Bows smiling*). Ya, doomo.

FISBY. Now for the ladies. We intend to organize a Ladies' League for Democratic Action. We'll want to elect a League President.

SAKINI. Oh, ladies never vote before—they like that. (*He turns to the* LADIES.) Kondowa Ladies' League for Democratic Action!

(*This announcement is greeted by excited chatter. The* LADIES *push* MISS JIGA *forward.*)

LADIES. Higa-Jiga-san—Higa-Jiga-san!

SAKINI. They say they elect Miss Higa Jiga. They think she make classy president.

MISS HIGA JIGA (*points to her head*). Ano, watashi nimo ano booshio . . .

FISBY (*laughs*). All right, I'll see that she gets a helmet, too. Now ask them if they have any question they'd like to ask *me*.

SAKINI. Sa, nanka kikitai koto ga attara.

OLD WOMAN. Sakini-san, ima nanji kaina?

SAKINI. They say they like to know what time is it?

FISBY (*puzzled*). Time? (*Glances at his watch.*) Quarter of five, why?

SAKINI. They say they got to hurry then. They not like to miss sunset. This is time of day they sit in pine grove, sip tea and watch sun go down.

FISBY. All right, thank them and tell them they can go have tea in the pine grove.

SAKINI. Ya, minna kaette mo iiyo.

(They bow and, chattering happily among themselves, go off right. FISBY *gathers up his gifts.)*

FISBY. How do you think we did, Sakini?

SAKINI. They co-operate, boss. Future look very rosy.

FISBY. Where do you think I can find a cricket?

SAKINI. One come along. May have one in house now and not know it.

FISBY. Well, I'll take these things in and get started on my Progress Report. *(He goes to the office hut.)*

SAKINI. I take a little snooze then. Public speaking very exhausting.

FISBY *(as he goes inside). I* think I handled it pretty well.

(He sits down at his desk. He examines his gifts and then, putting on his glasses, begins to study Plan B again. After a moment, MR. SUMATA *enters from the right. He carries a couple of battered suitcases. He is followed by* LOTUS BLOSSOM, *a petite and lovely geisha girl in traditional costume. When they are about center stage, young* MR. SEIKO *runs up after the geisha girl. She turns to him.)*

SEIKO. Ano, chotto . . .

LOTUS BLOSSOM. Ara! Nani?

SUMATA *(steps in front of* SEIKO *and points an angry finger under his nose).* Dame, dame, atchi ike. (SEIKO *bows head and retreats.* MR. SUMATA *then turns to* SAKINI.) Amerika-san doko?

SAKINI *(indicates the office).* Asco.

SUMATA *(indicates geisha girl).* Kore tsurete kitandayo.

SAKINI. Oh? Do-sunno?

SUMATA. Kore Taisho-san ni agetainja.

(He bows and goes off quickly, almost running. The GEISHA *remains with* SAKINI. SAKINI *smiles and steps inside the office. He stands behind* FISBY.)*

SAKINI. You busy, boss?

FISBY *(without turning around to him).* Yes, but what is it?

SAKINI. Mr. Sumata leave present for you, boss.

FISBY. Put it on the shelf where it'll be out of the way.

SAKINI *(glances back outside).* Not able to do, boss. Present get mad.

FISBY *(turns around).* What's this about, Sakini?

SAKINI *(motions to the* GEISHA, *who steps inside smiling. She bows).* Here you are, boss.

FISBY *(rising).* Who is *she!*

SAKINI. Souvenir.

FISBY. What are you talking about?

SAKINI. Present from Mr. Sumata.

FISBY. Wait a minute. Is he kidding? I can't accept a human present.

SAKINI. Oh, human present very lovely. Introducing Lotus Blossom, geisha girl first class. *(He turns to* LOTUS BLOSSOM.) Amerika-san no Captain Fisby.

LOTUS BLOSSOM *(smiling happily).* Ara, ii otokomaene! Watashi sukidawa.

SAKINI. She say she very happy to belong to handsome captain. She say she serve you well.

FISBY. She's not going to serve me at all. You get that Mr. Sumata and tell him I'm returning his present.

SAKINI. Impossible to do, boss. Mr. Sumata leave present and go up mountains to visit cousin. He say good-bye and wish you much success in Tobiki.

LOTUS BLOSSOM *(sweetly).* Watashi kokoni sumun desho?

SAKINI. She say, where do you want her to stay, boss?

FISBY. You tell her I don't care where she stays. She can't stay here.

SAKINI *(shocked).* Where she go then? She got no home. Mr. Sumata already gone away.

FISBY. Well, find her a place for the time being.

SAKINI *(grins).* Plenty of room in my house, boss. Just me and my grandpapa.

FISBY. No, I can't do that. Sit her over on that box until I can think where to put her.

SAKINI. You can put her in business, boss.

FISBY. You keep a civil tongue in your head, Sakini.

(LOTUS BLOSSOM *comes over to* FISBY, *whom she has been watching with great interest).* Okimono to ozohri motte kimasune.

SAKINI. She like to put on your sandals and kimono for you. She trained to please you, boss.

FISBY. I know what she's trained to do. And I don't need any translation. *(He sits down at his desk again.)* Sakini . . . take my supplies out of the shack and bring them over here. We'll set her up there where I can keep an eye on her.

SAKINI. Not very democratic, boss. You make her lose face if she not make you comfortable, boss. She think she bad geisha girl.

FISBY. You tell her . . . I've got some face to save, too . . . so she can just forget this Oriental hanky-panky.

SAKINI. Anta irantesa!

LOTUS BLOSSOM (*waves him away*). Ara, nani ittennoyo. Imasara ikettatte ikarenai desho.

FISBY. Well, what did she say?

SAKINI. She say for me to go on home to grandpapa . . . she first-class geisha girl . . . she know her business. Good night, boss.

(FISBY *stands eyeing* LOTUS BLOSSOM *as* SAKINI *goes out. The lights go down quickly. During the brief blackout, the two center panels are lowered, shutting out the village street. The office of Colonel Purdy is swung into place in the last panel right. The lights come up on* PURDY *twisting the bell on his field telephone.*)

PURDY. What do you mean . . . there's no answer? Well, keep trying. I'm not the kind of a man to take "no answer" for an answer.

(*The lights come up on the opposite side of the stage in Fisby's office.* FISBY *is holding onto his jacket buttons.* LOTUS BLOSSOM *stands in front of him holding out his robe. She is gently persistent and puzzled at his reticence.*)

FISBY. It's *not* a kimono . . . it's a bathrobe. And I don't *want* to put it on.

LOTUS BLOSSOM (*reaches to unbutton his jacket*). Sa! Shizukani shimasho ne.

FISBY. No, it's against regulations. (*Phone rings. He takes the robe away from* LOTUS BLOSSOM *and sits on it. Then he picks up the phone.*) Hello!

PURDY (*jumps*). You don't have to shout. I can hear you. This is Colonel Purdy.

FISBY (*leaps to his feet and pushes* LOTUS BLOSSOM *behind him as if to hide her*). Yes, sir.

PURDY. Just thought I'd check up on you. How are things going?

(LOTUS BLOSSOM *begins to fan her master.*)

FISBY. Well, everything seems to be under control at the moment.

(*He sits down and takes out a cigarette.* LOTUS BLOSSOM *promptly lights it for him.*)

PURDY. Anything *I* can do for you?

FISBY (*pauses*). I can't think of anything, sir.

PURDY. I realize it's bound to get lonely for you down there . . . so you know what I'm going to do, my boy?

FISBY (LOTUS BLOSSOM *gets the geta and kneels before him.* FISBY *watches her apprehensively and asks . . .*). What are you

going to do?

PURDY. I'll tell you. I'm going to send you some of my old *Adventure Magazines*.

FISBY (*as* LOTUS BLOSSOM *starts to take off his shoes*). No, *no*. I don't want them. (*Into the phone.*) I mean . . . yes . . . thank you. (*He rises and twists about trying to pull his foot away from* LOTUS BLOSSOM.) I'd like something to read.

PURDY. How are you getting along with the natives?

FISBY (*his leg over the chair*). The problem here, sir, is a very old one. It seems to be a question of who's going to lose face.

PURDY. I understand. As Mrs. Purdy says, "East is East and West is West, and there can be no Twain." But you're making progress?

FISBY. Nothing I'd like to put on paper, sir.

(LOTUS BLOSSOM *gets his shoes off and slips the sandals on.*)

PURDY. Well, when things get moving down there, send in a detailed Progress Report.

FISBY. If that's what you want, sir.

(LOTUS BLOSSOM *recovers the robe. She reaches out to unbutton his jacket.*)

PURDY. You'll find these people lack the capacity for sustained endeavor. Don't hesitate to build a fire under them.

FISBY (*struggling to keep his jacket on*). That won't be necessary, sir.

PURDY. Don't forget . . . the eyes of Washington are on you, Fisby.

FISBY (*as* LOTUS BLOSSOM *tries to pull his jacket over his head*). I hope not, sir.

PURDY (*ponders*). Fisby, it just occurred to me. Have you given any thought to physical education?

FISBY. If I may say so, sir . . . (LOTUS BLOSSOM *gets one arm out.*) I consider the suggestion . . . (*He hugs the other sleeve.*) a masterpiece of timeliness. (*He gets down on one knee.*)

PURDY. Thank you, my boy. (*pauses.*) Could you use a deck of cards? Hello? Hello, Fisby . . . you're getting weak.

(*As* FISBY *looks back at the telephone and nods in complete agreement, the two scenes black out simultaneously. The panels fall. A spot picks up* SAKINI *as he steps from the wings.*)

SAKINI. Discreet place to stop now and sip soothing cup of jasmine tea.

Conclusion?

Not yet.

Continuation shortly.
Lotus Blossom not lose face!
(*He bows.*)

THE CURTAIN FALLS

ACT TWO

Scene One

SCENE: *Tobiki village.*
TIME: *A few days later.*
AT RISE: *All the panels are down.* SAKINI
*enters from the wings and crosses down to the
footlights center. He bows to the audience.*

SAKINI

Lovely ladies, kind gentlemen:
Most traveled person in history of world
   is summer sun.
Each day must visit each man no matter
   where he live on globe.
Always welcome visitor.
Not bring gossip.
Not stay too long.
Not depart leaving bad taste of rude
   comment.
But summer sun never tell topside of
   world what bottomside like.
So bottomside must speak for self.
We continue with little story of Tobiki.
Center of industry.
Seat of democracy.
   (*He beams.*)
Home of geisha girl.
   (*He goes to the right proscenium arch as
   all the panels are raised, revealing the
   empty street outside of Fisby's office.
   *FISBY *enters, starts across stage,* SAKINI
   falling in step behind him.*)
Was wondering what happened to you,
boss?

FISBY (*stops*). I went down to inspect
the sweet-potato fields. Sakini, no one
was there. The potatoes were piled up,
but no one was working.
SAKINI. Very hot day, boss.
FISBY. But I can't find my Chief of
Agriculture. Or the Mayor, or the Chief
of Police. Where is everybody?
SAKINI. Lotus Blossom leave belongings over at Awasi—got no way to bring
things here. So—everybody take wheelbarrow to help move Lotus Blossom to
Tobiki.

FISBY. And has she got so many things
that it takes my entire staff to move her
to this village?
SAKINI. No, boss, but Chief of Police
not trust Chief of Agriculture, and Mayor
not trust Mr. Oshira, so all go.
FISBY. Mr. Oshira? That old man!
SAKINI. He's old, boss, but not dead.
FISBY. A fine way for officials to behave!
You tell them I want to see them the
moment they come back. (*He starts for his
office.*) A fine thing!
SAKINI. Nothing to worry about, boss.
They not beat your time. You own Lotus
Blossom.
FISBY. I do *not* own her. It's not a question of—of—(*He sits down at his desk.*)
Well, this sort of nonsense isn't going to
stop my work. (*He shifts the papers on his
desk.*) I intend to get started on that
schoolhouse today. We've got the mate-
rials, so all we need now is some good
carpenters. (*He turns to* SAKINI, *who has
followed him inside.*) Who is the best carpenter in the village?
SAKINI. Mr. Sumata.
FISBY. Fine. Get hold of him. Wait a
minute! Isn't he the joker who gave me
Lotus Blossom?
SAKINI. Mr. Sumata has finger in lots
of pies, boss.
FISBY. Well, since he's vanished, who
is the next best carpenter?
SAKINI. Father of Mr. Sumata.
FISBY. Where is he?
SAKINI. Go on vacation with Mr. Sumata.
FISBY (*beginning to get annoyed*). Well,
who is the *third* best carpenter then?
SAKINI. No more, boss. Only Sumata
and son. They have what you call mo-
nopoly.
FISBY. There's something fishy about
their disappearing.
   (MISS HIGA JIGA, *wearing a red helmet with
flowers, followed by several other* LADIES,
*comes storming across the stage to the office
door.* SAKINI *hears them and goes to the door.*)
MISS HIGA JIGA (*angrily*). Watashitachi
sabetsu taigu desyo!
FISBY (*Goes to the door also*). What's the
matter with her?
SAKINI. Miss Higa Jiga say do you
know what we got in this village, boss?
Discrimination.
FISBY (*wearily*). Where?
   (SAKINI *turns to* MISS HIGA JIGA.)
MISS HIGA JIGA (*indignantly*). Watashi-

tachi hykyu matte itara Lotus Blossom ga kite clarku ga anata desuka ma dozo kochirae watashitachi nijikan mo machi mashita yo.

SAKINI. She says that Ladies' League for Democratic Action wait in line for rice rations. Along come Lotus Blossom and ration clerks say, "Oh, how do you do. Oh, please don't stand in line. You come inside and have cup of tea." Then clerks shut up warehouse and leave Ladies' League waiting in sun two hours.

FISBY. It's things like this that undermine the democratic ideal. You tell Miss Higa Jiga I intend to do something about it. (*He storms into his office.*)

SAKINI (*turns to* MISS HIGA JIGA). Nantoka shimasuyo.

FISBY. I can see right now we're going to have to get rid of the disrupting factor in our recovery. (*He picks up the field telephone and twists the handle.*) Get me Major McEvoy at Awasi.

SAKINI (*follows* FISBY *inside*). What are you going to do, boss?

FISBY. This village isn't big enough for Plan B and a geisha girl.

SAKINI. Oh, boss, Tobiki never have geisha girl before. We like very much.

FISBY. She has to go. (*Then into the telephone.*) Major McEvoy? Captain Fisby at Tobiki. I have a request from one of my people to transfer to your village. Yes, it's a female citizen. Profession? Well . . . (*He looks at* SAKINI.)

SAKINI. Oh, please not send her away, boss. Not democratic.

FISBY. As a matter of fact her name *is* Lotus Blossom. *How* did *you* know? What do you mean, what am I trying to put over on you? Oh, you did? (*He hangs up. Then he glares at* SAKINI.)

SAKINI (*with great innocence*). He knows Lotus Blossom, boss?

FISBY. Very well. She was at Awasi and damn near wrecked his whole plan for recovery. She's been booted out of every village by every commander on the island.

SAKINI. Oh, poor little Lotus Blossom.

FISBY. Poor little Lotus Blossom my eye. She upsets every village she's in.

SAKINI. Not her fault she beautiful, boss.

FISBY. No wonder that Mr. Sumata disappeared. The major paid him a hundred yen to get her out of his village.

SAKINI (*eagerly*). You keep her now,

boss?

FISBY. I have to. (*He points a finger at* SAKINI.) Well, she's not going to get away with causing dissension in *my* village!

(MISS HIGA JIGA, *weary of waiting outside, storms in.*)

MISS HIGA JIGA. Doshte itadakemasno Daitoryo ni tegami wo kakimasawayo.

FISBY (*pleads*). Tell her to go away.

SAKINI. She say she waiting for some democratic action. She say if she don't get it, she thinks she write this Uncle Sam you talk about.

FISBY. Now, look. I don't want complaints going into Headquarters. Tell her discrimination is being eliminated.

SAKINI. Sabetsu yamemasyo.

MISS HIGA JIGA. Yamenakutemo iinoyo, watashitachi nimo wakete itadakeba.

SAKINI. Miss Higa Jiga say please not eliminate discrimination. She say just give her some too.

FISBY. And just what does she means by that?

SAKINI. She say Lotus Blossom unfair competition.

FISBY. Granted.

SAKINI. She say you promise everybody going to be equal.

FISBY. I intend to keep my word.

SAKINI. Well, she say she can't be equal unless she has everything Lotus Blossom has.

FISBY. What Lotus Blossom's got, the Government doesn't issue.

SAKINI (*taking a piece of paper which* MISS HIGA JIGA *waves*). She make list, boss. Shall I read, boss?

FISBY. Go ahead.

SAKINI. She wants you to get her and ladies in League following items: A. Red stuff to put on lips like geisha. B. Stuff that smell pretty—

FISBY. Now, *just* wait a minute. What would H.Q. think if I requisitioned lipstick!

SAKINI (*hands list back to* MISS HIGA JIGA). Dame desuyo.

MISS HIGA JIGA. Jaa Daitoryo ni tegami wo dashimaswa.

SAKINI. She say she sorry, but now she guess she just have to write this letter to Uncle Samuel after all.

FISBY (*throws up his hands*). All right. *All right!* Tell her I'll call up the post exchange at Awasi and see if they have any shaving powder and toilet water.

SAKINI. Ya, katte agemasuyo.

MISS HIGA JIGA (*beams*). Ano wasure naidene bobby pin.

SAKINI. She say, not forget bobby pins for hair.

FISBY. I think I might have been happier in the submarine command.

MISS HIGA JIGA (*stops as she is about to go*). Mohitotsu onegai watashitachi mo mina geisha ni.

SAKINI. She say one more thing. Can you get Lotus Blossom to teach Ladies' League all to be geisha girls?

FISBY (*leaps to his feet*). Teach the innocent women of this village to be—*No!* (MISS HIGA JIGA *shrugs and goes outside. As* FISBY *sinks back at his desk,* MISS HIGA JIGA *talks excitedly to the* WOMEN *gathered outside. They run off giggling.* FISBY *sits at his desk and picks up Plan B.*) Plan B! (*He thumbs through its pages.*) Let's just see if Washington anticipated *this*.

(*He buries his chin in his hands.* SAKINI *sits quietly watching him. Outside in the village street,* LOTUS BLOSSOM *enters and starts daintily toward the office. She has only gotten halfway when* SEIKO *overtakes her.*)

SEIKO (*panting*). Ano, chotto.

LOTUS BLOSSOM (*stops and looks at him archly*). Nani?

SEIKO (*takes a chrysanthemum bud from his waist*). Ano korewo dozo.

LOTUS BLOSSOM (*takes it indifferently*). Ara, so arigato.

SEIKO (*strikes his heart passionately*). Boku no, kono, hato, o.

LOTUS BLOSSOM (*flicks her finger*). Anato no hahto? Ara shinzo ne.

SEIKO (*disembowels himself with an imaginary knife*). Harakitte shinimas.

LOTUS BLOSSOM (*yawns*). Imagoro sonnano hayaranai noyo.

SEIKO (*points toward Fisby's office*). Soka Amerika-san ga iinoka?

LOTUS BLOSSOM (*haughtily*). Nandeste! Sonnakoto yokeina osowa.

SEIKO (*laughs derisively*). Nanda rashamon janaika.

LOTUS BLOSSOM (*backs him up with an angry finger*). Watashimo kotoni kansho shinaideyo.

SEIKO (*bows his head*). Gomen nasai iisugi deshta.

LOTUS BLOSSOM (*points away*). Atchi, itte. (SEIKO *sighs, turns and plods off toward the sweet-potato fields, crushed and dejected.* LOTUS BLOSSOM *tidies her hair and continues to the office. She calls in coyly.*) Fuisbee-san!

SAKINI (*rises and looks out the door*). Oh, what do you think, boss? Lotus Blossom back. She come to see you.

FISBY. And high time. (*He turns to face the door as* LOTUS BLOSSOM *enters and bows.*) Where have *you* been all day? Never mind, I know—upsetting the agricultural horse cart.

LOTUS BLOSSOM. Fu-san no kao nikkori nasaruto totemo kawaii wa.

SAKINI. She say sun burst through the clouds now that you smile on her.

FISBY. I'm not smiling. (*She hands him Seiko's chrysanthemum bud.*)

SAKINI. Oh, boss, you know what she give you?

FISBY. The works.

SAKINI. When lady give gentleman chrysanthemum bud, in Okinawa that means her heart is ready to unfold.

FISBY. Well, this is one bud that's not going to flower.

LOTUS BLOSSOM (*offering a box she has brought*). Kore otsukemono yo. Dozo.

SAKINI. She say, you like to eat some tsukemono? Tsukemono nice thing to eat between meals.

FISBY. No.

LOTUS BLOSSOM (*takes geta and kneels beside him*). Dozo ohaki osobase.

FISBY. Tell her to *leave my feet* alone.

LOTUS BLOSSOM (*studies* FISBY). Kasa kaburu. Nisshabyo nanoyo.

SAKINI. She worried about you, boss. She say, when you go in hot sun, should wear *kasa*—that straw hat—on head.

FISBY. Tell her never mind about my feet or my head. I want her to stop interfering with the recovery program. To stop causing rebellion and making the men—ah—ah—discontented.

SAKINI (*turns to* LOTUS BLOSSOM). Jama shicha dame dayo.

LOTUS BLOSSOM (*smiles*). Fu-san ocha ikaga?

SAKINI. She say: You want some tea?

FISBY (*throwing himself down on his cot*). No.

LOTUS BLOSSOM. Shami demo hikimashoka?

SAKINI. She say: You want some music?

FISBY. No.

LOTUS BLOSSOM (*giggles*). Ara Fu-santara yaiteruno.

SAKINI. She say: You jealous, boss?

FISBY (*mirthlessly*). Ha!

LOTUS BLOSSOM. Honto ni doshita no?

SAKINI. She say: You want to tell her

your troubles, boss?

FISBY. Why should I tell her my troubles?

SAKINI. She geisha girl, that's her *business*, boss.

FISBY. Some business.

LOTUS BLOSSOM. Shoga naiwane. Mah soshite irasshai yo.

SAKINI. She say she hear about lack of co-operation here. She feel very bad. She say she want to help because you best boss she ever had. You not make her work and you not take money from her.

FISBY (*sits up on his cot*). Did the other men who owned her . . . hire her out and then take money from her?

SAKINI. Oh, sure.

FISBY. Well, where I come from we have a name for men who—who—do *that* sort of thing.

SAKINI. You have geisha business in America, too?

FISBY (*rises*). No! Sakini, you give her to understand I have no intention of putting her to—to work.

SAKINI. Why not, boss? She pay all her dues to Geisha Guild. She member in good standing.

FISBY. You mean they've got a union for this sort of thing?

SAKINI. Geisha girl have to be protected, boss. Must keep up rates.

FISBY. This is the most immoral thing I've ever heard of. Haven't you people any sense of shame?

SAKINI. We bad not to be ashamed, boss?

FISBY. Obviously, there is a fundamental difference between us that can't be reconciled. I don't say that where I I come from there's no such thing as prostitution. But, by God, we don't have unions, set rates and collect dues!

SAKINI. But geisha girl not prostitute, boss.

FISBY. At least we have the decency— (*He stops.*) What do you mean, geisha girls aren't prostitutes? Everybody knows what they do.

SAKINI. Then everybody wrong, boss.

FISBY. Well, what do they get paid for, then?

SAKINI. Hard to explain fundamental difference. Poor man like to feel rich. Rich man like to feel wise. Sad man like to feel happy. All go to geisha house and tell troubles to geisha girl. She listen politely and say, "Oh, that's too bad."

She very pretty. She make tea, she sing, she dance, and pretty soon troubles go away. Is not worth something, boss?

FISBY. And that's *all* they do?

SAKINI. Very ancient and honorable profession.

FISBY. Look, Sakini, I apologize. I guess I jumped the gun. And I'm glad you explained. It sort of puts a new light on things. (*He turns to* LOTUS BLOSSOM *and grins.*)

LOTUS BLOSSOM. Ara, kyuni nikkorisite, mada okotteru no.

SAKINI. She say: Why are you smiling at her all of a sudden? You mad or something?

FISBY. Tell her that I'm a dope. That I have a coconut for a head.

SAKINI. No use, boss. She not believe.

FISBY. Then will you ask her if she'd be kind enough to give geisha lessons to the Ladies' League for Democratic Action?

SAKINI. Odori ya shami Ladies' League ni oshiete?

LOTUS BLOSSOM. Er iiwa, demo kumiai-aga kowaiwane.

SAKINI. She say Geisha Guild closed shop, but she teach if you not report her.

(*At this point the men of the village come across the square and stop before the office.* LOTUS BLOSSOM *goes to the door. Immediately there are* ohs *and* ahs *from the men.*)

FISBY. What is that?

SAKINI. Sound like Okinawan wolf call, boss.

FISBY. Well, let's find out. (*He goes outside to face the group, followed by* SAKINI.) Ask what's the matter.

SAKINI. Doshtano?

MR. KEORA. Minna gakko nanka yori chaya ga ii soda.

SAKINI. They say they just held meeting in democratic fashion and majority agree on resolution. They want you to build them cha ya.

FISBY. A what?

SAKINI. Cha ya. That's teahouse, boss.

FISBY. A teahouse?

SAKINI. Yes, boss. They say now that this village have geisha girl just like big city, they should have teahouse like big city too.

FISBY. But I can't build them a teahouse . . . I have no authority to do that.

SAKINI. But you tell them will of majority is law. You going to break law?

FISBY. They're going to get a school . . .

that's enough.

SAKINI. But majority too old to go to school . . . they want teahouse.

FISBY. There is no provision in Plan B for a teahouse.

LOTUS BLOSSOM. Ano . . . ochaya sae tatereba mondai naija nai no.

SAKINI. Lotus Blossom say teahouse in Tobiki make recovery program work. Everybody make geta and cricket cages like crazy so they can spend money at teahouse.

FISBY. I haven't got any materials to build a teahouse.

SAKINI. Zairyo ga naiyo.

LOTUS BLOSSOM. Ara, kinoo renga ya zaimoku takusan kite orimashitayo.

SAKINI. She say Army truck come yesterday and leave beautiful brick and lovely paint.

FISBY. For the new *schoolhouse*. Tell them . . . it just can't be done.

SAKINI. Dame, dame, dame desuyo! (FISBY *looks down into the disappointed faces of the* VILLAGERS.)

VILLAGERS. Achara-san, iijiwaru dane.

SAKINI. They say you very mean to them after *all* the nice presents they give you.

FISBY. I'm sorry.

SAKINI. They very sorry too, boss. You know why?

FISBY. I think I do.

SAKINI. No, boss. When you leave here . . . Tobiki be forgotten village. Not have park, not have statue . . . not even lovely jail. Tobiki like to be proud. Teahouse give them face.

FISBY. It's going to be a fine schoolhouse. Five sides.

OSHIRA. May I speak, Captain-san?

FISBY. Of course, Mr. Oshira.

OSHIRA. There are lovely teahouses in the big cities. But the men of Tobiki have never been inside them. We are too poor and our clothes are too ragged. All of my life I have dreamed of visiting a teahouse where paper lanterns cast a light in the lotus pond and bamboo bells hanging in the pines tinkle as the breezes brush them. But this picture is only in my heart . . . I may never see it. I am an old man, sir. I shall die soon. It is evil for the soul to depart this world laden with envy or regret. Give us our teahouse, sir. Free my soul for death.

FISBY (*unhappily*). But . . . we haven't got any carpenters!

SAKINI (*calls over the heads of the group*). Oi! Daiku-san! Daiku-san! (MR. SUMATA and HIS FATHER *come trotting across the stage carrying their carpenter boxes.* SAKINI *turns to* FISBY.) Oh, what you think? Mr. Sumata and his papa just come down from mountains!

FISBY (*gives* SAKINI *a penetrating but defeated look*). All right. All right! I haven't got a chance. I guess Uncle Sam is going into the teahouse business.

(*He turns and goes back into his office, followed by* LOTUS BLOSSOM. *He picks up Plan B.* SAKINI *announces the decision from the steps.*)

SAKINI. Cha ya, tatete iiyo!

(*There is an outburst of cheers from the* VILLAGERS. *It sounds very much like* "Fisby-san, Banzai, Uncle Sam, Banzai!" *Inside* FISBY *begins tearing up Plan B.* LOTUS BLOSSOM *kneels before him, geta in hand.* FISBY *extends his feet and smiles down at her. The cheering outside continues. As the panels descend—*

THE SCENE BLACKS OUT QUICKLY

SCENE TWO

SCENE: *Colonel Purdy's office.*

TIME: *A few weeks later.*

AT RISE: *The right panel is lifted. A light picks up* COLONEL PURDY. *He sits at his desk fuming over a report. The rest of the stage remains dark. He calls* GREGOVICH *on his office inter-com.*

———

PURDY. Gregovich!

GREGOVICH'S VOICE. Yes, sir?

PURDY. Get me Captain Fisby at Tobiki.

GREGOVICH. Yes, sir.

(*The extreme left panel rises leaving the intervening panels lowered.* FISBY *sits with his feet propped up on his desk. He is wearing his bathrobe "kimono."* LOTUS BLOSSOM *stands at his side fanning him. Over the scene, the sound of hammering and sawing can be heard. Over this the phone can be heard to ring.* FISBY *lifts the receiver.*)

FISBY. Captain Fisby.

PURDY. Colonel Purdy.

FISBY (*over noise*). Who?

PURDY. Colonel Purdy!

FISBY. I can't hear you. Hold on a minute. (*He turns to* LOTUS BLOSSOM.) See if you can stop that hammering on the teahouse for a minute.

(*He goes through the motions.* LOTUS BLOSSOM *nods understandingly and goes out.*)

PURDY. What's going on down there, Fisby?

FISBY (*as the noises cease*). Now, who is it?

PURDY. Colonel Purdy.

FISBY (*wraps his robe about his legs quickly*). Oh, good afternoon, Colonel.

PURDY. I want to talk to you about your Progress Report.

FISBY. I sent it in.

PURDY. I have it. I have it right in front of me. I've read it twice. Now, suppose *you* tell *me* what it says.

FISBY. What would you like to have me explain, sir?

PURDY. I'd like you to explain why there's nothing in here about the schoolhouse. Didn't you get the lumber?

FISBY (*uneasily*). Yes, sir ... it's being used right now. But we'll need some more, I'm afraid.

PURDY. I sent ample, according to specifications. How big a structure are you building?

FISBY. Well ... we ought to consider expansion. Populations increase.

PURDY. We don't need to consider expansion. Our troops will be out of here by the next generation. Which brings me to another point. (*He refers to the report.*) What's this about six kids being born last week?

FISBY. Well, there wasn't much else to fill the Progress Report, sir.

PURDY. Then you've failed at your indoctrination. Don't you know yet that births are entered under "Population Increases"? They are not considered progress.

FISBY. But they weren't children, sir. They were kids ... goats.

PURDY. There must be something wrong with this connection. It sounded just as if you said "goats."

FISBY. I did, sir. Kids ... goats. You see, we're trying to increase the livestock herd down here. I thought ...

PURDY. Goats! I don't care what you thought. Look here, Fisby. Suppose some congressman flew in to inspect our team. How would I explain such a report?

FISBY. Well, goats will breed, sir. Congress can't stop that. And I've been concerned with ...

PURDY. The population of civilians alone concerns us. I want to know exactly what progress you've made as outlined in Plan B.

FISBY. Well ... I'm getting along fine with the people.

PURDY. In other words, nothing. Listen to me. Do you realize what Major McEvoy has accomplished in his village?

FISBY. No, sir.

PURDY. Well, I'll tell you. His fourthgraders know the alphabet through "M," and his whole village can sing "God Bless America" in English.

FISBY. Yes, sir. That's real progress, sir. I wish I could say the same.

PURDY. See that you do. I don't want any rotten apples in my barrel. Now ... I want to know exactly what you have accomplished in the five weeks you've been down there.

FISBY. Well, sir ... I've started an industry. I'm sending our first shipment out for sale this week.

PURDY. What are you making?

FISBY (*looks down at his feet*). Oh, getas and ...

PURDY. Wait a minute ... what in God's name is a *geta?*

FISBY. Not "a" geta ... *getas* ... you have to have two.

PURDY. Are you breeding some *other* kind of animal?

FISBY. You wear them on your feet, sir. Excellent for strengthening the metatarsal muscles. Then ... I have a group busy building cricket cages. ...

PURDY. Captain Fisby!

FISBY. Yes, sir.

PURDY. What kind of cages did you say?

FISBY. Cricket. Like in cricket on the hearth. I think we'll find a great market for them. Of course, we don't supply the crickets.

PURDY. Naturally not. Captain Fisby ... have you been taking your salt pills?

FISBY. Yes, sir ... I take them at cha ya ... with my tea.

PURDY. Have you been going out in the sun without your helmet?

FISBY. I wear a kasa, sir ... it's more practical ... wind can blow through the straw.

PURDY. I see. I see. That will be all, Captain. (*He hangs up quickly.*)

FISBY. Hello ... hello ...

(*He hangs up and sits looking at the phone rather puzzled. The lights go down in his office and the panel descends.* COLONEL PURDY *also sits looking at the phone in his office. He calls* SERGEANT GREGOVICH *on the inter-com.*)

PURDY. Sergeant! What is the name of that psychiatrist over at Awasi?

GREGOVICH. Captain McLean?

PURDY. Get him on the phone. My man at Tobiki has gone completely off his rocker!

THE SCENE BLACKS OUT QUICKLY

SCENE THREE

SCENE: *Captain Fisby's office.*

TIME: *A few days later.*

AT RISE: *The office is empty as the panel rises. After a moment* CAPTAIN MC LEAN *enters. He is an intense, rather wildeyed man in his middle forties. He glances about furtively, then begins to examine the papers on Fisby's desk. He makes several notes in a notebook. He picks up Fisby's cricket cage and is examining it intently when* FISBY *enters behind him. He halts upon seeing* MC LEAN. FISBY *is wearing his blue bathrobe, his geta and a native straw hat.*

FISBY. Well, who are you?

MC LEAN (*gasps in surprise*). Oh, you startled me.

FISBY. Can I do anything for you? I'm Captain Fisby.

MC LEAN. I'm Captain McLean. There was no one here . . . so I came in.

FISBY (*he looks at his insignia*). Oh, medical corps. What brings you to Tobiki?

MC LEAN. Well, I'm—I'm on leave. Thought I'd spend it making some—some—ethnological studies. (*He adds quickly.*) Of the natives.

FISBY. Well, you couldn't have come to a more interesting spot. Sit down, Captain.

MC LEAN (*sits*). Thank you. Would you have any objection to my spending a week or so making my studies, Captain?

FISBY. Not at all. Make yourself at home. I'll take that if it's in your way.

(*He reaches out to relieve* MC LEAN *of the cricket cage he still holds.*)

MC LEAN (*glances at the cage in his hand and laughs awkwardly*). Oh, yes. I was just examining it.

FISBY (*pleased at his authority on the subject*). It's a cricket cage.

MC LEAN (*pauses*). You . . . like crickets?

FISBY. I haven't found one yet. But at least I've got the cage. I've got two . . . if you want one.

MC LEAN. Thank you, no. Thank you very much. (*He looks at* FISBY's *attire.*) What happened to your uniform. Captain?

FISBY. It's around. I find getas and a kimono much more comfortable in this climate.

MC LEAN. But isn't that a bathrobe?

FISBY (*shrugs*). It passes for a kimono. Would you like to take off your shoes, Captain?

MC LEAN. Thank you . . . no. I'll keep them on if you don't mind.

FISBY. Can I offer you some tsuke-mono? You eat these during the day between meals. (*He extends a platter.*) Tsukemono means fragrant things.

MC LEAN. I just had a chocolate bar, thank you. (*He rises and looks out the door.*) May I ask what you're building down the road?

FISBY (*proudly*). That's my cha ya. (*He pops a few tsukemonos into his mouth.*) It's really going to be something to write home about.

MC LEAN. Cha ya?

FISBY. Well, it just so happens, Captain, that I own a geisha girl. That might sound strange to you, but you get used to these things after a while. And if you have a geisha, you've got to have a cha ya. Sure you don't want some tsukemono?

MC LEAN. I really couldn't eat a thing. (*He glances out the door again.*) May I ask what the men are doing down there wading in that irrigation ditch?

FISBY. They're not wading, they're building a lotus pond. You can't have a cha ya without a lotus pond.

MC LEAN (*sits opposite* FISBY). How have you felt lately, Fisby?

FISBY. McLean, I'll tell you something. I've never been happier. I feel reckless and free. And it all happened the moment I decided not to build that damned pentagon-shaped school.

MC LEAN. That what?

FISBY. The good colonel ordered me to build a pentagon-shaped schoolhouse down here. But the people wanted a teahouse. Believe it or not, someone gave me a geisha girl. So I'm giving this village what it wants. That must all sound pretty crazy to you, Mac.

MC LEAN. Well, yes and no.

FISBY. These are wonderful people with a strange sense of beauty. And hard-working . . . when there's a purpose. You should have seen them start out day before yesterday, great bundles of things they'd made piled high on their heads. Getas, cricket cages, lacquer ware—things to sell as souvenirs up north. Don't let anyone tell. you these people are lazy.

MC LEAN. Oh. I see. I see.

FISBY. No, you don't. But you'll have a chance to study them.

MC LEAN. So you're building them a teahouse.

FISBY. Next thing I'm going to do for them is find out if this land here will grow anything besides sweet potatoes. I'm going to send for fertilizers and DDT and—

MC LEAN (leaps to his feet). Chemicals!

FISBY. Sure, why not?

MC LEAN. Do you want to poison these people?

FISBY. No, but—

MC LEAN. Now you've touched on a subject that is very close to me. For years I've planned to retire and buy a farm—raise specialties for big restaurants. So let me tell you this. Chemicals will kill all your earthworms, and earthworms aerate your soil.

FISBY. They do?

MC LEAN. Do you know an earthworm leaves castings eight times its own weight every day?

FISBY. That much!

MC LEAN. Organic gardening is the only thing. Nature's way—compost, manure, but no chemicals.

FISBY. Hey! You know a lot about this.

MC LEAN (modestly). I should. I've subscribed to all the farm journals for years.

FISBY. Say, you could help these people out while you're here—if you would. Do you think you could take over supervision—establish a sort of experimental station for them?

MC LEAN. Well, I—no—no—I haven't time.

FISBY. Take time. This is a chance for you to put some of your theories into practice.

MC LEAN (haughtily). They are not theories. They are proven facts.

FISBY. I'll give you a couple of men to help, and all you'd have to do is tell us how.

MC LEAN (hesitates). Is your soil acid or alkaline?

FISBY. Gosh, I don't know.

MC LEAN. Well, that's the very first thing you have to find out. Do you have bees?

FISBY. I haven't seen any.

MC LEAN (shakes his head sadly). People always underestimate the importance of bees for pollinating.

FISBY (slaps him on the back). Mac, you're just the man we've needed down here. You're a genius!

MC LEAN. I'll want plenty of manure.

FISBY. You'll get it.

MC LEAN. And I'll want to plan this program scientifically. I wish I had some of my books . . . and my seed catalogues. (He measures from the floor.) I've got a stack of catalogues that high.

FISBY. Why don't you make a list, and I'll get the boys over at the airstrip to fly us in seeds from the States.

MC LEAN (the gardener fever possesses the doctor as he begins to make his list). Every spring I've made lists of seeds and never had any soil to put them in. And now . . . I could actually germinate. (He writes.) Corn—Golden Bantam. (Then adds enthusiastically:) And Country Gentleman! Hybrid.

FISBY. Why don't I just leave you with your list while I check on the lotus pond? (MC LEAN doesn't hear him.) Well, I'll be back for tea. We have tea in the pine grove and watch the sun go down. (He goes out.)

MC LEAN (continues with his list reading aloud). Cucumbers—Extra Early Green Prolific. (His enthusiasm mounts.) Radishes—Crimson Giant! (The telephone begins to ring; he ignores it as he writes.) Tomatoes—Ponderosa Earliana. (The telephone rings insistently.) Watermelon! (He closes his eyes ecstatically.)

(The panel rises on the opposite side of the stage revealing Colonel Purdy's office. The intervening panel remains down. COLONEL PURDY sits at his desk jiggling his telephone hook.)

PURDY. What's the matter with this connection! Ring again!

MC LEAN (*ignores the ringing*). Watermelon—All-American Gold Medal! (*He writes it down as the phone rings. He looks up impatiently and lifts the receiver.*). Hello!

PURDY (*confidentially*). Who is this?

MC LEAN. This is Captain McLean.

PURDY. This is Colonel Purdy. Can you talk?

MC LEAN. Why not?

PURDY. I was anxious to hear your report on you-know-who.

MC LEAN. On *who?*

PURDY. *Captain Fisby!* The man I sent you down to examine.

MC LEAN. Oh. (*He weighs his problem quickly.*) Oh. Well . . . I'll have to stay down here several weeks for some . . .

PURDY. Several weeks!

MC LEAN. Rome wasn't built in a day.

PURDY. What?

MC LEAN. I said, Rome wasn't built in a day.

PURDY (*digests this*). Well . . . you're the doctor.

MC LEAN. I'll send in a report . . . from time to time. I can tell you now I expect to work miracles down here.

PURDY. Splendid . . . splendid. Is there anything I can send? Some old *Adventure Magazines* or anything?

MC LEAN. There are a couple of books I'd like, but I don't think you could get them.

PURDY (*picks up pencil*). You name them.

MC LEAN. Well . . . one is *Principles of Pea Production*, and the other is *Do's and Don'ts of Cabbage Culture.* (PURDY *starts to write . . . then stops.*) And do you think you could lay your hands on a soil test kit?

PURDY (*looks at earphone*). A what?

MC LEAN (*enunciating*). A *soil test kit.* I want to see if the soil is sour down here.

PURDY. Sour, did you say?

MC LEAN. Yes . . . if your soil is sour your seeds won't germinate. And I sure wish I had some bees.

PURDY. There *is* something wrong with this connection!

MC LEAN. I'm going to take time out here to build up the soil with manure.

PURDY (*unbelieving*). Did you say manure?

MC LEAN. I've lost faith in chemicals. You kill all your worms. I can tell you, when you kill a worm, Colonel . . . you're killing a friend. (*There is a long pause.*)

Hello . . . hello.

PURDY (*puts down the phone and turns to the squawk box*). Gregovich, where is Plan B!

GREGOVICH'S VOICE. What did you want, sir?

PURDY. I want to see who I send to analyze an analyst.

THE PANELS FALL QUICKLY ON
EACH SIDE OF THE STAGE

SCENE FOUR

SCENE: *Village square.*

TIME: *A few weeks later.*

AT RISE: *The panels rise to reveal the village square and Fisby's office. Natives are seated in the square, great bundles beside them. Others arrive and sink into positions of dejection.* FISBY *works at his desk.* SAKINI *enters and looks at the* VILLAGERS.

SAKINI (*to* MR. KEORA). Doshtano?

KEORA. Hitotsu mo unremasenna.

SAKINI. Oh, oh . . . too bad. (SAKINI *crosses and enters Fisby's office.*) Boss!

FISBY. Yes.

SAKINI. Mr. Keora and everybody back from Big Koza.

FISBY. Good. Let's see how they made out. (*He steps outside followed by* SAKINI. *He stops as he sees his* VILLAGERS *sitting dejectedly before their large bundles. He turns to* SAKINI.) What's the matter?

SAKINI. Mr. Keora very tired. Walk two days with bundle on back to sell straw hats to American soldiers at Big Koza. Nobody buy, so walk back. Too many damn hats now, boss.

FISBY. He couldn't sell *any?* (SAKINI *shakes his head.*) Why not?

SAKINI (*shrugs*). Soldiers not want. Soldiers say . . . what you think we are . . . hayseed? So come home.

FISBY (*sees old* MR. OSHIRA *and crosses to him.* OSHIRA *rises*). Mr. Oshira . . . did you take your lacquer ware to Yatoda?

OSHIRA. Oh, yes . . . but come back . . . not go again.

FISBY. But I don't understand. . . . The Navy always spends money.

OSHIRA. Sailors say, "Oh, pretty good . . . how much you want?" I say, "Twenty-five yen." They say, "Oh, too much . . . can get better in five-and-ten-cent store.

Give you one nickel."

FISBY. Did you explain how many years it took you to learn how to turn out such work?

OSHIRA (*nods*). They say, "What you want us to do, cry?"

FISBY (*angrily*). Damn stupid morons! (*He turns back to* OSHIRA.) Did you tell then that each cup was handmade?

OSHIRA. They say . . . not care. They say . . . at home have big machines that turn out ten cups every minute. They say . . . take nickel or jump in lake.

FISBY (*unhappily*). So you had to carry them all the way back?

SAKINI. Poor Mr. Oshira. No one want his lacquer ware.

FISBY. Well, he's wrong. He's a great artist and I'll buy everything he's made myself.

SAKINI. But you not able to buy everything from everybody in Tobiki, boss.

FISBY (*sits down on steps*). Tell them that they should all be proud of their work. And that I'm proud of all of them.

SAKINI. Gokro, gokro san.

FISBY. I'll think of something . . . I'll hit on an idea to bring money to this village yet.

SAKINI. Boss . . . you stop work on teahouse now?

FISBY. No! You'll get a teahouse if I give you nothing else.

SAKINI. They sure wish they could make some money to spend at teahouse, boss. Not like to go like beggars.

FISBY. Give me a little time, Sakini. (*As they sit around, each deep in his personal problems,* MC LEAN *enters. His uniform is gone. He is wearing his bathrobe, a straw hat and geta.*)

MC LEAN. Fisby! You're just the man I want to see. Can I have a couple of boys to help me? The damn Japanese beetles are eating up my Chinese peas.

FISBY (*dispiritedly*). Sure . . . I'll get a couple for you.

MC LEAN (*looks around*). What's the matter?

FISBY. There's no market for our products.

MC LEAN. Oh . . . that's too bad. What are you going to do? (*He sits down.*)

FISBY. Try to think of something.

OSHIRA. The world has left us behind. (*The* VILLAGERS *begin to rise and pick up their handiwork.*)

SEIKO. Amerika-san no seija naiyo. Sa, sa, kaette yakezake da!

SAKINI. They say . . . tell you not your fault no one wants to buy, boss. They say guess they go home now and get drunk.

FISBY. Tell them I don't blame them. If I had anything to drink . . . I'd do the same. (*As they start to file out, both* MC LEAN *and* FISBY *have a delayed reaction. They leap to their feet together.*) Wait a minute! (*The* VILLAGERS *stop.*) What are they going to get drunk *on?*

SAKINI. They got nothing but brandy.

MC LEAN. Nothing but *brandy!*

FISBY. How did they manage to get brandy?

SAKINI. We make very fine brandy here, from sweet potatoes. Been making for generations.

FISBY. You make a brandy *yourselves?*

SAKINI. Oh, yes. We make for weddings and funerals.

FISBY (*looks at* MC LEAN). What does it taste like?

SAKINI. You want some, boss? (*He turns to* HOKAIDA.) Imozake, skoshi!

FISBY. Sakini, if this stuff is any good at all, we're in business. This is one thing I *know* our men will buy.

SAKINI. Oh . . . I think we not like to sell brandy. Only make for ceremony.

MC LEAN. It may not be any good anyhow. There are some things even the troops won't drink.

HOKAIDA (*returns with an earthen jug*). Hai, imozake. (*He hands the jug to* FISBY.)

SAKINI. There you are, boss. You like taste now?

FISBY. I'd like to smell it first. (*He gives it a sniff and jerks his head back.*)

MC LEAN. Obviously, it has a kick.

FISBY. How old is this brandy, Sakini?

SAKINI (*turns to Hokaida*). Kore itsuno?

HOKAIDA (*Holds up seven fingers*). Is-sukan mae dayo.

FISBY. Seven years old?

SAKINI. Oh, no, boss. He make last week.

FISBY. It couldn't smell like that in only a week.

SAKINI. Is village secret. You try now?

FISBY (*hands it to* MC LEAN). You try it, Mac. You're a medical man.

MC LEAN (*backs away*). You first.

FISBY. I insist. You're my guest.

MC LEAN. I waive the honor.

FISBY (*Turns to* SAKINI). Has anyone ever gone blind or died from this?

MC LEAN. He said they make it for

funerals.

SAKINI. Oh, no, boss. We not blind. We not dead.

FISBY. There, you see.

MC LEAN. They've worked up an immunity over the years.

FISBY. Well, I don't want to kill any of my countrymen. Couldn't you make some sort of test, Doc? (*As* MC LEAN *considers this, the bleat of a goat is heard offstage.* FISBY *and* MC LEAN *exchange looks and nod.*) Sakini, get Lady Astor. (*To* MC LEAN.) That's Miss Higa Jiga's goat. She asked me to give it a classy name.

(SAKINI *goes to get* LADY ASTOR.)

MC LEAN. I'm not sure what we'll prove. Goats have hardy stomachs.

SAKINI (*returns leading a goat*). Boss, you make guinea pig of goat?

FISBY. If this passes the goat-test, it's all right. No Marine would ever admit he had a weaker stomach than a goat.

MC LEAN. May I borrow this a moment?
(*He takes* MR. HOKAIDA's *red helmet and pours into it from the jug.*)

SAKINI. Lady Astor very lucky goat.

FISBY. You hold her, Sakini. Proceed, Doctor . . . in the name of science. (*The goat sniffs the contents of the helmet.*) We're either going to have an industry or goat meat for dinner.

(LADY ASTOR *begins to drink the concoction. They watch her lap up the liquor and lick her lips with relish.*)

MC LEAN (*stands back*). It doesn't seem to affect her. (*Draws his fingers back and forth in front of the goat's eyes.*) Reflexes all right.

FISBY. Let's watch her a minute. The future of Tobiki and the health of the Army are at stake here. (FISBY *and* MC LEAN *and the* VILLAGERS *stand watching the goat.* LADY ASTOR *is quite content.* FISBY *rises.*) Well, here goes. (*He takes the jug and samples the contents himself.* MC LEAN *watches him. Then he, too, tests from the jug. They look at each other and grin.*) Whee! (*He dashes for his office.*)

SAKINI (*follows*). What you going to do, boss?

FISBY. I am about to form the Cooperative Brewing Company of Tobiki. (FISBY *is followed by* SAKINI, MC LEAN, *and some of the* VILLAGERS. *He picks up the phone.*) Get me the Officers' Club at Awasi.

SAKINI. We going to make brandy, boss?

FISBY. I'll tell you in a minute. (*He turns back to telephone.*) Hello . . . Officers' Club, Awasi? This is Captain Fisby at Tobiki. Oh, hello, Major, how are you? Major, when I was with your unit, I could never keep a supply of liquor in the club, and I stumbled onto something and wondered if you'd be interested. Tobiki, as you know, is the heart of the brandy industry and— (*He takes the phone away from his ear as the word brandy is shouted back at him.*) Yes . . . brandy. . . . (*He turns to* MC LEAN.) Doc, look up the word "sweet potato" and see if it has another fancier name. (*He turns back to the phone.*) Yes . . . I'm here . . . yes . . . I could get you some if you could pay their price and keep the source secret. Oh, yes, it's been made here for generations. Why, you never tasted anything like it.

MC LEAN. The Haitian word for sweet potato is *b-a-t-a-t-a*. (*He spells it out.*)

FISBY (*into the phone*). You've heard of Seven Star Batata, haven't you? Well, Tobiki is where it's made. (*He turns to* MC LEAN.) The Seven Star did it.

SAKINI. Brandy much better if eight or ten days old, boss.

FISBY. We also have Eight Star and Ten Star. Well, naturally the Ten Star comes a little higher. It sells for— (*He looks at* SAKINI *desperately.* SAKINI *holds up ten fingers.*) A hundred occupation yen a gallon.

SAKINI. I mean *ten* yen, boss.

FISBY. Delivered. All right, we'll send up five gallons in about a week. It'll be delivered by our Department of Agriculture. You're welcome. (*He hangs up and turns to* SAKINI.) Sakini, if every family in Tobiki starts making brandy, how much can we turn out in a week?

SAKINI. Oh, maybe . . . forty . . . fifty gallons.

FISBY. Better aim for eighty. (*He lifts the receiver again.*) I'd like to get the naval base at Big Koza, Officers' Club, Commander Myers.

SAKINI. Maybe if everybody build private stills, Tobiki can turn out hundred gallon.

FISBY. I'll know better after I talk to the Navy. (*He speaks into the phone.*) Commander Myers? Captain Fisby at Tobiki. Commander, we've got a surplus of brandy down here and I was wondering . . . (*Again he takes the phone away from his ear as the word brandy is blasted back.*)

Yes. Brandy. Ten Star Batata. Well, Lady Astor won't drink anything else. Oh . . . we could supply you with as much as you want at a hundred yen a gallon. Fifteen gallons? Right! It will be delivered Horse Cart Special in ten days. (*He hangs up and turns to the others crowding into his office.*) Sakini, tell them to all start making brandy, and in a week or two everyone in this village is going to have more money than he ever dreamed of.

SAKINI. Ah, dondon kaseide sake tsukreba minna kanega mokaruyo!

MR. KEORA. Minna shiroi koto katte moii darone?

SAKINI. They say . . . if they work like the dickens, can they all have white coats like the mayor?

FISBY. Yes. I'll get the cloth somewhere. That's a promise. (*The telephone rings.*) Wait a minute. Hello? Well, word gets around fast. (*He picks up his order blank.*) Twenty gallons? PX, GHQ, C.O.D. O.K. (*He hangs up.*) Get to work, boys! (*As they turn to leave,* FISBY *suddenly leaps to his feet.*) Wait! (*They stand frozen as he crouches and starts toward them. He slaps his hand on the floor and then rises triumphantly.*) I got my cricket!

(*The* VILLAGERS *cheer for* FISBY.)

THE PANELS FALL QUICKLY

ACT THREE

SCENE ONE

SCENE: *Teahouse of the August Moon.*
TIME: *Several weeks later.*
AT RISE: *All the panels are down.* SAKINI *steps from the wings to address the audience.*

SAKINI
(*Bows*)
Ability of Americans for mass production equaled only by American capacity for consumption.
Fortune often comes in back door while we look out front window.
Prosperity not only smile on Tobiki.
Prosperity giggle like silly girl.
Very strange.
Things we do best . . . not wanted.
Things we think least of . . . wanted most.
No conclusion.

Tobiki now village of beautiful houses. But loveliest of all is Teahouse of August Moon.

(*He goes off extreme left, signaling for the panels to rise. Offstage the music of string instruments can be heard playing softly. The panels go up. The ugly thatched huts are gone. In the center of the stage, exquisite in its simplicity, stands the teahouse. Small bells tinkle from its pagoda roof. Soft lights glow through the colored paper panels. Dwarf pines edge the walk leading to a small bridge. An August moon hangs in the autumn sky. The silhouette of* LOTUS BLOSSOM *is framed in the center panel by the soft back lighting. She slides the panel open and steps into the almost bare center room of the teahouse. She crosses and lights the lanterns hanging from the eave extensions. As she goes through this ceremony, the* GUESTS *wander in. Before they enter the teahouse, they remove their shoes and rinse their fingers in the ceremonial bamboo basin. Then they enter and seat themselves on green floor mats. The* WOMEN *are dressed in silk kimonos of varying hues and the majority of the men wear spotless white suits.* LOTUS BLOSSOM *bows to them and returns through the sliding door again.* FISBY *and* MC LEAN, *followed by* SAKINI, *enter.* SAKINI *wears a white suit and the* AMERICANS *wear their bathrobes and geta. They are greeted enthusiastically by the* GUESTS.)

SAKINI. I tell Lotus Blossom you here, boss. (*He disappears through the sliding panel in the center of the teahouse.*)

FISBY (*as they walk around inspecting the grounds*). It's really something, isn't it?

MC LEAN. Where did they all get their white suits?

FISBY. They made them.

MC LEAN. Where'd they get the cloth?

FISBY. I got it from the naval base at Awasi for ten gallons of brandy. It's target cloth.

MC LEAN. Those kimonos aren't target cloth.

FISBY. Parachute silk. Six gallons' worth.

(LOTUS BLOSSOM *enters, followed by* SAKINI. *She hurries down to* FISBY *and bows. She extends a yellow chrysanthemum to him.*)

SAKINI. Chrysanthemum bud in full bloom, boss.

LOTUS BLOSSOM (*she bows as* FISBY *accepts*

the gift). Hop-pee. (*Her eyes almost disappear in a great smile of pride.*)

FISBY. What did she say?

SAKINI. I try like the dickens to teach her to say "happy birthday," but she can't say "birthday," boss.

LOTUS BLOSSOM. Hop-pee.

FISBY. Well . . . I'm floored! (*He bows to her.*) Thank you, Lotus Blossom. (*To* SAKINI.) How did you know?

MC LEAN. I gave you away.

SAKINI. Everybody in village like to show appreciation, boss.

FISBY. I should have had a kimono made. When you said "formal," I thought this would do.

LOTUS BLOSSOM. Hop-pee. Hop-pee.

FISBY. And a hop-pee hop-pee to you.

GUESTS (*murmur in the background*). Hayaku oiwai hajimeyo, soda, soda.

SAKINI. Everybody impatient to get on with the party, boss.

LOTUS BLOSSOM. Hop-pee. (*She indicates the center mat.*)

SAKINI. You sit down now, boss. Lotus Blossom going to dance in your honor.

FISBY. You hear that. . . . She's going to dance! (*Quickly sits down.*) Sit down, you farmer. . . . This is in my honor.

MC LEAN. My, my! How am I going to stall Purdy so I can stay down here?

FISBY. I'll have a relapse for you. (*They turn to watch* LOTUS BLOSSOM *as she takes her position and the first notes are struck by the musicians present.* LOTUS BLOSSOM *performs for them a traditional dance of infinite grace and delicacy. She finishes, concluding her performance in front of* FISBY, *who rises and bows to her.*) What a lovely little thing you are! This belongs to you. (*He returns the chrysanthemum with a flourish.* LOTUS BLOSSOM *accepts it and seats herself quickly on a mat and hides her head.*)

SAKINI. Oh, boss . . . you know what you do!

FISBY. It called for flowers.

SAKINI. That mean you give your heart to her.

FISBY (*lightly*). Well, I do. We all do. (*Turns to* MC LEAN.) Wasn't that beautiful, Mac!

MC LEAN. She can dance in my cha ya any day.

SAKINI. You sit beside Lotus Blossom now, boss. You guest of honor and referee.

FISBY (*starts to sit down*). *Referee!* I thought this was a birthday party.

SAKINI. Lotus Blossom now putting on

wrestling match for you, boss.

FISBY. *Wrestling* match?

LOTUS BLOSSOM (*stands and claps hands*). Sa, osumo hajime mashoyo.

(*Immediately two men bring in four poles which they set up downstage center to mark a square. Each pole has colored cloth hanging from it.*)

MC LEAN. Who is wrestling? (*He sits next to* FISBY.)

SAKINI. Wrestling match between Chief of Agriculture and Chief of Police.

FISBY (*to* LOTUS BLOSSOM). Hokaida and Seiko? (*She nods.*)

SAKINI. Grudge fight, boss.

FISBY. Really?

SAKINI. Whoever win match get to haul sweet potatoes for Lotus Blossom.

FISBY (*watching the poles being set up, he indicates them to* LOTUS BLOSSOM). Why have they wrapped colored cloth around the poles?

LOTUS BLOSSOM. Kuro wa fuyu, Ao wa haru, Akaga natsu de, Shirowa akiyo. Wakkatta?

SAKINI. She explain, boss, that black cloth remind us of winter, green cloth remind us of spring, red is the summer and white the autumn.

LOTUS BLOSSOM (*claps her hands*). Osumo, osumo!

(MR. HOKAIDA, *bare except for a pair of black shorts, enters and crosses to one corner of the ring, where he squats on his heels. An outburst of approval greets his entrance. He smiles with fatuous pleasure, and makes a desperate effort to hold in his fat stomach.*)

MC LEAN. Do his black shorts mean anything?

SAKINI. Just easy to clean.

(LOTUS BLOSSOM *claps her dainty hands again.* MR. SEIKO *enters, lean and wiry, also wearing black shorts and a sweat shirt reading* U.S.S. Princeton.)

FISBY. Where did he get *that?*

SAKINI. Sailor at naval base. Some class, eh? (MR. SEIKO *peels off the shirt to great applause and squats in the opposite corner. He glares across at* HOKAIDA, *who thrusts his jaw forward.*) They waiting on you to give signal now, boss.

FISBY. Waiting on *me?*

SAKINI. Oh, yes . . . you are Honorable Referee.

LOTUS BLOSSOM (*hands her fan to* FISBY). Korede aizu shite kudasai.

FISBY. What do I do with this?

SAKINI. Now you cover face with fan.

FISBY. Why?

SAKINI. That mean you not take sides. Now you go to center of ring and drop fan from face.

MC LEAN. And get the hell out in a hurry.

FISBY. How many falls?

SAKINI. No falls, boss. First one to throw other out of ring—winner. (FISBY *covers his face with the fan and walks down center. The two wrestlers crouch, poised to leap, their eyes on the fan.* FISBY *whips the fan away from his face and dashes back out of range. The protagonists circle each other slowly. Suddenly all hell breaks loose. The teahouse guests cheer their favorite. The fat* MR. HOKAIDA *picks up* MR. SEIKO *and subjects him to a series of head spins and thumpings. But he exhausts himself; and it is* SEIKO *who ends by tossing* HOKAIDA *out of the ring. A cheer rises from the guests.* FISBY *sighs with relief.*) Now the judges must decide who win.

FISBY. Decide! Is there any doubt?

(*The three judges confer. They then turn to* MR. HOKAIDA *and bow.*)

SAKINI. Mr. Hokaida! The winner . . .

(*This startling announcement is greeted with approval.* SEIKO *beats his head and wails.*)

FISBY. How *could* he be the winner! He was thrown out of the ring.

SAKINI. Maybe so, but judges all cousins of Mr. Hokaida.

FISBY. But the judges are wrong.

SAKINI (*confidentially*). We know who really win . . . but this way nobody lose face.

(SEIKO *and* HOKAIDA *exit.*)

LOTUS BLOSSOM. Sa kondo wa Fu-san no ban yo.

SAKINI. Lotus Blossom say guests now wish *you* to perform.

FISBY. Perform what?

SAKINI. They like now for you and doctor to sing song or something.

FISBY. Sing!

SAKINI. Must do, boss. Bad manners to refuse.

FISBY (*repeats in alarm*). Sing! (*He turns to* MC LEAN.) Get on your feet, Mac, we've got to sing something.

MC LEAN. What?

FISBY. We could sing the national anthem.

MC LEAN. No, we couldn't—I don't know the words.

FISBY. How about "Deep in the Heart of Texas"?

MC LEAN. Why not? There're no Texans here. (*They step forward.*)

FISBY. Mac, let's have some fun. (*He turns to* SAKINI.) Sakini, you tell them they must all help us. They must clap and sing "Deep in the Heart of Texas" every time *we* do.

SAKINI (*beaming*). Tewo tataite Deep in the Heart of Texas. (*Demonstrates clapping.*) Koshte, Deep in the Heart of Texas.

(*The* VILLAGERS *chaiter and agree with enthusiasm.* FISBY *and* MC LEAN *stand close together and begin singing. Each time they come to the designated phrase,* SAKINI *gives a signal and the* VILLAGERS *join in lustily. Lost in their eager concentration, no one observes the entrance of* COLONEL PURDY. *He looks from the "kimono"-clad figures of* FISBY *and* MC LEAN *to the assemblage. As he shouts at* FISBY, *his voice is drowned out by the chorus of "Deep in the Heart of Texas." The song continues.* PURDY *signals offstage.* GREGOVICH *enters and is instructed by* COLONEL PURDY *to end the objectionable noises.*)

GREGOVICH. Captain Fisby!

(*Again the voice coincides with the shouts of "Deep in the Heart of Texas" and is lost.* COLONEL PURDY *stalks downstage center, followed by* GREGOVICH.)

PURDY. Captain Fisby! What in the name of Occupation is going on here?

(FISBY *gasps and backs away. Suddenly aware of his bathrobe, he stoops down to cover his bare legs.* MC LEAN *surrenders completely to panic. He runs to hide behind guests. The* GUESTS, *alarmed by the sudden intrusion, scatter in all directions. In the midst of this bedlam—*

THE PANELS ARE LOWERED

SCENE TWO

SCENE: *Office of Captain Fisby.*

TIME: *Next morning.*

AT RISE: *The four bamboo panels are down.* SAKINI *enters from the wings right and crosses down to the footlights.*

SAKINI

(*Bows*)

When present is blackest,
Future can only be brighter.
Okinawa invaded many times.
Not sink in ocean yet.

Survive Chinese.

Survive Japanese.

Survive missionaries and Americans.

Invaded by typhoon.

Invaded by locust.

Invaded by cockroach and sweet-potato moth.

Tobiki now invaded by Honorable Colonel.

Not sink in ocean.

(He goes to the left side of the stage and raises the panels in front of Fisby's office. He then exits. COLONEL PURDY *is seated at Fisby's desk going through his papers.* FISBY *stands behind him nervously watching.* MC LEAN *sits on the cot biting his nails. He rises.)*

PURDY *(without looking up)*. Sit down! *(*MC LEAN *sits down again.* PURDY *turns to* FISBY *and glares at him.)* Where are your bimonthly Progress Reports?

FISBY. I—I think they should be right here under the cricket cage, sir.

PURDY *(takes some papers from under the cage and glances at them)*. These are all completely blank. *(He turns to* FISBY.*)* Fisby, you can't convince me that you've been down here for two months doing absolutely nothing.

FISBY. Oh, no, sir. I mean yes, sir, I have not been doing "nothing."

PURDY. You're beginning to sound like a native.

MC LEAN *(rises)*. The tendency is always to descend to the level of the environment, sir. It's a primary postulate of psychology.

PURDY *(turns on him)*. Well, it's a primary regulation of the Army to make out reports! *(Back to* FISBY.*)* Now, I want to know exactly what you've accomplished here from the moment you arrived.

FISBY. Well, let me think. . . .

MC LEAN. Could I—

PURDY. Sit down! *(He turns to* FISBY.*)* How many lectures have you delivered to the village children on democratic theory?

FISBY. Well, let me see.

PURDY. Four-five?

FISBY *(thinks)*. Not that many, sir.

PURDY. Three?

MC LEAN *(hopefully)*. Two?

FISBY. N-no.

PURDY. You only delivered *one* lecture?

FISBY. None, sir.

PURDY. Don't tell me you haven't de-

livered a single lecture!

FISBY. Yes, sir, I haven't delivered no lecture. I mean . . . any lecture.

PURDY. Did you organize a Ladies' League for Democratic Action?

FISBY *(beaming)*. Yes, sir. I sure did. I did that all right!

PURDY. And how many lectures on democratic theory have you given *them?*

FISBY *(deflated again)*. None, sir.

PURDY. You can't mean none. You must mean one or two.

FISBY. No, sir, none.

PURDY. I refuse to believe it.

FISBY. I'm glad, sir.

MC LEAN *(rises in desperation)*. Sir, I *must* go.

PURDY. Where!

MC LEAN My *seedlings* are wilting. I have to transplant them.

PURDY. Captain, you will pack your gear and transplant yourself to your unit at once.

MC LEAN. Yes, sir. *(He turns to* FISBY.*)* They'll die. It's murder. *(He goes to the door and turns sadly to* FISBY *again.)* Please take care of my beans. *(He exits.)*

PURDY *(turns back to* FISBY*)*. Now! Is the schoolhouse finished?

FISBY *(sighs)*. No, sir.

PURDY. *Why* isn't it finished?

FISBY. It isn't finished, sir, because it isn't started.

PURDY. I have a splitting headache, Fisby. I ask you not to provoke me needlessly. Now, where is the schoolhouse?

FISBY. I never built it.

PURDY. Don't stand there and tell me you never built it. I sent the lumber down two months ago.

FISBY *(impressed)*. Is it *that* long, sir?

PURDY. What did you do with the lumber I sent?

FISBY. Well, I built a teahouse.

PURDY *(stares at him)*. I don't suppose you have any aspirin here?

FISBY. No, sir, I haven't.

PURDY. Now, sit down. Fisby. I want to be fair. *(*FISBY *sits down.)* I'm a patient man. When I run into something that defies reason, I like to find the reason. *(Explodes.)* What in the name of Occupation do you mean by saying you built a *teahouse* instead of a *schoolhouse!*

FISBY. It's a little hard to explain, sir. Everybody in the village wanted one . . . and Lotus Blossom needed it for her work.

PURDY. And just what is your relationship with this woman?

FISBY. Well, she was a present. So to speak. She's a geisha girl—after a fashion.

PURDY. You built this teahouse—this place for her to ply her trade—with lumber belonging to the Army of Occupation of the United States Government?

FISBY. Well, it just seemed like lumber at the time.

PURDY. Fisby, are you operating a house of prostitution here on Government rice?

FISBY. No, sir! Geishas aren't what you think.

PURDY. Don't tell me what to think. Army Intelligence warned me I'd find something mighty peculiar going on in Tobiki.

FISBY. What's Army Intelligence got to do with it, sir?

PURDY. You're not very cunning, Fisby. With all the Occupation money on the island finding its way to this village, did you think it wouldn't come to the attention of Intelligence?

FISBY. Oh.

PURDY. Why did you do it, Fisby, why!

FISBY. Well, Lotus Blossom had to have a place to teach the Ladies' League how to become geishas and—

PURDY. Fisby! You mean to say you've turned all the decent women of this village into professional . . . (He slumps into the chair.) How could you sink to such depths, man!

FISBY. I was only giving in to what the majority wanted, sir.

PURDY. I don't doubt that statement—not at all. It is a sad thing that it took a war to convince me that most of the human race is degenerate. Thank God I come from a country where the air is clean, where the wind is fresh, where—

FISBY (interrupts). For heaven's sake, sir, would you please listen to me instead of yourself! There is not a thing goes on in that teahouse that your mother couldn't watch.

PURDY (leaps to his feet and points a warning finger). You be careful how you use my mother's name, Fisby.

FISBY. Well, my mother then. I swear there's nothing immoral about our tea-house.

PURDY. Then answer me this. What is bringing all that Occupation money to this particular village? There is only one thing that attracts that kind of money.

FISBY. Well, evidently there are two things.

PURDY. And if it isn't honor that you sell here, what is it?

FISBY (sighs unhappily). We . . . make things.

PURDY. What?

FISBY. Mats . . . and hats . . . and cricket cages.

PURDY. One hundred and fifty thousand yen finds its way to this village every month. You can't convince me that the American soldier is spending that much on "cricket cages."

FISBY. Well, naturally . . . not all of it. (The telephone rings. FISBY looks at it apprehensively.)

PURDY. Answer it.

FISBY (pauses). It's nothing important, sir.

PURDY. It might be for me. Answer it.

FISBY (airily). Oh, it rings all day, sir. Pay no attention.

PURDY. Then I'll answer it! (He picks up the telephone. FISBY covers his face.) Hello? What do you want? Who is this? Well, Commander Myers, I think you have the wrong connection. This is not a brewery. Yes . . . yes . . . yes! (He turns to look at FISBY.) Oh . . . I see. I see. I see. (He hangs up. He turns to FISBY, who smiles weakly.)

FISBY. It was the only thing we could make that anyone wanted to buy, sir.

PURDY. Brandy! (Sadly.) I don't know which is worse. Putting your country in the white slave trade or the wholesale liquor business. Congress will have to decide.

FISBY. We've the most prosperous village on the island, sir.

PURDY. This ends my Army career. I promised Mrs. Purdy I'd come out a general. You've broken a fine woman's heart, Fisby.

FISBY. You said to make the village self-supporting, sir.

PURDY. I didn't tell you to encourage lewdness and drunkenness. You've sullied the reputation of your nation and all the tears—

FISBY. All right, sir, shall I kill myself?

PURDY. Oh, don't minimize this. You don't know the enemy's genius for propaganda.

FISBY. Does anyone have to know, sir? We're doing all right.

PURDY (*explodes*). Yes, they have to know! I requested an investigation myself. I've notified the Inspector General. Now I'll have to radio the whole story to Washington.

FISBY. Oh.

PURDY (*calmer*). Well, what have you done with all this money you've made so dishonestly?

FISBY. Banked it in Seattle.

PURDY. Oh, that's despicable—making a personal fortune off the labor of these ignorant people.

FISBY. I haven't touched a cent for myself, sir. It's been deposited in the name of the Tobiki Cooperative. The whole village are equal partners. Share and share alike.

PURDY (*leaps up*). That's *Communism!*

FISBY. Is it?

PURDY (*sinks down again*). I'll be lucky to get out of this war a private. (*He is a beaten man.*) Well, there is only one thing for me to do.

FISBY. What is that, sir?

PURDY. First, you are to consider yourself under technical arrest. You will proceed to H.Q. at once to await court-martial.

FISBY. Yes, sir.

PURDY (*steps to the door*). Gregovich! (*He turns back to* FISBY.) I must go on to Awasi this afternoon on an inspection tour. But before I leave, I intend to wipe this stain from our country's honor.

(SERGEANT GREGOVICH *enters and salutes.*)

GREGOVICH. You called, sir?

PURDY. I did. We have some business to attend to here before going on to Awasi.

GREGOVICH. Yes, sir. I'm glad to hear it. (*He turns to* FISBY.) May I congratulate you on what you've done to this village, sir. It's a dream.

FISBY. Thank you, Sergeant.

PURDY. It is an alcoholic dream. It is one vast distillery. I want you to take a detail and some axes and smash every still in this village.

GREGOVICH. Destroy them?

PURDY. Beyond repair. I want you take another detail and rip down that teahouse.

GREGOVICH. But, Colonel—

PURDY. Pile the lumber beside the warehouse. That is an order. Do you understand?

GREGOVICH. Yes, sir! (*As he turns to follow orders,* FISBY *sinks into his chair and the scene blacks out quickly.*)

CURTAIN

SCENE THREE

SCENE: *Teahouse of the August Moon.*
TIME: *A few hours later.*
AT RISE: *All the panels are down. Behind the sceens can be heard the destruction of the stills and the dismantling of the teahouse.* SAKINI *comes out from the wings and crosses down to the footlights. He flinches at the sound of an ax falling on wood.*

SAKINI
    (*Sadly*)
Oh, no comment.
    (*He walks back into the wings as all the panels are raised simultaneously. Only the frame of the teahouse has been spared. The paper panels have disappeared, the pagoda roof is gone with its tinkling bells. There are no colored lanterns and no dwarf pines to grace the path. The bare supports stand stark and ugly. Resting at the edge of the frame is a wheelbarrow.* LOTUS BLOSSOM *is collecting the last of her possessions. She takes a brass brazier down to place in the wheelbarrow. Then she stands with her back to the audience surveying all that remains of the teahouse.* FISBY *comes on, and, seeing* LOTUS BLOSSOM, *hesitates. Then he crosses to stand beside her. He takes her hand, and the two of them stand looking at the ruins.* LOTUS BLOSSOM *walks to the center of the teahouse and sits on the bare floor.* FISBY *comes up and sits on the floor facing her. She goes through the ceremony of pouring him an imaginary cup of tea.* FISBY *accepts with mock formality. As he takes the cup and pretends to drink it,* LOTUS BLOSSOM *covers her face with her hands.* FISBY *sits watching her mutely.*)

SAKINI (*entering*). Jeep all loaded, boss.
FISBY. I'll be along in a minute.
SAKINI. Oh, pretty soon have nice

schoolhouse here.

FISBY (*bitterly*). Pentagon-shaped.

SAKINI. Not be too bad. You take Lotus Blossom with you?

FISBY. No.

SAKINI. What happen to her then?

FISBY. What would have happened to her if we'd never come along?

SAKINI. Not know. Maybe someday she meet nice man and give up Geisha Guild.

FISBY. Ask her if there is anything I can do for her before I go.

SAKINI (*comes up to stand behind them*). Nanika iitai?

LOTUS BLOSSOM (*softly*). Fu-san, watas-hito kekkon shite chodai.

SAKINI (*scolding*). Sonna bakana koto.

LOTUS BLOSSOM (*persistent*). Iikara hay-aku itte!

FISBY. What does she want?

SAKINI. Oh, that crazy Lotus Blossom. She want you to marry her.

FISBY. Why should she want to marry me?

SAKINI. She think you nicest man she ever see, boss.

FISBY. Tell her that I am clumsy, that I seem to have a gift for destruction. That I'd disillusion her as I have disillusioned her people.

SAKINI. Kokai suruyo.

LOTUS BLOSSOM. Ikitai noyo. Amerika ni. Ikitai noyo.

SAKINI. She say she think she like to go to America. There everybody happy. Sit around and drink tea while machines do work.

FISBY. She wouldn't like it, Sakini. I should hate to see her wearing sweaters and sport shoes and looking like an American looking like an Oriental.

SAKINI. But she want to be an American, boss. She never see an American she not like, boss.

FISBY. Some of them wouldn't like her. Sakini. In the small town where I live, there'd be some who would make her unhappy.

SAKINI. Why, boss?

FISBY. She'd be different.

SAKINI. Dame dayo.

LOTUS BLOSSOM (*takes Fisby's hand*). Sonna koto naiwa, Amerikatte minshu shugi desumono ne.

SAKINI. She say not believe that. In America everybody love everybody. Everybody help everybody; that's democracy.

FISBY. No. That's faith. Explain to her that democracy is only a method—an ideal system for people to get together. But that unfortunately . . . the people who get together . . . are not always ideal.

SAKINI. That's very hard to explain, boss. She girl in love. She just want to hear pretty things.

FISBY. Then tell her that I love what she is, and that it would be wrong to change that. To impose my way of life on her.

SAKINI. Tassha dene!

FISBY. Tell her that I shall never forget her. Nor this village. Tell her that in the autumn of my life—on the other side of the world—when an August moon rises from the east, I will remember what was beautiful in my youth, and what I was wise enough to leave beautiful.

SAKINI. Issho wasurenai kara ne. Man-getsu no yoru niwa anata o omoidashim-asu.

LOTUS BLOSSOM (*remains silent a moment*). Watashi mo Fu-san no koto issho wasurenaiwa. Fu-san no koto uta ni shite, Okinawaju ni hirome masu.

SAKINI. She say she always remember you, boss. She say she guess maybe she be what she is—first-class geisha girl. She want you to know she make up long song-story about you to sing in teahouse. And maybe hundred years from now, you be famous all over Okinawa.

FISBY (*rises*). I'd like that.

LOTUS BLOSSOM (*rises*). Iinoyo. Fu-san damedemo Seiko-san ga irun dakara.

SAKINI. She say, since you not marry her, maybe you suggest somebody here. (FISBY *laughs*.) She say that Mr. Seiko been looking at her like sick goat. She say what you think of him?

FISBY. Well, he took an awful beating just so he could carry her sweet potatoes.

LOTUS BLOSSOM. Fu-san, Seiko-san iito omouno?

SAKINI. She say you think she ought to marry him?

FISBY. I think she ought to decide for herself.

(*And* MR. SEIKO *enters. He is dressed in his white suit and his hair is slicked down tight. He crosses to* LOTUS BLOSSOM. *They all turn to look at him.*)

SEIKO (*bows to* LOTUS BLOSSOM).A, boku, oshimasho.

SAKINI (*to* FISBY). Mr. Seiko tell Lotus Blossom he sure like to push her wheelbarrow for her.

LOTUS BLOSSOM. Iikara sakini itte cho-dai.

SAKINI. She say, oh, all right, but not to think that means she's his property.

(MR. SEIKO *beams like a schoolboy and, picking up the handles of the wheelbarrow, he trots off stage with* LOTUS BLOSSOM'S *possessions. She turns to* FISBY *and hands him her fan.*)

LOTUS BLOSSOM. Korede aizu shite cho-dai. Soremade watashi dokonimo ikima-sen kara.

SAKINI. She say she go now, but you still her boss. She not go until you give signal.

(FISBY *takes the fan and puts it before his eyes. Without waiting for him to drop it,* LOTUS BLOSSOM *runs off right. When he lowers the fan, he knows she's gone. He sits down on the platform that had been the teahouse veranda.*)

SAKINI. You go now, boss?

FISBY. Shortly.

SAKINI. Since you not take Lotus Blossom, maybe you take me, boss?

FISBY. Major McEvoy is coming down to take charge. You'll work with him.

SAKINI. Would rather work with you.

FISBY. You'll like Major McEvoy.

SAKINI. I'll work for you for half price, boss.

FISBY. Major McEvoy will need your help in getting this village on its feet again.

SAKINI. You very hard man to bargain with, boss. If you want, I work for rice rations only.

FISBY. No.

SAKINI. You mean you going to make me work for *nothing*, boss?

FISBY. I mean *yes*, you're *not* going to work for me at all. And you belong here.

SAKINI. You know what I think happen when Americans leave Okinawa?

FISBY. What?

SAKINI (*grins*). I think maybe we use pentagon-shaped schoolhouse for tea-house.

(FISBY *laughs. He gives* SAKINI *a slap on the shoulder.*)

FISBY. Good-bye, Sakini, you're a rare rascal and I'll miss you.

SAKINI. Good-bye, boss. (FISBY *starts off left. He has gone halfway when* SAKINI *calls.*) Boss—

FISBY (*stops*). Yes?

SAKINI. You not failure.

FISBY (*laughs*). I'll tell you something,

SAKINI. I used to worry a lot about not being a big success. I must have felt as you people felt at always being conquered. Well, now I'm not so sure who's the conqueror and who the conquered.

SAKINI. Not understand, boss.

FISBY. It's just that I've learned from Tobiki the wisdom of gracious accept-ance. I don't want to be a world leader. I'm making peace with myself some-where between my ambitions and my limitations.

SAKINI. That's good?

FISBY. It's a step backward in the right direction. (*He throws* SAKINI *a salute.*) Take care.

(*He walks off and* SAKINI *watches him go. Then, with a sigh,* SAKINI *turns to survey the skeleton of the teahouse. The silence is broken by the stormy entrance of* COLONEL PURDY.)

PURDY. Sakini! Where is Captain Fisby?

SAKINI (*points*). Just leaving, boss.

PURDY (*shouts*). Fisby! Fisby! (*Gestures frantically.*) Come back here at once! (*He goes to the platform and sinks down gasping.*) I'm not in shape—too much paper work. (FISBY *returns from the left.*) Where in hell have you been, Fisby? I've been looking all over for you.

FISBY. I'm ready to leave, sir.

PURDY. You can't leave. You've got to stay here. You've got to help me, Fisby.

FISBY. Help doing what, sir?

PURDY. Pulling this village back to-gether again. All hell has broken loose, Fisby. (*He sits down to wipe his brow.*) Where is Gregovich!

FISBY. Breaking up the last of the stills, sir.

PURDY. Oh, *no!* (*He holds his head.*)

FISBY. What's happened, sir?

PURDY. I radioed the report to Wash-ington. Some fool senator misunder-stood. He's using this village as an exam-ple of American "get-up-and-go" in the recovery program. The Pentagon is boasting. Congress is crowing. We're all over the papers.

FISBY. But that's wonderful, sir.

PURDY. No, it's not wonderful. A Con-gressional Committee is flying over to study our methods. They are bringing in photographers for a magazine spread. Today, Fisby, today!

FISBY. Oh, that's bad, sir.

PURDY (*wails*). Gregovich!

FISBY. Isn't there any way to stall

them off, sir? Quarantine the place or something?

PURDY. You can't quarantine a congressman. They have immunity or something. (*He takes* FISBY *by the jacket.*) Fisby, help me. I don't ask for my sake. I ask for Mrs. Purdy. I could be a brigadier yet.

(*Before* FISBY *can answer,* GREGOVICH *comes in from the left and salutes.*)

GREGOVICH. You called, sir?

PURDY (*hurries over to him*). Gregovich! Gregovich! You haven't destroyed all the stills, have you, Gregovich? No, of course you haven't.

GREGOVICH. Yes, sir, I have. I carried out orders to the letter.

PURDY (*turns away shouting*). Why can't someone disobey orders once in a while! What has happened to the American spirit of rebellion! (GREGOVICH *hiccups, smiles sillily and folds up on the floor.* FISBY *and* PURDY *race over to kneel beside him.*) Sunstroke?

FISBY. Potato brandy.

PURDY. Sergeant, wake up. Do you hear me? That's an order.

FISBY. I'm afraid he's passed out, sir.

PURDY. It's desertion. I need every man. Gregovich, get to your feet!

(*With* FISBY'S *help he gets* GREGOVICH *to his feet.*)

GREGOVICH. Sorry, sir.

PURDY. I want to ask you some questions. Stop weaving.

GREGOVICH. *You're* weaving, sir. *I'm* perfectly still.

PURDY. You smell like a brewery.

GREGOVICH. I fell in a vat.

PURDY. You got drunk.

GREGOVICH. No, sir. I fell in a vat. Naturally, I had to open my mouth to yell for help.

PURDY. Go to the office and sober up at once.

GREGOVICH. Yes, sir. (*He salutes with a happy smile, jogs off.*)

PURDY. I'm a sinking ship . . . scuttled by my own men.

(*He sinks.* SAKINI, *who has been sitting with arms folded and a fatuous grin on his face, speaks up.*)

SAKINI. Colonel Purdy?

PURDY. Don't bother me.

SAKINI. Stills not all destroyed.

PURDY. I haven't got time to . . . What did you say?

SAKINI. We not born yesterday. Get sergeant drunk . . . and give him water

barrels to break.

PURDY. Sakini, my friend, you're not just saying that to make me feel better?

SAKINI. Oh, stills all good as ever. Production not cease yet.

FISBY (*fondly*). You really are a rogue, Sakini.

PURDY. No . . . he's really an American. He has get-up-and-go.

FISBY. Sakini, if everybody in the village worked together . . . how long would it take to rebuild the teahouse?

PURDY. We don't ask the impossible.

SAKINI. Oh, maybe three minutes . . . maybe five.

PURDY. That's impossible.

SAKINI. We not destroy. Just take away and hide. You watch now, boss. (*He turns and calls.*) Oi, mo iiyo, mo iiyo. (*From the wings, right and left, the* VILLAGERS *step out.*) Oi, haba, haba. (*The* VILLAGERS *respond with happy cries and dash off.*) Country that has been invaded many times soon master art of hiding things.

PURDY. You think we can pull it off, Sakini?

SAKINI. You watch now.

(*And even as he speaks, the sections of the teahouse are carried in and the swift work of putting them together progresses before our eyes. Music is heard in the background. The pagoda roof with its tinkling bells is lowered. The dwarf pines and the arched bridge are brought back. The colored panels are slipped into place and the lanterns are hung.* LOTUS BLOSSOM *comes on with flowers which she arranges.* SAKINI *snaps his fingers and the August moon is magically turned on in the sky. When the final lantern is hung,* MC LEAN *comes in. He stops. His mouth falls open.*)

PURDY. Close your mouth, Captain—haven't you ever seen a cha ya before? (*He turns back to* FISBY.) Fisby, this is a land of adventure . . . a land of jade and spices . . . of Chinese junks and river pirates. . . . Makes a man's blood pound.

FISBY. Colonel . . . I consider what you just said pure . . . (*He pauses.*) . . . poetry.

PURDY. Thank you . . . thank you, boy. (*He sighs ecstatically.*) It's the mystery of the Orient.

FISBY. It's beautiful. Simply beautiful.

PURDY. There's only one thing wrong. It needs a sign to tell people what it is. And I think we ought to put a sign up over there naming this Grace Purdy Avenue. And another sign . . .

FISBY. Colonel Purdy. Won't you have

a cup of tea? (*He takes his arm. As he propels him toward the teahouse, he speaks over his shoulder to* SAKINI.) Twenty Star for the colonel, Sakini.

(*As the bamboo panels begin to descend on the teahouse,* SAKINI *steps down to the audience.*)

Little story now concluded.
History of world unfinished.
Lovely ladies . . . kind gentlemen—
Go home to ponder.

What was true at the beginning remains
    true.
Pain makes man think.
Thought makes man wise.
Wisdom makes life endurable.
Our play has ended.
May August moon bring gentle sleep.
    (*He bows.*)

THE CURTAIN FALLS

THE DIARY OF ANNE FRANK

Dramatized by

Frances Goodrich and *Albert Hackett*

(based upon the book, *Anne Frank: Diary of a Young Girl*)

The Diary of Anne Frank was first presented by Kermit Bloomgarden at the Cort Theatre, New York City, on October 5, 1955. It was staged by Garson Kanin, with setting designed by Boris Aronson. The cast was as follows:

MR. FRANK . . . . Joseph Schildkraut
MIEP . . . . Gloria Jones
MRS. VAN DAAN . . . . Dennie Moore
MR. VAN DAAN . . . . Lou Jacobi
PETER VAN DAAN . . . . David Levin
MRS. FRANK . . . . Gusti Huber
MARGOT FRANK . . . . . . Eva Rubinstein
ANNE FRANK . . . . Susan Strasberg
MR. KRALER . . . . Clinton Sundberg
MR. DUSSEL . . . . Jack Gilford

THE TIME: During the years of World War II and immediately thereafter. THE PLACE: Amsterdam. There are two acts.

Copyright as an unpublished work 1954 and 1956, and © Copyright 1956 by Albert Hackett, Frances Goodrich Hackett and Otto Frank. Reprinted by permission of Random House, Inc.

All rights including the right of reproduction in whole or in part, in any form, are reserved under International and Pan-American Copyright Conventions. Published in New York by Random House, Inc., and simultaneously in Toronto, Canada, by Random House of Canada, Limited.

CAUTION: *The Diary of Anne Frank* is the sole property of the dramatists and is fully protected by copyright. It may not be acted by professionals or amateurs without written permission and the payment of a royalty. All rights, including professional, amateur, stock, radio broadcasting, television, motion picture, recitation, lecturing, public reading, and the rights of translation into foreign languages, are reserved. All inquiries should be addressed to the dramatists' agent: Leah Salisbury, 234 West 44th Street, New York, N.Y.

The Diary of Anne Frank, one of the outstanding productions of the American stage in the 1950's, is in every respect a work of collaboration. It is based on the posthumous book *Anne Frank: The Diary of a Young Girl*, an intensely moving record of a young girl's life while hiding with her family in Amsterdam before the Nazi conquerors of the Netherlands herded them off to a German concentration camp. The book itself is the product of an individual situation and a social reality; Anne Frank's sensibility collaborated with the crisis of the Nazi occupation of Europe in producing the *Diary*. Then Frances Goodrich and Albert Hackett collaborated on a dramatization authorized by the girl-author's father, Otto Frank, the sole survivor of the family.

The playwrights started collaborating successfully in 1930, married a year later, and became a permanent literary partnership, accounting for *Up Pops the Devil* (1930), *Bridal Wise*, and *The Great Big Doorstep* as well as for numerous motion pictures, including *The Thin Man, Father of the Bride*, and *Lady in the Dark*. Miss Goodrich, born in Belleville, New York, came to the theatre after exposure to the stage at Vassar, where the celebrated Hallie Flanagan Davis conducted her Vassar Experimental Theatre courses with distinction. Miss Goodrich also took postgraduate work at the New York School of Social Service, but became an actress rather then a social worker.

Albert Hackett, who was born in New York in 1900, began his career as actor at the age of six and attended the Professional Children's School, a suitable start for the son of a theatrical family that ran and performed in the Lubin Stock Company of Philadelphia.

Mr. Hackett summarized the inception of his career delightfully in an article in the January 4, 1961 issue of *Variety*. "Fifty-five years ago," he wrote, "when *Variety* was starting, I was starting. I was playing in *Lottie the Poor Saleslady, or Death before Dishonor. Variety* has changed a lot since. So have I. I was playing a little girl." He added to this reminiscence that he died in the second act, and after extricating himself from the leading lady (presumably the stage mother), who had collapsed on top of him with simulated grief, he would rush offstage, adjust wings over his nightgown, reappear on the kitchen table, and wing his way to heaven against a background of moving clouds. On tour, during one-night stands, he would also assist the stage crew, hold a smoke pot in the fire scene, roll buckshot on a drumhead in the storm scene, and perform other necessary chores, before he joined the ranks of unemployed actors at the age of nine and was sent to a convent school. One season, if his memory is accurate, he played three hundred one-night stands.

Nothing the collaborators had accomplished proved to be so distinguished and materially successful as their work on the *Diary*. Louis Kronenberger's comment is especially true and relevant: "They brought off, by a right approach, what might easily have been ruined through a lachrymose or stagy one. They took an adolescent girl's real-life chronicle of Jews hiding out in an Amsterdam garret and contrived vivid stage pictures of their huddled, muffled, strangely commingled existence. They portrayed it as a weird blend of the brightly ordinary and the hideously abnormal . . . of comic fault-finding and heroic adjustment."

In the New York production, impeccably staged for Kermit Bloomgarden by Garson Kanin, the collaborators' efforts received noteworthy support from Joseph Schildkraut's Otto Frank, Gusti Huber's Mrs. Frank, Eva Rubinstein's young Margot Frank (Anne's elder sister), and Susan Strasberg's immensely appealing Anne. Rising from little human realities to nobility in the Friday evening lighting-of-the-candles scene, and to controlled heroism in the next to the last scene when the elder Frank fetches the bags he has kept in readiness for the time when the Nazis would discover them, declaring, "For the past two years we have lived in fear. Now we can live in hope," the dramatization made a profound impression on audiences on both sides of the Atlantic, and perhaps nowhere more strongly than in postwar Germany itself.

It may be niggling to try to apportion credit to the play as distinct from the stage production, or as distinct from its appeal as an historical document. Creative imagination as well as craftmanship entered into the work, and there is no reason to treat a living document as a second-class citizen in the realm of art. As for the collaborators, the adaptation brought them to the ranks of our most successful playwrights, and it was of little consequence to the public to what degree they got to their destination on their own steam. In playwriting, success is usually determined by circumstance and luck as well as by intrinsic merit, and it does not matter to audiences whether or not the achievement is exclusively the playwright's.

The Diary of Anne Frank was indeed an event rather than ordinary play. The *Diary*, begun by Anne when she was thirteen and discovered in 1945 after its young author's death at the age of fifteen in the concentration camp, was published in 19 languages. The play founded on it, though with much independent creation and organization by the adapting team, was performed in more than twenty countries. It was seen by some two million playgoers in Germany alone. It opened simultaneously in seven German cities, and the awed silence of the audiences as they filed out of the theatres was a tribute to the compelling reality of the play as well as the humanity of the gifted girl whose unmarked remains lay buried in one of the mass graves of Bergen-Belsen, about eighty miles from Hamburg.

A Berlin reviewer described the effect of the Berlin premiere in one typically sesquipedalian German sentence that nevertheless reflects the awesome experience: "When, after three hours, as if awakening from deepest embarrassment, the people in the stalls can hardly rise from their seats, will not permit applause, and leave silently with bowed heads, that marks the greatness of a moment which must rouse the slowest hearts and which must shake the most indifferent nerves." (*New York Times*, October 14, 1956.)

The adapters, aware of the importance of their assignment, made as many as eight drafts of their dramatization. Garson Kanin staged the work with a sense of dignified dedication which was reflected in the memorable New York production that started the wave of productions throughout the rest of the world.

ACT ONE

Scene One

The scene remains the same throughout the play. It is the top floor of a warehouse and office building in Amsterdam, Holland. The sharply peaked roof of the building is outlined against a sea of other rooftops, stretching away into the distance. Nearby is the belfry of a church tower, the Westertoren, whose carillon rings out the hours. Occasionally faint sounds float up from below: the voices of children playing in the street, the tramp of marching feet, a boat whistle from the canal.

The three rooms of the top floor and a small attic space above are exposed to our view. The largest of the rooms is in the center, with two small rooms, slightly raised, on either side. On the right is a bathroom, out of sight. A narrow steep flight of stairs at the back leads up to the attic. The rooms are sparsely furnished with a few chairs, cots, a table or two. The windows are painted over, or covered with makeshift blackout curtains. In the main room there is a sink, a gas ring for cooking and a woodburning stove for warmth.

The room on the left is hardly more than a closet. There is a skylight in the sloping ceiling. Directly under this room is a small steep stairwell, with steps leading down to a door. This is the only entrance from the building below. When the door is opened we see that it has been concealed on the outer side by a bookcase attached to it.

The curtain rises on an empty stage. It is late afternoon November, 1945.

The rooms are dusty, the curtains in rags. Chairs and tables are overturned.

The door at the foot of the small stairwell swings open. MR. FRANK *comes up the steps into view. He is a gentle, cultured European in his middle years. There is still a trace of a German accent in his speech.*

He stands looking slowly around, making a supreme effort at self-control. He is weak, ill. His clothes are threadbare.

After a second he drops his rucksack on the couch and moves slowly about. He opens the door to one of the smaller rooms, and then abruptly closes it again, turning away. He goes to the window at the back, looking off at the Westertoren as its carillon strikes the hour of six, then he moves restlessly on.

From the street below we hear the sound of a barrel organ and children's voices at play. There is a many-colored scarf hanging from a

nail. MR. FRANK *takes it, putting it around his neck. As he starts back for his rucksack, his eye is caught by something lying on the floor. It is a woman's white glove. He holds it in his hand and suddenly all of his self-control is gone. He breaks down, crying.*

We hear footsteps on the stairs. MIEP GIES *comes up, looking for* MR. FRANK. MIEP *is a Dutch girl of about twenty-two. She wears a coat and hat, ready to go home. She is pregnant. Her attitude toward* MR. FRANK *is protective, compassionate.*

MIEP. Are you all right, Mr. Frank?

MR. FRANK (*quickly controlling himself*). Yes, Miep, yes.

MIEP. Everyone in the office has gone home ... It's after six. (*Then pleading.*) Don't stay up here, Mr. Frank. What's the use of torturing yourself like this?

MR. FRANK. I've come to say good-by ... I'm leaving here, Miep.

MIEP. What do you mean? Where are you going? Where?

MR. FRANK. I don't know yet. I haven't decided.

MIEP. Mr. Frank, you can't leave here! This is your home! Amsterdam is your home. Your business is here, waiting for you ... You're needed here ... Now that the war is over, there are things that ...

MR. FRANK. I can't stay in Amsterdam, Miep. It has too many memories for me. Everywhere there's something ... the house we lived in ... the school ... that street organ playing out there ... I'm not the person you used to know, Miep. I'm a bitter old man. (*Breaking off.*) Forgive me. I shouldn't speak to you like this ... after all that you did for us ... the suffering ...

MIEP. No. No. It wasn't suffering. You can't say we suffered. (*As she speaks, she straightens a chair which is overturned.*)

MR. FRANK. I know what you went through, you and Mr. Kraler. I'll remember it as long as I live. (*He gives one last look around.*) Come, Miep. (*He starts for the steps, then remembers his rucksack, going back to get it.*)

MIEP (*hurrying up to a cupboard*). Mr. Frank, did you see? There are some of your papers here. (*She brings a bundle of papers to him.*) We found them in a heap of rubbish on the floor after ... after you left.

MR. FRANK. Burn them. (*He opens his*

rucksack to put the glove in it.)

MIEP. But, Mr. Frank, there are letters, notes . . .

MR. FRANK. Burn them. All of them.

MIEP. Burn *this?* (*She hands him a paperbound notebook.*)

MR. FRANK (*quietly*). Anne's diary. (*He opens the diary and begins to read.*) "Monday, the sixth of July, nineteen forty-two." (*To* MIEP.) Nineteen forty-two. Is it possible, Miep? . . . Only three years ago. (*As he continues his reading, he sits down on the couch.*) "Dear Diary, since you and I are going to be great friends, I will start by telling you about myself. My name is Anne Frank. I am thirteen years old. I was born in Germany the twelfth of June, nineteen twenty-nine. As my family is Jewish, we emigrated to Holland when Hitler came to power."

(*As* MR. FRANK *reads on, another voice joins his, as if coming from the air. It is* ANNE'S VOICE.)

MR. FRANK AND ANNE. "My father started a business, importing spice and herbs. Things went well for us until nineteen forty. Then the war came, and the Dutch capitulation, followed by the arrival of the Germans. Then things got very bad for the Jews."

(MR. FRANK'S VOICE *dies out.* ANNE'S VOICE *continues alone. The lights dim slowly to darkness. The curtain falls on the scene.*)

ANNE'S VOICE. You could not do this and you could not do that. They forced Father out of his business. We had to wear yellow stars. I had to turn in my bike. I couldn't go to a Dutch school any more. I couldn't go to the movies, or ride in an automobile, or even on a streetcar, and a million other things. But somehow we children still managed to have fun. Yesterday Father told me we were going into hiding. Where, he wouldn't say. At five o'clock this morning Mother woke me and told me to hurry and get dressed. I was to put on as many clothes as I could. It would look too suspicious if we walked along carrying suitcases. It wasn't until we were on our way that I learned where we were going. Our hiding place was to be upstairs in the building where Father used to have his business. Three other people were coming in with us . . . the Van Daans and their son Peter . . . Father knew the Van Daans but we had never met them . . .

(*During the last lines the curtain rises on the scene. The lights dim on.* ANNE'S VOICE *fades out.*)

SCENE TWO

It is early morning, July, 1942. The rooms are bare, as before, but they are now clean and orderly.

MR. VAN DAAN, *a tall, portly man in his late forties, is in the main room, pacing up and down, nervously smoking a cigarette. His clothes and overcoat are expensive and well cut.*

MRS. VAN DAAN *sits on the couch, clutching her possessions, a hatbox, bags, etc. She is a pretty woman in her early forties. She wears a fur coat over her other clothes.*

PETER VAN DAAN *is standing at the window of the room on the right, looking down at the street below. He is a shy, awkward boy of sixteen. He wears a cap, a raincoat, and long Dutch trousers, like "plus fours." At his feet is a black case, a carrier for his cat.*

The yellow Star of David is conspicuous on all of their clothes.

———

MRS. VAN DAAN (*rising, nervous, excited*). Something's happened to them! I know it!

MR. VAN DAAN. Now, Kerli!

MRS. VAN DAAN. Mr. Frank said they'd be here at seven o'clock. He said . . .

MR. VAN DAAN. They have two miles to walk. You can't expect . . .

MRS. VAN DAAN. They've been picked up. That's what's happened. They've been taken . . .

(MR. VAN DAAN *indicates that he hears someone coming.*)

MR. VAN DAAN. You see?

(PETER *takes up his carrier and his schoolbag, etc., and goes into the main room as* MR. FRANK *comes up the stairwell from below.* MR. FRANK *looks much younger now. His movements are brisk, his manner confident. He wears an overcoat and carries his hat and a small cardboard box. He crosses to the* VAN DAANS, *shaking hands with each of them.*)

MR. FRANK. Mrs. Van Daan, Mr. Van Daan, Peter. (*Then, in explanation of their lateness.*) There were too many of the Green Police on the streets . . . we had to take the long way around.

(*Up the steps come* MARGOT FRANK, MRS. FRANK, MIEP (*not pregnant now*), *and* MR. KRALER. *All of them carry bags, packages,* and so forth. *The Star of David is conspicuous on all of the* FRANKS' *clothing.* MARGOT *is eighteen, beautiful, quiet, shy.* MRS. FRANK *is a young mother, gently bred, reserved. She, like* MR. FRANK, *has a slight German accent.* MR. KRALER *is a Dutchman, dependable, kindly.*

As MR. KRALER *and* MIEP *go upstage to put down their parcels,* MRS. FRANK *turns back to call* ANNE.)

MRS. FRANK. Anne?

(ANNE *comes running up the stairs. She is thirteen, quick in her movements, interested in everything, mercurial in her emotions. She wears a cape, long wool socks and carries a schoolbag.*)

MR. FRANK (*introducing them*). My wife, Edith. Mr. and Mrs. Van Daan (MRS. FRANK *hurries over, shaking hands with them.*) . . . their son, Peter . . . my daughters, Margot and Anne.

(ANNE *gives a polite little curtsy as she shakes* MR. VAN DAAN'S *hand. Then she immediately starts off on a tour of investigation of her new home, going upstairs to the attic room.*

MIEP *and* MR. KRALER *are putting the various things they have brought on the shelves.*)

MR. KRALER. I'm sorry there is still so much confusion.

MR. FRANK. Please. Don't think of it. After all, we'll have plenty of leisure to arrange everything ourselves.

MIEP (*to* MRS. FRANK). We put the stores of food you sent in here. Your drugs are here . . . soap, linen here.

MR. FRANK. Thank you, Miep.

MIEP. I made up the beds . . . the way Mr. Frank and Mr. Kraler said. (*She starts out.*) Forgive me. I have to hurry. I've got to go to the other side of town to get some ration books for you.

MRS. VAN DAAN. Ration books? If they see our names on ration books, they'll know we're here.

MR. KRALER. There isn't anything . . . ⎫
MIEP. Don't worry. Your   ⎬ (*Together.*)
names won't be on them.   ⎭
(*As she hurries out.*) I'll be up later.

MR. FRANK. Thank you, Miep.

MRS. FRANK (*to* MR. KRALER). It's illegal, then, the ration books? We've never done anything illegal.

MR. FRANK. We won't be living here exactly according to regulations.

(*As* MR. KRALER *reassures* MRS. FRANK, *he takes various small things, such as matches, soap, etc., from his pockets, handing them to her.*)

MR. KRALER. This isn't the black market, Mrs. Frank. This is what we call the white market . . . helping all of the hundreds and hundreds who are hiding out in Amsterdam.

(*The carillon is heard playing the quarter-hour before eight.* MR. KRALER *looks at his watch.* ANNE *stops at the window as she comes down the stairs.*)

ANNE. It's the Westertoren!

MR. KRALER. I must go. I must be out of here and downstairs in the office before the workmen get here. (*He starts for the stairs leading out.*) Miep or I, or both of us, will be up each day to bring you food and news and find out what your needs are. Tomorrow I'll get you a better bolt for the door at the foot of the stairs. It needs a bolt that you can throw yourself and open only at our signal. (*To* MR. FRANK.) Oh . . . You'll tell them about the noise?

MR. FRANK. I'll tell them.

MR. KRALER. Good-by then for the moment. I'll come up again, after the workmen leave.

MR. FRANK. Good-by, Mr. Kraler.

MRS. FRANK (*shaking his hand*). How can we thank you?

(*The others murmur their good-bys.*)

MR. KRALER. I never thought I'd live to see the day when a man like Mr. Frank would have to go into hiding. When you think—

(*He breaks off, going out.* MR. FRANK *follows him down the steps, bolting the door after him. In the interval before he returns,* PETER *goes over to* MARGOT, *shaking hands with her. As* MR. FRANK *comes back up the steps,* MRS. FRANK *questions him anxiously.*)

MRS. FRANK. What did he mean, about the noise?

MR. FRANK. First let us take off some of these clothes.

(*They all start to take off garment after garment. On each of their coats, sweaters, blouses, suits, dresses, is another yellow Star of David.* MR. *and* MRS. FRANK *are underdressed quite simply. The others wear several things, sweaters, extra dresses, bathrobes, aprons, nightgowns, etc.*)

MR. VAN DAAN. It's a wonder we weren't arrested, walking along the streets . . . Petronella with a fur coat in July . . . and that cat of Peter's crying all the way.

ANNE (*as she is removing a pair of panties*). A cat?

MRS. FRANK (*shocked*). Anne, please!

ANNE. It's all right. I've got on three more.

(*She pulls off two more. Finally, as they have all removed their surplus clothes, they look to* MR. FRANK, *waiting for him to speak.*)

MR. FRANK. Now. About the noise. While the men are in the building below, we must have complete quiet. Every sound can be heard down there, not only in the workrooms, but in the offices too. The men come at about eight-thirty, and leave at about five-thirty. So, to be perfectly safe, from eight in the morning until six in the evening we must move only when it is necessary, and then in stockinged feet. We must not speak above a whisper. We must not run any water. We cannot use the sink, or even, forgive me, the w.c. The pipes go down through the workrooms. It would be heard. No trash . . . (MR. FRANK *stops abruptly as he hears the sound of marching feet from the street below. Everyone is motionless, paralyzed with fear.* MR. FRANK *goes quietly into the room on the right to look down out of the window.* ANNE *runs after him, peering out with him. The tramping feet pass without stopping. The tension is relieved.* MR. FRANK, *followed by* ANNE, *returns to the main room and resumes his instructions to the group.*) . . . No trash must ever be thrown out which might reveal that someone is living up here . . . not even a potato paring. We must burn everything in the stove at night. This is the way we must live until it is over, if we are to survive.

(*There is silence for a second.*)

MRS. FRANK. Until it is over.

MR. FRANK (*reassuringly*). After six we can move about . . . we can talk and laugh and have our supper and read and play games . . . just as we would at home. (*He looks at his watch.*) And now I think it would be wise if we all went to our rooms, and were settled before eight o'clock. Mrs. Van Daan, you and your husband will be upstairs. I regret that there's no place up there for Peter. But he will be here, near us. This will be our common room, where we'll meet to talk and eat and read, like one family.

MR. VAN DAAN. And where do you and Mrs. Frank sleep?

MR. FRANK. This room is also our bed-room.

MRS. VAN DAAN. That isn't right. We'll sleep here and you take the room up-stairs. } (*Together.*)

MR. VAN DAAN. It's your place.

MR. FRANK. Please. I've thought this out for weeks. It's the best arrangement. The only arrangement.

MRS. VAN DAAN (*to* MR. FRANK). Never, never can we thank you. (*Then to* MRS. FRANK.) I don't know what would have happened to us, if it hadn't been for Mr. Frank.

MR. FRANK. You don't know how your husband helped me when I came to this country . . . knowing no one . . . not able to speak the language. I can never repay him for that. (*Going to* VAN DAAN.) May I help you with your things?

MR. VAN DAAN. No. No. (*To* MRS. VAN DAAN.) Come along, *liefje*.

MRS. VAN DAAN. You'll be all right, Peter? You're not afraid?

PETER (*embarrassed*). Please, Mother.

(*They start up the stairs to the attic room above.* MR. FRANK *turns to* MRS. FRANK.)

MR. FRANK. You too must have some rest, Edith. You didn't close your eyes last night. Nor you, Margot.

ANNE. I slept, Father. Wasn't that funny? I knew it was the last night in my own bed, and yet I slept soundly.

MR. FRANK. I'm glad, Anne. Now you'll be able to help me straighten things in here. (*To* MRS. FRANK *and* MAR-GOT.) Come with me . . . You and Margot rest in this room for the time being. (*He picks up their clothes, starting for the room on the right.*)

MRS. FRANK. You're sure . . . ? I could help . . . And Anne hasn't had her milk . . .

MR. FRANK. I'll give it to her. (*To* ANNE *and* PETER.) Anne, Peter . . . it's best that you take off your shoes now, before you forget. (*He leads the way to the room, followed by* MARGOT.)

MRS. FRANK. You're sure you're not tired, Anne?

ANNE. I feel fine. I'm going to help Father.

MRS. FRANK. Peter, I'm glad you are to be with us.

PETER. Yes, Mrs. Frank.

(MRS. FRANK *goes to join* MR. FRANK *and* MARGOT.)

(*During the following scene* MR. FRANK

helps MARGOT *and* MRS. FRANK *to hang up their clothes. Then he persuades them both to lie down and rest. The* VAN DAANS *in their room above settle themselves. In the main room* ANNE *and* PETER *remove their shoes.* PETER *takes his cat out of the carrier.*)

ANNE. What's your cat's name?

PETER. Mouschi.

ANNE. Mouschi! Mouschi! Mouschi! (*She picks up the cat, walking away with it. To* PETER.) I love cats. I have one . . . a darling little cat. But they made me leave her behind. I left some food and a note for the neighbors to take care of her . . . I'm going to miss her terribly. What is yours? A him or a her?

PETER. He's a tom. He doesn't like strangers. (*He takes the cat from her, putting it back in its carrier.*)

ANNE (*unabashed*). Then I'll have to stop being a stranger, won't I? Is he fixed?

PETER (*startled*). Huh?

ANNE. Did you have him fixed?

PETER. No.

ANNE. Oh, you ought to have him fixed—to keep him from—you know, fighting. Where did you go to school?

PETER. Jewish Secondary.

ANNE. But that's where Margot and I go! I never saw you around.

PETER. I used to see you . . . sometimes . . .

ANNE. You did?

PETER. . . . in the school yard. You were always in the middle of a bunch of kids. (*He takes a penknife from his pocket.*)

ANNE. Why didn't you ever come over?

PETER. I'm sort of a lone wolf. (*He starts to rip off his Star of David.*)

ANNE. What are you doing?

PETER. Taking it off.

ANNE. But you can't do that. They'll arrest you if you go out without your star.

(*He tosses his knife on the table.*)

PETER. Who's going out?

ANNE. Why, of course! You're right! Of course we don't need them any more. (*She picks up his knife and starts to take her star off.*) I wonder what our friends will think when we don't show up today?

PETER. I didn't have any dates with anyone.

ANNE. Oh, I did. I had a date with Jopie to go and play ping-pong at her house. Do you know Jopie deWaal?

PETER. No.

ANNE. Jopie's my best friend. I wonder what she'll think when she telephones and there's no answer? . . . Probably she'll go over to the house . . . I wonder what she'll think . . . we left everything as if we'd suddenly been called away . . . breakfast dishes in the sink . . . beds not made . . . (*As she pulls off her star the cloth underneath shows clearly the color and form of the star.*) Look! It's still there! (PETER *goes over to the stove with his star.*) What're you going to do with yours?

PETER. Burn it.

ANNE (*she starts to throw hers in, and cannot*). It's funny, I can't throw mine away. I don't know why.

PETER. You can't throw . . . ? Something they branded you with . . . ? That they made you swear so they could spit on you?

ANNE. I know. I know. But after all, it *is* the Star of David, isn't it?

(*In the bedroom, right,* MARGOT *and* MRS. FRANK *are lying down.* MR. FRANK *starts quietly out.*)

PETER. Maybe it's different for a girl.

(MR. FRANK *comes into the main room.*)

MR. FRANK. Forgive me, Peter. Now let me see. We must find a bed for your cat. (*He goes to a cupboard.*) I'm glad you brought your cat. Anne was feeling so badly about hers. (*Getting a used small washtub.*) Here we are. Will it be comfortable in that?

PETER (*Gathering up his things*). Thanks.

MR. FRANK (*opening the door of the room on the left*). And here is your room. But I warn you, Peter, you can't grow any more. Not an inch, or you'll have to sleep with your feet out of the skylight. Are you hungry?

PETER. No.

MR. FRANK. We have some bread and butter.

PETER. No, thank you.

MR. FRANK. You can have it for luncheon then. And tonight we will have a real supper . . . our first supper together.

PETER. Thanks. Thanks.

(*He goes into his room. During the following scene he arranges his possessions in his new room.*)

MR. FRANK. That's a nice boy, Peter.

ANNE. He's awfully shy, isn't he?

MR. FRANK. You'll like him, I know.

ANNE. I certainly hope so, since he's the only boy I'm likely to see for months and months.

(MR. FRANK *sits down, taking off his shoes.*)

MR. FRANK. Annele, there's a box there. Will you open it?

(*He indicates a carton on the couch.* ANNE *brings it to the center table. In the street below there is the sound of children playing.*)

ANNE (*as she opens the carton*). You know the way I'm going to think of it here? I'm going to think of it as a boarding house. A very peculiar summer boarding house, like the one that we—(*She breaks off as she pulls out some photographs.*) Father! My movie stars! I was wondering where they were! I was looking for them this morning . . . and Queen Wilhelmina! How wonderful!

MR. FRANK. There's something more. Go on. Look further.

(*He goes over to the sink, pouring a glass of milk from a thermos bottle.*)

ANNE (*pulling out a pasteboard-bound book*). A diary! (*She throws her arms around her father.*) I've never had a diary. And I've always longed for one. (*She looks around the room.*) Pencil, pencil, pencil. (*She starts down the stairs.*) I'm going down to the office to get a pencil.

MR. FRANK. Anne! No!

(*He goes after her, catching her by the arm and pulling her back.*)

ANNE (*startled*). But there's no one in the building now.

MR. FRANK. It doesn't matter. I don't want you ever to go beyond that door.

ANNE (*sobered*). Never . . . ? Not even at nighttime, when everyone is gone? Or on Sundays? Can't I go down to listen to the radio?

MR. FRANK. Never. I am sorry, Anneke. It isn't safe. No, you must never go beyond that door.

(*For the first time* ANNE *realizes what "going into hiding" means.*)

ANNE. I see.

MR. FRANK. It'll be hard, I know. But always remember this, Anneke. There are no walls, there are no bolts, no locks that anyone can put on your mind. Miep will bring us books. We will read history, poetry, mythology. (*He gives her the glass of milk.*) Here's your milk. (*With his arm about her, they go over to the couch, sitting down side by side.*) As a matter of fact, between

us, Anne, being here has certain advantages for you. For instance, you remember the battle you had with your mother the other day on the subject of overshoes? You said you'd rather die than wear overshoes? But in the end you had to wear them? Well now, you see, for as long as we are here you will never have to wear overshoes! Isn't that good? And the coat that you inherited from Margot, you won't have to wear that any more. And the piano! You won't have to practice on the piano. I tell you, this is going to be a fine life for you!

ANNE'S *panic is gone.* PETER *appears in the doorway of his room, with a saucer in his hand. He is carrying his cat.*)

PETER. I . . . I . . . I thought I'd better get some water for Mouschi before . . .

MR. FRANK. Of course.

(*As he starts toward the sink the carillon begins to chime the hour of eight. He tiptoes to the window at the back and looks down at the street below. He turns to* PETER, *indicating in pantomime that it is too late.* PETER *starts back for his room. He steps on a creaking board. The three of them are frozen for a minute in fear. As* PETER *starts away again,* ANNE *tiptoes over to him and pours some of the milk from her glass into the saucer for the cat.* PETER *squats on the floor, putting the milk before the cat.* MR. FRANK *gives* ANNE *his fountain pen, and then goes into the room at the right. For a second* ANNE *watches the cat, then she goes over to the center table, and opens her diary.*

In the room at the right, MRS. FRANK *has sat up quickly at the sound of the carillon.* MR. FRANK *comes in and sits down beside her on the settee, his arm comfortingly around her.*

Upstairs, in the attic room, MR. *and* MRS. VAN DAAN *have hung their clothes in the closet and are now seated on the iron bed.* MRS. VAN DAAN *leans back exhausted.* MR. VAN DAAN *fans her with a newspaper.*

ANNE *starts to write in her diary. The lights dim out, the curtain falls.*

In the darkness ANNE'S VOICE *comes to us again, faintly at first, and then with growing strength.*)

ANNE'S VOICE. I expect I should be describing what it feels like to go into hiding. But I really don't know yet myself. I only know it's funny never to be able to go outdoors . . . never to breathe fresh air . . . never to run and shout and jump. It's the silence in the nights that frightens me most. Every time I hear a creak in the house, or a step on the street outside, I'm sure they're coming for us. The days aren't so bad. At least we know that Miep and Mr. Kraler are down there below us in the office. Our protectors, we call them. I asked Father what would happen to them if the Nazis found out they were hiding us. Pim said that they would suffer the same fate that we would . . . Imagine! They know this, and yet when they come up here, they're always cheerful and gay as if there were nothing in the world to bother them . . . Friday, the twenty-first of August, nineteen forty-two. Today I'm going to tell you our general news. Mother is unbearable. She insists on treating me like a baby, which I loathe. Otherwise things are going better. The weather is . . .

(*As* ANNE'S VOICE *is fading out, the curtain rises on the scene.*)

SCENE THREE

It is a little after six o'clock in the evening, two months later.

MARGOT *is in the bedroom at the right, studying.* MR. VAN DAAN *is lying down in the attic room above.*

The rest of the "family" is in the main room. ANNE *and* PETER *sit opposite each other at the center table, where they have been doing their lessons.* MRS. FRANK *is on the couch.* MRS. VAN DAAN *is seated with her fur coat, on which she has been sewing, in her lap. None of them are wearing their shoes.*

Their eyes are on MR. FRANK, *waiting for him to give them the signal which will release them from their day-long quiet.* MR. FRANK, *his shoes in his hand, stands looking down out of the window at the back, watching to be sure that all of the workmen have left the building below.*

After a few seconds of motionless silence, MR. FRANK *turns from the window.*

MR. FRANK (*quietly, to the group*). It's safe now. The last workman has left.

(*There is an immediate stir of relief.*)

ANNE (*her pent-up energy explodes*). WHEE!

MRS. FRANK (*startled, amused*). Anne!

MRS. VAN DAAN. I'm first for the w.c.

(*She hurries off to the bathroom.* MRS. FRANK *puts on her shoes and starts up to the sink to prepare supper.* ANNE *sneaks* PETER'S *shoes from under the table and hides them behind her back.* MR. FRANK *goes in to* MARGOT'S *room.*)

MR. FRANK (*to* MARGOT). Six o'clock. School's over.

(MARGOT *gets up, stretching.* MR. FRANK *sits down to put on his shoes. In the main room* PETER *tries to find his.*)

PETER (*to* ANNE). Have you seen my shoes?

ANNE (*innocently*). Your shoes?

PETER. You've taken them, haven't you?

ANNE. I don't know what you're talking about.

PETER. You're going to be sorry!

ANNE. Am I?

(PETER *goes after her.* ANNE, *with his shoes in her hand, runs from him, dodging behind her mother.*)

MRS. FRANK (*protesting*). Anne, dear!

PETER. Wait till I get you!

ANNE. I'm waiting! (PETER *makes a lunge for her. They both fall to the floor.* PETER *pins her down, wrestling with her to get the shoes.*) Don't! Don't! Peter, stop it. Ouch!

MRS. FRANK. Anne! . . . Peter!

(*Suddenly* PETER *becomes self-conscious. He grabs his shoes roughly and starts for his room.*)

ANNE (*following him*). Peter, where are you going? Come dance with me.

PETER. I tell you I don't know how.

ANNE. I'll teach you.

PETER. I'm going to give Mouschi his dinner.

ANNE. Can I watch?

PETER. He doesn't like people around while he eats.

ANNE. Peter, please.

PETER. No!

(*He goes into his room.* ANNE *slams his door after him.*)

MRS. FRANK. Anne, dear, I think you shouldn't play like that with Peter. It's not dignified.

ANNE. Who cares if it's dignified? I don't want to be dignified.

(MR. FRANK *and* MARGOT *come from the room on the right.* MARGOT *goes to help her mother.* MR. FRANK *starts for the center table to correct* MARGOT'S *school papers.*)

MRS. FRANK (*to* ANNE). You complain that I don't treat you like a grownup. But when I do, you resent it.

ANNE. I only want some fun . . . someone to laugh and clown with . . . After you've sat still all day and hardly moved, you've got to have some fun. I don't know what's the matter with that boy.

MR. FRANK. He isn't used to girls. Give him a little time.

ANNE. Time? Isn't two months time? I could cry. (*Catching hold of* MARGOT.) Come on, Margot . . . dance with me. Come on, please.

MARGOT. I have to help with supper.

ANNE. You know we're going to forget how to dance . . . When we get out we won't remember a thing.

(*She starts to sing and dance by herself.* MR. FRANK *takes her in his arms, waltzing with her.* MRS. VAN DAAN *comes in from the bathroom.*)

MRS. VAN DAAN. Next? (*She looks around as she starts putting on her shoes.*) Where's Peter?

ANNE (*as they are dancing*). Where would he be!

MRS. VAN DAAN. He hasn't finished his lessons, has he? His father'll kill him if he catches him in there with that cat and his work not done. (MR. FRANK *and* ANNE *finish their dance. They bow to each other with extravagant formality.*) Anne, get him out of there, will you?

ANNE (*at* PETER's *door*). Peter? Peter?

PETER (*opening the door a crack*). What is it?

ANNE. Your mother says to come out.

PETER. I'm giving Mouschi his dinner.

MRS. VAN DAAN. You know what your father says.

(*She sits on the couch, sewing on the lining of her fur coat.*)

PETER. For heaven's sake, I haven't even looked at him since lunch.

MRS. VAN DAAN. I'm just telling you, that's all.

ANNE. I'll feed him.

PETER. I don't want you in there.

MRS. VAN DAAN. Peter!

PETER (*to* ANNE). Then give him his dinner and come right out, you hear?

(*He comes back to the table.* ANNE *shuts the door of* PETER's *room after her and disappears behind the curtain covering his closet.*)

MRS. VAN DAAN (*to* PETER). Now is that any way to talk to your little girl friend?

PETER. Mother . . . for heaven's sake . . . will you please stop saying that?

MRS. VAN DAAN. Look at him blush! Look at him!

PETER. Please! I'm not . . . anyway . . . let me alone, will you?

MRS. VAN DAAN. He acts like it was something to be ashamed of. It's nothing to be ashamed of, to have a little girl friend.

PETER. You're crazy. She's only thirteen.

MRS. VAN DAAN. So what? And you're sixteen. Just perfect. Your father's ten years older than I am. (*To* MR. FRANK.) I warn you, Mr. Frank, if this war lasts much longer, we're going to be related and then . . .

MR. FRANK. *Mazeltov!*

MRS. FRANK (*deliberately changing the conversation*). I wonder where Miep is. She's usually so prompt.

(*Suddenly everything else is forgotten as they hear the sound of an automobile coming to a screeching stop in the street below. They are tense, motionless in their terror. The car starts away. A wave of relief sweeps over them. They pick up their occupations again.* ANNE *flings open the door of* PETER's *room, making a dramatic entrance. She is dressed in* PETER's *clothes.* PETER *looks at her in fury. The others are amused.*)

ANNE. Good evening, everyone. Forgive me if I don't stay. (*She jumps up on a chair.*) I have a friend waiting for me in there. My friend Tom. Tom Cat. Some people say that we look alike. But Tom has the most beautiful whiskers, and I have only a little fuzz. I am hoping . . . in time . . .

PETER. All right, Mrs. Quack Quack!

ANNE (*outraged—jumping down*). Peter!

PETER. I heard about you . . . How you talked so much in class they called you Mrs. Quack Quack. How Mr. Smitter made you write a composition . . . " 'Quack, quack,' said Mrs. Quack Quack."

ANNE. Well, go on. Tell them the rest. How it was so good he read it out loud to the class and then read it to all his other classes!

PETER. Quack! Quack! Quack . . . Quack . . . Quack . . .

(ANNE *pulls off the coat and trousers.*)

ANNE. You are the most intolerable, insufferable boy I've ever met!

(*She throws the clothes down the stairwell.* PETER *goes down after them.*)

PETER. Quack, quack, quack!

MRS. VAN DAAN (*to* ANNE). That's right, Anneke! Give it to him!

ANNE. With all the boys in the world ... Why I had to get locked up with one like you! ...

PETER. Quack, quack, quack, and from now on stay out of my room!

(*As* PETER *passes her,* ANNE *puts out her foot, tripping him. He picks himself up, and goes on into his room.*)

MRS. FRANK (*quietly*). Anne, dear ... your hair. (*She feels* ANNE'S *forehead.*) You're warm. Are you feeling all right?

ANNE. Please, Mother.

(*She goes over to the center table, slipping into her shoes.*)

MRS. FRANK (*following her*). You haven't a fever, have you?

ANNE (*pulling away*). No. No.

MRS. FRANK. You know we can't call a doctor here, ever. There's only one thing to do ... watch carefully. Prevent an illness before it comes. Let me see your tongue.

ANNE. Mother, this is perfectly absurd.

MRS. FRANK. Anne, dear, don't be such a baby. Let me see your tongue. (*As* ANNE *refuses,* MRS. FRANK *appeals to* MR. FRANK.) Otto ... ?

MR. FRANK. You hear your mother, Anne.

(ANNE *flicks out her tongue for a second, then turns away.*)

MRS. FRANK. Come on—open up! (*As* ANNE *opens her mouth very wide.*) You seem all right ... but perhaps an aspirin ...

MRS. VAN DAAN. For heaven's sake, don't give that child any pills. I waited for fifteen minutes this morning for her to come out of the w.c.

ANNE. I was washing my hair!

MR. FRANK. I think there's nothing the matter with our Anne that a ride on her bike, or a visit with her friend Jopie deWaal wouldn't cure. Isn't that so, Anne?

(MR. VAN DAAN *comes down into the room. From outside we hear faint sounds of bombers going over and a burst of ack-ack.*)

MR. VAN DAAN. Miep not come yet?

MRS. VAN DAAN. The workmen just left, a little while ago.

MR. VAN DAAN. What's for dinner to-night?

MRS. VAN DAAN. Beans.

MR. VAN DAAN. Not again!

MRS. VAN DAAN. Poor Putti! I know. But what can we do? That's all that Miep brought us.

(MR. VAN DAAN *starts to pace, his hands behind his back.* ANNE *follows behind him, imitating him.*)

ANNE. We are now in what is known as the "bean cycle." Beans boiled, beans en casserole, beans with strings, beans without strings ...

(PETER *has come out of his room. He slides into his place at the table, becoming immediately absorbed in his studies.*)

MR. VAN DAAN (*to* PETER). I saw you ... in there, playing with your cat.

MRS. VAN DAAN. He just went in for a second, putting his coat away. He's been out here all the time, doing his lessons.

MR. FRANK (*looking up from the paper*). Anne, you got an excellent in your history paper today ... and very good in Latin.

ANNE (*sitting beside him*). How about algebra?

MR. FRANK. I'll have to make a confession. Up until now I've managed to stay ahead of you in algebra. Today you caught up with me. We'll leave it to Margot to correct.

ANNE. Isn't algebra *vile*, Pim!

MR. FRANK. Vile!

MARGOT (*to* MR. FRANK). How did I do?

ANNE (*getting up*). Excellent, excellent, excellent, excellent!

MR. FRANK (*to* MARGOT). You should have used the subjunctive here ...

MARGOT. Should I? ... I thought ... look here ... I didn't use it here ...

(*The two become absorbed in the papers.*)

ANNE. Mrs. Van Daan, may I try on your coat?

MRS. FRANK. No, Anne.

MRS. VAN DAAN (*giving it to* ANNE). It's all right ... but careful with it. (ANNE *puts it on and struts with it.*) My father gave me that the year before he died. He always bought the best that money could buy.

ANNE. Mrs. Van Daan, did you have a lot of boy friends before you were married?

MRS. FRANK. Anne, that's a personal question. It's not courteous to ask personal questions.

MRS. VAN DAAN. Oh I don't mind. (*To* ANNE.) Our house was always swarming with boys. When I was a girl we had ...

MR. VAN DAAN. Oh, God. Not again!

MRS. VAN DAAN (*good-humored*). Shut up! (*Without a pause, to* ANNE. MR. VAN DAAN *mimics* MRS. VAN DAAN, *speaking the first few words in unison with her.*) One summer we had a big house in Hilversum. The boys came buzzing round like bees around a jam pot. And when I was sixteen! . . . We were wearing our skirts very short those days and I had good-looking legs. (*She pulls up her skirt, going to* MR. FRANK.) I still have 'em. I may not be as pretty as I used to be, but I still have my legs. How about it, Mr. Frank?

MR. VAN DAAN. All right. All right. We see them.

MRS. VAN DAAN. I'm not asking you. I'm asking Mr. Frank.

PETER. Mother, for heaven's sake.

MRS. VAN DAAN. Oh, I embarrass you, do I? Well, I just hope the girl you marry has as good. (*Then to* ANNE.) My father used to worry about me, with so many boys hanging round. He told me, if any of them gets fresh, you say to him . . . "Remember, Mr. So-and-So, remember I'm a lady."

ANNE. "Remember, Mr. So-and-So, remember I'm a lady."

(*She gives* MRS. VAN DAAN *her coat.*)

MR. VAN DAAN. Look at you, talking that way in front of her! Don't you know she puts it all down in that diary?

MRS. VAN DAAN. So, if she does? I'm only telling the truth!

(ANNE *stretches out, putting her ear to the floor, listening to what is going on below. The sound of the bombers fades away.*)

MRS. FRANK (*setting the table*). Would you mind, Peter, if I moved you over to the couch?

ANNE (*listening*). Miep must have the radio on.

(PETER *picks up his papers, going over to the couch beside* MRS. VAN DAAN.)

MR. VAN DAAN (*accusingly, to* PETER). Haven't you finished yet?

PETER. No.

MR. VAN DAAN. You ought to be ashamed of yourself.

PETER. All right. All right. I'm a dunce. I'm a hopeless case. Why do I go on?

MRS. VAN DAAN. You're not hopeless. Don't talk that way. It's just that you haven't anyone to help you, like the girls have. (*To* MR. FRANK.) Maybe you could help him, Mr. Frank?

MR. FRANK. I'm sure that his father . . . ?

MR. VAN DAAN. Not me. I can't do anything with him. He won't listen to me. You go ahead . . . if you want.

MR. FRANK (*going to* PETER). What about it, Peter? Shall we make our school coeducational?

MRS. VAN DAAN (*kissing* MR. FRANK). You're an angel, Mr. Frank. An angel. I don't know why I didn't meet you before I met that one there. Here, sit down, Mr. Frank . . . (*She forces him down on the couch beside* PETER.) Now, Peter, you listen to Mr. Frank.

MR. FRANK. It might be better for us to go into Peter's room.

(PETER *jumps up eagerly, leading the way.*)

MRS. VAN DAAN. That's right. You go in there, Peter. You listen to Mr. Frank. Mr. Frank is a highly educated man.

(*As* MR. FRANK *is about to follow* PETER *into his room,* MRS. FRANK *stops him and wipes the lipstick from his lips. Then she closes the door after them.*)

ANNE (*on the floor, listening*). Shh! I can hear a man's voice talking.

MR. VAN DAAN (*to* ANNE). Isn't it bad enough here without your sprawling all over the place?

(ANNE *sits up.*)

MRS. VAN DAAN (*to* MR. VAN DAAN). If you didn't smoke so much, you wouldn't be so bad-tempered.

MR. VAN DAAN. Am I smoking? Do you see me smoking?

MRS. VAN DAAN. Don't tell me you've used up all those cigarettes.

MR. VAN DAAN. One package. Miep only brought me one package.

MRS. VAN DAAN. It's a filthy habit anyway. It's a good time to break yourself.

MR. VAN DAAN. Oh, stop it, please.

MRS. VAN DAAN. You're smoking up all our money. You know that, don't you?

MR. VAN DAAN. Will you shut up? (*During this,* MRS. FRANK *and* MARGOT *have studiously kept their eyes down. But* ANNE, *seated on the floor, has been following the discussion interestedly.* MR. VAN DAAN *turns to see her staring up at him.*) And what are you staring at?

ANNE. I never heard grownups quarrel before. I thought only children quarreled.

MR. VAN DAAN. This isn't a quarrel! It's a discussion. And I never heard children so rude before.

ANNE (*rising, indignantly*). *I,* rude!

MR. VAN DAAN. Yes!

MRS. FRANK (*quickly*). Anne, will you get me my knitting? (ANNE *goes to get it.*) I must remember, when Miep comes, to ask her to bring me some more wool.

MARGOT (*going to her room*). I need some hairpins and some soap. I made a list.

(*She goes into her bedroom to get the list.*)

MRS. FRANK (*to* ANNE). Have you some library books for Miep when she comes?

ANNE. It's a wonder that Miep has a life of her own, the way we make her run errands for us. Please, Miep, get me some starch. Please take my hair out and have it cut. Tell me all the latest news, Miep. (*She goes over, kneeling on the couch beside* MRS. VAN DAAN.) Did you know she was engaged? His name is Dirk, and Miep's afraid the Nazis will ship him off to Germany to work in one of their war plants. That's what they're doing with some of the young Dutchmen . . . they pick them up off the streets—

MR. VAN DAAN (*interrupting*). Don't you ever get tired of talking? Suppose you try keeping still for five minutes. Just five minutes.

(*He starts to pace again. Again* ANNE *follows him, mimicking him.* MRS. FRANK *jumps up and takes her by the arm up to the sink, and gives her a glass of milk.*)

MRS. FRANK. Come here, Anne. It's time for your glass of milk.

MR. VAN DAAN. Talk, talk, talk. I never heard such a child. Where is my . . . ? Every evening it's the same, talk, talk, talk. (*He looks around.*) Where is my . . . ?

MRS. VAN DAAN. What're you looking for?

MR. VAN DAAN. My pipe. Have you seen my pipe?

MRS. VAN DAAN. What good's a pipe? You haven't got any tobacco.

MR. VAN DAAN. At least I'll have something to hold in my mouth! (*Opening* MARGOT's *bedroom door.*) Margot, have you seen my pipe?

MARGOT. It was on the table last night.

(ANNE *puts her glass of milk on the table and picks up his pipe, hiding it behind her back.*)

MR. VAN DAAN. I know. I know. Anne, did you see my pipe? . . . Anne!

MRS. FRANK. Anne, Mr. Van Daan is speaking to you.

ANNE. Am I allowed to talk now?

MR. VAN DAAN. You're the most aggravating . . . The trouble with you is, you've been spoiled. What you need is a good old-fashioned spanking.

ANNE (*mimicking* MRS. VAN DAAN). "Remember, Mr. So-and-So, remember I'm a lady."

(*She thrusts the pipe into his mouth, then picks up her glass of milk.*)

MR. VAN DAAN (*restraining himself with difficulty*). Why aren't you nice and quiet like your sister Margot? Why do you have to show off all the time? Let me give you a little advice, young lady. Men don't like that kind of thing in a girl. You know that? A man likes a girl who'll listen to him once in a while . . . a domestic girl, who'll keep her house shining for her husband . . . who loves to cook and sew and . . .

ANNE. I'd cut my throat first! I'd open my veins! I'm going to be remarkable! I'm going to Paris . . .

MR. VAN DAAN (*scoffingly*). Paris!

ANNE. . . . to study music and art.

MR. VAN DAAN. Yeah! Yeah!

ANNE. I'm going to be a famous dancer or singer . . . or something wonderful.

(*She makes a wide gesture, spilling the glass of milk on the fur coat in* MRS. VAN DAAN's *lap.* MARGOT *rushes quickly over with a towel.* ANNE *tries to brush the milk off with her skirt.*)

MRS. VAN DAAN. Now look what you've done . . . you clumsy little fool! My beautiful fur coat my father gave me . . .

ANNE. I'm so sorry.

MRS. VAN DAAN. What do you care? It isn't yours . . . So go on, ruin it! Do you know what that coat cost? Do you? And now look at it! Look at it!

ANNE. I'm very, very sorry.

MRS. VAN DAAN. I could kill you for this. I could just kill you!

(MRS. VAN DAAN *goes up the stairs, clutching the coat.* MR. VAN DAAN *starts after her.*)

MR. VAN DAAN. Petronella . . . *liefje!* *Liefje!* . . . Come back . . . the supper . . . come back!

MRS. FRANK. Anne, you must not behave in that way.

ANNE. It was an accident. Anyone can have an accident.

MRS. FRANK. I don't mean that. I mean the answering back. You must not answer back. They are our guests. We must always show the greatest courtesy to them. We're all living under terrible tension. (*She stops as* MARGOT *indicates that* VAN DAAN *can hear. When he is gone, she continues.*) That's why we must control ourselves . . . You don't hear Margot getting into arguments with them, do you? Watch Margot. She's always courteous with them. Never familiar. She keeps her distance. And they respect her for it. Try to be like Margot.

ANNE. And have them walk all over me, the way they do her? No, thanks!

MRS. FRANK. I'm not afraid that anyone is going to walk all over you, Anne. I'm afraid for other people, that you'll walk on them. I don't know what happens to you, Anne. You are wild, self-willed. If I had ever talked to my mother as you talk to me . . .

ANNE. Things have changed. People aren't like that any more. "Yes, Mother." "No, Mother." "Anything you say, Mother." I've got to fight things out for myself! Make something of myself!

MRS. FRANK. It isn't necessary to fight to do it. Margot doesn't fight, and isn't she . . . ?

ANNE (violently rebellious). Margot! Margot! Margot! That's all I hear from everyone . . . how wonderful Margot is . . . "Why aren't you like Margot?"

MARGOT (protesting). Oh, come on, Anne, don't be so . . .

ANNE (paying no attention). Everything she does is right, and everything I do is wrong! I'm the goat around here! . . . You're all against me! . . . And you worst of all!

(She rushes off into her room and throws herself down on the settee, stifling her sobs. MRS. FRANK sighs and starts toward the stove.)

MRS. FRANK (to MARGOT). Let's put the soup on the stove . . . if there's anyone who cares to eat. Margot, will you take the bread out? (MARGOT gets the bread from the cupboard.) I don't know how we can go on living this way . . . I can't say a word to Anne . . . she flies at me . . .

MARGOT. You know Anne. In half an hour she'll be out here, laughing and joking.

MRS. FRANK. And . . . (She makes a motion upwards, indicating the VAN DAANS.) . . . I told your father it wouldn't work . . but no . . . no . . . he had to ask them, he said . . . he owed it to him, he said. Well, he knows now that I was right! These quarrels! . . . This bickering!

MARGOT (with a warning look). Shush. Shush.

(The buzzer for the door sounds. MRS. FRANK gasps, startled.)

MRS. FRANK. Every time I hear that sound, my heart stops!

MARGOT (starting for PETER'S door). It's Miep. (She knocks at the door.) Father?

(MR. FRANK comes quickly from PETER'S room.)

MR. FRANK. Thank you, Margot. (As he goes down the steps to open the outer door.) Has everyone his list?

MARGOT. I'll get my books. (Giving her mother a list.) Here's your list. (MARGOT goes into her and ANNE's bedroom on the right. ANNE sits up, hiding her tears, as MARGOT comes in.) Miep's here.

(MARGOT picks up her books and goes back. ANNE hurries over to the mirror, smoothing her hair.)

MR. VAN DAAN (coming down the stairs). Is it Miep?

MARGOT. Yes. Father's gone down to let her in.

MR. VAN DAAN. At last I'll have some cigarettes!

MRS. FRANK (to MR. VAN DAAN.) I can't tell you how unhappy I am about Mrs. Van Daan's coat. Anne should never have touched it.

MR. VAN DAAN. She'll be all right.

MRS. FRANK. Is there anything I can do?

MR. VAN DAAN. Don't worry.

(He turns to meet MIEP. But it is not MIEP who comes up the steps. It is MR. KRALER, followed by MR. FRANK. Their faces are grave. ANNE comes from the bedroom. PETER comes from his room.)

MRS. FRANK. Mr. Kraler!

MR. VAN DAAN. How are you, Mr. Kraler?

MARGOT. This is a surprise.

MRS. FRANK. When Mr. Kraler comes, the sun begins to shine.

MR. VAN DAAN. Miep is coming?

MR. KRALER. Not tonight.

(KRALER goes to MARGOT and MRS. FRANK and ANNE, shaking hands with them.)

MRS. FRANK. Wouldn't you like a cup of coffee? . . . Or, better still, will you have supper with us?

MR. FRANK. Mr. Kraler has something to talk over with us. Something has happened, he says, which demands an immediate decision.

MRS. FRANK (fearful). What is it?

(MR. KRALER sits down on the couch. As he talks he takes bread, cabbages, milk, etc., from his briefcase, giving them to MARGOT and ANNE to put away.)

MR. KRALER. Usually, when I come up here, I try to bring you some bit of good news. What's the use of telling you the bad news when there's nothing that you can do about it? But today something has happened . . . Dirk . . . Miep's Dirk, you know, came to me just now. He tells me that he has a Jewish friend living near him. A dentist. He says he's in trouble. He begged me, could I do anything for this man? Could I find him a hiding place? . . . So I've come to you . . . I know it's a terrible thing to ask of you, living as you are, but would you take him in with you?

MR. FRANK. Of course we will.

MR. KRALER (rising). It'll be just for a night or two . . . until I find some other place. This happened so suddenly that I didn't know where to turn.

MR. FRANK. Where is he?

MR. KRALER. Downstairs in the office.

MR. FRANK. Good. Bring him up.

MR. KRALER. His name is Dussel . . . Jan Dussel.

MR. FRANK. Dussel . . . I think I know him.

MR. KRALER. I'll get him.

(He goes quickly down the steps and out. MR. FRANK suddenly becomes conscious of the others.)

MR. FRANK. Forgive me. I spoke without consulting you. But I knew you'd feel as I do.

MR. VAN DAAN. There's no reason for you to consult anyone. This is your place. You have a right to do exactly as you please. The only thing I feel . . . there's so little food as it is . . . and to take in another person . . .

(PETER turns away, ashamed of his father.)

MR. FRANK. We can stretch the food a little. It's only for a few days.

MR. VAN DAAN. You want to make a bet?

MRS. FRANK. I think it's fine to have him. But, Otto, where are you going to put him? Where?

PETER. He can have my bed. I can sleep on the floor. I wouldn't mind.

MR. FRANK. That's good of you, Peter. But your room's too small . . . even for you.

ANNE. I have a much better idea. I'll come in here with you and Mother, and Margot can take Peter's room and Peter can go in our room with Mr. Dussel.

MARGOT. That's right. We could do that.

MR. FRANK. No, Margot. You mustn't sleep in that room . . . neither you nor Anne. Mouschi has caught some rats in there. Peter's brave. He doesn't mind.

ANNE. Then how about this? I'll come in here with you and Mother, and Mr. Dussel can have my bed.

MRS. FRANK. No. No. No! Margot will come in here with us and he can have her bed. It's the only way. Margot, bring your things in here. Help her, Anne.

(MARGOT hurries into her room to get her things.)

ANNE (to her mother). Why Margot? Why can't I come in here?

MRS. FRANK. Because it wouldn't be proper for Margot to sleep with a . . . Please, Anne. Don't argue. Please.

(ANNE starts slowly away.)

MR. FRANK (to ANNE). You don't mind sharing your room with Mr. Dussel, do you, Anne?

ANNE. No. No, of course not.

MR. FRANK. Good. (ANNE goes off into her bedroom, helping MARGOT. MR. FRANK starts to search in the cupboards.) Where's the cognac?

MRS. FRANK. It's there. But, Otto, I was saving it in case of illness.

MR. FRANK. I think we couldn't find a better time to use it. Peter, will you get five glasses for me?

(PETER goes for the glasses. MARGOT comes out of her bedroom, carrying her possessions, which she hangs behind a curtain in the main room. MR. FRANK finds the cognac and pours it into the five glasses that PETER brings him. MR. VAN DAAN stands looking on sourly. MRS. VAN DAAN comes downstairs and looks around at all the bustle.)

MRS. VAN DAAN. What's happening? What's going on?

MR. VAN DAAN. Someone's moving in with us.

MRS. VAN DAAN. In here? You're joking.

MARGOT. It's only for a night or two . . . until Mr. Kraler finds him another place.

MR. VAN DAAN. Yeah! Yeah!

(MR. FRANK hurries over as MR. KRALER and DUSSEL come up. DUSSEL is a man in his late fifties, meticulous, finicky . . . bewildered now. He wears a raincoat. He carries a briefcase, stuffed full, and a small medicine case.)

MR. FRANK. Come in, Mr. Dussel.

MR. KRALER. This is Mr. Frank.

DUSSEL. Mr. Otto Frank?

MR. FRANK. Yes. Let me take your things. (He takes the hat and briefcase, but DUSSEL clings to his medicine case.) This is my wife Edith . . . Mr. and Mrs. Van

Daan ... their son, Peter ... and my daughters, Margot and Anne.

(DUSSEL *shakes hands with everyone.*)

MR. KRALER. Thank you, Mr. Frank. Thank you all. Mr. Dussel, I leave you in good hands. Oh ... Dirk's coat.

(DUSSEL *hurriedly takes off the raincoat, giving it to* MR. KRALER. *Underneath is his white dentist's jacket, with a yellow Star of David on it.*)

DUSSEL (*to* MR. KRALER). What can I say to thank you ... ?

MRS. FRANK (*to* DUSSEL). Mr. Kraler and Miep ... They're our life line. Without them we couldn't live.

MR. KRALER. Please, Please. You make us seem very heroic. It isn't that at all. We simply don't like the Nazis. (*To* MR. FRANK, *who offers him a drink.*) No, thanks. (*Then going on.*) We don't like their methods. We don't like ...

MR. FRANK (*smiling*). I know. I know. "No one's going to tell us Dutchmen what to do with our damn Jews!"

MR. KRALER (*to* DUSSEL). Pay no attention to Mr. Frank. I'll be up tomorrow to see that they're treating you right. (*To* MR. FRANK.) Don't trouble to come down again. Peter will bolt the door after me, won't you, Peter?

PETER. Yes, sir.

MR. FRANK. Thank you, Peter. I'll do it.

MR. KRALER. Good night. Good night.

GROUP. Good night, Mr. Kraler. We'll see you tomorrow, etc., etc.

(MR. KRALER *goes out with* MR. FRANK. MRS. FRANK *gives each one of the "grownups" a glass of cognac.*)

MRS. FRANK. Please, Mr. Dussel, sit down.

(MR. DUSSEL *sinks into a chair.* MRS. FRANK *gives him a glass of cognac.*)

DUSSEL. I'm dreaming. I know it. I can't believe my eyes. Mr. Otto Frank here! (*To* MRS. FRANK.) You're not in Switzerland then? A woman told me ... She said she'd gone to your house ... the door was open, everything was in disorder, dishes in the sink. She said she found a piece of paper in the wastebasket with an address scribbled on it ... an address in Zurich. She said you must have escaped to Zurich.

ANNE. Father put that there purposely ... just so people would think that very thing!

DUSSEL. And you've been *here* all the time?

MRS. FRANK. All the time ... ever since July.

(ANNE *speaks to her father as he comes back.*)

ANNE. It worked, Pim ... the address you left! Mr. Dussel says that people believe we escaped to Switzerland.

MR. FRANK. I'm glad. ... And now let's have a little drink to welcome Mr. Dussel. (*Before they can drink,* MR. DUSSEL *bolts his drink.* MR. FRANK *smiles and raises his glass.*) To Mr. Dussel. Welcome. We're very honored to have you with us.

MRS. FRANK. To Mr. Dussel, welcome.

(*The* VAN DAANS *murmur a welcome. The "grownups" drink.*)

MRS. VAN DAAN. Um. That was good.

MR. VAN DAAN. Did Mr. Kraler warn you that you won't get much to eat here? You can imagine ... three ration books among the seven of us ... and now you make eight.

(PETER *walks away, humiliated. Outside a street organ is heard dimly.*)

DUSSEL (*rising*). Mr. Van Daan, you don't realize what is happening outside that you should warn me of a thing like that. You don't realize what's going on ... (*As* MR. VAN DAAN *starts his characteristic pacing,* DUSSEL *turns to speak to the others.*) Right here in Amsterdam every day hundreds of Jews disappear ... They surround a block and search house by house. Children come home from school to find their parents gone. Hundreds are being deported ... people that you and I know ... the Hallensteins ... the Wessels ...

MRS. FRANK (*in tears*). Oh, no. No!

DUSSEL. They get their call-up notice ... come to the Jewish theatre on such and such a day and hour ... bring only what you can carry in a rucksack. And if you refuse the call-up notice, then they come and drag you from your home and ship you off to Mauthausen. The death camp!

MRS. FRANK. We didn't know that things had got so much worse.

DUSSEL. Forgive me for speaking so.

ANNE (*coming to* DUSSEL). Do you know the deWaals? ... What's become of them? Their daughter Jopie and I are in the same class. Jopie's my best friend.

DUSSEL. They are gone.

ANNE. Gone?

DUSSEL. With all the others.

ANNE. Oh, no. Not Jopie!

(*She turns away, in tears.* MRS. FRANK *motions to* MARGOT *to comfort her.* MARGOT *goes to* ANNE, *putting her arms comfortingly around her.*)

MRS. VAN DAAN. There were some people called Wagner. They lived near us . . . ?

MR. FRANK (*interrupting, with a glance at* ANNE). I think we should put this off until later. We all have many questions we want to ask . . . But I'm sure that Mr. Dussel would like to get settled before supper.

DUSSEL. Thank you. I would. I brought very little with me.

MR. FRANK (*giving him his hat and briefcase*). I'm sorry we can't give you a room alone. But I hope you won't be too uncomfortable. We've had to make strict rules here . . . a schedule of hours . . . We'll tell you after supper. Anne, would you like to take Mr. Dussel to his room?

ANNE (*controlling her tears*). If you'll come with me, Mr. Dussel?

(*She starts for her room.*)

DUSSEL (*shaking hands with each in turn*). Forgive me if I haven't really expressed my gratitude to all of you. This has been such a shock to me. I'd always thought of myself as Dutch. I was born in Holland. My father was born in Holland, and my grandfather. And now . . . after all these years . . . (*He breaks off.*) If you'll excuse me.

(DUSSEL *gives a little bow and hurries off after* ANNE. MR. FRANK *and the others are subdued.*)

ANNE (*turning on the light*). Well, here we are.

(DUSSEL *looks around the room. In the main room* MARGOT *speaks to her mother.*)

MARGOT. The news sounds pretty bad, doesn't it? It's so different from what Mr. Kraler tells us. Mr. Kraler says things are improving.

MR. VAN DAAN. I like it better the way Kraler tells it.

(*They resume their occupations, quietly.* PETER *goes off into his room. In* ANNE'S *room,* ANNE *turns to* DUSSEL.)

ANNE. You're going to share the room with me.

DUSSEL. I'm a man who's always lived alone. I haven't had to adjust myself to others. I hope you'll bear with me until I learn.

ANNE. Let me help you. (*She takes his briefcase.*) Do you always live all alone?

Have you no family at all?

DUSSEL. No one.

(*He opens his medicine case and spreads his bottles on the dressing table.*)

ANNE. How dreadful. You must be terribly lonely.

DUSSEL. I'm used to it.

ANNE. I don't think I could ever get used to it. Didn't you even have a pet? A cat, or a dog?

DUSSEL. I have an allergy for fur-bearing animals. They give me asthma.

ANNE. Oh, dear. Peter has a cat.

DUSSEL. Here? He has it here?

ANNE. Yes. But we hardly ever see it. He keeps it in his room all the time. I'm sure it will be all right.

DUSSEL. Let us hope so. (*He takes some pills to fortify himself.*)

ANNE. That's Margot's bed, where you're going to sleep. I sleep on the sofa there. (*Indicating the clothes hooks on the wall.*) We cleared these off for your things. (*She goes over to the window.*) The best part about this room . . . you can look down and see a bit of the street and the canal. There's a houseboat . . . you can see the end of it . . . a bargeman lives there with his family . . . They have a baby and he's just beginning to walk and I'm so afraid he's going to fall into the canal some day. I watch him. . . .

DUSSEL (*interrupting*). Your father spoke of a schedule.

ANNE (*coming away from the window*). Oh, yes. It's mostly about the times we have to be quiet. And times for the w.c. You can use it now if you like.

DUSSEL (*stiffly*). No, thank you.

ANNE. I suppose you think it's awful, my talking about a thing like that. But you don't know how important it can get to be, especially when you're frightened . . . About this room, the way Margot and I did . . . she had it to herself in the afternoons for studying, reading . . . lessons, you know . . . and I took the mornings. Would that be all right with you?

DUSSEL. I'm not at my best in the morning.

ANNE. You stay here in the mornings then. I'll take the room in the afternoons.

DUSSEL. Tell me, when you're in here, what happens to me? Where am I spending my time? In there, with all the people?

ANNE. Yes.

DUSSEL. I see. I see.

ANNE. We have supper at half past six.

DUSSEL (*going over to the sofa*). Then, if you don't mind . . . I like to lie down quietly for ten minutes before eating. I find it helps the digestion.

ANNE. Of course. I hope I'm not going to be too much of a bother to you. I seem to be able to get everyone's back up.

(DUSSEL *lies down on the sofa, curled up, his back to her.*)

DUSSEL. I always get along very well with children. My patients all bring their children to me, because they know I get on well with them. So don't you worry about that.

(ANNE *leans over him, taking his hand and shaking it gratefully.*)

ANNE. Thank you. Thank you, Mr. Dussel.

(*The lights dim to darkness. The curtain falls on the scene.* ANNE'S VOICE *comes to us faintly at first, and then with increasing power.*)

ANNE'S VOICE. . . . And yesterday I finished Cissy Van Marxvelt's latest book. I think she is a first-class writer. I shall definitely let my children read her. Monday the twenty-first of September, nineteen forty-two. Mr. Dussel and I had another battle yesterday. Yes, Mr. Dussel! According to him, nothing, I repeat . . . nothing, is right about me . . . my appearance, my character, my manners. While he was going on at me I thought . . . sometime I'll give you such a smack that you'll fly right up to the ceiling! Why is it that every grownup thinks he knows the way to bring up children? Particularly the grownups that never had any. I keep wishing that Peter was a girl instead of a boy. Then I would have someone to talk to. Margot's a darling, but she takes everything too seriously. To pause for a moment on the subject of Mrs. Van Daan. I must tell you that her attempts to flirt with father are getting her nowhere. Pim, thank goodness, won't play.

(*As she is saying the last lines, the curtain rises on the darkened scene.* ANNE'S VOICE *fades out.*)

SCENE FOUR

It is the middle of the night, several months later. The stage is dark except for a little light which comes through the skylight in PETER'S room.

Everyone is in bed. MR. *and* MRS. FRANK *lie on the couch in the main room, which has been pulled out to serve as a makeshift double bed.*

MARGOT *is sleeping on a mattress on the floor in the main room, behind a curtain stretched across for privacy. The others are all in their accustomed rooms.*

From outside we hear two drunken soldiers singing "Lili Marlene." A girl's high giggle is heard. The sound of running feet is heard coming closer and then fading in the distance. Throughout the scene there is the distant sound of airplanes passing overhead.

A match suddenly flares up in the attic. We dimly see MR. VAN DAAN. *He is getting his bearings. He comes quickly down the stairs, and goes to the cupboard where the food is stored. Again the match flares up, and is as quickly blown out. The dim figure is seen to steal back up the stairs.*

There is quiet for a second or two, broken only by the sound of airplanes, and running feet on the street below.

Suddenly, out of the silence and the dark, we hear ANNE *scream.*

———

ANNE (*screaming*). No! No! Don't . . . don't take me!

(*She moans, tossing and crying in her sleep. The other people wake, terrified.* DUSSEL *sits up in bed, furious.*)

DUSSEL. Shush! Anne! Anne, for God's sake, shush!

ANNE (*still in her nightmare*). Save me! Save me!

(*She screams and screams.* DUSSEL *gets out of bed, going over to her, trying to wake her.*)

DUSSEL. For God's sake! Quiet! Quiet! You want someone to hear?

(*In the main room* MRS. FRANK *grabs a shawl and pulls it around her. She rushes in to* ANNE, *taking her in her arms.* MR. FRANK *hurriedly gets up, putting on his overcoat.* MARGOT *sits up, terrified.* PETER'S *light goes on in his room.*)

MRS. FRANK (*to* ANNE, *in her room*). Hush, darling, hush. It's all right. It's all right. (*Over her shoulder to* DUSSEL.) Will you be kind enough to turn on the light, Mr. Dussel? (*Back to* ANNE.) It's nothing, my darling. It was just a dream.

(DUSSEL *turns on the light in the bedroom.* MRS. FRANK *holds* ANNE *in her arms. Gradually* ANNE *comes out of her nightmare, still trembling with horror.* MR. FRANK *comes into the room, and goes quickly to the window, looking out to be sure that no one outside has heard* ANNE'S *screams.* MRS. FRANK *holds* ANNE, *talking softly to her. In the main room* MARGOT *stands on a chair, turning on the center hanging lamp. A light goes on in the* VAN DAANS' *room overhead.* PETER *puts his robe on, coming out of his room.*)

DUSSEL (*to* MRS. FRANK, *blowing his nose*). Something must be done about that child, Mrs. Frank. Yelling like that! Who knows but there's somebody on the streets? She's endangering all our lives.

MRS. FRANK. Anne, darling.

DUSSEL. Every night she twists and turns. I don't sleep. I spend half my night shushing her. And now it's nightmares!

(MARGOT *comes to the door of* ANNE'S *room, followed by* PETER. MR. FRANK *goes to them, indicating that everything is all right.* PETER *takes* MARGOT *back.*)

MRS. FRANK (*to* ANNE). You're here, safe, you see? Nothing has happened. (*To* DUSSEL.) Please, Mr. Dussel, go back to bed. She'll be herself in a minute or two. Won't you, Anne?

DUSSEL (*picking up a book and a pillow*). Thank you, but I'm going to the w.c. The one place where there's peace!

(*He stalks out.* MR. VAN DAAN, *in underwear and trousers, comes down the stairs.*)

MR. VAN DAAN (*to* DUSSEL). What is it? What happened?

DUSSEL. A nightmare. She was having a nightmare!

MR. VAN DAAN. I thought someone was murdering her.

DUSSEL. Unfortunately, no.

(*He goes into the bathroom.* MR. VAN DAAN *goes back up the stairs.* MR. FRANK, *in the main room, sends* PETER *back to his own bedroom.*)

MR. FRANK. Thank you, Peter. Go back to bed.

(PETER *goes back to his room.* MR. FRANK *follows him, turning out the light and looking out the window. Then he goes back to the main room, and gets up on a chair, turning out the center hanging lamp.*)

MRS. FRANK (*to* ANNE). Would you like some water? (ANNE *shakes her head.*) Was it a very bad dream? Perhaps if you told me . . . ?

ANNE. I'd rather not talk about it.

MRS. FRANK. Poor darling. Try to sleep then. I'll sit right here beside you until you fall asleep. (*She brings a stool over, sitting there.*)

ANNE. You don't have to.

MRS. FRANK. But I'd like to stay with you . . . very much. Really.

ANNE. I'd rather you didn't.

MRS. FRANK. Good night, then. (*She leans down to kiss* ANNE. ANNE *throws her arm up over her face, turning away.* MRS. FRANK, *hiding her hurt, kisses* ANNE'S *arm.*) You'll be all right? There's nothing that you want?

ANNE. Will you please ask Father to come.

MRS. FRANK (*after a second*). Of course, Anne dear. (*She hurries out into the other room.* MR. FRANK *comes to her as she comes in.*) Sie verlangt nach Dir!

MR. FRANK (*sensing her hurt*). Edith, Liebe, schau . . .

MRS. FRANK. Es macht nichts! Ich danke dem lieben Herrgott, dass sie sich wenigstens an Dich wendet, wenn sie Trost braucht! Geh hinein, Otto, sie ist ganz hysterisch vor Angst. (*As* MR. FRANK *hesitates.*) Geh zu ihr. (*He looks at her for a second and then goes to get a cup of water for* ANNE. MRS. FRANK *sinks down on the bed, her face in her hands, trying to keep from sobbing aloud.* MARGOT *comes over to her, putting her arms around her.*) She wants nothing of me. She pulled away when I leaned down to kiss her.

MARGOT. It's a phase . . . You heard Father . . . Most girls go through it . . . they turn to their fathers at this age . . . they give all their love to their fathers.

MRS. FRANK. You weren't like this. You didn't shut me out.

MARGOT. She'll get over it . . .

(*She smooths the bed for* MRS. FRANK *and sits beside her a moment as* MRS. FRANK *lies down. In* ANNE'S *room* MR. FRANK *comes in, sitting down by* ANNE. ANNE *flings her arms around him, clinging to him. In the distance we hear the sound of ack-ack.*)

ANNE. Oh, Pim. I dreamed that they came to get us! The Green Police! They broke down the door and grabbed me and started to drag me out the way they did Jopie.

MR. FRANK. I want you to take this pill.

ANNE. What is it?

MR. FRANK. Something to quiet you.

(*She takes it and drinks the water. In the main room* MARGOT *turns out the light and goes back to her bed.*)

MR. FRANK (*to* ANNE). Do you want me to read to you for a while?

ANNE. No. Just sit with me for a minute. Was I awful? Did I yell terribly loud? Do you think anyone outside could have heard?

MR. FRANK. No. No. Lie quietly now. Try to sleep.

ANNE. I'm a terrible coward. I'm so disappointed in myself. I think I've conquered my fear . . . I think I'm really grown-up . . . and then something happens . . . and I run to you like a baby . . . I love you, Father. I don't love anyone but you.

MR. FRANK (reproachfully). Annele!

ANNE. It's true. I've been thinking about it for a long time. You're the only one I love.

MR. FRANK. It's fine to hear you tell me that you love me. But I'd be happier if you said you loved your mother as well . . . She needs your help so much . . . your love . . .

ANNE. We have nothing in common. She doesn't understand me. Whenever I try to explain my views on life to her she asks me if I'm constipated.

MR. FRANK. You hurt her very much now. She's crying. She's in there crying.

ANNE. I can't help it. I only told the truth. I didn't want her here . . . (Then, with sudden change.) Oh, Pim, I was horrible, wasn't I? And the worst of it is, I can stand off and look at myself doing it and know it's cruel and yet I can't stop doing it. What's the matter with me? Tell me. Don't say it's just a phase! Help me.

MR. FRANK. There is so little that we parents can do to help our children. We can only try to set a good example . . . point the way. The rest you must do yourself. You must build your own character.

ANNE. I'm trying. Really I am. Every night I think back over all of the things I did that day that were wrong . . . like putting the wet mop in Mr. Dussel's bed . . . and this thing now with Mother. I say to myself, that was wrong. I make up my mind, I'm never going to do that again. Never! Of course I may do something worse . . . but at least I'll never do that again! . . . I have a nicer side, Father . . . a sweeter, nicer side. But I'm scared to show it. I'm afraid that people are going to laugh at me if I'm serious. So the mean Anne comes to the outside and the good Anne stays on the inside, and I keep on trying to switch them around and have the good Anne outside and the

bad Anne inside and be what I'd like to be . . . and might be . . . if only . . . only . . .

(She is asleep. MR. FRANK watches her for a moment and then turns off the light, and starts out. The lights dim out. The curtain falls on the scene. ANNE'S VOICE is heard dimly at first, and then with growing strength.)

ANNE'S VOICE. . . . The air raids are getting worse. They come over day and night. The noise is terrifying. Pim says it should be music to our ears. The more planes, the sooner will come the end of the war. Mrs. Van Daan pretends to be a fatalist. What will be, will be. But when the planes come over, who is the most frightened? No one else but Petronella! . . . Monday, the ninth of November, nineteen forty-two. Wonderful news! The Allies have landed in Africa. Pim says that we can look for an early finish to the war. Just for fun he asked each of us what was the first thing we wanted to do when we got out of here. Mrs. Van Daan longs to be home with her own things, her needle-point chairs, the Beckstein piano her father gave her . . . the best that money could buy. Peter would like to go to a movie. Mr. Dussel wants to get back to his dentist's drill. He's afraid he is losing his touch. For myself, there are so many things . . . to ride a bike again . . . to laugh till my belly aches . . . to have new clothes from the skin out . . . to have a hot tub filled to overflowing and wallow in it for hours . . . to be back in school with my friends . . .

(As the last lines are being said, the curtain rises on the scene. The lights dim on as ANNE'S VOICE fades away.)

SCENE FIVE

It is the first night of the Hanukkah celebration. MR. FRANK is standing at the head of the table on which is the Menorah. He lights the Shamos, or servant candle, and holds it as he says the blessing. Seated listening is all of the "family," dressed in their best. The men wear hats, PETER wears his cap.

MR. FRANK (reading from a prayer book). "Praised be Thou, oh Lord our God, Ruler of the universe, who has sanctified us with Thy commandments and bidden us kindle the Hanukkah lights. Praised be Thou, oh Lord our God, Ruler of the universe, who has wrought wondrous deliverances for our fathers in days of old. Praised be Thou, oh Lord our God, Ruler of the universe, that Thou has given us life and sustenance and brought us to this happy season." (MR. FRANK *lights the one candle of the Menorah as he continues.*) "We kindle this Hanukkah light to celebrate the great and wonderful deeds wrought through the zeal with which God filled the hearts of the heroic Maccabees, two thousand years ago. They fought against indifference, against tyranny and oppression, and they restored our Temple to us. May these lights remind us that we should ever look to God, whence cometh our help." Amen. [Pronounced O-mayn.]

ALL. Amen.

(MR. FRANK *hands* MRS. FRANK *the prayer book.*)

MRS. FRANK (*reading*). "I lift up mine eyes unto the mountains, from whence cometh my help. My help cometh from the Lord who made heaven and earth. He will not suffer thy foot to be moved. He that keepeth thee will not slumber. He that keepeth Israel doth neither slumber nor sleep. The Lord is thy keeper. The Lord is thy shade upon thy right hand. The sun shall not smite thee by day, nor the moon by night. The Lord shall keep thee from all evil. He shall keep thy soul. The Lord shall guard thy going out and thy coming in, from this time forth and forevermore." Amen.

ALL. Amen.

(MRS. FRANK *puts down the prayer book and goes to get the food and wine.* MARGOT *helps her.* MR. FRANK *takes the men's hats and puts them aside.*)

DUSSEL (*rising*). That was very moving.

ANNE (*pulling him back*). It isn't over yet!

MRS. VAN DAAN. Sit down! Sit down!

ANNE. There's a lot more, songs and presents.

DUSSEL. Presents?

MRS. FRANK. Not this year, unfortunately.

MRS. VAN DAAN. But always on Hanukkah everyone gives presents . . . everyone!

DUSSEL. Like our St. Nicholas' Day.

(*There is a chorus of "no's" from the group.*)

MRS. VAN DAAN. No! Not like St.

Nicholas! What kind of a Jew are you that you don't know Hanukkah?

MRS. FRANK (*as she brings the food*). I remember particularly the candles . . . First one, as we have tonight. Then the second night you light two candles, the next night three . . . and so on until you have eight candles burning. When there are eight candles it is truly beautiful.

MRS. VAN DAAN. And the potato pancakes.

MR. VAN DAAN. Don't talk about them!

MRS. VAN DAAN. I make the best *latkes* you ever tasted!

MRS. FRANK. Invite us all next year . . . in your own home.

MR. FRANK. God willing!

MRS. VAN DAAN. God willing.

MARGOT. What I remember best is the presents we used to get when we were little . . . eight days of presents . . . and each day they got better and better.

MRS. FRANK (*sitting down*). We are all here, alive. That is present enough.

ANNE. No, it isn't. I've got something . . . (*She rushes into her room, hurriedly puts on a little hat improvised from the lamp shade, grabs a satchel bulging with parcels and comes running back.*)

MRS. FRANK. What is it?

ANNE. Presents!

MRS. VAN DAAN. Presents!

DUSSEL. Look!

MRS. VAN DAAN. What's she got on her head?

PETER. A lamp shade!

ANNE (*she picks out one at random*). This is for Margot. (*She hands it to* MARGOT, *pulling her to her feet.*) Read it out loud.

MARGOT (*reading*).
"You have never lost your temper.
You never will, I fear,
You are so good.
But if you should,
Put all your cross words here."

(*She tears open the package.*) A new crossword puzzle book! Where did you get it?

ANNE. It isn't new. It's one that you've done. But I rubbed it all out, and if you wait a little and forget, you can do it all over again.

MARGOT (*sitting*). It's wonderful, Anne. Thank you. You'd never know it wasn't new.

(*From outside we hear the sound of a streetcar passing.*)

ANNE (*with another gift*). Mrs. Van Daan.

MRS. VAN DAAN (*taking it*). This is awful ... I haven't anything for anyone ... I never thought ...

MR. FRANK. This is all Anne's idea.

MRS. VAN DAAN (*holding up a bottle*). What is it?

ANNE. It's hair shampoo. I took all the odds and ends of soap and mixed them with the last of my toilet water.

MRS. VAN DAAN. Oh, Anneke!

ANNE. I wanted to write a poem for all of them, but I didn't have time. (*Offering a large box to* MR. VAN DAAN.) Yours, Mr. Van Daan, is *really* something ... something you want more than anything. (*As she waits for him to open it.*) Look! Cigarettes!

MR. VAN DAAN. Cigarettes!

ANNE. Two of them! Pim found some old pipe tobacco in the pocket lining of his coat ... and we made them ... or rather, Pim did.

MRS. VAN DAAN. Let me see ... Well, look at that! Light it, Putti! Light it.

(MR. VAN DAAN *hesitates.*)

ANNE. It's tobacco, really it is! There's a little fluff in it, but not much.

(*Everyone watches as* MR. VAN DAAN *cautiously lights it. The cigarette flares up. Everyone laughs.*)

PETER. It works!

MRS. VAN DAAN. Look at him.

MR. VAN DAAN (*spluttering*). Thank you, Anne. Thank you.

(ANNE *rushes back to her satchel for another present.*)

ANNE (*handing her mother a piece of paper*). For Mother, Hanukkah greeting.

(*She pulls her mother to her feet.*)

MRS. FRANK (*She reads*). "Here's an I.O.U. that I promise to pay. Ten hours of doing whatever you say. Signed, Anne Frank." (MRS. FRANK, *touched, takes* ANNE *in her arms, holding her close.*)

DUSSEL (*to* ANNE). Ten hours of doing what you're told? *Anything* you're told?

ANNE. That's right.

DUSSEL. You wouldn't want to sell that, Mrs. Frank?

MRS. FRANK. Never! This is the most precious gift I've ever had!

(*She sits, showing her present to the others.* ANNE *hurries back to the satchel and pulls out a scarf, the scarf that* MR. FRANK *found in the first scene.*)

ANNE (*offering it to her father*). For Pim.

MR. FRANK. Anneke ... I wasn't supposed to have a present!

(*He takes it, unfolding it and showing it to the others.*)

ANNE. It's a muffler ... to put round your neck ... like an ascot, you know. I made it myself out of odds and ends ... I knitted it in the dark each night, after I'd gone to bed. I'm afraid it looks better in the dark!

MR. FRANK (*putting it on*). It's fine. It fits me perfectly. Thank you, Annele.

(ANNE *hands* PETER *a ball of paper, with a string attached to it.*)

ANNE. That's for Mouschi.

PETER (*rising to bow*). On behalf of Mouschi, I thank you.

ANNE (*hesitant, handing him a gift*). And ... this is yours ... from Mrs. Quack Quack. (*As he holds it gingerly in his hands.*) Well ... open it ... Aren't you going to open it?

PETER. I'm scared to. I know something's going to jump out and hit me.

ANNE. No. It's nothing like that, really.

MRS. VAN DAAN (*as he is opening it*). What is it, Peter? Go on. Show it.

ANNE (*excitedly*). It's a safety razor!

DUSSEL. A what?

ANNE. A razor!

MRS. VAN DAAN (*looking at it*). You didn't make that out of odds and ends.

ANNE (*to* PETER). Miep got it for me. It's not new. It's second-hand. But you really do need a razor now.

DUSSEL. For what?

ANNE. Look on his upper lip ... you can see the beginning of a mustache.

DUSSEL. He wants to get rid of that? Put a little milk on it and let the cat lick if off.

PETER (*starting for his room*). Think you're funny, don't you.

DUSSEL. Look! He can't wait! He's going in to try it!

PETER. I'm going to give Mouschi his present!

(*He goes into his room, slamming the door behind him.*)

MR. VAN DAAN (*disgustedly*). Mouschi, Mouschi, Mouschi.

(*In the distance we hear a dog persistently barking.* ANNE *brings a gift to* DUSSEL.)

ANNE. And last but never least, my roommate, Mr. Dussel.

DUSSEL. For me? You have something for me? (*He opens the small box she gives him.*)

ANNE. I made them myself.

DUSSEL (*puzzled*). Capsules! Two capsules!

ANNE. They're ear-plugs!

DUSSEL. Ear-plugs?

ANNE. To put in your ears so you won't hear me when I thrash around at night. I saw them advertised in a magazine. They're not real ones ... I made them out of cotton and candle wax. Try them ... See if they don't work ... see if you can hear me talk ...

DUSSEL (*putting them in his ears*). Wait now until I get them in ... so.

ANNE. Are you ready?

DUSSEL. Huh?

ANNE. Are you ready?

DUSSEL. Good God! They've gone inside! I can't get them out! (*They laugh as* MR. DUSSEL *jumps about, trying to shake the plugs out of his ears. Finally he gets them out. Putting them away.*) Thank you, Anne! Thank you!

MR. VAN DAAN. A real Hanukkah!

MRS. VAN DAAN. Wasn't it cute of her?

MRS. FRANK. I don't know when she did it.

MARGOT. I love my present.

(*Together.*)

ANNE (*sitting at the table*). And now let's have the song, Father ... please ... (*To* DUSSEL.) Have you heard the Hanukkah song, Mr. Dussel? The song is the whole thing! (*She sings.*) "Oh, Hanukkah! Oh Hanukkah! The sweet celebration ..."

MR. FRANK (*quieting her*). I'm afraid, Anne, we shouldn't sing that song tonight. (*To* DUSSEL.) It's a song of jubilation, of rejoicing. One is apt to become too enthusiastic.

ANNE. Oh, please, please. Let's sing the song. I promise not to shout!

MR. FRANK. Very well. But quietly now ... I'll keep an eye on you and when ...

(*As* ANNE *starts to sing, she is interrupted by* DUSSEL, *who is snorting and wheezing.*)

DUSSEL (*pointing to* PETER). You ... You! (PETER *is coming from his bedroom, ostentatiously holding a bulge in his coat as if he were holding his cat, and dangling* ANNE'S *present before it.*) How many times ... I told you ... Out! Out!

MR. VAN DAAN (*going to* PETER). What's the matter with you? Haven't you any sense? Get that cat out of here.

PETER (*innocently*). Cat?

MR. VAN DAAN. You heard me. Get it out of here!

PETER. I have no cat. (*Delighted with his joke, he opens his coat and pulls out a bath towel. The group at the table laugh, enjoying the joke.*)

DUSSEL (*still wheezing*). It doesn't need to be the cat ... his clothes are enough ... when he comes out of that room ...

MR. VAN DAAN. Don't worry. You won't be bothered any more. We're getting rid of it.

DUSSEL. At last you listen to me.

(*He goes off into his bedroom.*)

MR. VAN DAAN (*calling after him*). I'm not doing it for you. That's all in your mind ... all of it! (*He starts back to his place at the table.*) I'm doing it because I'm sick of seeing that cat eat all our food.

PETER. That's not true! I only give him bones ... scraps ...

MR. VAN DAAN. Don't tell me! He gets fatter every day! Damn cat looks better than any of us. Out he goes tonight!

PETER. No! No!

ANNE. Mr. Van Daan, you can't do that! That's Peter's cat. Peter loves that cat.

MRS. FRANK (*quietly*). Anne.

PETER (*to* MR. VAN DAAN). If he goes, I go.

MR. VAN DAAN. Go! Go!

MRS. VAN DAAN. You're not going and the cat's not going! Now please ... this is Hanukkah ... Hanukkah ... this is the time to celebrate ... What's the matter with all of you? Come on, Anne. Let's have the song.

ANNE (*singing*).

"Oh, Hanukkah! Oh, Hanukkah!
The sweet celebration."

MR. FRANK (*rising*). I think we should first blow out the candle ... then we'll have something for tomorrow night.

MARGOT. But, Father, you're supposed to let it burn itself out.

MR. FRANK. I'm sure that God understands shortages. (*Before blowing it out.*) "Praised be Thou, oh Lord our God, who hast sustained us and permitted us to celebrate this joyous festival."

(*He is about to blow out the candle when suddenly there is a crash of something falling below. They all freeze in horror, motionless. For a few seconds there is complete silence.* MR. FRANK *slips off his shoes. The others noiselessly follow his example.* MR. FRANK *turns out a light near him. He motions to* PETER *to turn off the center lamp.* PETER *tries to reach it, realizes he cannot and gets up on a chair. Just as he is touching the lamp he loses his balance. The chair goes out from under him. He falls. The iron lamp shade crashes to the floor. There is a sound of feet below, running down the stairs.)*

MR. VAN DAAN (*under his breath*). God Almighty! (*The only light left comes from the Hanukkah candle.* DUSSEL *comes from his room.* MR. FRANK *creeps over to the stairwell and stands listening. The dog is heard barking excitedly.)* Do you hear anything?

MR. FRANK (*in a whisper*). No. I think they've gone.

MRS. VAN DAAN. It's the Green Police. They've found us.

MR. FRANK. If they had, they wouldn't have left. They'd be up here by now.

MRS. VAN DAAN. I know it's the Green Police. They've gone to get help. That's all. They'll be back!

MR. VAN DAAN. Or it may have been the Gestapo, looking for papers . . .

MR. FRANK (*interrupting*). Or a thief, looking for money.

MRS. VAN DAAN. We've got to do something . . . Quick! Quick! Before they come back.

MR. VAN DAAN. There isn't anything to do. Just wait.

(MR. FRANK *holds up his hand for them to be quiet. He is listening intently. There is complete silence as they all strain to hear any sound from below. Suddenly* ANNE *begins to sway. With a low cry she falls to the floor in a faint.* MRS. FRANK *goes to her quickly, sitting beside her on the floor and taking her in her arms.)*

MRS. FRANK. Get some water, please! Get some water!

(MARGOT *starts for the sink.)*

MR. VAN DAAN (*grabbing* MARGOT). No! No! No one's going to run water!

MR. FRANK. If they've found us, they've found us. Get the water. (MARGOT *starts again for the sink.* MR. FRANK, *getting a flashlight.)* I'm going down.

(MARGOT *rushes to him, clinging to him.* ANNE *struggles to consciousness.)*

MARGOT. No, Father, no! There may be someone there, waiting . . . It may be a trap!

MR. FRANK. This is Saturday. There is no way for us to know what has happened until Miep or Mr. Kraler comes on Monday morning. We cannot live with this uncertainty.

MARGOT. Don't go, Father!

MRS. FRANK. Hush, darling, hush. (MR. FRANK *slips quietly out, down the steps and out through the door below.)* Margot! Stay close to me.

(MARGOT *goes to her mother.)*

MR. VAN DAAN. Shush! Shush!

(MRS. FRANK *whispers to* MARGOT *to get the water.* MARGOT *goes for it.)*

MRS. VAN DAAN. Putti, where's our money? Get our money. I hear you can buy the Green Police off, so much a head. Go upstairs quick! Get the money!

MR. VAN DAAN. Keep still!

MRS. VAN DAAN (*kneeling before him, pleading*). Do you want to be dragged off to a concentration camp? Are you going to stand there and wait for them to come up and get you? Do something, I tell you!

MR. VAN DAAN (*pushing her aside*). Will you keep still!

(*He goes over to the stairwell to listen.* PETER *goes to his mother, helping her up onto the sofa. There is a second of silence, then* ANNE *can stand it no longer.)*

ANNE. Someone go after Father! Make Father come back!

PETER (*starting for the door*). I'll go.

MR. VAN DAAN. Haven't you done enough?

(*He pushes* PETER *roughly away. In his anger against his father* PETER *grabs a chair as if to hit him with it, then puts it down, burying his face in his hands.* MRS. FRANK *begins to pray softly.)*

ANNE. Please, please, Mr. Van Daan. Get Father.

MR. VAN DAAN. Quiet! Quiet!

(ANNE *is shocked into silence.* MRS. FRANK *pulls her closer, holding her protectively in her arms.)*

MRS. FRANK (*softly, praying*). "I lift up mine eyes unto the mountains, from whence cometh my help. My help cometh from the Lord who made heaven and earth. He will not suffer thy foot to be moved . . . He that keepeth thee will not slumber . . ."

(*She stops as she hears someone coming. They all watch the door tensely.* MR. FRANK *comes quietly in.* ANNE *rushes to him, holding him tight.)*

MR. FRANK. It was a thief. That noise must have scared him away.

MRS. VAN DAAN. Thank God.

MR. FRANK. He took the cash box. And

the radio. He ran away in such a hurry that he didn't stop to shut the street door. It was swinging wide open. (*A breath of relief sweeps over them.*) I think it would be good to have some light.

MARGOT. Are you sure it's all right?

MR. FRANK. The danger has passed. (MARGOT *goes to light the small lamp.*) Don't be so terrified, Anne. We're safe.

DUSSEL. Who says the danger has passed? Don't you realize we are in greater danger than ever?

MR. FRANK. Mr. Dussel, will you be still!

(MR. FRANK *takes* ANNE *back to the table, making her sit down with him, trying to calm her.*)

DUSSEL (*pointing to* PETER). Thanks to this clumsy fool, there's someone now who knows we're up here! Someone now knows we're up here, hiding!

MRS. VAN DAAN (*going to* DUSSEL). Someone knows we're here, yes. But who is the someone? A thief! A thief! You think a thief is going to go to the Green Police and say . . . I was robbing a place the other night and I heard a noise up over my head? You think a thief is going to do that?

DUSSEL. Yes. I think he will.

MRS. VAN DAAN (*hysterically*). You're crazy!

(*She stumbles back to her seat at the table.* PETER *follows protectively, pushing* DUSSEL *aside.*)

DUSSEL. I think some day he'll be caught and then he'll make a bargain with the Green Police . . . if they'll let him off, he'll tell them where some Jews are hiding!

(*He goes off into the bedroom. There is a second of appalled silence.*)

MR. VAN DAAN. He's right.

ANNE. Father, let's get out of here! We can't stay here now . . . Let's go . . .

MR. VAN DAAN. Go! Where?

MRS. FRANK (*sinking into her chair at the table*). Yes. Where?

MR. FRANK (*rising, to them all*). Have we lost all faith? All courage? A moment ago we thought that they'd come for us. We were sure it was the end. But it wasn't the end. We're alive, safe. (MR. VAN DAAN *goes to the table and sits.* MR. FRANK *prays.*) "We thank Thee, oh Lord our God, that in Thy infinite mercy Thou hast again seen fit to spare us." (*He blows out the candle, then turns to* ANNE.)

Come on, Anne. The song! Let's have the song! (*He starts to sing.* ANNE *finally starts falteringly to sing, as* MR. FRANK *urges her on. Her voice is hardly audible at first.*)

ANNE (*singing*).
"Oh, Hanukkah! Oh, Hanukkah!
The sweet . . . celebration . . ."

(*As she goes on singing, the others gradually join in, their voices still shaking with fear.* MRS. VAN DAAN *sobs as she sings.*)

GROUP.
"Around the feast . . . we . . . gather
In complete . . . jubilation . . .
Happiest of sea . . . sons
Now is here.
Many are the reasons for good cheer."

(DUSSEL *comes from the bedroom. He comes over to the table, standing beside* MARGOT, *listening to them as they sing.*)

"Together
We'll weather
Whatever tomorrow may bring."

(*As they sing on with growing courage, the lights start to dim.*)

"So hear us rejoicing
And merrily voicing
The Hanukkah song that we sing.
Hoy!"

(*The lights are out. The curtain starts slowly to fall.*)

"Hear us rejoicing
And merrily voicing
The Hanukkah song that we sing."

(*They are still singing, as the curtain falls.*)

CURTAIN

ACT TWO

SCENE ONE

In the darkness we hear ANNE'S VOICE, *again reading from the diary.*

———

ANNE'S VOICE. Saturday, the first of January, nineteen forty-four. Another new year has begun and we find ourselves still in our hiding place. We have been here now for one year, five months and twenty-five days. It seems that our life is at a standstill.

(*The curtain rises on the scene. It is afternoon. Everyone is bundled up against the cold. In the main room* MRS. FRANK *is taking down the laundry, which is hung across the back.* MR. FRANK *sits in the chair down left, reading.* MARGOT *is lying on the couch with a blanket over her and the many-colored knitted scarf around her throat.* ANNE *is seated at the center table, writing in her diary.* PETER, MR. *and* MRS. VAN DAAN, *and* DUSSEL *are all in their own rooms, reading or lying down.*

As the lights dim on, ANNE'S VOICE *continues, without a break.*)

ANNE'S VOICE. We are all a little thinner. The Van Daan's "discussions" are as violent as ever. Mother still does not understand me. But then I don't understand her either. There is one great change, however. A change in myself. I read somewhere that girls of my age don't feel quite certain of themselves. That they become quiet within and begin to think of the miracle that is taking place in their bodies. I think that what is happening to me is so wonderful . . . not only what can be seen, but what is taking place inside. Each time it has happened I have a feeling that I have a sweet secret. (*We hear the chimes and then a hymn being played on the carillon outside.*) And in spite of any pain, I long for the time when I shall feel that secret within me again.

(*The buzzer of the door below suddenly sounds. Everyone is startled;* MR. FRANK *tiptoes cautiously to the top of the steps and listens. Again the buzzer sounds, in* MIEP'S *V-for-Victory signal.*)

MR. FRANK. It's Miep! (*He goes quickly down the steps to unbolt the door.* MRS. FRANK *calls upstairs to the* VAN DAANS *and then to* PETER.)

MRS. FRANK. Wake up, everyone! Miep is here! (ANNE *quickly puts her diary away.* MARGOT *sits up, pulling the blanket around her shoulders.* MR. DUSSEL *sits on the edge of his bed, listening, disgruntled.* MIEP *comes up the steps, followed by* MR. KRALER. *They bring flowers, books, newspapers, etc.* ANNE *rushes to* MIEP, *throwing her arms affectionately around her.*) Miep . . . and Mr. Kraler . . . What a delightful surprise!

MR. KRALER. We came to bring you New Year's greetings.

MRS. FRANK. You shouldn't . . . you should have at least one day to yourselves. (*She goes quickly to the stove and brings down teacups and tea for all of them.*)

ANNE. Don't say that, it's so wonderful to see them! (*Sniffing at* MIEP'S *coat.*) I can smell the wind and the cold on your clothes.

MIEP (*giving her the flowers*). There you are. (*Then to* MARGOT, *feeling her forehead.*)

How are you, Margot? . . . Feeling any better?

MARGOT. I'm all right.

ANNE. We filled her full of every kind of pill so she won't cough and make a noise.

(*She runs into her room to put the flowers in water.* MR. *and* MRS. VAN DAAN *come from upstairs. Outside there is the sound of a band playing.*)

MRS. VAN DAAN. Well, hello, Miep. Mr. Kraler.

MR. KRALER (*giving a bouquet of flowers to* MRS. VAN DAAN). With my hope for peace in the New Year.

PETER (*anxiously*). Miep, have you seen Mouschi? Have you seen him anywhere around?

MIEP. I'm sorry, Peter. I asked everyone in the neighborhood had they seen a gray cat. But they said no.

(MRS. FRANK *gives* MIEP *a cup of tea.* MR. FRANK *comes up the steps, carrying a small cake on a plate.*)

MR. FRANK. Look what Miep's brought for us!

MRS. FRANK (*taking it*). A cake!

MR. VAN DAAN. A cake! (*He pinches* MIEP'S *cheeks gaily and hurries up to the cupboard.*) I'll get some plates.

(DUSSEL, *in his room, hastily puts a coat on and starts out to join the others.*)

MRS. FRANK. Thank you, Miepia. You shouldn't have done it. You must have used all of your sugar ration for weeks. (*Giving it to* MRS. VAN DAAN.) It's beautiful, isn't it?

MRS. VAN DAAN. It's been ages since I even saw a cake. Not since you brought us one last year. (*Without looking at the cake, to* MIEP.) Remember? Don't you remember, you gave us one on New Year's Day? Just this time last year? I'll never forget it because you had "Peace in nineteen forty-three" on it. (*She looks at the cake and reads.*) "Peace in nineteen forty-four!"

MIEP. Well, it has to come sometime, you know. (*As* DUSSEL *comes from his room.*) Hello, Mr. Dussel.

MR. KRALER. How are you?

MR. VAN DAAN (*bringing plates and a knife*). Here's the knife, *liefje.* Now, how many of us are there?

MIEP. None for me, thank you.

MR. FRANK. Oh, please. You must.

MIEP. I couldn't.

MR. VAN DAAN. Good! That leaves one

... two ... three ... seven of us.

DUSSEL. Eight! Eight! It's the same number as it always is!

MR. VAN DAAN. I left Margot out. I take it for granted Margot won't eat any.

ANNE. Why wouldn't she!

MRS. FRANK. I think it won't harm her.

MR. VAN DAAN. All right! All right! I just didn't want her to start coughing again, that's all.

DUSSEL. And please, Mrs. Frank should cut the cake.

MR. VAN DAAN. What's the difference?

MRS. VAN DAAN. It's not Mrs. Frank's cake, is it, Miep? It's for all of us. *(Together.)*

DUSSEL. Mrs. Frank divides things better.

MRS. VAN DAAN *(going to* DUSSEL*)*. What are you trying to say?

MR. VAN DAAN. Oh, come on! Stop wasting time! *(Together.)*

MRS. VAN DAAN *(to* DUSSEL*)*. Don't I always give everybody exactly the same? Don't I?

MR. VAN DAAN. Forget it, Kerli.

MRS. VAN DAAN. No. I want an answer! Don't I?

DUSSEL. Yes. Yes. Everybody gets exactly the same ... except Mr. Van Daan always gets a little bit more.

*(*VAN DAAN *advances on* DUSSEL, *the knife still in his hand.)*

MR. VAN DAAN. That's a lie!

*(*DUSSEL *retreats before the onslaught of the* VAN DAANS.*)*

MR. FRANK. Please, please! *(Then to* MIEP.*)* You see what a little sugar cake does to us? It goes right to our heads!

MR. VAN DAAN *(handing* MRS. FRANK *the knife)*. Here you are, Mrs. Frank.

MRS. FRANK. Thank you. *(Then to* MIEP *as she goes to the table to cut the cake.)* Are you sure you won't have some?

MIEP *(drinking her tea)*. No, really, I have to go in a minute.

(The sound of the band fades out in the distance.)

PETER *(to* MIEP*)*. Maybe Mouschi went back to our house ... they say that cats ... Do you ever get over there ...? I mean ... do you suppose you could ...?

MIEP. I'll try, Peter. The first minute I get I'll try. But I'm afraid, with him gone a week ...

DUSSEL. Make up your mind, already

someone has had a nice big dinner from that cat!

*(*PETER *is furious, inarticulate. He starts toward* DUSSEL *as if to hit him.* MR. FRANK *stops him.* MRS. FRANK *speaks quickly to ease the situation.)*

MRS. FRANK *(to* MIEP*)*. This is delicious, Miep!

MRS. VAN DAAN *(eating hers)*. Delicious!

MR. VAN DAAN *(finishing it in one gulp)*. Dirk's in luck to get a girl who can bake like this!

MIEP *(putting down her empty teacup)*. I have to run. Dirk's taking me to a party tonight.

ANNE. How heavenly! Remember now what everyone is wearing, and what you have to eat and everything, so you can tell us tomorrow.

MIEP. I'll give you a full report! Goodby, everyone!

MR. VAN DAAN *(to* MIEP*)*. Just a minute. There's something I'd like you to do for me.

(He hurries off up the stairs to his room.)

MRS. VAN DAAN *(sharply)*. Putti, where are you going? *(She rushes up the stairs after him, calling hysterically.)* What do you want? Putti, what are you going to do?

MIEP *(to* PETER*)*. What's wrong?

PETER *(his sympathy is with his mother)*. Father says he's going to sell her fur coat. She's crazy about that old fur coat.

DUSSEL. Is it possible? Is it possible that anyone is so silly as to worry about a fur coat in times like this?

PETER. It's none of your darn business ... and if you say one more thing ... I'll, I'll take you and I'll ... I mean it ... I'll ...

(There is a piercing scream from MRS. VAN DAAN *above. She grabs at the fur coat as* MR. VAN DAAN *is starting downstairs with it.)*

MRS. VAN DAAN. No! No! No! Don't you dare take that! You hear? It's mine! *(Downstairs* PETER *turns away, embarrassed, miserable.)* My father gave me that! You didn't give it to me. You have no right. Let go of it ... you hear?

*(*MR. VAN DAAN *pulls the coat from her hands and hurries downstairs.* MRS. VAN DAAN *sinks to the floor, sobbing. As* MR. VAN DAAN *comes into the main room the others look away, embarrassed for him.)*

MR. VAN DAAN *(to* MR. KRALER*)*. Just a little—discussion over the advisability of selling this coat. As I have often reminded Mrs. Van Daan, it's very selfish of her to keep it when people outside are in such desperate need of clothing . . . (*He gives the coat to* MIEP.) So if you will please to sell it for us? It should fetch a good price. And by the way, will you get me cigarettes. I don't care what kind they are . . . get all you can.

MIEP. It's terribly difficult to get them, Mr. Van Daan. But I'll try. Good-by.

(*She goes.* MR. FRANK *follows her down the steps to bolt the door after her.* MRS. FRANK *gives* MR. KRALER *a cup of tea.*)

MRS. FRANK. Are you sure you won't have some cake, Mr. Kraler?

MR. KRALER. I'd better not.

MR. VAN DAAN. You're still feeling badly? What does your doctor say?

MR. KRALER. I haven't been to him.

MRS. FRANK. Now, Mr. Kraler! . . .

MR. KRALER (*sitting at the table*). Oh, I tried. But you can't get near a doctor these days . . . they're so busy. After weeks I finally managed to get one on the telephone. I told him I'd like an appointment . . . I wasn't feeling very well. You know what he answers . . . over the telephone . . . Stick out your tongue! (*They laugh. He turns to* MR. FRANK *as* MR. FRANK *comes back.*) I have some contracts here . . . I wonder if you'd look over them with me . . .

MR. FRANK (*putting out his hand*). Of course.

MR. KRALER (*he rises*). If we could go downstairs . . . (MR. FRANK *starts ahead,* MR. KRALER *speaks to the others.*) Will you forgive us? I won't keep him but a minute. (*He starts to follow* MR. FRANK *down the steps.*)

MARGOT (*with sudden foreboding*). What's happened? Something's happened! Hasn't it, Mr. Kraler?

(MR. KRALER *stops and comes back, trying to reassure* MARGOT *with a pretense of casualness.*)

MR. KRALER. No, really. I want your father's advice . . .

MARGOT. Something's gone wrong! I know it!

MR. FRANK (*coming back, to* MR. KRALER). If it's something that concerns us here, it's better that we all hear it.

MR. KRALER (*turning to him, quietly*). But . . . the children . . . ?

MR. FRANK. What they'd imagine would be worse than any reality.

(*As* MR. KRALER *speaks, they all listen with intense apprehension.* MRS. VAN DAAN *comes down the stairs and sits on the bottom step.*)

MR. KRALER. It's a man in the storeroom . . . I don't know whether or not you remember him . . . Carl, about fifty, heavy-set, nearsighted . . . He came with us just before you left.

MR. FRANK. He was from Utrecht?

MR. KRALER. That's the man. A couple of weeks ago, when I was in the storeroom, he closed the door and asked me . . . how's Mr. Frank? What do you hear from Mr. Frank? I told him I only knew there was a rumor that you were in Switzerland. He said he'd heard that rumor too, but he thought I might know something more. I didn't pay any attention to it . . . but then a thing happened yesterday . . . He'd brought some invoices to the office for me to sign. As I was going through them, I looked up. He was standing staring at the bookcase . . . your bookcase. He said he thought he remembered a door there . . . Wasn't there a door there that used to go up to the loft? Then he told me he wanted more money. Twenty guilders more a week.

MR. VAN DAAN. Blackmail!

MR. FRANK. Twenty guilders? Very modest blackmail.

MR. VAN DAAN. That's just the beginning.

DUSSEL (*coming to* MR. FRANK). You know what I think? He was the thief who was down there that night. That's how he knows we're here.

MR. FRANK (*to* MR. KRALER). How was it left? What did you tell him?

MR. KRALER. I said I had to think about it. What shall I do? Pay him the money? . . . Take a chance on firing him . . . or what? I don't know.

DUSSEL (*frantic*). For God's sake don't fire him! Pay him what he asks . . . keep him here where you can have your eye on him.

MR. FRANK. Is it so much that he's asking? What are they paying nowadays?

MR. KRALER. He could get it in a war plant. But this isn't a war plant. Mind you, I don't know if he really knows . . . or if he doesn't know.

MR. FRANK. Offer him half. Then we'll soon find out if it's blackmail or not.

DUSSEL. And if it is? We've got to pay it, haven't we? Anything he asks we've got to pay!

MR. FRANK. Let's decide that when the time comes.

MR. KRALER. This may be all imagination. You get to a point, these days, where you suspect everyone and everything. Again and again . . . on some simple look or word, I've found myself . . .

(*The telephone rings in the office below.*)

MRS. VAN DAAN (*hurrying to* MR. KRALER). There's the telephone! What does that mean, the telephone ringing on a holiday?

MR. KRALER. That's my wife. I told her I had to go over some papers in my office . . . to call me there when she got out of church. (*He starts out.*) I'll offer him half then. Good-by . . . we'll hope for the best!

(*The group call their good-bys halfheartedly.* MR. FRANK *follows* MR. KRALER, *to bolt the door below. During the following scene,* MR. FRANK *comes back up and stands listening, disturbed.*)

DUSSEL (*to* MR. VAN DAAN). You can thank your son for this . . . smashing the light! I tell you, it's just a question of time now.

(*He goes to the window at the back and stands looking out.*)

MARGOT. Sometimes I wish the end would come . . . whatever it is.

MRS. FRANK (*shocked*). Margot!

(ANNE *goes to* MARGOT, *sitting beside her on the couch with her arms around her.*)

MARGOT. Then at least we'd know where we were.

MRS. FRANK. You should be ashamed of yourself! Talking that way! Think how lucky we are! Think of the thousands dying in the war, every day. Think of the people in concentration camps.

ANNE (*interrupting*). What's the good of that? What's the good of thinking of misery when you're already miserable? That's stupid!

MRS. FRANK. Anne!

(*As* ANNE *goes on raging at her mother,* MRS. FRANK *tries to break in, in an effort to quiet her.*)

ANNE. We're young, Margot and Peter and I! You grownups have had your chance! But look at us . . . If we begin thinking of all the horror in the world, we're lost! We're trying to hold onto some kind of ideals . . . when everything . . . ideals, hopes . . . everything, are being destroyed! It isn't our fault that the world is in such a mess! We weren't around when all this started! So don't try to take it out on us! (*She rushes off to*

her room, slamming the door after her. She picks up a brush from the chest and hurls it to the floor. Then she sits on the settee, trying to control her anger.)

MR. VAN DAAN. She talks as if we started the war! Did we start the war?

(*He spots* ANNE's *cake. As he starts to take it,* PETER *anticipates him.*)

PETER. She left her cake. (*He starts for* ANNE's *room with the cake. There is silence in the main room.* MRS. VAN DAAN *goes up to her room, followed by* VAN DAAN. DUSSEL *stays looking out the window.* MR. FRANK *brings* MRS. FRANK *her cake. She eats it slowly, without relish.* MR. FRANK *takes his cake to* MARGOT *and sits quietly on the sofa beside her.* PETER *stands in the doorway of* ANNE's *darkened room, looking at her, then makes a little movement to let her know he is there.* ANNE *sits up, quickly, trying to hide the signs of her tears.* PETER *holds out the cake to her.*) You left this.

ANNE (*dully*). Thanks.

(PETER *starts to go out, then comes back.*)

PETER. I thought you were fine just now. You know just how to talk to them. You know just how to say it. I'm no good . . . I never can think . . . especially when I'm mad . . . That Dussel . . . when he said that about Mouschi . . . someone eating him . . . all I could think is . . . I wanted to hit him. I wanted to give him such a . . . a . . . that he'd . . . That's what I used to do when there was an argument at school . . . That's the way I . . . but here . . . And an old man like that . . . it wouldn't be so good.

ANNE. You're making a big mistake about me. I do it all wrong. I say too much. I go too far. I hurt people's feelings . . .

(DUSSEL *leaves the window, going to his room.*)

PETER. I think you're just fine . . . What I want to say . . . if it wasn't for you around here, I don't know. What I mean . . .

(PETER *is interrupted by* DUSSEL's *turning on the light.* DUSSEL *stands in the doorway, startled to see* PETER. PETER *advances toward him forbiddingly.* DUSSEL *backs out of the room.* PETER *closes the door on him.*)

ANNE. Do you mean it, Peter? Do you really mean it?

PETER. I said it, didn't I?

ANNE. Thank you, Peter!

(*In the main room* MR. *and* MRS. FRANK *collect the dishes and take them to the sink, washing them.* MARGOT *lies down again on the couch.* DUSSEL, *lost, wanders into* PETER'S *room and takes up a book, starting to read.*)

PETER (*looking at the photographs on the wall*). You've got quite a collection.

ANNE. Wouldn't you like some in your room? I could give you some. Heaven knows you spend enough time in there . . . doing heaven knows what . . .

PETER. It's easier. A fight starts, or an argument . . . I duck in there.

ANNE. You're lucky, having a room to go to. His lordship is always here . . . I hardly ever get a minute alone. When they start in on me, I can't duck away. I have to stand there and take it.

PETER. You gave some of it back just now.

ANNE. I get so mad. They've formed their opinions . . . about everything . . . but we . . . we're still trying to find out . . . We have problems here that no other people our age have ever had. And just as you think you've solved them, something comes along and bang! You have to start all over again.

PETER. At least you've got someone you can talk to.

ANNE. Not really. Mother . . . I never discuss anything serious with her. She doesn't understand. Father's all right. We can talk about everything . . . everything but one thing. Mother. He simply won't talk about her. I don't think you can be really intimate with anyone if he holds something back, do you?

PETER. I think your father's fine.

ANNE. Oh, he is, Peter! He is! He's the only one who's ever given me the feeling that I have any sense. But anyway, nothing can take the place of school and play and friends of your own age . . . or near your age . . . can it?

PETER. I suppose you miss your friends and all.

ANNE. It isn't just . . . (*She breaks off, staring up at him for a second.*) Isn't it funny, you and I? Here we've been seeing each other every minute for almost a year and a half, and this is the first time we've ever really talked. It helps a lot to have someone to talk to, don't you think? It helps you to let off steam.

PETER (*going to the door*). Well, any time you want to let off steam, you can come into my room.

ANNE (*following him*). I can get up an awful lot of steam. You'll have to be careful how you say that.

PETER. It's all right with me.

ANNE. Do you mean it?

PETER. I said it, didn't I?

(*He goes out.* ANNE *stands in her doorway looking after him. As* PETER *gets to his door he stands for a minute looking back at her. Then he goes into his room.* DUSSEL *rises as he comes in, and quickly passes him, going out. He starts across for his room.* ANNE *sees him coming, and pulls her door shut.* DUSSEL *turns back toward* PETER'S *room.* PETER *pulls his door shut.* DUSSEL *stands there, bewildered, forlorn.*

The scene slowly dims out. The curtain falls on the scene. ANNE'S VOICE *comes over in the darkness . . . faintly at first, and then with growing strength.*)

ANNE'S VOICE. We've had bad news. The people from whom Miep got our ration books have been arrested. So we have had to cut down on our food. Our stomachs are so empty that they rumble and make strange noises, all in different keys. Mr. Van Daan's is deep and low, like a bass fiddle. Mine is high, whistling like a flute. As we all sit around waiting for supper, it's like an orchestra tuning up. It only needs Toscanini to raise his baton and we'd be off in the Ride of the Valkyries. Monday, the sixth of March, nineteen forty-four. Mr. Kraler is in the hospital. It seems he has ulcers. Pim says we are his ulcers. Miep has to run the business and us too. The Americans have landed on the southern tip of Italy. Father looks for a quick finish to the war. Mr. Dussel is waiting every day for the warehouse man to demand more money. Have I been skipping too much from one subject to another? I can't help it. I feel that spring is coming. I feel it in my whole body and soul. I feel utterly confused. I am longing . . . so longing . . . for everything . . . for friends . . . for someone to talk to . . . someone who understands . . . someone young, who feels as I do . . .

(*As these last lines are being said, the curtain rises on the scene. The lights dim on.* ANNE'S VOICE *fades out.*)

SCENE TWO

It is evening, after supper. From outside we hear the sound of children playing. The "grownups," with the exception of MR. VAN DAAN, *are all in the main room.* MRS. FRANK *is doing some mending,* MRS. VAN DAAN *is reading a fashion magazine.* MR. FRANK *is going over business accounts.* DUSSEL, *in his dentist's jacket, is pacing up and down, impatient to get into his bedroom.* MR. VAN DAAN *is upstairs working on a piece of embroidery in an embroidery frame.*

In his room PETER *is sitting before the mirror, smoothing his hair. As the scene goes on, he puts on his tie, brushes his coat and puts it on, preparing himself meticulously for a visit from* ANNE. *On his wall are now hung some of* ANNE's *motion picture stars.*

In her room ANNE *too is getting dressed. She stands before the mirror in her slip, trying various ways of dressing her hair.* MARGOT *is seated on the sofa, hemming a skirt for* ANNE *to wear.*

In the main room DUSSEL *can stand it no longer. He comes over, rapping sharply on the door of his and* ANNE's *bedroom.*

ANNE (*calling to him*). No, no, Mr. Dussel! I am not dressed yet. (DUSSEL *walks away, furious, sitting down and burying his head in his hands.* ANNE *turns to* MARGOT.) How is that? How does that look?

MARGOT (*glancing at her briefly*). Fine.

ANNE. You didn't even look.

MARGOT. Of course I did. It's fine.

ANNE. Margot, tell me, am I terribly ugly?

MARGOT. Oh, stop fishing.

ANNE. No. No. Tell me.

MARGOT. Of course you're not. You've got nice eyes . . . and a lot of animation, and . . .

ANNE. A little vague, aren't you?

(*She reaches over and takes a brassière out of* MARGOT's *sewing basket. She holds it up to herself, studying the effect in the mirror. Outside,* MRS. FRANK, *feeling sorry for* DUSSEL, *comes over, knocking at the girls' door.*)

MRS. FRANK (*outside*). May I come in?

MARGOT. Come in, Mother.

MRS. FRANK (*shutting the door behind her*). Mr. Dussel's impatient to get in here.

ANNE (*still with the brassière*). Heavens, he takes the room for himself the entire day.

MRS. FRANK (*gently*). Anne, dear, you're not going in again tonight to see Peter?

ANNE (*dignified*). That is my intention.

MRS. FRANK. But you've already spent a great deal of time in there today.

ANNE. I was in there exactly twice.

Once to get the dictionary, and then three-quarters of an hour before supper.

MRS. FRANK. Aren't you afraid you're disturbing him?

ANNE. Mother, I have some intuition.

MRS. FRANK. Then may I ask you this much, Anne. Please don't shut the door when you go in.

ANNE. You sound like Mrs. Van Daan! (*She throws the brassière back in* MARGOT's *sewing basket and picks up her blouse, putting it on.*)

MRS. FRANK. No. No. I don't mean to suggest anything wrong. I only wish that you wouldn't expose yourself to criticism . . . that you wouldn't give Mrs. Van Daan the opportunity to be unpleasant.

ANNE. Mrs. Van Daan doesn't need an opportunity to be unpleasant!

MRS. FRANK. Everyone's on edge, worried about Mr. Kraler. This is one more thing . . .

ANNE. I'm sorry, Mother. I'm going to Peter's room. I'm not going to let Petronella Van Daan spoil our friendship.

(MRS. FRANK *hesitates for a second, then goes out, closing the door after her. She gets a pack of playing cards and sits at the center table, playing solitaire. In* ANNE's *room* MARGOT *hands the finished skirt to* ANNE. *As* ANNE *is putting it on,* MARGOT *takes off her high-heeled shoes and stuffs paper in the toes so that* ANNE *can wear them.*)

MARGOT (*to* ANNE). Why don't you two talk in the main room? It'd save a lot of trouble. It's hard on Mother, having to listen to those remarks from Mrs. Van Daan and not say a word.

ANNE. Why doesn't she say a word? I think it's ridiculous to take it and take it.

MARGOT. You don't understand Mother at all, do you? She can't talk back. She's not like you. It's just not in her nature to fight back.

ANNE. Anyway . . . the only one I worry about is you. I feel awfully guilty about you. (*She sits on the stool near* MARGOT, *putting on* MARGOT's *high-heeled shoes.*)

MARGOT. What about?

ANNE. I mean, every time I go into Peter's room, I have a feeling I may be hurting you. (MARGOT *shakes her head.*) I know if it were me, I'd be wild. I'd be desperately jealous, if it were me.

MARGOT. Well, I'm not.

ANNE. You don't feel badly? Really? Truly? You're not jealous?

MARGOT. Of course I'm jealous . . . jealous that you've got something to get up in the morning for . . . But jealous of you and Peter? No.

(ANNE *goes back to the mirror.*)

ANNE. Maybe there's nothing to be jealous of. Maybe he doesn't really like me. Maybe I'm just taking the place of his cat . . . (*She picks up a pair of short white gloves, putting them on.*) Wouldn't you like to come in with us?

MARGOT. I have a book.

(*The sound of the children playing outside fades out. In the main room* DUSSEL *can stand it no longer. He jumps up, going to the bedroom door and knocking sharply.*)

DUSSEL. Will you please let me in my room!

ANNE. Just a minute, dear, dear Mr. Dussel. (*She picks up her Mother's pink stole and adjusts it elegantly over her shoulders, then gives a last look in the mirror.*) Well, here I go . . . to run the gauntlet. (*She starts out, followed by* MARGOT.)

DUSSEL (*as she appears — sarcastic*). Thank you so much.

(DUSSEL *goes into his room.* ANNE *goes toward* PETER's *room, passing* MRS. VAN DAAN *and her parents at the center table.*)

MRS. VAN DAAN. My God, look at her! (ANNE *pays no attention. She knocks at* PETER's *door.*) I don't know what good it is to have a son. I never see him. He wouldn't care if I killed myself. (PETER *opens the door and stands aside for* ANNE *to come in.*) Just a minute, Anne. (*She goes to them at the door.*) I'd like to say a few words to my son. Do you mind? (PETER *and* ANNE *stand waiting.*) Peter, I don't want you staying up till all hours tonight. You've got to have your sleep. You're a growing boy. You hear?

MRS. FRANK. Anne won't stay late. She's going to bed promptly at nine. Aren't you, Anne?

ANNE Yes, Mother . . . (*To* MRS. VAN DAAN.) May we go now?

MRS. VAN DAAN. Are you asking me? I didn't know I had anything to say about it.

MRS. FRANK. Listen for the chimes, Anne dear.

(*The two young people go off into* PETER's *room, shutting the door after them.*)

MRS. VAN DAAN (*to* MRS. FRANK). In my day it was the boys who called on the girls. Not the girls on the boys.

MRS. FRANK. You know how young

people like to feel that they have secrets. Peter's room is the only place where they can talk.

MRS. VAN DAAN. Talk! That's not what they called it when I was young.

(MRS. VAN DAAN *goes off to the bathroom.* MARGOT *settles down to read her book.* MR. FRANK *puts his papers away and brings a chess game to the center table. He and* MRS. FRANK *start to play. In* PETER's *room,* ANNE *speaks to* PETER, *indignant, humiliated.*)

ANNE. Aren't they awful? Aren't they impossible? Treating us as if we were still in the nursery. (*She sits on the cot.* PETER *gets a bottle of pop and two glasses.*)

PETER. Don't let it bother you. It doesn't bother me.

ANNE. I suppose you can't really blame them . . . they think back to what *they* were like at our age. They don't realize how much more advanced we are . . . When you think what wonderful discussions we've had! . . . Oh, I forgot. I was going to bring you some more pictures.

PETER. Oh, these are fine, thanks.

ANNE. Don't you want some more? Miep just brought me some new ones.

PETER. Maybe later. (*He gives her a glass of pop and, taking some for himself, sits down facing her.*)

ANNE (*looking up at one of the photographs*). I remember when I got that . . . I won it. I bet Jopie that I could eat five ice-cream cones. We'd all been playing ping-pong . . . We used to have heavenly times . . . we'd finish up with ice cream at the Delphi, or the Oasis, where Jews were allowed . . . there'd always be a lot of boys . . . we'd laugh and joke . . . I'd like to go back to it for a few days or a week. But after that I know I'd be bored to death. I think more seriously about life now. I want to be a journalist . . . or something. I love to write. What do you want to do?

PETER. I thought I might go off some place . . . work on a farm or something . . . some job that doesn't take much brains.

ANNE. You shouldn't talk that way. You've got the most awful inferiority complex.

PETER. I know I'm not smart.

ANNE. That isn't true. You're much better than I am in dozens of things . . . arithmetic and algebra and . . . well, you're a million times better than I am in algebra. (*With sudden directness.*) You like Margot, don't you? Right from the start you liked her, liked her much better than me.

PETER (*uncomfortably*). Oh, I don't know.

(*In the main room* MRS. VAN DAAN *comes from the bathroom and goes over to the sink, polishing a coffeepot.*)

ANNE. It's all right. Everyone feels that way. Margot's so good. She's sweet and bright and beautiful and I'm not.

PETER. I wouldn't say that.

ANNE. Oh, no, I'm not. I know that. I know quite well that I'm not a beauty. I never have been and never shall be.

PETER. I don't agree at all. I think you're pretty.

ANNE. That's not true!

PETER. And another thing. You've changed . . . from at first, I mean.

ANNE. I have?

PETER. I used to think you were awful noisy.

ANNE. And what do you think now, Peter? How have I changed?

PETER. Well . . . er . . . you're . . . quieter.

(*In his room* DUSSEL *takes his pajamas and toilet articles and goes into the bathroom to change.*)

ANNE. I'm glad you don't just hate me.

PETER. I never said that.

ANNE. I bet when you get out of here you'll never think of me again.

PETER. That's crazy.

ANNE. When you get back with all of your friends, you're going to say . . . now what did I ever see in that Mrs. Quack Quack.

PETER. I haven't got any friends.

ANNE. Oh, Peter, of course you have. Everyone has friends.

PETER. Not me. I don't want any. I get along all right without them.

ANNE. Does that mean you can get along without me? I think of myself as your friend.

PETER. No. If they were all like you, it'd be different.

(*He takes the glasses and the bottle and puts them away. There is a second's silence and then* ANNE *speaks, hesitantly, shyly.*)

ANNE. Peter, did you ever kiss a girl?

PETER. Yes. Once.

ANNE (*to cover her feelings*). That picture's crooked. (PETER *goes over, straightening the photograph.*) Was she pretty?

PETER. Huh?

ANNE. The girl that you kissed.

PETER. I don't know. I was blindfolded. (*He comes back and sits down again*). It was at a party. One of those kissing games.

ANNE (*relieved*). Oh. I don't suppose that really counts, does it?

PETER. It didn't with me.

ANNE. I've been kissed twice. Once a man I'd never seen before kissed me on the cheek when he picked me up off the ice and I was crying. And the other was Mr. Koophuis, a friend of Father's who kissed my hand. You wouldn't say those counted, would you?

PETER. I wouldn't say so.

ANNE. I know almost for certain that Margot would never kiss anyone unless she was engaged to them. And I'm sure too that Mother never touched a man before Pim. But I don't know . . . things are so different now . . . What do you think? Do you think a girl shouldn't kiss anyone except if she's engaged or something? It's so hard to try to think what to do, when here we are with the whole world falling around our ears and you think . . . well . . . you don't know what's going to happen tomorrow and . . . What do you think?

PETER. I suppose it'd depend on the girl. Some girls, anything they do's wrong. But others . . . well . . . it wouldn't it wouldn't necessarily be wrong with them. (*The carillon starts to strike nine o'clock.*) I've always thought that when two people . . .

ANNE. Nine o'clock. I have to go.

PETER. That's right.

ANNE (*without moving*). Good night.

(*There is a second's pause, then* PETER *gets up and moves toward the door.*)

PETER. You won't let them stop you coming?

ANNE. No. (*She rises and starts for the door.*) Sometime I might bring my diary. There are so many things in it that I want to talk over with you. There's a lot about you.

PETER. What kind of thing?

ANNE. I wouldn't want you to see some of it. I thought you were a nothing, just the way you thought about me.

PETER. Did you change your mind, the way I changed my mind about you?

ANNE. Well . . . You'll see . . .

(*For a second* ANNE *stands looking up at* PETER, *longing for him to kiss her. As he makes no move she turns away. Then suddenly* PETER *grabs her awkwardly in his arms, kissing her on the cheek.* ANNE *walks out dazed. She stands for a minute, her back to the people in the main room. As she regains her poise she goes to her mother and father and* MARGOT, *silently kissing them. They murmur their good nights to her. As she is about to open her bedroom door, she catches sight of* MRS. VAN DAAN. *She goes quickly to her, taking her face in her hands and kissing her first on one cheek and then on the other. Then she hurries off into her room.* MRS. VAN DAAN *looks after her, and then looks over at* PETER'S *room. Her suspicions are confirmed.*)

MRS. VAN DAAN (*She knows*). Ah hah!

(*The lights dim out. The curtain falls on the scene. In the darkness* ANNE'S VOICE *comes faintly at first and then with growing strength.*)

ANNE'S VOICE. By this time we all know each other so well that if anyone starts to tell a story, the rest can finish it for him. We're having to cut down still further on our meals. What makes it worse, the rats have been at work again. They've carried off some of our precious food. Even Mr. Dussel wishes now that Mouschi was here. Thursday, the twentieth of April, nineteen forty-four. Invasion fever is mounting every day. Miep tells us that people outside talk of nothing else. For myself, life has become much more pleasant. I often go to Peter's room after supper. Oh, don't think I'm in love, because I'm not. But it does make life more bearable to have someone with whom you can exchange views. No more tonight. P.S. ... I must be honest. I must confess that I actually live for the next meeting. Is there anything lovelier than to sit under the skylight and feel the sun on your cheeks and have a darling boy in your arms? I admit now that I'm glad the Van Daans had a son and not a daughter. I've outgrown another dress. That's the third. I'm having to wear Margot's clothes after all. I'm working hard on my French and am now reading *La Belle Nivernaise.*

(*As she is saying the last lines—the curtain rises on the scene. The lights dim on, as* ANNE'S VOICE *fades out.*)

SCENE THREE

It is night, a few weeks later. Everyone is in bed. There is complete quiet. In the VAN DAANS' *room a match flares up for a moment and then is quickly put out.* MR. VAN DAAN, *in bare feet, dressed in underwear and trousers, is dimly seen coming stealthily down the stairs and into the main room, where* MR. *and* MRS. FRANK *and* MARGOT *are sleeping. He goes to the food safe and again lights a match. Then he cautiously opens the safe, taking out a half-loaf of bread. As he closes the safe, it creaks. He stands rigid.* MRS. FRANK *sits up in bed. She sees him.*

———

MRS. FRANK (*screaming*). Otto! Otto! Komme schnell!

(*The rest of the people wake, hurriedly getting up.*)

MR. FRANK. *Was ist los? Was ist passiert?*

(DUSSEL, *followed by* ANNE, *comes from his room.*)

MRS. FRANK (*as she rushes over to* MR. VAN DAAN). *Er stiehlt das Essen!*

DUSSEL (*grabbing* MR. VAN DAAN). You! You! Give me that.

MRS. VAN DAAN (*coming down the stairs*). Putti ... Putti ... what is it?

DUSSEL (*his hands on* VAN DAAN's *neck*). You dirty thief ... stealing food ... you good-for-nothing ...

MR. FRANK. Mr. Dussel! For God's sake! Help me, Peter!

(PETER *comes over, trying, with* MR. FRANK, *to separate the two struggling men.*)

PETER. Let him go! Let go!

(DUSSEL *drops* MR. VAN DAAN, *pushing him away. He shows them the end of a loaf of bread that he has taken from* VAN DAAN.)

DUSSEL. You greedy, selfish ... !

(MARGOT *turns on the lights.*)

MRS. VAN DAAN. Putti ... what is it?

(*All of* MRS. FRANK's *gentleness, her self-control, is gone. She is outraged, in a frenzy of indignation.*)

MRS. FRANK. The bread! He was stealing the bread!

DUSSEL. It was you, and all the time we thought it was the rats!

MR. FRANK. Mr. Van Daan, how could you!

MR. VAN DAAN. I'm hungry.

MRS. FRANK. We're all of us hungry! I see the children getting thinner and thinner. Your own son Peter ... I've heard him moan in his sleep, he's so hungry. And you come in the night and steal food that should go to them ... to the children!

MRS. VAN DAAN (*going to* MR. VAN DAAN *protectively*). He needs more food than the rest of us. He's used to more. He's a big man.

(MR. VAN DAAN *breaks away, going over and sitting on the couch.*)

MRS. FRANK (*turning on* MRS. VAN DAAN). And you . . . you're worse than he is! You're a mother, and yet you sacrifice your child to this man . . . this . . . this . . .

MR. FRANK. Edith! Edith!

(MARGOT *picks up the pink woolen stole, putting it over her mother's shoulders.*)

MRS. FRANK (*paying no attention, going on to* MRS. VAN DAAN). Don't think I haven't seen you! Always saving the choicest bits for him! I've watched you day after day and I've held my tongue. But not any longer! Not after this! Now I want him to go! I want him to get out of here!

MR. FRANK. Edith!
MR. VAN DAAN. Get out of here? } (*Together.*)
MRS. VAN DAAN. What do you mean?

MRS. FRANK. Just that! Take your things and get out!

MR. FRANK (*to* MRS. FRANK). You're speaking in anger. You cannot mean what you are saying.

MRS. FRANK. I mean exactly that!

(MRS. VAN DAAN *takes a cover from the* FRANKS' *bed, pulling it about her.*)

MR. FRANK. For two long years we have lived here, side by side. We have respected each other's rights . . . we have managed to live in peace. Are we now going to throw it all away? I know this will never happen again, will it, Mr. Van Daan?

MR. VAN DAAN. No. No.

MRS. FRANK. He steals once! He'll steal again!

(MR. VAN DAAN, *holding his stomach, starts for the bathroom.* ANNE *puts her arms around him, helping him up the step.*)

MR. FRANK. Edith, please. Let us be calm. We'll all go to our rooms . . . and afterwards we'll sit down quietly and talk this out . . . we'll find some way . . .

MRS. FRANK. No! No! No more talk! I want them to leave!

MRS. VAN DAAN. You'd put us out, on the streets?

MRS. FRANK. There are other hiding places.

MRS. VAN DAAN. A cellar . . . a closet. I know. And we have no money left even to pay for that.

MRS. FRANK. I'll give you money. Our of my own pocket I'll give it gladly.

(*She gets her purse from a shelf and comes back with it.*)

MRS. VAN DAAN. Mr. Frank, you told Putti you'd never forget what he'd done for you when you came to Amsterdam. You said you could never repay him, that you . . .

MRS. FRANK (*counting out money*). If my husband had any obligation to you, he's paid it, over and over.

MR. FRANK. Edith, I've never seen you like this before. I don't know you.

MRS. FRANK. I should have spoken out long ago.

DUSSEL. You can't be nice to some people.

MRS. VAN DAAN (*turning on* DUSSEL). There would have been plenty for all of us, if *you* hadn't come in here!

MR. FRANK. We don't need the Nazis to destroy us. We're destroying ourselves.

(*He sits down, with his head in his hands.* MRS. FRANK *goes to* MRS. VAN DAAN.)

MRS. FRANK (*giving* MRS. VAN DAAN *some money*). Give this to Miep. She'll find you a place.

ANNE. Mother, you're not putting *Peter* out. Peter hasn't done anything.

MRS. FRANK. He'll stay, of course. When I say I must protect the children, I mean Peter too.

(PETER *rises from the steps where he has been sitting.*)

PETER. I'd have to go if Father goes.

(MR. VAN DAAN *comes from the bathroom.* MRS. VAN DAAN *hurries to him and takes him to the couch. Then she gets water from ʾ.e sink to bathe his face.*)

MRS. FRANK (*while this is going on*). He's no father to you . . . that man! He doesn't know what it is to be a father!

PETER (*starting for his room*). I wouldn't feel right. I couldn't stay.

MRS. FRANK. Very well, then. I'm sorry.

ANNE (*rushing over to* PETER). No, Peter! No! (PETER *goes into his room, closing the door after him.* ANNE *turns back to her mother, crying.*) I don't care about the food. They can have mine! I don't want it! Only don't send them away. It'll be daylight soon. They'll be caught . . .

MARGOT (*putting her arms comfortingly around* ANNE). Please, Mother!

MRS. FRANK. They're not going now. They'll stay here until Miep finds them a place. (*To* MRS. VAN DAAN.) But one thing I insist on! He must never come down here again! He must never come to this room where the food is stored! We'll divide what we have . . . an equal share for each! (DUSSEL *hurries over to get a sack of potatoes from the food safe.* MRS. FRANK *goes on, to* MRS. VAN DAAN.) You can cook it here and take it up to him.

(DUSSEL *brings the sack of potatoes back to the center table.*)

MARGOT. Oh, no. No. We haven't sunk so far that we're going to fight over a handful of rotten potatoes.

DUSSEL (*Dividing the potatoes into piles*). Mrs. Frank, Mr. Frank, Margot, Anne, Peter, Mrs. Van Daan, Mr. Van Daan, myself . . . Mrs. Frank . . .

(*The buzzer sounds in* MIEP's *signal.*)

MR. FRANK. It's Miep! (*He hurries over, getting his overcoat and putting it on.*)

MARGOT. At this hour?

MRS. FRANK. It is trouble.

MR. FRANK (*as he starts down to unbolt the door*). I beg you, don't let her see a thing like this!

MR. DUSSEL (*counting without stopping*). . . . Anne, Peter, Mrs. Van Daan, Mr. Van Daan, myself . . .

MARGOT (*to* DUSSEL). Stop it! Stop it!

DUSSEL. . . . Mr. Frank, Margot, Anne, Peter, Mrs. Van Daan, Mr. Van Daan, myself, Mrs. Frank . . .

MRS. VAN DAAN. You're keeping the big ones for yourself! All the big ones . . . Look at the size of that! . . . And that! . . .

(DUSSEL *continues on with his dividing.* PETER, *with his shirt and trousers on, comes from his room.*)

MARGOT. Stop it! Stop it!

(*We hear* MIEP's *excited voice speaking to* MR. FRANK *below.*

MIEP. Mr. Frank . . . the most wonderful news! . . . The invasion has begun!

MR. FRANK. Go on, tell them! Tell them!

(MIEP *comes running up the steps, ahead of* MR. FRANK. *She has a man's raincoat on over her nightclothes and a bunch of orange-colored flowers in her hand.*)

MIEP. Did you hear that, everybody? Did you hear what I said? The invasion has begun! The invasion!

(*They all stare at* MIEP, *unable to grasp what she is telling them.* PETER *is the first to recover his wits.*)

PETER. Where?

MRS. VAN DAAN. When? When, Miep?

MIEP. It began early this morning . . .

(*As she talks on, the realization of what she has said begins to dawn on them. Everyone goes crazy. A wild demonstration takes place.* MRS. FRANK *hugs* MR. VAN DAAN.)

MRS. FRANK. Oh, Mr. Van Daan, did you hear that?

(DUSSEL *embraces* MRS. VAN DAAN. PETER *grabs a frying pan and parades around the room, beating on it, singing the Dutch National Anthem.* ANNE *and* MARGOT *follow him, singing, weaving in and out among the excited grownups.* MARGOT *breaks away to take the flowers from* MIEP *and distribute them to everyone. While this pandemonium is going on* MRS. FRANK *tries to make herself heard above the excitement.*)

MRS. FRANK (*to* MIEP). How do you know?

MIEP. The radio . . . The B.B.C.! They said they landed on the coast of Normandy!

PETER. The British?

MIEP. British, Americans, French, Dutch, Poles, Norwegians . . . all of them! More than four thousand ships! Churchill spoke, and General Eisenhower! D-Day they call it!

MR. FRANK. Thank God, it's come!

MRS. VAN DAAN. At last!

MIEP (*starting out*). I'm going to tell Mr. Kraler. This'll be better than any blood transfusion.

MR. FRANK (*stopping her*). What part of Normandy did they land, did they say?

MIEP. Normandy . . . that's all I know now . . . I'll be up the minute I hear some more! (*She goes hurriedly out.*)

MR. FRANK (*to* MRS. FRANK). What did I tell you? What did I tell you?

(MRS. FRANK *indicates that he has forgotten to bolt the door after* MIEP. *He hurries down the steps.* MR. VAN DAAN, *sitting on the couch, suddenly breaks into a convulsive sob. Everybody looks at him, bewildered.*)

MRS. VAN DAAN (*hurrying to him*). Putti! Putti! What is it? What happened?

MR. VAN DAAN. Please. I'm so ashamed.

(MR. FRANK *comes back up the steps.*)

DUSSEL. Oh, for God's sake!

MRS. VAN DAAN. Don't, Putti.

MARGOT. It doesn't matter now!

MR. FRANK (*going to* MR. VAN DAAN). Didn't you hear what Miep said? The invasion has come! We're going to be liberated! This is a time to celebrate! (*He embraces* MRS. FRANK *and then hurries to the cupboard and gets the cognac and a glass.*)

MR. VAN DAAN. To steal bread from children!

MRS. FRANK. We've all done things that we're ashamed of.

ANNE. Look at me, the way I've treated Mother ... so mean and horrid to her.

MRS. FRANK. No, Anneke, no.

(ANNE *runs to her mother, putting her arms around her.*)

ANNE. Oh, Mother, I was. I was awful.

MR. VAN DAAN. Not like me. No one is as bad as me!

DUSSEL (*to* MR. VAN DAAN). Stop it now! Let's be happy!

MR. FRANK (*giving* MR. VAN DAAN *a glass of cognac*). Here! Here! *Schnapps! Locheim!*

(VAN DAAN *takes the cognac. They all watch him. He gives them a feeble smile.* ANNE *puts up her fingers in a V-for-Victory sign. As* VAN DAAN *gives an answering V-sign, they are startled to hear a loud sob from behind them. It is* MRS. FRANK, *stricken with remorse. She is sitting on the other side of the room.*)

MRS. FRANK (*through her sobs*). When I think of the terrible things I said ...

(MR. FRANK, ANNE *and* MARGOT *hurry to her, trying to comfort her.* MR. VAN DAAN *brings her his glass of cognac.*)

MR. VAN DAAN. No! No! You were right!

MRS. FRANK. That I should speak that way to you! ... Our friends! ... Our guests! (*She starts to cry again.*)

DUSSEL. Stop it, you're spoiling the whole invasion!

(*As they are comforting her, the lights dim out. The curtain falls.*)

ANNE'S VOICE (*faintly at first and then with growing strength*). We're all in much better spirits these days. There's still excellent news of the invasion. The best part about it is that I have a feeling that friends are coming. Who knows? Maybe I'll be back in school by fall. Ha, ha! The joke is on us! The warehouse man doesn't know a thing and we are paying hi. all that money! ... Wednesday, the second of July, nineteen forty-four. The invasion seems temporarily to be bogged down. Mr. Kraler has to have an operation, which looks bad. The Gestapo have found the radio that was stolen. Mr. Dussel says they'll trace it back and back to the thief, and then, it's just a matter of time till they get to us. Everyone is low. Even poor Pim can't raise their spirits. I have often been downcast myself ...

but never in despair. I can shake off everything if I write. But ... and that is the great question ... will I ever be able to write well? I want to so much. I want to go on living even after my death. Another birthday has gone by, so now I am fifteen. Already I know what I want. I have a goal, an opinion.

(*As this is being said—the curtain rises on the scene, the lights dim on, and* ANNE'S VOICE *fades out.*)

SCENE FOUR

It is an afternoon a few weeks later ... Everyone but Margot is in the main room. There is a sense of great tension.

Both MRS. FRANK *and* MR. VAN DAAN *are nervously pacing back and forth,* DUSSEL *is standing at the window, looking down fixedly at the street below.* PETER *is at the center table, trying to do his lessons.* ANNE *sits opposite him, writing in her diary.* MRS. VAN DAAN *is seated on the couch, her eyes on* MR. FRANK *as he sits reading.*

The sound of a telephone ringing comes from the office below. They all are rigid, listening tensely. MR. DUSSEL *rushes down to* MR. FRANK.

DUSSEL. There it goes again, the telephone! Mr. Frank, do you hear?

MR. FRANK (*quietly*). Yes. I hear.

DUSSEL (*pleading, insistent*). But this is the third time, Mr. Frank! The third time in quick succession! It's a signal! I tell you it's Miep, trying to get us! For some reason she can't come to us and she's trying to warn us of something!

MR. FRANK. Please. Please.

MR. VAN DAAN (*to* DUSSEL). You're wasting your breath.

DUSSEL. Something has happened, Mr. Frank. For three days now Miep hasn't been to see us! And today not a man has come to work. There hasn't been a sound in the building!

MRS. FRANK. Perhaps it's Sunday. We may have lost track of the days.

MR. VAN DAAN (*to* ANNE). You with the diary there. What day is it?

DUSSEL (*going to* MRS. FRANK). I don't lose track of the days! I know exactly what day it is! It's Friday, the fourth of August. Friday, and not a man at work. (*He rushes back to* MR. FRANK, *pleading with him, almost in tears.*) I tell you Mr. Kraler's dead. That's the only explanation. He's dead and they've closed down the building, and Miep's trying to tell us!

MR. FRANK. She'd never telephone us.

DUSSEL (*frantic*). Mr. Frank, answer that! I beg you, answer it!

MR. FRANK. No.

MR. VAN DAAN. Just pick it up and listen. You don't have to speak. Just listen and see if it's Miep.

DUSSEL (*speaking at the same time*). For God's sake . . . I ask you.

MR. FRANK. No. I've told you, no. I'll do nothing that might let anyone know we're in the building.

PETER. Mr. Frank's right.

MR. VAN DAAN. There's no need to tell us what side you're on.

MR. FRANK. If we wait patiently, quietly, I believe that help will come.

(*There is silence for a minute as they all listen to the telephone ringing.*)

DUSSEL. I'm going down. (*He rushes down the steps.* MR. FRANK *tries ineffectually to hold him.* DUSSEL *runs to the lower door, unbolting it. The telephone stops ringing.* DUSSEL *bolts the door and comes slowly back up the steps.*) Too late. (MR. FRANK *goes to* MARGOT *in* ANNE'S *bedroom.*)

MR. VAN DAAN. So we just wait here until we die.

MRS. VAN DAAN (*hysterically*). I can't stand it! I'll kill myself! I'll kill myself!

MR. VAN DAAN. For God's sake, stop it!

(*In the distance, a German military band is heard playing a Viennese waltz.*)

MRS. VAN DAAN. I think you'd be glad if I did! I think you want me to die!

MR. VAN DAAN. Whose fault is it we're here? (MRS. VAN DAAN *starts for her room. He follows, talking at her.*) We could've been safe somewhere . . . in America or Switzerland. But no! No! You wouldn't leave when I wanted to. You couldn't leave your things. You couldn't leave your precious furniture.

MRS. VAN DAAN. Don't touch me!

(*She hurries up the stairs, followed by* MR. VAN DAAN. PETER, *unable to bear it, goes to his room.* ANNE *looks after him, deeply concerned.* DUSSEL *returns to his post at the window.* MR. FRANK *comes back into the main room and takes a book, trying to read.* MRS. FRANK *sits near the sink, starting to peel some potatoes.* ANNE *quietly goes to* PETER'S *room, closing the door after her.* PETER *is lying face down on the cot.* ANNE *leans over him, holding him in her arms, trying to bring him out of his despair.*)

ANNE. Look, Peter, the sky. (*She looks up through the skylight.*) What a lovely, lovely day! Aren't the clouds beautiful? You know what I do when it seems as if I couldn't stand being cooped up for one more minute? I *think* myself out. I think myself on a walk in the park where I used to go with Pim. Where the jonquils and the crocus and the violets grow down the slopes. You know the most wonderful part about *thinking* yourself out? You can have it any way you like. You can have roses and violets and chrysanthemums all blooming at the same time . . . It's funny . . . I used to take it all for granted . . . and now I've gone crazy about everything to do with nature. Haven't you?

PETER. I've just gone crazy. I think if something doesn't happen soon . . . if we don't get out of here . . . I can't stand much more of it!

ANNE (*softly*). I wish you had a religion, Peter.

PETER. No, thanks! Not me!

ANNE. Oh, I don't mean you have to be Orthodox . . . or believe in heaven and hell and purgatory and things . . . I just mean some religion . . . it doesn't matter what. Just to believe in something! When I think of all that's out there . . . the trees . . . and flowers . . . and seagulls . . . when I think of the dearness of you, Peter, . . . and the goodness of the people we know . . . Mr. Kraler, Miep, Dirk, the vegetable man, all risking their lives for us every day . . . When I think of these good things, I'm not afraid any more . . . I find myself, and God, and I . . .

(PETER *interrupts, getting up and walking away.*)

PETER. That's fine! But when I begin to think, I get mad! Look at us, hiding out for two years. Not able to move! Caught here like . . . waiting for them to come and get us . . . and all for what?

ANNE. We're not the only people that've had to suffer. There've always been people that've had to . . . sometimes one race . . . sometimes another . . . and yet . . .

PETER. That doesn't make me feel any better!

ANNE (*going to him*). I know it's terrible,

trying to have any faith . . . when people are doing such horrible . . . But you know what I sometimes think? I think the world may be going through a phase, the way I was with Mother. It'll pass, maybe not for hundreds of years, but some day . . . I still believe, in spite of everything, that people are really good at heart.

PETER. I want to see something now . . . Not a thousand years from now!

(*He goes over, sitting down again on the cot.*)

ANNE. But, Peter, if you'd only look at it as part of a great pattern . . . that we're just a little minute in the life . . . (*She breaks off.*) Listen to us, going at each other like a couple of stupid grownups! Look at the sky now. Isn't it lovely? (*She holds out her hand to him.* PETER *takes it and rises, standing with her at the window looking out, his arms around her.* Some day, when we're outside again, I'm going to . . .

(*She breaks off as she hears the sound of a car, its brakes squealing as it comes to a sudden stop. The people in the other rooms also become aware of the sound. They listen tensely. Another car roars up to a screeching stop.* ANNE *and* PETER *come from* PETER'S *room.* MR. *and* MRS. VAN DAAN *creep down the stairs.* DUSSEL *comes out from his room. Everyone is listening, hardly breathing. A doorbell clangs again and again in the building below.* MR. FRANK *starts quietly down the steps to the door.* DUSSEL *and* PETER *follow him. The others stand rigid, waiting, terrified.*

In a few seconds DUSSEL *comes stumbling back up the steps. He shakes off* PETER'S *help and goes to his room.* MR. FRANK *bolts the door below, and comes slowly back up the steps. Their eyes are all on him as he stands there for a minute. They realize that what they feared has happened.* MRS. VAN DAAN *starts to whimper.* MR. VAN DAAN *puts her gently in a chair, and then hurries off up the stairs to their room to collect their things.* PETER *goes to comfort his mother. There is a sound of violent pounding on a door below.*)

MR. FRANK (*quietly*). For the past two years we have lived in fear. Now we can live in hope.

(*The pounding below becomes more insistent. There are muffled sounds of voices, shouting commands.*)

MEN'S VOICES. *Auf machen! Da drinnen! Auf machen! Schnell! Schnell! Schnell! etc., etc.*

(*The street door below is forced open. We hear the heavy tread of footsteps coming up.* MR. FRANK *gets two school-bags from the shelves, and gives one to* ANNE *and the other to* MARGOT. *He goes to get a bag for* MRS. FRANK. *The sound of feet coming up grows louder.* PETER *comes to* ANNE, *kissing her good-by, then he goes to his room to collect his things. The buzzer of their door starts to ring.* MR. FRANK *brings* MRS. FRANK *a bag. They stand together, waiting. We hear the thud of gun butts on the door, trying to break it down.*

ANNE *stands, holding her school satchel, looking over at her father and mother with a soft, reassuring smile. She is no longer a child, but a woman with courage to meet whatever lies ahead.*

The lights dim out. The curtain falls on the scene. We hear a mighty crash as the door is shattered. After a second ANNE'S *voice is heard.*)

ANNE'S VOICE. And so it seems our stay is over. They are waiting for us now. They've allowed us five minutes to get our things. We can each take a bag and whatever it will hold of clothing. Nothing else. So, dear Diary, that means I must leave you behind. Good-by for a while. P.S. Please, please, Miep, or Mr. Kraler, or anyone else. If you should find this diary, will you please keep it safe for me, because some day I hope . . .

(*Her voice stops abruptly. There is silence. After a second the curtain rises.*)

SCENE FIVE

It is again the afternoon in November, 1945. The rooms are as we saw them in the first scene. MR. KRALER *has joined* MIEP *and* MR. FRANK. *There are coffee cups on the table. We see a great change in* MR. FRANK. *He is calm now. His bitterness is gone. He slowly turns a few pages of the diary. They are blank.*

———

MR. FRANK. No more. (*He closes the diary and puts it down on the couch beside him.*)

MIEP. I'd gone to the country to find food. When I got back the block was surrounded by police . . .

MR. KRALER. We made it our business to learn how they knew. It was the thief . . . the thief who told them.

(MIEP *goes up to the gas burner, bringing back a pot of coffee.*)

MR. FRANK (*after a pause*). It seems strange to say this, that anyone could be happy in a concentration camp. But Anne was happy in the camp in Holland where they first took us. After two years of being shut up in these rooms, she could be out . . . out in the sunshine and the fresh air that she loved.

MIEP (*offering the coffee to* MR. FRANK). A little more?

MR. FRANK (*holding out his cup to her*). The news of the war was good. The British and Americans were sweeping through France. We felt sure that they would get to us in time. In September we were told that we were to be shipped to Poland . . . The men to one camp. The women to another. I was sent to Auschwitz. They went to Belsen. In January we were freed, the few of us who were left. The war wasn't yet over, so it took us a long time to get home. We'd be sent here and there behind the lines where we'd be safe. Each time our train would stop . . . at a siding, or a crossing . . . we'd all get out and go from group to group . . . Where were you? Were you at Belsen? At Buchenwald? At Mauthausen? Is it possible that you knew my wife? Did you ever see my husband? My son? My daughter? That's how I found out about my wife's death . . . of Margot, the Van Daans . . . Dussel. But Anne . . . I still hoped . . . Yesterday I went to Rotterdam. I'd heard of a woman there . . . She'd been in Belsen with Anne . . . I know now.

(*He picks up the diary again, and turns the pages back to find a certain passage. As he finds it we hear* ANNE'S VOICE.)

ANNE'S VOICE. In spite of everything, I still believe that people are really good at heart.

(MR. FRANK *slowly closes the diary*.)

MR. FRANK. She puts me to shame.

(*They are silent*.)

The CURTAIN *falls*.